P9-CIU-836

6011538560115385601 1

CURRENT
BIOGRAPHY

CURRENT
BIOGRAPHY

WHO'S NEWS AND WHY
1 9 5 3

EDITED BY

Marjorie Dent Candee

THE H. W. WILSON COMPANY
NEW YORK, N. Y.

Fourteenth Annual Cumulation—1953

Printed in the United States of America

Copyright 1954

by

The H. W. Wilson Company

International Standard Book No. 0-8242-0119-1

Library of Congress Catalog Card No. (40-27432)

Preface

During 1953 CURRENT BIOGRAPHY published an average of thirty biographical articles in eleven monthly issues. Of the total of 330 biographies, here cumulated in one alphabet, fifty were of women, and eighty were of individuals in foreign countries. They represent people in some thirty varied fields including art, agriculture, aviation, business, diplomacy, education, government and politics, military, literature, journalism and publishing, labor, law, medicine, motion pictures, radio, television, theatre, religion, philosophy, science, social science, social service, and technology.

Also in this Yearbook are twenty biographies of authors which were originally published during 1953 in the *Wilson Library Bulletin*. These are indicated in the Index by (WLB).

CURRENT BIOGRAPHY continues to publish superseding articles about people still prominent in the news whose biographies first appeared in the 1940, 1941 or 1942 Yearbook (which volumes are now out of print). Among these are Winthrop W. Aldrich, Chiang Kai-Shek, Sir Winston Churchill, John Foster Dulles, Albert Einstein, Oveta Culp Hobby, Clare Boothe Luce, Luis Muñoz Marín, Bing Crosby, Shirley Booth and Leopold Stokowski.

The assembling of material for these biographies requires painstaking research. When a name is selected for inclusion in CURRENT BIOGRAPHY a questionnaire is sent to the subject. A research writer is then assigned who consults *Readers' Guide to Periodical Literature* and many other indexes which lead to a mass of information; "Who's Who's," encyclopedias and other reference works are also culled for biographical and background facts. Information is obtained from Government offices and from commercial and educational organizations. Subjects of the biographies are sometimes interviewed, and asked to confirm or correct facts. The result of these endeavors is biographical information often unavailable elsewhere. It should be pointed out, however, that these are objective rather than authorized biographies. For the Yearbook these have been revised to include any major changes in an individual's position in the course of the year.

On the pages following are **Explanations** of this Yearbook, **Key To Pronunciation** and **Key To Abbreviations.** At the rear of this volume will be found these indexes:

Biographical References Consulted
Periodicals and Newspapers Consulted
Necrology
Classification by Profession
Cumulated Index, 1951-1953

NOTE: The index for 1940-1950 is published in the 1950 Yearbook. Separate copies of this index, including the 1951-53 supplement, are available. Inquire of the publisher for price.

M.D.C.

Explanations

Authorities for biographees' full names, with some exceptions, are the bibliographical publications of The Wilson Company. When a biographee prefers a certain name form, that is indicated in the heading of the article: for example, "Anderson R(obert) B(ernerd)" means that he is usually referred to as R. B. Anderson. When a professional name is used in the heading, as, for example, "Crosby, Bing," the real name, in this case Harry Lillis Crosby, appears in the article itself.

The heading of each article includes the pronunciation of the name if it is unusual, date of birth (if obtainable), and occupation. The article is supplemented by a list of references to sources of biographical information, in two alphabets: (1) newspapers and periodicals and (2) books. See the section **Biographical References Consulted.**

References to newspapers and periodicals are listed in abbreviated form; for example, "Sat Eve Post 217:14-15 S 30 '44 por" means **Saturday Evening Post,** volume 217, pages 14-15, September 30, 1944, with portrait. (For full names, see the section **Periodical and Newspaper Abbreviations,** in the rear of this volume.) The reference following each obituary notice is to the New York **Times**; these notices appear for persons whose biographies have been published in **Current Biography.**

KEY TO PRONUNCIATION
(Based on Webster's Guide to Pronunciation*)

ā	āle	N	Not pronounced, but indicates the nasal tone of the preceding vowel, as in the French *bon* (bôN).	û	ûrn; French eu, as in *jeu* (zhû); German ö, oe, as in *schön* (shün), *Goethe* (gû′tĕ)
â	câre				
ă	ădd				
ȧ	ȧccount				
ä	ärm				
à	àsk				
ạ	sofạ				
		ō	ōld	ŭ	tŭb
		ô	ôrb	ů	circŭs
ē	ēve	ŏ	ŏdd	ü	Pronounced approximately as ē, with rounded lips: French u, as in *menu* (mē-nü′); German ü, as in *grün*.
ĕ	ĕnd	oi	oil		
ẽ	makẽr	o͞o	o͞oze		
g	go	o͝o	fo͝ot		
		ou	out		
ĭ	īce				
ĭ	ĭll	th	then	zh	azure
		th	thin	′ = main accent
к	German ch as in *ich* (ĭк).			″ = secondary accent
		ū	cūbe		

(*Exceptions : th in then ; main and secondary accents.)

KEY TO ABBREVIATIONS

AAA — Agricultural Adjustment Administration
A.A.A.A. — Amateur Athletic Association of America
A.A.U. — Amateur Athletic Union
ABC — American Broadcasting Company
A.C.L.U. — American Civil Liberties Union
ADA — Americans for Democratic Action
AEC — Atomic Energy Commission
AEF — American Expeditionary Force
AFL — American Federation of Labor
A.L.A. — American Library Association
A.M.A. — American Medical Association
AMG — Allied Military Government
A.P. — Associated Press
ASCAP — American Society of Composers, Authors and Publishers
ASNE — American Society Newspaper Editors
AVC — American Veterans Committee

b. — business address
B.A. — Bachelor of Arts
BBC — British Broadcasting Corporation
B.D. — Bachelor of Divinity
B.L.S. — Bachelor of Library Science
B.S. — Bachelor of Science

CAA — Civil Aeronautics Administration
CAB — Civil Aeronautics Board
C.B. — Companion of the Bath
C.B.E. — Commander of (the Order of) the British Empire
CBS — Columbia Broadcasting System
CCC — Civilian Conservation Corps
C.E. — Civil Engineer
CEA — Council of Economic Advisers
C.E.D. — Committee for Economic Development
CIO — Congress of Industrial Organizations
C.M.G. — Companion of (the Order of) St. Michael and St. George
Com. — Commodore
CWA — Civil Works Administration
CWS — Chemical Warfare Service

D.A.R. — Daughters of the American Revolution
D.C.L. — Doctor of Civil Law
D.D. — Doctor of Divinity
D.Eng. — Doctor of Engineering
D.F.C. — Distinguished Flying Cross
D.J. — Doctor of Jurisprudence
D.Lit. — Doctor of Literature
D.Mus. — Doctor of Music
DP — Displaced Person
D.Pol.Sc. — Doctor of Political Science
D.Sc. — Doctor of Science
D.S.C. — Distinguished Service Cross
D.S.M. — Distinguished Service Medal
D.S.O. — Distinguished Service Order

ECA — Economic Cooperation Administration
ECOSOC — Economic and Social Council
ERP — European Recovery Program
ESA — Economic Stabilization Administration

FAO — Food and Agriculture Organization
FBI — Federal Bureau of Investigation
FCA — Farm Credit Administration
FCC — Federal Communications Commission
FEPC — Fair Employment Practice Committee
FERA — Federal Emergency Relief Administration

FHA — Federal Housing Administration
FSA — Federal Security Agency
FTC — Federal Trade Commission

G.B.E. — Knight or Dame Grand Cross Order of the British Empire
G.C.B. — Knight Grand Cross of the Bath
GHQ — General Headquarters

h. — home address
H.M. — His Majesty; Her Majesty
HOLC — Home Owners' Loan Corporation

ICC — Interstate Commerce Commission
I.C.F.T.U. — International Confederation of Free Trade Unions
I.L.A. — International Longshoremen's Association
I.L.G.W.U. — International Ladies' Garment Workers' Union
I.L.O. — International Labor Office
I.L.P. — Independent Labour Party
INS — International News Service
IRO — International Refugee Organization
I.T.U. — International Typographical Union

J — Journal
J.C.B. — Juris Canonici Bachelor
J.D. — Doctor of Jurisprudence
j.g. — junior grade

K.B.E. — Knight of (the Order of) the British Empire
K.C. — King's Counsel
K.C.B. — Knight Commander of the Bath

L.H.D. — Doctor of Humanities
Litt.D. — Doctor of Letters
LL.B. — Bachelor of Laws
LL.D. — Doctor of Laws
LL.M. — Master of Laws
M.A. — Master of Arts
M.B.A. — Master of Business Administration
MBS — Mutual Broadcasting System
M.C.E. — Master of Civil Engineering
M.D. — Doctor of Medicine
M.E. — Master of Engineering
MGM — Metro-Goldwyn-Mayer
M.Lit. — Master of Literature
M.P. — Member of Parliament
M.P.P.D.A. — Motion Picture Producers and Distributors of America
MRP — Mouvement Républicain Populaire
MSA — Mutual Security Agency
M.Sc. — Master of Science
Msgr. — Monsignor, Monseigneur
MVA — Missouri Valley Authority

NAACP — National Association for the Advancement of Colored People
NAB — National Association of Broadcasters
NAM — National Association of Manufacturers
NATO — North Atlantic Treaty Organization
NBC — National Broadcasting Company
N.E.A. — National Education Association
NLRB — National Labor Relations Board
N.M.U. — National Maritime Union
NRA — National Recovery Administration
NRPB — National Resources Planning Board
NWLB — National War Labor Board
NYA — National Youth Administration

OCD — Office of Civilian Defense

OEEC — Organization for European Economic Cooperation
OPA — Office of Price Administration
OPRD — Office of Production Research and Development
OSRD — Office of Scientific Research and Development
OWI — Office of War Information

PAC — Political Action Committee
P.C. — Privy Councilor
PCA — Progressive Citizens of America
P.E.N. — Poets, Playwrights, Editors, Essayists and Novelists (International Association)
Ph.B. — Bachelor of Philosophy
Ph.D. — Doctor of Philosophy
por — portrait, -s
PWA — Public Works Administration

Q.C. — Queen's Counsel

R — Review
RAF — Royal Air Force
RCA — Radio Corporation of America
REA — Rural Electrification Administration
RFC — Reconstruction Finance Corporation
RKO — Radio-Keith-Orpheum
ROTC — Reserve Officers' Training Corps

SEC — Securities and Exchange Commission
s.g. — senior grade
SCAP — Supreme Command for the Allied Powers
SHAEF — Supreme Headquarters, Allied Expeditionary Force
SHAPE — Supreme Headquarters, Allied Powers Europe
S.J.D. — Doctor of Juridical Science
SPA — Surplus Property Administration
SSB — Social Security Board
S.T.B. — Bachelor of Sacred Theology
S.T.D. — Doctor of Sacred Theology

T.U.C. — Trades Union Congress
TVA — Tennessee Valley Authority
T.W.U.A. — Textile Workers Union of America

U.A.W.A. — Union Auto Workers of America
UMT — Universal Military Training
U.M.W.A. — United Mine Workers of America
U.N. — United Nations
UNESCO — United Nations Educational, Scientific, and Cultural Organization
UNRRA — United Nations Relief and Rehabilitation Administration
U.P. — United Press
USO — United Service Organizations
U.S.S.R. — Union of Socialist Soviet Republics
U.S.W.A. — United Steel Workers of America

VA — Veterans Administration
V.F.W. — Veterans of Foreign Wars

WAA — War Assets Administration
W.C.T.U. — Woman's Christian Temperance Union
WFA — War Food Administration
W.F.T.U. — World Federation of Trade Unions
WHO — World Health Organization
WLB — War Labor Board
WMC — War Manpower Commission
WPA — Work Projects Administration
WPB — War Production Board

CURRENT BIOGRAPHY

1953

ADKINS, BERTHA S(HEPPARD) Aug.
24, 1906- Political leader
Address: b. c/o Republican National Committee,
Washington, D.C., h. 3040 Idaho Ave.,
Washington, D.C., 321 Park Ave., Salisbury,
Md.

Succeeding Mrs. Ivy Baker Priest as assistant chairman of the Republican National Committee, Bertha Adkins (whose appointment was
announced on January 18, 1953) has as her
main task the development of activities for
Republican women on a nation-wide basis.
Active for many years in the Republican party
in Maryland, she was named in March 1950
executive director of the Women's Division of
the Republican National Committee, having
earlier relinquished her college administrative
work to enter politics.

She is a firm believer in developing political
work at the grass-roots level. To accomplish
this, she considers it her responsibility "to in-
form and educate women on the entire range
of party politics, as well as the actual know-
how of government." (New York *Herald Tribune,* January 29, 1953).

Bertha Sheppard Adkins, daughter of Frederick Paul and Edna May (Sheppard) Adkins,
was born on August 24, 1906 in Salisbury,
Maryland, where she still maintains residence.
After attending Salisbury High School, she
entered the Baldwin School in Bryn Mawr,
Pennsylvania, from which she was graduated
in 1924. She holds the B.A. degree from Wellesley College (1928) and the M.A. degree
from Teachers College, Columbia University
(1943); she also took graduate courses at the
University of Chicago (1937).

At the end of her fourth year as a teacher
in a private school in Salisbury, Miss Adkins in
1932 turned to secretarial work for two years
in the office of E. S. Adkins and Company,
also in Salisbury. In 1934 she accepted the
post of dean of women of Western Maryland
College in Westminster, where she remained
until 1942 when she began a four-year period
as dean of residence at Bradford (Massachusetts) Junior College.

An active participant in local politics in
Maryland, Miss Adkins has been the Republican committeewoman from Maryland since
1948. After helping to draft the party's special
declaration of principles in March 1950, she
was named executive director of the Women's
Division of the Republican National Committee.
Her principal work in association with Mrs.
Gilford Mayes, Assistant National Chairman,
was to mobilize women's votes for the 1950
Congressional elections, which were regarded as
a proving ground for the 1952 Presidential campaign.

Chase Photo.

BERTHA S. ADKINS

As Guy G. Gabrielson, then Republican National chairman, said at the time, Miss Adkins'
services were to be of "immeasurable value to
the party and to the building of a stronger
women's unit in every precinct of the country."
To this end, she trained speakers and organizers and prepared educational material. Traveling about the country to debate campaign
issues, Miss Adkins spoke in May of that year
in Missouri, Illinois, Wisconsin, Michigan and
Pennsylvania, telling women that they must
work through an organized party if they want
their influence felt in national life. She urged
them to press for equal representation with
men in State and local party organizations.

Working for the Republican victory in the
1952 Presidential campaign, the Women's Division director stated that before the Republican Convention in July 1952 in Chicago, she
had to remain officially "neutral" until her
"favorite candidate, General Eisenhower" was
nominated (New York *Times,* July 13, 1952).

On January 17, 1953 she was appointed assistant to the new national chairman of the
Republican National Committee, C. Wesley
Roberts (who has since resigned and is succeeded by Leonard W. Hall). Miss Adkins
succeeded Mrs. Ivy Baker Priest of Utah, who
became Treasurer of the United States.

On the basis of reports from Republican
leaders across the country, Miss Adkins, whose
counterpart in the Democratic party is Mrs.

ADKINS, BERTHA S.—*Continued*

India Edwards, said that there was "no question but that the interest of women was the motivating force that gave General Eisenhower his tremendous majority" (New York *Herald Tribune*, January 31, 1953). Republican women members of State legislatures, Miss Adkins has pointed out, now number 197, a gain of forty-one over 1951.

In a debate with Mrs. Edwards, Miss Adkins stated that "the Democrats failed to understand the Far East which led to war and they grossly neglected national defense."

The task in 1953 for Miss Adkins and her colleagues on the Republican National Committee is to consolidate the party's gains of November 1952 and increase the number of Republicans in both Houses of Congress in the 1954 elections. To accomplish this, Miss Adkins has announced, an expanded Women's Division planned to hold a nationwide conference of Republican women in Washington which would be followed by a series of regional conferences in the fall. The division is also setting up an information service for women in which their questions about the Eisenhower Administration will be answered by members of the Cabinet and Congress, Republican Governors and other public officials.

During the January inauguration activities in Washington, Miss Adkins mapped out the 1953 program with Republican women leaders including committeewomen from Republican national and State organizations, officers and members of the National Federation of Women's Republican Clubs, women workers with the Citizens for Eisenhower-Nixon Clubs, Young Republicans, and the organized women of nonpartisan groups instrumental in turning out the vote. Among the projects in which their cooperation was enlisted were radio and television programs, a "Young Citizens Award" contest, various types of conferences, schools of politics and visual aids. Miss Adkins is cooperating with Mrs. D. Ray Murdock, Pennsylvania's National Committeewoman in arranging political sight-seeing tours of Washington for groups of women from all over America to see government-in-action. Various members of the President's Cabinet gave reports to the first contingent of 1,000 women who visited the nation's Capitol in April.

Miss Adkins, who has brown eyes and brown-gray hair, is five feet eight inches tall and weighs 145 pounds. She belongs to the Methodist Church, and is a member of the American Association of University Women, the Maryland Federation of Women's Clubs, and Pi Lambda Theta. Golf is her favorite sport.

References

N Y Herald Tribune II p2 Mr 19 '50 por
N Y Times p8 Ja 26 '53
Washington (D.C.) Post p48 F 22 '53

American Women, 1939-40
Who's Who in America, 1952-53

ALDRICH, WINTHROP W(ILLIAMS)
Nov. 2, 1885- United States Ambassador to Great Britain; banker
Address: b. c/o United States Embassy, London, England; h. 960 5th Ave., New York 21

> NOTE: This biography supersedes the article which appeared in *Current Biography* in 1940.

The new United States Ambassador to the Court of St. James, Winthrop W. Aldrich, designated on November 30, 1952, has long been regarded as a warm friend of Great Britain, having been president of the British War Relief Society from 1940 to 1943 and a strong advocate of the United States loan to Britain. To accept the diplomatic appointment, Aldrich resigned from the chairmanship of the board of the Chase National Bank of the City of New York, which he had held since 1933. Earlier he had practiced law in New York before entering the banking field in 1929.

The tenth of eleven children, Winthrop Williams Aldrich was born in Providence, Rhode Island, on November 2, 1885. His parents, Nelson Wilmarth and Abby Pierce Chapman (Greene) Aldrich, made their home part of the time in Washington, D.C., where his father served as a United States Senator from Rhode Island from 1881 to 1911. The Senator, a conservative Republican and exponent of high tariffs, was well known as chairman of the National Monetary Commission, the forerunner of the Federal Reserve System. Having completed his preparatory training at the Hope Street High School in Providence, young Aldrich studied at Harvard University, where he took his B.A. degree in 1907. He then entered Harvard Law School and, after graduating tenth in his class in 1910 with the LL.B. degree, he joined the New York law firm of Byrne, Cutcheon and Taylor, was admitted to the bar in 1912, and became a junior partner in 1916.

Interested in the sea and yachting since his boyhood, Aldrich took a course in navigation and in 1917 was commissioned a lieutenant in the United States Naval Reserve. During World War I he served as commander of patrol boats, the navigating officer of the *Niagara*, and then, with the rank of lieutenant, as assistant navigating officer on the cruiser *New Orleans*, which convoyed troop ships.

In January 1919 he joined the firm of Murray, Prentice and Howland. From 1922 to 1930 he devoted most of his time to handling legal matters for the Equitable Trust Company of New York, an institution in which John D. Rockefeller, Jr., the lawyer's brother-in-law, was interested. An important case which he undertook outside of the firm was that of the proxy dispute in which the Rockefeller interests conflicted with those of Colonel Bob Stewart of Standard Oil of Indiana. After a complex legal contest, Aldrich won the case and succeeded in ousting Stewart, who had been connected with the Teapot Dome affair, from the chairmanship of the oil company (*Fortune*, January 1936).

Since Aldrich had handled the legal details of the merger of the Equitable Trust Company with the Seaboard National in 1929, he was

WINTHROP W. ALDRICH

regarded as having the most thorough knowledge of the bank's affairs and was prevailed upon to become temporary president of the combined organizations in December 1929, following the death of Chellis A. Austin. While at first reluctant to leave the practice of law, he remained in the post through the bank's merger with the Chase National Bank of New York in June 1930 and then assumed the title of president of the consolidated organization. The banker soon found himself in disagreement with the chairman of the board, Albert H. Wiggin, on basic policy. The two points of view were presented to the Chase's board of directors, and the decision given in favor of Aldrich, who was named chairman of the governing board in January 1933 on Wiggin's resignation. In January of the following year he assumed the title of chairman of the board of directors and as such has served as head of the Chase National Bank, as well as of the Chase Bank and the Chase Safe Deposit Company, until resigning in January 1953 to become Ambassador to Great Britain.

During the bank moratorium, on March 8, 1933, Aldrich made an important and influential statement on banking, recommending that "the spirit of speculation should be eradicated from the management of commercial banks" (*Literary Digest*, March 25, 1933). He proposed the complete separation of banking and security selling and suggested that banks be allowed to underwrite only State, municipal, and Federal securities and that all be brought under the Federal Reserve System. The statement provoked the criticism from Wall Street associates that he had broken tradition by not consulting them before presenting his views. The press, however, received it as a healthy indication that banking interests would support reform measures in their structures. The Chase National Bank carried out Aldrich's policy by discontinuing the Chase-Harris-Forbes securities, an affiliate

of the bank. After the passage of the Glass-Steagall Banking Act, which contained many of the provisions that the banker had suggested, Aldrich appeared before the Senate Committee on Banking and Currency in November 1933 to detail the ways in which he thought the law could be perfected.

Aldrich, who had become president of the American Society for British Medical and Civilian Aid, Inc., and the American Society for French Medical and Civilian Aid, Inc., in October 1939, was named president of the Allied Relief Fund in June 1940 when the two organizations were merged under that name. The fund supported such relief measures as the American Ambulances of Great Britain and the American Hospitals of France and Great Britain. The financier also acted from 1940 to 1943 as the president of the British War Relief Society, the largest relief group for Britain in the United States. When all war relief agencies' campaigns for funds (except that of the Red Cross) were coordinated in one annual drive, the National War Fund, Inc., Aldrich became the organizing chairman of this group, taking over the post in January 1943.

The financier in May 1947 attended a meeting in Montreux, Switzerland, of the International Chamber of Commerce, of which he was then president. In October he proposed, in an address before the American Bankers' Association, the creation of a United States Corporation for European Reconstruction, which would supervise American aid to Europe. In 1950 Aldrich made a two-month tour of Europe to survey the financial situation abroad.

Replying to a letter from a stockholder who had requested that holders of bank stock carry on an "educational campaign" to promote certain ideas critical of Administration policies, Aldrich expressed his views as follows: "As a private citizen I believe that I am free to speak and vote on political questions and political candidates as I may think best. On the other hand, I feel that my trust as chairman of the board of this bank requires me to exert every effort to guard the bank . . . from taking part in any activities that could fairly be characterized as political" (quoted by the New York *Times*, February 4, 1951). In a discussion of his political philosophy, the New York *Herald Tribune* (December 1, 1952) said, "A devotee of the Adam Smith laissez-faire economy, Mr. Aldrich is a believer in the founding principles of America, in individual enterprise, and in a free economy." Aldrich's proposal for a reappraisal of Government's role in reality credit, made in an address before the Austin, Texas, Chamber of Commerce in November 1951, was termed by the New York *Herald Tribune* as "perhaps the more significant coming from one of the nation's leading financial authorities without a direct or extensive interest in real estate activity" (December 9, 1951). Commenting in January 1952 upon the proposed merger of the Chase National Bank and the Bank of the Manhattan Company, Aldrich stated that he would "like Chase to have a city-wide branch bank system."

Long active in New York's Fifteenth Assembly District Republican Club, Aldrich favored

ALDRICH, WINTHROP W.—*Continued*

the nomination of General Eisenhower as the Republican candidate for President in 1952 and worked throughout the campaign to raise funds. His Republican finance committee was reported by *Newsweek* to have raised $2,250,000 in New York. At the Republican convention, which he attended, the possibility of his appointment as Ambassador to Great Britain was foreseen by some observers. Aldrich has said that he regarded Britain as his "second home abroad" and is accorded equal friendliness by the British, who remember his work in war relief and his strong support of financial aid to Britain. He also favored the Marshall Plan and Point IV Program, is regarded as an internationalist in his economic views by his associates, and advocates expanding world trade and lower tariffs, now an important issue with the British people. When it was announced, therefore, on November 30, 1952, that Aldrich had been designated by President-elect Dwight D. Eisenhower as the new Ambassador to the Court of St. James, the news was given a highly favorable reception in the British press. The banker succeeds Ambassador Walter S. Gifford, who resigned in January 1953. Aldrich presented his credentials to Queen Elizabeth II on February 20, 1953.

Aldrich has been a director of the American Telephone and Telegraph Company, the New York Central Railroad, the Metropolitan Life Insurance Company, the Westinghouse Electric and Manufacturing Company, the Discount Corporation of New York, Rockefeller Center, Inc., and the International Paper Company. He is chairman and director of the Chase Safe Deposit Company, chairman of the board of trustees of the Banking Research Fund of the Association of Reserve City Bankers, and a member of the American Bankers Association and the advisory committee of the American Institute of Banking. Philanthropic and civic organizations for which Aldrich has acted as a director include the American Association for the Control of Cancer, the Nassau Hospital Association, and the Henry Street Visiting Nurse Service; he is a trustee of Riverside Church, the United Hospital Fund, the New York Orthopedic Hospital and Dispensary, the General Education Board, the Rockefeller Foundation, the New York Community Trust, and the Police Relief Association of Nassau County, Inc. The financial leader is also the president of the board of managers of the State Charities Aid Association, a member of the board of managers of the Home for Incurables, treasurer and member of the executive committee of the Welfare Council of New York City, and treasurer of the Girl Scout Federation of Greater New York.

Former president of the International Chamber of Commerce (1945-47), Aldrich has also served as a member of the United States Council of the International Chamber of Commerce, Inc., president of the New York Clearing House Association (1947-49) and of the New York

State Chamber of Commerce (1936-38), and he is a director of the Swedish Chamber of Commerce of the United States of America. He is the vice-president of the National Institute of Social Sciences and a member of the Academy of Political Science. Other organizations with which he has been associated are the Holland House Corporation of the Netherlands (director), the Navy League of the United States (director), the American Merchant Marine Library Association, the National Foreign Trade Council, and the Japan Society. Aldrich is a member of the finance committee of the Tuskegee Normal and Industrial Institute and a trustee of Barnard College; he maintains membership in the Harvard Fund Council, the Harvard Board of Overseers, and the Two Hundred and Fifty Associates of the Harvard Business School. Honorary LL.D. degrees have been awarded him by the following universities: Colgate (1937), Northeastern (1938), Brown (1944), Lafayette (1945), Columbia (1946), Bryant (1947), and Georgetown (1952), and by Washington and Jefferson College (1939). He also holds the degree of Doctor of Commercial Science from New York University (1950).

Decorated by the Governments of the Netherlands, Belgium, Luxembourg, and France, Aldrich was also twice honored by the late King George VI of England, becoming the first holder of the King's Medal for Service in 1945 and receiving the Knight Grand Cross of the British Empire in 1948 for the work he had done for British war relief. On June 18, 1945, Pope Pius XII bestowed on him the decoration of Knight Commander of the Order of Pope Pius IX, with Star. He is the recipient of the United States Medal of Merit (October 3, 1946) and of the Goodrich Award for distinguished public service. Aldrich's clubs are the Harvard, the Knickerbocker, the Bond, the Broad Street, the Union, the River, the Pilgrims, the Piping Rock, the National Golf, The Brook, the Century, the Links, the Creek, and the New York Yacht in New York; the Harvard in Boston; the Hope in Providence; the Tarrantine in Dark Harbor, Maine; the Spee in Cambridge; the Faculty Club of Harvard, Beaver Dam, and Southside Sportsmen's Club of Long Island.

Aldrich and Harriet Alexander were married on December 7, 1916. Their children are Mary (Mrs. Robert Homans), Harriet (Mrs. Edgar Bering, Jr.), Lucy Truman (Mrs. David W. Devens), Elizabeth Brewster (Mrs. J. Woodward Redmond), and Alexander; one son, Winthrop Williams, is deceased. An amateur watercolorist and musician, Aldrich also enjoyed golf before his business duties forced the suspension of his hobbies. His principal nonprofessional interest has always been yachting. In his schooner *Flying Cloud* he won the Astor Cup in 1923 and some years later managed the New York Yacht Club syndicate that built the cup-defender *Enterprise* (he was navigator on the ship when it defeated Sir Thomas Lipton's *Shamrock V* in 1930).

The banker stands five feet eleven inches tall and has been described in the New York *World-Telegram* as "not the shoulder-thumping type" and as "deliberate, precise, and well-tailored."

References

Fortune 13 :54-60+ Ja '36 pors
N Y Herald Tribune p3 D 1 '52
N Y Times p1 D 1 '52 por
International Who's Who, 1952
Mirrors of Wall Street (1933)
Smith, A. D. H. Men Who Run America (1936)
Who's Who, 1951
Who's Who in America, 1952-53
Who's Who in Commerce and Industry (1951)
Who's Who in the East (1951)
World Biography (1948)

Wide World Photos

ALEXEI, PATRIARCH OF RUSSIA

ALEXEI, PATRIARCH OF RUSSIA

Oct. 27, 1877- Leader of the Russian Orthodox Church

Address: Moscow, U.S.S.R.

The spiritual leader of the one hundred million communicants of the Holy Orthodox Eastern Catholic and Apostolic Church (Russian Orthodox Church) is the Patriarch of Moscow and All Russia. The present Patriarch, the thirteenth to hold the title, is the former Metropolitan Alexei of Leningrad and Novgorod, who became Acting Patriarch following the death of his predecessor Sergei in May 1944 and was formally crowned in February 1945. Western observers have frequently commented upon the loyalty of Patriarch Alexei to the Stalin regime in the Soviet Union.

Patriarch Alexei was born Sergei Vladimirovich Simansky in Moscow, Russia, on October 27, 1877. His forebears were aristocrats, and he attended a school for sons of the nobility before entering the University of Moscow, where he studied jurisprudence and received the Doctor of Canon Law degree from the Faculty of Law in 1899. Shortly thereafter he turned to the religious life and in 1902 became a monk and a deacon of the Russian Orthodox Church, at that time taking the name by which he has since been known. Brother Alexei, who became a priest-monk in the following year, received his Doctor of Theology degree from the Moscow Ecclesiastical Seminary in 1904. Engaged in theological teaching and seminary administration for the next seven years, he became successively inspector at the Pskov Theological Seminary (1904), rector and archimandrite (abbot) of Tula Ecclesiastical Seminary (1906) and rector of Novgorod Ecclesiastical Seminary and prior of St. Antony Monastery (1911). In 1913 he became Bishop Alexei of Tikhvin and Vicar of Novgorod, ecclesiastic posts which he occupied at the time of the Bolshevik revolution and the 1917-18 Sobor (Orthodox Church Congress).

The 1917-18 Sobor was the last to be held for eighteen years; for on January 23, 1918, two months or so after seizing power, the new Communist Government of Russia formally separated Church and State and launched its policy of "extirpating" religion. That policy was being carried out when, in 1921, Alexei became Vicar of Petrograd (formerly St. Petersburg and later Leningrad) and Bishop of Yamburg, and when, in 1926, he was elevated to Archbishop. In 1933 Alexei became Metropolitan of Leningrad and Novgorod. Four years later (1937) a new census surprised the Soviet authorities by its revelation of the continuing faith of the Russian people. With the attack on the U.S.S.R. in 1941 by the Nazis, "Stalin, in his efforts to rally all Soviet citizens to the defense of the fatherland, relaxed his strong opposition to the Church, and put a quietus on the activities of atheist organizations, particularly the 'Godless League'" (*Ten Eventful Years*).

From his retreat at Ulianovsk on the Volga, the acting Patriarch Sergei issued a call to the faithful to rally to the defense of Russia and himself refused to accept Hitler's "crusade" to "liberate" the Russian Church. The Metropolitan Alexei was particularly conspicuous in response, remaining in Leningrad throughout the two months of the Nazi siege early in 1942, to organize the Church in support of the Red armies; and when in September of the same year the Moscow Patriarchate issued (with Soviet approval) a widely distributed book entitled *The Truth About Religion in Russia*, it included sermons by Alexei. "The book also contained," noted Alexander Werth in the New York *Times*, "an epistle sent in the summer of 1942 to Orthodox believers in the occupied territories reminding them that they must never forget they were Russians and must never do anything, wittingly or unwittingly, by which they would betray their homeland." Such (continued the New York *Times* correspondent) was "some of the background of the developments which led up . . . to the re-establishment" on September 12, 1943, of the Church Patriarch and the Holy Synod and the return of Sergei

ALEXEI, PATRIARCH—*Continued*

to Moscow from Ulianovsk. The latter was regularly elected Patriarch at this time, while Alexei was one of those made permanent members of the Holy Synod. The following month (October) Metropolitan Alexei was the principal among several of the Orthodox clergy to be awarded the Leningrad Defense Medal "for their help in the defense of Leningrad, including their collection of funds for armaments and for presents for the Red Army" (New York *Times*).

The last will and testament of the Patriarch Sergei, who died on May 15, 1944, directed that Metropolitan Alexei become "guardian of the throne," and on May 21, 1944, the latter was named Acting Patriarch by the Holy Synod. In accepting his appointment, Alexei directed a personal letter to Premier Stalin, in which he stated that in his future work he would "unfailingly and unalterably keep the principles which characterized the clerical activity of the late Patriarch: to follow the canons of Church regulations on the one side and constant faithfulness to the motherland and the Government headed by [Stalin] on the other" (quoted by the New York *Times*, May 22, 1944).

Alexei was formally crowned as the thirteenth Patriarch of Moscow and All Russia at the Bogoyavlensky Cathedral in Moscow on February 4, 1945, at which time the Holy Orthodox Eastern Catholic and Apostolic Church (Russian Orthodox Church) was estimated to have 16,000 churches open in the Soviet Union (as against about 54,000 in the last years of the Czar) and around 100,000,000 communicants in various parts of the world. Many Metropolitan Districts (notably the American, which had refused to recognize the Soviet Government and had been put under interdict, or suspension, by the Moscow Patriarchate on January 4, 1935) had split from Moscow for one reason and another. The new Patriarch, as nominal spiritual leader, at once sought to reunify the Eastern Orthodox Church and to renew his predecessor's challenge to the strongest of its religious competitors. Thus a statement by the Russian Orthodox Church broadcast from Moscow on February 9, 1945 (less than one week after the coronation of Alexei), called on Church delegates assembled in the Soviet capital to "lift their voice against those, particularly the Vatican, who . . . in their utterances" had attempted "to absolve Hitler Germany from responsibility for all the abominable deeds she has committed." At about the same time the Moscow Patriarchate responded to a request by the American Metropolitan Districts for reunion under terms of semiautonomy with a "ukase" (decree) stipulating "abstention from political activities against the U.S.S.R." as a condition of readmission.

In late May and early June Patriarch Alexei made a personal tour of the Near East, visiting Palestine, Syria, Lebanon, and Egypt; then he visited England at the invitation of the Archbishop of Canterbury. In the early fall of 1945, the Patriarch sent Archbishop Alexei of Yaroslav and Rostov to New York to confer with local churchmen on terms for reconciliation.

The result was that in November of that year the American Sobor (General Council) meeting at Cleveland, Ohio, adopted a resolution requesting the Patriarch "to continue the Russian Orthodox Church in America in his fold as its spiritual head" provided the American Church retained full administrative autonomy (New York *Times*). At the end of January 1947 Patriarch Alexei cabled the Metropolitan Theophilus of San Francisco that he had accepted the decisions of the American Sobor, and lifted the 1935 suspension of the American Church by declaring that "from now on . . . spiritual and prayerful communion is reinstated."

In Europe, meanwhile, the Russian Church had scored a triumph at the expense of the Vatican. A 10,000 word encyclical by Pope Pius XII (dated December 23, 1945 but not publicized until the middle of the following month) charged the Soviet Union with trying to stamp out Catholicism in Ruthenia (the former eastern tip of Czechoslovakia, which had been annexed to the Soviet Ukraine) and the Patriarch Alexei with having "by means of letters . . . openly and publicly invited the Ruthenian faithful to desert the Church of Rome." On March 17 the Moscow radio reported that the Council of the Uniate Church of the Western Ukraine had voted to return to the Russian Orthodox Church, thus causing a loss of 3,000,000 Catholics to Rome (*Newsweek*). Leaders of eight Eastern Orthodox Churches meeting in July 1948 in Moscow, voted "to establish close relations with Anglican and Protestant Churches throughout the world" but "decided not to approach the Roman Catholic Church, which they considered incompatible and hostile" (Joseph Newman in the New York *Herald Tribune*). Alexei, whose personal loyalty to Stalin was on many occasions reiterated, formally endorsed the Soviet-sponsored World Congress for Peace in April 1949, by designating two high Russian Orthodox churchmen to attend the Congress in Paris; and in August 1950 he identified himself with the Soviet position in regard to the Korean war by cabling the United Nations in protest against the "inhuman destruction of the peaceful population of Korea by American aircraft" and calling for "withdrawal of foreign troops from Korea and for the complete ending of the illegal war."

Alexei has been awarded the Bulgarian St. Alexandre Nevsky First Degree Order, Serbian For Deliverance Order, Syria First Degree, Liban Ordre Du Cedre, First Degree, and the Alexandria Patriarchate St. Apostle Marc Order First Degree. He also holds the Valorous Labor Medal of the Soviet Union and the Defense of Leningrad Medal for refusal to leave that city while it was under German siege. More recently, November 9, 1952, the Supreme Soviet conferred on the Primate the Order of the Red Banner of Labor for "outstanding patriotic activity during the great war for the Fatherland and after the war." "He would be a handsome cleric even without the rich garments of pre-eminence," wrote Delos W. Lovelace of Alexei shortly after he became Acting Patriarch. "He is tall and strong with a broad forehead, a wide bold mouth and a carefully trimmed spade beard." The New York *Sun* writer further observed that he "is familiarly fond of both the music and literature of the West"; and *Time* has spoken of him as "fastidious, ascetic, and persistently optimistic."

References
> Life 19:35-6+ Jl 2 '45 pors
> N Y Sun p18 O 16 '44
> N Y Times p21 My 22 '44 por; p9 F 3 '45 por; p7 N 10 '52 por
> Time 45:63-4 F 12 '45 por
> Britannica Book of the Year (1946)
> International Who's Who, 1952
> International World Who's Who (1949)
> Ten Eventful Years (1947)
> World Biography (1948)

ALLEN, WILLIAM L. April 17, 1896-
Labor union official
Address: b. c/o Commercial Telegraphers Union, 5913 Georgia Ave., Washington 11, D.C.; h. 812 Jefferson St. N.W., Washington 11, D.C.

As international president of the Commercial Telegraphers Union for the past twelve years, William L. Allen represents approximately 40,000 Western Union employees in the United States (except those in New York City). He had served as the international secretary-treasurer of the union (an affiliate of the American Federation of Labor) from 1928 to 1941. His work has included organizing, handling grievances, negotiating contracts, arbitration and conciliation. He also represents 250 United Press workers.

William L. Allen was born April 17, 1896 in Comnock, Ontario, Canada, the son of Gerard Allen, a teamster, and Mary (Cripps) Allen. After completing grade school, young Allen began his career in telegraphy in 1908 as a messenger, and soon became a Morse operator working chiefly in western Canada for various companies including the Canadian Northern Telegraphs, Grand Trunk Telegraphs, Canadian Pacific Telegraphs, and Canadian National Telegraphs.

In World War I Allen served with the Canadian forces in France and Belgium. After the war he resumed his former occupation and became a member of the Canadian National general committee of the CTU. He was one of the leaders in the struggle against that committee's attempt from 1925 to 1928 to withdraw from the CTU. According to the *Commercial Telegraphers Journal* (November 1941) Allen "represented the pro-International sentiment of Canada, as contrasted with the Communist-inspired 'Canada for Canadians' slogan which caused considerable bitterness during the mid-20's." In 1928 Allen became the chairman of the Western District, Canadian National System Division No. 43 of the CTU in Winnipeg, Canada.

In this post Allen served as local chairman, organizer and international representative in Canada. He also attended several AFL conventions and served as a member of committees on Post-War Planning, Education, and Transportation. He was also a delegate to the Trades

Wide World Photos
WILLIAM L. ALLEN

and Labor Congress convention in Canada in 1928.

After he was elected international secretary-treasurer of the CTU Allen undertook the editorship of the *Commercial Telegraphers Journal*, the official organ of the union, for which he wrote a number of articles. He has also written bulletins and a pamphlet entitled "The CTU and Why?"

Having served as deputy international president on many occasions, he was elected international president October 28, 1941, succeeding Frank B. Powers, who took over the offices of editor and statistician. As head of the CTU, Allen is the spokesman for all Western Union employees in the nation except the employees of Western Union in New York City, where the company's workers are members of the American Communications Association. When the CTU made an attempt in May 1953 to establish jurisdiction in New York City in a National Labor Relations Board election, the 5,000 Western Union workers in that city again voted, as they had in previous elections, to remain a part of the American Communications Association.

The CTU in 1948 secured an eight-cent increase per hour for its Western Union employees without resorting to a strike. Joining with the American Communications Association and the Child Labor Committee, the CTU in March 1950 opposed the efforts of Western Union to receive permission from the Wage-Hour Administration to pay their messengers less than the seventy-five-cent hourly minimum; the Western Union request was subsequently refused.

The first strike against the United Press that had occurred in forty-three years of contract relations between that company and the CTU was called in 1950. The dispute, involving tele-

ALLEN, WILLIAM L.—*Continued*

type operators and maintenance men, was settled after the UP granted a weekly raise estimated at $3.50. This was an increase over the company's offer of a general wage advance of $2.21 a week across the board. The company's demand for open shop was dropped.

When the Western Union division demanded a twenty-five cent hourly wage raise for the telegraph employees in 1951, Adolph Brungs, the president of the Western Union division, asserted that the Korean war had enabled the union to reopen negotiations on their contract because of a clause which stated that in the event of war the contract could be renegotiated. A strike was scheduled for July 2 but a tentative agreement was reached on July 1, and a decision (approved later by the union members) gave them a thirteen-cent hourly raise immediately, and a further four-cent increase to take effect September 1.

The CTU then called a strike in April 1952 against Western Union because that company would not grant its demand for a sixteen-cent hourly increase, a shorter work week with no decrease in pay, and other contract revisions. (The New York City Western Union employees were not involved in the strike as they had voted on April 2 to retain their membership in the American Communications Association).

The telegraph company asserted that the CTU's demands would cost $50,000,000 a year and could not be met without "jeopardizing its survival as a private enterprise." On April 17 Western Union proposed that the strikers return to work for sixty days to allow time for further bargaining. The union policy committee met to consider this proposal and after the meeting Allen stated that it was "lack of realism to expect the employees to return without a contract—with nothing at all but a ghost in the sky. Surely, before any return to work can realistically be expected, the company should make a realistic offer."

On April 18 the union definitely rejected the company's plan, Allen terming it "silly" and "ridiculous." He suggested that the dispute be referred to arbitration, but Western Union would not agree to this. On May 7, however, the company announced that their representatives would attend a Government-sponsored mediation session with the union. A new contract was agreed upon by the company and the union officials on May 23; Western Union offered a ten-cent increase to workers on a forty-hour week and a 20 per cent increase to employees who work forty-five and one third hours a week. The two-year contract also provided for a reopening of negotiations on a cost-of-living basis at the end of the first year.

On July 15, 1932 Allen married Ruth Delilah Smithburg. The labor leader is a member of the Eagle-Humboldt Lodge, the Independent Order of Odd Fellows and the Royal Arcanum, Illinois Council. The sports in which he is interested are golf, hunting, and hiking.

Reference

Who's Who in Labor (1946)

ALLEN, WILLIAM M(CPHERSON)
Sept. 1, 1900- Aircraft manufacturer

Address: b. c/o Boeing Airplane Company, Seattle 14, Wash.; h. "The Highlands," Seattle, Wash.

President of the Boeing Airplane Company since 1945, William M. Allen has guided the organization through the less busy postwar years into the period which again brought large Government orders for aircraft. Boeing, whose employees number 55,000, was recently chosen by the Air Force to manufacture intercontinental jet bombers to replace the B-36s, and the new plane, the B-52 Stratofortress eight-jet bomber, will soon be in production. A lawyer for twenty years, Allen acted until 1945 as counsel for the Seattle aircraft firm and for fourteen years as a director.

Born in the orchard community of Lolo, Montana, on September 1, 1900, William Mc-Pherson Allen is the son of Charles Maurice Allen, a mining engineer, and Gertrude Maud (Hughes) Allen. After receiving his B.A. degree from Montana State University in 1922, Allen continued his education at Harvard Law School, where he took the LL.B. degree in 1925. He then joined the law firm of Donworth, Todd and Higgins, in Seattle, Washington, the counsel for the Boeing Airplane Company, and in 1925 he was admitted to the Washington bar. The young lawyer quickly became familiar with the corporate structure of the airplane manufacturing company by handling details of the various organizational changes which took place, such as the setting up of Boeing Air Transport, Inc., in 1926 to carry transcontinental airmail. A company director since 1931, Allen several years later took charge of contracts and financing. At the beginning of World War II Allen drew up the first "cost plus fixed-fee" contract for war production, a form which was widely used thereafter.

The Boeing Airplane Company was founded in 1916 by William Edward Boeing, son of a wealthy lumberman. Boeing's interest in airplanes, which began as a hobby, became a business when he finished construction of an improved seaplane, the "B. & W.," in 1916. In 1917 Boeing moved his company to Seattle, Washington, where he began the commercial manufacture of planes. In World War I Boeing produced Model C trainers and flying patrol boats for the Government. The company met its first postwar reconversion by producing Hickman sea sleds and bedroom furniture; then in 1921 came its first big order, for 111 observation planes. For the next six years Boeing's production was exclusively military, including trainers, pursuit planes, and patrol bombers. In the 1920's and early 1930's Boeing led all other companies in aircraft innovations, producing an all-welded steel frame in place of wood, an all-metal monoplane with retractable landing gear, and an all-metal transport with the first automatic pilot and de-icing equipment. The Boeing four-engine "299," prototype of the B-17, was built in 1935, and the Stratoliner, the first pressurized cabin passenger plane, went on the market four years later. Heavy production schedules were maintained during the war when the B-29 Superfortresses were fabricated.

When urged to accept the presidency of the Boeing company after the death of Philip G. Johnson in September 1944, Allen was unwilling to leave his law firm, Holman, Sprague and Allen, because two important firm members were then serving with the armed forces. The chairman of Boeing, C. L. Egtvedt, headed the company for some months while the directors continued the search for a president. Persuaded after a time to accept the position, Allen took office on September 5, 1945.

The day before Allen became president, the Army Air Force advised Boeing to cease work at the Wichita, Kansas plant and on September 5 the number of Superfortresses to be delivered from the Seattle plant was reduced from 658 to 179. The company was forced to close temporarily and 25,000 employees were dismissed. There were no civilian orders for aircraft and while Boeing had been prepared for a decrease in Government orders, it had been expected that there would be a tapering-off period for reconversion.

In the crisis Allen was faced with the necessity for a quick decision and, according to *Business Week* (September 29, 1951), lived up to his reputation as "a man who pulls things together." He announced to a special staff meeting on September 6 that the Boeing Airplane Company would start construction on fifty Stratocruisers (a commercial version of the B-50) although there were no orders for the planes. A year later fifty-five Stratocruisers had been ordered by a number of airlines, among them British Overseas Airways and Pan American Airways. Boeing lost $13.5 million on these planes (*Business Week*), but Allen achieved his objective of holding together the engineering staff and providing the "continuity" which he felt was indispensable in his business. As quoted by the New York *Herald Tribune* (September 16, 1945), he maintained: "From the standpoint of national defense alone, it's necessary that the Boeing organization, possessing recognized skills and know-how should be kept together."

Under Allen's leadership, Boeing's engineering staff designed the B-47 Stratojet medium bomber, for which, along with guided missiles, some $17,000,000 in orders was secured. The Stratojet can attain speeds up to 600 miles an hour, can carry more than ten tons of bombs, and is characterized in its design by swept-back wings and tail surfaces. Allen warned against public complacency in November 1947, stating that people tend to depend on "paper" planes which are as yet only in the experimental stage and which require many years to be developed into real defense weapons. In 1948, at a time when shortages of material and strikes throughout the country had already slowed production on Stratocruisers and military orders, some 15,000 machinists at Boeing went on strike, demanding a union shop and a strict seniority clause. Boeing's president called the strike illegal and was upheld in his stand by the United States Court of Appeals, which stated that the International Association of Machinists had lost its right to bargain by striking. After five

WILLIAM M. ALLEN

months the strikers returned to work, under a contract which did not provide for a union shop or seniority provisions. Allen reorganized his management system, providing a rating system for every employee, and an incentive system for 2,000 of the workers. A profit-sharing plan which had been set up for some 300 officers of the company was extended to cover supervisors who had sided with management during the strike.

By 1951 Boeing had a backlog of $1,250,000,-000 in orders, employed 50,000 workers, and was engaged in filling Government orders for B-47 Stratojets, B-50 Superfortresses, and C-97 Stratofreighters. To help meet the production problem and to avoid overexpanding his company, Allen gave out much of the work on subcontracts. The cost of the expansion of the Boeing company itself was estimated at $15,000,000. Planning was also made for products to take up the slack should defense orders decline; these included guided missiles which could be used for peacetime purposes, a jet transport, an analog computer, and a gas turbine engine. In an appraisal of the United States' arms program, Allen said in February 1952, "We had better ask ourselves a vital question: Can we rearm, sufficiently and within the desired time, under our present guns-and-butter program? The answer to me seems as simple as this: If we are to have 'butter' in present quantities we cannot at the same time have guns on the desired schedule." (New York *World-Telegram*, February 5, 1952).

After Boeing's B-52 Stratofortress eight-jet bomber was chosen by the Air Force in July 1952 as its intercontinental jet bomber, the airplane company was given a letter contract for some seventy planes. The B-52 is said to have a speed in excess of 600 miles an hour, a range of 8,000 miles, and a ceiling of 55,000 feet. Discussing the complexity of the huge bomber's construction, Allen remarked, "Comparing a

ALLEN, WILLIAM M.—Continued
World War II bomber and the B-52 is like comparing a kiddie-car and a Cadillac" (*Time*, August 4, 1952). The first two prototypes of the plane, which was designed over four years previously, were put through successful tests in the spring of 1952. In a report reviewing the activities of Boeing during 1952, its president named as high spots of the year the test performance of the B-52, the production record achieved on B-47s, and the decision to construct the United States' first jet transport. The last-named plane will be ready for demonstration by 1954 and will be usable by either the Air Force or commercial airlines. Boeing's sales and other operating revenues for 1952 totaled $529,468,131 as compared with $235,870,980 in 1951 (New York *Herald Tribune*, October 29, 1952).

By his marriage to Dorothy Dixon on April 15, 1927, Allen is the father of two children, Nancy Dudley and Dorothy Dixon. After the death of his first wife in 1943, Allen married Mary Ellen Agen on December 28, 1948. The executive is a member of the board of directors of the Boeing Airplane Company and belongs to the Seattle, Washington State, and American Bar associations. He is a member of Sigma Chi and his clubs comprise the Seattle Golf, Rainier, and University of Seattle. An expert on air law, Allen has written a number of articles on the subject. He is a Protestant and a Republican. He turns to golf for recreation.

References

Bsns W p106 S 29 '51
Time 60:67 Ag 4 '52 por
Blue Book of American Aviation (1942)
Business Executives of America (1950)
Who's Who in America, 1952-53
Who's Who in Commerce and Industry (1951)
Who's Who in the West (1951)

ALVAREZ, WALTER C(LEMENT) July 22, 1884- physician; physiologist; author
Address: b. 700 N. Michigan Ave., Chicago, Illinois; h. Hotel Pearson, Chicago, Illinois

A consultant in internal medicine for twenty-five years at the Mayo Clinic, and professor of medicine at the University of Minnesota from 1934 to 1950, Dr. Walter C. Alvarez is an authority on the physiology of the digestive tract and its diseases. He is, in addition, a popular lecturer and an author of several books for the layman, among which are *Danger Signals* (Wilcox & Follett 1953), *Nervous Indigestion* and *How to Live with Your Nerves*. He also writes a syndicated medical column. He is regarded as one of the nation's experts on migraine headaches.

His contributions to medical science include pointing out the effects of small, unnoticed strokes in older persons, and the necessity of recognizing the influence of the mind in producing symptoms of disease. Editor-in-chief of *Modern Medicine*, and editor of the specialists' magazine, *Geriatrics*, he has written about 1,000 medical articles and editorials.

Walter Clement Alvarez was born in San Francisco, California, on July 22, 1884, the son of Luis Fernandez and Clementina (Schuetze) Alvarez. His maternal ancestors were pioneer settlers in Minnesota and Chicago. His paternal grandfather was the business agent for Charles V, Infante of Spain, in charge of the royal palace and estates. When Walter was four years old, his father became a Government physician in Hawaii and took the family there.

He believes the fact that his father was a physician influenced him in choosing medicine for a career. He also states, "When I was eleven or twelve I started reading science voraciously with no urging from anyone." Two subjects which particularly appealed to him were archaeology and geology.

At the age of seventeen, Alvarez returned to California to enter Cooper Medical College, now Stanford University School of Medicine. Among the extracurricular activities he enjoyed were track and gymnasium. He received an M.D. degree in 1905, then remained at the college during 1906 and 1907 as an assistant in clinical pathology.

The next two years he spent practicing medicine in Cananea, Mexico. Returning to San Francisco in 1910, he went into medical practice in partnership with one of his college professors and received training in internal medicine.

While practicing as an internist in San Francisco, Dr. Alvarez was assistant in the medical school at Stanford University during 1911 and 1912. The following year he did postgraduate work in physiological research at Harvard University under the guidance of Dr. Walter B. Cannon. Returning to his practice in San Francisco he became an assistant in research medicine and later an instructor at the University of California. He was made an assistant professor in 1924, a post he retained until 1926.

In his physiological research Dr. Alvarez obtained the first adequate figures showing normal blood pressure from youth to old age. He was one of the first practicing physicians to point out the importance of using statistical methods in medical research, and his researches in the laboratory soon became nationally known.

Dr. Alvarez found that the increasing demands upon him as a physician encroached upon his research work, and in 1924 he became an associate in the division of internal medicine at the Mayo Clinic in Rochester, Minnesota. He was later advanced to head of this division, and ultimately senior consultant at the clinic. He was also an associate professor of medicine at the Mayo Foundation, University of Minnesota, from 1926 to 1934 when he became a full professor.

He became editor of the *American Journal of Digestive Diseases* in 1938 and served until 1942. He headed a group of eminent physicians in May 1941 who published the first five of a series of seventeen booklets on medical diseases, written for the layman to replace the "old-fashioned medical encyclopedia" (*Time*, May 5, 1941). These booklets were sold in bookshops, drugstores, newsstands, and railroad stations.

The internist served as editor of the medical publication *Gastro-enterology* from 1943 to 1950. During the wartime shortage of physicians, he proposed in an article, "Diagnostic Time Savers for Overworked Physicians," that doctors speed up the care of patients by more accurate diagnosis. He advocated a few shrewd questions in place of elaborate laboratory tests, and more effort toward distinguishing the chronic complainers from the actually ill (*Journal of the American Medical Association*, July 31, 1943).

In *Geriatrics* (May-June, 1946), Dr. Alvarez stated that the brain can experience thousands of "little strokes" with no symptoms except changes in personality, and that doctors too often dismiss these patients as neurotic or hypochondriac. The strokes are a series of tiny blood clots and are "one of the commonest diseases . . . a slow petering out towards the end of life." At the first annual scientific assembly of the American Academy of General Practice in Cincinnati on March 7, 1949, he declared that fatigue comprises "one of the biggest problems in medicine," and that it most often results from nervous breakdowns (New York *Times*, March 8, 1949).

After retirement from the Mayo Clinic in 1950, he became its consultant emeritus in internal medicine. Moving to Chicago, Illinois, he resumed the practice of medicine, and in 1951 was appointed professional lecturer in medicine at the University of Illinois Medical School. As editor of *Journal of General Practice*, a responsibility he assumed in 1950, Alvarez addressed 3,000 doctors in San Francisco at an assembly of the American Academy of General Practice. He discussed the need for "frankness and indulgence" when a patient has an inoperable cancer or a degenerative disease of old age (*Time*, April 2, 1951).

Dr. Alvarez has written a medical column four times weekly since 1952 for the New York *Herald-Tribune*, syndicated in the United States, Canada, and South America. In this column he discusses such subjects as the value of electric stimulus of the brain in aiding the mentally ill (June 22, 1953), the tendency of young doctors to avoid "poorer country districts" (June 15, 1953), and the fact that at least "one in five American children" is so retarded as to require some specialization in his education (May 29, 1953).

Among the books he has written are *Mechanics of the Digestive Tract* (1928); *An Introduction to Gastro-enterology* (1948); *Nervousness, Indigestion and Pain* (1943), *The Neuroses* (1951), and *The Emergence of Modern Medicine from Ancient Folkways.* His lecture relating to quackery and folk medicine, given for the laity at the New York Academy of Medicine, is included in a book *March of Medicine* (1940) compiled by Columbia University.

Nearly all of the technical books which Dr. Alvarez has written have been translated into Spanish and Portuguese. *Time* calls his book *Nervous Indigestion* a "medical best-seller" and states that "laymen like his cheerful, chatty style, free from scientific double talk, and full of Aesopic richness of anecdote and character sketches in which many a reader may recognize

Austen Field

DR. WALTER C. ALVAREZ

himself" (October 11, 1943). *Danger Signals* describes recognizable symptoms of common diseases and has been condensed in the author's syndicated newspaper column.

Dr. Alvarez was First Caldwell lecturer, American Roentgen Ray Society in 1920. Hahnemann Medical College in Philadelphia awarded him an honorary M.S. degree in 1939. He received in 1951 the Friedenwald Medal, the highest award of the American Gastro-enterological Association. The following year he was given the American Medical Writers' Association Honor Award for distinguished contributions to medical literature. He is described by *Time* (August 16, 1943), as "tall, twinkly, immensely popular . . . with a hardboiled attitude toward illness."

He is an honorary M.S. fellow of the American College of Physicians and the American Medical Society and is a diplomate of the American Board of Internal Medicine and of the board of Gastro-enterology. He holds honorary membership in many societies, including the Royal Society of Medicine of England, and is a member of the National Academy of Medicine in Spain and the Gastro-enterologic Society of Paris. Alvarez was elected to the honor fraternities Sigma Xi and Alpha Omega Alpha. Interested in anthropology, he is a member of the American Anthropologic Society and was a founding member of the American Association of Physical Anthropologists.

The physician married Harriet Skidmore Smyth on February 22, 1907. They have two sons, Dr. Luis Walter, a physicist, and Dr. Robert Smyth, head of the Nashville Public Library (Tennessee) and two daughters, Gladys (Mrs. Raymond Archibald), and Bernice (Mrs. Bradley C. Brownson). Alvarez is six feet tall, weighs 180 pounds, and has hazel eyes and gray hair. He is a Republican and a Congrega-

ALVAREZ, WALTER C.—*Continued*

tionalist, and belongs to the University Club in Chicago. A former mountain-climbing enthusiast and a collector of early medical books, Dr. Alvarez now enjoys photography and reading. He has a library of books by physically and mentally handicapped writers from which he says "I have learned a great deal."

References

Newsweek 36:39 D 25 '50
American Men of Science (1949)
Webster's Biographical Dictionary (1951)
Who's Who in America, 1952-53
World Biography (1948)

ANDERSON, GAYLORD W(EST) Dec. 31, 1901- Physician; public health administrator; educator; author

Address: b. c/o School of Public Health, University of Minnesota, Minneapolis 14, Minn.; h. 2261 Folwell St., St. Paul 8, Minn.

A noted authority on public health administration and education, Dr. Gaylord W. Anderson has been director of the School of Public Health of the University of Minnesota since 1944 and Mayo professor and director of the school since his discharge from the Army Medical Corps in 1946. Before going to Minneapolis in 1937 to head the university's department of preventive medicine and public health, he had held important administrative positions in the Massachusetts Department of Public Health. Anderson is president of the Association of Schools of Public Health and in 1951-52 was president of the American Public Health Association.

The younger of two sons of Frank Maloy and Mary Gertrude (Steele) Anderson, Gaylord West Anderson was born on December 31,

GAYLORD W. ANDERSON

1901, in Minneapolis, Minnesota. He is of Scotch and English descent with forebears on his mother's side who came to America in the seventeenth century. His father, who was teaching at the University of Minnesota in the early 1900's, later became professor of history at Dartmouth College, Hanover, New Hampshire, where from 1914 to 1916 Gaylord attended the public high school. From Worcester (Massachusetts) Academy, at which he was a student from 1916 to 1918, he entered Dartmouth College to major in chemistry. There, as in secondary school, his extrascholastic interests were mainly literary: he worked on the college paper and yearbook and was student editor of the alumni magazine. Upon his graduation from Dartmouth with his B.A. degree *summa cum laude* in 1922, Anderson studied for several months at the Sorbonne in Paris and from March to July 1923 at the University of Zurich in Switzerland. After a year, 1923-24, as a teaching fellow in chemistry at Harvard, he enrolled in Harvard Medical School, taking his M.D. degree *cum laude* in 1928. During this period of study he was considerably influenced in deciding upon his field of specialization by Dr. Milton J. Rosenan, professor of preventive medicine and public health at the medical school. (In 1942 Anderson received his Doctor of Public Health degree from Harvard.)

On completing his year's internship at the Albany (New York) Hospital in 1929, Anderson began his work in the field of public health as epidemiologist in the division of communicable diseases of the Massachusetts Department of Public Health. In 1930 he was promoted to assistant director and in 1931 to director of the division, a position he retained until 1937. Concurrently, from 1931 to 1937, he served as Deputy Commissioner of Public Health in Massachusetts and as assistant in public health administration at the Harvard School of Public Health. For two years (1935-37) he was executive secretary of the Massachusetts legislative commission to investigate public health laws and policies. On October 6, 1937, at a meeting of the epidemiology section of the American Public Health Association in New York he reported on experiments in scarlet fever immunization with formalinized toxin that he began in 1931 and carried on with the help of the divisions of biological laboratories and communicable diseases in the Massachusetts Department of Public Health.

Dr. Anderson left his administrative and educational work in Massachusetts in 1937 to accept an appointment as professor and head of the department of preventive medicine and public health at the University of Minnesota. During most of the years that he held this position he also served in the Medical Corps of the United States Army, which he joined in the rank of major in July 1942. Stationed in Washington, D.C., he was attached to the division of venereal disease control in the Office of the Surgeon General in 1942-43. Anderson outlined a program of venereal disease education in the Army (*Journal of Social Hygiene*, January 1944), in which he pointed out that the success of such a program was dependent upon the individual soldier's participation, and that instruction must be presented in such a form as to appeal to all levels of intellect, with special attention to those in the lower half of the intellectual range.

As a lieutenant colonel from 1943 to 1945, he filled the position of chief of the division of medical intelligence in the Office of the Surgeon General, working with thirty assistants to obtain a picture of world diseases. He and his staff checked enemy newspapers and inspected captured enemy medical equipment to discover health conditions in areas to be invaded by the United States Army. Before American troops undertook to invade or occupy any country, Anderson provided their medical officers with a health report on the region. For his work in this service, the *American Magazine* (July 1944) called him "Advance Man for Invasion" and noted: "Thanks largely to Anderson, the United States Army can go anywhere in the world and be fully prepared to cope with diseases more dangerous than human enemies—such as bubonic plague in Southeast Asia, sleeping sickness in Africa, black fever in China, leg-breaking clams in the Solomons, and rabies-infecting bats in the West Indies." Anderson left the Army in 1946 in the rank of colonel, which he had attained in 1945.

During his last two years in the Medical Corps (1944-46) Anderson had been director of the School of Public Health at the University of Minnesota. In 1946 he was named to the newly established Mayo professorship in the university's School of Public Health, continuing as the school's director. An outline of Anderson's concept of public health was presented in the article "The Political Impact of Modern Science on Public Health" (*Annals of the American Academy of Political and Social Science*, January 1947). He stated that "the mandate of the people seems clearly to place upon the health department a responsibility for concerning itself with all forces of mortality, whether due to environmental, communicable, nutritional, physiological, or psychological factors—not be a mere chronicler of illness and mortality within the community." The maintenance of health, he added, is so complicated that unless the Government participated actively in various fields formerly left to private initiative, the best interests of the community would not be served. In 1950, with his associates, Anderson made a comprehensive study, supported by the National Foundation for Infantile Paralysis and based on the poliomyelitis epidemic in Minnesota in 1946, which indicated that children who have tonsillectomies during an epidemic of infantile paralysis run "a three times greater risk" of contracting the disease than nontonsillectomized children (New York *Times*, December 7, 1950).

An elective member of the governing council of the American Public Health Association (1943-44 and 1947-49), Anderson was also a fellow (1934), vice-chairman (1942), and chairman (1944) of the epidemiology section and a member of the committee on professional education (1944-50). In 1950 he became president-elect of this association, an organization representing the public health movement in the United States and in Canada, Cuba, and Mexico. It is divided into thirteen sections, each with its own committees and major health specialty, including laboratory services, health officers, statistics, engineering, industrial hygiene, food and nutrition, epidemiology, maternal and child health, public health education, public health nursing, school health, dental health, and medical care. On October 31, 1951, Anderson was elected president of the A.P.H.A. at its seventy-ninth annual meeting in San Francisco, to succeed William P. Shephard.

In his presidential address at the eightieth annual meeting of the A.P.H.A. in Cleveland on October 21, 1952, Anderson affirmed his acceptance of the definition of public health established in 1869 by the Massachusetts State Board of Health to "take cognizance of the interests of health and life among the citizens." Asserting that this mandate covered all forms of ill-health and all causes of mortality, he protested the resolution presented to the House of Delegates of the American Medical Association by John W. Cline which would limit health department activities to vital statistics, health education, sanitation, communicable diseases, and exclude any diagnostic or therapeutic services outside the field of infectious diseases. If put into action, he said, such a concept would eliminate all programs in the field of maternal and child health, sight and hearing conservation, degenerative diseases, and mental health, and would "turn back the pages of public health half a century." In support of his belief in the need for further expansion of public health programs, Anderson pointed out: "Today the degenerative diseases—cancer, heart disease, diabetes, mental hygiene, and other diseases of adult life—present the chief causes of mortality and the major public health problems." Anderson retired from the A.P.H.A. presidency in late October 1952.

Among articles written by Anderson in the field of public health are "Foreign and Domestic Trends in Diphtheria" (*American Journal of Public Health*, January 1947); "Professional Training for Public Health" (*Canadian Journal of Public Health*, January 1948); and "Endemic and Epidemic Diseases, 1870-1950" (*Journal-Lancet*, February 1950). He is also author of the chapter entitled "Regulation in Public Health" in *Regulatory Administration* by G. A. Graham and H. Reining (1943). In collaboration with M. G. Arnstein, Anderson wrote *Communicable Disease Control*, called "an important reference for the health officer and public health nurse, also for lay members of public health organizations, parents, and instructors in nursing schools" (*American Journal of Nursing*, March 1942). Three years later (1944) came the publication of volume one of Anderson's *Global Epidemiology* (with J. S. Simmons, T. F. Whayne, and H. H. Horack), a book described by the *Natural History* reviewer (November 1944) as "an invaluable guide to medical men. Its style is such that the layman will enjoy it too, and anyone contemplating a visit to the Pacific or Far East

ANDERSON, GAYLORD W.—*Continued*

will do well to consult it." The second volume of *Global Epidemiology* appeared in 1952.

On several occasions Anderson has visited Latin American countries as a representative of the United States, concerned with medical and public health education and the training of graduate students. He has lectured on public health at the Universidade de São Paulo, Brazil (1948), Universidad Nacional del Litoral, Santa Fe, Argentina (1948), and Universidad de Chile, Santiago, Chile (1948 and 1950). In 1951 he acted as adviser to the United States delegation to the fourth World Health Assembly, Geneva. In other advisory posts he has been consultant to the Surgeon General, United States Public Health Service; Surgeon General, United States Army; the Institute of Inter-American Affairs; and to the World Health Organization. He was decorated with the Legion of Merit in February 1946 for his war service.

Other professional organizations in which the former president of the American Public Health Association maintains membership are the Association of Schools of Public Health (president 1952 and 1953), American Epidemiological Society (president 1950-51), American Medical Association, and Massachusetts Medical Society. His Greek letter societies are Phi Beta Kappa, Alpha Omego Alpha, Sigma Xi, Delta Omega, and Alpha Chi Sigma. He belongs to the Minneapolis Auto Club and the Campus Club. His church is the Congregational. On October 26, 1929, Anderson married Viola Dennis, a former piano teacher; their daughter is named Gail Elizabeth. The public health administrator, who has gray hair and blue eyes, weighs 140 pounds and stands six feet tall. He votes independently of political party.

References

Am J Pub Health 41:1550-1 O '51
American Men of Science (1949)
Who's Who in America, 1952-53
World Biography (1948)

ANDERSON, JOHN W(ILLIAM) February 14, 1899- Commodore, American Merchant Marine
Address: b. c/o United States Lines, 1 Broadway, New York 4; h. Bergenfield, N.J.

Appointed Commodore of the United States Lines' fleet of forty-eight ships on May 21, 1953, Captain John W. Anderson is also master of the company's superliner, *United States*, the world's fastest merchant vessel and the largest ever built in this country.

Recognized as one of the most popular skippers in the American Merchant Marine, he has served the United States Lines for twenty-eight years as master of many vessels. He was captain of the company's luxury liner *America* from 1949 to 1952, and in 1948 and 1949 was skipper of what was then the Lines' second largest ship, the *Washington*.

During World War II, Anderson commanded the motorship *John Ericsson* (formerly the Swedish liner *Kungsholm*), and transported 130,000 troops among enemy ships and under enemy plane attack without a major incident. In the first World War he was an officer in the United States Navy engaged in transport service. Anderson now holds the rank of Captain in the United States Naval Reserve.

John W. Anderson was born in Jersey City, New Jersey, on February 14, 1899. He attended the local schools, then entered the nautical school at Fort Schuyler, Bronx, New York City, now the New York State Maritime College. At the age of fourteen he went on his first training cruise on the schoolship *Newport*, and two years later in 1915 graduated from the nautical school. He then went to sea as a quartermaster and won both his master's ticket and his first command within six years.

During World War I, Anderson held officer rank in the United States Navy and was assigned to transport vessels. He was a cadet officer on the American Line's *St. Louis* during 1916-17, and subsequently a junior officer on the *Manchuria*, the *Kroonland*, and the *New York*. When this country entered the war, he became third officer and then second officer on the *Bantu* of the Isthmian Line. At the close of the War, he was second officer on the *Westhampton*, operated by the United States Army.

At the age of twenty-two Anderson was appointed captain of the *Lake Girth*, and for the first time sailed as a shipmaster. He joined the United States Lines in 1925 in the employ of their subsidiary, the American Pioneer Line, as a captain in the Far East-Australia service, and in 1927 became master of the *Easterling*, of the Roosevelt Steamship Company. Anderson commanded several American Pioneer Line vessels, including the *New Orleans*, and in 1934 the *American Importer*, a passenger-freight vessel operated between New York and Liverpool.

Appointed commander of the troopship *John Ericsson* in 1942, he saw action at the North African landings where many vessels were struck and sunk, but the *Ericsson* was spared. After the war his ship transported war brides to the United States.

The ship *John Ericsson* was severely damaged by fire at the New York City pier in 1947 while Captain Anderson was on leave. It was then withdrawn from service and Anderson was made commander of the *American Merchant* in April 1947. This vessel, which carried cargo and passengers in North Atlantic service, won the Naval Reserve pennant the following September.

Anderson remained in her command until January 1948, when he was named master of the 22,846 gross ton transatlantic liner *Washington*, then the United States Lines' second largest ship, also in war-bride transport service. Captain Anderson directed the rescue of five crew members of a Navy plane lost off Nantucket Shoals in 1948. He was promoted to command of the company's superliner *America* in May, 1949, then known as the "queen of the American Merchant Marine" (New York *Times*, April 16, 1950).

At Newport News, Virginia, Captain Anderson watched the final work on the 53,000 gross ton superliner *United States,* constructed in 1951 and 1952 at a cost of $73,000,000. He was also on board when the ship, the largest commercial vessel ever built in this country, made her trial run. Put in North Atlantic service as a passenger vessel operated by the United States Lines, the flagship could be converted into a troop ship capable of carrying 14,000 men, a full Division. On her maiden voyage in July 1952 the ship exceeded all transatlantic speed records. She took the blue ribbon from the English Cunard liner *Queen Mary* and gave the United States for the first time in a century the record for the world's fastest passenger vessel, a speed of over 35 nautical knots, or about 40 land miles per hour.

Already familiar with the ship's structure and operation, Captain Anderson succeeded Commodore Harry Manning as master of the *United States* when the superliner sailed for Europe on her third voyage on August 8, 1952. On a return trip to the United States, in a record-breaking run in September 1952, he veered "eight miles off course" to avoid appearing to race the Cunard liner *Queen Elizabeth* to the New York City port. "I'm sure any Cunard captain in the same position would do the same thing," he said (New York *Times,* September 3, 1952).

At the end of her first year the S.S. *United States* had carried over 70,000 passengers, had travelled a total of 146,000 nautical miles, had completed 22 voyages during which her propeller shafts had never been stopped by machinery derangement, and had operated at full speed for 190 24-hour days.

In February 1953 Captain Anderson aided the freshman science class of Harrison High School, Ohio, in an experiment tracing currents of the North Atlantic. About midway between New York and Southhampton he dropped overboard eighty-six sealed bottles containing messages inserted by the students about their experiment. Then he forwarded the high school class a pilot chart of the North Atlantic which he had marked with the exact position where he had dropped the bottles.

After Commodore Harry Manning retired on May 1, 1953, Captain Anderson was named to succeed him as Commodore of the United States Lines fleet of forty-eight ships which includes the *United States* and the *America,* six Victory type cargo vessels and forty C-2 type of ships.

Commodore Anderson is the recipient of several honors. For his rescue of five crew members of a Navy plane lost off Nantucket Shoals in 1948, he was highly commended by United States Navy Admiral Thomas C. Kinkaid, commander of the Eastern Sea Frontier. He praised Anderson's "invaluable service, understanding, prompt action and efficient rescue as well as his "consideration and courtesies extended to survivors."

At a dinner on March 10, 1950, of the Alumni Association of the New York State Maritime College, Anderson was guest of honor. A month later he was inducted into the "Quarter Century Club" of the United States Lines in

COMMODORE JOHN W. ANDERSON

recognition of twenty-five years' service with the Lines. The Downtown Manhattan Association awarded him a scroll of honor on December 9, 1952, for his role in making a record-breaking run of the liner *United States.*

Anderson advocates a strong United States Merchant Marine as a peacetime security measure and as an auxiliary of the Navy in any emergency. "In a world of unrest it would be a great tragedy if we didn't continue to produce replacement vessels and maintain our merchant seaman training program," he stated (*Scholastic,* November 5, 1952). As described in the New York *Times* (August 5, 1952), Anderson has a "warm and friendly manner that has rewarded him with a host of friends among the travelling public."

On his voyages across the Atlantic he is usually accompanied by his two dogs, Eric, an airedale, and Chotapeg, a little golden cocker spaniel.

During his troop transport service Anderson met Mary Beard, of the Women's Army Corps, whom he married. They have a son, Charles. More than six feet tall, the Commodore is referred to as a "slim but powerfully built" man (New York *Times,* August 5, 1952). As quoted by George Horne in *Scholastic* (November 5, 1952), Anderson expresses his personal code, built around the sound idea that it is a lot easier to do a good job than it is to try to avoid it. "You have to devote a lot of attention and energy to gold-bricking. It is so much easier, provided you are doing a job you are equipped for, to get the job done simply and well."

"Popular with the men of his crew, the fifty-three-year old mariner is in many respects the direct opposite of the old school of seafarers. He is easy-going in approach, quiet-spoken as a thoughtful professor, casual in manner. But his men have come to know that these characteristics are not the mark of a slipshod commander."

References

N Y Times p31 Jl 9 '34; V p8 Ap 16 '50; p43 Ag 5 '52; p45 My 22 '53
Scholastic 61:6 N 5 '52

ANDERSON, MAXWELL Dec. 15, 1888-
Playwright
Address: b. The Playwrights' Company, 630
Fifth Ave., New York 20; h. New City, N.Y.

> NOTE: This biography supersedes
> the article which appeared in
> *Current Biography* in 1942.

Now in his thirtieth year as a Broadway
playwright, Maxwell Anderson has completed
his thirtieth play, *The Devil's Hornpipe,* written in collaboration with Rouben Mamoulian,
which is scheduled for a Broadway production.

A great many of Anderson's plays have been
produced in European capitals and translated

Kugelmeyer
MAXWELL ANDERSON

into more than a dozen foreign languages—with
the exception of Russian. A champion of democracy, he makes many of his heroes spokesmen for his ideas of liberty and justice. He
won a Pulitzer Prize for his play, *Both Your
Houses,* in 1933, and the New York Drama
Critics' Circle Award for *Winterset* in 1935
and for *High Tor* in 1936.

The son of a Baptist minister, the Reverend
William Lincoln Anderson, and Premely
(Stevenson) Anderson, Maxwell Anderson was
born on December 15, 1888 in Atlantic, Pennsylvania. As his father and mother moved with
their four children from parsonage to parsonage
and from State to State, Anderson gained experience in all types of farm work in Pennsylvania, Ohio, Iowa, and North Dakota. He also
recalls that he attended eight primary schools,
three high schools and two colleges.

He attended the University of North Dakota
where he played right guard on the varsity football team and took part in all college athletics.
He remembers that he saw a stage play for the
first time while in college. It was Ibsen's *A
Doll's House,* in which Alla Nazimova was

starred. He also remembers seeing Walter
Hampden in Charles Rann Kennedy's play, *The
Servant in the House.* However, he wanted at
that time only to write poetry, although he did
join the college dramatic society and admits that
he wrote and acted in the senior class play, a
musical farce.

After graduating in 1911, he went to California and taught English while earning his
M.A. degree at Stanford University. For three
years he was an instructor in English in the
Polytechnic High School in San Francisco.

The urge to write became stronger, and he
decided on newspaper work for his career. He
worked first on the *Herald* in Grand Forks,
North Dakota, then as editorial writer on the
San Francisco *Bulletin,* and later on the San
Francisco *Chronicle.*

He was discharged from some teaching and
newspaper jobs during World War I because of
the ideas he expressed about the war; one dismissal was for having suggested that Germans
were people, and another that Germany should
not bear the whole blame for World War I.

Anderson went east in 1918, at the invitation
of Alvin Johnson, of the *New Republic* staff
who had liked one of his poems, *Sic Semper.*
He continued to write poems and articles and
occasionally dramatic criticisms for the *New
Republic,* then went to the New York *Evening
Globe* as an editorial writer, and finally joined
the editorial staff of the New York *World.*

At this time he read Keats and Shelley and
Shakespeare, and later read practically all of the
world's poetry. He was one of the founders of
the poetry magazine, *The Measure.* His collection of poems, *You Who Have Dreams,* was
published in 1925 by Simon and Schuster.

On the *World,* Anderson met Lawrence
Stallings, a book reviewer, to whom he showed
his first play, *The White Desert.* Stallings liked
it and showed it to Brock Pemberton who,
despite the fact it was written in blank verse,
decided to produce it. In 1923, Anderson
recalls, plays simply were not written in verse.

After having the lines retyped so that the
poetic divisions would not confuse the players,
the play was given a tryout in Stamford, Connecticut. Yet, when a snow-covered hero in a
North Dakota scene declaimed in an Othello-
like fit of jealousy the audience laughed. Anderson and Pemberton worked the play over for its
opening in New York, but the critics were un-
impressed.

"The theatre tugged at me thereafter," Anderson admitted, and despite this discouraging
reception, he intended to go right on writing
plays in verse.

While listening one day to Stallings remin-
isce about his war experiences in France, Anderson got an idea for a plot, and brought into
the *World's* editorial office one morning soon
after the script of a war play. Stallings went
to work to give the characters the language of
the dug-out, but Anderson's story of the struggle between the captain and the top sergeant of
a marine company for the affections of a girl
of the countryside was kept intact. The two
worked in a high pitch of enthusiasm, doing
most of their collaboration on a bench in the
New York Public Library.

When the play was finished, Stallings persuaded producer Arthur Hopkins to read it. Hopkins agreed, very reluctantly, but liked it and signed Stallings and Anderson to a contract. The play, *What Price Glory?* with its realistic language debunked the glories of war, shocked many, but it had a long run on Broadway in 1924.

Until the play became a box office success, Anderson had not dared to give up his editorial job, for he had a wife and three sons to support. Moreover, he owed the bank at Nyack, New York, the sum of $500 which he had borrowed in 1922 to purchase three acres and a waterfall in Rockland County. Today, he owns sixty acres and the same waterfall.

Anderson resigned from the *World* in 1925 and, freed from editorial deadlines, wanted to do something to celebrate his start as a playwright. He walked around, but couldn't think of anything to do. Finally, he bought a cane and spent an afternoon flourishing it up and down Fifth Avenue. After that, he settled down to work.

Anderson and Stallings collaborated on two historical plays, *First Flight* in 1925, dramatizing General Andrew Jackson's early years, and *The Buccaneer,* about Sir Henry Morgan's piratical career, in 1926, but both had short runs on Broadway. Anderson's next play, written alone, in prose, called *Saturday's Children,* (1927) was a sentimental comedy of love in the modern urban equivalent of a cottage. It drew moderate praise from the critics and audiences.

George Abbott, who had acted in *The White Desert* and in *Saturday's Children,* collaborated with Anderson on a play called *The Feud.* "John Golden paid me a thousand dollars for it, and called in a Broadway 'play doctor'. My name wasn't used," Anderson recalled. "The play was a quick failure, so I was the only one who made any money on it."

His next play, *Sea Wife,* written in 1926, explored the folk legend of the island woman who loved a merman. It was in verse, and never reached Broadway, but it had one notable production at the University of Minnesota in 1932.

"My enthusiasm for my plays cools very shortly after they are written," the dramatist said, "but *Sea Wife,* I think, contains some fairly good poetry." His next two plays in prose, *Forfeits* (1926) and *Gypsy* (1929) were "dismal flops." It was at this point that he began to develop an outer integument of what he calls "chain mail and horsehide" as protective armor for the slings and arrows of critics.

The play based on the Sacco-Vanzetti case, *Gods of the Lightning,* on which Anderson and Harold Hickerson collaborated in 1928, was a failure. Anderson's single-handed effort, *Winterset,* about the same case however, won the New York Drama Critics' Circle Award—the first offered by that group—a silver plaque made by the sculptor Henry Varnum Poor, in 1935. His characters spoke blank verse naturally, and the main character, Mio, consumed with the desire to revenge his father, was compared by critics with Hamlet.

After the failure of *Gods of the Lightning,* Anderson wrote *Elizabeth the Queen,* which

was produced by the Theater Guild in 1930, starring Lynn Fontanne as the Queen and Alfred Lunt as the Earl of Essex. It was an immediate success, and audiences felt an exhaltation hearing "blank verse well spoken." Then followed other hits, *Mary of Scotland* in 1933, starring Helen Hayes, and *Valley Forge* in 1934, also in blank verse. A forceful study of corrupt politics, *Both Your Houses,* in prose, was presented in 1933 and won the Pulitzer Prize for drama for that year.

High Tor, produced in 1936, starring Burgess Meredith, successfully combined blank verse with colloquial prose. Both audiences and critics liked this comic satirical fantasy and it won the Critics' Circle award. In accepting the award, Anderson told the critics: "I have learned some simple facts about the theatre, the first being that the better you think you are the harder the floor will seem to you when you hit it, as you surely will."

In 1938 Anderson and Robert Sherwood formed The Playwrights' Company, the culmination of a long-time dream of Anderson's. They invited Elmer Rice, S. N. Behrman and Sidney Howard to join them, each dramatist putting in $10,000; five friends pledged a like amount. The company has prospered, although Anderson commented: "It hasn't been *too* successful. I'm glad it hasn't grown into something monstrous and monolithic . . . I'm glad I have a home in the theatre—one in which the best craftsmen are also the best company and even the turmoil of pre-production can be part of a good life."

The present membership of The Playwrights' Company includes the dramatists Maxwell Anderson, Robert Sherwood, Robert Anderson, and Elmer Rice; Roger L. Stevens, a business man with a good deal of theatrical experience, and John Wharton.

The dramatist continued to turn out a play each season, most of which proved popular with audiences, although some received "mixed" reviews from the critics. These included *The Star Wagon* (1937) a fantasy about a time machine, starring Lillian Gish and Burgess Meredith; *Knickerbocker Holiday* (1938) which included the still-popular "September Song"; *Masque of Kings* (1936) a verse tragedy about the Crown Prince Rudolph of Austria; *Wingless Victory* (1936), starring Katharine Cornell, a tragic portrait of a South Sea island princess who married a New England sailing ship captain; *Journey to Jerusalem* (1940) starring Sidney Lumet in the role of the twelve-year old Jesus.

World events soon had their effect on Anderson, and he turned from writing verse-tragedies to plays dealing with contemporary rebel-heroes who defy tyrants and die for liberty. Among these were *Key Largo* (1939) concerning the Spanish Civil War; *Candle in the Wind* (1941), an anti-Nazi play and a strong plea against dictatorship of any kind; *Eve of St. Mark* (1942) with scenes on an island in the Pacific where American soldiers face the Japanese, and *Storm Operation* (1943), written after Anderson had been with the troops in the North Africa invasion, and which

ANDERSON, MAXWELL—*Continued*

said very clearly that men ought to be willing to die, if necessary, to preserve democracy.

As in *What Price Glory?* the playwright shows that there is no glory in war—only hunger, fatigue and pain. His main character in *Storm Operation,* First Sergeant Peter Moldau, a role played by Myron McCormick, told the men on his invasion barge, "We all want to go home. I haven't met a soldier yet who wanted to buy in on these foreign parts. America—that's for us. But do you suppose we'd be allowed to keep a place like that if we weren't willing to fight for it—and run our chance of dying among these ruins to keep it? Hell, no! The year we go soft enough to say we won't fight for it there won't be any United States. Only we haven't gone soft yet."

At the end of World War II Anderson wrote *Truckline Cafe* (1946), which dealt with wartime infidelity of married couples. The criticism of this play was so vitriolic that producers put large advertisements in newspapers defending the playwright and his play.

Undeterred by the critics, Anderson completed *Joan of Lorraine,* in both blank verse and colloquial prose. It starred Ingrid Bergman and was an outstanding hit of the 1946 season. Then followed another historical play, in verse, *Anne of the Thousand Days* (1948), starring Rex Harrison as King Henry VIII and Joyce Redmond as Anne Boleyn. This, too, proved extremely popular with theatre-goers and received fulsome praise from the critics as well.

When the playwright was asked why he did not quote these favorable statements in advertisements, he replied: "Whether they praise or condemn my plays it's still my honest conviction that the critics have too much power. . . When critics say 'no' to a play, that is final. They operate a censorship—an unhealthy state of affairs—whether the critics are learned or unlearned, witty or dull, just or unjust. It's unhealthy because it's undemocratic. The people of a democracy should decide for themselves what plays they will see."

Anderson collaborated with composer Kurt Weill to write a musical version of Alan Paton's novel, *Lost in the Stars* (1949), which starred Todd Duncan. Although it won plaudits from the critics it was an expensive production and lost money both in New York and on the road. Nevertheless, Anderson and The Playwrights' Company which produced it felt proud to have presented this play. His play *Barefoot in Athens* was presented in 1951 with Barry Jones in the role of Socrates. It had only a short run, but was chosen as a Fireside Theatre play-of-the-month selection.

Although he has written the scripts for a number of successful motion pictures including *All Quiet on the Western Front* and *Rain,* Anderson disclaims any association with the recent moving picture versions of *Key Largo* and *Winterset.*

The playwright has also written for radio and for television, recently for the Ford Foundation's program, *Omnibus. The Trial of Anne Boleyn* was highly praised by television critics. In the 1930's John Royal, a vice-president of

the National Broadcasting Company, signed Anderson to do three original plays at the unprecedented price of $3,000 for each play. However, the dramatist's primary devotion is to the theatre even though he knows he can make more money writing for other media.

Other plays for future production besides *The Devil's Hornpipe* (which is a musical drama about the New York waterfront rackets with music by Alli Wrubel), are: *Adam, Lilith and Eve; Huck Finn,* and *Cavalier King.*

The strong, adverse criticism which some of Anderson's plays elicit may be due to his own belief concerning the theatre and the function of a playwright in a democracy. Many think the theatre should simply entertain. Anderson's credo is: "The theater is a religious institution devoted entirely to the exaltation of the spirit of man. . ."

Sometimes Anderson's heroes who resent totalitarianism, fascism and communism and "all other political patent medicines" wear doublet and hose, sometimes Army field boots, or buckled shoes, or tennis sneakers or even go barefoot, as in his last play, *Barefoot in Athens,* about Socrates. Anderson's heroines have been burned at the stake (as *Joan of Lorraine*), beheaded in the Tower (*Mary of Scotland*), shot (*Winterset*), drowned or stabbed while speaking verse. In spite of what the critics call "his rich gift for comedy" he goes on writing verse tragedies because he believes that "the theatre is a temple of democracy" and requires the language of poetry.

Speaking at a luncheon given in his honor on February 2, 1950, by the National Conference of Christians and Jews, Anderson stated that he agreed with the historian, Dr. Arnold Toynbee, that the solution to the world's ills is brotherhood, amity, tolerance, and understanding "that crosses all boundaries." He declared, "So long as weapons of war were comparatively inefficient men could afford to hate each other . . . there were always survivors. But when we begin to use hydrogen bombs it's possible that the survivors will be few or none. There is one hope for us: if men have got to the point where they can achieve anything they can imagine, maybe they will begin to imagine the most difficult thing of all, *a way to get along without wars.*"

For the past seventeen years Anderson has written his plays in a wooden shack, ten by twelve feet, in the woods back of his home. His first drafts, written in a ledger book in longhand in ink, require very little rewriting. He usually spends six or seven months plotting a play in his mind before putting it on paper. Writers admire his neat mind which can store up so much. His principal research source for his historical plays has been an eight-volume *History of England* by George L. Craik and Charles MacFarlane, published in 1821.

The playwright's preference for his Rockland County home to the bistros of Manhattan accounts for the fact that his name is seldom mentioned by the columnists. During rehearsals he sits in the back of the theatre, making notes. Later, he quietly offers suggestions to the actors. Directors report that he rewrites dialogue with lightning speed as occasion requires it.

He seldom attends the openings of his own plays, and admits that he has not read the reviews in many years. "The critics took all the pride out of me", he said with a wry smile.

Maxwell Anderson has earned his pinnacle in the theatre by following what John Mason Brown called "the hard, bare, lonely life of a writer who is fighting with all his might and moral passion against the bloodless whimperers who spell death of everything worth saving in this world. Maxwell Anderson rebels at everything cheap, transitory and mean on Broadway. He is a playwright who believes in the beauty of great words nobly used, a philosopher who dares to ponder upon the imponderables, a dramatist who is neither the defeatist he has been accused of being, nor one of what he calls 'the jugglers and vendors of rose-colored spectacles.'"

Anderson is a member of The Players. He is described as "a shy and comfortable man, about six feet tall and broad shouldered. He has a ready smile, a pleasant manner, and a love for people for whom he writes, and their meeting-place, the theatre, which he diligently serves" (Walter Alford, *Lost in the Stars*).

His first wife, Margaret Haskett, whom he married in 1911, died in 1931, leaving three sons. In 1933 he married Gertrude (Mab) Maynard, who died in 1953. They had one daughter, Hesper. Anderson's oldest son, Alan, directed Anderson's recent television plays on *Omnibus,* and the play, *Barefoot in Athens.*

References

New Repub 89:328+ Ja 13 '37; 89:386 Ja 27 '37; 91:193+ Je 23 '37
PM p23+ N 29 '42 por
Scholastic 31:19E Ja 15 '38 por; 37:20 Ja 13 '41 por
Stage 13:32+ My '36 por; 14:54+ O '36 por; D '38
N Y Herald Tribune O 30 '49
N Y Times II p 3 O 10 '43
Anderson, M. The Essence of Tragedy (1939)
Anderson, M. Journey to Jerusalem (1940)
Anderson, M. Off Broadway (1947)
Clark, B. H. Maxwell Anderson, the Man and His Plays pam(1933)
Flexner, E. American Playwrights, 1918-1938 (1938)
Kunitz, S. J., and Haycraft, H. eds. Twentieth Century Authors (1942)
Who's Who in America, 1952-53
Who's Who in the Theatre (1953)

ANDERSON, R(OBERT) B(ERNERD)
June 4, 1910- Secretary of the Navy; lawyer
Address: b. c/o Department of the Navy, Washington 25, D.C.; h. 2831 Wilbarger St., Vernon, Tex.

A Texas Democrat-for-Eisenhower, R. B. Anderson, was named on December 19, 1952 to the post of Secretary of the Navy. Prior to this appointment, Anderson had been, since 1941, general manager of the W. T. Waggoner

estate of Texas, the second richest in the country, encompassing approximately 510,000 acres of ranch land, with extensive oil and livestock interests.

From the time of his introduction to public life in the Texas State Legislature in 1932, Anderson had served in various official capacities which included Assistant Attorney General, State Tax Commissioner, chairman and executive director of the Texas Unemployment Commission and chairman of the Texas State Board of Education.

Robert Bernerd Anderson was born on June 4, 1910, on a farm near Burleson, Texas, in Johnson County, the son of Robert Lee Anderson, who was mayor of the town, and Elizabeth (Haskew) Anderson. (His parents still live on a farm, which they operate, in Johnson County.) In his youth, Anderson combined cotton and dairy farming with acquiring an education at a rural grade school and Godly High School. He attended Weatherford College, Texas, and was graduated in 1927. In an effort to earn his tuition for a law degree, he accepted in 1929 a position at Burleson High School, teaching Spanish, history, and mathematics, and coaching the newly-formed football team. Knowing little about the game, he learned basic football formations out of a rule book and coached the team to an undefeated record.

He resumed his studies at the University of Texas Law School in 1930 and, in his senior year, became a candidate for the Texas State Legislature. He managed to carry on his campaign and study for his law examinations concomitantly. State Senator Warren McDonald, at that time his roommate at the University, described Anderson as a "prodigiously fast" reader who was able to absorb the contents of legal textbooks while riding trains during week-end campaign trips. On the day of his graduation in 1932 with high honors, Anderson was elected to the State Legislature.

While making a nominating speech in 1933 in the Legislature, Anderson impressed one of the gallery spectators, James V. Allred, then attorney-general of Texas. A few months later Allred appointed the young lawyer assistant Attorney General. In 1933, Anderson was a Professor of Law at the University of Texas. When Allred was elected Governor of Texas in 1934, he named Anderson State Tax Commissioner, and also a member, ex-officio, of the State Racing Commission.

During Anderson's tenure of office as Tax Commissioner, he originated a plan for a sixty-inch pipeline to start from the Texas panhandle and terminate in Detroit, Michigan, to be built and operated by a public corporation, but the State Legislature voted it down. His proposal may have originated the Federal Government's later Big and Little Inch pipeline projects. Recently defending criticism brought against his proposal of the pipeline as a public corporation venture, Anderson maintained that back in the 1930's he offered it as a "depression project" which would have opened up new jobs "more economically feasible" than those provided by W.P.A. He also introduced a bill to organize the first social security agency in

R. B. ANDERSON

Texas which was passed by the Legislature. Governor Allred appointed Anderson in 1936 chairman and executive director of the Texas Unemployment Commission.

In 1937 Anderson became general attorney for the W. T. Waggoner estate and signed a ten-year contract at a salary of $15,000 a year. Four years later, upon the death of Robert Moore, the estate's general manager, Anderson was named to succeed him at a salary of $60,000. Under Anderson's direction the estate which he has described as a "common-law or Massachusetts trust," increased its holdings and interests. Among modern ranching methods introduced by Anderson was the use of helicopters in herding cattle. The ranch encompasses half a million acres extending over six northwest Texas counties, and its operations include refining of oil, manufacture of gas, tilling of farm lands, raising of livestock, and handling stock and bond investments.

Unable to join the armed forces during World War II because of a slight limp, the effect of poliomyelitis in childhood, Anderson served as a civilian aide to the Secretary of the Army. Other posts to which he was named are vice-president of the Associate Refineries, Inc., since 1943; a director of the Vernon *Times* Publishing Company, the Northwest Broadcasting Company, the Vernon Transit Company, the Vernon Industrial Association, Inc., The American Petroleum Institute, the Texas and Southwestern Cattle Raisers Association, and trustee of the Texas Wesleyan College, Fort Worth, and McMurry College, Abilene, Texas. He became chairman in 1949 of the State Board of Education and was twice elected to that office.

When Anderson's appointment as Secretary of the Navy was first discussed, he protested, "I've never paced the deck of a battleship and I come from Texas where it doesn't even rain."

Assured that a good business organizer was needed to fill the office, he decided that he could make a contribution, since his inability to take an active part in World War II had always been a great disappointment to him.

Designated by President Eisenhower in December 1952 to be Secretary of the Navy, Anderson resigned as general manager of the Waggoner estate and voluntarily relinquished his directorships in all his other business organizations. This conformed with the Congressional law that all Government appointees having power over defense contracts should divest themselves of private business interests and holdings, particularly when those companies might be in direct competition with, or customers of, the United States Government. Anderson told the Senate Armed Services Committee, "So far as I am concerned, I have examined my own conscience very carefully, and I know of no ownership which I have in any company which would ever impose any restrictions whatsoever upon my doing a completely loyal job for the Navy" (*U. S. News & World Report,* February 6, 1953).

Anderson, who was sworn into office on February 4, 1953, is in charge of the task of policy control in the Navy Department and is directly responsible for relations with the public, for morale and the budget. Other functions of the Navy such as Naval command, logistics, administration and controls, and business administration, are distributed within his Department. The Secretary of the Navy (like the Secretaries of the Army and of the Air Force) does not have Cabinet rank or direct access to the President, but is responsible to the Secretary of the Department of Defense which was created by the National Security Act of 1947. In a speech before the Second Annual Texas Congressional Forum two weeks after the election of Eisenhower, Anderson stated "We are being compelled to look forward for a long, long time to the maintenance of a system of defense designed first to deter the Soviet Union from deliberately initiating a general war and, secondly, to protect as much of the rest of the world as possible from Communist invasion and from localized Communistic aggression. . .".

Formerly president of the Texas Mid-Continent Oil and Gas Association and director of the General Mid-Continent Oil and Gas Association, Anderson has been one of the oil industry's most persuasive witnesses before congressional committees. He has also been a director and a deputy chairman of the Federal Reserve Bank of Dallas.

Anderson has been characterized as a modest, friendly, quiet-mannered man who usually minimizes his achievements, and who will "move and talk only after study." He is six feet one inch in height. He married Ollie Mae Rawlings of Austin, Texas, on April 10, 1935, and they have two sons, James Richard and Gerald Lee. He and his family like horseback riding and hunting, and own a modern ranch house in Texas; in Washington they have moved into a Colonial home in Kenwood.

He has received the honorary LL.D. degree from McMurry College and Texas Christian

University in Fort Worth, the honorary Litt.D. degree from Mid-Western University in Wichita Falls, Texas, and was named "Vernon's Most Distinguished Citizen." A close friend of Texas Governor Allan Shivers, Anderson was an active Democrat-for-Eisenhower in last year's campaign.

His clubs are the Dallas Petroleum, the Dallas Athletic, the Cipango, the Austin, the Amarillo, the Forth Worth, the K.C.C.H., the Knights Templar, the Maskat Shrine Temple, and he is a 32nd Degree Mason. He served as president of the Vernon School Board and was active in the Boy Scouts of America and in the United States Chamber of Commerce, and also in the Vernon branch of that organization. He is an active member of Vernon's Methodist Church.

References

> N Y Herald Tribune p2 D 20 '52; II p1 D 28 '52 por
> N Y World-Telegram p9 D 19 '52
> N Y Times p32 D 20 '52; IV p6 D 21 '52
> Newsweek 40:17 D 29 '52
> Time 60:11 D 29 '52 por
> U S News 34:90 F 6 '53
> Washington (D.C.) Post p21 Ja 20 '53 por; p48 Ap 19 '53
> Who's Who in America, 1952-53

ANDERSON, SIGURD   Jan. 22, 1904-
Governor of South Dakota; lawyer
Address: h. State Capitol, Pierre, S.D.; h. Webster, S.D.

The nineteenth Governor of South Dakota, Sigurd Anderson, was elected in November 1950 and re-elected in 1952 for a second two-year term ending January 1955. Governor Anderson, a Republican, is Scandinavian by birth, but has lived in the United States since early childhood, and has been active in South Dakota State and County affairs since shortly after graduation in 1937 from the University of South Dakota Law School.

A United States Naval Reserve officer, he was on active duty during the last two years of World War II and served in the Philippine Islands. He was Attorney General of South Dakota for four years beginning in 1947.

Sigurd Anderson, the elder son of Karl August and Bertha Thorstenson (Broten) Anderson, was born January 22, 1904 on a mountain farm near Arendal in Norway. His father, who had been a sailor, immigrated to the United States in 1905 and sent for his wife and two sons in 1906. They settled on a farm in South Dakota, about ten miles from Canton, in the southeastern section of the state. Anderson acquired United States citizenship upon his father's naturalization in 1912, and began his education at the Pleasant Ridge School in District Number 11 of Lincoln County. He then attended the high school department of the Lutheran Normal School at Canton, where his extracurricular activities included speech, debating and dramatics. "My mother," he stated, "was instrumental in interesting me in getting an education, and my high school debate coach

SIGURD ANDERSON

urged me to follow a speaking career." Even today he candidly admits that he is prepared to be "a public speaker at any kind of occasion."

On graduating from high school in 1925, Anderson enrolled at the South Dakota State College of Agriculture and Mechanic Arts at Brookings and participated in public speaking, literary and journalistic activities. The effects of scarlet fever prevented his return in the fall of 1926.

After working one year as a farm hand at Bancroft in Kingsbury County (to which his family had moved in 1925), and teaching one year in a rural school at nearby Melham in Clark County, Anderson resumed his studies at the University of South Dakota in Vermillion. He majored in government and received a B.A. degree *cum laude* in 1931, after which he taught for one year at the high school in Rapid City and for two years at Webster in Day County, his present legal residence.

Anderson returned to the University of South Dakota in 1937 to enter the law school, from which he received the LL.B. degree *cum laude* two years later. The need to work at odd jobs in order to meet expenses did not deter Anderson from participating in varsity debating and journalism; he received the Edward Hope prize for the best scholastic record in his law school class, and was the university's extemporaneous speech champion. He was elected to Phi Beta Kappa, Pi Kappa Delta (speech) and Delta Theta Pi (legal) fraternities, becoming chapter president in the latter.

After he began to practice law at Webster in 1937, Anderson became a member of the Young Republican League; in 1938, he was a successful candidate for the office of State attorney for Day County. In association with Republican County Chairman Sam Buhler, he managed the local G.O.P. campaign with such vote-producing energy that Republicans were

ANDERSON, SIGURD—*Continued*

elected to almost all County offices in an area previously dominated by Democrats.

Anderson was re-elected attorney for Day County in 1940 after a similarly vigorous campaign; he did not, however, finish out his second two-year term, as in August 1941 he was appointed Assistant Attorney General of South Dakota by Attorney General Leo A. Temmey and moved to the State capitol of Pierre. In the same year he was elected president of the Lincoln Club (described as "a Republican Statehouse group").

Anderson was retained on the Attorney General's staff when Temmey was succeeded by George T. Mickelson in January 1943, but he served under the latter only until March, when he was called to active duty by the armed forces. (Anderson had joined the United States Naval Reserve the previous fall).

Indoctrinated at the Naval training station established on the campus of the University of Arizona at Tucson, Arizona, he was commissioned a lieutenant (junior grade) and served at both the Bremerton (Washington) Naval Ammunition Depot and the Camp Shoemaker Overseas Staging Area at Pleasanton, California, before transfer to the Philippine Islands as a legal officer in the Leyte Gulf Command. In the Philippines he was stationed successively at the Naval Operating bases at Tacloban on Leyte and at Guiuan, Samar Island. Released from active duty as a lieutenant commander, his terminal leave concluded in February 1946.

In the following March he resumed law practice at Webster, and a few weeks later was endorsed by the Republican State Convention as its candidate for Attorney General of South Dakota. After his election in November, he became a member of the Republican State Executive Committee.

During 1947 and 1948 Attorney General Anderson took what has been characterized as "a vigorous stand on law enforcement matters," and has been credited with the elimination of commercial gambling in his State. In 1949 he was elected to the executive committee of the National Association of Attorney Generals.

Elected in January 1949 to a second term as State Attorney General, Anderson had served only half of that term when Governor Mickelson indicated in February 1950 that he did not desire re-election. Five candidates then competed for the Republican gubernatorial nomination, including Anderson, a World War II Marine "ace" named Joe Foss, and Boyd Leedum, a Rapid City lawyer. To secure nomination a candidate is required in South Dakota to poll 35 per cent of the total vote at the primaries, and Anderson polled just over that amount.

In the gubernatorial race the Democrats' standard-bearer, Joseph H. Robbie, Jr., was extremely popular with the farmers and the young voters, and a close contest was foreseen. Anderson campaigned on a "sound business" platform stating "the best government is the kind of government that is sound, solid and progressive" (*Northwest Republic* August 1951). He carried his message to every section of

South Dakota, and at the election defeated Robbie by a margin of approximately 55,000 votes. He was inaugurated January 2, 1951.

South Dakota's Legislature convenes only in odd-numbered years, usually from January 1 to March 1, but despite the brevity of the session in 1951, appropriations reaching a record of nearly $44,000,000 were authorized, and much new highway construction, financed in part by raising the State gasoline tax from 4 per cent to 5 per cent, was undertaken.

In the field of education, it was made possible to initiate by petition a re-districting of schools, while repeal of the existing retirement law enabled South Dakota teachers to share in the benefits of the Federal Social Security Act. Salaries of State employees were raised about 10 per cent and State World War II benefits were extended to veterans of the Korean War. Despite these added costs, which included the payment of a soldiers' bonus, Governor Anderson was able on October 1 to reduce the South Dakota sales tax from 3 per cent to 2 per cent.

The Governor personally made the recommendation, which was adopted by the Legislature, that a Legislative Research Council be established to provide for a more careful study of State government. This council made itself distinctly heard during 1952 when, following the disaster of the Missouri River spring floods which inundated Pierre and other places, a subcommittee thereof recommended that the 1953 Legislature "consider the advisability of memorializing Congress" with a request that all funds be withheld from the Federal James River Valley dam project unless it could be shown to be "desired by the people of the area affected by the project." Anderson himself served as a member of the Missouri Basin Inter-Agency Committee and chairman of the Missouri River States Committee during his first gubernatorial term, and is now chairman of the Inland Governors' Conference. He is also vice-chairman of the Midwest Governors Conference.

In the 1952 election Governor Anderson defeated his Democratic opponent, Sherman Iverson, 203,070 to 86,396 votes.

He received an honorary LL.D. from Yankton College on June 1, 1953. He is a member of both the South Dakota and American Bar Associations, the Kiwanis, Masons (Shriner), and belongs to such service organizations as the American Legion, the Veterans of Foreign Wars and the Reserve Officers Association. He attends Lutheran Church services. His other interests include reading, geology, archeology, hunting and fishing.

The blond chief executive of South Dakota, who is still under fifty, is five feet eleven inches in height, and 165 pounds in weight, and has blue eyes. Mrs. Anderson, a journalist and teacher, is the former Vivian Dell Walz of Vermillion. The Andersons were married in Omaha, Nebraska, on April 3, 1937.

References

Northwest Repub p1 Ag '51 por

Who's Who in America, 1952-53

Who's Who in United States Politics (1952)

ANDRADE, VICTOR (MANUEL) (än-drä'dǐ věk'tôr mä-nwěl') Mar. 6, 1905-
Bolivian Ambassador to the United States

Address: b. c/o Embassy of Bolivia, 2220 Massachusetts Ave., N.W., Washington 8, D.C.; h. 3012 Massachusetts Ave., N.W., Washington 8, D.C.

For the second time heading his country's diplomatic mission in Washington, D.C., Victor Andrade presented his credentials on August 11, 1952, as the Bolivian Ambassador to the United States. In his earlier period of service in this post, from 1944 to 1946, Andrade had represented the Government of Major Gualberto Villarroel, in whose Cabinets he had previously been Minister of Public Health, Work and Social Welfare and Minister of Foreign Affairs. The new Ambassador has been spokesman in Washington for his country's views and policies on the recent nationalization of its tin mines—an issue of vital concern to the United States in buying tin for defense production.

A great-great-grandson of Bartolome Andrade, one of the leaders under Pedro Domingo Murillo in the fight for Bolivian independence in 1809, Victor Manuel Andrade was born in Chulumani, Bolivia, on March 6, 1905, the son of Manuel and Maria (Usquiano) Andrade. He was educated at the American Institute of La Paz, from which he was graduated in 1923, and at the University of San Andres in La Paz, where he majored in political sciences, taking his degree in law in 1930. At the institute he was a member of the glee club and enjoyed such sports as track, football, and basketball.

In his last years of study at the University of San Andres, Andrade also taught mathematics there until in 1930 he accepted the position of Under Secretary of Public Education. During the Chaco War he fought from 1932 to 1935 as an officer in the Bolivian Army, for which service he was awarded the Medalla de Guerra and the Mérito Militar. After being engaged for a year (1936-37) in a private mining business, Andrade became director general of the Savings and Security Bank, an office which he was to fill until 1943. Meanwhile, in 1940, he was elected a member of Cámara de Disputados (lower chamber of the Bolivian Parliament). Earlier (1939) chairman of the Bolivian delegation to the International Labor Organization in Havana, Cuba, Andrade also represented his country in the same capacity at the conference on social welfare held in Lima, Peru, in 1940 and at a similar conference in Santiago, Chile, in 1942.

As a member of the Movimiento Nacionalista Revolucionario, a political party formed in 1940, Andrade took part in December 1943 in the overthrow of the Government of President Enrique Pěnaranda by a group of army officers in cooperation with the MNR. In the Cabinet of Major Gualberto Villarroel, who was appointed by the revolutionary junta on December 20 of that year, Andrade was made Minister of Public Health, Work and Social Welfare. While visiting the United States in April 1944 as head of the Bolivian delegation to the International Labor Organization Con-

VICTOR ANDRADE

ference meeting in Philadelphia, he told newspaper reporters that the Bolivian Cabinet "was busy studying a plan whereby the excess profits of tin mine owners could be used to raise the standard of living among underpaid miners" (in the words of *PM*, April 20, 1944). At the same time he denied that the revolution of the previous December had been Nazi-inspired and blamed the failure of the United Nations to recognize the Bolivian Government for his country's inability to carry out social reforms among the tin miners.

In the election of July 1944 the MNR won a majority of seats in the Constituent Assembly, which immediately elected Villarroel Constituent President. To the post of Minister of Foreign Affairs in the new Cabinet the President on August 7, 1944, appointed Andrade, who shortly afterward was named Bolivian Ambassador to the United States. Andrade arrived in Washington, D.C., in November to take part in negotiations for American purchases of Bolivian tin. When he presented his letters of credence to Franklin D. Roosevelt on December 20, 1944, he said that his Government was then studying the Dumbarton Oaks plan "in order to contribute to the fullest measure . . . to the attainment of the ideal of collective peace and security" (quoted by the New York *Times*, December 21, 1944). In 1945 Andrade led the Bolivian delegation at the Inter-American Conference on Problems of War and Peace (February 21-March 8), held in Chapultepec, Mexico; and in April of that year was vice-chairman of the Bolivian delegation at the United Nations Conference on International Organization, which met in San Francisco. At the latter conference he introduced the subject of the revision of treaties, which he believed to be in the province of the General Assembly. In discussing this matter, before a commission of the conference, Andrade referred to a 1904 treaty with Chile which shuts off Bolivia from

ANDRADE, VICTOR—*Continued*

the sea. "My people, smothered by the Andes," he said, "look to the future with full faith that the world organization will one day study the problems which arise from Bolivia's geographical situation in the middle of the continent, and will recognize the right of its landlocked people to have contact with the rest of the world through its own outlet to the sea."

When, in the revolution of July 21, 1946, the Villarroel Government was deposed and the MNR party swept out of power, Andrade became a leader of the opposition to the new regime. In exile during the next few years, as were many of the prominent members of the MNR, he was from 1947 to 1949 a visiting professor at the New School for Social Research in New York City and from 1949 to 1952 a representative in Ecuador of the International Basic Economy Corporation. Following the election in the spring of 1951, the MNR, now the largest political party in Bolivia, was returned to power, this time under Victor Paz Estenssoro. In June 1952 Andrade was again appointed Ambassador to the United States, succeeding Ricardo Martinez Vargas.

Assuring President Harry S. Truman that Bolivia would make its mineral resources available for "peace" and "inter-American solidarity," Andrade presented his credentials on August 11, 1952. During that month he headed the Bolivian group negotiating with officials of the Reconstruction Finance Corporation, which buys tin for the United States Government. The action of the Estenssoro Government in nationalizing Bolivia's tin mines caused some concern. Andrade stated the case for Bolivia in a letter to the New York *Times*, November 28, 1952, and a letter to the Washington *Post*, December 2, 1952, pointing out in the latter communication: "The failure of the people of Bolivia to get real benefit from the sale of its mineral wealth lies behind the persistent unrest in my country, and is one explanation for the unstable political situation." On December 9, 1952, he reiterated an earlier assurance that Bolivia intended to deal fairly in compensating Americans who had invested in the mines nationalized by his Government. In a joint statement issued on January 16, 1953, Ambassador Andrade and the chairman of the Reconstruction Finance Corporation announced that an agreement had been concluded for the first United States purchase of tin from Bolivia since the nationalization of the mines.

Andrade is the author of the textbook *Aritmética aplicada* (1931), written when he was Under Secretary of Public Education for use in high schools. His other books are *Derrumbamiento* (1937), which deals with the Chaco War, and *Elementos de las condiciones sociales de Bolivia* (1943). One of Andrade's decorations is the Cóndor de los Andes. He is a member of the board of trustees of the American Institute of La Paz and of the Inter-American Committee of Social Security; he also belongs to the Ateneo de Bolivia, Círculo de la Union, and Club de Tennis.

Andrade and his wife, Blanca Salmon Tapia Andrade, whom he married on October 17,

1937, have two children, Lupita and Mario Victor. The "amiable" diplomat is dark-eyed and dark-haired, stands five feet nine inches tall, and weighs 184 pounds. Andrade, who plays the piano, regards music as his favorite recreation. He attends the Roman Catholic Church.

References

International Who's Who, 1952
World Biography (1948)

ANDREWS, BERT June 2, 1901—Aug. 21, 1953 Journalist; headed New York *Herald Tribune* Washington bureau since 1941; graduate of Stanford University; worked for Sacramento (California) *Star*; San Diego *Sun*; Paris *Herald*; was Albany correspondent of *Herald Tribune*; received Raymond Clapper and Heywood Broun awards; and Pulitzer Prize (1947). See *Current Biography*, 1948.

Obituary

N Y Times p15 Ag 22, 1953

ANDREWS, ROY CHAPMAN Jan. 26, 1884- Explorer; author; naturalist

Address: h. Colebrook, Conn.

> NOTE: This biography supersedes the article which appeared in *Current Biography* in 1941.

Explorer of the Gobi Desert, leader of the expedition which discovered the eggs of the dinosaur, associated for forty-seven years with the American Museum of Natural History, Roy Chapman Andrews knew from boyhood what he wanted to do, and his life is a prime example of the fulfillment of his early ambition. "Exploritis", he once said, "is a congenital disease and one is born an explorer."

His book, *Nature's Ways* (Crown, 1951) with illustrations by Andre Durenseau, enjoyed wide popularity among high school students. His autobiography, *Under A Lucky Star* (1943), was high on the best-seller lists for months. A book for younger readers, *All About Dinosaurs,* was published by Random House (1953).

Fond of quoting statistics on accidents in bathtubs, Andrews has always considered life in New York more dangerous than that encountered on any of his numerous expeditions. Tense moments with mutinous natives, hairbreadth escapes from tigers and lions in the Frank Buck tradition, never fazed him nor dimmed his enthusiasm. Now retired from active explorations, he spends his time writing books full of lively incident and graphic descriptions of animals and insects.

Roy Chapman Andrews was born January 26, 1884 in Beloit, Wisconsin, the son of Charles Ezra and Cora May (Chapman) Andrews. His father was a wholesale druggist. Young Andrews first owned a gun when he was nine years old and learned from a book how to mount the birds and animals he shot. He became the best taxidermist in the locality before he had finished grammar school. School subjects did not interest him except nature lore, and he preferred to study the animals and record the migrations of birds in the fields around his home. Among Andrews' favorite books were *Robinson Crusoe* and Frank M. Chapman's *A Handbook of North American Birds.*

Upon his graduation from Beloit High School in 1902 he entered Beloit College, majoring in science and paying his way by taxidermy. His sport was baseball, and his fraternity Sigma Chi. He was graduated in 1906 *cum laude* and was elected to Phi Beta Kappa. While in college he heard William Jennings Bryan speak and from him learned his first lesson in the technique of public speaking. Andrews later became a very popular lecturer.

Encouraged by a letter from the director of the American Museum of Natural History, he went to New York, arriving with only $30, and learned that there was no job for him. Undeterred, he offered to scrub the floors. The director suggested that a man of Andrews' education would not want to scrub floors. "Not *any* floors," said the determined young scientist, "but the Museum floors are different."

His earnestness and persistence were rewarded with a job in the preparations department of the Museum where he washed floors and mixed clay. One of his first important tasks was the construction and assembling of the model whale that still hangs by wire in the Museum and delights countless children.

Andrews' progress as a naturalist was swift. Sent to fetch the skeleton of a whale buried in sand on Long Island, he worked in freezing salt water and did his work so well that he was sent in the spring of 1908 on a one-man whaling expedition to Vancouver Island and Alaska. Later he was a special representative of the Museum aboard the U.S.S. "Albatross" on a voyage to the Dutch East Indies, the Celebes and Borneo to study whales. Then, as on later voyages, he was tormented by constant seasickness. He became assistant curator of the department of mammals at the Museum in 1911.

He studied whales in the waters surrounding Korea and Japan in 1911 and 1912 and discovered the California gray whale, until then believed extinct. For his thesis on this subject he received his master's degree from Columbia in 1913. Not yet thirty, he was the leading authority on the subject of whales and had filled a large hall in the Museum with specimens. During the first World War the naturalist served the Naval Intelligence in China and Mongolia.

Andrews was influenced by Dr. Henry Fairfield Osborn's theory that Central Asia would prove to have been the "dispersal center" of mammalian life, including man. After an expedition into the unexplored forests of Northern Korea and along the border of Manchuria, Andrews began a series of preliminary expeditions into Central Asia in 1916 and continued them through 1919. He then began to prepare for the American Asiatic Expedition which he led. The Museum did not have sufficient funds to meet the expenses, and, therefore, Andrews solicited financial aid from business men. He once spent half an hour talking to J. P. Morgan about the expedition to the Gobi Desert and was given fifty thousand dollars by the financier.

Wide World Photos

ROY CHAPMAN ANDREWS

The expedition, which consisted of forty men, 150 camels, and eight motor cars, started out in 1921 and the researches extended into the year 1932. The cost of the project was $700,000. The explorers uncovered the partial skeleton of the Baluchitherium, the largest known mammal, a species of rhinoceros, and the largest carnivore which was named the Andrewarches in honor of its discoverer. They studied the geology, fossil life, former climate and vegetation of the area. Orville Prescott wrote that their discoveries "widened immeasurably the sphere of man's scientific knowledge about prehistoric life on the high plateaus of [Central] Asia" (New York *Times*, September 10, 1943).

Important as were these findings and also the mapping of the Gobi desert and opening it to modern motor traffic, they were overshadowed by the discovery of twenty-five dinosaur eggs, each of which was nine inches long, and perfectly preserved.

On various expeditions Andrews had been shipwrecked, eaten monkey's flesh in order to survive; been lost chasing wolves, witnessed secret rites in a Buddhist temple, undergone bombing, fought off Chinese bandits, and escaped the accidental discharge of his own revolver. But his expeditions were generally free of mishap.

Because war conditions made explorations impossible and financing of Museum projects difficult, Dr. Andrews retired as director January 1, 1942. He is now an honorary director.

While a director of the American Museum of Natural History, he was the narrator on the *"New Horizons"* geography and science program of Columbia Broadcasting System's "American School of the Air."

Andrews' second profession is that of author. In addition to numerous articles, he has produced many books written in a brisk, non-technical style and all successful. They include

ANDREWS, ROY C.—*Continued*

Whale Hunting with Gun and Camera, 1916; *Camp and Trails in China*, 1918; *On the Trail of Ancient Man*, 1926; *The New Conquest of Central Asia* (1932); *This Amazing Planet* (1940); *Under a Lucky Star* (1943); *Meet Your Ancestors* (1945); *An Explorer Comes Home* (1947); *Heart of Asia* (1951), described by the *Library Journal* as a "rough, gory and extremely exciting adventure tale", and *Nature's Ways* (1951). Rex Lardner in the New York *Times* called this "the most fascinating non-fiction book I have come upon in a long time". On the other hand, the *Saturday Review* critic described it as "essentially innocuous", stating that full appreciation of nature required a blending of Dr. Andrews' style and Dr. Will Cuppy's.

The recipient of many honors, Dr. Andrews won the Elisha Kent Kane Gold Medal of the Philadelphia Geographic Society in 1928, the Hubbard Medal of the National Geographic Society in 1931, the Explorers' Club Medal in 1932, the Charles P. Daly Gold Medal of the American Geographical Society, the Medal of the Sigma Chi Fraternity in 1935, and the Loczy Medal of the Hungarian Geographical Society in 1937. He is the third American ever to win the Vage Gold Medal of the Royal Swedish Geographical Society (1937).

He is a fellow of the American Geographical Society, the American Association for the Advancement of Science, the New York Zoological Society, the National Geographic Society, the American Philosophical Society of Philadelphia, and a member of the Biological Society of Washington, the California Academy of Sciences, and many other societies. He was president of the Explorers' Club from 1931 to 1935.

He has received two honorary degrees of Doctor of Science, one from Brown University in 1926 and one from Beloit College in 1928.

He married Wilhelmina Anderson February 21, 1935. The couple live at "Pondwood," a farm in Colebrook, Connecticut, where they personally cleared every foot of ground. They spend the winters in Arizona. Andrews has two children, George Borup and Roy Kevin, by his first marriage, to Yvette Borup. His hobbies formerly included polo (which he taught the Tibetans to play) and fox-hunting, but he lists his present avocations as bird shooting and fly fishing.

Andrews has "a sense of humor, a zest for experience, and a keen appetite for the give and take of life," said Louis D. Froelick in *Asia*, and described him as "a remarkable organizer," and "a generous sharer with his associates in the credit for the achievement of the expeditions."

Roy Chapman Andrews is six feet tall and weighs 170 pounds. He has blue eyes, and hair which he reports with proper scientific exactness as "brown (bald)." In politics he is a Republican.

References

Am Mag 107:46+ My '29
Asia 24:638+ Ag '24
Fortune 15:101 Ap '37

Nat Geog Mag 63:653+ Je '33
Natur Hist 45:118+ F '40 pors
Science 99:16+ F 7 '44
American Men of Science (1949)
Andrews, R. C. An Explorer Comes Home (1947)
Andrews, R. C. Under a Lucky Star (1943)
International Who's Who, 1952
Who's Who Among North American Authors (1939)
Who's Who in America, 1952-53
World Biography (1948)

ARBENZ GUZMAN, JACOBO (ärbĕnz gōōz-män jä-kō'bō) Sept 14, 1913- President of Guatemala

Address: b. Palacio Nacional, Guatemala City, Guatemala; h. Casa del Presidente, Guatemala City

Inaugurated as President of Guatemala on March 15, 1951, Lieutenant Colonel Jacobo Arbenz took office at the age of thirty-seven, the youngest Chief Executive of any country in the Americas. He was also the second President of Guatemala to be elected by popular vote. His Administration has been marked by difficulties between capital and labor, and controversies involving Communists and anti-Communists, but he is still confident that he can restore his country's economy.

Because of Arbenz' efforts to reconcile these divergent elements, there has been a greater willingness to unite behind this President than previous leaders. He has also attempted to reorganize the national economy and raise production. On July 7, 1953, he signed the largest budget in the history of Guatemala, $73,000,000 which was approved by Congress for the fiscal year of 1953-1954. Of this amount, $10,000,000 will be spent on public education and $6,000,000 on national defense.

According to Sydney Gruson in the New York *Times*, (March 1, 1953), the Communists have been Arbenz's "most ardent supporters." He writes: "Whether he wanted to or not—and he has never indicated that he was willing to throw them over—Arbenz would have had difficulty in doing without the Communists. By the time he came to power they were in control of the unions, the Government's radio and newspaper propaganda organs, and various other key jobs that gave them power far beyond their numbers. . . He has had to pay the price of giving them more and more power. . . It is now a question in Guatemala whether Arbenz uses the Communists for his ends or the Communists use him."

Jacobo Arbenz Guzmán was born Sept. 14, 1913 in Quetzaltenango, Guatemala, the only son of Jacobo Arbenz and Octavia (Guzmán) de Arbenz. The elder Jacobo Arbenz was born in Switzerland, but he migrated to Guatemala at an early age where he later became a druggist. He sent his son to several small private schools and the West National Institute for Men in Quetzaltenango before entering him in the Escuela Politécnica, the nation's military academy, in Guatemala City. After graduation, Arbenz remained as an instructor.

With other young Army officers, Captain Arbenz took part in forcing General Jorge Ubico Casteñada to resign in July of 1944 after a thirteen-year regime. Dissatisfaction with Casteñada's successor, General Federico Ponce, led Arbenz to resign from the academy in July and go to El Salvador where he and his friends could work for the revolution with more freedom. On October 20 these officers and a small group of students ousted General Ponce and installed a Junta, comprised of Arbenz, Major Francisco Javier Arana and Jorge Toriello Garrido, a civilian, and ruled the country until their candidate, Professor Juan José Arévalo, won the presidency in the next election which was held in December 1944.

Dr. Arévalo, known as a "spiritual socialist," had been in voluntary exile in Argentina since 1935. His Administration, characterized by social security programs and an extensive labor code, met with opposition. Captain Arbenz became his War Minister and later National Defense Minister and Major Arana became chief of the armed forces. Dr. Arévalo recognized Arbenz and Arana as the strong men in his Cabinet and "played one against the other as his possible successor" (New York *Times,* March 1, 1953). On July 18, 1949 Arana was assassinated at Lake Amatitlán. This was followed by a short rebellion, the twentieth against Arévalo. "After that, Arbenz seemed to be the undisputed heir of the revolution. . . . Opportunist Arbenz, who has acquired $500,000 worth of real estate . . . and often downs highballs with some of Guatemala's richest capitalists, readily accepted the backing of the Communist-line labor political-action committee" (*Time* May 8, 1950). Upon resigning as Defense Minister in June 1950 to campaign for President, Arbenz received strong support from the anti-Communist Army as well as from the large left wing Partido Accion Revolucionario and, shortly before the election, the Popular Front party. He won the three-day election held November 11th through the 13th of 1950 with 267,234 votes out of a total of 407,596 and was officially proclaimed President by Congress on December 11, 1950.

The *Christian Science Monitor* (March 3, 1951) quoted Arbenz as stating " 'Communism is not a problem in Guatemala. . . . Guatemala is an undeveloped, agricultural country. Communism does not prosper in that kind of economy . . . As for misinformation, there is an unjust propaganda in the United States which creates the bad impression.' He explained the bad press as a conspiracy on the part of 'economic interests.' " The writer of the article saw a similarity "between the days when North China was being communized and the present official view of what has been going on in Guatemala." Discussing the same issue, Herbert L. Matthews in the New York *Times,* (March 27, 1952) wrote: "There are two reasons why decent, well-meaning and patriotic Guatemalans still think of the Communists as social reformers, and not as destructive revolutionaries. One is the way that these Guate-

Wide World Photos

JACOBO ARBENZ GUZMAN

malans have insulated themselves against developments of the outer world . . . An even stronger reason lies in the powerful and dominating sense of nationalism."

Upon taking office March 15, 1951 for a six-year term, President Arbenz and his coalition Cabinet promised to continue the "spiritual socialism" of the Arévalo Administration. In his inaugural address, he emphasized that his economic policy was based on private initiative with Guatemalan capital in the hands of Guatemalans. However, he soon realized that Government finances would not cover his program and he encouraged the International Bank for Reconstruction and Development to make a study of the country's economy. This group suggested foreign loans as one of the possible remedies for these difficulties.

Arbenz's Government also allocated $50,000 for institutional advertising in the press of the United States to offset "biased reporting" concerning alleged infiltration of Communists into the Guatemalan Government and into labor unions. Many officials believe that these reports have had detrimental effects upon their efforts to interest foreign investments in their Republic. During the summer of 1951 Guatemala was placed under a partial "state of siege" in order to control the dispatches by foreign correspondents.

One of the President's principal problems has been a series of labor strikes inspired by Victor Manuel Gutierrez, leader of the Guatemalan Confederation of Labor. Soon after he was inaugurated, 6,000 railroad workers went out on strike paralyzing the banana industry, the second biggest in Guatemala. Almost all of the union's demands were fulfilled.

It was also demanded that the Federal coffee *fincas* (representing forty per cent of the total acreage in coffee) raise their minimum wage from 40 cents a day to 80 cents, and that the

ARBENZ, GUZMAN J.—*Continued*

United Fruit Company (in control of the banana industry) increase its wage from $1.36 to $2.50 per day. Arbenz delegated his Economy Minister Dr. Manuel Noriega Morales, to review the labor problems, but when Federal customs workers struck for more pay the President ordered them to go back to work or be fired without severance pay. The customs workers returned to work without a raise, but the demands of coffee workers were met.

In the case of the United Fruit Company, (the country's biggest employer) the work stoppage was prolonged because of the September 1951 hurricane, which destroyed 10,000 acres of bananas at Tiquisate on the Pacific coast.

The company threatened to liquidate its holdings, a move which would have spelled disaster for the country. The Government drew up new contracts, but these included extra taxes and lower freight rates on the rail networks built and controlled by the company. Controversy over these left 4,000 workers unemployed.

The date of March 5, 1952 was set by a labor court to auction the company's Tiquisate properties to satisfy the union's claim for back wages. At the last moment, a labor pact was signed which halted the auction. It provided that the United Fruit Company was to have the right to cancel contracts whenever banana production costs were increased but that they would pay salary arrears.

Reviewing the conflict in his message to Congress on March 1, 1952, Arbenz said that no animosity existed toward foreign capital and he urged that the recent measures be reconsidered for greater harmony. (The settlement had been severely criticized by the General Confederation of Labor, headed by Victor Manuel Gutierrez.)

President Arbenz proposed a bill by which land worked by the share-crop system, and *fincas* of more than 220 acres having less than two-thirds of the land under cultivation be subject to nationalization. The right to use this land and other State farms was to be given peasant families without land, although ownership was to remain with the national Government. The maximum grant would be fifty-five acres per family. In proposing this, Arbenz stated that 2 per cent of the agricultural population owned 70 percent of the arable land. The expropriated owners were to be compensated by non-negotiable Government bonds.

The program was presented to Congress in May 1952, and passed as the Agrarian Reform Law on June 17, 1952, which exempts farms of less than 667 acres from expropriation. The new laws threw the country into a mild panic. Peasants began measuring off parcels of land listed by the National Peasants Union for expropriation, while angry small farmers created minor violence and large landowners wondered how funds would be raised to repay them for expropriated lands. The Export-Import Bank had refused to loan the Government funds for this purpose.

A Department of National Agronomy to supervise expropriations was created under the direction of Captain Alfonso Martinez, former

secretary to Arbenz. Plans were outlined for raising the funds by new taxes and percentages from coffee shipments.

In his annual message to Congress on March 1, 1953, Arbenz said (New York *Times*, March 3, 1953) that national and privately owned property had been distributed to over 5,000 peasants and that further expropriation of over 155,000 acres of United Fruit Company's Pacific coast holdings would help the nation's prosperity and benefit thousands of landless workers. On June 17, a report on the first year of the land reform laws announced that to date 110 Federal *fincas* had been distributed to the landless and 300,000 acres of private lands had been expropriated for distribution, for which $1,500,000 compensation had been paid in non-negotiable bonds. On July 14, 1953 the Government announced 8,000 acres confiscated from the United Fruit Company will be distributed to 1,500 peasants.

As an Army man President Arbenz has never considered himself a member of any political party. Although his regime has been widely noted for its susceptibility to Communist pressure, it has generally been willing to let anti-Communist groups express their opposition and campaign for civil liberties. According to *Newsweek* (July 6, 1953) it is the public market women of Guatemala City, under the leadership of Concha Estevez, who are the most effective anti-Communist force in the country.

The President is a Roman Catholic. He is described as a "quiet man who prefers to listen rather than talk . . . on the blond side, medium height, slim and well-built."

He was married in February 1939 to María Cristina Vilanova, whom he met while he was an Army cadet in 1935. They have three children, two girls, Arabella and Leonora, who are at school in Switzerland, and a son. Señora Arbenz is thirty-four years old, was born in El Salvador and educated in a convent near San Francisco. She is described (San Francisco *Chronicle*, March 4, 1951) as "an attractive combination of Eva Perón and Eleanor Roosevelt, being both beautiful and active in widely divergent civic and social affairs."

References

Christian Sci Mon p9 Mr 3 '51 por
N Y Herald Tribune p5 F 13 '50 por
San Francisco Chronicle p11 Mr 4 '51 por
Time 55:31 Je 8 '50 por
U N World 5:37+ S '51 por

ARCHIPENKO, ALEXANDER May 30, 1887- Sculptor; professor of art

Address: b. 1947 Broadway, New York 23; h. 274 W. 19th St., New York 11; Woodstock, N.Y.

In the forty-five years since Alexander Archipenko left Russia to enroll at the Ecole des Beaux Arts in Paris, he has introduced many of the plastic innovations in modern sculpture. The first to experiment in the cubist-abstract idiom by using both convex and concave surfaces, he has modeled space and has pioneered in combining many materials such as terra-cotta, papier-mâché, cement, wood and plastic in one figure. His sculptures are exhibited in many public museums as well as in private art collections.

Archipenko is now preparing for his 111th one-man exhibition. Recently his sculpture and drawings have been displayed in museums in Guatemala City, Guatemala, in São Paolo, Brazil, and in the Museum of Modern Art *Sculpture of the Twentieth Century*, on view in the summer of 1953 in New York City.

Alexander Archipenko was born in Kiev, Ukraine, Russia, on May 30, 1887, to Porfiry Antonovich and Poroskovia Wassilievna Machova Archipenko. His paternal grandfather had been a painter of church murals. His father was a mechanical engineer and inventor, and for many years was professor of engineering at the University of Kiev.

Archipenko was privately tutored until the age of nine when he entered the Kiev Gymnasium from which he was graduated in 1905. He began studying painting and sculpture at the Kiev art school, but was expelled in 1905 because he criticized his teachers for being "too old-fashioned and academic."

During his youth, he enjoyed the mechanical and scientific problems of the workshop and laboratory, but was influenced by the rich emotionalism of art, particularly by the mystic appeal of the St. Sophia Cathedral in Kiev with its Byzantine frescoes and ancient ikons. He was impressed by the writings of Leonid Andreyev, and the revolution of 1905, which left its stain of blood and butchery in the streets of Kiev. Later he moved to Moscow where he worked and participated in many exhibitions.

The young artist, already a trained engineer and a sculptor of accomplishment, left Russia at the age of twenty to study at the Ecole des Beaux-Arts. This school, however, claimed his interest for only two weeks.

He set up a studio in a converted monastery off the Boulevard Montparnasse near the Hôtel des Invalides which also housed the school of Henri Matisse's and a studio of Rodin's. Archipenko spent much time studying ancient art at the Louvre, and a number of his pieces dating from this period indicate his interest in Egyptian, early Greek and Gothic sculpture.

Gene Lux, in *Creative Art*, wrote that "had Archipenko never again given proof of the strength of his genius, it would nevertheless have been amply demonstrated by his early realization (at twenty-one) that impressionism, with its softening influence, . . . could not express the aims of an age of science. and technological evolution."

Paris in 1908 was excited by the cubistic paintings of Picasso and Braque which stressed abstract form to produce a specific aesthetic sensation rather than merely to represent nature. Archipenko saw the possibility of applying the painters' cubistic technique to sculpture, and in his work of that period he introduced pure geometric form and abstraction. His sculpto-expressionism was first mentioned

Arman V. Wall
ALEXANDER ARCHIPENKO

in art journals in 1909, when he introduced it in Paris.

In 1910 Archipenko held his first one-man show at the Hagen Museum in Berlin which was followed by exhibitions in other cities of Germany; several of his works from this group were purchased by German museums. Two years later he opened his own school in Paris and created sculpto-painting, a process of grading materials with coloring so as to obtain new combinations of form and color and to emphasize new lighting effects. Professor Hildebrandt of the University of Stuttgart called him "the sole creator of the new idea of combining sculpture and painting as one art. . . . "Several plastic pieces dating from 1912 "represent a cross between man and machine, and are the first productions of constructivism now being developed by Russian, Hungarian and German artists in a purely abstract form."

C. J. Bulliett in his *Introduction to Archipenko's Exhibition* at the Ukrainian Pavilion at the Chicago World's Fair in 1933, wrote: "The French and Germans became excited over his sculptured figures that eliminated faces from heads and introduced great concave spaces where nature has thought best to mould convexities. Archipenko explained that he had a right to alter the plans of nature as he saw fit so long as he kept within bounds of an artistic unity of his own devising."

Archipenko worked on the problem of deepening the concave in modeling. One of his outstanding examples of concave sculpture is the *Madonna*, which though apparently without face reveals the Madonna's form through the outlining of cloak and figure. According to *The Art Digest* (October 1, 1936) his 25-inch-high marble *Madonna* "illustrates the revolutionary treatment of form which Archipenko uses. . . . In it he has literally turned the human figure 'inside out,' and presented concave masses

ARCHIPENKO, ALEXANDER—*Cont.*

where the curves of nature are convex. Nevertheless, the sculptor has retained a feeling of reality." In the terra cotta *The Bride*, now in the Seattle Art Museum, "he has conveyed his thought through the use of long graceful lines and the play of reflected light on the immaculate surface of his material. Here again the subject itself, a chaste woman, emerges from the abstract conception."

His *Circus Medrano*, constructed in 1913 in glass, metal and wood, and portraying a mechanistic, kneeling performer in a style reminiscent of Picasso, exemplifies how he resolved the technological challenge which the modern age presents to creative art. In the construction of the *Woman Before the Mirror* Archipenko used a real mirror in which the figure was reflected; together they formed one rhythmic entity.

He spent the war years, 1915 to 1918, in a Villa at Sumié, a suburb of Nice, loaned him by a wealthy friend. Modigliani was also in Nice at the time, and the two artists, who were close friends, were the first of the modernists to settle on the Riviera. Archipenko made an extensive tour in 1919 exhibiting his new work in various European cities including Zurich, Geneva and London.

Archipenko established himself in Berlin in 1921, organized a school of art (his school in Paris had been disbanded during World War I), and gave a number of one-man shows. In 1923 he went to New York City, established the Ecole d'Art, and has remained in America ever since. He became an American citizen in 1928.

He opened a summer art school in Woodstock, New York, and expanded it in 1929 on a new property; it now consists of several modern, handsome buildings in which he and his students live and work. Among the teachers in his New York school (which he has maintained for three decades) were the late John Sloan, and Constantin Alajalov, best known for his stage designs and magazine covers.

The sculptor invented a machine in 1924 which he called "Archipentura," or movable painting (Patent 1,626,496). Based on Einstein's theory of relativity, the device displayed a screen on which was painted a pure abstract form. By pressing a button, the abstraction gradually changed in form and assumed the particular shapes of many of Archipenko's sculptures. The machine was exhibited at the New School for Social Research in 1939, and has since been dismantled.

In 1935 and 1936 Archipenko taught at the University of Washington. He also worked and resided intermittently in California from 1933 to 1937. In the latter year he established a school of creative fine arts in Chicago and was associate instructor at the New Bauhaus School of Industrial Arts.

Archipenko created a statue of *Moses* for the benefit of artists exiled by the Fascist regimes of Europe. The seven-foot-high sculpture was completed in Chicago in 1939, but its planned tour was cancelled due to the delays of wartime railroad transportation. Twenty-two

of his paintings and most of his sculpture then owned by German museums were confiscated during the Nazi purge of "decadent modern art." His paintings are generally of the female nude and are a direct development of his sculpture, striking the same emotional note found in his bronzes and marbles.

Archipenko taught at the University of Kansas City in 1950, and created for the entrance to the University grounds two abstract statues in iron, twenty-one feet high. After touring with an exhibition of his work in southern cities in 1950, he exhibited at the Milwaukee Art Institute, the Art Institute of Chicago, the Universities of Oregon, Washington, and Delaware, and Rutgers University. He has had 110 one-man shows in the Americas, Europe and Japan. He has over 1000 of his works in many museums and private collections throughout the world.

He has also been active as a lecturer; in the last two years he has given lectures at the University of Delaware, Amherst College, Rutgers University, the University of New Hampshire, and Allegheny College. In 1952 he was a delegate to the United Nations Educational, Scientific and Cultural Organization in New York.

Among work which he is creating and collecting for his 111th show are *Venus,* an example of his sculpto-painting, an abstract figure of obtruding colored wood and mother-of-pearl shells; an Egyptian-style mummy of terra cotta, and pieces in carved plastic, demonstrating his principles of modeling light in which space becomes the sculpture itself. As he phrases it, "Space is an element of sculpture. This is a psychological thing: those parts which are absent have the form of the absent object . . . which I want to present. I draw a parallel between space problems and the pause in music, which has as much meaning as sound itself. These sculptures are more lucrative for the imagination, and it is only through imagination that we can build a civilization. Since photography, representation is unnecessary. Now the imagination seeks to express nature through the use of symbol and abstract form."

A retrospective showing was given in 1948 at the Associated American Artists Galleries in New York. Of this, the New York *World-Telegram* (May 11, 1948), said, "Archipenko is at his best in his great monumental pieces, powerful, heroic expressions that are almost Biblical in their dignity and strength. These small works tend to be decorative and superficial."

Archipenko scorns the idea of artistic periods. "It is difficult to classify an artist into periods," he says. "I never belonged to schools; I was expelled from schools. I did research, I invented and experimented, I was then imitated. . . .Art is one creative flow upward, to discovery of truths in nature's forms, for each individual artist, and periods are simply pigeonholes in the minds of the critics."

Robert Coates, art critic of *The New Yorker,* wrote (May 15, 1948): "Archipenko has never attained the sublimities of simplification that Brancusi achieved, but he has come close to doing so, and his investigations of the possibilities of contrasting forms and textures have helped widen the scope of sculpture considerably. On the other hand, C. J. Bulliett described him in *Art News* (July, 1937) "the world's greatest sculptor since Rodin". Archipenko has never subscribed to the "cult of the ugly", Bulliett continued. He "sought and found new aesthetic laws and stylistic innovations that ever conformed to the universal urge for grace and rhythm."

Archipenko married Angelica Bruno-Schmitz, a sculptress, on July 21, 1921. He has no political, church or club affiliations. He is five feet eight inches tall, weighs 162 pounds, and has blue eyes and brown hair. He has a ruddy complexion and a stocky, muscular build. His New York art school and studio is small and crowded with examples of his prolific output. On opposite walls he has photographs of the work of his students.

References

Art Digest 11:16 O 1 '36; 14:17 Ja 1 '40
Illus Arts 5:31+ Ja '24
Illus Mag Art 31:103+ F '38
Bulliet, C. J. Apples and Madonnas; Emotional Expression in Modern Art (1930)
Columbia Encyclopedia (1950)
Who's Who in America, 1952-53
Who's Who in American Art, 1940-47

ARDEN, EVE April 30, 1912- Comedienne
Address: b. c/o Columbia Broadcasting System, 485 Madison Ave., New York 22.

The character "Our Miss Brooks" on radio and television is played by comedienne Eve Arden, who has worked in all the entertainment media including stock companies, Broadway revues, motion pictures, summer theatres as well as on network programs. Currently appearing Friday evenings on the Columbia Broadcasting System's TV show sponsored by General Foods, she plays the part of an unmarried high school teacher, beset by humorous and romantic difficulties. In a poll conducted by *Radio-Television Daily* in 1952, Eve Arden was chosen the Woman of the Year on radio. In a tour of the summer theatres in 1950 and 1951, she appeared in Ruth Gordon's plays *Over 21*, and *Here Today*. Her annual income is reported to be $200,000.

Eve Arden, whose real name is Eunice Quedens, was born on April 30, 1912, in Mill Valley, on the outskirts of San Francisco, California. An only child of divorced parents, Eunice was raised by her mother and aunts. Her mother is reported to have had some stage experience and both she and the aunts encouraged the girl's theatrical ambitions. From the Mill Valley grammar school Eunice went to Tamalpais High School where she appeared in school theatricals, playing the lead in a production of *Dulcy*.

Her theatrical career began at the age of sixteen when, she said, "I was dumped by my mother and aunt at the Henry Duffy office in San Francisco and told to get a job acting,

Columbia Broadcasting System
EVE ARDEN

which I did." Henry Duffy, who operated a stock company in the Alcazar Theatre in San Francisco and the El Capitan Theatre in Los Angeles, engaged the young aspirant, whose debut was made in *Alias the Deacon*. Eunice at one time worked as a clerk in the San Francisco department store, the White House.

For eighteen months Eunice acted with the Duffy company. Then she became one of a group of young players who, calling themselves the Bandbox Repertory Theater, toured the "citrus circuit" in an old Ford, carrying their "props" in a trailer. Managed by Katherine Turney, subsequently a screen writer, the troupe played in desert resorts and hotels from Palm Springs to Del Monte.

After a year and a half on the road, still using the name Eunice Quedens, she got a part in the Leonard Sillman revue, *Lo and Behold*, which opened at the Pasadena Community Playhouse and later moved to larger quarters at the El Capitan. Kay Thompson, Tyrone Power, and Teddy Hart were also in the cast. While in this show she was noticed by Lee Shubert who engaged her for the Billie Burke show, *Ziegfeld Follies*, which opened at the Winter Garden, New York, on January 4, 1934. Miss Quedens said that it was at this time that she took the name of Eve Arden, choosing it after looking over her cosmetics, combining Evening in Paris with Elizabeth Arden.

Her next theatrical engagement was in a Theatre Guild production, *Parade*, featuring Jimmy Savo, which opened at the Guild Theatre in May 1935, and in which Eve's work received favorable recognition. Of it, Brooks Atkinson wrote in the *Times*, "Count on the credit side. . . . Eve Arden's lorgnette humor which turns a song entitled 'Send for the Militia' into highly amusing satire."

This engagement was followed by one in another edition of the *Ziegfeld Follies*, also at

ARDEN, EVE—*Continued*

the Winter Garden, opening in January, 1936, in which Miss Arden was among the featured members of the cast and served as understudy for Fannie Brice.

Eve's mother died the following year and Eve returned to Hollywood to settle the estate. While there, she appeared in her first film, as a gun moll, in *Oh, Doctor* (1937), a Universal picture starring Edward Everett Horton.

Eve continued in pictures and soon established a reputation for ingenuity in building up "bit" parts. When Gregory La Cava cast her for a Radio Keith Orpheum (RKO) picture, *Stage Door,* Eve played her part wearing a live cat as a fur piece. Her work soon became typed, and the comedienne played for some time in roles with caustic, brittle humor. After *Stage Door,* she is reported to have worked in twenty-three pictures in three years.

Returning to Broadway in 1939, she played the part of Minnie Spofford in the Jerome Kern-Oscar Hammerstein musical, *Very Warm for May,* which opened at the Alvin Theatre in November. Her next appearance was in *Two For the Show,* at the Booth Theatre in 1940.

She then played the role of Maggie Watson in *Let's Face It* (1941), a Cole Porter show presented by Vinton Freedly, starring Danny Kaye, which had its première at the Imperial Theatre.

It was with her characterization of the Russian sniper in *The Doughgirls* (1944), a Warner Brothers' picture with Ann Sheridan and Charles Ruggles, that Eve Arden became one of the foremost comediennes in motion pictures. The year after, she began her career in radio, appearing with Jack Haley on the NBC Village Store program.

Other radio engagements followed, including work with Ken Murray and Russ Morgan, a featured role on the CBS Danny Kaye show, and work with Jack Haley and Jack Carson. In 1945 Eve was combining motion picture work and radio with appearances in summer stock at La Jolla, California, where she was with the Gryphon Players in *The Road to Rome.* In July of 1948 she opened in a CBS radio show entitled *Our Miss Brooks.*

Press opinion was divided at the inception of the program. Jack Gould wrote in the New York *Times* (July 25, 1948), "Eve Arden, who can deliver a line with a decidedly sophisticated and acerbic wallop, finally has won a program of her own . . . which has the makings of a Hooper hit." Harriet Van Horne of the New York *World Telegram* (August 11, 1948) conceded "the part is capably played by Eve Arden."

John Crosby of the New York *Herald Tribune* (July 23, 1948) wrote "although Miss Arden wisecracks indefatigably and courageously, still the program just isn't very funny." By March of the next year, however, he said: "I'll have to revise those churlish remarks to some extent . . . it is a very amusing program . . . there just isn't anyone in the business who can handle feline dialogue as well as Miss Arden."

Miss Arden's dander goes up and her eyes flash when she sees teachers caricatured as crabby, tired old maids. "It just isn't so," says Eve. She told a writer in *American Magazine* July, 1953: "Sure, Miss Brooks is just a make-believe teacher. Yet to me she's a warm, romantic, realistic, attractive woman. Teachers are like Miss Brooks. She's typical. I know many teachers now. I remember with affection those who taught me. I recall my third-grade teacher, umpteen years ago—Miss Ruth Waterman—she had dimples, big brown eyes, and was always smiling. I try to give Miss Brooks that same smiling quality."

Eve has said that about half of her fan mail comes from teachers. One in Maine wrote: "Thank you for recording the human side of our profession. We're not all social left-overs, nor withered gnomes."

The Alumni Association of Teachers College of Connecticut in 1952 cited Eve Arden for her "contribution toward humanizing the American Teacher." An article in *Collier's* (January 5, 1952) states that Miss Arden "has addressed the Los Angeles Federation of Teachers, and has received invitations to appear before PTA groups." Jack Gould of the *Times,* however, questions the service performed by the program, saying that "what that service could be defies any conceivable rationalization, because *Our Miss Brooks* is strictly tired theatrics having no discernible relationship to the classroom."

Miss Arden has appeared in more than forty pictures. Some of the best remembered are: *No, No, Nanette,* 1940, *Manpower,* 1941, *The Doughgirls,* 1944, *Mildred Pierce,* 1945, *Unfaithful,* 1947, *Voice of the Turtle,* 1948, *The Lady Takes a Sailor,* 1949, and *Three Husbands,* 1950.

Others include: *Oh, Doctor,* 1937, *Stage Door, Cocoanut Grove, Having Wonderful Time, Forgotten Woman, A Child was Born,* 1940, *She Couldn't Say No,* 1941, *She Knew All the Answers,* 1941, *Let's Face It,* 1941, *One Touch of Venus,* 1941, *Bitter Victory,* 1941, *Last of the Duanes, Slightly Dishonorable, Whistling in the Dark, Sing For Your Supper, San Antonio Rose, Bedtime Story, Obliging Young Lady, Road to Utopia, Cover Girl,* 1944, *A Day at the Circus, Letter of Introduction, Comrade X, Eternally Yours, My Reputation* 1944, *Patrick the Great,* 1945, *Pan Americana* 1945, *Earl Carroll Vanities,* 1945, *Tea for Two, The Kid from Brooklyn, Night and Day, My Dream is Yours,* 1947, *Goodby My Fancy,* 1952, and *We're Not Married,* 1952.

Miss Arden was married to Edward Bergen, a Hollywood literary agent, in 1939, and was divorced July 27, 1947. She was married for the second time on August 25, 1951, to the actor Brooks West, portrayer of Richard Rhinelander on the CBS television series, *My Friend Irma.* Her husband was Miss Arden's leading man in *Here Today.* Miss Arden has two adopted daughters, Liza and Connie. After undergoing a psychoanalysis Miss Arden said: "My real reason for getting my psyche explored was to avoid making major mistakes in raising our children." Her home in the Outpost Drive section of Hollywood exemplifies her two major hobbies, interior decorating and the collection of antiques. A dachshund and two Siamese cats are members of the household.

Miss Arden has been described by Edmund Leamy in the *World-Telegram* as "tall, slender, blue-eyed, blonde and glamorous in real life. Eve is as friendly and unpretentious as she is in *Miss Brooks,* and even more human." She is five feet seven inches in height and weighs 129 pounds.

References

Collier's 185:50 Ja 5 '52 por
Cue p21 S 27 '52
Look 16:52 N 4 '52 por
N Y Times II p5 F 4 '51
Motion and Television Almanac, 1952-53
Who's Who in the Theatre (1953)

ASAF, ALI May 1888—Apr. 2, 1953 Indian Minister to Switzerland; former Ambassador to Washington; lawyer; worked for thirty years for Indian independence, spending in that time a total of seven years in prison; served in Delhi Municipal Council (1923-46); held seat in Central Legislative Assembly (1934-46); on achievement of Indian independence, held first Transport portfolio in Nehru's cabinet (1946), and was appointed India's first Ambassador to United States (1947); delegate to special session of United Nations General Assembly in spring of 1947; accredited Minister to Switzerland (1952), Austria, and Vatican; outstanding Urdu poet. See *Current Biography,* 1947.

Obituary

N Y Times p23 Ap 3 '53

ASIMOV, ISAAC (ăz'ĭm-ŏv) Jan. 2, 1920- Author
Address: h. 265 Lowell St., Waltham, Mass. b. 80 East Concord St., Boston 18, Mass.

Reprinted from the *Wilson Library Bulletin,* Jan. 1953

Apologists for the detective story used to point defensively to the presidents and prime ministers who found their relaxation therein. Science fiction addicts are more brazen, but even so they take comfort in the fact that scientists themselves not only enjoy but even perpetuate the species. They point with particular pride to one distinguished American biochemist, Isaac Asimov, whose "sf" novels and stories have met with the approval of critics, the reading public, and scientists themselves.

Isaac Asimov is now professor of chemistry at the Boston University School of Medicine. He was born in a small Russian town, Petrovichi, on January 2, 1920, the eldest son of Judah Asimov and Anna Rachel (Berman) Asimov. Isaac, his parents, and his sister arrived in the United States as immigrants— they are all citizens now—in February 1923. A second son was born in 1929. The elder Asimovs have jointly owned a retail newspaper, magazine, cigar, candy and ice-cream store in Brooklyn since 1926, and Isaac was kept happily

busy reading the stock, besides "supplementary matter from every public library within ten miles." But, as one interviewer put it, "Isaac, alas, was not long for Earth. At the tender age of nine he became a science fiction fan."

It was his father, in fact, who gave him a copy of *Science Wonder Stories,* thinking such reading matter was educational. Later he bought the aspiring author a typewriter. When Isaac Asimov wrote the successful *Pebble in the Sky* (1950), he dedicated the novel "To My Father, Who First Introduced Me to Science Fiction."

After graduation in 1935 from Boys' High School in Brooklyn, young Asimov majored in chemistry at Columbia University, on scholarships in his freshman and senior years, receiving his B.S. in 1939, M.A. in 1941, and Ph.D. in 1948. During the war he was a chemist at the Philadelphia Navy Yard, performing chemical analyses. He was assigned to KP duties in such varied places as Virginia and Hawaii, although classified by the Army as a "critically-needed specialist."

He received a score of 160 in the Army General Classification Test (a score of 110 was required to take officers' training).

Asimov had begun to write science fiction at Columbia, with eight rejections in four months before making his first sale. He soon "got the hang of it," and has had little trouble placing his work since 1942. About fifty short stories of his have appeared in various science fiction magazines, most frequently in Street and Smith's *Astounding Science Fiction,* "to whose editor, John W. Campbell, I owe a great deal," he has stated.

Asimov is well and favorably known at Oak Ridge, Tennessee, and at Massachusetts Institute of Technology as author of a burlesque research article in this publication, about a mythical compound that reacted so fast it dissolved before water was added. During his doctor's orals at Columbia, the final question asked by one of the seven examining professors ("Please tell us something about the thermodynamics of thiotimoline") concerned an incident in one of his own stories. He managed to answer satisfactorily, and got his degree!

Pebble in the Sky (1950) tells the odd story of Joseph Schwartz, who raised one foot in the 20th century and lowered it in Galactic Era 827, some crude uranium having intervened. Margaret Scoggin called it "nice satire" and "well plotted," and the San Francisco *Chronicle* verdict was "adult entertainment." The year before its publication the Asimovs (he married Gertrude Blugerman July 26, 1942, and they have a son, David born August 20, 1951) moved to Boston. Besides teaching, "my field of research is cancer—a big field. No sensation of being crowded at all," he has said.

I, Robot was also published in 1950, *The Stars, Like Dust* in 1951, and a juvenile, *David Starr, Space Ranger* (under the pseudonym of "Paul French") in 1952 (Doubleday).

Asimov is now working on another David Starr story, and a new novel with the tentative title *The Littlest Robot.* Of *The Stars, Like Dust,* Virginia Kirkus wrote, "Top writing with a welcome interspersion of humor often rare in the field." Other Asimov novels are

ISAAC ASIMOV

Foundation (1951), and *Foundation and Empire* (1952), a selection of the Unicorn Mystery Book Club.

Dr. Asimov, described as a breezy, thickset young man, is blue-eyed and brown-haired. His favorite recreation is sitting still, his favorite sport making after-dinner speeches. He is a Democrat. In collaboration with Burnham Walker and William C. Boyd, he is the author of *Biochemistry and Human Metabolism* (1952), a textbook for medical students. In writing his sociological science fiction, he does not "worry so much about scientific gadgets as about the reactions of human beings in a scientifically advanced society."

Reference

American Men of Science (1949)

ATKINSON, ORIANA (TORREY) Sept. 4, 1894- Author

Address: h. 120 Riverside Drive, New York 24; Durham, N.Y.

Reprinted from the *Wilson Library Bulletin*, Jan. 1953

Oriana Atkinson was born in New York City, September 4, 1894, the daughter of Irving Torrey and his wife, Mary Ann Armstrong. On August 18, 1926, she married the drama critic and journalist (Justin) Brooks Atkinson. She has one son, Bruce Torrey MacIlveen, by a former marriage.

These facts are perhaps the only run-of-the-mill events characteristic of the career of the author who wrote the best selling account of her ten months' residence in Soviet Russia, *Over at Uncle Joe's*, and the novels *Big Eyes* and *The Twin Cousins* (Bobbs, 1951).

When queried about her ancestry, she wrote recently that nine generations back on her father's side and three on her mother's were American—"before that, Scotch and Irish." School teaching and writing were popular professions in her father's family.

An only child, Oriana was raised in the Greenwich Village section of New York and attended the Metropolitan Methodist Church from earliest childhood. "I added a pure soprano voice to the children's and young people's choir for ten years. I wrote poetry from an early age and all of it was published in New York magazines or newspapers. I was a great reader always and was allowed to read anything I wished. I loved to dance and had dancing lessons; I loved to draw and it was thought that I might be an artist. But I never deviated from my love of literature and writing."

Summers, she recalls, were spent at her grandfather's home in East Dorset, Vermont, "which was crawling with cousins of my own age and relatives of all ages. My mother was an expert needlewoman and reveled in all kinds of beautiful handwork. My father, a hearty, humorous, very gentle and kind man, was enormously popular. He was a civil service clerk and spent all his spare time reading and laughing."

In 1912 Oriana graduated from Washington Irving High School in New York City. She continued to write poetry for publication and also did occasional newspaper stories. Her stories and articles have appeared in the *Woman's Home Companion*, the *New Yorker*, *McCall's*, *Holiday*, and the New York *Times* and *Herald Tribune*. She has also done personnel and social service work, as well as a stint in a munitions plant.

During World War II Brooks Atkinson took a leave from his duties as drama critic for the New York *Times* to serve as foreign correspondent for the paper. He was sent to Moscow in 1945 and Mrs. Atkinson accompanied him. The account of her life among the Russians appeared in 1947 as *Over at Uncle Joe's*. A reviewer for the New York *Times* called it "an impious and witty book." Her literary chatting about the personal side of housekeeping, dining out, the life of women, etc., in the U.S.S.R. induced the Chicago *Sun* to comment: "There is nothing very profound about the book. It is light and enjoyable. Unless you are violently pro- or anti-Russian, you will enjoy it for what it is—a rambling, pleasant account of what the Russian people are like and why."

Mrs. Atkinson's novel *Big Eyes*, a story of a Catskill mountain village in the early 1900's, was published in 1949 with generally favorable reviews. The New York *Times* stated: "A large part of the novel's charm derives from the authentic backwoods which the author creates through vividly drawn minor characters. Mrs. Atkinson brings to her novel the same kind of astute observation of mores which marked her account of everyday life in Soviet Russia." A reviewer for the New York *Herald Tribune* commented favorably on her "excellent ear for local speech and a suitably brisk, ironic narrative style."

A romance of life in and around Catskill. New York, after the American Revolution, *Twin Cousins*, published in 1951, is the story of

ORIANA ATKINSON

Luther Ware and his wife Content, of the widowed Dutch wife of Luther's cousin, and of the inn they built on the Susquehanna Turnpike. Mary Ross described the book in the New York *Herald Tribune* as "an unassuming and unabashedly romantic tale that will please grownup readers, who, like most children, prefer their stories straight and active, uncomplicated by nuances." Carl Carmer considered it "an honest attempt at a realistic re-creation of a time and a place in our lives. . . . It is so convincing in its detail, so adept in its characterizations, so charming in its style that it deserves a place near the top of the list in recent historical fiction."

The last novel to complete this Catskill trilogy is now in progress. Mrs. Atkinson, whose interest in the Catskill area of New York State began some twenty years ago when her husband bought a farm in Durham, has traveled extensively in the region, visited museums, and studied old records, newspapers and books. Even more important in her research is getting to know the people of the area and their folklore.

The latest list of her recreations includes rose gardening and travel. She and her husband went around the world on a freighter in 1933; she has traveled widely in Europe and Asia. She loves the sea, the seashore, and sea bathing, but also enjoys living in the mountains. She collects old fashioned, heavy, dark ruby red Bohemian glass. She is a member of the Overseas Press Club, a political independent, and a member of the Methodist Episcopal Church. Blue-eyed and brown-haired, Mrs. Atkinson is five feet two inches tall.

References

    Atkinson, O. Over at Uncle Joe's; Moscow and Me (1947)

AURIOL, JACQUELINE Nov. 5, 1917-
Aviatrix
Address: Elysee Palace, Paris, France

Daughter-in-law of the President of France, and that country's most distinguished aviatrix, Madame Jacqueline Auriol broke her own international women's speed record on December 21, 1952 by flying a Mistral jet fighter an average speed of 534.375 miles an hour over a measured 100 kilometer course.

For her previous record, established May 12, 1951, when she took the title of "fastest woman in the world" from Jacqueline Cochran of the United States, she was awarded the Cross of Chevalier of the French Legion of Honor in September 1952, and the 1952 Harmon International Trophy for an Aviatrix. For her last record she was again announced the winner of the Harmon Trophy for 1953.

Yet Mme. Auriol took up flying only seven years ago, and in 1949 was so severely injured in a plane crash (in which she was a passenger) that she spent almost two years in hospitals. On August 29, 1953 she flew faster than the speed of sound in the new French jet interceptor, the Mystère IV, at 687.5 miles per hour. She is one of her country's best test pilots, and the only woman in her country engaged in that extremely hazardous occupation. Mme. Auriol hopes to start a women's flying service modelled after the American wartime W.A.S.P.S.

Jacqueline Douet was born on Nov. 5, 1917, at Challans, a small town in the Vendée, part of the French coastal section along the Bay of Biscay. Her father, Pierre Douet, was a wealthy shipbuilder and importer of wood from Scandinavia. She spent most of her childhood, which was carefully disciplined, at Nantes, where she attended school. She then studied art in Paris at L'Ecole du Louvre. On weekends she would go skiing with friends in the French Alps.

Through Jacqueline Martel, a ski champion, she met Paul Auriol whose father, Vincent Auriol (see *Current Biography*, 1947), at that time was one of the most prominent leaders of the Socialist party and had served a number of years in the Government.

Both families deemed the match of a wealthy shipowner's daughter to a Socialist leader's son inappropriate and they also decided that the couple were too young to marry. Jacqueline was sent to Sweden on one of her father's cargo ships while Paul Auriol toured Italy with his mother. However, two years after their first meeting, in February 1938, they were married in a small mountain chapel. They have two sons, Jean-Claude, and Jean-Paul.

When World War II broke out, Mme. Auriol refused to leave France while her husband was in the French Resistance movement, and lived out the war quietly in the country under an assumed name, chiefly concerned with avoiding the Gestapo and finding enough food for her baby son.

When the war ended and Vincent Auriol was elected President of the Republic, Paul became his father's press secretary, and he and

JACQUELINE AURIOL

Jacqueline went to live with M. and Mme. Auriol at the Palais Elysee, the French White House, in Paris.

Reacting against her long wartime retirement and anxieties, Mme. Auriol became her father-in-law's emissary at many social functions. She organized balls and receptions, and attended charity bazaars and fashion shows. Her beauty, wit, and fashionable clothes struck a bright note in the first dreary days of postwar France. She was initiated as a Chevalière du Tastevin, a society of wine connoisseurs, restricted usually to literary lights and statesmen, at the historic Abbey of Beaune in a ceremony attended by Winston Churchill and President Auriol who agreed that "the ancient ceremony had never been so gala."

Mme. Auriol at that time had already been flying for a few months. She had met Commander Raymond Guillaume, one of the most famous French pilots, at a dinner, and remarked that flying must be a job like any other. In reply, the aviator agreed, but added that it was also the closest thing he knew to being free. She became so interested that she and her husband, a former pilot in the French Air Force, accepted his offer to take them flying.

"All of a sudden", the aviatrix says, "I discovered a world where, no matter what your name, the only things that count are merit, skill and courage." She took flying lessons at Villacoublay, a large private airfield outside Paris, and received her pilot's license, first degree, on March 10, 1948, and second degree on April 20, having soloed in the required ten hours. She then wanted to learn stunt flying, but it was only after President Auriol had given her written permission that Commander Guillaume agreed to instruct her.

"Jacqueline makes Demosthenes inarticulate," explained M. Auriol after he consented.

At an Air Show outside Paris in July 1949, she exhibited her new skill before 30,000 spectators, the only woman among twenty famous French fliers. Three days later, a test seaplane in which she and Commander Guillaume were flying as passengers crashed into the Seine. Although the pilot suffered only a ·concussion and her teacher several broken ribs, every bone in Mme. Auriol's face, including both jaws, was broken, and her skull was fractured in three places.

She spent a year in French hospitals, and to take her mind off her mangled appearance, she assiduously studied algebra, trigonometry, aerodynamics and other theoretic courses necessary to obtain military and commercial pilot licenses. She qualified for these on September 26, 1950 and November 25, 1950.

After fourteen facial operations by French plastic surgeons, she came to New York with her husband, and at the Manhattan Eye, Ear and Throat Hospital underwent eight further operations to acquire a new face. At this time a psychiatrist convinced her family that her tenacious desire to fly again must be acceded to if they wished her to recover fully.

Mme. Henri Bonnet, wife of the French Ambassador to the United States, introduced her to Lawrence Bell, president of the Bell Aircraft Corporation in Buffalo, who gave her permission to take helicopter flying lessons at his plant. She soloed after eight hours and forty minutes and qualified for a helicopter pilot's license on January 23, 1951, after twenty-three hours of dual and solo instruction combined with very demanding classwork.

Mr. Bell calls her "the most extraordinary woman in the world. She has met fear head-on and conquered it. She has a complete passion for flying. . . In the four weeks she spent with us, even with her poor English and our poor French, she became the First Lady of Buffalo, the best Ambassador France ever had." (*Collier's*, January 12, 1952).

Returning to France in February 1951, after six months in the United States, a French newspaper said of her reconstructed face: "The nose is American but the smile is still French" (quoted by Blair Clark, New York *Times* Magazine, March 2, 1953). Lifetime friends failed to recognize her and Mme. Auriol found that she no longer wished to participate in the social whirl.

She became reacquainted with her two sons, and drove out daily to Villacoublay to watch the building of the Havilland Vampire jet fighter plane in which she planned to try for the new women's flying record. When she landed after her first solo flight in this plane, she burst into tears, her first display of emotion in two years.

"That day I experienced a sense of completeness, an extraordinary sense of power, . . . a sense of being in complete possession of myself," she told her family.

She went to Marignane, a large airfield near Marseille and the Istres airfield, and stayed there for three weeks preparing for her speed test. Finally, on May 12, 1951 she took off from Istres and flew her Vampire jet 818.181

kilometers an hour (509.245 miles) in a 100-kilometer (62.1 miles) closed-circuit flight between Istres and Avignon, officially breaking the world speed record for women of 469.549 miles an hour for the same distance set by Miss Jacqueline Cochran of the United States on December 10, 1947.

After her achievement, Mme. Auriol said, "I am very touched and very happy at having brought back to France the women's world speed record for a closed circuit. I want women who have the same ideals as myself to know that they can also cooperate, if necessary, in the renaissance of our aviation. I am also happy to have beaten this world record in a plane built by French engineers." (New York *Herald-Tribune,* May 13, 1951).

Commenting on Mme. Auriol's achievement, Jacqueline Cochran said, "The splendid French flying woman did not beat my record, which I obtained with a plane of a different type." She added, "The record obtained with a jet-propelled plane cannot annul the record obtained by a plane with a motor-explosion type of engine." (New York *Times,* May 18, 1951).

At the presentation ceremonies for the Harmon Award in the White House garden, Mme. Auriol handed a letter of introduction from her father-in-law to President Truman and "suddenly froze at the controls and couldn't think of a thing to say" (*Christian Science Monitor* November 22, 1952). "The President turned to Ambassador and Mme. Bonnet. 'Tell her I am no one to be afraid of,' he laughed. And the ice was broken." When asked by a Washington *Post* reporter "Why speed flying?" Mme. Auriol laughed and said, "It came naturally."

Three days afterwards, she visited the Manhattan Eye, Ear and Throat Hospital in the role of "most grateful patient" to thank the trustees and surgeons there for restoring her countenance. Walter C. Baker, President of the Hospital, returned his thanks and extended best wishes for happy landings. Mme. Auriol's former nurse remarked that "she is the only patient I ever saw who smiled when she came out of the anesthetic." (New York *Times,* November 22, 1952).

Returning to France, the aviatrix beat her own record on December 21, over the same measured 100-kilometer course, attaining an average time of 855.920 kilometers (534.375 miles) an hour on the second attempt. This time she flew a Mistral jet fighter of the French nationalized aircraft industry, powered by a Nene-Hispano Suiza motor.

Two days later, she christened the first French-produced Comet liner at LeBourget airport. Her next attempt will be to fly faster than the speed of sound (761 miles an hour) in a Mystère IV, the new French jet interceptor. (Recently in California, Miss Jacqueline Cochran became the first woman pilot to fly faster than sound)

She has been one of France's top dozen test pilots (and the country's only female test pilot) for the last two years, and has tested more than fifty different kinds of planes, ranging from the four-motored American Constellation to the tiny French sports planes. Her job is strictly full-time professional work, and she drives daily to Paris' Bretigny airport from the Palais Elysee to test and make reports on any type of planes seeking a governmental flying certificate.

Her associates at Bretigny call her "Auriol" and regard her as a very good test pilot. Her clothes now range from Jacques Fath creations for evening to aviation outfits, white from helmet to shoes, which become covered with grease during one day's work.

Mme. Auriol's great dream now is to form a woman's international flying corps which would free men for combat duty by enabling women to handle ferrying and transport assignments on the plan of America's wartime W.A.S.P.S. President Auriol supports her plan, as does General François Lechères. However, so far she has been unable to obtain official sanction.

Mme. Auriol spends most of her spare time with her two sons. The older one, Jean Paul, has already taken over the controls of a plane, and Claude loves to fly with his mother. On holidays, the family goes skiing at some small resort in the French Alps.

Mme. Auriol has an eager smile and boyish look. Since her accident, she has limited her friendships "to very few and all good": Jacqueline Martel, Edith Piaf, General Lechères, Lawrence Bell, Commander Guillaume, other pilots and some Buffalo friends.

Mme. Auriol once said: "When I began to fly I discovered suddenly that my life before had not been full and joyous but empty and superficial. . . Suddenly I wanted to know the truth, to find out what was important to me. And the truth is with me when I fly. Now I know that only life and death are important. When I am in the air, close to both, things finally take on their proper perspective. Nonsense becomes nonsense. The big things stand out, become alive" (*Collier's* January 12, 1952).

References

  Am W p11 S 30 '51
  Christian Sci Mon p16 N 22 '52
  Collier's 129:30+ Ja 12 '52 por
  N Y Herald Tribune p23 My 13 '51;
    p15 N 22 '52
  N Y Times p10 My 13 '51; S 21 '52;
    D 22 '52; D 24 '52
  N Y Times Mag p20+ My 2 '53
  Washington (D.C.) Post p28 N 1 '52

BAKER, GEORGE T(HEODORE) Dec. 21, 1900- Airline executive
Address: b. c/o National Airlines, Aviation Bldg., 3240 N. W. 27th Ave., Miami 42, Fla.; h. 4521 Sabal Palm Rd., Miami 37, Fla.

A pioneer in the popularizing of low-cost tourist air travel, George T. Baker is the founder and president of National Airlines, Inc., which operates a passenger and cargo fleet northward to New York City, and southward to New Orleans, Havana and Mexico City, from Miami, Florida, a system extending 2,829 miles. His company, established in 1934, carried air mail from St. Petersburg to Daytona Beach, using two small single-engined planes

GEORGE T. BAKER

and five employees. Nineteen years later it has a personnel of 2,705 and a fleet of aircraft which comprises eleven Lodestars, eight DC-6B's, six DC-6's, three DC-4's and two C-46's.

Baker has retained his position as president, director, and chairman of the board since the airline was incorporated October 8, 1937. He is credited with being responsible for placing Florida on a year-round basis "by introducing low-cost off-season flights, and inducing hotels in Miami to remain open during the summer and to cut prices to cost levels. It has paid off handsomely both for the airline and the hotels" (New York *Times,* August 12, 1951).

George Theodore Baker was born in Chicago, December 21, 1900, the son of George Henry and Emma (Langguth) Baker. He attended Senn High school, and during summer vacations worked on an Illinois farm. The owner was an amateur pilot who took the boy on short flights in his plane. By the time Baker was sixteen, he was able to operate the plane himself. However, he did not become interested in airline operation until after World War I, in which he commanded an Army tank unit.

After the Armistice he worked in the Northwest as a ranch hand. Later, he took courses at the Montana State School of Mines and obtained a job with the Forestry Service. When he returned to Chicago he "sold everything from candy bars to calculating machines and autos" (New York *World-Telegram,* December 30, 1950). His youthful interest in airplanes continued, and, reasoning that the best way to get a plane was to sell them, he found employment with Eastman flying boats.

By 1925 he had qualified for a pilot's license and had purchased the two single-engine Ryan cabin planes which nine years later were to launch him in the air transportation business. Today Baker still holds a commercial license with a multi-engine rating, and his personal achievement as a pilot includes the establish-

ment on November 2, 1940 of what was then a transcontinental flight record of 9 hours and 29 minutes.

He built up an investment brokerage business which was wiped out in the stock market crash of 1929, and this experience turned Baker to aviation as a livelihood. Using his two small planes, he began to fly charter flights for wedding parties, groups attending football games and for newspaper reporters and newsreel photographers flying films of the Kentucky Derby. This provided him with a modest income from 1930 to 1933.

When the Civil Aeronautics Board cancelled some airmail contracts in the South and invited new bids, Baker submitted the lowest bid of seventeen cents a mile for the 142-mile route from St. Petersburg to Daytona Beach, Florida. He was awarded the contract, and with four associates, two planes and a capital of $2,000 began operations on October 15, 1934. Describing the first year of Baker's airline, *Time* (June 26, 1944) reported, "Passengers were devil-may-care businessmen or vacationers. Baker kept his line going by doing everything himself. When a passenger arrived at the field, George [Baker] stopped sweeping up the hangar and tinkered with the motor a bit, opened the office, sold the ticket, and finally hedge-hopped his passenger to the other end of the line."

In its first year of operations National Airlines flew 400 paying passengers. Within two months the line had been extended to Jacksonville, and in 1937 added new air routes between St. Petersburg and Miami, and between Sarasota and Fort Myers.

Routes to Mobile, Gulfport and New Orleans were inaugurated by June of 1938. In 1944, the opening of a Miami-Key West run marked complete air service for Florida by National. With the permission of the Civil Aeronautics Board, routes were extended on October 1st of that year to Havana, and to New York City, via Savannah, Wilmington, and Norfolk. This expansion was made possible by increased revenue, a large new stock issue, and by adding five new Lockheed Lodestars to the National fleet. Baker was at the controls on the maiden flight to New York where Mayor LaGuardia met him and announced that National was the first to sign a contract for space at Idlewild International Airport. The effect of this new route was to "break potent Eastern Airlines' fifteen-year virtual monopoly on the rich north-south run along the Atlantic coast" (*Time,* June 26, 1944).

Rivalry between Eastern and National Airlines has been intense. In August 1950 CAB approved lower fares on the Miami-New York line. The order was suspended when Eastern protested that the new rates were "unrealistic." In 1951 Baker requested a new authorization for low-cost coach and special excursion fares on this line. Approval was granted July 30, 1951 for daylight air coach service at $58 between Miami and New York. This enabled Baker to promote his off-season tourist travel.

Another problem began for Baker in 1945 when NAL dismissed a union pilot. Lengthy negotiations between the company and the Airline Pilots' Association, an AFL affiliate, were begun in September 1945 but failed to produce an agreement, and on February 3, 1948 the union called a strike. Simultaneously, two other strikes occurred, based upon other issues, one by the maintenance group and one by the clerical workers, both of which lasted approximately nine months. The company responded by hiring non-union pilots, and in the ensuing ten month period was successful in maintaining its schedules.

Meanwhile, a Presidential Emergency Board which had been appointed to investigate the dispute, recommended reinstatement of the strikers, found National in violation of the Railway Labor Act, and criticized the company for a "lack of the responsibility consistent with the duties imposed by Congress upon carriers in interstate commerce." The recommendation was rejected by Baker on August 2 on the ground that the Board's action was tantamount to a "tacit endorsement of a strike instituted during the mediation process."

The airline was by now in a precarious financial position, and in September 1948, CAB announced that it would seek to revoke National's charter and order it to sell its routes and equipment to Pan-American, Delta, and Eastern Airlines. NAL officials "hinted that CAB's move was political and designed primarily to pressure NAL into settlement of its pilot strike." On November 24, the company agreed to mediation, the outcome of which was the rehiring of the striking employees. (*Aviation Week,* March 20, 1950). National's net loss in 1948 was $1,876,000.

In an attempt to resolve its financial difficulties, NAL signed an agreement in March 1949 with W. R. Grace and Company providing for the purchase of 174,000 shares of National stock which gave the former a forty-eight per cent interest in National. This marked the beginning of an upward swing for National, which has continued to the present time, chiefly credited to innovations introduced by Baker. These include coach fares along the East coast; luxury service; reduced family fares for businessmen who take their families with them; music for passengers, and open double-end hangars for repair work at Miami.

National instituted the Great Circle route by which 130 miles are eliminated from the run between New York and Miami. By such means, National was able to report a profit in 1949 of $38,963 during which year the company carried 335,000 passengers. By 1951 the airline ranked an estimated fifth in net operating income among domestic lines. With this stabilization of National's economic position, CAB terminated its actions against the line.

Baker also lowered rates of summer tours to Havana, Nassau, Jamaica, Mexico City, Haiti and Puerto Rico, introduced low-cost, off-season rates to Miami, and persuaded hotels to reduce their rates and to remain open during the summer months.

National's labor relations have improved, and in January 1950 when a second strike of the Airlines Pilots Association was threatened, it was averted because of the president's and the personnel's "acceptance of the human relations

tenets of Buchmanism," the Moral Rearmament Movement (*Pathfinder,* April 18, 1951).

In 1951 Baker asked the Civil Aeronautics Board to reduce National's mail pay from the Government to forty-five cents a ton per mile, the same rate paid the big four in the industry. He made the request "in view of National's growth and increasing economic self-sufficiency" (New York *Herald Tribune,* September 7, 1951). Baker and his associates were also in a position to re-purchase, over the objections of a strong minority of stockholders, the 174,000 shares held by W. R. Grace and Company, of which 68,000 were immediately resold at a higher price.

National Airlines, which receives no governmental subsidy, reported that its net revenue for the twelve months ending March 31, 1953, was $3,666,184. Attempts have been made to effect a merger which is now under consideration by CAB, of the National system with Colonial Airlines. National and Eastern have each been bidding for Colonial since 1951. Baker has said, "As soon as jets become available for commercial use in this country, we hope to pioneer in the field" (Washington *Post,* October 15, 1950).

George Baker and the former motion picture actress Irma Wilson were married March 21, 1941 and they have one daughter, Barbara Irma. He is a director of the First National Bank of Miami and a director of the Air Transportation Association of America. The airline executive enjoys deep sea fishing, golf, bridge, and poker. His clubs are the Indian Creek Golf, Bath, Key Largo Anglers in Miami and the Wings in New York City. Baker is an Episcopalian.

References

N Y Herald Tribune p22 Ap 16 '51 por
N Y Times III p3 Ag 12 '51 por
N Y World-Telegram p19 D 30 '50 por
Pathfinder 58:30 Ap 18 '50 por
Time 43:84 Je 26 '44 por; 52:96+ O 11 '48 por
Aircraft Year Book, 1951
Business Executives of America (1950)
Who's Who in America, 1952-1953
Who's Who in Aviation, 1942-43
Who's Who in Commerce and Industry (1951)
World Biography (1948)

BAKKE, E(DWARD) WIGHT (bä'-kē) Nov. 13, 1903   University professor

Address: b. 333 Cedar St., New Haven, Conn.; h. Rimmon Rd., Woodbridge, Conn.

Dr. E. Wight Bakke of Yale University established and developed at that university the Labor and Management Center where representatives of both work together in clinical sessions. He was selected by the Conference Board of Associated Research Councils, which supervises Fulbright Scholarship awards, to lecture during 1953 at the Copenhagen (Denmark) Graduate Business School.

While in Denmark he is assisting in training specialists for research in the structure

Anrod

E. WIGHT BAKKE

to take economics out of the cap and gown, and garb it in the overalls and blue serge of the workaday world. In 1940 he became Sterling Professor of Economics and director of post-graduate studies in economics. He interested Yale's Institute of Human Relations in his plan for a labor-management program, and in 1943 obtained a fellowship which permitted him to bring five labor and five management representatives to the university for joint studies.

The Labor and Management Center was established in December 1944. Dr. Bakke says labor-management differences are to be expected. He believes labor peace comes after there has been an understanding of why each side acts as it does. He said, "I am convinced that the lack of a theory of human behavior is our most serious handicap in the development of policy in labor relations. Management, union leaders and workers all must have a working knowledge, validated by experience, of such questions as: (1) why does the other person behave as he does? (2) why does he change from one kind of behavior to another? (3) how will this proposal or this action affect him—and why?"

Labor and management, Dr. Bakke says, "must cease viewing each other as mirror images. Many a squabble has resulted from management's desire to have unions behave as though they were businesses or from labor's desire that management behave as though it were a union."

Before starting the Center, Bakke studied a number of serious labor situations. He went to nine major centers of industry, including Detroit during a General Motors strike and Pittsburgh during a steel strike. In these centers, he talked to sixty labor leaders and sixty top spokesmen for management. In order to broaden his background, he made a list of the grievances, philosophies, fears, and hopes of both groups.

He reported after his investigating tour that management was anxious about the future, and that it fears not so much what labor's demand is now, but where it will end. "Every year it is something new. Will management eventually become employees of the union?" Labor's fears he summed up this way: "The boss has his job and we can't do it for him. He's got to have enough rope to work with. But if he starts using that slack to hang the union—then we just take the rope away!"

A nine-man policy committee supervises the Center, with Yale, management and labor each represented by three members. Bakke has insisted that an ivory tower approach to labor problems would be impracticable. He has not only established research listening posts in industrial centers from Detroit to Charlotte, North Carolina, but has brought in labor and management men.

Dr. Bakke lists his favorite recreations as music, tennis and hiking. He lists his politics as "Independent". He is a Quaker, although while attending the Yale Divinity School from 1926 to 1929 he served as a pastor of the Park Methodist Episcopal Church. In 1926 he married Mary Sterling. They have three children, Karl Edward, Carolyn and William.

and dynamics of human relations in organizations and in collaborating with those so trained on a pilot study in a Danish factory.

Edward Wight Bakke was born on November 13, 1903 in Onawa, Iowa, to Oscar Christian and Harriet Frances (Wight) Bakke. His paternal grandparents came from Norway in 1865 and his maternal ancestors came from England to Massachusetts in 1630. His father was a shoe merchant in Onawa. He has two brothers, one associated in business with his father, and the other an electrical contractor. Edward attended Onawa high school where his activities showed a wide range of interest—the glee club, debating society, and the baseball and track teams; he was also editor of the yearbook and president of the senior class.

He majored in philosophy at Northwestern University and received his B.A. in 1926, as well as a cup for public speaking and first prize in the National Oratorical contest. He was president of the Delta Sigma Rho fraternity, the debating and oratory society; he was also class orator, and a member of the Young Men's Christian Association and the glee club.

He went to Yale University for post-graduate study and was advised by Professor Albert G. Keller to change from philosophy to social science. He began his labor relations work by living on the dole in London.

"For nine months," he recalls, "I was the most unemployed man in England." While there he was influenced by Sir William Beveridge, John Hilton, Sir Llewellyn-Smith and by the many workers with whom he lived. A paper he wrote on this experience constituted part of the work toward his Ph.D. degree at Yale which he received in 1932.

He joined the Yale faculty in that year, was loaned to Harvard in 1936, and returned to Yale's economics department in 1937. He told the university's officials then that he intended

He states in his book, *Bonds of Organization*; *an Appraisal of Corporate Human Relations* (Harper, 1950), "You could call in the psychologist, the anthropologist, the economist, the political scientist, the doctors, the ministers. But practical men don't understand their jargon. They don't analyze the kind of human relations with which management and labor are familiar. It's too big a jump from findings having to do with the rat cage, the Hottentot society, or the 'free competitive' market to the factories, union halls or the picket line.

"The practical man is too close to details of daily operations to generalize effectively. The academic man is too far away from the details of daily operations to make their generalizations realistic. The former has too many fires to put out, the latter is not concerned with putting them out."

The titles of his books reveal his major interests. Among them are: *The Unemployed Man* (1934); *After the Shut Down* (1934); *Insurance or Dole* (1935); *The Unemployed Worker* (1940); *Mutual Survival: The Goal of Unions and Management,* (1946).

Government boards and bureaus on which he has served are: Social Security Board, Governor's Commission on Re-employment, Collective Bargaining Associates, National War Labor Board, Panel on Human Relations, Navy Department, President's Emergency Board, and the Pennsylvania Railroad and Brotherhood of Locomotive Firemen and Enginemen.

References

Look 12:23 S 14 '48
Nation's Bsns 34:41+ D '46
Who's Who in America, 1952-53

BALL, ZACHARY June 16, 1897- Author
Address: b. c/o Little Brown & Co., 34 Beacon St., Boston 6, Mass, h. 2130 N.W. 105 Ter., Miami, Fla.

Reprinted from the *Wilson Library Bulletin* April, 1953

"What actually decided me to become a writer? *Gone with the Wind.* I liked it so much that I decided to try to write like Margaret Mitchell." Thus Kelly R. Masters, actor, met the challenge of the decline of the stock company; thus he became Zachary Ball, author of short stories, the novel *Piney,* and the popular and the authentic books for teen-agers, *Joe Panther* and *Swamp Chief.*

Zachary Ball was born Kelly Ray Masters, June 16, 1897 in a log cabin near Millgrove, Missouri, the son of Abelino W. Masters, a farmer, and his wife, the former Iva Adelia Herrick. His boyhood was spent first on farms in Missouri and later in Kansas; then in the cities of St. Joseph and Kansas City, Missouri. He had had only seven years of formal education before he had to leave school to go to work. However, he had taken part in all the activities a country boy enjoys, and the vivid remembrance of these days makes his understanding of boys and animals so keen.

ZACHARY BALL

It was when he was working as a bellhop in a hotel in St. Joseph that he went to see an airdome stock company. This experience was a revelation. He was suddenly consumed with the desire to be an actor. Therefore, equipped with a new suit, a derby, and a potato-bug mandolin, he joined his first "rag opry," as dramatic repertoire companies playing under canvas were called. For the next thirty-three years he trouped in virtually every state in the Union. He acted in stock companies. He played with orchestras, and with an instrumental quartet which performed in night clubs, made records, and appeared on the major radio networks. Then came Pearl Harbor. "Rag opry" which had been hit hard first by talking pictures, then by radio, was dealt the final blow by the war.

During these years in show business Ball had written plays which he and others had produced, but not until he read *Gone with the Wind* did he realize that he *must* write! War began, and this compulsion became imperative. Zachary Ball, his wife, and child went to Austin, Texas. Here for three years he wrote all day and delivered newspapers most of the night. Some western pulp writers taught him the "angles" so well that in a few months he sold his first piece, a true detective story. By the end of eighteen months, he had sold short stories to both *The Saturday Evening Post* and *Collier's.* With the change of occupation, came the change of name, and he has written under the name Zachary Ball ever since.

Ball's short stories have been published in twenty-seven American magazines, as well as in periodicals in England, France, Germany, Australia, and the Scandinavian countries. He prefers writing novels. His first book was a collaboration, *Pull Down to New Orleans* (1946), a novel set against the background of the Mississippi River in 1802. He himself feels that it is probably his least successful effort and

BALL, ZACHARY—*Continued*

agrees with Harnett T. Kane in *Book Week* who felt that "it has some of the merits as well as the drawbacks of readymade, ready-to-wear fiction."

He brought out *Piney* in 1950. Based on many of his boyhood experiences, it is the story of a teen-aged Mississippi backwoods boy, and tells of how he grew into manhood the hard way. *Piney* was liked by the critics. Jules Bergman of the New York *Times Book Review* wrote that Ball "has written in lucidly poetic prose of a freshly conceived character."

Joe Panther (1950), written for teen-agers, is the story of the exciting summer that a Seminole Indian boy spent working as a helper on a deep-sea fishing boat in Miami. Siri Andrews in the New York *Herald Tribune Book Review* called this book "a well written, vivid, fast moving story with a new setting, for boys and girls"; the New York *Times* wrote "Mark this down as one of the most thrilling, satisfying teen-age books of the year."

The sequel, *Swamp Chief* (1952), portrays the struggle of Joe between two loyalties—to his own people and to his friend, Captain Harper. A. B. McCreary in the *Library Journal* described it as having "a likeable hero, a tropical setting, good writing and plot that holds one's attention."

Ball often works on as many as six books at one time. At present he is concentrating on novels: one the third book in the Joe Panther series, a period novel about the New Orleans river bar pilots, one based on his boyhood on a Kansas farm, one with his show business experience as background, and two adventure novels.

In his novel about his experiences on a Kansas farm, he is writing about the frustrations of the "hard-pan" farmers of those days, the droughts, storms and hot winds, and of the cockleburs and sunflowers that grew higher than the corn.

Golfing, fishing, hunting are his favorite sports. His favorite books include everything by Ernest Hemingway, and, of course, Margaret Mitchell's *Gone with the Wind*.

Ball, a brown-haired, hazel-eyed man, lives in Miami, Florida, with his wife Gladys and his son Kelly Ray, Jr. He is a member of the Methodist church. He also belongs to the Authors Guild. He is five feet ten inches tall, and weighs 185 pounds. Radiating geniality and kindness, Zachary Ball seems strangely non-temperamental for an ex-actor turned author. Actually, he is an introvert who is very serious about his writing. The Miami Public Library's Florida Author Collection is the depository of many gifts from Ball—the manuscript and galleys of *Piney,* theatre programs, his musical comedy and night club photographs, and autographed books.

References

Atlanta Constitution Je 22 '50
Atlanta J Je 23 '52
Miami Herald N 18 '51
Miami News p8-E D 10 '50

BANKHEAD, TALLULAH (BROCKMAN) Jan. 31, 1903- Actress

Address: b. c/o Actor's Equity Association, 45 W. 47th St., New York 19; h. "The Windows," Bedford Village, N.Y.

> NOTE: This biography supersedes the article which appeared in *Current Biography* in 1941.

The stage, motion picture and radio actress Tallulah Bankhead won applause in 1952 for her achievements in two other forms of entertainment: in September her autobiography *Tallulah* was published by Harper and she appeared for the first time on television as a regular star on the National Broadcasting Company program *All Star Review*. Beginning her acting career in New York in 1918, she played on the stage there for four years. In England she achieved her first great success, becoming in 1923 a London favorite in her first play, *The Dancers*. After returning to the United States in 1931 and making several motion pictures, Miss Bankhead again turned to the stage, where she twice received the New York Drama Critics award as the best actress of the year; in 1939 for her part in *The Little Foxes* and in 1942 for her role in *The Skin of Our Teeth*. Her most recent Broadway success was *Private Lives* (1948). Also recognized for her motion picture acting, Miss Bankhead won the New York Film Critics award in 1944 for her performance in *Lifeboat*. She first entered radio on a regular basis in 1950 as mistress of ceremonies on NBC's *Big Show*.

Born in Huntsville, Alabama, on January 31, 1903, Tallulah Brockman Bankhead is one of two daughters of William Brockman and Adeline Eugenia (Sledge) Bankhead, a well-known Virginia beauty. Her father, serving in Congress for nearly a quarter of a century, was Speaker of the House of Representatives for four years, and her grandfather, John Bankhead, was a long-time member of the Senate. Her mother died shortly after Tallulah's birth, and the future actress and her older sister Eugenia were brought up by relatives in Montgomery and Jasper, Alabama. While a child, Tallulah was subject to bronchial ailments which deepened her voice and gave it its unique quality. Spending some time in Washington, D.C., with her father, she attended Fairmont Seminary and the Convent of the Visitation. She also received schooling in New York at the Convent of the Sacred Heart and in Virginia at the Mary Baldwin Seminary and at the Convent of the Holy Cross, during which time she took piano and violin lessons and played at the commencement exercises.

At fifteen Tallulah Bankhead, having decided that she wanted to be an actress, submitted her photograph to a motion picture magazine contest. The winner, she was given the opportunity to appear in the silent picture *Thirty a Week* with Tom Moore. Her father, who had once wanted to be an actor himself, permitted Tallulah to go to New York City to try for a career in the theater. There, living at the Algonquin Hotel, she soon became a member of the "Algonquin set," which included such celebrities as Alexander Woollcott, Heywood Broun, and Dorothy Parker. Her first appearance on the stage was in the play *Squab Farm* in March 1918. A number of New York plays followed: *Footloose* (1919; her first big part), *39 East* (1919), *Nice People* (1921), *Everyday* (1921), *Danger* (1922), *Her Temporary Husband* (1922), and *The Exciters* (1922).

In 1923 Miss Bankhead went to London to appear with the English actor, director, and playwright Sir Gerald du Maurier in *The Dancers*. An immediate success, for the next eight years (1923-31) she starred in more than fifteen London productions and came to be identified by her first name only. Many critics considered her greatest role of this period to be that of Iris March in Michael Arlen's *The Green Hat* (1925). Other plays in which she appeared were *Conchita* (1924), *This Marriage* (1924), *The Creaking Chair* (1924), *Fallen Angels* (1925), *They Knew What They Wanted* (1926), *Scotch Mist* (1926), *The Gold Diggers* (1926), *Garden of Eden* (1927), *Blackmail* (1928), *Mud and Treacle* (1928), *Her Cardboard Lover* (1928), *He's Mine* (1929), *The Snob* (1929), *The Lady of the Camellias* (1930), and *Let Us Be Gay* (1930). While in London at her West End home, she entertained such notables as Noel Coward, Ethel Barrymore, and Lawrence of Arabia. Augustus John, the English artist, painted her portrait, which hung for a time in the Royal Academy in London.

After she had signed a motion picture contract with Paramount Studios, Miss Bankhead returned to the United States in 1931 and made several films, including *Tarnished Lady, My Sin, Devil and the Deep, The Cheat,* and *Faithless,* none of which won high acclaim. Going back to the stage in 1933 to appear in *Forsaking All Others,* she spent the next five years playing roles which the critics in general regarded as unequal to her ability. She toured in the summer of 1934 in *The Snob* and that fall appeared in *Dark Victory.* The following year she fulfilled an old ambition to portray Sadie Thompson in a revival of *Rain.* Several months later, in 1935, she appeared in *Something Gay* and the next year played the lead in *Reflected Glory.* A low point in her acting career was reached in 1937 with her performance in Shakespeare's *Antony and Cleopatra,* this role evoking the often-quoted criticism by John Mason Brown: "Miss Bankhead barged down the Nile last night as Cleopatra—and sank." The revival of *The Circle* in April 1938 provided Miss Bankhead with a more suitable vehicle and found her giving "a performance of poise and grace." In August of that year she starred in *I Am Different.*

With her interpretation of the role of Regina Giddens in Lillian Hellman's *The Little Foxes* (1939), Miss Bankhead became recognized as an actress of some talent in the American theater. The critics agreed that she had found a play suited to her "special brand of magic," one reviewer describing her performance as a "superb example of mature acting fully under control." *The Little Foxes* brought the star, who rated the play and her role in it as the

TALLULAH BANKHEAD

finest she had ever had, the New York Drama Critics Circle award for the best acting of the year. In the summer of 1940 she toured in Pinero's *The Second Mrs. Tanqueray* and the following summer appeared in a revival of *Her Cardboard Lover.* About her performance in 1941 in Clifford Odets' *Clash by Night,* Richard Watts, Jr., wrote in the New York *Herald Tribune,* "Although Miss Bankhead hardly manages to seem the rebellious Staten Island housewife, she plays with that vibrant air of excitement which always makes her so fascinating to watch." In 1942 Miss Bankhead received her second New York Critics award as the best actress of the year for her performance in Thorton Wilder's *The Skin of Our Teeth.* In the symbolic fantasy she took the part of Sabina, who was variously a maid, a bathing beauty, and a camp follower, and who often stepped out of the play to comment about the stage goings-on. Lewis Nichols described her in the New York *Times:* "Miss Bankhead is magnificent—breezy, hard, practical by turns. She can strut and posture on broad comedy, she can be calmly serene."

Miss Bankhead's first motion picture in more than ten years, *Lifeboat,* written by John Steinbeck and directed by Alfred Hitchcock, was received with much critical applause in 1944. Of Miss Bankhead in the role of Connie Porter, a "war correspondent deluxe," Eileen Creelman of the New York *Sun* wrote: "Tallulah Bankhead has never given such a sound and vivid characterization on the screen. She makes the most of the comedy. She also, without any apparent softening, brings to the film a real emotion." The New York Film Critics voted her portrayal the best screen performance of the year. Her role in her last film to date, *Royal Scandal* (1945), a comedy about Catherine the Great of Russia, was said to fit "Miss Bankhead's brittle talent to perfection." In the opinion of Alton Cook of the New

BANKHEAD, TALLULAH—Continued

York World-Telegram: "Sweeping over everything is the gale of laughter Tallulah Bankhead spreads around herself, full of a tempestuous earnestness. . . .Miss Bankhead is genuinely regal as actress, as comedienne, and as Catherine."

Foolish Notion, the Philip Barry comedy produced on Broadway in March 1945, disappointed the critics as a sample of that author's work, but the attitude of the reviewers on Miss Bankhead's performance was typified by Howard Barnes's statement in the New York Herald Tribune: "Only Miss Bankhead, I think, could have made so many of his ragtag, bobtail notions about life, love, truth, and beauty stand up in a dramatic structure. As the central character of a fable which confronts a 'personality' actress with a husband who had been legally declared dead, a man she is about to marry, an adopted daughter and the girl whom the husband really loves, she is serene and magnificent. . . .Her performance is a veritable triumph of the season." When The Eagle Has Two Heads by Jean Cocteau was presented on the New York stage in March 1947, critical reaction to Miss Bankhead as the queen was mixed. The New York Herald Tribune reviewer thought she was "more radiant and resourceful than ever. It is a personal triumph against considerable odds. A PM writer remarked that "even the electrical personality of Tallulah Bankhead fails to be very important particularly since Miss Bankhead provides something less than an electrical performance." The play closed after twenty-nine performances.

Preceded by a fifty-three week cross-country tour, the revival of Noel Coward's Private Lives opened on Broadway in October 1948. Most reviewers found Coward's comedy dated and slight, but called Miss Bankhead's performance "a fascinating one-woman show." Ward Morehouse in the New York Sun observed: "Bankhead is changeless and unchanging and by her sheer gusto she succeeds in turning a dated comedy into a rather satisfactory entertainment." About a month later, Time (November 22, 1948) commented that "last week, as it has for the past six weeks, Private Lives was packing the Plymouth Theater with as many standees as the New York Fire Department will allow. What the customers were crowding to see was not so much a play as a remarkable personality with a remarkable name: Tallulah Bankhead." Time went on to report that the contract for the show gave Miss Bankhead some extraordinary privileges—the right to pass on who would be the play's directors, players, company manager, stage manager, press agent, and costumer, and the stipulation that the management must provide her with footlights (which had been going out of fashion on the New York stage) because she insisted that they "offset overhead lights that throw unflattering shadows."

Tallulah Bankhead began her career in radio in November 1950 as mistress of ceremonies on the new NBC ninety-minute variety show on Sunday nights, the Big Show. Wrote Harriet Van Horne

in the New York World-Telegram: "I wish radio had thought of it years ago." The New York Herald Tribune critic found that Miss Bankhead, as mistress of ceremonies, "was sharp as a knife and succeeded somehow in outshining even the most glittering names on that glittering roster." The New York Newspaper Guild presented her with its Page One Award for "putting new life into radio." The actress became known for her exchanges of repartee with such guest stars as Margaret Truman, Jimmy Durante, Fred Allen, Judy Holliday, Danny Kaye, Ethel Merman, Robert Merrill, Dean Martin, Jerry Lewis, and Ezio Pinza. The first program in the 1951 fall season of the Big Show was broadcast from London over BBC's light program channel on September 16 and recorded for rebroadcast in the United States several days later. On Miss Bankhead's first visit to England since 1935, she was greeted by public enthusiasm, but the show itself received varying criticisms in the press. The final performance of the Big Show was given April 2, 1952, NBC having been unable to find enough sponsors to continue the program.

The same year that Miss Bankhead entered radio—1950—Columbia released her first commercial American singing recording, "I'll Be Seeing You" and "You Go to My Head," with Joe Bushkin at the piano. In 1951 the actress embarked on a lecture tour, giving her first talk before 3,000 persons on the campus of Southern Methodist University. Her autobiography Tallulah, written with the aid of a dictaphone and with the editorial assistance of her long-time press agent Richard Maney, was published in September 1952 and shortly afterward became a national best-seller. Reviewers commented on the candor of the book and on its effective presentation of the actress's wit and vitality.

The fall of 1952 saw Miss Bankhead's first undertaking in another medium new to her—television—as a regular star on NBC's new All-Star Revue. After her initial appearance Jack Gould said in the New York Times (October 13, 1952): "Tallu is eminently videogenic. . . . From the moment of her entrance. . .it was a Tallulah joyously and overwhelmingly alive." John Crosby later wrote in the New York Herald Tribune (November 16, 1952) that the first show contained "a lot of dead spots . . . still, it was a wonderful show because it demonstrated beyond the shadow of an option that Tallulah was a great television personality. . . .She is a magnificent comedienne and NBC, I think, has corralled a really great success."

Miss Bankhead was married to John Emery on August 31, 1937; they were divorced in 1941. She "adopted" Barbara Nicholai, a Greek war orphan, and has contributed to her support in England. One of the actress's enthusiasms is keeping an assortment of pets, which has included a lion cub named Winston Churchill, a mynah bird, a rhesus monkey, a golden marmoset, a parakeet, a Pekingese, a Sealyham terrier, two poodles, and a sheep dog. Another of her pastimes is "rooting" for the New York Giants baseball team. (Originally a Southerner, she has said: "I just couldn't root for a team named Yankees.") She also likes to swim, dance, and listen to jazz and classical music. Since 1942 Miss Bankhead has lived in a white-washed brick country house that, she once told Ward Morehouse of the New York *World-Telegram*), has "thousands and thousands of windows." She is five feet three inches tall and has been described by Maurice Zolotow (*Saturday Evening Post*) as follows: "Her face is large and strong, with a sharply prominent aquiline nose, voluptuous down-drawn lips, and luminous china-blue eyes with eyelids that flutter frequently. . . .Her face is crowned with soft, thick, shoulder-length hair of a tawny, leonine color."

References

Coronet 31:56-60 N '51
Cue 21:12 S 27 '52 por
Life 14:46 F 15 '43; 30:90 Je 25 '51 por
Look 15:50 F 13 '51 por
Sat Eve Post 219:15-17+ Ap 12 '47
Time 52:76+ N 22 '48
Who's Who in America, 1952-1953
Who's Who in the Theatre (1952)
World Biography (1948)

BARNES, MARGARET CAMPBELL

Feb. 27, 1891- Author

Address: b. c/o Macrae Smith Co., 225 S. 15th St., Philadelphia 2, Pa., h. Norton Cottage, Yarmouth, Isle of Wight, England

Reprinted from the *Wilson Library Bulletin* February, 1953

Looking back to her English childhood, Margaret Campbell Barnes (not to be confused with the American author, Margaret Ayer Barnes), counts among her blessings the fact that she was the youngest in a big family, that her parents, George and Emily (Roberts) Wood, were not overburdened with money, and that what they had was spent on giving their children good schooling and happy holidays in a rambling old schoolhouse, once part of the manor of Firstead Keynes, and mentioned in her first book, *The Passionate Brood*. They made their own fun, getting up plays and otherwise stimulating their imaginations, and she believes her bent for writing historical novels may have been formed when she was taken, as a little girl, to see old castles and cathedrals. "My eldest sister," she says, "made these things live for me."

Margaret Wood was born in London, February 27, 1891. She was educated in boarding schools: St. Ronan's, Hedley Wood, Middlesex, and at the Pension Collot in Paris.

Her entrance into the field of fiction was by way of buying silent French and American films for an English agency and translating French titles into English. She well remembers that her first short story was sold for two guineas when she was twenty-one to a small magazine, the morning after a Zeppelin raid in World War I. The happiest event during that difficult time was her marriage to George Alfred Campbell Barnes, Registrar of the London Company (now retired).

MARGARET CAMPBELL BARNES

In the interval between wars, Mrs. Barnes earned money to help educate her two sons by writing travel articles, getting material for them the hard way by touring the Near East, for example, in a cargo boat and on mule back. Her writing apprenticeship served, and the rejection period over, she sold her stories to the better English magazines as fast as she could turn them out.

The start of the second World War ended this peaceful existence, with one boy in khaki and the other at Oxford prior to joining the Navy, her husband fighting fires in London during the bombings, and herself driving an ambulance for both military and civilian wounded. Because many magazines had to discontinue publication during the war, she turned to writing novels. Following *The Passionate Brood* and *Like Us They Lived,* came her first marked success, *My Lady of Cleves* (1946), chosen as Book-of-the-Month for Canada that year. Based on the life of Anne of Cleves, fourth wife of Henry VIII, it portrays her as a woman of character and understanding. Said Ben Ray Redman, in the *Saturday Review (of Literature)*: "The important . . . thing is that these historical characters . . . come alive in a succession of memorable scenes; not only Anne, but Henry and Holbein and Cranmer and Tom Culpepper and Thomas Seymour. . . . This is a real achievement in a difficult kind of writing. And the whole of *My Lady of Cleves* is as good as its parts." When Mrs. Barnes was half through writing this book, she received the tragic news that her older son, Michael Campbell Barnes, lieutenant in the Royal Armoured Corps, had been killed in Normandy, leading a night attack in his tank, with the famous 51st Highlanders.

In *Within the Hollow Crown* (1947), she presents a vivid life of Richard II, and his turbulent fourteenth century reign, from the time he

BARNES, MARGARET C.—*Continued*

was an idealistic youth to his murder. Compressed into this compact story are manifold intrigues and crises of wars, plagues, heavy taxes, with a background of medieval pageantry and color. The Philadelphia *Inquirer* called it " a distinguished novel that is a welcome addition to . . . historical fiction," although the New York *Times* commented: "Mrs. Barnes takes some pains to show that Richard was a nicer fellow than Shakespeare made him out to be. When all the swordplay is over, her Richard seems a little too good to be true."

After triumphing over a long and critical illness, Mrs. Barnes turned for inspiration to the brief but spectacular life of the fascinating Anne Boleyn, Henry VIII's second wife, to marry whom he braved papal ire and made England a Protestant country. The book *Brief Gaudy Hour,* deals with her love affair and her vengeance on Cardinal Wolsey. ". . . light fiction, despite a sturdy historical background and almost exclusive use of historical characters," wrote a reviewer for the New York *Herald Tribune Book Review.*

Next, she resolved to present the complex character of Charles II from a new viewpoint —that of his consort, Catherine of Braganza. How, the author wondered, must it have felt to be the wife of this philanderer, overshadowed by his showy mistresses, yet loving him nevertheless. She had found a different Charles revealed in his letters to his young sister, and felt that his real story needed telling. The result was *With All My Heart* (Macrae Smith, 1951).

Mrs. Barnes has twice visited America, appearing on radio and television, and is eloquent on American warmth and hospitality. Several of her books have been translated into other languages. Her own favorite, although it won no awards, is *Within the Hollow Crown.*

She loves the woods and the sea, rich colors in fabrics and flowers, and her many friends, although she must desert them for long intervals while living in the "two worlds" of a period writer. For such concentration, she retires to a 500-year-old cottage on the Isle of Wight.

Her self-description lists grey hair and green eyes, a height of 5 feet, 6 inches, and a weight of "9 stones, 6 pounds" (132 pounds).

Reference

Who's Who in America, 1952-53

BARNES, STANLEY N(ELSON) May 1, 1900- United States Government official; judge

Address: b. Department of Justice, Washington 25, D.C.; h. 1780 Ramiro Rd., San Marino 9, Calif.

Appointed by President Eisenhower as Assistant Attorney General in charge of the Anti-trust Division of the Department of Justice, Stanley N. Barnes took office on May 1, 1953. He resigned as presiding Judge of the Superior Court of Los Angeles County, of which he had been a member since 1947, to assume his new duties

of administering the controversial anti-monopoly laws of the United States Government.

Admitted to the bar in 1925, Barnes practiced law in San Francisco and later in Los Angeles. Governor Earl Warren appointed him to the bench in Los Angeles County in 1946, and he was twice elected presiding judge. He has also taught law at the University of Southern California.

One of the three sons of the Reverend Charles L. and Janet (Rankin) Barnes, Stanley Nelson Barnes was born in Baraboo, Wisconsin, on May 1, 1900. One of his ancestors, Timothy Barnes of Connecticut, fought in the Revolutionary War, and his grandfather, Joseph Rankin, served as a Congressman from Wisconsin. His mother died of typhoid fever when he was one year old, and his father moved the family to San Diego, California.

Stanley attended San Diego High School, participating in debate and football, and graduated in 1918. He served with the United States Navy in that year and was a member of the Naval Reserve from 1918 to 1921. While a student at the University of California in Berkeley, he majored in law and philosophy. He was an all-Pacific lineman on the "wonder" football teams of that period, playing center, tackle and guard. He won his letter four years, and played in the Rose Bowl twice. Elected president of Sigma Chi and the junior class, he was a member of the Winged Helmet, junior honorary society, and president of the Golden Bear, the senior honorary society.

To help pay his way through school Barnes held jobs as an athletic instructor at boys' camps, a pipefitter's helper, an asbestos handler, and a shipyard worker. He also coached at the University of California and worked as a seaman for the Matson Line. After receiving his Bachelor of Arts degree in 1922 from the University he entered Harvard Law School as a special student. He returned to the University of California Law School in 1924 and received the degree of Juris Doctor from that institution one year later. His doctoral thesis was entitled *The Historical Development of the Doctrine of Equitable Servitudes in Chattels.*

After his admission to the California bar in 1925, Barnes practiced law in San Francisco, specializing in corporate finance. Three years later he moved to Los Angeles, became a member of the firm of Chase, Barnes and Chase, and turned his attention to trial work.

On December 12, 1946 Governor Earl Warren appointed him a member of the Superior Court of Los Angeles County.

The Republican "California Volunteers for Good Government," the group which supported Richard Nixon in his Senate contest with Helen Gahagan Douglas, attempted to persuade Barnes to run for State Attorney General in 1950, but he preferred to remain on the bench. In 1952 the sixty members of the State Superior Court chose him as the presiding Judge of that body and he was unanimously re-elected in November of the same year. The chairman of the Judicial Council of the State of California found his court the most efficiently run in the country.

After announcement, April 1, 1953, of his appointment to the Department of Justice, Barnes stated that his selection could probably be ascribed to a recommendation from Vice-President Richard Nixon, a long-time friend (New York *Times*, April 4, 1953). After Senate confirmation of the appointment he was sworn in on May 1.

The division which he directs handles cases involving monopolies who use their power for unreasonable restraint of trade. Indicating the policy his office will follow, Barnes stated, "The attitude of the President and the Attorney General, in which I concur, is that the anti-trust laws should be enforced absolutely—that there should be no recess from prosecution, but that the laws should not be used to persecute big business or anybody else" (New York *Times*, April 4, 1953). He went on to say that he hoped to çarry out Attorney General Herbert Brownell's expressed desire that the Antitrust Division operate as efficiently as "any good law office" and that a thoroughgoing reorganization would probably be carried out to effect this.

Businessmen expect the Anti-trust Division to discontinue the policy of the former Administration, which, according to an article in *Business Week* (April 11, 1953), consisted of filing suits against companies simply on the grounds of bigness. California oil companies involved in a suit said that they expected to get "clearer, fairer treatment" from Barnes and to have an opportunity for a more extensive presentation of their side in the dispute. Action on pending suits will be suspended until Barnes can review the cases and decide on procedures. It is also expected that anti-trust procedure will be simplified and companies will be advised how to conform to antitrust legislation (*U.S. News & World Report*, April 17, 1953).

Judge Barnes does not consider himself a "trustbuster." He believes that "We have certain laws, unpopular in certain places, but under our concept of civilization they must be enforced. I mean to enforce them with good judgment, to accomplish the purpose of the legislative enactments, and I mean to do it without persecution" (Washington *Post*, May 23, 1953). He took a $1,500 cut in salary to accept the Assistant Attorney General post.

Barnes is a past president of the University of California Alumni Association and served as regent of the university from 1946 to 1948. After serving as a national trustee of Sigma Chi fraternity from 1950 to 1952, he was elected president in 1952. He is a trustee of the Southwest Museum of Los Angeles and a director of the California Institute for Cancer Research and the Daniel William Cooper Foundation, both of Los Angeles. He is a member of the American Bar Association, the California State Bar and the Los Angeles Bar Association. Other organizations to which he belongs are the International Association of Insurance Counsel and Phi Delta Phi.

Married on October 19, 1929, Judge Barnes and his wife, the former Anne Fisk, have three daughters, Janet, Judith and Joyce. The Assistant Attorney General has one of the finest general collections of primitive masks in the country and gives lectures on the subject; he also reads extensively on judicial administration. He

Wide World Photos

JUDGE STANLEY N. BARNES

is an Episcopalian and a Republican. He has brown eyes, brown and grey hair, is six feet one and one-half inches tall, weighs 249 pounds, and "still has the build of a varsity tackle."

References

Bsns W p32+ Ap 11 '53 por
U S News 34:64 Ap 17 '53
N Y Times p17 Ap 2 '53; p14 Ap 4 '53
Washington (D.C.) Post p3B My 24 '53 por
Who's Who in the West (1951)

BARRAULT, JEAN-LOUIS Sept. 8, 1910-
Actor; director; producer

RENAUD, MADELEINE Feb. 21, 1903-
Actress
Address: Théâtre de Marigny, Paris, France

In September 1946 at the Théâtre Marigny in Paris, Jean-Louis Barrault and Madeleine Renaud, France's famous husband and wife dramatic team, established a permanent, unsubsidized repertory company, alternating classic with modern and experimental plays. Since the inception of this company, they have offered twenty-eight plays to the Parisian public, toured Western Europe and South America, and in October-November 1952 visited Canada and the United States in their third foreign venture sponsored by the French Government to promote international goodwill. Barrault and Miss Renaud had earlier (1940-46) been associated with the Comédie Française and both have appeared in French motion pictures. Barrault is known to American audiences for his performance in the film *Les Enfants du Paradis*.

Jean-Louis Barrault was born in Vésinet, France, on September 8, 1910, the son of a pharmacist of Burgundy ancestry. At the age

JEAN-LOUIS BARRAULT

of six he began to develop an interest in acting and in his autobiography, *Réflexions Sur Le Théâtre*, he states that he spent his entire childhood "living out imaginary stories." Barrault attended public school in Paris, then entered the Collège Chaptal, where he studied mathematics, philosophy, and drawing. After receiving his degree upon graduation from the Collège Chaptal, he returned to the Collège in 1931 as an undermaster in drawing and study-hall supervisor and during the same period attended painting classes at l'École du Louvre.

His decision to make acting, rather than painting, his vocation has been attributed by Barrault to an interview with Charles Dullin, actor-director of the Atelier dramatic school and theater, who accepted him as a scholarship pupil. Having left his position in July 1931 at Collège Chaptal, he was reportedly too poor to rent a room, so that he slept in the wardrobe room or in the wings of the Atelier stage. Dullin soon admitted him as a member of his company at a salary of 15 francs a day. Playing the role of the servant in Ben Johnson's *Volpone*, Barrault made his stage debut at the Atelier theater on September 8, 1931, his twenty-first birthday. From 1931 to 1935 he continued to study the techniques of his master, Dullin, learning "how to live a situation sincerely" (*France in New York Monthly*, November-December 1952). From a fellow pupil, Étienne Decroux, he received his first lesson in the art of the mime. He discovered, he has stated in his autobiography, "the whole problem of the theater is to make *silence* vibrate."

With a troupe comprising several of his friends, Barrault in 1935 produced his own adaptation of William Faulkner's *As I Lay Dying*, in pantomime drama at the Atelier theater, on which he spent his entire inheritance of 12,000 francs. His powerful production won for him a contract with the motion picture producer, Marc Allégret, for the film *Les Beaux*

Jours. Barrault's film experience, apart from the theater, represented to him "a kind of exaltation in the void"; but it convinced him of a need to concentrate on a professional plan. He formed an experimental theatrical company, called Le Grenier des Augustins, with a friend, Jean Dasté, but produced little before 1937. In 1936 he met his future business associate and marital partner, Madeleine Renaud, while both were starring in the film *Hélène*. The following year he staged a successful production at the Théâtre Antoine of Cervantes' *Numance*, in which he took several roles. In bringing this work to the stage, at a cost to himself of over 40,000 francs, he has said that he rediscovered the human heart and was replanted from the nursery in the solid earth. In 1937 he appeared in the films *Drôle de Drame, Les Perles de la Couronne,* and *Le Puritain.* Two years later, in 1939, while playing in the motion picture *L'Or dans la Montagne,* he adapted and staged Jules Laforgue's *Hamlet,* and Knut Hamsun's *La Faim* at the Atelier theater. The outbreak of World War II in Europe called him into the army to serve until 1940.

Madeleine Renaud was born in Paris on February 21, 1903, a cousin of the noted artist and stage designer, Christian Bérard. She was educated in the Paris public schools. When, as a child, she recited a poem at a party, an actor present suggested that she become an actress. Her mother told the young girl, "Very well; but it will be done properly. . . .You will go to the Conservatoire and the Comédie Française" (*Theatre Arts*, November 1952). At her mother's advice, therefore, Madeleine trained for the stage as a scholarship student at the Conservatory of Dramatic Art in Paris. In 1923 she joined the Comédie Française, where she made her debut as Agnes in *L'École des Femmes* by Molière. In the Comédie's repertory and in tours throughout Europe, she subsequently played the ingénue parts in plays by Molière, Marivaux, and Musset, giving "brilliant interpretations" (*Dictionnaire Biographique Français Contemporain*).

In her first film appearance in 1932, Miss Renaud played in the important picture *Jean de la Lune.* Later, under contract to Paramount she made the films *La Belle Marinière, La Couturière de Lunéville,* and *Mistigri,* while in the theater at about this time she portrayed Ophelia in the production of *Hamlet* staged by Charles Granval. Her film performance in *La Maternelle* (1933), by Jean Benoit-Lévy, was called "a sensitive portrayal of a nursery school charwoman" (*Theatre Arts*, November 1952), and in 1934 she received the Grand Prize of the French Cinema for her interpretation of *Maria Chapdelaine.* After playing roles as leading lady and coquette in the stage productions *Le Chandelier* and *Les Fausses Confidences,* Miss Renaud starred in Vicky Baum's *Hélène* on the screen in 1936, in association with her future husband, Barrault. She was the choice of Jean Grémillon for a part in his realistic film *L'Etrange M. Victor* (1938) and in his *Remorques* (1940). Critics noted that her restrained and sensitive playing added to her apparent fragility, enabled her to excel in tragedy and drama but did not hinder her from giving spirited interpretations in comedy and vaudeville.

Following Barrault's demobilization from the army, he and Madeleine Renaud in 1940 became costars and a husband and wife team at the Comédie Française. As Rodrique in Corneille's classic *Le Cid*, Barrault rediscovered the resources of the classics and subsequently enhanced his development in the theater by staging Racine's *Phèdre* and André Gide's interpretation of Shakespeare's *Hamlet*. At the Comédie, as producer-director, he brought to the stage François Mauriac's *Les Mal Aimés,* in which Miss Renaud starred; she also starred in his five-hour production of Paul Claudel's *Le Soulier de Satin* (1943), staged for the first time, with music by Arthur Honegger. The couple played together in Salacrou's *Les Fiancés du Havre*. During their six years at the Comédie Française, Barrault and Renaud continued their individual motion picture careers. Barrault appeared in *La Symphonie Fantastique* among other films in 1941, and in *Les Enfants du Paradis* in 1944, playing the clown in love and attaining world-wide fame for his extraordinary miming. His 1945 films were *Le Cocu Magnifique* and *D'Homme à Hommes*, the latter a portrayal of Henri Dunant, the Red Cross pioneer. Meanwhile, Miss Renaud was the leading lady in Grémillon's *Lumière d'Été* (1942) and in his *Le Ciel est à Vous* (1943), a story dealing with athletic success.

When the Comédie Française was reorganized in 1946, at the instigation of the French Government, Barrault and Miss Renaud resigned to undertake in the fall of that year the joint management of the Marigny theater with the formation of the Madeleine Renaud-Jean-Louis Barrault Company. Here they were responsible for the production of the successful Gide-Barrault adaptation of Franz Kafka's *The Trial* and of plays by Salacrou, Anouilh, Camus, and Claudel, interspersed with Molière and Shakespeare classics. In these Barrault amply illustrated his belief that the theater requires experiments that combine respect for tradition and audacious innovation. *Les Nouvelles Littéraires* found *The Trial* (1947) : "A surprising and almost unhoped for success. . . . The prodigious miming of Barrault is the soul of the entire play" (quoted by *Time*, November 10, 1947). Commenting upon Madeleine Renaud in *Les Fausses Confidences*, Albert Camus wrote in *Caliban* (February 1949), "Effacing herself, characteristically, behind Marivaux—so quietly the audience was unaware of the fact—while subordinate emotions assume their proper places behind the principal passion, that precise and tender creature illustrated in her own way the only thing which is indestructible on this relentless earth, namely beauty."

The Madeleine Renaud-Jean-Louis Barrault Company appeared twice at the Venice Festival and in August 1948 presented *Hamlet* and *Les Fausses Confidences* at the Edinburgh Festival. For three weeks in October 1951 in London at the St. James's Theater, the company played to crowded audiences. Barrault was described as a "bomb . . . a force of tremendous explosive power that blows into nothingness the cobwebs,

MADELEINE RENAUD BARRAULT

the conventions, and the drearinesses that develop in a theater when it begins to lose its vitality" (*Christian Science Monitor*, November 10, 1951). At the Marigny theater in Paris in December 1951, Miss Renaud and Barrault produced Jean Cocteau's *Bacchus*. On its third foreign tour sponsored by the French Government to advance international relations, the Renaud-Barrault company visited Canada and the United States in the fall of 1952. The Montreal critics, as reported by the *Saturday Review (of Literature)* (November 8, 1952), were divided in their evaluation of the company's production of *Hamlet*, after giving unanimous applause to *Les Fausses Confidences* and *Les Fourberies de Scapin*. The arrival of the French troupe of thirty players, three-fourths of whom are charter members, at the Ziegfeld Theater in New York on November 12, 1952, was termed by the *Saturday Review (of Literature)* "the most ambitious theatrical project of our time."

For its initial presentation in New York the company chose Marivaux's *Les Fausses Confidences* and Prévert's *Baptiste* pantomime-ballet, a part of which Barrault had played in the film *Les Enfants du Paradis*. "We begin with Marivaux," Barrault explained, "because we were born with him and we think he will protect us" (New York *World-Telegram*, November 14, 1952). Of *Les Fausses Confidences*, Brooks Atkinson, the drama critic for the New York *Times* (November 13, 1952) wrote, "The performance is a thorough delight. The amazing plasticity of Barrault's acting is rooted in pantomime. Mme. Renaud looks every inch a lady of grace and breeding." The *Christian Science Monitor* critic commented that "Barrault plays the valet in an extravagant style—but it is a neat and disciplined extravagance. As the lovely Araminte, Mme. Renaud is exquisitely radiant—mystery in the midst of light." *Baptiste*, in the opinion of *Variety* (November 19,

BARRAULT, JEAN-LOUIS, and REN-AUD, MADELEINE—*Continued*

1952), "showed Barrault to be perhaps the most flexible and versatile comic artist alive."

Reviewing the American production of the Gide-Barrault adaptation of Kafka's *The Trial*, the New York *World-Telegram* critic remarked that the company "reveals an uncanny coordination in performance, through its sensitive, co-operative timing; it also continues its series of penetrating characterizations, wholly illuminated by shrewd tones and selective postures" (November 18, 1952). Of Madeleine Renaud's performance, he wrote that "her few moments count . . . and fragmentary impressions become quietly memorable ones."

The New York success of the French company resulted, the sponsor Sol Hurok reported, in the turning away of 5,000 to 6,000 patrons at the end of the opening week. The players offered as their third repertory production a double bill including two plays by Molière: *Amphitryon*, a court comedy, and *Les Fourberies de Scapin*, a farce. On November 24, 1952, Renaud-Barrault company introduced at the Ziegfeld Theater the bedroom farce *Occupe-Toi d'Amélie* by Georges Feydeau, a favorite with French audiences; and during the second half of that week presented *La Répétition ou L'Amour Puni*, which Barrault had encouraged the author, Jean Anouilh, to write and which had become one of the Marigny theater's greatest successes. New York critics were divided in their comments on the company's *Hamlet*, with *Variety*, in early December 1952, calling it a "loose three-and-a-half hour production that lacks power and drive, though interesting in individual scenes." Other critics thought the acting "brilliant" and the interpretation "intelligent."

Originally scheduled to close its New York appearance on December 6, 1952, the French company, because of its popularity, extended its stay at the Ziegfeld Theater through December 20, 1952. On December 22, Miss Renaud and Barrault, with their company, gave a single performance of *Les Fausses Confidences* in Washington, D.C., before sailing for France.

Among articles Barrault has written are "L'Acteur: cet instrument du Théâtre," appearing in *Elites Françaises* (December 1946) and "Entretiens sur le Théâtre," compiled by Jean-Marie Conty for *La Revue Théâtrale* (November 19, 1952). He is the author of the autobiographical *Reflections on the Theatre* (English translation by Barbara Wall, 1951), and *Une Troupe et Ses Auteurs* (1950). For his work in the theater, Barrault received the 1952 merit award of the Catholic Stage Guild of Ireland. Miss Renaud was awarded the Grand Prize of the French Cinema in 1934 for her performance in the film *Maria Chapdelaine*.

Jean-Louis Barrault and Madeleine Renaud are "perfectly complementary to each other," Harold Hobson, London drama critic of the *Christian Science Monitor* has written; "if M. Barrault is volcanic and restless, Mme. Renaud is quiet, gentle, prudent, and patient." Miss Renaud was formerly the wife of Charles Grandval; she was married to Barrault in 1940. She is slight and graceful and speaks in what Albert Camus calls "flutelike, melodious tones"; Barrault is thin and slight, with dark curly hair, and black eyes in a pale, gaunt, and intellectual face. André Gide, as quoted by the New York *Herald Tribune*, has said in his *Journals* that Barrault possesses a "wonderful face, instinct with enthusiasm, passion, genius."

References

Christian Sci Mon p9 O 12 '52
France in N Y Monthly N-D '52
Sat R 35:28-9 N 8 '52
Theatre· Arts 31:24-8 O '47; 36:21-3 N '52
This Week p7 N 2 '52
Dictionnaire Biographique Français Contemporain (1950)
International Who's Who, 1952
Who's Who in the Theatre (1952)
Winchester's Screen Encyclopedia (1948)

BARTON, GEORGE A(RTHUR) Feb. 20, 1885- Sports columnist; president National Boxing Association of America

Address: b. Minneapolis Star and Tribune, Minneapolis 15, Minn.; h. 1642 Hubbard Ave., St. Paul 4, Minn.

A veteran reporter who for fifty years has covered sports news for St. Paul and Minneapolis dailies, George A. Barton is the president of the National Boxing Association of America. He is the recipient of the James J. Walker Memorial Plaque awarded in January 1953 by the Boxing Writers Association of New York for "meritorious service" to the sport. Barton, a professional boxer at the turn of the century and a YMCA instructor, has been chairman of the Minnesota Athletic Commission for the past ten years and for thirty-five years served as referee of more than 12,000 bouts in which many of the fighters were world champions. Barton has recently been appointed chairman of the Commission for another three year term.

Born in Northfield, Minnesota, on February 20, 1885, George Arthur Barton was one of the five children of George Washington and Mary Ellen (Ryan) Barton, the former of Anglo-Irish and the latter of pure Irish descent. He has two brothers, Richard and William, and a sister, Alberta; another, Sadie, is deceased. When he was a child his family moved to St. Paul where at Central High School he won letters in baseball and track. At the age of seventeen, while still a junior in high school, Barton began a career as a professional boxer in order to be self-supporting. He describes the purses as "pitifully small" in those days because boxing was illegal in Minnesota from the late nineties until 1915. Fights were held in small gymnasiums, halls, and barns during the winter and along the shores of the Mississippi river during the summer. Tickets were sold under cover because any advance publicity would cause the local police departments to stop the fights. However, the sport was popular, and the police did not interfere unless stories appeared in the newspapers and "the clergy demanded that such brutal affairs be stopped." In his seven years as a professional boxer, Barton was matched in the bantamweight and featherweight divisions.

On his graduation from high school in 1903 Barton was offered a job at $10 a week as assistant to J. Alec Sloan, then sports editor of the St. Paul *Daily News*. At the end of the same year, he became sports editor of the Minneapolis *Daily News*, but his salary was not increased and he continued to make extra money by boxing. What he regards as his "most notable achievement as a fighter" came in 1904 when he won a decision over Terry McGovern, who had been national bantamweight champion in 1899-1900 and featherweight champion the following year. He also fought and lost decisions to Maurice Rauch and to Tommy Thomas, who later became a noted Illinois referee and officiated at the Braddock-Louis World Heavyweight Championship fight in 1936. Barton boxed exhibitions with Joe Gans and Battling Nelson when each, as current national lightweight champion, appeared with touring shows in both Minneapolis and St. Paul. During his years as a professional fighter he also taught boxing at the St. Paul YMCA. Among his pupils were Mike Gibbons, later a claimant to the middleweight title, Henry Hoppe, a lightweight who fought under the name of Young Jack Redmond, and, Barton remembers, "a handsome young fellow named Ernest Brimmer who later gained fame in the movies as Richard Dix."

A raise in his salary as sports editor to $35 a week made it possible for Barton to retire as a professional boxer early in 1910, but he continued to occupy a place in the ring as one of the northwest's well-known referees, officiating for the next thirty-five years at more than 12,000 professional and amateur bouts. In those years Barton refereed complete professional cards of from six to eight bouts, starting with the first preliminary and going through with the main event. Among the boxers were twenty-four world champions in all eight weight classifications, including the heavyweights Jack Dempsey, Gene Tunney, Jimmy Braddock, and Primo Carnera; the lightweights Benny Leonard and Sammy Mandell; and the featherweights Johnny Dundee and Freddie Miller.

Barton's long connection with the Minneapolis *Daily News* came to an end in February 1923, when he was engaged by the Minneapolis *Tribune* as executive sports editor of the morning, evening, and Sunday editions. He held that post until May 1941, when John and Gardner Cowles bought the papers and combined them with the Minneapolis *Star* and *Journal*. Since then Barton has been sports columnist for the *Tribune*. He has also contributed articles on boxing, baseball, football, and horse-racing to such periodicals as *Look, Esquire*, and *Sporting News*.

Since the Golden Gloves contests for amateur boxers were jointly established in 1928 by the New York *Daily News* and the Chicago *Tribune*, Barton has officiated at all twenty-four of the New York-Chicago Intercity Tournaments, as a referee from 1928 to 1940, and

GEORGE A. BARTON

after that as a judge. He has also refereed several national intercollegiate tournaments.

Appointed chairman of the Minnesota Athletic Commission by Governor Harold Stassen in 1943, Barton was subsequently reappointed to the post by Governor Edward Thye, and by Thye's successor, Luther Youngdahl. This made him a member of the National Boxing Association which had been formed in January 1921, after professional boxing had been legalized in individual states, to provide uniform regulations among the states. By 1947, the NBA represented the boxing commissions of all states except New York, Massachusetts, and Maryland, and also held jurisdiction over the District of Columbia, Cuba, Puerto Rico, Venezuela, the City of Montreal, the Province of Quebec, the provinces of western Canada, and the British Board of Boxing Control. Meeting in Montreal, Canada on September 9, 1952, the NBA, which elects its president for a one-year term at an annual convention, chose Barton to succeed Dave Rochon of Montreal as President. When the Association issued its quarterly ratings the following month, President Barton predicted a dim future for boxing in America, pointing out that currently the United States was supreme in only four of the eight weight categories, with the world welterweight, lightweight, bantamweight, and flyweight championships being held by Cuba, Mexico, South Africa and Japan respectively.

After ten years as chairman of the Minnesota Athletic Commission, Barton was reappointed for three additional years by the new Governor, C. Elmer Anderson, in January 1953. He was also awarded the James J. Walker Memorial Plaque for "meritorious service to the sport" in the course of "fifty years as boxer, referee, and critic" by the Boxing Writers Association on January 15. On the following day, Barton participated in the first official action of the newly-created Boxing Board of Review, which

BARTON, GEORGE A.—*Continued*

was set up to reconcile differences between the New York State Athletic Association and the NBA.

A member of the Minneapolis Athletic Club, he keeps in good physical trim by playing handball and golf. For indoor recreation he enjoys both theater and movies, particularly musical comedies. His religion is Roman Catholic, and his political affiliation is Republican. Mrs. Barton, *née* Kathryn Elizabeth Riley, was an office secretary before her marriage on September 17, 1908; the Bartons are the parents of two sons, George Arthur, Jr. and Kenneth, and have five grandchildren. The NBA president and erstwhile bantamweight and featherweight fighter stands at five feet six inches and today weighs around 162 pounds. His eyes are brown, and his now white hair was formerly black.

Reference

N Y Times p27 Ja 16 '53 por

BECKER, MRS. HARRY *See* Freeman, L. (G.)

BELL, BERNARD IDDINGS, REV. Oct. 13, 1886- Clergyman; educator; writer

Address: h. 1321 E. 56th St., Chicago 37, Ill.

For more than forty years through his sermons, books, articles, and lectures the Reverend Dr. Bernard Iddings Bell has been known as a vigorous critic of materialism, complacency, and hazy thinking in the religious, educational, home, political, and economic life of the nation. Bell, honorary canon of the Protestant Episcopal Diocese of Chicago, is a former university professor, and author of some twenty books, the latest of which is *Crowd Culture* (Harper, 1952).

Bernard Iddings Bell was born on October 13, 1886, in Dayton, Ohio, son of Charles Wright and Vienna Valencia (Iddings) Bell. Of his father, a small manufacturer, Bell has said, "He was a great educator because he taught me the meaning and satisfaction of doing any job well" (quoted by Wambly Bald, New York *Post Magazine,* July 1, 1949). Bell received his B.A. degree in 1907 from the University of Chicago, where he had majored in social history. Most of his extracurricular activities centered around dramatics and work on college publications. "During his college years he underwent a long siege of secularistic skepticism," according to the *Post* article. "His probing led him to ordination as a priest of the Episcopal Church." For his religious training he enrolled at the Western Theological Seminary (which later became a part of Seabury-Western Seminary) in Chicago; here he also continued his studies in historical and sociological subjects and was graduated in 1912 with the degree of Bachelor of Sacred Theology. Meanwhile, in 1910, in which year he became deacon and priest of the Episcopal Church, he served as assistant curate of Christ Church in Chicago and from 1910 to 1913 held the post of vicar of St. Christopher's Church in Oak Park, Illinois, where within two years he built a church. During the latter part of this period he also initiated a Sunday night forum at Grace Church, Chicago, to which he invited people representing many different points of view to express their ideas freely.

Leaving Chicago in 1913, Bernard Bell went to Fond du Lac, Wisconsin, to become dean of St. Paul's Cathedral Church and examining chaplain to the bishop. Before the end of his five years there, Bell in 1917 entered World War I service as senior aide to the head chaplain at the Great Lakes Naval Training Station. It was at this time that he wrote his first books, *Right and Wrong After the War* (1918) and *Work of the Church for Men at War* (1919). On completing duty at the training station in 1919, he took the post of warden of St. Stephen's College at Annandale-on-the-Hudson, New York, then "a dying college." With the help of Haley Fiske, president of the Metropolitan Life Insurance Company, and Edward Albee, a "vaudeville impresario," Bell, according to *Time*, raised about a million dollars "to revolutionize the St. Stephen's faculty and methods." Bell has characterized the experiment as one which encouraged the student's individuality and withstood the tendency of American education to standardize its products. Since one million dollars was not adequate to meet the needs of the college, during the depression St. Stephen's was taken over by Columbia University. The property was later used by Bard College. In his last three years with St. Stephen's (1930-33), Bell was a professor of religion at Columbia University.

In Providence, Rhode Island, Bell occupied the position of preaching canon of St. John's Cathedral from 1933 to 1946, when he became consultant on education to the Right Reverend Wallace E. Conkling, Protestant Episcopal Bishop of Chicago. In 1946 he was also made honorary canon at the Cathedral of St. Peter and St. Paul, a post which required his representing the church in its relations with the University of Chicago and other schools in the diocese. At the same time he assumed the post of lecturer on religious education and preaching at Seabury-Western Theological Seminary in Evanston, Illinois, from which he resigned in January 1948 to devote his time to lecturing, preaching, and writing. A delegate in May 1949 to the Protestant Episcopal Church Congress meeting in Boston, Bell pointed out in a discussion on the question of unity with other Protestant churches that the Episcopal Church was itself divided. The faction to which he belonged, he said, conceived of Episcopalianism as based upon a theology which regards man as "diseased within himself . . . needing God's direct intervention and help for salvation" (quoted by *Pathfinder,* May 18, 1949).

A frequent guest preacher at Trinity Episcopal Church in New York City, Canon Bell in 1945 presented a group of sermons which he had delivered there in *God Is Not Dead,* a book dealing with spiritual problems of man in modern society. "Those who have learned to expect from Dr. Bell a searching analysis of contemporary civilization," noted the Virginia Kirkus review, "a trumpet call to real faith in God, couched in epigrammatic language and a gripping style, will not be disappointed in the sermons (or essays) which constitute this volume." Other of his sermons have appeared in *Best Sermons* (1946 and 1947), edited by G. P. Butler.

Among Bell's chief targets of criticism in his writings have been modern education and the failure of the schools to teach people to think clearly and to understand what constitutes happiness. An early work on the subject, *Common Sense in Education*, which was published in 1928 when he was warden of St. Stephen's College, has been called "timeless in the pure clarity and wisdom of its presentation of education's aims" (M. Whitcomb Hess in *Catholic World*, May 1951). In *Crisis in Education; A Challenge to American Education* (1949) Bell attacked the educational system at every level for secularism, materialism, and mediocrity of standards, and in the final chapter suggested measures for reform. Generally well received by reviewers, *Crisis in Education*, was a "wise and frightening book" in the opinion of H. A. Overstreet, the *Saturday Review* critic. For the New York *Times Magazine*, Bell has written several articles on educational problems, "We Are Indicted for Immaturity" (July 20, 1947), "We Lack Leaders; Is Education at Fault?" (January 18, 1948), and "Schools Can't Take the Place of Home" (May 9, 1948). His article on American education for *Life* magazine (October 16, 1950), which has been described as "a blast at our schools as criminally superficial and undisciplined," was said to have raised "a storm" in educational circles (M. Whitcomb Hess). In the *Life* article Bell charged that American youth are permitted to believe that "one may eat one's cake and have it too, that there can be reward without quest, wages without work, a master's prestige without a master's skill, marriage without fidelity, national security without sacrifice."

Sharing the blame with the schools for "religious illiteracy" is, in the view of Bell, the Christian Church itself. In *The Church in Disrepute* (1943), he explains why the influence of the church is weak in contemporary society and shows how this much-needed influence can be strengthened. A "slashing tract" was the comment of *Christian Century*; while *Commonweal* considered it "a stirring and well-written book . . . full of shrewd aphorisms and striking observations." Elsewhere, Bell has deplored the practice of regarding the church as a "social club" and has criticized the Episcopal Church for a tendency "to exalt itself and minimize God." Failures of the school and church were again scored by Bell in *Crowd Culture, An Examination of the American Way of Life* (1952), which describes America as dominated by the "mass man," the majority which insists that the individual conform to the standards of the crowd. Bell's hope is that a democratic "elite" will emerge from the masses to rescue the nation from its immaturity and mediocrity. Of *Crowd Culture*, which received mixed reviews,

Wide World Photos
REV. BERNARD IDDINGS BELL

the *Library Journal* critic wrote, "Some recommendations impractical, e.g., church schools supported by public funds; categorical observations make book banal; description of 'elite' is infantile . . . but recommended, of course."

Canon Bell has held a number of lectureships in the United States and abroad; he was the William Vaughan Moody lecturer at the University of Chicago (1931), Coleman lecturer at Lafayette College (1935), Yarnall lecturer in the British public schools (1939), and Gates lecturer at Grinnell College (1941). Five lectures that Bell delivered at Lafayette were published in *Preface to Religion* (1935), a survey of the origins and development of religious behavior; another series of lectures, *A Catholic Looks at His World* (1936), examines the social philosophies of various dominant religious groups and compares them with the Anglo-Catholic view. *A Man Can Live* (1947) includes more recent lectures given by Bell on teaching missions in various parts of the United States. Besides writing some twenty books and many articles and pamphlets, he edited *Affirmations* (1938) and *St. James Lessons in Religion* (1940-45).

Honorary doctorates awarded to Bell are the D.D. degree from Western Theological Seminary (1921), the Doctor of Sacred Theology degree from the University of the South (1923), the Litt.D. degree from Columbia University (1929) and from Colorado College (1931), and the Doctor of Pedagogy degree from the University of the State of New York, Coe College, and Ohio Wesleyan University. His fraternities are Phi Beta Kappa and Kappa Sigma. He is a Mason and belongs to the University Club, the Quadrangle Club in Chicago, and the Authors' Club in London. On April 24, 1912, he married Elizabeth Wood Lee; their only son, Bernard Lee, is deceased.

(Continued next page)

BELL, BERNARD I.—*Continued*

In manner, observed the New York *Post*, the Episcopal canon "is chatty and comfortable as if he likes gentle argument."

References

Cath World 173:98-104 My '51
N Y Post Mag p27 Jl 1 '49 por
Religious Leaders of America, 1941-42
Who's Who in America, 1952-53
World Biography (1948)

BELL, ELLIOTT V(ALLANCE) Sept. 25, 1902- Editor; publisher

Address: b. c/o Business Week, 330 W. 42d St., New York 36; h. 150 E. 73d St., New York 21; "Quaker Hill," Pawling, N.Y.

Since his resignation as New York State Superintendent of Banks in late 1949, Elliott V. Bell has been chairman of the executive committee of the McGraw-Hill Publishing Company and editor and publisher of *Business Week* magazine. A noted expert on banking

ELLIOTT V. BELL

and finance, Elliott had earlier been economic adviser to Thomas E. Dewey and had been associated with the New York *Times* as a financial writer (1929-39) and later as a member of the editorial board.

Elliott Vallance Bell, a life-long resident of the State of New York, was born in New York City on September 25, 1902, the son of William and Harriet (Elliott) Bell. After attending a public elementary school and the DeWitt Clinton High School, he enrolled at Columbia University, where he became captain of the fencing team and president of the Philolexian Society. As a Columbia undergraduate, he was a contemporary of the future New York State Governor Thomas E. Dewey, with whom, however,

he had no personal acquaintance until about three years after his graduation. Bell, who had taken his B.A. degree in 1925 and had been meanwhile engaged in study, travel, and free-lance writing, was editing a house organ for the Consolidated Edison Company when, following a meeting in 1928 at the Columbia University Club, Dewey talked with him. (According to Edward Angly in his article "Tom Dewey's First String Eleven" in the *Saturday Evening Post* of August 2, 1947, the occasion was a political rally of Young Republicans during the Smith-Hoover Presidential campaign. Joseph and Stewart Alsop, writing for the October 16, 1948, issue of the same magazine, reported that Dewey "introduced himself to Elliott Bell on the way out of a Columbia lecture by Rexford Guy Tugwell.") It is generally agreed that on this evening stroll the two discovered what Alden Hatch has called "a mutual taste for serious discussion on the Romanesque politics and fantastic finance of the bull market days" (*Harper's Magazine*, October 1948) and that they later became close friends.

In January 1929 Elliott Bell secured his first position on a metropolitan newspaper staff, as a banking and money market specialist for the New York *Herald Tribune*. "In that capacity," stated a biographical sketch in the same paper, "he scored one of the famous 'beats' of the stock market boom era by writing of the succor which Charles E. Mitchell, then chairman of National City Bank, gave the call money market in March 1929, when the supplies of call money, under Federal pressure, seemed on the point of drying up completely."

The New York *Times,* in the following summer, asked Bell to join its financial news staff. He accepted, and worked with that paper for the next ten years, becoming in due course the assistant financial news editor. For seven years, beginning in 1932, he was also the American correspondent of the London financial journal *The Banker*, and in the same period contributed on several occasions to *Banking* (the official journal of the American Banking Association), *The Analyst*, and *Current History*, which was at that period published by the New York *Times*. Titles of his *Current History* articles include "Bankers Sign a Truce" (December 1944), "Who Shall Rule the Money Market?" (July 1935), and "Silver Fiasco" (February 1936). His view of the silver bloc, then and later, has been "laughingly described" by Bell as "uncomplimentary" (New York *Times*). He became in 1938 the first president of the New York Financial Writers' Association and in the same year contributed the chapter entitled "The Decline of the Money Barons" to the volume *We Saw It Happen*, described by the editors Hanson W. Baldwin and Shepard Stone as an attempt "to present through the eyes of thirteen of the outstanding correspondents and critics of the New York *Times* a cross-section of twentieth century civilization."

Throughout the ten-year period ending in 1939 Dewey frequently sought in an informal way the advice of Bell when confronted with some key decision. "It was Bell he telephoned," the Alsops have stated, "when the late George Medalie, United States Attorney, offered him his first chance at racket busting, as assistant United States attorney, in 1931." Bell is said to have advised Dewey to reject Medalie's offer unless he was looking forward to a political career. Dewey's acceptance of Medalie's offer led to his appointment as special rackets prosecutor in 1935 and to his election in 1937 as District Attorney of New York County. At lunch one day in the spring of 1939, as related by Edward Angly, Dewey and Bell "began an enduring political partnership." Dewey reportedly told his friend that although he had been defeated the previous autumn in his race for the New York Governorship, he felt there was "just . . . the chance the Republicans might tap him the following year with their Presidential nomination." He asked Bell to become his economic consultant and to head a research team to be devoted to stockpiling facts which might provide the material for effective speeches on fiscal and other issues.

Having agreed to Dewey's request, Bell shortly afterward sent in his resignation as assistant financial editor of the New York Times. He wrote a "20,000 word monograph on money" for Dewey and also, with the research economist John Edward Burton drafted many of Dewey's most effective preconvention addresses in 1940. When in July Dewey lost the Republican nomination to Wendell L. Willkie, he "lent" Bell to the latter as research consultant in the Presidential campaign. Bell "guided Willkie's policy statements on domestic and foreign affairs" (Sylvia F. Porter in the New York Post) with such authority that after the campaign he was invited to rejoin the New York Times as a member of the editorial board. In the spring of 1942, when Dewey was planning his second campaign for the Governorship of New York, he again called on his friend for practical aid. After Dewey's election in November, Bell accepted an appointment by the Governor-elect as consulting economist on the Committee on Unemployment in New York City and, at the persuasion (it was said) of Dewey's foreign affairs adviser John Foster Dulles, agreed to take the post of State Superintendent of Banks in succession to Jackson S. Hutte. The appointment, effective when Dewey assumed office at the beginning of the following year, was announced December 21, 1942.

As State Superintendent of Banks from 1943 to 1949, a longer period than any of his predecessors', Bell was identified with opposition to excessive governmental regulation of business and to lavish governmental spending. "Money for government doesn't come from an endless source," he was quoted as saying early in 1947. "It comes from the people themselves, who are the real little fellows." He further maintained that the housing shortage was "the artificial product of inflation" and preferred a "long-range program for veterans" to payment of a State bonus (Nate White in the Christian Science Monitor). His influence extended beyond his own office, for—as the Alsops wrote just before the 1948 election—"although he is officially banking superintendent, Bell's specialty

is general wisdom and speech-drafting." Considered, along with Paul Evans Lockwood, the closest to the Governor of all members of the "Dewey team" (noted Alden Hatch), he was again a key figure in Dewey's 1944 and 1948 campaigns for the Presidency. At the end of October 1949 Bell was elected President of the National Association of State Bank Supervisors, about six weeks before his resignation on December 13 as New York State Superintendent of Banks was made public.

The position accepted by Elliott Bell after withdrawal from the Dewey "cabinet" (effective on December 31, 1949) was that of chairman of the executive committee of the McGraw-Hill Publishing Company, Inc., of which he had been a director since December 1947. At the same time he became chairman of a new three-man board of editors created for McGraw-Hill's Business Week. The other members of this board, the magazine announced in its December 24, 1949, issue, would be Edgar A. Grunwald and Kenneth Kramer, who would "work as an executive team under Bell's supervision." Bell subsequently became publisher also of the magazine. A weekly news periodical, Business Week, which was founded in 1929 and had in 1952 a circulation of 206,577, is devoted to reporting, analyzing, forecasting, and interpreting information in various fields of public interest related to business. Some of the subjects with which it is concerned are finance and markets, labor, production, management, industrial research, new products, and conditions in foreign countries as well as the United States. As a writer and speaker on finance, Bell has continued to oppose what he regards as inflationary theories and practices. Thus in his farewell statement as New York State Superintendent of Banks, he urged the Federal Reserve System to abandon the practice, "necessary and proper" in wartime of pegging the Government bond market. In April 1951 in an address to the Federal Reserve Bank of Minneapolis, he called for an end to the "phony war" against inflation by a new four-point program calling, among other things, for "speedy increases of taxes on persons, instead of on business." Following the November 1952 election Bell predicted, to the Economic Club of New York, an economic recession in 1953 or 1954. He added, however, that the recession was not expected to be "deep or disastrous" and that in any case the threat would be met successfully by the Eisenhower Administration.

Bell, who was made a director of the New York Life Insurance Company in January 1950, also holds a directorship in the New York Telephone Company, the Bank of . Manhattan Company, the Dime Savings Bank of Brooklyn, the Tri-Continental Corporation, the American Agricultural Chemical Company, Revere Copper and Brass, Inc., and the Carrier Corporation. He is vice-chairman of the Power Authority of the State of New York; a member of the State Banking Board and of the research and policy committee of the Committee for Economic Development; and a trustee of Vassar College, the Lenox School, John Simon Guggenheim Memorial Foundation, and the Community Service Society of New York. Other

BELL, ELLIOTT V.—*Continued*

organizations with which he has been associated are the New York Heart Association (director), Rockefeller Distinguished Service Award (member of the selection committee), Fulbright Awards (member of the national selection committee), Boy Scouts of America (member of the Greater New York Council), and Columbia University (member of the university development plan committee). He also belongs to the Century Association, the University Club Council, the Council on Foreign Relations, and the Economic Club of New York, and is a member of the board of governors of the Bankers Club of America. Bell holds an honorary LL.D. degree from Bard College, conferred in 1950.

Married on November 23, 1927, Elliott and Amelia (Lange) Bell are the parents of a daughter, Nancy Melissa. He has been described by Alden Hatch as "an energetic man, with crisp coppery hair," and as a good skier and athlete. He attends Christ Church on Quaker Hill at Pawling, New York.

References

Bsns W p20 D 24 '49 por
Christian Sci Mon Apr 1 '47 por
Comm & Fin Chr 156:2327 Dec 31 '42
Harper 197:38-46 O '48
Look 8:25 Jl 11 '44 por
N Y Herald Tribune p9 D 22 '42
N Y Post p26 Je 25 '48
N Y Times p21 D 22 '42 por; VI p10-
    11+ S 12 '48 por; p1 D 14 '49 por;
    p13 F 20 '52 por
N Y World-Telegram p25 O 19 '48 por
Newsweek 23:46 Je 26 '44 por
Sat Eve Post 220:18-19+ Ag 2 '47 por;
    221:17 O 16 '48 por
Time 42:16 N 1 '43 por
Baldwin, H. W., and Stone, S., eds. We
    Saw It Happen (1938)
International Who's Who, 1952
International World Who's Who (1949)
Who's Who in America, 1952-53
Who's Who in the East (1951)
Who's Who in New York, 1952
Who's Who in United States Politics
    (1952)
World Biography (1948)

BEN-ZVI, ISAAC (bĕn-tsvē') Nov. 24, 1884- President of Israel
Address: 10 Ibu Gabirol Rd., Rahavia, Jerusalem, Israel

A member of "the small band of legendary pioneers" responsible for the establishment of Israel and leader of the Labor (Mapai) party, Isaac Ben-Zvi was elected second President of the young nation on December 8, 1952, to succeed the late Dr. Chaim Weizmann. As head of Vaad Leumi, the organization that represented the Jewish community under the British mandate, Ben-Zvi was the principal spokesman for Palestine Jewry for almost thirty years. He was a founder of the Jewish defense organization that later developed into the Haganah, and in World War I he helped recruit the Jewish Legion that fought on the side of the British to push the Turks and Germans out of the Holy Land. A noted Orientalist, Ben-Zvi is the author of books and articles on archaeology, ethnology, history, and jurisprudence of the Near East.

Isaac ("Yitzhak" is the Hebrew form) Ben-Zvi was born Isaac Shimshelivitz in Poltava, the Ukraine, Russia, November 24, 1884. His father, a prosperous businessman, was an ardent Zionist who inspired his son to dedicate himself to the movement. He received his education at a traditional Hebrew school (*Heder Metukan*), at the Government high school at Poltava, and at the University of Kiev, where he studied natural science. Influenced while he was at the university by the Zionist writer Azar (Alexander Ziskind Rabinowitz), Ben-Zvi taught Hebrew and Russian to earn enough money to go to Palestine. A three months' visit there in 1904 impressed him with the achievements of the early Zionist pioneers, and he returned to Russia to become a founder of the Zionist Labor Movement in that country.

In the Russian pogroms of 1905 Ben-Zvi helped to create Jewish self-defense units which were the first attempts of pogrom victims to organize to defend themselves. As a result of this activity, he and his family were placed on the Czarist blacklist. His father was deported to Siberia, but Ben-Zvi succeeded in escaping and, spurred by experiences in Russia, traveled through Germany and Switzerland working for the Zionist movement. In 1907 he returned to Palestine to make it his home. Together with David Ben-Gurion and Josef Springzak, he was a founder of Hashomer ("the Guardsmen"), the first Jewish self-defense organization in Palestine, which after World War I developed into the Haganah, the underground army of the Zionist movement in the period of the British mandate. Since 1908, when he represented the Palestine labor movement at the Zionist congress at The Hague, Ben-Zvi has been the delegate of the Israel Labor party at all Zionist congresses. In 1909 he helped establish the first Hebrew high school in Jerusalem and became one of its teachers. With Ben-Gurion he edited a journal, *Haachdut*, from 1910 to 1914, and in 1912 the two men, so closely associated in their work that they were called "the twins," went to Constantinople to study law at Istanbul University. There they also made contact with Jewish groups, especially with the Jewish port workers of Salonika, who later immigrated to Palestine to become the first Jewish stevedores in the port of Haifa.

When Ben-Zvi and Ben-Gurion returned to Palestine on the outbreak of World War I and attempted to organize a Jewish militia in Jerusalem, they were exiled by Jemal Pasha, then Turkish Governor of southern Syria. In 1916 the two Zionist leaders reached the United States, where they organized the Hechalutz (pioneer) movement, and, after the United States entered the war, recruited the American Battalion of the Jewish Legion. In 1918 Ben-Zvi returned to Palestine to fight with the Legion in the British army which ousted the Turks from Palestine. With the end of the war, Jewish efforts to establish a national State were intensified. In 1919 Ben-Zvi became a member of the provisional committee of the Jewish community in Palestine, the first national body of Jewish self-government in that country. When the provisional committee became Vaad Leumi (the Jewish National Council) in the next year, Ben-Zvi was elected to its presidium and was made the official spokesman for the Jewish community, which he represented for the next thirty years before British, Anglo-American, and later United Nations commissions. He was elected chairman of Vaad Leumi in 1931 and president in 1944.

In the postwar years Ben-Zvi's activities were concentrated in four major fields—civic government, where he served nearly twenty years (beginning in 1927) in the Municipal Council of Jerusalem; the labor movement, in which in 1920 he helped establish Histadrut, the General Federation of Jewish Labor in Palestine; Zionism, working to finance Jewish immigration and settlement in Palestine; and in foreign relations, primarily in dealing with the British. Sir Herbert Samuel, first British High Commissioner, appointed him in 1920 to the Palestine Government Advisory Council, from which a year later Ben-Zvi resigned in protest against the British order temporarily suspending Jewish immigration. He took part in the Zurich Conference of 1929, which established the Jewish Agency for Palestine, recognized in Article IV of the Palestine Mandate of the League of Nations as the representative body of the Jewish people. In 1937 he represented Jewish Palestine at the coronation of King George VI.

Ben-Zvi, who was one of the thirty-seven signers of Israel's Declaration of Independence, was elected to the provisional state council of Israel on May 14, 1948, when the British withdrew their armies from Israel. In the elections of the following January he won a seat in the first Knesset (Parliament) and was later re-elected to the second Knesset.

After a thirty-day period of mourning, the Knesset met to elect a successor to President Chaim Weizmann, who died on November 9, 1952. By a majority vote, on the third ballot, Ben-Zvi, the candidate of Mapai, was elected to the office for a five-year term. Two days later his inauguration took place, with representatives of all the Western powers witnessing the simple traditional ceremony held in the Knesset building. Also present was the new President's ninety-year-old father.

Ben-Zvi took his pledge of office on the Bible, a gesture interpreted by observers "as lending a welcome Jewish touch to the ceremony." The President of the Israeli Government is the symbolic leader of the country, but has little political power. His duties are to sign laws (all official papers require countersignatures of Cabinet members concerned); make diplomatic appointments and receive diplomats from abroad; and mediate between heads of parties when necessary. "An attempt may be made in the Knesset to broaden the powers of the President," reported the New York Times in December 1952, "giving him, among other things, a temporary suspension veto over legislation."

I.S.I. Photos

ISAAC BEN-ZVI

A few days after Ben-Zvi assumed office, Prime Minister Ben-Gurion submitted the resignation of his Government, a coalition of the Mapai party and religious parties, which no longer had the required majority in the Knesset. A new coalition between Mapai and the conservative General Zionist party was approved and Ben-Gurion introduced his new Cabinet on December 22, 1952. The coming of the General Zionists into the Israeli Government was viewed as "a substantial shift to the right."

Throughout his political career Ben-Zvi has continued his work as a Near East scholar, studying Palestine lore and Arab and Jewish history. His published works include several books on the history of Palestine: *Eretz Israel in Past and Present* (with David Ben-Gurion) (1918); *The Book of the Samaritans* (1935); five volumes of *Researches and Articles* (1937); and *The Moslem World and the Arab World* (1937). He was chief of the Institute for the Research of Jewish Communities in the Middle East (1947-52), established within the Hebrew University. For his scholarly work he has been awarded the title of doctor *honoris causa* by the Jewish Theological Seminary of America. In recognition of his public service, the British Government conferred on him the Order of the British Empire. In March 1953 Ben-Zvi was elected honorary president of Hebrew University in Jerusalem.

The President's wife, Rachel Yanait Ben-Zvi, is a former agricultural engineer, for many years the director of an agricultural training farm for girls and the founder and director of the Youth Aliya Village of Ein Karem in Jerusalem. One of their sons was killed in 1947 in the Israeli-Arab fighting. They have another son and a daughter. The Ben-Zvis continue to live in the austere ways of the early settlers of their country. For twenty-six years their home was a tar-papered wooden

BEN-ZVI, ISAAC—*Continued*

shack in Rahavia, Jerusalem, and they have chosen as the official residence of the President a three-room prefabricated bungalow of the type being erected for immigrant families in work villages. Ben-Zvi is described as tall and thin, "simple of manner and dignified in bearing."

References

N Y Herald Tribune p1 D 9 '52; p3 D 11 '52; II p1 D 14 '52
N Y Times p1 D 9 '52
N Y World-Telegram p24 D 10 '52
Washington (D.C.) Post D 9 '52
International Who's Who, 1952
Who's Who in the State of Israel, 1949

BENAVENTE (y MARTíNEZ), JACINTO
(bä′nä-vän′tä) Aug. 12, 1866- Dramatist
Address: The Spanish Academy, Madrid, Spain

With the recent deaths of George Bernard Shaw and Maurice Maeterlinck, the Spanish playwright Jacinto Benavente becomes the oldest living dramatist of world stature. Since the production of his first play at the age of twenty-eight, he has, in the prolific tradition of the Spanish theatre, written over 170 plays. He

Courtesy, Hispanic Institute
JACINTO BENAVENTE

is best known to the non-Spanish world for two plays: *The Bonds of Interest* (1907) and the powerful peasant tragedy, *Malquerida* (1913). Today, at eighty-seven, he is still an active figure in Madrid's literary and theatrical circles.

Last year from his tireless pen came five new plays which were produced in Madrid and written in the satirical tradition in which he has so long been a master. His achievements

received international recognition in 1922, when he was awarded the Nobel Prize for Literature "for the happy way in which he has pursued the honored traditions of the Spanish drama." He is also regarded as Spain's most eminent literary critic, and is still an occasional contributor to Madrid journals. His work has been translated in many languages and produced in cities all over the world.

Benavente has been successful in all *genres*: peasant drama, tragedy, romantic comedy, romantic drama, rococo spectacles and imaginative fairy tales. "His versatility is not confined to technique, but appears in the extraordinary range and complexity of human feeling and motive which is invariable throughout his theatre" (*Poet Lore*, March 1918).

Jacinto Benavente (y Martínez) was born in Madrid on August 12, 1866, the only child of a distinguished pediatrician, Dr. Mariano Benavente, to whom a statue was subsequently erected in the Buen Retiro Gardens of Madrid. Benavente was educated at the fashionable San Isidro Institute, where he demonstrated a precocious brilliance. As a child he had his own puppet theatre for which he wrote short skits. He studied with the Faculty of Law at the University of Madrid, but after his father's death in 1885, Benavente determined to devote the rest of his life to literature. He became a frequenter of the theatres of the capital and began to read systematically the works of the great dramatists, especially Shakespeare.

For a while he travelled with a circus and with it visited France, Germany and Russia. Eventually, he became its impresario and acquired his lifelong fascination for clowns and their art. Subsequently, he became an actor in the company of Maria Tubau, where his first role was that of a sportsman, at that period an unfamiliar and ridiculous figure in Spain. In an interview in the Spanish periodical, *La Esfera* (1916), Benavente stated that he would rather have been a great actor than a writer of plays. Throughout his life he has been an occasional performer: in 1920 he assayed, with critical success, the role of Don Juan in Zorilla's play of the same name.

Benavente's earliest literary experiments were four little romantic fantasies, published under the title *Teatro Fantástico* in 1892. These showed the strong influence which Shakespeare, even then, exerted over his imagination. The next year he produced a slim volume of poems, *Versos*, which were "sensual, but cruel and Mephistophelean," as W. Starkie terms them in his biography of Benavente. Also in 1893 he wrote *Cartes de Mujeres*, described as "tender, subtle, satiric," which exhibited an extraordinary insight into the complexity of women's emotions.

The dramatist's first full-length play *El Nido Ajeno* was acted in 1894 and failed to attract attention. But on the performance of his second work, *Gente Conocida*, at the Teatro de la Comedia, Madrid, in 1896, it was at once recognized that an extraordinary talent had appeared. It was followed by a brilliant succession of satirical comedies, dealing with Madrid society or with the fortunes of political adventurers from the capital condemned for a while to serve in the provinces. Of these, the finest were *The Governor's Wife* (1901), *Saturday Night* (1903) and *Brute Force* (1908), all with a strong undercurrent of serious and symbolic import which was often obscured by the brilliance of the dialogue. This same scintillating wit, which Starkie calls "Benavente's Toledo blade of satire," was responsible for his unpopularity with theatre-goers who felt his lash and gave rise to the criticism that his plays were devoid of action. In reply to all criticism, the dramatist said, "I make the public for my plays, not the plays for the public."

He reached the height of his fame and power with two plays of widely-varied tone: the satiric comedy, *The Bonds of Interest* (1907), a deft and facile work which portrays the two irreconcilable selves of every man, the good and the bad, which are inextricably mixed. Of this play Barrett H. Clark in *A Study of Modern Drama* (1936) wrote: "It is a striking proof of the fact that a man of genius can use the oldest and most hackneyed forms provided he has something to say and can say it well." The other play to attain an international reputation was *La Malquerida*, a grim, naturalistic peasant drama with Freudian overtones. Nance O'Neill starred in the English version of this play in New York and on tour for 866 performances from 1920 to 1922. Of all Benavente's plays, only *La Malquerida* and *His Widow's Husband* (which was presented for 100 performances by the Washington Square Players on the same bill with O'Neill's *In the Zone*), have been commercially successful in the United States. *The Bonds of Interest* was presented by the Theater Guild (1919), Everyman Theatre (1920), Walter Hampden (1929), and Loft Players (1951), but none of these had long runs.

Like his father, Benavente had an intense love of children which manifested itself in countless donations to charity and the writing of a score of special children's plays. In 1909 he and the actor Porredon founded a short-lived Children's Theatre, to which he contributed, among other pieces, *The Prince Who Learned Everything Out of Books* (1909), an allegorical fairy-tale of great delicacy. In 1913 he was admitted to the Royal Spanish Academy after the successful presentation of *La Malquerida*. He refused demonstrations in his honor and arranged that all sums subscribed for such fetes be invested in a school breakfast fund. In 1917 he brought out a book, *Los Niños,* devoted entirely to the discussion of child problems.

From 1908-12 the dramatist wrote weekly articles for the Madrid newspaper, *El Imparcial,* on any subject which came to mind; these later were collected in the five-volume *De Sobremesa (Table-Talk).* At the outbreak of the first World War, although he owed a great deal of his quality as a writer to his assimilation of the French and English spirit, Benavente chose to be on the side of Germany, along with the Spanish army, clergy and aristocracy, and edited a symposium, *El Ano Germanófilo* (1916), in defense of his decision.

He devoted much time to translating Shakespeare's and Molière's plays into Spanish, and in editing the intellectual magazine, *La Vida Literaria,* which was mainly responsible for giving a voice to the young writers of the post-Spanish-American war movement who were vigorously attempting to resurrect Spain from the classical and early nineteenth-century romantic grave into which its art had fallen.

In 1920 he became director of the Teatro Español, the national theatre of Spain, and ran unsuccessfully for a seat in the Chamber of Deputies. When he received the Nobel Prize for Literature in 1922, a new generation of artists objected vociferously to this honor, but ironically, the aristocracy he had lampooned mercilessly for many years rose to his defense. In the wake of his revived world fame, he launched a long tour of the United States and Latin America with his own theatrical company.

Various reports were circulated about Benavente during the Spanish Civil War. He was reported killed by the Loyalists at the outbreak of hostilities in Barcelona in 1936, but a dispatch to the New York *Times* (October 3, 1936) stated that he had been living quietly in Valencia. The same dispatch revealed the execution of the younger dramatist, Garcia Lorca, in Granada. Barrett H. Clark and George Freedley in *A History of Modern Drama* (1947) wrote that Benavente "had fled Madrid with the Republic, was captured in Valencia and taken back to Madrid by Franco forces, and kept under guard in his own house. Later he made his peace with Franco." The July 31, 1939 issue of the *Daily Worker* reported that he was one of the 3,170 intellectuals detained in a French concentration camp. After the Civil War, Benavente returned to Valencia, where he played the role of Crispin in his *Bonds of Interest* for the benefit of the war's victims (New York *Herald Tribune,* November 1, 1939).

J. Van Horne, in his *Tres Comedias de Benavente,* describes the dramatist as a "Spaniard of the Golden Age. He is a small, neat, refined man. His manners have an air of feminine elegance. His aquiline profile and pointed beard give a typically Spanish appearance to his countenance, but his character lies above all in his brow which is broad and spacious like that of Cervantes and in his bright witty eyes, in which there nevertheless lurks a faint shadow of melancholy." Dr. Julius Brouta in *The Drama Magazine* (May 1915) calls Benavente "in many respects the Bernard Shaw of Spain. Like Shaw he is a disciple of Ibsen; like him an iconoclast, reformer, teacher, preacher, and his dialectics are hardly less efficient or his spirit less brilliant." A devout Catholic, and a bachelor, Benavente has been repeatedly honored publicly by Generalissimo Francisco Franco's Government.

"It has been said that every idea of Benavente's is an idea and a half," wrote John G. Underhill, who translated many of his plays into English. "We see not only the thought, but its reverse and its ramifications, its genesis, as well as the nature by which it was conceived."

BENAVENTE, JACINTO—*Continued*

The Spanish dramatist's work was appraised by Horatio Smith in the *Columbia Dictionary of Modern European Literature* (1947): "Benavente's plays show that kindness, pity, generosity, tolerance are stronger than brute force. . . .This essentially Christian conception of life is in no wise in contradiction to the skeptical, pessimistic, critical, negative character which is found in his first works and which will always be the dominant characteristic of his writings, for his eye catches with greater precision, fidelity and acuteness the weaknesses of human nature. The fact that there is a touch of sweetness in his bitterness, of sadness and melancholy in his laughter, entitles him to a place among the great modern satirists." John G. Underhill in his preface to Benavente's plays (1924) believes that in the comedy, *The School of Princesses,* Benavente expresses his personal viewpoint. "My philosophy is . . . to accept my position in life with all its obligations, to realize that only by fulfilling them completely, that of my own free will can I be happy. . . .The government of oneself is a most difficult matter, but when once it is achieved, what splendid liberty!"

A recent comment on Benavente's six decades of work was written by Dore Ogrizek in *Spain and Portugal* (1953): "He skillfully adapts every European theatrical trend: Maeterlinck's symbolism, Ibsenian anxiety, Shavian wit, Porto-Riche's preciosity, Bernstein's turbulence. He widened the scope of Spanish drama and opened fresh sources of inspiration."

Whatever place we or posterity may assign him, his art is related to that of Cervantes, Shakespeare and Molière, in the opinion of Horatio Smith. "The idealism, kindness and optimism in his work counterbalance his critical, negative vision of life and humanity and elevate it to the plane of profound, consoling irony."

References

The Criterion Magazine Ap '23
Drama Magazine N '15
N Y Herald Tribune O 28 '17; F 3 '35; N 1 '39
N Y Times p4 N 10 '22; III p3 Ja 28 '23; II p6 III p8 Ap 1 '23; 3 Jl 29 '36; p3 Ag 22 '36; p20 O 3 '36
Times Lit Sup Ja 11 '23, S 18 '24
Bell, A. F. G. Contemporary Spanish Literature
Barrett, H. C. and Freedley, G. A History of Modern Drama (1947)
Columbia Encyclopedia (1950)
Diccionario Biógrafico (1950)
Freedley, G., and Reeves, J. A. A History of the Theatre (1941)
Hoehn, M. ed. Catholic Authors, 1930-47
Living Authors (1931)
Oxford Companion to the Theatre (1951)
Kunitz, S. J. and Haycraft, H. eds. Twentieth Century Authors (1942)
Underhill, J. C. Plays of Benavente (Scribner's 1917)
Who's Who, 1952

BENCHLEY, NATHANIEL (GODDARD) Nov. 13, 1915- Author
Address: h. 103 E. 86th St., New York 28

Although he has written only one book, Nathaniel Benchley, son of the late humorist, is a well known writer, chiefly of short stories and articles.

His novel *Side Street* (Harcourt, 1950) has been dramatized by Benchley and entitled *The Frogs of Spring.* The play is scheduled for a Broadway production by Lynn Austin and Thomas Noyes. and directed by Burgess Meredith.

Nathaniel Goddard Benchley is the son of Robert Benchley and Gertrude (Darling) Benchley. The fact that his father was a writer, Nathaniel Benchley has said, "influenced me as much as anything else; at any rate, I never seriously considered doing anything but writing."

He was born in Newton, Massachusetts, on November 13, 1915 and brought up in Scarsdale, New York. He attended Philips Exeter Academy in New Hampshire, where he worked on the school yearbook and belonged to the dramatic society. Graduating in 1934, he entered Harvard University, majored in English, and continued his interest in writing and dramatics. He was a member of the Hasty Pudding-Institute of 1770, the Signet Society and D.U. Club, worked in the Hasty Pudding shows of 1937 and 1938, and was president of the Harvard *Lampoon.* In 1938 Benchley received his B.S. degree.

Like his father, Benchley began his writing career as a newspaperman. His first job, which he had for four weeks, was writing a weekly feature story for Heywood Broun's *Connecticut Nutmeg.* In 1939 he became a city reporter for the New York *Herald Tribune,* a job he held until 1941 when he joined the Navy. From 1941 to 1943 he was with the Navy Public Relations Department, and from 1943 to 1945 he was on anti-submarine and escort duty in PC boats.

After discharge from the Navy Benchley became in 1946 an assistant editor on *Newsweek* in the drama and movie department. Meanwhile, he had begun selling articles and short stories, and in 1947 gave up his job to devote his time to free lance writing.

Benchley's short stories have appeared in *Good Housekeeping, Ladies Home Journal,* the *Nation's Business, This Week, Cosmopolitan, McCall's,* and the *New Yorker.* He has published articles in these journals and also in *Holiday, Collier's,* and *House and Garden.* His novel *Side Street* was based on his short stories in the *New Yorker* and other journals on the Beldens and the Allens, the two families who live next door to each other on New York's fashionable East Side and share a series of diverting and sometimes mildly harrowing adventures. His numerous magazine articles include "This Is Garbo" (*Collier's,* March 1, 1952), a portrait of the actress based on Benchley's interviews of a number of people who know her—from actors and directors to a hat-check girl; "Cool Friend" (*Holiday,* September 1950), an aesthetic appreciation of beer

Kay Bell

NATHANIEL BENCHLEY

and a history of the beverage; "Look Up To The Young" (*House and Garden*, July 1952), a candid and resigned bit of advice to parents, in which Benchley says that "children's minds, unencumbered by the complexities of adult society, are terrifyingly keen and well-ordered;" "Insanity Ahoy," (*Nation's Business*, April 1953), a discouraged account of his attempts to build a model sailboat for his sceptical young son; and "Birds, Beasts, and Benchley" (*Good Housekeeping,* November 1948), a reminiscence of his father's difficulties in getting along with animals.

From June 1951 to February 1952 Benchley wrote a regular feature, "Offstage," for *Theatre Arts* magazine. In these articles he reviewed plays and movies and one book (Tallulah Bankhead's autobiography), interviewed celebrities of the entertainment world, and reported on backstage life.

Side Street received praise from the reviewers, although some of them questioned whether the incidents in the book were closely enough connected to call it a novel. John K. Hutchens of the New York *Herald Tribune* commended Benchley for "his neat writing, his steady good humor, and a way he has with dialogue." Gilbert Millstein, writing in the New York *Times*, pointed out that the stories in *Side Street* "have been stitched together with pretty thin thread—but that shouldn't diminish anybody's enjoyment. The son of the late Robert Benchley, who was a very funny man himself, has gotten off to a smooth, free-wheeling start."

In general, reviewers and the public agreed that Nathaniel Benchley is not a humorist like his father, but like him he is a chronicler of modern society and its minor but maddening frustrations. The Benchley hero is an affable, well-meaning man, prosperous, reasonably sophisticated, and utterly bemused. Intelligent,

and successful in his business, he is constantly being outwitted by his wife, his alarmingly precocious children, gadgets, and by civilization in general. He falters and fumbles, but never actually collapses. Part of the heart-warming good humor of Benchley's stories is that the reader is confident that the hero will come through each of these distressing experiences, if not unscathed, at least triumphant and ready for more. For this reason, although *Side Street* takes place in New York, it is not limited to New York readers in its appeal.

Benchley was married to the former Marjorie Bradford in May 1939. They have two children, Bradford Goddard and Nathaniel Robert. Of his private life he said in 1951 in *Nation's Business*: "I'm married, have two children and an intelligent dog. My hobby is going to saloons where, I tell myself, I get good ideas for stories." His recreations and hobbies are "baseball and football as a spectator; saloon dialectics; drawing and painting." He is a Democrat. His church affiliation is Episcopalian. He is a member of the Coffee House Club. In appearance, Benchley bears a striking resemblance to his father. He has brown hair and blue eyes, is six feet two inches tall, and weighs 205 pounds.

References

Nation's Bsns 39:7 Ja '51

BENNETT, W(ILLIAM) A(NDREW) C(ECIL) Sept. 6, 1900- Canadian government official

Address: b. Parliament Buildings, Victoria, British Columbia, Canada; h. 1979 Ethel St., Kelowna, British Columbia, Canada

"A political phenomenon unequalled in Canadian history" was the way *Maclean's Magazine* characterized the June 12, 1952 election in British Columbia, in which the Social Credit Party won control of the provincial legislature and W.A.C. Bennett became Premier. After representing the Progressive Conservative Party in the Legislature for ten years, Bennett had become affiliated with the Social Credit movement in December 1951, and was one of the two representatives of the party who had political experience when it unexpectedly came into power. At that time the Social Credit party did not have a majority, and soon after taking office Premier Bennett scheduled an election for early in June 1953 in the hope that the electorate would give a clear mandate to his party. He was re-elected by "a clear majority".

William Andrew Cecil Bennett was born September 6, 1900 in New Brunswick, Canada, the son of A. H. and Mary (Burns) Bennett. After beginning his career in the hardware business in St. John, New Brunswick, Bennett moved to western Canada and, settling in the Okanagan Valley of British Columbia, became the owner of five hardware stores (Bennett's Stores, Ltd.) located at Penticton, Vernon, Kelowna, Westbank, and Kamloops. Elected to the British Columbia Legislature in 1941 as a Progressive Conservative, Bennett attempted several times to wrest leadership of his party

W. A. C. BENNETT

from Herbert Anscombe, who was then its head. When in the spring of 1951 the coalition Government composed of Conservatives and Liberals raised the premiums of its compulsory hospital insurance program nine dollars a year, Bennett left the Government ranks to sit as an Independent in protest against this added burden in the already unpopular plan. Later that year he announced his affiliation with the Social Credit party, which advocates social credit monetary theories as a solution to provincial and Federal problems. Established in 1935 in Alberta, Canada, where it has since been the majority party, the Social Credit movement had been limited chiefly to that province.

The theory of Social Credit maintains that insufficient money exists for the purchase of goods produced and that credit should be issued to prevent this discrepancy and consequent depressions. Against the wishes of its founder, Major C. H. Douglas, the Alberta Social Credit organization entered politics and took over the Government of the province. Legislation on monetary reform which the Social Crediters passed was declared unconstitutional by the Federal Government on the ground that it alone has the power to control credit. The movement gained converts in British Columbia and in April 1949 the British Columbia Social Credit League received its charter from the international organization. With the election of 1952 British Columbia became the second Canadian province (Alberta was the first) to be governed by Social Crediters.

In accordance with a British Columbia tradition, the Conservative-Liberal coalition Government, which could have remained in power until 1954, called an election for June 1952, and the Social Credit Party decided to run a full slate of candidates. Dissatisfaction with the coalition administration's compulsory hospital insurance plan, a widespread opinion that large corporations were receiving an undue share of

the profits from British Columbia's natural resources, and a split between the two parties in which Herbert Anscombe went into opposition to the Government, had impaired the older parties' popularity with the electorate.

The Social Credit program, adopted at a convention held April 26, called for abolition of the hospital insurance program and its replacement by a voluntary plan, monetary reforms, greater profits from natural resources for British Columbians, and the encouragement of free enterprise and discouragement of monopolies. The Reverend Ernest Hansell, national president of the Social Credit Association of Canada and a member of the Parliament in Alberta, was appointed to direct the campaign.

In the election which took place June 12, the four major parties, Conservative, Liberal, Social Credit and Cooperative Commonwealth Federation, ran candidates. The outcome was not official for thirty days, because the alternative system of voting, used for the first time in British Columbia, made tabulation long and difficult. Despite the complicated election system, in which the voter lists a number of choices in preferred order, it was evident by June 14 that Bennett had been returned by South Okanagan, and it later became apparent that he was one of only five candidates who had been elected by a majority on the first count of the ballots. In July, the tabulation was complete and it was announced that the Social Credit party had elected 19 members to the Legislature, the CCF 18, the Liberals 6, the Conservatives 4, and Labor 1, thus giving the Social Credit party the responsibilty for forming a minority Government.

With twenty-five seats required for a majority, the balance of power was held by the Liberal Party. As an advocate of free enterprise, the Social Credit party, which strongly opposes the CCF program for the socialization of industry, received the support of both Liberals and Conservatives in the Legislature.

After victory in the election, the Social Credit party, which had gone to the polls without a party leader, met in a caucus called by Lyle Wicks, president of the Provincial Social Credit League, to select the future Premier of British Columbia. Bennett, the only member of the party with previous legislative experience except for Mrs. Tilly Rolston, was selected for the post.

Taking office in August after the resignation of Liberal Premier Byron Johnson, he formed his Cabinet and announced that orders-in-council would be open to public scrutiny and that Government purchasing would follow an "open and above the table" policy. The Montreal *Star* reported on August 29 that Bennett was planning to call an election before the new session of the Legislature in an effort to gain a definite majority for the Social Crediters. However, the election was put off until June 1953, and when Bennett's Government lost control of the Legislature early in April, the *Christian Science Monitor* reported that he was pleased with the defeat, because he was certain that the new election would give his party a clear majority. Bennett had expressed the same assurance in the fall of 1952 when two Social

Credit candidates for the Legislature scored an overwhelming victory. Bennett, who had campaigned for them vigorously on the issue of the administration's achievements in its short term of office, commented on their election, "If there was ever any doubt in anyone's mind that the Social Credit government had the confidence of the people . . . that doubt can no longer exist" (Montreal *Star*, November 25, 1952).

Bennett was the first public figure to oppose the altered exchange rate of Canada's money. In September 1952 he asked the Government to devaluate the dollar to avoid harmful effects on the export industry. However, the *Christion Science Monitor* reported that the Canadian Government had "no intention of tampering with the value of the nation's currency (September 26, 1952).

G. V. Ferguson, editor of the Montreal *Star*, has said of the Social Crediters that when in power "They do not try to implement Social Credit. They talk Social Credit . . . [but] behave otherwise like what they are—very sturdy conservatives who do not believe in a welfare state and are anxious to foster private enterprise in every way possible" (April 12, 1953).

The Premier is five feet eleven inches tall, and has blue eyes and brown hair. He married Annie Elizabeth May Richards on July 11, 1927 and they have three children, Anita Mary, Russell J., and William. Bennett has served as a member of the British Columbia Post-War Rehabilitation Committee, is a member of the Shriner and Gyros organizations, the Phi Delta Kappa and Kappa Delta Pi societies, and is affiliated with the United Church of Canada (comprising members of the Congregationalist, Methodist and Presbyterian denominations).

Reference

Maclean's Mag p7 S 1 '52

BENSON, EZRA TAFT Aug. 4, 1899- Secretary of Agriculture; marketing specialist

Address: b. c/o Department of Agriculture, Washington 25, D.C.; 47 E. South Temple St., Salt Lake City, Utah; h. 1389 Harvard St., Salt Lake City, Utah

Three weeks after the Republican victory in the 1952 election, President-elect Dwight D. Eisenhower, on November 24, 1952, announced that he had selected Ezra Taft Benson for the post of Secretary of Agriculture in the new Cabinet to be set up following the inauguration in January. A farm marketing specialist with firsthand experience in virtually all phases of agriculture, Benson was born and raised on a farm, studied agriculture at several institutions, operated his own farm from 1923 until 1929, and was employed as a county agricultural agent and farm marketing specialist for the University of Idaho's extension service. For many years he has been prominently associated with the farmer cooperative movement: in 1930 he helped organize the Idaho Cooperative Council, from 1939 until 1944 he was executive secretary of the National Council of Farmer Co-

Wide World Photos
EZRA TAFT BENSON

operatives, and since 1943 has been a member of the executive committee of the board of trustees of the American Institute of Cooperatives. A Mormon, he has held high positions in the Church of Jesus Christ of Latter-day Saints, including membership in the Quorum of Twelve Apostles, the Church's governing body.

Great-grandson of a pioneer Mormon, for whom he was named, and grandson of Heber C. Kimball, who was an advisor to Brigham Young during the Mormon migration to Utah in 1847, Ezra Taft Benson was born on the family farm at Whitney, Idaho, on August 4, 1899, to George Taft and Sarah S. (Dunkley) Benson. (He is remotely related to Senator Robert A. Taft of Ohio.) It has been told that by the time he was five he could drive a team of horses. "My parents and grandparents were deep lovers of the soil and farming," Benson has said regarding early influences on his interest in agriculture; "my father always gave us boys an opportunity to try out new methods and practices learned in school." He received his early education at an elementary school in Whitney and from 1914 to 1918 attended Oneida Stake Academy in Preston, Idaho ("stake" is the Mormon equivalent of parish), a school founded and operated by the Mormons (according to the account of Melvin K. Jennings in the *Christian Science Monitor*) "to meet the Three-R and Bible-learning needs of what was then a community of pioneer Mormon settlers of Idaho's Bear Lake country."

After taking a correspondence course in farming, Benson entered Utah State Agricultural College (Logan) to study from 1918 until 1921. He spent the following two years in Great Britain and on the Continent on a mission for the Church of Jesus Christ of the Latter-day Saints. On his return to the United States he and his brother Orval bought their

BENSON, EZRA T.—*Continued*

father's farm, each alternating active operation with studies at Brigham Young University (Provo, Utah), where Benson received his B.S. degree in 1926. On a scholarship awarded by Gamma Sigma Delta, honorary agricultural society, he attended Iowa State College (Ames) to take his M.Sc. degree in agricultural economics in 1927. Some time later (1937-38) he pursued graduate studies in agriculture at the University of California.

"Drafted" into county agent work by the local county commissioner, Benson in 1929 became county agricultural agent in Preston of the extension service of the University of Idaho and in 1929-30 was employed as extension economist and marketing specialist of the university's extension division. When this division the following year inaugurated a department of agricultural economics and marketing, Benson accepted the position of head of the new department. He was instrumental at about this time in organizing the Idaho Cooperative Council, of which he was secretary from 1933 to 1938. In Washington, D.C., where he represented this group, his work attracted national attention and led to his appointment in the spring of 1939 as executive secretary of the National Council of Farmer Cooperatives, a post he retained until 1944. The organization then comprised 4,600 member cooperatives whose annual business amounted to $1,300,000,000. "He was supported for the secretaryship," reported the New York *Herald Tribune*, "by many farm organizations, in addition to the cooperatives." As spokesman for the N.C.F.C., Benson recommended in July 1940 that the Democratic party platform support, among other measures, "a program for extension of agricultural cooperatives, management of surplus farm commodities . . . establishment of the 'commodity dollar,' [and] exemption of agricultural labor from the Wage-Hour Act." During World War II President Franklin D. Roosevelt called upon Benson, who in 1940-41 had been a member of the National Farm Credit Committee, to serve on the National Agricultural Advisory Commission.

In November 1942 Benson was a signer of a statement issued jointly by the National Grange, the American Farm Bureau Federation and the N.C.F.C. protesting against what were termed "misdirected efforts" by Government agencies to establish "far-reaching bureaucratic controls and restrictions" over farmers and farm workers. A year later he issued a statement criticizing Roosevelt's policy of farm subsidies: "The virus of subsidies," he said in part, "permeates the economic body and eats it up once it gets its proboscis under the skin." He proposed to the Senate Banking Committee an alternative program of wage subsidies of $482 million in four industries—food processing, petroleum products, clothing, and machinery—as a means of reducing inflationary pressures. Otherwise active in agricultural matters, Benson in 1942 became a member of the executive committee of the board of trustees of the American Institute of Cooperation, an aggregation of "farm cooperatives, farm organizations and land grant colleges, educational in purpose and financed by voluntary contributions." (In 1952 he was made chairman of the board of trustees of A.I.C.)

While engaged in the nation's capital in work relating to agriculture, Benson, who had been president of the Boise stake of the Church of Jesus Christ of the Latter-day Saints in the late 1930's, headed the Washington stake from 1940 to 1943. Upon his being selected in July 1943 as a member of the Quorum of Twelve Apostles, the ruling group of the Mormon Church, Benson returned to Salt Lake City, "disappeared from the national spotlight and devoted himself almost exclusively to the Mormon Church" (*Business Week*). Appointed president of the European Mission of the Church, with headquarters in London, on January 15, 1946, he spent nearly a year abroad and was responsible for postwar distribution of food, clothing, and other supplies through the Mormon welfare program and for reorganization of the work of the Church. In 1946 he was also a United States delegate to the first International Conference of Farm Organizations, held in London. Even "as a leader in his church," Jennings has noted, "Mr. Benson hasn't lost sight of agriculture and its problems. His counsel as a farm-marketing specialist often has been sought by officials and laymen alike." From 1946 to 1950 he was the director of the Farm Foundation.

At the twenty-fifth convention of the American Institute of Farmer Cooperation, held in Madison, Wisconsin, in August 1949, Benson urged, as quoted by the New York *Times*, that one of the goals of the cooperatives should be "to put more emphasis on service and less on price and patronage dividends. It should be clearly recognized that the cooperative movement will be judged more by the quality of its performance than by its size in membership or volume." He recommended that cooperatives "establish as their major goal the preservation of free enterprise." On other occasions he has expressed the idea that "farm cooperatives are not an end in themselves. In the hands of farmers, wisely used, they may prove to be a very useful tool in accomplishing worthwhile objectives." He believes that farmers have, in the past, done only "half a job" in their unorganized state, and that they could improve their position particularly in their farming methods and marketing practices. Benson made known his economic views in speeches "studded with reference to 'eternal' truths which he says are violated by the present overemphasis on 'security' and the trend toward 'paternalistic government'" (Kenneth S. Davis, New York *Times Magazine*, January 4, 1953).

President-elect Dwight D. Eisenhower's designation of Benson as Secretary of Agriculture, announced on November 24, 1952, was considered by many observers as nonpolitical in character, since the Mormon apostle, who supported Senator Taft in his bid for the Republican nomination, had been prevented by his Church duties from taking an active role in party affairs. (For the period that he will serve in Washington Benson was granted a leave of absence from his duties as eighth ranking apostle of the Church).

The *U. S. News* and *World Report* expressed the belief that Mr. Benson "was recommended for the post by General Eisenhower's brother, Milton Eisenhower, president of Pennsylvania State College and long interested in farm problems. The appointment was also warmly approved by Senator Taft, and there are suggestions that Mr. Benson may have had a place on the list of Cabinet recommendations submitted by the Senator at Ike's request." The New York *Times,* noting that Eisenhower had selected a man acceptable and friendly to both the American Farm Bureau Federation and to the National Farmers Union, pointed out: "This was regarded as a considerable achievement, since the two farmers' organizations, the right wing and left wing respectively of organized agriculture, have often been poles apart on such matters as the Brannan Plan, parity prices, crop controls, agricultural tariffs, and similar fundamentals."

As part of his preparation for his cabinet duties, Benson in December 1952 undertook a country-wide tour in order to renew acquaintances with agricultural leaders and to hear suggestions for possible appointment to his department staff. In the course of the tour Benson expressed his opinion at a press conference in Oregon that the farmers did not "want to be the ward of the Government." The New York *Times* also reported him as saying that he foresaw no necessity for additional price supports that would raise the present guarantee of 90 per cent of parity. His nomination approved by the Senate, Benson took the oath of office of Secretary of Agriculture on January 21, 1953.

Active in the Boy Scouts of America, Benson has been a scoutmaster (1918-29), scout commissioner (1930-33), a member of the national council of the organization (since 1939), member of Region Twelve Executive Committee (since 1945), and member of the national executive board (since 1948). He was awarded the Silver Antelope in 1951. Other memberships are on the board of trustees of Brigham Young University, the American Marketing Association, Farm Economics Association, and Delta Nu. He formerly belonged to the Kiwanis and Rotary clubs. Among his awards are the Distinguished Service Award of the Alumni Association of Brigham Young University (1950), an honorary Doctor of Humanities degree conferred by the College of Osteopathic Physicians and Surgeons in Hollywood, California (1951), a testimonial by the University of Wisconsin for his distinguished service to Agriculture (1952). Benson is the author of several articles on agriculture and on religion.

Benson's wife is the former Flora Smith Amussen, whom he married on September 10, 1926. The Bensons have six children, two sons and four daughters—Reed, Mark, Barbara, Beverly, Bonnie, and Flora Beth. *Time* has described the brown-eyed, brown-haired agriculture expert as "a big (six feet, 220 lbs.) farmer-like man, with huge hands, an open, oval red face and a direct, purposeful manner." In his leisure time Benson enjoys recreation with his family and outdoor activities like camping and hunting.

On Secretary Benson's recommendation, President Eisenhower allocated $8,000,000 in the summer of 1953 in emergency funds for drought relief of farmers in the Southwest.

References

Bsns W p30+ N 29 '52 por
Christian Sci Mon p15 D 6 '52
Deseret N p1+ N 24 '52 por
N Y Herald Tribune p1+ N 25 '52 por
N Y Times p24 N 25 '52
N Y World-Telegram p10 N 25 '52
Newsweek 22:59 O 11 '43 por; 40:19 D 1 '52 por
Salt Lake Tribune p1+ N 25 '52 por
Salt Lake Tribune Mag D 14 '52 por
Time 60:15 D 1 '52 por
U S News 33:39 D 5 '52 por
Who's Who in America, 1952-53

BETTIS, VALERIE (ELIZABETH) Dec. 20, 1919- Dancer; choreographer

Address: h. 125 W. 11th St., New York 11

After performing for ten years in the intimacy of the concert hall before small audiences of modern dance devotees, Valerie Bettis came into the Broadway limelight in May 1948, winning several awards with two dances in the musical revue *Inside U.S.A.* Since then Miss Bettis has been creating and performing dances for musical comedies, television, and motion pictures, and at the same time has created several major works, including a dance-drama inspired by William Faulkner's novel, *As I Lay Dying.* Her full-scale ballet in 1952 based on Tennessee Williams' play, *A Streetcar Named Desire,* used theatrical and "cinematic" techniques in a serious vehicle, and her choreography for Rita Hayworth's highly publicized dances in the films *Affair in Trinidad* and *Salomé* employed the techniques of modern dance in simplified, easily recognizable form.

Valerie Elizabeth Bettis Segall was born in Houston, Texas, on December 20, 1919, one of the two children of Royal Holt and Valerie Elizabeth (McCarthy) Bettis. Her father, a well-to-do business man, died when she was thirteen. While attending elementary school and San Jacinto High School in Houston, she participated in musical and dramatic productions and also won scholarships in painting and music.

Valerie began her dancing lessons at the age of ten at Rowena Smith's School of the Dance in Houston, where a ballet-type of dance was taught, with emphasis, however, on teaching the pupil to move in terms of phrases rather than in steps. She also took a six-week course in Houston with Tina Flade, a former student of the Mary Wigman School. At that time, she told a *World-Telegram and Sun* reporter, her body was "big and strong, but not flexible." She went through "agonies" trying to achieve a high kick and said that to this day she en-

VALERIE BETTIS

vies youngsters in dancing classes who do so with ease.

After a year "collecting frat pins" (*Collier's*) at the University of Texas, the Houston debutante set off for New York in September 1937 to study with Hanya Holm, who taught a "free" type of ballet which "attempted a discovery of the ballet premise" rather than a strict set of exercises and offered no conflict with the modern dance. Miss Bettis made her first professional appearance as a member of this group in Miss Holm's composition, *Trend*, in 1937, and earned her first money as a dancer in the *Railroads on Parade* Company at the New York World's Fair in 1939.

Miss Bettis' first solo performance, which took place in November 1941 at the Carnegie Chamber Music Hall after a year of intensive study, brought her little attention. In December of the following year she caused excitement in modern dance circles when she presented her "ritualistic yet passionate" solo *And the Earth Shall Bear Again* to music by John Cage, on a triple bill at the YMHA Dance Center shared with Erick Hawkins and Sybil Shearer (New York *Herald Tribune*, June 27, 1946).

Full recognition as a major figure on the modern dance scene came to Miss Bettis in March 1943 with her presentation of *The Desperate Heart*, a solo composition to a poem especially written for the dance by John Malcolm Brinnin. In a "soft dove-colored gown with a cut-out crimson heart as part of the bodice" and making use of long passages of silence, she "blew the roof" off the intimate Humphrey-Weidman Studio Theater in one of the *Dance Observer* series of concerts, and won John Martin's coveted award for outstanding solo composition (Lloyd, *Borzoi Book of Modern Dance*).

As head of the Perry Mansfield Summer Camp at Steamboat Springs, Colorado, during the summers of 1942 and 1943, Miss Bettis choreographed her first group works, *Vain Shadows* and *Study*. In the summer of 1942 she was also a guest artist at the Colorado Springs Fine Arts Center.

With money she made by accepting a commission to arrange the dances for a musical revue (which never reached Broadway), Miss Bettis financed her own company's Broadway debut at the Adelphi Theatre in May 1945. Although she was acclaimed by most critics, Edwin Denby, who admired her dance virtuosity, complained of the limitation of her subject matter to the writhings of unhappy young women. (New York *Herald Tribune*, May 14, 1945).

Miss Bettis' next important work was *Yerma*, a trio dance based on Garcia Lorca's tragedy about a barren woman whose only desire in life is to bear a child, performed for the first time in June 1946, at the Barbizon-Plaza Concert Hall in New York City. The quality of this dance, with its earthbound movements, was conveyed by Miss Bettis' statement that "the soil is between your toes all the time."

In the summer of 1946 the dancer went on a joint piano-dance recital tour of Central and South America with her husband, Bernardo Segall, whom she had married on September 29, 1943. Segall, Brazilian concert pianist and composer who came to the United States at the age of sixteen on a music scholarship, has been her composer and accompanist since 1941.

The historic occasion when, "for the first time a modern dance choreographer . . . created a work for a major ballet organization" (Walter Terry, New York *Herald Tribune*, March 5, 1947), took place in March 1947, with the presentation of Miss Bettis' *Virginia Sampler* by the Ballet Russe de Monte Carlo in New York City. A piece of Americana based on the struggle between a decadent aristocracy and the rough, lusty frontiersmen, the experiment was unsuccessful, partly, Miss Bettis believed, because the ballet company did not appreciate the "gauche-classic-naive" mood in which the dance was conceived and because the ballet dancers thought in terms of steps, while she thought in terms of movement.

The dancer continued to appear with her group at the YMHA Dance Center and in June 1947 she performed five solo modern dances at the Jacob's Pillow Dance Festival in Lee, Massachusetts.

Miss Bettis' sudden emergence from the dedicated atmosphere and small audiences of the concert hall to fame on Broadway came in May 1948 when she was acclaimed for her two dance numbers choreographed by Helen Tamiris for *Inside U.S.A.*, a revue starring Beatrice Lillie. For her dancing in *Tiger Lily*, a tabloid ballet trial of an enchantress who pushes her lovers off cliffs, and *Haunted Heart*, in which she played a waterfront belle, she received the Donaldson Award that year for both the Best Danseuse and the Season's Best Musical Comedy Debut, and also the *Mademoiselle* Award for Outstanding Women. Walter Terry wrote in the *Herald Tribune* (May 9, 1948) that after ten years "one of the best concert dancers of our generation has just been discovered by Broadway" and remarked that for this larger audience she had not changed her original dance techniques at all.

When Miss Bettis returned to the concert stage after her musical comedy success to present her hour-long dance-drama based on William Faulkner's novel *As I Lay Dying*, her afternoon performance at the YMHA theatre on January 6, 1949 was sold out and a special evening performance was added, an unprecedented occurrence for this specialized series. Considered her masterpiece by dance critics, this composition uses speech freely and takes "dance farther from its own medium into drama than ever before without getting lost" (John Martin in the New York *Times,* August 21, 1949).

One critic who admired *As I Lay Dying* took the dancer to task for other compositions she performed at the Connecticut College Dance Festival the following August, accusing her of getting involved in "modern dance clichés, litterary pretensions, and the collaboration of word-infatuated poets." Cecil Smith in *Musical America* (September 1949) stated that "so unbridled an inner originality as Miss Bettis'" needed better ideas and materials and a bolder organization than appeared in most of her works.

When Valerie Bettis appeared in a program with other modern dance stars in December 1949 at the City Center in a group effort to organize a New York City Dance Theater, Walter Terry wrote in the New York *Herald Tribune* on her performance of *The Desperate Heart,* "If modern dance had a system of ranking its performers, Valerie Bettis would wear the insignia of a prima ballerina."

For her choreography on Paul Whiteman's television show in a series beginning in November 1949, Miss Bettis received the Critics' Award for creating the best TV dances of the season. She has also danced, acted, and choreographed for other television shows, including the *Colgate Comedy Hour,* the *Philco Playhouse, Your Show of Shows,* the *Chevrolet Hour, Studio One,* and *Omnibus,* for which she staged a neglected George Gershwin operetta, *135th Street,* in March 1953.

In *Great To Be Alive* in March 1950 Miss Bettis danced, acted, and sang, and in her next musical comedy appearance, in *Bless You All* the following December, her twelve-minute *Desert Flame* solo won audience approval. A month later, in January 1951, a streamlined version of *Peer Gynt* with John Garfield in the leading role featured Valerie Bettis' choreography, which Walter Terry found "served the drama itself beautifully" (New York *Herald Tribune,* February 18, 1951).

The second dance which Miss Bettis created for a ballet company represented a culmination of her previous tendencies to combine dance with theater, modern with ballet movements, and "highbrow" with popular techniques. In a ballet based on Tennessee Williams' play *A Streetcar Named Desire,* performed in December 1952 by the Slavenska-Franklin Ballet Company in New York City, she produced what Walter Terry called "an independent theater piece of enormous power and urgency" (New York *Herald Tribune,* December 9, 1952).

In the summer of 1952 Miss Bettis went to Hollywood to choreograph the dances for Rita Hayworth in *Affair in Trinidad* and *Salomé* for Columbia Pictures. Her only previous experience with motion pictures had been a direct filming of her dance *The Desperate Heart.* Against opposition by Miss Hayworth's producer, who preferred the star in high-heeled shoes, Miss Bettis insisted on her dancing barefoot in *Affair in Trinidad,* and created simplified modern dance movements that Walter Terry found similar to the "earthiness" in some of Miss Bettis' own concert works. She appeared in the film in a non-dancing role, as a "slinking villainess." She is scheduled to appear in another Columbia Pictures film not yet titled or released.

Blond, green-eyed, "volcanically expressive" Miss Bettis is five feet five and one-half inchs tall and weighs 125 pounds. Her hobbies are painting and stud poker, which she plays in all-night games with her husband and other dancers. The Russian ballerina Alexandra Danilova, who was appearing with the Slavenska-Franklin company when they performed Miss Bettis' ballet, told a *Collier's* reporter, "Here is very elegant . . . woman with so-supple feline body . . . like ready to leap or pounce. Very extraordinary woman."

References

Collier's 128:21 Ag 4 '51
Chujoy, A. ed. Dance Encyclopedia (1949)
Lloyd, M. Borzoi Book of Modern Dance (1949)

BEVIS, PALMER (bē'vĭs) Mar. 19, 1892-
Public relations counsel
Address: b. c/o American-Korean Foundation, Inc., 303 Lexington Ave., New York 16; h. Garth Road, Scarsdale, N.Y.

As executive director and co-founder of the American-Korean Foundation, Inc., Palmer Bevis administers a nonprofit organization which aids large numbers of destitute Koreans in their immediate needs and which seeks to establish a long-range policy of friendship and understanding between Korea and the United States. Bevis, who at one time was executive secretary and treasurer of Yale-in-China, has been a public relations counsel for several charitable and educational organizations and has served as director of community relations for the National Association of Manufacturers. Prior to the founding of the American Korean Foundation in June 1952, he was for two years director of national information for American Relief for Korea, Inc.

On March 19, 1892, Palmer Bevis was born in Macomb, Illinois, one of three children (two sons and a daughter) of Philemon and Leura (Palmer) Bevis. His father was Secretary of the Young Men's Christian Association in St. Louis, Missouri, and in Duluth, Minnesota, where young Bevis attended the Duluth Central High School until 1911. To complete his college preparatory training he enrolled at the Hotchkiss School in Connecticut, where he

PALMER BEVIS

joined the football team, the debating team, and the glee club, and edited the literary magazine; he was graduated in 1914. While working his way through Yale University, Bevis studied history as his major subject and was a member of Beta Theta Pi, Dwight Hall, the glee club, the college choir, and the student council. He left college for one year (1918) to serve in World War I as a lieutenant in the United States Field Artillery, and returned to take his B.A. degree in June 1919. From the year of his graduation until 1923 he held the position of sales manager of the Yale University Press in New Haven, Connecticut.

For the next seven years (1923-30) Bevis was executive secretary and treasurer of Yale-in-China, an institution established in 1906 by graduates of Yale University and supported by Yale alumni, their friends, and other co-operating agencies. Located in thirty buildings on forty-two acres of land in Changsha in the Province of Hunan, this educational organization possessed equipment valued at $500,000, including one of the most modern hospitals in China. With a faculty of forty Americans and Western-educated Chinese, most of whom were graduates of Yale, in 1923 Yale-in-China had about 450 students. Traveling back and forth between Changsha and New Haven, Bevis handled both the financial and administrative problems of the institution, which operated on an annual budget of about $150,000. In 1927 he spent six months in China at a time when the Government of Hunan exerted pressure upon the school to teach the Communist ideology, making it difficult for the faculty to maintain its standards of work and discipline. Yale-in-China was closed in 1929.

A public relations counsel from 1930 to 1945 in New York for various philanthropic and educational groups, Bevis was also occupied with projects such as the exchange of young

ambassadors of good-will between France and the United States in 1935 on the first voyage of the French steamship, the *Normandie.* In 1940-41 he acted as a special consultant to the Office of Civilian Defense in Washington, D.C., on a program commemorating the 150th anniversary of the Bill of Rights.

In World War II Bevis was a member of the Aircraft Warning Service of the United States Army. After four years (1941-45) as director of public relations for St. Georges & Keyes in New York City, Bevis was from 1945 to 1947 president of his own firm, Palmer Bevis, Inc. He directed group and community relations for the public relations division of the National Association of Manufacturers (1945-49) and worked with civilian leaders representing church, educational, youth, and other public welfare groups to educate the American people on various economic and political issues.

In June 1952, after two years in the post of director of national information of American Relief for Korea, Inc., Bevis founded, with Dr. You Chan Yang, Korean Ambassador to the United States, the American-Korean Foundation, Inc., a nonprofit organization to aid millions of people in the devastated areas of Korea and to establish mutual understanding between the United States and Korea on social, economic, and political problems. The American-Korean Foundation estimated that more than 100,000 Korean children were completely separated from their homes and parents, and were without adequate food, housing, clothing, schools, and recreation. Large numbers of aged and infirm individuals, as well as wounded Korean soldiers, were in need of care. Educational facilities, especially trade schools, are high on the Foundation's agenda. As executive director of the Foundation, Bevis is the administrative head of the organization, handling its finances and its public relations, while Dr. Yang is honorary chairman and Dr. Milton S. Eisenhower is chairman. Organizers of the Foundation include Nelson Rockefeller, Herbert Hoover, Arthur Hays Sulzberger, Henry R. Luce, William G. Brady, Thomas J. Watson, and Chester I. Bernard. Bevis made a visit to Korea in March 1953 with Dr. Howard A. Rusk, an international authority on prosthetics, and other members of the rehabilitation mission.

Bevis is active in the alumni associations of the Hotchkiss School and Yale University, and takes a strong interest in helping the Boy Scouts and other boys' clubs. He is a one-time Trustee of the village of Ocean Beach, New York (Fire Island), a member of the American Institute of Science, Beta Theta Pi, the Yale Club of New York, the Army and Navy Club (Washington, D.C.), the Newcomen Society, and the Fire Island Beach Club. Writer of a number of magazine articles and booklets, he is co-author of the pamphlet, *Footprints of the Trojan Horse* (1939), on Nazi infiltration tactics; author of *Your Bill of Rights and Mine* (1939); and co-author of *The Spirit of Paul Revere* (1945).

On December 28, 1937, Bevis married Margaret Firth (now deceased); they had one child, Peggy Anne. Bevis had two children by a previous marriage—Palmer L., and William D.

His favorite sports are deep-sea fishing, sailing, swimming, and tennis. Fond of traveling, he has made three voyages to Europe and trips to Mexico, Bermuda, Nassau, Cuba, Canada, and the Orient. Bevis has blue eyes and brown hair, is five feet eleven inches tall, and weighs 190 pounds. He is a member of the Scarsdale Community Baptist Church, and votes Republican.

Reference

Who's Who in Commerce and Industry (1951)

Harris & Ewing

J. W. BEYEN

BEYEN, J(OHAN) W(ILLEM) (bā'ĕn yō-hän' vil'ĕm) May 2, 1897- Minister for Foreign Affairs of the Netherlands

Address: b. Plein 23, The Hague, the Netherlands; h. Plein 1813, No. 2, The Hague, the Netherlands

The Netherlands Minister for Foreign Affairs Dr. J. W. Beyen, long known as an expert in international finance, was appointed to the Cabinet of Premier Willem Drees on September 1, 1952, to assume with Joseph M. A. H. Luns, Minister without Portfolio, joint responsibility for foreign policy. Beyen, who from 1927 to 1935 held the office of director-manager of the Rotterdam Bank, was for two years (1935-37) president of the Bank for International Settlement in Basel and for six years (1940-46) financial director of Lever Brothers and Unilever, Ltd., in London and Rotterdam. A participant in a number of monetary conferences, including that at Bretton Woods, New Hampshire, in the summer of 1944, Dr. Beyen became an executive director of the International Bank for Reconstruction and Development in 1946 and of the International Monetary Fund in 1948.

Born to Karel Hendrik and Louise Maria (Coenen) Beyen on May 2, 1897, Johan Willem Beyen is a native of Utrecht, the Netherlands. Here he was reared and educated, for his advanced training attending the University of Utrecht, where he received his Doctor of Jurisprudence degree in 1918. He then joined the Ministry of Finance at The Hague, became deputy treasurer general three years later, and resigned at the end of 1923 to serve as legal adviser to Philips Incandescent Lamp Company. On April 1, 1925, just before the simultaneous return of Great Britain and Holland to the gold standard, Beyen became one of the two "delegates" (managers) in charge of the Amsterdam branch of the Javasche Bank, the central bank for the Dutch East Indies, and as such "undertook in 1926 to reorganize in that area the banking institutions furnishing credit to small businessmen" (*Commercial and Financial Chronicle*). In this post he was the Java Bank's principal contact with the Government, the Bank of the Netherlands, and other central banks of Europe. Also in 1926 Dr. Beyen saw published in Holland the first of his two books, a work on municipal taxation entitled *Het plaatselijk belastinggebied*.

The next year (1927) Beyen was made managing director of the Rotterdamsche Bank-vereeniging (Rotterdam Bank, Inc.), one of the six largest banking institutions in the Netherlands, and was to retain this position for the next eight years. Following agreement of the principal creditor powers to the so-called "Hoover moratorium" on World War I reparations by Germany and Austria, Beyen became in the summer of 1931 a member of the Bankers Stabilization Conference in Berlin, and helped, under the auspices of the Bank for International Settlements at Basle, Switzerland, to conclude the first "Standstill Agreement" pertaining to war debts. The Bank for International Settlements, which had begun to function in 1930 and later served as a general clearing house of the central banks of Europe, is defined in the *Encyclopaedia Britannica* as "an institution created for the handling of all reparations transactions arising from the operations of the Young Plan." Beyen served as Netherlands delegate to the World Economic and Monetary Conference at London in 1933, and in the same year was named vice-chairman of Philips Incandescent Lamp Company and a director of Handels Vereeniging in Amsterdam and of other corporations. When Dr. L. A. J. Trip, the president of the Bank of the Netherlands, was chosen to succeed Leon Fraser of the United States as president of the Bank for International Settlements, Beyen on March 11, 1935, was elected as his alternate. A little over two years later, on May 3, 1937, he replaced Trip as president. He resigned from that office in late 1939.

On leaving the B.I.S. presidency, Beyen accepted an appointment in January 1940 as financial director of the manufacturing concern, Lever Brothers and Unilever, Ltd., in London and Rotterdam. He was out of Holland at the time of the Nazi invasion (May 10, 1940), but

BEYEN, J. W.—*Continued*

not out of danger, and it was the end of May before he reached London again safely, after a period of delay in Belgium and France. By that time the Royal Netherlands Government had also taken refuge in the British capital. When Beyen was appointed its financial adviser, one of his first actions was to negotiate a monetary understanding with the British Government in relation to the Dutch colonies. Later he participated in reaching other international agreements and in April 1943 was jointly invited by the British and United States Governments "to submit suggestions for the reconciliation of the currency plans of Lord Keynes and Harry D. White" (*New York Times*). Beyen's suggestions helped to make feasible the Bretton Woods Conference in New Hampshire, at which he headed the Netherlands delegation and which on July 22, 1944, produced "articles of agreement" for the creation of both the International Bank for Reconstruction and Development and the International Monetary Fund.

The main purpose of the International Bank for Reconstruction and Development is "to make available from its own resources, or by other means, international investment capital for productive purposes" (*United States Government Manual*). This task "includes the guidance of such financing into rehabilitation expansion, and modernization of industrial and agricultural facilities both in areas whose economies have been disrupted by the war and in underdeveloped areas." The International Bank with headquarters in Washington, D.C., has a membership of about fifty nations and a subscribed capital of $8,338,500,000 (as of May 15, 1951); it has approved loans to France, the Netherlands, Belgium, Luxembourg, Yugoslavia, Denmark, India, and several Latin-American countries. Closely allied, but with a separate organization, is the International Monetary Fund, created "to promote international monetary cooperation through a permanent institution which provides machinery for consultation and collaboration on international monetary problems" and "to give confidence to members by making the fund's resources available to them under adequate safeguards (*United States Government Manual*). The International Monetary Fund's membership approximates that of the International Bank, and its capital is also around $8,000,000,000. Beyen, who had represented the Netherlands at the Reparations Conference of 1945, was elected an executive director of the International Bank for Reconstruction and Development at the Savannah, Georgia, Conference in March 1946, at which time he severed his connection with Lever Brothers. In July 1947 he represented the Netherlands at the fifth session of the United Nations Economic and Social Council and in April 1948 was also elected an executive director of the International Monetary Fund, to represent the Netherlands and South Africa.

Beyen's views on the functions and problems of the International Bank for Reconstruction and Development are set forth in an article in the October 1948 issue of *International Affairs*, while his general explanation of what has been called "the mysteries of international finance" is to be found in his book *Money in a Maelstrom*. George Soule, reviewing the latter work for the *Nation*, observed that "out of his experience" Dr. Beyen had "learned many things that others need to know, and states them with both assurance and moderation." Commenting in the *Canadian Forum*, Henry Kreisel was not so impressed by Beyen's examination of "the causes of the 'maelstrom,'" but found him "at his best when he writes about the numerous international conferences which tried so hard and often failed so miserably to bring order out of financial chaos."

On September 1, 1952, Labor Premier Willem Drees of the Netherlands announced the formation of a new Cabinet, with Beyen as Foreign Minister and Joseph M. A. H. Luns, a Roman Catholic, as Minister without Portfolio. At a press conference on the same day, Premier Drees revealed that Ministers Beyen and Luns "would exercise 'joint responsibility' for foreign policy, but would divide their duties 'on a functional basis'" (*New York Times*). This unusual arrangement, which was not expected to reflect any change in policy, was viewed as "a compromise settlement" of "a conflict over this increasingly important post," and the Premier's desire to include a Catholic in his Cabinet. Dr. Beyen belongs to no political party.

By his marriage to Petronella Hymans on March 28, 1922, Beyen is the father of three children, Karel Herman, Frédérique and Jan Willem. After the dissolution of this marriage in October 1945, Beyen on November 14, 1945, married the former Margaretha Antonia Lubinka of Vienna. (He has one stepson, John Alexander Bult.) The blue-eyed, blond-haired Foreign Minister is a member of the St. James' Club in London, the Union Interalliée in Paris, and the Congressional Country Club in the District of Columbia.

References

Comm & Fin Chr 163:3236 Je 13 '46 por
U N Bul 3:313 S 2 '47 por
Beyen, J. W. Money in a Maelstrom (1949)
International Who's Who, 1952
International World Who's Who (1949)
Who's Who, 1952
Who's Who in America, 1952-53
Who's Who in Commerce and Industry (1951)
Who's Who in the United Nations (1951)
Wie is dat? 1948
World Biography (1948)

BHAVE, VINOBA (bä-vä) 1894?- Indian mystic

Address: c/o Puanar, Madhya Pradesh, India

A social and spiritual revolution without violence has been instigated in India by Acharya (teacher) Vinoba Bhave. Called by many the "new Gandhi" or "the son of Gandhi," the emaciated mystic has walked barefoot from village to village across India, covering 6,500 miles, and gathering gifts of arable land from the rich and redistributing it to the poor. The goal of his land-gift movement is 50,000,000 acres, or one-sixth of all the arable land of India, which he hopes to achieve by 1957.

Prime Minister Jawaharlal Nehru calls this *Bhoomidan-yagna* (land-gift sacrifice) move‧ment the "beginning of a social and economic revolution." Bhave himself explains the success of his method as follows: "In India the ideal of *Ahimsa* (non-violence) has deeply influenced people's minds. We can successfully bring about peaceful social revolution by gentle persuasion. If we adopt violent means, as has been done in China and Russia, the whole world will face calamity."

According to Robert Trumbull (New York *Times*, December 22, 1952), Bhave is credited with being "the most powerful single influence against the Reds in rural India." His campaign received the unanimous official backing of both houses of Parliament in India on March 27, 1953. Some members gave land in their own home towns, while others contributed a month's parliamentary allowance to the cause. The central Ministry of Food and Agriculture also offered him ten million acres of Government-owned cultivable wasteland for distribution among the landless.

Born to a high-caste (Brahmin) family in Gangoda, a village in Baroda State in western India, Vinayak Bhave became a Hindu devotee at an early age and he determined upon lifelong celibacy, gave up sweets and began going barefoot. At twenty, he was sent to study in Bombay; instead of remaining there he ran away to Bengal, where he joined the nationalist movement.

In the holy city of Benares, on the sacred Ganges River, he studied Sanskrit, Hindu theology and philosophy. In 1916 he journeyed to Mahatma Gandhi's *ashram* (religious retreat) at Sabarmati, near Abmedabad. Too shy to approach the Mahatma, Bhave wrote him a letter and was invited to join the *ashram*. Gandhi, who changed his protegé's given name from Vinayak to Vinoba, wrote to Bhave's father: "Your Vinoba is with me. His spiritual attainments are such as I myself attained only after a long struggle."

Still restless, Bhave went away to study more Sanskrit, after telling Gandhi that he would be back in a year if he did not find peace of soul. He returned on the appointed day, and from that time on became one of Gandhi's favorites. In 1921, when a rich patron offered to finance a new *ashram*, Gandhi sent Bhave to set it up in Sewagram, in central India; later it also became Gandhi's headquarters.

In 1932, Bhave was arrested for participation in the Mahatma's civil disobedience movement. This was the first of six terms, totaling two years, spent in British prisons. He was selected by Gandhi to lead the passive resistance against India's part in World War II, which was undertaken because entrance into the war had not had the consent of the people.

After Gandhi died in 1948, Bhave, already an Acharya, or teacher, to his followers, remained in relative retirement at Sewagram. He wrote occasional articles against money, which, he

Govt. of India Inf. Services

VINOBA BHAVE

said, "tells lies and is like a loafing tramp." Instead of money he favored the use of scrip showing the number of hours a person had worked to earn it.

Bhave became concerned in April 1951 about violent civil war in Telengana, in Hyderabad, where eight million oppressed peasants were harassed by Communist guerrillas. Disregarding police warnings and offers of protection against the Communists he set out on foot with a few followers, to preach *ahimsa* (non-violence). Seeing, however, that the root of the civil violence lay in the unequal distribution of the land, he launched his plea to landlords to contribute some of their holdings for the landless as a way of counteracting communism. "The land is a Mother. Everybody has a right to approach her. Hence, a proper distribution of land should take place. If landlords will donate their lands willingly and with pleasure, they'll transform the entire outlook of the people."

Some 35,000 acres were collected, including a donation from the Nizam of Hyderabad. Gradually, the revolt died down, as Bhave's words were heard: "The Communist path of violence is not in theme with the culture of India. The notion that the Communists serve the poor is wrong. . ." Bhave distributed the donated land to those without land on the basis of one acre for each member of the family.

In September 1951, after Bhave's method proved so successful in Telengana, Prime Minister Nehru invited him to come to New Delhi to discuss *Bhoomidan-yagna* with the National Planning Commission. Refusing Nehru's offer to send a plane for him, Bhave replied: "I will come, but in my own time, and as always." For two months, he walked the 795 miles to the capital. At every village on the way, villagers turned out to welcome him with shouts of "the God who is distributing land has come!" They garlanded him, touched and

BHAVE, VINOBA—*Continued*

bathed his feet. He held a prayer meeting at each stop, asking the rich to give land to the poor. He collected 25,000 acres from eager donors, many of whom owned less than five acres. Arriving in New Delhi on November 13, he was met by sixty members of Parliament at the outskirts who walked the remaining miles with him. He spent eleven days in a thatched bamboo hut at Rajghat, adjoining the spot where Gandhi's body had been cremated. Nehru visited him twice. Five members of the Commission listened as he pleaded for village wells (instead of irrigation projects), local, small-scale industries (instead of factories), and more small farms. On hearing Bhave's plea, President Rajendra Prasad contributed his Bihar estate.

Vinoba Bhave's land-distribution campaign received the support, in April 1952, of the five thousand delegates to the annual conference of Gandhi's followers. They called it a "peaceful revolution" to stem the tide of communism.

Since then, Bhave has trained younger men to work with him in collecting land for India's poorest peasants. He has journeyed on foot through the six states of Madhya Pradesh, Madhya Bhattar, Rajasthan, Delhi, Uttar Pradesh, and Bihar. His entourage consists of a dozen or more young Hindu men and women, who stay three months to a year with him. Bhave's only permanent companion is Damadar Das, who acts as his secretary, mails copies of Bhave's speeches to the newspapers, and keeps track of the land deeds. According to a recent report, the largest gift of 100,000 acres was recently made by the Rajah of Ramgarh, a small principality merged with Bihar.

Bhave's day, like Gandhi's, begins at 3 a.m., when he leads his followers in an hour and a half of prayers and meditation. By 5 a.m. he starts the day's walk, averaging about five miles an hour. Along the dusty roads, Bhave holds conferences with local officials, his disciples, and interviewers. At noon they stop at a village and prepare a frugal vegetarian breakfast without tea or coffee. Bhave himself eats only buttermilk and *gur*, an unrefined sugar, by which diet he controls a duodenal ulcer from which he suffers. In all, he eats five bowls of such curds a day.

After a rest and a half hour of spinning *khaddar* or homespun cloth (he is an excellent spinner and weaver), Bhave holds an informal court to hear and settle village grievances. At five he leads a daily prayer meeting with readings from India's major religions.

When he explains the land-gift movement, his most persuasive plea to landlords is: "Regard me as your additional son, and give me my share for the poor." Bhave transfers an average of about 300 acres a day. Deeds to the land gifts are made at the time of the transfer, and the villagers themselves are asked to choose the most needy families to receive the land. A committee later returns to see that the redistribution is actually carried out. Gifts have varied from hundreds of acres to a single *gunta* or one-fortieth of an acre from a poor man. Cash donors are asked to buy either land or a

pair of bullocks, or to pay for digging a well.

While walking through Bihar in December 1952, Bhave fell sick with malignant malaria. He continued his journey in a bullock cart despite a temperature of 103. He collapsed in the village of Chandil, but refused medical care, saying: "God either wants to free me or desires to pacify this body for employing it again in His work." Government officials, among whom was President Prasad, who flew to his bedside, persuaded Bhave to accept medication after he was assured it contained no animal matter. All India awaited reports of his condition. When he was able to walk, he set out again to collect land; donations came in faster than they could be recorded.

Bhave translated the Hindu's *Bhagavad Gita*, which he regards as his supreme book of guidance, into Marathi (a Sanskritic language). It sold about a quarter of a million copies in western India. He also reads and re-reads Euclid's *Elements*, Aesop's *Fables*, and the scriptures of various religions. A practitioner of *karma-yoga*, the way of God through action in the world, Bhave says his object "is to transform the whole of society. . . . The people are going to solve their problems, not I. I am simply creating an atmosphere. The beginning is always small, but when the atmosphere spreads, somebody will ask—and somebody will give." His appeal is solely on the basis of right and wrong. He shows little concern with criticisms raised by some who say the *Bhoomidan-yagna* only aggravates the existing problem of over-fragmentation of land into economic holdings. He also continues to advocate cottage industries, while many Indian economists plead for large-scale industrialization for India. Many persons, however, even though the results of the land-gift movement are still small, find inspiring this "peaceful revolution in which love and self-sacrifice take the place of Communist hatred and violence." Donald Harrington (*Saturday Review*, May 9, 1953) calls it "a miracle of the spirit."

Like Gandhi too, according to Gordon Graham (*Christian Science Monitor*, November 14, 1951), "he is deeply moral, humble, and ascetic in his approach to human problems and, like Gandhi, he is not afraid of small beginnings and of setting a personal example." One of India's most learned men, he has studied in addition to Sanskrit, Persian, Urdu, Hindi, Marathi, Gujarati, Bengali, Telugu, Kanarese, Mayalam, and English. His present *ashram* retreat is at Puanar in Madhya Pradesh, about six miles from Gandhi's former *ashram* at Wardha. Unless it is raining, he sleeps outdoors. Bhave weighs only eighty-six pounds.

References

Christian Sci Mon p2 N 14 '51
N Y Herald Tribune II p5 N 25 '51
N Y Times p3 Mr 28 '53
N Y Times Mag p13+ F 10 '52
Reader's Digest 60:88+ My '52
Sat Rev 36:5 My 9 '53
Time 57:36 Je 4 '51; 58:40 N 26 '51;
    61:32 My 11 '53 por
U N World 6:20+ My '52

BLACKALL, FREDERICK S(TEELE), JR. Nov. 26, 1896- Industrialist

Address: b. c/o Taft-Peirce Manufacturing Company, Woonsocket, R.I.; h. "Orchard House," West Wrentham Rd., Cumberland Hill, R.I.; "The Lighthouse," Harwich Port, Mass.

For twenty years, beginning in 1933, Frederick S. Blackall, Jr., has served as president and treasurer of the Taft-Peirce Manufacturing Company, producer of machine tools, in Woonsocket, Rhode Island. Joining this firm in 1922, Blackall advanced gradually to his present post, while gaining a reputation as an energetic promoter of New England industry. An active member of many professional associations, during 1951-52 he served as the president of the National Machine Tool Builders Association and for 1953 he was selected as president of the American Society of Mechanical Engineers. On several occasions Blackall has acted as the industry spokesman on current problems affecting the machine tool manufacturers in the United States defense program.

On November 26, 1896, Frederick Steele Blackall, Jr., was born in Roselle, New Jersey, the son of Frederick Steele and Bertha Gates (Brown) Blackall, of English and Scottish ancestry and descendants of Governor Bradford and Bradford Steele. Young Frederick attended the Abbott School in Farmington, Maine for some time and was graduated in 1913 from the Phillips Academy in Andover, Massachusetts. At Yale University, he became chairman of the *Courant*, the undergraduate magazine, and received his B.A. degree in 1919. (His studies were interrupted by service in the war, and he was classified with the class of 1918). While in college Blackall joined the Yale Naval Training Unit, in which he took part in the training cruise of the S.S. *Ansantawe* from May to September 1917. The next month he was placed in command of the U.S.S. *Acoma*, receiving a commission in December 1917 as ensign in the United States Naval Reserve Force and serving on this ship until January 1918. After entering the Third Reserve Officers' School at the United States Naval Academy, in February, he was commissioned in May 1918 as an ensign in the United States Navy and assigned from June 1918 to February 1919 as turret officer on the U.S.S. *Pennsylvania*.

Having completed his World War I service, Blackall attended the Massachusetts Institute of Technology, where he joined Sigma Alpha Epsilon and Theta Tau fraternities and in 1922 received his B.S. degree. In May of that year he became supervisor of heat treatment at the Taft-Peirce Manufacturing Company in Woonsocket, Rhode Island. For a while during 1923 he served as the Detroit branch sales manager and for a year (1923-24) as the assistant to the general manager. From 1925 to 1928 he occupied the post of assistant manager before being promoted in 1929 to be the company's general manager and vice-president. In 1933 he was named to his present position as president and treasurer of the firm. Employing about 800 workers and having a capital and surplus in excess of $3,000,000, the company which Black-

FREDERICK S. BLACKALL, JR.

all heads was described by *Fortune* magazine as a "machine and precision-tool shop . . . largely owned by his family and two others . . . [which], if anyone asked it to, could build a combination mousetrap-victrola in any quantity from one to fifty thousand."

During World War II the industrialist became a member of the Boston Ordnance District Advisory Board, the United States Navy War Manpower Commission, and the Machine Tools and Precision Tools Advisory Committee of the War Production Board. In 1946 he was chairman of a technical mission to England to help standardize English and American screw threads. Blackall has also sponsored a proposal to build a steel mill in New England.

As a chief spokesman for the machine tool industry in problems relating to the United States defense program, Blackall has been concerned with the metal-working equipment required by ordnance, aircraft, tank, and atomic energy plants to turn out the finished products. These tools are made by a highly specialized group of less than four hundred United States manufacturers, aided by about four hundred producers of less intricate metal-working devices. One of the industry's main problems is the extreme fluctuation in orders resulting from varying needs of the economy. After World War II sales of machine tools declined severely, but with the beginning of the Korean war the backlog of machine tool orders mounted "incredibly," according to the New York *Times* (December 10, 1951). When critics charged that the industry was a "bottleneck" which was holding back defense preparedness, manufacturers pointed out that many of them had been forced to reduce their facilities after World War II because of the lack of buyers. Blackall said at this time that the machine tool industry needed to select the appropriate industries for subcontracting, but could use only

BLACKALL, FREDERICK—*Continued*

those producers who were accustomed to precision work.

With the accumulation of a large backlog of orders, a crisis in machine tool production occurred in the summer of 1951. In July Charles E. Wilson, Director of the Office of Defense Mobilization, issued a directive for "clarification of the machine tool price situation" so that "machine tool builders might devote their entire energies to production and be provided with genuine incentives" (New York *Times,* July 23, 1951).

Blackall, then vice-president of the National Machine Tool Builders Association, attacked a regulation on prices issued a short time previous to Wilson's directive, charging that it was "not of price control but one of outright profit control" and that it was a "dangerous excursion into socialistic philosophy" with "sinister" implications (New York *Times,* July 23, 1951). He stated that the ruling, by putting a floor under the earnings of the inefficient and high-cost manufacturers, helped this type of producer but gave no incentive to the efficient manufacturer to increase operations and profit beyond his own convenience.

In February 1952 machine tool order cancellations totalling $30,000,000 or around 30 per cent of the new order volume, caused anxiety in the industry about future business. The New York *Times* reported in April 1952 that the Government and the manufacturers were becoming increasingly concerned about how to maintain a strong machine tool industry during peacetime. Blackall urged on April 1 that a stand-by priority plan should be prepared which by executive order could quickly increase the industry to full strength in case of a national emergency. He emphasized the necessity of overhauling present tax laws, which, he said, "prevent recovery, within a reasonable period, of capital invested in productive equipment" (New York *World-Telegram,* April 1, 1952). Depreciation allowances, he said, should be so authorized that they encourage the continual modernization of "our national industrial plant."

Machine tool producers complained in June 1952 that the Government restriction limiting their shipments to only buyers with priority ratings was causing them to have idle productive capacity, while the importation of machine tools from Europe to the United States was increasing. Blackall attributed this rise in European competition to the Mutual Security Agency's policy of developing European production and of discouraging customers abroad from purchasing American machine tools, with the result that the United States export market had shrunk from "an historical average of about 25 per cent of output" to 3.2 per cent in February 1952 (New York *Times,* June 15, 1952). During this same month, the National Machine Tool Builders Association, of which Blackall was then president, reported that there had been a large cancellation of orders resulting from "a second stretch-out in the defense program since January and tardy recognition of injudicious over-ordering" (New York *Times,* July 11, 1952). The Association charged that

"the on-again-off-again policy of ordering machine tools as though they were canned goods from a shelf has, as usual, resulted in putting an impossible strain upon the nation's machine tool industry, which is the very keystone of a nation's defense."

After representatives of the machine tool industry and of the National Production Authority met in Washington, the Government eased its regulation requiring buyers of tools to have a priority rating, and the New York *Times* (July 27, 1952) reported that the danger of a crisis in this industry had "all but disappeared." The following November at the annual fall meeting of the National Machine Tool Builders Association, President Blackall recommended "progressive decontrol for machine tools" as "the surest way to strengthen the industry for the future defense of the country" (New York *Times,* November 14, 1952).

Blackall is vice-president, director, and a member of the executive committee of the American Wringer Company, Woonsocket, Rhode Island, and its subsidiaries—the American Wringer Company of Canada, Farmham, Quebec; the Chamberlain Corporation, Waterloo, Iowa; the American Wringer Company of (Raeford) North Carolina; and the Para Thread Company, Woonsocket, Rhode Island. He is a member of the Rhode Island Advisory Board of the Liberty Mutual Insurance Company; a director of the Federal Reserve Bank of Boston, the New England Transportation Company, and the American Research and Development Corporation (Boston); and a director and member of the executive committee of the New York, New Haven and Hartford Railroad Company.

The president in 1953 of the American Society of Mechanical Engineers, Blackall also served during 1951-52 as president of the National Machine Tool Builders Association and was a director of the National Association of Manufacturers. From 1944 to 1946 he was president of the New England Council and "did much to build that organization to its present position of eminence" (*Iron Age*); from 1946 to 1951 he was a term member of the Corporation of the Massachusetts Institute of Technology. The Rhode Island manufacturer is a member of the American Gage Design Committee, acting as chairman of the editorial committee and as a member of the standing committee. He belongs to the Gage Industry Advisory Committee of the United States Army Industrial College, the Machine Tools Advisory Committee of the National Production Authority, and the Boston Ordnance District Advisory Board. He is also a member of the American Society for Metals, the American Society of Tool Engineers, the Providence (Rhode Island) Engineering Society, the Army Ordnance Association, and the Newcomen Society.

Blackall has written articles for magazines, newspapers, and trade and technical journals on such topics as machinery and tool manufacturing, gages and gaging, standardization, banking, industrial history, and depreciation. He was the author of the text of the *Re-*

port of the *American Gage Design Committee* (published in 1930 by the United States Bureau of Standards) and has been editor of all later editions. His book, *Invention and Industry Cradled in New England*, a history of the development of the machine tool industry in New England, was published by the Newcomen Society (1946). Active in civic organizations, Blackall is a trustee of the Woonsocket Taxpayers' Association, the Woonsocket Community Fund, the Rhode Island Community Chests, Inc.; he is president of the Woonsocket Hospital and vice-president of the Rhode Island Public Expenditure Council. Blackall is a Mason. His clubs are Agawam Hunt, Hope, and Terrace (Providence, Rhode Island); Stone Horse Yacht (Harwich Port, Massachusetts); Yale (New York); and the Detroit Athletic Club.

On August 19, 1922, Blackall married Hazel White; their children are Frederick Steele 3d and Marilyn White, now Mrs. K. G. Wheeler. One of his proudest possessions is Orchard House Farm, a 200-acre commercial apple farm in Cumberland Hill, Rhode Island. His favorite sports are riding, sailing, and fishing; his hobby is stamp collecting. Blackall has brown eyes and brown hair, is five feet seven inches tall, and weighs 165 pounds. He is an Episcopalian and votes as an independent Republican.

References

Fortune 41:83 Mr '50 por
Iron Age 168:51 D 27 '51 por
Business Executives of America (1950)
Who Knows—and What (1949)
Who's Who in America, 1952-53
Who's Who in Commerce and Industry (1951)
Who's Who in Engineering, 1948
Who's Who in New England (1949)
World Biography (1948)

BLISS, HENRY E(VELYN) Jan. 29, 1870- Librarian, author
Address: h. 602 E. Front St., Plainfield, N.J.

One of America's foremost contributors to the systemizing of bibliographic classification, Henry E. Bliss, retired Associate Librarian of the College of the City of New York, has devoted over fifty years to this study. The object of his system, as the term *bibliographic* implies, is service to the scholar and the librarian in arranging collections of books and documents.

His first book, *The Organization of Knowledge and the System of the Sciences* was introduced by John Dewey in 1929 as a "monumental work" and an "important and much-needed contribution" to the unification of knowledge. This volume was followed by two others, *The Organization of Knowledge in Libraries* and *A System of Bibliographic Classification*. The latter was expanded in the four-volume work, *A Bibliographic Classification*, which was completed early in 1953. In these books Bliss has undertaken to systemize all the branches of

HENRY E. BLISS

knowledge and study in accordance with the consensus of modern scientific and educational thought.

Henry Evelyn Bliss was born on January 29, 1870 in New York City. His parents, Henry Hale and Evelina Matilda (Davis) Bliss were both descended from English families who had settled on the Eastern seaboard during the Colonial period. His first seven years were spent mostly in New York City, the next six on his mother's estate in Tom's River, New Jersey.

Until he was eleven years old, Bliss was educated at home by his mother who "taught him to read, write, sing, and recite the catechism". He was later tutored by governesses in French, Latin, arithmetic, grammar and history. In 1883 his family moved back to New York City. He attended grammar schools at 69 West 54th Street and at 68 West 128th Street; he was graduated from the latter in 1885 as Salutatorian of his class.

The school which was to influence his career most markedly was the College of the City of New York. In 1885 he enrolled in the classical course, but he left in 1888 without graduating because his father urged him to go into business, and also because he was dissatisfied with the course of study.

His separation from City College was of short duration. After three years in business and a brief period of teaching, he was invited in 1891 to take the post of Deputy Librarian at the college, and he remained there until his retirement in 1940. During his first years his duties included advice on reading, and thus he became acquainted with numerous students who later became prominent in law, literature, philosophy and the sciences; among these were Upton Sinclair, Robert Wagner, Louis Anspacher, Joel Spingarn, Stephen Wise, James

BLISS, HENRY E.—Continued

K. Hackett, Paul Radin, Angelo Patri, Felix Frankfurter and Montrose J. Moses.

The particular phase of librarianship which has become his life work first engaged Bliss' attention about 1900 when he found that the classification system used by the City College library was inadequate for classifying the rapidly developing fields of science, social science, technology, literature, and other subjects. Finding none of the three systems in use at that time—Dewey, Cutter, Library of Congress —suitable to his needs, Bliss proceeded to develop his own system. When the college was being moved, from 1905 to 1908, to the Convent Avenue campus which it now occupies, Bliss had the opportunity to re-classify the library collections.

Bliss' system resulted from an extensive and intensive program of study to which he devoted himself in all his spare time. His only formal library school training was a course in classification at a summer session at Amherst College in 1903 given by Professor William I. Fletcher. He also discussed classification that summer with Charles A. Cutter, then director of the Forbes Library. Bliss notes in his memoirs that, as a result of his studies, "I came to comprehend that *subject matters* are interrelated as the existent *realities* evidently are in the universe. Moreover, there is interdependence of parts, of particular things. Furthermore, the universe is entirely developmental. So is our knowledge of it. . . .Realities exist and subsist in a system of relations."

With this thought and purpose, "to discover the relations, and to systemize the knowledge of the realities and their relations," Bliss developed his system. He termed the process "the organization of knowledge," which is the title of the book that introduced his ideas to the library world. Assuming that for the classifier and cataloger the main problem is the organization of subject matter, Bliss recommended that book-stacks be arranged so as "to serve the principle of *collocation* as well as efficiency in *location*."

He reasoned that the reader and the researcher are best served by a classification which places in proximity the subject matters that are most likely to be wanted together (the principle he calls "collocation for maximal efficiency") ; which groups smaller, related subjects under the relevant, more general subjects ("subordination") ; and which provides for revision according to changes or new developments in various subject matters ("adaptability").

Many years ensued between the inception of the Bliss Classification and its publication in book form. In 1910 he prepared an epitome and sent a copy to Dr. Ernest Cushing Richardson, Librarian of Princeton University, himself a specialist in classification, who regarded Bliss' system even in this early stage as "the most usable scheme yet invented . . . easily the best thing to date." Eleven years later he encouraged Bliss to publish his work.

During the interim Bliss contributed articles to the *Philosophical Review,* the *Educational Review,* and the *Library Journal* in which he presented some of his views on the philosophy of knowledge, on departmental libraries in universities, and on classification for libraries. His criticisms of the Dewey Decimal Classification (originated by Melvil Dewey in 1876 and to this date the most widely used library classification scheme) were regarded as shockingly heretical by many of his more conventional colleagues for whom the perfection of the Dewey system was an article of professional faith.

In 1917 Bliss participated in a symposium on classification conducted by the Catalog Section of the American Library Association. Four years later, at the Conference of Eastern College Librarians at Columbia University, in response to Dr. Ernest Richardson's inquiry about the progress of his classification, Bliss revealed that he was at work on "a broader undertaking", namely, the organization of knowledge, which he planned to be universal in scope, international in application. This project came to the attention of President Mezes of City College, who was interested in international bibliography. Bliss, then Assistant Librarian, was granted a leave of absence to complete the work. This leave was renewed for the two years following.

By June 1924 he had completed a draft of more than a thousand pages on the organization of knowledge and a 150-page outline of his system of classification. In the following half-year he recast the manuscript so that it could be published as two separate but connected volumes. There followed a delay of several more years owing to the difficulty of finding a publisher for the first volume, *The Organization of Knowledge and the System of the Sciences.* The university presses and commercial publishers whom Bliss approached were unwilling to undertake its publication, believing that it could not sell enough copies to cover its costs. But when the most eminent living American philosopher commended the work, the position changed : in 1929 Henry Holt brought the book out with a laudatory introduction written by John Dewey.

After he resumed active service at the College of the City of New York in 1925, Bliss was appointed Head of Departmental Libraries, in which position he worked on the consolidation of the several departmental libraries into a unified system. In 1928 he was named Associate Librarian. Among the other activities of his long career at City College was his co-editing of the *City College Quarterly,* with Professor Lewis Freeman Mott. A volume of his poems, *Better Late than Never,* was published in 1937.

In 1929 Bliss was ready with his second volume, *The Organization of Knowledge in Libraries and the Subject-Approach to Books,* which was intended to show the specific relevancy of the theoretical principles of the introductory volume to the problems of librarianship and bibliography. Again he encountered obstacles to publication. After negotiations lasting several years, the American Library Association's Publishing Board refused to undertake publication of the work without a generous subsidy of the author sufficient to cover all publishing costs. Bliss then offered the volume to the H. W. Wilson Company, which accepted it, issued it in 1933, and has since been his publisher.

This second volume sold out in six months, making necessary a reprint and a second edition in 1939. With this success came an increased market for the first volume, the remaining stock of which was purchased from Holt by the Wilson Company.

Most of the reviews of the second volume were favorable but it provoked some controversy in the influential *Library Quarterly*. An article in the April 1934 issue questioned Bliss' deductive approach to the problem of classification, whereas an equally authoritative contributor to the October 1934 issue called Bliss' learning "truly impressive" and maintained that his book would help to establish librarianship as a true scholarly discipline.

A Bibliographic Classification, setting forth detailed schedules of all branches of knowledge for the use of classifiers in libraries, completes Bliss' project. An introductory version appeared in 1935, promptly sold out, and was re-issued in a revised edition two years later. It was then decided to publish the classification in an extended four-volume edition. Volume I (Introduction, Synopsis, Tables, Systematic Schedules, Classes A-G) appeared in 1940, followed by Volume II (Classes H-K) in 1947. The last volumes, III (Classes L-Z) and IV (the Index) appeared in 1953.

Among the reviewers, Susan Grey Akers, describing the first two volumes in the *Library Quarterly* of April 1948, commended in particular Bliss' up-to-date treatment of various special fields, the logical arrangements of his subdivisions, his introduction of new topics. A feature of the Bliss Classification which she felt should make librarians especially confident of its soundness was his enlisting of the co-operation of authorities in such fields such as medicine, psychology, and sociology.

The work has been received with enthusiasm by some of the outstanding British classification specialists, such as W. C. Berwick Sayers of the Croydon Public Libraries; in the 1944 edition of his authoritative *Manuel of Classification* he stated that the Bliss system was "more comprehensive and accommodating than any other published scheme whatsoever."

The Bliss classification has been adopted by about fifty libraries in England and in English-speaking countries overseas. In the United States an early form of the system, with some modifications, is still in use at the College of the City of New York, but elsewhere in this country the system has been studied only from a theoretical point of view, the heavy expense of re-classification having precluded any attempt to apply it.

The most recent English tribute to Bliss is an editorial in the June 1953 *Library Association Record* which concludes: "We should all feel indebted to Bliss for the wealth of scholarship and the careful architecture of his life's work . . . The number of libraries in this country who are resolute enough to adopt the Bliss scheme is mounting, and there is surely no more fitting tribute to his achievement."

Bliss married Ellen de Koster, a teacher at Hunter College, June 1, 1901. They had four children, Enid Evelyn (who died in 1918), Margaret (Mrs. Wolcott Treat), John Hale and Conrad de Koster. After Mrs. Bliss' death in 1943, Bliss lived until 1946 in Pasadena, California, near his daughter and her family. He lived in Winter Park, Florida, from 1947 to 1952.

In June 1948 a paper by Bliss was presented before the Conference of the International Federation for Documentation which was assembled to consider revision of the Universal Decimal Classification. In 1952 he moved to Plainfield, New Jersey, where he now resides.

At eighty-three, Bliss is at work currently on his autobiography, tentatively titled "Lest We Forget." He has given up his favorite activities, gardening and cabinet-making, but continues his daily hikes, "nearly 1,000 miles in a year," he estimates.

He is a member of the Special Libraries Association; Library Association of the United Kingdom; Poetry Society (British). He contributes articles to Library and educational periodicals.

References

Who's Who in America, 1940-41

BLOCH, ERNEST (blok) July 24, 1880-
Composer
Address h. Agate Beach, Ore.

Ranked among the foremost living composers, Ernest Bloch has won renown for his *String Quartet No. 2* and his *Quintet for piano and strings*. The *Nigun* from his *Baal Shem* suite is in the repertory of nearly every concert violinist. His *Schelomo, Israel Symphony*, and *Trois poemes juifs* are widely admired, and the *Sacred Service* and *Concerto Grosso* are frequently performed.

Ernest Bloch was born July 24, 1880 in Geneva, Switzerland, the son of Maurice and Sophie (Brunschwig) Bloch. Although it is said that neither music nor religion played a large part in the household, Maurice Bloch, a clock merchant, loved to sing songs from the ancient Jewish religious service, and Ernest gave his first public performance at the age of ten. When he was eleven, he made a solemn vow to devote his life to composing.

Ernest's first music teachers were Louis Rey for violin and E. Jacques Dalcroze for composition. Before he was fifteen he had composed a string quartet and the *Oriental Symphony*. Completing his academic education at Geneva College in 1896, he spent the next eight years studying violin in Brussels with F. Schorg and Eugène Ysaye, and composition with R. Rasse, with Ivan Knorr in Frankfort and with Ludwig Thuille in Munich. When the youth realized that his violin study was not allowing enough time for composing, he gave up the violin.

Settling in Paris, he wrote the *Symphony in C Sharp Minor*, for great orchestra (1901-02). *Historiettes au crépuscule* (1903) was the first of his works to be published. This was followed

ERNEST BLOCH

by the symphonic poems *Vivre et Aimer* and *Hiver-Printemps* (1905).

Bloch was unable to have his symphony performed either in France or Germany, and this fact, together with his family's financial problems, caused him to return to Geneva in 1904 and enter his family's business. "I will write music as I feel I must," he said, "and if it is good it will be heard."

The twenty-four-year-old composer settled down as a businessman, working in his father's shop, keeping the books and traveling as a salesman. He continued composing and lectured on metaphysics at the University of Geneva several nights a week. Since he never required more than a few hours' sleep, he could devote many night-time hours to composing. He composed an opera *Macbeth* on a libretto by Edmund Fleg. In 1909 he began conducting a series of subscription concerts at Lausanne and Neuchatel.

After that, until 1916 he lectured on esthetics at the Geneva Conservatory of Music, giving a total of some 120 lectures. Of his compositions at that period, David Ewen has written, "Bloch's early works reveal none of the groping and blundering that generally characterize immature creations; they are compositions of definite importance and of artistic stature."

To Bloch's surprise, the Paris Opéra-Comique accepted his *Macbeth* and presented it on November 30, 1910. It was, says Gdal Saleski, "the most discussed première of the season." Critic Arthur Pougin called it "an indescribable rebus rhythmically and tonally" and the harmonic sequence "savage," but the general verdict was favorable. (*Macbeth* did not return to the repertory, however, and was not heard anywhere again until a 1938 revival. Reviewers of the 1953 performance in Rome found the opera "strongly influenced by Wagner and Debussy, written with skill and dramatic force, but a bit "sprawling").

Romain Rolland, the novelist and musicologist, called *Macbeth* "one of the most important works of the modern school," and made a "pilgrimage" to Geneva to see the author. Rolland's surprise and indignation at finding the composer working at business accounts influenced Bloch to give up business and devote himself entirely to music. (The composer's struggles are said to have provided Rolland with material for his ten-volume Nobel prize-winning novel about a musician, *Jean-Christophe*).

Bloch during this period became imbued with the idea of creating music expressive of his race. "Racial consciousness is absolutely necessary in music even though nationalism is not," he announced in his esthetic creed. By 1916 he had completed the *Two Psalms,* for soprano and orchestra, *Trois Poèmes Juifs,* for orchestra, and *Psalm 22,* for baritone and orchestra, *Schelomo,* for violoncello and orchestra, a portrait in tone of the Biblical Jew, and *Israel Symphony.*

Early in 1916 Ernest Bloch went to America as conductor for the touring dancer Maud Allen. The bankruptcy of this enterprise left Bloch stranded in a strange country, without resources, and unable to speak the language. He experienced a few months of near-starvation before his plight became known to local musicians. Olin Downes has recorded his memory of Bloch then—"In a stuffy little bedroom with an upright piano in it . . . a [man] with blazing eyes, jet-black hair and a face lined with suffering and will and vision sat at the piano, beating it as a madman his drum and, bawling, singing, shouting, released a torrent of music which poured out of him like lava from a volcano . . . bitter, passionate, exalted, and all purple and gold."

Soon Bloch was appointed teacher of composition at the David Mannes School of Music in New York. A performance of his String Quartet in B Minor by the Flonzaley Quartet on December 27, 1916 made a strong impression. The *Musical America* reviewer called it "one of the greatest pieces of music composed in the last twenty years." Dr. Karl Mück, conductor of the Boston Symphony Orchestra, invited the composer to conduct his *Trois poèmes juifs* at two concerts in March 1917, and in May the Society of the Friends of Music presented an all-Bloch concert under the baton of Artur Bodansky. Some were repelled by what they called the cacaphonic ugliness of Bloch's music, but many admired it. Then, as later, the adjectives constantly used to describe Bloch's work were rich, vigorous, barbaric, Oriental, colorful, intense, individual, passionate, vehement.

The turning point in Bloch's career came when he won the $1,000 Elizabeth Sprague Coolidge Prize in the international competition in 1919, with his Suite for Viola and Piano (which he later expanded for orchestra). This was described by *Musical America's* Herbert Peyser as "not only great music, it is epochmaking," and by *Musical Quarterly's* O. G. Sonneck as "the greatest work for viola in musical literature, and what is more important, one of the most significant and powerful works of our time."

The next year, Bloch became the founding director of The Cleveland Institute of Music, starting with six students. This grew to more than 700 by 1925, the year he resigned.

For the next five years the composer was director of the San Francisco Conservatory, but could not arouse the public support he had hoped for. Among the composers who have studied with Bloch are Roger Sessions, George Antheil, Bernard Rogers, Randall Thompson, Frederick Jacobi, and Quincy Porter. He has also been interested in the musical education of children; lectures by him at an experimental summer school are recorded in *A School in Action* (1922).

Having become an American citizen in 1924, Bloch wrote his epic rhapsody *America,* he said, "in love for this country—in reverence for its past—in faith in its future." Very ill of heart trouble, he wept for hours thinking that he would die before it was finished. Submitted anonymously in the *Musical America* contest in 1928, it was the unanimous choice of the five judges from the 93 scores entered. Bloch was awarded the $3,000 prize and the work was premièred by the New York Philharmonic and performed the next day by the Boston, Chicago, Philadelphia, and San Francisco symphonies. Two years earlier, Bloch's *Four Episodes for Chamber Orchestra* had won the Beebee Prize.

An endowment by a San Francisco music lover in 1930 enabled Bloch to devote himself entirely to composing for ten years. "Starved for companionship," he said, he returned to Geneva and spent the next decade in Europe, composing and conducting. For a year he studied pathology hoping to find a cure for a skin disease which doctors had not been able to relieve. Then Bloch told his conclusions to a Swiss doctor uncle of his, and together, D. Ewen recounts in *Composers of Today*, they effected a cure. Bloch lived in Italy until Fascism and anti-Semitism made him uncomfortable, then he moved to France and later to Sweden.

A major work of this period was the Jewish Sacred Service, *Avodath Hakodesh,* commissioned by cellist Gerald Warburg of the New York banking family. It has been called "a masterpiece of modern liturgical music." Another project of Bloch's was the restudying of counterpoint—he went back to the 16th-century masters and wrote thousands of contrapuntal exercises.

The Ernest Bloch Society was formed in 1937 in London, with the composer's friend Albert Einstein as honorary president. It was from Einstein's stepdaughter Margot that Bloch's daughter Suzanne first learned to play the 19-string flute on which she is now a leading performer.

Bloch returned to the United States in 1939 and has since been associated with the University of California at Berkeley as professor of music, teaching during summer sessions only. In 1941, at the age of sixty, he moved to Agate Beach, Oregon, with his wife and six cats and has lived there in virtual isolation ever since, gardening, growing mushrooms, polishing beach stones, and continuing to compose. His 1944 *Symphonic Suite* was performed by the major orchestras and nationally broadcast; his recent works include the *Second String Quartet,* 1945, *Concerto Symphonique,* 1948, *Scherz Fantasque,* 1948, *Concertino,* 1950, *Rhapsodie Hebraïque,* 1951.

In his seventy-second year, 1952, Bloch completed the *String Quartet No. 3* in April, *Concerto Grosso No. 2* in August, *Sinfonia Breve* and *In Memoriam* in December, and then left for Rome to hear the revival of his *Macbeth.* In the year 1947 his *Second String Quartet* was voted the most outstanding chamber work premiered in New York that season, and the following November the Juilliard School and the League of Composers co-sponsored a two-day "festival" of three all-Bloch concerts. Commented Miles Kastendieck, "There is no doubt that his music wears exceedingly well. If he has not been quite in fashion, the reason is simply that in writing music he has spoken from the heart." Bloch's return to Britain in 1949 for the first time in a decade was honored by wide performances of his works, and he conducted an all-Bloch program at the opening concert of the London Philharmonic season.

Bloch is the first composer ever to receive the gold medal of the American Academy of Arts and Letters; he is a member of the Academy and an honorary member of the Academia di Santa Cecilia in Rome. In 1948 he was awarded a doctorate of Hebrew letters by Linfield College. Short and solidly built, he is a man of great energy and nervous gestures, "savagely honest" and outspoken, and has said, "passion and violence are characteristic of my nature." The music division of the Library of Congress accepted his collection of manuscripts, sketches, correspondence, and family papers in 1926. Bloch is passionately fond of mountains and forests. In the arts, he has said, "I live mostly in the past and find the deepest satisfaction with the old masters."

In August 1904 Ernest Bloch was married to Marguerite Schneider in Hamburg, Germany. Their children are Ivan, an engineer and division chief in the Bonneville Power Administration; Lucienne, a painter married to artist Stephen Dimitroff; and Suzanne, whose husband, Paul Smith, is head of the Columbia University mathematics department. Suzanne Bloch gives concert performances on the 19-string lute, the virginals, and other Renaissance instruments, and is an expert on the music of the period and one of the few persons who can read tablature, the complicated notation then used for lute music. "Father lives each of our lives intensely," she has said, "and expects us to share his own life with equal intensity."

Selected References

Menorah J 36 :196+ Spring '48
Mus Q 33 :443+ O '47
N Y Times Mag p17 Jl 16 '50 por
Newsweek 31 :84 F 16 '48
Time 53 :82+ Mr 7 '49; 50 :74+ N 24 '47; 61 :80 Ja 19 '53

Baker, T. ed. Biographical Dictionary of Musicians (1940)
Brook, D. Composers' Gallery (1946)
(Continued next page)

BLOCH, ERNEST—*Continued*

Ewen, D. The Book of Modern Composers (1950)

Ewen, D. American Composers Today (1949)

Howard, J. T. Our American Music (1946)

International Cyclopedia of Music and Musicians (1949)

Reis, C. Composers in America (1947)

Saleski, G. Famous Musicians of Jewish Origin (1949)

Tibalda Chiesa, M. Ernest Bloch (1933)

Who's Who in America, 1952-53

World Biography (1948)

BOLES, EWING T(HOMAS) May 4, 1895- Business executive; banker

Address: b. c/o Ohio Company, 51 N. High St., Columbus 15, Ohio; c/o Investment Bankers Association of America, 33 S. Clark St., Chicago 3, Ill.; h. 2750 Crafton Court, Columbus 8, Ohio

The Investment Bankers Association of America, an organization of individuals, partnerships, and corporations connected with the sale and purchase of securities, concluded its forty-first annual convention on December 5, 1952, with the inauguration of Ewing T. Boles of Columbus, Ohio, as its president for the en-

EWING T. BOLES

suing year. President of the Ohio Company, a leading Middle Western investment banking concern, Ewing Boles has been active since 1941 in the committee work of the association, of which he was vice-president in 1951.

A descendant of the John Boles who came to Jamestown, Virginia, from England and later settled at Warwick Cove, Ewing Thomas Boles is one of the three children (two sons and a

daughter) of John Robert Boles, an independent tobacco buyer and farmer, and Sarah Sheriff (McGowan) Boles. He was born on May 4, 1895, at Williamstown in northern Kentucky and was reared "in the rough, rugged region of Grant County" (as he has described it), where he attended the Williamstown grade school and high school, graduating as class valedictorian in 1913. At the small liberal arts Centre College of Kentucky (established at Danville, Kentucky, in 1819 and affiliated with the Presbyterian Church), from which he received his B.A. degree in 1916, Boles was vice-president and salutatorian of his class. In his senior year he was captain of the football team, popularly known as the "Praying Colonels" because of Centre College's long religious tradition, and was also a member of Ye Round Table, a scholastic society, and president of the Phi Kappa Tau social fraternity. During the summer of 1915 he had taken special courses at the University of Illinois. After a year at the Law School of the University of Kentucky in Lexington, which he entered in the fall of 1916, he gave up his legal studies to serve in World War I as an ensign in the United States Navy (1917-19).

Boles's career in the investment business began in 1926 when he was appointed Central Ohio representative of Halsey, Stuart and Company, Inc., a Chicago brokerage house, for which he sold securities until 1929, when he joined the BancOhio Securities Company at Columbus. After six years as sales manager, Boles was elected president and in 1942, when the name of the BancOhio Securities Company was changed to the Ohio Company, continued as president of the reorganized concern, becoming also a member of its board of directors. Boles is a director of several business and industrial enterprises, including Federated Publications, Inc., the White-Haines Optical Company, the Ohio Valley Baking Company, the Universal Concrete Pipe Company, and the Tiffin Art Metal Company. He is a member of the Investment Dealers of Ohio, Inc., of which he was president in 1945, and of the National Association of Security Dealers, Inc., of which he was a governor from 1949 to 1952. In his own firm, the Ohio Company, he participates regularly in Saturday morning sales meetings and has been described by an associate in the Investment Bankers of America as one who "ardently advocates . . . modern merchandising techniques" and is especially interested in the financing of small business. Besides national underwriting, this associate points out, "the Ohio Company specializes in new capital issues sold intra-state to provide capital for small Ohio companies . . . the Ohio Company played a leading role in developing the largest municipal issue ever sold, to provide $326,000,000 to finance the Ohio Turnpike," the issue having been offered in June 1952 through 410 investment banking houses.

Since 1941 Ewing Boles has been active in the affairs of the Investment Bankers Association of America, an organization founded in 1912 to further the interests of both the bankers and the public "through mutual cooperation, through the maintenance of high standards of service, through self-regulation, and through the support of appropriate legislation." Boles served as a member of the Association's railroad securities committee (1941-43), as chairman of the Ohio Valley Group, one of the eighteen regional divisions of the I.B.A. (1945-47), and thus as a member on the Association's group chairmen's committee. For the next two years he was on the Federal legislation, public education, and railroad securities committees, and was chairman in 1949 of the savings bond committee. Named a member of the board of governors in 1950 and chairman of the group chairmen's committee in the same year, he continued in both capacities until his election as president of the Association. He has also been active on the public education and nominating committees (1949-50) and the administrative review committee (1950-51). On November 30, 1951, when Joseph T. Johnson of Milwaukee, Wisconsin, was elected president of the I.B.A., Boles became one of the Association's five vice-presidents and a member of the executive committee. As a member of the education committee he helped to conduct a campaign which included the issuance of a film (*Opportunity-U.S.A.*) on investment banking processes and a portable exhibit ("Money Tells Its Own Story") for use by member firms and other organizations.

The president of the Investment Bankers Association of America, who holds office for a single year, is technically selected at the end of each annual convention, though nomination by the board of governors is tantamount to election. Boles's nomination, accepted by him in May 1952, was made public at I.B.A. headquarters in Chicago on October 30. At his formal election in Hollywood Beach, Florida, on December 4, the last day of the I.B.A.'s forty-first convention, Boles's inaugural address to more than 1,500 delegates and their wives pledged to the incoming Eisenhower Administration the Association's cooperation in "returning this nation to a . . . policy of sound dollars and balanced budgets." He emphasized the need to replace with the "products of peace" the "part of our prosperity that comes from war," and made use of the slogan-like phrase "We must sell prosperity." Pointing out that the economy needs two or three times as much capital as private investors are now supplying, Boles emphasized the need for public education to recruit more investments, to prevent the Government from taking this responsibility away from private enterprise. The new I.B.A. president announced that the Association would undertake a nation-wide survey in an attempt to learn why some people invest and why some do not. He commended the Federal Reserve System for "the objective manner" in which it carried out its responsibilities in the past twenty months and cautioned that "monetary policy alone cannot be wholly effective in dealing with the problems of inflation that arise from other than monetary causes" (Paul Heffernan in the New York *Times*).

In his home city of Columbus, Boles is a trustee of White Cross Hospital and chairman of its finance committee, as well as president of Gladden Community House, a center for some two thousand adults and young people in one of the poorer sections of Ohio's capital city. Social organizations to which Ewing Boles belongs are the Columbus Club and the Columbus Athletic Club, and he is a past national president of the Phi Kappa Tau fraternity. He is an Episcopalian in creed, and he has been described politically as "a consistent Republican." Mrs. Boles, a teacher before her marriage on June 19, 1920, is the former Katherine Dwyer, of Charleston, Illinois; the couple, who met while both were students at the University of Illinois, are the parents of Dr. Ewing Thomas Boles, Jr., chief resident in surgery at University Hospital in Columbus, and Mrs. Helen Anne Hardy, wife of Wofford B. Hardy, Jr., of Big Spring, Texas. (Their other daughter, Mary Katherine, is deceased.) Standing six feet in height, Boles weighs 185 pounds; he has gray eyes and dark brown hair. He takes a keen spectator interest in football and all other sports and is an avid reader, particularly of publications in the business field. He is said to possess "effervescent humor and a ready fund of pertinent stories."

References

Burroughs Clearing House 37:54 D '52
    por
Who's Who in America, 1952-53
Who's Who in Commerce and Industry (1951)
Who's Who in the Midwest (1949)

BOOTH, SHIRLEY Aug. 30, 1907- Actress

Address: b. c/o Actors' Equity Association, 45 W. 47th St., New York 19; h. 25 W. 54th St., New York 19

NOTE: This biography supersedes the article which appeared in *Current Biography* in 1942.

Before achieving stardom in the Broadway success *Come Back, Little Sheba* and four major acting awards in 1950, Shirley Booth was a featured comedienne and a character actress on the New York stage for twenty-five years, giving more than 3,500 performances in twenty-two plays. Her versatility was developed by a long apprenticeship in stock companies in the years between 1919 and 1935. Besides performing in the theater, she appeared on radio as Miss Duffy in the popular program *Duffy's Tavern* (1940-42) and in motion pictures in 1952 in a film version of the stage play *Come Back, Little Sheba*, winning with her first screen role the New York Film Critics award for the best feminine acting of the year and the award of the Academy of Motion Picture Arts and Sciences for the best actress. When she starred in the Broadway play *The Time of the Cuckoo*, which opened in October 1952, for the first time her name appeared alone on the Empire Theatre marquee.

Born Thelma Booth Ford in New York City on August 30, 1907, Shirley Booth is the eldest daughter of Albert J. and Shirley (Wright) Ford. Shortly after her birth, her father, a district manager of the International Business

SHIRLEY BOOTH

Machines Corporation, moved his family from Manhattan's Morningside Drive to the Flatbush section of Brooklyn. There, reportedly, Thelma gave her first public performance at the age of three, singing "In the Good Old Summertime" in a Sunday School show, an experience she has described as "heady" (*Life*, December 1, 1952).

At Public School 152 in Brooklyn, Miss Booth has recalled, her English composition "Autobiography of a Thanksgiving Turkey" was chosen to be read in the auditorium. It is said that she was a shy and lonely child who liked to imagine herself someone else and that she thereby developed an attitude which she believes contributed to her success in character parts on the stage. When she was seven years old, her family established a temporary residence in Philadelphia, where the child was given her first contact with the theatre in the person of J. Hammond Daly, a young local stock company actor who became a friend of the family. After her family had moved to Hartford, Connecticut, five years later, where Daly was appearing with a theatrical stock company, he helped the young girl get her first part on the stage, at the age of twelve, in *Mother Carey's Chickens.* After a summer season with the stock company in Hartford, she returned to school; her withdrawal the following year marked the end of her formal education.

Against her father's wishes, Thelma Ford left Hartford at the age of fourteen to seek a stage career in New York, where she lived with a friend of her mother's. Obtaining an ingénue's part with the Poli stock company, she was assigned to its unit playing in New Haven, Connecticut, at a small salary out of which she had to furnish her own wardrobe. During the fifty-four weeks that she played in New Haven she adopted the professional name Shirley Booth. With the Poli stock company, she toured the principal cities of the

Eastern United States, appearing in a number of minor roles through which she acquired versatility as an actress. Miss Booth's first part on Broadway was that of the ingénue in *Hell's Bells* (1925), in which she played opposite Humphrey Bogart. After the play completed its run of four months, she returned to stock until November, when she was again seen on the New York stage, in a minor part in *Laff That Off.* For the next ten years she interspersed her stock engagements with appearances in short-lived Broadway plays. Explaining why she remained in stock, she has pointed out, "I was big in stock. I had a reputation and a public. I could afford to hang around New York and take my chances, but I had to go where people believed in me. . . .I had to keep acting, so I could believe in myself" (*Life*).

Among the nearly 600 productions in which Miss Booth appeared in stock from 1925 to 1935 were such dissimilar plays as *Lady Windermere's Fan* by Oscar Wilde and *The Wild Duck* by Henrik Ibsen. Her favorite role, Sadie Thompson in *Rain,* Miss Booth called "the hardest working part [she] ever had" (New York *Herald Tribune*). She has said that she has never forgotten the working motto of stock, "You get your cue and you come out acting" (*Collier's*). During this decade in stock she also appeared on Broadway in many plays including *Buy, Buy, Baby* (1926), *High Gear* (1927), *The War Song* (1928), *The School for Virtue* (1931), *The Mask and the Face* (1933), and *After Such Pleasures* (1934). Referring to this period, James Poling has commented in *Collier's*: "For years, as a featured player, Shirley has taken tired, minor roles and made them incandescent."

After watching her play a Dorothy Parker character in *Sunday Nights at Nine* (1934) at the Barbizon-Plaza Hotel's little theater, producer George Abbott gave Miss Booth her first substantial part on Broadway in *Three Men on a Horse* (1935), a hit comedy in which she played an inane but good-hearted "gangster's moll" called Mabel. Abbott, who was later associated with Shirley Booth in other productions, has said: "I have worked with more actresses than I can count, and to me Shirley is easily tops." With her two-year success in *Three Men on a Horse,* Miss Booth left stock permanently. The next two plays in which she appeared on Broadway, *Excursion* (April 1937) and *Too Many Heroes* (November 1937), were short-lived, and in 1938 she moved to the West Coast to take a year's vacation from the theatre and be a homemaker. She returned to New York in 1939 to act the part of Elizabeth Imbrie in the Theatre Guild's *Philadelphia Story,* receiving almost as much praise from the critics as Katherine Hepburn, the star of the play, which ran for more than a year.

Shirley Booth's next role was that of Ruth Sherwood, the less attractive and somewhat stocky sister in *My Sisteen Eileen* (1940), a Broadway hit that had a two-year run. At that time Miss Booth told a reporter, "I want to keep improving, to keep acting and to play many character parts" (New York *World-Telegram*). While appearing in *My Sister*

Eileen, Miss Booth also performed on radio from 1940 to 1942 as Miss Duffy in the popular program *Duffy's Tavern,* which was conceived and produced by her husband, Ed Gardner. Like Mabel in *Three Men on a Horse,* Miss Duffy gave opportunity for display of Shirley Booth's talents as a comedienne, which were further employed in the similar character of Dottie Mahoney, in several top radio variety shows. On the National Broadcasting Company's *Theatre Guild of the Air,* she acted various dramatic roles.

Tomorrow the World, in which Shirley Booth was seen on Broadway in 1943-44, had 499 performances, a record in the New York theatre for any drama dealing with war problems, and was a notable financial success. As the school teacher who is concerned with how German children may be untaught the Nazi philosophy, Miss Booth played opposite Ralph Bellamy in a performance called "warmly human" and "utterly convincing" (New York *World-Telegram*). In her first musical comedy, *Hollywood Pinafore* (1945), a satire on Hollywood, she played the part of a chatterbox movie-columnist named Louhedda Hopsons, who sings of herself at one point as "Little Miss Butter-up," George Kaufman's version of Gilbert and Sullivan's "Buttercup." Howard Barnes described her as "the bright, particular star of the new musical at the Alvin. There are some who knew that she could sing like a lark. . . .Those who did not know it will derive tremendous pleasure from her handling of the lovely songs" (New York *Herald Tribune*). Two short-run plays followed, *Land's End* (1946) and *The Men We Marry* (1948). *Land's End* closed after its fifth performance, but the *World-Telegram* praised Miss Booth's "job of infinite expertness as Susan. Never obvious or heavy, she suggests the innate toughness and earthiness of a girl who would like to be free and frank as a wind, but is forced into intricacy by her relentless fervor." Miss Booth's role in *The Men We Marry* was described by the same critic as "the only pleasant character" among useless and decadent people.

For her part in *Goodbye, My Fancy* (1948) Miss Booth received the Antoinette Perry Award for the best feminine supporting role of the season. Living at this time on a farm in Bucks County, Pennsylvania, she commuted to Broadway to play the part of an acid-tongued secretary in a role that "brought so many laughs from the audience that she was asked to give some of her lines to the star, Madeleine Carroll" (*Collier's*). This exchange was, however, unsuccessful because the lines were not suited to the other actress. The New York *World-Telegram* reviewer wrote that "as · a Congresswoman's secretary, Shirley Booth has the sort of cynical role she can seemingly let slide off the back of her hand." *Love Me Long,* in which the actress appeared in 1949, closed after seven performances.

Starring in the part of Lola Delaney, a dowdy, middle-aged housewife, in the Theatre Guild drama *Come Back, Little Sheba* (1950), Miss Booth won the Antoinette Perry Award, the Donaldson Award, the Drama Critics Circle Award, and the Barter Theater Award. Richard Watts, Jr., in the New York *Post* found that "she is as fine at straight characterization as she has long been at slightly sardonic comedy. . . .To her other immense virtues, Miss Booth now adds the valuable quality of variety." The reviewer for the *Christian Science Monitor* observed, "She admirably realizes the loneliness and ineffectuality of a dowdy ex-flapper whose surface humor accentuates an inner pathos," while Daniel Mann, director of the play, has been quoted as remarking that she "doesn't act, she lives on the stage" (*Collier's*).

When she had completed a successful nationwide tour in *Come Back, Little Sheba,* Shirley Booth took the role of Cissy in Broadway's musical production of *A Tree Grows in Brooklyn* (1951) by George Abbott and Betty Smith, based on the latter's best-selling novel. Her performance brought acclaim from all critics, with the New York *World-Telegram* stating that "the jewel of the evening . . . is Shirley Booth's miraculous handling of the salty life and loves of Cissy," and the New York *Herald Tribune* that Miss Booth's singing "is better than good enough; she stops the show with a number called 'Love Is the Reason.'" The consensus of opinion was summed up in John Mason Brown's comment: "Miss Booth is one of the most gifted actresses our theater boasts. She is one of the few who, to my knowledge, has never been guilty of a bad performance" (*Saturday Review of Literature,* May 5, 1951). In her most recent New York play, the successful *The Time of the Cuckoo,* which began its run on Broadway in October 1952 and which closed in June, 1953 (when it was announced that the Empire Theatre was to be razed) she depicted a frustrated, romantic middle-aged American secretary in Italy. Shirley Booth "conquers an unfamiliar type of role in this serious romantic character" (New York *World Telegram*). Her acting in this production brought her the Antoinette Perry Award in March 1953.

Miss Booth made her first motion picture appearance in a film version of the play *Come Back, Little Sheba* (1952), for which she received the Best Actress of the Year Award from both the National Board of Review and the New York Film Critics. On March 19, 1953, she won the award of the Academy of Motion Picture Arts and Sciences as the best actress in a 1952 picture. Alton Cook (New York *World-Telegram*) credited her with the increase in warmth and pity the play acquired in its transition to a new medium, while Bosley Crowther (New York *Times*) admired "her skillful and knowing creation of a depressingly common type—the immature, mawkish, lazy housewife."

On November 23, 1929, Shirley Booth was married to Edward Gardner, from whom she was divorced in 1942. The following year, on September 24, she was married to William H. Baker, Jr., a New York investment counselor who died in 1951. The actress is five feet three and one-half inches in height, slightly stocky, and has brown eyes and brunette hair which she sometimes colors to suit her roles. Her religious affiliation is Episcopal. Among her

BOOTH, SHIRLEY—*Continued*

hobbies are interior decorating and reading novels set in the English countryside. "Someday," she has said, "I'd like to go on a walking tour of Devon."

On April 29, 1953 Miss Booth was named "the world's best actress" at the sixth International Film Festival at Cannes, France, for her performance in the film *Come Back, Little Sheba.* She also received the 1953 Delia Austrian Medal of the Drama League of New York for her performance in Arthur Laurent's play *The Time of the Cuckoo.*

References

    Collier's 127:22-3 Je 16 '51 pors
    Life 33:128+ D 1 '52 pors
    Sat R 34:23-24 My 5 '51
    N Y Herald Tribune Jl 20 '41
    N Y World-Telegram p10 Mr 2 '42 por
    This Week p14 Ja 18 '53 pors
    Who's Who in the Theatre (1952)

BORGESE, G(IUSEPPE) A(NTONIO) Nov. 12, 1882—Dec. 4, 1952 Italian-American author; educator; taught literature, aesthetics, history of criticism at University of Rome (1910-17) and at University of Milan (1917-31); literary and foreign editor of *Corrière della séra* (1912-31); head of Press and Propaganda Bureau (1917-18); denouncing fascism, came to United States in 1931; taught at University of California, New School for Social Research, Smith College, and University of Chicago; helped organize Committee to Frame a World Constitution (1946); returned to Italy and was reinstated at University of Milan (1948); author of many books on government, history, and literature. See *Current Biography,* 1947.

Obituary

    N Y Times p27 D 5 '52

BOWDITCH, RICHARD L(YON) Oct. 11, 1900- President of the Chamber of Commerce of the United States; coal and shipping executive

Address: b. Chamber of Commerce of the United States, Washington 6, D.C.; 10 Post Office Sq., Boston 1, Mass.; h. 31 Fayerweither St., Cambridge 3, Mass.

The twenty-fifth president of the Chamber of Commerce of the United States, elected April 29, 1953 for one year, is Richard L. Bowditch, head of C. H. Sprague and Son Company, a coal mining and distributing concern, and president of the Sprague Steamship Company, both of Boston. Long active in regional affairs in New England, he has been a vigorous exponent of various measures to keep that area's economy healthy and expanding.

Bowditch had previously headed the Foreign Commerce committee of the Chamber of Commerce, which represents about 1,600,000 Americans, most of whom are engaged in small business. He had also served as a vice-president

and a director of special committees in the fields of United States and Canadian relations, transportation, communications and natural resources.

He has served as a member of the Solid Fuels Advisory War Council and of the Emergency Solid Fuels Administration of Massachusetts. For some months in 1951 he was director of the transportation, public utilities, fuel, service, import and export division of the reorganized Office of Price Stabilization.

Richard Lyon Bowditch was born in Milton, Massachusetts, October 11, 1900, to Ernest William Bowditch, a civil engineer and landscape architect, and Margaret (Swann) Bowditch. He is a great-grandson of Nathaniel Bowditch, who compiled a book of navigation tables still in use and known as "the seamen's bible". He is a descendant of English seafarers who settled in Salem in the Colonial period.

After attending Milton Academy, Hotchkiss School, and Massachusetts Institute of Technology, Bowditch made an eight-months tour of Japan, China, Korea and India. He returned with eight dollars in his pocket and suffering from jaundice which he had contracted in the Orient. Upon recovering, he decided to obtain a job instead of studying for an engineering degree.

He applied to Phineas Sprague, of the C. H. Sprague and Son Company, who put him to work as a trapper boy in a Sprague-controlled mine. His job was to open and close by hand the heavy doors separating mine compartments to admit the men and trains.

Bowditch still maintains that he would rather work in a mine than a factory "because there's something new to do in the mines every day." He was quickly advanced from trapper boy to tracklayer, then to hand-loader of coal, and later to operator of a mine locomotive.

Bowditch served with the United States Army Engineers Reserve in 1922. After studying at the Massachusetts Institute of Technology for a period in 1923, he obtained work with the Logan County Coal Corporation of Lundale, West Virginia. During a Christmas vacation in Massachusetts in 1924, he had another interview with Sprague, the result of which was that he resumed his association with the Sprague company.

Starting as a member of the sales department, he advanced in eleven years to the presidency of the firm. The two principal Sprague companies are now the largest coal dealers in the nation. By 1953, under the presidency of Bowditch, they were handling coal and fuel oil shipments to twenty-three foreign countries and to twenty-seven states.

In March 1950 Bowditch was elected a director of Pacific Mills, and in the following month was promoted from president to chairman of the board of the Imperial Smokeless Coal Company of Quinwood, West Virginia, a subsidiary of the Sprague Company.

Other directorships currently held by Bowditch are in the First National Bank of Boston, the Boston and Maine Railroad, the Liberty Mutual Insurance Company, the Ludlow Manufacturing and Sales Company, the New River Company of Mt. Hope, West Virginia, the Sylvania Electric Products Company, and the New England Steel Development Corporation.

He was president of the New England Council of the Chamber of Commerce from 1946 to 1948. Before his election as a vice-president to the national organization in 1949, he served on the executive, public relations and education committees. Subsequently, he became interested in promoting a better understanding between United States and Canadian businessmen which prompted him to accept the chairmanship of the United States section of the Canada-United States committee of the Chamber of Commerce.

He was also the chairman of the Foreign Commerce committee which submitted a report recommending a unified foreign assistance program, and urging the "elimination of discriminating trade practices aimed at United States production and the restoration of free convertibility of currencies" (New York *Times,* November 24, 1950). In February 1952 the board of directors of the Chamber of Commerce voted to adopt his recommendation for the establishment of a single independent Government agency to direct all foreign economic operations.

A new policy on trade and tariffs was advocated by members of the United States Chamber of Commerce meeting in Washington on April 29th at which session they elected Richard L. Bowditch to succeed retiring president Laurence F. Lee. This policy approves trade with "Iron Curtain" countries for non-strategic items, and favors increased imports rather than tax-supported foreign aid to free nations.

In favor of a low tariff, Bowditch declared, "Under a free enterprise system increased competitive pressure (whether from foreign or domestic sources) impels capital and labor toward more productive, and hence more profitable, activities" (*Newsweek,* May 4, 1953). Protective tariff should be instituted only when national security requires it, he has stated.

In addition to his business activities, Richard L. Bowditch served from 1941 to 1945 as a member of the board of the Massachusetts Institute of Technology, and has been a trustee since 1950 of Northeastern University in Boston. He was awarded an honorary LL.D. by Northeastern in 1949, and has also received an honorary degree from Marlboro College.

He is a member of the American Institute of Mining and Metallurgic Engineers, the American Military Engineers, and the American Society of Naval Architects and Marine Engineers.

He married the former Mabel Lowell Rantoul on May 11, 1929, and they have three sons, Richard Lyon, Jr., Nathaniel and James. "Amiable" and "husky" are adjectives applied to Bowditch by *Newsweek.* He is a recipient of the Naval Order of the United States. Bowditch enjoys vacationing in Maine and skiing.

Fabian Bachrach

RICHARD L. BOWDITCH

References

Christian Sci Mon p7 Ap 29 '53 por
N Y Herald Tribune p9 Ap 30 '53
Newsweek 41:70+ My 4 '53 por
Business Executives of America (1950)
Poor's Register of Directors and Executives (1952)
Who's Who in America, 1952-53

BRACKMAN, ROBERT Sept. 25, 1898-
Artist

Address: b. Noank, Connecticut

A member of the National Academy of Design since 1932, Robert Brackman has remained a staunch defender of realism in painting. One of the most sought-after artists for his ability as a portrait and nude painter, and as a teacher, he has been commissioned by some of the best-known personalities in the United States and has sold his work to many of the leading museums and collectors in this country.

Brackman painted the portrait of Jennifer Jones used in the motion picture *Portrait of Jenny,* based on Robert Nathan's novel. Among the many prizes he has won, two of the most recent are the $1,000 first prize at the Art Festival at Laguna Beach, California, and the Gold Medal of Honor, Allied Artists of America, in 1952.

Robert Brackman was born September 25, 1898, in Odessa, Russia, the son of Moycée and Celia (Miners) Brackman, who immigrated to America when the artist was ten years old. Brackman's first studies in art were begun at the Ferrer School in San Francisco, and were later continued at art classes in a settlement house in the Harlem section of New York, where he came under the supervision of Robert Henri and George Bellows, two members of

ROBERT BRACKMAN

the *Five* who had made art history as the founders of the *Ashcan School*. George Bellows in particular took special interest in Brackman, and urged him to apply for admission to the National Academy of Design in New York. Brackman did so and was accepted at the age of fourteen. He supported himself while studying by working as a photoengraver and lithographer apprentice, and in 1932 was accepted as an associate member of the Academy.

Although the period in which Brackman was learning was largely dominated by the expressionist and cubist schools of France and Germany, he studied the sound objective techniques of the 'realist' school. Coming under the influence of Picasso only for a brief period, he soon developed his own style of restrained figure painting.

Recognition came to the artist in 1929 when he was awarded the Anonymous Prize at the Chicago Art Institute. Three years later he received the Thomas B. Clarke Prize and the Athenaeum Prize. He became a member of the faculty of the Art Students League in New York City in 1934, a position which he has since held. The Noel Flagg Prize was given to him in 1936.

As his commissions for portraits increased, Brackman was able to choose from about twenty persons a year the three or four who interested him most as subjects. Planning his pictures in his mind in detail, he painted on canvas without preliminary sketches such famous personalities as Helen Morgan, the singer (the portrait was commissioned by Flo Ziegfeld, the theatrical producer), John D. Rockefeller, Jr., for Colonial Williamsburg, Inc., and other members of the Rockefeller family. Other portraits, for which the artist received about $3,500 each (*Life*, February 5, 1940) were of President-Emeritus Charles Seymour of Yale University, Governor Herbert H. Lehman of New York (now Senator), Peter M. Frazer, of the Connecticut

Life Insurance Co., Hartford, and the late Rabbi Stephen S. Wise.

Brackman was on the faculty of the Brooklyn Museum from 1936 to 1938, and in the last year excited considerable curiosity when it was rumored that he had painted portraits of Charles Lindbergh and his wife, Anne. The rumor proved true, but the portraits, exhibited only once in the United States, in 1938, were carefully guarded at that showing and photographs were not permitted.

Moving to Connecticut in 1939, he settled in the old fishing village of Noank, near the art colony at Mystic, because he feels at home living in a New England atmosphere. His fourth one-man show was held at the Macbeth Gallery in New York City in January, 1940. In the summer of that year, he taught fifty-three students and painted a considerable number of nude portraits which sold at top prices.

During World War II he was commissioned to do a portrait of Henry L. Stimson, then Secretary of War. Although his reputation was for quiet nudes and portraits, the hectic Pentagon atmosphere did not disrupt him. "It didn't bother me," he recalled cheerfully, "nothing bothers me when I am working. I'm too interested in painting to notice anything else. If I did, however could I have painted Stimson in his office with six generals, all gold braid, having conferences all day?" (*New York Sun*, December 18, 1948) The portrait of Stimson now hangs in the Pentagon Building collection, Washington, D.C.

In a review of Brackman's exhibit of paintings in May 1946 at the Grand Central Galleries Henry McBride, wrote in the New York *Sun*: "Brackman's new pictures show him to be clinging to all the well-known rules with undiminished faith. His technic answers to the demands he makes upon it but he does not demand much. He shuns the passions and does not approach very near to life. . . " (May 11, 1946).

Described as "boyish-faced," an artist who lives modestly and has little regard for money, Brackman was elected a National Academician in 1940. He is represented in the permanent collections of the Toledo (Ohio) Museum of Art, Municipal Gallery (Davenport, Iowa), Georgia University, Brooks Memorial (Memphis, Tennessee), Houston (Texas) Art Museum, New Britain (Connecticut) Museum, University of Connecticut, Rockford (Illinois) Art Association, Canajoharie (New York) Museum, Minneapolis Institute of Arts (where he has been a guest lecturer), Wilmington Society of Arts, New Haven Library, High Museum (Atlanta, Georgia), Montclair (New Jersey) Museum, Newark (New Jersey) Museum, Metropolitan Museum of Art (New York City), Pasadena Museum, Honolulu Museum, Rhode Island School of Design, Brooklyn (New York) Museum.

He received the Saltus Gold Medal of the National Academy in 1941, the first prize at the Connecticut Academy in 1947, honorable mention at the Carnegie Institute in 1949, and the Gold Medal of Honor awarded by the Allied Artists of America in 1952. Brackman has been affiliated with the American Art School since 1950.

In 1936 Brackman married Francis Davis, an art student. They have two daughters, Celia D., and Roberta F. Among the organizations in which he holds membership are the Mystic (Connecticut) Art Association of which he is president, Audubon Society of Artists, Paint and Clay Club, the American Watercolor Society, the International Society of Arts and Letters, the Allied Artists of America, the Connecticut Academy of Fine Arts, the Wilmington Society of Arts, and the Grand Central Art Galleries.

Brackman is five feet six inches tall, has brown hair and eyes, and weighs 160 pounds. He has no political or religious affiliations. "Few artists in America combine integrity and popularity with so much success," commented *Life* (February 5, 1940).

His painting *After the Masque* is in the Encyclopedia Brittanica collection; *Roberta and Celia* (a portrait of his daughters) is in the International Business Machines collection. Others are included in the collections of the DuPont Company, Harvard Club of New York, Princeton University and Milton Academy.

References

Life 8:58 F 5 '40

N Y Sun p5 D 18 '48

Boswell, P. Modern American Painting (1948)

Who's Who in America, 1952-53

Who's Who in American Art, 1940-47

BRADBURY, RAY (DOUGLAS) August 22, 1920- Author

Address: 10750 Clarkson Rd., Los Angeles 64, California

One of the major forms of escape reading in America today is that curious phenomenon known as "science-fiction," and one of the most successful writers in this field is thirty-three-year-old Ray Bradbury. He has had 170 short stories published and twenty-three radio dramas and five television plays produced. All of these deal with imaginative themes which combine advanced technology with subtle fantasy and have what has become known as "the Bradbury twist." His stories were first published in science fiction and fantasy magazines, but the freshness and power of his writings has lifted him out of this restricted category and has brought him publication in magazines of broader interests such as *Collier's, Saturday Evening Post* and the *New Yorker*.

One result of Bradbury's achieving a wider audience is that while distinguished critics are "discovering" him and suggesting that he is too good to be called a science fiction writer, the science fiction fans, who hail Bradbury as among their best, are pointing with pride to his work as an example of what science fiction can produce.

His most recent work, *The Golden Apples of the Sun,* is the fourth of his published books, the others being *Dark Carnival* (1947), *The*

RAY BRADBURY

Martian Chronicles (1950) and *The Illustrated Man* (1951). Two of his stories have been included in O. Henry Awards *Prize Stories* volumes. He has also done much writing for the moving pictures and radio, especially for the Columbia Broadcasting System program *Suspense*. His work has been compared with that of Poe, Saki, Shirley Jackson and John Collier.

Of Bradbury's prolific output *Punch* (August 1952) has written: "It is hard to speak with restraint of these extraordinary tales which raise Ray Bradbury to a secure place among the imaginative writers of today." *The Saturday Review (of Literature)* concurred with this: "Bradbury deserves special attention . . . his stories are memorable not only for the ideas they embody but also for their legitimate human values" (July 28, 1951).

Ray Douglas Bradbury was born on August 22, 1920 to Leonard Spaulding and Esther M. (Moberg) Bradbury in Waukegan, Illinois. His younger brother, Leonard, is also a writer. His father was a lineman for Public Service. His ancestors came to Salisbury, Massachusetts, in 1630, later settling in Illinois, and his great-grandfather and grandfather were publishers of books and newspapers in Chicago and in Waukegan. His mother's family came from Stockholm, Sweden. He attended public school in Waukegan until 1934, when his family moved to California and he entered Los Angeles High School. The year before his graduation he joined the Los Angeles Science-Fantasy Society and started writing science fiction in his own magazine, *Futuria Fantasia* which ran for four issues.

He has been writing stories for his own amusement since the age of twelve. He recalls that his aunt, Neva Bradbury, read Poe to him, and gradually through his reading of the *Oz* books, *Tarzan, Alice in Wonderland* and *Grimms' Fairy Tales,* his sense of the fantastic

BRADBURY, RAY—*Continued*

was stimulated. "But I stopped reading fantasy when I began to write," he said recently, "because I wanted to bring back to science fiction something fresh and new. It needed revivifying," so out into space he ventured for the locale of many of his stories (New York *Times Book Review,* August 5, 1951).

Graduating from high school in 1938, he sold newspapers and took other jobs which allowed him time to devote to writing. A year and a half of acting with a little theatre group convinced him that the stage was not his métier. His first story, entitled "It's Not the Heat, It's the Hu,' was published in *Script* (1940), a California magazine. It was a whimsical treatment of what might happen to an individual who reiterates irritatingly vapid phrases about the heat and the humidity. This theme of social irritation has been used in subsequent Bradbury stories. The clash between society and the individual in an over-developed civilization has motivated a number of his protagonists. The most brilliant example of this is "The Fireman" (*Galaxy* 1951), which with savage cynicism exposes the substitution of social mores and mechanisms for individual thought. The fireman was a warden whose duty was to destroy books and learning, thus preventing man from thinking for himself.

By 1942 Bradbury was able to earn enough money from his writing so that he could relinquish his job selling newspapers. He spent the war years writing radio appeals for the Red Cross, and short dramas for blood donor drives. His work was represented in *The Best American Short Stories of 1946,* edited by Martha Foley. The story, "The Big Black and White Game," originally published in the *American Mercury* (August 1945), was of a non-fanciful nature.

In the same year, *Mademoiselle* purchased his story "Homecoming," which later appeared in the O. Henry *Prize Stories* (1947). Arkham House published in 1947 a collection of twenty-seven of his stories entitled *Dark Carnival,* and from then on Bradbury's reputation steadily mounted, and he has become an important name in fantasy and science fiction today. These stories were characterized by a theme of return, not quite to the womb, but to an unrealistically recalled golden childhood, a desire to escape from the gray burdens of adult life. The Best One-Act Plays of 1947-48 included one of his radio plays.

The editors of the O. Henry *Prize Stories* selected "Power House" for a third prize award in 1948. Two years later, a collection of Bradbury's short stories, *The Martian Chronicles,* lifted him to national recognition, and a second edition published by Bantam Pocket-books sold over 200,000 copies. This book dealt with the development and exploitation of Mars and its effect upon mankind and its home world, and the stories were connected by the repeated theme that earthmen are despoilers, not developers. The collection was organized chronologically, beginning with the first intrepid explorer, continuing through the early Mars colonists, to the final phase in which the earth-

men had to adjust to the conditions on Mars, and in so doing, became Martian.

One of his stories, "Forever and the Earth," published in 1950 in a collection by Groff Conklin called *The Big Book of Science Fiction,* illustrates an idea that has often intrigued Bradbury. This is a tale of an age which has no lyric poet to sing of its legends and its heroes. Men have become like their machines, and though masters of a far-flung interplanetary empire, they are troubled by their lack of emotional and aesthetic experience. In an effort to remedy this, a novelist of the past, whose giant grasp of life is capable of dealing with the new civilization, is stolen, via time machine, from his death-bed 300 years before. Thomas Wolfe is selected, and he provides the giant empire of the future with a lyric poet who can sing the songs of the Spaceman.

Bradbury defines the difference between science fiction and fantasy: "Science fiction is really sociological studies of the future, things that the writer believes are going to happen by putting two and two together. . . .Fantasy fiction is the improbable. . . .If you had a leprechaun or a dinosaur appearing in the streets of New York—that's highly improbable. But science fiction is a logical or mathematical projection of reality" (New York *Times Book Review,* August 5, 1951).

Questioned as to the literary value of science fiction Bradbury admitted frankly that "the form has a bad name because of the space operas. You say science fiction and people think of Buck Rogers and Flash Gordon." However, he stated that there are some science fiction writers who are trying to think in human terms of real human problems, and the field can only come of age when good writers contribute their talents to it. "The mechanical age is crushing people," he concluded.

A third collection of his stories, *The Illustrated Man,* published in 1951, told of a man covered by tattoos, each of which came to life to form a tale of horror.

Reviewing this collection, *Punch* wrote: "It is true that the quality of art depends on the treatment, and not the choice of subject: but to take the paraphernalia of 'science fiction,' the rocket-ships, the robot, the great engines, the cosmic wars and galactic explorations that popularly belong to the American 'comic' and film-serial, and fashion from them stories as delicate as Faure's songs, or Cezanne's water-colours, is a very considerable achievement" (August 1952).

On September 27, 1947 Bradbury married Marguerite Susan McClure, an English instructor at the University of California in Los Angeles, and shortly thereafter he ceased to write stories of "golden childhood" and, instead, began to describe children as "dangerous little monsters," beginning with "The Small Assassin." His own children, Susan Marguerite, and Romona Anne, are not, however, responsible for this change of attitude toward the younger generation.

Ray Bradbury has been described as "a pretty big fellow, looking more like football material than like interplanetary stuff." He is five feet and ten inches tall, and weighs 180 pounds.

He has blue eyes and blond hair. An independent thinker as far as politics and religion are concerned, he is active in poetry, drama and art clubs. He is president *pro tem* of the Science Fiction and Fantasy Writers of America, vice-president of the Pacific Art Foundation, and a member of the Screen Writers' Guild. His hobbies are oil and watercolor painting, ceramics, and collecting tribal dance masks.

The young science fiction author told a *Current Biography* writer: "I have often been misquoted as disliking 'science.' I would like to be quoted as saying I think science is a glove, so much depends upon what kind of hand is put into it. The hand of man himself can be good or bad. I have nothing against the 'glove,' only the hand. A story like 'The World the Children Made' is a protest not at science, but at the way we *use* science."

His latest book, *The Golden Apples of the Sun* (1953), a collection of twenty-two stories, was reviewed by Charles Poore in the New York *Times* (March 19, 1953) as written "in a style that seems to have been nourished on the poets and fableists of the Irish literary renaissance." Charles Lee in the *New York Times Book Review* (March 22), commented: "Depending on his story, Bradbury is whimsical, poetical, allegorical, editorial, or macabre. . . . The delicate poetry of *The April Witch* contrasts pleasantly with the boisterous humors of his teen-age piece, *The Great Fire*. Ace practitioner of this special type of tale, he is at his startling best in this collection."

Novelist Christopher Isherwood wrote of Bradbury's work: "The sheer lift and power of a truly original imagination exhilarates you . . . he has a very great and unusual talent."

Reference

N Y Times Book R p11 Ag 5 '51

BRENTON, W(OODWARD) HAROLD

Feb. 27, 1899- Organization official; banker; farm executive

Address: b. c/o American Bankers Association, 12 E. 36th St., New York 16; 333 Insurance Exchange Bldg., Des Moines 9, Ia.; h. 10 W. 35th St., Des Moines 12, Ia.

W. Harold Brenton was elected president of the American Bankers Association on October 1, 1952, after having served the preceding year as vice-president. Since 1947 he has held important offices in this association: for two terms vice-president for Iowa, then a member of the executive council, and later a member of the commerce and marine commission. Brenton entered the field of banking in 1920 in his native town of Dallas Center, Iowa, advancing by 1931 to become president of the Iowa-Des Moines National Bank and Trust Company. After a period during the 1930's in which he was occupied in banking affairs in Minneapolis, he returned to Iowa to assume his present post as president and director of eleven Brenton banks in that State. He is also president of Brenton Brothers, Inc., owners and operators

Townsend

W. HAROLD BRENTON

of several thousand acres of Iowa farm land for the production of grain and livestock.

Born in Dallas Center, Iowa, on February 27, 1899, Woodward Harold Brenton is the son of Charles R. and Carrie Alicesta (Woodward) Brenton, whose families had been residents of Iowa for nearly a century. Harold's great grandfather, the first country doctor in Iowa west of Des Moines, settled in Dallas County; his grandfather, William Brenton, was a farmer who during the 1870's started the first of the Brenton banks and organized the firm later to be named Brenton Brothers, Inc. Having completed his preparatory training at the Dallas Center High School in 1916, Harold Brenton attended Iowa State College in Ames, where he chose farm crops and soils as his major subjects and received his B.S. degree in 1920.

After graduation Brenton returned to Dallas Center to begin his career in banking. "When I started out in a little country bank thirty-two years ago," he has told, "the territory I had to know was ten to twenty miles in every direction." He pointed out that in those days he did not need to know about international situations, "$80 billion budgets and $257 billion debts," matters that the banker today in even the smallest community must understand (*Banking*, October 1952). In 1929 Brenton was elected vice-president of the Iowa National Bank in Des Moines; later when the bank, in a merger, became the Iowa-Des Moines National Bank and Trust Company, he was chosen its president in 1931, retaining this office until 1934 and serving as a director until January 1951.

Entering the banking field in Minneapolis, Minnesota, in 1933, Brenton became vice-president of the Northwest Bancorporation. Two years later he assumed the responsibilities of the additional posts of treasurer and director, remaining in all three capacities until 1941.

BRENTON, W. HAROLD—*Continued*

Upon his return to Iowa, he assumed the presidency and directorship of the eleven Brenton banks in that State: Brenton State Bank, Dallas Center; Jefferson State Bank, Jefferson; Poweshiek County National Bank, Grinnell; First National Bank, Perry; Dallas County State Bank, Adel; Palo Alto County State Bank, Emmetsburg; Benton County Bank & Trust Company, Vinton; Warren County Bank & Trust Company, Indianola; Wright County State Bank, Clarion; Eagle Grove National Bank, Eagle Grove; and State Bank of Des Moines, Beaverdale, Des Moines. All are located within 150 miles of Des Moines, where Brenton maintains his principal offices. Each bank is independently operated and its executive officers meet with Brenton one day each month to discuss problems, operating policies, and loan actions. Brenton believes that his bank officers should have a background and understanding of agriculture, as well as banking, in order to shape effective bank policies in farming communities.

As president of Brenton Brothers, Inc., a family-owned corporation, Brenton is responsible for the management of several thousand acres of farm land owned by the firm in a concentrated area mostly in Dallas County. The principal crops include corn, oats, and alfalfa, used to raise and fatten about 5,000 hogs yearly and a great many cattle. Brenton has called his weekly inspection trips of these farms his "Saturday golf" (*Banking*, October 1952).

In 1945 Brenton was chosen president of Wood Brothers Thresher Company in Des Moines, Iowa, which had run ahead of its schedule in reconversion planning as a result of overexpansion to prepare for large postwar production of corn pickers, combines, and other farm implements. Production of such machinery continued to be frozen at controlled levels, although the company no longer had any war contracts. To adjust the ensuing financial tangle, Brenton and the company's general manager reduced the executive and office payroll $100,000 a year (*Newsweek*, April 30, 1945). Union leaders and the War Labor Board approved a six-month trial contract that reduced the average wartime wages about five or seven cents an hour. This wage reduction, which still left the level of company wages above average for the Des Moines area, was the first one ever ordered by the War Labor Board.

After a year (1946) as president of the Iowa Bankers Association, Brenton assumed office in the American Bankers Association as vice-president for Iowa, serving in this post for two terms (1947-48 and 1948-49), then becoming a member of the executive council (1948-49) and a member of the commerce and marine commission (1950-51). On October 3, 1951, Brenton was elected vice-president of the American Bankers Association at its seventy-seventh annual convention in Chicago. In this capacity he gave the opening address at a March 1952 meeting of the Consumer Credit committee of the American Bankers Association, declaring: "Bankers have a responsibility to protect the value of the currency and to lead people toward financial soundness. . . .Prosperity was brought about through our free, competitive, productive production ingenuity. It was not brought about by excessive spending, which creates inflation instead of goods and real income" (New York *Times*, March 25, 1952). He stated that installment credit had helped to develop the economy of the United States and raise the standard of living "to where it is the envy of the rest of the world."

At the seventy-eighth annual convention in Atlantic City, New Jersey, members of the American Bankers Association elected W. Harold Brenton president, to succeed C. Francis Cocke. The association, established in 1875, represents nearly 15,000 banks of all sizes in the rural areas as well as in the big cities throughout the country. It is the parent organization of the American Institute of Banking, which conducts educational programs for bank personel, and of the Graduate School of Bankers, which has an enrollment of approximately 1,000 bank officers and meets annually at Rutgers University in New Brunswick, New Jersey.

Brenton came to the presidency at a critical time, as the week preceding his election a staff report of the subcommittee of the Judiciary Committee of the United States House of Representatives called for "a sweeping investigation of the banking industry and legislation to halt the unrelenting merger trend" (New York *Times*, September 28, 1952). The report suggested that credit facilities of banks were inadequate and were not meeting the needs of smaller businessmen.

In his acceptance speech as president of the American Bankers Association, Brenton pledged the organization to stimulate a competitive program for savings deposits and to strengthen its activities at the State level. In urging a program of competition for savings deposits, Brenton supported an association resolution to increase its efforts to secure legislative clarification of the place of the savings and loan associations in the banking field. Brenton also agreed with another resolution charging that the United States Government had engaged in excessive spending, in inflationary monetary policies, and in the production of unbalanced budgets, all of which threaten the economy. "Inflation is already imbedded to a great extent in our economy," he has stated; "the problem now is to prevent it from proceeding further. . . .Price increases have a definite relationship to deficit financing" (*Banking*, October 1952). The association's charge that the excess profits tax was a most harmful method of raising Government funds and that it should be allowed to die at its expiration date June 30, 1953, was also supported by Brenton, who has expressed the belief that increases in personal and corporate taxes would do more harm than good.

W. Harold Brenton has been quoted by the *U. S. News and World Report* (October 10, 1952) as stating that "the United States debts, spending, foreign aid, and magnitudinous responsibilities have been gaining at a terrific pace and they have gone beyond the ordinary person's knowledge of how to cope with them."

Because of this, Brenton has advocated a broad and continuing education in banking, not only for the bankers themselves but also for the public—an education which goes beyond the local level to the national and international spheres. In favoring the maintenance of an independent central banking system, Brenton has said that he believes the United States Treasury and the Federal Reserve System should work "harmoniously but independently" on the financial policies of Government (*Banking*, October 1952).

Brenton is a member of the board of directors of Swift and Company of Chicago, Illinois, in which association he makes use of his knowledge of livestock gained from his experience as president of Brenton Brothers, Inc. He is a trustee of the Committee for Economic Development, of Grinnell College, of the Iowa Methodist Hospital in Des Moines, of the Iowa Economic Council, and of the Good Government Association of Des Moines. During World War I he served in the United States Navy. Brenton is a Mason and a member of the Iowa Bankers Association and the Newcomen Society of England. His clubs are the University Club of Chicago, the Des Moines Club, and the Wakonda Club of Des Moines. His fraternity is Delta Tau Delta, of which he was national president from 1948 to 1950. He is a Republican and a Presbyterian.

On June 18, 1921, Brenton married Etta Spurgeon of Adel, Iowa. Their children are Mary Elizabeth, William Henry, Carolyn Ruth, Sarah Jane, Charles Robert, and twins Junius Clyde and Juliette. His oldest son, William, is a cashier in the State Bank of Des Moines and an assistant in the management of the Brenton farms. Brenton is six feet tall, weighs 200 pounds, and has brown hair. Of banking he has said, as quoted by *Banking*, (October 1952), "I am proud to belong to a business that is making such strides in public relations, human relations, or, in other words, in the field of just knowing folks and liking them and having them like you."

References

Banking p36+ O '52
Business Executives of America (1951)
Who's Who in America, 1952-53
Who's Who in Commerce and Industry (1951)

BREWER, ROY M(ARTIN) Aug. 9, 1909- Labor union official

Address: b. International Alliance of Theatrical Stage Employees and Motion Picture Machine Operators of the United States and Canada, 6636 Hollywood Blvd., Hollywood 28, Calif.; h. 716 N. Curson Ave., Los Angeles 46, Calif.

Representing more than 22,000 members of the Hollywood Film Council and 15,000 members of the International Alliance of Theatrical Stage Employees (American Federation of Labor), Roy M. Brewer has been much concerned with keeping films out of this country's

Wide World Photos

ROY M. BREWER

theatres which have been made by Communists, and the unemployment situation created by "runaway" American producers who make pictures abroad to avoid paying the high costs of production at home and production cutbacks made to await technical changes in picture-making necessary for the new three-dimensional movies. More than half of the Film Council's workers have lost their jobs, and between 25 and 30 per cent of the I.A.T.S.E. members are out of work, according to Brewer (New York *Times*, April 19, and June 7, 1953).

The resignation of Roy M. Brewer as international representative in Hollywood for the International Alliance of Theatrical Stage Employees was accepted formally on September 13, 1953 by Richard F. Walsh, the international president of the union.

"Roy M. Brewer who rose from obscurity to national prominence during his eight years as leader of Hollywood craft labor, had advocated broad expansion of operations by the Hollywood office. Mr. Walsh opposed the plan, reportedly on the ground that it might tend to lessen his control over the union members" (New York *Times,* September 14, 1953). Brewer was brought into the labor picture at the height of the 1945-46 strike and earned prestige for his handling of the explosive situation. He then led the fight to rid the union of Communist elements and subsequently attained national prominence by his leadership in the broader effort to expose Communists and fellow traveler factions in all branches of the motion picture industry.

Of pioneer Nebraska family, Roy Martin Brewer is the son of Martin M. Brewer, a blacksmith and mechanic, and Lottie (Woodworth) Brewer. He was born August 9, 1909, in Cairo, Hall County, and spent his childhood in small Nebraska towns. After graduation from high school in Grand Island in 1926,

BREWER, ROY M.—*Continued*

Brewer began his career as a silent film projectionist at the Capitol Theatre there, becoming a member of Local 586 of the International Alliance of Theatrical Stage Employees and Motion Picture Machine Operators in August 1927.

In 1928, at the age of nineteen, Brewer was elected vice-president of the Nebraska State Federation of Labor. He became its president in 1932, and was re-elected in 1937 and 1943. He also served as president of his own Local 586 for fifteen years, and during the short lifetime of the National Recovery Act of the 1930's he was labor compliance officer for the State of Nebraska.

He held the post of secretary of an I.A.T.S.E. district covering nine States from 1940 to 1948. He was on loan from the AFL union from 1943 to 1945 to the War Production Board where he served as chief of the plant community facilities division of the Office of Labor Production in Washington. He was also a member of the Nebraska Defense Council.

Brewer was named international representative of his union and assigned to the Hollywood movie studios in 1945 when jurisdictional strikes between the Conference of Studio Unions and the I.A.T.S.E. were creating much havoc on Hollywood sets. He arrived in Hollywood on March 12, the day painters of the CSU walked off a set. Brewer has stated "Within a month we knew the Commies lay behind the strike. And we realized it was either them or us!"

In a truce arranged by Eric Johnston, head of the Motion Picture Producers Association, the rival unions agreed to let the jurisdictional question be settled by a three-man committee appointed by the AFL Executive Council. The committee awarded the right to build parts of sets to the CSU carpenters and painters, and the right to assemble the parts into complete sets to the I.A.T.S.E. craftsmen.

Then Richard F. Walsh, I.A.T.S.E. president, decided that 350 jobs held by CSU carpenters constituted setbuilding, and succeeded in having producers replace CSU members with his own men. The studios proceeded to fire all CSU members who refused to work on the same sets with I.A.T.S.E. replacements, and seven thousand CSU members went out on a strike that lasted for eighteen months. The I.A.'s Laboratory Workers Local No. 683 refused to cross CSU picket lines and Walsh suspended its officers and appointed Roy M. Brewer to administer its affairs.

That October, while the strike continued and clashes occurred daily, Brewer announced wage agreements made for Local 683 with ten producers, giving the laboratory technicians $5,500,000 in wage increases over a two-year period, and $2,320,000 in wages retroactive to January 1, 1946.

In July 1949, when Ronald Reagan, president of the AFL Screen Actors Guild, succeeded to the chairmanship of the Motion Picture Industry Council, Roy Brewer was elected his co-chairman and successor-elect. As chairman, in March 1950, Brewer denounced Senator Edwin

C. Johnson's bill to apply a "purity test" to moviemakers as "the first step toward totalitarianism."

As head of the seventeen-union AFL Hollywood Film Council, Brewer was concerned with the fact that by 1950, employment among the members had dropped to about 67 per cent of what it was in 1940, and 57 per cent of its 1946 level. In May 1950 the Film Council wrote to Secretary of State Dean Acheson, asking that the Government intervene in the Anglo-American film agreement negotiations to protect "the living standards of American motion-picture workers." The letter stated, "If all other appeals fail, American labor may be forced against its will to adopt prohibitions or boycotts against American films made abroad."

The first step in this direction was taken in January 1953, when the Film Council resolved that no member of affiliated unions should accept assignments for work on such films without union approval.

In October 1951 Brewer won for workers of I.A.T.S.E. a three-month wage increase of 24 cents an hour or 10 per cent, whichever was greater; after this, the wage rates were to advance with increases in the Bureau of Labor Statistics consumer price index, but not to decrease with decreases in the index. The studios were also to pay 5 cents an hour on all straight time earnings to establish a health and welfare fund, but they rejected demands for a pension fund and a five-day week.

In opposing the showing of films made, in Brewer's words, by "those who refuse to declare themselves when called upon by Congress to answer Commie charges," he asked the House Un-American Activities Committee in August 1952 to initiate legislation to ban the showing of the films made abroad. He added, "This type of police work is a responsibility which should not rest upon private citizens. It is the duty of the Government."

The union leader has been described in the New York *Times* (May 4, 1952) as "a power in the anti-Communist campaign, who wields a big stick over producers if they inadvertently hire a person of alleged Communist connections or sympathies."

Some of his time is devoted to what he terms an educational program, of which he says, "It often takes a good deal of time and patience to show people just how they were duped by Commie friends into supporting Commie causes."

In February 1953, he and the Film Council called for a Federal investigation of the filming of a picture in New Mexico by a group of persons named by the council as Communists at Congressional hearings.

Roy Brewer has written a number of articles, as well as the Hollywood I.A.T.S.E. information bulletin and, for four years, the presidential column in the Omaha *Unionist*. His pamphlet, *Collective Bargaining Agreement*, was published by the Nebraska Bar Association.

In July 1929, Brewer was married to Alyce J. Auhl; their children are Roy Martin, Jr., and Ramona Rae. He is five feet ten inches tall and weighs 190 pounds; he has been described as "deceptively mild, bespectacled, roly-poly." He is a member of the Masquers Club, and his favorite recreations are golf, reading, and photography. A New Deal Democrat, Brewer was co-chairman of the Hollywood Stevenson-Sparkman committee in 1952.

References

International Motion Picture and Television Almanac, 1952-53
Who's Who in Labor (1946)
Who's Who in the West (1951)

BRICK, JOHN January 1, 1922- Author
Address: b. c/o Doubleday & Company, Inc., 575 Madison Ave., New York 22; h. Hollow Brook Lake, Peekskill, New York

Reprinted from the *Wilson Library Bulletin*, Sept. 1953

One of the younger American historical novelists—he was born on New Year's Day, 1922—John Brick already has four books to his credit, and shows no signs of finding his upper New York State milieu and its history exhausted. He was born in Newburgh, New York, the Highland Landing of his first novel, *Troubled Spring* (Farrar, Straus 1950), the son of John T. Brick, of Irish descent, and Elizabeth (Connell) Brick. He had "a pretty ordinary life as a boy in a small Hudson Valley city," attending Newburgh Free Academy and holding a variety of jobs in his spare time as caddy, delivery boy, paper boy, grocery clerk, and bellhop. One of his English teachers, the late Marghita MacDonald, was the first to persuade him that he should write. Later John Farrar's encouragement and advice were of great benefit to him, says Mr. Brick.

Before he was caught up by the war, John Brick was night traffic clerk in a road transport company, and secretary to the professor of military topography and graphics at West Point. What he did in the war was "nothing useful to anyone," he thinks, though some experiences along the Alaskan Highway may prove of value to him as a writer. He was discharged for medical disability before the end of the war; married Mary Helen Yakim in December 1943; worked in a shipyard, was a clerk in an Army prison, and timekeeper for a firm of naval architects in New York City. In 1945 Brick became editorial assistant on a weekly business magazine, *Export Trade & Shipper*. He was promoted to managing editor in 1947, and resigned two years later to move to the country and put into practice the writing courses he had absorbed at Columbia. John and Mary Brick, the children—Johnny, Martha, and Janice—and two Irish setters, one of them named for Timothy Murphy, hero of *The Rifleman* (Doubleday, 1953) all live together at Hollow Brook Lake, Peekskill, New York.

Troubled Spring (1950) won the writer a Farrar Straus Regional Fellowship of $2,000 in 1949, and was a Doubleday Dollar Book Club selection. The story of a soldier's return from the Confederate prison at Andersonville to a Hudson River town, it was praised by Virginia Kirkus for taut narration and dramatic values, while John Cournos in the New York

JOHN BRICK

Times thought that the hero, in Flaubert's phrase, "rises to the dignity of a type." As a study in the problem of the returned veteran, it seemed especially timely. In *The Raid* (Farrar, Straus, 1951) events parallel the Battle of Minisink in July 1779, when Joseph Brant, with a party of Indians and Tories, attacked this Orange County hamlet. Shirley Barker, herself a historical novelist, recommended the tale in the *Library Journal*; other reviewers thought the writer better in scenes of conflict than of comedy, but agreed that the reader "is carried along on a high tide of suspense." (The book was dedicated "For Johnny, who wanted the Indian book for his own.")

The hero of *Homer Crist* (Farrar, Straus, 1952) is a farm boy in Brick's mythical Highland County in 1833-1872. Critics attacked his third novel, although the *Herald Tribune* praised the subtleties of Homer's character. Edmund Fuller in the Chicago *Sunday Tribune*, however, objected to "minor and useless vulgarities," and Oriana Atkinson in the New York *Times* described it as "a lifeless and completely incredible book." The *Library Journal* reviewer called it a little thin and not up to standard, then recommended its purchase. The *New Yorker* thought the ending was "abrupt and unreasonable."

The Rifleman, in 1953, was better received, and was picked by the Book League of America. Its hero, Timothy Murphy, was a real though forgotten Revolutionary hero who fired an "impossible" 200-yard sniper shot at British General Fraser, which laid that dignitary low. One result was the surrender of Burgoyne. Richard Match wrote in the New York *Times* that Timothy's "love life isn't very convincing, but everything else in this soundly researched story is."

John Brick is blue-eyed and brown-haired, weighs 148 pounds, and admits that he is a "bug" on trout-fishing. He also reads, hunts,

BRICK, JOHN—*Continued*

plays baseball, ties trout flies, and paints "bad pictures in oils." He was a Stevenson Democrat (and "proud of it"), is a member of the Authors League and P.E.N., and chairman of the special committee on paper-covered reprints for the Authors Guild, of whose council he is a member. He takes pride in his collection of William Faulkner firsts, purchased before Faulkner won the Nobel Prize. *Troubled Spring* was bought for the movies by Metro-Goldwin-Mayer; the money the author received was another factor in his becoming a free-lance writer. Brick has written some short stories, but still concentrates on novels. The next, a novel of Loyalists in New York state during the Revolution, is tentatively titled *We Band of Brothers*.

BUBER, MARTIN (boo'-ber) Feb. 8, 1878-
Philosopher; writer; editor; university professor
Address: h. Talbiyeh, Jerusalem

Contemporary philosophers throughout the world in their efforts to reconcile modern scientific attitudes with religious experience have been influenced by Martin Buber. The Christian theologian, Reinhold Niebuhr, calls him "the greatest living Jewish philosopher."

Dr. Buber was professor of social philosophy at Hebrew University in Jerusalem from 1938

MARTIN BUBER

until 1951. Since he became professor-emeritus he has lectured in universities throughout the United States. His latest book (1953) is *Good and Evil: Two Interpretations.*

Buber's "staggering output" of books, essays and lectures is divided into five groups: philosophical and sociological studies; writings on Zionism and Hasidism (Jewish mysticism); Biblical studies; translations; and essays and addresses compiled into "four slender but most important volumes dealing with his theory of relationship" (*Commonweal*, August 6, 1948).

This theory is described in Buber's chief work, *I and Thou* (1937), in which he wrote that man is engaged in a "dialogue" with God, in which man is "I" and God is "Thou." Most men, Buber stated, live in an "I-It" relationship with the universe which depletes it of meaning. When man realizes God as a "Thou" rather than an "It" the universe becomes meaningful, and he also begins to see human beings as "Thou" rather than "It." From this perception, wrote Buber in *Between Man and Man* (1947), a new relationship between people is created, which he believes should lead to a form of society in which the political superstructure of a too-powerful State would be succeeded by a decentralistic socialism in which small, personal groups of men would live in a direct relationship with one another, and the ideas motivating the group would be religious rather than political.

Born in Vienna February 8, 1878, Martin Buber was taken at the age of three to Lemberg, Galicia (at that time a part of Austria), to the home of his grandfather, Salomon Buber, a noted Hebrew scholar and a leader of the Jewish *Haskalah* or Enlightenment. The boy went with his father on occasional visits to the neighboring town, Sadagora, and saw the Hasidic rabbis, descendants of the *Zaddikim* or "perfect men," acting as advisers and soothsayers to people who appeared more superstitious than religious. Despite the debased state of the *Zaddik* tradition, the boy perceived the earlier authority of the holy man who could lead a community united by its love of God and its veneration for a noble wise man. "This luminous idea I found in the dirty little town of Sadagora," Buber wrote (in a memoir, *My Road to Hasidism*, 1943).

These perceptions lay dormant, however, through his early youth, when in addition to his training in the ideas of the Jewish Enlightenment, he was steeped in the West European intellectual tradition of reason, logical criticism and historical research. He spent several unhappy years, he tells in his memoir, alienated not only from Hasidism, but from Judaism as a whole. During this period he studied philosophy and the history of art at the Universities of Vienna, Berlin and Zurich from 1896 to 1899. The next year, at the University of Leipzig, he was converted to Zionism, in which he found not only a political movement, but a religious idea which resolved his spiritual confusion. He attended the third Zionist Congress at Basel, Switzerland, in 1899, and became editor of the Zionist journal *Die Welt* in 1901. The following year he assisted in founding Jüdischer Verlag, a prominent Jewish publishing house.

Zionism led Buber to an interest in Hasidism, a mystical movement in which he found the essence of the Jewish national character. Memories of the *Zaddik* he saw in his childhood were awakened, and at the age of twenty-six he gave up his activities as a journalist and lecturer for the Zionist cause to retire into solitude for five years, to study the Hasidic literature which was regarded as occult and disreputable by most enlightened thinkers.

Buber found the neglected Hasidic writings in a crude state, many of them obscured by superstitious additions and commentaries, but he saw in them an experience of direct communion with the Divine that he wanted to translate for the modern world. His studies resulted in the publication of 100 Hasidic tales and parables retold in his own words, and *The Legend of the Baalshem,* which he based on traditional stories about the life of a Hasidic spiritual leader.

He spent the next few years in Florence, Berlin and Vienna, studying the philosophy of religion. Strongly influenced by German mysticism, he wrote his doctoral dissertation on this subject, and received his Ph.D. at the University of Vienna in 1904. He was active in Jewish journalism, editing from 1916 to 1924 *Der Jude,* the leading periodical of German-speaking Jewry, and from 1926 to 1930 co-operating with Wittig, a Catholic, and Weizsacker, a Protestant, in editing the journal *Die Kreatur.* Dr. Buber also held the only chair of Jewish philosophy in a German university, as professor of Comparative Religion at Frankfort, from 1923 to 1933.

When Jewish students were excluded by the Nazis from all German educational institutions in 1933, Buber became Director of the Central Office for Jewish Adult Education in Germany. In 1938 the philosopher fled Germany and went to Palestine, where he was Professor of Social Philosophy at the Hebrew University, until 1951, when he became professor-emeritus. He founded and became the director of the Institute for Adult Education in 1949, an Israeli institution which trains teachers in the instruction of newly-arrived immigrants.

The Jewish philosopher is one of the main figures in contemporary religious existentialism. His thinking, according to the *Yale Review,* has "entered as a vital ingredient into the newer Christian theology as well as into a good deal of the most significant social philosophy of our day." In his *Good and Evil,* published in 1953, Buber develops the premise that the basic evil is that of having no direction, of refusing to take the only possible direction, which is towards God. *Between Man and Man* is a development and application of the "dialogical" motif in terms of contemporary social problems, while *Eclipse of God* discusses the "I-Thou" theme in the context of such modern thinkers as Sartre, Heidegger, and Jung, seeking to distinguish what he calls the *"living God"* from the images and ideas of the Deity erected by the philosophers.

Buber's theological position is closely related to his political ideas. He opposes Soviet socialism and the large-scale centralist collectivism of European social democratic thought, and espouses a decentralized socialism, which he believes is workable if each member of the community is inspired with the desire for "cre-

ative companionship" stemming from the "I-Thou" feeling. In his work, *Die Frage an den Einzelnen* Buber expresses his belief that the only salvation of the modern world lies in men learning and applying the "I-Thou" relation in their human and divine emotional interactions. The book *Paths in Utopia* discusses these philosophical conceptions in terms of the village communities in the modern State of Israel.

When Professor Buber visited the United States for the first time in 1951, he delivered lectures which were later published in his books *Eclipse of God* and *At the Turning* (1952). Will Herberg wrote in *Commentary* (December 1952) that students who heard Buber felt that they were "in the presence of authentic greatness and were participating in something altogether outside the bounds of academic routine."

The distinguished philosopher also addressed an audience of 2,500 in Carnegie Hall in New York City on April 6, 1952. Shortly afterward he was presented with an award at the Second Annual World Brotherhood dinner of the Union Theological Seminary in New York City. Buber has received an honorary doctorate from the University of Aberdeen in Scotland, from Hebrew Union College in Cincinnati, Ohio, and from the Hebrew University in Jerusalem. He received the Goethe Prize from the University of Hamburg in Germany.

Buber has had, *Commonweal* states, an "immense influence on diverse thinkers of all faiths, including Denis de Rougemont, Father d'Arcy, Eric Przywara, Arnold Zweig and Paul Tillich. Ronald Gregor Smith has predicted that Buber's *I and Thou,* which contains his central philosophical ideas, "will rank as one of the epoch-making books of our generation." Max Lerner in 1949 placed Buber on a list of twenty-five men who constitute "the political, intellectual, and moral rulers" of the world, and Herman Hesse, who in 1949 nominated the Jewish philosopher for the Nobel Prize, stated that Buber is "one of the leading and most valuable personalities in contemporary world literature." In 1927 Ludwig Lewisohn classed Buber with Einstein, Freud, and Bergson as one of the world's great living geniuses.

Dr. Buber is the author of a large number of books and essays. His most important works translated into English comprise: *Jewish Mysticism and the Legends of the Baalshem* (Dent, Ltd., 1931) ; *I and Thou* (Edinburgh, Clark, 1937) ; *For the Sake of Heaven* (Jewish Publication Society of America, 1945) ; *Mamre* (Oxford, 1946) ; *Moses* (Müller, 1948; Scheider, 1952) ; *Ten Rungs, Hasidic Sayings* (Schocken, 1947) ; *Between Man and Man* (London, Paul, 1947; Macmillan, 1948) ; *Tales of the Hasidim, the Early Masters* (1947) and *Tales of the Hasidim, the Later Masters* (1948), both published by Schocken; *Israel and the World* (Schocken, 1948) ; *Hasidism* (McLeod, 1948) ; *The Prophetic Faith* (Macmillan, 1949) ; *Paths in Utopia* (Routledge, 1949; Macmillan, 1950) ; *The Way of Man* (Routledge and Paul, 1950) ; *Two Types of Faith* (Routledge and Paul, 1951) ; *Israel and Palestine* (Artemis-Verlag, 1950; London, East and West Library, 1952) ; *Eclipse of God*

BUBER, MARTIN—*Continued*
(Harper, 1952); and *Good and Evil* (Scribner, 1953).

Martin Buber was married to Paula Winkler in 1899. The philosopher's wife is a well-known fiction writer under the pseudonym of George Mundt. Dr. Buber has brown eyes and white hair, and is about five feet two inches high. He has been described as a "tiny man with a huge head and a flowing white beard, who resembles a prophet of old."

Dr. Greta Hoyt in her introduction to *Mamre* (1946), a collection of Buber's essays on religion, stated that although he writes philosophy and theology, "the only valid name we can give to Dr. Buber's writing is teaching," in the manner of the *Zaddiks* he admired, the "perfect men" who could bring the word of God to the people.

References

Menorah J 26:185 Ap '38
Agus, J. B. Modern Philosophers of Judaism (1941)
International Who's Who, 1952
Kohn, H. Martin Buber: Sein Werk und Seine Zeit (1930)
Lewisohn, L. Cities and Men (1927)
Liptzin, S. Germany's Stepchildren (1944)
Robinson, D. The 100 Most Important People (1953)
Schwarz, L. W. Memoirs of My People (1943)
The Universal Jewish Encyclopedia, vol. 2 (1940)
Who's Who, 1952
Who's Who in the State of Israel (1949)

BUGHER, JOHN C(LIFFORD) (boo'hûr)
Sept. 26, 1901- United States Government official; physician
Address: b. c/o United States Atomic Energy Commission, Washington 25, D.C.; h. 510 21st St., Washington, D.C.

On June 30, 1952, Dr. John C. Bugher became director of the Division of Biology and Medicine of the United States Atomic Energy Commission in Washington, D.C., after having served for a year as deputy director of the division. An authority on tropical disease, he conducted research on yellow fever for fourteen years, in South America and Africa for the international health division of the Rockefeller Foundation (1937-48) and in the New York laboratories of the foundation (1948-51). He had earlier been on the faculty of Taylor University and the University of Michigan.

Now on leave of absence from the Rockefeller Foundation, Dr. Bugher is responsible for co-ordinating nearly 400 projects in more than 160 colleges and universities and supervising the Division of Biology and Medicine's atomic research centers at Brookhaven, Oak Ridge and Argonne National Laboratories; Los Alamos Scientific Lavoratory, and university installations in Rochester, New York; New York

City; Chicago; Knoxville, Tennessee; Los Angeles and Berkeley, California.

The long-range research program which he directs may lead to the development of more effective treatment for cancer and other diseases, photosynthesis (the use of the sun's energy) to build tissue for plants and to supply food for livestock, and to convert heat from atomic piles into industrial power.

John Clifford Bugher was born in Upland, Indiana, on September 26, 1901, the son of Anson Clifford and Sallie Ann (Pugh) Bugher. At Taylor University, in his native town, he studied mathematics and physics as his major subjects and during his senior year became an instructor in physics, a position he held for two years, until 1922. Meanwhile, in 1921, he received both the B.A. degree from Taylor University and the B.S. degree from the University of Michigan.

For the next three years (1922-25) he remained at the University of Michigan as assistant in bacteriology, before assuming the post of director of public health in South Haven, Michigan (1926-28). Having in the meantime studied medicine at the University of Michigan, he was awarded the M.D. degree in 1929 and in the same year appointed senior instructor in pathology in the medical school. He took his M.Sc. degree at Michigan University in 1931. Engaged at this period in a study of electrode reactions, Bugher developed a quinhydrone-collodion electrode useful for pH measurements in yellow fever research, giving an account of his work in the article "Quinhydrone-collodion Electrode of Special Applicability in Experimental Pathology" (*Journal of Biological Chemistry*, August 1931). In 1933 the University of Michigan promoted him to assistant professor of pathology.

Four years later (1937) Dr. Bugher began his research in tropical medicine as a staff member of the international health division of the Rockefeller Foundation. For the next decade he did extensive medical research, especially in yellow fever, in South America and Africa. His articles for professional publications on his research include "Micromortar Especially Adapted to Virus Studies in Insects" (*Proceedings of the Society of Experimental Biology and Medicine*, February 1940) and "Use of Baby Mice in Yellow Fever Studies" (*American Journal of Tropical Medicine*, April 1941). As a result of his research on jungle yellow fever in Colombia, South America, Bugher prepared in collaboration with A. Gast-Galvis an article on the effects of vaccination in the prevention of the disease, published in *Revista de la Facultad de Medicina*, Bogotá, November 1944. In his tropical disease studies, Bugher examined the susceptibility of South American vertebrates to yellow fever and demonstrated yellow fever antibodies in animal sera by intracerebral protection tests in mice. Results of this research and of a later investigation of the effect of prolonged storage of sera on yellow fever protection tests were published in the *American Journal of Tropical Medicine*.

At the Yellow Fever Research Institute in Lagos, Nigeria, Africa (supported jointly by the Medical Department of Nigeria and the international health division of the Rockefeller Foundation), Bugher carried on studies in the use of radioactive isotopes for marking mosquitoes. His findings in this research were reported in *Science* magazine (August 5, 1949) in an article entitled "Radiophosphorus and Radiostrontium in Mosquitoes" (with Marjorie Taylor). In additional investigations he examined the effects of radioaction on the yellow fever virus, as well as on the mosquito's ability to transmit the virus; his research also included studies of mosquito sounds. Bugher returned from Africa to the United States in 1948 to work in the New York laboratories of the Rockefeller Foundation.

From New York Bugher moved to Washington, D.C., in 1951 to become deputy director of the Division of Biology and Medicine of the United States Atomic Energy Commission. The work of the division at this time included a study of the delayed effects of atomic bomb radiation on the populations of Hiroshima and Nagasaki, Japan, calling for examination of cases of leukemia and a report on the birth rate in these cities. On May 7, 1952, the AEC announced the appointment of Bugher as director of the Division of Biology and Medicine, to succeed Dr. Shields Warren, of Boston, who resigned, and to assume office on June 30, 1952. Among his responsibilities is the supervision of the research program in treatment of malignant diseases with radioactive materials. At the dedication at Montefiore Hospital (the Bronx, New York) in February 1953 of a $50,000 device that uses cobalt in cancer treatment, Bugher said that the use of the machine, which was developed through atomic research in Canada, marked "one of the more significant moments in the medical history" of the country.

In an interview with Richard Witkin in *This Week* (August 2, 1953) Dr. Bugher stated that the Brookhaven Laboratory at Upton, Long Island was conducting what he considered one of the most exciting experiments in the whole field of atomic medicine—the treatment of brain cancer. "This is perhaps the most significant new development in cancer in the last twenty years," he said. "So far it has not resulted in a cure. But the treatment has brought marked temporary improvement and the research is just beginning."

Dr. Bugher is the author of a book entitled *Yellow Fever* (1951, in collaboration with George King Strode and others), prepared by the international health division of the Rockefeller Foundation. Describing the foundation's achievements during more than thirty years of research on yellow fever, the volume was cited in the *American Journal of Public Health* (September 1951) for telling its story in a "simple, straightforward way" and being "beautifully illustrated, well-indexed, and . . . a great book," and in the New York *Times* as "a broad and exciting adventure in biology, with much accomplished and much ahead."

In recognition of his services in medical research, Bugher was awarded the Cruz de Boyacá from the Republic of Colombia (1943) and the decoration of Commander of the British Empire (1948). He is also the recipient of an

Wide World Photos

DR. JOHN C. BUGHER

honorary doctor of science degree from Taylor University, conferred in 1951. In the Michigan State Pathology Society, Bugher has held the office of president (1938) and secretary-treasurer (1933-35). Other organizations of which he is a member are the Royal Society of Tropical Medicine, the American Medical Association, the Michigan State Medical Society, the American Association of Pathologists and Bacteriologists, the American Society of Tropical Medicine, the American Association for Cancer Research, and the American Society of Clinical Pathology. His clubs are the Cosmos Club, Washington, D.C., and the Larchmont (New York) Yacht Club; his fraternity is Alpha Omega Alpha. On April 1, 1926, Bugher married Elizabeth Foust. The director is five feet and ten inches in height, weighs 180 pounds, and has black hair and hazel eyes. His church affiliation is Protestant, and he is an independent voter. His hobby is yachting.

References

This Week p11 Ag 2 '53 por
American Men of Science (1949)
Who Knows—and What (1949)
Who's Who Among Physicians (1938)

BURNS, SIR ALAN (CUTHBERT MAXWELL) Nov. 9, 1887- British Diplomat and Colonial Civil Servant

Address: b. United Kingdom Delegation to the United Nations, 350 Fifth Avenue, New York; h. 27 Wildcroft Manor, Putney Heath, London, England

As Permanent United Kingdom Representative on the Trusteeship Council of the United Nations, Sir Alan Burns is now in his forty-eighth year of continuous service to the British Crown. He has been a Colonial civil servant

United Nations

SIR ALAN BURNS

since 1905, starting in the Treasury Department of the Leeward Islands Government.

Twenty-two years of his official duty were spent in West Africa, where he initiated many of the forward steps in self-government and eradication of racial prejudice in Nigeria and the Gold Coast. Sir Alan held other colonial posts in British Honduras and the Bahamas, and during World War II he was recalled to England to act as Assistant Under Secretary for the Colonies. From 1941 to 1947 he was Governor and Commander-in-Chief of the Gold Coast.

Among Sir Alan's written works are an analysis of color prejudice, a history of Nigeria, and an autobiography which gives much discussion of the problems in colonies in which he has served. He has also written a book about bridge for beginners.

Alan Cuthbert Maxwell Burns was born on November 9, 1887 at Basseterre, the chief town of St. Kitts (St. Christopher) Island in the Leeward Islands group of the West Indies. He was one of four sons of James and Agnes Delisle Burns; there was also a daughter. His grandfather, Patrick Burns, had been active in the Colonial Civil Service of the Islands, as Auditor-General, Colonial Secretary and Administrator of various islands in the group; he died in the year of Alan's birth. His father was Treasurer of St. Kitts and Nevis Islands and died when Alan was nine years old.

At the age of twelve Alan Burns was sent to England to attend St. Edmund's College in Ware, the oldest Catholic school in England. Owing to the family's critical financial condition he returned to the Leewards when he was seventeen, and on February 15, 1905 began his career with an appointment to the Treasury and Customs Department at St. Kitts-Nevis. He acted as Revenue Officer and, at times, Harbour Master. He was appointed Clerk to the Magistrate at Basseterre in 1909 and soon afterwards

was made a Justice of the Peace. Having risen to the rank of regimental sergeant-major in the local volunteer force, he was chosen in 1911 as one of the local contingent which attended the coronation of King George V.

In the summer of 1912, Burns accepted an appointment as Supervisor of Customs, Southern Nigeria, against the advice of friends who regarded West Africa as the white man's grave. He assumed duty in the Central Secretariat in 1915.

Feeling the need for an up-to-date Handbook of Nigeria, and the Government being unwilling to subsidize one, he compiled and published one himself in 1917; the Government bought the Handbook in 1924 and re-issued it as an official publication. In 1918 Burns was appointed Aide-de-Camp to the Governor-General, Lord Frederick Lugard, the unifier and creator of modern Nigeria.

During the first World War Sir Alan served with the Cameroons Expeditionary Force as a commissioned officer of the West African Regiment which was involved in many skirmishes and boat expeditions against military stations in Togoland and Cameroon which at that time were German territories.

Recalled to Lagos, the capital of Nigeria, for civil duties, he was also made Adjutant of the Nigeria Land Contingent. When the Egba tribe rebelled in 1918, besieged a small police force in Lagos and threatened to cut off the water supply there, Sir Alan went with troops and relieved the garrison.

Early in 1924 he accepted the post of Colonial Secretary of the Bahamas. He also served as Governor four times (May-Oct. 1924, Sept.-Nov. 1925, Sept. 1926-Mar. 1927, June-Sept. 1928) when the Governor, Sir Harry Cordeaux, was on leave and during the interregnum between Sir Harry's resignation and the appointment of a new Governor. He was one of the two representatives of the Bahamas at the London West India Conference in 1926, and in 1927 was appointed a Companion of the Order of St. Michael and St. George.

Sir Alan served five years in the Bahamas and then was appointed Deputy Chief Secretary of Nigeria, "the colony to which I had hoped, all through my service in the Bahamas, to return, and in which I still continue to take the greatest interest." While at Nassau, he had written a *History of Nigeria* for which he had long been collecting notes. After trying unsuccessfully to interest serveral publishers in it, George Allan and Unwin, Ltd. (London, 1929) "decided to take the risk." The book received complimentary reviews ("a valuable book", *West Africa*) and is regarded as a definitive work on Nigeria (by the *Columbia Encyclopedia*); it has more than once been quoted in Nigerian courts and has now gone through four editions.

While the Chief Secretary of Nigeria was administering the Government during the protracted illness of the Governor, Sir Alan spent most of his second tour of duty there acting as Chief Secretary, which he terms "the most responsible and interesting job in the Civil Service." He made great efforts to integrate Nigerian natives into the Government and to establish closer social relations between the Europeans and Africans by founding joint libraries, sports and dining clubs.

When Sir Alan left Lagos on June 23, 1934 to become Governor and Commander-in-Chief of British Honduras, the Nigerian *Daily Times* (May 19, 1934) commented "he has made more contributions towards an understanding between man and man than any officer similarly placed can boast of. . . .The greatest or perhaps the best service which could be rendered in this country toward the removal of racial misunderstandings is the latest institution created by Mr. Burns, namely, the Lagos Dinner Club. . . ."

In replying to speeches made in his honor at a farewell banquet, Sir Alan said ". . . I am particularly glad that my hosts this evening are of both races, and from both the official and non-official community, and that the last public function which 1 shall have the honor of attending in Nigeria should provide so noteworthy an example of that cooperation in which I am so interested. . . ."

Sir Alan remained in Belize, the capital of British Honduras, for the normal five-year term. In 1936 he was appointed a Knight Commander of the Order of St. Michael and St. George. At the outbreak of the second World War, he was on leave in England and returned hurriedly to the colony to place it on a wartime footing. In October 1939, only a few weeks after he had resumed his duties, he was selected to be Assistant Under Secretary for the Colonies, in which service he was responsible for the business of the Far East, Pacific and West Indies Departments.

When British and American Governments held a Conference in 1941 on the proposed exchange of fifty American destroyers for bases in the West Indies and Newfoundland, Sir Alan was vice-chairman of the meetings. After the Agreement had been signed in the Cabinet Room at 10 Downing Street on March 27, 1941, "Mr. Churchill then shook hands with me and congratulated me on having, as he put it, brought my ship safely to port," Sir Alan records in his autobiography, *Colonial Civil Servant,* (1949).

Appointed Governor and Commander-in-Chief of the Gold Coast, in 1941, Sir Alan with Lady Burns lived at Accra, its capital, in Christiansborg Castle, formerly a fort protecting Danish slave traders. From February to June 1942 he also acted as Governor of Nigeria (and Chairman of the West African Governor's Conference) during the absence on leave of the Nigerian Governor, and for his expeditious and tactful manner in handling a serious strike of railway and dock workers there, which threatened the war effort in West Africa, he received a personal citation from the Secretary of State for the Colonies.

Feeling it "better to anticipate the demand for African membership to the Executive Council" of the Gold Coast, Sir Alan was the first West African Governor to appoint Africans, on September 29, 1942, to his Council, an action imitated shortly after bv the Nigerian Governor. This forward step has since been followed by the establishment, in 1951, of universal suffrage, a legislative assembly and a Cabinet, provided for by a new Constitution, and the election of the first Negro Prime Minister (Kwame Nkrumah) inside the British Empire. *Life* Magazine, (May 4, 1953), commented, "Britain's hardest try to set itself a half tick ahead of history's racing clock is taking place on the Gold Coast."

Responsible for many legislative improvements in the Colony before the adoption of its Constitution, Sir Alan was created a Knight Grand Cross of the Order of St. Michael and St. George in 1946. No previous Governor had received this honor while serving in the Gold Coast and, as he states, "it was regarded by the inhabitants as proof of the increasing status of the Colony."

In June 1947 he was appointed Permanent United Kingdom Representative of the Trusteeship Council of the United Nations.

The Trusteeship Council of the United Nations supervises territories that are not self-governing, all of which are former mandates of the League of Nations (British and French Togoland, British and French Cameroons, Tanganyika, Western Samoa, etc.) or former possessions of Italy and Japan (Italian Somaliland, Japanese Islands in the Pacific). The Council consists of members of the United Nations administering Trust Territories, an equal number of other member nations which do not, and members of the Security Council.

Sir Alan "protested vigorously" against the Philippine proposal that the British colonies of Uganda and Kenya should be placed under United Nations Trusteeship (New York *Times,* July 1, 1948) because Mr. Carpio of the Philippines Delegation regarded Britain's recently-formed administrative union between those two Colonies and Tanganyika as having "unfavorable repercussions on the Trust Territory."

Two weeks later, Sir Alan, replying to the Soviet delegate's attack on British policy in her colonies, accused Communist agitation of responsibility for recent riots in the Gold Coast, reminded Mr. Tsarapkin, the Russian delegate, of the Russian seizure of the Baltic countries and said "there is no Iron Curtain shutting off Trusteeship Territories or British colonies from public inspection." He warned that "irresponsible criticism" of administering powers could do "real harm" in Trust Territories. (New York *Herald Tribune,* July 14, 1948). In April 1950, Sir Alan was Chairman of the first United Nations visiting mission to the Trust Territories of the Western Pacific.

At the ninth session of the Council, Sir Alan was elected President by a secret ballot vote of ten to one on June 5, 1951. At this same meeting, when Russia claimed that the "illegal representative of the Kuomintang regime" should not be seated, Sir Alan supported the United States proposal to postpone further discussion of the issue. Although the United Kingdom regarded the Peking Government as the Government of China, "from which view it did not digress," he said, the United Nations had condemned Peking as the aggressor in Korea, "an aggression in which Peking is still engaged"; therefore his delegation would support the American proposal. (United Nations *Bulletin,* June 15, 1951).

At the tenth session of the Council, Feb. 27, 1952, the first in the new Conference Building

BURNS, SIR ALAN—*Continued*

at United Nations Headquarters in New York City, a similar Soviet bid to seat the Peking Government met with a similar overruling vote, and a warning to the Russian Delegate from Sir Alan against further application of the term "Kuomintang" to the Nationalist Chinese Government.

On Jan. 18, 1952, he presented the Trusteeship Council's report of progress of the Trusteeship System to the General Assembly. Replying to criticism of the report, he held that no one possessing any knowledge of the Territories, unless blinded by prejudice, could sincerely believe that all existing difficulties could be wiped out overnight. Nor could anyone fail to recognize that considerable progress had been and is continuing to be made, in dependent territories throughout the world. In none of the Trusteeship countries was the position of the backward groups so simple that it could be cleared up in a short time. The Trusteeship Council by careful study of the problems and through collective experience it had gathered over a period of years, took a balanced view of the situation in the Territories. Extremists were seldom right; it was, said Sir Alan, the moderate man, appreciating both sides of the question and criticizing with restraint, who won the respect of his fellow men. (United Nations *Bulletin*, February 1, 1952).

He called the United States annual progress report on the Trust Territories of the Pacific Islands "a creditable achievement by the administering authority". (New York *Times*, March 25, 1952). Reporting later in the same year to the General Assembly Trusteeship Committee on British admiinstration in Tanganyika and two other Trust colonies in East Africa, Sir Alan warned that "the best will in the world applied to the best of all policies" could not hasten the development of "those peoples who have, through accidents of history and geography, remained over-long in a backward state." British control over the Trust Territories had been leading the people "surely toward the goal of self-government or independence." (New York *Times*, November 20, 1952).

Other works written by Sir Alan are *Index to the Laws of the Leeward Islands* (joint compilation), *History of Nigeria* (Allen and Unwin, 1948), and *Colour Prejudice; with Particular Reference to the Relationship between Whites and Negroes* (Allen and Unwin, 1948), in which he pleads for mutual courtesy and consideration between races.

In 1942 he was made a Knight, and Lady Burns a Commander, of the Order of St. John of Jerusalem. They have two daughters, Helen Benedicta and Aileen Barbara, both of whom now work in London. Sir Alan stands five feet eleven inches tall and weighs 195 pounds; he has blue eyes and grey hair. He is a Roman Catholic. His club is the Athenaeum.

Sir Alan's two favorite recreations in Nigeria were sailing and tennis, but he became interested as well in auction bridge and for two years wrote a weekly article on the game for the London *Daily Telegraph*, the substance of which was later published in book form (*Auction Bridge for Beginners*). Today he professes to take less interest in bridge, because of the multitude of conventions used and the too serious manner in which players approach it.

References

N Y Times 7:1 Je 6 '51 por
U N Bul 10:597 Je 15 '51; 11:156 Ag 15 '51
Burns, Sir A. Colonial Civil Servant (1949)
International Who's Who, 1952
Who's Who, 1951
World Biography (1948)

BURNS, ARTHUR F(RANK) April 27, 1904- United States Government official; economist

Address: b. c/o Council of Economic Advisers, Executive Office Building, Washington 25, D.C.; h. 4808 Chevy Chase 15, Md.; 270 Central Park West, New York 24, N.Y.

The first member to be named to the Council of Economic Advisers by President Dwight D. Eisenhower is Arthur F. Burns who has been given the task of reorganizing the Council for the Republican Administration and of presiding over the Advisory Board on Economic Growth and Stability. His nomination, announced on March 6, 1953, was confirmed by the Senate on March 18. On August 8 he was appointed chairman.

Burns succeeds Leon H. Keyserling to the post of chairman and he reports directly to the President. The Council, established as a part of the Employment Act of 1946, was designed as a three-member board of experts to administer the employment act and to "formulate and recommend national economic policy to promote employment, production and purchasing power under free competitive enterprise."

An expert in the field of business cycles, Professor Burns has taught economics at both Rutgers and Columbia Universities. He is the author of three books, two of which are concerned with business cycles, and one of which is a critique of the theories of John Maynard Keynes, the British economist. Burns' previous Government positions were as consultant to the United States Treasury Department in 1937 and as chief economist for the President's Railway Emergency Board in 1941.

Arthur Frank Burns was born April 27, 1904 in Stanislau, Austria, the son of Nathan and Sarah (Joseph) Burns. While he was still a boy, his family immigrated to the United States and settled in Bayonne, New Jersey. As a student at Bayonne High School, from which he was graduated in 1921, he was chiefly interested in debating.

At Columbia University, however, he did not participate in extracurricular activities because of the necessity of earning his way. He worked successively as a waiter, salesman, post office clerk, and seaman. He majored in economics, was elected to Phi Beta Kappa, and was awarded a dean's scholarship. He received both B.A. and M.A. degrees in 1925.

During the school year of 1926-1927, Burns was a Gilder Fellow in political science and taught economics in the extension division of Columbia. While studying for a Ph.D. degree at Columbia, Burns became associated with Rutgers University, where from 1927 to 1930 he was an instructor in economics, an assistant professor from 1930 to 1933, and an associate professor until 1943 when he was named a full professor. Burns had received his Ph.D. from Columbia in 1934 and in 1941 returned to his alma mater as a visiting professor. In 1944 he became a full professor at that university.

In addition to teaching, Burns has served since 1930 on the staff of the National Bureau of Economic Research, an organization founded in 1920 for the purpose of conducting impartial research, largely statistical, in the social sciences, with particular emphasis on such subjects as national economy, production, capital formation, and banking credit. He became its director of research in 1945, succeeding the economist, Wesley C. Mitchell, by whom Professor Burns believes he has been principally influenced.

In a report prepared by the Bureau for the Government in 1948, Professor Burns pointed out that statistical offices of the Government employed ten thousand persons at a cost to taxpayers of approximately $40,000,000; he went on to emphasize the need for expanding statistical services. In 1950 the Bureau completed a study of eight hundred statistical series, measuring indicators in periods of recessions and revivals since 1854, which produced findings helpful in recognizing approaching trends.

Professor Burns, in 1951, declared that a conspicuous change had taken place in the distribution of income among Americans and called the change "one of the great social revolutions of history." (New York *Herald Tribune* May 29, 1951). If future reductions in income inequalities are to be achieved, Burns emphasized that they must come from "raising the productivity of those at the bottom of the income scale rather than by transferring income from the rich to the poor." To this end he would encourage increased competition and small business by amending the tax laws which now favor large business firms. Dr. Burns was critical of the "free money" of the Truman Administration and, though a registered Democrat, voted for Eisenhower in 1952.

The Bureau's report of that year stressed the role of the consumer in checking inflation, and Burns commented that "largely as a result of the lull in consumer buying, the past year was characterized by a degree of over-all stability that few economists had anticipated." He added that the consumer, "rarely a heroic figure in economic affairs, scored a modest but noteworthy success."

Professor Burns and Dr. Benjamin H. Beckhart, economist, at the American Assembly meeting at Harriman, New York, in May 1953 presented the view that "those who believe inflation a present danger are apt to emphasize rearmament expenditures, foreign aid, high level of personal incomes, and the economic power of certain groups to bring about increases

Wide World Photos

ARTHUR F. BURNS

in costs as among the primary causes of the inflation. Those who believe inflation not dangerous are likely, they said, to stress current expansion in plant capacity and lessening of fears of shortages in civilian supplies."

After his nomination to the Council of Economic Advisers, Dr. Burns said he would accept the position and attempt to avoid speechmaking and political activities, to concentrate upon giving technical information to the President and to stress business competition as a basic determinant of high productivity.

Dr. Burns was also designated chairman of the Advisory Board of Economic Growth and Stability, a new board devised by the Eisenhower Administration. The purpose of this board is to apply the findings of the Council of Economic Advisers in a consistent fashion to top level Administrative departments, namely, the Treasury, Commerce, Agriculture, Labor, and the Budget Bureau.

In respect to the relationship between the political and economic institutions, Burns believes that economists have not yet evolved a technique for making dependable long-range forecasts and therefore, Government must make its plans so as to allow for various contingencies (Washington *Post*, March 13, 1953).

The *Christian Science Monitor* summarized Professor Burns' views, thus: ". . . a lot of people who think America has conquered the economic cycle and ended depressions are overoptimistic; that many today are seeking economic "stability" when they ought to look for something more dynamic. . ." (March 12, 1953).

In answering questions asked by the Senate Banking and Currency Committee concerning the economic theories which would guide him in his office, he said, "The people of this country believe, and genuinely believe, in a free economic society. . . . That belief I share fully"

BURNS, ARTHUR F.—*Continued*

(*Newsweek,* March 23, 1953). He has said that he is "pre-disposed" to favor indirect controls over direct measures by the Government to control economic conditions, reserving such controls as those of price and wage for grave emergencies.

Under the publishing aegis of the National Bureau of Economic Research, Burns in 1934 wrote *Production Trends in the United States Since 1870* which was credited by the *American Economic Review* with being "an example of fact-finding in its highest form. . . The results will go into that well of information which, some day, will be drawn on to formulate the new economics."

His second work, *Measuring Business Cycles,* of which Wesley C. Mitchell was co-author, was published in 1946. According to the *United States Quarterly Bulletin,* the volume gave "valuable materials" on the various phases of business cycles, with numerous tables and charts which "much enhanced" the value of the book.

In the same year, *Economic Research and the Keynesian Thinking of our Times,* was published, a work in which Burns acknowledged the important contributions Lord Keynes had made by calling attention to the need for maintaining high employment.

Professor Burns' academic societies are the American Statistical Association, the Academy of Political Science, the American Economic Association, and honorary membership in the American Philosophical Society. He is a member of the Research Council for the Institute of World Affairs, the board of directors for Rutgers University, the administrative board of the Institute for Urban Land Use and Housing Studies, and of the editorial and advisory board of the American Palestine Institute. He is also a correspondent for the Institute de Science Economique Appliquée. His social club is the Men's Faculty Club of Columbia University.

Burns was married on January 25, 1930 to Helen Bernstein, a student at the time of her marriage and a teacher for a few years after. They have two sons, David and Joseph. Blue-eyed, five feet eleven inches in height, and weighing 180 pounds, the economist has been described as having "a fine shock of iron gray hair". He speaks in a "voluble and informative manner accompanied by rapid gestures."

For recreation Burns enjoys baseball, and reading detective stories and eighteenth century English prose works. In 1952 he was given an honorary LL. D. degree from Lehigh University.

References

Bsns W p43+ Jl 18 '53
Christian Sci Mon p1 Mr 12 '53
N Y Herald Tribune p7 Mr 7 '53; II p1 Mr 15 '53
Washington (D.C.) Post p30 Mr 13 '53; p1B Mr 29 '53
Directory of American Scholars (1951)
Who's Who in America, 1952-53

CABOT, JOHN M(OORS)   Dec. 11, 1901-
United States Government official
Address: b. Department of State, Washington 25, D.C.; h. 2339 S St., N.W., Washington 8, D.C.

Beginning his career in the United States foreign service as vice-consul in Lima, Peru, John M. Cabot steadily rose until he became Assistant Secretary of State for Inter-American Affairs on February 28, 1953, succeeding Edward G. Miller, Jr., who had held the post for three years. When Dr. Milton Eisenhower undertook a goodwill tour of Latin America in June 1953, he was accompanied by Cabot.

The career diplomat, who is a member of the well-known Cabot family of Boston, has also had assignments in Europe and in the Far East.

John Moors Cabot was born in Cambridge, Massachusetts, on December 11, 1901, one of five children of Dr. Godfrey Lowell Cabot and Maria Buckminster (Moors) Cabot. His father was a manufacturer of carbon black, and headed the Cabot Carbon Company, among other enterprises. He is well known as a philanthropist.

John Moors Cabot entered Harvard University, from which he received an A.B. degree, *magna cum laude,* in 1923. He continued his studies at Oxford, where he attended Brasenose College, receiving a Bachelor of Literature degree in 1925. His thesis concerned the Hungarian-Rumanian boundary.

Cabot served in Callao, Lima, Peru, as vice-consul in 1927 and 1928. Later, in 1930 he attracted attention to himself, as third secretary to the Dominican Republic, when he intercepted a band of revolutionaries who were threatening bloodshed in the outlying districts. He persuaded this group to make a peaceful settlement. Cabot was transferred as third secretary to Mexico in 1931, and served in that post to 1932. The young diplomat, who speaks fluent Spanish and adequate Portuguese, won a promotion to second secretary while serving in Rio de Janeiro, Brazil, from 1932 to 1935, and maintained this rank during subsequent assignments in The Hague, from 1935 to 1938, and in Guatemala from 1939 to 1941.

Cabot was next promoted to assistant chief of the Division of American Republics, with headquarters in Washington, D.C., serving in this capacity from 1942 to 1944. In that year he was appointed chief of the Division of Caribbean and Central American Affairs, with headquarters also in Washington, D.C.

His next diplomatic mission was that of chargé d'affaires to Argentina, during the tense pre-election campaign of 1945. While serving in that country Cabot stated that the United States Government intended to fulfill the treaties it had entered into, while refraining from interference in the purely internal affairs of other nations. He also warned that the "Nazi menace that still exists in Argentina is properly a matter of international concern," adding further that it was "a self-evident truth that the Government and people of the United States cannot help but feel . . . warmer friendship for those Governments that rest on the periodically and freely expressed consent of the governed."

On January 18, 1946, Cabot released thirteen of 400 German documents, top secret telegrams sent between 1942 and 1943, to the foreign office in Berlin by the chargé d'affaires to the German Embassy in Buenos Aires. In making public these documents to the newspapers of Argentina, Mr. Cabot expressed a belief that it was time the public learned the identity of some of the *vendepatrias*, or traitors (New York *Herald Tribune* January 18, 1946). When, on July 22, 1946, Cabot left Buenos Aires for reassignment, the New York *Times* commented "Cabot . . . had a thankless and difficult task. Despite . . . the failure of a mission in which he acted under strict supervision without the benefit of plenipotentiary powers, Mr. Cabot at all times maintained a calm and friendly manner."

Cabot was next assigned as chargé d'affaires in Belgrade, Yugoslavia, succeeding Richard C. Patterson, Jr. During his service there the Yugoslavians became critically short of food, and a delegation called on Cabot at the United States Embassy, requesting aid. Without committing himself, he promised to consider the request.

Although published reports from Belgrade stated that the United States Embassy had agreed to the request, the State Department threw considerable doubt on the need for relief grain and stated that Cabot had been unable to make the necessary recommendations as of March 11, 1947. Cabot further figured in the tense Yugoslavian situation when, during a pleasure trip on May 2, 1947, his camera and identification card were confiscated by a militia captain and a youthful civilian who demanded a "special check" of Cabot's camera. The State Department called the affair a "disagreeable incident," demanding and receiving an apology for this violation of diplomatic immunity. It was during Cabot's assignment that permission was finally given to the United States Army Graves Registration Units to enter Yugoslavia in search of American bodies lost in the war.

Cabot's next assignment was to another trouble-spot, Shanghai. Early in 1949, it became evident that Shanghai was a possible battlefield in the revived Chinese Civil War. As consul general he issued a warning to all Americans to leave Shanghai while it was still possible to do so with safety, since he had been informed that Shanghai would be defended, come what may.

While he was stationed at Shanghai, Cabot was appointed Career Minister, and in 1950 he became Minister to Finland. Upon being asked whether the "warm temperature" awaiting him there would be disturbing to him, he reminded his questioners of his Shanghai assignment, and stated that he was looking forward to the post.

When President Truman put into effect a $15,000,000 dollar loan to Pakistan on September 18, 1952, he simultaneously announced the appointment of John M. Cabot as Ambassador to that country, succeeding Avra M. Warren, who had held the position for three years. However, Cabot did not proceed to the post, and on February 10, 1953 he was named chief

Wide World Photos

JOHN M. CABOT

of the United States delegation to the Inter-American Economic and Social Conference held in Caracas, Venezuela, he was subsequently elected first vice-president of the Conference.

In his address to the Conference, whose delegates listened attentively for signs of the Eisenhower Administration's policy regarding the American republics, Cabot stated that although limits existed to United States' economic aid, Washington desired to know the needs of the Latin American countries. This statement was enthusiastically received by the attending Republics.

As the Eisenhower Administration continued its policy of appointing career diplomats in key posts throughout the world, John Moors Cabot was confirmed as Assistant Secretary of State for Inter-American Affairs, on February 28, 1953. In a speech before the Export Managers' Club in New York City on March 17, 1953 he gave a revealing summary of his views on the future of the Latin American countries, "There is nothing more dangerous from the viewpoint of long-range American policy than to let Communists, with their phony slogans, seize the leadership of social reform. We simply cannot afford to identify ourselves with the elements which would tie down the social safety valve. That wouldn't protect our national interests. It wouldn't even for long protect our investments." Commenting editorially on this speech, the Buenos Aires newspaper *La Prensa* stated, "If his views represent those of the Republican Administration we must assume that the Administration is well prepared to examine a serious plan for future movements of capital."

In applying a progressive approach to the problems of Latin America, Cabot toured eleven Latin American nations, including Cuba, to study prevailing conditions. Returning to this country, he warned that proposed import curbs on Latin American goods would only cause "re-

CABOT, JOHN M.--*Continued*

sentiment and despair" in those republics. "That is not the road to cooperation, friendship and Pan-Americanism," he further declared.

Recently American labor leaders were concerned over the possibility that Bolivian workers were suffering over reported refusals of the United States Government to buy Bolivian tin. Cabot, in a sharp letter published by the Inter-American Regional Organization, refuted the charges, and maintained that the record showed that the United States Government had purchased all tin offered up until May 1, 1953.

The six foot three inch Cabot weighs 195 pounds, has brown hair and gray-green eyes. He married Elizabeth Lewis on April 2, 1932. The Cabots have four children, Marjorie Moors, John, Lewis Pickering, and Elizabeth Tracy. He has no political or church affiliations. His favorite recreations are tennis, squash, and swimming. He is a member of the Metropolitan Club, Chevy Chase Club, and University Club, all of Washington, D.C. He is the author of the book *The Racial Conflict in Transylvania,* 1926.

References

Christian Sci Mon p14 My 15 '53
N Y Times p7 F 28 '53
Time 61:44 F 16 '53
Who's Who in America, 1952-53

CALDWELL, MRS. LESLIE GODFREY
See Caldwell, S. C.

CALDWELL, SARAH C(AMPBELL)
Dec. 31, 1904- Organization official; educator
Address: b. c/o National Education Association, 1201 16th St., N.W., Washington 6, D.C.; c/o Garfield High School, Akron 1, Ohio; h. 121 Eastgay Dr., Akron 13, Ohio

Mrs. Sarah C. Caldwell, who had earlier held a number of administrative offices in the Ohio Education Association and the National Education Association, was elected to the presidency of the National Education Association for the term 1952-53 and is also now serving a three-year term as vice-chairman of the Educational Policies Commission. A high school biology teacher, she has a record of twenty-nine years of experience in education, including both small town and large city classroom instruction at elementary and secondary levels.

One of three daughters in a family of four children, Sarah Campbell Caldwell was born to Robert Walker and Mary Mabel (Patrick) Campbell on December 31, 1904, in Newton County, Georgia. After attending the local elementary school, she enrolled at Covington (Georgia) High School, from which she was graduated in 1921. At the Georgia State College for Women, Sarah Campbell majored in biology and education and received her Bachelor of Science degree in 1928 in the latter course of study. For her postgraduate work, she attended Columbia University, Pennsylvania

State College, and the Universities of Akron and Miami.

About two years after beginning her teaching career in a primary school in Sparta, Georgia, in 1923, Sarah Campbell moved to Atlanta, where as a critic in a training school she was engaged in demonstration work. From 1927 to 1929 she taught in the same capacity in Ashley Hall, a private school for girls in Charleston, South Carolina. Since 1929, in which year she moved to Ohio, she has been teaching in the primary and secondary schools of Akron, and is now a biology instructor at the Garfield High School.

At the local professional level Mrs. Caldwell helped organize the Akron Classroom Teachers Association in 1940, serving as its first president until 1942. She has also been a member of the executive committee (1947-48) and of the board of directors of this organization, which was renamed the Akron Education Association. From 1942 to 1946 Mrs. Caldwell was president of the Ohio Council of City Teachers Association and for the following two years (1946-48) was on the executive committee of the Ohio Education Association's department of classroom teachers. Of her work as president of the National Education Association's department of classroom teachers, which office she held in 1948-49, it has been said, "In all capacities Mrs. Caldwell has fearlessly championed the cause of the classroom teacher and has worked tirelessly for teacher welfare and advancement" (*Ohio Schools,* official journal of the O.E.A.).

In the summer of 1949 Mrs. Caldwell represented the National Education Association's department of classroom teachers at a meeting in Berne, Switzerland, of the World Organization of the Teaching Profession. After this meeting the American educator traveled as an ambassador of goodwill in Germany, Greece, Malta, Italy, and Egypt. Upon her return she was frequently called on to speak for the department in the United States. In his column in the Akron *Beacon Journal* of September 3, 1950, Keith Spriggel wrote of Mrs. Caldwell, "Her colleagues swear that this drawling daughter of Georgia did more on one trip overseas to promote international understanding than many ambassadors do during a whole term." (Mrs. Caldwell has also traveled in Holland, Belgium, France, England, Scotland, and Canada.) At N.E.A.'s San Francisco convention in July 1951, Mrs. Caldwell was elected as the association's first vice-president for the period 1951-52. Prior to filling this post she had been elected to a three-year membership on the N.E.A. Educational Policies Commission. As chairman of this Commission subcommittee on moral and spiritual values, she delivered a speech at the annual meeting of the National Education Association on July 2, 1952, in which she made a report on the Commission's 100-page study of the function of the public schools in teaching moral and spiritual values.

The National Education Association of the United States, which was founded in 1857, is dedicated to the upbuilding of democratic civilization and supported by the co-operation of the teachers of the United States to advance

Paul T. Esselburn Studio

SARAH C. CALDWELL

the interests of the teaching profession, promote the welfare of children, and foster the education of all the people. At the annual presidential election of the N.E.A., in September 1952, Mrs. Caldwell was chosen to succeed J. Cloyd Miller, for the term 1952-53. In her acceptance speech, Mrs. Caldwell urged that the teaching profession "uncover potential leadership which is needed at all levels to help build a greater teaching profession through recruiting and selecting its own prospective members, develop, determine, and enforce its own standards, establish and govern its own code of ethics, and constantly strive to improve its services." As a representative of the National Education Association, Mrs. Caldwell delivered a welcome address at the seventh National Conference on Citizenship in Washington, D.C., on September 17, 1952. The association in cooperation with the United States Department of Justice sponsored this conference, in which more than one thousand public and private organizations from all over the world participated. In October 1952 N.E.A. conducted a two-day conference in New York City to discuss the subject "The Teaching Profession and the American Future," during which Mrs. Caldwell presided at all general sessions.

In the summer of 1952, as president of the N.E.A., Mrs. Caldwell headed the delegation in Copenhagen and took an active part in the inauguration of the newly formed World Confederation of Organizations of the Teaching Profession. She was appointed by President Truman a member of the U.S. Delegation to the Seventh Conference of UNESCO which met in Paris, November 12 to December 12, 1952. She was the first classroom teacher ever to receive such an appointment.

Other contributions of Mrs. Caldwell in the field of education include her activities as a member of the Northeastern Ohio Teachers Association, a member of O.E.A. legislative planning and Federal relations committees, and program participant at the North Central Regional and Classroom Teachers National Conferences. She is a member of the World Organization of the Teaching Profession and a life member of the O.E.A. and the N.E.A. In 1949 she was made honorary president of the Malta Union of Teachers. In June 1952 the University of Akron bestowed upon Mrs. Caldwell the honorary degree of Doctor of Letters. She holds honorary membership in Delta Kappa Gamma (first vice-president for Ohio from 1948 to 1950); Kappa Kappa Iota, national social and professional teachers group; and Kappa Delta Pi, an honor society in education. She was elected the first honorary member of Phoenix, an honorary society for outstanding students, by the faculty of Georgia State College for Women. She is a member of League of Women Voters and the Akron Interclub Council of Business and Professional Women. In 1948 she was chosen for the "Woman of the Year" award of the latter organization. Mrs. Caldwell, in addition to her regular curriculum, has taught Red Cross first aid.

Mrs. Caldwell is married to Leslie Godfrey Caldwell, an advertising copy chief of the Firestone Tire and Rubber Company. A daughter Arline, a licensed physician, is a resident in psychiatry at Hillside Hospital, Glen Oaks, New York. A son Leslie, Jr., died in a Navy airplane accident in 1949. Mrs. Caldwell is a member of the Episcopal Church. She has brown hair and brown eyes, is five feet four inches tall, and weighs 126 pounds. A colleague of the educator (quoted in *Ohio Schools*) has described her as "a progressive thinker with sound judgment, broad vision, keen understanding, unusual personal charm, and great skill in management of human relations."

On June 5, 1953 Bowling Green, Ohio State University conferred on her the honorary degree of Doctor of Pedagogy.

CAMPANELLA, ROY   Nov. 19, 1921-
Baseball player

Address: b. c/o Brooklyn National League Baseball Club, 215 Montague St., Brooklyn 2, N.Y.; h. 114-10 179th St., St. Albans, L.I.

Sportswriters and other baseball experts generally agree that the ablest catcher currently active in the National League is Roy Campanella of the Brooklyn Dodgers. "Campy," as he is often called, joined the Ebbets Field club in the middle of the 1948 season and had his most brilliant year in 1951, when his skill in the handling of pitchers and a high batting average brought him the Baseball Writers of America award for the league's "most valuable player." Campanella, who throws and bats right-handed, spent eight years in Negro professional baseball before being signed for a Brooklyn-owned minor league team in 1946.

(Continued next page)

Wide World Photos
ROY CAMPANELLA

Roy Campanella was born in November 19, 1921 in Homestead, Pennsylvania, the son of an Italian immigrant and a Negro mother. His father, John Campanella, peddled fruits and vegetables. "There never was much money in John Campanella's house," Ed Fitzgerald has written, "and neither waste nor shiftlessness was encouraged. 'From the time I was nine or ten,' the ball player recalls, 'I used to earn my spending money by helping my older brother Lawrence deliver his milk route. . . .I got a quarter a day for the job.' "

The family moved to North Philadelphia when Roy was a child, and at the Simon Gratz High School there, which he attended for three years, the boy won "letters" in football, basketball, and track, as well as in baseball. Roy showed such proficiency "behind the plate" that during his junior year he was paid fifty dollars by the Bacharach Giants to catch for that Philadelphia Negro team on a week-end tour of the suburbs of New York City. While staying with the team at the Woodside Hotel in New York Campanella was invited by the manager of the Baltimore Elite Giants, to play for his club in the Negro National League. Three days later, he caught both games of a double-header for the Elites in Baltimore. When he returned to school, the coach of a rival team said Roy had become a professional and should no longer be permitted to play in school games. Campanella dropped out of the Simon Gratz High School team but continued to catch for the Elites, with whom he became so well established that by the beginning of the 1937-38 school year he decided not to return to his studies.

In the opinion of *Time* (May 16, 1949), Campanella became a catcher for two reasons: he was a born athlete, and none of the other boys in his Philadelphia neighborhood wanted to catch. The young player spent the years between 1937 and 1945, with one interruption, in the Negro National League as backstop for the Baltimore Elites. Like most Negro players, "Campy" supplemented his meager pay by taking winter engagements in Cuba, Puerto Rico, Venezuela, and other places; he estimates that he used to catch about 220 games a year and played ball for all but two weeks of each year. On one notable occasion Campanella "caught" two double-headers in one day. He was an excellent "power" hitter as well, and not only helped the Elites to a Negro League championship in 1939 but made five hits in five times at bat in a subsequent "play-off" contest.

Deferred for World War II service, he played with the Baltimore team until the summer of 1942, when he joined the Monterey club of the Mexican League at more than double the salary the Elites had paid. However, when the owner of the Elites offered Campanella $3,000 a summer to play again for the Baltimore team, the catcher returned to the Negro National League and backstopped so effectively in 1945 that he was asked by Mrs. Effie Manley, owner of the Newark, New Jersey club, to play a post-season series between an all-star Negro team and a squad of barnstorming major-leaguers. The white team included second baseman Eddie Stanky and pitcher Hal Gregg of the Brooklyn Dodgers and was managed by Charlie ("Chuck") Dressen, then a coach with the Brooklyn National League team.

After Campanella had caught two games at Ebbets Field and a third in Newark, he was sent for by General Manager Branch Rickey of Brooklyn. The "Mahatma," as Rickey is nicknamed, tried to interest the Negro catcher in the Brown Dodgers team to play at Ebbets Field while the regulars were on tour. When Campanella refused, Rickey asked him as a favor "not to sign any contract for next year until he had a chance to talk . . . again." A short time afterwards, in October 1945, the news came that Rickey had breached the color line in organized baseball by signing infielder Jackie Robinson of the Kansas City (Negro) Monarchs for the Dodgers' most important "farm," the Montreal club of the "Triple A" International League. Campanella, who played with Robinson in Venezuela during the ensuing winter, recounts that he was more delighted than surprised when he was again contacted by Rickey and given a contract with the Dodgers' organization. With pitcher Don Newcombe, another Negro prospect for Ebbets Field, he was sent to the Nashua, New Hampshire, team of the Class "B" New England League where, although he made 15 errors, he established a season's record with 687 put-outs and 64 assists, and drove in 96 runs with his timely hitting. Sent to Montreal in 1947, Campanella improved his fielding average to .988 (the best in the International League), batted .273 and established the season's records for putouts and assists.

In the spring of 1948 Campanella went to Florida with the Dodgers, but since Brooklyn already had at least one first-rate catcher in Bruce Edwards, he was "farmed out" to the St. Paul, Minnesota, team of the **American**

Association not long after the regular season had begun. In his debut with St. Paul on May 22 Campanella struck out twice and made a throwing error; but thereafter showed his true form, hitting 11 home runs in his first 24 games. The Dodgers meanwhile had fallen into a batting slump and at the end of June he was recalled by manager Leo Durocher to Brooklyn, where he made his major league debut against the New York Giants on July 2, hitting a double and two singles, and going on to make two resounding home runs in the next Giants' series. "Campy" finished his first half season with Brooklyn with a mere .258 batting average, but came decidedly into his own in the early summer of 1949, when he batted around .400 and began regularly to display that intelligence and insight in the handling of battery-mates which alone would cause him to stand out from the rank and file of catchers. By mid-season Campanella was behind the plate more frequently than Bruce Edwards, and in the All-Star Game of that year was used by the National League team's manager, Billy Southworth of the Boston Braves, through most of the contest in preference to Andy Seminick of Philadelphia. He has caught for the National League in every subsequent All-Star Game. Campanella's fine teamwork with his pitchers, his .985 fielding average (best in the league) and his respectable all-season hitting percentage of .287 were key elements in Brooklyn's successful 1949 pennant drive. In that year's World Series with the New York Yankees, the Dodgers' catcher played errorless ball and made 4 hits, one a home run and another for a double.

One of the memorable games of 1950 was the contest on August 26 between Brooklyn and Cincinnati in which Roy Capanella hit three 400-feet home runs. The Dodgers lost to the Philadelphia Phillies in that year's struggle for first place, but Campanella led all other National League catchers in chances and put-outs and hit 31 home runs. The latter figure rose to 33 in 1951, the year in which Roy made his greatest successes and won the New York Baseball Writers' award as the "most valuable player" in the National League. This distinction was achieved despite a slow start (it was not until some time in May that his batting percentage rose to .300, although shortly thereafter he made nine hits in ten times at bat in a two-game series with the Boston Braves) in which he was hindered by a series of physical handicaps. These included a "spiked hand, a leg and hip injury, and (in a game at Chicago on September 17) a blow behind the ear from a pitched ball which kept him out of the Dodgers' lineup for four days and impaired his efficiency in the remainder of the regular season, in which the Dodgers and the Giants finished in a dead heat for first place. To determine the winner of the pennant, the first three-games "play-off" in the history of the National League became necessary; but because of an aggravation to his leg injury Campanella was able to appear in only the first of these games, and was thus in no way concerned with the series-ending home-run ball pitched by Ralph Branca to Bobby Thomson

which gave the victory (and the pennant) to the Giants. Altogether "Campy" missed about a dozen games in 1951 because of injuries, but went to bat 505 times (the greatest number of his career) and made 164 hits during the regular season, including 33 doubles and one triple as well as his 33 homers. He batted .325 (fourth in the league standings) and drove in 108 runs.

In the October, 1951 voting by the Baseball Writers Association to decide the recipient of the Kenesaw Mountain Landis plaque given annually to the "most valuable player" in the National League, Campanella led Stan Musial of the St. Louis Cardinals by 243 points to 191 and had 11 first-choice votes to 2 for Musial. The catcher won a salary increase to an estimated $25,000 a season for 1952, but injuries of one kind or another continued to plague him from time to time. He played in only 128 games as compared with 143 in 1951, and although he hit 22 home runs, his batting average dropped to .269. His fielding percentage was .994 and in the seven games of the 1952 World Series between the Dodgers and the Yankees he played errorless baseball and made 6 hits.

"Campy," who operates a liquor store in the Harlem area of Manhattan during the winter, is considered by Dodger President Walter O'Malley to have five more years as "the best catcher and one of the greatest clutch hitters in baseball" still ahead of him (New York Times, October 11, 1952). When his playing days are over he will probably become a coach.

Roy Campanella and Ruthe Willis, who met at the New York World's Fair, were married January 3, 1939 and are the parents of five children. They make their home at St. Alban's, Long Island. Roy enjoys fishing and is an expert raconteur of fishing yarns, both "tall" and true; another of his hobbies is his model railway. The Brooklyn catcher, who has brown eyes and black hair, is heavily built, weighing 190 pounds to his five feet nine inches of height, but sports writer Ed Fitzgerald calls him "deceptively fast."

In the 1953 season Campanella continued to set the pace for his teammates. On May 9th, he knocked three home runs in one day.

References

Baseball Stars 1952 1:58 pors
Baseball's Best p15-21 '52 pors
Christian Sci Mon p13 Je 22 '50 por
Collier's 130:44-6 S 6 '52 por
Look 15:77-8 S 25 '51 pors
N Y Herald Tribune p27 Ja 24 '51 por; p31 N 1 '51 por; p16 O 11 '52; III p5 F 22 '53 por
N Y Times p39 N 11 '51; p25 O 11 '52
Newsweek 35:79 F 13 '50
Sport 12:76 Je '52 por
Sport Life 5:15-17 Je '52 pors
Sport Stars 4:34-36 My '52 pors; 4:24-5 N '52 pors
Time 53:43-5 My 16 '49 por
Baseball Register (1952)
Hopkins, L. Real Book About Baseball (1951)

(Continued next page)

CAMPANELLA, ROY—*Continued*

Reichler, J. Inside the Majors (1952)
Turkin, J. and Thompson, S. C., Official Encyclopedia of Baseball, Jubilee Edition (1950)
Who's Who in Baseball (1953)
Who's Who in Colored America, 1950
Who's Who in Major League Baseball (1951)
Young, D. Roy Campanella (1952)

CANTINFLAS (MARIO MORENO)

(căn′tĭn-flăs) Aug. 12, 1911 Comedian

Address: b. Balderas 32, Mexico, D. F.; h. Rincón del Bosque 15, Mexico, D. F.

The central figure in the huge mural recently painted by Diego Rivera for Mexico's newest and most modern theatre is Cantinflas, often called Latin America's Charlie Chaplin. Cantinflas, who ran away from school to join a traveling tent show, won international success over a decade ago with his bedraggled though high-spirited characterization of the *pelado*, the underdog of the Mexican slums.

CANTINFLAS

He gained notice in the United States in 1942 when his second full-length film, *Ni Sangre, Ni Arena (Neither Blood Nor Sand)* outgrossed in Mexico such record money-makers as *The Great Dictator* and *Gone With the Wind.* Since then he has enjoyed continuous success throughout Latin America, both in personal appearances and on the screen. Although he has discussed making English-speaking films in Hollywood, none have materialized because of the largely untranslatable flavor of his patter and his dissatisfaction with the roles offered. In his most recent films, and in political

and union activities, he has prompted programs for social reform.

Cantinflas was born Mario Moreno August 12, 1911 in a house on Santa María La Redonda Street in Mexico City in a "poor but respectable neighborhood." According to an article in *Américas* (March 1953) he was the son of José and María Guizar Moreno, and the sixth in a family of twelve sons and three daughters. His father, a post office employee, tried to keep him in the Bartolomé de las Casas School, but instead, Mario got his learning, including dancing and singing, in the streets. His father eventually sent him to the national agricultural school at Chapingo, but Mario never finished his course. He ran away to Jalapa and joined a *carpa,* or traveling tent show, as a dancer.

The audiences of the *carpas* were a mixed lot of peasants, workers and soldiers who paid the equivalent of from one to three cents for admission and enjoyed slapstick and political satire that was colloquial, relatively artless and peppered with allusions to local conditions. George Creel related in *Collier's* (May 30, 1942) that Moreno, dissatisfied with the dollar a day he earned in these shows, left them in the hope of making more as a touring boxer. He returned to the *carpa* circuit when he was offered three dollars a day.

Moreno accidentally discovered the characterization of Cantinflas when on one occasion he substituted for an announcer at a *carpa.* Suffering a spell of stage fright, he garbled his speech, and became even more incoherent as he tried to correct it. This so convulsed the audience that he found himself doing a frantic combination of gibberish and pantomime. When someone in the audience yelled, "*Callate,* (Shut up) *Cantinflas,*" the meaningless word caught the public's fancy and came to be Moreno's nickname. Since then, Cantinflas has generally played to audiences who begin to laugh the moment he appears or his name is flashed on the screen.

By 1940 Cantinflas had graduated from the *carpa* circuit. When he was to appear at the Folies Bergères Theatre in Mexico City in a skit satirizing the election scandals, the Government closed the theater before the show opened (*Time,* August 26, 1940). Cantinflas persuaded the officials to relent and thereupon "joyously needled the Government more sharply than ever." His popularity had grown to the point where a new verb had come into the language—"*cantinflear,*" meaning to talk much, say little and indulge in wild *non sequiturs.*

Santiago Reachi, who was in the advertising business, used Cantinflas to sell reluctant Mexican truck drivers on the advantages of cab-over-engine trucks. So successful were these skits on trucks that Reachi organized Posa-Film to make them and other advertising skits into movie shorts. Constant requests for them by theater owners soon indicated that Cantinflas had possibilities as a star entertainer. Reachi experimented with several two-reelers, then produced the full-length *Ahí Está el Detalle (Here's the Point)* and *Ni Sangre Ni Arena (Neither Blood nor Sand)* (1941) both of which broke box office records for Mexican-made films throughout Latin America. Other popular successes followed, including *Los Tres Mosqueteros (The Three Musketeers)* and *El Gendarme Desconocido (The Unknown Gendarme)*.

Cantinflas' costume is modeled on that of the Mexican *cargador* or porter. With trousers hanging around his hips and held up by a piece of rope, he wears a long undershirt, a battered felt hat, a handkerchief around his throat, and a ragged coat over his shoulder, which he treats with great care. His patter has been described in the New York *Herald Tribune* (January 25, 1942) as a "madcap gibberish often delivered in solemn earnestness. It is a hash of ad-libs, double-talk, innuendoes, words that don't exist or are mispronounced." Whether he is playing a bullfighter, a fireman or a politician, the patter and the costume are adapted accordingly. Raoul Fournier Villada has described this garrulity as influenced by the environment, "an age of words; everyone was making speeches and issuing declarations, leaders multiplied . . . Hitler and Mussolini raved. The climate existed and the artist was born of external circumstances" (*Américas*, March 1953).

John McManus, reviewing Cantinflas' *El Circo (The Circus)* in *PM* (November 24, 1944), wrote that audiences laughed at his "unquenchable effrontery, his try-anything-once daring." Unlike Chaplin, the tramp who usually meets frustration, Cantinflas is the gutter type who has the gall to push himself into any situation and triumph in spite of himself. In the course of his struggle, he enjoys a good whack at authority and is not afraid to risk drowning himself in big words or whatever opportunity for satire is at hand. Verna Carleton Millan in *Inter-American Monthly* (June 1942) commented that his audiences identify themselves closely with his predicaments and revel in his triumphs.

Ni Sangre Ni Arena was a satire on bullfighting in which the confused Cantinflas fumbled his way through without the bullfighter's art, yet managed to win. Its spoofing seemed especially pointed because a Hollywood version of Blasco Ibañez' *Blood and Sand*, starring Tyrone Power as a serious bullfighter, came out about the same time. The enthusiasm over Cantinflas' "bullfighting," which the New York *Herald Tribune* (January 25, 1942) reported grossed 75 per cent better in Mexican box offices than any of the contemporary American imports, surpassing the popularity of *Gone With the Wind* and Chaplin's *The Great Dictator*, brought him to the attention of Hollywood.

Cantinflas' discussions in Hollywood have so far not produced an English-speaking picture. He was at one time under contract to RKO and negotiated at various times with Columbia and MGM. When he returned from a European trip in 1949, there were reports that his first role would be that of Sancho Panza with Cary Grant as Don Quixote, a technicolor film to be made in Spain and Mexico. However, the next year, *Variety* (June 14, 1950) reported Cantinflas' first English-language picture would be a specially designed story aimed at introducing him to American audiences.

Cantinflas, who now owns Posa-Film with Reachi, has a financial relationship with Columbia Pictures. According to *Variety* (June 14, 1950), Columbia advances Posa about $115,000 before the start of each new Spanish-language production, then handles world-wide distribution, except in the United States. Posa has averaged three productions every two years between 1940 and 1950 and *Variety* estimated the Posa share in the profits was about $230,000 a picture.

Cantinflas has also taken an active part in union activities of the Mexican film industry and has reportedly put a good deal of his own money into it. In 1944 he helped organize the Cinema Production Workers Union when he and his group were outvoted by the more numerous studio and theater laborers in the existing Cinema Industry Workers Union. The Government had recognized Cantinflas' new group and permitted it to take over in three major studios, resulting in the ouster of the rival union (*Variety*, August 18, 1944). In 1946 the Government had to step in again when Cantinflas threatened to quit work and leave Mexico because the rival union members tried to bar his films from the theaters where they worked. *Newsweek* reported that President Avila Camacho felt impelled to intervene to save the whole film industry, since it was so dependent on Cantinflas' prestige.

In 1952, the comedian launched a large-scale social improvement program with the help of the newspaper *Ultimas Noticias*. The plan, as reported by the New York *Times* (June 23, 1952), was to raise some twenty million pesos a year to solve the problems of the poor by building hospitals, maternity clinics, housing and restaurants exclusively for their use. When the newspaper urged certain millionaires personally to contribute, charges of blackmail were raised but the controversy died down when President Miguel Alemán gave the fund the blessing of the Government by pledging large contributions.

The social improvement message has become increasingly important in Cantinflas' latest pictures, particularly in *Si Yo Fuera Diputado (If I Were a Member of Congress)* and *El Bombero Atómico (The Atomic Fireman)*. Although this trend has continued to make his mass audiences laugh, some critics feel that as a propagandist he is undermining his value as an artist. S. Leon in *Mañana* (June 11, 18, 25, 1949) warns Cantinflas that his pictures have degenerated and that he has begun to belong to yesterday because there is a personality clash between Moreno, the glamorous movie star who is looking out for the little people, and Cantinflas the lovable bum, who really *is* one of the little people, and unfortunately, Moreno is winning.

After more than a decade of success, however, Cantinflas seems secure in his place as Mexico's foremost comedian. In the new *El Teatro de los Insurgentes*, where he is seen in the big mural by Rivera, he is also slated (New York *Times*, March 29, 1953) to star in its first production, a heavily financed musical com-

CANTINFLAS—*Continued*

edy, *Yo, Colon (I, Colombus)* which was especially designed for him.

Cantinflas is of medium height and athletic build. In 1937, he married Valentina Zubareff, a dancer of Russian descent who was a fellow performer on the *carpa* circuit. Cantinflas is an expert bullfighter. He is president of the Association of Mexican Actors and has been honored with a gold medal by the actors of Chile.

"When it comes to comedians, there's only one man who counts—a little guy who made himself a millionaire, and Mexico's best-loved citizen. . . .Many have called him Mexico's Charlie Chaplin, but Chaplin himself has called him the world's greatest comedian" (*Theatre Arts*, November 1, 1951).

References

> Americas 5:6+ Mr '53 pors
> Collier's 109:62+ My 30 '42 por
> Inter Am Mo 1:29 Je '42 por
> N Y Herald Tribune VI p5 Ja 25 '42
> N Y Post Mag p8 O 23 '49
> N Y Star p24 Jl 21 '48
> N Y Times IX p3 Je 15 '41 por
> Time 9:34 Ag 26 '40
> Theatre Arts 25:86 N '51
>
> Columbia Encyclopedia (1950)
> Who's Who in Latin America (1946-51)

CAROL II Oct. 16, 1893—Apr. 4, 1953

Former King of Rumania; marriage of state to Princess Helen of Greece (1921) ended in divorce (1928); one son, later King Michael, born of this marriage; renounced throne (1925); went into exile in Paris with Magda Lupescu; restored to Rumanian throne (June 1930); compelled to abdicate in September 1940 in favor of his son because of popular unrest; interned in Spain six months at Hitler's request; escaped to Portugal, where he lived in exile since 1947 with Magda Lupescu, whom he married in Brazil. See *Current Biography*, 1940.

Obituary

N Y Times p13 Apr 4 '53

CHAMPION, GOWER June 22, 1921- Dancer; choreographer

CHAMPION, MARGE (MARJORIE CELESTE BELCHER) Sept. 2, 1923- Dancer

Address: b. c/o Metro-Goldwyn-Mayer, Hollywood, Calif.

The first dance team to win nation-wide popularity through the medium of television is Marge and Gower Champion. Since their marriage six years ago, the Champions have appeared together in motion pictures and nightclubs as well as on the *Admiral Broadway Revue* on the National Broadcasting Company television network.

John Crosby described the Champions as "light as bubbles, wildly imaginative in choreography, and infinitely meticulous in execution. Above all, they are exuberantly young . . . the best dance team of its kind in the world."

Before they became a team, Gower Champion danced with another partner, and did the choreography for Broadway musical shows, winning several major awards for his work. Marge Champion began her professional career at an early age, and appeared in west coast musical productions and Broadway revues before becoming Gower's partner.

Marjorie Celeste Belcher was born in Los Angeles on September 2, 1923 to Ernest and Gladys (Basquette) Belcher. Her father is a Hollywood ballet master who has taught many well-known movie stars, from Vilma Banky in the early days of the films to Betty Grable today. He coached Marjorie in acrobatic, tap, ballet and Spanish dancing, starting her lessons when she was three years old.

Changing her name to Marjorie Bell, she made her movie debut in 1938 in a small part in the Astaire-Rogers film, *The Castles*. In the same year she modelled for Walt Disney's cartoon heroines in *Snow White* and the blue fairy in *Pinocchio*.

While attending public schools and Hollywood High School in Los Angeles, Marjorie appeared in local Civic Opera musical productions, making her stage debut at the age of thirteen before an audience of 23,000 in the Hollywood Bowl.

An early marriage to Art Babbitt, a commercial artist, was terminated by divorce after two years, and in 1947 the young dancer went to New York to appear in the Broadway musicals, *Dark of the Moon*, and Duke Ellington's *Beggar's Holiday*.

At this point Gower Champion, recently discharged from the United States Coast Guard, was looking for a dancing partner and asked Marjorie to team up with him. They had both attended Bancroft Junior High School in Los Angeles, and Gower had been a star pupil of her father's. Their careers did not converge until April 1947, when Marjorie Bell refused an offer to appear in the Rodgers and Hammerstein musical show *Allegro* and chose to become Gower's partner.

Gower Champion was born in Geneva, Illinois, on June 22, 1921. When he was two years old, his parents, John W. Champion, an advertising executive, and Beatrice (Carlisle) Champion were divorced. His mother took Gower and his brother John to Los Angeles, where she is now a well-known custom dressmaker and creates Marge Champion's costumes.

Gower, who was named after a grandmother, Belle Gower, attended grade school, Bancroft Junior High School and Fairfax High School in Los Angeles. While in his junior year there, he won an amateur dance contest at the Cocoanut Grove with a classmate, Jeanne Tyler. The nightclub awarded them a 13-weeks engagement and they did not return to school. As "Gower and Jeanne—America's Youngest Dancers" (they were both sixteen) they appeared in west coast supper clubs, and then went to New York to appear in the Waldorf-Astoria for two engagements that brought them dancing parts in several Broadway musical revues. Between 1939 and 1941 they performed in *Streets of Paris, The Lady Comes Across*, and *Count Me In*. They were also featured dancers at the Radio City Music Hall. Throughout this tour they were chaperoned by Gower's mother.

While making professional appearances, Gower decided to study dancing seriously. He took ballet classes with Ernest Belcher in Hollywood, and while on tour and on the east coast, he took lessons in modern dance, acting and voice.

Immediately after Pearl Harbor, he entered the Coast Guard, where he served for three years. He toured in the Coast Guard musical show, *Tars and Spars*, and then did transport duty on both oceans.

When he returned to civilian life, he found that his former partner had married and retired from show business. Looking for a new partner, he wrote to Ernest Belcher, his former teacher, who suggested that Champion talk to his daughter, Marjorie, in New York. After contacting her, however, he was offered a movie contract by Metro-Goldwyn-Mayer, which required him to return to Hollywood. The studio kept him idle while paying him a regular salary, with only one small role in *Till the Clouds Roll By*. After eight months of inactivity, Gower broke the contract and returned to New York.

He teamed up with Marjorie Bell as Gower and Bell, and their first professional appearance together took place in Montreal in April 1947. They made their debut in New York at the Persian Room of the Hotel Plaza, a few days after their marriage on October 5, 1947.

They toured nightclubs throughout the country, but returned to New York the following year, when Gower staged the dances for the Broadway revue *Small Wonder*. Back in Hollywood a few months later, he did the choreography for *Lend an Ear*, in which the dances satirized the style of the 1920's. The show was brought to New York for a successful run, and won him the Donaldson, Antoinette Perry, and *Dance Magazine* awards for the creation of the best dances on the Broadway stage for that year. In 1951, assisted by his wife, Champion staged the dances for the revue *Make a Wish*, including a ballet satirizing bargain day in a department store which the New York *Post* critic called "a fine triumph of rowdy slapstick hilarity" (April 29, 1951).

The young couple became nationally known in 1949 with their weekly appearance on the *Admiral Broadway Revue* with Sid Caesar and Imogene Coca on the Dumont and NBC television networks. Their story-dances and pantomime were well-suited to the television medium, and the small following they had built up in their appearances in supper clubs across the country grew into an audience of millions of admirers.

A highly successful appearance at the Mocambo night club in Hollywood in 1950 brought the team a screen assignment to appear in Paramount's *Mr. Music* with Bing Crosby. They were then signed by Metro-Goldwyn-Mayer to make two pictures a year for five

MARGE AND GOWER CHAMPION

years. Their first important roles came the following year in *Show Boat*, in which they played Ellie and Frank, parts for which the New York *Times* reviewer thought they were too sophisticated in their manners. They performed four dances in their next film *Lovely To Look At*, a remake of Jerome Kern's *Roberta*.

A two million dollar movie based on their own story, *Everything I Have Is Yours* (1952), in which the pair played themselves, gave them their first real acting parts. The New York *Times* reviewer found the script and the acting poor, and objected to Gower's "snootiness," but enjoyed the dancing (October 30, 1952). In the same year they made another film, *Give a Girl a Break*. The *Christian Science Monitor* reported on March 31, 1953 that Metro-Goldwyn-Mayer released the team because they refused to sign a new high-salaried contract that stipulated no television shows. In June 1953 the dancers appeared on Ed Sullivan's *Toast of the Town* TV program. In a joint biography, "The Marge and Gower Champion Story," they performed the outstanding dances of their career.

"Each of the Champions' dances tells a story; and virtually every leap, every move, every gesture tells part of that story," wrote John Crosby (New York *Herald Tribune*, June 12, 1953). They use speech and pantomime as well as dance in their performances. "Our work is as near creative theatre as we dare make it," they told a reporter (*PM*, October 12, 1947).

Offstage, one writer stated, they look like "a pair of fresh scrubbed teen-agers" (*Cosmopolitan*, July 1953). Gower is six feet tall and weighs 150 pounds, and Marge is five feet one and one-half inches tall and weighs 102 pounds. Both have dark brown eyes and light brown hair. Gower wears a crew cut.

The pair has a six-room home in the Hollywood hills with a large practice room. Gower

CHAMPION, MARGE and GOWER—
Continued

has done most of the decoration in the house, and collects works of art. He and Marge share the hobbies of collecting classical music records and miniature china cats. They also have five live cats in their home.

In working out their dances, Gower is the choreographer and Marge is the editor. The dancers will make one film a year, and are making frequent night club and television appearances.

References

> Cosmopolitan 135:11+ Jl '53 pors
> Life 76:82 Mr 7 '49 por
> N Y Post p15 S 15 '52 pors
> This Week p20 Mr 25 '51 pors
> Motion Picture and Television Almanac, 1952-53

CHASE, MRS. HAMILTON   *See* Seton, A.

CHIANG KAI-SHEK (chĭ-äng' kĭ-shĕk')
Oct. 31, 1886-   President of China
Address: Taipei, Formosa

> NOTE: This biography supersedes the article which appeared in *Current Biography* in 1940.

Shortly after the transfer of the Chinese Nationalist Government to its capital on Formosa, Generalissimo Chiang Kai-shek in February 1950 resumed the Presidency of China, an office which he had resigned a year earlier following military reverses in the civil war with the Communists. Chiang, who was a member of a revolutionary secret society prior to the declaration of the first Chinese Republic by Dr. Sun Yat-sen in 1912, became the effective head of the Chinese state in 1926 and was the leader of his country's military forces throughout the Sino-Japanese War of 1937-1945 and World War II. He has been considered the most controversial Asiatic figure in the history of America's relations with the Far East.

Chiang Kai-shek was born on October 31, 1886, in Chikow, a village in the Chekiang province of eastern China, the oldest son in the family of five children of the wine merchant Chiang So-an and his third wife. He was given a temporary name in accordance with Buddhist custom and in adolescence adopted for permanent use the name Kai-shek. His father having died when Chiang was nine years old, he was sent to relatives for schooling and apprenticeship to a trade.

At fifteen Chiang married a local girl of the Mao famiy (this marriage, which had been "arranged" by his relatives, was terminated by divorce in 1911). Leaving home to become a soldier, he made his way to Japan when he was nineteen, in the hope of being admitted to a military academy. Finding that this was not possible without a recommendation from the Imperial Chinese Government, he returned to China. He took first place in tests for entrance to the newly established National Military Acad-

emy at Paoting, where his record was such that by the end of a year he was among the cadets sent to Tokyo by the Chinese Government for advanced and specialized military training. He spent four years (1907-11) in Japan, as a student in the Imperial Military Staff College and as Japanese artillery officer.

Having meanwhile met Dr. Sun Yat-sen, known as the "father of the Chinese Revolution," Chiang joined the revolutionary secret society, the Teng-men-hui, in 1907. He was in Japan in October 1911 when the so-called "Wunchang Uprising" took place which led to the abdication of the Manchu dynasty and the proclamation on February 12, 1912, of a Chinese Republic with Dr. Sun as Provisional President. At once he deserted the Japanese Army and sailed for home. As leader of a revolutionary force Chiang gave proof of his military ability at the capture of Shanghai, but he broke with Yuan Shi-kai, in whose favor Dr. Sun had resigned as President.

In 1915 Chiang was a leader in an anti-Yuan conspiracy to sieze the Kiangnan arsenal at Shanghai, and when this was frustrated "disappeared somewhere into Shanghai's murky underworld" (Theodore H. White and Annalee Jacoby in *Thunder Out of China*). The death of Yuan in 1916 brought new chaos of civil war (sometimes among the war lords of the North and sometimes between the latter and Dr. Sun's Republicans in the South.)

Chiang is said to have been occupied at one time or another as second-in-command to a Fukien guerrilla leader, as a brokerage clerk, and as a speculator on the Shanghai stock exchange until one of his patrons, a wealthy revolutionist, sent him to Canton where he was attached to general headquarters from 1917 through 1920.

In 1921 Dr. Sun, who had received little or no encouragement from the Western powers having territorial concessions in China, established contact with Nikolai Lenin, with the consequence that a Chinese Communist party was formed in 1922 and a U.S.S.R. political mission arrived in Canton in August 1923. As a part of the diplomatic exchange, Chiang was sent as a liaison officer to Moscow to study "the military and social system of Soviet Russia."

On his return in 1924 he organized, and became the first principal of, the Whangpoa Military Academy, and a Soviet marshal was assigned as his chief adviser. Unlike Dr. Sun, Chiang was not attracted by the Communist ideology.

Sun Yat-sen's death in March 1925 left control of the Kuomintang to a Central Executive Committee consisting of a right wing leader, Hu Han-min, the Borodin-supported Wang Ching-wei, and Chiang Kai-shek who was also chairman of the Military Affairs Commission. Hu Han-min died shortly, and in March 1926 Chiang staged a military coup which was followed by the flight of Wang Ching-wei and the naming of Chiang as Commander-in-Chief, Northern Expeditionary Force. He faced the task of uniting China by arms. The Cantonese armies started northward in July, and in the following month captured Hankow, where a left-wing Government was set up in November; but about one month after the capture of Nanking in March 1927, Chiang named that city the new capital of China and immediately issued a proclamation denouncing Communism (Victor A. Yakhontoff, *The Chinese Soviets*).

Chiang Kai-shek and Soong Mei-ling, youngest of the three Soong sisters (all of whom were Christians and graduates of American colleges) were married December 1, 1927. Chiang was converted to Christianity and received into the Methodist church October 23, 1930. He is reported to be very devout in his daily prayers and Bible readings.

The Nanking Government was recognized by both the United States and Great Britain during 1928, and in October of that year Chiang was named Chairman of the State Council and Generalissimo of all Chinese Fighting Forces. The Generalissimo "resigned all Government offices in the interest of conciliation of groups at Canton and Shanghai" during 1931, the year of the Japanese occupation of Manchuria.

Soon back in power, Chiang with his brother-in-law T. V. Soong and certain British and American advisers, shared the credit for putting the Chinese currency and budget on a sound basis. With Madame Chiang, he launched in 1934 at Nanking a regimen described in their 1937 book, *New Life Movement*. His policy toward Japan at this period was conciliatory, but he fought Reds and war lords alike until after his kidnapping by the "Young Marshal" Chang Hsueh-liang at Sian in December 1936 prompted, it was said, by the Communist intermediary Chou En-lai. Chang Hsueh-liang confronted his prisoner with eight "demands," the second of which was to "end all civil war and initiate resistance against Japan." Chiang never officially accepted the eight points, but they seem to have been the basis of the agreement with Chou En-lai which led to his release.

When Japan invaded China in July 1937, there was accordingly a common "National Salvation" front in existence. Chiang remained commander-in-chief. His strategy, both before and after the Third Sino-Japanese War became a part of World War II, was not to waste substance on the defense of positions which he knew could not be held indefinitely. Peiking, Shanghai, and Nanking were lost before the year was over, and the Chinese capital was moved to Hankow. That city, as well as Canton, fell in 1938, when the capital was moved, this time to remote Chungking, where Chiang settled down to a holding-delaying action in the avowed belief that "if China held on, powerful allies would come to her side" (*Time*).

Following the Japanese attack in December 1941 on Pearl Harbor, President Franklin D. Roosevelt sent Major General Joseph W. ("Vinegar Joe") Stilwell to China in January 1942. Stilwell, who was soon named Chief of Staff to the Generalissimo, commanded a large body of Chinese troops, as well as American forces, and was often in disagreement with Chiang as to the conduct of the war, as reported by Joseph Alsop in the *Saturday Evening Post* series of articles "Why We Lost China" (January 1950).

Wide World Photos

GEN. CHIANG KAI-SHEK

In the Kuomintang (Nationalist) Government Chiang was throughout World War II president of the Executive Yuan. The Central Executive Committee of the Kuomintang party elected him President of China on September 13, 1943, in succession to Lin Sen. In November of that year the Generalissimo met President Roosevelt and Prime Minister Churchill in Cairo to discuss plans for the defeat of Japan.

In the last years of the war, domination of the Kuomintang passed to reactionary elements, a development which strengthened the prestige of the Chinese Communists, who were at the time widely regarded as primarily agrarian reformers and foes of landlordism and corruption. Stilwell and the Far Eastern Division of the United States Department of State favored a coalition Chinese government in which the Communists would be represented, but an agreement between the two political forces was not achieved.

When China's first National Assembly under the new Constitution convened in the spring of 1948, Chiang became the first constitutional President of China. Because the Communists and one other minority party were not included in the new "committee type" Government, the civil war continued. The Communists took Mukden in Manchuria on November 1, 1948, and two months later were threatening Nanking. Chiang resigned as President on January 21, 1949.

Recalled from retirement in his native province of Chekiang to head the Supreme Policy Council at Canton later in 1949, Chiang resumed command of the Kuomintang's army, but suffered staggering defeats. Canton was lost to the Communists on October 15 and Chungking six weeks later. On December 8, 1949, Chiang had to abandon any further attempt to hold a portion of the mainland and he moved to Tapei,

CHIANG KAI-SHEK—*Continued*

on the island of Formosa, the capital of what is now known as Nationalist China.

On January 4, 1950, President Truman announced that the United States, while continuing recognition of the Nationalist régime as the *de jure* government of China, would give no further military aid to Generalissimo Chiang. Two days later Great Britain, following the example of India, transferred her recognition to the Communist People's Republic of Chou En-lai and Mao Tse-tung.

Chiang resumed the Presidency at Taipei on February 28, 1950, and the following March named as his Premier Chen Cheng, who, with Chiang himself and other officials, is credited with cleaning up much of the inefficiency, corruption, and abuse of privilege which brought the old Kuomintang into bad international repute.

The invasion of South Korea by Communist forces in June 1950 brought a general re-estimation by the United States of the Far Eastern situation. American aid "began flowing into Formosa" until the United States "was spending about $300,000,000 a year in Formosan assistance—two thirds military and one third economic" (Robert Sherrod in the *Saturday Evening Post*, January 10, 1953). A United States Military Assistance Advisory Group was sent to Taipei and the small Nationalist air, naval, and marine forces were strengthened.

Interviewed in the spring of 1951 by Major General Claire Lee Chennault, Chiang had said, "We can retake the mainland of China, given adequate supplies and technical assistance . . . my Chinese forces can recover the mainland with the co-operation and assistance of the Chinese people who will rebel against the Communists" (New York *Herald Tribune*, April 1, 1951). The Nationalists in 1952 made 380 raids on the mainland, while their army of nominally 600,000 men (about 150,000 fully equipped) was said to be "in a fine state of training" (*Time*, July 28, 1952). Early in 1953 when President Dwight D. Eisenhower announced his decision to withdraw the United States Seventh Fleet from the Strait of Formosa, thereby allowing Nationalist China to attack the mainland, Chiang called the action "militarily and morally sound."

The *Collected Wartime Messages of Chiang Kai-shek, 1937-1945* was published by The John Day Co. in 1946, and some of the Generalissimo's speeches are also to be found in *All We Are and All We Have* (Day, 1943). Chiang is the author of *China's Destiny*, Macmillan, 1947), and *China's Destiny and Chinese Economic Theory* (Roy, 1947) ; he was the editor of a new Chinese translation of the *New Testament* completed in the latter year. The Chinese leader has one son, Chiang Ching-hui, by his first wife ; another son, Chiang wei-ju, is adopted. Slight and wiry, Chiang stands five feet seven inches tall and weighs 130 pounds. Some observers have commented on his tenacity of purpose and faith in his crusade to unite China.

Selected References

See also Magazine and Newspaper Indexes.

Berkov, R. Strong Man of China (1938)
Burbidge, W. F. Rising China (1943)
Chang, H. H. Chiang Kai-shek, Asia's Man of Destiny (1944)
Chen, T. General Chiang Kai-shek, the Builder of the New China (1929)
Chiang, K. China's Destiny 1946; Collected Wartime Messages, 1937-45 (1946)
Chiang, K. and M. New Life Movement (1937)
Chiang, M. General Chiang Kai-shek (1937)
China Handbook (1951)
Clark, E. T. The Chiangs of China (1943)
Crain, M. Rulers of the World (1940)
DeWeerd, H. A. Great Soldiers of World War II (1941)
Fernsworth, L. A. ed. Dictators and Democrats (1941)
Gunther, J. Inside Asia (1939)
Hedin, S. Chiang Kai-shek, Marshal of China (1940)
Hsiung, S. Life of Chiang Kai-shek (1948)
International Who's Who (1952)
Kuo, C. Giants of China (1944)
Linebarger, P.M.A. The China of Chiang Kai-shek (1941)
McCabe, J. The Picturesque and Adventuous Career of Chiang Kai-shek (1944)
Mathews, B. Wings Over China (1940)
Michener, J. B. Voice of Asia (1951)
Miller, B. W. Generalissimo and Madame Chiang Kai-shek (1943)
Paneth, P. The Generalissimo Chiang Kai-shek (1943)
Reynolds, E. E. Four Modern Statesmen (1944)
Salter, Sir J. Personality in Politics (1947)
Soward, F. H. Moulders of National Destinies (1940)
Steel, J. Men Behind the War (1943)
Tong, H. T. Chiang Kai-shek (1937)
White, T. H. and Jacoby, A. Thunder Out of China (1946)
Who's Who in America, 1952-53
World Biography (1948)

CHURCHILL, (CLEMENTINE OGILVY HOZIER SPENCER) LADY 1885- Dame, Grand Cross Order of the British Empire.

Address: 10 Downing St., London S.W. 1; 28 Hyde Park Gate, London, S.W., 7; Chartwell, Westerham, Kent

Lady Churchill, of whom her husband, Sir Winston, once wrote: "My most brilliant achievement was . . . to persuade my wife to marry me," has appeared on the honors list of two monarchs and been an active supporter of her husband's political career. She acquired her title when her husband was knighted on April 24, 1953.

Lady Churchill has at times campaigned for her husband and contributed suggestions for many of his most famous speeches. In January 1918 she was made a Commander Order of British Empire (C.B.E.) by King George V for services to the nation in World War I, and in 1946 she was elevated to the rank of Dame, Grand Cross Order of the British Empire (G.B.E.) by George VI for services during World War II.

Born Clementine Ogilvy Hozier in 1885, Lady Churchill is a daughter of the late Sir Henry Montague Hozier, K.C.B., and Lady Blanche (Ogilvy) Hozier. Her father, a retired Colonel, was the third son of James C. Hozier, laird of Newlands and Mauldslie Castle in the Scottish county of Lanarkshire; her mother was a daughter of the seventh Earl of Airlie of Airlie Castle near Dundee, Forfarshire (now Angus County). When his daughter Clementine was nine years old Colonel Hozier resigned his commission to accept the post of secretary-general of the Lloyds interests.

Clementine Hozier, who received her early education from governesses, was later enrolled at the Berkhamstead School in Hertfordshire, not far from London, and subsequently studied at the Sorbonne in Paris. (She speaks French fluently, and has a good command of four other foreign languages). In school, she played championship tennis as well as a good game of croquet, and also enjoyed skiing, horseback riding and long walks in the country.

Her first meeting with her future husband occurred in the spring of 1908 during a by-election in Dundee, where young Winston Spencer Churchill, then a member of the Liberal Party, was seeking a new seat in Parliament after having been appointed President of the Board of Trade. Lady Blanche Hozier and Mrs. George Cornwallis-West, mother of Winston Churchill, were close friends, and the Countess of Airlie, Lady Hozier's mother, offered her Dundee house to Churchill as a campaign headquarters.

The new President of the Board of Trade won his political fight against an independent Liberal "temperance" candidate, about 7000 votes to 4000, but lost his heart in the process. After a comparatively short engagement, Churchill and the Honorable Clementine Hozier were married in St. Margaret's Church, Westminster, on September 12, 1908, in a ceremony at which Lord Hugh Cecil officiated as best man and was attended by the entire Cabinet.

Soon after the newlyweds had honeymooned at Blenheim Palace and Lake Maggiore, and established their first London home, young Mrs. Churchill was called upon to pour oil on political waters agitated by her husband's forthright expressions of opinion. The Dundee by-election, which had brought the two together, had been necessitated by Churchill's loss of his previous parliamentary constituency in Manchester partly as a consequence of his denunciation of the excesses of the suffagette movement. In February, 1909, accordingly,

British Inf. Services

LADY CHURCHILL

Mrs. Churchill returned to Dundee for an address in which she declared that both she and her husband were "ardently in favor of votes for women" in due course, and warned Liberal women against "hostility to their party."

Throughout the pre-World War I period, in which her husband was successively President of the Board of Trade, Home Secretary and First Lord of the Admiralty, Mrs. Churchill made numerous non-political speeches in support of charities, at prize-givings, and at the dedication of buildings. During the war she organized, on behalf of the Young Men's Christian Association, canteens for munition workers in the northeastern area of London. For this service she was created a Commander Order of the British Empire by King George V.

After the war, Winston Churchill was returned to Parliament from Dundee by a large majority in the "Khaki Election" of December 1918, but three years later his popularity had waned. Shortly before the general elections of 1922, Churchill was stricken with appendicitis. Mrs. Churchill filled his speaking engagements with acknowledged ability, but her husband lost his seat for Dundee.

Out of Parliament until the Spring of 1924, Churchill spent the time writing his four-volume work, *The World Crisis* (Butterworth, Ltd., Scribner's, 1923-29) an achievement greatly facilitated by his wife's constant encouragement.

Shortly after the outbreak of World War II in September, 1939, Mrs. Churchill became active in the British Red Cross, and in the following year, when her husband succeeded Neville Chamberlain as Prime Minister, she was named Chairman of the Council of the Fulmer Chase Maternity Hospital for the Wives of Junior Officers. She became President of the Young Women's Christian Association War

CHURCHILL, LADY—*Continued*

Time Fund in 1941, a member of the advisory committee of the British War Relief Society of America, handling the "Bundles for Britain" service in 1942, and director of the depot for Knitted Garments for the Royal Navy. It was for her acceptance of the chairmanship of the British Red Cross Aid to Russia Fund in 1939 that King George VI sanctioned her admission as a Commander of the Order of St. John.

In the summer of 1942 Mrs. Churchill and her daughter Mary accompanied the Prime Minister to the Quebec Conference and to Washington. In April 1945 Mrs. Churchill visited the Near East and Russia to inspect medical institutions under the auspices of the Turkish Red Crescent Society, the Red Cross and the Soviet Government. At Moscow on May 7 she was decorated with the Order of the Red Banner of Labor by N.M. Shverkin, first vice-chairman of the "Supreme Soviet."

For the general election of July 1945 the Epping Division of Essex was partitioned, and Churchill sought re-election to Parliament in the new Wanstead and Woodford Division. Mrs. Churchill toured the constituency on the eve of the polling and delivered six addresses in behalf of her husband. The constituency responded, but the nationwide result of the election was a landslide for Labor and the displacing of Churchill by Clement Attlee as Prime Minister.

In the King's Birthday Honors List issued June 12, 1946, Mrs. Churchill was elevated to the rank of Dame, Grand Cross Order of the British Empire (G.B.E.) for her World War II services. A week later she received an honorary LL.D. from Glasgow University and on June 26 the D.C.L. degree from Oxford, where the Earl of Halifax, Chancellor of the University, introduced her, saying, "She watched over and sustained her husband while he sustained a tottering world" (New York Times, June 27, 1946).

Since 1945 her activities in politics have been limited, although on April 20, 1948, she made a speech at the Conservative Women's Conference in which she predicted that the Conservatives would return to power in the next general election. Actually, however, the Conservatives did not return Churchill to power until the autumn of 1951.

The Churchills have one son, Major Randolph Churchill, and three daughters: Diana (Mrs. Duncan Sandys), Sarah (Mrs. Anthony Beauchamp), and Mary (Mrs. Christopher Soames). Lady Churchill is chairman of the National Hostels Committee of the Young Women's Christian Association. Her present-day recreations include the growing of roses at their country home near Westerham in Kent, and tramping the countryside with the collection of Churchill dogs.

She has a flair for interior decoration, with emphasis on light panelling, chintzes and simple English and French furniture. "She knows all about 'cordon bleu' cooking, and the right wines, too," Kay Halle of the NEA

Service once wrote: "One of the charming things about the Prime Minister's wife is her girlish delight in fashions. She has a bandbox neatness and a knack of putting together nothings to make a very smart something. Her upswept . . . white hair, which she curls herself, frames a strongly modeled face. Her slim figure, large blue eyes and smiling, youthful mouth make it hard to guess her age."

Sir Winston's pet name for his wife is "Clemmie," and possibly the finest tribute ever paid her was his rhetorical query of many years ago: "what can be more glorious than to be united in one's way through life with a being incapable of an ignoble thought?"

References

Christian Sci Mon p10 Ag 25 '43
N Y Herald Tribune pl Ag 11 '43;
   II p3 S 17 '44 por
N Y Post Mag p21 Ag 13 '43 por
N Y Sun p7 Ag 13 '43; p20 Jl 17 '46
   por
N Y Times IV p2 S 28 '41 por
N Y World-Telegram p38 Ag 18 '44
Debrett's Peerage, Baronetage, Knightage and Companionage (1952)
Kraus, R. Winston Churchill in the Mirror (1944)
Who's Who, 1952

CHURCHILL, SIR WINSTON (LEONARD SPENCER) Nov. 30, 1874- British Prime Minister; statesman; author

Address: b. 10 Downing St., London, S.W. 1, England., h. 28 Hyde Park Gate, London S.W. 7; Chartwell, Westerham, Kent

> NOTE: This biography supersedes the article which appeared in *Current Biography* in 1942.

Universally regarded as one of the outstanding statesmen of the twentieth century, Prime Minister Winston Churchill of Great Britain was called upon for the second time to form and head his country's Conservative Government following the general election of October 1951. First elected to Parliament as a Conservative in 1900, Churchill afterwards served in the House of Commons as a Liberal as well as a Tory, and by 1940 had held eight offices and was twice the First Lord of the Admiralty. In 1940 he succeeded Neville Chamberlain and became Britain's wartime Prime Minister.

A master of oratory and literary style, Churchill was named to the Order of Merit in 1946. He became Sir Winston on April 24, 1953 when Queen Elizabeth II knighted him and presented him with the insignia of the Most Noble Order of the Garter.

Born on November 30, 1874, at Blenheim Palace near Woodstock in Oxfordshire, he was registered as Winston Leonard Spencer Churchill. His father was Lord Randolph Henry Spencer Churchill, third son of the seventh Duke of Marlborough, whose long political career reached its climax in 1886, when he became Chancellor of the Exchequer in the government of Lord Salisbury and Conservative leader in the House of Commons. His mother was the American-born Jennie Jerome, daughter of Leonard Jerome, proprietor and owner of the New York *Times*. Winston was the elder of two sons (his brother was Major John Strange Churchill).

Winston spent his first two winters at Blenheim, the palace which had been presented to his ancestor, the first Duke of Marlborough, the victor of the Battle of Blenheim in 1704. Winston's earliest recollections, however, are of Dublin, where Lord Randolph Churchill served for three years beginning in 1876 as secretary to his father who had been appointed Lord Lieutenant of Ireland.

Young Winston learned his letters from a beloved nurse, a Mrs. Everest. At seven he was entered at St. James' Preparatory School at Ascot in Berkshire, an institution modelled on the nearby Eton College and where the birch rod was freely applied to recalcitrant pupils. A sensitive child, with a slight speech impediment, and far from robust, Winston was transferred after a serious illness to a school at Brighton where the sea air and kindly treatment helped to build up his health.

In the summer of 1887 when he was twelve years old, he was admitted to Harrow School, the headmaster having decided to overlook the blank paper he turned in for Latin in the entrance examination. Winston could not or would not muster an interest in Latin or mathematics, and it consequently took him three full terms to get out of the lowest "form." During this period, however, he received from an inspiring teacher, a Mr. Somerville, a thorough grounding in English grammar and sentence structure. His only distinction was to win a prize for reciting 1,200 lines of Macaulay's *Lays of Ancient Rome* and the Public School Championship in fencing.

Lord Randolph Churchill had hoped that his elder son would become a barrister, but the boy's school record caused him to suggest the Army instead. Even so, young Winston Churchill failed three times to pass the entrance examinations for Sandhurst, the West Point of Britain, before coaching by a "crammer" and luck in the questions asked enabled him to pass eventually.

Once admitted, however, he applied himself to his studies, especially tactics and fortification, and completed the course with honors in December 1894 standing eighth in a class of one hundred and fifty.

Appointed in the following March to the Fourth (Queen's Own) Hussars as a sublieutenant, Churchill was on duty at the Aldershop camp in Hampshire through the spring and summer of 1895.

He got himself attached as an "observer" to a Spanish force sent to Cuba in 1895 to put down an insurrection, and sent back reports to the *Daily Graphic* in London. In the spring of 1896 he was with the Fourth Hussars at Bangalore, India, where he alleviated garrison duty by playing polo and reading Plato, Aristotle, Malthus, Darwin, Gibbon's *Decline and Fall of the Roman Empire*, and Macaulay's *History of England*.

British Inf. Services

SIR WINSTON CHURCHILL

When General Sir Bindon Blood headed a punitive expedition in 1897 against the Pathans in the area of the Malakand Pass, Churchill wanted to go but there were no vacancies on the General's staff. When he learned that he could go as a newspaperman, he entered into an arrangement with the London *Daily Telegraph*, and joined the expedition as a war correspondent.

Early in 1898 Churchill served as orderly officer to Sir William Lockhart on the Tirah Expeditionary Force, and later in the same year he completed the first of his military histories, *The Story of the Malakand Field Force* (Longmans, Green, 1898), which elicited praise from the future King Edward VII and Prime Minister Lord Salisbury but criticism from high Army officials. His next military service was with the Nile Expeditionary Force, headed by General Sir Herbert Kitchener, in the famous cavalry charge at Omdurnam. On his return to England he wrote *The River War* (Longmans, Green, 1902; Eyre and Spottiswood, 1933) a two-volume history of the campaign, and a novel, *Savrola* (Longmans, 1900). He also made his political debut, running as a Conservative in a by-election in the Oldham Division of Lancashire, but was defeated by his Liberal opponent.

After the outbreak of the Boer War, Churchill went to South Africa as a correspondent for the London *Morning Post*, and on November 15, 1899, was taken prisoner by Louis Botha, the young Boer officer who later became a general and prime minister. He was imprisoned at Pretoria from which he made a dramatic escape, full details of which were not revealed until his autobiography *A Roving Commission* (Scribner's, 1930; 1939) was published. (Books by Churchill dealing with the Boer War include *London to Ladysmith via Pretoria* and *Ian*

CHURCHILL, SIR WINSTON—*Continued*

Hamilton's March, both published in 1900 by Longmans, Green.

Churchill returned to England in time for the so-called "khaki election" of 1900, when he again ran, this time successfully, as a Conservative in Oldham. He made his first speech in the House of Commons in February 1901 after lecturing in both Britain and the United States on his South African experiences.

In *A Roving Commission,* Churchill has recorded that he made only three speeches in about two years on the Conservative benches. He found himself increasingly out of sympathy with the "protectionist" high tariff policy championed by Joseph Chamberlain, and more and more in accord with a young Conservatives' "free trade" bloc headed by Lord Hugh Cecil nd nicknamed "the Hughligans."

In June 1904 accordingly, he made the dramatic gesture of "crossing the aisle" to the opposition benches in the House of Commons, thus initiating an affiliation with the Liberal "free trade" party which was to last for over twenty years.

In 1906 his two-volume memorial to his father, *Lord Randolph Churchill* (Macmillan), was published, and in that year he fought and won, in the North West Manchester constituency, his first election under his new party label.

Churchill was named Under-Secretary for the Colonies by the new Liberal Prime Minister Sir Henry Campbell-Bannerman, and in 1907 a Privy Councillor. The resignation of Campbell-Bannerman in April 1908 and the accession of Herbert Henry Asquith to the premiership and leadership of the Liberal Party brought Churchill advancement to President of the Board of Trade.

Because this was a Cabinet post he was required, by the practice of that time, to seek re-endorsement by his constituency. In the ensuing by-election in North West Manchester he alienated sympathizers with the suffragette movement, and was defeated by a Conservative opponent; but a few weeks later he was returned to Parliament through a second by-election in Dundee. It was during his electioneering in that Scottish constituency that he met the Honorable Clementine Hozier, whom he married in September 1908.

As a Liberal Cabinet member the thirty-four-year-old aristocrat paradoxically found himself more in harmony with the ideas of Chancellor of the Exchequer, David Lloyd George, than with Asquith. As President of the Board of Trade (1908-1910) and Home Secretary (1910-1911) Churchill authored progressive legislation such as that which established the British Labor Exchanges and Old Age Pensions.

He was made First Lord of the Admiralty in 1911, and being one of the comparatively few Britons who accepted the possibility of war with Germany, had the British fleet ready for action in 1914. In the spring of 1915, amid a storm of criticism because he had sponsored the British landings in 1912 on Gallipoli resulting in heavy casualties, he was demoted in the Cabinet to the "well-paid inactivity" of the Chancellory of the Duchy of Lancaster.

Early in 1916 Churchill relinquished this office and went to the front as a lieutenant-colonel in command of the 6th Royal Fusiliers, but in July he was recalled to Westminster by David Lloyd-George, (who had just succeeded Asquith as Prime-Minister) to become Minister of Munitions.

Retaining his Dundee seat at the "khaki election" of December 1918 Churchill continued in the Lloyd-George Cabinet as Secretary of State for War and for Air (1918-21) and for the Colonies (1921-22).

By the time of the general election of 1922, however, his popularity was at its lowest, partly because a new Anglo-Turkish crisis had revived memories of the Gallipoli disaster, and he lost his Dundee seat to an Independent candidate by a decisive margin of 10,000 votes. In the country at large the Conservatives were returned to power under the leadership of Andrew Bonar Law.

Out of Parliament for the next two years, Churchill devoted much of his time to laying bricks on his country estate, painting landscapes and compiling his four-volume work, *The World Crisis* (Butterworth, Ltd.; Scribner's, 1923-29), an admittedly personal analysis of the strategy of World War I, which Lord Balfour summed up as "Winston's brilliant autobiography, disguised as a history of the universe." The first volume was published in April 1923; others followed at intervals until 1929, and a one-volume abridgement was issued in 1931.

Still a Liberal at the time of the general election of 1923, Churchill contested one of the Leicester constituencies, but lost to a Socialist opponent. In the words of a biographer, Philip Guedalla, he was already "a little apt to view Socialism as half way to Moscow," and was so disgusted by the subsequent flirtation with Labor of the Asquithian bloc of his party, that when a by-election was called in the Abbey division of Westminster in 1924, he entered the lists as an "Independent Anti-Socialist" but failed by only a few votes to win this traditionally Conservative seat.

In the autumn of that year he ran again in the Epping Forest division of Essex under the label of "Constitutionalist," and easily defeated his Liberal and Socialist opponents.

Churchill's "modified acceptance of applied protection" in his campaign speeches paved the way for his readmission to the Conservative Party, and in all subsequent elections he has been returned to Commons as a Conservative. He represented Epping Forest until 1945, when the constituency was subdivided and he became the member for the Woodford and Wanstead part of the former division.

Having rejoined the Tories, he was promptly named Chancellor of the Exchequer in the Cabinet of Stanley Baldwin, who succeeded Bonar Law as Conservative leader. Churchill served for five years, during which period he "put Britain back on the gold standard . . . and helped to break the General Strike of 1926" (*Time* January 2, 1950).

After the Labor victory in 1929 Churchill was able to engage in much personal and literary activity. He completed *A Roving Commission,* the autobiography of his first thirty-four years, in 1930, and in the following year made another lecture tour in the United States. His books *The Eastern Front* and *Thoughts and Adventures* (Butterworth) were published respectively in 1931 and 1932, and from 1933 to 1936 he was at work on *Marlborough, His Life and Times* (Harrap, 1933; Scribner's 1933-38), the biography of his ancestor.

Following the Lausanne Conference of 1932 Churchill warned that "Britain's hour of weakness is Europe's hour of danger." But his predictions of a second World War were ignored by Baldwin, who did not ask Churchill to join his Cabinet when he returned to power in 1935. Churchill further alienated Baldwin in the following year when he espoused the cause of King Edward VIII in the controversy which led to the King's abdication.

However, with the outbreak of World War II, public opinion forced Neville Chamberlain, who had succeeded Baldwin in 1937, to reappoint Churchill on September 3, 1939, as First Lord of the Admiralty. In the following April, Churchill became Chairman of the Armed Services Committee, thus controlling the Army as well as Navy, and on May 10, 1940, he succeeded Chamberlain as Prime Minister. On taking office, he told the House of Commons, "I have nothing to offer but blood, sweat and tears." He defined the national aim as "victory at all costs" since "without victory there is no survival."

When the collapse of France made a Nazi invasion of England almost a certainty, he declared, "We shall defend our island, whatever the cost may be. . . .We shall never surrender." In June, on the eve of the air battle over Britain, the Prime Minister called upon his countrymen to bear themselves in such wise that "if the British Empire and its Commonwealth last for a thousand years, men will say, 'This was their finest hour.'"

Collections of speeches and articles by Churchill were published from 1938 to 1941 under the titles: *Arms and the Covenant* (Harrop, 1938) *Step by Step* (Butterworth, 1939); *Blood, Sweat and Tears (Into Battle)* (Putnam, 1941); *The Unrelenting Struggle* (Little, Brown, 1942).

The British war leader met with President Franklin D. Roosevelt at sea in August 1941 and drew up a joint Anglo-American declaration of peace aims known as the Atlantic Charter. Shortly after the Pearl Harbor attack, Churchill came to the United States to confer with Roosevelt and other American officials on Allied strategy, and on the 26th of December he became the first British Prime Minister invited to address a joint session of Congress.

He returned to Washington in June 1942 for conferences on strategy, at which time he made a joint statement with Roosevelt confirming their agreement on the opening of a second front in Europe. Other important policy and strategy conferences attended by Churchill included those with Roosevelt in 1943 at Casablanca (January), with Roosevelt and Chiang

Kai-shek at Cairo (November), and with Roosevelt and Stalin at Teheran (November); with Roosevelt and Stalin at Yalta (February 1945); and with President Harry S. Truman and Stalin at Potsdam (July 1945) (at which he was replaced by Clement Attlee, who became Prime Minister while the conference was being held).

After the surrender of Germany, Churchill tendered his resignation to the King on May 23, 1945. A general election was called in July 1945, which resulted in an overwhelming victory for Labor and the formation of a new Government under Clement Attlee. Churchill felt the repudiation of his leadership so keenly that he declined the knighthood in the Order of the Garter proposed at that time by King George VI on the recommendation of Attlee.

During his six-year period as leader of His Majesty's Loyal Opposition from July 1945 to October 1951. Churchill devoted much of his time outside Parliament to the compilation and writing of *The Second World War,* of which five volumes have so far been published by Houghton, Mifflin: *The Gathering Storm* (1948), *Their Finest Hour* (1949), *The Grand Alliance* (1950), *The Hinge of Fate,* (1950) and *Closing the Ring* (1951), the latter carrying the narrative up to June 5, 1944, just before the Normandy landings. Houghton-Mifflin published in November 1953 *Triumph and Tragedy,* the sixth and final volume of Churchill's World War II memoirs.

Speaking at Fulton, Missouri, in March 1946 at the invitation of President Harry S. Truman, Churchill used the phrase "Iron Curtain" for the first time. He warned the Western democracies to stand firm behind the United Nations and to suffer no division or faltering in their duty, asserting that there is nothing the Russians "admire so much as strength, and there is nothing for which they have less respect than for weakness, especially military weakness."

By the general election of February 1950 the Attlee Government was continued, but with a small majority. A new election was called for October 25, 1951, and Churchill, nearing his seventy-seventh birthday, appealing to British sporting instincts ("It is the last big prize I seek to win") again sought the premiership. His campaign resulted in the election of the Conservatives by a small margin.

On the domestic front, Prime Minister Churchill moved with caution during the next eighteen months, and while steps were taken to return the steel and motor transport industries to private control, he made no move to denationalize the railways or the Bank of England or to repeal such popular Socialist measures as the National Health Act.

A firm supporter of both the North Atlantic Treaty Organization and of the Council of Europe, that nucleus of an eventual European federation which he himself had taken a lead in founding, Churchill had almost continuously to cope with criticism from Aneurin Bevan and his wing of the Labor party.

Commenting on the Russian "peace offensive" launched after the death of Stalin, he stated that he would "be very glad to learn that in-

CHURCHILL, SIR WINSTON—*Continued*
formal talks could be held at the highest level"
(New York *Herald Tribune,* April 30, 1953).

His highest academic honor was conferred on
him in 1925, when he was made an honorary
Doctor of Civil Law by Oxford University. He
was Lord Rector of the University of Edinburgh in 1929-31 and Chancellor of Bristol
University in 1930. Between 1941 and 1952
Churchill was the recipient of seventeen honorary degrees from British and foreign Universities, including Cambridge, Columbia, McGill,
Oslo and Copenhagen. He has been Lord
Warden of the Cinque Ports since 1941.

His chief hobby for the past quarter of a
century has been landscape painting; he wrote a
short book on the subject, *Painting As a
Pastime* (Whittlesey; McGraw, 1949), and he
is an honorary Academician Extraordinary of
the Royal Academy. In his younger days he
was an expert polo player, fencer and tennis
player.

At his country home, Chartwell Manor, he
keeps fit by daily walks and frequent dips in the
swimming pool. Always an excellent showman,
the short, gruff British Premier has long made
the fat black cigar an adjunct of his personality. In Parliament he has frequently created a
good dramatic effect with the hearing aid which
oncoming deafness now requires him to use.

Selected References

    See also Magazine and Newspaper
    Indexes
    Arthur, Sir G. C. A. Concerning Win-
    ston Spencer Churchill (1941)
    Ausubel, H. and others Some Modern
    Historians of Britain (1951)
    Begbie, H. Mirrors of Downing Street
    (1923)
    Broad, C. L. Winston Churchill (1951)
    Churchill, W. L. S. War Speeches;
    comp by C. Eade (1952)
    Cowles, V. Winston Churchill: The Era
    and the Man (1953)
    Davenport, B. ed. Great Escapes (1952)
    Davenport, J. and Murphy, C. J. V. The
    Lives of Winston Churchill (1945)
    Dawson, R. M. Winston Churchill at the
    Admiralty (1940)
    De Weerd, H. A. Great Soldiers of
    World War II (1944)
    Eden, G. Portrait of Churchill (1945)
    Gardiner, A. G. Portraits and Portents
    (1926)
    Germains, V. H. Tragedy of Winston
    Churchill (1931)
    Guedalla, P. Mr. Churchill (1942)
    Gunther, J. Inside Europe (1940)
    Hawthorne, H. Long Adventure: the
    Story of Winston Churchill (1942)
    Hilditch, N. comp. In Praise of Church-
    ill (1946)
    Hughes, E. Winston Churchill in War
    and Peace (1950)
    Keynes, J. M. Essays in Biography
    (1951)
    Kraus, R. Winston Churchill (1940)
    Lockhart, J. G. Winston Churchill
    (1951)

    MacNalty, Sir A. S. The Three Church-
    ills (1949)
    Martin, H. Battle: the Life Story of
    Winston Churchill (1940)
    Moir, P. I was Winston Churchill's
    Secretary (1941)
    Nicolson, H. Winston Churchill (1948)
    Nett, S. Young Churchill (1941)
    Roberts, C. E. B. Winston Churchill
    (1940)
    Roosevelt, E. This I Remember (1949)
    Sherwood, R. E. Roosevelt and Hopkins
    (1948)
    Taylor, R. L. Winston Churchill; an In-
    formal Study of Greatness (1952)
    Thompson, W. H. I Was Churchill's
    Shadow (1951)
    Thomson, M. Life and Times of Win-
    ston Churchill (1949)
    Wingfield-Stratford, E. C. Churchill;
    the Making of a Hero (1942)

CHURCHILL, MRS. WINSTON. *See*
Lady Churchill, C.O.H.S.

CLARK, EUGENIE May 4, 1922- Ich-
thyologist
Address: b. c/o American Museum of Natural
History, Central Park West and 79th St., New
York 24; h. 817 West End Ave., New York 25

Popular interest in undersea life has been
considerably stimulated in the past two years
by the publication of Rachel Carson's *The
Sea Around Us* and J. Y. Cousteau's *The Silent
World*. In the summer of 1953 a new book,
Lady With a Spear (Harper) introduced to
armchair readers who take deep sea thrills
vicariously Dr. Eugenie Clark, ichthyologist
and research associate of the American Museum of Natural History.

Dr. Clark has studied fish in tropical waters
of the Atlantic and Pacific. For this task
she prepared herself not only with the conventional college and graduate degrees but with
an underwater mask and, where necessary, a
spear or net. She has explored the waters
around the West Indies, the Palau and Caroline
Islands of the South Pacific, and the Red Sea,
collected numerous specimens of rare and
poisonous fish, and, in a number of articles in
journals, made valuable contributions to the
science of ichthyology.

Eugenie Clark was born in New York City
on May 4, 1922, the daughter of Charles Clark,
who died when she was two, and Yumico
(Mitomi) Clark, now Mrs. Masatomo Nobu.
Her interest in fish began when she was a
little girl. Her Japanese mother, who worked
in lower Manhattan, would often leave her at
the old Aquarium, near the Battery, on Saturday mornings. There Eugenie first discovered
the wonders and delights of the undersea world.
She persuaded her mother to buy her a fifteen-
gallon aquarium for a Christmas present and
then began her own collection of fish. Her
collection extended to many other forms of
animal life, and she managed at one time or

another to keep an alligator, a toad and a friendly snake in her family's apartment.

When she graduated from Bryant High School in Queens, New York, and entered Hunter College, she had no problem in choosing her major field—zoology. In summers during her college years she did further study in zoology at the University of Michigan's biological station in northern Michigan.

After her graduation from Hunter College, Miss Clark worked for a while as a chemist with the Celanese Corporation in Newark, New Jersey, and she enrolled in evening courses in the Graduate School of New York University. There she did specialized study for the Master's degree in the anatomy and evolution of the puffing mechanism of the blowfish.

In 1947 she went to La Jolla, California, to work as research assistant to Dr. Carl Hubbs of the Scripps Institute of Oceanography of the University of California. At La Jolla she did her first diving in a helmet and learned to swim underwater with a face mask. Miss Clark relates in *Lady With a Spear* that she found the helmet clumsy and confining, but with the face mask she was free to explore the waters comfortably and thoroughly. She is inclined to minimize the dangers of her underwater research, although she admits to several slightly disconcerting encounters with sharks, barracuda, and giant clams. "Once you are familiar with the sea's dangers," she writes, "and know where to expect them and how to avoid them, you can roam with safety and assurance in a world of wonder that otherwise you will never really know."

Miss Clark spent a brief period in Hawaii in 1947, where she bought her own face mask and did independent research. She then returned to New York as research assistant at the Museum of Natural History. Simultaneously she began work for a Ph.D. degree at New York University. Her special research project was on the reproductive behavior of platies and swordtail species (her friends called her work the Kinsey Report on fish), and she made the first successful experiments in the United States on the artificial insemination of fish. This project was supported by the department of animal behavior, the New York Zoological Society, and the Atomic Energy Commission. Eugenie Clark's articles, "Artificial Insemination in Viviparous Fishes," which appears in *Science*, December 15, 1950 is an account of these experiments.

She did additional study at the Marine Biological Station at Woods Hole, Massachusetts, and at the Lerner Marine Laboratory in the West Indies. At Bimini, in the West Indies, she worked with Roger Sperry, a neuroanatomist, on experiments testing the vision of fish, especially the question of whether a fish can transfer to one eye the image it has seen with the other. The results of this study were published in *Physiological Zoology* for October 1949.

In June 1949 Dr. Clark was sent to the South Seas under the sponsorship of the Office of Naval Research to study the identification of poisonous fish. *Lady With a Spear* describes her visits to Kwajalein, Guam, Saipan, the

EUGENIE CLARK

Palaus, and other islands of the area. At each island she explored the surrounding waters with native fishermen from whom she learned the technique of underwater spear-fishing, and she collected and identified many specimens of poisonous fish.

Her studies were of special interest to the United States Navy-sponsored research program at the Loma Linda, California, School of Tropical Medicine, and it was to collect specimens of the "puffer" or blowfish type of poisonous fish for their research that she received a Fulbright Scholarship in 1950 to work at the Ghardaqa Biological Station of Fuad University in Egypt. Her headquarters was an isolated desert outpost at the edge of the Red Sea. The first woman to work at this station, and the first ichthyologist to complete a study of Red Sea fish since 1880, she collected some three hundred species of fish, three of them entirely new, thirty or forty of their poisonous. The results of her work were described by Dr. Lester Aronson, chairman of the department of animal behavior of the Museum of Natural History, as "adding materially to existing knowledge of poisonous fishes."

Dr. Clark received a Ph.D. from New York University in 1951. She has published many scientific papers. Of more popular interest was her article describing her field trip to the South Pacific (*Natural History* January 1951). In February 1952 she won the twenty-eighth fellowship of the Eugene F. Saxton Memorial Trust, sponsored by Harper and Brothers. Under this fellowship she wrote *Lady With a Spear* which Harper published in 1953 and the Book-of-the-Month Club named as a summer alternate selection. Clifton Fadiman praised *Lady With a Spear* as "not merely interesting and informative but a . . . story that exhales a quite special personal flavor."

(Continued next page)

CLARK, EUGENIE—*Continued*

In her book, Dr. Clark describes her encounter with a particular species of filefish found at Saipan Island "that could only come from the underwater fairyland one finds in tropical coral reefs. It was a golden-spotted, emerald fish, the minutest of the monacanthids, a toy-like jewel. . . . It wore bright yellow lipstick around a little mouth situated at the end of an elongated, tubelike snout. The eyes had remarkable irises: twelve radiating spokes of blue and orange. When we picked it up . . . it fluttered its delicate fins in rippling movement, stretched its tail into a tense fan, erected its long, sharp, dorsal spine, and lowered a little flap from its belly. It was a wrench to leave Saipan. So little is known about the fishes around this island that I could have spent my whole time there profitably."

Part of the personal story recorded in the book is Dr. Clark's account of her marriage to Dr. Ilias Konstantinu, a Greek-American orthopedic surgeon, of whom she says, "He had a personality that could tempt a female ichthyologist's interests away from fish." They were married in a Greek Orthodox Church in Cairo in June 1951 and on their honeymoon they went spear-fishing in the Red Sea. Dr. Clark, her husband, and their baby daughter, Hera, now live in New York City.

References

Coronet 33:122 Ap '53
N Y Herald Tribune p21 N 6 '51
N Y Times p 31 N 6 '51
Time 58:68 N 19 '51
Clark, E. Lady with a Spear (1953)

COLEMAN, JOHN S(TRIDER) Oct. 12, 1897- Business executive
Address: b. c/o Burroughs Adding Machine Company, 6071 2d Ave., Detroit 32, Mich.; h. 700 Seward Ave., Detroit 2, Mich.

A prominent advocate of an alert attitude of social and international responsibility on the part of American business management is John S. Coleman, president of the Burroughs Adding Machine Company, leading manufacturer of business machines. Associated with Burroughs since 1920, Coleman, who was trained in law and accounting, advanced in the company through sales and managerial positions in the Washington and Detroit offices to become president in 1946.

Born on October 12, 1897, in Charlestown, West Virginia, John Strider Coleman is the son of Charles Nelson Coleman, a hardware merchant and director of several local companies, and Nellie (Strider) Coleman. Having completed his early education at Charlestown's elementary and high schools, Coleman took a private course at the Emerson Institute in Washington, D.C. After a brief period of employment by the Guaranty Trust Company of New York, where he was assigned to the bond trading floor, he enlisted in the Army Ordnance Training School Reserves in 1917, and when he had finished seven weeks of training at Watervliet Arsenal, Troy, New York,

he was sent to France for two years' service as an ordnance sergeant.

For a short time after being mustered out of the Army in 1919, Coleman was employed in Washington, D.C., as an accountant in the payroll compensation division of the Federal Board of Vocational Guidance. When the Washington branch manager of the Burroughs Company visited Coleman's office at the guidance board on a sales call, Coleman became so much interested in the company's work that he joined the Washington sales staff of Burroughs in April 1920. He had meanwhile enrolled at Georgetown University Law School to study at night for his LL.B. degree, which was granted in 1924, graduating fifth in his class.

Manufacturer of business machines and machine supplies, the Burroughs Adding Machine Company, incorporated in 1905, produces portable adding-subtracting and bookkeeping machines; calculators; high-speed bookkeeping, accounting, and statistical machines; microfilm systems; and similar equipment. For the armed services it makes accelerometers, gyrosyns, aircraft instruments, and electronic fire control devices. With a staff of some 20,000 employees, it maintains executive offices in Detroit, Michigan; operates plants in a number of cities in the United States and abroad; and has eighteen marketing subsidiaries in foreign countries.

Coleman's rapid rise in the Burroughs organization has been attributed to his ability as a salesman, particularly on Government contracts, his training in law, and his proficiency as an accountant. After four years as a junior salesman and then as salesman in the Washington branch of the company, Coleman secured for Burroughs a million dollar Government order for machines to compute the veterans' benefits, when the first soldiers' bonus bill was passed in 1924. He was then made Government representative for Burroughs and in 1930 became assistant manager of the Washington branch. While in the posts of Burroughs' division manager for the East (1934-39) and assistant to the executive vice-president of the company (1939-42), he divided his time between Washington and company headquarters in Detroit. With his promotion to executive assistant of the company in 1942, Coleman moved to Detroit to make that city his permanent residence. In this position he directed Burroughs' contribution to the war effort, including the manufacture of the famous Norden bomb-sight on which, by standardization of parts, he was able to reduce the original cost of the process by two-thirds. After serving as vice-president and a director of the firm (1944-46), Coleman was elected president of Burroughs in October 1946 and in 1947 a member of the company's executive commission.

When Coleman took over the presidency of the firm, Burroughs was emerging from the war period with no government orders on hand and much obsolescent machinery on inventory. By scrapping and replacing seven-eighths of the company's machines, reducing the variety of models, and doubling the working force to a total of 15,000 employees, with a program for improved employee-management relations, Coleman doubled Burroughs' production from about 50,000 machines per year before the war to 100,000 business machines in 1947. A corresponding rise in profits in the first half of 1948 brought the company a net profit of $1.27 per share of stock. Burroughs' decline in profits since then has been attributed by Coleman to "the high rate of taxation and inflation." Commenting on the future of the company he has said, "I've learned that the adaptability of our machines to a wide variety of computing jobs is their greatest asset . . . Burroughs is essentially an expanding industry."

As an exponent of an enlightened industrial statesmanship, Coleman has addressed himself to the larger world of American business. In speeches before business and community organizations, he has repeatedly pointed out that the great power of corporate management implies great responsibilities to American society. Speaking at Iowa State Teachers' College in 1952, Coleman stated that "management has a twofold job. One has to do with production and distribution, the other with people . . . the function of management is to operate a successful organization both economically and humanly . . . to give every man a sense of function. Men will strive, but they must see the significance of their striving." In the employee relations program which he inaugurated at Burroughs, Coleman has tried to put this theory into practice. Applying the principles of "human engineering," the Burroughs organization has made an extensive effort to explain to its workers the significance for the individual employee of the company's industrial processes and financial policy. An attempt has been made to create an atmosphere of mutual cooperation in union-management relations, and the company takes an active part in the work of local community organizations.

An application of Coleman's ideas on business responsibility in the field of foreign trade was seen in his October 1950 announcement that the total equipment for manufacturing one line of calculators had been moved to a new Burroughs factory in Strathleven, Scotland, to make Burroughs products available to customers in dollar-short countries. Since some of the British-produced machines are imported into the United States, Coleman has argued, the Strathleven factory's dollar earnings can be made available to foreign customers for the purchase of American-made Burroughs parts. As president of the Detroit Board of Commerce, Coleman, who is an advocate of free trade, directed a ten-year study of America's foreign trade, which resulted in a report (November 1952) that called for the abolition of all United States tariffs as impediments to prosperity. "World trade is vital to Burroughs, and to the free world," Coleman wrote. "The strength of our allies depends on trade, largely with the United States. By buying from them we make it possible for them to buy from us." At the Chicago World Trade Conference in February 1953, he urged

JOHN S. COLEMAN

a gradual reduction of tariffs and simplification of the custom laws by the United States.

Regarding the Republican victory of 1952 as a challenge to the American business community to exercise its responsibility to the nation and the world, Coleman called on business and agriculture to help the new administration in the prevention of economic disturbances: "No sale of free enterprise will stick in the face of another depression." He told the Economic Club of Detroit in November 1952 that to retain leadership the businessman must have "the ability and willingness to make constructive proposals for the solution of the problems of the day. . . .Today we may indeed congratulate ourselves on our good fortune, but tomorrow we will be judged by our use of this opportunity."

He is president of the Employers' Association of Detroit and of the Detroit Board of Commerce, Vice-chairman of the United Foundation of Metropolitan Detroit, and is also class "C" director and deputy chairman of the Board of the Federal Reserve Bank of Chicago, and a director of the following organizations: the Michigan Bell Telephone Company; the Fruehauf Trailer Company; the Michigan Post of the American Ordnance Association; the Economic Club of Detroit; the Greater Detroit Hospital Fund; the Institute for Economic Education, Inc.; and the U.S.O. of Metropolitan Detroit. Other business and civic groups with which he is associated are the Michigan State Economic Development Commission, the advisory committee of the Wayne University School of Business Administration, the board of trustees of the Detroit Industrial Safety Council, the National Industrial Conference Board, the Detroit Advisory Committee, Junior Achievement, the industries advisory committee of the Advertising Council, and the lay board of trustees of the University of Detroit.

(Continued next page)

COLEMAN, JOHN S.—*Continued*

Coleman belongs to the University Club of New York, the Chicago Club, the Detroit Club, the Recess Club, the Engineering Society of Detroit, and the Newcomen Society of Great Britain, and is a member of the Free and Accepted Masons. Gamma Eta Gamma is his fraternity. In 1952 he was awarded an honorary degree of LL.D. by the University of Detroit. Married on March 15, 1921, Coleman and his wife, the former Elsie Hudson, of Cedar Rapids, Iowa, are the parents of a son, John Hudson Coleman. The business executive votes as a Republican; his church is the Episcopal.

References

> Business Executives of America (1950)
> Who's Who in America, 1952-53
> Who's Who in Commerce and Industry (1951)

COSTAIN, THOMAS B(ERTRAM) May 8, 1885- Author
Address: h. Lakeville, Conn.

At the top of the list of fiction best sellers for 1952 was *The Silver Chalice* (Doubleday) by Thomas B. Costain. This historical romance of the early days of Christianity is the seventh of Costain's novels and was published just ten years after his first novel appeared. In this decade Costain's books—among them *The Black Rose, The Moneyman, High Towers, Son of a Hundred Kings,* all published by Doubleday, have all held secure places on best seller lists, and each has been a selection of one of the major book clubs. He has also written two volumes of a popular history of England as part of a projected twelve-volume series, *The Pageant of England.*

Fifty-seven when his first novel was published, Costain had already had a long and successful career as an editor, including fourteen years on the staff of the *Saturday Evening Post* and several as fiction editor for Twentieth Century-Fox Films and for Doubleday and Company.

Thomas Bertram Costain, the son of John Herbert and Mary (Schultz) Costain was born in Brantford, Ontario, Canada on May 8, 1885. He was educated in the public schools of Brantford and before he had finished high school was the author of three ambitious but unpublished novels, one a 70,000-word romance about Maurice of Nassau. A mystery story which he submitted to the local newspaper, the Brantford *Courier,* while he was still in high school won him a job as a reporter on the paper. The job paid five dollars a week, and he took it, he told an interviewer in 1949, mainly so that he could follow Brantford's lacrosse team on their out-of-town games. "I started as a reporter on a little Canadian paper," Costain recalled, "and I think I was a good one. I still think of myself as a reporter in the sense that a reporter tries to be accurate and interesting . . . a writer has no right to be dull."

In 1908 Costain became editor of the Guelph (Ontario) *Daily Mercury.* Two years later he joined the staff of the Maclean Publishing Company and edited·three trade journals— *Plumber and Steamfitter, Hardware and Metal,* and *Milliner and Drygoods Review.* He became editor of *Maclean's Magazine* in 1910, a post he·retained for ten years until he came to the United States in 1920 to be an associate editor of the *Saturday Evening Post.*

In his fourteen years with the *Post* working under its famous editor, George Horace Lorimer, Costain served as both editor and talent scout, discovering and encouraging such newcomers as J. P. Marquand and Earl Derr Biggers. He became eastern story editor for Twentieth Century-Fox in 1934. With E. H. Ellis and P. Hal Sims he launched in 1937 a pocket-size magazine, *American Cavalcade,* to publish short fiction and general articles. Costain described it as "a promising infant, but it died young."

He resumed his editorial activities but they left Costain only a little time for his personal writing. During these years he published some stories and articles, some of them under a pseudonym, but there was scant opportunity for sustained periods of writing. In 1939 he joined Doubleday and Company as an advisory editor, a part-time arrangment which allowed him at least some time to write. It was not until 1946, however, after he had published four books, that Costain gave up his editorial duties and began to devote full time to his novels.

Costain turned to the writing of historical novels after trying four short modern novels which he never submitted to a publisher. He put into practice the advice which he had given so many beginning writers when he was a fiction editor. "Write about what interests you most," he had told them. His own interests had long been history and biography. He therefore prepared a non-fiction manuscript which he called "The Stepchildren of History,"—sketches of six colorful but little-known figures in history. His literary agent suggested that there was enough material in this manuscript for at least six books. Acting upon that suggestion, Costain began work on his first historical novel. So far, he has used four of these personalities—the pirate John Ward in *For My Great Folly* (Putnam, 1942); the English diplomat-general Sir Robert Wilson in *Ride With Me* (Doubleday, 1944) the Mongolian warrior Bayan of the Hundred Eyes in *The Black Rose*; and the French financier Jacques Coeur in *The Moneyman.*

Costain's first published novel was *For My Great Folly* (1942) and it became a selection of the Book League of America. It set the pattern for the novels which were to follow— historical romance based on extensive research, colorful detail, intrigue, swift pace, rousing action—all the ingredients, in short, of an entertaining adventure story. The author's intention in this tale of seventeenth century England and its relations with Spain was "to present a full picture of the life of those crucial times." To do this he studied in detail not only the history and manners but also the language, and especially the slang, of the time. The result was described by the *New Yorker* as "a better-than-average tale, with pretty ladies, dashing men, and the usual martial trimmings."

His second novel, *Ride With Me* (1944), became a Sears People's Book Club Selection, and to write it Costain spent more than fifteen months in research. He selected the Napoleonic era as the setting, his central character England's "forgotten hero," Sir Robert Wilson. Into his story Costain wove great scenes of battle and adventure—the fight on the Iberian peninsula, the retreat of the French armies from Moscow. Richard Match, in the New York *Times*, called it "a rousing and thoroughly entertaining tale, oversized perhaps, but not flabby, unashamedly but not lushly romantic."

The most ambitious and colorful of Costain's novels is probably *The Black Rose* (1945). Launched with a first printing of 650,000 copies, and a Literary Guild selection, its sales reached and have now topped the 2,000,000 mark in all editions. It was sold to Twentieth Century-Fox for a reported $125,000 and made into a film starring Tyrone Power.

Set in the thirteenth century against a background that ranges from England to Cathay and a set of characters which includes Roger Bacon and Kubla Khan, *The Black Rose*, wrote Orville Prescott of the New York *Times*, "swashbuckles with the best of them." Several reviewers compared it with the novels of H. Rider Haggard. Others suggested that it had something of the spirit of Sir Walter Scott's novels.

From the early Middle Ages Costain moved to the early Renaissance with his next book, *The Moneyman* (1947), the story of Jacques Coeur, the financier who directed the battle against the English at the end of the Hundred Years' War. This novel was a Book-of-the-Month alternate selection.

His next historical novel, *High Towers* (1949), a Dollar Book Club selection, was based on seventeenth century Canadian history, and Canada was also the scene of *Son of a Hundred Kings* (1950). Unlike his earlier novels, however, *Son of a Hundred Kings* is a novel of almost contemporary times. Its scene is a small Canadian town in the 1890's, and it is the story of the rising fortunes of a young orphan immigrant boy. Elaborately plotted and subplotted, the novel reminded several of its reviewers of the work of Charles Dickens. It was a selection of both the Literary Guild and the People's Book Club.

With *The Silver Chalice* (1952) Costain returned to the form of the historical novel. His subject is the making of the chalice which was to hold the sacred cup from which Christ drank at the Last Supper. This was a subject that had long held Costain's interest. He consulted more than 1,000 volumes in research, but the idea was crystallized for him, he has written, by a visit to the Cloisters in New York where the renowned Chalice of Antioch, which many believe was used at the Last Supper, was on display. Inspired by its beauty, Costain developed the character of the young artisan Basil, the craftsman who makes the chalice, and in the course of his adventures participates in many of the most stirring moments in the history of early Christianity. The novelist moves

Karsh, Ottawa

THOMAS B. COSTAIN

the action from Antioch to Rome to Jerusalem, and among the characters are Paul and Joseph of Arimathea.

The Silver Chalice was the selection of several book clubs—the Literary Guild, the People's, the Dollar, and Family Book Clubs—and was a book dividend of the Book-of-the-Month Club. It was also reported by *Publishers' Weekly* as the best-selling novel of 1952, both in "trade" and total sales.

Costain's works of non-fiction include a biography, *Joshua: Leader of a United People* (1943), which he wrote with Roger MacVeagh, and two volumes in the "Pageant of England" series—*The Conquerers* (1949) and *The Magnificent Century* (1951)—which cover the period from 1066 through the reign of Henry III. Of *The Conquerers* the historian Geoffrey Bruun wrote in the New York *Herald Tribune*: "Thomas Costain belongs to the school of Michelet in his conviction that history ought to be a resurrection of the flesh, and he is in the great tradition of Scott and Dumas in his ability to make it fascinating."

Costain was married in 1910 to Ida Randolph Spragge of Guelph, Ontario. They have two daughters, Molly (Mrs. Howard Haycraft) and Dora (Mrs. Henry D. Steinmetz). For many years the Costains lived in Bethayres, Pennsylvania. They live now in Lakeville, Connecticut, where they both sketch, collect antique furniture, and where Costain writes from three to four hours a day, seven days a week, averaging about 3,000 words a day. His current writing projects are a volume of Canadian history, an outline for a new historical novel, and a third volume of "The Pageant of England" series.

Thomas B. Costain has snow-white hair, a fair complexion, and blue eyes. Nona Balakian of the New York *Times* describes him as an "amiable, communicative personality." He holds an honorary degree of D. Litt. con-

COSTAIN, THOMAS B.—*Continued*

ferred by the University of Western Ontario. The distinguished author was reared a Baptist. He now attends the Protestant Episcopal Church.

A verbal portrait of Costain was penned by his daughter, Molly Costain Haycraft, in a publication of the Sears People's Book Club. She wrote: "His success story is not that of a man retiring and turning his hobby into a gold mine. It is that of a man doing two jobs at once to make a life dream come true . . . What is he like? I find him understanding and tolerant, as much friend as father. . . .He is delightful company and young in looks and heart. . . .He loves animals and won't even kill bugs, but his live-and-let-live policy does not, alas, extend to his bridge partners! He likes the theater and good movies, and they send him to his typewriter refreshed."

References

Book-of-the-Month Club News p4 Jl '47
N Y Herald Tribune Book Review p2 D 11 '49; p9 O 8 '50; p3 Aug 10 '52
N Y Times Book Review p15 Aug 17 '52
Newsweek 9:96 Ap 24 '37
Wilson Library Bulletin 20:186 November '45
Warfel, H. R. American Novelists of Today (1951)
Who's Who in America, 1952

COTHRAN, JAMES W. Jan. 6, 1915-
Veterans organization official; lawyer
Address: h. 16 Cousar St., Bishopville, S.C.

Elected as commander in chief of the Veterans of Foreign Wars at that organization's fifty-third national encampment in Los Angeles, California, in August 1952, James W. Cothran

Leo Stern
JAMES W. COTHRAN

has been active in the V.F.W. since his discharge from the Navy at the end of World War II during which he saw combat action in the Pacific Theatre. His first office with the V.F.W. was that of junior vice-commander for the Department of South Carolina, and after serving in several other posts was made senior vice-commander in chief in 1951. An attorney in Bishopville, South Carolina, Cothran participates in civic and church activities and other veterans' organizations.

The son of M. C. Cothran, James W. Cothran was born at Cartersville, South Carolina, on January 6, 1915. He received his grade school education in Timmonsville, South Carolina, and attended Timmonsville High School, where he was president of the junior and senior classes and a member of the debating team. After his graduation from high school in 1932, he enrolled in the University of South Carolina at Columbia.

While in college he was elected vice-president of the sophomore class, president of the junior class, and president of the Blue Key, national leadership fraternity. He was also the business manager of "Garnet and Black," the university annual, and a member of Kappa Sigma fraternity, the Interfraternity Council, the Clariosophic Literary Society, the Selden Society, the Cotillon Club, and the German Club. From the university he received the degrees of Bachelor of Arts in 1937 and Bachelor of Laws in 1939.

Cothran set up his law practice in Bishopville in 1940 and is a member of the firm of Baskin, Cothran and Lane. He saw three years service as an officer with the United States Navy during World War II, acting as communications officer during much of that period. Combat actions in which he took part were those of Matsuwa, Kurabu Zaki, Paramushiro, and the Kurile Islands, and he was a member of the invasion and occupation forces which took Leyte, Luzon and Okinawa.

On his return from the Navy, Cothran became a member of the Veterans of Foreign Wars and in 1946 was made junior vice-commander for the Department of South Carolina. The next two years he served as senior vice-commander, assuming the office of department commander in 1949. His next post was that of junior vice-commander in chief for the national organization, which he undertook in 1950, and the following year he became the senior vice-commander in chief.

Expressing the strongly anti-Communist tone of the convention which elected him commander in chief, Cothran refused to take office in the Los Angeles hall where the veterans had assembled because it had been used previously for a meeting of the Civil Rights Congress.

After an apology by Mayor Fletcher Bowron of Los Angeles in which he regretted that the veterans had been subjected to the "indignity" of using a hall which had been used for "the rantings of Communists," (*Christian Science Monitor,* August 19, 1952) the new commander in chief was sworn in at a new meeting place at the Biltmore Hotel. "I pledge you," he said, "that we will fight the Commies wherever they raise their heads—both at home and abroad."

He also asked that "the 55,000 known Commies be deported from the shores of America."

Another threat to America is inflation, Cothran continued. and he asked for a return to Francis Bacon's "four pillars of government—religion, justice, council, and treasure." He expressed the V.F.W.'s position that the United States must continue to assume its share in world responsibility, saying, "There is no bargain basement saving and short cut to national security in our role of world leadership. And with commitments to our allies, the cost will be a staggering one. But let us all insist that every dollar appropriated for the military shall become a dollar honestly and effectively spent on defense."

On his return from Europe, where he attended the dedication of an American monument at Suresne, France, under the auspices of the American Battle Monuments Commission, Cothran called on President Truman at the White House on October 13, 1952. He told the President that he had found that the progress of the European defense program and the organization of the joint military headquarters was excellent, and that the morale of American military personnel was high. In an Armistice Day message the V.F.W. commander stressed the unity of a large part of the peace-loving people of the world against Soviet aggression.

Speaking at a dinner on February 18, 1953 given by the V.F.W. to honor members of Congress who had served in the armed forces, Cothran stated that the veterans' organization favors universal military training and a foreign policy that makes it clear that although the United States will strive for peace it is prepared to defend its heritage with force if necessary.

On April 26, 1953 he attacked Representative John Phillips of California for "casting a shadow of suspicion" on the Government program of hospitalization and medical care for veterans, stating that the Congressman's desire for economy had led him to this viewpoint.

Cothran gave the 1953 Bernard M. Baruch Distinguished Service Award, with gold certificate of merit (highest honor of the Veterans of Foreign Wars) to Francis Cardinal Spellman, Roman Catholic Archbishop of New York on August 3.

In addition to the V.F.W. Cothran holds membership in the Military Order of World Wars and the American Legion. A member of the Bishopville Presbyterian Church, he is active in church affairs. He belongs to the Bishopville Masonic Lodge and Sumter Lodge of the Elks and is a past director of the Bishopville Kiwanis Club. His legal affiliations include the South Carolina Bar Association and the Lee County Bar Association.

The lawyer is a member of the University of South Carolina BAM Club, the South Carolina Wildlife Federation, and the Advisory Board of the State Forestry Commission of South Carolina. After serving as secretary of the Lee County Fair Association for 1947-1948, he became its vice-president in 1948 and its

president in 1949. He acted as chairman of the county Christmas Fund for 1948-1949 and 1949-1950.

He and his wife, the former Dorothy Parke of Columbia, South Carolina, have three children, James W., Jr., Thomas Parke, and Julia Lea.

References

N Y Times p22 O 14 '52

COUSTEAU, J(ACQUES-)Y(VES) 1911-

French naval officer; undersea explorer; author; photographer

Address: b. 48 Ave. de la Motte-Picquet, Paris XV, France; h. Villa Boabab, Sanary (Var) France

Co-inventor of the Aqualung, a portable breathing device which permits divers to swim about like fish at depths of 300 feet in the ocean without the use of cables or hoses to the surface or the burden of a heavy diving suit, Captain J.-Y. Cousteau has contributed much to the knowledge of life beneath the sea as well as to diving techniques. He has made six motion picture records of his underseas expeditions and is a pioneer of submarine color photography, being the first to take color pictures in the ocean's twilight zone.

A member of the French Underground during World War II Captain Cousteau and a group of Aqualung divers worked in 1948 to clear portions of the French Mediterranean coast of mines. *The Silent World* (Harper), written with Frédéric Dumas, published in February 1953, is an account of his experience during fifteen years of diving. His latest project involves the raising and duplicating of a Greco-Roman vessel, the oldest known cargo ship in the world, for the National Geographic-Calypso Marine Archeological Expedition, which he heads.

The son of Daniel P. Cousteau, Jacques-Yves Cousteau was born in 1910 in St. André-de-Cubzac, France. He spent his boyhood in his native country, with the exception of one year in the United States. After his graduation from the Naval Academy at Brest, France, he entered the French Navy as a midshipman, later serving as a gunnery officer on the cruiser *Dupleix* and other vessels.

Cousteau's interest in the world beneath the ocean was awakened one day in 1936 at Le Mourillon when, wearing diving goggles, he saw undersea life for the first time. He spent many hours "goggle-diving" and fishing with spears, arbalests, and soring guns, activities which he recorded in his first submarine movie, *Par Dix-huit Metres de Fond* (1942).

Goggle-diving soon became unsatisfactory because it did not allow him to penetrate deeply enough into the ocean nor to remain there long enough. After trying Le Prieur's independent diving gear, he designed an oxygen re-breathing outfit which allowed him more freedom of movement but which soon had to be discarded because the oxygen caused convulsions. During the German occupation of France in World War II Cousteau carried on

National Geographic Society
J. Y. COUSTEAU

his diving experiments to conceal the work he was doing for the French Underground.

Late in 1942 he went to Paris to find an engineer to aid him in the construction of a diving lung he had designed. The device would feed compressed air to the diver from three tanks fastened to his back. When Captain Cousteau discovered that Émile Gagnan had designed an automatic valve for feeding gas which embodied the desired principle, he worked with Gagnan to create the first model of the Aqualung.

Captain Cousteau satisfactorily tested in June 1943 in the waters of the French Riviera an improved Aqualung which has since made it possible for divers to descend to 300 feet and to remain under water up to an hour. The Aqualung was first manufactured commercially by the French Air Liquids company in 1946 and has since been sold to many divers in the United States.

The decision to test the Aqualung at depths lower than sixty feet was prompted by the desire of Cousteau and Dumas to investigate a sunken British steamer, the *Dalton*. After discovering that it was safe to work at the depth of the vessel, the two men decided to make experimental dives to determine the maximum depth to which a free diver could descend. Dumas reached a depth of 210 feet in October 1943, but it was not until four years later that the present world record of 306 feet was set. His experience with sunken ships provided the material for Cousteau's second movie, *Épaves* (1945).

With the end of World War II Cousteau was assigned to direct a collecting center for returning sailors in Marseilles. He became convinced that his diving experience could be useful to the Navy, and after showing the Marine Ministry his films he was commissioned to continue his experiments. He thereupon established the Undersea Research Group in 1946 which he headed with Phillipe Tailliez and which employed Frédéric Dumas as civilian specialist.

The undersea researchers assisted the French Government in 1946 in clearing German mines from the harbors of Toulon, Sète, and the Gulf of the Lions in the Mediterranean, using a team system of divers devised by Captain Cousteau to spot the mines. When they were requested by the French Navy to film a submarine maneuver, the men became interested in its cinematographic possibilities, and photographed the submarine *Rubis* laying mines and firing torpedoes in an escape-hatch sequence.

The group also made voyages in the Mediterranean and Atlantic to study oceanography, and conducted a series of experiments, using themselves as underwater guinea pigs, on the effects of explosives on the submerged human body. In these tests they discovered that the danger of such explosions had been over-rated.

The most dangerous moment in Cousteau's career came when he attempted to solve the mystery of the Fountain of Vaucluse, near Avignon, a pool which erupts once a year for no known reason and floods the River Sorgue. Dumas and Cousteau descended into the fountain in August 1946 and almost perished at a depth of 200 feet after nearly losing consciousness. They managed to struggle to the surface and discovered that the compressed air contained carbon monoxide.

In 1947 Cousteau set the world's record for a free dive by reaching 300 feet. This was broken in 1948 by his colleague Dumas, who reached 306 feet. The research group experimented with underwater television in 1947, and a year later went on an archeological expedition in which they recovered ancient art treasures from a Roman galley believed to have sunk in 80 B.C. off the coast of Tunisia, near Mahdia. The color movies which they took of the divers at work were the first to be taken at a depth of 127 feet.

Captain Cousteau and Professor Auguste Piccard were scheduled to descend in October 1948 in the latter's invention, the *Bathyscaphe*, to a depth of 13,000 feet in the ocean after the Undersea Research Group had assisted in the metal balloon's preparation. Although the vessel survived an experimental descent without men aboard, it was destroyed beyond repair on its ascent by the buffeting of surface waves.

The first color photographs to be taken at a depth of 150 feet were produced by Cousteau in 1951, when he served as the director of the Calypso Red Sea Expedition (1951-1952). In September 1952 the National Geographic Society announced that it would support a four-year expedition led by Cousteau. The principal interest of the expedition is oceanography, exploring the depths to learn the physical and chemical properties of ocean water. The expedition, supported also by the French Academy of Sciences, the French Navy, Education Nationale and the city of Marseille, was temporarily diverted from its schedule by a rare archeological find, a sunken Greco-Roman argosy of the third century B.C. which was discovered off the coast of southern France. The ship contained many treasures of ancient culture. Melville Bell Grosvenor of the *National Geographic Magazine* stated that "Their startling discoveries promise to add much to mankind's knowledge of the ancient world." Cousteau plans a movie of the salvage operations, and will sail a duplicate vessel on the course taken before the ship foundered.

Published in February 1953, *The Silent World* was written by Cousteau and Dumas as a record of their undersea adventures and explorations. A reviewer in *Saturday Night* (March 21, 1953) wrote, "Awe and beauty are two sides of wonder; therefore this book is truly wonderful." Cousteau wrote the original version in English, then rewrote it in French for publication in his native country; it has also been published in other languages. *The Silent World* was an April choice of the Reader's Digest Book Club and an alternate selection for July in Book of the Month Club.

Cousteau is the author of two previous books in French, *Par Dix-huit Metres de Fond* (1946) and *La Plongée en Scaphandre* (1949), and has published an article, "Fish Men Explore a New World Undersea" in the *National Geographic Magazine* (October 1952). His films are *Par Dix-huit Metres de Fond* (1942); *Épaves* (1945), English version *Full Fathom Five* (1946) and American version *Danger Under the Sea* (1952); *Paysages du Silence* (1947); *Autour d'un Recif* (1948), American version *Rhythm on the Reef* (1952); *Une Plongée de Rubis* (1949); and *Carnets de Plongées,* in color (1949).

Captain Cousteau has received the Légion d'Honneur for his aid to the Underground in World War II and he is a Capitaine de Corvette in the French Navy. He also holds the Personal Award for Creative Film-making of the Cannes Festival of 1946, and film awards in Venice, Nice, and Paris. His wife Simone and sons, Jean-Michel and Phillipe, also dive with the Aqualung. He has blue eyes, dark hair, weighs 145 pounds and is five feet eleven inches tall. James Dugan, his assistant, describes him as "a lean, bronzed man with a bold Mediterranean profile."

His explorations are oriented towards utilizing the sea's wonders for mankind. He stated that in the new under-water agriculture, animals will be bred in spaces fenced in by nets. He believes that when chemists find a cheap method to remove salt from the ocean, the soils accumulated in salt water estuaries can be purified and made available to man. In offering his color pictures to the world, Cousteau stated. "By the Aqualung, photoflash and hand-held camera, we have been able to pull aside more fully the dense sea curtain which, since the dawn of time, has shrouded from man's eyes a world of vibrant color—the world of the twilight depths, (*National Geographic Magazine,* October 1952).

References

Christian Sci Mon p2 Mr 6 '53
N Y Herald Tribune Book Rev p3 F 22 '53 por
N Y Times Book Rev p20 F 22 '53 por
Nat Geog Mag 102:431+ O '52 pors
Sci Illus 3:20+ D '48

COX, E(DWARD) EUGENE Apr. 3, 1880

—Dec. 24, 1952 United States Representative from Georgia; began law practice in Camilla, Georgia (1902); judge of the Superior Court of Albany Circuit (1912-16); Democratic member of the Sixty-ninth to Eighty-second Congresses (1925-52); opponent of the Roosevelt-Truman Administration. See *Current Biography*, 1943.

Obituary

N Y Times p29 D 25 '52

CROCE, BENEDETTO Feb. 25, 1866—

Nov. 20, 1952 Italian philosopher; historian; writer, in 1903 founded *La Critica,* which he edited for many years; made Senator for life (1910); in early 1900's wrote many articles and books on philosophy and the meaning of history; Minister of Public Information (1920-21); removed by fascists from the Senate and from his chair of philosophy at the University of Naples; after 1943 took part in activities for restoration of friendly relations between Italy and Western nations. See *Current Biography*, 1944.

Obituary

N Y Times p25 N 21 '52

CROCKETT, LUCY HERNDON Apr. 4, 1914- Author

Address: c/o Henry Holt & Co., 257 Fourth Ave., New York 10; h. Seven Mile Ford, Va.

Reprinted from the *Wilson Library Bulletin* May, 1953

Whether as author, artist, illustrator, designer, lecturer, or Red Cross worker, Lucy Herndon Crockett devotes her whole energy to the thing of the moment.

Her five books for children, and one nonfiction for adults, have been well received. She is proprietress now of the Wilderness Trading Post, a shop planned to give more expression to her gift for design. She has revived the almost forgotten art of *découpage,* popular on the continent and in England in the eighteenth century. She has traveled around the world extensively, living in army posts that were temporarily home, and in 1943 was sent by the American Red Cross to New Caledonia in a public relations post. Later it was Guadalcanal and the Philippines, then a year and a half assignment in Japan and a brief one in Korea.

Lucy Herndon Crockett was born April 4, 1914, to Nell (Johnson) and Cary Ingram Crockett in Honolulu, Hawaii, where Colonel Crockett was stationed with the United States Army.

The family background is old Virginia, where Miss Crockett and her mother now live at Seven Mile Ford, in the old Preston house, built in 1842 as a stage coach inn. One hundred years later Colonel Crockett, distant cousin of the original family, purchased the historic property and restored it. Now his daughter writes there and attends her shop which is becoming internationally known.

The oriental flavor in Miss Crockett's books comes first from her childhood. Later, after

LUCY HERNDON CROCKETT

schooling in Switzerland, England, and the United States, instead of going to college, she chose to follow her father to the Philippines where he had been assigned to the staff of Colonel Theodore Roosevelt, Jr., then Governor General of the Islands. The experiences of travel, life on army posts in Europe, Central and South America, and the Far East stimulated her latent desire to write.

In 1936 Miss Crockett came to New York, hoping to become a commercial artist. Her search for a commission to do book jackets led to the writing and illustrating of her first book, *Lucio and His Nuong, a Tale of the Philippine Islands* (Holt), published early in 1939. It was later chosen one of a group of thirty in an international graphic arts show at the Metropolitan Museum of Art.

Each of Miss Crockett's books has a definite relation to a place and her own experiences there. *That Mario* (1940), also with a setting in the Philippines, won a New York *Herald Tribune* award. *Capitan, the Story of an Army Mule* was published in October of the same year by Henry Holt.

While assigned to the Red Cross headquarters in Tokyo, Miss Crockett was asked to do a book on the American occupation of Japan. *Popcorn on the Ginza*, the author's first and only book, as yet, for adults, was published subsequently (1949). It is an informal portrait of social and economic adjustments among the Japanese.

Teru, a Tale of Yokohama (1950) grew out of the author's interest in Japanese children as sketching subjects. They made the first approaches to the strange foreigners who were changing their accustomed way of life and helped their parents in that adjustment. The New York *Herald Tribune* said,"No bare outline can suggest the wealth of information, of details of Japanese ways and difficulties in comprehending ours, that enrich these pages."

Pong Choolie You Rascal! (1951) is about a Korean boy who attaches himself to an Ameri-

can unit in the epic retreat from the Manchurian border. Eleanor Brent wrote in the New York *Times*: "This is a well knit, breathless adventure; it is also an important picture of the betrayal into tyranny and slavery that follows allegiance to Communist precepts. Subtle humor threads the story; Korean superstitions, prejudices, and daily customs are seen through Korean eyes."

Ruth Hill Viguers commented in the *Saturday Review*: "The author has . . . obviously done careful research for this book, and she writes with a light touch in spite of the grimness of the setting. The result is a bitter testimony against the futility of war and hatred. There is no idealization of any group. The sensitive child will not read this book; and will the child who is tough enough minded to read it see behind the filth, disease, and fantastic superstitions of the Koreans pictured here, the human spirit worthy of understanding and help?"

Tall and slender, Miss Crockett has brown hair and eyes and a distinctive speech, the original Virginian accent finely linked with those of the other cultures in which she grew up.

A book called *David Ingram* is tentatively scheduled for publication early in 1954. It is based on the life of the author's father in the mountains of Virginia. At present Miss Crockett is working on her first adult novel, a story of the Marines in the South Pacific, entitled "The Magnificent Bastards." Her time is divided between writing and carrying on the shop at Seven Mile Ford. Of this she comments: "I opened the shop to get away from the typewriter, because writing is such lonely work and also to be an outlet for my life-long desire to design." It is her purpose to give others an outlet also, for she is encouraging country crafts, reviving and rejuvenating many, and helping her friends in the Far East to find markets for their work. "Yet is it impossible," she adds, "to leave it [writing] alone and I hope I shall never be able to."

References

Atlanta Constitution p17 Ap 5 '50
Bristol Virginia-Tennessean p8 Jl 28 '50
Chicago Sun-Times Je 8 '51
Chicago Sunday Times My 27 '51
Los Angeles Daily N Je 21 '52
Roanoke Times N 5 '50; F 2 '52

Mahony, B. E. and others. Illustrators of Children's Books (1947)

CROSBY, BING May 2, 1904- Singer; radio, motion picture entertainer
Address: b. c/o Paramount Pictures, Hollywod, Calif., Bing Crosby Enterprises, 9028 Sunset Blvd., Hollywood, Calif.

NOTE: This biography supersedes the article which appeared in *Current Biography* in 1941.

One of the first "crooners," Bing Crosby started his career as a member of Paul Whiteman's trio, the Rhythm Boys, in the late twenties. He attained nationwide popularity in 1932 with his first broadcast over the Columbia Broadcasting System, and has since become one of radio's top-ranking entertainers, and the first to record his programs on tape. *College Humor,* his first important motion picture, was released in 1933 and is one of over forty movies he has made for Paramount Pictures, including the series of six *Road* comedies co-starring Bob Hope, and *Going My Way* (1944), which won Crosby an "Oscar" for his portrayal of Father O'Malley. His singing has changed with the years from his early "crooner" or "scat" style to a relaxed, easy delivery which has enabled him to include in his repertoire everything from cowboy songs to hymns.

During World War II, Crosby entertained troops overseas in England and France, while the fighting was still in progress. "The look on the faces of the men we entertained was better than money from Paramount. They were so glad to see us," he said (*Saturday Evening Post,* March 28, 1953).

Born in Tacoma, Washington, on May 2, 1904 as Harry Lillis Crosby, the singer earned the nickname of Bing by his fondness for a comic strip called the *Bingville Bugle,* according to "Call Me Lucky", an autobiographical sketch in the *Saturday Evening Post* (February 21, 1953). He was one of seven children of Harry Lowe and Catherine Helen (Harrigan) Crosby. Both of his parents were musically talented, and his father gave the boy an early introduction to music by purchasing a phonograph.

The family moved to Spokane, Washington, in 1906, where the elder Crosby became a bookkeeper for the Inland Brewery. The boy attended Webster grade school in Spokane and continued his education at Gonzaga High School. His first and only singing lessons ended when the teacher tried to make him do breathing and tone exercises, and refused to let him sing popular numbers. In high school he engaged in athletics, which has always been one of his strongest interests, playing basketball, baseball, handball and football. Elocution and oratory were stressed in Gonzaga, which was a Jesuit school, and in his study of these subjects Crosby developed the "phrasing" which has made his singing style clear and easy to understand.

The jobs at which young Crosby worked during his school days included delivering papers, thinning apples, work at a lumber camp and on a farm. His favorite job was as an assistant in the prop department of the Auditorium Theater where he had his first encounter with show business. At Gonzaga University in Spokane, which he entered in 1921, he joined a local band called the Musicaladers which played at high school dances and private parties. After playing the drums and singing with the band at a Spokane movie theatre, Crosby and Al Rinker, the band's piano player, were hired by the manager to carry on the show by themselves. In 1922 Crosby switched to the study of law at Gonzaga and worked part-time for a local law firm, but he soon decided that his future did not lie in the legal field and in 1925 he and Al Rinker started out for Los Angeles,

BING CROSBY

where Rinker's sister, Mildred Bailey, was a successful singer.

In Los Angeles the "Two Boys and a Piano", as they were billed, got a job at the Boulevard Theater with Mildred Bailey's help, and travelled the rest of the Fanchon and Marco circuit on the west coast. With Croby still playing the drums, they signed with the Morrisey Music Hall Revue. After the show closed, the team was booked into the Metropolitan Theater in Los Angeles, where Paul Whiteman heard them in 1927 and hired them as a singing act for his band. When they had finished their contract in Los Angeles, the team joined Whiteman at the Tivoli Theater in Chicago and audiences liked them. In New York they were less successful, however, and Whiteman was forced to drop them from the show, working them at odd jobs to keep them with the band.

When Harry Barris joined Crosby and Rinker to form the Rhythm Boys, the group was an immediate success. They sang at the Whiteman Club and made a number of recordings, now collectors' items, including "Mississippi Mud," 'From Monday On," and "My Suppressed Desire." Whiteman then booked the Rhythm Boys on a vaudeville tour of the Keith-Orpheum circuit, and on their return in 1930 they went to Hollywood with the bandleader to appear in his famous picture, *The King of Jazz.* After the movie's completion, the trio toured theatres on the west coast with Whiteman's band. When Whiteman fired Crosby in Seattle for not having a sufficiently serious attitude about his work, the trio left the band and returned to Los Angeles to score a success at the Montmartre Café. Their next engagement was at the Coconut Grove with Gus Arnheim's orchestra, where Crosby first sang on the radio over a two-hour nightly outlet.

While working at the Montmartre, Crosby had met Dixie Lee (Wilma Winifred Wyatt), a rising movie star, and they were married on

CROSBY, BING—*Continued*

September 29, 1930 despite the many warnings of Miss Lee's friends that the singer would never be successful. "Well-known Fox Star Married Bing Croveny," one headline read, testifying to Crosby's comparative obscurity at that point. After a disagreement with the manager of the Coconut Grove, the Rhythm Boys disbanded and Crosby made a number of movie shorts for Mack Sennett. Shortly after Crosby's brother Everett, who had taken over the management of his business affairs, sent Columbia Broadcasting System President William Paley a record of Bing crooning "I Surrender, Dear" early in 1932, the singer was heard over CBS from New York and immediately became a nationwide favorite. He appeared at the Paramount Theatre in New York for a record run of twenty consecutive weeks.

The success of Crosby's radio program prompted Paramount Pictures, whose star he has been since that time, to include him in *The Big Broadcast* of 1932, a movie featuring prominent radio entertainers. In the following year he had a starring role in *College Humor*. He also appeared in *Too Much Harmony* and *Going Hollywood,* which was one of Marian Davies' last movies. He made three more films in 1934, *We're Not Dressing, She Loves Me Not,* and *Here is My Heart.*

Crosby also signed a contract in 1934 with the newly-formed Decca Records, whose head, Jack Kapp, had worked with the singer for three years previously on records made for another company. Kapp is given the credit for toning down Crosby's singing style (getting rid of the "boo-boo-boos," for example) and for inducing him to sing many different types of songs, including Hawaiian, cowboy, Irish, patriotic, semi-classical, blues, ballads, and hymns. Crosby's records have been consistent best sellers and include such favorites as his theme song "When the Blue of the Night Meets the Gold of the Day," "Swinging on a Star," "Sweet Leilani," "Sunday, Monday and Always," and "Don't Fence Me In." "White Christmas" and "Silent Night," which have had the largest sale of his records, have become standard Christmas numbers.

Mississippi and *The Big Broadcast of 1936* were Crosby movie releases in 1935, and the following year he appeared in *Anything Goes, Rhythm on the Range,* and *Pennies from Heaven.* He left CBS in 1936 to star on NBC's *Kraft Music Hall,* which soon became one of the ten most popular programs on the air and on which he appeared for ten years. Part of his radio popularity is attributed to the relaxed, conversational style with which he conducts his programs and interviews guests and which is said to be identical with his off-mike personality. His 1937 movies were *Waikiki Wedding* and *Double or Nothing,* and in 1938 he made *Doctor Rhythm* and *Sing You Sinners.* The following year he starred in *Paris Honeymoon, Eastside of Heaven,* and *The Star Maker.*

The first appearance of Crosby and Bob Hope as a comedy team came in 1940 with the production of the *Road to Singapore.* Their comedy styles complemented each other and they departed from the script frequently, ad-libbing many of the best lines. Five more *Road* pictures have subsequently appeared, featuring Dorothy Lamour: *Road to Zanzibar* (1941), *Road to Morocco* (1924), *Road to Utopia* (1946), *Road to Rio* (1948), and *Road to Bali* (1952). Otis L. Guernsey commented in the New York *Herald Tribune* (February 8, 1953), "The Crosby and Hope style is flip, easygoing, whimsical and breezily paced, with perfect teamwork substituted for loud noise."

Crosby also appeared in *If I Had My Way* and *Rhythm on the River* in 1940, *Birth of the Blues* in 1941, and *Holiday Inn* in 1942. *Star Spangled-Rhythm* and *Dixie* were seen in 1943, and *Here Come the Waves* in 1944. One of his most highly-praised movies, *Going My Way,* was also made that year and co-starred Barry Fitzgerald. *Time* (May 1. 1944) said of his performance, for which he received the Academy Award that year, "Father O'Malley . . . might have been one of those brisk, bland, up-and-comers who have made an impure science of 'not acting like a priest at all.' Instead he is subtle, gay, debonair—a wise young priest whose arresting resemblance to Bing Crosby never obscures his essential power." During the war years he sang at service camps, hospitals, and on overseas short wave broadcasts, and in the summer of 1944 gave shows for the troops in Europe.

Duffy's Tavern, made in 1945, marked the first appearance of Crosby's four sons in a movie with the actor, and in that year he also repeated his role of a priest in *Bells of St. Mary's* with Ingrid Bergman. He created a precedent in 1946 by becoming the first major radio star to record his programs on tape in advance of broadcasting. He left NBC, which did not allow the recording of network shows, to move to the ABC network and a new sponsor. The experiment gave Crosby the freedom he desired, and proved successful in producing better programs by making it possible to weed out dull spots before broadcasting.

Crosby made *Blue Skies* and *The Emperor Waltz* in 1946 and *Welcome Stranger* the following year. *A Connecticut Yankee* was released in 1949, and Crosby films of 1950 were *Top o' the Morning, Riding High,* and *Mr. Music.* He returned to the Columbia Broadcasting System in 1949. In 1950 another Crosby, Gary, Bing's eldest son, achieved sudden popularity after several appearances on his father's radio show and the two made a record of "Sam's Song" and "Play a Simple Melody," which became a best seller. All four of Crosby's sons have appeared with him in an album of Christmas carols. In 1951 Crosby made *Here Comes the Groom* and the next year *Just For You.*

Crosby's long-awaited television debut occurred in June 1952 when he appeared on a "telethon" with Bob Hope to raise money for the United States Olympic Fund. "Bing's relaxed style and easy-going ways were made to order for home viewing," said Jack Gould in the New York *Times.* The singer sailed for Europe in September 1952 to make his latest film, *Little Boy Lost.* The first autobiographical material ever written by Crosby appeared in the *Saturday Evening Post* in eight installments from February 14 through April 4, 1953 entitled "Call Me Lucky." The work was published in cloth and paper-backed editions in June 1953 by Simon and Schuster.

Named as the greatest box office motion picture star in 1944 and 1945, Crosby has been one of the ten best money-making stars in the *Motion Picture Herald* Fame Poll in 1934, 1937, 1940, and 1943-1951. In *Motion Picture Daily's* Radio Poll in 1951 he was voted the best master of ceremonies and the most popular male vocalist and finished far ahead in a Gallup Poll of 1950 to determine the nation's favorite male singer. Gonzaga University gave him the honorary degree of Doctor of Music in 1937. He wrote the lyrics for "Waltzing in a Dream," "At Your Command," "From Monday On," "Where the Turf Meets the Surf," and "A Ghost of a Chance." Three biographies of the singer have been published: *The Story of Bing Crosby* by Ted Crosby (1937); *Bing* by Dr. J. T. H. Mize (1946); and *The Incredible Crosby* by Barry Ulanov (1948).

In addition to the income from his voice, Crosby makes a considerable financial profit from various business enterprises. His brother Everett manages Bing Crosby Enterprises and his brother Larry, the Crosby Research Foundation, which develops a variety of items to be marketed through another Crosby organization. Crosby Enterprises is one of the foremost producers of films for television. The singer owns a large amount of real estate, including a ranch in Argentina and a cattle ranch in Elko, Nevada, a home in Palm Springs, a place at Hayden Lake, Idaho, and a Beverly Hills home. Interested in horses and racing, Crosby was at one time part owner of the Del Mar Race Track and still owns and races some horses. An expert golfer, scoring in the low seventies, he was presented with the William D. Richardson Memorial Trophy in 1950 for his contribution to the game, including many benefit exhibitions. His home at Pebble Beach, California, is located near the famous golf course of that name. He is also an enthusiastic hunter and fisherman.

Crosby and his wife, Dixie Lee Crosby, who died November 1, 1952, had four sons, Gary Evan, Philip Lang, Dennis Michael, and Lindsay Harry. His clubs include the Bel-Air Country Club, the Lakeside Golf Club, the Friars, and the North Hollywood Marching and Chowder Club. He is a Roman Catholic. He is five feet nine and one-half inches tall, weighs 175 pounds, and has blue eyes and brown receding hair.

Bing signed on August 21 with CBS to resume his radio series, but agreed to accept a $500 penalty for every week in which he does not go on television. The singer's salary, less the $500 fine, is said to be $15,500 weekly. General Electric, his radio sponsor, hopes the deduction will hasten Crosby's entry into television.

References

Sat Eve Post 215:9-10 O 31 '42 pors; 215:26+ N 7 '42 pors; 225:17 F 14 '53 pors; 225:22 F 21 '53 pors; 225:30 F 28 '53 pors; 225:36 Mr 7 '53 pors; 225:40 Mr 14 '53 pors; 225:36 Mr 21 '53 pors; 225:38 Mr 28 '53 pors; 225:30 Ap 4 '53 pors

Crosby, T. The Story of Bing Crosby (1937)

Mize, Dr. J. T. H. Bing (1946)

Motion Picture and Television Almanac, 1952-53

Ulanov, B. The Incredible Crosby (1948)

Who's Who, 1952

Who's Who in America, 1952-53

CROSBY, HARRY LILLIS   See Crosby, Bing

CROSBY, JOHN C(AMPBELL) May 18, 1912- Radio and television reviewer
Address: b. c/o New York Herald Tribune, 230 W. 41st St., New York 36

Regarded as one of the most astute critics of radio and television, columnist John Crosby has brought to millions of readers the reactions of "the discontented listener." For seven years his column of provocative comments has been appearing in the New York *Herald Tribune,* and is also nationally syndicated in seventy newspapers. His efforts to raise the standards of air-wave communication have been recognized by several official awards, and some of his suggestions for improving programs have been adopted by broadcasting companies.

John Campbell Crosby was born in Milwaukee, Wisconsin, on May 18, 1912, the son of Fred G. and Edna (Campbell) Crosby. He was reared in his native city and in Oconomowoc, Wisconsin. He attended Milwaukee Country Day School and later Phillips Exeter Academy in New Hampshire where his principal extra-curricular activity was hockey. After he was graduated from the Academy in 1931, he attended Yale University for two years, where he was honored by being the first freshman to have a play performed by the Yale Dramatic Club.

The Milwaukee *Sentinel* gave Crosby a chance to be a reporter in 1933, and he covered police news and politics. Through his friendship with a fellow-member of the Yale swimming team, Whitelaw Reid, whose family published the New York *Herald Tribune,* he obtained a job as reporter on that newspaper. He was assigned to police stations and wrote occasional news stories, at a salary of five dollars a day. He admits that in this period he wrote a play, *The Mirror Cracked,* which interested Theresa Helburn of the Theatre Guild, who invited him to join the Guild's playwriting course. His play was optioned to five producers but was never produced.

He entered the Army in 1941 as a private, and reached the rank of captain. During the

Herald Tribune—Warman
JOHN CROSBY

latter half of the war, he wrote newscasts for the Army News Service. Returning to the *Herald Tribune* in 1946, he was asked to write a radio column. At that time he did not own a radio and knew very little about the programs. He was just as surprised as his editors were by the immediate success of his "five-a-week" columns, the first of which was published May 6, 1946. In September, he was signed by the *Herald Tribune* for national syndication, and the first paper to buy his column was the *Philadelphia Record*.

Avoiding press agents and radio people, Crosby began writing his columns away from the *Herald Tribune* office, refusing to be influenced by anything but what he heard on the air waves. He soon developed a reputation for frank criticism and fair analysis. Sixty per cent of his reviews were unfavorable, and several of his attacks ran in series. He wrote eight columns criticizing breakfast programs. Commentator Gabriel Heatter also drew some pointed criticism. He attacked "give-away" programs built on the "questionable theory that philanthropy is an adequate substitute for talent." He commended broadcasts of great music, dramatizations of the world's great books, and praised the Fred Allen and Arthur Godfrey and Henry Morgan programs, and sports broadcasts.

Within approximately three months after beginning his "Radio in Review" column for the *Herald Tribune,* Crosby received four increases in salary. He refused a request to appear in a radio show. Of his job as a radio reviewer he finds the most unpleasant aspect is the monotony. He wrote that, "A radio columnist is forced to be literate about the illiterate, witty about the witless, coherent about the incoherent" (*Out of the Blue,* Simon and Schuster, 1952.).

When Crosby completed his first year as a radio critic in 1947, his column had gained sufficient prestige to be moved from the classified section to the New York *Herald Tribune's* entertainment page. He wrote at this time that radio was showing an increased vitality and an awakening of refreshing ideas which had not been apparent when the column began. He spent several weeks listening to radio in the Mid-West to discover whether it differed from programs originating in Hollywood and New York. He looks and listens conscientiously, and seldom writes a review until he has monitored a program at least three times.

He rarely praises with a flow of adjectives, preferring to indicate his enthusiasm mildly. He wrote that Ed Gardner of *Duffy's Tavern* had "restored to honorable estate the comedy of insult." Of *The Author Meets the Critics* radio program, Crosby commented that "as a literary discussion it lacks the urbanity usually associated with books and the detachment that ought to accompany criticism; but if it had these qualities it probably wouldn't be such a good show" (New York *Herald Tribune,* January 23, 1948). He believes that the type of program "with a lead in listenership over all others, is news." In Crosby's opinion, Governor Thomas E. Dewey was the first political candidate to use televison properly.

Discussing the impact of television on our culture, Crosby wrote that it is destroying both the art of conversation and the art of dining. The only bright side to this, he believes, is that it will force competing media to greater cultural effort. He favors a limited number of non-commercial educational television stations which will be used by schools, museums and art galleries. "Television is the greatest challenge ever presented to an educator," he wrote in his November 27, 1950 column.

"They are letting go by default the greatest educational medium ever devised as they let radio go by default to the commercial interests. . . . .Television demands of an educator imagination, integrity, resource and plain hard work. . . . .Educators are the hardest people in the world to educate. They have been using a blackboard and eraser since the University of Bologna was founded in the twelfth century; they accepted with some reluctance the invention of type and, with even greater reluctance the development of visual education, used with such great success by the Army, Navy and Air Force."

The presidential campaign of 1952 drew penetrating comment from Crosby. "I can't recall any previous election year in my short, grief-spattered history," he wrote, "in which so many respectable people were called liars right out on the air for all of us to see. . . . .Senator Joseph McCarthy . . . is being used on any new program that deals in controversy—not to shed enlightenment, which doesn't command much interest—but to throw mud, which does." He stated on April 3, 1953 that "Ever since Adlai Stevenson turned in such an extraordinary performance as a laugh-maker during the campaign, all the other politicos have been aching to get into the act . . . how are you going to keep the politicians down in city hall after

tion and, along with Representative William Gordon of Ohio, he was one of the twenty-four Congressmen who voted against conscription. He also "offered to Mr. Wilson's Espionage Bill an amendment for the behoof and protection of 'philosophical anarchists' " as well as other conscientious objectors; and to finance the war proposed a national single tax for the raising of revenue (New York *Times*, August 16, 1918). Having lost the support of the Cleveland Democratic political organization, both Crosser and Gordon were defeated for renomination by organization candidates in the August 1918 primaries. Two years later (1920) Crosser lost by a single vote.

Early in 1920 the former Ohio Congressman formed with Alvord Bishop and Edward Blythin the new Cleveland law firm of Crosser, Bishop and Blythin and continued in practice until shortly after his re-election to the Sixty-eighth Congress convening March 4, 1923. Crosser had the support of the powerful railroad brotherhoods as well as other labor groups, and has held his seat through every subsequent election, while challenged biennially in the primaries from the Cuyahoga County Democratic organization. For ten years he was technically a member of the opposition party and as such had only meager opportunity to carry to success any personally sponsored legislation of controversial character. In March 1931 he was prominent in an attack on the Capper-Kelly price-fixing bill, and in February 1932 he introduced a bill to encourage operation of American passenger airship lines between the United States, Europe, and the Orient by "amending the Merchant Marine Act to enable the Postmaster General to make mail contracts with air lines similar to those of the ocean liners." (Crosser discussed the whole matter of "construction in the United States by private capital of airships for use in foreign commerce" in his article "For An Air Marine" in the New York *Times* of June 26, 1932.) The Air Line Pilots Association, an affiliate of AFL, was to confer on Crosser six years later an honorary membership carrying the title of "Chief Pilot (International)" in recognition of "meritorious and unselfish service" repeatedly rendered to the air line pilots "when their horizons were beclouded with trouble and uncertainty."

With the return of his party to control of Congress in March 1933, Robert Crosser was named to the new Democratic Steering Committee in the House of Representatives; he became its first chairman and was again to serve as chairman in the Seventy-eighth Congress (1943-44). As a member of the House Committee on Interstate and Foreign Commerce, the Cleveland legislator played a prominent role in the passage in 1934 of amendments to the Railroad Labor Act, which (in the words of President D. B. Robertson of the Brotherhood of Locomotive Firemen and Enginemen five years later) established "the right of railroad workers to organize and bargain collectively." Also in 1934, in association with Senator Robert F. Wagner of New York, he sponsored the original Railroad Retirement Bill, passed by both houses and signed by President Franklin D. Roosevelt, but invalidated by the Supreme

Court early in the following year on the ground that it violated the "due process" clause of the Constitution. A revision intended to meet the Court's objection was brought forward by Wagner and Crosser soon afterward, and was accompanied in the House by a proposal by Crosser that a three-quarters majority should be required in the Supreme Court to invalidate Federal legislation.

Completion by Robert Crosser of twenty-five full years as a member of Congress was celebrated at a testimonial dinner in Cleveland on April 22, 1939, when Speaker Sam Rayburn delivered the principal address. At this time an editorial in the Cleveland *Plain Dealer* called the Scottish-born legislator "an uncommon Congressman" who "with Caledonian tenacity sticks to his convictions, whether or not they are popular at the moment." President Robertson of the Firemen's and Enginemen's Brotherhood expressed his belief that Crosser's name would be "forever identified" not only with the Railway Labor and Railroad Retirement Acts but with the Railroad Unemployment Compensation Act, the passage of which he attributed "in large measure to the fact that it bore the name and carried the endorsement of Robert Crosser."

During the Republican-controlled Eightieth Congress (1947-48) Crosser's votes were recorded against the banning of portal-to-portal pay suits (February 1947), and overriding President Truman's vetoes of the Taft-Hartley law (June 1947) and the railroad antitrust exemption bill (June 1948); and in favor of the $6,000,000,000 appropriation for Marshall Plan aid (March 1948) and the displaced persons bill (June 1948).

Upon the return of the legislative branch of the Federal Government to Democratic control on January 3, 1949, Robert Crosser became Chairman of the House Committee on Interstate and Foreign Commerce, which post he held throughout the Eighty-first and Eighty-second Congress. In September 1949, with eighteen members of the thirty-man committee, he visited Great Britain to study the national health programs of England and other countries and British developments in transportation and jet propulsion. Earlier in the year, with Senator Dennis Chavez of New Mexico and Representative Charles A. Wolverton of New Jersey, he had visited Mexico in connection with proposals to grant a $200,000,000 loan to that country for the development of its petroleum fields, and on return had recommended such a loan.

Following the outbreak in June, 1950 of the Korean War, Crosser named a subcommittee of the Interstate and Foreign Commerce Committee to check on the preparedness of American industry to meet the new emergency; another subcommittee appointed by Crosser was that designated in August 1951 to conduct a broad investigation of the Securities and Exchange Commission.

Meanwhile, in the Eighty-first Congress Crosser had voted in favor of extension of the trade agreement act (February 1949) and extension of the rent control act (March 1949), and against a 50 per cent cut in European arms aid (August 1949). He opposed cutting Federal spend-

CROSSER, ROBERT—Continued

ing by $600,000,000 (May 1950) and upheld a bill to increase farm price supports of $2,000,-000,000 (June 1950). During the Eighty-second Congress he voted "nay" on the tidelands oil bill (July 1951) and on a proposal to use the Taft-Hartley law to end the steel strike (June 1952), and supported the $7,500,000,000 foreign assistance bill (August 1951) and the measure for keeping 90 per cent farm price supports (June 1952). The Ohio Representative, who lost the chairmanship of the Interstate and Foreign Commerce Committee as a result of Republican control of the Eighty-third Congress convening in January 1953, had the gratification of winning election to his nineteenth term by a majority of 99,520 votes to 49,947 for his opponent. (Even the Cuyahoga County organization had given him "token support" in the 1952 primaries.) "Today," remarked the New York *Times,* "he stands as one of the nation's political marvels—a man who cannot be beaten."

The seventy-eight-year-old Congressman has long been the president of the National Popular Government League; other organizations to which he belongs are the St. Andrew's Scottish Benevolent Society in Washington, D.C., and the City Club and Western Reserve Historical Association in Cleveland. Honored by Kenyon College with the Master of Civil Laws degree in 1929, he was also awarded an honorary LL.D. degree from that college in 1942. In a ceremony in Mexico City on December 6, 1951, he had conferred upon him the Aztec Eagle Medal from the Government of Mexico. Crosser also holds honorary life membership in the Brotherhood of Railroad Signalmen of America. Married on April 18, 1906, Crosser and his wife, Isabelle Dargavel (Hogg) Crosser, before her marriage secretary of an industrial company, had four children: Justine (deceased), Barbara (Mrs. Sweeny), Robert, and James (deceased). The gray-haired Congressman stands six feet tall and weighs about 165 pounds. His chief intellectual diversion from his Congressional duties is in the study·of philosophy, on which subject he would like some day to complete and publish his own treatise.

References

Cincinnati Enquirer p16 Ja 24 '44
Congressional Record p6798-7803 Ap 27 '39
N Y Times IV p10 N 16 '52
Biographical Directory of the American Congress, 1774-1949 (1950)
Congressional Directory (1952)
International World Who's Who (1949)
Who's Who in America, 1952-53
Who's Who in the Midwest (1949)
Who's Who in the Nation's Capital, 1938-39
Who's Who in United States Politics (1952)
World Biography (1948)

CUNNINGHAM, MRS. JAMES L. *See* Jenkins, S.

CURTICE, HARLOW H(ERBERT) Aug. 15, 1893- President of General Motors Corporation

Address: b. c/o General Motors Corporation, Detroit, Mich.; h. 1810 Overhill Dr., Flint, Mich.

Elected president of General Motors Corporation on February 2, 1953, Harlow H. Curtice succeeds in that office Charles E. Wilson, who became Secretary of Defense in the Cabinet of President Dwight D. Eisenhower. Curtice, who also holds the chairmanship of the corporation's operations policy committee and administration committee, first became associated with General Motors in 1914 as bookkeeper of its AC Spark Plug Company. After fifteen years as president of the Buick Motor Division, beginning in 1933, during which time he was responsible for developing Buick into one of the corporation's highest selling companies, he was named executive vice-president of General Motors in 1948.

Harlow Herbert Curtice was born near Eaton Rapids, Michigan, on August 15, 1893, the son of Marion Joel and Mary Ellen (Eckhart) Curtice. During his vacations from study at Eaton Rapids High School, he took care of his father's books and attended to car lot shipments of fruit that his father, a commission merchant, had purchased from local growers. Later Curtice worked as a shipping clerk in a small Eaton Rapids woolen mill, from which position he resigned in 1912 to study accounting and allied business subjects at Ferris Business College in Big Rapids, Michigan. A few months after ·graduation in 1914, he went to Flint, Michigan, to begin his career with General Motors in the AC Spark Plug Division, having answered a newspaper advertisement for a bookkeeper.

Within a year at AC Spark Plug, Curtice was made comptroller, thus enjoying the distinction at the age of twenty-one of being the youngest executive in the automotive industry. For a time during World War I he served in the United States Army; then he returned to his former position and in 1923 was made assistant general manager while retaining his duties as comptroller. Four years later he became AC Spark Plug's vice-president and assistant general manager engaged in manufacturing management and in 1929 he was named president of the company. Under Curtice's leadership in the depression years, the company's product line expanded and employment increased.

When, in the fall of 1933, Curtice was chosen president and general manager of Buick Motor Division, oldest division of General Motors, Buick was selling only 2.9 per cent of the auto industry's total. Production had fallen off to a low of 40,621 units, less than one-sixth of Buick's 1926 peak of 266,753 cars and less than its output of 43,946 cars in 1915, at which time it had begun its climb to leadership as a volume producer. Under Curtice's management the first step taken to offset this decline was the introduction of a new car, the Series 40 Buick, which was 550 pounds lighter and 150 dollars cheaper than the preceding model. This car, brought into production by May of 1934, raised

Buick sales to 63,067 units that year, an increase of almost 50 per cent over 1933. Meanwhile, more than $8,000,000,000 was spent for new machinery, equipment, and plant rearrangement, and in November 1934 the Buick factory sales organization was set up exclusively to distribute Buick production. Toward the end of 1935 Buick introduced a completely redesigned line of 1936 model cars, contributing such features as a convex front fender, a sloping roof, and an engine that enabled the shift from ten to sixty miles per hour in thirty seconds. The result was a production increase to 179,533 units in 1936, raising Buick's percentage of the industry's volume to 4.9. In 1938 the company rose from sixth to fourth place in the industry and accounted for 8.5 per cent of the total automobile sales. In 1940 Buick produced 311,403 units, the greatest volume to that date in Buick's history, in 1941 surpassing this record by the production of 377,428 cars.

The threat of war having arisen in 1940, Curtice offered Buick's facilities to William S. Knudsen, who had left the presidency of General Motors to direct the National Defense Advisory Committee. Late in the year Knudsen selected Buick to build and operate a Pratt and Whitney aircraft engine plant near Chicago. Curtice took personal charge of this project, which, under his guidance, saw automobile production methods adapted to the airplane engine to give the Army the one thousand a month volume it needed. In March 1941 construction was begun on Buick's new engine plant at Melrose Park, Illinois, and in January 1942 the first engine was completed and accepted months ahead of schedule. The plant, keeping ahead of schedule, during the war delivered to the Army 74,797 engines, enough for 18,699 four-motored Liberator bombers. Buick undertook more than thirty other war assignments, one of its most notable achievements being the development and production of the M-18 Hellcat tank destroyer, reportedly the first mobile Allied weapon to prove a match for heavy German tanks.

With the return of peace in 1945, Curtice guided Buick's reconversion program, rebuilding, expanding, and modernizing facilities to enable Buick to produce more than 500,000 cars a year. In an address before a meeting of southern California Buick dealers held in Los Angeles on March 10, 1947, he described Buick's then nearly completed expansion and modernization program as including the production of seventeen new buildings and the provision of 2,325,000 additional feet of floor space. In March 1948, while on a five-thousand-mile tour to discuss factory sales, manufacturing, and engineering plans with dealers in the Western States, he made known at a meeting of Buick representatives in Chicago that Buick orders had reached "record level."

In September 1948 Curtice was appointed to the newly created position of executive vice-president of General Motors in charge of general staff activities, including distribution, styling, engineering, manufacturing, research, personnel, employee relations, public relations, business research, procurement and schedules, facilities and processes, real estate, and the Motors Holding Division. This position, which he as-

HARLOW H. CURTICE

sumed on November 1, made him "C. E. Wilson's right hand," in the words of Charles M. Sievert of the New York *World-Telegram*; he sat in "on labor policy, later negotiating defense contracts, almost commuting to Washington in his private plane to tackle material restrictions and price ceilings." Concerned with the manufacturing scope of the entire industry, he had a responsibility for all divisions of the corporation: Oldsmobile, Chevrolet, Pontiac, Buick, Cadillac, Allison, Fisher Body, Delco Radio, and Truck and Coach. When Charles Erwin Wilson, president of the corporation since 1940, resigned on December 1, 1952, to become Secretary of Defense in Dwight D. Eisenhower's Cabinet, Curtice succeeded to the top position at G.M.C., being formally elected, after a short period as acting president, on February 2, 1953.

In Detroit in late December he had spoken optimistically of the ensuing year, predicting that the easing of Government restrictions on basic materials and an expanded market of prospective new car buyers would mean a "substantial market" for automobiles in 1953. *Time* magazine reported him as stating that General Motors' sales would advance from 1952's $7,500,000,000 to a record of $9,000,000,000 or more in 1953. The objective of the corporation, one of its officials has said, is to regain its pre-World War II sales volume of 47 per cent of all cars on the street.

Discussing his formula for success in an address at Olivet College, Michigan, Curtice advised: "Do it the hard way. Think ahead of your job. Then nothing in the world can keep the job ahead from reaching out for you. Be bold, knowing that finally no one can cheat you but yourself." Curtice is a director and secretary of the Automobile Manufacturers Association, a member of the Business Advisory Council for the Department of Commerce, a member of the board of trustees and the research policy committee of the Committee for

CURTICE, HARLOW H.—*Continued*

Economic Development, a member of the advisory council for the School of Industrial Management of Massachusetts Institute of Technology, a member of the industry advisory committee of the Advertising Council, director of the United Foundation of Detroit, director of the Economic Club of Detroit, and a member of the Detroit Board of Commerce.

His clubs are the Recess, the Detroit, the Detroit Athletic, the Elks, and the University of Michigan Club of Detroit. He has also been active in the civic affairs of Flint, Michigan, the city in which he has maintained his residence since he joined General Motors in 1914. There he is chairman of the Board of the Genesee County Savings Bank, Trustee of the Clara Elizabeth Maternal Health Fund, a past president of the Flint Community Association, which formerly headed all civic activities in the city, and a member of the Flint Chamber of Commerce, the Flint City Club, and the Flint Golf Club. In 1938 he was awarded an honorary LL.D. degree from Olivet College.

By his marriage on May 5, 1927, to Dorothy Biggs of Sherman, Texas, Curtice is the father of three daughters, Mary Leila, Dorothy Anne, and Catherine Dale. Living with his family in the Woodcroft section of Flint, he commutes the sixty-seven miles to Detroit almost every weekday by company plane. For recreation he prefers hunting or fishing or attending a football or baseball game. Curtice is a Republican, and a Presbyterian. The G.M.C. executive, who has pale blue eyes and graying red hair, has been described by *Fortune* as "a rather slight man, of erect, graceful carriage, careful dress, and natural reserve . . . [who] speaks softly and to the point, but with a subtle sense of humor."

References

Fortune 36:93+ N '47
N Y Herald Tribune p1 N 21 '52; p24 F 3 '53 por
N Y Times p33 F 3 '53 por
N Y World-Telegram p6 Ja 24 '53 por
Newsweek 40:61-2 D 1 '52
Time 60:68 D 1 '52
Business Executives of America (1950)
Who's Who in America, 1952-53

DALRYMPLE, JEAN Sept. 2, 1910- Theatrical publicist; producer; director

Address: b. & h. 110 East 55th St., New York 22, N.Y.

Of the leading dozen Broadway publicists, only one is a woman, Jean Dalrymple, who has also gained further distinction as a producer of a number of successful plays. Beginning as a writer, she has since been a vaudeville actress, a publicist, producer, and tour manager.

Miss Dalrymple, has written a play *Seven Women*, which is scheduled for an early production by Gilbert Miller. She will produce *October Gal*, a comedy by Charles Robinson.

One of the founders and members of the board of the New York City Center, she has been very active in raising funds for the Center's productions, and obtained permission from the late George Bernard Shaw to produce several of his plays there.

Jean Dalrymple was born in Morristown, New Jersey, on September 2, 1910. Her parents, George and Elizabeth (Collins) Dalrymple, were well-to-do. Her grandfather had been an officer in the Civil War, who afterwards founded a coal and lumber business in New Jersey. Raised in Morristown, Jean's public school education was limited to six months in a Newark school, and thereafter she was tutored by a governess and a cousin. She taught herself French and Spanish, which she speaks fluently.

At the age of nine she sold her first short story, "The Spinning Top," to a Newark newspaper for $1. Later she wrote a series of stories in a Philadelphia paper for which she received $5 each. Her earliest ambition, which dates from the first play she ever saw, *Snow White and the Seven Dwarfs*, was to be a stage director (Helen Colton in *Film and Radio Discussion Guide*, Volume XI, No. 1). So enamoured was she of this play that she went around giving performances of it for her playmates, playing almost all the parts herself. By the time she was twenty-one she had written vaudeville sketches and helped to "doctor" several produced plays.

After taking a course in a business school in New York, Miss Dalrymple obtained a stenographer's job in a Wall Street brokerage firm at $12 a week. She said that she was only sixteen at the time, but gave her age as four years older. By the time she was eighteen, she was earning $75 a week as secretary to one of the executives of Dominick and Dominick, 115 Broadway. She admits that she had made a substantial profit in the stock market at the end of four years, when she left Wall Street to become an actress in a vaudeville sketch for Thomas E. Shea.

She toured as a comedienne in an act which she wrote with the late Dan Jarrett, and among the actors whom they employed were James Cagney and Cary Grant (then known as Archie Leach). In collaboration with Jarrett she also wrote a play, *Salt Water*, which was produced by John Golden.

Golden launched her on her career as a publicist by giving her a job in his office handling publicity, reading scripts, casting, doctoring plays and assisting him in the general business of play production. In the early 1930's Jean Dalrymple and her former husband, Ward Morehouse, the New York *Sun* drama critic, collaborated on a screen story, *It Happened in New York*, for Universal Pictures. With Nedda Harrigan (Mrs. Joshua Logan) she is co-author of the play *Destination Unknown*.

In 1940 Jean Dalrymple opened her own publicity office in New York. Plays for which she has done publicity include *Mr. and Mrs. North, The Green Pastures, Early to Bed, Porgy and Bess, One Touch of Venus, The Voice of the Turtle,* and *Anna Lucasta.* In addition, she has publicized the Maplewood Theatre of Cheryl Crawford, the Ballet Russe of Monte Carlo, and the New York City Center opera, ballet and theatre companies, which she helped to organize. Stage and concert personalities for whom Jean Dalrymple has acted as manager or press representative include José and Amparo Iturbi; the late Grace Moore, Lily Pons, André Kostelanetz, Vera Zorina, Tito Guizar, Nathan Milstein, Tallulah Bankhead, Bidu Sayao, Margo, Margaret Sullavan, Mary Martin, Paula Laurence, Marc Connelly, Leopold Stokowski, Norman Bel Geddes, and many others. As a Latin America concert tour manager, she accompanied the singer, the late Grace Moore, and the concert pianist, Jose Iturbi, on several trips throughout South America as well as Europe.

Her first venture as a producer came in 1945 when she presented *Hope for the Best,* a comedy by William McCleery, formerly Sunday editor of *PM* Magazine. The play starred Franchot Tone and Jane Wyatt and ran a little over three months. Her next venture as a producer, late in the same year, was with John Cecil Holm's comedy, *Brighten the Corner,* starring the late Charles Butterworth in his last Broadway role. The following year she presented a revival of the George Manker Watters-Arthur Hopkins comedy, *Burlesque,* the great hit of 1927. Starring Bert Lahr and Jean Parker, it had 437 performances in New York and had a successful run on the road. Miss Dalrymple, "who looks about as businesslike as an anemone" according to William Hawkins in the New York *World-Telegram* (October 28,1947) said, "This show was a natural for Bert Lahr, and I can't stand seeing great talent lie around doing nothing."

Jean Dalrymple visited Europe in the spring of 1948, at which time she got permission from Shaw to do several of his plays at the New York City Center. She also went to France to obtain the rights to Jean-Paul Sartre's *Les Mains Sales* (*Red Gloves*) and visited Spain, where she obtained Joaquin Calvo-Sotello's play, *La Carcel Infinita,* known here as *The Eternal Prison.*

Jean Dalrymple's fourth Broadway presentation was the controversial production of *Red Gloves,* with Charles Boyer in the lead-role. The American adaptation by Daniel Toradash provoked a storm of protest on the part of the French existentialist playwright and his supporters who claimed that it was "vulgar" and had introduced a strong anti-Communist bias. Sartre brought suit against his agent, Louis Nagel, for authorizing the translation without his permission. Miss Dalrymple nevertheless went ahead with the American production as scheduled, and even sent copies of the French text of *Les Mains Sales* to all the critics in order to

JEAN DALRYMPLE

support her contention that the American version retained substantially the flavor and the key points of the original play.

In the summer of 1950 Miss Dalrymple launched three "package" shows for the summer theatre circuit—Ella Raines in *The Voice of the Turtle,* Burgess Meredith in *Harvey* and Franchot Tone in *The Second Man.* These proved very successful, and in the summers of 1952 and 1953 she again sent Franchot Tone on a tour of summer playhouses starring in *Jason, The Second Man, A Play for Mary,* and *The Petrified Forest.*

She also took charge of the ANTA Album presentation on May 6, 1951 which was the fourth of an annual series of one-night shows presenting highlights from the American theatre for the benefit of the American National Theatre and Academy.

The press agent was divorced from Morehouse in 1937. She was married on November 1, 1951 to Colonel Philip de Witt Ginder (now a Brigadier-General in the 45th Division in Korea), whom she met in Berlin, Germany, while she was representing ANTA at the Berlin Arts Festival. She lives and works in a remodeled brownstone house on East 55th Street in New York City, designed by the artist Ben Ali Haggin. She spends her week-ends on her Connecticut farm, where her neighbors are Gilbert Miller and Joshua Logan.

Miss Dalrymple has been described by the Cleveland *Plain Dealer* as "a petite, long-haired, piquant-faced woman, fragile as a Fragonard painting, but hep and with a sense of timing like a Garrand rifle." Elsa Maxwell has compared her to the "Mona Lisa of Leonardo da Vinci," and Franchot Tone has characterized her as "the tenderest little lady."

(Continued next page)

DALRYMPLE, JEAN—*Continued*

Jean Dalrymple believes that everyone has some calling as urgent as a missionary's. Hers is to bring exciting talent before the public. "I can do absolutely nothing I don't believe in," she states, "but I can do *anything* I do believe in."

References

Newark (N.J.) *Sunday Call*, Aug 22 '43
N Y World-Telegram p22 O 28 '47
Film and Radio Discussion Guide 11:60 O '44 por
Read Mag p36+ D '44
Theatre World (1949/50)
Who's Who in the Theatre (1953)

DANGERFIELD, GEORGE (BUBB) Oct. 28, 1904- Author

Address: b. c/o Harcourt, Brace and Co., 383 Madison Ave., New York 17, N.Y.; h. 3599 Padaro Lane, Carpinteria, Calif.

The 1953 Pulitzer Prize for history was awarded to George Dangerfield for his book, *The Era of Good Feelings* (Harcourt, Brace, 1952), which deals with the presidential administrations of James Monroe and John Quincy Adams. The book also received one of the anual Bancroft Prizes given by Columbia University for outstanding writing in American history.

A native of Great Britain and a graduate of Oxford, Dangerfield has lived in the United States since the early 1930's, and became an American citizen while serving with the Army in World War II. He is the author of three other historical works: *Bengal Mutiny* (Harcourt, Brace, 1933), *The Strange Death of Liberal England* (Smith and Haas, 1935), and *Victoria's Heir* (Harcourt, Brace, 1941).

George Bubb Dangerfield was born in Newbury, Berkshire, England, on October 28, 1904, one of the four children of George and Ethel Margaret (Tyrer) Dangerfield. His father, a Church of England clergyman, served as rector of Mixbury-cum-Finmere, in the diocese of Oxford. "My first memory is one of being held up to a window and shown Halley's Comet," Dangerfield has recalled.

As a boy of fourteen, he used to spend his pocket money at Harold Munro's famous Poetry Bookshop in London. After graduating in 1923 from the Forest School in Walthamstow, a suburb of London, he entered Hertford College at Oxford University. He received his Bachelor of Arts degree from Oxford in June 1927, with honors in English literature.

Beginning his career as a poet, Dangerfield taught at the English Institute in Prague, Czechoslovakia, from 1928 to 1929, and subsequently at the English College in Hamburg, Germany. In 1930 he settled in the United States, and served as a reader and editor for the New York publishing house of Brewer, Warren, and Putnam, for the next two years.

His first book, *Bengal Mutiny: The Story of the Sepoy Rebellion,* was published early in 1933. This volume described what Dangerfield

has termed "one of the darkest chapters in the long history of India"—the revolt of the Bengal sepoy, or native army, against British authority in 1857-58, centering in Delhi, Cawnpore, and Lucknow. "Mr. Dangerfield has done an excellent piece of work and given us a big history in a little book," observed the Boston *Transcript* reviewer. "It is compelling and it is thrilling. The detail is handled with great skill; there is enough to show in a series of flashes all that transpired, yet not enough to clog the movement and become cumbersome."

According to Edward Thompson in *The Spectator,* Dangerfield had written "the best popular account of the Mutiny. . . .He is vivid and easily read without being slipshod or melodramatic or big-drum; he is fair-minded and feels the intense pity of the story. He knows his stuff, and is at pains to set it out accurately and in proportion."

From 1933 to 1935, Dangerfield held the post of literary editor of *Vanity Fair* magazine, and it was in the latter year that his second historical work, *The Strange Death of Liberal England,* appeared. He had long believed that between the death of Edward VII in 1910 and the outbreak of World War I in 1914 there was "a considerable hiatus" in English history. "When I first thought of writing this book," he explained in the foreword, "I had in mind a mixture of *Cynara* and *Sophocles*—the madder music, the stronger wine, and the approaching catastrophe of which the actors themselves were unaware."

But as soon as he began to look into the subject, he found himself confronted with a "far more curious drama." By the end of 1913, in Dangerfield's opinion, "true pre-war Liberalism —supported, as it still was in 1910, by Free Trade, a majority in Parliament, the ten commandments, and the illusion of Progress . . . was killed, or it killed itself."

Several critics expressed their doubts about this thesis. Reviewing the book for the New York *Herald Tribune.* William MacDonald commented: "One can enjoy Dangerfield's jaunty manner and sparkling style, and linger over his unforgettable pictures of stirring episodes, and yet feel compelled to ask whether, after all, he has quite made out his case."

Stanley Pargellis in the *Saturday Review (of Literature),* however, ranked Dangerfield among "the newest of the 'new' historians." "It is the clear authentic voice of the new young England which speaks in this book," Pargellis continued, "the voice of those young Englishmen . . . with the will not to let any sentiment for the beauties of that England which is gone, or any compromise with the unreal thinking of the men who enjoyed it, stand in their way as they mold the England that shall be."

This book was followed in 1941 by *Victoria's Heir: The Education of a Prince,* a biography of Albert Edward, Prince of Wales from 1841 to 1901, who reigned as Edward VII from 1901 to 1910. Writing in the New York *Times,* P. W. Wilson thought that Dangerfield's Edward was "a man of flesh and blood, authentic and intimate," but he found the book more a vast panorama of the times than a portrait of a single figure.

A few other critics objected to what they called the "cinematic treatment" or "disjointed, kaleidoscopic" manner of presentation. L. P. Curtis in the *Saturday Review (of Literature)* stated that the author had "made himself at home in an epoch of western history peculiarly congenial to his talents." In the opinion of G. F. Whicher (New York *Herald Tribune*), Dangerfield's "lucidity of mind and his sardonic wit" entitled him to "immediate recognition as Lytton Strachey's heir," and *Time's* reviewer considered this biography "almost worthy to be a sequel to Strachey's *Queen Victoria.*"

Dangerfield served with the 102nd Infantry Division of the United States Army from 1942 to 1945, and while stationed at Paris, Texas, in April 1943, he became an American citizen.

After the war, Dangerfield wrote his first book dealing with American history—*The Era of Good Feelings,* from 1817 to 1829. The author's preface states that the book is "essentially a description of some of the personalities and experiences, American and European, which assisted in or were necessary to the political transition from Jeffersonian democracy to Jacksonian democracy: from the great dictum that central government is best when it governs least to the great dictum that central government must sometimes intervene strongly in behalf of the weak and the oppressed and the exploited."

The "era of good feelings" is the name traditionally given to the eight years of Monroe's presidency (1817-25), because it was a period of nationalism and one-party government. Dangerfield has attempted to show how this designation is appropriate to only the first two years of Monroe's administration, and that after the panic of 1819 the "era of good feelings" came to an end. For the succeeding decade, a time of significant change, he has suggested the title "the era of suspense."

When *The Era of Good Feelings* was published in January 1952, many critics credited Dangerfield with giving this crucial and hitherto largely neglected period its proper attention. "The book throws new and fresh light on an important transitional period in our history," remarked F. M. Green (*Social Forces*). Wayne Andrews declared in *Commonweal*: "Though the writing of history has never been and never will be reduced to a science . . . it has on occasion been disguised as an art, and seldom more successfully than by Dangerfield . . . whose study is as delightful as it is profound."

Similar praise came from Charles Poore (New York *Times*), who found it "an exceptionally well-written narrative of remarkable personalities in an astonishing time." Although he criticized the author for not attempting a much-needed new interpretation of the era, and for approaching the period too exclusively from the standpoint of national politics, Richard Hofstader (*New Republic*) regarded the book as "one of the solidest works of historical writing in years." Without any predecessors in the field, Dangerfield, in Hofstader's estimation, had written "a general synthesis of the history of the period that is almost certain to endure as a standard work."

On April 20, 1953, Dangerfield was awarded one of the Bancroft Prizes for *The Era of*

Shreve Ballard

GEORGE DANGERFIELD

Good Feelings. The prizes, carrying stipends of $2,000, are given annually by Columbia University to the authors of the two best works published in the field of American history, diplomacy, or international relations. Announcement of the Pulitzer Prize winners two weeks later, on May 4, revealed that he had received the $500 award in history for the same volume.

Dangerfield, who had come East for the Bancroft presentation, had just returned to his home in California when he heard the news of the second honor. He told a Chicago *Tribune* interviewer who asked about his future plans that he wanted to do a book on the visits to the United States of three Englishmen in the 19th century—Anthony Trollope, Herbert Spencer, and Matthew Arnold. "I like best to write biography and tie it up with a period," he said. "There is a large field of untouched material."

In an article for the *North American* (March 1937), Dangerfield said he believed "the American past could be given an enormous vitality by a body of historical writing which—while not dishonest or irreverent as regards the sanctity of fact—tended to look upon the past as a tale of which the plot had already been dictated, but which had still to be provided with character and color." Such a tradition would be essentially "popular"; relying more upon "an artistic than a scientific integrity, selecting, condensing, omitting, in a somewhat arbitrary manner, it would not attempt to compete with the close world of scholarship."

The reality that this kind of popular history aimed at would, with due concern for fact, also be an "inventive reality"; it would attempt to make "a happy marriage between the economic and the psychological motive." If the novel can go to history, Dangerfield concluded, history can go to the novel, "at least to the extent of bringing creative imagination to bear upon its characters." History, he has said, "is a combi-

DANGERFIELD, GEORGE—*Continued*

nation of taste, imagination, science, and scholarship; it reconciles incompatibles, it balances probabilities; and at last it attains the reality of fiction, which is the highest reality of all."

Dangerfield has lectured widely throughout the United States, and has contributed numerous book reviews, and articles on such writers as Strachey, E. M. Forster, Archibald MacLeish, and Rosamond Lehmann, to the *Saturday Review of Literature, New Republic, Virginia Quarterly Review, North American, Life, Bookman, Commonweal, Scribner's Magazine,* and other periodicals.

On June 29, 1941, he married Mary Lou Schott; they have one daughter, Mary Jo. The historian, who is five feet ten inches tall and weighs 142 pounds, has blue eyes and gray hair. He is a Democrat, and holds membership in Americans for Democratic Action. Among his favorite forms of recreation are reading and watching sports.

References

N Y Times p29 Ap 21 '53; May 5 '53 pors
Wilson Lib Bul 16:202 N '41 por

DAVIS, BETTE Apr. 5, 1908- Actress
Address: b. c/o Warner Brothers Studios, Hollywood, Calif.; h. Malibu, Calif.

NOTE: This biography supersedes the article which appeared in *Current Biography* in 1941.

After an absence from the legitimate stage of twenty-three years Bette Davis, well-known screen actress and winner of two awards from the Academy of Motion Picture Arts and Sciences, returned to Broadway in December of 1952 to star in a musical revue—a medium new to her and one utilizing talents rarely shown in her Hollywood productions. She was first seen by motion picture audiences in 1931; since then Bette Davis, considered by many critics the leading actress in the American cinema, has appeared in 74 films, her 1953 release being *The Star*, a story of an aging film actress who fails to make a "comeback." Among her most successful screen productions are *Of Human Bondage, Dangerous, Jezebel, Juarez, Dark Victory,* and *All About Eve.*

Bette Davis was born Ruth Elizabeth Davis on April 5, 1908, in Lowell, Massachusetts, the elder daughter of Harlow Morrell and Ruth (Favor) Davis. She was known as Bette by her family and friends and she kept the name when she began her professional career. During the first eight years of her life she lived in the New England town of her birth, where her father had a law practice. After the divorce of her parents in 1916 she and her sister, Barbara, and their mother, who had taken up photography as a profession, lived in a number of communities in New England and in New York City. For a time Bette and her sister attended a boarding school in the Berkshires and also studied at the Newton (Massachusetts) High School. Miss Davis completed her educa-

tion at Cushing Academy, a finishing school in Ashburnham, Massachusetts, where she met part of her expenses by waiting on tables—a task she thought would mean social ostracism, but which, instead, gained her many friends among the students. At both Newton and at Cushing Academy the future star had shown some interest in school dramatics, but it was not until the summer of 1925, when she enrolled in the Mariarden School of Dancing in Peterborough, New Hampshire, that she gave real attention to acting. Here she was seen by Frank Conroy, a Broadway actor, who urged her to concentrate on a career as an actress and who later befriended her when she made her first visits to theatrical agents.

Upon graduation from Cushing Academy, Miss Davis remained for a short while in her mother's home in Newton and then, with the theatre still her chief interest went to New York City for an interview with Eva LeGallienne. The established actress found the young woman lacking in seriousness, (as related in a biographical sketch released by Twentieth Century-Fox) and advised her to study in some other field. Not discouraged by this judgment, Miss Davis succeeded in being accepted as a student in the John Murray Anderson Dramatic School and later won a scholarship there. Before completing her studies, Miss Davis was given her first professional assignment—bit parts in George Cukor's stock company, playing at the Lyceum Theatre in Rochester, New York.

From here she moved on to the Cape Playhouse in Dennis, Massachusetts, where she was an usherette and where she occasionally was permitted to take small roles. Following another period with the Rochester players, she was chosen by James Light, then the director and producer for the Provincetown Playhouse, for her first major role, in *The Earth Between.* Brooks Atkinson of the New York *Times* commented that she played an "interesting character" in "a soft, unassertive style." Miss Davis then toured for a brief time in Ibsen's *The Wild Duck,* appeared again at the Cape Playhouse, and in the fall of 1929 was given a part in the Broadway production of *Broken Dishes,* which opened at the Ritz Theater on November 5 and ran for six months. Her performance in her next play, *Solid South,* which ran for four weeks during October of 1930, won her a screen test with Universal Pictures and a contract.

Those who saw Miss Davis' screen tests are said to have considered her lacking in cinema appeal, and her first motion picture performances, in *Bad Sister* and *Seed,* both released in 1931, gained her no critical recognition. At the end of 1931 she was ready to leave the film capital when George Arliss offered her the opportunity to play opposite him in a Warner Brothers picture, *The Man Who Played God.* On the basis of her work in this film she received an eleven-year contract with Warner Brothers. As a featured player in a number of subsequent Hollywood productions, she failed to attract critical approval until she was seen as the slatternly cockney waitress in the RKO production of W. Somerset Maugham's *Of Human Bondage.* Released in July 1934, the picture immediately established Miss Davis as a brilliant young screen actress with a unique ability to portray individual character. *Newsweek* observed: "In her thankless role, [she] proves herself a really capable actress. . . . Harshly cruel, repulsively vulgar, she speaks her lines with an inimitable cockney accent."

For her next important role, a dipsomaniac ex-Broadway star in the film *Dangerous* (1935), Miss Davis won an award from the Academy of Motion Picture Arts and Sciences as the best woman actress of that year. She subsequently appeared in *Golden Arrow, Kid Galahan,* and *That Certain Woman.* Her second citation as the best woman actress of the year was awarded for her acting in *Jezebel* (1938), in which Miss Davis created a tempestuous woman of the South during the Civil War. *Time,* which devoted its March 28, 1938, cover to a painting of Miss Davis and carried a two-column biographical sketch of the actress, wrote that she has "as wide a dramatic range as any cinema actress in the business." Of her performance in Jezebel, the *Time* critic wrote: "By force of personal intensity and able acting, actress Davis gives her emotional crises a convincing importance." In 1939 she again triumphed in *Juarez,* a film which some critics rated as poor in content and dramatic appeal, but interesting because of the "real cinematic excitement" achieved by Miss Davis. Her reputation as a versatile artist was in the next year strengthened by her creation of the role of the doomed heroine in *Dark Victory,* winning for her the Annual Gold Medal for the best feminine performance of the year from *Picturegoer,* a leading film magazine of Great Britain. Among other notable motion pictures released at about this time were *The Private Lives of Elizabeth and Essex, All This and Heaven Too, The Letter,* and *The Little Foxes.*

While achieving what *Life* described as "an eminence unique in her profession today," Miss Davis was at times in disagreement with Warner Brothers. Complaining about poor story material, low salary, and inadequate rest periods between films, she attempted to break her contract by going to England in 1936 and making a film there. The American producers contested the action, won the suit, and Miss Davis was forced to fulfill her contract. Subsequently, her relations with Warner Brothers having improved, she received a salary increase, longer vacation periods, and a wider choice of scripts. When her contract was concluded she continued to make most of her films under Warner Brothers, while working occasionally for other Hollywood and British producers. By 1947 Miss Davis had, according to Peter Noble, completed 56 films; by 1952 the figure had reached 73 by a count made by Gilbert Millstein, writing of the star in the New York *Times Magazine.* The same writer calculated that during her twenty years in the film world she had earned approximately three million dollars.

Judging by reviews of her work from 1941 to 1952, Miss Davis suffered at times from mediocre material, but in those films with strong dramatic content her talents were readily admitted by the critics. In *Watch on the Rhine* (1943) her portrayal of the wife, wrote the

BETTE DAVIS

New York *Times* reviewer, showed "a gentle restraint and warm devotion such as Miss Davis has seldom revealed." The same year her characterization in *Old Acquaintance* was considered by the New York *Times* as "fluid and full of contrivance" and by the New York *Herald Tribune* as "modulated and believable." Two years later, in the 1945 screen version of the play *The Corn is Green,* she also won critical praise: "A worthy addition to Miss Davis' gallery of notable cinema portraits" (New York *Herald Tribune*); "Miss Davis gives a clear and warm conception of the middle-aged spinster . . . [with] quiet dignity in manner and a human graciousness in her voice" (New York *Times*). During the 1940's she also appeared in *Now, Voyager* (1942), *Mr. Skeffington* (1944), *Hollywood Canteen* (1944), *A Stolen Life* (1946), and *Deception* (1946).

With her performance in *June Bride* (1948), described by the New York *Times* as "a delightful vehicle," Bette Davis showed "a lovely talent for the comic touch." The next important films in which she starred—*Winter Meeting* and *Beyond the Forest*—were less well received. In 1950 Miss Davis made, reported *Look,* a comeback "with the superiority of a champion" in *All About Eve,* a "withering satire" on Hollywood. The New York film critics granted her their annual award as the best actress of the year and the New York *Times* commented that she gave "a superb illumination of the spirit and pathos" of the character of the aging actress. *Variety* found the movie "a literate, adult film . . . wherein Miss Davis does not spare herself, makeup-wise, in the aging star assignment." When her seventy-fourth film, *The Star,* was released in 1953, Otis L. Guernsey, Jr., of the New York *Herald Tribune,* remarked: "Miss Davis' crisp, definite acting style keeps the picture from wilting into an emotional collapse. . . .She gets the elements of a real woman into her character [of a fading

DAVIS, BETTE—*Continued*

screen star]. . . .There is nothing faded about Miss Davis' abilities, and she pulls every ounce of possible dramatic value out of the role." Alton Cook of the New York *World-Telegram* praised Miss Davis as a "wisely controlled and subtle actress, giving a stirring and convincing performance."

In 1952 Miss Davis also starred in a Broadway musical revue—*Two's Company,* which opened on December 15, 1952, marking her return to the stage, her first attempt at singing and dancing and one of her infrequent attempts at comedy. A "turbulent history" of changes in performers, lyrics, and sketches, as well as the star's attack of laryngitis had delayed the Broadway opening of the show, a box office success, but regarded by some New York critics as not a happy vehicle for Miss Davis. Wolcott Gibbs of *The New Yorker* described her as "probably the most determined player ever to come out of Hollywood," but found her material poor and suggested that she "confine her talents to Maugham's pale green and despicable Mildred and leave humor to girls who just play for quick laughs." The critic for the New York *World-Telegram* wrote: "Her dancing is likely to consist of hip rolls, marching, and none too steady lifts by a whole corps of male partners. Her singing is deep, husky, very articulate and rhythmic, but not very musical. In sketches she can do almost anything better than whip off a laugh line. But . . . Miss Davis is electric, as she has always been on the screen. . . .Somewhere along the line you are dazzled, and in the end awed." The star's own reaction to her musical revue efforts was quoted in a New York *Herald Tribune* article as follows: "This has been the roughest, quickest, most wonderful experience of my life. . . . I'm a ham. That is, a good ham. A good ham is an actor who really enjoys giving pleasure to people." The revue closed on March 11, 1953 after 89 performances because of Miss Davis's illness.

She has been president of the Academy of Motion Picture Arts and Sciences and in 1942 founded and served as first president of the Hollywood Canteen. Known also to radio audiences, she has been heard frequently in dramatic productions on the air, and in April 1951 she made her television debut on Jimmy Durante's program.

Bette Davis was first married in 1932, to Harmon Oscar Nelson, Jr., a school friend, and was divorced in 1938. Two years later she was married to Arthur Farnsworth, a Boston businessman, who died in 1943. By her marriage in 1945 to William Grant Sherry, an artist, she has a daughter, Barbara. She is also the mother of two adopted children, Michael and Margo. After her divorce in 1950, she was married to Gary Merrill, a film actor whom she had met when both were engaged in making *All About Eve.* Described by one reporter as "just as beautiful at forty-four as when she went to the West Coast in late 1930," Miss Davis has blue eyes, dark blond hair, and stands five feet three and one-half inches tall. She prefers to live in the country, near open water, and is said

to dislike air travel and people who are slow or late to an appointment. *Life* reported that she is a "voracious" reader and "a highly animated, eloquent conversationalist."

References

Life N 20 '44
N Y Post Mag p9 D 26 '42; p5M F 8 '53 por
N Y Times Mag p22 O 19 '52
N Y World-Telegram p25 S 30 '52
Time 31:33 Mr 28 '38
International Motion Picture Almanac, 1952-53
Noble, P. Bette Davis, A Biography (1948)
Who's Who in America, 1952-53
World Biography (1948)

DAVIS, MRS. FLOYD (MACMILLAN)
See Davis, G. R.

DAVIS, GLADYS ROCKMORE May 11, 1901- American artist
Address: h. and b. 1 West 67th St., New York 23

An artist who has succeeded in both commercial and fine arts, Gladys Rockmore Davis gave up a career in advertising art to devote herself to creative painting, and about seven years later in 1940, the Metropolitan Museum of Art purchased *August Afternoon,* one of her paintings reminiscent of the richness and vibrant color of Renoir. This was followed by a number of prizes in museums throughout the country, and in 1941 she gave her first show at the Rehn Gallery in New York City.

. . Later she exhibited at the Midtown Gallery with which she is associated today. Her work in pastels ranks with her oils, and although her chief subjects are children, nudes and still-lifes, she has also painted ballet dancers, vignettes of liberated Paris, and scenes of Spain.

Born in New York City, on May 11, 1901, the daughter of David William Rockmore and Jeanette (Richman) Rockmore, she lived in New York until she was nine years old when her father, a lawyer and metallurgist, moved the family to Canada. She and her brother spent the next five years getting used to new schools as the family moved from place to place. The Rockmores eventually settled in San Francisco where Gladys attended the Girls' High School.

Miss Davis tells about her early background in an article, *"My Desire to Paint,"* which appeared in the January 1940 issue of *Magazine of Art,* saying, "I was completely absorbed with the business of drawing from the first minute I was able to hold a pencil. I can remember as a child being intensely interested in drawing almost to the exclusion of everything else. That interest has continued uninterruptedly." Although neither of her parents had any artistic inclinations, they encouraged her and sent her to the California School of Fine Arts.

At the age of sixteen she entered the Art Institute of Chicago where she studied with John Norton and George Bellows. She speaks affectionately of Norton who "taught me to look, to see, really to use my eyes. He showed me the vast difference between the actual distortion of reality and the 'pretty' distortion of the average point of view." She praised the Institute, not only for its teaching, but for having a museum where the students could compare their work with the works of masters. "Great paintings put us in our places," she said.

After graduation from the Art Institute in 1920 she began her career as a commercial artist and worked in the advertising and fashion fields for eleven years. She feels this was an important phase of her career because it was then that she learned judgment, discipline and facility. In 1925 she married Floyd MacMillan Davis, well-known illustrator, and combined painting with caring for her children, Noel and Deborah.

The Davises went to Europe in 1932. While in France Mrs. Davis visited Renoir's home and studio and studied his paintings. After touring the continent the family settled in Cannes, France, where Mrs. Davis started to paint as a creative artist.

The transition was not so noticeable from day to day, but on her return to the United States in 1933 she found she had completely lost her flair for commercial work. Abandoning her former methods, she studied at the Art Students League in New York and with George Grosz for a year; then she started on her own as an artist.

Recognition came soon. She won the William R. French Gold Medal at the Chicago Institute of Art in 1937 and was recommended for the 1938 purchase prize by the Virginia Museum of Fine Arts at Richmond, Virginia. In 1939 she received honorable mention from the Pennsylvania Academy of Fine Arts, and third honorable mention from the Corcoran Gallery of Art, Washington, D.C. The Metropolitan Museum of Art in New York bought her *August Afternoon* in 1940, and she gave her first one-man show at the Rehn Gallery in New York in 1941. After two additional one-man shows at the Midtown Gallery in New York an art critic called Gladys Rockmore Davis "the ten-year wonder of United States art".

Mrs. Davis always set out to paint the things with which she was familiar. Her two children, Noel and Deborah, posed for many paintings from their babyhood through their youth. Among her best known works are *Noel with Violin, Emma, Girl Braiding Her Hair, Letter,* and *Carousel.* Her nudes and figures have been praised as "richly plastic figures" and her work was described by a critic of the *Art Digest* (May 1, 1943) as that of "one of our strongest women artists who is not so much concerned with fantasy as she is with painting a good solid, professional picture"

On the other hand, after her 1949 show at the Midtown, an art critic from *Art News* spoke of Davis as "a gifted and facile realistic painter who has permitted her expression to

George Karfiol

GLADYS ROCKMORE DAVIS

descend to the easy reference of commercial art. Her wistful little children have already promoted a number of products in national advertisements and wide eyes and puppy-like gestures are absolutely irresistible to the average housewife. It is a pity that her more serious paintings—some of them are extremely ambitious metaphorical works—have become infected by this soap-opera disease."

At the Metropolitan Opera House in 1944 Mrs. Davis made many intimate sketches of the ballet from backstage and other studies in the dressing rooms. In painting the ballet scenes, she captured the drama of contrasts resulting from the intense lighting on the stage and darkness of the wings where the dancers waited their entrances. In the dressing rooms she sketched the ballerinas while they made their changes. She selected scenes from *Petrouchka, Swan Lake, Les Sylphides, Giselle* and *Aleko.*

During the war her ballet sketches were exhibited in Bonwit Teller store windows while she worked inside sketching ballerinas and giving her pictures away for the purchase of $100 war bonds. She received a citation from the Government in 1945 in recognition of this service.

Mrs. Davis and her husband were commissioned by *Life* magazine to paint liberated Paris in 1944 and 1945. Floyd Davis concentrated on the wartime city with American soldiers, while she painted the familiar and nostalgic scenes. Reviewing the show which was exhibited in the foyer of the Time-Life Building in 1945, the critic from the New York *World-Telegram* commented, "This was an uncertain, frightened city Gladys Davis was painting. Only the children seemed happy, well-nourished, at ease. The merry-go-rounds, the Luxemborg gardens, the

DAVIS, GLADYS—*Continued*

puppet shows, are quite as they have always been. Everything else had a furtive, unreal look about it in those uncertain days before the Rhine was crossed." Parisian scenes painted by Mrs. Davis were the *Chez Suzy, Bookstalls, Joan of Arc Statue* and *Flower Stalls.*

Mrs. Davis was one of the artists participating in the first art show sponsored by the Encyclopædia Britannica in 1945; in the same year she won the Pepsi-Cola Portrait of America Show popular prize. She was represented in the Portraits, Inc., in 1947 of Family Life in the United States during the past hundred years with her paintings of the children of Mr. and Mrs. John P. Marquand. Some art lovers compare her portraits of children to those of Mary Cassatt, American painter of a previous generation.

In 1951 Mrs. Davis won the Gold Medal from the Pennsylvania Academy of Fine Arts. She is a full Academician at the National Academy of Design.

When Mrs. Davis visited Spain in 1952 she was stimulated, as in France, to new work, which resulted in her most recent one-man show held in April 1953, called "Paintings of Spain." One critic spoke of the "vibrant color of her brush work" and "her classic virtues applied in a contemporary way."

Calling herself "a conservative modern" she writes that her husband's "unfailing interest and flawless taste have been a continuous source of inspiration." The artist is five feet one inch tall, and weighs 103 pounds.

References

Art Digest 17:9 My '43
Art News 48:51 N '49
Life Jl 16 '52-Ap 19 '43 Mr 27 '44
Magazine of Art Ja '40
Newsweek Jl 21 '52
N Y Herald-Tribune Mr 26 '44
N Y World-Telegram Jl 14 '45
Time Mr 27 '44

Who's Who In America, 1952
Who's Who in Art (1953)
World Biography (1948)

DAVIS, HARVEY N(ATHANIEL) June 6, 1881—Dec. 3, 1952 Educator; engineer; scientist; professor of mechanical engineering at Harvard University (1904-28); held several engineering positions in private industry; during World War I did research on helium gas for armed forces; invented improved steam turbine (patented 1918) and process for liquefaction and rectification of air (patented 1922); president of Stevens Institute of Technology, Hoboken, New Jersey (1928-51); during World War II directed Office of Production Research and Development of the War Production Board (1942-44); led mission to London to establish closer liaison with British research authorities (1943). See *Current Biography*, 1947.

Obituary

N Y Times p27 D 5 '52

DAVIS, JOHN W(ILLIAM) Apr. 13, 1873- Lawyer

Address: b. 15 Broad St., New York 5; h. Locust Valley, N.Y.

The noted lawyer John W. Davis, who was a member of the West Virginia and Federal Legislatures, Solicitor General of the United States, and Ambassador to Great Britain prior to his nomination for the United States Presidency in 1924, is today regarded as one of the country's leading authorities on both international and constitutional law. As an avowed Jeffersonian he has been a champion of States' rights and a guardian of constitutional checks and guarantees. It was Davis who in the spring of 1952 convinced the Supreme Court that President Harry S. Truman had exceeded his rights in ordering seizure of the steel mills under alleged "inherent" powers, and later in the same year undertook to defend, before the same tribunal, the right of the State of South Carolina to maintain a segregation system in its schools.

On April 12, 1953 John W. Davis was appointed by Queen Elizabeth II an honorary Knight Grand Cross of the Most Excellent Order of the British Empire, the highest civilian distinction the Queen could bestow on a United States citizen.

John William Davis, the only son but not the only child of John James and Anna (Kennedy) Davis, was born on April 13, 1873; his birthplace was Clarksburg, West Virginia, to which his paternal grandfather, John Davis, had migrated from the Shenandoah Valley in Virginia to follow his trade as a saddler. The latter's son, John J. Davis, became one of the two leading lawyers at Clarksburg, served in the State legislature and represented his district in the United States Congress from 1870 to 1875. The mother of John W. Davis, of Scots-Irish ancestry, held a B.A. degree from the Baltimore College for Women, and it was from her that the boy received his early education in Latin, English composition, and literature.

At the age of thirteen John Davis was sent to Pantops Academy, Charlottesville, Virginia, to prepare for Washington and Lee University, Lexington, Virginia, which he entered when he was sixteen. Four years later, in 1892, he took his B.A. degree in literature, *summa cum laude.* Davis then taught school for about a year before returning to Washington and Lee to study for the LL.B. degree, received in 1895. He was admitted to the West Virginia bar the same year, taught as assistant professor of law at Washington and Lee in 1896-97, and in 1897 began the law partnership with his father which lasted until his election to Congress in 1911. One of his early court appearances was in defense of one of three groups of strikers who had been arrested for marching near a colliery while an antipicketing injunction was in force. "By stipulation," stated *World's Work*, "judgment in all three cases was joined in one decision, which was favorable to the laboring men largely as the result of a four-hundred-word brief prepared by young Davis."

Davis entered politics in 1899, when he was elected on the Democratic ticket to represent

Clarksburg in the West Virginia House of Delegates, becoming in that year chairman of the Judiciary Committee. As a Democratic candidate for Presidential elector-at-large in 1900, Davis attended his first Democratic National Convention four years later. In 1906 he was chosen president of the West Virginia Bar Association and in 1909 became a member of the State's commission on uniform tax laws.

When he ran for Congress the first time in 1910, he was supported by both mine-owners and union, and was elected Representative of the hitherto Republican First West Virginia District by a heavy majority. Seated in the Sixty-second Congress in April 1911, he was assigned to the House Judiciary Committee, wherein he was respected for his work on the Clayton Act, which exempted unions from the Sherman Anti-Trust Law. Also in the Sixty-second Congress, the West Virginia Representative denounced the wool schedule of the Payne Tariff Act and was active in support of reforming Federal court procedure. Davis appeared before the Senate as one of the managers for the House in the impeachment proceedings initiated July 11, 1912, against Robert W. Archbald of Pennsylvania, Associate Judge of the Commerce Court, who was found guilty of corrupt collusion and removed from office. Davis was re-elected to the Sixty-third Congress, but served only until August 30, 1913, when President Woodrow Wilson appointed him Solicitor General of the United States. He served until late 1918 and in the course of nearly six years argued sixty-seven cases before the Supreme Court, a greater number than any other Solicitor General except John G. Johnson, his briefs helping to validate the Federal Reserve Act, the income tax and selective service laws, the Adamson eight-hour law, and other important legislation.

Toward the end of World War I, in September 1918, Davis, who had been counselor to the American Red Cross since 1913, was sent to Berne, Switzerland, as the American delegate to a conference with the Germans on treatment and exchange of prisoners. Later in the year, when Walter Hines Page resigned as envoy to Great Britain, the President named Davis to succeed him. As United States Ambassador to the Court of St. James, Davis was notably successful, especially in difficult negotiations over oil concessions in Mesopotamia. He also attended the Versailles Peace Conference and is credited with a major role in drafting regulations for the control of occupied territory.

On May 23, 1920, in a three-and-one-half-column editorial which carried the title "A Great Democrat," the New York *Times* recommended the nomination of John W. Davis as Democratic candidate for President of the United States. At this time his name, presented to the Democratic National Convention in connection with both the presidency and the vice-presidency, created little stir. Following the election of Republican Warren Harding in November, Davis resigned as Ambassador to Britain, and on return to the United States settled in New York City, practicing law first as a member of the firm of Stetson, Jennings, Russell and Davis and later as a partner of Davis,

Wide World Photos
JOHN W. DAVIS

Polk, Wardwell, Gardiner and Reed (now Davis, Polk, Wardwell, Sunderland and Kiendl); his clients included Standard Oil, the United States Rubber Company, the Guaranty Trust Company of New York, and a number of corporations in which the J. P. Morgan banking concern held stock. The former Ambassador became president of the American Bar Association in 1922.

At the Democratic National Convention meeting in New York City in July 1924, in which Governor Alfred E. Smith of New York and William G. McAdoo of California were deadlocked for over one hundred ballots, Davis seemed scarcely even a "dark horse," but when it became clear that neither of the leading contestants could get the two-thirds vote necessary for nomination, there was a swing to Davis, who was nominated on the 103d ballot. In the ensuing November election Davis was defeated, gaining only 8,391,431 votes to 15,729,060 for Calvin Coolidge. After an extensive foreign tour, Davis resumed law practice in New York City.

Davis also wrote, during the next few years, a number of articles on international law, such as "Anglo-American Relations and Sea Power" (*Foreign Affairs*, April 1929), "Permanent Bases of American Foreign Policy" (*Foreign Affairs*, October 1931), and "The World Court Settles the Question" (*Atlantic Monthly*, January 1932) on the Austro-German customs agreement. Davis supported the candidacy of Franklin D. Roosevelt for President in 1932, but two years later, when he felt that the Administration was departing from Jeffersonian principles, he joined with John J. Raskob and other conservative Democrats in forming the anti-New Deal American Liberty League. In 1936 he opposed Roosevelt's re-election; in 1940 testified before a Senate subcommittee in favor of a resolution which would limit the Presidency to a single six-year term; and in October of

DAVIS, JOHN W.—*Continued*

that year announced his formal support of Wendell L. Willkie against Roosevelt, who was then seeking a third term. In May 1941 he joined two other former Democratic candidates for President, James Cox and Alfred E. Smith, in a radio appeal to the nation to support the Roosevelt foreign policy; and on December 9, 1944, at a Metropolitan Opera Victory Rally in New York City, urged American acceptance of "the Dumbarton Oaks proposal for an organization to be known as the United Nations."

Elected vice-president of the Carnegie Endowment for International Peace in 1942, Davis in 1947 was advanced to vice-chairman of the board. Another position of international significance accepted by the lawyer (April 1946) was the presidency of the Pilgrims of America, which is influential in fostering Anglo-American relations. As a director of the Guaranty Trust Company of New York, and the American Telephone and Telegraph Company, trustee of the Mutual Life Insurance Company of New York, and general counsel as well as a director of the United States Rubber Company, Davis argued numerous important cases in State and Federal courts. A high point in his career as a constitutional authority came in May 1952, when the Supreme Court heard and upheld his reasons, advanced as chief counsel for various steel companies, why United States District Judge David A. Pine should be held correct in ruling that President Truman had exceeded his powers in ordering seizure of the steel mills on April 8, and why, accordingly, the Government should be "dispossessed." The following October Davis announced his support of General Dwight D. Eisenhower as the Republican candidate for President.

During the first part of December, 1952 Davis, as counsel for the State of South Carolina, appeared before the Supreme Court on another constitutional issue, namely the right of States to enact and enforce school segregation laws. In what Don Irwin of the New York *Herald Tribune* called "a closely reasoned argument," Davis maintained that the Fourteenth Amendment does not debar segregation provided that "separate but equal" educational facilities are maintained. A few days after he had made this plea, the New York State Bar Association announced, on December 16, that its second annual Gold Medal "For Distinguished Service to the Legal Profession" would be presented to John W. Davis at the end of January 1953.

Theodore A. Huntley's *Life of John W. Davis* (Duffield, 1924) contains 150 pages of speeches by Davis, while other of his addresses such as *The Treaty-Making Power of the United States* (Milford; Oxford, 1920) and *Party Government in the United States* (Princeton, 1929), have also appeared in book form. In England in January 1919, Davis was made an honorary bencher of the Middle Temple; he was awarded an honorary LL.D. degree by the University of Birmingham (1919) and by the University of Glasgow (1920). Other honorary LL.D. degrees held by Davis are from Washington and Lee (1915), the University of West Virginia (1919), Union University in

Schenectady, New York (1921), Yale University (1921), Dartmouth College (1923), Brown University (1923), Princeton University (1924), and Oberlin College (1947). Oxford University made him an honorary Doctor of Civil Law in 1950.

On June 20, 1899, Davis married Julia T. McDonald, who died August 17, 1900. One daughter, Julia West, was born of this marriage. Ellen G. Bassel, whom Davis married on January 2, 1912, died July 13, 1943. The former Ambassador is a member of a number of clubs in New York, Washington, and London, and of the Phi Beta Kappa and Phi Kappa Psi societies. He is a Presbyterian in faith and a thirty-second degree Mason. Six feet in height, he weighs 190 pounds; he has white hair and a ruddy complexion.

References

    Cur Hist 20:734-6 Ag '24
    Cur Opinion 65:294-5 N '18 por; 77: 290-2 S '24
    Lit Digest 82:35-40 Jl 26 '24 pors
    N Y Herald Tribune II p1 My 18 '52 por
    N Y Times II p2 My 23 '20; p1+ Jl 10 '24 pors; VIII p1 Jl 13 '24 por; p25 D 17 '52 por
    Nation 119:94-5 Jl 28 '24
    Outlook 137:59-60 My 14 '24 por; 137: 466-9 Jl 23 '24 por
    R of Rs 70:149-56 Ag '24 pors
    Sat Eve Post 197:3-4 Ag 30 '24
    This Week p13 D 7 '52 por
    Time 59:25-6 My 26 '52 por
    World's Work 48:491-7 S '24 pors; 48: 605-12 O '24 pors

    Biographical Directory of the American Congress, 1774-1949 (1950)
    Huntley, T. A. Life of John W. Davis (1924)
    National Cyclopædia of American Biography Current vol A (1926)
    Poor's Register of Directors and Executives (1951)
    Stone, I. They Also Ran (1945)
    Who's Who, 1952
    Who's Who in America, 1952-53
    Who's Who in Law, 1937
    Who's Who in New York, 1952
    Who's Who in the East (1951)
    Willson, B. America's Ambassadors to England, 1785-1929 (1929)
    World Biography (1948)

DAY, LARAINE Oct. 13, 1920- Motion picture actress; radio and television commentator

Address: b. c/o William Morris Agency, 1740 Broadway, New York 19. h. 715 Park Ave., New York 21; "The Sycamores," Santa Monica, Calif.

Since her motion picture debut in 1937, Laraine Day has achieved film stardom, acted on the legitimate stage, conducted her own radio and television shows, written a book, and won the reputation of being "the First Lady of Baseball." Among the thirty-five pictures in which she has appeared are *My Son, My Son,*

Foreign Correspondent, Journey for Margaret, Mr. Lucky, The Locket, and the Dr. Kildare series.

After her marriage, in 1947, to Leo Durocher, the present manager of the New York Giants Baseball Club, the actress developed into one of the game's foremost women enthusiasts. She has recently limited most of her professional activity to television interview shows during the baseball season and to TV film shorts about sports.

Laraine Day was born La Raine Johnson in Roosevelt, Utah, on October 13, 1920, the daughter of Clarence Irwin Johnson and Ada M. Johnson. She has two brothers (one of whom, Lamar, is her twin) and four sisters. Her maternal great-grandfather, Charles C. Rich, was an important leader in the Mormon Church who had tried unsuccessfully to establish a Mormon colony on the Pacific Coast. Her grandfather had settled in Roosevelt, and her father, who served as mayor of the town, worked as a grain dealer and Government agent among the Ute Indians for over twenty years. The family moved from Utah to Long Beach, California, in 1931, and it was there that Laraine attended George Washington Junior High School and was graduated from Polytechnic High School.

Laraine had wanted to become an actress ever since she was taken to her first movie at the age of six. In Long Beach, she joined the Players' Guild, managed by the late Elias Day, and was eventually given leading roles in such plays as Growing Pains, Call It a Day, Flyaway Home, Winterset, Private Lives, Victoria Regina, and, in addition, toured the West in the road company of Conflict. The young actress received most of her dramatic training from Day, and in gratitude she took his surname for her own in 1938.

According to Collier's (June 7, 1941), Laraine Johnson was "discovered" by talent scout Marty Martyn. She was given the part of a girl who sat at a soda fountain and spoke four lines in Samuel Goldwyn's production of Stella Dallas (1937). Then Paramount signed her to play a small role in Scandal Street (1938); later, when her six months' option came up for renewal, the studio dropped her for "lack of talent."

Her next screen appearances were as George O'Brien's leading lady in three Westerns made by RKO-Radio: Border G-Man (1938), Painted Desert (1938), and Arizona Legion (1939).

Taking the name Laraine Day, she signed a seven-year contract in 1938 with Metro-Goldwyn-Mayer. Her initial assignment for the studio was a subordinate role in I Take This Woman, starring Hedy Lamarr and Spencer Tracy, which was not released until 1940. Actually, Miss Day was first seen under Metro's auspices as an Irish lass adopted by a New York policeman, played by Wallace Beery, in Sergeant Madden (1939).

The public came to know Miss Day chiefly through her portrayal of the young nurse, Mary Lamont, in the Dr. Kildare series. She first created this role in Calling Dr. Kildare (1939), and along with Lew Ayres and Lionel Barrymore became a permanent member of the cast

LARAINE DAY

in each succeeding picture, which included The Secret of Dr. Kildare (1939); Dr. Kildare's Strange Case, Dr. Kildare Goes Home, and Dr. Kildare's Crisis (1940); and The People vs. Dr. Kildare (1941). Studio officials finally decided that Miss Day was becoming too closely identified with this character in the public's mind. Therefore, in Dr. Kildare's Wedding Day (1941), the script writers arranged to have Mary Lamont killed by a truck and Miss Day was free to go on to more ambitious productions.

Her first big opportunity came on a loan-out to United Artists for the Edward Small production of My Son, My Son (1940), in which she was cast as Maeve, a sensitive young girl who wanted to become an actress. She was tested for this role, but did not get it until Frances Dee collapsed on the set. Critical praise for this part won her the feminine lead in Alfred Hitchcock's Foreign Correspondent, which Walter Wanger produced for United Artists later that year. A nationwide poll of motion picture exhibitors in 1941 designated Miss Day as the most promising of all the younger players in Hollywood.

At MGM, Miss Day had appeared in Tarzan Finds a Son! (1939); And One Was Beautiful (1940); The Trial of Mary Dugan and The Bad Man (1941). Following her release from the Dr. Kildare series, her studio assigned her to Unholy Partners (1941) and Kathleen (1941). These were followed in 1942 by A Yank on the Burma Road, Fingers at the Window, and Journey for Margaret (a story of war-torn Britain which featured Robert Young and Margaret O'Brien). The New York Herald Tribune critic found Miss Day "moving" in the serious role of a young matron suffering from emotional shock.

On May 16, 1942, Miss Day married James Ray Hendricks, a former dance-band singer

DAY, LARAINE—*Continued*

who became an executive of the Santa Monica airport. They adopted two girls and a boy.

Miss Day's favorites among the films in which she has starred are *Mr. Lucky* (1943) in which she played a sophisticated Park Avenue socialite, and *The Locket* (1946), a psychological melodrama in which she portrayed "a sweet-faced wanton." Critic Eileen Creelman in the New York *Sun* felt the actress made the neurotic girl "a very real person." During the period between these two pictures, Miss Day was loaned to Paramount for Cecil B. De Mille's *The Story of Dr. Wassell* (1944); returned to RKO for *Bride By Mistake* (1944) and *Those Endearing Young Charms* (1945); and *Keep Your Powder Dry* (1945).

Released from her MGM contract at her own request in May 1946, Miss Day signed a contract in December with RKO to make one film a year for five years, at a salary reported to be $100,000 a picture. She was co-starred with John Wayne in *Tycoon* (1947), and then lent to United Artists for *My Dear Secretary* (1948), with Kirk Douglas and Keenan Wynn. She played opposite Robert Ryan in RKO's *The Woman on Pier 13* (1949), and was again borrowed by United Artists for *Without Honor* (1949), with Dane Clark and Franchot Tone.

After she had obtained a divorce in Mexico, Miss Day on January 21, 1947, married Leo Durocher, then manager of the Brooklyn Dodgers Baseball Club. (They went through a second ceremony on February 15, 1948, when her California divorce became final). It was in April 1947 that Durocher was suspended by Baseball Commissioner A. B. (Happy) Chandler from participating in professional baseball for the rest of that season. He returned as manager of the Dodgers early in 1948, but during the summer made his surprise move to the managership of the Dodgers' arch-rivals in the National League—the New York Giants. "The move from Brooklyn to New York marked a definite change in my life," Miss Day has observed. "Before that I had been commuting between Hollywood and New York and now I settled down to baseball."

At school, as a young girl, Miss Day had hated baseball, and had never seen a regularly scheduled game. When she was first introduced to Durocher, she didn't know who he was or even what the Dodgers were. "After I married Leo, I *had* to learn about baseball," she has explained (*Collier's*, March 8, 1952). "I read everything I could, with the exception of the rulebook." Before Durocher even took her to a game, he told her stories about all the players—little incidents about their careers, their families. When she did see the players in action, she felt she knew them so well that she was interested in their playing.

Miss Day, in turn, has used this same method —of stressing the human interest angles, the personalities of the individual players, instead of statistics—in her various efforts to stimulate further interest in the game. "Baseball is not a lot of statistics to me," she has said, "it's blood and tears." Although she quickly developed into one of the game's most ardent fans,

she never quite believed she belonged "to the great fraternity of baseball" until 1951, when she was invited to appear at the annual dinner of the New York chapter of the Baseball Writers Association—the first woman ever to be so honored.

In May 1950, Miss Day initiated her fifteen-minute sports interview television show preceding all home games of the Giants which the New York Station WPIX carried that year. At first, she had misgivings about the prospect of exchanging "bright baseball quips with famous players before an audience that knew more about the sport than I would ever know," but she soon found that having followed the players' careers closely, she knew just about what to ask them. *Variety's* reviewer of the first telecast commented on "her good looks, infectious personality, and better-than-speaking acquaintance with baseball."

Her aim was to interest people in the Giants and in baseball (in that order), with particular emphasis on encouraging new fans among women. The program was entirely unrehearsed and originated from a special booth underneath the stands at the Polo Grounds. *Variety's* reviewer of the first telecast commented on "her good looks, infectious personality, and better-than-speaking acquaintance with baseball."

Miss Day's other activities included a tour of the summer theatre circuit in 1950 as the star of *Angel Street*. This marked her first stage work in the East, although she had appeared in the play with Gregory Peck for ten weeks at the La Jolla (California) Playhouse in the preceding year. In May 1951 the *Laraine Day Show* made its debut over ABC-TV; it was a half-hour program of variety turns and interviews (not connected with baseball) every Saturday afternoon. Also in May, the première of *Daydreaming with Laraine*, a fifteen-minute video show, was given on Thursday evenings over ABC-TV. The premise of this program was that sports figures have unexpected non-athletic avocations. Miss Day extended her broadcast activities in May 1952 with a nightly interview series over New York Station WMGM from midnight to 3:00 A.M. That same year her book, *Day with the Giants,* (edited by Kyle Crichton) was published by Doubleday. The *Herald Tribune* reviewer found it "an amusing, informative book, the first . . . to report on baseball from the viewpoint of the wife," while Aline B. Louchheim (*Times*) commented: "Every day is Ladies' Day for Laraine Day and she makes a good story of it."

In 1953 Miss Day has been appearing in films made for television, some forty fifteen-minute video shorts. The series is called *Double Play with Durocher and Day* and features the couple interviewing personalities from baseball and other sports. It was announced in May 1953 that Miss Day's new ABC series, *White Collar Girl,* would soon go into production at the Hal Roach Studios. Shortly before this, the actress told an interviewer that for the first time in six years she had set up her life so she could return to the major studios for feature film work. "Pictures are still second with me, though," she added. "My life as Mrs. Leo Durocher and baseball come first."

The screen and video star, who is five feet five inches tall and weighs 112 pounds, has light brown hair and blue-green eyes. As a Mormon, she does not drink alcoholic liquors, coffee, or tea, and does not smoke. The Durochers live in California during the winter, spend six weeks in spring training and exhibition tours, and make New York their headquarters during the regular season. (Their two adopted children, Michele, and Christopher Ray, usually accompany them.) She sees every home game at the Polo Grounds and is careful to do all her rooting *for* the Giants, and not *against* the opposing team, which she thinks is both tactless and unsporting.

The social life of the Durochers depends entirely upon the outcome of the ball game; they never go out nights following a lost game but stay home and watch television. For recreation, Miss Day enjoys reading mystery stories, has taken up weaving, and writes poetry and children's stories. She likes television and the movie work, but does not care much for stage acting, finding it boring to do the same show over and over again. "Let someone else be the world's greatest actress," she remarked after her conversion to the game, "I'll be the world's greatest baseball fan."

References

Collier's 107:14 Je 7 '41; 129:23+ Mr 8 '52 pors
Cue 21:12+ Ag 16 '52 pors
N Y Herald Tribune X p10 D 14 '41 por
N Y Times II p9 My 21 '50
Day, L. Day with the Giants (1952)
Motion Picture and Television Almanac, 1952-53
Winchester's Screen Encyclopedia (1948)

DEBUTTS, HARRY A(SHBY) Oct. 13, 1895- Railroad president
Address: b. Southern Railway Bldg., McPherson Sq., Washington, D.C.; h. Upperville, Va.

Beginning his career in railroad as a "pick and shovel" track apprentice on the Southern Railroad System, Harry A. DeButts advanced through almost every type of position in the company to become president on January 1, 1951, succeeding the retiring Ernest Eden Norris. DeButts had been elected vice-president in charge of operations in October 1937, after more than twenty years employment with the Southern system, which with its subsidiaries operates about 8,000 miles of track and constitutes the largest rail transportation network in the Southeastern United States.

One of the eight children of Dulany Forrest and Emma Virginia (Ashby) DeButts, Harry Ashby DeButts was born at Delaplane, Virginia on October 13, 1895. His forebears on both sides were members of old Southern families, his paternal grandfather Richard Earle DeButts (a descendant of Dr. Samuel DeButts who came to the United States from County Sligo, Ireland, in 1790) and his mother's father, Harry S. Ashby, having fought for the Confederate States as members of Mosby's Rangers. His maternal grandfather was the Southern Railway's station agent at Delaplane, Fauquier County, Virginia, and Harry DeButts' father, a farmer and horse-breeder, had worked on the

railroad until injured in a freight train derailment.

During the years that Harry DeButts attended Fauquier County grade schools, from 1903 to 1908, he often visited his grandfather at the station, where, for helping the local crew unload freight, he was rewarded by a free boxcar ride to the next town. His boyhood ambition was to be a conductor, and when he completed high school in 1912 at Front Royal in adjacent Warren County, he chose Virginia Military Institute in Lexington for his college because he believed that its course in civil engineering "would be good training for a railroad man." A month after receiving his B.S. degree in June 1916, he began a career with the Southern Railway System which has been interrupted only by a year's service with the armed forces in World War I. Starting at Culpeper, Virginia, as a student track apprentice working with pick and shovel, he later became foreman of a six-man gang assigned to four or five miles of double track near Buena, Virginia. He was promoted to general yard foreman at Alexandria, Virginia, in June 1917, and to assistant track supervisor at Strasburg, Virginia, in November.

For a year, beginning June 1, 1918, Harry DeButts fought in World War I in the United States Marines, advancing in rank from a private to a first lieutenant. He then rejoined the Southern Railway as assistant track supervisor at Manassas, was promoted to track supervisor at Strasburg in October 1919, and was appointed assistant trainmaster at Birmingham, Alabama, in December 1920, and trainmaster at Sheffield, Alabama, in June 1921. The role of trainmaster, he has observed with amusement, was the closest he ever came to realizing his boyhood dream of being a conductor. From his position in Sheffield as assistant superintendent (1923-24), he rose to division superintendent on June 18, 1924, and during the next five to six years was employed in that capacity in Selma (Alabama), Macon (Georgia), Alexandria (Virginia), and Greensboro (North Carolina). In April 1930 he was advanced to the position of general superintendent (which has since been abolished) in Danville, Virginia. "I didn't miss a single rung of the ladder," he has recalled, "including one that isn't there now."

The Southern Railway System's main line runs from Washington, D.C., to New Orleans, Louisiana, with major terminals at Jacksonville, Memphis, Louisville, and Cincinnati. The Southern has also controlled the Mobile and Ohio (running northward from the Gulf of Mexico to St. Louis), the Alabama Great Southern, the Georgia Southern and Florida, and several minor lines which collectively brought the system trackage up to about 8,000 miles. Since the railway serves a primarily agricultural area, its annual financial status is closely linked to the price of cotton and the size of the cotton crop. Thus from 1897 to 1924 the road paid no dividends on common stock, but for seven years after that enjoyed a period of relative prosperity. In 1931 payment of dividends again ceased, and two years later Ernest Eden Norris, who had built up

HARRY A. DEBUTTS

a notable record as vice-president of the subsidiary Mobile and Ohio, was recalled to Southern headquarters at Washington, D.C., to be the parent road's vice-president in charge of operations. In August 1934 vice-president Norris named DeButts to the post of general manager, with headquarters at Charlotte, North Carolina. During the next three years Norris coupled operating economies with technological, servicing, and public relations improvements, with the result that by 1936 the line's net operating income was more than double that of 1931, while the gross income in the same category fell below the 1931 figure (*Time*, November 1, 1937).

When Ernest Eden Norris succeeded Fairfax Harrison as fourth president of the railway in January 1937, DeButts was summoned to Washington to take Norris' position as vice-president in charge of operations. During the thirteen years in which he held this post, DeButts was responsible for an almost complete conversion on the Southern from steam to diesel locomotives, for instituting safety devices, for launching extensive improvements in the system's freight terminal facilities, especially at Knoxville, Birmingham, and New Orleans. With a view to "humanizing" the system's organization, he and seven of his associates personally purchased a mountain camp at Asheville, North Carolina, which is used for frequent conferences of supervisory personnel. He has become known among his colleagues as "an alert and foresighted recruiting officer and educator" (*Railway Age*, December 31, 1951). As a result of the economies effected by DeButts, according to *Railway Age*, "in 1950 the Southern hauled just twice as many tons of revenue freight as in 1938, with an even larger increase in ton-mileage." The line's passenger-miles in 1950 were 52 per cent greater than in 1938; operating revenue in 1938 was $89,400,000, and in 1950, $239,900,000, an increase of 168 per cent.

On the retirement from the presidency of Norris, who then became chairman of Southern's board of directors, Harry DeButts was elected the fifth president of the Southern Railway. Taking office on January 1, 1952, DeButts, who simultaneously became vice-president of the Southern's various subsidiaries, pledged completion of dieselization as quickly as funds would permit, as well as continuation of the yard improvement program, then about 50 to 60 per cent achieved. Looking forward to a reorganization which would make it possible to move freight in solid blocks and to have modern yards, DeButts also advocated fewer and better passenger trains, stating that "those anemic local passenger trains which nobody rides and which are losing us barrels of money have got to come off." A year later, as a result of careful management, DeButts was able to report (January 1953) that Southern Railway net income had risen to $27,834,900 in 1952, or 47 per cent above the $18,856,597 of 1951, and to announce a forthcoming dividend of $1.25 a share on common stock.

Harry DeButts is a director of the Association of American Railroads, chairman of the Southeastern Presidents' (railroad) Conference, a governor of the National Industrial Conference, a director of both the Equitable Life Assurance Society of the United States and the Riggs National Bank at Washington, and a member of the American Society of Sales Executives, the American Railway Engineering Association, and International House. His fraternity is the Kappa Alpha, and his clubs are the Chevy Chase and Metropolitan in Washington, the Blue Ridge Country in Millwood (Virginia), and the Pendennis in Louisville.

DeButts married Margaret Rose Blair on June 7, 1922; he is now a widower. His daughter, the former Frances Van Meter DeButts, is the wife of George M. Page, of Austin, Texas. The railroad executive is an Episcopalian and a Mason. He has been described in the Knoxville *News-Sentinel* as "a big man with a kind and understanding smile." For recreation he may turn to hunting, fishing, golf, or the raising of white-faced cattle on his farm in Upperville, Virginia, near his birthplace.

References

   Knoxville (Tenn.) News-Sentinel D 9
     '51 por
   Manuf Rec 120:37 D '51 por
   Newsweek 38:73 D 10 '51 por
   Railway Age 131:43-45 D 31 '51 por
   Time 59:86 Ja 14 '52
   Washington (D.C.) Post p8 D 1 '51; D
     3 '51
   Business Executives of America (1950)
   International World Who's Who, 1948-49
   Poor's Register of Directors and Executives (1951)
   Who's Who in America, 1952-53
   Who's Who in Commerce and Industry
     (1951)
   Who's Who in Railroading (1946)
   World Biography (1948)

DE KIEWIET, CORNELIS W(ILLEM)

(dě kē'vēt) May 21, 1902- University president; historian

Address: b. c/o University of Rochester, 15 Prince St., Rochester, N.Y.; h. 22 Berkeley St., Rochester, N.Y.

Beginning his career as an educator thirty years ago in Southern Rhodesia, Cornelis W. de Kiewiet is now president of the University of Rochester. At the time he accepted the presidency in October, 1951, he was acting president of Cornell University.

Expressing his concern for "the academic spirit and intellectual coherence," Dr. de Kiewiet has said that these have gradually diminished and that education is being replaced by interest in special subjects. "The highest function of education," he has stated, "is to make human experience contemporary; that is, to make it available for use in the life of a man or a nation" (*Scientific Monthly,* February 1953).

Cornelis Willem de Kiewiet was born in Rotterdam, Netherlands, on May 21, 1902, the son of Arie Willem and Maria A. R. (Van Vugt) de Kiewiet. He has a twin brother and two sisters. His father was construction supervisor on the railroad between Johannesburg, South Africa, and Delagoa Bay, and in the corps of engineers on the Republican side during the Boer War. Young Cornelis was reared in both Rotterdam and Johannesburg.

After graduating from Jeppe High School in Johannesburg in 1919 de Kiewiet attended the University of Witwatersrand there and received his A.B. degree in 1923 and M.A. in 1924. He saw military service in the Imperial Light Horse, emergency enlistment, during 1922, and taught Afrikaans and history at Prince Edward High School, Salisbury, Southern Rhodesia, from 1923 to 1925.

He went to the University of London as a Herbert Ainsworth scholar and received his Ph.D. degree in 1927. He studied at the University of Paris from 1927 to 1929 and the University of Berlin. Deciding to come to the United States in 1929, he joined the faculty of the State University of Iowa as an assistant professor of history. He became full professor in 1937, and in 1941 accepted an appointment at Cornell University as professor of modern history. He became dean of the College of Arts and Sciences in 1945, provost in 1948, and acting president in 1949.

In helping the university settle a strike of building service workers, he recognized union membership as "voluntary" and declared membership or non-membership to be "without prejudice to any employee" (New York *Times,* December 7, 1950).

While Dr. de Kiewiet was serving as acting president, Cornell University established an association with the Sloan-Kettering Institute for Cancer Research and the Cornell Medical College in New York. It also received an endowment for its first professorship of American Values, and established the Daniel and Florence Guggenheim Aviation Safety Center in New York City.

At the eightieth annual commencement of Cornell University on June 14, 1948, de Kiewiet

Loulen Studio

CORNELIS W. DE KIEWIET

delivered an address "Communism Sets a Trap" (*Vital Speeches* August 1, 1948). He declared that to select some of life's elements, qualities and potentialities and to reject others "is to decree that life shall be unfruitful and limit its capacity for continuous adjustment. That is the trap that Communism has set for the world."

The selection of Dr. de Kiewiet as president of the University of Rochester was announced October 20, 1950 by M. Herbert Eisenhart, chairman of the university's board of trustees. Addressing a convocation commemorating the 100th anniversary of the University of Rochester, he advised that "universities have a moral obligation to fight cynicism, resignation and despair in this generation" (New York *Herald Tribune,* November 5, 1950).

Addressing the December 1952 conference on scientific manpower held in St. Louis by the American Association for the Advancement of Science (AAAS), he said "never in modern times has a nation possessed so much physical power and yet been so baffled in the conduct of its foreign policy" (*Scientific Monthly,* February 1953). He advocated a more generous immigration policy for the United States, less hurling of loose charges of subversiveness against higher education, and more emphasis in education upon skills in human relations.

At his installation on June 11, 1951, as president of the University of Rochester, de Kiewiet advocated "a reciprocal pledge between the university and society to support one another in discerning the highest interests of our civilization" (New York *Times,* June 12, 1951). Since he took office he has established one curriculum for men and women undergraduates in a co-educational College of Arts and Sciences. He has also favored State-operated educational television channels.

(Continued next page)

DE KIEWIET, CORNELIS—*Continued*

Dr. de Kiewiet is a member of an advisory committee of educators and economists who reported on June 13, 1953 to Harold E. Stassen, Director for Mutual Security, and urged a long-range program for building up the economies of "undeveloped areas" in Asia and Latin America by means of technical aid and investments to curb Communist domination.

Dr. de Kiewiet's public services have included a study in 1947 of South African educational institutions for the Carnegie Corporation, adviser in 1951 on a development program for the Institute of Social and Economic Research of the University College of the British West Indies, and director, in the same year, of a study of political and social conditions in East Africa financed by the Carnegie Corporation and administered by the Institute of International Education. During World War II he had been a director of Army Specialized Training Programs in Areas and Languages, comprising Russian, Italian, German, and Chinese, and a special consultant to the Department of the Navy.

Author of several articles for professional journals, de Kiewiet has also written three books on historical subjects: *British Colonial Policy and the South African Republics, 1848-1872* (1929), a doctoral thesis on the South African history of isolation; *The Imperial Factor in South Africa* (Cambridge 1937), analyzing British policy in relation to racial, social, and economic issues in South Africa from 1870-90; and *A History of South Africa* (Oxford, 1941).

He edited *Studies in British History* (1941) and contributed the chapter "United States and the British Empire: Past and Present" to *Impact of War on America* (1942); the chapter "United States and the United Kingdom" to *Foreign Policy for the United States* (1947), and the chapter "Frontier and the Constitution in South Africa" to *Constitution Reconsidered* (1938).

De Kiewiet received an honorary LL.D. degree from Syracuse University in January 1951. A scholarship in history was set up at Cornell University in 1953 in his honor. Since 1950 he has been a director of the Lincoln-Rochester Trust Company. His organization memberships include Phi Beta Kappa, the American Historical Association, the American Council of Learned Societies (chairman finance committee), and the University, Genesee Valley, and Rochester Country Clubs.

He married Lucea Marian Hejinian, a university instructor, on August 22, 1930, and their children are Marie, Christine, and John. De Kiewiet is five feet eleven inches tall, weighs 180 pounds, and has light hair and grey eyes. He became a United States citizen in 1939. His hobbies are hunting and fishing.

References

Sci Mo 76:57 F '53

Directory of American Scholars (1951)
International Who's Who, 1952
Who's Who in America, 1952-53
Who's Who in American Education, 1951-52

DIBELIUS, OTTO (FRIEDRICH KARL) BISHOP (dē-bā′lē-ŏŏs) May 15, 1880- German religious leader; author

Address: Faraday Weg 10, Berlin-Dahlem, Germany

Regarded as one of the world's great churchmen and the foremost Protestant leader in Germany, the Reverend Doctor Otto Dibelius has been Lutheran Bishop of Berlin and Brandenburg since the end of World War II. He was elected Presiding Bishop of the newly constituted Evangelical Church in January, 1949, and he is also a member of the Central Committee of the World Council of Churches. With Pastor Martin Niemöller, he received world-wide attention in 1937 when both defied the National Socialists, criticizing the racial and doctrinal ukases, and thereby became defendants in celebrated trials.

Three-quarters of the members of his Diocese live behind the Iron Curtain in the Soviet zone of East Germany. The Bishop has been outspoken in opposing recent totalitarian abuses. He is the author of about twenty books on ecclesiastical history, Christian practice, and Government.

Friedrich Karl Otto Dibelius, the son of Otto Andreas and Margarete (Käuffer) Dibelius, was born in Berlin, Germany, on May 15, 1880. His father, a privy councilor, was the brother of Dr. Franz Dibelius, who became vice-president of the Evangelical-Lutheran consistory in Saxony. After attending the Berlin Lichterfeld Gymnasium, he entered the University of Berlin, where he majored in theology and received his Ph.D. degree in 1901. At the University of Berlin the future bishop was greatly influenced in the choice of a lifework by Professor Adolf von Harnack, author of numerous works on New Testament and early ecclesiastical history, and president of the Evangelical Congress from 1902 to 1912. Under the guidance of von Harnack, Dibelius prepared his first important, if brief, work of scholarship, *Der Vaterunser* (1903), the subtitle of which may be translated as Outline for a History of Prayer in the Early and Mediaeval Church. Dibelius became a Licentiate in Theology at the University of Berlin in 1904, and subsequently pursued his ecclesiastical studies at the University of Wittenberg and for a year at the University of Edinburgh.

Ordained to the Lutheran Church in Berlin in 1906, Dibelius began his ministry as a pastor at Crossen-on-the-Oder in the following year. He was called as a pastor to Danzig in 1910 and in that year published his second important treatise, *Unsere Grosstadtgemeinden*, dealing with the problems confronting municipal corporations. The next book completed by Dibelius, *Das Kirchliche Leben Schottlands* (The Spiritual Life of Scotland), was published in 1911, just after his call to Lauenburg in Pomerania as rector. Returning to Berlin as a rector in 1915, he finished his *Das Königliche Priesterseminar zu Wittenberg, 1817-1917* (The Royal Seminary at Wittenberg, 1817-1917) two years later and in 1921 became a member of the Council of Churches. In 1925 Dibelius was appointed general superintendent of the Kurmak

(East Prussia) and was officiating as such when his *Das Jahrhundert der Kirche* (First Century of the Church) appeared in 1927. He contributed the chapter entitled "The Protestant Churches in Germany" to Sir James Marchant's anthology *The Reunion of Christianity* (1929) and during 1929 also wrote *Friede auf Erden?* (Peace on Earth?), which was published in 1930.

When Adolf Hitler became Chancellor of Germany in 1933, Dibelius was suspended from his office for failure to concur in National Socialist racial theories, but continued what he has described as "illegal resistance" against the Nazis, and in 1934, after having been arrested three times, he hired a 'non-Aryan' secretary. "The administrative building of the Church having been seized and turned over to the Nazi puppet 'Reichsbischof' Ludwig Müller," wrote E. R. Turner of the *Christian Century* (October 11, 1950), "Dibelius worked in a one-room office of the Brandenburg Council of the Confessional Church. . . .Believing that every great religious movement is carried on the wings of song, Dibelius wrote several hymns and found publishers for the hymns of Heinrich Vogel and Otto Reithmüller." As a fellow member with Pastor Martin Niemöller of the Confessional Council's Brotherhood Synod, Dr. Dibelius was a signatory of the 1935 manifesto which read in part: The State's power and sovereignty are wholly a gift of God, who alone founded and preserves human authority. Whoever puts blood and race in the place of God, the creator, destroys the State's foundation." In February 1935 Dr. Dibelius addressed an "open letter" to Hanns Kerrl, the Nazi Minister for Church Affairs. "You have demanded that Protestant preaching must change," he charged. "You said further that priests declare Jesus is a Jew, and that they talk of the Jew Paul and assert that salvation comes from Jews—that this must cease. When you declare Evangelical pastors shall not repeat these things you forbid them to say that which stands in the New Testament."

About six weeks later the Nazi secret police confiscated a pamphlet jointly written by Niemöller and Dibelius entitled *We Summon Germany to God*; and at the beginning of July Niemöller and about fifty other Evangelical pastors were arrested. Dibelius, who was not one of the fifty, took over Niemöller's pulpit in the Berlin suburb of Dahlen on the following Sunday, pronounced the arrest "a blow aimed consciously at the Christian Church in Germany," and "scornfully referred to 'the vanity of temporary rulers'" (New York *Times*). The "open letter" to Hanns Kerrl had meanwhile been brought to the personal attention of Hitler, and on August 2 Dr. Dibelius was arrested and charged with "malicious misrepresentation" of the Church Minister. Four days later (August 6) he was tried by an emergency court which found him "not guilty." The controlled German press made no mention of this verdict, which was probably a major cause of the postponement of the trial of Pastor Niemöller for several months to permit gathering of "new evidence." New works by Dibelius continued

BISHOP OTTO DIBELIUS

to be published in Germany, at least until 1941. These include *Bericht über Jesus aus Nazareth* and *Die werdende Kirche,* both dated 1938, and *Die Jünger,* an account of the youth movement past and contemporary (1941), all published by Furche-verlag, Berlin.

On conclusion of World War II, Dr. Dibelius became, in 1945, the Lutheran Bishop of Berlin and Brandenburg, and a member of the Ecumenical Council. In 1948 Bishop Dibelius was named a member of the Central Committee of the World Council of Churches, and in July was a delegate to a conference in Eisenach held to consider the proposed constitution for a new united Evangelical Church in Germany which had been drafted by the venerable Lutheran Bishop Theophil Wurm of Württemberg and which was adopted after five days of debate. (In the words of *Time,* the new constitution, "while allowing each church to retain its own viewpoint on Holy Communion," stated that "all German Protestants can partake of the sacrament in any German Protestant church.")

Dibelius' belief that "on freedom depends all faith and all genuine inner life," together with the doctrine of his 1949 book *Grenzen des Staats* (Limitations of the State) published by Tübingen, Furche-verlag, displeased Soviet authorities, but in general he refrained from direct criticism of Soviet methods until the early summer of 1949, when activation of both the West German Federal Republic and the East German Democratic (Soviet) Republic was in the offing. Then in a Whitsuntide pastoral letter read from all pulpits of the EKID on June 5, 1949, he attacked police state methods in the Russion zone and denounced what

DIBELIUS, OTTO KARL, BISHOP—
Continued

amounted to one-party, Nazi-type balloting for the Volkskongress as "based on internal dishonesty." The Soviet-controlled Berlin radio demanded his removal as head of the Evangelical Church in Berlin and Brandenburg, but he was quickly confirmed in his position by the clergy of his diocese, and continued to preach in the Marienkirche at least once a month. Bishop Dibelius, who added *Vom Erbe der Vater* to his round score of books in 1950, wrote to the late Josef Stalin in September 1952 what the *Christian Century* described as "a letter . . . protesting against the universal violations of justice in the Eastern zone," and followed this up in London on the following November 19 with a speech attacking slave-labor conditions in the Soviet zone.

During the next month Bishop Dibelius visited the United States to attend the biennial meeting of the National Council of Churches at Denver, Colorado, and in a speech there (December 11) declared that Communism could be conquered only by the Christian faith. "God," he asserted, "has made Germany a battlefield in this big fight. We realize that it is a fatal question for all the world whether we Christians in Germany withstand and finally win, or whether we will succumb to the materialistic philosophy of the East." A week later (December 19) J. Emlyn Williams of the *Christian Science Monitor* reported that the East German Ministry of the Interior was believed to be "studying how it can legally refuse to recognize Dr. Dibelius as Bishop in those parts of his diocese inside East Germany," and that he might not "be allowed to appear in Brandenburg 'on grounds of State security.'"

What United Press Staff Correspondent Joseph Fleming characterized as "a violent attack" on the Bishop by East German Communists ·(December 26) was widely regarded as heralding "open war on the Church" and the formation of a "Government-controlled Soviet church zone," since much was made of a statement by Deputy Premier Walter Ulbricht to the effect that "the East German church may not take orders from the West." On March 1, 1953, following the arrest of the pastor of the Marienkirche on undisclosed charges, Bishop Dibelius again crossed into the Soviet zone to occupy the arrested pastor's pulpit.

Although Bishop Dibelius has denounced Communism, according to *Time* (April 6, 1953) Americans find him "a hard man to understand. He is one of Germany's few consistent fighters against the totalitarian state, yet . . . to Dibelius' mind, the democracies are at root the same 'power states' as the dictatorships, because, he thinks, they do not base their authority on God."

During his recent visit to the United States, Bishop Dibelius was awarded (December 15, 1952) the honorary degree of Doctor of Humane Letters by Gettysburg College in Pennsylvania and he has also received the same degree from the University of Toronto as well as an LL.D. from the University of Marburg.

He had earlier been awarded an honorary Doctor of Theology degree by the University of Giessen (1925) and an honorary Doctor of Divinity degree by Eden College at Webster Grove in Maryland (1935). The Bishop is considered an authority on Goethe, about whom he has lectured from the ecclesiastical point of view.

Bishop Dibelius stands at a little over five feet six inches; his eyes are brown, his hair is described as "dark-blond," and he wears a mustache and small goatee beard. He is a widower; his wife, the former Armgaard Frieda Josephine Wilmanns, died December 2, 1952. The couple, married November 13, 1906, became the parents of six children, Otto, Wolfgang, Hanna, Christes, Margarete, and Franz. (Wolfgang and Franz were killed in World War II.) Dibelius' party is the Christian Democratic Union. History is his favorite reading; for outdoor recreation he turns to golf and tennis.

References

Christian Cent 67:1199-1201 O 11 '50
N Y Herald Tribune p20 D 10 '52 por
Time 53:61-3 Ja 24 '49 por; 53:60+ Je 20 '49; 55:43-4+ My 8 '50 por; 60:56 D 8 '52 por; 61:66+ Ap 6 '53 por
Bartlett, R. M. They Dared to Believe (1952)
Deutschland-Jahrbuch (1949)
Grosse Brockhaus, Ergänzungsband (1935)
International Who's Who, 1952
Kleine Brockhaus (1949)
Kürschners Deutscher Gelehrten-Kalendar (1950)
Meyers Lexikon, Ergänzung (1931)
Neue Herder (1949)
Schweitzer Lexicon (1946)
Wer Ist Wer? (1951)
World Biography (1948)

DIETRICH, MARLENE Dec. 27, 1904-
Motion picture and radio actress
Address: c/o Columbia Broadcasting System, 485 Madison Ave., New York 22

Twenty-nine years of acting in motion pictures have not dimmed the sparkle of Marlene Dietrich, whose popularity has proved more durable than that of many of her contemporaries. Her most recent screen success was in RKO's *Rancho Notorious* in 1952 and her present radio appearance is in a weekly program on the Columbia Broadcasting System entitled *Time for Love,* patterned after her successful *Cafe Istanbul* program on the American Broadcasting Company network last year. For her services in World War II in entertaining troops overseas she received the Medal of Freedom, the highest honor the War Department can award to a civilian.

Marlene Dietrich was born on December 27, 1904 in Berlin, Germany. Her father, Louis Dietrich, was a major in the Uhlan cavalry. She was christened Maria Magdalena (which was elided into Marlene). Her mother, Josephine Felsing Dietrich, was the daughter of Conrad Felsing, a wealthy Berlin jeweler. Three years after Major Dietrich died Marlene's mother married Colonel Edward von Losch of the Hussars. The family lived in various garrison towns in eastern Germany. Marlene attended a private school at Weimar. From governesses she learned French and English before she was seven years old. In the. Dietrich-von Losch household, a Prussian-Spartan regime was enforced, and Marlene learned "such character-building disciplines as how to go without an overcoat when you feel cold, and how to refrain from asking for a glass of water when you feel thirsty" (*Life*, August 18, 1952). At seven she began to study the violin, and looked forward to becoming a concert violinist. After receiving her early education at the Augusta Victoria School in Berlin, she entered the *Hochschule fur Musik*, but an injury to her wrist when she was eighteen years old compelled her to abandon her hope for a musical career.

She then enrolled in Max Reinhardt's school of dramatic art, using the name of Marlene Dietrich because of the von Losch family's opposition to her going on the stage. After playing several walk-on parts she was given a minor role in *Midsummer Night's Dream* which elicited favorable comment on her looks, but no mention of her acting.

She was sent from the Reinhardt school in 1924 with a group of students to the UFA studios (Universum-Film Aktien-Gesellschaft) to apply for jobs as extras in a film. Marlene met Rudolf Sieber, the assistant casting director, who advised her to put her long, blond hair for a gambling scene being screened. She followed his advice and won the part. She was married to Sieber on May 13, 1924, and settled down to being a Hausfrau.

Their daughter, Maria (now Maria Sieber Riva, a dramatic actress frequently seen on television programs), was born in 1925. Marlene did not stay in this domestic background very long. She began to appear in German motion pictures and she made her stage appearance as Pearl in the German translation of the successful play, *Broadway* (by Philip Dunning and George Abbott). She subsequently appeared in musical comedies including *The Great Baritone* (1925), *It's in the Air* (1927), *Two Neckties* (1929) and in George Bernard Shaw's play, *Misalliance* (1929). Among the German films in which Dietrich appeared were *Tragedy of Love* (1923), *Princess Ohlala* (1928), *The Ship of Lost Men* (1929) *I Kiss Your Hand, Madame* (1929), and *Three Loves* (1929); the latter two were released in the United States.

Josef von Sternberg, who was in Germany in 1929 to direct Emil Jannings in *The Blue Angel*, saw Marlene Dietrich while she was appearing in the satirical revue, *Two Neckties*. He signed Dietrich immediately and painstakingly coached her in the part of a glamorous café singer who ensnares a middle-aged professor. When the picture was completed in 1930, Dietrich was catapulted to stardom and the film was acclaimed as the greatest made in Germany since the first World War.

MARLENE DIETRICH

On the strength of this success, von Sternberg brought Marlene Dietrich to the United States and obtained a contract for her with Paramount Pictures. She played opposite Gary Cooper and Adolph Menjou in *Morocco* (1930), and again portrayed the role of a seductive café singer. The picture won plaudits from critics and public alike, assuring Marlene a place in Hollywood. Recognizing von Sternberg's genius as a director, Marlene submitted compliantly as he built her up as a great glamour personality, creating what *Life* magazine described as "the magic myth; the low, sultry voice, the insolently displayed legs, the sleepy, mocking manner, the bony, strangely angelic, strangely vulgar face with the penciled eyebrows."

A publicity campaign by Paramount enhanced the legend instituted by von Sternberg, and she became a symbol of glamour during the 1930's. She made other pictures directed by him: *Dishonored* (1931) a war story in which she played a beautiful spy set to entrap an enemy soldier; *Shanghai Express* (1932), in which she outwitted a Chinese bandit leader, played by Akim Tamiroff, to save her lover, played by Clive Brook; *Blonde Venus* (1932) with Herbert Marshall and Cary Grant; *Scarlet Empress* (1934), in which she portrayed Catherine II of Russia; and *The Devil is a Woman* (1935), regarded by some critics as second only to *The Blue Angel*.

Following *Shanghai Express*, Dietrich's contract was rewritten to give her $125,000 a picture; she thus became Paramount's highest-paid star. She made a picture, *Song of Songs*, in 1934 under director Rouben Mamoulian.

While the prestige of Director von Sternberg declined, according to *Life* (August 18, 1952), "that of his greatest pupil persisted indestructibly, and after they had separated by mutual consent Miss Dietrich worked for a series of other directors," including Ernest Lubitsch, Alexander Korda and Billy Wilder.

(Continued next page)

DIETRICH, MARLENE—*Continued*

Marlene broke many traditions of the film capital; she readily admitted that she was a mother, something which most actresses of that era did not publicize for fear it would detract from their glamour. She also admitted that she admired Greta Garbo and had no intention of trying to be her rival. She started a vogue for mannish dress "that had women wearing slacks from morn till night, but so hauntingly lovely was Dietrich herself that no ascetic clothing could hide her essential womanliness." In 1936 she appeared in *Desire,* with Gary Cooper and in her first color picture, *The Garden of Allah,* with Charles Boyer. Then followed *Knight Without Armor* (1937), with Robert Donát, filmed in England by Alexander Korda, and *Angel* (1938), with Herbert Marshall and Melvyn Douglas.

This last picture marked the low point in a steady decline in the quality and popular appeal of Dietrich's pictures. She was regarded by many as having reached the end of her career in films. The general criticism was that Dietrich's glamour had become "stereotyped, cold and slightly absurd," and that producers had neglected her natural acting ability and her vibrant personality.

The producer, Joseph Pasternak, of Universal Pictures engaged Miss Dietrich in 1939 to play in a Western, the now famous *Destry Rides Again* (1940), with James Stewart. Her performance as a boisterous dance-hall girl and her rendition of such songs as "The Boys in the Back Room," brought her to the fore again as a top box-office attraction. She made two other pictures for Pasternak, *Seven Sinners* (1940) and *The Flame of New Orleans* (1941), both of which were successful. Then followed in quick succession: *Manpower* (1941), *The Spoilers* (1942), *Pittsburgh* (1942), *The Lady is Willing* (1942), and *Kismet* (1944). She also appeared briefly in *Follow the Boys* (1944).

Marlene calls her three years of wartime work entertaining American troops from Anzio to the Aleutians "the only important thing I've ever done." She paid her own expenses much of the time and worked far from cameras and close to front lines. "Bundled in . . . GI overcoats," wrote *Life* (August 18, 1952) "her hands often freezing, standing patiently in chow lines with her mess kit, sleeping in rat-infested ruins and dugouts, Trouper Dietrich put on a performance that was a triumph of sheer stamina." She entertained the soldiers by singing songs from her old pictures and mindreading ("it's not difficult to read a GI's mind overseas" she said), and playing on a musical saw. She was on the Anzio beachhead in Italy when it was learned that the Allied armies had landed in France, and she was given the privilege of announcing the news during a performance.

When she sang for captured German soldiers she expected them to show bitterness toward her, since she was a strong anti-Nazi. But they gazed at her adoringly as she sang songs from *The Blue Angel* film. According to *Life* her

"consistent and deep-rooted loathing for the Nazi regime, though she never capitalized on it for publicity purposes, had started as soon as Hitler came to power. Many of her friends suffered from Nazi persecution. She flatly refused all of Hitler's offers and showed von Ribbentrop the door."

After the war, Marlene Dietrich made her first French film, *Martin Roumagnac* (1946), with Jean Gabin, which was released in the United States two years later as *The Room Upstairs.* She was scheduled to make another picture in France with the French actor Raimu, but when Raimu died the picture was cancelled. Her first postwar picture in the United States was *Golden Earrings* (1947), in which she was miscast as a gypsy, according to most of the critics.

She appeared in *A Foreign Affair* in 1948, in the role of a nightclub singer and former associate of a high-ranking Nazi officer. Critic Bosley Crowther of the New York *Times* admired "her subtle suggestion of mocking scorn, her singing of 'Illusions' and 'Black Market Song.'"

Her next film was a murder-mystery story, *Stage Fright* (1950), directed by Alfred Hitchcock. She was cast as a glamorous motion picture actress in *No Highway in the Sky* (1951) with James Stewart. RKO's *Rancho Notorious* (1952) gave her the role of a husky-throated charmer who owns a ranch where desperadoes of the Old West hide from the law.

Marlene Dietrich became an American citizen in 1937. She was awarded a special citation by the Treasury Department for her successful war bond selling tour. Following the war, she received the Medal of Freedom, the highest award given by the United States Army to civilians, for the "extraordinary record in entertaining troops overseas." In October, 1951 Henri Bonnet, the French Ambassador to the United States, presented her with the French Legion of Honor on behalf of her services to France during the war. The actress has made a Decca album of recordings including "Symphonie," "Lili Marlene' and other ballads. Recordings of eight other songs (German Polydor records) which she made before World War II are now in a Vox album.

The actress is five feet five inches tall and weighs 120 pounds. Although glamour is Dietrich's stock-in-trade, she genuinely enjoys cooking, "glories in the possession of two grandchildren . . . cultivates her interest in highbrow books and collecting paintings, has an almost incredible reputation for generosity . . . an incessant helper of every Tom, Dick and Harry who is in need" (*Life*, August 18, 1952).

The novelist Ernest Hemingway wrote that Dietrich is "brave, beautiful, loyal, kind and generous . . . if she had nothing more than her voice she could break your heart with it. But she has that beautiful body and the timeless loveliness of her face." Hemingway also said: "She loves writing and is an intelligent and scrupulous critic. . . .I value her opinion more than that of many critics."

Dietrich is now acting in a radio drama *Time for Love* on the Columbia Broadcasting System network, which, like the very popular *Cafe Istanbul* program in 1952, is a series of international adventure plots with Marlene playing what *Time* called "the same romantic *Weltschmerz* role with whispered snatches of French and German songs."

References

Coronet 32:101-16 My '52 pors
Liberty 18:18 My 31 '41
Life 25:59+ Ag 9 '48 por; 33:86+ Ag 18 '52 pors
N Y Post Mag p9 Ap 3 '43 por
Pict R 32:4+ Ag '31 por; 34:16-17 Jl '33 por
Time 28:40-1 N 30 '36 por
American Women, 1939-40
Hughes, E. Famous Stars of Filmdom (Women) (1931)
International Motion Picture Almanac, 1950-51
Who's Who in America, 1950-51
Winchester's Screen Encyclopedia (1948)
World Biography (1948)

DILLON, C(LARENCE) DOUGLAS Aug. 21, 1909- United States Ambassador to France; banker

Address: b. c/o American Embassy, Place de la Concorde, Paris, France; 46 William St., New York 5; h. Far Hills, N.J.

For the critical diplomatic post of United States Ambassador to France, President Dwight D. Eisenhower in January 1953 named C. Douglas Dillon, who resigned as chairman of the board of Dillon, Read & Company to accept the appointment. With his twenty-two years of experience in international investment companies and knowledge of the financial problems involved in building a military defense program, Dillon has the task, among other duties, of advancing the Republican Administration's new economic and mutual aid policies in France. Chairman of the executive committee of the New Jersey Republican State Committee since 1949, Dillon actively supported Eisenhower's candidacy for President in 1952.

Clarence Douglas Dillon was born in Geneva, Switzerland, on August 21, 1909, one of two children (a boy and a girl) of Clarence and Anne McEldin (Douglass) Dillon, American citizens who at the time of their son's birth were traveling in Europe. The elder Dillon, an investment broker and later founder of the banking firm Dillon, Read & Company, returned to the United States with his family in 1910. Graduated with high honors from Groton School in Massachusetts in 1927, young Dillon entered Harvard University, where his major subjects were American history and literature and where he became manager of the varsity football team and a member of the student council before receiving his B.A. degree *magna cum laude* in 1931.

About a month after joining his father's firm in September 1931, Dillon left to become a floor trader on the New York Stock Exchange, on which he acquired a seat, reported the New York *Times*, for $185,000. During the five years of his membership on the exchange (1931-36), he was also an associate member of the New York Curb Exchange. Rejoining Dillon, Read & Company, Inc., in January 1938, Dillon held the vice-presidency of the firm and membership on the board of directors from that year to 1941. In January 1946, after his return from World War II service, he became chairman of the board. (Dillon, Read & Company, a firm of investment bankers with world-wide interests, grew out of the banking firm of William A. Read & Company. In 1916 Clarence Dillon became president of the organization and kept that position when the firm took its present name, in 1920, and launched what have been described as "some of the most spectacular financial operations of the 20's.")

In January 1938 Dillon was also made a director of two investment houses with which he had become associated a year earlier, the United States and Foreign Securities Corporation and its subsidiary United States and International Securities Corporation. These corporations, of which Dillon was elected president in November 1946, were organized by Dillon, Read & Company in 1924 as publicly owned investment trust concerns with far-flung domestic and foreign holdings in chemicals, metals, natural gas, oil, and public utilities. In 1951 they showed a net income of $4,712,414. Dillon accepted responsibilities in a third major business affiliation when he became a director in May 1947 of the Amerada Petroleum Corporation, which was established in 1921 (its present name dates from 1941) to develop and exploit petroleum in the United States and the Province of Alberta, Canada. Nearly eight million acres are owned or controlled by the firm, which in 1951 produced 23,271,654 barrels of crude oil.

Commissioned an ensign in the United States Navy on October 26, 1940, Dillon soon afterward gave up his business associations for the period of his service in World War II. In the Naval Reserve from May 1, 1941, to November 4, 1945, when he returned to inactive duty with the rank of lieutenant commander, he mainly fought with the air arm of the Seventh Fleet stationed in the Southwest Pacific and took part in a number of major operations. Dillon was awarded the Air Medal, the Legion of Merit Medal, and the Navy Commendation Ribbon.

Since his discharge from the Navy Dillon has been an active member of the Republican party, working with John Foster Dulles on the foreign policy team in the 1948 Presidential campaign of Governor Thomas E. Dewey. The next year the county of Somerset, where he resides, elected him to the New Jersey Republican State Committee, on which he served as chairman of the executive group. In December 1951 he initiated the "draft Eisenhower" movement in his State and took part in the appeal to New Jersey voters to participate in the Republican primary elections regardless of their previous political affiliations, and in this effort clashed with supporters of Senator Robert A. Taft. Dillon was an alternate delegate-at-large

Karsh, Ottawa
C. DOUGLAS DILLON

to the National Republican Convention in Chicago in the summer of 1952, which nominated Dwight D. Eisenhower for the Presidency. The New York *Herald Tribune* reported that Dillon had expected a place in the new Administration, but was "surprised" when President Eisenhower designated him United States Ambassador to France in January 1953. Dillon's only previous Government experience was in 1940 when he made a special study of the Navy Department for the then Under Secretary of the Navy, James Forrestal, who was his close friend. After accepting his diplomatic appointment, Dillon resigned as head of Dillon, Read & Company.

As outlined by *United States News,* Dillon's Ambassadorship carries with it the responsibility of advancing "President Eisenhower's plan for a closely integrated, well-armed Europe, prepared, with United States help, to rise to its own defense against any Russian attack." Dillon's task is to "combat the trend [in France] against European unity, away from cooperation, and toward French nationalism." His knowledge of international finance is expected to be useful in the proposed possible "examination" of United States foreign aid policies, as they affect France. Before leaving for his post in Paris, Dillon told a group which held a luncheon in his honor that France and its ministers had been leaders in creating the idea of European economic and military unity, and stated that antagonism to the United States in France was fostered by Communists. His mission, he said, would be to try to make the French people see "what we are really trying to do." One aspect of Dillon's role as Ambassador, as viewed by Drew Middleton of the New York *Times,* is to mediate, if necessary, between France and West Germany in any difference that might arise to threaten ratification of the Bonn peace contract with the Western Allies and the European Defense Community

Treaty. The new Ambassador presented his credentials in Paris on March 13, 1953.

Charitable and public organizations Dillon has served are the United Hospital Fund and two New York hospitals, the State Charities Aid Association, the Metropolitan Museum of Art, and the United States Council of the International Chamber of Commerce. He is an overseer of Harvard and permanent treasurer of the Harvard class of 1931. His clubs are the Racquet and Tennis, the Links, Knickerbocker River, and Recess in New York; and the Metropolitan in Washington, D.C. Married on March 10, 1931, to Phyllis Chess Ellsworth, Dillon is the father of two daughters, Phyllis Ellsworth and Joan Douglas. His religious affiliation is Episcopal. Dillon, who has been described as "handsome," has brown hair, blue eyes, stands an inch over six feet, and weighs 180 pounds. His taste in reading reflects his interest in history and current events. His other forms of recreation are golf, tennis, small-boat sailing, enjoyment of art, and management of his family's 300-acre farm in the foothills of Somerset County, New Jersey. The Ambassador, who speaks French, has traveled in France on business and vacation trips.

References

Newsweek 41:35 Ja 26 '53
N Y Herald Tribune p3 Ja 26 '53; II p1 F 22 '53 por
N Y Times p60 Ja 18 '53
U S News 34:62 Ja 30 '53
Who's Who in America, 1952-53
Who's Who in Commerce and Industry, 1952-53

DOUGLAS, MARJORY STONEMAN
April 7, 1890- Author
Address: h. 3744 Stewart Avenue, Coconut Grove, Florida

When Marjory Stoneman Douglas' book *The Everglades: River of Grass* (Rinehart) was published in 1947 and became a best seller, she achieved national recognition in a career devoted primarily to fictional and factual writings on Florida.

Prior to this achievement, Mrs. Douglas was already recognized as a writer of short stories approximately forty of which appeared in the *Saturday Evening Post* over a period of fifteen years. *Collier's, Woman's Home Companion, Reader's Digest,* and other national magazines have carried her writings. She received the second prize in the O. Henry Memorial Collection of 1928.

Road to the Sun (Rinehart, 1951) was Marjory Stoneman Douglas's first novel. In the making ten years, it is a "tense Florida drama." Her accurate knowledge of Florida history in this and *The Everglades* made her the logical choice for a representative story in the new "The State of the Union" series. This historical story, with teen-age characters, is laid in 1845, the year Florida joined the Union. This is her first book for young people.

Marjory Stoneman Douglas was born in Minneapolis, Minnesota, on April 7, 1890. Her father was Frank Bryant Stoneman, an attorney who later became a judge in Miami, and her mother, Lillian Trefethen, was a concert violinist. When her mother died, her French grandmother took over her care. She was brought up in Taunton, Massachusetts, and influenced in the choice of her career by her grandmother who was an inveterate and inspired story teller.

Marjory attended the public schools in Taunton, and Wellesley College, in Wellesley, Massachusetts, where she majored in English composition, graduating in 1912 with an A.B. degree. Her English teachers in high school and in college encouraged her to write.

When her father moved to Miami he founded the *Miami Herald*. Marjory joined the staff in 1914 as a reporter and three years later was promoted to the position of society editor. She served overseas in the American Red Cross in France, Belgium, Italy and the Balkans in World War I. Married in April, 1914, she was divorced in April, 1917.

Returning to Miami in 1920, she became assistant editor of the *Herald,* writing editorials and a literary column, "The Galley" which included a daily original poem. Some of these called forth favorable comment from prominent publishers and writers, notably a poem entitled "The Builders". Her editorial writing was concerned with what she describes as "regionalizing southern Florida". She called attention to the geographic uniqueness of this area, urged the development of its native resources and opposed any influences which would alter its distinctive character.

Leaving the *Miami Herald* to become a free lance writer, in 1923, Marjory sent one of her first short stories to the *Saturday Evening Post*. It was accepted. The locale was Florida. Editors of the *Post* noted that this area had not been "discovered" by writers, and urged her to capitalize on the Florida scene. She took their advice and has made a successful career, devoting many years almost exclusively to short stories. Her piece "He Man" was included in the *O. Henry Memorial Collection of 1927*. The following year Mrs. Douglas' "Peculiar Treasure of a King" was awarded second prize in the *O. Henry Memorial Collection of 1928*. The *Post Stories of 1937*, a selection of the best short stories to appear in the *Saturday Evening Post* for that year, included her "Story of a Homely Woman".

Twenty-five years ago Marjory Stoneman Douglas built a roomy, breeze-swept study across the street from her father's home in Coconut Grove. She later added a kitchen and sleeping quarters, and transformed it into a thatched cottage. Here she lives now and works, writing in long-hand on a lapboard before an open door which looks out on a tropical garden. She shuns such modern conveniences as a telephone and a car.

When working on research she finds little occasion for trips to the public library. Her own walls are lined with just what she needs, choice and rare books. Yet for years she has worked toward an adequate Coconut Grove Library and is a member of the board of directors of its Library Association.

Park Madison Studio

MARJORY STONEMAN DOUGLAS

She spent four years in research and exciting exploratory trips, often of discovery, gathering material for her book, *The Everglades: River of Grass,* one of the American River series. In canoes, row boats, swamp-buggies and on foot, she made her field trips into this mighty river of saw-grass and water. Here was a topic dear to her heart, for she had been one of the original crusaders for the creation of an Everglades National Park.

She has lived most of her adult life near this comparatively unknown and primeval area, and has long been fascinated by the cruelty of the terrain and of the men who have inhabited it and impinged upon it. No other writer had attempted to put into one volume the whole subject of the Everglades. Her volume is a complete guide book, description, story, and history in which she has had the privilege of incorporating recent and remarkable first studies and findings of naturalists, geologists, ethnologists, archeologists, horticulturists. She has delved into the difficult subject of the history of the Indians in the Everglades today, the early African slaves, and the Spaniards who discovered the land. The New York *Herald Tribune* described her achievement as "a fabulous book of a fabulous Florida", and recommends it to "all readers concerned with American life and the general relation of man to nature."

Mrs. Douglas is the author of *Gallows Gate* (1931), a play in one act. She was an associate professor at the University of Miami from 1925 to 1929, directed a winter Institute of Literature there, lectured on the history of the short story at Pennsylvania State College, 1929, was the book review editor of the *Miami Herald* 1942 to 1949, and the editor of the Fairchild (Florida) Tropical Garden Bulletin, 1945 to 1950.

(Continued next page)

DOUGLAS, MARJORY S.—*Continued*

She is a member of the editorial board of the University of Miami Press, and also of *Tequesta*, the publication of the Historical Society of Southern Florida. She has been writing book reviews for the New York *Herald Tribune* since 1949.

Her other activities include serving as a director of the Junior Museum of Miami, director of the Coconut Grove Slum Clearance Association, Secretary of the Fairchild Tropical Garden, and a member of the Society of Woman Geographers.

This petite, energetic authoress advocates work and eating fish in place of rum and loafing, to keep vigorous in the tropics. She loves swimming, gardening, living alone, and most of all, Florida. Everything which will preserve its unique identity has her vital and active support.

The honorary Doctorate of Letters was conferred upon her by the University of Miami, and a Certificate of Merit at the Centennial Celebration of the University of Florida. She is an honorary member of Theta Sigma Chi. "Hers is the voice of authority about Florida", states the *Miami Herald*.

References

 Miami Herald N 2 '47: D 9 '51; D 30
  '51; F 14 '52; F 15 '53
 Miami Daily N Mr 20 '52; Je 10 '52
 N Y Herald Tribune N 30 '47

 American Women, 1939-40
 Who's Who in America, 1952-53
 Who's Who in the South and Southwest
  (1952)

DUFY, RAOUL (ERNEST JOSEPH)
June 3, 1877—Mar. 23, 1953 Modernist French painter; studied at École des Beaux Arts in Paris; first exhibited at Salon des Artistes in Paris in 1901; became associated with "Les Fauves" (1901-09); designed prints for fabrics in association with couturier Paul Poiret; painted giant fresco for Paris Exposition of 1937 depicting the story of electricity; came to United States in 1950; crippled by arthritis, and after cortisone treatment resumed his work, painting American scenes; won first prize at International Art Show in Venice (1952). See *Current Biography,* 1951.

Obituary

 N Y Times p31 Mr 24 '53

DU JARDIN, ROSAMOND (NEAL) July 22, 1902- Author

Address: b. c/o J. B. Lippincott Co., E. Washington Sq. Philadelphia 5, Pa., h. 670 Kenilworth Ave., Glen Ellyn, Ill.

 Reprinted from the *Wilson*
 Library Bulletin, June 1953.

A busy mother, and, at fifty, a grandmother, Rosamond (Neal) du Jardin began her writing career while her "first two babies were taking their naps." Today, one hundred short stories and eleven novels later, she is most widely known as the author of junior fiction noted for its honesty, naturalness, humor, and authentic teen-age accent.

Rosamond Neal was born in the small town of Fairland, Illinois, on July 22, 1902, the daughter of Ida May (McConkey) and Edgar Neal. She was of Scotch and Irish descent on her mother's side, English and Welsh on her father's. When she was two, her father, who earlier had taught school, moved the family to Chicago, where he went into detective work, and she has lived in that city and its suburbs ever since.

Mrs. du Jardin recalls her childhood with pleasure. She became "what amounted to an only child" when her only brother died in infancy, but says she was "never conscious of the loneliness often associated with that situation." Her choice of a writing career, she feels, may have been affected by life in a family of readers, where she read freely of everything from Sherlock Holmes to Shakespeare.

In Chicago, she attended the Barnard Elementary School and was graduated in 1919 from the Morgan Park High School (she was a reporter and art editor on the school paper) "into the billing department" of Charles A. Stevens and Company. Here she remained until her marriage, on August 28, 1925, to Victor du Jardin, a Chicago business executive.

Mrs. du Jardin's first writing was humorous verse. Encouraged by her husband's insistence that she hire household help and devote more time to writing, she decided to try her hand at fiction, which sold at first to the Chicago *Daily News* and other syndicated markets. Since then, about a hundred of her short stories have appeared in such magazines as *Red Book, American, McCall's, Good Housekeeping, Liberty, Cosmopolitan, Mademoiselle,* and foreign publications, English, Swedish, Danish, and Austrian among them. She has also written several short plays presented on such radio programs as "Sil-

ROSAMOND DU JARDIN

ver Theater," Stars Over Hollywood," and "Aunt Jenny's Stories," and for a time wrote, though she did not originate, a radio serial script called "Arnold Grimm's Daughter."

Her early novels, the first of which appeared in 1935, were for adults. *All Is Not Gold, Only Love Lasts* (1937), *Honorable Estate* (1943), *Brief Glory* (1944), *and Tomorrow Will Be Fair* (1946), met with fair but reserved reviews.

They were succeeded, in 1949, by *Practically Seventeen,* a first-person account of Tobey Heydon, her family, and her first beau, which marked Mrs. du Jardin's departure into the junior novel. The book, which was recommended by May Lamberton Becker and praised by Esther Gorey in the *Library Journal* for the "welcome spontaneity" produced by its first-person technique, has had six printings and appeared in Braille and Swedish, as well as in the American edition.

Wait for Marcy (1950), Mrs. du Jardin's second teen-age novel, received uniformly favorable reviews, among them Margaret Scoggin's reference to it in the New York *Herald Tribune Book Review* as "a completely authentic report on the teen age with its hopes and fears —and in its very accents . . . a wise and amusing presentation of the changing relationships in one family as brother and sister grow up."

In *Class Ring* (1951), a sequel to *Practically Seventeen,* E. E. Frank commented in the *Library Journal,* the subject "is treated practically and sanely and will exert far more influence than innumerable lectures by parents and teachers. . . . It is well written and wholesome. . . ." The *Saturday Review* commented: "A thread of humor gives Tobey's story lightness and proportion." Other critical comment was unanimous in praise of the book, and of its successor, *Double Date* (1952), describing the lives of twin teen-age girls.

Marcy Catches Up (1952), a sequel to the first Marcy book, also met with consistently favorable comment, including the remark of Polly Goodwin in the Chicago *Sunday Tribune* that "the author again shows why she is such a favorite. For she seems to know just what makes them tick and writes about what is close to their teen-age hearts."

Boy Trouble (1953), Mrs. du Jardin's most recent publication, is another Tobey Heydon book and reviews of it were generally enthusiastic. "As in other stories," commented Polly Goodwin, "the author shows her love and understanding of the modern teen-ager, her knowledge that all the fun and foolishness, the waverings and wonderings, are part of growing up."

Mrs. du Jardin, who is currently at work on *Double Feature,* a new book about twins Pam and Penny of *Double Date* which is to be published in the fall, is a vivacious woman five feet four inches tall, and weighing 130 pounds, with blue eyes and light brown hair. She has three children, Jacqueline Neal (Mrs. F. William Clemenson, Jr.), Victor, Jr., and Judith Carol, "a built-in critic" for her mother's books who is now her 'teens.

A Presbyterian in her church affiliation and a Republican in politics, Mrs. du Jardin is a member of the Midland Authors and Scribblers

groups. Her favorite recreations are sports, hobbies—golf, bridge, dancing, badminton and travel, especially leisurely motor trips to off-the-beaten-path places. As reading, she says she has too many favorite authors and books to list, her tastes being "broad and not too discriminating."

References

    Chicago Sun Mr 27 '52
    International Who's Who, 1952
    Who's Who in America, 1952-53

DULLES, JOHN FOSTER (dŭl'les) Feb. 25, 1888- Secretary of State of the United States; lawyer

Address: b. Department of State, Washington, D.C.; h. 72 E 91st St., New York 28, N.Y.; Cold Spring Harbor, L.I., N.Y.

Note: This biography supersedes the article which appeared in *Current Biography* in 1944.

The fifty-third Secretary of State of the United States, John Foster Dulles, has had a long and distinguished career as a participant in formulating his country's foreign policies. He took office in the Cabinet of President Dwight D. Eisenhower in January, 1953, succeeding Dean Acheson.

A lawyer by profession, Secretary Dulles has had diplomatic experience dating from the Hague Convention in 1907. He was a member of the American delegation to the Versailles Peace Conference in 1919 and the San Francisco organizational conference for the United Nations in 1945.

An active supporter, both during and after World War II, of a bi-partisan foreign policy, Secretary Dulles has been an American delegate to most of the sessions of the United Nations General Assembly. He also negotiated the peace treaty with Japan, which was concluded in September 1951. He is regarded as one of the most influential of Presbyterian laymen.

John Foster Dulles was born in Washington, D.C., on February 25, 1888, one of the five children of the Reverend Allen Macy and Edith (Foster) Dulles. His father was a Presbyterian pastor at Watertown, New York, who later took the chair of apologetics at Auburn Theological Seminary. His grandfather was the Reverend John Welsh Dulles. Other ancestors were Joseph Dulles, one of the founders of the Academy of Sciences in Philadelphia and manager of the American Sunday School Union, and John Welsh, who served as United States Minister to Great Britain from 1877 to 1879. His mother was the daughter of General John Watson Foster, a Civil War soldier who became Secretary of State in the Cabinet of President Benjamin Harrison (1892-1893) and negotiated the Treaty of Shimonoseki of 1895 after the Sino-Japanese War.

Dulles received his early education in Watertown public schools, except for a period of six months in Lausanne, Switzerland, where he acquired fluency in French and German. Upon

Dept. of State

JOHN FOSTER DULLES

graduation from Watertown High School, he entered Princeton University, of which Woodrow Wilson was then President. In his junior year he accompanied his grandfather, General Foster, to the Second Hague Peace Conference in 1907, and observed the drawing up of the international code of warfare and of the rights and obligations of neutrals.

Dulles was a quick and brilliant student. He was elected to Phi Beta Kappa and was the valedictorian of his graduating class in 1908. After a year of post-graduate work at the Sorbonne in Paris, studying philosophy with Henri Bergson, and international law, he received a LL.D. degree. Two years later he received a LL.B. degree from the Law School of George Washington University in Washington, D.C., graduating at the head of his class.

Admitted to the New York State bar in the same year, he was accepted (through the recommendation of General Foster) into the offices of the New York law firm of Sullivan and Cromwell, specialists in international law.

Only a few months after he joined this firm, Dulles was selected to go to British Guiana in behalf of the New York Produce Exchange, in a matter concerning tariff discrimination against the United States. The trip, which had the approval of the Department of State, led to other semi-official assignments, including missions to England and the Netherlands shortly before the outbreak of World War I.

Robert Lansing, Dulles' uncle by marriage, became Secretary of State in 1915 and early in 1917 he assigned Dulles to represent the United States at the second Pan-American Scientific Congress. He was also a special agent of the Department of State in Central America where he assisted in aligning Panama and her neighbors to defend the Panama Canal.

Dulles had been rejected by the Army for active duty in World War I because of im-

paired eyesight, but was later commissioned a captain and directed the economic section of the military intelligence division of the General Staff. Early in 1918 he became assistant to Chairman Vance C. McCormick of the War Trade Board and represented the Army General Staff on that board. In this capacity he worked out the legal justification for requisitioning 980,000 tons of Dutch shipping in American ports, which the President ordered in March 1918. He held the rank of major when he was discharged from service.

On the joint recommendation of Bernard Baruch, Thomas W. Lamont and McCormick, Dulles was appointed by President Woodrow Wilson as counsel to the reparations section of the American Commission to Negotiate Peace. At the Versailles Conference in 1919 he was a member of both the Reparations Commission and the Supreme Economic Council.

When he returned to the United States Dulles was advanced, at the age of thirty-one, to a full partnership in the Sullivan and Cromwell law firm. His "Versailles prestige," states John Chamberlain, "caused a rush among American banking houses to retain him as their legal counsel," but what Dulles "particularly enjoyed going after in the early 1920's and 1930's was the legal work connected with governmental financing by Germany, Norway, Poland, Denmark, France, Argentina, Uruguay, Chile and Colombia" (*Life*, August 21, 1944).

He served in 1927 as legal adviser on the Polish Plan of Financial Stabilization. Following the collapse of the various foreign exchanges in 1932, Dulles represented American bondholders in three successive international conferences called by Dr. Hjalmar Schacht in Berlin, and was an American representative at the Berlin Debt Conference of 1933. On another occasion Dulles was chief counsel for the American creditors of Kreuger & Toll, recovering seventy to eighty cents on the dollar for his clients after that company had collapsed.

At Paris in 1937 Dulles served as chairman of a League-sponsored conference to consider the question of "peaceful change". He became dismayed with the timidity and nationalist bickering displayed there. From Paris, he went to England where he participated in the Oxford conference of churchmen who discussed the same topic. "The freedom with which the ministers faced up to the menacing international situation made Dulles think that maybe the Protestant churches were on the threshold of a spiritual renaissance that would have its effect on the political world. He returned to America with a conviction that the nations of the West must recover their lost sense of spiritual purpose" (*Life*, August 21, 1944). In respect to the League of Nations and the Versailles system, Dulles has maintained that they failed primarily because they did not make adequate provision for peaceful alteration of the international status quo.

During the following year (1938) he made a detailed study of the political and economic situation in the Far East, and wrote his first book, *War, Peace and Change* (Harper's, 1939), a philosophical analysis of war in which he expounded his belief that war had been tolerated as a means of settling disputes only because no procedures were available whereby changes in international relations could be made effective. In July 1939 Dulles participated (at Geneva, Switzerland) in the World Council of Churches Conference which strove in vain to prevent the outbreak of World War II.

In the early part of 1941 he was elected the first chairman of the Commission on a Just and Durable Peace of the Federal Council of Churches of Christ in America. This commission, in a statement entitled "The Six Pillars of Peace," supported the idea of a world governmental organization and of a new "order" in which the exploitation of subject or colonial peoples should be ended and religious and intellectual freedom guaranteed. The commission also issued an "Interfaith Statement" outlining the common ground on which Protestants, Catholics and Jews could take a stand in reference to world peace.

Despite his early admiration of President Wilson and the League ideal, Dulles had remained a Republican in political affiliation. Governor Thomas E. Dewey appointed him a member of the New York State Banking Board in 1943. He attended the Republican Post-War Policy Association meeting (the Mackinac Conference) in that same year and became acquainted with Senator Arthur Vandenberg of Michigan, who at that time persuaded a majority of Republicans to support a bipartisan foreign policy. Not long afterwards he accepted the chairmanship of the Carnegie Endowment for International Peace.

Dulles was a delegate to the Republican National Convention of July 1944 and supported Thomas E. Dewey for the presidential nomination. (The international lawyer had known Dewey since the middle 1930's, and at one time had invited him to join the firm of Sullivan and Cromwell). Dulles served as Dewey's "adviser" on foreign policy in the 1944 campaign.

On recommendation of Senator Vandenberg, Dulles was named in the summer of 1945 to accompany the latter to San Francisco for the organizational and charter-writing conference for the United Nations, and at which "his special contribution was a formula to safeguard Latin-American regional interests" (Time August 13, 1951).

"My troubles with the Russians started when I went to San Francisco . . . ," Dulles wrote in an article in Collier's (March 12, 1949). "Molotov and Gromyko were there and I soon learned they had ideas very different from the sweetness and light of the Atlantic Charter and the Four Freedoms."

In September 1945, at the personal invitation of Secretary of State James F. Byrnes, Dulles attended the first meeting of the Council of Foreign Ministers at London, and in the same city early in 1946 was a member of the United States delegation to the first General Assembly of the United Nations. Later in the same year, when the United Nations met in New York, Dulles served as United States representative on the Trusteeship Committee of the General Assembly.

In March 1947 he accompanied General George C. Marshall, who had succeeded Byrnes as Secretary of State, to the Council of Foreign Ministers meeting at Moscow, and on his return home made an important radio address in which he warned against the Soviet policy of penetrating foreign political parties and trade unions, asserting that "it is up to us to show, in every available way, that free institutions are the means whereby men can save themselves from the sea of misery in which they find themselves."

Dulles, who was again a United Nations delegate in 1947, made a study of Stalin's book concerning Leninism which he characterized as "the 'bible' which is taught to Communists" (Collier's March 12,1949).

In the 1948 presidential campaign he again served the Republican nominee, Governor Dewey of New York, as adviser on foreign relations. He also attended, as chairman of the Commission on a Just and Durable peace of the Federal Council of Churches of Christ in America, the World Council of Churches assembly at Amsterdam, Holland. Here he stressed that the "sharp division" of the world into pro- and anti-Communist alignments had taken place "most of all because even the good practices of the West no longer seem to be the expression of a great faith." He further maintained "The most important response to the Soviet challenge will be in effecting peacefully the reforms which Soviet leaders contend can only be effected by violent means."

With the re-convening of the United Nations in Paris in October 1948, Dulles was again a representative. After the defeat of Governor Dewey by President Truman in the presidential election, Dulles received an unexpected promotion. He writes in his book, War or Peace (Macmillan, 1950): "After the election Secretary Marshall felt it necessary to return to the United States for an operation. That would leave the Delegation without a chairman. Then, on November 18, President Truman designated me to be Acting Chairman of the United States Delegation. That was a fine and generous gesture, made at the moment of victory toward one of the defeated opposition. I was, and always shall be, grateful for this action." The appointment was viewed as "doubly significant" in that it "serves notice on the rest of the world, and especially Russia, that the bipartisan props would remain under United States foreign policy" (New York Times, November 19, 1948). In the spring of the following year, Dulles accompanied Dean Acheson, General Marshall's successor and his own predecessor as Secretary of State, to Paris as Republican foreign policy adviser at the meeting of the Council of Foreign Ministers.

Dulles was serving as chairman of the Rockefeller Foundation and of the Carnegie Endowment for International Peace when Governor Dewey appointed him on July 7, 1949 to fill the vacancy left by Senator Robert F. Wagner, who resigned from the Senate because of ill health. Dulles had succeeded William Nelson Cromwell as the senior partner of Sullivan and Cromwell but resigned to serve the interim ap-

DULLES, JOHN FOSTER—_Continued_

pointment. He said at that time he had "no expectations" of being a candidate for the following special election.

It was widely assumed that the Eighty-first Congress would make use of the interim Senator's specialized experience by placing him on the Foreign Relations Committee. However, his speech on July 12 defending the North Atlantic Pact precipitated a debate in which Dulles clashed with Senator Robert A. Taft of Ohio over whether the Treaty committed the United States to rearm Western Europe. Dulles said it did not, Taft said that it did.

Two days later the Republican leadership stated that it had been unable to find committee assignments worthy of Dulles' talents that "do not invade seniority rights of other members" (New York _Times_ July 15, 1949). On July 26 he was appointed to the Post Office, Civil Service and District of Columbia Committees.

Dulles stated on September 7 that he had reconsidered and would "gladly" run in the special election in November of 1949 if approved by the Republican State Committee, which nominated him by a unanimous vote. He resigned his chairmanship of the Commission on a Just and Durable Peace in order not to involve the Federal Council of Churches of Christ in America "in the rough and tumble of political controversy".

His ensuing campaign was largely waged on the issue of the Fair Deal and the welfare state. He lost the election by a substantial margin to the Democratic candidate, former Governor Herbert H. Lehman. Yielding his Senate seat in December, Dulles was appointed by Governor Dewey to a second three-year term on the New York State Banking Board.

In his first public address after the election, Dulles criticized the "defensive tactics" of a United States foreign policy which failed to exploit the likelihood that "the Communist political structure is over-extended, over-rigid and ill-founded" and might well be "shaken by a moral offensive." This idea was also embodied in his book, _War or Peace_ (1950), a survey of foreign relations since the end of World War II.

He was appointed a consultant to the Department of State in 1950 and again represented the United States in the General Assembly of the United Nations. Dulles was assigned in 1951 (with the rank of Ambassador) to negotiate the peace treaty with Japan which was signed at San Francisco in September.

Several months later Dulles expressed in _Life_ (May 19, 1952) his views on challenging the Communist threat, saying that the basic goal should be to dislocate, by peaceful measures, the internal structure of the Soviet empire. His position was endorsed by Senator Taft as well as by those supporting General Eisenhower for the Republican presidential nomination, and he was entrusted with the writing of the foreign policy plank of the party's platform.

The appointment of Dulles as Secretary of State was the first Cabinet announcement made by General Eisenhower after his election. Shortly after being sworn into office in January

1953, Secretary Dulles made a series of trips to Europe and in the spring joined Mutual Security Director Harold E. Stassen on a goodwill tour of twenty Near and Middle East countries between Greece and India. He was the first American Secretary of State to have visited this area. On his return Dulles urged in a radio report to the nation an "impartial approach" to the Arab-Israel friction and suggested that Americans could earn much good will by spending funds to aid irrigation. He viewed "a Middle East defense organization," however, as "a future rather than an immediate possibility."

The Secretary of State on July 9, 1953 warned the Senate Appropriations Committee that a "substantial" cut in President Eisenhower's $5,222,000,000 foreign aid request would gravely affect the whole effort at collective security. "The entire Mutual Security Program will collapse," he declared. "All free countries will say they had better try to go it alone. But some countries will find they won't be able to go it alone and will fall prey to Soviet communism." When Senator Henry C. Dworshak, Republican of Idaho and Senator Allen J. Ellender, Democrat, of Louisiana, asked if "there is any value to America in having allies that have constantly to be supplied with crutches and bribes," Dulles retorted: "Would you expect countries like Norway or Denmark to fight alone against Soviet Russia? It would be suicide. . . .Such countries will fight as part of a common group and, as such, will contribute much to us and the whole free world."

The Secretary also contended that "there is not one dollar in this bill that is not there because our military authorities tell us it is the cheapest way to provide for our own security" (New York _Times_, July 10, 1953). (Congress passed and sent to the White House on July 14 a compromise Mutual Security bill authorizing $5,157,232,500 for military, technical and economic foreign aid in this fiscal year, with strings attached to more than $1,000,000,000 of military aid funds for Western Europe.)

When the State Department issued its new policy in regard to books in its overseas libraries, Secretary Dulles received a letter from Freedom House commending it. "The new policy should go a long way toward restoring our loss of prestige in the world caused by some of the confusion in recent weeks," the letter noted. "Far from being 'soft' on communism, it permits only those books by Communists which are useful in advancing the American cause in the world" (New York _Times_, July 14, 1953).

Secretary Dulles on July 21 said that he would put the United States on record against discussion of Chinese Communist membership in the United Nations at the political conference to be held ninety days after a truce in Korea had been reached. He said he did not think the question would be appropriate at the meeting.

On the same day he defended the State Department's International Information Administration and urged against sharply cutting its activities. He said the agency had done a splendid job despite its imperfections.

After the Korean armistice was announced on July 26, Secretary Dulles said: "In this hour let us recognize that the need for effort and for sacrifice has not passed. In war men make vast sacrifices for peace. And then, when peace is won, they fail to make the lesser sacrifices needed to keep the peace. Let us, this time, not relax, but mobilize for peace the resources, spiritual and material, which too often we reserve for war. Now more than ever we are bound irrevocably to press forward the goals of universal peace and justice."

Numerous academic honors have been conferred upon John Foster Dulles. They include LL.D. degrees from Tufts College (1939), Princeton University (1946), Wagner College and Northeastern University (1947), Union College (1948), the University of Pennsylvania (1949), Amherst College and Seoul National University (1950), the University of Arizona and St. Joseph's College (1951) and St. Lawrence College, John Hopkins, Fordham and Harvard Universities (1952).

His directorships have included the Bank of New York and the Fifth Avenue Bank, the American Bank Note Company, the International Nickel Company of Canada, Ltd., the American Agricultural Chemical Company, the Babcock and Wilcox Corporation, the Gold Dust Corporation, the Overseas Security Corporation, Shenandoah Corporation, the United Cigar Stores, the American Cotton Oil Company, the United Railways of St. Louis, and the European Textile Corporation.

Dulles married Janet Pomeroy Avery of Auburn, New York on June 26, 1912. They have two sons, John Walsh and Avery, one daughter, Lilias Pomeroy (Mrs. Robert Hinshaw), and seven grandchildren. His brother is Allen Welsh Dulles, head of Central Intelligence Agency.

Dulles is a member of the New York City Bar Association and of Phi Delta Phi. He is a trustee of the New York Public Library, Brick Presbyterian Church of New York City, Union Theological Seminary, Rockefeller Foundation, and Carnegie Endowment for International Peace. His clubs are the University, Piping Rock, Downtown and Century in New York and the Metropolitan in Washington, D. C. The books which he likes to read most often are the Bible, Shakespeare's sonnets and plays, Beveridge's *Life of John Marshall* and General Foster's *Diplomatic Memories*. His preferred outdoor recreations are sailing, fishing, tree surgery, and ornithology.

Selected References

Bsns W p27+ N 29 '52 por
Collier's 125:25+Mr 12 '49 por
Harper 197:38+ O '48; 203:88+ N '51
Life 17:84+ Ag 21 '44 pors; 25:130+ O 4 '48 pors; 27:72+ O 31 '49 pors; 34:59+ Mr 9 '53 pors
N Y Herald Tribune 11 p3 My 4 '47 por; 11 p3 Je 10 '49 por
N Y Post p19 Ap 10 '44
N Y Times Mag p10+ S 12 '48 por; pl Jl 8 '49 por

Newsweek 23:32 My 1 '44 por; 34:14 Jl 18 '49; 38:36+ S 10 '51 pors; 40:19 D 1 '52 por
Scholastic 45:10 O 2 '44 por
Time 44: 13+ Ag 28 '44 por; 54:29 S 19 '49 por; 58:18+ Ag 13 '51 pors; 60:13 D 1 '52 por
U N Bul 3:698 N 25 '47 por
U S News 25:36+ Ag 20 '48 pors; 33: 24+ N 28 '52 pors; 34:52+ Ja 2 '53 por
Washington Post p15 Mr 15 '53 pors
National Cyclopedia of American Biography Current Volume G (1943-46)
Ten Eventful Years (1947)
Who's Who, 1953
Who's Who in America, 1952-53
Who's Who in the United Nations (1951)
World Biography (1948)

DURKIN, MARTIN P(ATRICK) Mar. 18, 1894- Former Secretary of Labor; labor official
Address: b. c/o United Association of Journeymen and Apprentices of the Plumbing and Pipe Fitting Industry of the United States and Canada, Ring Bldg., 1200 18th St., N.W., Washington 6, D.C.; h. 5614 Kirkside Dr., Chevy Chase, Md.

With his appointment as Secretary of Labor in the Cabinet of President Dwight D. Eisenhower, announced on December 1, 1952, Martin P. Durkin became the first trade union member in twenty years to head the Labor Department. Durkin, who was made international president of the United Association of Journeymen and Apprentices of the Plumbing and Pipe Fitting Industry, American Federation of Labor in 1943, had been an official of that union since 1921, except for an eight-year leave of absence (1933-41) when he held the office of Director of Labor for the State of Illinois. A Democrat and a critic of the Taft-Hartley labor law, Durkin supported Adlai E. Stevenson in the November 1952 election.

On September 10, 1953 Durkin resigned as Secretary of Labor to resume his post as international president of the United Association of Journeymen and Apprentices of the Plumbing and Pipe Fitting Industry, A.F.L.

Martin Patrick Durkin was born in Chicago, Illinois, on March 18, 1894, to James J. and Mary Catherine (Higgins) Durkin. His father, an immigrant from Ireland, was a stationary fireman (boiler) and a strong believer in trade unions. While attending the Visitation parochial school in Chicago, Martin, at the age of thirteen, worked as a part-time runner in a department store. When he was seventeen he became an apprentice steam fitter and four years later a journeyman plumber in Chicago Local 597 of the United Association of Journeymen and Apprentices of the Plumbing and Pipe Fitting Industry of the United States and Canada. For three years he had studied heating and ventilation in evening technical schools. In World War I he served overseas for two years as a private in the 332nd Artillery and the Sixth Cavalry Corps. After his discharge from

MARTIN P. DURKIN

the Army, he became in 1921 business manager of the largest local of the plumbers' union, Local 597. He was made vice-president of the Chicago Building Trades Council in 1927..

Appointed Illinois State Director of Labor by Democratic Governor Henry Horner in 1933, Durkin served in that capacity, on leave of absence from the union, for eight years, retaining his office under the succeeding Republican Governor Dwight H. Green until 1941. During this period he is said to have "streamlined his department and gained recognition as an administrator." He initiated and successfully backed legislation setting up unemployment compensation, a State employment service, a State mediation and conciliation service, development of new safety rules for industrial employees, and regulation of minimum wages and maximum hours for women and children in industry. Toward the end of his otherwise noncontroversial tenure, he ruled that members of the United Mine Workers, then an affiliate of the Congress of Industrial Organizations, were not entitled to unemployment compensation because they held a six-week work stoppage during contract negotiations. Opposition from the CIO and from Republican forces were said to have been responsible for the termination of his appointment.

From his Illinois State office Durkin went to Washington, D.C., in 1941, as secretary-treasurer of the national office of the plumbers' union. Founded in 1889, the union has a reported membership of 225,000 in 829 locals (*Time*, December 8, 1952) and is affiliated with the American Federation of Labor. When George Meany, national president of the plumbers' union, resigned to take the office of secretary-treasurer of the AFL in 1943, Durkin succeeded him. In 1952 his salary was raised from $15,000 a year to $20,000 and expenses.

When Durkin was designated Secretary of Labor by President-elect Dwight D. Eisenhower on December 1, 1952, the appointment was reported in the press as the most surprising and controversial of Eisenhower's Cabinet selections. On the day following the announcement of the choice, Senator Robert Taft, chairman of the Senate Labor Committee, made a public statement calling the appointment "incredible" and "an affront to millions of union members and officers who had the courage to defy the edict of officials like Mr. Durkin that they vote for Stevenson." Favorable reactions were expressed by CIO and AFL leadership and by some management organizations, including the Associated General Contractors. Three objectives achieved by his appointment, as summarized in the column of Washington reporter David Lawrence, were the "unwritten laws" that at least one Catholic should be on the Cabinet, that the Secretary of Labor should be a pro-union man, and that the minority party should have representation. Durkin's predecessor, Maurice J. Tobin, pointed out that the new Secretary was "well-versed" in the functions of the Department of Labor because of his administrative experience in the Illinois labor department.

Business Week (December 20, 1952) noted that while management generally was disappointed at the selection of a trade union official, the new secretary "has a record of fairness, of competence in administration, of viewpoints well to the right of many other labor leaders." As a product of an era in which labor has achieved great importance in the national economy, Thomas L. Stokes wrote in the New York *World-Telegram*, Durkin has imposed upon him "a far bigger responsibility as a Cabinet member than any professional labor man ever had before. He speaks for millions beyond organized labor, and is a spokesman along a broad front, for 'social welfare' now covers a broad front."

The new Secretary of Labor took office in a department which was given independent status in 1913, after having been a bureau of the Department of the Interior (from 1884) and, a division of the Department of Commerce and Labor (from 1903). As defined by the *United States Government Organization Manual*, the Department of Labor has as its function "administering and enforcing statutes designed to advance the public interest by promoting the welfare of the wage earners of the United States, improving their working conditions, and advancing their opportunities for profitable employment." Under the jurisdiction of the department are the women's bureau, the wage and hour and public contracts division, the bureau of veterans' re-employment rights, bureau of labor statistics, bureau of labor standards, office of international labor affairs, defense manpower administration, bureau of employment security, employees' compensation appeals board, bureau of employees' compensation, and bureau of apprenticeship. Durkin has expressed the expectation that the Department would be strengthened under the Eisenhower Administration, notably by bringing within its management the National Labor Relations Board, the

Federal Mediation and Conciliation Service, the National (Railway) Mediation Board, and the Immigration Service (*Business Week*, December 20, 1952). He has also suggested that the department should have more jurisdiction over matters concerning industrial health and safety.

On the subject of the Taft-Hartley labor law, which as a trade union official he opposed, he has stated that his role as Secretary of Labor will be "to bring the interested parties together so they can make changes." He has also been quoted as saying that he believes that there is a good possibility for a merger of the CIO and the AFL, and that he favors early conferences to discuss this change. After his appointment had received Senate approval, Durkin on January 21, 1953, took office as Secretary of Labor.

At the National Conference on Labor Legislation held in Washington in 1939, Durkin headed a committee which recommended that wage earners not covered by the Federal wage and hour law be protected by State legislation. As a member of the National War Labor Board in World War II, he participated in setting wage policies during that period. He is vice-president of the Catholic Conference on Industrial Problems, a director of the Union Labor Life Insurance Company and of the National Safety Council, and holds the office of sixth vice-president of the American Federation of Labor.

The labor leader is about five feet ten inches tall, weighs 180 pounds, and has "white-streaked black hair and heavy eyebrows." He has been described as a "quiet executive who moves slowly but firmly" and who had been known to "achieve some heroic outbursts." On the occasion of his appointment to the Cabinet post, the New York *Times* called him, editorially, "an efficient administrator" who "has the reputation of seeing things in perspective . . . unorthodox, definitely not a routineer, and accessible to new ideas." Durkin and his wife, the former Anna H. McNicholas, were married on August 29, 1921. Their two older sons, Martin B. and William J. Durkin, alumni of the Catholic University in Washington, are now both practicing journeymen steam fitters. A third son is John F. Durkin. Durkin's preferred form of entertainment is attending prizefights.

References

Bsns W p30 D 6 '52 por; p118 D 20 '52
N Y Herald Tribune p17 D 2 '52; II p1 D 7 '52
N Y Times p34 D 2 '52; p36 D 21 '52
N Y World-Telegram p8 D 2 '52; p13 D 6 '52
Newsweek p21 D 8 '52
Time p21 D 8 '52 por
Washington (D.C.) Post p2 D 2 '52
Who's Who In America, 1951-52
Who's Who In Commerce and Industry (1951)

DUROCHER, MRS. LEO (ERNEST) *See* Day, L.

EATON, CHARLES A(UBREY) Mar. 29, 1868—Jan. 23, 1953 Former United States Representative from New Jersey; ordained a Baptist minister in 1893 and held a number of pastorates during the next twenty-six years; also engaged in newspaper work and became an industrial relations expert; Republican Representative from New Jersey to Congress (1924-53); supported bipartisan foreign policy; delegate at San Francisco conference in 1945; chairman of the House Foreign Affairs Committee in the Eightieth Congress. See *Current Biography*, 1945.

Obituary

N Y Times p15 Ja 24 '53

EDMAN, IRWIN Nov. 28, 1896- Philosopher; educator; author
Address: b. Columbia University, New York 27; h. 315 W. 106th St., New York 25

Chairman of the department of philosophy at Columbia University, where he has taught undergraduate and graduate students for thirty-five years, Professor Irwin Edman is a spokesman for the liberal tradition of William James and of John Dewey, and believes in the possibilities of social progress through education.

Occupied less with abstruse theory than with bringing the pleasures of philosophy and the arts to the layman, Edman writes widely in newspapers and magazines, appears on radio forums, and is the author of books which go into many editions. He was made vice-president of the National Institute of Arts and Letters in January, 1953.

His latest book is a collection of short philosophical reflections, *Under Whatever Sky* (1951). As a Fulbright professor he attended in the summer of 1953 the Second Annual Conference on American Studies at Oxford University, in which eminent American scholars engaged in round-table discussions with English professors.

A native New Yorker, Edman was born on November 28, 1896, on Morningside Heights, near Columbia Univerity. His father, Solomon Edman, was a manufacturer of shirts and blouses, and with his wife, Ricka (Sklower) Edman, provided a comfortable home for their son and daughter.

Young Edman attended public schools and Townsend Harris High School, from which he was graduated in 1912. When he entered Columbia College he chose English as his major study, but he soon changed to philosophy, believing that it offered a better key to understanding the world. Among his teachers at Columbia were Charles Beard, Carlton Hayes and John Erskine, and later, John Dewey. He was elected to Phi Beta Kappa, and when he received his B.A. in 1917, he was awarded the William Mitchell Fellowship for graduate work at Columbia and a trip to Europe, where he studied at the Sorbonne in Paris.

After two years as a lecturer in the philosophy department at Columbia, Edman received his Ph.D. degree in 1920. He has remained there since that time, advancing from lecturer

IRWIN EDMAN

to instructor (1920-24), to assistant professor (1925-31), to associate professor (1931-35). He became a full professor in 1935 and was appointed to his present position as executive officer of the department of philosophy in 1945. In 1950 he was designated chairman of Columbia's philosophy department, as Johnsonian Professor of Philosophy.

Dr. Edman regards himself as an educator not only of his students, but of the general reader. "The resources of the common man have only begun to be tapped," he wrote in *Fountainheads of Freedom* (1941), a book in which he traces the idea of democracy through the ages. Quick to defend the democratic ideal, Edman has used his polemical wit to attack opponents of the liberal tradition. In an essay, "The Renascence of Sin," in *Under Whatever Sky* (1951), he described contemporary theologians who insist upon the hopelessly sinful nature of man, and who conclude that there is no use fighting evil or trying to improve the world. "When we give up the battle," wrote Edman, "the devil must smile as he watches us relax—under the guidance of theologians."

Professor Edman has concentrated in the field of aesthetics, and is seriously interested in utilizing abstract theories of art in everyday problems. He recently told a group of educators that, "it may seem a far cry, but it is not, from a sense for beauty of form to a passion for slum clearance . . . to a sense for the need of dignity and beauty in the places where we work and live" (New York *Herald Tribune,* April 8, 1951). He believes that an understanding of the fine arts is "of equal importance at least with the social studies, and perhaps more decisive morally" (New York *Times,* March 7, 1953).

Addressing 200 Columbia alumni at a reunion, he told the graduates, a majority of whom had gone into business and the professions, that many of them were not enjoying the fruits of their education because they considered themselves too busy with their daily responsibilities. "It is rather as if one were going through life . . . attuned only to certain essential practical signals, like the sound of a buzzer or a telephone," he remonstrated. "Books and the arts," he added, make it possible "to live very richly indeed on a modest twenty-four hours a day" (New York *Times,* March 23, 1953).

Dr. Edman has been philosophy editor of the radio symposium *Invitation to Learning,* and has participated in *America's Town Meeting of the Air, Author Meets the Critics* and other radio forums, on one of which he stirred up a controversy by stating that he thought baseball was "a bore."

Although Edman is a strong defender of the American way of life, he has often criticized many aspects of modern American culture, usually using the light essay to make his points. Reflecting on the digest magazine called *Quick,* for example, he proposed that one be created called *S-L-O-W,* in which the articles would "be read, marked, and inwardly digested. "Then there might be a revival of the art of literature against the purveying of information," he wrote. "The pleasures of the epicure would be renewed, and we should learn to taste rather than to gulp" (*Under Whatever Sky,* 1951).

Professor Edman's works include *Poems* (1925), *The Contemporary and His Soul* (1931), *The Mind of Paul* (1935), *Philosopher's Holiday* (1938), *Candle in the Dark* (1939), *Fountainheads of Freedom* (with H. W. Schneider) (1941), *Philosopher's Quest* (1947), and *Under Whatever Sky* (1951). He was editor of *The Works of Plato* (1928) and *The Philosophy of Santayana* (1936).

He is a contributor to many magazines, including the *Nation, New Republic, New York Times, Harper's, Saturday Review, Atlantic Monthly* and the *New Yorker.* He is a member of the editorial board of the *American Scholar* and the *Columbia University Quarterly,* and book editor in the field of aesthetics for the *Journal of Philosophy.* Professor Edman recently edited a selection of the works of George Santayana (Scribner's).

The philosopher has been contributing light verse to periodicals since he was an undergraduate, when he was a regular contributor to Franklin P. Adams' *Conning Tower* in the New York *Tribune.* Today many of his humorous poems appear in the *New Yorker.*

Professor Edman was a Fulbright lecturer in France in 1951. He has been a visiting professor at Amherst (1935), the University of California (1939), Hamilton College (1942), Harvard University (1944) and Wesleyan University (1947). In 1945, the United States Department of State and the Brazilian Government sponsored a series of lectures by Dr. Edman at the University of Brazil in Rio de Janeiro. He was awarded an honorary LL.D. degree by Goucher College in 1949.

A member of the National Institute of Arts and Letters since 1941, Dr. Edman was elected its vice-president in January 1953. He was made a member of the board of directors of the American Council of Learned Societies in

April 1953. The New York University Society of Libraries presented him with a gold medal in 1949 for the "breadth of his interests and the charm and clarity of his writing." The philosopher's clubs are the Century, Columbia, and the Athenaeum in London. He is also a member of the American Philosophical Association and the New York Philosophy Club.

Dr. Edman is small in stature, has light-colored hair and dark eyes. He is unmarried. His favorite recreation is music, particularly that of Brahms.

Professor Edman is an admirer of his native city. In a recent issue of the New York *Times Magazine,* he wrote a paean to the city in which he affirmed that it is the cultural center of the world not only for its official cultural resources, but because of the variety of peoples with diverse interests who can be found there. In another essay he wrote that New York is the perfect place for a philosopher to live because in its "massive anonymity, committed to no group and no localism, one can contemplate all time and all existence."

References

    Time 32:81+ N 14 '38 por
    Wilson Lib Bul 6:676 Je '32 por; 13:236 D '38 por
    Columbia Encyclopedia (1950)
    Edman, I. Philosopher's Holiday (1938)
    Kunitz, S. J. and Haycraft, H. eds. Twentieth Century Authors (1942)
    Who's Who in Philosophy (1942)
    Who's Who in America, 1952-53

EDWARDS, JOAN Feb. 13, 1919- Singer; song writer

Address: b. c/o Columbia Broadcasting System, 485 Madison Ave., New York 22

The singing star of the Columbia Broadcasting System's morning radio program, *At Home with Joan* is Joan Edwards who is also a song writer with several current hits to her credit. As a singer she has shared the spotlight with Frank Sinatra and Lawrence Tibbett on the popular music program, *Your Hit Parade,* and has been the featured vocalist with the bands of Rudy Vallee and Paul Whiteman. She has made many personal appearances in movie theaters and night clubs, is an accomplished pianist and arranger, and has composed lyrics and music for several television shows.

Joan Edwards was born in New York City on February 13, 1919. She is the daughter of Ben and Ethel (Mendelson) Edwards, and niece of the late Gus Edwards, famous song writer and theatrical figure. Ben and Gus were boys when their parents came to the United States from Germany and settled in Brooklyn. The family name of Simon was legally changed to Edwards after Gus began to attract attention as a singer. Ben Edwards became a successful music publisher and Joan's brother, Jack, a composer.

As a child Joan Edwards planned to be a concert pianist and music teacher. While attending George Washington High School, she directed the school glee club and accompanied

JOAN EDWARDS

singers who auditioned for her uncle. At Hunter College, she majored in music and arranged her classes so that she might fill piano playing engagements on WOV and other radio stations.

Once, after she had accompanied a singer during a try-out the manager asked Joan if she could sing. She sang *Stormy Weather* so effectively that she was given the job instead of the girl who came for the audition. During her first engagement, and soon after graduating from Hunter, Joan was invited by Rudy Vallee to make a guest appearance on his show. This developed into an eight-month tour of the country with his band.

On her return to New York, Joan took over a sustaining network program, directing her own orchestra and singing. This led to a job as vocalist with Paul Whiteman's orchestra that lasted for two years and brought her guest appearances on several CBS programs. Following the Whiteman engagement, she entertained at several night clubs, where she did her own arranging, and CBS starred her in a radio series called *Girl About Town.*

While with the Paul Whiteman band, Joan met Jules Schachter, Whiteman's concertmaster and violinist whom she married on January 25, 1942. Shortly before her marriage, she became the girl singer on *Your Hit Parade,* a weekly CBS presentation of the nation's most popular songs.

After Joan's first child was born in 1943 and after Frank Sinatra replaced Barry Wood as the male vocalist on *Your Hit Parade, Time* (May 1, 1944) reported, "No one paid much attention to Joan until after she had a baby— then aping their shameless sisters, mewling boys began to give the same treatment to Sinatra's partner." A Moan-and-Groan-for-Joan Club started in a San Francisco hospital for wounded soldiers and spread across the country until there were seventeen of them. "They

EDWARDS, JOAN—*Continued*

screech, shriek, drool, whistle and shout," Earl Wilson wrote (New York *Post*, February 14, 1944) and called Joan, "radio's sweater girl."

Setting a record for salaries among girl singers, Joan appeared with Paul Whiteman in a George Gershwin memorial series at the Roxy Theatre in 1944 and received $2,225 a week. She later filled engagements at the Paramount Theatre and at the Waldorf Astoria Hotel, where she sang and improvised on the piano. *Tune In Magazine* awarded her a citation as the nation's outstanding singer of popular songs for 1944.

And So It Ended was Joan's first published song. *Darn It Baby, That's Love* won her a membership in ASCAP and *I'm Just the Girl Who Sings with Sinatra* got her into trouble with Sinatra fans. A photograph of her in *Life* (December 11, 1944) captioned "Joan imitates the emaciated cheeks of her partner in song," reportedly inflamed his fans still more. Later, when Joan was appearing at the Roxy (for $3,000 a week) and Sinatra had been replaced on *Your Hit Parade* by Lawrence Tibbett, Sinatra fans accused her of edging him out.

Republic Pictures made *The Hit Parade of 1947* with Joan in one of the four featured parts. A review in the New York *World-Telegram* (May 3, 1947) credited Joan with holding her own in comedy as well as in song.

Joan and Jules Schachter and their daughter, Judith Ann, were the subject of an illustrated article in the *American Magazine* (May 1946), called *My Husband Won't Let Me*, by Joan Edwards. The article explained how Joan had made a success of marriage even though her earnings were three times her husband's. She realized how her uncle Gus and her father had "opened doors" for her in radio, while Jules had not had the same advantages. Jules wouldn't let her spend her money on their living expenses and before their marriage they had agreed to keep the budget within the limits of his income. Under this set-up, Joan invested part of her income in "the business," which included glamour clothes, a secretary, press clipping services, a maid for Judy Ann and other job promotion essentials. The balance went into securities, trust and educational funds and savings. Judy Ann had begun modeling at fourteen months and might be able to pay for her own education.

In an article called *Smarter Than They Look,* in the *Woman's Home Companion* (July 1946), Joan was quoted as saying, "Building a career in show business is no cinch and a girl usually gets along much better if she camouflages her fast-working brain. Then all the shrewd operators underestimate her ability and she has a fine opportunity to come out two jumps ahead of them."

When George Washington Hill, president of the American Tobacco Company—*Your Hit Parade's* sponsor—died in September 1946, Joan had been on the show for five years. Hill was said to have ruled the program with an iron hand and Joan's salary had risen from $500 a week to four figures. *Newsweek* (February 3, 1947) reported that at the time of Hill's death

the company had agreed to make no changes for a year. In November 1946, however, the show moved to Hollywood and Joan was replaced by a series of guest stars.

Joan made her television debut in a musical series presented by WABD and the Du Mont networks on June 27, 1950. In July the program, *Songs for Sale,* starring Jan Murray, featured Joan on the panel of experts. Other guest appearances on television followed.

In collaboration with Lyn Duddy, Joan wrote a successful score for a show presented at New York's Copacabana night club. Their song, *You Can't Take It With You,* was featured in *Tickets Please,* the 1950 Broadway revue starring Grace and Paul Hartman, and another, *Let's Make Up Before We Say Goodnight,* is a current success. At present, they are working on the books and scores of two projected musical shows for Broadway.

On television, Joan has written with Duddy the music and lyrics for *Godfrey's Calendar Show* (1952) and many advertising jingles used by the network. *At Home with Joan,* the current CBS radio show, which had its première on March 3, 1952, is multi-sponsored, with commercials given by Joan herself. Both her daughter and her husband have appeared as guests several times. The program theme song was written and composed by Miss Edwards and Duddy.

Joan and Jules Schachter have three children: Judith Ann, born October 1943, David, July 1947 and Linda, January 1953. Outside her career, Joan's main interest is her home and family and she enjoys cooking creatively. Her hobbies are collecting perfume bottles, wearing glamour clothes and new hair styles. Her favorite sport is fishing. She is five feet five and blonde. *Time* has described her as "delectable and showbusinesslike."

References

> Am Mag 141-36+ My '46 por
> N Y Post p26 F 14 '44; p16 Jl 24 '45 por
> N Y World-Telegram p11 My 16 '44 por; p8 Ja 27 '45; p25 Mr 1 '51
> Newsweek 29:55 F 3 '47 por
> PM p17 Mr 21 '44 por; p20 Jl 21 '46 por
> Time 43:48 My 1 '44 por

EGLEVSKY, ANDRÉ   Dec. 21, 1917-
Ballet dancer

Address: b. c/o New York City Ballet, City Center of Music and Drama, 130 W. 56th St., New York 19; h. 126 Rumson Rd., Massapequa, N.Y.

Russian-born André Eglevsky, a premier danseur in the classic ballet tradition who is now a member of the New York City Ballet, has an international reputation in the field of ballet for his technical virtuosity, which has been widely acclaimed for its style and brilliance. Associated for more than twenty years with outstanding ballet companies in Europe and the United States, he has performed with the Colonel de Basil's Ballet Russe de Monte Carlo, American Ballet, Marquis de Cuevas'

Grand Ballet de Monte Carlo, and others, before joining the New York City Ballet in 1951. Among his best-known roles are those in *Les Sylphides, Swan Lake,* and *Apollo, Leader of the Muses.*

André Eugenovitch Eglevsky was born in Moscow, Russia, December 21, 1917, the son of Eugene and Zoe (Obranoff) Eglevsky. His father was a colonel in the White Russian Army, commanding Cossack troops in World War I. As the Russian Revolution spread, Mrs. Eglevsky disguised herself and fled with her son, André, and her daughter to Constantinople and later to Bulgaria. After considerable privation and wandering, they settled in a small fishing village near Nice, France. The boy was frail, his lungs weakened by pneumonia; with the hope of improving his physical condition, his mother sent him, at the age of eight, to a ballet teacher in Nice, Madame Maria Nevelskaya—or Nevelska, as she is now known—a graduate of the Imperial Ballet of the Bolshoi Theatre, Moscow. She has since stated that after one week she knew the boy had the ability to become a great dancer.

As Eglevsky grew older and his technique developed, Madame Nevelska persuaded his mother to arrange an audition for him with Michel Fokine, the well-known choreographer of the Diaghileff Ballet Russe, who was then in Paris. Fokine's opinion having been highly favorable, André's future profession was decided upon. From then on, while he attended French high school, the boy's education was primarily a matter of study under a succession of renowned ballet teachers: Lubov Egorova (Princess Troubetzskoy), Mathilde Kchessinska (Princess Krassinska-Romanovska), Alexandre Volinine (one-time partner of Anna Pavlova), and Nicholas Legat—all products of the Russian Imperial Ballet School and distinguished exponents of their art.

On a visit to Egorova's studio, Leonide Massine, a former member of the Diaghileff Ballet and well known on both sides of the Atlantic as dancer, choreographer, and entrepreneur, was impressed by Eglevsky and arranged for him, at the age of fourteen, to make his debut as a member of the corps de ballet in Colonel de Basil's Ballet Russe de Monte Carlo in an engagement at the Alhambra, London, in the summer of 1931. Six months later, he was being given principal parts in such classical ballets as *Swan Lake, Les Sylphides,* and *Présages.* When the Ballet Russe de Monte Carlo came to the United States in 1934, Eglevsky was a member of the company. His next professional engagement was with the short-lived Epstein Ballet, touring Italy and South Africa. After an interval of study in Paris, he accepted an engagement in a company headed by the Polish dancer, Leon Woicikowski, which toured the continent for nearly two years, with Eglevsky in starring roles.

In 1936 Eglevsky came under the direction of Fokine in the René Blum-Michel Fokine Ballet Company, which was an outgrowth of the original Ballet Russe de Monte Carlo, a company that had undergone a number of organizational changes since its inception under the direction of René Blum in 1931. The asso-

Walter E. Owen

ANDRÉ EGLEVSKY

ciation with Fokine in a season at the Alhambra left a lasting impression on the young dancer: "Fokine always said, 'Let the hand follow the arm.' I don't forget," Eglevsky told a writer for the *Christian Science Monitor* in 1944. "You know, it's how you use your arms that makes a jump look bigger on the stage than it really is." Eglevsky appeared in the Fokine ballets *Les Sylphides, Prince Igor, Spectre de la Rose,* and *Petrouchka.* In 1937 Eglevsky returned to the United States with Massine, who had drawn largely on the Fokine-Blum ballet in the formation of a new company. This season saw Eglevsky's first association with the American Ballet, an outgrowth of the School of American Ballet founded in 1933-34 by Lincoln Kirstein and Edward M. M. Warburg, with the invited assistance of George Balanchine and Vladimir Dimitriew. During 1937 Eglevsky also appeared at the Radio City Music Hall in *Great Lady,* his one venture into the musical comedy field. Of this experience he has said, "It is too routine. There is more collaboration in ballet. You work with great artists. You have fine audiences. Every time we do *Princess Aurora* it is new. New personnel in the company, changes in the cast, new stage, new audiences—all this helps to make a ballet new every time it is performed" (*Christian Science Monitor,* June 10, 1944).

Since 1937 the record of Eglevsky's engagements is a record of the ballet renaissance in the United States with its kaleidoscopic formations of one ballet company after another, their amalgamations and rebirths, and the recurrent exchange of personnel (*Newsweek,* November 13, 1950). Being much in demand as an established star and a great virtuoso, Eglevsky has appeared with the following companies, at times as a member of the company, at other times as a guest artist: American Ballet, 1937-38; Ballet Russe de Monte Carlo, 1939-42; Ballet Theatre, 1942-46; Ballet International, 1944; Mas-

EGLEVSKY, ANDRÉ—Continued

sine's Ballet Russe Highlights, summer of 1945; Original Ballet Russe, 1946-47; Grand Ballet Russe de Monte Carlo, 1947; New York City Ballet, 1948. Touring Europe in 1949 Eglevsky danced with the Marquis de Cuevas' Grand Ballet de Monte Carlo. In the 1950-51 season he was back in the United States with the Marquis de Cuevas' Grand Ballet. Since 1951 he has been associated with the New York City Ballet, which, under the artistic direction of Balanchine, has as its "home theater" the New York City Center of Music and Drama. During the summer of 1952 the company engaged in a five months' tour of Europe which has been described as "triumphal."

Among the famous ballerinas Eglevsky has partnered are: Alicia Alonso, Irina Baronova, Alexandra Danilova, Rosella Hightower, Nora Kaye, Alicia Markova, and Maria Tallchief. Some of his outstanding roles are Paris in *Helen of Troy* (which he created), Apollo in Balanchine's *Apollo, Leader of Muses,* and the Prince in Balanchine's *Swan Lake.* To John Martin of the New York *Times,* Eglevsky's part in Balanchine's *A La Francaix,* first performed on September 11, 1951, seemed the best role of the dancer's life: "It is light years away from the old-fashioned pas de deux, which has thus far been his principal type of vehicle; yet it provides him with an opportunity to reveal his technical prowess quite as well as any of his exhibition pieces." Commenting on Eglevsky's performance in the Balanchine-Minkus *Pas de Trois* on November 7, 1952, Martin found him "in superb form this season, and certainly his famous batterie never has been more impeccably neat and brilliant." In the Charles Chaplin film, *Limelight,* released in 1952, Eglevsky appears with Melissa Hayden in the dance sequences and is also credited with being one of the four choreographers for the film production.

Eglevsky has said of himself, "I'm a classical dancer but not the 'cold' classical. I'm what is called technically 'bravura' classical—that's dancing with more dramatic character than the purely classical dance" (New York *Post,* October 10, 1946). Referring to Eglevsky as "one of the foremost male classic dancers in the world," Paul V. Beckley of the New York *Herald Tribune* has commented also on his "phenomenal ability" and his "prodigious technical equipment." John Martin, whose opinion is that "there are few dancers . . . who can match Mr. Eglevsky in his own particular field," has praised his "fine modesty" in the portrayal of a ballet role, "acted with taste and sincerity and danced wonderfully," his famed elevation, and his "easy technical command." The *Christian Science Monitor* critic, Margaret Lloyd, has pointed out, "Eglevsky dances the classical roles with clearness, force and ease. . . .His high mastery of dance rhetoric is not for him a means of emotional expression; but in the cool, aloof atmosphere of the classic dance, he conveys something better—the intangible communication of the spirit."

While appearing in *Great Lady,* Eglevsky in 1938 married Russian-born Leda Anchutina,

also a member of the company, whom he had met previously in the American Ballet. They have two sons and a daughter: André, Jr., Paul, and Mariana. Eglevsky's religion is Russian Orthodox. He became an American citizen in 1939. In physical appearance the dancer has been described as "a big, strapping fellow with the physique of a football player . . . piercing blue-grey eyes with faun-slanting eyebrows." His hobbies are carpentry, leather-tooling, photography, and fishing.

References

Christian Sci Mon p5 Je 10 '44
Dancing Times Jl '50
N Y Herald Tribune p15 N 28 '52
Chujoy, A. The Dance Encyclopedia (1949)

EINEM, GOTTFRIED VON   January 24, 1918- composer

Address: h. Festspielhaus, Salzburg, Austria

The world première of Gottfried von Einem's latest opera, *Der Prozess,* was given at the Salzburg Festival August 1953 under the direction of Karl Boehm. Based on Franz Kafka's novel, *The Trial,* the opera is also scheduled for production by the New York City Opera Company.

Einem's opera, *Danton's Tod,* (Danton's Death) adapted from the play by Georg Büchner, was first performed at the Salzburg Festival in 1947 with Paul Schoeffler of the Metropolitan Opera House in the title role. This has since been given in many European opera houses and has done much to establish von Einem as a composer of rank.

In the 1952-53 season the New York Philharmonic Orchestra introduced to New York audiences his *Orchestermusik.* Among other works of this young composer are *Capriccio for Orchestra, Concerto for Orchestra, Hymnus for alto solo, chorus and orchestra, Princess Turandot* and *Pas de Coeur.*

Gottfried von Einem was born January 24, 1918 in Berne, Switzerland to William von Einem and Gerta Luise Aiess von Scheurer. His father was the Austrian military attaché. He received his early education in Holstein, Germany, and was graduated from the Gymnasium. During these early years he showed considerable interest in music and was fortunate in being able to attend regularly the festivals at Salzburg and Bayreuth. He did some composing of chamber music and small orchestral works which merited the encouragement of Bruno Walter and Jan Sibelius.

He visited England in 1937 and was recalled to Austria for military service. Rejected after taking the physical examination, he left for Berlin, planning to study composition with Paul Hindemith. He was disappointed to discover that Hindemith's differences with the Nazi regime had caused his suspension from the Hochschule and he was forced to leave the country. Einem then coached singing at the Berlin State Opera House under Heinz Tietjen. Later he assisted Karl Elmendorff at the Dresden Opera House where he remained until 1944.

He found in Boris Blacher, whose noted works had been banned by the Nazis, the teacher of composition for whom he had been looking, and settled down to years of regular study with him. Blacher introduced him to the music of Stravinsky, Milhaud, Prokofieff and other modern composers, most of whom were in disfavor with the Nazis. It was in such an atmosphere of antagonism and suspicion that he and Blacher collaborated on *Danton's Tod*.

Einem's first orchestral work, *Capriccio for Orchestra* is divided into three parts marked Allegro, Adagio and Allegro. It was first performed by the Berlin Philharmonic under Leo Borchard in 1943. Music critics have generally conceded that this is the weakest and least interesting of his major compositions. The young composer showed in it his unquestionable musical gifts, but also illustrated the need for further study.

His *Concerto for Orchestra* which was first performed in Berlin in 1944 demonstrated a marked advance both melodically and rhythmically, with more expert orchestration. Apparently its rhythmic pattern suggesting jazz did not appeal to the Nazis. The Goebbels propaganda ministry became definitely unfriendly at this point. Both von Einem and his mother were arrested by the Gestapo but had to be released for lack of evidence.

His next large work, *Princess Turandot*, a ballet in two scenes, achieved some success in Dresden. It was followed by *Danton's Tod*, a far more ambitious work based on a play by Georg Büchner, written in 1834 and consisting of four acts with twenty-nine scenes. Boris Blacher worked with von Einem in combining scenes for greater dramatic effect as well as cohesiveness. They finally achieved an opera in two acts with six scenes. The setting is the French Revolution, and the story tells of Danton's fall and his execution at the hand of Robespierre.

It has been said that von Einem was inspired to write this opera by the Nurnberg trials and the plot on Hitler's life. The music critic for *Time*, stated: "Few [listeners] could forget the sheer violence of Einem's orchestral onslaught on dictatorship." However, according to *Musicology* (November, 1948), Einem thought of Danton as a dramatic character rather than a political symbol. The young composer is quoted as follows: "The well-nigh archaic effectiveness of Büchner's character sketches render it possible for me to feel, over the hundred years span, those burning heartbeats."

In spite of this strong identification with the protagonist, von Einem's music in no way sentimentalizes Danton. Those who have heard it sense in the writing the composer's reaction to the conflicts in the world about him. "What was left unsaid by the orchestra was sung by the chorus, which Einem employed as Mussorgsky did in *Boris Godunov*, as the real protagonist of the drama" (*Time*, August 18, 1947).

According to Hans Rutz (*Musicology* November 1948) the opera takes place on two planes: "the plane of the voice (stage), and the plane of the instruments (orchestra). There is hardly any thematic relationship between voice

Erna Stoll

GOTTFRIED VON EINEM

and orchestra, no world repetition . . . no leitmotifs. Each tableau is a thematic unity . . . the drama always arising from contrasts."

Henry Pleasants, reviewing the Salzburg premiere for the New York *Times* on August 7, 1947, wrote of "a violent, noisy and somehow extraordinarily effective opera", "a good opera for singing actors" of which "the best writing is for the chorus".

The Intercollegiate Broadcasting System arranged for listeners in America to hear the records of this first performance on October 1, 1947. *Musical America* for that month reviewed it as follows: "*Danton's Tod*, if rather unrelieved in its expressive moods, offers a modern score, searing in its idiom and amazingly ingenious in its construction."

The new work, *Der Prozess*, is based on Franz Kafka's novel, *The Trial*. Blacher and Heinz Von Cramer collaborated on the libretto which retains the original wording. Of this opera von Einem says "As I did before, when I composed Danton, I let the libretto rest in my desk for more than a year. I felt I needed that time to get fully acquainted with the plot, its symbolic meaning, and its . . . musical form."

He began composing it in the twelve-tone system, but after three scenes were finished, he realized the impossibility of continuing in that idiom. "I had to start anew," von Einem recalls, "and I composed the complete work in old-fashioned tonal form, without motifs and illustrations, every scene being a rounded entity in itself. Many of the roles were given to the same singers, not to save money, but to illustrate their similarity of character; the three female parts for instance, to be sung by the same soprano, simply show the 'woman' in the accused man's life."

(Continued next page)

EINEM, GOTTFRIED VON—*Continued*

"The orchestration calls for a normal-sized orchestra and a piano," he explains, "there is no chorus, no music between the scenes, no overture and no epilogue. The staging has to be done in a way that allows the fastest change of scenery, and in this respect the work calls for the most modern technical apparatus of an operatic stage" (*Musical America,* February 1953). Here von Einem's great sense of theatre is clearly manifested.

Attempts have been made to classify the young composer in various "schools"; while professing admiration for both Mahler and Stravinsky, he prefers to think of himself as a creator of his own style.

The State Department arranged for von Einem to visit this country during the winter of 1952-53 to observe American music at first hand. Dimitri Mitropoulos gave his *Orchestermusik* a brilliant and sympathetic reading and the composer a warm welcome to our musical scene. He subsequently toured the country, met a number of our most distinguished conductors and heard many of our symphony orchestras.

Einem married, in 1944, the former Liane von Bismarck. They have one son, Casper, and live for a part of the year in Salzburg. In recent years he has travelled a great deal in Switzerland, England and Italy.

Einem is six feet tall, has grey eyes and brown hair. He is a Protestant and has no avowed political affiliations. His hobbies are reading and painting.

In 1948 von Einem was appointed to the five-member Board of Directors of the Salzburg Festivals.

Einem's opera, *The Trial,* was effectively produced at the Salzburg Festival, August 17; according to *Time,* "critics noted, the von Einem score was derivative—now a dash of Puccini, now Tchaikovsky, now Stravinsky . . . although its overall effect was suitably uncanny, at times it sounded like a good movie sound track rather than full-blooded, dramatic music" (August 31, 1953).

Henry Pleasants in the New York *Times* wrote: "[This opera] will hardly survive on its music, and it has no dramatic situations. . . . What [it] has is an uncanny atmosphere sustained over a series of episodes" (August 18, 1953).

References

Mus Am 71:5 My '51; 73:227 F '53
Mus Courier p28 My 15 '53
N Y Times Je 15 '47

EINSTEIN, ALBERT (īn'stīn) Mar. 14, 1879- Theoretical and mathematical physicist
Address: b. c/o Institute for Advanced Study, Princeton, N.J.; h. 112 Mercer St., Princeton, N.J.

NOTE: This biography supersedes the article which appeared in *Current Biography* in 1941.

The world's number one scientist and America's pre-eminent refugee is Albert Einstein. A Nobel Prize winner in physics in 1921, he has made contributions to science which are unequalled by any other man. His theories of Relativity, introduced in 1905 and developed in 1916, brought him world-wide recognition. Equally important was his development of the Quantum theory. With these tools science was advanced in its search for knowledge of the universe. In March 1953 Einstein presented a possible solution to the most important question confronting theoretical physicists: a unified logical concept enabling men to explain both the quantum construction of matter and the relativistic nature of the universe. This solution is the Unified Field theory.

Albert Einstein was born in Ulm, Germany, on March 14, 1879, to Hermann and Pauline (Koch) Einstein. The family moved to Munich in 1881, where the elder Einstein opened an electrical business which proved successful for fourteen years. However, in 1895 the business failed, and the Einsteins moved to Milan, Italy, where they lived with their cousins who, unlike them, were orthodox Jews. Young Albert was left behind in school at Munich and by purposely doing poorly in his examinations, he managed to get permission—on the grounds of a nervous breakdown—to rejoin his family in Milan.

Recalling his childhood, Dr. Einstein wrote in his brief autobiographical memoir (edited by Dr. Paul Arthur Schilpp under the title *Albert Einstein, Philosopher-Scientist* (1949): "A wonder of . . . nature I experienced as a child of four or five years, when my father showed me a compass. That this needle behaved in such a determined way did not fit into the nature of events which could find a place in the unconscious world of concepts (effect connected with direct 'touch'). I can still remember—or at least I believe I can remember—that this experience made a deep and lasting impression upon me. Something deeply hidden had to be behind things . . . at the age of twelve I experienced a second wonder of a totally different nature: in a little book dealing with Euclidian plane geometry. This lucidity and certainty made an indescribable impression upon me."

For six months without the restrictions imposed by formal schooling, Albert taught himself calculus and higher mathematics. With this preparation he was admitted to the Polytechnic Academy in Zürich, Switzerland, where from 1896 to 1900 he studied mathematics and physics. He became a Swiss citizen and in 1901 began teaching in Winterthur Technical School. A year later he secured the substantial position of patent examiner at the Swiss Patent Office in Berne, which he held for seven years. While in this protective atmosphere, he obtained his Ph.D. degree from the University of Zürich and began publication of a series of epochal papers which were destined to revolutionize the science of physics and to elevate the name of Albert Einstein to world eminence. These five papers were all published in 1905, although he had begun work on some of them as early as 1902.

The first of these was *The Special Theory of Relativity,* which dealt with the relativistic attributes of motion, time and space. Einstein postulated that all these parameters cannot be absolute because they are measured relative to the observer. This approach gave form to the theory of matter which included the Lorentz-Fitzgerald contraction and explained the results of other work such as the Michaelson-Morley experiment which had hitherto been a stumbling block to the formation of any comprehensive theory.

Einstein's second paper *The Quantum Law of the Emission and Absorption of Light* provided the base for, and a proof of, the Quantum theory (propounded by Max von Planck in 1901) which regards energy to be in the form of little packets or "quanta." This paper gave substance to the concept of energy states or levels, and one of the subsequent developments of this theory was the atomic bomb. It is usually conceded among physicists that this was one of the most important papers Einstein ever published.

A third paper entitled *Theory of Brownian Movement* gave a mathematical formula predicting the path distance and relative speed of minute particles suspended in liquid, as first observed by the British botanist, Robert Brown, in 1827. This movement was assumed to be caused by atomic motion, and Einstein by his brilliant analysis, confirmed this assumption, giving the atomic theory a major piece of corroborative evidence.

The fourth piece in this series, *The Inertia of Energy,* provided the basis for Einstein's later theories of relativity. Here Einstein gave voice to the postulate that matter and energy have many properties in common and may be interconvertible. The modern view that the energy of the sun and stars arises from the destruction of matter within these radiating bodies leans heavily upon this postulate.

The final paper was a brief one entitled *On the Electrodynamics of Moving Bodies,* also published in 1905. Planck, the famous German physicist, called this "an impressive piece of work".

Einstein read his paper *The Special Theory of Relativity* before a congress of scientists meeting in Salzburg, Austria, in 1908 and it attracted such attention that by 1909 he was professor-extraordinary of theoretical physics at the University of Zurich. This allowed him to continue his work on relativity which resulted in his appointment to the Chair of Physics at the German University of Prague in 1911. The following year he returned to Zurich to become the professor of physics at his old school, the Polytechnic Academy. In 1912 he was named professor of physics at the University of Leyden.

By 1913 Einstein's fame was so great that the Kaiser Wilhelm Institute named him its director and early in 1914 he was elected a member of the Prussian Academy of Sciences. The extra salary received from this appointment permitted him to devote all his time to research. It was in this period that he developed his *General Theory of Relativity,* which was published late in 1915 and "was destined to bring Einstein to the attention of the world at large as well as to the world of science" (*The Story of Science* by David Dietz).

Alan W. Richards, Princeton Univ.
ALBERT EINSTEIN

The First World War prohibited immediate astronomical proof of the theory which led Einstein to remark wryly, "If my theory is proved correct, Germany will hail me as a great German, and the French will hail me as a citizen of the world. If it is proved false, the French will call me a German and the Germans will call me a Jew" (*The 100 Most Important People* by Donald Robinson).

This was a forerunner of his Unified Field theory announced on March 30, 1953. The *General Theory of Relativity* contained a prediction that light would be bent by a gravitational field because of the disruptive effect such a field has on the nature of space. Hence, photographs of solar eclipses would show surrounding star images to be displaced. On May 29, 1919, a group of British astronomers including Arthur Stanley Eddington, Davison and Cottingham verified Einstein's work during a solar eclipse. The results were re-checked in 1952 and found to be comparatively accurate.

This theory relates mass, space and time one to the other, by making time a fourth dimension and thus making all physical phenomena relative to the observer. Einstein further showed that energy is related to matter by the now-famous equation: $E = M c^2$ where c is the infinite velocity of light, the only absolute constant according to his 1905 theory of Relativity. He carried this further and suggested that electro-magnetic and gravitational fields of force are different expressions of similar factors.

The Lick Observatory in 1922 under Dr. W. W. Campbell verified the Einstein prediction with greater precision. This was good news to Einstein who had received the 1921 Nobel Prize in physics (and had given all the prize money to charity). He had won this honor for his work on the photo-electric effect of light as described in his 1905 paper *The Quantum*

EINSTEIN, ALBERT—*Continued*

Law of the Emission and Absorption of Light. This later check of his astronomical predictions resulted in his being awarded the Copley Medal of the Royal Society (1925) as well as the Gold Medal of the Royal Astronomical Society.

A heart attack resulting from overwork caused Einstein to resign his professorship at the University of Leyden in 1928. After recovering his health he published two short papers in 1929 giving what he called A Unified Field theory. These papers were an attempt to develop further his previous ideas on electromagnetic and gravitational fields with the resulting single mathematical formula from which they could both be derived. This work led to his being given the Franklin Institute medal in 1935.

Despite his great personal popularity in Germany during the Weimar Republic, he was branded a Jew and an exile with a price on his head by Adolph Hitler in 1933. He escaped to America, abandoning his house in Berlin which had been a gift to him from the citizens. He settled in Princeton, New Jersey, at the Institute for Advanced Study of Princeton University, where he collaborated with Leopold Infeld on a book, *On the Method of Theoretical Physics* (1933). In the same year he headed a committee which issued *The Brown Book of the Hitler Terror.*

The next years were devoted to scientific research until in September 1939 he wrote an historic letter to President Franklin Delano Roosevelt advising him on the possibilities of atomic warfare. On October 2, 1940, Einstein became a citizen of the United States, remarking that "as long as I have any choice I will stay only in a country where political liberty, toleration and equality of all citizens before the law is the rule."

In May of the same year Einstein stood before the Eighth Scientific Conference and admitted failure to achieve application of the Unified Field Theory to the atomistic nature of matter. "All attempts to represent the particle and wave features displayed in the phenomena of light and matter by direct recourse to a space-time model have so far ended in failure," Dr. Einstein told his colleagues.

All his past work had shown that while Newton's observations on space and time were true for the few particles in reference to our own system, when dealing with the giant numbers of the universe, and when working in the macrocosm of celestial bodies or the microcosm of the atom, the relativistic phenomenon becomes obvious. William L. Lawrence in the New York *Times* (May 16, 1940) wrote: "Einstein's past work, the relativistic approach regarding the structure of the universe as a whole, and the concept which serves a similar function for the complex universe within the atoms, are separate logical constructs neither of which can explain the other."

Einstein spent the time from 1940 to 1953 trying to resolve this conflict in approach. He said, "I cannot believe that God plays dice with the cosmos, as the non-deterministic theory of relativity would seem to indicate." In the intervening years he served as an adviser to the United States Navy and devoted much time to raising money for war relief organizations by giving violin concerts accompanied by Mrs. Robert Casadesus at the piano.

For several years after World War II Dr. Einstein was a leading figure in the World Government Movement with other prominent scientists. During this period he also sponsored the Zionist Movement, and he was rewarded by the State of Israel in November 1952 when he was asked to accept the presidency of the new Jewish State (following the death of the founder and first president, Dr. Chaim Weizmann). He declined, saying that he was deeply touched by the offer, but was not suited for the position. He said that he had a little comprehension of the natural and physical world and his ardent wish was uninterrupted contemplation of that world (New York *Times,* November 19, 1952).

His published books include: *Meaning of Relativity* (1923); *Sidelights on Relativity* (1923); *Investigation on the Theory of the Brownian Movement* (1926); *About Zionism* (1931); *Living Philosophies* (with others) (1931); *Builders of the Universe* (1932); *On the Method of Theoretical Physics* (1933); *Why War?* (1933, with Sigmund Freud); *The World As I See It* (1934); *Evolution of Physics* (with Leopold Infeld, 1938), and *Out of My Later Years* (London, Thames; McLeod, 1950).

On his 74th birthday (March 14, 1953) Dr. Einstein was notified that the Yeshida University Medical School in New York had been named the Albert Einstein College of Medicine. Two weeks later, on March 30th, the great scientist announced that he had resolved his previous difficulties with the Unified Field theory by using mathematical expressions which treat atoms as "singularities in the field." He went on to say, "One cannot keep side by side the concepts of field and particle as elements of physical description." As General Relativity depends upon a field theory, "and relativity explains away the no-thing inertial system" of particle theory, the conclusion is inescapable: "The field theory is inevitable." With this conclusion, he predicts that scientists will be forced to abandon their quantum approach as they delve deeper into the mysteries of the universe.

Dr. Einstein was married in 1901 to a Serbian fellow student, Mileva Marec, a gifted mathematician by whom he had two sons, Albert, Jr., and Edward. Divorced fifteen years later, he married in 1917 his cousin Elsa Einstein, who acted as the buffer between him and the world until her death in America in 1936. This man who changed the concept of the universe has long waving white hair which he covers with a knitted cap while on his daily walks in Princeton. He is a better-than-average violinist and improvises on the piano for his own amusement.

Skilled in many fields of endeavor, he is dedicated to his work in science: "What is really beautiful is science!" he has said. "It is a great gift if one is permitted to work in science for his whole life."

References

Christian Sci Mon II p9 Ja 30 '51; p3
    Mr 16 '53
Christian Sci Mon Mag p5 S 30 '50
Ladies' Home J 68:47 Ap '51
Life 34:55 Mr 29 '53
N Y Herald Tribune p1 Mr 30 '53
N Y Times p27 Mr 14 '40; p37 O 5 '52
Newsweek 34:53-4 D 26 '49
Sat R Lit 32:9-12 N 26 '49

American Men of Science (1950)
de Broglie, L. Matter and Light (1937)
Dietz, D. The Story of Science (1942)
Einstein, A. and Infeld, L. The Evolu-
    tion of Physics (1938)
Harrison, G. Atoms and Action (1939)
Infeld, L. Quest (1941)
Moszkowski, A. Einstein the Searcher
    (1922)
Who's Who in America, 1952-53
World Biography (1948)

MRS. DWIGHT D. EISENHOWER

**EISENHOWER, MRS. DWIGHT D(A-
VID)** Nov. 14, 1896- Wife of the President
of the United States.

Address: The White House, Washington, D.C.

After thirty-seven years of establishing
households in military posts throughout the
world, Mrs. Dwight D. Eisenhower, wife of
the thirty-fifth President of the United States,
has taken over her duties as mistress of
the White House. Although the First Lady
considers herself "non-political," she accompanied her husband on his 50,000-mile Presidential campaign tour and with her short bangs
and warm smile became a familiar figure to
the electorate. "Mamie," as she is known to
the press and public, brings to her role of
White House hostess her experience entertaining leading European political figures while her
husband was Supreme Commander of the
forces of the North Atlantic Treaty Organization. As First Lady, she has initiated press
conferences of her own, at which questions of
a political nature are barred.

Mamie Geneva Doud Eisenhower was born in
Boone, Iowa, November 14, 1896, one of four
daughters in the family of John Sheldon and
Elivera Mathilda (Carlson) Doud. One sister,
Mrs. Frances Moore, is married to an air transport executive; the other two died while in
their teens. Mrs. Eisenhower's ancestry is English on her father's side and Scotch on her
mother's. The Doud family of Guilford, England, first came to the United States in the
early 17th Century and in 1639 helped to establish the town of Guilford, Connecticut. Her
paternal grandfather, Royal H. Doud, established a meat-packing business in Chicago which
he later transferred to Boone, Iowa, where her
mother's father, Carl Carlson, a Swedish immigrant, had settled as a farmer and operated
a grain mill. The Doud family's meat-packing
business was sufficiently prosperous for Mamie's
father, John Sheldon Doud, to retire at the age
of 36 and establish for his family a comfortable
home in Denver, Colorado, where Mamie attended the elementary and high schools, and

Miss Wolcott's School. Her father owned the
first automobile in town, in 1904, a green Ram-
bler in which he took his wife and daughters
on many family picnics. Mamie liked to sing
the popular songs of the day, and according to
her mother was "always dressing up" for entertainments (*Collier's*, October 4, 1952).

When late in the year 1915 Miss Doud accompanied her family to San Antonio, Texas,
for their usual winter vacation, she met among
the young army officers stationed at Fort Sam
Houston second lieutenant Dwight D. Eisenhower. On St. Valentine's Day in 1916 Eisenhower gave Mamie, as an engagement ring, a
full-sized copy of his West Point class ring,
and on the first of July, when he was promoted to first lieutenant, they were married in
the Denver home of the Doud family. There
followed a ten-day wedding trip and the establishment of the first of their many temporary
homes in a two-room officers' quarters at Fort
Sam Houston. Eisenhower, who still likes to
cook, taught his 19-year-old bride how to prepare meals, though it is said that she has never
become interested in this phase of homemaking.

Their first child, Doud Dwight, born September 24, 1917, died at the age of three of
scarlet fever while the Eisenhowers were stationed at Fort Oglethorpe, Georgia. On August
3, 1922, their second son, John Sheldon Doud,
was born. The younger Eisenhower was graduated from West Point and served overseas
during World War II, after which he studied
at Columbia University, where he received a
Master of Arts degree in English. He was
married in June 1947 to Barbara Jean Thompson and they have three children, Dwight David
Eisenhower 2d, Barbara Anne, and Susan
Elaine. John Eisenhower is now a Major in
the United States Army and was attached to
the Third Division on Korea.

From the time of her marriage Mrs. Eisenhower moved with her husband from one army

EISENHOWER, MRS. DWIGHT D.—
Continued

post to another establishing households, according to a calculation made by *Time*, in some twenty different quarters during more than three decades. "She learned to clean, decorate, move out," *Time* wrote in its January 19, 1953, issue, "to clean and decorate again; to pay bills and dress on Army pay; and to catch yet another train." These quarters were in widely scattered parts of the world, including Paris, the Panama Canal Zone, the Philippines, where Eisenhower was on the staff of General Douglas MacArthur, and army posts throughout the United States.

Wherever she has moved, Mrs. Eisenhower has carried with her samples of the rose and green shades in which her childhood bedroom in Denver was decorated, and has duplicated the color scheme in her various temporary homes. "I guess you could say that my hobby is fixing up homes for other people to live in," she told a reporter (*Collier's*). "We'd be jogging along, like any other young couple, then suddenly Ike would be tapped on the shoulder for some new and terrifying job. It would mean abandoning all our plans, plunging into the unknown"— and, usually, setting up another household.

During World War II, while her husband was Supreme Commander of the Allied forces in the European Theatre of Operations, Mrs. Eisenhower stayed at the Wardman Park Hotel, and contributed to the war effort her services as a hostess for the Stage Door Canteen and as a waitress at the Soldiers, Sailors, and Marines Club.

Another official residence became Mamie Eisenhower's responsibility when "Ike" was chosen president of Columbia University in June 1948. From the president's house on Morningside Drive the Eisenhowers moved on to France, when the General was appointed Supreme Commander of the North Atlantic Treaty forces in Europe. Their new residence was a fourteen-room French mansion at Marnes-la-Coquette, where Mrs. Eisenhower officiated at formal dinners and parties for military leaders, government officials, and royalty, which afforded her "a unique apprenticeship for life in the White House" (*Time*). She also joined the General on several tours of Great Britain, the Scandinavian countries, and Holland.

With the Presidential campaign in the fall of 1952 Mrs. Eisenhower first became a public figure when she joined her husband on his nation-wide tour, traveling almost 50,000 miles in the Eisenhower train, appearing with him at large political rallies. Often, at the conclusion of his prepared remarks at whistle-stops and at political meetings Eisenhower would say: "And now I want you to meet my Mamie," and the crowd would welcome her enthusiastically. She began to receive from 200 to 300 letters a day, and most commentators believe that her presence aided in her husband's victory.

As First Lady, Mrs. Eisenhower is now in charge of the largest quarters she has yet had to supervise. In addition to managing the fifty-four room White House, she is required on some evenings to entertain as many as 2,000 persons, and every year to preside over numerous official receptions and official dinners at which members of the Cabinet and their wives, ambassadors from foreign countries and United States Senators and Representatives will be the guests of honor. Mrs. Eisenhower will also be expected to receive delegates from women's groups at the White House and to attend numerous luncheons, teas, conferences, and benefit affairs. Shortly after moving into the White House, the First Lady announced her intention of holding press conferences from time to time, where reporters will be permitted to ask direct questions, but where politics will not be discussed.

After her first press conference on March 11 with a group of men and women reporters, the New York *Herald Tribune* said editorially: "This one dealt with things that everybody, at least every woman, can understand—curtains and closets, meal times and menus . . . this information was elicited from Mrs. Eisenhower with her unfailing grace and good humor," and the Washington *Post* commented on the number of "American beauty and festival queens representing American agriculture and industry" and groups of people whom Mrs. Eisenhower has been receiving, "managing to have something to say to make each guest feel welcome."

Since coming into the limelight, Mrs. Eisenhower has influenced fashions. Her short bangs have become a fad, and her dresses have become an important influence in the fashion industry. Although she owns a few gowns styled in Paris or by leading American designers, the First Lady is known to favor moderately-priced dresses and hats purchased in department stores. Suits form the basis of her daytime wardrobe, but in the evenings she likes to wear feminine dresses in bright colors. The New York Dress Institute named her one of the world's twelve best-dressed women in December 1952. In clothing as in decoration, pink is her favorite color; pearls are the jewels she likes best.

The Eisenhowers' ultimate home may be the 114-acre farm with a rambling old farmhouse near Gettysburg, Pennsylvania, which they purchased in 1950 and which they plan some day to convert into their permanent residence.

The President's wife is five feet four inches tall, weighs 138 pounds, has blue eyes, and brown hair tinged with gray which she wears in a style that features her famous bangs on her high forehead. "An extrovert who likes to surround herself with old, familiar friends," Mrs. Eisenhower has been described as "cheerful and direct in her talk." An editorial in the Washington *Post* said of her: "She is still fresh, enthusiastic and, to the delight of photographers, she can smile easily. . . . [She] has a friendly, informal attitude toward people that complements that of her husband." When not fulfilling her official duties the First Lady likes to read mystery novels and to baby-sit with her three grandchildren, who are frequent visitors to the White House.

Reluctant to make public speeches, she is described as "completely nonpolitical." Her food tastes are standard American, with a preference for Iowa corn-on-the-cob, Southern fried chicken, home-baked beans, apple pie, and cornbread. She enjoys bridge, canasta, and playing the piano. Mrs. Eisenhower and the President are of the Presbyterian faith. She holds two foreign decorations, the Order of Malta and the Southern Cross from Brazil.

References

Christian Sci Mon p9 Ja 15 '53
Collier's 130:46 O 4 '52
Ind Woman 32:3 Ja '53
N Y Times p64 N 9 '52
N Y Times Mag p7 D 28 '52
Newsweek 40:29 O 13 '52
Time 61:17 Ja 19 '53
U S News 34:17 Ja 23 '53; 35:52 Ag 21 '53
Washington (D.C.) Post p31 O 15 '52; p24 Ja 20 '53

EISENHOWER, MAMIE (DOUD) *See* Eisenhower, Mrs. D. D.

EMERSON, LEE E(ARL) Dec. 19, 1898- Governor of Vermont; lawyer

Address: b. State House, Montpelier, Vt.; h. Barton, Vt.

Among the Republican Governors re-elected in November 1952 was Lee E. Emerson of Vermont, whose second term will expire in January 1955. A lawyer by profession and a former speaker of the State House of Representatives, he served as Lieutenant-Governor from 1945 to 1946, and he was elected Vermont's sixty-seventh Governor in November 1950. He is an advocate of a greater regional forest conservation program, continued promotion of New England as a recreation area and the development of highway and rail transportation in his State.

Lee Earl Emerson, who is of Scotch-Irish descent, was born December 19, 1898 at Hardwick, Caledonia County, Vermont. His father, who was a granite cutter, manufacturer and farmer, later moved his family to Barton in Orleans County, where Lee attended Barton Academy. Graduated in 1917, he entered Syracuse University in New York State. He majored in English and for three months during 1918 prepared for World War I service in the Students' Army Training Corps.

After receiving his A.B. degree from Syracuse in 1921, Emerson taught school until his entrance into the Law School at George Washington University, Washington, D.C., where he obtained his LL.B. in 1926. He was admitted to the bar in 1937 and began practice as an attorney in his home town, Barton. (Even after his inauguration as Governor, he continued to maintain his partnership with James E. Knapp in the Barton law firm of Emerson and Knapp).

Emerson was elected to the lower chamber (House of Representatives) of the Vermont General Assembly in November 1938 and again in November 1940; he was Speaker of the House in 1941. (The Vermont Assembly meets

The Huff Studio

LEE E. EMERSON

only in odd-numbered years). In 1943 he served as a member of the State Senate. On November 5, 1944 Emerson was elected Lieutenant-Governor of Vermont for the two-year term beginning in January 1945.

A Republican State since the formation of that party in 1856, Vermont has never had a Democrat as Governor, and in 1945 still had a firmly entrenched political "escalator system" by which the Lieutenant-Governor advanced to the governorship at the end of the incumbent's second term. Thus Emerson would have had every expectation of becoming his State's chief executive in January 1949, had not a reaction set in during 1946 against the "Old Guard" Republican group which supported Governor Mortimer R. Proctor and himself.

Ernest W. Gibson, Jr., who had completed the term of his deceased father in the United States Senate in 1940 decided to contest the renomination of Governor Proctor. With the support of the "liberal" wing of the local Republican party, Gibson defeated Proctor in the primaries and with a running mate of his own persuasion was elected to the governorship in November.

In the September 1948 primaries, Emerson challenged the renomination of Gibson, and was actually ahead of him in early tabulations but defeated in the final count. Gibson, however, resigned the governorship a year later to accept an appointment on the Federal bench. His successor, Harold J. Arthur, decided not to seek the gubernatorial nomination in the September 1950 primary and to campaign for nomination for Vermont's single Congressional seat. Meanwhile on May 20 Emerson had announced his candidacy for the Republican gubernatorial nomination, which he won in a three-cornered primary contest, with 30,868 votes to 24,886 for former Speaker J. Harold Stacey and 15,788 for former Chairman Peter A. Bove

EMERSON, LEE E.—*Continued*
of the State Liquor Control Board. At the
November general election, Emerson, with his
running mate Joseph E. Johnson, defeated his
Democratic opponent, Mayor J. Edward Moran
of Burlington, by 64,915 votes to 22,227.

Early in Emerson's first gubernatorial term
beginning January 1951, the Vermont General
Assembly carried out recommendations made
by former Governor Gibson in his second inaugural message to increase the salaries of
legislators and other State employees, and to
liberalize the State's Workmen's Compensation
law. Medical and hospital benefits were extended, and an Occupational Diseases law was
passed. A special State Taxation Commission
was established, while to meet an augmented
budget the Vermont income tax law was altered to provide for a 15 per cent surtax to be
withheld at the source.

In July, Vermont threatened to stop withholding Federal income taxes from the salaries of State employees in retaliation for refusal by Federal agencies to deduct the Vermont income tax from salaries paid to Federal
employees resident in the State. Absentee voting by members of the Armed Forces was
facilitated; a Civil Defense law was passed
and a Vermont State Guard instituted, while
during the same year Vermont "conducted a
survey of lakes and streams in the interest of
pollution elimination.

In his welcoming address to the 103rd
quarterly meeting of the New England Council, Governor Emerson emphasized the common language, waterways and transportation
resources of the six New England states, and
cited efforts of New York granite manufacturers to bar Vermont granite from that
State in contrast to the free trade of granite
between the New England states. The Vermont Executive stressed the growth of New
England as a recreation area, and emphasized
"the need for better rail transportation and
the expansion of interconnecting highways"
(*Christian Science Monitor,* June 25, 1951)

The Iroquois Indian tribe confronted, in
1951, the General Assembly with claims to
the title of five of Vermont's sixteen counties as part of the old tribal hunting grounds.
The claims were scheduled for hearings by
the 1953 Assembly, with counsel for the Indians indicating that they might settle for
about $1,200,000. In the summer of 1952,
New Hampshire charged Vermont, as well as
New York and Michigan, with using New
Hampshire scenes to illustrate promotional bro-
chures. Governor Emerson replied that Vermont had "scenery enough for the whole
country" (New York *Times,* July 26, 1952).

In the September 1952 Republican primary
Governor Emerson's renomination was challenged by State Senator Henry D. Vail, who
"filed for the race thirty minutes before the
deadline." The contest was close, with Emerson defeating Vail by fewer than 2,500 votes;
and in November his Democratic opponent,
Robert W. Larson, displayed impressive
strength, polling 60,551 votes to 78,338 for
Emerson.

Lee Emerson was sworn in for his second
two-year term on January 8, 1953, at which
time the forty-second biennial Assembly convened for one of the busiest sessions in many
years. Among the bills considered was one
authorizing the sale of colored oleomargarine,
and one which would provide for the observance of most legal holidays on the nearest Monday. Lively controversy followed
the proposal by Governor Emerson later in
January of a budget of $60,767,198, the larg-
est in the State's history, for the new bien-
nium beginning in July. He recommended
balancing the budget by using an estimated
accumulated surplus of $6,602,458, even
though "some of those in the Legislature
. . . recalled that his former philosophy was
to use surplus only for capital or non-recur-
ring expenses" (New York *Times,* February
1, 1953). Use of the surplus was opposed
by the influential Senator Vail, Emerson's
challenger in the 1952 primary, and the substitution of a sales or other temporary tax
was widely predicted.

The Governor, in July 1953, proposed a
meeting for the week of July 20th of officials
from Vermont, Maine and New Hampshire
to explore the feasibility of regional programs for providing college educations in
New England.

Governor Emerson has been awarded honorary LL.D. degrees by the University of
Vermont and State Agricultural College at
Burlington and Norwich University at Northfield, Vermont, as well as by the University
of Syracuse at the ninety-seventh commencement exercises on June 2, 1952. He was
named Syracuse University's "most distinguished graduate" for the year 1951. The
Vermont Governor is an American Legion-
naire and a Mason; his religious affiliation is
with the Baptist Church. Mrs. Emerson,
the former Dorcas M. Ball, was a secretary
before her marriage. The Emersons have
two daughters, Cynthia M. and Nancy Lee.
The blue-eyed, black-haired Governor is five
feet three inches in height and weighs around
160 pounds. His favorite outdoor exercise is
hiking.

References

N Y Times p23 N 8 '50

Martindale-Hubbell Law Directory,
1952

**EMMET, EVELYN (VIOLET ELIZA-
BETH)** British delegate to the United Nations

Address: b. c/o United Nations Delegation of
the United Kingdom, 350 5th Ave., New York
1; c/o National Union of Conservative and
Unionist Associations, 2-8 Victoria St., Westminster, London, S.W. 1, England

By appointing the Honorable Mrs. Evelyn
Emmet to be a member of the United Kingdom
delegation to the United Nations General Assembly session opening in October 1952, the
Churchill Government of Great Britain established two precedents. Mrs. Emmet, who

has been a member of the Conservative Party National Executive since 1948, is the first woman to represent her country in the U.N. as a full delegate, and is the first British full delegate appointed who is not a Government minister or a member of Parliament. Since 1936 Mrs. Emmet has been a member of either the London County Council or the West Sussex County Council; she is a Justice of the Peace (county magistrate) for Sussex and has served on numerous county and Home Office committees and commissions. She has made a special study of child welfare, juvenile delinquency, and probation questions.

Evelyn Violet Elizabeth Rodd Emmet is the elder of the two daughters born to James Rennell and Lilias (Guthrie) Rodd, who were also the parents of three sons. Her father, subsequently knighted and later elevated to the peerage as the first Baron Rennell of The Rodd, took his title from his family's estate in the west of England county of Hereford, while the Guthries come from Forfarshire in Scotland. Lord Rennell entered the British foreign service in 1884, became secretary of the Legation in Cairo ten years later, and was appointed first secretary of the Embassy in Rome in 1901, Minister in Stockholm in 1905, and British Ambassador in Rome in 1908. His elder daughter, accordingly, received a large part of her early education in Swedish and Italian (also German, French, and Swiss) schools, and speaks several European languages fluently. At St. Margaret's School at Bushey in the English county of Middlesex she was prepared for matriculation at Lady Margaret Hall, one of the three women's colleges at Oxford, where she took her baccalaureate degree with honors. Later she was granted the master's degree from Oxford and also took courses at the London School of Economics.

As His Britannic Majesty's Ambassador in Rome from 1908 to 1919, Sir Rennell Rodd was in Italy when that country broke the Triple Alliance with Germany and Austria-Hungary and entered World War I on the side of Britain and France. His elder daughter served as his secretary during the war years; then following his resignation in 1919, she spent several months in London's East End slum area as a social service worker for the Toynbee Hall University Settlement. In June 1923 she became the wife of Thomas Addis Emmet, heir to Amberley Castle in Sussex, and in the following year (1924) young Mrs. Emmet was elected to the London County Council as member for North Hackney. During the nine years that she held this seat, she was chairman of a number of the Council's committees including its supplies committee. "Many of the committees and subcommittees of which she was chairman," noted a biographical sketch supplied by the British Information Service, "were concerned with public health and with hospitals, including the hospital management subcommittee which was responsible for 73 hospitals."

Following the death of her husband on June 3, 1934, Mrs. Emmet left London for Sussex to become the mistress of Amberley Castle pending the coming of age of the elder of her two sons, who was then only nine years old,

United Nations

EVELYN EMMET

and there operated a dairy farm and bred Jersey and Dexter cattle. "Under Mrs. Emmet's personal supervision," stated Melita Knowles in the *Christian Science Monitor*, "the old castellated manor house was turned from a dreary ruin into a modern comfortable home." (Amberley Castle, half way between Arundel and Pulborough, dates from Norman times; remains of the old castle walls still surround the manor house, while the keep also survives and was used during World War II as a guard tower.) Mrs. Emmet did not withdraw from public service; while no longer an elected member of the London County Council, she has been a "co-opted" member of that body continuously since 1934. In 1936 she was appointed a Justice of the Peace (county magistrate) for Sussex, and from 1935 until 1944 served as chairman of the Children's and Matrimonial Courts of Sussex. Especially concerned with problems of juvenile delinquency, she held for several years the chairmanship of the Home Office Approved School for Girls at Shermanbury. Mrs. Emmet, who is a member of the Quarter Sessions Appeals Committee, is said to be the only woman ever to preside at Quarter Sessions.

Having in 1938 become County Organizer for Sussex of the Women's Voluntary Services, with the outbreak of World War II Mrs. Emmet was made "responsible for all women's war work in the county outside the purview of the Red Cross and the St. John War Organization" (British Information Service). In this activity, while she had not yet visited the United States, she developed many friendships with Americans. "I have never lost a chance of making friends through correspondence," Melita Knowles has quoted her as saying, "since I had to handle generous gifts of clothing and food from America to West Sussex during the war." The same writer further pointed out that Mrs. Emmet's elder son trained in the United States in the war, that she entertained many young

EMMET, EVELYN—*Continued*

Americans at Amberley, and that later, as a member of the West Sussex Education Committee, she used "her influence to get American exchange schoolteachers into its schools." The war over, Mrs. Emmet was elected to the West Sussex County Council as the member for Pulborough and served as such until 1952, when she became an alderman. She has been chairman of the Child Guidance Committee, of the Children's Committee, of the Further Education Committee, and vice-chairman of the Education Committee and of the Finance and General Purposes Committee. From 1945 to 1951 she was chairman of the Sussex County Advisory Probation Committee. Mrs. Emmet is a member as well of the Home Office Probation Advisory Committee and sat on the special Government "Cinema and the Child" commission which studied and reported on the relation of motion pictures to delinquency.

Named for the first time to membership in the National Executive of the Conservative party in 1948, Mrs. Emmet served on its General Purposes Committee. Two years later she was made vice-chairman of the Women's National Advisory Committee; then on June 13, 1951, she was elected chairman. The presiding member of the special committee which produced the so-called "True Balance Report" on women's problems, Mrs. Emmet also served with the Maxwell Fyfe committee on party reorganization and on the political education committee. She spoke widely in support of Conservative candidates in the election campaigns of 1950 and 1951 and presided over the Conservative Women's Conferences of May 1952. A series of lectures that she delivered in Germany for the Foreign Office was said to have demonstrated a gift for interpreting British policy to alien audiences and to have been a possible factor in Prime Minister Winston Churchill's decision to appoint her as a full delegate to the United Nations General Assembly meeting at New York City in October 1952. In this post, which carries ministerial rank, Mrs. Emmet enjoys the dual distinction of being both the first Englishwoman to attend the U.N. as a full delegate and the first British full delegate who is not also technically a Minister of the Crown, that is to say, a minister with a seat in Parliament. She was appointed to the Third (Social, Humanitarian, and Cultural) Committee of the General Assembly. In New York Mrs. Emmet has devoted some of her time to a study of the work of the city juvenile courts, and of the probationary system as a deterrent of crime.

Evelyn Violet Elizabeth Rodd and Thomas Addis Emmet were married on June 9, 1923; their children are Gloria Lavinia Eileen (Mrs. Mark Fleming), Christopher Anthony Robert, David Alistair Rennell, and Penelope Ann Clare. Mrs. Emmet, who has several grandchildren, is described by Melita Knowles as a "slight, curly-haired woman, with composure and charm."

References

Christian Sci Mon p9 N 1 '52 por
U N Bul 13:454 N 15 '52
Burke's Landed Gentry (1952)
Kelly's Handbook to the Titled, Landed and Official Classes, 1951

EMMET, MRS. THOMAS ADDIS *See* Emmet, E. V. E.

ERIKSON, LEONARD F. June 4, 1897- United States Government official

Address: b. International Broadcasting Service, 251 W 57th St., New York 19; United States Information Agency, 1778 Pennsylvania Ave., N.W., Washington 25, D.C; h. Greenwich, Conn.

Active in the radio and advertising fields for more than twenty years, Leonard F. Erikson was appointed head of the International Broadcasting Service (which directs the *Voice of America*) on July 27, 1953. He succeeded Alfred M. Morton, now chief consultant of the Department of State's tele-communication program, to this post of directing the broadcasting division of the United States Information Agency. Established August 1, 1953, this agency replaces the Office of International Information of the Department of State, and it serves as an instrument of America's foreign policy in presenting "a true picture of American aims."

Erikson was a director and a vice-president of McCann-Erikson, Inc., an international advertising agency, since 1949, and was formerly an executive of the Columbia Broadcasting System for fourteen years. As chief of the *Voice of America* he supervises more than 100 radio programs which are broadcast daily in forty-one languages to countries in Europe, the Near East, South Asia, and Africa.

Leonard F. Erikson was born June 4, 1897, the son of Selma (Dahlstrom) and C. F. Erikson. His father immigrated to America from Sweden. After attending public schools in Madison, Wisconsin, he enrolled in the school of journalism of the University of Wisconsin. He served in the Navy as a petty officer until the end of World War I, when he resumed his studies, graduating in 1920. He received his master's degree from the graduate school of business administration at Harvard University in 1922.

Following a year of study abroad, Leonard F. Erikson obtained his first experience in the newspaper publishing fields in Chicago, working for his father who had purchased two Swedish-language newspapers and had combined them into the *Swedish Tribune-News*. In 1930, he joined the staff of the Columbia Broadcasting System as western sales manager, in the Chicago office. He specialized in automotive industry accounts.

After fourteen years of service with Columbia Broadcasting System, during which time he had been promoted to the position of general sales manager in CBS's New York office, Leonard Erikson became associated with the New York advertising firm of Batten, Barton,

Durstine, and Osborn. Here he was assistant to the president, Bernard C. ("Ben") Duffy, and was responsible for liaison between management and the agency's radio department.

Erikson later became manager of the radio department where he supervised, among other programs, the United States Steel Corporation's *Theater Guild of the Air*, an hour-long radio dramatic show. Erikson left Batten, Barton, Durstine, and Osborn to become associated with Kenyon & Eckhardt, Inc., another large New York City advertising agency, where he served as vice-president, director of radio and television, in addition to being a member of the agency's plans board. During his association with Kenyon & Eckhardt, Inc., Erikson pioneered in the development and production of one of the first series of hour-long television dramas.

Erikson remained with Kenyon & Eckhardt until 1949, when he joined McCann-Erickson, Inc., an advertising agency, where, in addition to being a director of the agency, Erikson (who is not related to one of the founders of the company, the late Alfred W. Erickson) also functioned as vice-president in charge of radio and television, in which capacities he continued until his association with the *Voice of America*.

At the time of his appointment it was announced by Dr. Robert L. Johnson, administrator of the Office of International Information, that Leonard F. Erikson had been brought in "to reorganize the entire radio effort" of the overseas information program. Erikson, upon being sworn in to his new post as director, stated "I am deeply conscious of the responsibility that goes with the new post I am assuming as head of the *Voice of America*, but I am encouraged by the fact that there are hundreds of capable and dedicated people in the organization who have been doing an excellent job and will continue to do so (New York *Herald Tribune*, July 28, 1953). He also declared that the new post holds out a "great opportunity to any one interested in serving the best interests of the United States."

The *Voice of America* began in February 1942 as a wartime project, was later taken over by the Office of War Information, and in 1948 under Public Law 402 was administered under the Office of International Information of the Department of State. Since August 1, 1953, it has been under the direction of the United States Information Agency, an independent agency. The sum of $80,000,000 was requested but this was cut by members of the House of Representatives in the Eighty-third Congress to $60,000,000; the Senate restored $15,000,000 of this cut, so that the annual budget is $75,000,000.

The New York *Times* commented editorially on July 29, 1953: "The Senate Appropriations Committee was well-advised in restoring most of the cuts made by the House in funds for the Government's overseas information activities . . . what the Eisenhower Administration is said to consider [$80,000,000] is 'the least possible amount necessary' to continue this important program."

The agency will move all its divisions, radio, press, films, and library to its new offices at

LEONARD F. ERIKSON

1778 Pennsylvania Avenue, Washington, D.C. by June 30, 1954. The agency's head is Theodore Streibert. The function of each division is to "work for the attainment of the foreign policy objectives of the United States by presenting a true picture of American aims, by creating psychological strength and resistance to Soviet imperialism, by counteracting anti-American slanders, and by exposing the fraud of international communism."

As of August 1, 1953 the *Voice of America* operated more than 100 separate programs, ranging from fifteen minutes to one hour, and amounting to about thirty-four program hours and about 300,000 words, broadcast daily in forty-one languages.

Among these programs are eight hours daily broadcasting to the USSR and to Soviet-controlled areas, in ten different languages. Erikson indicated his special interest in these particular broadcasts when he said, upon taking office, that the importance of the *Voice of America* stems from the fact that it is "the only means of reaching behind the Iron Curtain" thereby providing the millions under Soviet domination with "unbiased news, clear up misunderstandings and answer enemy propaganda."

Erikson also stated that "there have been indications that the Voice can carry on more effectively and economically than ever before."

The *Voice of America* has frequently been the subject of debate in Congress and has stirred up controversy in the press. Recently, Walter Lippman wrote in his column in the New York *Herald Tribune* (April 27, 1953) "For any Government agency to call itself the Voice of America is an impertinence. In a democratic society where opinions are free, a government propaganda agency which is a monopoly is an inherent contradiction that must cause confusion at home and abroad . . . the people overseas should have available to them

ERIKSON, LEONARD F.—*Continued*

substantially the same news that we have available to us . . . the selection should be entrusted to men chosen by our own broadcasting companies and the press services."

On the other hand, Dr. Wilson Compton, an administrator of Office of International Information, delivered on January 30, 1953 an address before the Congressional Club, Washington, D.C. (*Vital Speeches,* March 1, 1953) saying, "The *Voice of America* is perhaps our most important single service because it is not only the best, but the *only* dependable means available to us to reach behind the Iron Curtain. RIAS, our potent radio service in Berlin, is coming close to blanketing Germany including communist-controlled East Germany. It is having a powerful political effect."

Erikson was married to Lorraine Thompson on February 14, 1928 and they have a son, Gilmore.

References

Broadcasting Mag p44 D 25 '44; p24 Ja 26 '48 por; p24 Ag 1 '49 por; p28 Ag 15 '49; p54 Jl 6 '53 por
N Y Herald-Tribune p8 Jl 2 '53
N Y Times p12 Jl 28 '53 por
Time 62:87 Jl 13 '53

ESTENSSORO, VÍCTOR PAZ *See* Paz Estenssoro, V.

EWING, (WILLIAM) MAURICE May 12, 1906- Scientist; educator

Address: b. c/o Lamont Geological Observatory, Palisades, N.Y.; h. Torrey Cliff, Palisades, N.Y.

As a research associate on the National Defense Research Committee projects and as director of research at the Woods Hole Oceanographic Institute during World War II, Maurice Ewing devised and designed the SOFAR system—a sonic method for rescuing men lost at sea. Simultaneously, in directing the first concrete experiments in underwater photography since 1893, Ewing devised a camera that could take underwater pictures at a depth of more than three miles. Since becoming a full professor of geology at Columbia University in 1947, Ewing has every summer led an expedition to study the Atlantic Ocean bottom. He and his associates study the sediments they collect from the ocean floor at Columbia's Lamont Geological Observatory, of which Ewing has been the director since 1949.

Descended from Scotch, Irish, and English ancestry, William Maurice Ewing was born on May 12, 1906, in Lockney, Texas, the son of Floyd Ford Ewing, a farmer and merchant, and Hope (Hamilton) Ewing. The youth and his three brothers and three sisters were reared in Lockney, where Ewing was graduated in 1922 from the Lockney High School. He left his native town that year to enter Rice Institute in Houston, Texas, at which from 1923 to 1926 he was a Hohenthal Scholar. Majoring in

physics and mathematics at school, Ewing worked winters as a library assistant and summers as a member of geophysical prospecting crews of various oil companies. He received his B.A. degree with honors in physics and mathematics in 1926; whereupon he became a fellow at the institute for the next three years, earning his M.A. degree in 1927.

After a year (1929-30) as an instructor in physics at the University of Pittsburgh, Ewing was employed in the same capacity at Lehigh University, Bethlehem, Pennsylvania. There he stayed for the next six years (1930-36), during which time he finished writing his doctor's thesis, *Calculation of Ray Paths from Seismic Time Curves,* and received his Ph.D. degree from Rice Institute in 1931. In 1936 Ewing was promoted on the Lehigh University staff to be an assistant professor of physics, that same academic year (1936-37) acting as the chief scientist on an expedition sponsored by the American Geophysical Union and the United States Navy. From 1938 to 1941 he was a lieutenant in the United States Naval Reserve. Also in 1938 he won a Guggenheim Memorial Foundation fellowship for the next two years for seismic investigations of the ocean basins.

In 1940 Ewing moved from the physics department to the geology department of Lehigh University to become an associate professor of geology, and that same year took a leave of absence to work as a research associate at the Woods Hole (Massachusetts) Oceanographic Institution, a post he retains. For the next five years (1940-45) during World War II, he worked at Woods Hole both as a research associate on the National Defense Research Committee projects and as the director of research in physics. While he was there doing research for the Navy with the civilian rank of chief scientist, Ewing's appointment as associate professor of geophysics at Columbia University was announced in July 1944—his new post to be assumed at the end of the war. At the time of this announcement the New York *Sun* (July 18, 1944) reported that "Dr. Ewing's studies of the ocean floor have proved of value to the war effort."

What those studies involved, however, was kept secret until after the war. Early in 1946 came the announcement of Ewing's discovery and invention—the SOFAR system, short for "Sound Fixing and Ranging," a method used to rescue men from ships or planes lost at sea. The survivor drops a TNT charge underwater, timed to explode at a depth of 3,000 to 4,000 feet, which sets up underwater sound waves that are picked up by hydrophones at shore stations. "Survivors can be located within a square mile of sea as far as 2,000 miles from shore" (New York *Times,* January 20, 1946). How long it would take for the rescue would depend on the survivor's positon, Ewing pointed out: "In the Pacific I would estimate roughly the maximum time required for rescue as around eight hours. Compare that with the twenty-two days it took to find Eddie Rickenbacker!" (*Newsweek,* May 27, 1946).

The idea for SOFAR first came to Ewing in the summer of 1937 while he was aboard the research ship *Atlantis* exploring the ocean's bed by exploding small bombs. He noticed that simply by holding his ear to the rail he could hear bombs explode on the ocean floor three miles below and that the blasts were followed by three echoes about six seconds apart. Ewing's discovery, which "four years later was to revolutionize underwater sound transmission" (*Newsweek*), was that deep in the ocean there existed a natural sound channel in which relatively faint sounds could be detected thousands of miles from their source, because of "speaking-tube" effect set up by a peculiar set of temperature and pressure conditions.

The scientist first tested his theory by dropping bombs from one ship, the explosions of which were picked up by a hydrophone on the end of a 4,000 foot line suspended from a second ship up to 1,000 miles away. The Navy later set up an experimental listening station which picked up explosions of bombs dropped by a ship 3,100 miles away. By January 1947 the Navy Underwater Sound Laboratory at Fort Trumbull, Connecticut, announced the completion of five stations in the Pacific to rescue fliers downed at sea, "based on a principle that the Navy called the most spectacular discovery made during the war in the field of sound physics" (New York *Herald Tribune*, January 26, 1947). The Navy also announced its intention to equip its ocean-flying planes with a special one-pound bomb that could be dropped overboard by the survivor and that would explode exactly three-quarters of a mile down. Besides its value as a rescue aid, SOFAR is helpful as a means by which the depths of the ocean can be explored, the existence of shoals determined, the geological nature of the bottom ascertained, and underground volcanoes detected.

Simultaneously with his work on SOFAR, Ewing was engaged in deep water photography, partly as a hobby and partly to help the Government identify ships lost to the German U-boats. Ewing and his associates began their experiments while occupied with other research on the *Atlantis* during the winter of 1938. Their first camera, enclosed in a pressure resistant aluminum case and designed to take a series of pictures on striking bottom, was lost on its third trial.

Ewing and his associates designed a second camera, enclosed in a pyrex glass tube five feet long and six inches in diameter, to take two pictures on each lowering, one on striking the bottom and another thirty seconds later. With this camera, by 1940 they had taken more than one hundred successful pictures showing the ocean bottom and various forms of marine life to depths of 500 fathoms. Later, using another camera, Ewing reported that "pictures were now being taken at a depth of 2,700 fathoms—more than three miles—a feat never before performed" (*Newsweek*, October 30, 1944). This same month—October 29, 1944—he told a New York *Herald Tribune* reporter: "Photography furnishes a more satisfactory means for studying deep-sea life than efforts to obtain samples by drags and raising the animal forms to the surface, because usually when the animals are taken from the tre-

MAURICE EWING

mendous pressures at the mile-deep levels to the shallower levels they explode."

Although the ocean's floor contains many marvels, among them prairies wider than those of the midWest, peaks higher than most mountains, and subterranean rivers, according to Ewing, there is no evidence of the fabled cities of the lost continent, Atlantis (*Pathfinder*, December 1, 1948).

After World War II, Ewing served on the counseling committee of the Geological Society of America, in New York City, from 1945 to 1948. He was promoted to be a full professor of geology at Columbia in 1947, his present position, and that same year became a member of the panel on seismology of the Research and Development Board, Washington, D.C., another post he still holds. In July 1947 Ewing set out as director of the first expedition to survey the hitherto unexplored Mid-Atlantic Ridge—a narrow S-shaped chain of undersea mountains extending from Iceland nearly to Antarctica. On this undertaking, sponsored by the National Geographic Society, Columbia University, and the Woods Hole Oceanographic Institution, he and his colleagues sailed aboard the research ship *Atlantis*, a 146-foot ketch, to explore the ridge, too deep for a diver to reach. To chart a 50,000 square mile area of the Atlantic roughly halfway between America and Europe, the scientists employed several methods including: underwater photography, sonic measurements, and the collection of samples of sediments from the ocean floor. Using the last method in trying to find out when and how the ridge was formed, the scientists collected sediment samples by driving steel tubes, ten to fifteen feet long, into the mud by means of heavy weights. Trapping a cross-section of the sediment, they brought these "cores" to the surface, dried them, and then studied them.

Since no method had been found to examine the solid rock underlying the softer sediments, the scientists had to use sonic measurements to study these structures. Ewing employed sound detectors near the surface of the water to record the echoes from the explosion of a bomb—also near the surface. He could then calculate the thickness of the mud layer and

EWING, MAURICE—*Continued*

consequently its age by studying the difference between reflections from the ocean floor and from the bedrock below the mud sediments. In the summer of 1948 Ewing, with eight other scientists and his regular crew of seventeen, took the second two-month cruise, for the first time using tubes 60 feet long in the hope of getting at sediments one million years old. They also used an improved camera in an attempt to take colored pictures of marine life two miles or more down, and black-and-white pictures at even greater depths. Later Ewing reported that he and his associates had taken photographs as deep as 18,000 feet (more than three miles).

In 1949 Ewing was named director of Columbia University's newly established Lamont Geological Observatory in Palisades, New York, a laboratory which is supported by both private and Government funds and has a staff of seven professors and more than thirty students. At the laboratory Ewing and his associates study specimens collected on their summer voyages. Also on the estate is an old root cellar converted into an earthquake seismograph vault housing nine sensitive seismometers, three of them built by the scientists and their students, and designed to detect and plot earth tremors within a few minutes. After his third cruise on the *Atlantis*, in the summer of 1949, Ewing reported that the explorers had traced the Hudson River Valley 225 miles into the Atlantic Ocean—105 miles beyond the point where it previously was believed to stop—and indicated that it might extend even further. In 1950 Ewing was named an associate in geophysics at Woods Hole Oceanographic Institution, a post he continues to fill. In the summer of 1951 in explorations off the Massachusetts coast, Ewing's party reported the discovery of an underwater mountain more than a mile high and a mile under the surface.

The following summer Ewing made a three-month cruise, his sixth and longest such expedition, this time under the sponsorship of Columbia University, the Office of Naval Research, the Navy's Bureau of Ships, and the Woods Hole Oceanographic Institution. When he returned to port on October 5, 1952, Ewing reported the discovery in the Western Atlantic of a vast new hitherto unknown ocean canyon, linked to a system of undersea channels comparable in extent with the Mississippi River and its tributaries. For part of this 10,000 mile expedition, the *Kevin Moran* and the *Atlantis* teamed up on a project of seismic refraction measurements, with one vessel listening while the other dropped TNT charges about fifty miles away. Ewing said that the preliminary evidence appeared to refute the idea still held by some European geologists that the eastern ocean was a foundered continent, because, he said, his explorers had found that the base of the Atlantic east of the Mid-Atlantic Ridge was identical geologically with the west base.

The author of the book *Propagation of Sound in the Ocean*, Ewing has since 1926 written nearly seventy articles for scholarly journals and for such periodicals as *Science*, *Nature*, and the *National Geographic Magazine*. About those who influenced his choice of a career Ewing has said: "Professors H. A. Wilson, C. W. Heaps, G. C. Evans, and L. R. Ford at Rice Institute influenced me to choose a scholar's life in mathematics and physics; Dr. William Bowie and Professor R. M. Field stimulated my work at sea." Ewing received an honorary D.Sc. degree from Washington and Lee University in 1949; that same year he was named the Arthur L. Day Medalist by the Geological Society of America. He is a member of two honorary fraternities, Phi Beta Kappa and Sigma Xi. He also holds membership in the American Academy of Arts and Sciences, the American Association for the Advancement of Science, the American Geographical Society, the American Geophysical Union, the American Mathematical Society, the American Physical Society, the Bermuda Biological Association, the Geological Society of America, the National Academy of Science, the National Geographical Society, the New York Academy of Science, the Seismological Society of America, and the Society of Explorational Geophysicists. His clubs are the Cosmos of Washington, D.C., and the Explorers and the Century in New York City.

On October 31, 1928, Ewing married Avarilla Grace Hildenbrand of Houston, Texas; they had one son, William Maurice, Jr. This marriage was terminated by a divorce in 1941. On February 19, 1944, Ewing married Margaret Sloan Kidder, a former secretary of New York; their children are Jerome Henry Kidder, Hope Hamilton, Peter Duryee, and Margaret Ewing. The scientist is six feet two inches tall, weighs 210 pounds, and has blue eyes and brown hair.

References

N Y World-Telegram p21 F 28 '47
Newsweek 24:87 O 30 '44; 27:58 My 27 '46
American Men of Science (1949)
Who Knows—and What (1949)
Who's Who in America, 1951-52
Who's Who in American Education, 1951-52

FAIRCHILD, DAVID (GRANDISON)
April 7, 1869—Botanist; agricultural explorer; author
Address: 4013 Douglas Rd., Coconut Grove, Fla.

Fifty-five years ago, on New Year's eve, 1897, off the island of Penang, David Fairchild made a promise which not only turned the course of his own life but eventually benefited much of the population of the United States. Fired by the vision and enthusiasm of his benefactor, Barbour Lathrop, with whom he was travelling at the time, Fairchild vowed to dedicate his life to the introduction of unknown plants into the United States.

From that day on, Fairchild, a young botanist, turned from his scientific papers and research in fungi, molds, and termites, to the study of fruits, drug plants, grains, and all types of plants useful to man and to methods of introducing their culture into a new environment.

Recognized today as the dean of horticulturists, he has successfully established the growth of over 200,000 named species new to his native land which he brought from many parts of the world. Some of these now yield yearly crops estimated at millions of dollars. Because of David Fairchild's diligence, valuable fruits, trees, grains and flowers unknown before he began his work nearly seventy years ago, are now a part of the American scene. A son-in-law of Alexander Graham Bell, he was in touch with early developments in the field of invention, particularly aviation. He is an expert photographer, as the pictures in his books attest. As an agricultural explorer, he spent the better part of his life walking, riding and sailing around the world in search of tropical foods for the American table, flowering plants, trees, and ornamentals to beautify American gardens. He also established proper receiving, distribution and experimental stations in the United States.

In his widely read book, *The World Was My Garden,* through which many Americans have come to know him and his botanical travels, David Grandison Fairchild tells of his youth at Michigan State College of Agriculture where his father held a professorship of English. He was born in Lansing, Michigan, on April 7, 1869, the son of George Thompson and Charlotte Pearl (Halsted) Fairchild. His was a family of educators. His grandfather, Grandison Fairchild, was one of the founders of Oberlin College where David's uncle James later became president. Another uncle, Henry Fairchild, was president of Berea College in Kentucky.

When David was ten, his father accepted the presidency of the Kansas State College of Agriculture in Manhattan, Kansas. His mother's brother, Bryon, who had considerable influence on David's later life and education, was a professor of botany at Iowa State College of Agriculture and at Rutgers University in New Jersey. Thus, David was reared in an environment adapted to the development of a naturalist.

His work in botany at the Kansas State College of Agriculture, where he was graduated in 1888, and graduate studies at Iowa State College of Agriculture and Rutgers University led to an invitation to join the staff of the newly formed Section of Plant Pathology of the Department of Agriculture in Washington.

After a successful association with the Department, he returned to Kansas State College of Agriculture to complete his work for a master's degree. He pursued his studies in Naples, Italy, as the first representative of the Smithsonian Institution to occupy a research table at the Naples Zoological Station, the outstanding laboratory of its kind in the world, at the time.

On the ocean-crossing to fill this assignment, Fairchild met Barbour Lathrop, world traveller, man of means, and gourmet, who was soon to change the whole course of his life. Because Lathrop was familiar with Java, Fairchild con-

DAVID FAIRCHILD

fided his ambition to visit that country. When some weeks later Lathrop generously offered to send Fairchild to Java, he decided that he should first prepare himself for the momentous trip with two years of study in Germany, at Breslau, Berlin and Bonn.

At last, in 1895 he set out for Java and studies in the famous Buitenzorg Botanical Gardens. From that time on, impressed with the variety and luxuriance of growth in the tropics, David Fairchild began his world wanderings to little frequented lands in search of the unusual, the new, the appetizing, the rare, and the beautiful. For eight years, he circled the globe and toured the world with Barbour Lathrop visiting South Sea islands, Australia, New Zealand, New Guinea, Japan, China, the Persian Gulf, Africa, the West Indies and South America.

His travels through the South Seas, the Dutch East Indies, Sumatra, Java and Penang, inspired a brief visit in 1898 to Florida to establish a small Plant Introduction Garden in a six-acre clearing near Miami. Although little attention was given in Washington at that time to tropical agriculture, eventually the Spanish-American War created a wave of interest in the fruits and foods which returning American soldiers had learned to like in Cuba and Puerto Rico. Fairchild fell in love with southern Florida, foresaw its phenomenal future, and envisioned its development with fruits and plants which would thrive in its climate, be of economic value, and add to the beauty of its tropical growth.

Afterwards he went to Washington, D.C., and worked in the Forestry Division and helped to found the Section of Foreign Seed and Plant Introduction at the Department of Agriculture which he directed from 1906 to 1928. It was this Government division which designated him its Special Agent, a title later changed to Agricultural Explorer, when he went abroad in

FAIRCHILD, DAVID—*Continued*

the interest of developing the newly formed agency. He also headed the Office of Cereal Investigation.

While in Washington, Fairchild met Alexander Graham Bell, and on April 25, 1905 married his daughter, Marian, who accompanied him on many of his journeys. The couple have three children, Graham Bell, Barbara (Mrs. Leonard Muller), and Nancy Bell (Mrs. Marston Bates).

At the end of World War I, Fairchild persuaded the Secretary of War to turn over to the Department of Agriculture Miami's Chapman Field, an abandoned air-training field of 800 acres, a wasteland of rocky white soil so impregnated with salt that scarcely a blade of grass grew there. Introducing thousands of trees, palms, and fruit plants into 200 acres of the area, Fairchild transformed them into the United States Plant Introduction Garden.

In the mid-twenties Allison V. Armour refitted the cargo vessel *Utowana* into a yacht equipped with laboratory, special seed-drying apparatus, and a library of reference books. With Fairchild the scientific leader of the expedition, the yacht nosed into Mediterranean and African ports, explored the fjords of Norway and the coasts of Mexico, the Canary Islands, the Balearic Islands, from 1925 to 1927, and again in 1930 and 1932.

Another scientific expedition in 1939 and 1940 took him on an air-conditioned Chinese junk, *Cheng Ho,* to Celebes, Bali, the Moluccas Islands, a voyage described in his book, *Garden Islands Of The Great East.* This expedition was halted when Dutch East Indies ports were closed because of World War II.

From all of these far places poured plants and seeds into the Plant Introduction Gardens which Fairchild had established in California, the State of Washington, Georgia, Maryland, North Dakota, and Florida. These were sent to experimenters in various localities especially equipped to test them, that they might become a permanent part of American horticulture and create new industries.

Among successful crops in the million-dollar category are the highly nutritive *durum* wheat from Russia, Japanese rices, Sudan grass, feterita sorghum from Egypt, soy beans, Peruvian hairy alfalfa and Mexican cotton.

While in contact with many varieties of unaccustomed foods, and realizing the limitations of the average North America's taste and diet, Fairchild went to work to cultivate them and to substitute for the monotonous "ham and eggs, grits and bacon" an appreciation of avocados, mangos, dasheen, chaya, wampi, mangosteens, and a host of other foods common to other parts of the world.

The project for which he is probably best known nationally and internationally, is the Fairchild Tropical Garden on Old 'Cutler Road, twelve miles south of Miami. Named in his honor, the Garden was formally dedicated on March 23, 1938 on ground presented by the late Colonel Robert H. Montgomery, long a plant collector himself. The global collection of plant

life here has made it one of the finest Botanical Gardens in the world and the largest in the United States.

David Fairchild serves now as President Emeritus of the eighty-five acre tract of shrubs, three hundred species of palms, flowering vines and trees, introduced from tropical areas. In informal arrangement, they grow in the open in the only area of the United States mainland where this is possible. In the garden are history, humor, and most of all, beauty. Unique are the cycads, a plant which flourished a hundred million years ago among the first vegetation on earth, and fast vanishing. A dazzling display of 15,000 orchids, an outstanding botanical library, and a Palm Products Museum, are other features of this garden tribute to a pioneer botanist.

David Fairchild todays lives in a Shangri-la in Cocoanut Grove (part of Greater Miami), named "Kampong", the Malayan word for "a little village or cluster of houses enclosed by a wall." Here, on the shores of Biscayne Bay, he is surrounded by one of the most remarkable gardens in the world planted to his liking with scores of the plants and trees he loves so well. He has fully described this "dream place" in his book, *The World Grows Round My Door* (Scribner, 1947).

Logically, high honors and medals of distinction have been bestowed lavishly on David Fairchild over the years. A modest and retiring celebrity, he has been awarded the George Robert White medal of the Massachussetts Horticultural Society in 1930, the Harvard Travellers Club medal in 1931, the bronze medal of the Societé d'Acclimatation de France, the Hartley public welfare gold medal of the National Academy in 1933, the Garden Club of America Medal of Honor, the Johnny Appleseed Medal of the Men's Garden Club of America, the medal of the National Council of State Garden Clubs, the Meyer Medal of Plant Introduction of the American Genetic Association, the Thomas Barbour Medal of the Fairchild Tropical Garden in 1948. He holds the highest award to American horticulturists, the Gold Seal of the National Council of State Garden Clubs. In 1952 he was named to the "South's Hall of Fame for the Living," an annual award to the region's man or woman of the year.

He is a member of the Board of Directors of the National Geographic Society, past president of the American Genetic Association, former chairman of the University of Miami Board of Regents, and an honorary member of the Committee of One Hundred in Miami Beach. Dr. Fairchild holds honorary degrees from Oberlin College, Florida State University and Kansas State College of Agriculture.

Fairchild is the author of several books including *Yams in the West Indies* (1899), *Exploring for Plants* (1930) *and Garden Islands of the Great East* (1945). He wrote, "Never to have seen anything but the temperate zone is to have lived on the fringe of the world. Between the Tropic of Capricorn and the Tropic of Cancer live the majority of all the plant species, the vast majority of the insects, most of the strange . . . quadrupeds, all of the great and most of the poisonous snakes and large lizards, most of the brilliantly colored sea fishes, and the strangest and most gorgeously plumaged of the birds" (*Exploring for Plants*).

References

Am Home 14:492 N '35
Asia 30:400+ Je '30
Atlan 174:77+ S '44; 174:91+ N '44
Christian Sci Mon Mag p20 Ap 2 '49
Miami Daily N Ag 10 '41; Ag 24 '41; Ap 30 '50
Miami Herald D 3 '50; Mr 24 '52; Ap 21 '52; D 5 '52; F 17 '53; Mr 22 '53; Mr 24 '53; Ap 24 '53
Nature Mag 35:13+ Ja '42
Pop Sci 121:35 Ag '32
Sat R 18:15 O 1 '38; 19:13 N 12 '38
Sci M 39:89 Jl '34
Sci N L 36:116 Ag 19 '39
Time 32:51 O 17 '38
American Men of Science (1949)
Dies, E. J. Titans of the Soil (1949)
Milne, L. J. and Milne, M. J. G. Famous Naturalists (1952)
Who's Who in America, 1951-52

FALKENBURG, JINX *See* McCrary, J. F.

FATEMI, HOSSEIN (fä´im-ĭ hōō-sän´) 1918- Former Minister of Foreign Affairs of Iran

Address: c/o Ministry of Foreign Affairs, Tehran, Iran

After a nine-hour coup in which the Iranian army ousted Premier Mohammed Mossadegh on August 19, 1953, it was reported that his chief lieutenant, Foreign Minister Hossein Fatemi, was also deposed.

A major figure in the Iranian oil-nationalization campaign, Dr. Hossein Fatemi was appointed in October 1952 by Premier Mohammed Mossadegh of Iran as Minister of Foreign Affairs. At the time of the pleading of Iran's case in the oil dispute with Great Britain before the United Nations Security Council in October 1951, Fatemi held the post of Deputy Premier, assistant to Mossadegh. He was one of the founders of the National Front party, the "Vatan," created under the leadership of Mossadegh to further oil nationalization in Iran.

Hossein Fatemi was born in Nain, the province of Yezd, Iran, in 1918, one of four sons of Ali Mohammed Fatemi, who was engaged in religious work, and Tooba Fatemi. In Isfahan, young Fatemi, who also spent part of his boyhood in Nain and Tehran, attended Saadi High School, from which he was graduated in 1936.

Entering newspaper work two years later, Fatemi contributed literary articles to the Isfahan newspaper *Bakhtar*, published by his brother Dr. Nasrollah Seyf-Pour Fatemi, who later became a professor of Persian literature at Princeton University. Hossein Fatemi went to Paris to study at the École des Sciences

Politiques, but before completing his college studies, he returned to Isfahan to become editor of *Bakhtar*. After resuming his advanced education, he received his degree (*licencié*) in 1947 and a year later obtained from the University of Paris his Ph.D. degree in social sciences, for which he submitted a thesis on the history of labor in Iran.

For many years a supporter of the policies of Dr. Mossadegh, Fatemi became a collaborator in establishing the National Front and made his newspaper, *Bakhtar Emrooz*, the organ for that movement. In 1950 he prepared for the National Front a formula for the nationalization of the properties of the British-owned Anglo-Iranian Oil Company. When Mossadegh became Premier of Iran in April 1951, he appointed Fatemi Deputy Premier. Among the initial steps of the new Government were the passage of the Oil Nationalization Act, based upon Fatemi's formula, and the creation of the Iranian National Oil Company. Fatemi in early June 1951 accompanied the three provisional directors of the company on an inventory tour to Khuzistan, Iran's vital oil-producing province, after a stop-over at the summer palace of Shah Mohammed Riza Pahlevi, who gave his sanction to the nationalization program.

In the ensuing discussions in Tehran on the future of British oil interests in Iran, Fatemi acted as spokesman for the Iranian group that met with the British delegation under Richard R. Stokes. These talks, at which W. Averell Harriman was present as mediator, failed to reach agreement on operation of the industry and division of profits. With the expiration of the deadline for British customers to renegotiate contracts, Fatemi announced that Iran would sell oil at a discount to any other country offering to buy. Several weeks later the Deputy Premier, who reported step-by-step developments of the oil crisis in daily press conferences, announced a deadline of October 4, 1951, for British oil technicians to leave Iran. As a result of the expulsion order, Britain charged before the United Nations that such an order was a violation of a ruling of the International Court of Justice. Fatemi in October 1951 accompanied Mossadegh in a seventeen-man delegation to the United States, where Iran's Premier pleaded his country's right to oil nationalization before the United Nations Security Council, which ruled that the dispute was not within its jurisdiction. During an interview with a reporter in Washington, D.C., Fatemi said, "We have ended the era of defeatism in Iran. We say to the Iranian people: 'You can do whatever you want to do, if you want it enough.'" (*Herald Tribune,* November 18, 1951).

Back in Tehran, Fatemi announced on December 6, 1951, in a nation-wide broadcast that Iran intended to take immediate action to sell oil throughout the world. At this time he also ordered the expulsion of a New York *Times* correspondent, Michael Clark, whom he charged (as quoted in the *Times*) with "activities in favor of the former British-controlled Anglo-Iranian Oil Company," an accusation that Clark denied. Fatemi, who resigned in December his

HOSSEIN FATEMI

Deputy Premiership to run as a candidate for Parliament, was elected in January 1953, thereby becoming one of eleven members of Mossadegh's party to win a Parliamentary seat in the Tehran constituency. The following month his work in the legislature came to an end when an attempt was made on his life. Shot by a fifteen-year-old member of a terrorist group, Fatemi sustained severe wounds that necessitated a long convalescent period.

When Fatemi returned to Iran, he was appointed on October 11, 1952, by Mossadegh as Minister of Foreign Affairs to succeed Hossein Navab. He was also named official spokesman for the Government. Immediately after taking office he announced a change in foreign policy whereby Iran's top diplomats would be sent to missions in Asia and neighboring countries instead of Western nations. On May 24, 1953 Iran and Syria signed a friendship treaty. He also made an effort to gain a favorable press abroad for Iran and in a news conference spoke abroad for Iran and he requested that all correspondents check with him to get facts straight. On October 13, after Iran authorities arrested four men for activities that Fatemi denounced as "a plot against the Government" backed by a foreign Embassy, the new Foreign Minister announced the tightening of discipline in Iran's Foreign Office by barring all visitors except diplomats who had appointments and reporters with special press passes.

Meanwhile, the oil dispute with Britain, which had continued for nineteen months without settlement, was brought to a crisis in early October 1952 with the British refusal to accept Mossadegh's latest offer of terms. On October 22 when Iran formally severed diplomatic relations with Great Britain, Fatemi explained that "for the moment" the break held only diplomatic significance and did not pertain to economic and commercial ties. The Foreign Minister denied in March 1953, as reported by

the New York *Times*, that Iran was showing increased friendliness toward the Soviet Union because of dissatisfaction wtih the United States in matters of economic aid to Iran and support of the British in the oil dispute.

Fatemi has been described as a man of "dynamic personality, forceful and fiery" in manner. He is a prolific writer whose literary articles number several thousand. The Foreign Minister, who does not speak English, usually conducts his interviews in French. Of medium height, he weighs about 150 pounds; he has dark hair and black eyes. He and his wife Parivash Setvati, who at the time of their marriage in December 1950 was a student, are the parents of a son, Cyrus. Dr. Fatemi's faith is the Moslem. His recreation is reading: "I am a happy man," he has said, "if I can manage to spend several days on end just reading."

References

N Y Times p1 F 16 '52; p4 O 13 '52
Time 59:38 F 25 '52

FELLER, ABRAHAM H(OWARD) Dec. 24, 1904—Nov. 13, 1952 General counsel to the United Nations; lecturer in law at Harvard University (1931-34 and 1937-38), later at Yale University; special assistant to United States Attorney General (1934-40); named consultant to Lend-Lease Administration and to National Defense Mediation Board (1941); deputy director and general counsel of Office of War Information (1942-44); appointed general counsel to the United Nations Relief and Rehabilitation Association (1944); served as alternate on United States delegation to the U.N. Preparatory Commission (1945). See *Current Biography*, 1946.

Obituary

N Y Times p1+ N 14 '52

FERRER, JOSÉ (PEPE) FIGUERES *See* Figueres Ferrer, J. (P.)

FERRIER, KATHLEEN Apr. 22, 1912— Oct. 8, 1953 British concert singer; in 1943 sang in the *Messiah* at Westminster Abbey; made her opera debut in 1946; sang in festivals at Glynedebourne, Edinburgh, Salzburg, Zürich, Vienna, and Amsterdam, and in major cities in Europe, England, America, and Canada. See *Current Biography*, 1951.

Obituary

N Y Times O 9 '53

FIGUERES FERRER, JOSÉ (PEPE) (fê-ga′rês fĕr-rĕr′) 1908?- President of Costa Rica; farmer
Address: San José, Costa Rica

Following his election as President of Costa Rica on July 27, 1953, José Figueres Ferrer declared his intention to "establish a regime of equal treatment for all" (New York *Times*, July 28, 1953). The leader of the National Liberation party received an overwhelming 121,108 votes against 65,625 for his only opponent, Fernando Castro Cervantes, candidate of the Opposition coalition consisting of outlawed Communists, extreme right wingers, and conservative right-of-center forces. It was the first election in the Republic in which women were allowed to vote.

After his election, Figueres pledged that United States investment capital would find "an environment of safety and honesty" in Costa Rica. He is quoted in *Time* (August 10, 1953) as follows: "There is one thing I want to make clear: this is going to be a pro-United States government. That is definite." He has stated that the middle-of-the-road socialist government of Denmark is what he would like for his country. "Our movement is not in any sense a Marxian revolution," he explained. "It is really a revolution of the middle class."

Figueres led a victorious civilian revolution in March and April of 1948 against Communist and extreme-rightists control of Costa Rica. He became provisional President of the Founding Junta of the Second Republic from May 1948 to November 1949. Known as a progressive employer in his management of his plantation, Figueres calls himself a "farmer-Socialist" (Washington *Post,* December 12, 1948).

José (Pepe) Figueres Ferrer was born a first-generation Costa Rican of Spanish ancestry in 1908. He was the son of a physician who came to the South American republic from Spain. Young José received his academic education in the United States, where he studied engineering at the Massachusetts Institute of Technology, and learned English and something of North American culture.

Returning to Costa Rica, he became a successful coffee grower and rope manufacturer, with more than 1,000 sharecroppers and laborers working on his plantations and in his factory. He called his *finca (land) La Lucha Sin Fin (Struggle Without End)* which describes the farmer's continual struggle against nature. Figueres built bungalows for his employees, established a community vegetable farm and a dairy which provides free milk for the children of workers. (*Time,* August 10, 1953.) His interest in human relations exceeded his concern with farming and engineering problems. His "colonos" (sharecroppers) could sell to him at market price, or elsewhere if they could get more, the cabuya, or raw material for rope, they produced on his plantations. Provision was made for the medical needs and recreation of his employees. He dislikes "politicians who are in politics only for the sake of holding office" (New York *Times,* April 27, 1948).

In a radio broadcast in 1942, Figueres attacked the regime of Dr. Rafael Ángel Calderón Guardia and claimed that the extreme right-wing President was collaborating with the Communist party. Figueres was ordered to leave Costa Rica and spent a two-year exile in Mexico. He returned when Licenciado Teodore Picado Michalski became President. Four years later, after Picade influenced the Congress to invalidate on March 1, 1948 the Presidential election of Otilio Ulate Blanco, Figueres and

. JOSÉ FIGUERES

a group of followers revolted and forced the Government's Army to surrender on April 19. Thus, the Communist allies of Guardia who controlled San José, Congress, the police, and rural barefoot troops were defeated. Picado then capitulated and went into exile in Nicaragua, and Guardia fled to Mexico.

Figueres described his revolutionary coup as an effort to set up a "second republic to end the spectacle of the majority impoverished by inefficiency and special privilege" (New York *Times,* April 4, 1948). Following his victory on April 20, 1948, he installed a provisional Government headed by Acting President Santos León Herrera. Figueres was in charge of foreign affairs, justice and public security in Herrera's Cabinet. He announced on April 22, 1948 that there would be no dictatorship.

In order to form a constituent assembly and a new constitution, Figueres declared on April 30, 1948, that beginning May 8, 1948 he would head an eleven-man junto to take over the Government of Costa Rica from interim-President Herrera. Figueres remained provisional President of the founding junta of the Second Republic for eighteen months. During this period Figueres outlawed the Vanguardia (former Communist) party and all other parties opposing representative democratic rule.

On June 19, 1948, he suspended constitutional guarantees for thirty days because of economic and political conditions, and levied a 10 per cent tax. On September 26, 1948 Figueres appealed to the people by radio to increase production and enhance banking operations by avoiding retention of cash and heavy withdrawals from banks.

The new Constituent Assembly was elected in December and the following month unanimously ratified Ulate as President-elect. Figueres demobilized the Army in order to avoid Army revolts. He stated that "the many hundred thousands of dollars saved from having

FIGUERES, JOSÉ—*Continued*

no army would be used for public schools and education" (*Newsweek,* December 13, 1948). Shortly thereafter, the Republic was invaded from Nicaragua by a group of exiles planning to reinstate ex-President Guardia. We're not a bit worried," said Figueres; "a people is much harder to conquer than an army" (*Time,* December 20, 1948).

Within seven days he had mobilized an Army and, wearing his "lucky boots and a silver-mounted .45 automatic," rode with Ulate to inspect his border troops (*Time,* December 27, 1948). He informed the Organization of American States of the invasion, and on December 11 asked for assistance in restoring peace under terms of the newly-formed Inter-American Treaty of Reciprocal Assistance.

The thwarting of the Nicaraguan invasion established Figueres and his junta more solidly in the Government of Costa Rica. The provisional President successfully disrupted a revolt on April 2, 1949 by his Minister of Defense, Edgar Gardona, who seized two leading fortresses of San José. When soldiers of the poorer class heard Figueres' radio plea for loyalty, they turned against Gardona. He surrendered on April 3, 1949, and two days later Figueres again ordered demobilization of Costa Rica's Army.

One diplomat said of Figueres' leadership, "Don Pepe was like the Pied Piper of Hamlin—with a tommy gun instead of a pipe." (*Newsweek,* May 2, 1949). The provisional President declared an amnesty on June 10, 1949, for all participants under arrest for the attempted Cardona military coup.

According to *Newsweek,* August 8, 1949, moneyed groups objected to the social reforms instituted by Figueres and considered him a traitor to his class. In a reply to his critics over a nationwide broadcast on July 28, 1949, Figueres said: "Costa Rica should not be a social club." He declared that he wanted the country made up of "prosperous, hard-working citizens." He admitted he would consider the Vice-Presidency when Ulate became President, in order to assure the continuation of the new social program.

However, he withdrew on August 9, 1949, as a candidate for that office in the October 1949 elections, and disbanded his National Coalition party, after Costa Rica's Constitutent Assembly called his candidacy constitutionally ineligible. *Caballeros* in the Republic compared Figueres' fortune to Churchill's and said: "He saved his country, but when the shooting was over they kicked him out" (*Newsweek,* August 8, 1949). He threatened to resign with his entire Cabinet in October 1949 just before the inauguration of President-elect Ulate, due to a Constituent Assembly measure to discharge all upper-grade civil servants without compensation. The assembly retracted the bill and Figueres remained until November 8, 1949, when Ulate took over the Government as President of Costa Rica with a majority of his Union Nacional right-of-center party in Congress.

A plot against the life of Figueres was discovered by Costa Rican police when the politician was about to leave the airport for a visit to the United States in the spring of 1951. In his lectures at American colleges and institutions during his trip, Figueres attributed his attempted assassination to a plot to destroy Latin-American democratic leaders. These leaders, like himself, were associated in the Inter-American Association for Democracy and Freedom, composed of democratic governments and opposition parties in exile, which were working for free trade union movement and a uniform political system of democratic Governments in the Americas. Their principles, he affirmed, were "true to the ideals of the United Nations and the Organization of American States" (New York *Times,* April 22, 1951).

At the opening of a three-day conference given to the appraisal of economic aid and technical assistance to Latin America, at Stanford University, California, Figueres said on June 18, 1951 that through "autonomous, or public corporations of Latin America" its economic development could be fostered. He declared that private enterprise in the American republic, unlike its counterpart in the United States, would "never be an improvement of conditions for the majority of population" (New York *Times,* June 19, 1951).

Figueres announced his candidacy for the post of President of Costa Rica on March 9, 1952 in a nationwide radio broadcast, and urged political unity. He stated that his National Liberation party would remain independent and would not form a coalition with any other parties. The anti-Figueres front was a coalition of National Union and Democratic parties aided by outlawed Communists. Figueres said on July 25, 1953: "It is unimportant whether or not I gain the Presidency; the important thing is whether the majority of Costa Ricans have realized yet the time has come for great changes in the country" (New York *Times,* July 26, 1953).

A victor in the July 27, 1953 Presidential election by a margin of nearly twice the votes received by his opponent, Fernando Castro Cervantes, Figueres promised "a regime for all Costa Ricans and not alone for a party" (New York *Times,* July 28, 1953). Almost two-thirds of the seats in the assembly were won by members of his National Liberation party. This was the first election in which women voted and three Congresswomen were elected to represent Figueres' party. He said his Administration would make "a general effort to invigorate the economy" and raise living standards.

President Figueres was married to an American, Henrietta Boggs, of Birmingham, Alabama. They were recently divorced. They have two children, one a boy named for José Marti, the Cuban patriot. On a wall in his home Figueres keeps a picture of Abraham Lincoln. He is described as an "energetic, personable man . . . with dark wavy hair," who is a "frank, forthright speaker" (*Christian Science Monitor,* May 5, 1951). The leader of the South American republic neither smokes nor drinks.

References

Christian Sci Mon Mag II p13 My 5 '51
N Y Times p14 Ap 27 '48; IV p2 D 19
'48
Newsweek 34:32 Ag 8 '49
Time 52:30 D 27 '48; 62:35 Ag 10 '53
Washington (D.C.) Post p2M D 12 '48
por

FISCHER, JOHN Apr. 27, 1910- Editor;
author

Address: b. c/o Harper's Magazine, 49 E. 33d
St., New York 16; h. 55 Sterling Ave., White
Plains, N.Y.

Working for *Harper's Magazine* since 1944,
John Fischer was named editor-in-chief in
January 1953 to succeed Frederick Lewis Allen
in September. A Rhodes scholar at Oxford
(1933-35), Fischer also served as a United
Press and Associated Press correspondent in
Europe and in Washington, D.C., before joining the United States Department of Agriculture staff. During World War II (1943-44)
he toured India as an economic representative
of the United States. Upon his return to Washington, he became an associate editor of *Harper's Magazine,* serving in that capacity until
1947 when he was appointed to the post of
editor-in-chief of the General (Trade) Books
Department of Harper & Brothers. He is the
author of *Why They Behave Like Russians*
(1947) and *Master Plan, U.S.A.* (1951), both
published by Harper.

John Fischer, one of two sons of John Simpson and Georgie (Caperton) Fischer, was born
on April 27, 1910, in Texahoma, Oklahoma, on
the Texas-Oklahoma state border. His ancestors were German, Scotch, and Irish, and
his grandfathers fought in the Civil War—one
with the Union, the other with the Confed-
eracy. His mother, a former teacher and
rancher, and his father, who supported the family through his farming, real estate and farm-
loan business, took their son to Idaho where he
attended high school in Boise (1924-26). During the summers Fischer worked on farms and
as a drug store delivery boy. He completed his
high school education at Amarillo, Texas, in
1928, serving on the school newspaper, the debating team and the boxing squad.

He entered the University of Oklahoma in
Norman in 1928 to major in journalism and
economics and was subsequently elected to two
honorary fraternities—Phi Beta Kappa in his
junior year and Sigma Delta Chi, a journalism
society. He held a variety of jobs on the *Oklahoma Daily,* the university newspaper which
also serves the local community, including editor, proofreader, and managing editor, using
the pay from this employment to work his way
through school and supplementing his income
by serving as a correspondent for out-of-town
papers. During the summers (1928-32) he
worked as a reporter on the Amarillo, Texas,
Globe-News, and the Carlsbad, New Mexico,
Current-Argus. Receiving his B.A. degree from
the University of Oklahoma in 1932, he worked
for the next year as a full-time reporter on the
Daily Oklahoman, in Oklahoma City. About

Lotte Jacobi

JOHN FISCHER

his work on Southwest newspapers the *Saturday Review of Literature* (April 26, 1947)
commented: "With the dust-bowl depression
rampant, [his] assignments were equal parts
society luncheons and murders."

Winning a Rhodes Scholarship in 1933, Fischer left reporting to study economics at Lincoln College, Oxford, England, where for the
next two years he also worked for the United
Press as a part-time Oxford correspondent
during the school term and a full-time European reporter during vacations. He wrote
articles for various periodicals including *Harper's Magazine.* Fischer wrote his thesis, *Modern Greats: Philosophy, Politics, Economics,*
but did not complete the requirements for a
degree because in 1935 he accepted a cabled
offer for a position with the United States Department of Agriculture with "an impulsiveness
not characteristic of him" (*Saturday Review of
Literature*). The next year he became a Washington correspondent for the Associated Press,
and in 1937 returned to work again at the
Department of Agriculture.

Becoming interested in the Board of Economic Welfare in 1939, Fischer, as organization chief of one of its three major divisions,
helped to organize its intelligence service, being put in direct charge of a department of
some hundreds of economists, business executives, and experts in various fields. He was
sent to India in July 1943 as the chief representative in charge of economic intelligence and
lend-lease for the board and for the Foreign
Economic Administration and wrote most of
the United States Government reports on the
1943-44 famine in India.

Five months after he returned to Washington he began work for *Harper's Magazine,*
first as a part-time Washington correspondent
and in October 1944 joining the staff as an
associate editor. Among his assignments was
the developing of new writers of articles and

FISCHER, JOHN—*Continued*

of fiction. In August 1947 he became editor-in-chief of the General (Trade) books department of Harper & Brothers.

Fischer took a leave of absence from Harper's in March 1946 to become recording officer for a United Nations Relief and Rehabilitation Administration mission in the Ukraine to check on the distribution of supplies there. Remaining in Russia for two months, Fischer and the other members of the mission were "by prior agreement between UNRRA and the Soviet Government, granted exceptional freedom of movement, observation and conversation with Russians (using their own American interpreter), more freedom, in fact, than any foreign diplomats or correspondents have been permitted for many years (*Christian Science Monitor,* August 6, 1946).

Fischer's first article on Russia was published in *Harper's* August 1946 and was followed by others in subsequent issues and also in *Reader's Digest* and *Life.* Harper & Brothers published Fischer's observations on his Russian trip in book form and it became the Book-of-the-Month Club selection for May, 1947.

Brooks Atkinson, former Moscow correspondent of the New York *Times,* called Fischer's book "a first-hand study of contemporary Russia . . . a thoroughly documented book about Russia and about the Ukraine by an exceptionally able reporter whose judgment is sound."

In essence, Fischer's proposal for dealing with Russia is to "speak firmly and carry a big stick. For a generation," he suggests, "Russia and the Western world must live in an armed truce. Then may come understanding" (H. E. Salisbury, New York *Times Book Review,* April 27, 1947).

The book's title was changed from *Scared Men in the Kremlin* to *Why They Behave Like Russians,* and it received varying reviews. *Time* magazine (May 5, 1947) commented: "As if to answer former UNRRA colleagues who attacked 'inaccuracies' in his *Harper's* articles, Fischer admits that he hardly qualifies as a full-fledged Soviet expert. But he thinks he learned why the Russians act as they do and puts his case plainly and without rancor." Lewis Gannett in the New York *Herald Tribune* (April 23, 1947) called Fischer "a shrewd and competent journalist making an obvious effort to understand what he saw and to report it fairly. [The book] is obviously what publishers call a 'quickie.' But it is a refreshing and an honest quickie, deserving neither a book club's half-million circulation nor violent attack." Foster Rhea Dulles wrote in the New York *Herald Tribune Book Review* (April 27, 1947) that "among books on Soviet Russia this volume is one of the most readable as well as one of the most unprejudiced that has appeared since the close of the war. Its descriptive chapters . . . reveal both shrewd observation and penetrating insight. The more significant discussion of the basic problem of Russian-American relations is at once realistic and hopefully constructive."

In the light of recent events, Fischer's opening chapter "The Scared Men in the Kremlin"

is interesting. "He listed an inner circle of Stalin, Beria, Malenkov and Zhdanov. The latter died in 1948. Malenkov and Beria subsequently split, and in October 1952 the Communist party congress approved a new secretariat headed by Stalin, Malenkov and Nikita Khruschchev which meant victory for Malenkov over Beria" (New York *Herald Tribune,* March 8, 1953).

Besides this highly controversial book, Fischer has written another, *Master Plan, U.S.A.* (1951), a study of American foreign policy, and also many magazine articles for *Harper's Magazine, Life,* the *New Yorker,* and *Reader's Digest.* When he succeeded Frederick Lewis Allen as editor-in-chief of *Harper's Magazine* on September 30, 1953, he became the seventh editor since the magazine was established in 1850.

Retiring editor Allen commented on Fischer's appointment: "He is the logical man for the job. *Harper's* is primarily a magazine of political and international affairs; Jack Fischer is a very good man in those fields" (*Time,* February 9, 1953).

Among Fischer's articles which appeared in *Harper's* were "The German Booby Trap" (May 1951), in which he stated his reasons for opposing the concept of a neutral Germany. "Small, unambitious countries like Switzerland and Sweden can make neutrality work. The biggest—and potentially the strongest—in Europe, cannot." In "Truman & Co. Limited" (July, 1949) Fischer predicted that Harry Truman "might easily be remembered as a kind of poor man's Calvin Coolidge," and in June 1951 he wrote: "The only leadership to which the country seems to respond is that of General Eisenhower. . . On those rare occasions when Eisenhower tugs the halter, we move; the rest of the time we sit back . . . and relax, until we get another prod from the Kremlin. It might also be said that the Russians have been making our foreign policy for the last four years—and that if they were only smart enough to act sweet for a few months, they would wreck the whole structure."

His article "Insomia in Whitehall," in *Harper's* January 1950, described British industry and he recommended that "change—swift, deep-cutting change—is the only thing that can save Britain. The brutal needs of survival demand shifts throughout the whole economy—shifts from the easy sterling customers to the tough dollar market, shifts from high-cost producers to the more efficient, shifts to meet the new pattern of demand caused by a massive redistribution of income, shifts to new products and new methods."

Fischer was an aide to Adlai E. Stevenson during the campaign in 1952, and he recently expressed the hope "that Stevenson may restore politics to the honored place it has held during the best days of our history" (*Harper's,* March 1953) and predicted that the Democrats in Congress will help the Eisenhower Administration in the "trade, not aid" program to support our European allies.

On January 11, 1936, Fischer married Scotch-born Elizabeth Wilson; they have two children, Nicolas and Sara Caperton. At the time he first became a *Harper's* editor, the *Saturday Review of Literature* reported that he planned to commute to his office from White Plains and in his spare time to "putter around with carpentry" and raise vegetables. His favorite recreations are boxing, travel, and music. He is a Democrat and a Unitarian and belongs to the Century Association, the Council on Foreign Relations, and the American Association of Rhodes Scholars. Fischer is five feet eleven and one-half inches tall, has brown eyes and black hair. He has been described in *Time* magazine as "scholarly, able."

References

Sat R 30:9 Ap 26 '47
Time 61:82 F 9 '53
Who's Who in America, 1952-53

FLEMING, (JILES) BERRY Mar. 19, 1899- Author
Address: b. c/o J. B. Lippincott Co., E. Washington Sq., Philadelphia 5, Pa.; h. 3050 Walton Way, Augusta, Ga.

BERRY FLEMING

Reprinted from the *Wilson Library Bulletin,* February 1953.

A middle-of-the-road southern novelist, Berry Fleming "is not a writer who speaks to all places and all times," a reviewer once wrote, "but he does speak honestly and with talent. None but the most unperceptive or the most snobbish will ignore *The Fortune Tellers* or continue to ignore his earlier books." At least two of his novels have had the wider circulation insured by a book club selection. *Colonel Effingham's Raid* (Duell, 1945) was a Book-of-the-Month choice, and *The Fortune Tellers* (Lippincott, 1951) was picked by the Literary Guild.

(Jiles) Berry Fleming was born March 19, 1899, at Augusta, Georgia, where he now lives after sojourns of varying lengths in New York City and France. He is the son of Porter Fleming and Daisy Belden (Berry) Fleming—hence the name so often mistakenly called Barry. In 1790 his great-great-grandfather brought his family to Georgia from Virginia, to settle near the Savannah River about 20 miles northwest of Augusta. His grandfather Porter was a cotton factor in Augusta, and the writer's father carried on the business till his death in 1926. Berry attended the Academy of Richmond County (later he was a trustee there), and graduated from Middlesex School, Concord, Massachusetts in 1918. Cambridge was an easy step from Concord, and in 1922 Fleming was graduated from Harvard with a B.S. degree. During his junior year he sold many short pieces to the New York *Evening Post,* then managed by the "scholar in action," Edwin F. Gay, and they were printed on the "Back Page" edited by Harry Dounce. (This is probably not what an AP interviewer meant by calling Fleming a man "who got into the newspaper business through the back door.") For a year after graduation he was a reporter on

the Augusta *Chronicle,* other employers having declined his services with unflattering speed. *The Conqueror's Stone* (Day, 1927), his first novel, was "historical," dealing with a Carolinian pirate of 1766. Will Cuppy called it "real seagoing stuff, agreeably written."

From 1923 to 1931 Fleming lived in New York, spending much of his time in the library of the Harvard Club. He married Anne Shirley Molloy on August 12, 1925, and they have a daughter, Shirley, in late 1952 a student at Smith College.

A year and a half in Europe produced *Visa to France* (Doubleday, 1930), "cut to the pattern of facile sophistication," according to the *Bookman,* and called "engaging" by more than one reviewer. *The Square Root of Valentine* (Norton, 1932), a fantasy about a young New York bond salesman, seemed "delightful and utterly crazy" to the New York *Times,* and "mildly boring" to the *New Republic. Siesta* (1935) showed a Southern town in time of drought.

To the Market Place (1938), a long novel, centered on a group of Southerners in the New York of the 1920's; was highly praised in *Books,* but called "consistently dull" by the late Herschel Brickell, and "too traditional, too familiar," by the *Nation.*

Fleming retired to Augusta to write a weekly column for the *Chronicle,* and soon became embroiled in local politcs. He objected to the political machine's razing the old courthouse, and eventually had the satisfaction of seeing the boss resign because of "ill-health." *Colonel Effingham's Raid* (1943) was the result of this lively experience. Clifton Fadiman thought it a good satiric comedy of local (Southern) mores; the *New Republic* called the style artificial, "an affected mélange of Confederate history and the Manual of Arms." Stephen Benét liked it, with reservations. *The Lightwood Tree* (Lippincott, 1947), intricately con-

FLEMING, BERRY—*Continued*

structed, described a Georgia community during three centuries, and was considered by Edward Weeks to be Fleming's best novel. The *New Yorker* called it readable and humane "in spite of a dozen structural faults."

Some newspaper clippings sent to Fleming by a friend in 1929, describing a Georgia flood, were the genesis of *The Fortune Tellers*. Since Fleming, in New York, was "living in a city that nobody feels responsible for," it was "hard to imagine one of those smaller communities that sometimes face their people with cries for help." For eighteen years, he writes, the clippings collected dust, "the oily dust of New York, the gray dust of Kentucky, and finally the pink dust of Georgia," till the writer abandoned another novel and wrote this one. Joseph Henry Jackson termed it "a moving and vigorous story of men in conflict with themselves and with each other, and the whole embraced by the dark and desperate struggle against nature in the form of a threatening flood."

Fleming's latest novel, *Carnival*, is the story of Johnny Croshow, who went to the carnival as a young man with his grandfather. Orville Prescott of the New York *Times* (August 14, 1953) wrote: "Johnny, it becomes apparent at once, is Everyman, in search of the answers to all the great questions. . . ." Prescott added that Fleming has "stuffed it with cryptic phrases and obscure symbols. Without humor or wit or fanciful charm *Carnival* stands or falls on its allegorical significance." On the other hand, the New York *Herald Tribune* reviewer called it "a fascinating performance . . . it is poetry in substance and pitch."

Two of his stories were included in *Best American Short Stories of 1944* and in *O. Henry Memorial Award Prize Stories of 1944*. He has been president of the Augusta Citizens Union, and the Young Men's Library Association. Tall, brown-eyed, balding, and soft-spoken, he writes on the typewriter, from 9 till noon, and again from 3 to 4. "Sometime I hope to write a book in longhand and at night. I suspect that it would be my best book and my most unpopular."

References

> Warfel, H. R. American Novelists of Today (1951)
> Who's Who in America, 1952-53
> Who's Who in the South ad Southwest (1952)

FLETCHER, C(YRIL) SCOTT July 28, 1904- Educational organization official

Address: b. c/o Fund for Adult Education, Ford Foundation, 914 E. Green St., Pasadena 1, Calif.; h. 1194 Oxford Rd., San Marino, Calif.

When the Ford Foundation established the Fund for Adult Education in April 1951, it chose as president of the new educational program C. Scott Fletcher, who resigned from the presidency of Encyclopaedia Britannica Films, Inc., to accept the appointment. During World War II he had been director of the Field Development Division of the Committee for Economic Development, becoming in 1944 executive director of the committee itself. For many years, from 1926 to 1943, an employee of the Studebaker Corporation, Australian-born Fletcher traveled in a number of countries promoting automobile sales and carrying out managerial assignments.

Born July 28, 1904, in Sydney, Australia, son of Michael Scott and Winifred Sara Anne (Davis) Fletcher, Cyril Scott Fletcher comes of a family of Methodist clergymen and educators. His paternal grandfather founded schools in Australia and New Zealand, and his father was the founder and first master of Kings College, University of Queensland, and Wesley College, University of Sydney. Fletcher's mother was a nurse; he has one sister. The boy's first schooling was at Oxford, England, where the family lived while the father studied for his M.A. degree previous to taking his doctorate in divinity and literature at Melbourne University, Australia.

Before entering the University of Sydney after his graduation in 1922 from Newington College, a private preparatory school in Sydney, Fletcher took a summer job with Cayce-Paul, the local Studebaker distributor (wholesaler), and became so much interested in the business that he decided to continue working there at the same time that he attended the university. While studying for his diploma in political economics and commerce, Fletcher took part in football, swimming, cricket, and was on the rifle team. During this period he also advanced from the Cayce-Paul assembly line to the position of automobile agent (assistant sales manager). In 1926, the year after Fletcher's graduation, Studebaker Corporation bought the Cayce-Paul distributorship and renamed it Studebaker Corporation of Australia; C. Scott Fletcher was appointed its advertising manager. For the next three years he served successively as manager of the used car department, manager of all dealer operations, and special factory representative traveling all over Australia.

On his first trip to the United States, in 1929 Fletcher was special Australia representative at the Studebaker head office in South Bend, Indiana. Later that year he was appointed sales promotion manager of the Studebaker Export Corporation and subsequently was sent to the West Indies as special representative of the company and then to the Far East to develop markets for Studebaker products in the Philippines, Japan, China, and Korea. By 1931 he was back in his native land as managing director of the Studebaker Corporation of Australasia, Ltd. The next year Fletcher and his wife and daughter moved again—this time to South Africa, where the Australian executive was to be regional director for Studebaker. Fletcher, who had bought his first 16-millimeter motion picture camera in Hong Kong in 1929, made full use of an advertising film sent out by the corporation. As related in a *Christian Science Monitor* article (July 22, 1952), he rented a Capetown theater, scheduled a presentation for five o'clock (an hour when there would be no competition), advertised it as showing "cars smashing head-on at 60 miles an hour," and distributed twice as many tickets as the number of seats. The result was successful beyond his hopes: five hundred had to be turned away, and Fletcher found it necessary to publish an apology.

From South Africa, Fletcher was sent in 1934 to Canada as the general sales manager for that Dominion. In September of the next year (toward the beginning of Paul G. Hoffman's tenure as president of Studebaker), Fletcher again arrived in South Bend, to become the sales promotion manager. Thus began the longest stay in one place of his career—six years, during which he rose to assistant sales manager in 1936 and general sales manager a year later. In that year of economic recession, the corporation had undertaken to "crack a new market" by entering the low-price field with the Studebaker Champion line of automobiles. Confident of the effectiveness of film as a medium of persuasion, sales manager Fletcher presented the new Champion to the public by means of an advertising motion picture; he sent out crews in eighteen different directions with as many copies and instructions to show it to a million people within six months. At the end of the six months, the film had been seen by a million and a half persons. In 1939-41 the Studebaker sales manager was an associate faculty member of the Indiana University School of Business. While in South Bend, he was chairman of the local Safe Drivers' League and of the local Red Cross special war fund committee.

During the ensuing years Fletcher took part in the development which, at the end of World War II, raised Studebaker from the fourth largest independent (non-General Motors) automobile manufacturer—behind Ford, Chrysler, and Hudson—in 1935 to the largest. He was also giving his attention to other matters. When Paul Hoffman accepted the chairmanship of United China Relief in 1941, he appointed Fletcher executive vice-president in charge of fund-raising campaigns, on leave from his regular position. One of Fletcher's first recommendations reportedly was, "We must make a film." When that campaign came to a successful end in 1942, after raising some $9 million, Hoffman and Fletcher took on another public task.

At the suggestion and with the cooperation of Secretary of Commerce Jesse Jones, in June 1942 a group of top-ranking American businessmen and industrialists formed the privately financed nonprofit Committee for Economic Development (the Department of Commerce provided office space), with Hoffman as board chairman. After the C.E.D.'s professional research staff reported that seven to ten million more jobs than had existed in 1940 would be needed to provide full employment after the war, the C.E.D. set about starting local committees of businessmen to make postwar expansion plans for each community. Scott Fletcher was appointed director of the Field Development Division. Within three years there were nearly 3,000 local committees with more than 75,000 volunteer members, and, as reported *Fortune*, the C.E.D. survey check-sheets were "the first real spur to postwar thinking among

C. SCOTT FLETCHER

many employers." Having resigned in 1943 as Studebaker sales manager, Fletcher in September of the next year advanced from C.E.D. field development director to the committee's executive director, a position he retained until the fall of 1946. He often stressed the point that it was easier to persuade a businessman to open a meeting by showing a film than by making a speech on the subject and that the audience was likely to respond more favorably.

In October 1946 Fletcher became president of Encyclopaedia Britannica Films, Inc., in Wilmette, Illinois, which, as ERPI Films, had been the pioneer producer of educational sound films. While the actual production was continued by the same group as before, the company, under Fletcher, experienced considerable expansion. Adding the 250-film library of Eastman Kodak 16-millimeter films to the more than 300 titles already in the E.B.F. vaults, E.B.F. became much the largest business in its field. A British subsidiary was established (presumably with the use of blocked funds) to produce and distribute motion pictures in the sterling area. Production was expanded to include more than 100 filmstrips (slide films), educational phonograph records (for music and language teaching), and educational films intended for adult audiences. From 1946 to 1950 Encyclopaedia Britannica Films released more than 200 new sound movies for classroom use and established a film-reader program, in cooperation with two textbook publishers. Sales increased by more than 25 per cent. Fletcher served also as a member of the board of editors of the *Encyclopaedia Britannica* and as director in charge of the original publication of the Great Books of the Western World. He has been described as a leading figure in the development of the Film Council of America, on the finance committee of which he was chairman for two years.

(Continued next page)

FLETCHER, C. SCOTT—*Continued*

About the same time that Fletcher resigned his position with Encyclopaedia Britannica Films to become head of the new Fund for Adult Education, in May 1951, he terminated other connections by resigning from the boards of the Muzak Corporation, the China Institute in America, and the C.E.D., of whose information committee he had been chairman since 1946. In his new post Fletcher again worked with Paul G. Hoffman, then director of the half-billion-dollar Ford Foundation, and associate director Robert Maynard Hutchins, who had been closely associated with the Great Books Foundation. One of the first grants made by Fletcher's fund was $90,000 to the National Association of Educational Broadcasters, to promote educational television; and in August $1,200,000 was made available for a radio and television workshop, under the supervision of James Webb Young, to produce programs of high quality to be offered without charge to commercial broadcasters. The fund announced plans to work with the new Adult Education Association in publishing a magazine for adult clubs and in making a moving picture. One million dollars was spent on the encouragement of community group discussions in 1951 and a like sum was alloted for 1952. After the New York Public Library began an American Heritage program for people who wanted something closer to the problems of citizenship than the Great Books program, the fund gave the American Library Association $150,000 to set up such programs experimentally in six widely separated areas. In sixty · towns enthusiastic groups met to discuss "Great Men and Great Issues in Our American Heritage"; Fletcher expressed the hope that the discussions would cause the participants to realize "the tremendous effort man has had to make to live in a free society." Opposed to the lecture method in adult education, he feels that the most fruitful adult education is discussion "between equals of different life experiences" (*Christian Science Monitor*, June 24, 1952).

Fletcher, who became a naturalized citizen in 1941, has served the United States Government as a member of advisory committees to the Department of Commerce and the Department of State (on commercial activities of the foreign service). He belongs to the Film Council of America and the American Society of Sales Executives. His church is the Methodist.

"Ebullient," energetic Fletcher is five feet ten inches, weighs 175 pounds, has hazel eyes and brown hair. On October 23, 1929, he married Olga Noreen Brigg of Sydney, Australia, and is the father of Barbara, Douglas, and Wendy. With fishing as one of his recreations, he is a director of the Izaak Walton League. His other hobbies are golf, gardening, photography, and flying.

References

Christian Sci Mon p9 Jl 22 '52 por
Fortune 44:117 D '51 por
Who's Who in America, 1952-53
Who's Who in Commerce and Industry (1950)
World Biography (1948)

FLYNN, EDWARD J. Sept. 22, 1891—August 18, 1953

Democratic National Committeeman and Bronx County leader in New York; graduated Fordham Law School, 1912; admitted to New York bar, 1913; Assemblyman of Bronx County from 1918 to 1921; sheriff of Bronx County from 1922 to 1925; LL.D., Fordham, 1925; Chamberlain of the City of New York from 1926 to 1928; Secretary of State of New York from 1929 to 138; appointed by President Franklin D. Roosevelt as Commander General of the United States World's Fair Commission, 1939; became Democratic National Committeeman· in 1940; an early and constant supporter of both President Roosevelt and Truman; stood for the New Deal-Fair Deal wing of his party; supported Manhattan Borough President Robert F. Wagner for the 1953 mayorality race in New York City. See *Current Biography*, 1940)

Obituary

N Y Times p1+ Ag 19 '53

FOOT, SIR HUGH (MACKINTOSH)
Oct. 8, 1907- Governor of Jamaica

Address: b. King's House, Kingston, Jamaica, British West Indies

As Governor-in-Chief of the island of Jamaica, Great Britain's largest Caribbean possession, Sir Hugh Foot has been faced with two challenging tasks since he took office in 1951. He is seeking solutions to the colony's grave economic situation and endeavoring to administer the political affairs of Jamaica amid native demands for a greater degree of independence.

The problem of colonial peoples striving for national sovereignty is not, however, a new one for Sir Hugh, since in both Nigeria and Palestine, where he served as an administrator for the British Government, he was confronted with similar situations.

Hugh Mackintosh Foot was born October 8, 1907 in Plymouth, England, to Isaac and Eva (Macintosh) Foot. His father, the Right Honorable Isaac Foot, was for many years a Liberal member of Parliament, Secretary of Mines and Privy Councillor. His brother, Dingle Foot, a Liberal, represented Dundee in Parliament from 1931 to 1945. Another brother, Michael Foot, a Laborite, currently represents Devonport.

Hugh Foot began his education at Leighton Park School in Reading, Berkshire. He was graduated in 1925 and then entered St. Johns College, Cambridge, where he studied history and law. As a member of the Cambridge University debating team he visited the United States in 1927. He was president of the Cambridge Union Society and the Cambridge University Liberal Club. After he was graduated in 1929, receiving the B.A. degree with honors, he entered the colonial service and was sent to Palestine as a junior assistant secretary. By 1932 he had been advanced in the service to assistant district commissioner. Foot was attached to the Colonial Office from 1938 to 1939.

He was sent in 1939 to Transjordan where he served as assistant resident until 1942.

At this time British interests in the Mediterranean were seriously threatened by the Axis Powers, and Transjordan was a key point in Britain's Middle East defense network. In January 1943 he was named chief secretary to the Cyrenaica Administration in Libya, North Africa.

From 1943 to 1945 he served as chief colonial secretary and acting-Governor at Cyprus. During his administration, the island, located in a strategic position, was the base and embarkation point of large numbers of troops. Because of the influx of men, Cyprus experienced a temporary wartime prosperity with a resultant increase in the cost of living. The British Government was then faced with strikes and labor dissension. This serious situation was alleviated under Hugh Foot's administration by taxing higher incomes, subsidizing essential goods and raising low wages. He was assigned to Jamaica in 1945, where he served as colonial secretary and acting-Governor (August 1945 to January 1946). In 1947 he was transferred to Nigeria, Britain's largest colony (population about 25,000,000), to serve as chief secretary, and from 1947 to 1951 as acting-Governor. One of the most difficult problems he encountered was the growing restlessness of the Nigerians for self-government. Aware of both the needs of England and the pressure of the Nigerians, Foot attempted to recognize the rights of native Africans. He introduced the training of native Nigerians for positions of responsibility.

In an interview in 1950 he expressed his point of view, "We believe that the only way to train people in responsibility is to give it to them, and not to give it to them reluctantly, but deliberately as a matter of positive policy. However good our plans for economic, social and political advance, they can succeed only to the extent that we can achieve the authoritative cooperation of Nigerians—not in a subordinate capacity, but in a leading capacity." In Nigeria, Sir Hugh improved colonial relations by going directly to the people and consulting with them; he was able to gain the confidence of Nigerians of all persuasions.

Knighted in 1951 by King George VI, Sir Hugh Foot was named captain-general and Governor-in-Chief of Jamaica succeeding Sir John Huggins. The island is different from most West Indies tourist resorts because, of its 4,450 square miles, only about 646 are level. The highest of its numerous ranges and peaks is Blue Mountain Peak (7,388 feet). Its original name, "Xaymaca," given by the Carib Indians, meant "Isle of Springs." It was owned and governed by the Spanish until 1655 when Admiral Penn and General Venables took it for England and it became a British Crown Colony. During the seventeenth century it was a rendezvous for buccaneers who made their headquarters at Port Royal, destroyed by an earthquake in 1692. Admiral Lord Nelson was Governor in 1779.

On taking office Governor Foot recognized that the economic situation in Jamaica was his most critical problem. The population of the island is about 1,400,000, of which about 15,000

British Inf. Services

SIR HUGH FOOT

are white, the remainder being colored, many of whom are descendants of African slaves brought there in the seventeenth century. The colony, whose main exports are sugar, bananas, rum, and coffee, has had a negative trade balance for several years. In 1949 and 1950, exports amounted to £22,329,233 while Jamaica's imports totalled £14,633,988. A further economic loss occurred in August 1951, when a severe hurricane destroyed property estimated at over £15,000,000.

Sir Hugh, shortly after assuming the governorship, began to revitalize the island's economic condition and its morale. In his "throne speech" to the joint Legislature (May 22, 1951) he said, "The first and most pressing need is for capital. . . .It is of first importance, if the objects we all support are to be achieved, that private capital should come to Jamaica in ever-increasing amounts. The vital need imposes a special obligation in everything we say or do: an obligation to create confidence, confidence in our good faith, confidence in our financial position; confidence in the future of Jamaica."

Sir Hugh's program to alleviate the financial distress with its concomitant unemployment and widespread poverty, depends on three vehicles: The newly created Industrial Development Commission and its sister organization, the Agricultural Development Commission; and the International Bank for Reconstruction and Development. The Governor was successful in finding prominent, capable Jamaicans to accept the non-paying posts on the new commissions.

The International Bank, in response to Sir Hugh's applications, sent to Jamaica a team of experts, headed by John C. DeWilde, who surveyed the economic situation and reported that "timid half-measures" would not solve the island's problems. They proposed a ten-year

FOOT, SIR HUGH—*Continued*

program which aimed at an increase in production of goods from £85,000,000 in 1950 to £150,000,000 in 1962. The International Bank report called for Government expenditures of £34,324,000 over a period of ten years. Opportunity for increased revenue existed, according to the report, in the expansion of tourist trade, in industry and in agriculture. The program it suggested includes planned soil conservation, irrigation of the plains and valleys, and reclamation of swampland. Such measures would provide 150,000 additional acres for development.

A second concern of Sir Hugh's is the internal political situation of Jamaica. There are two main political parties on the island, the Jamaica Labour party, and the People's National party. The Jamaica Labour party, headed by Alexander Bustamente, is a non-Socialistic party which favors the expansion of capitalism, emphasizes the interdependence of the laborer and the employer, and seeks close and cordial relations with Great Britain rather than self-government. It now has a working majority in the Legislature.

The People's National Party, headed by Norman K. Manly, a successful Jamaica lawyer, is an orthodox Socialist party closely resembling the British Labour party in its ideology. The PNP has aggressively demanded self-government and Dominion status for Jamaica. There is some evidence that there is a trend away from Bustamente's JLP and toward the PNP (*The Journal of Politics,* August 1952). On May 5, 1953, however, Foot appointed the Jamaican Labour party's Bustamente Chief Minister of an eight-minister cabinet under the provisions of a new Jamaican Constitution.

In April 1953 the foundation was laid for a British Caribbean Federation, which would include Jamaica, Trinidad, Tobago, Barbados, and the Windward and Leeward Islands. It is held by the proponents of the federation that this is the only way that the West Indies will be able to get a voice in the British Commonwealth of Nations.

Sir Hugh married Florence Sylvia Tod in 1935; they have four children, Paul, Sarah, Oliver, and Benjamin. He is a Methodist. The Governor holds the Officer Order of the British Empire (1939), and is Companion of St. Michael and St. George (1946), Knight Commander of St. Michael and St. George (1951) and Knight of the Order of St. John of Jerusalem (1952). His clubs are the Traveller's and the West Indian. Sir Hugh was commended for bravery in the British campaign in Syria.

References

International Who's Who, 1952
Who's Who, 1952
Who's Who in Jamaica, 1941-46

FRANKENBERG, MRS LLOYD *See* MacIver, L. (N.)

FREEMAN, LUCY (GREENBAUM) Dec. 13, 1916- Journalist
Address: b. New York Times, 229 W. 43rd St., New York 36; h. 1350 Lake Shore Dr., Chicago, Ill.

New York *Times* reporter Lucy Freeman decided, as her five-year psychoanalysis was being completed, that a full and frank description of her treatment would encourage others to seek help if they needed it. In her book, *Fight Against Fears,* she related how she came to try psychoanalysis, and how her own analysis progressed in a long, discouraging, but finally successful series of visits that revealed to her the sources of her physical and emotional difficulties.

Published in 1951 by Crown Publishers, Inc., the book became a national best-seller, was a selection of the Book Find Club, and was issued in a pocket-size edition by Pocket Books, Inc. A writer in the *Saturday Review* (August 25, 1951) said of it: "This is something new— a candid and intimate account of a young woman's psychoanalytic experience signed with the author's true name."

This year, on leave from the New York *Times,* Miss Freeman has had a second book published by Crown. *Hope for the Troubled* is a guide to the various types of aid available to those in need of help, from the guidance of the social worker to the treatment by a psychoanalyst.

According to the *Saturday Review* (August 15, 1953) Miss Freeman gives "a courageous appraisal of the confusion of present-day psychiatry and psychoanalysis, and the added problems of correlating their services with those of social workers and psychologists. . . .She is a reporter, trying to bring to the public a deeper understanding of the 'art of healing the psychic wounds that keep many from happiness.' The hope she holds out is that 'Freud gave to every man the right to become aware of his inner agony.' "

Lucy Greenbaum Freeman Becker was born in New York City on December 13, 1916, the daughter of Lawrence S. and Sylvia (Sobel) Greenbaum. She is the eldest of four children, one boy and three girls. Her father was a lawyer, and her paternal grandfather was a Supreme Court judge in New York City.

When Lucy was six years old, her family moved from their apartment just off Central Park to Larchmont, New York, where she attended a private school. She was graduated from Rye Neck High School in Rye, New York, in 1934 having earned most of the scholastic honors and medals awarded by the school.

Her interest in writing began in high school, where she received encouragement from a teacher and was given an opportunity to work on the schol newspaper. She also played tennis, golf and baseball.

At Bennington College in Bennington, Vermont, Lucy majored in social studies. During one of the winter work-study periods which the college includes in its curriculum she served as a volunteer worker in a New York settlement house. This was her first contact with slum problems, which later became one of her special interests as a reporter.

Her other winter working periods and her summer vacations were spent in newspaper work. She also contributed feature stories to the local town newspaper, and for her thesis she did research on an early founder of the paper. The essay was bound and put into the town's library.

While in college she edited a news sheet for a class in modern dress design, and served as a member of the college editorial board of *Mademoiselle* magazine. She also continued with her favorite sports, golf and tennis.

When she was graduated from Bennington in June 1938, a friend helped her to get her first job, on the weekly Tuckahoe *Record* in Tuckahoe, New York, at ten dollars a week. A year later she received a call from an acquaintance who was leaving the post of woman's editor of the *Daily Times* in Mamaroneck, New York, and suggested that she take the job. The paper covered the area in which she had lived most of her life, and the young reporter wrote social news, feature stories and a weekly column.

Her big opportunity came in 1941, when she was hired as assistant to the fashion editor of the New York *Times*. From fashions, Lucy Greenbaum went on to do general news and feature stories, and also wrote book reviews and articles for the Sunday book and magazine sections of the paper.

The New York Newspaper Women's Club cited her coverage of the Texas City explosion in April 1947 as the best news story of the year. She happened to be in Dallas at that time, covering an annual meeting of the American Association of University Women, and flew to the scene of the explosion. In the lead paragraph of her prize-winning story, she described the destruction she had witnessed, and told of a lone cow which "munched away at the scrubby grass, no one around to milk *him.*"

When she returned to New York a few days later, she met William Freeman, the young copy reader on the *Times* who had fortunately caught and corrected the error. A few months later they were married.

Writing under the name Lucy Freeman, she began to specialize in mental health and social welfare news. In 1951 she received the first annual award of Theta Sigma Phi, the national professional society for women in journalism, for coverage of news in this field.

Miss Freeman's interest in mental health news came as a result of her psychoanalytic treatment, which began in 1946. Plagued by emotional difficulties and physical ailments, including a sinus condition which seriously impeded her breathing, and she found no relief in medical treatment, and decided to undergo a psychoanalysis.

In the fifth year of her analysis, she wrote a book describing its course, in the hope of helping others who might need similar therapy. She reported in the book, *Fight Against Fears,* that soon after her treatment began, her sinus condition, which was psychosomatic in origin, dramatically cleared in the midst of a session with her analyst, Dr. John C. Thurrott.

Alegre

LUCY FREEMAN

"Analysis for me was continuous discovery, sometimes shocking discovery," she wrote. "I felt like the intended victim in a murder, with the analyst as hero-detective trying to rescue me from a life of inner terror."

Dr. Karl Menninger, reviewing the book in the New York *Times,* stated that it "shows clearly that psychoanalysis, far from being an 'escape' or 'indulgence,' is more in the nature of an ordeal in which the patient must struggle unceasingly against self-deception and rationalization in the long and painful search to know himself" (July 8, 1951).

In her new book *Hope for the Troubled,* Miss Freeman wrote, "It is proper that we save ourselves first. Those who save themselves first are more likely to save others. Self-appointed saviors who do not look within, but who must save the world out of their own desperate needs, may lead men to brimstone and fire."

Her marriage to William Freeman having been terminated, Miss Freeman on December 24, 1952 married Harry J. Becker of Chicago. He is associate director of the Commission on Financing Hospital Care, consultant to CIO President Walter Reuther on health, welfare and social security, and professor of hospital medical economics at Northwestern University.

The newspaperwoman has also written articles for *Mademoiselle,* the *American Mercury* and other national magazines. During World War II she was on loan from the *Times* to the Department of the Treasury for two months, to write stories about the war bond drive.

The blue-eyed, brown-haired reporter is five feet two inches tall and weighs 130 pounds. She is an ardent fan of the New York Giants baseball team. Her hobbies, in addition to tennis and golf, are dancing, boating and attending horse races. She is of the Jewish faith; is an independent Democrat; belongs to the New York Newspaper Women's Club, P.E.N.,

FREEMAN, LUCY—*Continued*
and the National Association of Science Writers.

Now a strong advocate of psychoanalysis, Miss Freeman concluded in her account of her own therapy, "I do not feel it indecent to expose inner thoughts if I believe some one else may be spared misery by knowing what helped me."

References

N Y Times D 24 '52
Freeman, L. Fight Against Fears (1951)

FROST, LESLIE M(ISCAMPBELL) Sept. 20, 1895- Prime Minister of Ontario; lawyer
Address; b. Parliament Bldgs., Toronto, Ont.; Temple Bldg., 142 Kent St. W., Lindsay, Ont.; h. 17 Sussex St. N., Lindsay, Ont., Canada

Prime Minister and President of the Council of the Province of Ontario since May 1949, the Honorable Leslie M. Frost likes to refer to himself as a "backwoods lawyer" and his province as "Old Man Ontario." His administration has been marked by many progressive measures, and he is a strong advocate of the St. Lawrence seaway which would open the Great Lakes to ocean-going ships.

A Progressive Conservative when that party came into power in 1943, he was named to the Cabinet as Provincial Treasurer. He has been a member of Ontario's Legislature since 1937, when he was elected by the constituency of Victoria to represent it at Toronto, the provincial capital, and was re-elected four times.

The second of the three sons of William Sword and Margaret Jane (Barker) Frost, Leslie Miscampbell Frost was born September 20, 1895, in Orillia, Ontario. His father, a Scotsman, had settled there in 1867, the year

Donald McKague

LESLIE M. FROST

of Confederation, and had taken an active part in the development of the town, founding its Young Men's Christian Association in 1906, and was elected its mayor in 1910 and 1911. The boy was named in honor of Andrew Miscampbell, at one time member of the Ontario Legislature for East Simcoe, the riding in which Orillia is located. With his older brother, Grenville, and his younger brother, Cecil Gray, Leslie attended the local public school and Orillia Collegiate Institute, then the University of Toronto. As a schoolboy his chief sports were swimming, canoeing and basketball.

On the outbreak of World War I, Leslie Frost and his brother, Cecil, enlisted in the Simcoe Regiment. Leslie served in France and Belgium as assistant adjutant, and later as company commander of the Twentieth Canadian Infantry Battalion. Wounded March 1918 at Neuville Vitasse (near Arras) in the left hip, he spent seventeen months in a hospital. His rank on discharge from the Army was that of captain. He has maintained his military interests, joining the Sir Sam Hughes branch of the Canadian Legion on its formation, and at one time serving as zone representative. He is a member of the Royal Canadian Military Institute.

Deciding to enter the legal profession, Frost attended Osgoode Hall in Toronto, and read law with the Honorable William Finlayson. He was called to the bar in June 1921, and that year established a firm with his brother Cecil, whose studies had paralleled his own. The brothers chose to locate in the town of Lindsay, Ontario. On June 3, 1933, Leslie Frost became a King's Counsel. He was called upon a number of times to act as Crown Counsel at assizes throughout the province. A prominent member of the profession, he has served as president of the Victoria County Law Association.

Brought up to take an interest in public affairs, the Frost brothers early took part in the activities of the Conservative party. Leslie was at one time president of the Conservative Association for South Victoria, the constituency in which Lindsay is located, and Cecil was president of the provincial association from 1937 to 1943.

In 1934 Leslie Frost was Conservative candidate for the provincial Legislature, but was defeated. In 1937 he won the seat, and has represented Victoria riding in Ontario's capital, Toronto, since that date, having been returned in the provincial general elections of 1943, 1945, 1948, and 1951.

His party, which was the opposition party at the time of his election, appointed him Financial Critic for the Opposition, and in 1938 he was appointed to the Select Committee to Investigate Contracts and the General Position of the Ontario Hydro-Electric Power Commission; he was also appointed to the Select Committee on the Administration of Justice.

When the Conservatives came into power in 1943 Frost was named both Treasurer and Minister of Mines in the Cabinet of Premier George Drew on August 17, portfolios which he continued to hold in successive Conservative ministries. In 1944 he was elected first president of the newly formed Provincial Mines Ministers Association of Canada. Frost's administration of the treasury was characterized by D. P. O'Hearn, writing in *Saturday Night* (May 10, 1949), as conservative in policy with debt reduction as his aim, and "a series of nice surpluses" as his achievement.

When the Ontario Progressive Conservative Party met in Toronto in April 1949 to choose a party leader to succeed Drew, who had become leader of the national party, Leslie Frost was elected on the first ballot, defeating three other nominees, Attorney General Leslie Blackwell, Kelso Roberts, and the Minister of Education, Dana Porter. Frost became Prime Minister and was sworn into that office, as well as that of the presidency of the council, on May 4, 1949. He retained the post of treasurer.

Some of the reasons behind the choice of Frost, according to the D. P. O'Hearn *Saturday Night* article, were that the party hoped his strong rural support would be of aid to Drew in a national election, that he could give greater unity within the party, and could cooperate with Drew to strengthen relations between the provincial and national parties. These estimates were based on the new Prime Minister's character. He has been described as "a man who is very easy for anyone to work with."

Prime Minister Frost assumed office at the second session of the Twenty-third Legislature. Legislation introduced by his administration has been called "sound, if not spectacular." The lack of bickering in sessions was attributed by Hugh Ross (*Saturday Night*, December 15, 1951) to two reasons: "The administration was to a large extent doing what it said it was, giving good government; and the Opposition was finding it difficult to fight with a man who wouldn't get mad."

After two and a half years in office Prime Minister Frost called a general election for November 22, 1951. His party was returned to power with a majority of seventy-nine seats, the largest majority ever held in the Ontario ninety-member house. At that time Ontario was the only province with a Progressive Conservative administration.

In his *Saturday Night* articles on the election, which he entitled "'Backwoods Lawyer' Wins Solid Urban Support," Ross attributed this success to Frost's "personal mixture of rural candor, metropolitan suavity, and solid political ability." The Prime Minister's speeches, said Ross, were effective because of "the impression of sincerity he creates. He is not an issue-of-the-day, pound-the-table orator, but more a conversational type of speaker."

Among the bills passed by the Twenty-third and Twenty-fourth Legislatures under Frost's leadership have been a fair employment practices act; an act establishing the principle of equal pay for equal work irrespective of sex; an act admitting women to jury duty; an act to promote the improvement, extension, and co-ordination of the rural telephone system; an act extending allowances to disabled persons not covered by other assistance acts; an act to pro-

vide financial assistance for the building of houses in rural areas.

Agreements were reached with the Government of Canada and assented to by the Ontario House with respect to the collection of income tax, and with respect to the development of power projects on the Niagara and St. Lawrence rivers (subject to ratification of international treaties between Canada and the United States by their respective Governments, and to the approval of the International Joint Commission). Premier Frost has been prominent in urging the building of the St. Lawrence Seaway, which would open the Great Lakes to deep-sea shipping, and has expressed confidence that if the United States refuses to participate in a joint project, Canada will proceed on her own.

The Ontario statesman has been awarded the LL.D. degree (*honoris causa*) by Queen's University (Kingston, Ont., 1946), Ottawa University (1948), and the University of Toronto (1952); and the D.C.L. degree by the University of Western Ontario (London, 1950). His clubs include: in Lindsay, the Rotary (past president), and the Curling; in Toronto, the Albany, Garrison, and Twenty. He is a Freemason, and belongs to the Loyal Orange Lodge. His religious affiliation is with the United Church of Canada, and he is a member of the Cambridge Street Church in Lindsay and chairman of tis board of management. On June 2, 1926, Frost married Gertrude Jane Carew of Lindsay, whose father was at one time Member of the Provincial Parliament for South Victoria. He and Mrs. Frost maintain their home in Lindsay, where they spend most week-ends during parliamentary sessions. They have an old pioneer cabin built over 125 years ago, which they have had reassembled on the shore of Sturgeon Lake; the life of the early settlers is one of Premier Frost's interests. His recreations are curling, hunting and fishing. He is five feet eleven inches tall.

References

Sat Night 64:11 My 10 '49; 67-13 D 15 '51
Canadian Who's Who, 1949-51
Who's Who in Canada, 1951-52

FRUEHAUF, ROY (AUGUST) Oct. 1, 1908- Business executive

Address: b. c/o Fruehauf Trailer Co., 10940 Harper Ave., Detroit 32, Mich.; h. 5330 Middlebelt Rd., Birmingham, Mich.

As president of the Fruehauf Trailer Company, which designed the first modern trailer, Roy Fruehauf heads the world's largest trailer manufacturing business, with sales totaling $161 million in 1951. Having worked his way up gradually in the business started by his father in 1915, Fruehauf has observed almost every phase of trailer growth and served apprenticeship in nearly every department of the Fruehauf plant. Before becoming president of the company in 1949, he held the positions of salesman in Chicago, Western sales manager, vice-

ROY FRUEHAUF

president in charge of sales, and vice-president in charge of all operations.

The youngest of four sons of August Charles and Louise (Schuchard) Fruehauf, Roy August Fruehauf was born in Fraser, Michigan, on October 1, 1908. As a child he frequented the blacksmith shop and wagon factory of his father, on a small dirt road in Detroit. He was seven years old when, because automobile expansion threatened to put the family horse-drawn vehicle trade out of business, the senior Fruehauf hooked his wagon to a Model T roadster, and the Fruehauf trailer company was started. Young Roy learned the motor transport business from the beginning, at first running errands for the eight employees and, when he was old enough, driving the truck-trailer unit that was used in the plant. Frequently he was called upon by his father to demonstrate the ease of operation of the trailers manufactured at the Fruehauf factory. In 1923 he left Detroit to attend Principia College in Elsah, Illinois, but withdrew in 1927 before graduation to return to the trailer business.

For several years working in the now expanded family concern as an apprentice in the service, parts, machine shop, and engineering departments, Fruehauf learned, as he has said, "every nut and bolt that went into the trailers." His first experience in selling the Fruehauf trailers was gained in Chicago, where he was sent as a $100-a-month salesman. "I used to make frequent demonstrations of the easy pulling and flexibility of our products and these helped a lot to clinch sales," Fruehauf told in an address before the Cleveland Advertising Club in November 1951. He once drove a large trailer all the way to Davenport, Iowa, and back to interest a potential buyer and often would bring the trailers to the very end of the Chicago docks to illustrate their maneuverability. From Chicago he was sent to Des Moines

and later to Kansas City to develop markets for Freuhauf. Promoted in 1933 from salesman to Western salesmanager, he opened the Western territory to the use of trailer trucks. Two years later, in 1935, he was made vice-president in charge of the Western division, advancing in 1938 to vice-president in charge of sales and in 1940 to vice-president in charge of operations. After four years as executive vice-president, Roy Freuhauf in April 1949 was elected President of the then $8.5 million Fruehauf Trailer Company.

The efficiency and economy in operation of the truck trailer is based on the principle that the same power can pull a greater load than it can carry. "Actually," Roy Freuhauf has explained, "it was my brother, Harvey, who took hold of the trailer idea, caught a vision of what this useful tool could mean to American industry, and set out to pioneer it." During the nearly forty years of its expansion, the Fruehauf company has remained largely a family undertaking, with the oldest of the Fruehauf brothers, Harry C., now (in 1953) chairman of the board and another brother, Harry R., the first vice-president. By 1951 the company had eight plants located in the United States and Canada and eighty-five factory branches, employing some 9,000 men and women. The largest of Fruehauf's trailers is thirty-two feet three and three-eights inches and carries 25,000 pounds (as of 1951). Among the company's thirty different models, ranging from two to fifty tons, are liquid tank carriers, log haulers, live-stock vans, and refrigerator cars, as well as several trailers exclusively constructed for Government and military use. "During World War II," reported *Time*, May 21, 1951, "Fruehauf made everything for the Army and Navy from front-line field hospitals to portable command posts and searchlight carriers, Fruehauf's latest model for the Government: a truck post office."

With war and postwar Government restrictions and material shortages, the Fruehauf Company has encountered a number of obstacles in its growth. One of the difficult problems that Roy Fruehauf has had to face since assuming the presidency was the default of a Columbus, Ohio, prefabricated house contract in 1950. Lustron had contracted for 810 "rolling warehouses and assembly lines" to be delivered by Fruehauf. When the Reconstruction Finance Corporation withdrew its support from Lustron, Fruehauf was able to realize only $1.5 million on a $4.4 million contract. Reconversion of the trailers at Fruehauf's Avon Lake, Ohio, assembly line to fill back orders for regular commercial vans enabled the president to say that the company would not lose money on the transaction.

Supplying an estimated 55 per cent of the nations' trailer market demands, the Fruehauf Trailer Company is the world's largest trailer manufacturing concern. From a volume of $22,000 in its first year of operation, its sales grew to $700,000 in four years (*Time*). When sales reached $132 million in 1950, about 71 per cent better than in 1949, Fruehauf had a $50 million Government order, a back-log of $50 million in civilian orders, and $50 million in military contracts. In November 1952 the company was reported in the New York *Times* to be a $161 million unit of the transportation industry as compared with $19,512,145 in 1940. Confident of similar expansion in the future, president Roy Fruehauf told his stockholders in 1951 that "everything America eats, wears and uses, travels today at least part of the way to the consumer in trucks and truck trailers. . . fuel . . . raw materials . . . merchandise . . . . All these necessities of life depend on motor transport to keep them moving." Anticipating changing requirements and developing its models accordingly, the Fruehauf Company has produced a midget trailer which it expects will open a greater future in the industry.

On July 18, 1953 it was announced that George J. Kolowich, president of the Detroit and Cleveland Navigation Company, had acquired 131,000 shares of the Freuhauf Trailer Company. Financial officials said "the Freuhauf family still holds 156,927 shares" (New York *Times*).

Married on November 30, 1935, Roy and Catherine M. (Meacham) Fruehauf had four children, Catherine Gail, Mary Carolyn, Roy Lawrence and William Meacham. Fruehauf was married a second time, on June 16, 1950, to Ruth Horn, formerly a secretary. His clubs are the Detroit Athletic, Detroit, Grosse Pointe Yacht Club, Grosse Pointe Hunt Club, Lochmoor, The Old, The Tavern, and the Recess. He also belongs to the Society of Automotive Engineers. Fruehauf has a height of five feet nine and one half inches, weighs 220 pounds, and has brown hair and blue eyes. He is a Republican. Robert H. Fetridge of the New York *Times* has described him as "big, energetic", "dynamic, interesting, exciting, friendly." The trailer industry executive likes boating, golf, horseback riding, and tennis when he has time for recreation.

References

Bsns W p72 Ap 7 '51
Finance p45+ Ap 15 '51
Pathfinder 58:30 Ap 18 '51
Tide 14:17 F 1 '40
Time 51:108 My 21 '51
N Y Herald Tribune p31 Ap 6 '51
N Y Times p33 Mr 30 '51; III p3 N 9 '52
N Y World-Telegram p19 O 14 '50
Business Executives of America (1950)
Who's Who in America, 1952-53
Who's Who in Commerce and Industry (1951)

GAITHER, H(ORACE) ROWAN, JR.

Nov. 23, 1909- Foundation executive; lawyer
Address: b. 914 E. Green St., Pasadena 1, Calif.; 333 Montgomery St., San Francisco 4, Calif.; h. 149 LaSalle Av., Piedmont, Calif.

H. Rowan Gaither, Jr., the new president of the Ford Foundation, is, like his predecessor, Paul G. Hoffman, a long-time resident of California. On March 1, 1953 he took office as

J. Allen Hawkins

H. ROWAN GAITHER, JR.

president and a trustee of what is generally conceded to be the largest public trust in the world. He had been associated with the Foundation since November 22, 1948 when he accepted an assignment from Henry Ford II to serve as Chairman of the Foundation's Study Committee on Policy and Program. Gaither is also Chairman of the Board of Rand Corporation which he organized in 1948, and of the Pacific National Bank of San Francisco.

As president of the Ford Foundation, Gaither now heads an organization which owns 3,089,908 shares of non-voting Class "A" stock in the Ford Motor Company valued at $417,137,580.

Established by the late Edsel Bryant Ford and his father Henry Ford in 1936, the Foundation became active in September 1950 in projects to "further the cause of peace, advance education, strengthen democratic institutions, promote economic stability, and increase knowledge about individual behavior and human relations." In 1953 the Foundation has granted funds for projects concerned with furthering adult education, studies of human behavior, village development in Pakistan, guarding civil liberties, and the television program *Omnibus*.

Horace Rowan Gaither, Jr., the elder son of the late Horace Rowan and Marguerite (Chamberlain) Gaither and the brother of Andrew Gaither, was born at Natchez, Mississippi on November 23, 1909. His family moved to the West Coast in 1919 when his father became an officer of the Pacific National Bank of San Francisco. Young Gaither attended the University of California at Berkeley, where he received his B.A. degree in 1929, and his LL.B. degree from the Law School four years later. Admitted to the California bar in 1933, Gaither served for three years as special assistant to the general counsel of the Farm Credit Ad-

(Continued next page)

GAITHER, H. ROWAN, JR.—*Continued*

ministration in Washington, D.C., before taking up his private practice.

Returning to California in 1936, Gaither joined the San Francisco law firm of Cooley, Crowley and Supple, gaining experience in corporation and insurance law, wills and administration, and litigation. Frederic E. Supple died in 1944, and the name of the firm was changed to Cooley, Crowley and Gaither in 1947. Gaither became a lecturer at the University of California Law School in that year.

With the entry of the United States into World War II, Gaither took a leave of absence from both law firm and law school. He became the assistant director in 1942 of the Radiation Laboratory at the Massachusetts Institute of Technology (1942-45), a position equivalent to that of business manager, in which his legal-administrative talents attracted the attention of Army Air Force chiefs and civilian scientists including President Karl T. Compton of M.I.T. After returning to his San Francisco law firm in 1945, Gaither was awarded in 1948 the Presidential Certificate of Merit for wartime services.

Gaither was one of the three organizers and incorporators of Rand, a California non-profit corporation engaged in scientific research for the United States Air Force. The Ford Foundation made a non-interest-bearing loan of $100,000 to Rand in October 1948. In 1950 an additional $900,000 was loaned for the purpose of providing Rand with working capital. In 1952 the $1,000,000 indebtedness was forgiven by the Foundation, thereby making a grant of that amount to Rand. (Rand is reimbursed by the Air Force for its services.)

With the death of Edsel Ford in 1943 and Henry Ford in 1947, the Foundation had acquired additional funds of between $200,000,000 and $500,000,000 making it probably "the largest public trust in the world." To determine the best means of using these vast resources, the Foundation trustees named a Study Committee on Policy and Program with Gaither as chairman in December 1948.

After two years of study, the Committee recommended in September 1950 that the Foundation support activities in five fields: the furtherance of world peace; promotion of the basic principles of freedom and democracy; advancement of the economic well-being of peoples everywhere; the expansion and improvement of educational facilities and methods; and scientific activities designed to increase knowledge of factors which influence or determine human conduct.

Paul G. Hoffman, president of the Foundation and former head of ECA, announced the appointment of Gaither as associate director in February 1951 in charge of the disbursement of funds in the field of scientific investigation of human behavior and conduct, which he administered on a part-time basis. When the trustees of the Foundation voted to move its offices from Pasadena, California to New York City for convenience in transacting its affairs, Hoffman resigned as president and Gaither was named acting president February 1953, and assigned the task of

gradually consolidating the operations of the Foundation in New York. On March 1, 1953 Gaither was elected President, Director and a Trustee of the Ford Foundation.

Among grants approved by the trustees for 1953 were $4,000,000 to the Adult Education Fund; $300,000 to American universities for studies of human behavior and $200,000 for pilot projects in connection with research into human behavior; $1,250,000 to assist Pakistan in a three-year program of village development; $1,825,000 to the support of various exchange-of-persons activities; and the largest grant of $15,000,000 to the new Fund for the Republic, to promote civil liberties.

H. Rowan Gaither, Jr. and Charlotte Cameron Castle were married July 18, 1931 and have two sons, Horace Rowan III and James Castle. He is a director of the Chromatic Television Laboratories, Inc., and is a member of the American and California Bar Associations. His fraternities are the Delta Upsilon, the Phi Delta Phi, and the Order of the Coif.

References

> Christian Sci Mon p4 Mr 18 '53 por
> Fortune 42:102 Mr '51 por; 44:116 D '51 por
> Los Angeles Daily N p19 F ' 53
> N Y Herald Tribune p14 F 2 '51
> N Y Times p21 F 6 '53
> American Bar (1947)
> Who's Who in America, 1952-53

GALLAGHER, BUELL GORDON Feb. 4, 1904- President of City College of New York

Address: b. City College of New York, 139th and Convent Ave., New York 31; h. "The Gatehouse," 133d St. and Convent Ave., New York 27

Shortly after his election in June 1952 to the presidency of City College of New York, Buell Gordon Gallagher remarked: "This is the thing I've been getting ready for all my life." His career, which began with the teaching of economics in 1925, has embraced two years' active service as a Congregational minister, ten years as president of a Southern college for Negroes, five as professor of Christian ethics and three years in Federal educational posts. He has also been a candidate for Congress and is the author of three outspoken, and widely read books dealing with racial problems.

Buell Gordon Gallagher was born on February 4, 1904, in Rankin, Illinois, the son of the Reverend Elmer David and Elma Maryel (Poole) Gallagher. His boyhood was spent in Minnesota, Nebraska, Montana, and North Dakota. He attended Wabasha High School in Wabasha, Minnesota, and was graduated in 1919 at the age of fifteen. At Carleton College in Northfield, Minnesota, he majored in economics, was on the track team, and received his B.A. in 1925. He taught economics at Doane College, Crete, Nebraska, for a year. Continuing his studies at Union Theological Seminary in New York, he received his B.D. degree in 1929. He then spent a year at the London School of Economics at London, England. From 1930 to 1931 he was National Secretary of the Interseminary Movement.

In his 27th year, Gallagher was called to the ministry of the First Congregational Church in Passaic, New Jersey, where he served two years. He was appointed in 1933 president of Talladega College, a liberal arts college for Negroes in Alabama. In his own words, "in the heart of the deep South we lived together, Negroes and Whites, without any distinction of any kind, defying Jim Crow."

In his ten years at Talladega, from 1933 to 1943, Gallagher's accomplishments included the furthering of tolerance in what he characterized as "a not too friendly white community," the financing and building of a library to be shared on equal terms by Negroes and Whites, and the creation of what he described in an article in *The Christian Century* as "an island of sanity and decency in the midst of an indecent and unconscionable caste system." He adds, "With the coming of Executive Order 8802 and the FEPC we managed to break the Jim Crow pattern of employment in local war plants. There was I, a publicly acknowledged pacifist . . . using my energies to get Negroes integrated in the war effort!"

In order to find some of the answers to his problems as an educator, Gallagher took leave from Talladega in his first year and attended classes at Columbia University. He studied there for five summers, obtaining his Ph.D. degree in 1939. His thesis was published in 1938 as a book with the title *American Caste and the Negro College* (Columbia). It was called by the *New Republic* "the soundest work in this field to date," and Theophilus Lewis in *The Commonweal* wrote, "For a complete anatomy and physiology of the race problem this is the best book written by anybody in our time."

In 1943, his last year at Talladega, Dr. Gallagher received his D.D. degree from Oberlin. From 1944 to 1949 he was professor of Christian ethics at the Pacific School of Religion in Berkeley, California. At the urging of local heads of labor and of liberal groups, he ran for Congress on the Democratic ticket in the strongly Republican Seventh District of California and polled 49 per cent of the total vote, losing by only 3,000. Upon his acceptance of the nomination he had resigned at the request of the college authorities. After his defeat he was asked to resume his post on the faculty and consented to do so.

Meanwhile Dr. Gallagher had written two more successful books on race relations—*Color and Conscience: the Irrepressible Conflict* (Harper, 1946) and *Portrait of a Pilgrim: A Search for the Christian Way in Race Relation* (Friendship Press, 1946) which sold 70,000 copies and was widely adopted as a college textbook.

Dr. Gallagher left the Pacific School to join the staff of the United States Office of Education. He became consultant to the Federal Security Administrator (1949-52), consultant to

BUELL GORDON GALLAGHER

the United States Commissioner of Education (1950-51), Assistant Commissioner for Program Development and Coordination from February 1951 to April 1952.

While serving as Assistant Commissioner for Higher Education, he was elected head of City College by unanimous vote of New York City's Board of Higher Education to succeed Dr. Harry N. Wright, who was facing mandatory retirement. The election concluded a sixteen-months' search in which some 100 candidates were considered. Dr. Wright was among the members of a special committee which had recommended Dr. Gallagher for the presidency.

To his post as president of the largest municipally-supported college in the world, which has an enrollment of 32,000 students, Dr. Gallagher brought a reputation as an independent thinker, a liberal, a foe of religious and racial intolerance, and a maker of phrases. After his election he told reporters on June 18 that he had a "prejudice" against communism and fascism but supported the right of faculty members to think for themselves.

He declared, "No one surrenders his right to be a citizen by virtue of being a member of a college faculty." Asked about the question of loyalty oaths, he gave his opinion that since disloyal persons, with no hesitation about perjury, would willingly swear to them, "the conclusion is that such oaths are not the most effective device for discovering the disloyal or preventing disloyalty."

President Gallagher has expressed himself as an advocate of complete intellectual freedom and of the resistance to pressures outside the institution of learning, but he has upheld the section of the New York City Charter which provides that city employees who refuse to answer the questions of Government committees automatically vacate their jobs. He had previously headed a group of educators who agreed that "membership in the Communist

GALLAGHER, BUELL—*Continued*

party should not be sufficient evidence to warrant dismissal of members of college and university faculties and staffs," asserting that "evidence must include individual identification of subversive acts on the part of the accused."

Dr. Gallagher on another occasion clarified his stand by saying, "No man should be put in jeopardy for holding an opinion: that is the meaning of academic freedom. But when an opinion holds a man, freedom for him has become impossible because there is no integrity in him. . . .His treasonable presence within the college does not give him the right to claim the protection of the academic freedom which he has violated." It is his conviction that "A college should teach its students the difference between making a living and making a life," and he believes that "Education has got to come out of its ivory tower and be an active force in all phases of community life."

Dr. Gallagher, who had assumed office on September 1, 1952, was formally inaugurated on February 19, 1953 as the seventh president of City College. The educator is a member of Phi Beta Kappa and of Delta Sigma Rho, vice-president of the National Association for the Advancement of Colored People, a director of the Manhattanville Neighborhood Center, New York, a member of the board of directors of Union Theological Seminary, and Chairman of the World Student Service Fund. He has also participated in the promotion of publicly supported educational television.

Standing six feet tall, Gallagher weighs 160 pounds; he has green eyes, brown hair, and a face characterized by the New York *Post* as "Lincolnesque." His manner is described as relaxed and informal.

On September 1, 1927, Dr. Gallagher married a former classmate, June Lucille Sampson. They have two daughters, Helen Maryel and Barbara Lucille. The college president's only hobby is carpentry, a wrist injury having made him give up golf, and he spends most of his spare time reading and writing. He lives with his family in the old gatehouse on Manhattanville College property recently acquired by City College.

The New York *Times* commented (February 20, 1953) editorially on Dr. Gallagher's address when installed as president of the 106-year-old college: "His utterances mark him as a man of tolerance, conviction, and high ideals."

In a recent address of Dr. Gallagher (as reported in The Barnard Alumnae Magazine, April, 1953) on developing educational resources, he said:

"Our national venture into higher education on a grand scale has proved itself so well that it would be a very good thing if *every* individual had the opportunity to pursue his educational right up to the limits of his potential." He recommended that we move "toward reducing financial barriers which so frequently determine who goes to college and who goes to what kind of college. We must begin to provide many more scholarships on the basis of merit and need."

Under the auspices of the World University Service Dr. Gallagher spent two months during the summer of 1953 visiting India, Pakistan, Turkey, Greece and Italy. The educator reported that this nation must continue to do all it can to help the needy peoples of the world. He expressed the belief that this policy would pay off in friendlier relations and better international conditions. There was no general anti-American feeling in the countries he visited, he asserted (New York *Times,* August 22, 1953).

References

N Y Herald Tribune 6:6 F 15 '53 por; p21 Mr 23 '53 por
N Y Post Je 22 '52 por
Newsweek 41:82 Mr 2 '53

GALLAGHER, WILLIAM M. Feb. 26, 1923- News photographer
Address: b. c/o Flint Journal, 501 Harrison St., Flint 2, Mich.; h. 2239 Corunna Rd., Flint 3, Mich.

"For an outstanding example of news photography" in 1952, William M. Gallagher, staff photographer of the Flint (Michigan) *Journal,* was awarded a Pulitzer Prize in May 1953. The photograph, which was taken on Labor Day 1952 shows the Presidential candidate Adlai E. Stevenson with a hole in the sole of his shoe. Given wide publication in United States and foreign papers, the picture received a number of other awards for excellence in news photography. Gallagher, a free-lance photographer since he was in high school, had served in the United States Army from 1943 to 1945 as a teletype operator and photographer before joining the staff of the Flint *Journal* on January 17, 1947.

William M. Gallagher is a native of Hiawatha, Kansas, and the son of George P. and Anna Marie (Bowmaker) Gallagher. He was born on February 26, 1923; he has one sister. His forebears were also Kansans, his mother's parents having been early farmers in that State and his paternal grandfather a police officer in Horton who was killed in the line of duty. While the family traveled over the United States with George Gallagher, who was a salesman, William attended school in Lake Charles and New Orleans, Louisiana, Topeka, Kansas, and Dallas and Houston, Texas. In his childhood he visited and lived in almost every Southern and Midwestern State. After the Gallaghers had moved to Flint in the summer of 1936, the boy studied at the St. Matthew's High School, from which he was graduated in January 1943.

During his high school years in Flint, young Gallagher worked as a clerk and delivery boy in a drugstore, sold magazines, and was otherwise occupied in free-lance photography. He has recalled that as a reward for selling a certain number of magazines he won a box camera with which he snapped a picture of the Detroit sky line. After receiving the first prize of five dollars with this photograph in a local contest, he invested the money in a home-developing kit and began developing and printing his own pictures.

At about this time the amateur photographer was saving money to buy an airplane with a friend. "But after a little thought," Gallagher has said, "I decided that I would be better off in photography. So instead of buying the airplane I invested my roll in photographic equipment. This in itself was a mistake because I got a lot of stuff that I didn't really need. But nevertheless I was interested in it and stuck it out."

When Gallagher enlisted in the United States Army in January 1943, he was assigned first to the medical corps in Walla Walla, Washington; from there he was transferred to the signal corps and sent to Redmond, Oregon, as a photographer. After a period in which he was attached to the air corps, he went to Boise, Idaho, as a teletype operator. Later from a station in Kansas he was shipped overseas with the Twentieth Air Force to North Africa and then to the China-Burma-India theater, again as a photographer. He afterward saw duty on Tinian Island in the Pacific Ocean before being returned to the United States for his discharge at Fort Sheridan, Illinois, on November 24, 1945.

In January 1946, Gallagher became photographer on the staff of the Flint *Sporting Digest,* a weekly newspaper covering sports events. Early in the following year he accepted a position with the Flint *Journal* (circulation 80,555) as wirephoto operator—receiving and transmitting Associated Press wirephotos—and part-time news photographer. He was made the *Journal's* staff photographer in April 1947.

Sent by his newspaper on Labor Day of 1952 to cover the visit to Flint of Adlai E. Stevenson, Democratic candidate for President, Gallagher was on a routine assignment when he snapped the picture which brought him national acclaim. The photographer, in describing his experience on that occasion, has related that he was on the platform waiting for Stevenson to be introduced at a rally at Flint Park. "I squatted down there almost directly in front of him. As I was kneeling there he started going over the notes of his speech and casually crossed his legs. This brought the shoe up right in front of me and just a litttle below my eye level. I couldn't miss seeing the hole. As quietly as I could I pre-focused my camera and set it on the floor at arm's length. I had to spot the camera by guess work because it was impossible for me to lie on the floor. . . .I was lucky because if I had moved the camera a fraction of an inch either way I would have ruined the picture. . . .It scares me a little now when I think that I could have missed the shot as easily as I got it."

As soon as the picture appeared in the Flint *Journal,* it was wireplated over the United States and abroad and was given much comment. "Adlai Bares His Sole," as the photograph was called, inspired the manufacture of small campaign pins in the form of a shoe with a hole in it, which were sold by the Democratic headquarters in Michigan as a symbol of the party. Autographing the picture, the Illinois Governor wrote, "To Wm. M. Gallagher, from a candidate who is really not holier than thou. Adlai E. Stevenson, Sept. 1952." In an

WIILIAM M. GALLAGHER

accompanying letter he told the Flint photographer, "I am glad you accomplished your heart's desire—even with the bottom of my foot!" (Flint *Journal,* May 5, 1953).

The first award won by Gallagher with his Stevenson picture was in the Michigan Associated Press Contest, receiving in January 1953 first place and best in show. He later took first place in the Michigan Press Photography Contest at Michigan State College, fifth place in the Graflex contest, and third place in the Associated Press national news photography contest. In other contests he was given honorable mention by *Editor and Publisher, Encyclopaedia Britannica,* and Kent State University (Ohio) Short Course in News Photography.

Announcement of the Pulitzer Prize to Gallagher for his "hole in the shoe" photograph was made in May 1953 by trustees of Columbia University, who annually select winners of the awards, each of which carries a prize of $1,000, for achievement during the previous year in journalism, letters and music. Among earlier recipients of the award in news photography were Max Desfor of the Associated Press (1951) and John Robinson and Don Ultang of the Des Moines *Register and Tribune* (1952). Commenting on his having been chosen a Pulitzer Prize winner, Gallagher said, "I have reached the acme of my profession on just one picture. . . .It was solely a trick of fate and mighty lucky on my part."

Gallagher belongs to the National Press Photographers Association and the Michigan Press Photographers Association. A member also of the Lightning Class Association, he enjoys sailboating as his favorite sport. Another of his hobbies is fishing. He is a merit badge counselor in photography for the Boy Scouts of America and is active in the Flint Youth Bureau, a "big brother" organization. Weighing 145 pounds, the photographer is six feet tall;

GALLAGHER, WILLIAM—*Continued*
he has blue eyes and blond hair. His church is the Catholic and his political party the Republican.

References

Flint J p1 My 5 '53
N Y Herald Tribune p16 My 5 '53
N Y Times p24 My 5 '53

GALLOWAY, IRENE O(TILLIA) Sept 1, 1908- United States Army officer

Address: b. c/o United States Women's Army Corps, The Pentagon, Washington 25, D.C.

The fourth director of the Women's Army Corps (WAC), Colonel Irene O. Galloway, was sworn into office on January 3, 1953, succeeding Colonel Mary A. Hallaren. Until her new appointment, Colonel Galloway was the commander of the Women's Training Center at Fort Lee, Virginia. During her ten years

U. S. Army
COL. IRENE O. GALLOWAY

with the Army she has served at various military·posts in the United States and Europe. She now supervises approximately 11,000 women who are members of the women's branch of the Army.

Irene Otillia Galloway was born on September 1, 1908 in the county of Carroll, Iowa. On the completion of her primary and secondary education she became a student at the Boyles Business College at Omaha, Nebraska. Later, after World War II, Miss Galloway studied at the University of Maryland's extension classes in Heidelberg, Germany.

With the entrance of the United States into World War II and with the establishment of the Women's Army Auxiliary Corps (WAAC) in May of 1942, Miss Galloway enlisted as a volunteer in the military service and became a

member of the second class of army women to train for the rank of officers of the WAAC. She graduated with her class in September 1942 and received the rank of second lieutenant. A year later, on November 10, 1943, she was promoted to the position of major, which she held until August 1948. Her rank was changed in December 1948 to that of major in the regular army. On February 5, 1950, she received the permanent rank of lieutenant colonel.

She later stated that she had decided to enter the WAC one Sunday morning as she was leaving St. Patrick's Cathedral in New York City. Her brother was among the first group of troops to be sent to the Pacific area. "I felt that I wanted to do my part to help. I never planned to stay in after the war was over, but here I am."

Irene Galloway's first major assignment was in the office of the Assistant Chief of Staff for personnel, at the Pentagon building in Washington, D.C. During 1944 she spent two months overseas, visiting the WAC detachments in Europe and the Middle East. After the war, in July 1948, she was again sent to Europe, to serve as WAC staff adviser for the European Command, where she remained until October 1952. On her return to the United States she was appointed commander of the Women's Training Center at Fort Lee, Virginia, serving there until December 1952 when she was appointed Director of the Women's Army Corps by Secretary of the Army Frank Pace, Jr. She was sworn in on January 3, 1953 and at the same time had the silver eagles of a full colonel pinned on her uniform.

In taking over the direction of the women's branch of the army, Colonel Galloway becomes the fourth woman in United States history to head a contingent of regular army women. Her predecessors have been Oveta Culp Hobby, Westray Battle Boyce, and Mary A. Hallaren. Of her predecessor she said, "Colonel Hallaren was one of the finest women to work under. If I can live up to the principles and standards set by Colonel Hallaren it will be a great satisfaction to me."

The organization which Colonel Galloway commands was established by act of Congress on May 14, 1942 as the Women's Army Auxiliary Corps. The act of June 12, 1948 integrated what had become known simply as the Women's Army Corps into the regular army, thus permitting women for the first time in United States history to serve as members of the regular army, rather than the army reserves. Approximately 11,000 women are serving in the WAC, thus replacing and releasing for combat service enlisted men and officers performing noncombatant duties. Some of these women are doctors, lawyers, dietitians, supply and ordnance personnel; others fill positions in the finance, transportation, signal, and adjustment departments of the army. In addition to directing these soldiers, Colonel Galloway serves as a member of the General Staff, which is the advisory and planning section of the Department of the Army. All plans and policies for the enlistment, reception, classification, utilization, training, logistical support, assignment, and separation of WAC personnel are under the immediate supervision of the WAC director. In the course of her duties, Miss Galloway makes regular inspections of all WAC units, detachments, and individuals in both the United States and in overseas posts.

Colonel Galloway on her first official trip since her appointment told the press: "The WAC is accepted and respected by all European women, especially those in occupied Germany. Our work with organized groups in that sector has made up a part of life there. German women have adopted our way of dress and our customs. There has also been a successful exchange of ideas during conferences with Danish, British and French auxiliaries in NATO." She added that "there is a very definite place for women in national affairs today. It may be in the service, or in business, but the world is becoming more aware of feminine abilities."

Colonel Galloway stated that the Army would like to have more WACs. She pointed out that in the early days of the Corps a woman had to be 21 years of age before she could enlist. Today, she can enlist at 18 upon obtaining her parents' consent. However, other qualifications are generally higher than during World War II. Opportunities for travel are extensive in the WAC, she said. Thirty per cent of the WACs are serving overseas in Germany, Austria, France, Italy, Japan, Okinawa, Panama, and Hawaii.

She recalled that when she was in Heidelberg, Germany, "the WACs took a Catholic orphanage under their wing and helped the nuns. To buy shoes and warm clothing for the orphans, 115 WACs raised $800. They also donated a stained glass window to the new Church" (*Catholic Standard,* February 6, 1953).

The WAC director has been awarded the Commendation Ribbon of the Army of Occupation, WAAC, and the World War II American Theater and European Theater ribbons. Described as an "attractive brunette who retains her femininity even while in uniform," the 44-year-old colonel likes to cook, and collect china and porcelain.

References

Catholic Standard F 6 '53
N Y Herald Tribune p7 D 10 '52
N Y Times p19 D 10 '52
Time 60:17 D 22 '52
Official Army Register, 1951

GAMBLE, RALPH A(BERNETHY) May 6, 1885- United States Representative from New York; lawyer

Address: b. House Office Bldg., Washington 25, D.C.; c/o McInnes and Gamble, 551 5th Avenue, New York 17; h. Albee Court, Larchmont, N.Y.

The Twenty-fifth, Twenty-sixth, and Twenty-eighth New York Congressional districts, comprising Bronx and part of Westchester counties in the south-eastern portion of the State, have since 1937 successively been represented in the United States Congress by Ralph A. Gamble of Larchmont, lawyer and former member of the State Assembly. Representative Gamble has

RALPH A. GAMBLE

served on the House Banking and Currency Committee for fifteen years and is the ranking Republican member. Since 1949 the Republican "whip" for New York in the House, he is also the ranking Republican House member of the Joint House-Senate Committee under the Defense Production Act and of the House subcommittee on banking and currency to investigate defective housing under Federal Housing Administration and Veterans' Administration loans. Representative Gamble is a member of the law firm of McInnes and Gamble in Manhattan.

Ralph Abernethy Gamble was born May 6, 1885, in Yankton, South Dakota, the son of the Honorable Robert Jackson and Carrie (Osborne) Gamble. His father, a lawyer in Yankton, was district attorney for the Second Judicial District of the Territory of Dakota, a Republican Representative from South Dakota to the Fifty-fourth and Fifty-sixth United States Congresses, and United States Senator from 1901 to 1913. Ralph Gamble's uncle, John Rankin Gamble, was a Representative from South Dakota to the Fifty-second United States Congress. Young Gamble, who obtained his elementary school education in Yankton public schools, was graduated in 1905 from Tome School for Boys in Port Deposit, Maryland, and in 1909 received a Litt.B. degree from Princeton University, where he was a member of the track team. After attending George Washington University Law School in Washington, D.C., from 1909 to 1911, he entered Columbia University to take his LL.B. degree in 1912. The following year he was admitted to the New York State bar and in 1916 was granted the right to practice in United States District Courts of South Dakota and Southern District of New York.

In New York City, where Gamble began his practice of law, he became secretary to Marlin

GAMBLE, RALPH—*Continued*

Rockwell Corporation, manufacturers of ball bearings. From 1918 to 1934 he was counsel for the town of Mamaroneck in New York and from 1926 to 1928, counsel for the village of Larchmont in New York. Representing the Second District (Westchester County) in New York State, he served in the State Assembly from 1931 to 1937, where he was chairman of the committee on taxation and a member of the rules committee. Meanwhile, he practiced law as a member of the Manhattan firms of Truesdale, Durkin and Gamble (1924-32); Metcalf, McInnes and Gamble (1932-34); and McInnes and Gamble (beginning in 1934). During 1933-34 he was on the New York State Commission for the Chicago World's Fair.

On November 15, 1937, Gamble was sworn in as United States Representative from the Twenty-fifth District of New York to the Seventy-fifth Congress to fill a vacancy caused by the resignation of Charles D. Millard, and on November 24 he was made a member of the House Committee on Banking and Currency. The following month he presented a petition to the House Committee on Foreign Affairs signed by residents of White Plains, New York, asking that the United States keep out of foreign entanglements. On domestic issues coming before the House in December 1937, he voted in favor of amendments to the farm bill and amendments to the National Housing Act. In opposition to the majority of House of Representative members, in May 1938 the Republican Representative supported an amendment to the Agricultural Adjustment Act of 1938, which would grant additional acreage for production of corn in the United States. He was against a Senate bill to provide for the appointment of additional judges to certain United States district courts and circuit courts of appeals and against an amendment authorizing temporary detail of United States civilian employees to the American republics or to the Commonwealth of the Philippines. He voted "yea" on a bill which extended for two and one-half years the 3½ per cent interest rate on certain Federal land bank loans and provided for a 4 per cent interest until July 1, 1940, on Land Bank Commissioner's loans.

Re-elected to the Seventy-sixth Congress in 1939 and renamed to the House Banking and Currency Committee, Representative Gamble presented to the House an editorial from the New York *Times* (April 20, 1939) indicating his opposition to a bill that would extend beyond June 30, 1939, the authority of the President to determine the gold content of the dollar and certain of his powers relating to the stabilization fund. On a bill calling for $2,660,000,000 credits in public works, termed self-liquidating projects by the Administration, Representative Gamble voted "nay." In 1940 he favored passage of a bill for a system of compulsory military training and service, and a bill providing appropriations to expedite strengthening of national defense. In voicing his opposition to the extension of classified executive civil service of the United States, he presented to the House an editorial from the Mamaroneck

Daily Times (October 7, 1940) which compared the increase in Government executive department employees between the years 1933 and 1939. During the Seventy-seventh Congress the New York Representative supported a resolution to continue the committee of investigation of un-American activities, a bill to provide supplemental appropriations for aid to Great Britain, and a bill to further national defense and security by checking excessive price rises and inflationary tendencies.

Gamble's votes and speeches in the House in World War II years, as reported in the *Congressional Record*, show him favoring legislation to curb unions and opposing Government subsidies (1942), arguing against the Civilian Conservation Corps and National Youth Administration (March 1942), and opposing in July 1943 the subsidy bill of the Commodity Credit Corporation, a part of the Price Control Act of 1942. Also in 1943 he voted in favor of the Lend-Lease Act extension for one year (March); a bill to increase the national debt to $125 billion—an increase of $60 billion—to amend the Second Liberty Bond Act (March); extension of the Reciprocal Trade Act for two years (May). Among "yea" votes cast by Gamble in 1944 were those on a bill to permit the regulation of business of insurance to remain within the control of the States; an amendment to the Emergency Price Control and Stabilization Act of 1942 which reduced the fee to landlords for making an overcharge on rents; and an appropriations bill for participation by the United States in the work of UNRRA. In September 1944 he introduced to the House Committee on Military Affairs a bill authorizing appointments to United States Military Academy and Naval Academy of sons of members of land or naval forces of the country who were killed in active service in World War II.

In the first session of the Seventy-ninth Congress in 1945 Representative Gamble voted for the nurses selective service bill to insure adequate nursing care for the armed services (March), a bill to outlaw the poll tax (June), a measure providing antitrust exemption for railroads (December). Manifesting a marked interest in housing problems in the United States, Gamble in 1946 was recorded as in favor of a bill to amend the National Housing Act by adding a new title to prevent speculation and excessive profits in sale of housing, and to make real estate available for housing purposes at fair and reasonable prices. He also voted for a bill to provide 100,000 temporary additional houses for veterans and their families. Other measures supported by Gamble in 1946 were draft extension to 1947 and the $3.75 billion loan to Great Britain. In June 1946 he was named by House Speaker, Sam Rayburn, as a member of the Government committee to participate in the celebration of the Princeton University Bicentennial.

The years 1947 and 1948 were two of the most active Representative Gamble had known in Congress. In January 1947 he was appointed to the Committee on House Administration and to the Joint House-Senate Committee on Printing, while retaining his membership in the House Banking and Currency Committee. As a member of the last-named committee, he was appointed on July 31, 1947, to a fourteen-member Joint House-Senate Committee on Housing, which conducted the first major investigation of housing. Its aim, as stated by Gamble, was "to promote the production of more and better housing at lower prices in the shortest possible time and to submit legislative recommendations to the full Congress by March 15, 1948" (New York *Herald Tribune,* January 11, 1948). The recommendations and data supplied by this committee, of which Gamble was named chairman on August 19, 1947, became the basis of a revision of the general housing laws.

On November 29 Gamble protested to the Export-Import Bank and Secretary of State George C. Marshall that completion of 350,000 American homes was being delayed by shipment to Italy of pig iron which was needed for soil pipe. At a conference of the New York Metropolitan Association of Real Estate Boards, on December 12, 1947, he stated that materials were the greatest increase, 221 per cent, had occurred in lumber. He said that lumber producers were prepared to reduce prices perhaps as much as 25 per cent and that Congress would act, if required, to legalize an industry-wide agreement for such a reduction. Addressing a conference of the National Association of Mutual Savings Banks in 1948, he pointed out that the solution of housing must eventually be a State and local responsibility and that democracy and the capitalist system are inseparable.

By his votes in the first session of the Eightieth Congress (1947) Gamble indicated that he was in favor of the rent control extension bill (May), the Greek-Turkish Aid bill (May), and the *Voice of America* bill (July). During 1947 he introduced a bill to the House Committee on Banking and Currency to end the rationing of sugar for home consumption. In the second session of that Congress (1948) he supported the $6 billion foreign aid authorization (March), the tidelands oil bill (April), the displaced persons bill (June), and the repeal of oleomargarine taxes (April). Gamble in 1949, in which year he was appointed Republican whip for New York in the House, voted "yea" on the trade agreements act extension (February) and on cutting European arms aid 50 per cent (August); and "nay" on the long-range housing bill (June). The following year, in the Eighty-first Congress, he was appointed a member of the Joint House-Senate Committee on Defense Production and a member of the board of visitors to the United States Military Academy. During that Congress he gave his support to a bill to admit Hawaii into the Union, but opposed Statehood for Alaska (March); he was for a $600 million cut in Federal spending (May) and for the Defense Production Act (August).

Gamble's record in the Eighty-second Congress shows his favoring in 1951 a cut in government civil payrolls (April), a measure limiting public housing to 5,000 units (May), a $350 million cut in European economic aid

(August); he voted against a $5.7 billion tax increase (October). During that year he introduced a bill (which was shelved) to abolish the Reconstruction Finance Corporation. In the next session (1952) he cast his votes in support of cutting Federal jobs 10 per cent (April), cutting economic aid for Europe (May), using the Taft-Hartley Act in the steel strike (June), and ending rent controls (June). Reading editorials from the Larchmont *Times* before the House on June 18, 1952, Gamble expressed his agreement with a measure to cut public debt, by a strict curtailment of public improvements in all except necessary cases, and with a Senate joint resolution, introduced by Senator Taft, to provide a constitutional amendment which would limit nonmilitary spending by the Government in any fiscal year to 5 per cent of the estimated national income.

Among articles on housing written by Representative Gamble are "The Federal Government's Fiscal Position in Housing", "A New Housing Policy," and "Housing in America." His organization and club memberships comprise the Larchmont Men's Club, the Larchmont Masonic Lodge, the Princeton University Cottage Club, the Princeton Club of Washington, D.C., the National Republican Club of New York, and Phi Delta Phi. The legislator is secretary and director of Pourier and Lindemen Company and of Forty-two Naught Two Twenty Street Corporation. His church is the Episcopal.

An editorial in the New York *Sun* (October 26, 1946), described Gamble as a "conscientious and hard-working legislator with a record in the House of a man neither reactionary nor radical." On April 19, 1911, he married Virginia Nesbitt (now deceased). His height is five feet nine inches and his weight is 132 pounds. He has blue eyes and gray hair, and speaks with a firm, confident tone. For recreation, he enjoys attending track meets.

References

Biographical Directory of the American Congress, 1774-1949 (1950)
Congressional Directory (1952)
Who's Who in America, 1952-53
World Biography (1948)

GIBSON, HUGH (SIMONS) Aug. 16, 1883- United States Government official; diplomat; author

Address: b. c/o Doubleday & Company, 575 Madison Ave., New York 22; h. 277 Park Ave., New York 17

A veteran of forty-five years of active participation in the field of international affairs, Hugh Gibson now holds as his most recent appointment the directorship of the Provisional Intergovernmental Committee for the Movement of Migrants from Europe, a twenty-nation body formed in December 1951. During the twenty years between the two world wars, Gibson served in many American diplomatic missions in Europe and South America, holding the posts of Minister to Poland, Minister to Switzerland, Ambassador to Belgium, Minister

HUGH GIBSON

to Luxembourg, and Ambassador to Brazil. He has represented the United States at numerous international conferences, including the disarmament talks in the 1920's. During World War II Gibson, while engaged in relief work for war-ravaged countries, also wrote several books and articles (some in collaboration with former President Herbert Hoover) about American foreign policy. In 1943 he became an editor for Doubleday, Doran and Company.

The son of Frank Asbury and Mary (Simons) Gibson, Hugh Simons Gibson was born in Los Angeles, California, on August 16, 1883. Frank Gibson, whose father had emigrated from Scotland, left his native Iowa to go to Los Angeles, where he became a bank cashier. Hugh was educated by private tutors before entering the École Libre des Sciences Politiques in Paris, from which he was graduated in 1907. Gibson's diplomatic career began in July 1908 when he was appointed secretary of the American legation at Tegucigalpa, Honduras. The following year he was assigned to London as second secretary in the American Embassy and then in 1910 returned to the United States to be private secretary to the Assistant Secretary of State in Washington.

At the end of two years (1911-13) in the post of secretary of the United States Legation in Havana, Cuba, Gibson went to Santo Domingo in December 1913 as a member of a special mission to observe elections in that country. Early the next year he was sent as an American legation secretary to Brussels, Belgium, where, following the outbreak of the European war, he helped organize and became a charter member of the Commission for Relief in Belgium, of which he was later named a director. It was also during this Brussels assignment that Gibson took part in the defense of Edith Cavell, the English nurse, who was executed by the Germans despite efforts by the

United States Minister to Belgium, Brand Whitlock, and Gibson to secure a reprieve. He returned to the American Embassy in London in May 1916. Again assigned, in 1917, to the Department of State in Washington, he served as attaché to the British Secretary of State for Foreign Affairs during his United States tour (April-June 1917) and then in the same capacity to the visiting Belgian War Mission (June-August 1917). In March 1918 he was appointed first secretary of the American Embassy in Paris, where he remained until the end of the war.

When Congress in 1918 appropriated $100 million to establish the American Relief Administration to provide food supplies for war-ravaged European countries, Gibson was named director general under chairman Herbert Hoover and was engaged in this work from the time of the Armistice until April 1919. In the eight months before the peace treaty was signed the American Relief Administration distributed nearly five million tons of foodstuffs, valued at $1 billion in twenty-three countries. During this period (1918-19) Gibson was also a member of the first Inter-Allied Mission to investigate conditions in Balkan countries which had been created from the former Austro-Hungarian Empire.

After the signing of the Armistice, Hugh Gibson on April 16, 1919, was appointed Envoy Extraordinary and Minister Plenipotentiary to Poland, where for the next five years (1919-24) he administered much-needed relief measures, assisted American technical advisers on railroads, finances, agriculture, and industry, and informally helped the Polish Government establish itself. Being transferred in the same capacity to Switzerland in 1924, he stayed there for three years (1924-27), during which time he participated in several international conferences concerned primarily with disarmament. As vice-chairman of the American delegation he attended the International Conference for Control of the Traffic in Arms, in Geneva, in 1925; he was chairman of the American delegation to the conference of the Preparatory Commission for Disarmament, which met in 1926-27; in 1927 he was a delegate to the Conference on the Private Manufacture of Arms and chairman of the United States delegation to the Conference for Limitation of Naval Rearmament.

In 1927 Gibson left Switzerland to become the American Ambassador to Belgium and simultaneously Envoy Extraordinary and Minister Plenipotentiary to neighboring Luxembourg, posts that he held until 1933 and again in 1937-38. During the early years of his assignment there, he was a delegate to the London Naval Conference (1930) and two years later was acting chairman of the American delegation to the Disarmament Conference in Geneva. In the mid-1930's Gibson, having been transferred from Europe to South America, occupied the post of United States Ambassador to Brazil (1933-37). As such he became his nation's representative on a mediatory group which met in Buenos Aires in 1935 to end the then seven-year-old Chaco War between Bolivia and Paraguay. Successful where the League of Nations and individual states had failed, this mediatory group arranged a truce, and a peace agreement was signed in August 1936.

Using his knowledge of South America, Gibson wrote the book *Rio* (1937), which the New York *Times* reviewer found "witty, unpretentious, sophisticated, appreciative, and alive," and the *Christian Science Monitor* critic thought could hardly have been written "with more enthusiasm, more understanding or more appreciation for a people and a city." Two years later came the publication of his *Belgium* (1939), described by the New York *Herald Tribune*, as "the best guide to acquaintance with Belgium that the present reviewer has ever seen." Gibson had previously written another book *A Journal from Our Legation In Belgium* (Doubleday, Page, 1917). With the advent of World War II, Gibson left America to become director-general for Europe of both the Commission for Polish Relief and the Commission for Relief in Belgium (1940-41). In 1942 another Gibson book was published, *The Problems of Lasting Peace*, written in collaboration with former President Herbert Hoover. *Time* magazine said the book provided a "sense-making frame to help clarify postwar thinking," while Anne O'Hare McCormick (New York *Times Book Review*) called it "an honest, courageous and comprehensive contribution to a debate that will determine the future of our own country and the world." The thesis of the book was that the Allies could have either peace or revenge—not both.

Among the articles by Gibson which have appeared in popular magazines are "Food Is a Weapon" (*Saturday Evening Post*, February 21, 1942), "Our Diplomatic Mess" (*Collier's*, July 22, 1944), "Senate and Foreign Affairs" (*American Mercury*, August 1944). In collaboration with Hoover he wrote a series of articles, "New Approaches to Lasting Peace," for the June 1943 issues of *Collier's*. "World Peace: Women Can Win It," also written with Hoover, was published in the *Woman's Home Companion* (February 1944).

In 1943 Gibson became an editor on the staff of his publisher, Doubleday, Doran and Company, to work with authors writing about contemporary events.

His book, *The Road to Foreign Policy* (Doubleday, Doran, 1944), stressed the need for more consistent and inclusive American foreign policy and a closer study of the United States' position in world affairs. The New York *Sun* reviewer commented: "No great plan or panacea is offered. It is a realist speaking, one who knows the ropes and wants many more of the American people to get to know them, too." The *Political Science Quarterly* thought that the book was "eclectic," and that "in spots" it was "a wise and mature commentary." Again in collaboration with Hoover, Gibson produced a booklet, *The Basis of Lasting Peace* (1945), about which Harry Hansen wrote in the New York *World-Telegram*: "With commendable brevity and clarity

[the authors] place before the public their views of the essential issues before the San Francisco security conference. . . .Their suggestions are deserving of close study at San Francisco." The New York *Times* critic, remarking that the book "strikes to the heart of the problem before us," pointed out that "behind its persuasive simplicity there is a stateman's vision." Early in 1946 two books appeared in which Gibson had a part: *The Ciano Diaries, 1939-43*, which he edited, and *Soldier of Liberty: Casimir Pulaski* by Clarence A. Manning, to which he wrote the preface.

Gibson, who had given numerous lectures on international subjects before the war, delivered the commencement address at Haverford College (Pennsylvania) in June 1944. Here he repeated a proposal (made in his *Road to Foreign Policy*) for a permanent autonomous Council of National Defense—which would includes representatives of all Government branches dealing with foreign affairs—to maintain and formulate a more coherent American foreign policy. Suggesting that such a council include majority and minority representatives of both Senate and House committees on foreign affairs, he declared: "Under present conditions . . . the Senate is largely ignored until agreements are reached, then is faced with the alternative of accepting a *fait accompli* or being held up to public scorn for obstruction." In the same speech, as reported in the New York *Times* (June 4, 1944), Gibson urged a greater emphasis in schools and colleges on the study of American and world history so that citizens might vote intelligently for men who influence the formulation of policy.

Late in the summer of 1952 Hugh Gibson made a six-week tour of South America, as director of the Provisional Intergovernmental Committee for the Movement of Migrants from Europe, organized by twenty nations in Brussels in December 1951. With a yearly budget of about $40 million, the committee during the first six months moved some 58,040 persons. Since American, Canadian, and Australian immigrations policies have become more restrictive, the committee has been forced to expand its original goal of merely arranging transportation for migrants to include the discovery of new "markets" for them. Seeking such outlets, Gibson made his South American trip and later reported that several South A.`merican countries, eager for an increase in skilled agricultural labor, had expressed an interest in taking as many migrants as could practically be arranged. In an editorial published in September 1952 when Gibson returned from his tour, the New York *Herald . Tribune* called him "well fitted by his long and distinguished career to handle affairs of this sort. . . .The United States and the world can be reassured in having any part of the migration problem intrusted to his capable hands."

In behalf of the Inter-governmental Committee for European Migration, Gibson appealed to the Governments of the United States, Canada and Australia to admit as many immigrants as possible from the Greek islands who

(Continued next page)

GIBSON, HUGH—*Continued*

were forced from their homes by the August 11, 1953 earthquakes.

While in Brussels, Gibson on February 27, 1922, married Ynés Marie Marcelle Reyntiens, a native of that city and daughter of Major Robert Reyntiens, one time head of the military household of Belgian King Leopold II. Mrs. Gibson died on March 19, 1950. There is one son, Michael F. The diplomat holds honorary degrees from Pomona College, Claremont, California, (the M.A. and LL.D.), Louvain University in Belgium (Doctor of Diplomacy and Political Science), the University of Brussels (LL.D.), and Yale University (LL.D.). He is a director of the Belgian-American Educational Foundation and a trustee of the French Institute in America. His clubs are University, Links, and Dutch Treat in New York; Metropolitan in Washington, D.C.; University, Sunset, and Friday Morning in Los Angeles; and Royal Golf in Brussels.

References

International Who's Who, 1952
National Cyclopaedia of American Biography Current vol A (1926)
Who's Who in America, 1952-53
World Biography (1948)

GIDNEY, RAY M(ILLARD) Jan. 17, 1887-
United States Government official

Address: b. Treasury Building, Washington 25, D.C.; h. Hotel Jefferson, 1200 16th St. N.W., Washington 6, D.C.; 19101 Van Aken Blvd, Shaker Heights 22, Ohio

A banker during his entire business career, and president of the Federal Reserve Bank of Cleveland since 1944, Ray M. Gidney was nominated by President Dwight D. Eisenhower to be Comptroller of the Currency on March 27, 1953, succeeding Preston Delano. In addition to banking, Gidney has participated in civic affairs, and was president of the Cleveland Community Fund in 1952.

Ray Millard Gidney was born January 17, 1887 in Santa Barbara, California, the son of Charles Montville and Clara Maude (Jones) Gidney. His father was ninth in descent from John Gidney, who settled in Salem, Massachusetts, in 1637. His mother was also of an old American family. Her ancestors were given a grant of land in Hodgdon, Maine, just after the Revolution.

The Gidneys had moved to Santa Barbara in 1886, where the elder Gidney was active in the real estate and insurance fields, edited a local newspaper and for many years was secretary of the Santa Barbara Chamber of Commerce. Ray Gidney began his banking career at the age of sixteen as a clerk in the Commercial Bank of Santa Barbara. After' five years, he resigned to major in economics at the University of California in Berkeley, and work as a stenographer for the Department of Irrigation. Gidney was elected to Phi Beta Kappa in his junior year, and received a Bachelor of Science degree in 1912.

He joined the First National Bank of Bakersfield, California, where he was employed for two years. In 1914 he went to Washington as secretary to A. C. Miller, a member of the Federal Reserve Board, and subsequently became deputy settling agent and Federal Reserve examiner. He was appointed assistant Federal Reserve agent in the Federal Reserve Bank of New York in 1917, and in 1919 went to Buffalo, New York, to open the Federal Reserve branch in that city and serve as its manager. Gidney returned to New York in 1921, and for nearly two years was controller-at-large in the New York Federal Reserve Bank.

Entering the private banking world in 1923, Gidney became vice-president and director of the Citizens Trust Company in Buffalo and upon its merger with the Marine Trust Company of that city he continued as its vice-president for a short period.

Ray M. Gidney returned to the New York Federal Reserve Bank in 1924, beginning an association that lasted twenty years. In that period he advanced successively to controller-at-large, controller of loans, assistant deputy governor, deputy governor, assistant Federal Reserve agent and finally vice-president. He became president of the Federal Reserve Bank of Cleveland on September 16, 1944 and assumed his duties on November 1 of that year.

Gidney continued as president of the Cleveland branch of the Federal Reserve until he was nominated to his present post. He was confirmed without objection by the United States Senate on April 2, 1953, and took up his duties on April 16, 1953.

The office of the Comptroller of the Currency, which is under the supervision of the Secretary of the Treasury, examines and supervises all national banks, authorizes new national banks, branches, mergers, and consolidations, and the conversion of State banks into national banks. As Comptroller of the Currency, Gidney is one of the three members of the board of the Federal Deposit Insurance Corporation, and is a member of the Federal Reserve Board.

In the first report issued by Ray Gidney after his nomination, it was declared that the 4,890 national banks active in the United States and its possessions had assets amounting to $103,-939,000,000 as of April 20, 1953. Of this figure, Mr. Gidney's report showed that banks had deposits of $94,336,000,000, which was $4,922,-000,000 or 5 per cent less than deposits at the end of 1952. The deposit figure was 4½ per cent more, however, than the figure reported a year ago. Among the deposits were demand deposits of individuals, partnerships and corporations of $53,714,000,000; deposits of the United States Government of $2,376,000,000; net loans and discounts of $36,567,000,000. Investments of the banks in United States Government obligations were $33,471,000,000, or 32 per cent of total assets.

In his annual report on national banks issued August 18, 1953, Gidney criticized some banks which had liberalized personal loan policies "beyond the point of prudence." He also pointed out that some pay-off periods had been too long, and that some payments had been too

RAY M. GIDNEY

low. He added, however, that national banks were in "generally good condition."

Mr. Gidney's office raised objections to recent attempts to amend the Federal Reserve Act through passage of the Cordon-Ellsworth bill, which would permit national banks to make loans of up to ten years on timber tracts. W. M. Taylor, Deputy Comptroller, told a Senate Banking subcommittee, "The Office of the Comptroller of the Currency recommends that loans secured by mortgages on timberlands be restricted to those which will be liquidated from the immediate . . . utilization of mature timber, . . . such loans should not be made for a longer period than three years" (New York *Times,* July 21, 1953). Bankers and lumbermen endorsed the bill.

Gidney has been continuously interested in various civic, educational and welfare organizations. He was treasurer of the Ridgewood (New Jersey) Hospital Association, second vice-president of the Ridgewood Community Fund, and a member of the board of education of Ridgewood from 1930 to 1939 and its chairman from 1939 to 1942. Later Gidney became a trustee and the treasurer of the Cleveland Council on World Affairs, a member of the Cleveland Commission on Higher Education, which is now utilizing a grant of $75,000 by the Cleveland Foundation to study problems of educational institutions in Cleveland. He was also chairman of the 1951 Cleveland Commission to celebrate the 175th Anniversary of the Signing of the Declaration of Independence.

Gidney was a member of the board of trustees and the treasurer of the Cleveland Community Fund, becoming president in 1952. He resigned upon his appointment as Comptroller of the Currency. During his term as president, the Cleveland Community Fund reached its 1952 campaign total of $7,059,000, exceeding its goal by $209,000.

Ray M. Gidney is a member of the American Forestry Association and a life member of the Ohio Forestry Association. He is also a member of the Friends of the Land, Cleveland Health Museum, Cleveland Academy of Political Science, the Philosophical Club, to which he has presented papers on Caudillo or Chieftain in Spanish and Latin American History; and the Philosophy of Land Expropriation with special reference to Mexican History. He is a member of the Fifty and Rowfant Clubs.

His social memberships include the Union Club, Pepper Pike Golf Club, Shaker Heights Country Club, Midday Club, all of Cleveland; and the Burning Tree Club at Washington, D.C. The new Comptroller was the recipient of an honorary Doctor of Laws degree from Western Reserve University, Cleveland, 1953.

Ray M. Gidney was married to Jean Ellison Brock on September 6, 1913. They have three children, James Brock, Dean Robert, and John Archibald. His favorite recreations are golf and reading; he has blue eyes, white hair, is five feet ten inches 'tall and weighs 200 pounds. A Unitarian, he was trustee of the First Unitarian Church of Cleveland. His political affiliation is Republican.

References

N Y Times p12 Mr 28 '53
U S News 34:68 Ap 18 '53
Business Executives of America (1950)
Who's Who in America, 1952-53
Who's Who in Commerce and Industry (1951)

GOERTZ, ARTHÉMISE (gürtz är-tā-mĕs') Nov. 9, 1905- Author

Address: b. Box 177, Mandeville, La., Mc-Graw-Hill Book Co., 330 W. 42d St., New York 36; h. 4440 Lindell Blvd, St. Louis, Mo.

Reprinted from the *Wilson Library Bulletin,* Nov. 1953.

Arthémise Goertz has written of adventure and romance, of heroic men and women; but not one of her characters has had a more adventurous, more tragic, more stirring life than hers. And this almost entirely because of the war. She herself says, "The biggest event of my life was the war as it changed for me the entire course of my destiny. Somehow I ceased to be interested so much in places, and became vitally, earnestly interested in people."

Arthémise Goertz was born November 9, 1905 in New Orleans, Louisiana to John Goertz, of French and Alsatian descent, and Mary Helena (Miller) Goertz, whose parents came to the United States from Hanover, Germany. After attending grade and high school in New Orleans, she received the City of New Orleans scholarship to Newcomb College (Tulane University) and was graduated with a major in Latin and a Phi Beta Kappa key. Her activities in both high school and college included dramatics, debating and the monthly magazine, but "the most athletic thing I did at college

(Continued next page)

ARTHÉMISE GOERTZ

was to run to the library and read, which I did every spare moment."

Her first job was with a steamship company. Sea captains with their gifts of bamboo and teak aroused her interest in the East; and the daughters of the Japanese consul in New Orleans, whom she tutored, stimulated her desire to see the Orient.

Miss Goertz, in the meantime, had married Hector A. Alfonso. He believed in his wife's talent for writing (she herself was not sure, though she had published both stories and articles) and encouraged her to travel in Mexico·and learn to know the people. She wrote of this trip in *South of the Border* (1940), a part-fiction, part-travel narrative account of the visit, when she stayed with friends in small Mexican towns, and shared in their feasts and gaieties. The New York *Times* said of this book, "She has produced something. which is really original because it is open-eyed, individual, and sincere."

In 1939 Miss Goertz accepted a three-year scholarship to the International Student Institute in Tokyo, headed by the consul whose daughters she had tutored and with her mother (her husband planned to follow them as soon as his business allowed) went to Japan. Here, while studying all phases of oriental culture, she became well acquainted with students of all countries, races and creeds, both men and women. Then the war broke out, and all of her student activities ceased. She was forced to burn all of her notes, and two manuscripts. She and her mother were confined under police surveillance. In spite of this, many of their Japanese friends, often at great risk to themselves, continued to be loyal.

At the end of 1943 came repatriation and the trip home on the mercy ship *Gripsholm*. When Miss Goertz with her mother arrived in New York, she was discouraged, destitute, ill with beri-beri. Almost immediately she was told that her husband, who had been called back into service, had just been killed.

For the next two years in order to forget the past, she stayed in New York. Here she wrote *Give Us Our Dream* (1947), the story of Mrs. Marsan who lived happily, watching and meddling in the lives of her neighbors because of the real affection she had for them. Of this book, which became a Literary Guild selection, R. A. Cordell says in the *Saturday Review*: "The story passes swiftly from one vivid episode to another—most of them very funny indeed, the grand coffee party with Adrian's arty talk, Mrs. Marsan's malapropisms and Jessamine's mad irrelevant comments; the hilarious reading aloud of *Tess of the D'Urbervilles* with the sound literary criticism of the cleaning woman, who is listening . . . one could summarize the whole book at this point. But it is much better to read this novel than a summary of it."

In 1948 she published *The Moon is Mine,* the story of Pat Eagan who chose to marry poor Tom Hunter rather than rich Ford Harrison because the former needed her. This novel the New York *Herald Tribune* called "A sentimental little book, but the background is done with surprising realism."

In 1948 Miss Goertz returned to New Orleans, then went to Mandeville, the family summer home. There she wrote *New Heaven, New Earth* (1953), the story of Louisiana in 1909, in which an aristocratic Creole doctor returns from his work in the Canal Zone to face intense opposition when he endeavors to improve the lot of his own people. It was chosen as a Sears Readers Club Selection and Francis A. Klein of the St. Louis *Globe-Democrat* declared, "This story is not only well written, but colorful and exciting with plenty of love interest that is never allowed to get out of hand. The people and the locale have an authenticity that can come only from one who knows this area intimately and thoroughly."

Attractive, blue-eyed Arthémise Goertz is now living in St. Louis, happily keeping house for her second husband, Charles O. Roome, whom she married in 1950, and working on a book about her wartime experiences in Japan. She is five feet six inches tall, weighs 130 pounds and her hair was grayed by the war.

First and foremost her interest is people; that is why she is so interested in the Fulbright Scholarship movement. She hopes that it is a step toward world peace; because as she states, "My friends before the war are my friends today; in the world of ideas there is no room for enmity."

References

Warfel, H. American Novelists of Today (1951)

Author's & Writer's Who's Who, 1948-49

Who's Who (1948-49)

Who's Who in the South and Southwest (1952)

GOLDMAN, FRANK   Dec. 4, 1890-   Organization official; lawyer

Address: b. c/o National Jewish Monthly, 1003 K St., N.W., Washington 1, D.C.; 511 5th Ave., New York 17; 402-404 Sun Bldg., 8 Merrimack St., Lowell, Mass.; h. 30 Florence Rd., Lowell, Mass.

Since 1947 Frank Goldman has been president of B'nai B'rith, the world's largest and oldest Jewish service organization, which has contributed notably toward improving Jewish welfare, perpetuating Jewish culture, and eliminating anti-Semitism. Under Goldman's administration this Jewish fraternal order, of more than 300,000 members, has had an important influence in international affairs, helping to establish the new State of Israel and to obtain German reparations for Nazi persecutions of Jews. A lawyer by profession, Goldman has practiced law in Lowell, Massachusetts, since he was admitted to the bar there in 1912.

Frank Goldman, the son of Maurice and Sarah Goldman, was born in Lowell, Massachusetts, on December 4, 1890. From local public schools in Lowell, he entered Boston University Law School, where, before his twentieth birthday, he received his Bachelor of Laws degree *summa cum laude* in 1910. Since he was too young to practice law in his State, he remained at Boston University until 1912, as a fellow for one year (1910-11) and as an assistant instructor the next (1911-12). Upon being admitted to the Massachusetts bar in 1912, he returned to Lowell, where he established the law practice he still maintains. Later he was for one year (1920-21) Assistant District Attorney of Middlesex County, and for three years (1938-41) president of the Lowell Bar Association. Active also in civic affairs, Goldman was the founder in 1926 of the Lowell Community Center, of which he served as first president (1926-29) and since 1929 as honorary president.

Having joined B'nai B'rith, a Jewish fraternal organization, in 1920, Goldman was elected president of the Lowell lodge in 1926, 1927, and 1928. In 1933 he advanced to the presidency of the B'nai B'rith District, Grand Lodge Number 1 (comprising New York State, all of New England, and eastern Canada), and eight years later (1941) became this district's representative as well as one of three vice-presidents on B'nai B'rith's national executive committee. In this capacity in September 1943, Goldman was a member of the American Jewish Conference delegation which asked Secretary of State Cordell Hull to urge the United States to consider the plight of the German Jews under Hitler and to seek the admission of refugees to Palestine.

A week before the four hundred delegates to the convention of the Supreme Lodge of B'nai B'rith met in Washington, D.C., in May 1947, Henry Monsky, president of the order, died. Goldman, known to be a follower and admirer of Monsky, was chosen by a unanimous vote as the new leader of the organization. As president of B'nai B'rith (which means Sons of the Covenant), Goldman heads the world's largest

FRANK GOLDMAN

and oldest Jewish service organization, founded in New York City in 1843. With branches all over the world, the association has more than 205,000 male members in about 1,000 lodges and approximately 127,000 women members in 629 chapters. In keeping with its purpose of perpetuating and promoting Jewish culture as well as unifying Jewish people on a national and international scale, B'nai B'rith has actively championed the rights of Jews in the United States and abroad, and has made numerous contributions to social welfare on a world-wide basis. Divisions within the organization include: the Anti-Defamation League, whose aim it is to prevent anti-Semitism; the Hillel Foundations, which serve as cultural, social, and religious centers for Jews at 197 American colleges; the youth organizations, which stimulate Judaism among members in about 1,000 communities; and the Vocational Service Bureau, which gives vocational guidance and engages in research on the career problems of Jews. These divisions and the organization as a whole are active in supporting the United Nations, particularly the Human Rights Commission; giving aid to the Government of Israel; and publishing the *National Jewish Monthly*, said to have the largest Anglo-Jewish circulation in America.

A champion of European Jews since he became president, Goldman in his first major address told the delegates of B'nai B'rith's District Number 1 that emergency legislation should be enacted to admit the survivors of Nazi atrocities to the United States. In September 1947 the B'nai B'rith head was appointed to the interim board of directors of the United Service for New Americans (formerly the National Refugee Service), a social service group to aid Jewish refugees. At a testimonial dinner given in his honor by his hometown of Lowell, Goldman pledged the support of his group for the resettlement of displaced persons

GOLDMAN, FRANK—*Continued*

of all faiths, while scoring the "imperialism and politics" which he said was interfering with the establishment of a Jewish state in Palestine. In 1947 he also appeared before a Senate Labor and Public Welfare Committee hearing to urge the passage of a strong Fair Employment Practices Commission bill.

When the majority report of the United States Special Commission on Palestine in 1947 called for the partition of that country into independent Jewish and Arab States with the further recommendation that 150,000 European Jews be immediately admitted into Palestine, Goldman asked President Truman to give official support to this proposal. Later, after the United Nations had agreed to establish a Jewish state in Palestine, the *National Jewish Monthly*, of which Goldman had been editor since 1947, stated in an editorial that President Truman would "go down in history as one of those responsible for righting a historic wrong done to Israel." In an effort to overcome the difficulties and delays in effecting the partition brought about by increased violence in Palestine, Goldman played a leading role at the American Jewish Conference (May 1948), which passed a resolution urging the United States to aid the U.N. in implementing partition. He felt that the United States should, in helping the U.N., lift its arms embargo immediately in order that the people of Israel could have adequate tools for their "defense and survival".

On January 31, 1949, when President Truman signed the United States proclamation recognizing the State of Israel, Goldman was present and received one of the pens used by the President. Since that time, B'nai B'rith has worked to help Israel improve its economic and social conditions and to obtain United States aid toward that goal. Three years after the recognition of Israel, Goldman, who had been re-elected president of B'nai B'rith in 1950, was named a member of a presidium of the Conference on Jewish Material Claims Against Germany, which consisted of representatives from twenty-two leading Jewish organizations in eight Western nations. This group participated in the long discussions at The Hague that resulted in a treaty in September 1952, whereby West Germany agreed to pay $822 million worth of goods over a twelve-to-fourteen-year period to the state of Israel, as reparations for Nazi persecution of European Jews. Out of this amount, the Israel Government promised to pay the conference $107 million, an agreement to which Goldman was one of the signers for the conference on September 9, 1952. He is also a vice-president and a member of the executive committee and the board of directors of this organization, which has been incorporated under the name of Conference on Jewish Material Claims Against Germany, Inc.

Goldman belongs to a number of other organizations concerned with Jewish and Zionist affairs. He is cochairman of the co-ordinating Board of Jewish Organizations for Consultation with the Economic and Social Council of the United Nations (consisting of members from B'nai B'rith, the board of deputies of British Jews, and the South African Jewish board of deputies) and in 1950 was its American spokesman at a London conference. He is on the board of governors of the Hebrew University in Jerusalem and of the Leo N. Levi Memorial Hospital in Hot Springs, Arkansas, and on the board of overseers of the Jewish Theological Seminary of America. Goldman holds the office of vice-president of the National Jewish Hospital in Denver. He is a member of the board of directors of the American Jewish Joint Distribution Committee of the Sara Delano Roosevelt House, and of the United Palestine Appeal. Other public service groups with which he is associated are the board of the American Heritage Foundation (which sponsored the Freedom Train); the National Citizens Committee to Promote Observance of United Nations Day; the executive committee of the conference group of United States National Organizations for the United Nations; the Hospitalized Veterans Foundation; the National Council for a Permanent Fair Employment Practice Commission; the National Association for the Employment of the Handicapped; the National Community Relations Advisory Council; the national committee of the Anti-Defamation League (B'nai B'rith); the Committee on Jewish Service; and the Boy Scouts of America.

At the twentieth triennial convention of B'nai B'rith on May 5, 1953, Frank Goldman retired as president and was succeeded by Philip M. Klutznick.

Married on June 24, 1915, Frank and Rose L. (Sydeman) Goldman have three sons, Robert H., Frederic G., and Edward S. He is a member of the following bar associations: the American, the Middlesex County, the Lowell, and the Massachusetts. He is a former president of Temple Beth El in Lowell, Massachusetts. He belongs to Zeta Beta Tau and is a thirty-second degree Mason.

References

Nat Jewish Mo p352 My '47 por; p134 D '50

Martindale-Hubbell Law Directory, vol I, 1952

Who's Who in America, 1952-53

Who's Who in New England (1949)

Who's Who in the East (1951)

GOTTWALD, KLEMENT Nov. 23, 1896—Mar. 14, 1953 President of Czechoslovakia; one of the founders of the Czech Communist party; became secretary of the party and member of Parliament (1929); Vice-Premier in Cabinet of Premier Fierlinger (1945-46); Premier of Czechoslovakia (July 1946); led Communist coup of February 1948 and replaced Beneš as President on June 1948. See *Current Biography*, 1948.

Obituary

N Y Times p1 Mr 15 '53

GOUGH, LEWIS K(ETCHAM) (gŏf)
Apr. 21, 1908- Veterans organization official;
tax appraiser

Address: b. c/o American Legion National
Headquarters, 700 N. Pennsylvania St., Indianapolis 6, Ind.; h. 737 Old Mill Road, Pasadena 9, Calif.

The fourth consecutive World War II veteran to hold the office, Lewis K. Gough was
unanimously elected national commander of the
American Legion at the organization's thirty-
fourth annual convention, held in New York
City in August 1952. Gough has been active in
Legion affairs since 1945 when he ended his
four-year tour of duty in the United States
Navy with the rank of commander. In the last
five years Gough has advanced in the Legion
from his position as commander of a local
Pasadena Post (1947-48) to become successively
a district commander, the department commander of California, and national vice-commander in 1950-51. While serving his year
(1952-53) as national commander, Gough is on
leave of absence from his position as State
inheritance tax appraiser for California.

Lewis Ketcham Gough was born April 21,
1908, in Los Angeles, the son of Robert Willard Gough, a salesman, and Hazel (Ketcham)
Gough, of Welsh and English ancestry. After
attending city schools and being graduated from
Los Angeles High School in 1926, he entered
the University of Southern California in the
same city. There elected to Phi Kappa Phi,
honorary scholastic fraternity, and awarded the
Trojan Diamond Medal for scholarship and
leadership, he also belonged to the Skull and
Dagger, Blue Key, and Trojan Knights (honorary society). He served as president of his
university student body and as vice-president
of the Western Student Body Presidents Association in 1931, the same year he received his
B.S. degree with honors in business administration.

For nine years (1931-40) following his graduation Gough remained on the University of
Southern California campus, working as an
assistant to the president, as a public relations
officer, and as executive director of the university's alumni association. (He is currently
serving on the association's board of directors.)
Joining the Navy in 1941, Gough was graduated
from the United States Naval War College,
became an instructor there, and later saw active
duty on the staffs of Vice-Admiral W. S. Pye
and Rear Admiral I. C. Johnson. When he
had completed his wartime service, with the
rank of commander, Gough returned to civilian
life in 1945 and took his present position as
California State inheritance tax appraiser
(from which he has been granted a year's
leave of absence to serve as 1952-53 national
commander of the American Legion). Gough,
whose interest in naval affairs continued, in
1946 organized and commanded the 11th Battalion of the United States Naval Reserve
(11th Naval District); two years later he was
appointed by Secretary of the Navy John L.
Sullivan as a member of the United States
Navy Civilian Research Commission. Con-

Maryland Studio

LEWIS K. GOUGH

cerned also with the welfare of former fighting
men, Gough served as a World War II consultant to the American Legion's executive committee and as vice-chairman of the National
Security Convention Committee. This interest
prompted his appointment to the California
State Veterans Board. In the last five years
Gough has risen in the American Legion from
his office as commander of the local Pasadena
Post No. 13 (1947-48) to become commander
of California's 18th District (1948-49) and
then department commander of California
(1949-50), where he was on the public relations and defense commissions. The first position held by Gough in the national Legion was
that of a vice-commander in the year 1950-51.

On August 28, 1952, Gough was elected national commander of the American Legion for
the 1952-53 year at the thirty-fourth annual
national convention held in Madison Square
Garden, New York City. Of the five candidates for the Legion's highest post, only one
was considered to be a major contender—Walter E. Alessandroni, a Philadelphia attorney
and former Marine captain. Alessandroni conceded defeat midway through the first roll call
of the States' representatives. After the first
ballot, with an unofficial count of 2,674 votes for
Gough and 435 for his opponent, Alessandroni
moved that the new commander's election be
made unanimous, and the delegates so voted.
As national commander of the American Legion, Gough heads the world's largest veterans'
organization, comprising about three million
members in approximately 17,000 local posts
Granted its national charter by Congress in
1919, the Legion is described as "an organization of World War veterans who served in the
armed forces of the United States or who as
American citizens entered the armed forces of
a Government associated with the United States
in the war" (*Encyclopedia Britannica*). The

GOUGH, LEWIS K.—*Continued*

Legion's activities include fostering educational projects, sponsoring boys' activities, giving emergency relief to flood sufferers, promoting various civic enterprises, and erecting community center buildings, athletic fields, and airports.

After outgoing Commander Donald R. Wilson placed the national commander's red cap on Gough's head, the new commander made a brief acceptance speech in which he stated that the United States "faces its greatest challenge—a life and death struggle with communism on , world-wide basis—and no quarter can be asked or given" (New York *Herald Tribune*, August 29, 1952). Gough pledged the Legion to continue its "all-out effort" to promote a program of universal military training, on the premise that military preparedness was the best insurance for world peace. He urged the United States to fight the "war of ideas" against the Soviet Union at home as well as abroad, by maintaining vigilance over the public school system. "We recognize that the problem of curriculum is primarily the concern of educators," he said, "but we also recognize the right and obligation that is ours to see that what is taught, and who teaches it, will lay the proper foundation which determines the future of America" (New York *Times*, August 29, 1952).

The month after his election the new American Legion commander addressed the seventy-first convention of the American Federation of Labor, at which he urged the 800 delegates to join the Legion in its fight against subversion. In discussing the Korean War, Gough recommended the use of atomic weapons, should it be necessary for victory, the employment of Chinese Nationalist troops, and the bombing of Manchurian bases beyond the Yalu River. "The only way to justify that war is to end it," Gough said. "That means carrying the war to the enemy with no holds barred" (New York *Herald Tribune*, September 18, 1952). The next month Gough flew to the Far East, arriving in Tokyo on October 25, 1952, for a five-day tour of the Korean battlefront. In the Japanese capital he expressed this opinion: "The United Nations should give the Communists in Korea an ultimatum and if the Reds fail to make peace we should use every weapon available" (New York *Times*, October 26, 1952). In Formosa on November 3, he recommended that the Nationalist air force be built up for offensive action.

Back in the United States later in November, Gough during American Education Week advised parents to "seek a better understanding and appreciation of the importance of the schools in building good American citizens." Emphasizing the need for continuing cooperation on educational problems by the Legion and the National Education Association, Gough declared: "Believing that an intelligent and informed citizenry is our best guarantee against every attempt to destroy freedom and liberty, our two organizations must continually work together in safeguarding and improving education in America." A few days later at the Armistice day ceremony in the amphitheater

beside the Tomb of the Unknown Soldier in Arlington National Cemetery, Gough repeated the idea that a time limit should be put on the Korean truce talks and then if the stalemate continues the United States should make a total effort to win the war.

Lewis K. Gough married Marguerite Shipley on April 14, 1937. He is five feet eleven inches tall, weighs 175 pounds, has brown hair and brown eyes. His Greek letter societies are Chi Phi (social fraternity), and Alpha Kappa Psi and Alpha Delta Sigma, (professional fraternities). In 1952 the French Government awarded him the Medal of Liberation of France. A Free and Accepted Mason (Carmelita Lodge), Gough belongs to the A.A.O.N.M. Shrine (Al Malaikah Temple). He belongs also to Native Sons of the Golden West and of the Forty and Eight (Voiture 104). He is a Methodist and a Republican. His favorite sports are swimming and golf.

The American Legion national commander returned from a twenty-three day tour of Europe on August 26, 1953, and urged the Western allies to take Spain and West Germany into "full partnership" in the North Atlantic Treaty Organization.

GRANT, GORDON (HOPE) N. A. June 7, 1875- Painter, etcher, lithographer
Address: 137 E. 66th St., New York 21, N.Y.

Few contemporary artists have equalled the skill of Gordon Grant as a painter of ships, harbors and men of the sea. He is represented in the major art museums of the United States and his painting of the frigate *Constitution* hangs in the President's office in the White House in Washington, D.C. For the past twenty-five years his pictures have been exhibited each year at the Grand Central Art Galleries in New York City. He has written and illustrated many books about the history of sailing ships.

Gordon Hope Grant was born in San Francisco, California, on June 7, 1875, of Highland Scottish ancestry. His father, George Grant, came from Scotland in 1866 as an agent of the Bank of British North America to Barkerville, the Cariboo mining country. His mother, Grace Adelaide (Griffin), was born in Australia, and was married to Grant in Victoria, B.C. They later settled in San Francisco, where the senior Grant became an officer of the Wells Fargo Nevada National Bank of San Francisco.

His father was closely connected with the sea, and with seafaring men, and Sunday dinner usually meant one or more sea captains as guests. When the elder Grant decided that his son should be educated in Scotland, Gordon made the voyage from San Francisco around the Horn on a big full-rigged Glasgow sailing ship. He was then thirteen years of age.

Recalling that experience in later years, Grant said, "I was not a member of the crew, simply a guest of the Captain, but I lacked not for odd jobs in the four-and-a-half month passage. What that voyage did to an imaginative youngster was not long in manifesting itself, for when my art training began, the salt in me came out and a stored-up fund of impressions has served me well through the subsequent years of paintings the sea and sailors."

After graduating from Kirkcaldy school in Tifeshire, Scotland, young Grant spent another two years studying in the Heatherly and the Lambeth Art Schools in London. In 1895 the budding marine painter spent one year as a staff artist on the San Francisco *Examiner* and *Chronicle*. In 1896 when he came to New York City he was engaged as staff artist by the old New York *World*. When the Boer War broke out *Harper's Weekly* sent him as a special artist to the front. From 1901 to 1909 the tall, sandy-haired, gray-eyed artist was on the staff of *Puck* where he did general illustrating and occasional painting.

His service to his country began in 1907 when he joined the Seventh Regiment National Guard and served on the Mexican border. During the First World War he did not go overseas with his regiment because of a foot disability. He was commissioned a Captain in the special branch of the General Staff in Washington, D.C., serving until 1918.

Since 1920 he has devoted his time to painting, etching and lithography. A judgment of the work of this artist is recorded in *Art Instruction* July 1937: "Grant has technical knowledge of seacraft which is the envy of many an old salt, and his drawings and paintings and prints have made him famous in the art world."

Carlyle Burrows, senior art critic of the New York *Herald Tribune* stated, "Gordon Grant who exhibits water colors regularly knows the harbor subjects and boats so well that he rarely misses giving a convincing and successful display of his work." He continued, "Grant's wide appeal is evident in show after show" not only by the quality of his work but by the quantity of little red stickers denoting 'sold' which were pasted on thirty of his forty new exhibits" (New York *Herald Tribune*, December 3, 1944). Art publications report that the sellout of Grant's pictures usually occurs in the very first week of each show.

His paintings have been exhibited in New York each year since 1928 at the Grand Central Galleries, the long-established home of contemporary artists of acknowledged repute. By virtue of the sales of his paintings over five decades, the artist is represented in innumerable private collections as well as in notable public collections.

Grant believes that a picture, to best fulfill its purpose, must be the playground for the spectator's imagination. In an article in *The Lookout* (September 1932) he wrote: "Many a man, carried off for the moment by the brilliant execution of a picture, has bought it and hung it in the best position in his house. In course of time he has wondered why it no longer interests him. The answer is not far to seek. It has no mystery. The painter put everything in and left nothing for the owner to supply."

The New York *Times*, in reporting Grant's annual show of watercolors in December, 1945, wrote: "The veteran Gordon Grant's work at

William Kahn

GORDON GRANT

the Grand Central Galleries for freshness and vigor holds up well with most of his more youthful competitors. The light in *Sailing Party*, the translucence of *Icing the Boat*, the fishing craft close-hauled and taking it white, the violence of *Surging Surf* and the small boat slugging back to the mother vessel . . . all show no falling off in the caliber of his work."

Of this prolific artist Burrows wrote, "Grant's subjects come from Gloucester and Rockport on the New England coast, a veritable happy hunting ground for the painter of boats and harbors. The pictures suggest the scene's picturesqueness, are well composed, full of atmosphere and luminous in color . . . the results are notably well achieved and without a trace of affectation."

Old Ironsides, a painting of the famous frigate *Constitution,* hangs in the President's office in the White House. The work was painted by Grant in 1927, and color reproductions were made and sold to raise funds to finance work on the repair of *Old Ironsides* which had been neglected for many years. Over a quarter of a million copies were sold.

Another of Gordon Grant's well known paintings is *Eternal Sea,* which is in the Chapel of the Seamen's Church Institute of New York. Commenting on this picture, the artist wrote: "I felt that the position of this painting—behind the altar—was too important to devote to an incident in Biblical history unless it were treated as pure design. Considering my (seafaring) audience, I was convinced that its treatment should be realistic and proclaim Space—Light—Creation—Eternity—Sky and Sea—the sailors' Be All and End All. Furthermore, the picture must light the chancel; therefore it must be warm in tone and harmonize with its surroundings—yellows—reds—bronze and gold. How many have seen a yellow sky—a bronze ocean—red clouds? What matter? Does it give you pleasure to look at it? Does it suggest

GRANT, GORDON—*Continued*

something beyond the mere works of man? I hope so. That's what I strove to put into it."

Grant has demonstrated his writing ability in a number of books which he also illustrated. He is the author of *Sail Ho, Greasy Luck, Ships Under Sail, The Secret Voyage,* stories of life on board square-riggers. He has illustrated others: *City Boy* by Herman Wouk, *Eternal Sea* by William M. Williamson, *There Go The Ships* by Robert Carse, and several juvenile books. In collaboration with Henry B. Culver he wrote *The Book of Old Ships,* which contains seventy drawings of historic vessels, and five color plates, and *Forty Famous Ships*; and *Ship Ahoy* with Harold Platt.

During his long career Grant has received many awards including the Silver Medal for Etching at the Paris Exposition of 1937, the Ranger Purchase Award of the National Academy of Design; the Chauncey F. Ryder prize of the American Water Color Society; the Shaw prize of the Salmagundi Club (1931 and 1936); the $500 prize Chicago Society of Etchers, 1936; the anonymous members' prize of the Society of Allied Artists of America, 1943. Two of his watercolors were purchased in 1950 by the Metropolitan Museum of Art.

In 1925 Grant made a voyage on an old windjammer, *Star of Alaska,* one of the Alaska Packers "Star" Fleet to Chignik, on the Aleutian peninsula. Many of the sketches in his book, *Sail Ho* (1931) were made on board, using as models the crew of salmon fishermen.

Some of his paintings hang in the Metropolitan Museum of Art, the Library of Congress, New York Historical Society, New York Public Library, and in Art Museums in Omaha, Nebraska; Madison, Indiana; Richmond, Indiana; Memphis, Tennessee; and New Britain, Connecticut.

He has been elected to membership in many organizations in the art world, among which are the National Academy of Design, American Society of Graphic Artists, Chicago Society of Etchers, Allied Artists of America, American Water Color Society, Audubon Artists, and others. He is an honorary member of the Dutch Treat Club and honorary life member of the Salmagundi Club, and a life member of the National Arts Club. He founded The Ship Model Society of New York, the parent of the present Marine Museum of the City of New York, of which he is a trustee and the curator.

Grant is a Presbyterian. In 1901 he married Violet Maude Goodall, an actress who had appeared with Augustin Daly and Olga Nethersole. The theatre has been one of his interests, and, as a member and officer of the Amateur Comedy Club of New York, he has designed scenery and costumes, written plays, acted in and directed many productions. He is known in the art world as a gifted raconteur. Another of his hobbies is building ship models in which he applies his technical knowledge of ships to the era of the whaling vessel and the windjammer.

References

Art Digest 9:12 O 15 '34
Creative Art O '27
The Lookout 23:1 S '32; 36:3 N '45
Grant, G. Sail Ho (1931)
Who's Who in New York, 1952
Who's Who in American Art 1940-47

GRANVILLE, WILLIAM SPENCER LEVESON-GOWER, 4TH EARL July 11, 1880—June 25, 1953 Former Governor of Northern Ireland, from 1945 to 1952; Lieutenant Governor of the Isle of Man from 1937 to.1945; retired as Vice-Admiral from British Navy in 1935 after serving forty-one years; uncle of Queen Elizabeth II by marriage to the former Lady Rose Bowes-Lyon, elder sister of Queen Mother Elizabeth. See *Current Biography*, 1950.

Obituary

N Y Times p19 Je 26 '53

GREEN, WILLIAM Mar. 3, 1873—Nov. 21, 1952 President of the American Federation of Labor; as a youth worked in Ohio coal mines; joined United Mine Workers union in 1890; U.M.W. subdistrict president (1900-06), Ohio district president (1906-10); served two terms in Ohio State Senate, where as Democratic floor leader won enactment of Ohio Workmen's Compensation Law; U.M.W. international secretary-treasurer (1912-24); became a vice-president and a member of the executive council of the AFL (1913); as president of the AFL since 1924 favored a policy of encouraging Government assistance; recipient of Roosevelt Memorial Association Medal for service in keeping industrial peace (1930). See *Current Biography*, 1942.

Obituary

N Y Times p1+ N 22 '52

GREENBAUM, LUCY *See* Freeman, L. G.

GUZMAN, JACOBO ARBENZ *See* Arbenz, J.

HAAS, FRANCIS J(OSEPH), BISHOP Mar. 18, 1889—Aug. 28, 1953 Bishop of the Roman Catholic diocese of Grand Rapids, Michigan; ordained St. Francis Seminary (Milwaukee), 1913; Ph.D. Catholic University, 1922; taught at St. Francis Seminary; Marquette University and at the School of Social Science at Catholic University; chairman of the President's World War II F.E.P.C. Committee; chairman of the Michigan Committee on Civil Rights; founder and co-chairman of the Council Against Intolerance in America; member of the National Recovery Administration and the National Labor Relations Board. See *Current Biography*, 1943.

Obituary

N Y Times p88 Ag 30 1953

HAGERTY, JAMES C. May 9, 1909- White
House press secretary
Address: b. The White House Office, Washington 25, D.C.; h. 5010 Reno Rd., Washington, D.C.

The designation by President-elect Dwight D. Eisenhower of James C. Hagerty to be Press Secretary to the President in the incoming Republican Administration was announced on November 27, 1952. On leave of absence as press secretary to New York's Governor Thomas E. Dewey, Hagerty had handled General Eisenhower's press relations since his return from Paris in June 1952 and had accompanied the Republican candidate on his campaign trips. As a writer for the New York *Times* from 1934 to 1943, he covered a number of State election campaigns and the 1940 Presidential campaign and gained a reputation as a top-ranking political correspondent before becoming Dewey's press secretary in 1943.

One of the three sons of James A. Hagerty, a newspaperman, and Katherine S. (Kearney) Hagerty, a school teacher, James C. Hagerty was born in Plattsburg, New York, on May 9, 1909. When he was three years old, the family moved to New York City, where his father joined the staff of the New York *Herald*. The elder Hagerty remained with that paper until becoming associated in 1920 with the New York *Times*, on the staff of which he is in 1953 a senior political writer. Young James attended grade school in the Bronx and the Evander Childs High School before enrolling at Blair Academy, Blairstown, New Jersey, for his last two years of high school training. After graduation in 1928 he went to work on the New York Stock Exchange, where, according to a statement made in the New York *Herald Tribune*, Hagerty "acquired a dubious feeling about the investment business as it stood in the early thirties." Deciding to continue his education in another field, he studied at Columbia University, from which he received his B.A. degree in 1934.

While at Columbia, Hagerty became a campus correspondent for the New York *Times*, and during the summers he worked for the City News Association as a district reporter. Upon graduation he secured a position as a reporter on the New York *Times* city staff, assigned to cover political news. In 1938 he was appointed to the position of legislative correspondent for that paper in Albany, a post he held until 1942. During this period he covered several State elections, Governor Thomas E. Dewey's preconvention campaign of 1940, and the Willkie Presidential campaign of the same year.

In Albany Hagerty's work had brought him into association with Governor Dewey, who in 1943 appointed the *Times* political correspondent to the position of press secretary to the Governor. Earlier as District Attorney in New York City, Dewey had acquired a reputation of being unpopular wth newsmen because of his "noncommital attitude." Hagerty is credited with having done much to improve Dewey's relationship with the press after the Governor had entered the field of national politics. With his understanding of the problems of jour-

Wide World Photos
JAMES C. HAGERTY

nalism, Hagerty made himself available to newspapermen at all times, handled news dispatches from the Governor's office in an orderly way, arranged for reporters to get speeches ahead of time, and after making an official release or announcement remained in the press room to answer questions or supply explanations. He served Dewey as press-contact man in the Presidential campaign in 1944 and the Gubernatorial campaign in 1946.

During the Presidential campaign of 1948 the *World-Telegram* said of him, "Newspapermen rate young Jim Hagerty one of the most efficient public relations men ever to run that side of a Presidential campaign . . . his counsel frequently is sought at top-level Dewey strategy conferences." One of Hagerty's duties in dealing with the 200 to 300 reporters covering national politics and the eighty newsmen traveling on the Dewey campaign train, was seeing to it that speeches were rushed to the mimeographing machines and from them to the correspondents. Hagerty's recipe for working with the press was a simple one, as reported in *Time*: "Make it as easy as possible for them to get what they want—and don't lie." He remained with Dewey after the election as press secretary in the Gubernatorial campaign of 1950.

Upon the return of Dwight D. 'Eisenhower from Paris in June 1952, Hagerty was "loaned" by Dewey to the General to take charge of press relations before and during the Republican National Convention in Chicago in the summer of 1952. After Eisenhower had been nominated as President of the United States, Hagerty accompanied the candidate to the Republican headquarters in Denver, traveled with him on a campaign tour throughout the country, and later set up an office at the New York headquarters. When President-elect Eisenhower took a vacation in Georgia after the Republican victory in the November election, he invited Hagerty, still

HAGERTY, JAMES C.—*Continued*

"on leave" from Governor Dewey, to accompany him in the post of press secretary. Here Hagerty was called upon by pressmen to discuss the matter of patronage, applications in the hundreds having been sent to Republican headquarters, and also such questions as the General's projected trip to Korea and the recent atom bomb explosion on Eniwetok atoll.

The announcement on November 27, 1952, of Eisenhower's selection of Hagerty for the post of White House press secretary in the new Republican Administration was well received by the press. In an editorial on November 29, the New York *Times* called the appointment, which demands expert handling of the details of liaison with press, radio, and television, "a tribute to Mr. Hagerty's ability, integrity, and intelligence, qualities that will go far in this confidential and sensitive position, to make the new Administration successful. . . . Hagerty is solidly grounded in Government and can be expected to give sound advice beyond the limits of his title of office." Since, in the view of newsmen, the number of Eisenhower's conferences during his campaign had been insufficient, one of the foremost questions confronting Hagerty after his appointment concerned the frequency and conditions under which the new President would make himself available to meet press correspondents. All rumors that Eisenhower intended to curtail Presidential press conferences were dispelled by Hagerty by an announcement on January 21, 1952, that Eisenhower would hold regular news conferences and would allow "live" broadcasts of television and radio in some of the sessions. He also disclosed the President's intention to have members of the Cabinet available to give information when questions pertaining to their offices were raised.

On February 17, 1953, the President's press aides Hagerty and Murray Snyder were the only members of the Government staff who accompanied Eisenhower at his first White House press conference. For a period after the inauguration Hagerty was called upon to act as Mrs. Eisenhower's social secretary, pending the appointment of a full staff for the First Lady.

Hagerty was married to Marjorie Lucas on June 15, 1937; they have two boys, Roger C. and Bruce C. The press secretary is an Episcopalian; he is a member of Delta Kappa Epsilon. He has been described as short, heavyset, and good-natured. Poker playing and golf are among his leisure time activities.

References

Christian Sci Mon p9 Ap 2 '47
Look 8:26 Jl 11 '44; 12:23 Ag 31 '48
N Y Herald Tribune II p3 N 16 '52 por; p6 N 28 '52
N Y Post Mag p2 Ja 25 '53
N Y Times p22 N 28 '52 por
Newsweek 46:23 D 8 '52; 23:46 Je 26 '44
Who's Who in America, 1952-53

HALL, JOYCE C(LYDE) Dec. 29, 1891-
Greeting card manufacturer

Address: b. Hall Brothers, Inc., 25th and Grand Ave., Kansas City, Mo.; h. 110th and State Line, R.R. No. 1, Kansas City, Mo.

Starting his career as a greeting card publisher forty years ago, Joyce C. Hall, President of Hall Brothers, Inc., has seen his company grow into the largest greeting card concern in the world, producing more than 1,500,000 cards a day, and employing about 2,500 people. Under Hall's leadership the firm pioneered in developing modern display racks for cards and fancy wrappings for gift packages, in advertising on radio and television, and in employee welfare. Hall Brothers was the first to present cards illustrated by well-known artists, and to sponsor an international fine arts contest. In 1950 Hall scored an industry "coup" by contracting with the Right Honorable Winston S. Churchill for the use of his paintings on Hallmark Christmas cards. Plans of the firm in 1953 include the construction of a six million dollar plant across the street from its main building in Kansas City, Missouri to keep up with its expanded production.

Joyce Clyde Hall was born on December 29, 1891, in David City, Nebraska, the son of George Nelson Hall and Nancy (Dudley) Hall. Joyce, his two older brothers, and his sister were brought up by their mother, a widowed semi-invalid. From the age of ten, he worked after school and on weekends in a stationery store owned by his brothers William and Rollie in Norfolk, Nebraska, and at fourteen pooled his savings of $158 with equal amounts contributed by his brothers to open an agency for selling cards. During school vacations young Hall went on the road as a salesman for scenic picture postcards, selling also a sawdust sweeping compound as a sideline, under the name "The Norfolk Brokerage Co., J. C. Hall, Manager."

By 1910, when he was graduated from high school, Joyce had accumulated a capital of $3,500 with which he established a business as a jobber of postcards while attending business college at night in Kansas City. Realizing that quality greeting cards were becoming increasingly popular, he went into partnership with his brother Rollie in 1913 to sell their own Christmas cards with the "Hallmark" label. However, after a year in which they were beset by financial difficulties, the plant was completely destroyed by fire, leaving them a deficit of $17,000. A further serious setback came when the firm's largest supplier of greeting cards discontinued the Hall brothers' services as jobbers at the beginning of the Christmas selling season. It became necessary to supply their own cards, and from this experience they concluded that there was a demand for more attractive, personalized greeting cards than those offered on the market at that time. In 1916 they bought a small engraving plant and began to manufacture cards under the name of "Hall Brothers Paper Craft."

Their business prospered, and when America entered World War I, a large demand for "missing you" cards and other greetings to soldiers overseas "rocketed the small business to industrial stature," according to *Coronet.* In 1921, the third brother, William, came from Nebraska to join the company as office manager, and the firm also opened a retail store on Petticoat Lane in Kansas City. The company continued to expand throughout the mid-West, and by 1922 they were operating with a staff of 120 employees. Rollie Hall's idea of using fancy wrappings for gift packages, (now standard marketing practice) was introduced, resulting in many important accounts in large retail stores. On entering the national greeting card market in Missouri on June 11, 1923, the concern was incorporated as the Hall Brothers Company, the three brothers being the stockholders.

By 1924 the company had achieved a nationwide reputation for its "Hallmark" cards. It had moved to a five-story building and, as it expanded, additional space was rented from a nearby building (*Swing* magazine). Observing during his business trips that greeting card counters were usually in disorder and placed in inconspicuous corners of stores, Hall developed the Eye-Vision Display Fixture, which proved an immense stimulus to sales. The Hall firm had become so large by 1936 that it purchased the Willys-Overland Building in Kansas City, a million dollar six-story structure, and by 1937 was employing 950 people.

Joyce Hall pioneered in the use of radio and television for advertising greeting cards. His firm sponsored the Tony Wons show in 1937 and numerous programs in later years, including the wartime "Meet Your Navy" show, the Hallmark Radio Readers' Digest, the Hallmark Playhouse, and the Hallmark Hall of Fame television program. The Hall Brothers were first to use Walt Disney characters on greeting cards, to utilize the work of noted artists like Norman Rockwell and "Grandma" Moses on Christmas cards, and also to make unfolding cards which tell a story. In 1949 the concern sponsored a Christmas theme art contest for French and American painters which *Cue* characterized as "the biggest international art competition ever held." Some $30,000 in prize money was awarded to the best among 10,000 artists. A second Hallmark Art Award Competition, sponsored by the United States National Commission for the United Nations' Educational, Scientific and Cultural Organization, was opened in 1952 to artists from North and South America and Western Europe, in the medium of water color.

Hall contracted with the Right Honorable Winston Churchill in 1950 for the use of his paintings on Christmas cards. He claims that there was no mystery about the deal. "We merely made him an offer which he graciously accepted," he explained. (*Pathfinder*, December 13, 1950).

Noted for his fatherly concern for the welfare of his company's employees, of whom about seventy-five per cent are women, Hall has introduced such benefits as low-cost balanced luncheons, group discussions, counsel on income tax problems, and a personal service department.

Wide World Photos

JOYCE C. HALL

The company's art department of 150 individuals designs about 5,000 different types of cards yearly. Approximately 500 varieties of St. Valentine's Day greetings have been manufactured in a single year, and in the same period six different cards for tonsillectomy patients were produced. Hall Brothers now produces about 1,500,000 cards every day. As an indication of the growth of the greeting card industry in the past two decades, the increase in sales of Hall Brothers in 1950 alone was greater than the company's total sales in 1935.

Joyce Hall is chairman of the board of Safety Federal Savings and Loan, and is a director of the Johnson County Bank. He is a member of the boards of the University of Kansas City, Pembroke Country Day School, the Helping Hand Institute, Drake University, the Midwest Research Institute, and the Eisenhower Foundation. He is a past president of the Kansas City Rotary Club, and is a member of the National Association of Greeting Card Publishers. Hall is a trustee of the Kansas City Art Institute, encouraging the students by maintaining thirty-eight scholarships and by frequently employing graduates. He received in 1946 the King's Medal for wartime services in the interest of the British Commonwealth, and in 1949 became a member of the American Society of the French Legion of Honor.

Hall is a Mason (Shriner), a member of the Rotary, Kansas City Country, River, and Saddle & Sirloin clubs. He married Elizabeth Dilday of Kansas City on March 25, 1922, and their three children are Barbara (Mrs. Robert Marshall), Elizabeth Ann (Mrs. Richard Schaffer), and Donald, who served in 1952 with the United States Army in Japan. Hall attends the Christian Church. His hobbies are horseback riding, badminton, boating, and fishing. His summer residence is at Echo Lodge, Colorado, located

HALL, JOYCE—*Continued*

on Grand Lake, 8,153 feet above sea level. In addition to his apartment in Kansas City, Hall has a farm on Indian Creek on which he has built a house in the style of a southern plantation manor. He makes occasional trips to Canada, Hawaii, and Europe. Hall has blue eyes and gray hair, is six feet tall, and weighs 175 pounds.

"More people use greeting cards than use coffee," Mr. Hall remarked in an interview (New York *Times*, December 11, 1949). "The purpose of the Hallmark contests is to encourage fine art, and to broaden and deepen public appreciation. The more art people see, the more they will understand it."

References

Bsns W p89 D 16 '50
Coronet 26:143-6 Ag '49
Kansas City Star O 23 '49 por
N Y Times III p2 Ag 13 '50 por; III p9 N 30 '52 por
Pathfinder 57:42 D 13 '50
Swing 8:430-44 '52 por
Time 55:78 F 13 '50 por
Who's Who in Commerce and Industry (1951)

Wide World Photos
LEONARD W. HALL

HALL, LEONARD W(OOD) Oct. 2, 1900-
Political party leader; lawyer
Address: b. Republican National Committee headquarters, Washington 25, D.C.; h. 147 Anstice St., Oyster Bay, New York

Unanimously elected chairman of the Republican National Committee on April 10, 1953, Leonard Wood Hall succeeded to the post left vacant by Charles Wesley Roberts, who resigned on March 27. Prior to his election as Republican party leader, Hall was Surrogate (probate judge) of Nassau County, New York, an office which he relinquished in order to serve the G.O.P. without pay. He had been a United States Representative from New York 2nd District from 1939 until 1952, and was elected chairman of the Republican Congressional Campaign Committee in 1947.

Other elective offices which he held included that of New York State Assemblyman from 1927 to 1928, and from 1934 to 1938, and Sheriff of Nassau County from 1929 to 1931. Known among his friends as a man eager for hard work and action, he has been described as "the Republican's Jim Farley" (*Time*, April 20, 1953).

Leonard Wood Hall, the son of Franklyn Herbert and Mary Garvin Hall, was born on October 2, 1900, at Oyster Bay, New York. Hall's father was a coachman for President Theodore Roosevelt, and later rose to the position of White House librarian. He named his son after General Leonard Wood, a hero of the Spanish-American War. Hall's godmother is Mrs. Ethel Roosevelt Derby, a daughter of Theodore Roosevelt.

Hall attended the public schools and then worked his way through Georgetown University, earning his LL.B. degree at its Law School in 1920. He served as a lawyer's clerk for a time before being admitted to the New York Bar Association (1921), and then began to practice in New York. In 1939 he joined in forming the firm of Hall, Robinson and Hogan in Oyster Bay, New York.

Reared in a Republican family, Hall began his political career in 1926 as a G.O.P. campaign worker. When President Coolidge appointed F. Trubee Davison Assistant Secretary of War, Hall was elected to succeed him in the New York State Assembly where he served in 1927 and 1928. A dispute arose over the nomination for sheriff, and Wilbur Doughty, Nassau County Republican leader, prevailed upon Hall to take the nomination in the interest of party harmony. In an interview with a representative of the New York *Times*, Hall related that he was elected sheriff, but "That was the only job I ever held that I didn't like."

He returned to the Assembly in 1934 and served until 1938, when he was nominated for Representative to Congress from the Second Congressional District of New York. As a Congressman, he introduced few bills and made few speeches, preferring to concentrate on committee work. Hall served on the Select Committee to Investigate and Study Problems of Small Business in 1945. He has also been a member of the Coinage, Weights, and Measures, and the Rivers and Harbors Committees. On March 27, 1941, he was elected chairman of the Republican Congressional Campaign Committee, succeeding Representative Charles A. Halleck of Indiana. This Committee was formed in 1866 to augment the strength of Republican members of the House in Congressional elections.

Eager for action and first-hand information, Hall made several airplane tours around the world. In 1945 he joined Representative Clare Booth Luce of Connecticut and John Kunkel of Pennsylvania on a tour of post-war Germany. Incensed over the conditions he viewed in Buchenwald and other prison camps, Hall said that every member of Congress should be permitted to examine them. "We should track down all Nazi criminals as we track down criminals here," he declared, "and they should be tried as just plain criminals" (New York *Time,* May 5, 1945).

The House Interstate and Foreign Commerce Committee, with Hall as acting chairman, went to Europe in the fall of 1947 to investigate the problems of American air carriers' operation in European, Mediterranean and Near East countries. The Committee inspected airports, communication installations, and search and rescue facilities, obtaining first-hand knowledge of the difficulties involved in carrying on international air commerce (New York *Times,* September 14, 1947).

As a member of a group of traveling Congressmen in 1949 Hall called on Dr. Charles Hill, secretary of the British Medical Society, in London to inquire about the progress of the British Labor Government's health program. Describing the interview, the New York *Post* (October 2, 1949) referred to Hall as a "vigorous foe" of the Truman plan for health insurance, on the ground that it is socialized medicine.

On the coal mine seizure bill, which came up before the House of Representatives in 1950, Hall opposed the President, stating: "Having himself created the coal crisis, Mr. Truman now asks the Congress to help extricate him from the appalling tragedy that faces the nation" (New York *Times,* March 4, 1950).

In July 1951 he introduced a bill prohibiting the release on bail, pending appeal, of anyone convicted of treason, espionage, sedition, and subversive activities (New York *Times,* July 16, 1951). That same month the House Judiciary Committee approved a bill designed to clear the way for the accident-ridden Long Island Railroad to obtain funds for new safety equipment. This measure, introduced by Hall, would amend the Federal Bankruptcy Law so that repayment priority over all other debts could be given to loans for the purchase of safety devices by bankrupt railroads (New York *Times,* July 20, 1951).

Representatives Hall and Joseph Martin, Jr. embarked in the fall of 1951 on an ambitious world-wide tour at their own expense, to study international problems. Speaking from Formosa on November 17, the two Congressmen concurred in finding that the funds allocated for military and economic aid in that area were "well spent" (New York *Times,* November 18, 1951).

They returned in December 1951 and asked that the Administration reverse itself and "fully support" the Chinese Nationalist regime of Generalissimo Chiang Kai-shek on Formosa. They stated emphatically that only in this way could all Asia be saved from Communist imperialism. During their trip they visited Hawaii, Japan, Korea, Formosa, the Philippines, Hong Kong, Thailand, Turkey, Israel, Greece, Italy, Spain, Portugal and France. They deplored what they called a "general apathy" in Europe toward the fighting in Korea (New York *Times,* December 21, 1951).

Hall's voting record in Congress from 1945 to 1952 indicates that he supported his party majority on 63 key issues, and opposed it on 14. He differed with them when he voted for the 1952 foreign aid measure, Korean aid in 1950, the British loan in 1946 and the 1945 extension of reciprocal trade agreements. The Republican chairman opposed recommittal of Universal Military Training proposals in 1951 and 1952 while the G.O.P. majority voted to reconsider UMT (*Christian Science Monitor,* April 10, 1953).

An amendment to create a permanent House Committee on Un-American Activities, a bill to eliminate the poll tax, and a bill to exempt the railroads from anti-trust laws which do not permit joint rates, were supported by Hall in 1945. He voted to shelve the Atomic Energy bill and thus to leave atomic energy in the control of the Army, and against the amendment to exempt teen-agers and fathers from the draft in 1946.

During the Republican-controlled 80th Congress of 1947, Hall did not differ with the Republican majority on any key issues; he favored the constitutional amendment to limit the presidency to two terms, the bill extending rent control for three additional months, and the Greek-Turkish Aid bill. In 1949, he voted to reduce European arms aid fifty per cent and to extend Marshall Plan appropriations.

Hall supported the Defense Appropriations Bill of 1951, and he voted to prohibit Government building of defense plants, to cut European economic aid by $350,000,000. He supported the bill to appropriate $7,500,000 dollars for foreign assistance, and against a conference report recommending a tax increase of $5,700,000,000.

In 1952 he voted for a $46,000,000,000 ceiling on military expenditures, and supported an amendment to a 1952 measure requesting the President to invoke the Taft-Hartley Law to enjoin steelworkers from striking. He has voted to limit public housing; for state control of the Tidelands; for 90 per cent parity on basic farm crops; for passage of the McCarran-Walker Immigration Act; and for the Social Security Bill which increased and extended insurance benefits.

In the 1950 Congressional campaign he accused the Administration of condoning Communist conquest of Asia for "five long years" and then of sending troops unprepared into Korea. In 1951 he warned that taxes can be used to "enslave a people" and that there is such a trend in this country. He called upon Americans to protect their heritage by stopping the drift toward "an all-powerful Federal Government" (New York *Herald Tribune,* December 31, 1951). Hall outlined the principal 1952 campaign issues as socialism, the Korean War, and political corruption. He denounced former President Truman's dismissal of General Douglas MacArthur from his command in the Far East.

In May 1952 Hall announced that he was giving up his $12,000 a year seat in Congress to

HALL, LEONARD—*Continued*

run for Surrogate, a position which pays an annual salary of $28,000. He replaced Surrogate Leone D. Howell of Mineola, who retired at the age of seventy. Arthur E. Summerfield, Republican National Chairman, announced in July that Hall had been appointed to a special campaign strategy board. At the National Convention in Chicago, Hall aroused comment by wearing a huge campaign button declaring, "I like Everybody."

When it was announced on April 10, 1953 that Hall had been elected the new chairman of the Republican National Committee, it was known that he had the support of all wings of the party, but was the particular candidate of the House Republican group. Governor Dewey of New York stated on April 3 that he would support Hall's nomination.

Hall's conference on April 9 with President Eisenhower, for whom he campaigned vigorously in 1952, made the appointment practically official, for the following day the session of the National Committee voted their unanimous approval of his nomination. The new chairman told a news conference on the day he took office, April 10, 1953, that he will serve without pay. In his new post, he will direct the 1954 Congressional elections campaign; he also faces various problems involving patronage, and relations between the White House and Congress (New York *Herald Tribune*, April 12, 1953).

The Republican chairman has stated that the national committee staff would be reduced in the interests of efficiency and economy and would operate with a force of approximately 100 instead of the present 139 with a net payroll saving of about $100,000 yearly (New York *World-Telegram*, May 2, 1953).

He is a member of the Nassau County Bar Association, Director of the North Shore Bank Trust Company, a Mason, an Elk, chairman of the Republican Committee for the Town of Oyster Bay, a member of the National Republican Club (New York), and a member of the Army and Navy Club in Washington, D.C. Woodworking and gardening are his chief hobbies. He is of the Episcopalian faith.

Leonard Wood Hall married Gladys Dowsey on May 10, 1934; he has two stepchildren, H. Wydol Carroll, and Patricia Carroll Ford. He has been described by *Time* (April 20, 1953) as "A big (6 ft. 2 in., 229 lbs.), bald, hearty, handshaking, backthumping man with a remarkable memory for names and numbers."

References

Christian Sci Mon p2 Ap 10 '53
N Y Herald Tribune p1 Ap 10 '53
N Y Times p12 Ap 10 '53
N Y World-Telegram p3 Ap 10 '53
Time 61:24 Ap 13 '53 por, Ap 20 '53
Congressional Directory (1951)
Who's Who in America, 1952-53
Who's Who in New York, 1952
Who's Who in United States Politics (1952)
World Biography (1948)

HALL, RAYMOND S(TEWART), REV. DR. July 6, 1908- Clergyman; seamen's organization official

Address: b. 25 South St., New York 4; h. 33 Horseshoe Dr., Northport, N.Y.

Known during World War II as "the parachute parson," the Reverend Dr. Raymond S. Hall now directs the Seamen's Church Institute of New York, the largest shore home, hotel and club in the world for active merchant seamen of all nationalities. The first Army chaplain to take training as a paratrooper, he jumped with his unit, the 502nd Parachute Infantry, 101st Airborne Division. He served in the European theatre where he was wounded, captured and imprisoned by the Germans. The Episcopal clergyman left the Army with the rank of major and with many decorations.

Raymond Stewart Hall was born in Lynn, Massachusetts, on July 6, 1908, the son of John Saunders and Edith Estelle (Mack) Hall. His father, a native of Nova Scotia, came to the United States as a boy and worked as a cabinet maker. His mother was born in New Hampshire. With his two brothers, Raymond grew up in Lynn and attended Classical High School, participating in rowing, track and football; he was a member of the YMCA swimming team. After graduating in 1927, he entered Brown University and majored in English. He worked his way through college at such jobs as waiting on table, dishwashing and being a lifeguard. He was captain of the Brown swimming team and received nation-wide mention as an All-American swimmer. He was champion of the New England Intercollegiate 50 and 100-yard dash, and was on the college freshman cross-country track team. Other activities included being vice-president of Brown University Christian Association, a member of the student government body, Junior Honorary Society, Camarian Club, Pi Kappa, and Delta Tau Delta.

Hall was influenced in the choice of his life work by the Right Reverend Dr. William Appleton Lawrence, Bishop of Western Massachusetts, who was rector of the church in Lynn that Hall attended. "I admired him very much," Hall states, "and entered the ministry because of his influence on my life." After receiving his Ph.D. degree from Brown University in 1931, he completed three years of study for the ministry at the Episcopal Theological School in Cambridge, Massachusetts. The young clergyman did his first work in the ministry as assistant minister of Christ Church, Fitchburg, Massachusetts, from 1934 to 1938. He then became rector of St. John's Episcopal Church in Lowell where he served until 1942.

In the summer preceding the Pearl Harbor attack he applied for a commission in the Chaplain's Reserve Corps, and was one of the first Episcopalian clergymen to be approved for service in the United States Army. Given the rank of first lieutenant, he was assigned in January 1942 to the Provisional Parachute Group at Fort Benning, Georgia.

Chaplain Hall was convinced that parachute troopers wanted "fighting" chaplains, and he did not want to stay "200 miles in the rear" while they went into combat (Toronto *Star Weekly,* May 16, 1942). He obtained permission to take the paratroopers' training course with his men and was the first chaplain to jump by parachute. After his first jump from the parachute tower at Fort Benning, his popularity with the men in his unit increased, and the church services he conducted had a record attendance. He said "the men can talk to me now because I've been through the same thing they have" (*Newsweek,* May 4, 1942). His success made the Army decide to have all paratroop chaplains jump with their men.

The chaplain was promoted to the rank of captain late in 1942, and assigned to the 502nd Parachute Infantry, 101st Airborne Division, at Fort Bragg, North Carolina. Recalling his initiation as a parachuter he said "I was really scared before the first jump. I had never been off the ground before. Yet it was the biggest thrill I've ever had."

Hall was in the lead plane on D-day and landed in Normandy several hours before H-hour, parachuting with his troops behind the lines. In battle he rescued wounded paratroopers, later declaring "the enemy was sniping at me, but their aim was bad" (*The Church Militant,* September 1, 1944). He received an eye injury from flying shrapnel in July 1944, while searching for "lost buddies" in combat, and was hospitalized in England. After this incident he could have returned to the United States but upon special request by his commanding general, he was retained with his division because his services were needed.

Reunited with the 101st Airborne Division, Chaplain Hall took part in the invasion of Holland in September 1944, and was captured and taken to a prison camp near Posen in Poland. He escaped four months later to Russia, where he joined the American authorities at Odessa. From there he returned to the United States and remained in active service until 1946, when he was discharged from the Army with the rank of major.

In that same year Dr. Hall was nominated for the directorship of the Seamen's Club of Boston by the Reverend Dr. Henry Knox Sherrill, presiding bishop of the Episcopal Church, and received the appointment to that post.

At a "Sailors' Day Service" held in the Cathedral of Saint John the Divine, New York City, in October 1946, Dr. Hall called for "aid to war-torn Europe as an assurance of peace," and termed the Merchant Marine "the lifeline of our armed forces" (New York *Times,* October 28, 1946).

Dr. Hall became assistant director of the Seamen's Church Institute of New York in 1947 and in 1949 was made the director after the retirement of the Reverend Dr. Harold S. Kelley. At his induction as head of the Institute in the presence of about 400 seamen and shipping officials he said: "I have been impressed with the high caliber of the men who sail our merchant vessels . . . and feel it is a challenge for the Institute to strive to serve these men in whatever way may be needed" (*Lookout,* March 1949).

REV. DR. RAYMOND S. HALL

The clergyman cited the club rooms, clinics, social service, and other facilities in the institute's thirteen-story building at 25 South Street, New York City, as examples of the many modern services available. "Seamen," he explained, "are self-supporting and are glad to pay the moderate charges for meals and beds, but the Institute does not charge for its other services which help to make it known in ports around the world as a friendly shore home in New York—particularly for men without families or far from their own homes."

Dr. Hall calls the Institute "the Church at work with its sleeves rolled up" (*Lookout,* October 1949). It is primarily a missionary work, he believes, "befriending men of the seven seas and helping to rid the waterfront of rackets aimed at seamen." For more than 110 years the institution has served the port of New York, and because every language is spoken there Dr. Hall describes it as "the junior United Nations" (New York *Herald-Tribune,* January 9, 1950).

In a paper presented at the Panel for Seamen's Welfare on October 20, 1949, held in the Waldorf-Astoria Hotel in New York City, Dr. Hall stated that unemployment had probably hit seamen harder than members of any other profession. Shipping has so decreased, he said, that many well-trained seamen are "thrown on the beach" (*Lookout,* May 1950). "We are living in days of great change and spiritual unrest," he added, "and there is a great job to be done along the waterfront . . . seamen have a strong need for friendship." He also warned that radical or subversive elements are a current threat to seamen.

The clergyman is the author of several articles in religious publications. He is called "a forceful preacher and a tireless visitor" (*Protestant Voice,* August 21, 1942). His World War II decorations include Pre-Pearl Harbor and American-European Theater Ribbons, Para-

HALL, RAYMOND S.—Continued

chute Wings, Gliderman Wings, Order of the Purple Heart, and Victory Medal, as well as many division decorations. He received an honorary Doctor of Divinity degree from Brown University in 1946.

Organizations in which Dr. Hall holds membership include the Holland Lodge of the Masons (chaplain), American Legion (chaplain), and the school board of Northport, New York. His clubs are the Propeller, Downtown Athletic, Navy League, Northport Yacht, Northport Tennis, and the clerical groups Clericus and the Cub. In politics he is an independent voter.

Raymond S. Hall married Mary Elizabeth Frankhauser, a schoolteacher, on September 1, 1934. Their children are Raymond S. Jr., A. Benjamin, and J. Thompson. Dr. Hall is five feet ten inches tall, weighs 185 pounds, and has blue-gray eyes and black hair. He is described by *Time* (March 9, 1942) as "soft-spoken." His hobbies are fishing, tennis, golf, hunting, and stamp collecting.

References

Am Mag 134:79 S '42
N Y Herald Tribune p19 Ja 9 '50
Newsweek 19:67 My 4 '42 por
Time 39:38 Mr 9 '42

HALLEY, RUDOLPH June 19, 1913- Lawyer; President of the City Council of New York

Address: b. City Hall, New York 7; h. 148 E. 48th St., New York 17

Television brought fame to Rudolph Halley, who became familiar to millions of Americans in 1951 when he was chief counsel during the televised hearings of the Senate's Special Committee to Investigate Organized Crime in Interstate Commerce ("Kefauver Committee"). The thirty-seven-year-old New York lawyer proved himself a calm, relentless inquisitor of the underworld. In November of that year, Halley was elected to New York's "second most important office"—the presidency of the City Council—winning over his Democratic opponent by a plurality of 163,492.

Halley has continued to be seen on television on a weekly program, *Public Report,* on ABC-TV (Channel 7), in which he presents to the public his views on the budget, taxes, subway fare, parking meters, housing, and other matters pertaining to the city's administration and economy.

Recently he invited bi-partisan support for a new effort to persuade Governor Thomas E. Dewey to call a special session of the State Legislature to deal with New York City's fiscal problems. His critics said that Halley was making a bid for the mayoralty by seeking headlines. In July 1953 the Liberal party unanimously selected City Council president Rudolph Halley as its candidate for mayor in the fall election.

Rudolph Halley was born on June 19, 1913, in Harrison, New York, where his father,

Henry Y. Halley, was a dentist. The family moved to New York City in that year. When his father died in 1918, Halley's mother, Pauline Shipman Halley, went to work as a secretary for her brother, Samuel Shipman, a Broadway playwright. Halley attended Townsend Harris High School, graduating at fourteen, and then enrolled in Morris High School. "I had to take a postgraduate course," he recalled, "because no one knew what to do with me. Finally, when I was fifteen, they let me into Columbia University" (*This Week,* January 6, 1952).

Entering Columbia in 1928, he completed his undergraduate studies in three years and was elected to Phi Beta Kappa. His major subject was mathematics, but while in college he became interested in the study of law, and decided to attend Columbia Law School. His extracurricular activities were chess, tennis, golf, and football, which he played despite the fact that he weighed only 160 pounds.

His high grades won him a Kent scholarship, and at Columbia Law School he edited the *Law Review.* On the recommendation of the faculty, after receiving his LL.B. degree in 1934, Halley was appointed secretary to Judge William Bondy of the United States District Court, a position he held until 1937. He was admitted to the New York State bar in 1935.

As secretary to Judge Bondy, young Halley spent much time in the courtroom observing the techniques of many great lawyers, including Joseph M. Proskauer and the late Max Steuer. After three years in this post, Halley rejected more remunerative offers from private law firms as well as from the Federal Government, and accepted a $2,600 a year position as an assistant in the United States District Attorney's office in the Southern District of New York, in which he served from 1937 to 1942.

Halley's next post was that of executive assistant for the Special Committee to Investigate Contracts under the National Defense Program, which was headed by the then Senator Harry S. Truman. In this position he had considerable success in developing investigation techniques, and in 1944 he was promoted to chief counsel of the Truman Committee.

He became a member of the United States Supreme Court Bar Association in that year, and the Washington, D.C., Bar Association in 1945. He worked with Hugh Fulton, chief counsel on the committee, who is now one of Halley's law partners in the firm of Fulton, Walter and Halley, which maintains offices in New York and Washington, D.C. Halley also served as chief counsel for the Senate Committee on Oil and Fuel Shortages.

Senator Estes Kefauver, chairman of the Crime Investigation Committee, asked Halley in May 1950 to becomes its chief counsel at a salary of $6,000. This was raised in January 1951 to $17,500, but Halley "accepted only $4,000 of it for eight months of work when the committee was strapped for funds" (New York *Herald Tribune,* May 2, 1951), and the money was used instead to hire additional investigators.

The Kefauver committee hearings in New York were sponsored by *Time* magazine over a nineteen-city television network and were also broadcast over many radio stations to "an audience estimated at twenty million persons."

Television-viewers and radio listeners neglected their daily tasks to follow the proceedings, which dramatically linked politics and business with organized crime. The stock market lagged and business generally marked time during the "crime show," which visited a number of cities to question local officials, underworld characters, and law enforcement officers. In a spectacular climax in New York City, witnesses from the world of organized crime were brought before the television cameras.

Rudolph Halley's name became almost overnight a household word. The New York *Times* called him "a new hero to take his place in American folk-lore along with the Private Eye, the G-Man, the racket-busting District-Attorney."

Describing his questioning of the witnesses *Life* (March 26, 1951) wrote: "dead-panned and patient . . . sometimes with an almost singsong repetition, sometimes with a rasping bite to his voice, but always with planned persistence, the 37-year-old Halley hacks away at evasive witnesses until he gets explicit answers." Among the 400 witnesses questioned by Halley about underworld activities were Frank Costello, Joe Adonis, Virginia Hill and Mickey Cohen.

Still another witness was William O'Dwyer, former Mayor of New York (1946-50), who was questioned on the relationship between criminals and politicians in that city. He testified that large-scale "'book-making' (taking of illegal bets on sport events) could not exist without police protection" (*Scholastic*, March 28, 1951).

In a symposium arranged by the American Television Society on June 19, 1951, Halley concluded that in Congressional hearings television was "an effective means of letting the public see for themselves." In criminal trials, with full press coverage, he believes that the video cameras should be permitted.

In the fall of 1951 Halley appeared on a weekly television program on CBS-TV, *Crime Syndicated*, which dramatized fictional cases based on the Committee's investigations. The proceeds from the sponsored show were donated to various charities.

Eight months after the crime investigations, Halley was elected President of the City Council of New York on the Liberal party ticket, with the endorsement of the Independent party and the City Fusion party. After being sworn in, Halley appointed a staff of fourteen experts to operate his office under a budget appropriation of $60,850. He receives a salary of $25,000 and is not permitted while in office to carry on his law practice (which *Collier's* states had earned him more than $70,000 yearly).

Halley presides over the meetings of the City Council, the chief law-making body of New York, and also has, he told *This Week* magazine (January 6, 1952), "a voice, three votes and unlimited power of debate on the Board of Estimate." Although he has the power to introduce legislation, he can vote only in the

Wide World Photos

RUDOLPH HALLEY

case of a tie in the Council. If the Mayor is out of town, Halley becomes acting Mayor.

When Halley was interviewed over Municipal Radio Station WNYC by student editors from colleges in the city, he offered a five-point program for New York. He proposed taking corruption out of politics; removing inefficient people from government; a city management plan; a long-term fiscal program; and a long-range plan of city services.

Submitting four proposed laws and resolutions to the City Council on December 16, 1952, Halley said they "would go a long way toward ending the gangsters' grip on the city's water front." He recommended the licensing of stevedores by the Police Department; eliminating the public loaders from the piers and requiring that the stevedoring companies which load and unload ships also load and unload the trucks that come to the piers; abolishing the shape-up method of hiring longshoremen and substituting a system of hiring less likely to be controlled by gangsters; and appointing a Council committee to study plans either to turn the waterfront over to the Port of New York Authority or to create a new authority "to eliminate the racketeer domination of the docks."

Recently, Halley has had verbal clashes with Mayor Vincent Impellitteri and Governor Thomas E. Dewey. On January 1953 he strongly criticized Dewey for a reduction of almost four million dollars in the State's appropriations to the city. He also opposed Mayor Impellitteri's new budget for the city, which was approved by the Board of Estimate after it rejected Halley's own budget plan. He spoke against the Transit Authority proposed by the Mayor, and the increase in subway fare he predicted it would bring.

Council President Halley also voted against the originally mapped but controversial section of the $86,000,000 Cross Bronx Expressway,

HALLEY, RUDOLPH—*Continued*

and pointed out that 1,400 residential buildings would have to be razed if such a route were authorized.

Halley has two children, Marian and Henry, by his first marriage to Grace Ralston. His second marriage to Marie Caruso was terminated in March 1949. He married Janice Brosh, a nurse, on December 27, 1951. They have a son, born on September 25, 1953.

He is the recipient of the Distinguished Service Award of the New York State Society of Professional Engineers for "extraordinary distinction in exposing the links between crime and politics," and the Knickerbocker award of the New York City Fusion party on May 23, 1951. He is also an ex-officio member of the Board of Trustees of the Museum of the City of New York, the New York Public Library and the Queens Borough Public Library.

Halley calls himself "an independent Democrat." The New York *Times*, commenting editorially on Halley's work as City Council president stated on July 22, 1953: "His opportunities as a watchdog for the forces of good government were great, but the net returns meager. On the other hand, he has played the rebel on the Board of Estimate in irresponsible fashion, currying popular favor on transit and tax issues while evading unpleasant realities of the city's budget problem."

References

American Mercury 75:87+ N '51
Collier's 127:24 My 19 '51
Life 30:37 Mr 26 '51
N Y Herald-Tribune p14 My 2 '51; p6
  My 4 '51; IV p7 O 7 '51 por; p38
  N 7 '51
N Y Times p24 O 30 '51; p24 N 7 '51
N Y World-Telegram p5 Mr 10 '51;
  p15 Mr 24 '51 por; p29 O 24 '51
Newsweek 38:79 O 1 '51; 38-28 N 19 '51
Pathfinder 58:36 Ap 18 '51 por
This Week p12+ Ja 6 '52
U S News 38:38 My. 26 '50

Martindale-Hubbell Law Directory (1952)
Who's Who in America, 1952-53
Who's Who in New York (1952)

HALLSTEIN, WALTER (häll'stīne) Secretary of State for Foreign Affairs of the Federal Republic of Germany, Nov. 17, 1901-
Address: b. Haus des Bundeskanzlers, Bonn, Germany; h. Lilienthalalle 16, Frankfurt a. M. Germany

The Federal German Republic's Secretary of State for Foreign Affairs is Walter Hallstein, a legal scholar and professor of law who entered the diplomatic service of West Germany as chairman of the German committee to the United Nations Educational, Scientific and Cultural Organization.

An advocate of European unity, Secretary Hallstein was one of the chief architects of the European Steel and Coal Community, (Schuman plan) the Treaty Establishing the Euro-

pean Defense Community, and a strong proponent of the Convention of Relations Between the Three Powers and the Federal Republic (Peace Pact of Bonn).

Walter Hallstein was born at Mainz, Germany on November 17, 1901, the son of J. Hallstein, a Government surveyor, and Anna (Geibel) Hallstein. He attended the Humanistische Gymnasium at Darmstadt and Mainz and was graduated in 1920. After studying law and economics at the universities of Bonn, Munich and Berlin, he received a Doctor of Jurisprudence degree in 1925.

He then became an assistant on the faculty of law at Berlin university and from 1927 to 1930 taught at the Kaiser-Wilhelm-Institut in Berlin. As a professor at the Universität Rostock from 1930 to 1941 and at the Johann Wolfgang Goethe Universität (Frankfurt-on-Main) in 1941 he taught civil, industrial and private commercial law.

During these years, Dr. Hallstein also devoted himself to writing such books as *Der Lebensversicherungsvertrag im Versailler Vertrag* (N. G. Elwert, 1926), *Die Aktienrechte der Gegenwart* (F. Vahlen, 1931), and *Die Berichtigung des Gesellschaftskapitals* (1942).

His academic career was interrupted by the war during which he was inducted into the *Wehrmacht* as a lieutenant. After being captured by the United States Army at Cherbourg, France. Hallstein was transferred to Camp Como, Mississippi. There he was permitted to set up a small university enabling the German prisoners of war to study American institutions. He was repatriated in 1946 and returned to his native country to become the *Rektor* of the university at Frankfurt and head of the conference of *Rektoren* in the American zone of Germany. Several years later he stated, ". . . when I left for home it was with the comforting feeling of how strong the good in man must be if a war, as terrible as the last one, was not able to destroy it" (*Vital Speeches*, May 15, 1952).

Georgetown University in Washington, D.C., invited Dr. Hallstein in 1948 to become a visiting professor. He accepted and spent a year teaching at the university and making a survey of American education. In March 1952 he returned to Georgetown University for several days to lecture on European integration and the Schuman plan as a means for such cooperation among the nations of Western Europe.

Dr. Konrad Adenauer. Chancellor and Foreign Minister of the Federal Republic, appointed Professor Hallstein chairman of the German committee to the UNESCO conferences held at Florence, Italy, in 1949 and 1950. Hallstein was later named the head of the German delegation to the Quai D'Orsay in Paris June 20, 1950, when deliberations began on Robert Schuman's plan to form a coal and steel community of six European nations. He was given the title of Secretary of State of the Federal Chancellery in August 1950. and in April 1951 was named Secretary of State for Foreign Affairs.

Hallstein is responsible for the relocation of a defeated nation in a new scheme of things in Western Europe. It consists in the reconciliation of the hopes of 50,000,000 Germans in the new Federal Republic for a revived *Vaterland* and the unification of East and West Germany. Other countries of the West have plans for an overall security system in Europe, which is dependent upon German divisions but the prevention of Germany as a military power.

Cognizant of the fact that German isolation and future peace are incompatible, Secretary Hallstein has consistently supported the Schuman plan, a fifty-year treaty which provides for pooling the basic industries of coal and steel of France, Germany, Italy, Luxembourg, Belgium and the Netherlands. It eliminates in that sphere all duties and levies; it also restricts private cartels.

To manage the community, provision was made for four governing bodies, a High Authority, the executive arm; a Council of Ministers to harmonize the High Authority with the member nations; a Common Assembly composed of members of the Parliament of each signatory nation; and a seven-member court.

Hallstein believes that by making these countries economically interdependent through the European Coal and Steel Community causes of conflict will be eliminated and there will also be a greater incentive for European political unity. In the governing bodies of the Schuman system, he sees the beginnings of the political organization of Europe. To assure Europe that Germany will not dominate the Schuman project, Secretary Hallstein agreed that the Ruhr will contribute one-half of the coal and one-third of the steel production and that Germany will have only two representatives on the High Authority.

In an effort to secure German ratification, he published on December 21, 1951 the Allied promise of October 19, 1951 to abolish the International Authority for the Ruhr, which allocated German coal to the nations of Western Europe, and to waive the 11,000,000-ton limit on German steel production after the implementation of the Schuman plan. The German Parliament ratified the system on February 1, 1952. It has also been ratified by the other member nations. Great Britain, although not participating, endorsed it in principle on March 17, 1951.

Michael L. Hoffman has written of the founders of the Schuman plan, "One cannot talk with men like M. Monnet or Prof. Walter Hallstein . . . without realizing that a new loyalty has taken hold of them—a loyalty to Europe" (New York *Times,* June 15, 1952).

Other important treaties during Hallstein's term of office have been the Convention of Relations Between the Three Powers and the Federal Republic which was signed May 26, 1952, and the Treaty Establishing the European Defense Community signed the following day. The former terminates the occupation of West Germany, the Allied High Commission and the land Commissions, and restores sovereignty to Germany. The European defense treaty, signed by the six Schuman plan nations, creates a European army which includes twelve German divisions, and a nine-man bureau to administer the forces. The Common Assem-

Wide World Photos

WALTER HALLSTEIN

bly of the European Coal and Steel Community is given the power to control the Army's budget. These treaties have not yet been ratified.

Secretary Hallstein stated on March 12, 1952, "We are, in fact, one world, and nothing of moment can take place in one continent without involving the rest of the world. It was formerly thought that conflicts could be localized. . . .Technical, economic, and communication developments have brought the peoples of the world too close together. It is therefore no longer a question of localizing . . . conflicts, but of preventing such conflicts from arising at all" (*Vital Speeches,* May 15, 1952).

Hallstein wrote in *Foreign Affairs,* "the German Federal Government has planned and developed its foreign policy to assist European integration. From the outset, its best energies have been directed to bringing about a united Europe which, in turn, is to be firmly bound to the Atlantic community. The Government has been especially active in collaborating in the two great plans which will form the foundation of the future European federation, the European Coal and Steel Community and the European Defense Community" (October 1952).

Since the war Dr. Hallstein has written *Wiederherstellung des Privatrechts* (1946), *Wissenschaft und Politik* (1949), *Der Schuman Plan* (V. Klostermann, 1951); and *Probleme des Schuman-Plans* (Kiel, 1951), a series of discussions between Hallstein, Andreas Predohl and Fritz Boade.

Secretary Hallstein, a bachelor, is a member of the Scientific Advisory Council to the German Ministry of Economics, Deutsche Gesellschaft für Rechtsvergleichung, Deutsche Vereinigung für Internationales Recht, and Deutscher Juristentag. For recreation he enjoys horseback riding and collecting sculpture.

(Continued next page)

HALLSTEIN, WALTER—*Continued*

References

N Y Herald Tribune II p2 Mar 18 '51
N Y Times p7 F 26 '52
Time 59:32 Mr 24 '52 por
Vital Speeches 18:458 My 15 '52
Handbuch der Deutchen Wissenchaft,
   1949
International Who's Who, 1952
Kürchners Deutscher Gelehrten-Kalender,
   1950
Wer ist Wer? (1951)

HAMBLET, JULIA E. May 12, 1916-
United States Marine Corps officer

Address: c/o Headquarters, United States Marine Corps, Washington 25, D.C.

Serving with the "lady leathernecks" since the women Marines were organized ten years ago, Colonel Julia E. Hamblet became director of this branch of the United States Marine Corps on May 1, 1953. The youngest director of women in the armed services, she has experienced almost every type of duty open to a woman Marine officer.

She succeeded Colonel Katherine A. Towle to her present appointment, which gives her the rank of a full colonel and the command of some 2,500 enlisted women Marines and 150 women officers stationed throughout the United States and overseas.

Julia E. Hamblet, the daughter of Abel and Marcia (Coburn) Hamblet, was born in Winchester, Massachusetts on May 12, 1916. She attended the Hartridge School, Plainfield, New Jersey, and majored in economics at Vassar College which awarded her a B.A. degree in 1937. After graduating she became associated with the United States Information Service in

Bradford Bachrach

COL. JULIA E. HAMBLET

Washington, D.C., where she was employed until 1943, when she joined the newly-organized women Marines. She was the first officer candidate from the capitol to enlist in the corps and graduated from the first Marine Corps Women's Reserve Officer Training Class at Mount Holyoke, Massachusetts. She was commissioned a first lieutenant on May 4, 1943.

Her first assignment was as adjutant to Colonel Towle at the first women's "boot camp" at Hunter College, in New York City. After that she was assigned to Marine bases at Camp Lejeune, North Carolina, Camp Pendleton and Quantico, Virginia, where she commanded a battalion.

At the end of the war Julia E. Hamblet, twenty-nine years old and a major, was in command of Aviation Women Reserve Group One, composed of 120 officers and 2,600 enlisted women at the Marine Corps Air Station, Cherry Point, North Carolina. For her service she was awarded a Letter of Commendation. Released from active duty in March 1946, she visited England and inspected the British women's services.

Miss Hamblet was recalled in September to succeed Colonel Towle as the third Director of the Women's Reserve. During the two years she held this post she guided a reserve program which brought women into the Marines on a part-time basis. When President Truman signed the Women's Armed Forces Integration Act in 1948, incorporating the Women's Reserve into the regular armed forces, Colonel Towle returned to duty as Director of the Women Marines and Julia E. Hamblet accepted a permanent commission with the Corps. On August 24, 1949 she was promoted to the rank of lieutenant colonel. She was sent by the Government to Ohio State University to take a master's degree in public administration, which she received in 1951; after that, she was ordered to Hawaii for a tour of duty in the personnel office at Fleet Marine Force Headquarters, Pearl Harbor.

Colonel Hamblet's next assignment placed her in charge of the Women Officers Training Detachment, Marine Corps Schools at Quantico, Virginia. Here she was able to carry out her theories of Marine training for women. "First," she told a writer for *This Week Magazine* (June 7, 1953), "we made our girls into Marines. Then we made them into Marine officers. Only then could we start training them to be women Marine officers."

Colonel Hamblet's training program required an indoctrination course for officer candidates which followed as closely as possible the program for male Marines. Boatloads of women trainees observed Marine amphibious games on the Potomac River. They became familiar with the fundamentals of individual small arms, and watched the male Marines give firepower demonstrations with live ammunition. Classroom instruction in command function emphasized a practical approach, for Colonel Hamblet believes that a knowledge of military regulations should be combined with an understanding of human nature. All this was in addition to training in details such as close order drill, deck-swabbing, bunk-tidying, and typing.

The new Director of Women Marines looks upon the integration of women in the military services as an indication that they are now being accepted as partners, rather than auxiliaries, of the men, performing duties at every military level that women can do best. The role of the new military woman, she feels, is to *help* a man to fight, giving her a position of greater responsibility than is implied in the World War II motto, *"Free a man to fight."*

Colonel Hamblet has her headquarters in the Navy annex above the Pentagon in Washington. She will hold her new post for a four-year term, the same as the tenure prescribed by law for a male Marine in a similar position. Even though she must take a reduction in rank after her term expires, she has made it known that she expects to stay with the Marines, hoping at that time to be stationed a good distance away from headquarters, so that her successor will be able to work without a feeling of constraint.

Colonel Hamblet is a brunette, and is five feet ten inches tall. She is fond of outdoor sports, particularly tennis and horseback riding. Her gift for leadership is shown in her ability to be very firm and decisive. As Colonel Towle, now Dean of women and Associate Dean of students at the University of California said, Julia Hamblet has "brains, ability, personality and looks." *Time* has described her as a "girl who was born to pose for a recruiting poster."

References

Collier's 131:38+ Ap 25 '53 pors
Newsweek 41.38 Mr 9 '53
This Week p13 Je 7 '53
Time 61:22 Mr 9 '53
Washington (D.C.) Post p27 F 26 '53

HAMMARSKJÖLD, DAG (HJALMAR AGNE CARL) (häm'är-shůld dåg) July 29, 1905- Secretary General of the United Nations; political economist; diplomat

Address: c/o United Nations Secretariat, United Nations, New York

Dag Hammarskjöld of Sweden was elected Secretary General of the United Nations by the General Assembly on April 7, 1953, for a term of five years, succeeding Trygve Lie of Norway to the $40,000-a-year tax-free post. He took oath of office three days later at the United Nations headquarters in New York City. Primarily a political economist, considered Sweden's leading monetary expert and one of her most brilliant diplomats, he has a strong background of international experience.

Previous to his new post, he participated in the United Nations General Assembly as chairman of the Swedish delegation at the seventh session, and as vice-chairman of this delegation at the sixth session. He became deputy Foreign Minister of Sweden in 1951 and a member of the Swedish Cabinet. Hammarskjöld served as vice-chairman of the executive committee of the Organization for European Economic Cooperation (OEEC) in 1948-49, and was Sweden's delegate at the organization meeting for the

United Nations
DAG HAMMARSKJÖLD

Marshall Plan in 1947. He was assistant Foreign Minister of Sweden in 1949, chairman of the board of governors of the Bank of Sweden in 1941-48, and under-secretary of the Department of Finance of the Swedish Government in 1936-45.

Dag Hjalmar Agne Carl Hammarskjöld was born in Jonkoping, Sweden, on July 29, 1905, the son of Knut Hjalmar Leonard and Agnes (Almquist) Hammarskjöld. He descends from a family of statesmen and military men dating back to the Swedish knight, Peder Hammarskjöld, who was given his title by Charles IX in 1610 for a defense against the Danes. The new Secretary General's father, a famous jurist and politician in Sweden and a university professor, was Prime Minister during World War I.

From Uppsala University in Sweden, Hammarskjöld obtained in 1925 what approximates the B.A. degree in the United States, and in 1928 the equivalent of the M.A. degree. Two years later he received a degree in law from this university. He was appointed secretary of the Swedish Government committee on unemployment, a post he held from 1930-34. Concurrently, during 1933, he was associate professor of political economics at the University of Stockholm. Uppsala University awarded him the degree of doctor of philosophy in 1934, with a major in political economy. His doctorate thesis, entitled *Konjunkturspridnisigen: en teoretisk och historisk undersökning* (A Theoretical and Historical Survey of Market Trends) was published in 1935.

Trained from the beginning of his adult life in financial and economic affairs, Hammarskjöld served as secretary of the Bank of Sweden in 1935. The following year, he became under-secretary of the Department of Finance of the Swedish Government, an office he retained until 1945. Concurrently, beginning in

HAMMARSKJÖLD, DAG—*Continued*

1937, he assumed the task of counselling the Swedish Government on the economic status and affairs of the country, as a member of its advisory board. This assignment, which Hammarskjöld held until 1948, is similar to the responsibilities in the United States of a member of the President's advisory committee. Hammarskjöld accepted the position of chairman of the board of governors of the Bank of Sweden during 1941-48, and was a member of the Board of Foreign Exchange from 1940-48.

During financial discussions between Great Britain and the United States in 1944-48, Hammarskjöld was a delegate for the Swedish Government to help bring about satisfactory negotiations. He entered the diplomatic service in 1946 as specialist in finance for the Swedish Foreign Office. In this post he discussed problems resulting from restrictions on sterling with representatives of Britain's Treasury in September 1947. He also visited the United States to explain to State Department officials in Washington the purpose of Swedish import bans imposed on March 15, 1947. The United States had protested that the trade restrictions violated the 1935 reciprocal trade agreement between this country and Sweden.

In replying to this criticism Hammarskjöld stated that his country's foreign exchange position permitted "no alternative to the restrictions Sweden had imposed on imports" (New York *Times,* April 22, 1947). He added that the "move neither discriminated against the United States nor favored European countries." He referred to bilateral trade agreements which Sweden had signed with neighboring countries, such as Poland, Norway, the Netherlands, and the Soviet Union, as a "negative guaranty" that his country would not cut off certain imports from these nations. Credits granted these countries, he explained, were "a postwar necessity" and a "farsighted means of restoring European economy."

At the Paris Conference in 1947, Hammarskjöld was Sweden's delegate at the organization meeting for the Marshall Plan. He became his country's chief delegate to the Organization for European Economic Cooperation (OEEC) in 1948, and served as vice-chairman of this organization's executive committee during 1948-49. While in this post, he stated in Paris that "rigid targets would be omitted" in the organization's long-term 4-year program, as "viability of European economy was the over-all target" (New York *Times,* August 12, 1948). He explained that the organization would endeavor to reach this target "through plans to insure increased production." Hammarskjöld added that "for the annual program definite production targets would be set." He predicted that answers provided by member governments on production affairs would "change the entire structure of European trade," and stated that one of the chief aims of the organization was "to make dollar savings."

Hammarskjöld was made assistant Foreign Minister of Sweden in 1949. He predicted in January 1950 that Sweden would surmount her post-war economic deficit "in two years" and be able to aid neighboring countries (New

York *Herald Tribune,* April 1, 1953). He became his country's deputy Foreign Minister and a member of the Swedish Cabinet in 1951. Because of his important role in Swedish foreign relations, political observers concluded that economic affairs would be a dominant factor in Sweden's foreign policy. Hammarskjöld was made chairman of UNISCAN in 1950, an organization comprising Scandinavian countries and England, set up to promote cooperation among these nations in economic projects and affairs.

As deputy Foreign Minister of Sweden, Hammarskjöld attended the biennial meeting in Stockholm on October 10, 1951, of the Foreign Ministers of Denmark, Norway, Iceland, and Sweden to approve a common policy on issues confronting the Scandinavian governments. An important problem discussed was Russia's demand for a 12-mile sea frontier which was strongly protested by Sweden and Denmark. Recommendations at the meeting were offered for endorsement by the International Court of Justice at The Hague.

Hammarskjöld was one of a committee of Foreign Ministers who met in Paris on July 18, 1952, to evaluate a report of financial experts in economics, and to advise the council of the Organization for European Economic Cooperation what action its member countries should take. He expressed his Government's view on a European Coal and Steel Community, provided in the Schuman plan, in Stockholm on November 4, 1952. "The Government," he said, "affirms that Sweden should contribute to making possible the common market envisaged by the Community, and yet, like other countries, not members of the Community, protect her own interests" (London *Times,* November 5, 1952). In the fall of 1952 Hammarskjöld came to the United States as vice-chairman of the Swedish delegation to the United Nations General Assembly, and in February 1953 he headed this delegation to the seventh session of the Assembly. In the spring of this year he attended conferences of the OEEC in Paris.

Following more than two years of disagreement over a successor for Trygve Lie, former Secretary General of the United Nations, the Security Council on March 31, 1953, nominated Hammarskjöld, who was considered the "darkest of dark horses for the post" (New York *Herald Tribune,* April 2, 1953). He was elected Secretary General of the United Nations on April 7, 1953, by a vote of fifty-seven of the sixty member states of the General Assembly. Referring to his new appointment, Hammarskjöld said: "My first move will be to learn the job," and added that he interpreted his election "as a sign of a more cooperative spirit on the part of the Big Five" (New York *Times,* April 2, 1953). He said that he was not advocating a "passive role" for the Secretary General but an active one—"active as an instrument, a catalyst, an inspirer." He stated that he wanted to do a job, not talk about it, and he shared the hope "that we are entering a period of less [international] tension" (New York *Times,* April 10, 1953).

In his short "inaugural speech" on assuming his U.N. post on April 10, 1953, Hammerskjöld said, "Ours is a work of reconciliation and realistic construction. This work must be based on respect for the laws by which human civilization has been built. It likewise requires a strict observance of the rules and principles laid down in the Charter of this organization" (New York *Times*).

Hammarskjöld has written various articles in Sweden on money and finance. Known among European statesmen for his ability to speak several languages, his ease in conducting personal relationships, and his wit in conversation, he is recognized as one of Sweden's "ablest negotiators," and is considered a brilliant orator (*Christian Science Monitor*, April 1, 1953). A luncheon was given in his honor by the Minister of State of Great Britain on July 22, 1952. He retains the family title of knight, not used as a formal title of address in Sweden.

The new Secretary General told a *New Yorker* reporter who interviewed him on his arrival in the United States: "My literary interests appear to invite misinterpretation. It's true I do like Thomas Wolfe very much . . . but I don't like being pinned down to any one phase of literature, or anything else. I would prefer, for example, to be known as an admirer of both Thomas Wolfe and Virginia Woolf."

The new Secretary General became vice-president of the Swedish Tourist Association in 1950, and has been a member of the board since 1940. He served for many years as president of the Swedish Alpinist Club. Although a member of the Labor Cabinet in Sweden, he is regarded as nonpartisan in politics. Hammarskjöld is of medium build and height, and has light hair and a fair complexion. His brother is Governor of the Swedish province of Sodermanland. "I have never satisfied a wish to go around the world," Hammarskjöld stated (New York *Herald Tribune*, April 2, 1953). He likes mountain climbing, modern French paintings, Swedish ceramics, and enjoys reading the works of Cervantes, Goethe and T. S. Eliot. He calls himself a "technician," but colleagues, reported in *Newsweek*, April 13, 1953 have called him a "realist who pricks balloons."

References

Christian Sci Mon p6 Ap 1 '53
N Y Herald Tribune p21 Ap 1 '53
N Y Times p9 Ap 1 '53; p4 Ap 3 '53
Ver Är Det (1951)
World Biography (1948)

HAMMOND, GODFREY Nov. 16, 1891-
Publisher

Address: b. Popular Science Publishing Co., 353 Fourth Ave., New York 10; h. 1 Carstensen Rd., Scarsdale, N.Y.

President of the Popular Science Publishing Company, publisher of *Popular Science Monthly* and *Outdoor Life* magazines, Godfrey Hammond has been in the publishing business since he began working as an office boy for the Munsey Publishing Company in 1907. He worked in the business office of the Hearst

GODFREY HAMMOND

Magazines in 1914 and later headed the promotion department of the New York *Tribune*. He joined the Popular Science Publishing Company as promotion manager in 1922, then left for an interval of nine years when he published the *Christian Herald,* and returned to the company in 1937. After serving for two years as vice-president of the company, he was elected president in 1939. In 1944 he was director of publicity for the Republican National Committee.

Godfrey Hammond was born in Patchogue, Long Island, on November 16, 1891, the son of Captain Charles Smith and Ezma (Godfrey) Hammond. He received his early training in the public schools and then attended Patchogue High School. After a year and a half he was compelled to leave high school because of the death of his father, a sea captain, who was lost off Cape Hatteras during a storm. A friend of the family, having observed young Hammond's fondness for reading, suggested that he try to get a job in publishing.

Hammond's first job, which paid $3.50 a week, was with the Frank A. Munsey Publishing Company as office boy. At that time, in 1907, Munsey was the largest magazine publisher in the country, producing *Munsey's Magazine, All Story, Cavalier, Argosy,* and others. Here Hammond rose successively to head office boy, assistant to the treasurer, and make-up man in the advertising department.

For a brief period Hammond was office manager of the advertising department of *Harper's Bazaar,* and later occupied the same post at Condé Nast. From 1914 until 1917 he was employed in the business office of the Hearst Magazines. During the first World War Hammond was a private in the United States Army. Upon his release from military service, he went to work for the New York *Tribune*, where he remained for three years, from 1919 until 1922,

(Continued next page)

HAMMOND, GODFREY—*Continued*

first as a statistician and then as promotion manager.

Deciding that he preferred magazine publishing to the newspaper business, Hammond in 1922 joined the Popular Science Publishing Company where he served several years as promotion manager in charge of circulation and advertising promotion. Hammond has said, "What a lot of people in the publishing field don't understand is that advertising is as much a part of the readable content of a magazine as the editorial matter. If you can't interest your type of reader in your type of advertising, your magazine hasn't much of a chance for success."

He left Popular Science in 1928 to become publisher of the *Christian Herald*. Nine years later he rejoined the former company as executive vice-president. He was elected president in March 1939, succeeding Albert L. Cole. The company he heads is one of the fifteen largest publishing firms in the country in terms of annual volume of business. *Popular Science Monthly,* one of its principal publications, had an advertising income of $250,000 and a circulation of 190,000 when Hammond joined the organization in 1922. According to the most recent figures, its circulation is now 1,260,025. The circulation of *Outdoor Life* mounted from about 150,000 in 1934 to the current figure of 903,200. But circulation increases are not, in Hammond's opinion, the most significant aspect of successful magazine publishing. "In the years I've been in this business," he has said, "no magazine has been successful that hasn't given a heaping editorial value to its readers . . .The most successful magazines have not necessarily been those of the largest circulation. It's not how big your circulation is, it's how adequately you occupy your field in comparison with competition—and how important your field is to advertisers—that makes a magazine profitable."

In addition to these two magazines, the Popular Science Publishing Company is part owner of the SM News Company, of which Hammond is a vice-president and director. This company operates an educational department for American schools and colleges and distributes many magazines including *Popular Science Monthly, Outdoor Life, Reader's Digest, McCall's, Redbook, Sunset,* and products of the Quality Comic Group.

Hammond likes to relate how "the New York *Times,* the United Press, International News Service and *Time* . . . telephoned *Popular Science Monthly* the morning after the first A-bomb dropped on Hiroshima "to ask how the blame thing worked."

In 1944 Hammond obtained a leave of absence from his publishing duties to accept an appointment from Herbert Brownell, Jr., then chairman of the Republican National Committee, as director of its public relations during that year's election campaign. Hammond served as the chairman of the magazine division of the American Red Cross in 1945 and 1946, and he is a director of the National Association of Magazine Publishers and a member of the Magazine Advertising Bureau.

The publisher's clubs are the Union League and the Manhattan, both of New York City, the Coveleigh Club and the American Yacht Club at Rye, and the Scarsdale Golf Club.

He married the former Irma Varian Gillespie on May 17, 1917. The Hammonds have five children, Marjorie Varian (Mrs. William Tracy Castimore), Robert Godfrey and Donald Gillespie, who are twins, and Philip Townsend and William Pierson, who are also twins. Hammond is a Republican and a Presbyterian. Hammond is five feet eight inches tall and weighs 190 pounds; he has brown eyes and graying brown hair. He enjoys collecting antiques.

References

N Y Herald Tribune p28 Ag 24 '44 por
N Y Times p32 Ag 24 '44
Business Executives of America (1950)
Who's Who in America, 1952-53
Who's Who in Commerce and Industry (1951)

HAMPDEN, WALTER (DOUGHERTY)
June 30, 1879- Actor
Address: b. The Players, 16 Gramercy Park, New York 3; h. Ridgefield, Conn.

Walter Hampden's acting career has spanned more than half a century and has included portrayals of over 150 roles on Broadway and on tour. Recognized as the dean of the American stage, he portrayed, in 1953, the role of Deputy-Governor Danforth in Arthur Miller's play, *The Crucible,* at the Martin Beck Theatre in New York City. He has also appeared in moving pictures and on radio and television networks. Older generations of theater-goers throughout the United States remember his Shakespearean touring companies and his role in Edmond Rostand's romantic drama, *Cyrano de Bergerac,* which he played 1,016 times.

Walter Hampden (Dougherty) was born in Brooklyn, New York, June 30, 1879, the son of John Hampden Dougherty and the former Alice Hill. His father was a lawyer, Commissioner of Water Supply under Mayor Seth Low, and was noted as a brilliant conversationalist whose avocation was reading dramas aloud. One of Walter's brothers, Paul Dougherty, became a painter; one sister, a sculptress, another a dancer. His mother was a proficient pianist.

Walter attended Brooklyn Polytechnic Preparatory School, spent one year at Harvard, then returned to New York, where he completed his studies at Brooklyn Polytechnic Institute. At sixteen he appeared as Shylock in his school production of *The Merchant of Venice.* After completing his academic education he went to Paris where he studied cello, singing, dancing and speech with Silvania of the Comedie Francaise. He crossed the Channel to England and at the age of twenty-two joined Sir Frank Benson's Company and learned to play over seventy parts in three years. He married Mabel Moore, an English actress in the troupe, in 1905.

When he played in *Hamlet* on the London stage in 1905 at the age of twenty-six he received such laudatory notices of his acting as "the most significant development in the English theatre since the advent of Sir J. Forbes-Robertson." Hampden while playing Laertes, had been understudying H. B. Irving (son of Sir Henry Irving) and when Irving's voice broke, he stepped into the Prince of Denmark's part and wore the original costume of the "melancholy Dane" worn by Sir Henry Irving.

The young actor chose to renounce an auspicious career in England and returned to New York, where he was soon playing supporting roles in Ibsen's plays which starred Alla Nazimova. Henry Miller gave him a year's contract on the strength of his voice. William Brady, Arthur Hopkins and other producers starred him in numerous plays. For three years, beginning in 1908, he played the role of the servant Manson in Charles Rann Kennedy's *The Servant in the House*, at the Savoy Theatre on West 34th Street. Some critics felt that the pontifical style of acting developed in this part hindered Hampden in subsequent roles.

He played in *Hamlet* at a special matinee in 1919 which "electrified audiences and critics" and created such a stir that it led to a long run and became the foundation of his own repertory company. His performance in *Macbeth* confirmed his position as the leading Shakespearean actor of his day. At the peak of his popularity he formed his own company in 1923, leased the National Theatre for $100,000, paid $50,000 for scenery and costumes and operated at a weekly cost of $13,000. He played in *Cyrano de Bergerac* for eight months and then took it on tour.

He opened his own theatre in 1925 and played Hamlet and Shylock with Ethel Barrymore as Ophelia and Portia.

He recalled that the only time he ever appeared in a play with John Barrymore was when he took over for an actor who did not show up, and thereby saved his job. Hedda Hopper once asked him which was his greatest play, and Hampden replied: "Who can choose the greatest? *Hamlet* was my mainstay. It gave me my chance. You might say *Hamlet* was the fulcrum, but *Cyrano* was the one which had the big run."

Throughout the ensuing decade Hampden played in various Shakespearean plays, introduced *Caponsacchi* and *Cardinal Richelieu* into his repertory and Ibsen's *An Enemy of the People*. He revived *Cyrano* in 1936, repeating its earlier success. "*Cyrano* is the gayest part Mr. Hampden ever ventured," wrote Brooks Atkinson in the New York *Times*. Hampden worked indefatigably, playing the triple roles of actor, director and producer, as he played monk, mountebank and cavalier in *Caponsacchi* while rehearsing his company in *Henry V*.

Mr. Hampden has displayed throughout his career a willingness to sacrifice fame and fortune for his ideals. He continued to produce Shakespeare's plays even when people did not always flock to see them. "To do one's bit for that beauty which is a joy forever is worth all the sacrifice, even the financial sacrifice," he

Wide World Photos

WALTER HAMPDEN

wrote in *Theatre*, April 1928. "Art does not always pay in coin."

He gave up his own theater in 1930 and played a variety of roles on tour: Svengali in *Trilby* (1938); Henry Wilton in *A Successful Calamity* (1938); the stage manager in *Our Town* (1939); *Ethan Frome* (1938); Thomas Jefferson in *The Patriots* (1943). He portrayed the butler in *The Admirable Crichton* (1931), Cardinal Wolsey in *Henry VIII* and Charles Venables in *What Every Woman Knows* in the American Repertory Company in New York (1946). He likes to recall that he departed from sword play and blank verse in such comedies as *Good Gracious, Annabelle* and *And Be My Love* and in the role of Sir Anthony Absolute in *The Rivals* (1942).

Of his many tours, Eleanor Hughes in *The Theatre Annual* 1948-1949 wrote: "Audiences everywhere esteem his name. In lean years and in fat, he has toured America, taking his fortune as he found it, never forgetting that the theatre should not limit itself to one city but should be part of the life of a nation." One of the dramatic critics who recognized Hampden's talents was H. T. Parker of the Boston *Transcript*, who wrote of *Cyrano* (April 30, 1929): "From outer semblance to inner spirit, from play with artifice to depths and heights of passion, is a personage well-rounded, many-shaded, in abundance achieved," and of *Macbeth* (January 5, 1923) "as with all his deeper-veined parts, Mr. Hampden assorts, adjusts, achieves in slowly ripening process. . . here sweeps the power that is yet born and reborn upon the tragic stage," and of *Hamlet* (December 26, 1922) "intrinsically romantic, a *Hamlet* of sensibility."

His film career began in 1939 in *The Hunchback of Notre Dame*. His most recent picture was the role of "an aging actor" in *All About Eve* (1950); the part of the British ambas-

HAMPDEN, WALTER—*Continued*

sador in *Five Fingers; The First Legion* with Charles Boyer (1950); *Adventures of Mark Twain* (1944) and others. He was in radio almost since the beginning and in 1945 had a popular Sunday night show playing a criminologist. In 1948 he was host on the Mutual network's radio series *Great Scenes from Great Plays,* sponsored by the National Council of the Protestant Episcopal Church, and he also played *Cyrano.*

He made his television debut on May 1, 1949, in the title role of *Macbeth,* a production by members of The Players (an actors' club founded in 1888 by Edwin Booth). When the columnist Hedda Hopper asked him how he managed the transition from the stage to video, he replied, "It's like everything else in life where things occur so gradually you don't stop to think" (Philadelphia *Bulletin,* November 4, 1951).

Returning to Broadway in 1949, he played the part of Professor Tobias Emanuel opposite Lee Tracy in Herman Wouk's play, *The Traitor.* Although seven of eight critics praised the play, it ran for only sixty-seven performances. On December 26, 1949, he portrayed an elderly monsignor opposite Grace George in *The Velvet Glove,* which ran for 152 performances. Brooks Atkinson in reviewing the play wrote: "Mr. Hampden gets mellower and more companionable through the years" (New York *Times*).

When asked who was the most beautiful woman he had ever known, Hampden replied: "After my wife and daughter, of course, I believe Modjeska was the most beautiful. She was also, in my opinion, the finest actress— better than Duse, better than Bernhardt" (*Cue,* February 24, 1945).

Walter Hampden is the fourth president of The Players, succeeding John Drew, Joseph Jefferson and Edwin Booth to this life-time honor. He is also a member of the Century and the Harvard Clubs.

He told the columnist Ward Morehouse (New York *Sun,* February 14, 1945), "*Cyrano* is one of the really tough parts, but the part that takes the most out of you is *Macbeth*— all those changes and that combat at the end. Hamlet is a long part but never so trying as Macbeth or Cyrano." Commenting on his most recent role in *The Crucible,* Hampden told Sidney Fields in the New York *Mirror* (February 21, 1953), "Now that I'm old it's exciting to act with hardy young talents like Arthur Kennedy and Beatrice Straight. I catch their fire."

Modesty has always been his mark, and although honors have come to him, he often says, "My wife would have done brilliantly in the theatre but she left the stage and busied herself with our home in Ridgefield, our son and daughter and later our four grandchildren. So you see, a husband is a handicap to a career."

For relaxation he still plays the cello. "But I keep a mute on it so no one will hear me," he said. When asked for his recipe for longevity he replied: "I follow Sarah Bernhardt's dictum for preserving energy: 'Never stand up when you can sit down, and never sit when you can lie down.'"

He told Sidney Fields of the New York *Mirror,* February 21, 1953, "An actor's prize is not to look at himself in the mirror every morning. . . .His chief reward is the opportunity to practice his craft in great roles. I've had that chance."

References

Cue 14:7 p8 F 24 '45
N Y Herald Tribune IV p 1 F 18 '45
N Y Post p24 F 20 '45
N Y Sun p30 F 14 '45
N Y Mirror F 2 '53
Theatre 47:19+ Ap 28 por
N Y Theatre Program (Martin Beck Theatre) J 22 '53
Who's Who in America, 1952-53
Who's Who in the Theatre (1953)
World Biography (1948)

HANNAGAN, STEVE Apr. 4, 1899—Feb 5, 1953 Publicity agent; began career as a newspaper reporter, later becoming sports writer; joined an advertising agency as copy writer in 1919; opened own publicity office in 1924; at first promoted vacation resorts (Miami Beach) and sports figures; afterward handled publicity for the Jack Benny radio show, the Stork Club, and for many corporations including the Union Pacific Railroad and the Coca Cola Company. See *Current Biography,* 1944.

Obituary

N Y Times p19 F 6 '53

HARP, EDWARD B(LAINE) JR. May 17, 1903- Chaplain

Address: b. Bureau of Naval Personnel, Washington, 25, D.C.; h. Falls Church, Va.

The ninth Chief of Chaplains of the Navy and assistant chief of Naval personnel, Rear Admiral Edward B. Harp, Jr., assumed office on February 1, 1953, upon the retirement of his predecessor, Rear Admiral Stanton W. Salisbury. For Chaplain Harp, this assignment culminates twenty-three years of experience as a Navy chaplain.

Admiral Harp has stated to the Chaplain Corps, "Amid all the confusion and uncertainty that exists, men and women everywhere are seeking light and truth and whatever else that will give stability and meaning to their lives . . .And though we all represent different religious traditions, our hearts should and must beat as one as we strive for the common objective of bringing the eternal riches of God to men." Harp served in the Southwest Pacific during World War II and was awarded a Letter of Commendation with combat "V" for his meritorious conduct when the aircraft carrier, the *Hornet,* was sunk in 1942.

Edward Blaine Harp, Jr., the son of Edward Blaine Harp, Sr., and Hadessa Martha (Stotelmyer) Harp, was born in Hagerstown, Maryland, on May 17, 1903. He was reared in Hagerstown, attending Smithburg High School from which he was graduated in 1920. Entering Franklin and Marshall College, Lancaster, Pennsylvania, Harp majored in sociology and participated in musical activities. He earned his A.B. degree in 1926. Harp's post-graduate study was conducted at the Reformed Theological Seminary in Lancaster, and in June 1929, he received his B.D. degree

Ordained June 24, 1929, he served as an assistant pastor of the Christ Reformed Church at Cavestown, Maryland. However, he soon decided to relinquish parish work and obtained a commission as a Navy chaplain in 1929.

Chaplain Harp's first assignment was to the hospital ship, U.S.S. *Relief,* where he served until 1931. He was then transferred to shore duty at the United States Naval Academy, Annapolis, Maryland. In 1933 he was returned to sea duty with an appointment to the battleship *Arkansas.* His next service, begun in 1936, was on the U.S.S. *Black Hawk,* a destroyer tender, where he remained until 1939, in which year he was again assigned to shore duty, this time at the United States Naval Hospital at Norfolk, Virginia.

Harp's next assignment was as chaplain of the aircraft carrier, the U.S.S. *Hornet,* in 1940. He saw Lieut. Gen. James Doolittle's fliers take off from this carrier to bomb Japan, went through the battles of Guadalcanal, Midway and Santa Cruz, and was aboard the vessel when it was struck and sunk off Santa Cruz Island on October 26, 1942.

As one of the twelve contributors to the book, *This Is It* (Vanguard, 1944), compiled by Harry Davis, Chaplain Harp recounted in the chapter, "God Stood Beside Us," his experiences during the attack upon the *Hornet,* begun in mid-morning, by seventy-two enemy planes, both bombers and torpedo carriers. He fell once by the striking of a demolition bomb upon the flight deck. Its explosion was so close that he could "smell the odor of white-hot steel."

At another time a torpedo hit the stern of the vessel and "the whole afterpart of the ship leaped up," lifting Harp into the air and hurling him along the deck. When the order was given to abandon ship, Harp recited the committal and the benediction for the dead, then went over the side on a knotted line. The Washington *Post* reported that Harp "swam for two hours before reaching a life raft" (January 4, 1953). For his conduct during the attack, the Chaplain was awarded a Letter of Commendation with Combat "V".

In *This Is It,* Harp also wrote of his work in conducting religious services at the small altar in the crew's main mess compartment, of the influence of these services upon the men, and of the counseling that he was called upon to give to those who turned to him for help.

Harp was on shore duty again in 1943, serving as executive officer and instructor in the Chaplains' School. Later he was transferred to service at St. Alban's Naval Hospital, New York, remaining there until 1945 when he was sent as chaplain to the United States Coast Guard Academy. From 1948 to 1950, Harp's

U. S. Navy

REAR ADM. EDWARD B. HARP, JR.

status was that of Pacific Fleet chaplain. His next service, undertaken in 1951, was as planning assistant to the Chief of Chaplains.

Upon his latest appointment, announced January 3, 1953, as Chief of Chaplains and assistant chief of Naval personnel, Chaplain Harp was also promoted to the rank of rear admiral. In his new office, he is in charge of the religious affairs of the Marines as well as the Navy, the Marines having no chaplains of their own. Since the formative years of many youths coincide with the period of military service, with one million entering and leaving it every year, and some 3½ million in the armed forces around the world, Harp commented on the fact that American churches may not be fulfilling their function towards these men. He stated that although he had not made a full study of the situation, he felt that churches "by and large, realize what is happening" (*Christian Science Monitor,* June 1, 1953).

Admiral Harp holds an honorary degree of Doctor of Divinity from Franklin and Marshall College, awarded in 1945. He is affiliated with the Evangelical and Reformed Church, and is a member of Phi Sigma Kappa, the Nucummen Society of England, and Rotary International. Harp married Laura Lee Cash of Spartanburg, South Carolina, on October 6, 1934. They have two children, Julia Lee and Edward Blaine, 3rd. The admiral is brown-haired, brown-eyed, weighs 164 pounds and is five feet eight inches tall. For relaxation he enjoys golf and listening to music.

References

N Y Times p4 Ja 4 '53 por
Washington Post p3M Ja 4 '53 por
Davis, H. ed. This Is It (1944)
Griffin, A. R. Ship to Remember; The Saga of the Hornet (Howell, Soskin, 1943)

HART, EDWARD J(OSEPH) Mar. 25, 1893- United States Representative from New Jersey

Address: b. House Office Bldg., Washington 25, D.C.; 591 Summit Ave., Jersey City, N.J.; Postoffice Bldg., Union City, N.J.; h. 63 Sherman Pl., N.J.

Edward J. Hart, Democratic Representative of the Fourteenth New Jersey Congressional District, is known nationally as the first chairman (January to July 1945) of the permanent House of Representatives Un-American Activities Committee and as a long-time member and later chairman of the House Merchant Marine

Wide World Photos
EDWARD J. HART

and Fisheries Committee. He joined the latter in January 1935, just after being seated in the Seventy-fourth Congress, and helped to draft the Merchant Marine Act of 1936. First elected chairman of the New Jersey Democratic State Committee in 1944, Hart won recognition from the Governor of New Jersey in March 1951 when his leadership was challenged by a rival group in the party. Hart was elected to the Eighty-third Congress in November 1952.

Born to Dominic J. and Margaret (Connelly) Hart in Jersey City, New Jersey, on March 25, 1893, Edward Joseph Hart is a native of the Congressional district he has so long represented in Washington. In Jersey City he attended local public grade and Roman Catholic parochial schools. He then entered St. Peter's High School, where he prepared for admission to St. Peter's (Jesuit) College, also in his native city. In September 1913, having received his B.A. degree the preceding June, young Hart began his career with a governmental appointment to the secretaryship of the Excise Commission of the District of Columbia, which he held until 1917. Hart continued

his academic studies and took his M.A. degree from St. Peter's in June 1914, became a chief field deputy of the United States Bureau of Internal Revenue in 1918, and continued as such until 1921, when the Republicans returned to power under President Warren G. Harding. The future legislator then enrolled in the Georgetown (Washington, D.C.) University School of Law, where he was awarded his LL.B. degree in June 1924 and was admitted to the District of Columbia bar.

Following his admission to the New Jersey bar in 1925, he was engaged in private law practice until he was appointed in late 1929 as assistant Corporation Counsel for Jersey City by the Democratic mayor and northern New Jersey political "boss," Frank Hague. With the support of Mayor Hague, Hart was elected to the Seventy-fourth Congress in November 1934 as representative of the Fourteenth New Jersey District. He has been re-elected to all subsequent Congresses by this strongly Democratic district, which today encompasses five Jersey City wards and several cities and towns in Hudson County.

Soon after being seated in the Seventy-fourth Congress (1935-36), Representative Hart was assigned to the House Merchant Marine and Fisheries Committee and to the committees on education and war claims. The United States shipping industry had declined alarmingly in the year subsequent to 1919, largely because of high American construction and operating costs in comparison with those of foreign countries. When, on March 4, 1935, President Franklin D. Roosevelt, in a special message to Congress, recommended legislation for the development of an adequate Merchant Marine, Representative Schuyler Otis Bland of Virginia authored a subsidy bill for American shipping which met strong opposition in the Senate, where it failed to reach a vote. During the second session of the Seventy-fourth Congress the House Merchant Marine and Fisheries Committee brought forth an improved bill which became the Merchant Marine Act of 1936. This act, in the drafting of which Congressman Hart took an active hand, provided for "payment of Government subsidies to builders and operators of American ships sufficient to make up the differences between United States and foreign costs," such ships "to serve as a naval and military auxiliary in time of war or national emergency" (*Collier's Encyclopaedia*). The fleet was to be owned and operated "in so far as practicable" by private citizens, subject to the authority of what later became the Maritime Commission.

On a majority of issues, especially domestic, Congressman Hart supported the Roosevelt Administration, voting for the Social Security, Eccles banking, and Guffey-Snyder coal bills in the Seventy-fourth Congress and for the President's Supreme Court retirement bill in the Seventy-fifth. He opposed investigation of sit-down strikes in 1937, though in the spring of the following year he was to defend Mayor Hague's opposition to the CIO in a radio speech. In February 1938 he proposed amendments to the 1936 Merchant Marine Act which, stated the New York *Times,* would regulate rates on the New York State barge canal system without extending the regulations to other inland waterways" (the proposed amendment was opposed by both the Shippers Conference of Greater New York and the New York Merchants Association, as discriminating in favor of Mississippi River traffic.) In the matter of foreign relations and pre-Pearl Harbor aid to the World War II Allies, Hart's position varied: in 1937 he voted against the peacetime embargo on exporting munitions, but favored its continuance two years later. On April 29, 1940, at the annual Americanization Day celebration in Jersey City, the Congressman stated, "No matter what pressure is brought to bear, I will never vote to send an American boy to engage in quarrels in Europe." The following September he favored passage of the conscription bill, supported lend-lease in February 1941 and repeal of the ban on arming merchant ships in October. Hart went on record against the Hatch pernicious political activities bill in both 1939 and 1940 and against the Smith anti-strike bill in November 1941. He attended his first Democratic National Convention in 1940, as an alternate delegate from New Jersey.

Early known as "an outspoken opponent of Communism" (New York Herald Tribune), the New Jersey legislator declined in August 1940 to address the American Youth Congress because he considered it Communist controlled. In 1942 he voted to extend the life of the House Special Committee on Un-American Activities (the Dies Committee) through 1943, and in July of the latter year served with Representative Richard D. Wigglesworth (Republican) of Massachusetts as one of a subcommittee of two which took testimony in New York for a special House committee investigating alleged "Gestapo phases" of the activity of the Federal Communications Commission. Hart, who attended the 1944 Democratic Convention as a delegate-at-large, was elected chairman of the Democratic State Committee of New Jersey a month later (August), and in his campaign for Congress in the same summer and fall received for the first time the support of the CIO (commentators pointed out at this time that Mayor Hague had ended his "feud" with the CIO earlier in the year). When, at the opening of the Seventy-ninth Congress (January 1945), the House voted to replace the Dies Committee with a permanent House Un-American Activities Committee, Hart was approved by the CIO to be the first chairman. In an editorial the New York Herald Tribune referred to Hart as "an able legislator" and applauded his credo of the committee's functions. "The first great need . . . is for a definition of what un-American activities are," Hart had said in an interview. "I deplore the attitude found in so many quarters that a thing is un-American because it is opposed to the personal views of those who are doing the denouncing." The balance of power on the committee was held by Representative John E. Rankin of Mississippi, with whom Hart disagreed on the desirability of a definition and on other matters. After about six months as chairman, Hart resigned on July 2, the reason given being the "recommendation of his physician" (New York Times).

During the Republican-controlled Eightieth Congress the Representative of the Fourteenth New Jersey District aligned himself with the Truman Administration on most issues of defense and foreign policy. He had favored the Fulbright world organization resolution in 1943, the authorization of UNRRA in the year following, and the 1946 loan to Great Britain; in 1947 he was to vote for Greek-Turkish aid (May) and the Voice of America bill (June), and in 1948 for $6 billion foreign aid authorization (March). On domestic issues Hart was not invariably a "Truman man"; he voted to limit the presidency to two terms (February 1947) and favored the Republican tax bill (February 1948) as well as the Mundt-Nixon subversive activities control bill (May 1948), which was denounced by the President. In the Eighty-first Congress Representative Hart (who had become the ranking Democrat in the House Merchant Marine and Fisheries Committee, under Chairman Schuyler Bland) headed the subcommittee which held public hearings on suggested long-range legislation including a CIO-supported proposal to extend construction subsidies to tramp vessels (July 1949). During the same summer he also headed the subcommittee on unemployment of the Joint Committee on the Economic Report. The final month of 1949 witnessed the beginning of the end of the long association of the Congressman with Frank Hague, who had been defeated in the New Jersey Democratic primaries (May) for renomination as Mayor of Jersey City by John V. Kenny. Kenny, on election in November, accepted Hart as chairman of the Democratic State Committee. "Mr. Hart broke with Mr. Hague," Robert M. Hallett of the Christian Science Monitor stated, "when he recommended a Kenny man for Hudson County elections commissioner to succeed a key Hague man. He also asked Mr. Kenny . . . to help insure his re-election in the Fourteenth Congressional District."

Following the death in February 1950 of Chairman Schuyler Otis Bland of the House Merchant Marine and Fisheries Committee, Representative Hart was elected his successor. Describing himself as "a student of Mr. Bland," the new chairman promised that the committee would "press progressive legislation furthering the Merchant Marine and including what the New York Times summarized as "machinery designed to set up a system of Government-financed war risk insurance against a future emergency" as well as a revived bill to subsidize tramp ships. He also endorsed "recovery" by the City of Hoboken of the old North German Lloyd and Hamburg-American Line piers, a recovery in practice effected in September 1952, when the piers were leased by the Maritime Commission to the Port of New York Authority for $1 a year. In September 1950 Hart led a successful fight on the floor of the House for revision of Panama Canal tolls; then in February 1951 he authorized a bill requiring licensed deck officers aboard all American vessels larger than 100 gross tons. The following month Congressman Hart, who had been re-elected by his district in the previous November by a majority of more than 20,000,

HART, EDWARD J.—*Continued*

was secured in the chairmanship of the New Jersey State Democratic Committee through "recognition" by Governor Alfred E. Driscoll, after his position had been challenged by State Senator Edward J. O'Mara, the nominee of former Mayor Hague. Hart, who declined an appointment to the Federal bench in New Jersey in the following October, was in that month the object of some criticism because he had failed to summon his committee to act on a long-range Merchant Marine bill passed by the Senate in August after some of its provisions, including tax-deferment benefits to shipbuilders, had been opposed by the President and the Treasury Department. In April 1952 Hart scheduled hearings on the controversial Senate bill, which included, among other provisions disapproved by the Administration, extension of construction subsidies to all American flag ships built for foreign trade.

The voting record of Hart in the Eighty-first and Eighty-second Congresses shows him supporting extension of the Marshall Plan (April 1949) and repeal of Federal margarine taxes (April 1949); he favored Korea-Formosa economic aid (February 1950) and opposed a $600 million cut in Federal spending (May 1950). In 1951 he was against a $10 million cut in reclamation funds (May) and against the tidelands oil bill. The following year he voted "nay" to using the Taft-Hartley law to stop the steel strike (June) and "yea" to retaining 90 per cent farm price supports (June). Hart was returned to Congress in the election of November 4, 1952.

Representative Hart is a member of the American, New Jersey, and Hudson County bar associations, the American Academy of Political and Social Sciences, the American Irish Historical Society, and the John Carroll Society, and is an honorary life member of both the Dante Alighieri Society and the Foresters. In religious affiliation he is a Catholic. On April 14, 1936, he married Loretta A. O'Connell, of Newark, New Jersey. The New Jersey Congressman, whose height is five feet eight inches and weight is about 214 pounds, has been described in the New York *Herald Tribune* as "a large, red-headed genial man."

References

N Y Herald Tribune II p3 Ja 21 '45 por
N Y Times p59 Mr 30 '50 por
American Catholic Who's Who, 1952-53
Biographical Directory of the American Congress, 1774-1949 (1950)
Who's Who in America, 1952-53
Who's Who in the Nation's Capital, 1938-39

HARTMAN, LOUIS F(RANCIS), REV.
Jan. 17, 1901- Religious leader; educator

Address: c/o Holy Redeemer College, Washington 17, D.C.

Since 1948 the Reverend Louis F. Hartman, C.Ss.R., has been chairman of the editorial board of the new Catholic translation of the Bible, the first volume of which was published in September 1952. Begun in 1943, this volume consisting of the first eight books of the Old Testament will be followed by four other volumes containing the rest of that Testament and all of the New Testament, to be finished by about 1955. The new Bible, translated from the original manuscripts into "the living language of today," was prepared by the Catholic Biblical Association of America, of which Hartman has been executive secretary since 1948. The association has headquarters at the Catholic University of America, Washington, D.C., where beginning in 1950 Hartman has been an assistant professor in the department of Semitic languages. Prior to his assignment in the nation's capital, he had taught Sacred Scriptures and Hebrew at the Redemptorist Seminary of Mount Saint Alphonsus in Esopus, New York.

The son of Louis Francis Hartman, a printer, and Josephine (Grennan) Hartman, the Reverend Louis Francis Hartman was born January 17, 1901, in New York City, the birthplace of his parents. (His elder brother died in childhood; of his five sisters, three are now married, one is a nun, and the fifth, now deceased, was also a nun.)

The boy was reared in the Bronx, in the parish of the Immaculate Conception, which is in charge of the Redemptorist Fathers. At his graduation from the parish school in 1915, Hartman went to the Redemptorist preparatory college (high school and junior college course) from September 1915 to June 1921, when he entered the Novitiate of the Redemptorist Fathers at Ilchester (near Baltimore), Maryland, the next year (August 22).

The Redemptorist Fathers (Congregation of the Most Holy Redeemer) is a society of missionary priests founded in 1732 by St. Alphonsus Maria Liguori in Scala, Italy, "for the purpose of laboring among the neglected country people in the neighborhood of Naples" (*Catholic Encyclopaedia*). The American province of the Congregation was established in Maryland in 1850, under the Reverend Bernard Hafkenschied. The Redemptorists (the *Catholic Encyclopaedia* explains) "take simple vows of poverty, chastity, and obedience, and by the vows of poverty they are bound to refuse all ecclesiastical dignities outside the Congregation." Thus Father Hartman uses only the letters, C. Ss. R., the abbreviations for his order, with his name.

For six years beginning in August 1922, Hartman was a seminarian at the Redemptorist Seminary of Mount Saint Alphonsus, Esopus, New York. Then from August 1928 to January 1929 he spent his second novitiate in Annapolis, Maryland. He remained for the spring semester of 1929 to take courses in Hebrew, Syriac, and Greek at the Catholic University of America, Washington, D.C. That fall he went to Rome, Italy, for three years (1929-32) to study Sacred Scripture and Semitic languages at the Pontifical Biblical Institute, from which he received the Licentiate in Sacred Scripture (equivalent to a master's degree). In September 1932 he returned to the United States and taught Sacred Scripture and Hebrew at the Redemptorist Seminary of Mount Saint Alphonsus, Esopus, until 1934 when he went back to Rome for two more years of study at the Pontifical Biblical Institute, this time specializing in cuneiform studies and receiving in 1936 the degree of the Licentiate in Oriental Languages. Having returned to the United States, Hartman in September 1936 resumed his teaching of Sacred Scripture at Mount Saint Alphonsus Seminary in New York.

This was also the year in which the Catholic Biblical Association was organized in Washington, D.C., "to promote scientific study of the Bible and the popular diffusion of Biblical knowledge" (*National Catholic Almanac*). At that time, the official Roman Catholic version of the Bible was the Vulgate (people's Bible)— the first translation of the Bible from its original language into Latin, completed by St. Jerome in 405 A.D. and officially accepted by the Roman Catholic Church through the action of the Council of Trent in 1546. The translation of this Latin version into English in 1609 was called the Douay Bible. It was to replace the Douay Bible that the Catholic Biblical Association set out to re-translate St. Jerome's Vulgate, without officially referring to the original Hebrew or Greek manuscripts. The association's revision—not a new translation—of the New Testament appeared in 1941 and work on the Old Testament had been in progress for about two years when the encyclical *Divino Afflante Spiritu*, issued by Pope Pius XII in 1943, caused the scholars to abandon the project and undertake an entirely new translation from the original languages.

In his encyclical His Holiness not only urged that a version of the Bible be made "in the language of the people" which would be "for the profitable use of the faithful and for a better understanding of the Word of God," but also declared that original Scriptural texts had "more authority and weight" than subsequent translations and that "the Biblical scholar who . . . would deprive himself of access to the original texts could in no wise escape the stigma of levity and sloth." The American Catholic Heirarchy, acting through the Episcopal Committee of the Confraternity of Christian Doctrine, asked the Catholic Biblical Association of America to prepare a translation of both the Old and the New Testaments from the original Hebrew, Aramaic, and Greek manuscripts into "the living language of today." Subsequently a committee of thirty-seven scholars, headed by the Reverend Louis F. Hartman, began work in 1943. They had the advantage of a greater volume of manuscripts as well as advances in textual criticism, which had not been available to St. Jerome.

Father Hartman continued his teaching at the Redemptorist Seminary in Esopus, until 1948 when he was named chairman of the editorial board of the new Catholic translation of the Old Testament, a position he retains. (The other members of the board are the Reverends Stephen Hartdegen, Patrick Skehan, Roland Murphy, and Edward Sigman.) At the same time he also accepted the office of general secretary of the Catholic Biblical Association

Ackad

REV. LOUIS F. HARTMAN

of America, with headquarters at the Catholic University of America, Washington, D.C., and has since been annually re-elected to this position, the title of which has now been changed to executive secretary. Since September 1948 he has been stationed at the Holy Redeemer College in the nation's capital, and since September 1950 he has been an assistant professor in the department of Semitic languages at the Catholic University of America, teaching Hebrew, Aramaic, Syriac, Akkadian (Assyrian-Babylonian), and Sumerian.

With Hartman heading the editorial board, the book of Genesis became the first part of the new Catholic translation of the Bible to be published in 1948; this was followed two years later by the book of Psalms. The first entire volume, containing the first eight books of the Old Testament (Genesis, Exodus, Leviticus, Numbers, Deuteronomy, Joshua, Judges, and Ruth), was published on September 30, 1952—a date coinciding with Catholic Bible week, with the feast of St. Jerome (patron of Roman Catholic Biblical studies), with the simultaneous publication of the new Protestant Revised Standard Version of the entire Bible, and with the celebration of the 500th anniversary of the first printing by Johann Gutenberg of the Latin Vulgate Bible, believed to have been the first sizable book printed in Europe on movable type. As one of the petitioners for the Gutenberg Anniversary postage stamp which the Post Office Department issued on September 30, 1952, Hartman served as chairman of the Gutenberg Anniversary Committee and presided at the Library of Congress ceremony at which this commemorative stamp was first presented by the Postmaster General to the Librarian of Congress.

Before the first volume was published Father Hartman had pointed out: "We are going further than the Protestant Revised Standard

HARTMAN, LOUIS F.—*Continued*

Version in avoiding every semblance of archaisms, including all 'thou' and 'thy' forms; our version will probably be the first to use 'you' and 'your' throughout" (New York *Times,* June 1, 1952). The work, which has been called "the greatest accomplishment to date of American Catholic Biblical scholarship," is marked by "improved English style, accuracy of thought and correctness of expression" without any "radical changes" (Washington *Post,* September 29, 1952). The volume published in September is the first of the projected five-volume work, known as the "Confraternity Bible" because of its sponsorship by the Episcopal Committee of the Confraternity of Christian Doctrine. The remainder of the Old Testament and a fresh translation of the New Testament will be published in four additional volumes, to be completed about 1955.

Hartman is the author of *Commentary on the New Testament* (1940) comprising his commentaries on Matthew, Mark, and Luke. His paper, "The Domestic Animals of Ancient Mesopotamia," written in collaboration with A. Leo Oppenheim and based on his interpretation of cuneiform inscriptions on tablets in the possession of the Metropolitan Museum of Art, appeared in the July 1945 issue of the *Journal of Near Eastern Studies.* Another of his papers, "On Beer and Brewing Techniques in Ancient Mesopotamia," was published in the December 1950 supplement of the *Journal of the American Oriental Society.* In 1951 his "Saint Jerome as an Exegete" appeared in the volume *A Monument to Saint Jerome.* Father Hartman is a member of the American Oriental Society and of the American Schools of Oriental Research. The gray-eyed and brown-haired Biblical scholar is five feet six inches in height and weighs 140 pounds. He names fishing and bird-watching as his recreations.

HARTNELL, NORMAN (BISHOP) June 12, 1901-　Couturier to Queen Elizabeth II of England

Address: b. 26 Bruton St., W.1, London, England; h. Lovel Dene, Windsor Forest, Berkshire, England

Recognized as a couturier with world influence on fashion, Norman Hartnell has been dressmaker by appointment to the royal family of England since 1938. He created the gowns which the Queen Mother wore on state visits to France in 1938, to the United States and Canada in 1939, and to South Africa in 1947. He designed the dress that Queen Elizabeth II wore at her wedding to the Duke of Edinburgh in 1947, and Her Majesty's coronation gown. Hartnell was also responsible for designing the new style robe worn by viscountesses and baronesses at the coronation on June 2, 1953. There was no copyright on his designs for the coronation robe nor for the cap of state worn as an "austerity" coronet.

He creates about 1,000 gowns each year, ranging in price from $300 to $5,000, and he also earns more than $1 million from Hartnell de-

signs used for mass production. As chairman of the Incorporated Society of London Fashion Designers, he helps Britain sell abroad mass-produced clothes worth several million dollars, and exclusive models netting several hundred thousand dollars. His perfume business includes a fragrance inspired by the coronation called "Hartnell 1st."

Norman Bishop Hartnell was born in the London suburb of Streatham on June 12, 1901, the son of a local grocer and his wife. He received his early education at Mill Hill, a small boarding institution. In 1921, he entered Magdalene College at Cambridge University, where he became one of the best "Rugby halfbacks" in football (*Maclean's Magazine,* January 1, 1951). He planned to be an artist, and during his second year won several prizes at the college arts show. A member of the University Footlights Club, he participated in revues, designing his own costumes. After two years he left Cambridge, foregoing his plans for an artist's career because he did not have enough money to study in Paris. Following the advice of a fashion editor, he went to work as a clerk in a London dress shop and endeavored to produce his own dress designs in his spare time.

With the aid of a loan from his sister, Hartnell opened his own dressmaking business in 1923, in an attic at 10 Bruton Street in London. He received encouragement from Lady Lucie Duff Gordon, a fashion editor, who published some of his designs in the *Daily Graphic.* His early patronage was largely comprised of his sister's friends, and wives and sisters of his classmates at Cambridge University. When Countess Mountbatten called and ordered a dress, Hartnell's reputation was made.

He soon became known for his creative use of tulle, embroidery, sequins, and furs, and was referred to as "one of the three leading London houses" in dress designing in the London *Times,* January 11, 1932, which stated that his efforts "aimed at establishing in London the counterpart of the *haute couture* in Paris," and helped British textile manufacturers display their products "under the most favorable auspices." Queen Mary became interested in the success of English fabrics and requested that some of Hartnell's designs be submitted to her for inspection.

His spring collection shown at Claridge's in London in 1933 was acclaimed "the first important fashion parade of the season" (London *Times,* March 6, 1933). The ball room was filled to capacity and "overflow parades" were held in adjoining rooms. Becoming celebrated for his distinctive and skillful use of embroidery and jewelry on evening frocks and court gowns, he received in 1935 his first royal commission from Lady Alice Christabel Montagu-Douglass-Scott for her wedding dress to be worn at her marriage to the Duke of Gloucester.

Through this commission he met the Duchess of York and two years later she requested Hartnell to make the train bearers' robes at the Coronation of George VI. In 1938 the couturier was made dressmaker by appointment to Queen Elizabeth (now Queen Mother).

By 1939 Hartnell had about 400 workers in his employ and was credited with making London "a fashion center for the world" (New York *Times,* April 26, 1939). Asked where he obtained his ideas, he is quoted by the *Times* as replying "from anything beautiful—a tree, maybe; a beautiful picture or scene." To get inspiration he studied Italian and French paintings in the National Art Gallery.

Queen Elizabeth (now Queen Mother) in 1939 commissioned Hartnell to create clothes for her state visits to Canada and the United States. The designs were closely guarded from style-pirates until the King and Queen sailed for North America. Included in the wardrobe, which reflected the pastel shade favorites of the Queen, were creations made from gifts of cloth from United States woolen manufacturers. Canadian and American women asked for British fashion styles and Hartnell sent an Australian film actress, Margaret Vyner, to Canada to model several of his designs, said to be indicative of the Queen's taste. The white satin dress with gold pearls worn by the Queen at the opening of Parliament in Ottawa during her royal tour of Canada was called "a glittering regal creation" (*Maclean's Magazine*). She presented it to Canada, where it is now displayed in the Royal Ontario Museum.

During World War II the British Ministry of Supply, upon the suggestion of Queen Elizabeth, commissioned Hartnell to design women's uniforms. The Government also sought his advice in 1942, together with that of other top English designers, concerning the production of utility clothes for mass consumption that would meet official "austerity" regulations. Hartnell submitted drawings of a basic wardrobe, from which many of the first utility coats, suits, and dresses were mass produced and the designer's opinion was that "austerity did much to improve taste." During the War, he also served as a member of the Home Guard.

The extent to which Hartnell's business suffered during the war could be judged by the shrinkage in his staff "from 400 to 103, with some still being called for service" (New York *Times,* May 15, 1945). Because of his export trade, he was allowed the use of "certain limited embellishments" and for those not permitted, such as embroidery, Hartnell substituted *clouté* (a kind of nailhead design).

A collection of his designs was first shown in Argentina in August 1946 to a crowded audience, including the late Señora Evita Duarte de Perón. Fashionable women, who previously responded only to French styles, were enthusiastic over his tea gowns and evening dresses. It was said that his "clever use of feathers and furs" had "an essentially Parisian stamp" *Christian Science Monitor,* August 5, 1946).

Upon his return to England in 1946, Hartnell received an order to prepare the wardrobe for Queen Elizabeth and in part that for Princesses Elizabeth and Margaret, for the royal tour of South Africa. Described by the New York *Times* (August 20, 1947) as standing "at the pinnacle of the fashion world,"

Wide World Photos

NORMAN HARTNELL

he was credited with fostering a trend to restore "peacetime femininity" and a return to the "feminine silhouette."

In his French Regency private salon in November 1947, Hartnell designed and fitted the wedding dress and going away suit for Princess Elizabeth, now Queen Elizabeth II, for her marriage to the Duke of Edinburgh. Austerity conditions in Britain prohibited a royal trousseau. As quoted by *Maclean's Magazine,* a London fashion expert said of the wedding gown: "In its design, Hartnell has probably reached the peak of his ability; it is a creation that needs the background of the Abbey, the splendor of the ceremony, and a princess to wear it." Following her marriage, Queen Elizabeth II, Hartnell states, "more or less continued" the Queen Mother's taste in clothes (New York *Herald Tribune,* November 27, 1951).

Hartnell's fall fashion show in London in 1948, emphasizing the "provocative bustle," was called the "most colorful" of Britain's season displays (New York *World-Telegram and Sun,* July 30, 1948). In 1950, together with about a dozen other members of the Incorporated Society of London Fashion Designers, Hartnell "netted Britain $300,000 from exclusive model exports to North America . . . and helped Britain sell abroad about $39 million worth of mass-produced clothes" (*Maclean's Magazine*). His royal patronage extended to the Duchess of Kent, considered one of the best-dressed women in the world. Then Princess Margaret gave Hartnell her custom, "assuring him attention of world debutantes" (*Maclean's Magazine*). Making dresses for the royal family, Hartnell says, "entails a great deal of work on the part of the designer . . . everything has to be of a completely special design" (New York *Herald Tribune*). His prominent customers in-

(Continued next page)

HARTNELL, NORMAN—*Continued*

clude Lady Churchill, Beatrice Lillie (Lady Peel) and Marlene Dietrich.

Hartnell was responsible for designing the streamlined robe and cap of state approved by Queen Elizabeth II, for wear by a viscountess or a baroness, at her coronation on June 2, 1953. It represented the first modifications in coronation dress "for 250 years" (*Christian Science Monitor,* February 3, 1953). The robe has a slender waistline, and a six-paneled skirt with short train. It requires six yards of material instead of twenty, as in the traditional robe, and . . . "crimson velveteen replaces silk velvet, while white coney replaces ermine" (*New York Times,* December 25, 1952). Women above the rank of viscountess or baroness were required to wear the traditional robe. In his design for the cap of state, Hartnell used velveteen sectioned in gold cord, edged with pointed white fur-fabric, and having five pearl drops suspended from a raised design of gold cord. For wear by commoners' wives at the ceremony in Westminster Abbey, Hartnell created a veil-like headdress.

Hartnell was awarded Officier d'Académie by the French Government in 1939. In 1940 he was granted the Royal Warrant. For distinguished service in the field of fashion, he received a Nieman-Marcus Award, the "Oscar" of American fashion industry, at Dallas, Texas, on September 8, 1947, in its first presentation on an international basis. Described by J. McKenzie in *Maclean's Magazine* as a "chunky—five feet ten inches, 170 pounds—" man "with rocky features, who looks like an athlete," Hartnell enjoys outdoor hobbies. He breeds horses, dogs, and homing pigeons, and finds recreation in riding, swimming, and painting. He professes little knowledge of the accounting side of his business, saying: "I am an artist, not a businessman." Of Queen Elizabeth II, and her preference in couture, Hartnell states her gowns "must have the magnificence that suits the occasion" (*New York Times,* February 3, 1953).

References

Maclean's Mag 64:20, 22, 34 Ja 1 '51
Who's Who, 1952

HAUGE, GABRIEL (SYLFEST) (hoúgē) Mar. 7, 1914- Administrative assistant to the President of the United States; economist

Address: b. The White House, Washington, D.C.; h. 3500 Lowell St., N. W., Washington 16, D.C.

A particularly valued and trusted adviser of President Dwight D. Eisenhower since early in the political campaign of 1952, Dr. Gabriel S. Hauge was named by the incoming Chief Executive about three weeks after the election to be his "administrative assistant in charge of domestic and economic affairs." The Minnesota-born Dr. Hauge, who acquired his Ph.D. at Harvard in 1947, had taught economics at both Harvard and Princeton Universities before his four years of World War II service with the United States Navy. He was chief

U. S. Army

GABRIEL HAUGE

of the research division of the New York State Banking Department from 1947 until 1950, when he joined the McGraw-Hill Publishing Company and the editorial staff of the magazine *Business Week.*

Born to the Reverend Soren Gabrielson and Anna B. (Thompson) Hauge on March 7, 1914, Gabriel Sylfest Hauge is a native of Hawley, Minnesota, where his father was the pastor of the local Lutheran church. Brought up in Hawley, "Gabe" Hauge entered Concordia College at Moorhead, Minnesota on completing Hawley High School and received his A.B. degree in 1935. He was valedictorian of his graduating class; was awarded the Wickey Prize for being the outstanding junior, earning 448 honor points out of a possible 456. He was president of the freshman, sophomore and junior classes, president of the student body in his senior year, active in the debating club, the newspaper, the college radio station and head of the student religious organization.

He remained at Concordia College for one additional academic year as assistant Dean of Men and coach of forensics before entering Harvard University in 1936 on a George C. Christian Fellowship. An M.A. in economics was conferred upon him by Harvard in June, 1938.

Following the acquisition of his master's degree, the young economist returned to Minnesota to work as a budget examiner in the office of the State commissioner of the budget. In the fall Hauge returned to Massachusetts to be an instructor in the department of economics at Harvard for two years. During the summer of 1939, Hauge was employed as a senior statistician by the Federal Reserve Bank in New York. From 1940 to 1942, he held an instructorship in economics at Princeton University. During the latter part of this period he was employed also as a research assistant for the fiscal policy conference of the National Bureau of Economic Research which was making a study of "Fiscal Planning for Total War."

The economist was on active duty with the United States Navy during World War II, mainly aboard battleships in the Pacific theatre. When he returned to civilian life in 1946 after four years service, he held the rank of lieutenant commander.

Hauge returned to Harvard as a Social Science Research Fellow to complete the requirements for the Ph.D. degree which he received in June, 1947. Here he was "influenced by Professor John H. Williams of Harvard to join Elliott V. Bell, New York State Banking Commissioner in 1947, which in turn led to a series of associations with Governor Dewey, Senator Lodge, and to association with General Eisenhower." Hauge's doctorate dissertation was entitled "Banking Aspects of Treasury Borrowing During World War II."

In 1947, he became a member of the technical advisory committee for the Corporate Bond Project. Bell appointed him in that year the chief of the division of research and statistics of the New York State Banking Commission (1947-1950). He also served on the economic commission to the New York State Joint Legislative Committee on Interstate Cooperation (1948 to 1949). Dr. Hauge, in addition, did much of the preparatory work for Governor Dewey's series of lectures at Princeton University on the American system of Government and was adviser to Dewey in his presidential campaign in 1948.

When Bell resigned his position at the end of 1949 to become chairman of the executive committee of the McGraw-Hill Publishing Company, Inc. and editor and publisher of *Business Week*, he selected Dr. Hauge as his chief assistant and the editor of the "Trend" editorial page in *Business Week*, which he conducted until December 1, 1952.

In one editorial, a discussion of President Truman's seizure of the steel industry, entitled "The High Court Clears the Air," Hauge declared, "The decision is memorable because it helps arrest the dangerous trend toward concentration of power in the executive branch of the Government toward a loose interpretation of the Constitution, and toward the subordination of Congress . . . the court makes clear that, under the Constitution, Congress, not the Chief Executive, makes the law" (June 7, 1952).

Hauge was awarded, for writing this editorial, the George Washington Honor Medal and a cash award by the Freedoms Foundation of Valley Forge, Pennsylvania, in February, 1953. It was selected by the Foundation's national awards jury composed of chief justices of State Supreme Courts and officers of national patriotic and service clubs.

Dr. Hauge joined the Citizens for Eisenhower staff as research director in November 1951 and in the following June became a member of General Eisenhower's personal staff as head of research. *Newsweek* characterized him as "the . . . man whose word on the content of whistle-stop speeches is just about the final one (October 6, 1952).

Shortly after the election on November 28, General Eisenhower announced the appointment of Dr. Hauge to the incoming presidential staff as "administrative assistant in charge of domestic and economic affairs." He took office with the rest of the new White House staff on January 20, 1953.

One of Hauge's principal responsibilities is as liaison between the White House and Government departments as well as between the White House and Congress. The administrative assistant is a member of the newly created Advisory Board on Economic Growth and Stability which is composed of representatives of the Cabinet officers and the Council of Economic Advisors. This board creates general administrative policies for the several departments.

Hauge has continued to collaborate with Emmett Hughes, President Eisenhower's "principal speech writer" on Presidential pronouncements, policy statements and addresses. "A typical operation would be for Mr. Hauge to write the domestic side of the message, while Mr. Hughes would do the foreign" (New York *Times*, January 25, 1953).

Dr. Hauge "favors classic economic controls— the indirect controls which the Republicans favor—but he is not a *laissez faire* economist. He can be expected to agree with the Eisenhower thesis that the whole resources of the Federal Government, if needed, will be used to stem any potential depression" (Washington *Post*, January 20, 1953).

The economist "neither wants to set the clock back nor chase rainbows. His experience with State governments makes him wary of Federal power. He opposes controls not as a negative reaction but because of a deep faith in the tremendous strength of the American economic system when free of shackles." He is considered "a key man in planning the move to lift price and wage controls," as well as being "next to Sherman Adams . . . the White House staffer with the readiest access to the Presidential Ear" (New York *Post*, May 3, 1953). *Newsweek* reported that Hauge "masterminded" the Governors' conference of May, 1953 and "marshalled the cold facts that were paraded before" the State executives (June 15, 1953).

Dr. Hauge is a member of the American Economic Association Council on Foreign Relations, Inc., United States Naval Institute, United States Naval Reserve, New York Young Republican Club, and a trustee of the Riverdale Children's Association. He belongs to the Harvard Club in New York. He is a Lutheran and has occasionally served as a lay preacher. Mrs. Hauge is the former Helen Lansdowne Resor. The couple, who were married November 6, 1948, are now the parents of four children—Ann Bayliss, Stephen Burnet and John Resor, twins, and Barbara Thompson.

The administrator has blue eyes, brown hair and is six feet one-half inch tall and weighs 210 pounds. *Newsweek* described him as a "big, scholarly-looking man with nervous hands and an infrequent smile," a "quiet, almost shy man." Dr. Hauge is interested in cathedral and church

HAUGE, GABRIEL—*Continued*

architecture. The pleasant décor of his office was chosen by him and his wife.

In a "Trend" editorial Hauge commented upon our present tariff problem. "No American looks forward to foreign aid forever. . . .Nor does any American like the prospect of Kremlin exploitation of the trade difficulties of our Allies. A starting point in this troubled matter must be the fact that a large volume of imports is a sensible objective of American commercial policy. Imports are what foreign trade is all about anyway. Exports are for the purpose of buying imports. One means to attain that end . . . is to see to it that America's economy runs at a high, steady level. Another is . . . a liberal trade policy. . . .And that means that, in the national interest, strains may be put upon certain industries and certain firms. . . .The question may properly be raised whether the alleviation of such injury is not a national responsibility. It is in this area that some fresh thinking on a stale subject needs to be done" (*Business Week,* May 3, 1952).

References

Morning Forum (Fargo, N.D.) Je 14 '53 por
N Y Herald Tribune p1 N 29 '52
N Y Post Mag p2 My 3 '53 pors
Newsweek 40:23 D 8 '52 por; 41:76+ Je 15 '53 por
St. Paul Dispatch Je 11 '53 por
Washington (D.C.) Post p20 Ja 20 '53 por

HAYES, A(LBERT) J. Feb. 14, 1900- Labor union President

Address: b. c/o International Association of Machinists, Machinists Building, Washington, D.C.; h. 10206 Greenacre Dr., Silver Springs, Md.

Representing more than 600,000 members and 984 local unions, Albert J. Hayes heads the International Association of Machinists. His union returned to the American Federation of Labor in December 1950 after a six-year absence because of jurisdictional differences. Hayes, who succeeded Harvey W. Brown to the presidency on July 1, 1949 when Brown retired on reaching the union's mandatory sixty-five year age limit, had been gradually assuming the presidential functions since his election to the vice-presidency in 1945.

On June 11, 1953 Hayes' (AFL) union and the United Auto Workers (CIO) renewed a four-year-old no-raiding agreement and broadened it to include cooperation in collective bargaining and strikes. The two union presidents, Walter P. Reuther of the United Auto Workers and Hayes of the Machinists, called the agreement "virtually unprecedented in American labor history." A strike of members of the machinists union in sixty West Coast shipyards was begun on July 1, 1953, but was settled on July 13, and the employees returned to work on July 15, having gained a three cents an hour raise to a $2.16 basic pay, seven and a

half cents contribution an hour per man by management to the union's health and welfare fund, and a five cents an hour allowance to workers using their own tools.

When Hayes became vice-president in 1945, the union, which was founded May 5, 1888, had become the third largest which had ever been affiliated with the American Federation of Labor. The union, however, after a jurisdictional dispute with the AFL's millwrights, a specialists' branch of the carpenters' union, quit paying AFL per capita tax in 1943 and were suspended. Although they went back into the Federation in 1945, they dropped out again after a few months.

Albert J. Hayes was born in Milwaukee, Wisconsin, February 14, 1900, and attended Milwaukee public schools. He started to work as an apprentice machinist at ten cents an hour in the Milwaukee railroad shops, and at the age of seventeen joined the I.A.M. and worked next seventeen years as a union machinist in various sections of the country.

Hayes' first office in the union was that of local committeeman, and he subsequently became local union officer and delegate to the national convention. Then he was president of District Seven, which included the Chicago and Northwestern Railroad, and in 1934 was made Grand Lodge representative. During World War II he served on the War Labor Board.

Hayes was the sole candidate for election to president by the union's 651,000 members in April 1949. While his predecessor had stood firmly against compromise in jurisdiction, Hayes was "considered a more willing bargainer" (*Business Week,* March 5, 1949). At a meeting of the AFL Executive Council in February 1950, Hayes said, "We believe in a united labor movement. Reaffiliation of the Machinists with the AFL is one way to work for it" (New York *Times,* February 7, 1950).

Again in April 1950 he reiterated his point of view that his union "has long felt that disunity in the labor movement is a tragic negation of the whole principle of collective action" (New York *Herald-Tribune,* April 8, 1950).

William L. Hutcheson, president of the United Brotherhood of Carpenters, threatened he would take his 600,000 carpenters out of the AFL if the 600,000 machinists were readmitted to good standing without settling their dispute with his group. Hutcheson was overruled, however, and the AFL decided to invite the Machinists to reaffiliate. On April 8, 1950, while the situation was pending, Hayes threw his union's support behind the plan of Phillip Murray, CIO president, for an immediate alliance of all labor unions, with a view to a future broadly inclusive labor council.

The Korean war put most unity talk in the background, however, and Hayes was one of nine union leaders whose names were submitted to W. Stuart Symington, chairman of the National Security Resources board, as spokesmen for labor in the crisis. On August 9, 1950, Symington announced that Hayes, along with William Green, AFL president, and Philip Murray would serve as labor members of the National Security Board.

When organized labor issued a statement on mobilization, Hayes was one of the nine-man delegation that conferred with President Truman to ask that any wage control plan permit pay increases to match rises in the cost of living. The union had been strongly anti-communist since 1924, when Communists were barred from it, and Hayes pledged the Machinists' unstinting support to the Government in a Labor Day speech in 1950 (New York *Times,* September 4, 1950).

During this time a referendum had taken place in the union, and on January 5, 1951 the I.A.M. returned to the AFL. The vote was three and one-half to one in favor of rejoining, and was official when the Machinists' check for $15,135.90 was presented to the AFL treasurer as dues payment for 504,530 machinists. The Union claims a total membership of 600,000, including unemployed members and those exempt from dues.

As the defense program expanded, the labor members of the Mobilization board soon found themselves disagreeing with Charles E. Wilson, chief of the Office of Defense Mobilization, who decided not to grant labor's request that one of their top leaders be represented at the highest level of decision. Hayes was part of the United Labor Policy Committee, which, on February 2, 1951, said it was "gravely concerned" at the way mobilization plans were developing. Wilson did, however, name a five-man labor advisory board, of which Hayes was a member. In addition to this post, Hayes was named special assistant in manpower and personnel problems by Mrs. Anna Rosenberg, Assistant Secretary of Defense.

When the labor leaders called a general walk-out of all its representatives in mobilization agencies on March 1, 1951, Hayes resigned from the Defense Department. At the same time he left the Advisory Committee to the Economic Stabilization Agency, and the Labor-Management Advisory Committee. When the two-month boycott by labor was ended, Hayes resumed his post as special assistant to Mrs. Anna Rosenberg, on May 1, 1951.

Hayes was one of three dissenters on the President's Commission on the Health Needs of the Nation, over which he presided in City Hall, Philadelphia on August 11, 1951. This led to the announcement that the machinists' union would set up a program of its own to assist in forming local health plans, in contrast to the voluntary health insurance plans preferred by the President's Commission.

During the strike of the United Steelworkers (CIO) against the steel industry in April 1952, Hayes supported the CIO and predicted that the court would rule in favor of the Government and uphold President Truman's seizure of the mills.

Hayes caused considerable controversy when, testifying before the Senate Labor Committee hearings on Taft-Hartley amendments, he proposed a compulsory arbitration plan instead of the eighty-day injunction against strikers. Hayes' plan called for a three-man board, composed of labor, management and public,

Harris & Ewing

A. J. HAYES

which would make binding decisions after deciding whether or not a "real emergency" existed.

George Meany, president of the AFL, took sharp issue with Hayes' plan. He called compulsory arbitration "unworkable, unconstitutional and dangerous to the maintenance of a free economy." On the other hand, the New York *Times* editorialized (March 26, 1953) "As the head of one of the nation's largest and most important unions, Mr. Hayes is to be commended . . . for an idea which has usually been fought by labor leadership generally."

Hayes was elected a vice-president of the A.F.L. at the 1953 annual convention. In September, 1953 Hayes and Hutcheson met and agreed to try to find a formula to end the jurisdictional dispute between the machinists' and carpenters' unions.

Hayes gained considerable attention by commissioning Gerald Marks, composer, and Milton Pascal, lyricist, to write labor songs. "All our best songs, like 'Solidarity Forever,' have been purloined by the Communists," he said.

When Hayes introduced the "Sing a Labor Song" booklet in February 1950, he said: "We in the Machinists' Union have long felt that working people needed music through which to express themselves—American music. We think these songs will help meet that need . . . they tell labor's story better, perhaps, than all the speeches we could make." The songbook is available to all unions for a nominal sum through Gerald Marks, Music, Inc., 1619 Broadway, New York City.

With his wife Lillian, Hayes lives in Silver Springs, Maryland.

References

Bus Week p99, Mr 5 '49; p145 Je 7 '52
Fortune 39:191 Ap '49 por
N Y Times p27 Ja 31 '51

HAYWARD, SUSAN June 30, 1919- Motion picture actress
Address: b. c/o Twentieth Century-Fox Film Corporation, 10201 Pico St., Los Angeles, Calif.

One of Hollywood's top money-making stars, Susan Hayward, has appeared in more than thirty pictures since her screen debut in 1939 and she has been twice nominated for an award from the Academy of Motion Picture Arts and Sciences. She did her most outstanding early work in *House of Strangers, My Foolish Heart* and *I Can Get It for You Wholesale*. Her most

SUSAN HAYWARD

recent appearances in three pictures, *The Lusty Men, The Snows of Kilimanjaro* and *With A Song in My Heart* drew a total of $10,000,000 into theatre box offices in 1952, according to a recent tabulation by Twentieth Century-Fox Film Corporation.

Born Edythe Marrener in the Flatbush section of Brooklyn, New York, June 30, 1919, Susan Hayward, of Swedish, Irish, and French descent, is the second daughter and third child of Ellen and Walter Marrener. Her father, at one time a Coney Island barker, was a wireman for the Brooklyn Rapid Transit Company. In press interviews Miss Hayward has compared her childhood with that of Francie in *A Tree Grows in Brooklyn*. The first eighteen years of her life were spent in that borough, where she attended the Girls' Commercial High School.

After leaving school, she took employment as a photographer's model. Some color photographs of Miss Hayward, taken by Ivan Dimitri, which appeared in the *Saturday Evening Post* were seen by George Cukor, who, in association with David O. Selznick, was then seeking a Scarlett O'Hara for *Gone With the Wind*. Mr. Selznick arranged for Miss Hayward to come to Hollywood for a screen test.

Although she did not receive the part and Selznick dropped his option on her after six months, Miss Hayward decided to remain in the film capital.

Through the motion picture agent, Benny Medford, Miss Hayward obtained a six-month contract with Warner Brothers at $50 a week, but she was employed only in the making of color photographs used in publicity. Miss Hayward worked alone to improve her speech. As reported in an article by Thomas Wood in *Collier's* in 1951. she went to Ronald Colman movies night after night. "I must have gone to see *Prisoner of Zenda* a hundred times," she recalled, "I'd memorize his speeches and then try to imitate them on the way home."

When her contract with Warner expired, her agent placed her with Paramount at a starting salary of $250 a week. She made her first motion picture appearance in *Beau Geste* (1939), which starred Gary Cooper and Ray Milland. In the same year she was seen in two other Paramount pictures, *Our Leading Citizen* and *$1,000 a Touchdown*.

The actress was cast in the Paramount production *Among the Living* (1941) and also appeared in two "loan-out" assignments to other studios, one a Republic picture, *Sis Hopkins*, the other, made by Columbia, *Adam Had Four Sons*, which starred Ingrid Bergman. In the latter vehicle, directed by Gregory Ratoff, Miss Hayward was cast in a vixenish role which gave her an opportunity to display a fresh aspect of her acting ability.

Relatively minor roles were assigned to her in the four motion pictures in which she worked in 1942, *The Forest Rangers, I Married a Witch, Reap the Wild Wind,* and *Star-Spangled Rhythm*. Miss Hayward's interpretation of a lesser role in *Reap the Wild Wind* (a Paramount picture starring Paulette Goddard and featuring Ray Milland, John Wayne, and Raymond Massey) was described by the New York *Times* as "in true romantic style."

More "loan-out" assignments followed, and Miss Hayward's roles ceased to be minor ones. In the Republic picture *Hit Parade of 1943* she played a singing part, and in the same year she appeared in two United Artists productions, *Young and Willing,* and *Jack London*; in the latter she was co-featured with Michael O'Shea. She was given the leading feminine role in a Republic picture, *The Fighting Seabees* in 1944 in which John Wayne and Dennis O'Keefe appeared. Miss Hayward's work received favorable comment: *Variety* spoke of a "workman-like job," and a performance "above average." Her appearance with Loretta Young and Alan Ladd in Paramount's *And Now Tomorrow* was followed by one in *The Hairy Ape*, produced by United Artists. Acting with William Bendix, Miss Hayward was again cast in the role of a vixen and received some favorable reviews.

Signing with an independent producer, Walter Wanger, in 1945 she played in *Canyon Passage*, a Technicolor Western in 1946 and was co-starred with Dana Andrews. *Deadline at Dawn*, made by RKO Radio Pictures, was another 1946 release in which Miss Hayward appeared, and in 1947 RKO presented her in *They Won't Believe Me.*

More important dramatic roles followed, as well as stardom, in the two 1947 Wanger productions, *The Lost Moment*, based upon Henry James' *The Aspern Papers*, and *Smash-up*. Playing a feminine counterpart of the leading character in *The Lost Weekend*, Miss Hayward won a nomination for an award from the Academy of Motion Picture Arts and Sciences for her handling of this role. The New York *Herald Tribune* thought that Miss Hayward's "acting job" proved her to be "one of the best actresses in town," and *Variety* referred to the picture as Miss Hayward's "biggest break to date." In an interview given to the New York *Times* in 1952, Miss Hayward said, "Mr. Wanger really gave me my start."

The *Saxon Charm*, with Robert Montgomery, was a 1948 presentation, as was *Tap Roots*, with Van Heflin, a Civil War picture which won press approval for Miss Hayward's portrayal of the role of a "latter-day Scarlett O'Hara." Her last picture under Wanger management was *Tulsa*, released in 1949, a presentation which cast Miss Hayward in a tempestuous part in a story dealing with the oilfields in the '20's.

Twentieth Century-Fox signed Miss Hayward in 1949 to a seven-year, no-option contract, starting at a sliding scale annual salary of $150,000. Her release from the remaining two years under the Wanger contract had been obtained for a reported $200,000. Miss Hayward's first picture for Twentieth Century-Fox was *House of Strangers*, with Edward G. Robinson and Richard Conte, a story which dealt with the enmities within an Italian family risen from the slums. The following year Miss Hayward appeared with Dana Andrews in *My Foolish Heart*, a Samuel Goldwyn production released by RKO. She was seen to advantage in the role of a naive college girl in an ill-starred wartime romance and was again nominated for the award of the Academy of Motion Picture Arts and Sciences.

The four Twentieth Century-Fox productions in which she was presented in 1951 gave Miss Hayward highly diversified roles. *Rawhide*, with Tyrone Power in the lead, was a Western; *I'd Climb the Highest Mountain*, with a Georgia setting, cast Miss Hayward as the wife of a preacher, played by William Lundigan. In this film, the *Herald Tribune* observed, Miss Hayward "photographs beautifully in Technicolor . . . in a part which gives her ample opportunity at comedy and pathos," while the *Times* thought she ran to "artifice and attitudes." *I Can Get It for You Wholesale*, with a cast that included Dan Dailey and George Sanders, depicted the world of the New York garment industry with Miss Hayward playing the role of a sophisticated and ambitious model; *Variety* commented that the three stars turned in "uniformly excellent trouping." In *David and Bathsheba* Miss Hayward shared honors with Gregory Peck in filling the title roles of the Biblical story. The *New Yorker* expressed a general press reaction when it said that Miss Hayward as Bathsheba "although extremely attractive . . . seemed too overwhelmed by the role to meet it head-on."

On November 8, 1951, the *Herald Tribune* stated that Miss Hayward had turned down a "loan-out" assignment to RKO Radio Pictures, objecting to the part offered to her. On November 14, 1951, the New York *Times* reported that the actress had settled the dispute by agreeing to star in a different RKO production.

One of her pictures in 1952 was RKO's *The Lusty Men*, with Robert Mitchum. Two others were Twentieth Century-Fox productions, *With a Song in My Heart*, a story based on the career of Jane Froman, and *The Snows of Kilimanjaro*, a "big-budget" screen dramatization of the Hemingway story in which Susan Hayward again shared honors with Gregory Peck. She was acclaimed for her skill in impersonating the singer, Jane Froman, whose voice was dubbed in for the songs in *With a Song in My Heart*. The press reaction to the Hemingway film was also favorable. *Variety* described Miss Hayward's work in the role of the rejected wife as "splendid, particularly in the closing sequence."

The Foreign Press Association of Hollywood, meeting on February 14, 1953, named Susan Hayward and John Wayne the most popular film stars of 1952, presenting them both with statuettes named "Henrietta's." Miss Hayward also won the 1953 *Photoplay* award as the most popular actress on the screen.

Joseph Schenck, executive production head of the Twentieth Century-Fox Film Corporation is quoted by Thomas Wood in *Collier's* as having said, "On the basis of investment alone, Miss Hayward is our most valuable player. We've tied up $12,500,000 in her—or nearly a quarter of the studio's production budget." Darryl Zanuck, head of the studio, is quoted in the same article as saying, "Susan is a rare combination of two elements so often sought and so seldom found: she's beautiful and she can act."

In 1944 Susan Hayward married Jeffrey (Jess) Thomas Barker in St. Thomas Episcopal Church in Hollywood. Barker, a motion picture and television actor who played in the Broadway production of *You Can't Take It With You*, met Miss Hayward in the Hollywood Canteen where they both volunteered in entertaining soldiers. Their twin sons are named Timothy and Gregory. The Barker family lives in the San Fernando Valley and enjoys swimming in their own pool as a hobby. Another interest of Miss Hayward's is astrology. She is five feet three and a half inches in height, weighs 112 pounds and has hazel eyes and red hair. In 1953 she played the role of Andrew Jackson's wife in *The President's Lady*, "with insight and restraint," and the role of "a noble nurse" in the Belgian Congo in *White Witch Doctor*.

References

Collier's 128:20 Ag 18 '51 por
Liberty p23 My 10 '47 por
Look 14:74 Ja 17 '50 por
Movieland 10:64 Ag '52
N Y Times II p5 Ap 20 '52
International Motion Picture and Television Almanac, 1952-53

HAYWOOD, ALLAN S(HAW) Oct. 9, 1888—Feb. 21, 1953 Labor union official; held various offices in United Mine Workers of America in Illinois (1906-36); adviser and organizer of unions in steel, utility, rubber, automobile, and other industries; president of New York State Industrial Union Council (1937-39); New York City regional director (1937), national director of organization (1939-53), vice-president (1942), head of Department of Industrial Union Councils (1950), and first executive vice-president (1951) of Congress of Industrial Organizations. See *Current Biography, 1952.*

Obituary

N Y Times p60 F 22 '53

HEDIN, SVEN ANDERS Feb. 19, 1865—Nov. 26, 1952 Swedish explorer; author; known as the "Marco Polo of our day," he opened Asia to modern exploration; for half a century (1885-1935) conducted expeditions to explore and map unknown areas in Central Asia; wrote about twenty books on his journeys including *Silk Road, Chiang Kai-shek,* and a *General Atlas of Central Asia;* one-time diplomatic representative from Sweden to the Shah of Persia. See *Current Biography, 1940.*

Obituary

N Y Times p31 N 27 '52

HEENEY, A(RNOLD) D(ANFORD) P(ATRICK) April 5, 1902- Ambassador from Canada to the United States
Address: b. c/o Embassy of Canada, 2825 Rock Creek Drive, Washington, D.C.

A three-way diplomatic shift, announced on June 9, 1953, sent A. D. P. Heeney to Washington as Canada's Ambassador, succeeding H. Hume Wrong who has returned to Ottawa as Under-Secretary of State. Heeney had been named on March 19, 1952 the permanent representative of Canada to the North Atlantic Council. L. Dana Wilgress, former Under-Secretary of State, succeeded Heeney at Paris, to this post which has the rank of Ambassador. For the preceding three years Heeney had served as Under-Secretary for External Affairs, rated the highest civil service office in Canada's foreign ministry. He had previously held the title of Clerk of the Privy Council and Secretary to the Cabinet, a post created for him in 1940.

Arnold Heeney, of Irish ancestry on his father's side, was born April 5, 1902, in Montreal, the elder of two children of the Reverend Canon (William) Bertal and Eva Marjorie (Holland) Heeney. The Canon's family lived temporarily at Belleville, Ontario, at Newport, Rhode Island (when Arnold was three to six years of age), and at Barrie, Ontario, before Canon Heeney was established in 1909 as rector of St. Luke's Anglican Church in Winnipeg, Manitoba.

Young Heeney attended St. John's College School in Winnipeg and after graduating, entered the University of Manitoba where he received honors in English and French, was captain of the football team, and edited a campus paper. After receiving his B.A. degree in 1921, he taught at St. John's while earning his M.A. at the University, specializing in Canadian history.

He was appointed to a Rhodes scholarship from Manitoba and attended St. John's College, Oxford University, three years. He became captain of the St. John's rowing team (according to one account, he was the best stroke the college had ever had), earned his B.A. degree in modern history in two years (1925) and devoted his remaining year to the study of Roman and constitutional law. These, and subsequent studies were rewarded by an Oxford M.A. degree eleven years later.

Returning to Montreal in 1926, Heeney enrolled at McGill University and won the Lieutenant-Governor's medal for leading his class. After receiving his B.C.L. degree with honors in 1929 he was admitted to the Quebec bar and began a distinguished legal career in the St. James Street firm of Meredith, Holden, Heward, and Holden. He concentrated on admiralty cases and simultaneously (from 1934) lectured on law at McGill. He was also active in the Montreal Board of Trade, an organization of some 500 young business executives, becoming the Board's third president in 1931. In 1933 Heeney, a member of the Anglican Church, acted as counsel and secretary to the Quebec Protestant Education Survey.

During Heeney's twelve years in Montreal the Dominion Government had passed temporarily (1930-35) into the control of the Conservative party. The Liberal leader, William Lyon Mackenzie King, was returned to the post of Prime Minister, which he had previously held, and assumed responsibility for preparing Canada for the possibility of an outbreak of war. It was under these circumstances that the Prime Minister, in October 1938, called the young Montreal lawyer to Ottawa to become his principal secretary.

For a year and a half Heeney administered the machinery of the Prime Minister's office, maintaining liaison between King and his Cabinet ministers, assigning duties to the staff of civil servants, organizing agendas, routing Cabinet decisions to the various departments. In September 1939 Canada became a belligerent in World War II; about the same time Ernest Lemaire, C.M.G., retired from the post of Clerk of the Privy Council (an office which allowed no access to Cabinet meetings). When Heeney was named to this post he was authorized to attend the Cabinet War Committee's weekly meetings. In 1941 he was also designated King's Council (Dominion). He became responsible for the smooth functioning of the Dominion departments to a greater degree than any other civil servant in Ottawa. More than 100,000 orders-in-Council are said to have been drafted under Heeney's supervision.

For nine years Heeney served in this capacity in the war and early postwar period. He attended all the major conferences: those at Quebec, 1943 and 1944; the inauguration of the United Nations at San Francisco, 1945; the Paris Peace Conference, 1946. The External Affairs ministry, which had employed a personnel of 174 in 1939, increased its 1950 staff to 1,250; the handful of pre-war diplomats in Ottawa became a corps of forty, and former ministers—such as those to the United States—became ambassadors. When Louis St. Laurent in 1948 succeeded King as Prime Minister, a new Under-Secretary was sought.

Heeney, the "only man outside the ministry to know the inner secrets of the Government," in the words of the Montreal *Standard* (February 12, 1949), was appointed to the vacancy on January 19, 1949. Shortly after Heeney assumed the most important career post in Canada's foreign office, the draft of the North Atlantic Treaty Organization was published (March 18); Prime Minister St. Laurent approved it as second in value only to that of the U.N.; on May 4 Canada was the first nation to send a completely ratified NATO membership to Washington.

The Under-Secretary recorded his approval of these events in an article, "Canada and the Atlantic Community," for *Public Affairs* (Spring, 1951): "The establishment of the North Atlantic Alliance . . . was the most important diplomatic event since the end of the war. . . . The rapid building up of the strength of that Alliance offers the most solid ground for hope that a third world war can be prevented. And, if Soviet aggression cannot be deterred, this combination of Atlantic nations affords the only firm basis for the successful defence of the free world." Heeney hoped that it would result in "something much greater and more positive—a genuine Community of the Atlantic."

Heeney's office in the foreign ministry was a non-political career post, but inevitably the question of advancement to Cabinet rank arose. Cross reported (*Canada's Weekly*, May 13, 1949) Heeney's reaction: "That is not my cup of tea. I have no ambition whatever to enter politics." But he was hailed by an important Ottawa newspaperman, Norman Smith, as "The New Watchman of our Foreign Policy," and in the Spring of 1950 he was sent on a tour of Canadian missions in western Europe. In 1949 and 1950 he served as an alternate to the fourth and fifth U.N. General Assembly. In March 1952 he was appointed (effective April 15) as Canada's Permanent Representative to the NATO Council, and on June 9, 1953 Ambassador from Canada to the United States.

Six feet in height, Ambassador Heeney weighs 178 pounds and has gray hair and blue eyes. He and Margaret Yuile of Montreal were married in 1931, and have a son, William Brian Danford, and a daughter, Patricia Jane. In Ottawa, Heeney often walked the three miles from his home at Rockcliffe to his office in the East Block. His favorite sports are golf (he is a member of the Rideau, Royal Ottawa, and Country clubs in Ottawa, of the St. Cloud Golf Club in Paris), tennis, and skiing.

Capital Press Service, Ottawa
A. D. P. HEENEY

He was awarded an honorary LL.D. degree in 1948 from the University of British Columbia, and from the University of Manitoba in 1950.

References

Can W My 13 '49 por
Can Bsns 15:6+ O '42
Can J of Econ 12:282 Ag '46
Montreal Gazette Ja 21 '50
Montreal Standard F 12 '49 por
Nat Home M 44:15 S '43 por
Pub Affairs 13:7+ Spring '51
Sat Night 58:2 F 20 '43; 67:7 Mr 22 '52 por

Canadian Who's Who, 1949-51
Who's Who in the United Nations (1951)

HEINTZLEMAN, B. FRANK—Dec. 3, 1888 —Governor of Alaska

Address: Governor's House, Juneau, Alaska

Taking office as Governor of Alaska on April 10, 1953, B. Frank Heintzleman is the first Republican chief executive of the Territory in twenty years. Before his present appointment, he was Regional Forester for sixteen years, directing the work of the Department of Agriculture's six bureaus in Alaska and acting as Commissioner. He was also instrumental in developing public library and recreational facilities in the territory.

Governor Heintzleman's service with the Alaska branch of the Forest Service dates back to 1918. He has directed and served on numerous Federal and territorial boards and commissions studying Alaska problems, has represented the Department of Agriculture in Congressional hearings concerning Alaska over a period of fifteen years, and has held such offices as Chairman of the Territorial Alaska Planning Board

B. FRANK HEINTZLEMAN

and Vice-President for Alaska of the Pacific Northwest Trade Association.

B. Frank Heintzleman was born in Fayetteville, Pennsylvania on December 3, 1888, the son of Andrew J. and Rebecca Jane Heintzleman. He attended local public schools and the Mont Alto School of Forestry in his native State, graduating as Bachelor of Forestry at the age of nineteen. He went to Yale University for graduate work, and in July 1910, shortly after he was awarded a Master of Forestry degree, he entered the Forestry Service of the Department of Agriculture. He was immediately assigned to the Northwest and served for eight years in the States of Washington and Oregon, then was transferred to Alaska in 1918 when the Government needed experts to direct lumber production during the first World War.

Heintzleman quickly rose to prominence in the Alaska Service. In 1921 he wrote the original version of the Forest Service bulletin, "The Forests of Southeastern Alaska," which he has revised several times over the years, and which was the first of his numerous important reports and articles on forest control in Alaska and related subjects.

Among his significant contributions during his early years in the territory were his encouragement of pulp and paper production and his assistance in drafting the long-term timber contracts to supply wood from Alaskan forests for sawmills, plywood plants, and pulp mills. During the early years of the Roosevelt adminstration, Heintzleman was called to Washington to serve as head of the forest conservation activities of NRA. In that post he organized the timber-using industries of the entire nation.

In 1937 Heintzleman was appointed Regional Forester, a position which made him represen-

tative of the Secretary of Agriculture in Alaska, general director of the Department's six bureaus in the Territory, particularly Agricultural Research, and custodian of 20,000,000 acres of national forest land. For the past sixteen years he has also served as representative of the Federal Power Commission for southeastern Alaska, directing the study of water power resources and assisting with the preparation of the Federal Power Commission bulletins on this subject.

Almost every national and local group concerned with development of the territory has benefited from Heintzleman's work. He was co-author of the report, "Alaska Planning," issued in 1937 by the National Resources Planning Board, and in 1939 he organized and became first chairman of the Territorial Alaska Planning Board. He has been in constant demand at Congressional hearings on Alaska matters, and his reports have always been invaluable to the national lawmakers.

As Regional Forester, Heintzleman has not confined his interests solely to the problems of forestry in Alaska and the related industries. Much of the national forest land is adjacent to small cities and towns, and he has been active in such matters as the encouragement of community expansion into undeveloped land, the planning of groups of home sites, and the construction of highways and roads. For public recreation, he has developed picnic areas, ski courses and rifle ranges near the existing communities. He has also participated in fish and game management activities. To aid in stimulating the mining industry, he has directed the building of hundreds of miles of prospector trails.

Another of Heintzleman's interests has been the development and improvement of public library facilities in Alaska communities. He acted as chairman of the board which solicited funds for the construction of the Juneau Public Library building, and initiated and directed the Southeast Alaska Circulating Library, financed by the Sears Roebuck Foundation, which serves twenty fishing villages and Indian settlements. In the fields of public health and social welfare, he has long been a member of the groups which direct the work in Alaska of such organizations as the American Cancer Society, The National Foundation for Infantile Paralysis, and the Salvation Army.

During the second World War, the new Governor directed the Alaska Spruce Log Program, a public agency formed at the request of the War Production Board to take Sitka spruce logs from Alaska forests for aircraft material. Heintzleman organized eight large logging camps in the Tongass National Forest which produced this lumber for processing in Seattle into the material used to build the British "Mosquito Bomber," an all-wood airplane.

Throughout the years, Heintzleman's interest in promoting industrial development has resulted in the establishment of many large mills and plants. He helped set up the Ketchikan Pulp Company operation, the largest such enterprise to date, which has a private investment of $46,000,000. Six years ago, he stated that he believed that Alaskan pulp and paper mills could compete commercially with those of Canada, Newfoundland, and other areas, and that southeastern Alaska could produce 3,500 tons of news-print a day—more than one-quarter the rate of consumption in the United States. Since 1947, he has been active in the affairs of an important group of industrialists, the Pacific Northwest Trade Association.

Unlike Ernest Gruening, his Democratic predecessor in the Governor's chair, Heintzleman feels that the immediate granting of statehood to Alaska would be somewhat premature and should await further industrial expansion. When Heintzleman's appointment was recommended on February 24, 1953, he said, "I think Alaska is on the verge of a large industrial development. We want to do everything possible for [this] development so we can smooth the way for statehood . . . when it can finance the services of State government." Asked what the Federal Government could do to help develop the territory, Heintzleman suggested "a review of antiquated land and homesteading laws, and revision of the terms of power licenses, mineral leases and timber contracts" (Washington Post, March 14, 1953). He also declared that he favors immediate enactment of a law permitting the people of Alaska to elect their own Governor, instead of the present system of appointment by the President.

The new Governor is the author of numerous articles in lumber and paper industry publications and technical forestry journals. In 1952, he was honored for his work in the Forestry Service with a Superior Service Medal, awarded to him by the Secretary of Agriculture. The Governor was made a fellow of the Society of American Foresters 1952, and belongs to the Cosmos Club of Washington, D.C., the Lutheran Church of Fayetteville, Pennsylvania, the Masons, the Elks, and the Pioneers of Alaska.

References

N Y Times p15 F 12 '47; p6 F 25 '53
Who's Who in America, 1952-53

HENDERSON, E(LMER) L(EE) Mar. 23, 1885—July 30, 1953 Surgeon; former president of American Medical Association and one of the founders of World Medical Association; graduated from University of Louisville Medical School in 1909; former president of Southeastern Surgical Congress and Southern Medical Association, and a diplomat of the American Board of Surgery; was active in the Pan American Medical Association, International Surgical Society and the International College of Surgeons. See *Current Biography* 1950.

Obituary

N Y Times p19 Jl 31 '53

HEPBURN, MITCHELL F(REDERICK) Aug. 12, 1896—Jan. 5, 1953 Former Premier of Ontario, Canada; leader of the Liberal party; elected to the Dominion Parliament in 1926 and re-elected in 1930; resigned in 1934 to become member of Ontario Legislature for Elgin; was made Prime Minister, President of the Council, and Provincial Treasurer of Ontario (July 10, 1934); resigned as Prime Minister (October 21, 1942); elected to Legislature as an Independent Liberal (1942); defeated in 1945 elections; retired to his farm in Elgin County. See *Current Biography*, 1941.

Obituary

N Y Times p29 Ja 6 '53

HERZOG, MAURICE Jan. 15, 1919- Mountain climber; engineer; author
Address: b. 76, Avenue Kléber, Paris 16 France; h. 17, rue Raynouard, Paris 16

Leader of the French expedition of 1950 which climbed Annapurna in the Central Nepal Himalayas, Maurice Herzog tells the story of the 26,493-foot climb and the hazardous downward retreat in his book *Annapurna* (Cape; Clark, Irwin, 1952). The book has been in either first or second place on the non-fiction best seller lists for many months.

James Ramsey Ullman, author of *The White Tower*, reviewing *Annapurna*, wrote: "It is a thrilling story, a gallant and a moving story, in some ways a terrible story, and long after higher summits are reached (which they will be) and Annapurna has become 'just another peak', it will be remembered and honored in the annals of mountaineering."

Until Mount Everest was successfully climbed on May 29, 1953, by a British expedition, led by Colonel H. C. John Hunt, Annapurna had been the highest mountain scaled by man. With his companion, Louis Lachenal, Herzog succeeded in reaching the summit of Annapurna in June 1950, but in so doing suffered permanent injuries which have kept him from engaging in greater climbing feats.

Maurice Herzog was born in Lyon, France, on January 15, 1919, the son of Robert and Germaine (Beaume) Herzog. He was one of eight brothers and sisters, all of whom were devoted to mountain climbing. The family spent their summers at Chamonix, a village at the foot of Mont Blanc, birthplace of their father, an engineer and also a mountain climber. In his youth, Maurice climbed the Matterhorn and later Mont Blanc.

He spent the eight years from 1931 to 1939 studying at the Collége Chaptal in Paris, the family's city home. In the Second World War he served three years in the artillery, after which he was transferred to the Alpine troops and was promoted to captain of a company in the distinguished 27th Battalion. He received the Croix de Guerre for his service.

Returning to his studies, Herzog attended the University of Lyon, the University of Paris and the École des Hautes Études Commerciales (School of Advanced Commercial Studies). He then began his career as an industrial engineer in Kleber-Colombes, a French associate of the B. F. Goodrich Company. He is now an assistant director.

(Continued next page)

Harcourt, Paris

MAURICE HERZOG

On his vacations Herzog visited many outlying parts of the world where he climbed various mountains. In 1950 he was selected to head the nine-man expedition sent by the French Alpine Club to attempt the ascent of either Dhaulagiri or Annapurna, two lofty Himalayan peaks in Central Nepal. After searching for a way up the first, they conferred with a lama who advised them that Dhaulagiri was "not propitious." Since Herzog and his eight companions concluded that they did not like the look of the mountain, either, they decided upon Annapurna, 26,493 feet high, and began a search for the mountain itself! When Annapurna was at last found, they established a base camp about 17,000 feet above sea level.

The expedition had left France in March 1950 but not until June 3 of that year was its objective attained. Herzog and Lachenal, after a tremendous struggle to establish successive camps, climbed the length of a small cornice of ice and reached the summit of Annapurna.

Herzog in his book described how he felt: "Above us there was nothing! Our mission was accomplished. But at the same time we had accomplished something greater. How wonderful life would now become! What an inconceivable experience it is to attain one's ideal and, at the same moment, to fulfill oneself. . . .Never had I felt happiness like this— so intense and yet so pure."

While taking photographs, Herzog's gloves had fallen and were swept away by the fierce mountain wind. By the time he reached Camp Number 5 on the downward trek, both his hands and feet were frozen. So were Lachenal's; the latter had, in addition, fallen over a precipice and suffered a concussion. In the final descent Herzog and his mate were carried

down by porters; the surgeon of the party amputated Herzog's fingers and toes on the way to prevent infection.

When the party reached Katmandu, the capital of Nepal, the Maharajah honored them with a ceremony of ancient ritual. Herzog and the others then went home to recuperate from the effects of their heroic achievement. At the American Hospital in Neuilly he wrote *Annapurna,* a circumstance which gives it an added dramatic significance. "One writes best," he has observed, "when one is suffering, when one is reduced to complete immobility."

His book, which has had great popular success in the United States, has also received high critical praise. Justice William O. Douglas, also a mountain-climbing enthusiast, described it in the *Times Book Review* as "the most beautiful chapter in mountain literature that I know," and Ullman, writing in the New York *Herald Tribune Book Review,* predicted that it would become "one of the classics of mountain-climbing literature." *Time* entered its dissenting opinion that Herzog was "no great shakes as a writer."

Some of those who met Maurice Herzog on his American lecture tour, undertaken with the backing of the French Government and other agencies, have described him as a slender man of medium height with dark hair and small dark mustache, smiling and humorous, and who expresses himself well in English. His height is just under six feet, and his weight about 140 pounds. He is apparently reconciled to the loss of his fingers and toes; he told reporters that their loss has made "hard climbing" impossible, but "hard climbing" is apparently a relative matter, because in the summer of 1952 he climbed the Matterhorn again.

Herzog's honors, in addition to the Croix de Guerre, include the ribbon of the Legion of Honor and the Ghurka War Cross of Nepal, and he is a Chevalier of the Crown of Belgium. He is unmarried, a Catholic, and has no political affiliations. He is vice-president of the Club Alpin Français (French Alpine Club) and president of the Groupe de Haute Montagne (High Mountain Group).

In the New York *Times* Magazine, May 31, 1953, Maurice Herzog wrote an article, *Earth's Third Pole—Everest,* in which he analyzed the motivations of mountain climbers: "Perhaps it is pride that makes men risk their lives to conquer the mountain; perhaps it is extreme curiosity, the compulsion to know all, to have touched everything. Perhaps in their effort the mountaineers represent mankind, which has increased its power over nature for centuries but which has a feeling of uncertainty and uneasiness, almost a sense of insecurity, so long as this point on the roof of the world flaunts its independence."

Shortly before the recent British expedition led by Colonel John Hunt in its successful "assault" upon Everest, Herzog wrote: "But the conquest of a mountain, even Everest, means nothing. Except . . . the satisfaction for the mountaineer of succeeding, of innovating, of discovering something new, and especially, in the end, of discovering himself. In making the ascent, he fulfills himself and frees himself."

References

New Yorker 28:93 Ja 17 '53
Sat Rev 36:32 Ja 24 '53
Time 61:96 Ja 12 '53

HEYMAN, MRS. MARCUS A. *See* Komarovsky, M.

HILSBERG, ALEXANDER Apr. 24, 1900-
Conductor; violinist
Address: c/o New Orleans Philharmonic-Symphony Society, New Orleans, La.

ALEXANDER HILSBERG

Director and conductor of the New Orleans Philharmonic Symphony Orchestra since May 1952, Alexander Hilsberg was recently engaged for three additional seasons. The Polish-born conductor is a violinist who had taught and concertized in Russia and the Far East before coming to the United States in 1923. Joining the violin section of the Philadelphia Orchestra in 1926, he has served as its concertmaster and associate conductor, leaving at the beginning of the 1952-1953 season to assume his present post. He has also been a member of the faculty of the Curtis Institute of Music for over fifteen years, and has served as guest conductor with a number of major American orchestras, including the NBC Symphony Orchestra.

Alexander Hilsberg was born on April 24, 1900, in Łódź, Poland (then under Russian domination), the son of Edward and Helen Hilsberg. A child prodigy, he began studying the violin at the age of seven. Two years later he gave his first public recital in Warsaw, and made his debut as a conductor leading a Cossack band through a march number. He toured Poland and Russia for a year and in 1910 entered the Imperial Conservatory of Music in St. Petersburg (now Leningrad). There he studied violin with the Hungarian teacher, Leopold Auer, and his assistant, Nalbandjan, as well as composition with Petrov. Among Hilsberg's classmates at the conservatory was Jascha Heifetz.

Following his graduation in 1917, Hilsberg obtained a position teaching violin at an affiliated conservatory in Tomsk, in West Siberia. He toured extensively and played in many cities, finally settling in 1919 at Harbin (Pinkiang), a city in Manchuria with a large Russian population.

Hilsberg remained there four years, teaching and playing before audiences of both Orientals and European-born music lovers. During this period, he founded and served as a member of the Skidelsky String Quartet, sponsored by Solomon Skidelsky, a wealthy Russian industrialist. The quartet won wide favor, not only in Eastern Siberia, but also in China and Japan.

In 1921, the year of the great Chinese famine, the group donated its proceeds to relief and, in recognition, each member was decorated with the personal order of Dr. Sun Yat-sen, founder and later president of the Chinese Republic. Hilsberg was offered a teaching position at the Tokyo Imperial Conservatory of Music in 1923, but the contract was cancelled as a result of the disastrous earthquake of that year, which he witnessed.

When Hilsberg heard a recording made by the Philadelphia Orchestra under the direction of Leopold Stokowski, he was so impressed that he decided that some day he would be associated with "this ideal orchestra." Encouraged by his friend, Heifetz, he sailed for America in 1923. He was reportedly offered the first chair with a major symphony orchestra, but turned it down to wait for an opening with the Philadelphia Orchestra, which eventually occurred in 1926. Hilsberg joined the orchestra as a member of the first violin section, and when Arturo Toscanini served as guest conductor in 1929, he promoted Hilsberg to the first violin desk. Two years later he was made concertmaster, and during the years that followed, he appeared on various occasions as soloist with the orchestra, both in its home city and on tour.

Hilsberg's principal ambition, however, was to become a conductor. Playing in an orchestra he has said, "is like being a painter and being handed a palette with only a few colors. Conducting, you have all the colors you could possibly want" (*Time*, November 5, 1951). He made his debut as a conductor with the Philadelphia Orchestra in 1936 during the first season of summer concerts at Robin Hood Dell in Fairmount Park, and was recalled to conduct there in subsequent seasons.

His first appearance as a conductor in New York took place on August 15, 1938, when he directed the New York Philharmonic-Symphony Orchestra in an outdoor concert at Lewisohn Stadium, with Josef Hofmann as soloist. According to the New York *Times*, the audience "responded cordially to the vigor, mus-

HILSBERG, ALEXANDER—*Continued*

cularity, and musicianship" of Hilsberg's interpretations. He returned as guest conductor at Lewisohn Stadium for a concert the following summer.

It was announced on May 7, 1945, that Hilsberg would succeed Saul Caston as associate conductor of the Philadelphia Orchestra, beginning with the 1945-1946 season. His first big opportunity came on December 10, 1946, when he led a Carnegie Hall concert substituting at short notice for the regular conductor, Eugene Ormandy, who was unable to appear because of a sprained shoulder. Hilsberg's interpretations of Beethoven's *Leonore Overture No. 3* and the Brahms First Symphony, both of which he conducted without score, won high praise from the New York critics. To Olin Downes, Hilsberg's reading of the Brahms symphony was "as classic in line as it was nobly lyrical in conception," and he went on to say: "With a fine self-effacement, but the most complete control of the orchestra and of the score, so clear in his head, Mr. Hilsberg led the composition and its interpreters to victory. A classic symphony was heard again, as it is heard so rarely, in its true proportions, at its full value" (New York *Times,* December 11, 1946).

Following this success, Hilsberg conducted at least one of the Philadelphia Orchestra's Carnegie Hall concerts each season. Reviewing Hilsberg's second New York appearance with the orchestra, Virgil Thomson stated that he revealed himself "not only a thoroughly aware technician of the orchestra but an interpreter of great force and originality. . . .His rhythmic adjustments are multiple and most delicately operated. He has a gift for elegance and a gift for drama. . . .Everywhere it was obvious that we were hearing a conductor of profoundly musical instincts" (New York *Herald Tribune,* February 4, 1948).

Hilsberg also directed concerts of the Philadelphia Orchestra in its home city, led the series of children's concerts presented each season, and conducted programs when the orchestra performed at the Worcester (Massachusetts) and Ann Arbor (Michigan) festivals. He received the C. Hartman Kuhn award for the 1948-1949 season given annually to the member of the Philadelphia Orchestra "who has shown ability and enterprise of such character as to enhance the standards and reputation of the orchestra." In addition he was made head of the orchestra department of the Curtis Institute of Music in January 1947 and conductor of the Curtis Symphony Orchestra. He also served as conductor of the Reading (Pennnsylvania) Symphony.

At the end of the 1950-1951 season, Hilsberg asked to be relieved of his duties as concertmaster of the Philadelphia Orchestra in order to devote his time entirely to conducting. The request was granted "with deepest regret" by the board of directors. He continued as the orchestra's associate conductor until January 21, 1952, when it was revealed that he had also resigned this post, because of an "increas-

ing number of engagements as guest conductor around the country."

Hilsberg has conducted the Minneapolis, Pittsburgh, New Orleans, and NBC orchestras. His appointment as musical director and conductor of the New Orleans Philharmonic-Symphony Orchestra for the 1952-1953 season, succeeding Massimo Freccia, was announced on March 10, 1952. This orchestra was organized in 1936 by Arthur Zack, a cellist.

Newsweek reported that the new conductor had eight rehearsals in which "to whip" the orchestra into shape. He added twenty-three new musicians, including several first-desk men and women, within a few days. The eighty-five-member orchestra has an annual budget of approximately $280,000. Among its musicians are twenty-one women, the largest number it has ever had. Most of them were selected by Hilsberg, who commented that they were "every bit as good as men musicians."

The New Orleans Philharmonic-Symphony Orchestra began its first season under Hilsberg's direction on October 2, 1952. *Musical America's* correspondent wrote that the ensemble gave "hearty co-operation to the new leader." Edward C. Brooks, Jr., of the *Times-Picayune,* called it an "inspiring debut. . . . There is every reason to believe that Hilsberg will bring to New Orleans and the Deep South a season of symphonic music which will transcend any it has known."

The 1952-1953 schedule provided for fifteen major concerts in the orchestra series, seventeen youth concerts (most of them led by the assistant conductor, Pierre Henrotte), twelve of which were broadcast on a State-wide radio network for the first time to some 600,000 school children of Louisiana, as an integral part of their school program, and an artists' series of eight concerts. In addition, two university concerts, a Negro church concert, and a road tour of the State were scheduled. After the fourth concert, Hilsberg was re-engaged as musical director for three additional years.

Among the long-playing records Hilsberg has made as conductor of the Philadelphia Orchestra are Tschaikovsky's *Violin Concerto,* Wieniawski's *Violin Concerto,* Bernstein's *Fancy Free,* Walter's *Façade Suite,* and Berlioz's *Roman Carnival Overture.*

On April 1, 1920, he married Neya Sheingesicht of Harbin. He became an American citizen in 1929. The conductor has been described by one interviewer as "an artist of intense, impressive personality, of medium height, and with an erect carriage and aristocratic bearing." He possesses a famous violin, the work of Giuseppe Antonio Guarneri "del Gesù" and dating from 1735, which he acquired from the Czech violinist, Jan Kubelik.

References

Newsweek 40:100 N 17 '52
Time 58:115 N 5 '51
Saleski, G. Famous Musicians of Jewish Origin (Bloch, 1949)
Thompson, O. (ed) International Cyclopedia of Music and Musicians (1949)
Who Is Who in Music (1951)
Who's Who in America Sup S '47

HOBBY, OVETA CULP Jan. 19, 1905-
Secretary of the Department of Health, Education and Welfare; publisher

Address: b. c/o Department of Health, Education and Welfare, Washington 25, D.C.; Houston Post, Houston, Tex.; h. 2 Remington Lane, Houston, Tex.

> NOTE: This biography supersedes the article which appeared in *Current Biography* in 1942.

To her new position as the First Secretary of the newly created Department of Health, Education and Welfare, Mrs. Oveta Culp Hobby brings experience as co-editor and publisher of Texas' largest morning newspaper, the Houston *Post,* and as former director of the Women's Army Corps.

As a member of the Cabinet, Mrs. Hobby is the first woman to be present at Cabinet meetings since the resignation of Mrs. Frances Perkins as Secretary of Labor in 1945.

Oveta Culp Hobby was born in Killeen, Texas, on January 19, 1905, to Isaac William and Emma (Hoover) Culp. From her father, a lawyer, young Oveta acquired a taste for law and as a schoolgirl spent many hours in his law office where she read the *Congressional Record* and listened to legal and political discussions. After her early education, partly in public schools and partly by private tutors, she studied at Mary Hardin-Baylor College in Belton, Texas, and at the University of Texas Law School.

At twenty Oveta Culp became parliamentarian of the Texas House of Representatives, a position which she held from 1925 to 1931 and from 1939 to 1941. She was also employed as legal clerk of the Texas State Banking Department, where she assisted in codifying Texas banking laws and in 1930 she was assistant to the city attorney of Houston. Having meanwhile become active in politics, she worked with the local Democratic organization in local elections and in the National Democratic Convention held in Houston in 1928. She became a candidate, at the age of twenty-four, for the Texas State Legislature, but was not elected.

On February 23, 1931, Oveta Culp was married to William Pettus Hobby, former Governor of Texas (1917-21) and publisher of the Houston *Post.* During the first year of her marriage she became research editor on the Houston *Post*; she then held the positions of book editor (1933-36), assistant editor (1936-38), and in 1938 was made executive vice-president, an office created for her at that time. As a newspaper woman Mrs. Hobby emphasized women's news and made a number of changes in the format and various departments of her paper. Because her husband's interests in banking and radio occupied much of his attention, she became full-time manager of the *Post.* She also worked for many civic and community welfare groups and was president of the Texas League of Women Voters, an executive director of radio station KPRC, director of the National Bank of Cleburne (Texas), member of the board of Regents of the Texas State Teachers College, and author of a book on

Wide World Photos
OVETA CULP HOBBY

parliamentary law, *Mr. Chairman* (1937), which has been used as a textbook in Texas and Louisiana. Visiting New York in May 1941 to attend a convention of the American Newspaper Publishers Association, Mrs. Hobby told a reporter for the New York *Herald Tribune,* "It is not so difficult to combine matrimony and a career in a small city like Houston." A few month later, in July, Mrs. Hobby went to Washington as head of the newly formed women's division of the War Department's Bureau of Public Relations. In this $1-a-year position her responsibility was to keep mothers and wives advised about the comfort, food, and recreation of men in the service. She was asked by General George C. Marshall, then Chief of Staff, to begin studying plans for establishing a women's auxiliary army, and in May 1942 when the Women's Auxiliary Army Corps was officially authorized by an act of Congress, Mrs. Hobby was made its director with the military rank of major, soon raised to colonel.

As the first officer of the first American women's army, Mrs. Hobby had as her problem the recruiting of officer candidates to be trained for administrative work in the WAAC. When officers were granted their commissions, after two months of training, in September 1942, the task of raising an initial quota of 12,200 volunteers was begun (the law provided for a corps of 150,000 ultimately). The response to early enlistment drives was encouraging. Regarding the flurry of interest in such matters as what the enlistees would wear and whether they might use make-up, Mrs. Hobby made it clear that "this is a serious job for serious women" and that regular army discipline and traditions would be maintained. In October Mrs. Hobby flew to England with Mrs. Franklin D. Roosevelt to study the war activities of British women. She inspected units of the Women's Royal Naval Service (WRENS) and the Auxiliary Territorial Service (ATS),

HOBBY, OVETA CULP—*Continued*

and commented to the press, "We're still, to use an American phrase, green to the army. But we're learning." The "Auxiliary" was dropped from the organization's name in 1943 when the WAC received full Army status; WACs were then serving in noncombat military posts both in the United States and overseas. Dwindling enlistments in the WAC in 1944, as reported by *Time*, was explained in part by the fact that other women's services like the WAVES and SPARS were recruiting and also by the fact that many American women were working in war plants, thereby releasing men for combat duty. When Mrs. Hobby in July 1945 retired from active service in the Army, stating that she had completed her mission, the WAC numbered 100,000.

Retirement from the Army did not mean withdrawal from a busy career for Mrs. Hobby, who returned to Houston, her duties on the Houston *Post* and a variety of professional and community activities: member of the boards of directors of the American Society of Newspaper Editors, Texas Newspaper Publishers Association, and Texas Medical Center. In March 1948 she went to Geneva, Switzerland, as a consultant-alternate of the Freedom of Information Conference; and in the same year served as consultant for the Hoover Commission for the Organization of the Executive Branch of the Government, later becoming a board member of the Citizens' Committee for the Hoover Report. Elected president of the Southern Newspaper Publishers in 1949, she also held the national vice-chairmanship of the American Cancer Society, and chairmanship of the newspaper advertising committee of that year's Opportunity Savings Bond Drive. In the fall of 1952 Mrs. Hobby was made co-editor and publisher of the Houston *Post* company.

While a regular voter of the Democratic State ticket, Mrs. Hobby backed the candidacy of Thomas E. Dewey on a national level in 1948 and announced herself for General Dwight D. Eisenhower some four months before the nominating convention of 1952. She supported the Republican candidate through the Houston *Post* and published a "political primer," which, reported *Time*, "was instrumental in getting pro-Eisenhower Texans into G.O.P. precincts." Working to organize Democrats for Eisenhower, she gave some of her time during the campaign to the activities of the Republican headquarters in New York City. Announcement that Mrs. Hobby had been designated to succeed Oscar R. Ewing as head of the Federal Security Agency was made on November 25, 1952. *Business Week* commented that the appointment "acknowledges Southern Democratic support and gives the South representation in the Cabinet." Senate approval of Mrs. Hobby as Federal Security Administrator was given on January 21, 1953.

The Federal Security Agency, created under the Reorganization Act of 1939, now comprises all those branches of the Federal Government concerned with health, education, and social and economic security of the individual citizen.

Among the agencies which make up FSA are the Public Health Service, the Food and Drug Administration, the Office of Education, and the Bureau of Old Age and Survivors Insurance. Plans have long been under way to reorganize the agency into a new Department with Cabinet status: President Truman called for such legislation in 1949 and the Hoover Commission also recommended reorganization. Such a plan was considered by the Eighty-third Congress in March, with the result that a joint resolution was passed on March 30 which transformed the Federal Security Agency into a Cabinet-rank Department of Health, Education and Welfare, effective April 11. Mrs. Hobby took the oath of office on April 11 before President Eisenhower.

In an interview for the *U. S. News and World Report* (December 26, 1952), Mrs. Hobby said that she believed that the Office of Federal Security Administrator should be made a Cabinet post "because of the growing concern over problems of education, health, and social welfare." Not an advocate of socialized medicine, she expressed full agreement with Eisenhower's statement that the solution to the problem of adequate medical care is to 'build on the system of voluntary, nonprofit insurance plans." Mrs. Hobby described her political philosophy as that of a "liberal Republican."

Mrs. Hobby holds honorary LL.D. degrees from Baylor University (1943), Sam Houston State Teachers College (1943), the University of Chattanooga (1943), and an honorary Doctor of Humane Letters degree from Bard College (1950). She has been awarded the Texas Press Association plaque for outstanding service in journalism and the honor medal for distinguished service in journalism from the University of Missouri. She is also the seventh woman in American history (and the first Army woman) to receive the Distinguished Service Medal; she was honored by the Philippine Government with the Philippine Military Merit Medal. "Service in nineteen groups is Mrs. Hobby's hobby," wrote Allen K. Tyler in *Editor and Publisher* in 1951. Among the organizations, not previously mentioned, with which she has been associated are the Houston Committee for Education on Alcoholism, Texas Safety Association, National Safety Council, Community Chest of America. She is a sponsor of the American Heart Association and the American Nurses Association, and a trustee of the Pacific War Memorial. Her clubs are the Houston, Bayou, Downtown, Ramada, and the Houston Junior League.

In a New York *Herald Tribune* editorial Mrs. Hobby was described as "an experienced and dynamic figure . . . [who] brings proven gifts of energy and administrative resourcefulness" to her new office. She is the mother of two children, William and Jessica. "Trim", "attractive" Mrs. Hobby has been voted one of the best dressed women in the United States. She collects antiques, old silver, and rare books. Her church is the Episcopal.

The new department of Health, Education and Welfare issued this announcement on April 17, 1953; "Secretary Hobby requests that she be referred to as 'Mrs. Secretary' and not as

'Madam Secretary.' Her request is based on the fact that she feels the title of 'Mrs.' is a fine American word and prefers this to the more formal protocol title of 'Madam'."

Mrs. Hobby spoke at the fifty-fifth annual convention of the American Hospital Association meeting in San Francisco on August 31, 1953, and stated that an overwhelming majority of American people had no desire whatsoever for socialized medicine in any form. The Federal Government would be going against the wishes of the American people if it were to enter the field of medical care.

But, she asserted, not only had the financial problem of catastrophic illness not been solved for the average family, but no sure way had been found "to see our retired senior citizens through the increased illnesses of age . . . which by their very duration can still wreck many a family's economy" (New York *Times,* September 1, 1953).

References

    Bsns W p30 D 6 '52
    Ed & Pub 84:20 F 24 '52
    N Y Herald Tribune p9 My 5 '41
    Time 38:52 Ag 11 '41; 39:72 My 25
      '42; 43:57-8 Ja 17 '44; 46:26 Jl 23 '45
    U S News 33:44 D 26 '52
    Washington (D.C.) Post p25 N 26 '52
    International Who's Who, 1952
    Who's Who in America, 1952-53
    Who's Who in the South and Southwest
      (1950)

HOBBY, MRS. WILLIAM P(ETTUS)
See Hobby, O. C.

HOGAN, FRANK S(MITHWICK) Jan. 17, 1902- District Attorney of New York County; lawyer
Address: b. 155 Leonard St., New York 13; h. 404 Riverside Drive, New York 25

District Attorney Frank S. Hogan's career in the service of New York County began in 1935 when he was chosen to work on the staff of Thomas E. Dewey, who had just been appointed as a Special Prosecutor to investigate rackets in New York County. When Dewey was elected to that post himself, in November 1937, Hogan became his administrative assistant. After Dewey announced in 1941 that he would not run again for District Attorney, Hogan won the support of all parties for his election to the office. He was re-elected in 1945, in 1949, and was unopposed in 1953.

Described by *Collier's* (July 7, 1951) as "the Horatio Alger type," Frank Smithwick Hogan was born January 17, 1902 in Waterbury Connecticut, the son of Michael F. and Anne (Smithwick) Hogan. His father, who retired at the age of seventy, was an immigrant from County Clare, Ireland, who became a buffer and polisher for the New England Watch Company. During summers after his thirteenth birthday, the youth worked at everything from

FRANK S. HOGAN

a job in a watch factory, to timekeeper, apprentice carpenter and collector for a clothing firm. After graduating from high school, he decided to become a journalist, and attended Columbia College in New York with this in mind, but he soon found himself becoming interested in law.

Hogan spent his first collegiate summer vacation selling a book called *The People's Home Library* and *The People's War Book and Atlas* to upper New York State farmers. "The next summer, Hogan worked as a Pullman conductor (heavy tips for changing people from uppers to lowers) . . . and the summer after his junior year he made a couple of round trips on the *Leviathan* as a steward in the steerage (tips light)" (*New Yorker,* April 14, 1951).

While working his way through school, he found time to become president of the senior class and president of his fraternity, Beta Theta Pi, and was on the backfield of the varsity football team. He received his B.A. degree in 1924 and entered Columbia Law School from which he graduated in 1928. He has said "I never liked law school . . . the law didn't excite me at all" (*Collier's,* July 7, 1951).

Hogan's first position in the field of law was with a Wall Street law firm, Gleason, McLanahan, Merritt, and Ingraham. However he joined with Anthony J. Liebler in their own law practice, specializing in insurance and real estate law. "What followed, Hogan recalls, "were certainly years of austerity."

The turning point in his life came in 1935— when he read a statement by Dewey, who had just been appointed a Special Prosecutor, saying that he was looking for young lawyers, both Republicans and Democrats, to help him in this special assignment. Hogan wrote a letter asking for one of the twenty available jobs, along with 3,000 other aspiring applicants. Dewey sent for him, hired him and together they

HOGAN, FRANK S.—*Continued*

went on to "convict Charlie (Luckie) Luciano for compulsory prostitution, and Democratic Leader James J. Hines for conspiracy to conduct a lottery" (*Collier's*, July, 7, 1951). When Dewey was elected New York County District Attorney in 1937, Hogan became his administrative assistant.

Hogan's duties were many and varied after he took this office. Budgets as well as cross-examinations took up his time, and men who worked with him say that he was as good at breaking down figures as he was at breaking down criminals. Despite his active role, he was the only assistant on Dewey's staff who did not have a secretary of his own.

When Dewey decided to run for the governorship of New York State, in 1941, he named four aides as logical successors. Three were Republicans and one, Hogan, was a Democrat. Hogan won the nomination of all three parties, the Democrat, Republican and Labor. This was the first time in the history of the city that the principal political parties agreed upon the same candidate for the county's prosecuting officer. He received the support of those three parties in 1945. In 1949, all parties backed him with the exception of the Communist.

District Attorney Hogan heads the biggest criminal law office in the world, and he is undoubtedly the world's busiest prosecutor. Through his office pass every year approximately 15,000 criminals, channeled through his chief assistant, Joseph A. Sarafite. The office, occupying four floors in the Criminal Courts Building, spends $1,000,000 annually to meet its running expenses. It requires a staff of seventy-two lawyers; and about 150 accountants, investigators and specialists. "We have a non-partisan staff," said Hogan, "and I think every one of my assistants is underpaid and overworked" (*New Yorker*, April 14, 1951).

According to Lester Velie (*Collier's*, July 7, 1951) the Senate crime investigation, which made such an enormous impression upon New Yorkers, was based on some of the reports which Hogan had unearthed in Grand Jury investigations. "It was Hogan's material that stole the show and helped make the Senate crime investigation a smashing success." During the entire affair Hogan "modestly" occupied a quiet seat by his television set.

Hogan's record speaks for itself: In 1942 he set six records in the prosecution of crime, on a budget that was $50,000 less than any other in recent years. Of the 2,788 defendants which he prosecuted, 97.4 per cent were convicted by juries or entered pleas of guilty. This percentage, according to the annual report submitted by the chief clerk of the District Attorney's office, excelled the 94.2 per cent record achieved by Hogan's predecessor. In August of 1943 the headlines on the front of every daily newspaper told of the Grand Jury investigation begun by Hogan into the activities of Frank Costello.

The District Attorney alleged that Costello had secured nominations of his chosen candidates for magistrates in New York City by exerting pressure upon Tammany politicians.

Taking time out from his busy schedule in 1945 to make a voyage on the Cunard Liner, *Queen Mary*, Hogan told reporters that he was going to London as an individual and was paying for his trip himself in order that he might study the problems of juvenile delinquency and adolescent crime in England.

In 1949 a "Hogan-for-Mayor" boom mushroomed into existence. The New York *Herald Tribune*, supported his candidacy and on June 20 paid him a tribute: "Few men in New York public life have such a full and intimate comprehension of the challenge that is constantly lurking at the municipal back door. . . . We believe that the Hogan candidacy has stature which rises above ordinary party lines."

He has stated, "I've been asked three or four times to go on the bench and I've had handsome private offers, but my work here is exciting, and I think it's important. I leave home every morning knowing that something new and different will probably happen" (*New Yorker*, April 14, 1951).

Hogan was awarded the Columbia University Medal in 1942 for exceptional public service, the Columbia Alumni Medal for conspicuous alumni service in 1946, and the Medal of Merit of the New York County Grand Jury Association in 1947. He was president of the Association of Alumni of Columbia College from 1946 to 1949 and the president of the Class of '42 for five years. From 1949 to 1951 he held the office of president of the Alumni Federation of Columbia University. Hogan is a member of the District Attorneys Association of the State of New York, and was elected its president in 1947. He is a member of the State Bar Association, and the Association of the Bar of the City of New York.

Organizations to which Hogan belongs include Columbia University, Manhattan, New York Athletic Club, and the Friendly Sons of St. Patrick. Hogan is especially fond of playing bridge, when he can find the time for it. He won a football letter at Columbia and is still very fond of sports, especially tennis and swimming. He also enjoys reading history and biography. He is a Roman Catholic.

Hogan was married to Mary Egan on November 11, 1936. According to most authorities, the Hogans live simply in a four room apartment on Riverside Drive.

He is five feet, nine and a half inches tall, and weighs 175 pounds. "His forehead is inclined to that convex sweep which cartoonists give to the brows of precocious youngsters." The first quality that shines through his reserve is an "ingratiating warmth which has won him some of his most notable successes." Governor Dewey described Hogan as the "most sweetly honorable man I've ever known." Last April the American Irish Historical Society presented him with a gold medal in recognition of his "outstanding ability, high courage, unqualified political independence, and incorruptible honesty."

Hogan attributes crime to environmental factors: "Delinquents rarely come from [those] homes where the foundation stones of family life are love, respect and understanding (N. Y. *Sunday News*, July 5, 1953).

HOGAN, FRANK S.—*Continued*

The raid on New York City's bookmakers and policy operators on July 7, 1953, instituted by Hogan, received mixed comments in the press. Some newspapers and political leaders criticized the District Attorney for "playing politics." On the other hand, the New York *Times* (July 9, 1953) commented editorially: "Of course showmanship was involved, but this need not be disparaged. It is always good to hear that the side of law and order is on the job. If this also happens to win additional friends for Mr. Hogan, what is wrong with that?"

References

Collier's 128:34+ Jl 7 '51 pors
N Y Times VII p11+ Ag 31 '41 por
New Yorker 27:25+ Ap 14 '51
P M p16 Ag 10 '41 por
Who's Who in New York, 1952

HONEYWELL, ANNETTE Apr. 13, 1904-
Commercial artist; designer
Address: b. 859 N. Lafayette Park Pl., Los Angeles 26, Calif.; h. 4865 Glencairn Rd., Los Angeles 27, Calif.

Muralist, illustrator and designer, Annette Honeywell is probably best known for her California historical series of Wedgwood din-

ANNETTE HONEYWELL

ner plates, her "Desert Rose", "Elsinore" and "California Poppy" informal dinner pottery patterns. She has also won renown in the interior decorating field for her designs and murals at Bullock's stores in Pasadena, and for her original textile patterns and dress fabrics for a number of New York and California firms.

Her illustrations of appetizing fruit, delectable pies and doughnuts, and lush tropical flowers have been pictured on billboards and in magazines all over the country. In 1951 she received the Woman of the Year Award from the Los Angeles *Times*. She has also been honored with the Frances Holmes awards in advertising and design.

Annette Honeywell was born Annette Olga Heidelbach in Oak Park, Illinois, on April 13, 1904, to Frederick and Anna (Bertung) Heidelbach, who came from Germany. While she was still a young girl her family moved to Coeur d'Alene, Idaho, and San Diego, California. She began drawing and designing even as a child, and after her graduation from high school in 1916, she returned to Illinois and attended the Chicago Academy of Fine Arts.

In September 1923, she married Clarence Honeywell, a disabled veteran of World War I, and they moved to Terre Haute, Indiana, where he was in the advertising business. Two days after the birth of their daughter, Avonne Owrien, in 1925, Mr. Honeywell suffered a stroke and was advised to return to the Veterans' hospital in California which was familiar with his case. The family arrived in Los Angeles with total assets of $20, and Mrs. Honeywell recalls how she "pounded the pavement" looking for work as a commercial artist.

Her husband was hospitalized for several years, and died in 1929. She managed to support her daughter by working as a free lance artist.

Her first commission was to design some "Hollyvogue" hand-painted ties, and she built up a clientele for her still-life illustrations among such companies as Sunkist (for whom she designed an elaborate orange and lemon recipe book still in use), and the Walnut Growers' Association.

With the development of color photography in the late 1930's, Mrs. Honeywell foresaw that the artist would be replaced by the photographer in advertising illustrations, and she began to look for commissions in the designing and interior decorating fields. Her first opportunity came in 1939 when she was assigned by Barker's, a chain of home furnishings stores, to design a series of twelve plates portraying California historical scenes, to be manufactured exclusively by Wedgwood.

Her next assignment was to design a wallpaper for Bullock's Wilshire store. In 1940 she was engaged to create designs for informal breakfast pottery, and her patterns are still among the country's best sellers. In that year, she began teaching her basic design course at Woodbury College in Los Angeles, which she continued until 1947.

Her first one-man show was given in Hollywood in 1943, and the exhibits of her floral water colors, portraits and commercial work of all kinds, in two and three dimensions, aroused much interest in her talents as both a fine artist and a commercial designer. Among her designs were "Victorian Valentine" greeting cards, California Handprint table linen, and "California Authentic" textile patterns, one of which, "The Swallows of Capistrano" was the best-selling dress print of 1945 and was cited as the greatest contribution of the decade to the textile industry.

During World War II she was one of the artists who devoted much time doing portrait sketches of patients at Veterans' hospitals.

When the new, block-long Bullock's store at Pasadena was being planned, Mrs. Honeywell was commissioned to design the tea room murals, carpeting, linen, china, menus, and to create mirror murals over the elevators, to cover 2,000 feet with murals in the Delmar foyer, and to design wallpaper for various departments, packaging and gift wrappings. Since the store's opening in September 1947, her designs have been applied to table mats, china, menus, match covers, and draperies.

For Bullock's store in Westwood, California, opened in September 1951, Mrs. Honeywell again designed three-panel murals. Executed in gold leaf in a special rough mat finish oil paint to create a humid, tropical atmosphere, they show five-foot figures of sarong-clad "lotus weavers," surrounded by giant Philodendron, Australian glacacia, Guatemalan strelitzia, and Javanese lotus blossoms.

Tropical motifs were also used in the Honeywell designs for dress fabrics by Cohama, Inc., of New York which contracted for twenty or more patterns a year, and sent her to Hawaii for inspiration in the fall of 1950. She is also a designer of fabrics for Seneca, a New York firm.

She was commissioned to do the murals for the executive offices of the Hercules Powder Company in Wilmington, Delaware, and these were completed in December 1952. They show the cotton fields and pine forests from which the company obtains its raw materials. In February 1953 Mrs. Honeywell designed a complete line of Royal Gouda hand-painted china for a manufacturer in Holland.

Now a grandmother, Mrs. Honeywell is five feet, seven inches in height, and a gray-eyed brunette, who is described as "attractive, witty and exuberant." The designer is a registered Republican, and attends Christ Church, Unity; she is a member of the National Business and Professional Women's Club and of the Los Angeles Advertising Women. Mrs. Honeywell lives in the Los Feliz hills, where she raises many of the lush plants portrayed in her designs.

"As an artist thinks, so he paints", Mrs. Honeywell claims. Since she loves nature and beauty, her work is evidence of her interests, and with each new design she says "a prayer that it bring happiness."

She especially enjoys what she calls the "odd jobs" that come her way—the one-of-a-kind things such as styling children's furniture, illustrating a story, designing a candy package for a new manufacturer. "As a free-lance artist, I find every new assignment a thrill, and an opportunity to grow," she said.

References

Christian Sci Mon Mag p5 My 27 '44
    pors; p10 O 22 '52 pors
Los Angeles Times IV p7 Ag 5 '51 por

HOOD, CLIFFORD F(IROVED) Feb. 8, 1894- Steel corporation executive

Address: b. c/o United States Steel Corporation, 525 William Penn Pl., Pittsburgh, Pa.; h. 5023 Frew St., Pittsburgh, Pa.

The president since January 1952 of United States Steel Corporation, or Big Steel, as it is often called, which produces about one-third of the nation's steel ingots, has been Clifford F. Hood, also a member of the corporation's finance committee. Hood, who is said to have been directly responsible for United States Steel's record-breaking expansion in recent years, is in charge of operations, while the man he succeeded in the presidency, Benjamin Fairless, continues as chairman of the board and chief executive officer to direct policy. Advancing to his present position over a period of some thirty-five years, Hood became in 1938 president of United States Steel's subsidiary American Steel and Wire Company, which he had joined as clerk in 1917, president of Carnegie-Illinois Steel Corporation in 1950, and the following year executive vice-president of United States Steel Company.

Born on a farm near Monmouth, Illinois, on February 8, 1894, Clifford Firoved Hood is the only child of Edward Everett and Ida Florence (Firoved) Hood. Shortly after his birth the family moved to another farm, near Cameron, Illinois, where in his boyhood he had a full schedule of farm chores and held his first paying job at the age of ten for fifty cents a day as water boy for a threshing crew. Young Hood walked three miles daily to a country schoolhouse, until he attended high school in Galesburg. He spent his summer vacations on the farm helping his father, and would possibly have become a farmer himself if he had not been influenced by a young electrical engineer, at work on a project in the area, who rented a room from the Hoods. Having become interested in electrical engineering through long conversations with the engineer, the youth decided to seek a career in that field and entered the University of Illinois to work for the Bachelor of Science degree in electrical engineering, which he received in 1915. As manager of the university's annual electrical show, in which manufacturers supplied equipment for display, Hood had his first contact with industry and was at this time influenced in his decision to take as his first job after graduation a position as sales engineer and assistant cable sales manager with the Packard Electric Company at Warren, Ohio.

Two years later, in 1917, Hood's work with cable led to his first association with United States Steel when he became an operating clerk with American Steel and Wire Company, a United States Steel subsidiary, producing electrical cable, wire rope, and steel cable. Six weeks after accepting this new post, he entered the Army (in 1917) as a private in the Coast Artillery. He returned from service overseas with the rank of first lieutenant and in 1919 rejoined American Steel and Wire as a foreman in the electrical cable department at Worcester, a position which added operating department experience to his sales and engineer-

Wide World Photos

CLIFFORD F. HOOD

new capacity. His job . . . makes him Number Two man in the field, outranked in the world of steel production only by his boss, Ben Fairless." Construction of the $450 million Fairless Works, described as the "largest single expansion of steel capacity ever undertaken anywhere," was begun in March 1951 near Morrisville, Pennsylvania, with more than 4,000 contractors in twenty-seven States and nearly 10,000 workers on the 3,939 acre site at the peak of operations. The construction time of twenty-one and a half months set an industry record.

Plans having been made for some time to reorganize the corporate structure and make changes in top management of United States Steel, at the beginning of 1953 the United States Steel Company, an operating company directly under the United States Steel Corporation, was dissolved, and the parent corporation became an operating rather than a holding company. Hood was elected president of the reorganized corporation as of January 1, 1953, succeeding Benjamin Fairless, who remained as chairman of the board and chief executive officer. The new president's responsibility was to direct production and sales, while Fairless was to continue to handle matters of public policy. In discussing the reorganization, *Business Week* commented, "Hood really is more the production type, although he is not unfamiliar with sales. [He] is inclined to have the engineer's approach to his job." The magazine also noted that Hood was "commercial minded" enough to realize a "competitive selling situation" was coming and "fortunately" had had experience with "lean years."

As an executive Hood is said to concentrate on finding new and better ways of operating. His five-fold program for progress, as reported in the New York *Times*, calls for employing competent aides, delegating authority, creating loyalty, hunting new methods, and taking an active part in community life. A *Newsweek* interviewer once quoted him as recalling that the job he liked best in his career was "dealing directly with men and materials, organizing them together."

The steel executive is a first vice-president and director of the Allegheny Conference on Community Development, director of the Chamber of Commerce of Pittsburgh, director of the Pittsburgh Branch of the Federal Reserve Bank of Cleveland, director and associate chairman of the Community Chest of Allegheny County, chairman of the Airport Advisory Committee, and member of the American Iron and Steel Institute. Hood is a Mason and belongs to the Chi Phi fraternity, the Rolling Rock Club, Fox Chapel Golf Club, Oakmont Country Club, Pine Valley (New Jersey) Golf Club, and Duquesne Club. Thiel College, in Greenville, Pennsylvania, awarded him the honorary LL.D. degree in June 1952. His church is the Baptist. In politics he has been called an "ardent Republican."

"A robust, broad-faced, genial man," Hood has brown hair and blue eyes, stands five feet ten and a half inches tall, and weighs 185 pounds. His first wife was Emilie R. Tener, whom he married on December 8, 1917. After

ing background. He became assistant superintendent of South Works, Worcester, in 1925 and superintendent three years later. At the end of a year (1932) as assistant manager of the Worcester district operations of American Steel and Wire Company, Hood was made manager of the district in 1933.

While district manager, Hood "piled up such a production record," *Time* reported, that in 1935 he was called to the company's headquarters in Cleveland to become vice-president in charge of operations and two years later was elected executive vice-president. On January 1, 1938, his eighteen years with American Steel and Wire were climaxed with his election to the post of president of the company. Twelve years later, on January 1, 1950, Hood became president of the Carnegie-Illinois Steel Corporation, the largest of United States Steel's subsidiaries, which had been formed in 1935 as a result of the merger of the Carnegie Steel Company and the Illinois Steel Company, both units of the United States Steel "community of companies." Hood's advancement at this time was regarded as the preliminary to his appointment as the next president of United States Steel (*Business Week*). Hood was also a director and a member of the executive committee of the United States Steel Corporation of Delaware. In January 1951 these companies and two other United States Steel Corporation subsidiaries were brought into a single company, the United States Steel Company, with Hood as executive vice-president in charge of operations, the top production post, and as a director of the new company.

In United States Steel's postwar expansion program which increased its steel-making capacity by five million tons in five years, Hood, according to *Fortune* (April 1951), was "the Big Steel official directly responsible for planning and building the corporation's tremendous

After her death he married, on May 6, 1943, Mary Ellen Tolerton. His sons, Randall F. and Richard E., were both serving as privates in the Army, the latter in Korea, when their father was elected president of United States Steel. In his leisure hours Hood is said to like to hunt and fish, and to do "a lot of reading." He has been called a man of "very few, but well-chosen words," and according to the *Newsweek* interviewer, "keeps a large jumble of metal odds and ends in his desk and likes to whip them out when he is talking about steel to visitors."

References

> Bsns Wk p42 D 31 '49; p27-8 D 6 '52
> Fortune 43:31 Ap '51; 47:37 Ja '53 por
> Iron Age 167:55 F 22 '51
> Newsweek 40:72+ D 8 '52
> N Y Herald Tribune p1+ N 26 '52 por; p26 N 27 '52
> N Y Times p1+ N 26 '52 por; III p1 D 21 '52 por
> Time 60:87 D 8 '52
> Business Executives of America (1950)
> International Who's Who, 1952
> Who's Who in America, 1952-53
> Who's Who in Commerce and Industry (1951)
> World Biography (1948)

HOPE, BOB May 29, 1903- Comedian
Address: b c/o Paramount Pictures, Hollywood, Calif.

> NOTE: This biography supersedes the article which appeared in *Current Biography* in 1941.

A rapid-fire comedy technique and an encyclopedic memory for jokes, which won Bob Hope the reputation of being one of the best ad-libbers in the country, have sustained his popularity as a comedian for eighteen years. During World War II he was the only entertainer among fifty persons voted into the Living Hall of Fame at the Smithsonian Institution.

Bob Hope made his radio debut on the *Atlantic Family* in 1935, his first movie, *The Big Broadcast,* in 1938, and his first television appearance in *Star Spangled Revue* in 1950. He has received more than one hundred citations from Government and military and civic groups for his work in entertaining. The Hollywood Chamber of Commerce gave him a trophy for creating good will for the city, and he was the first recipient of the Al Jolson Award of the Veterans of Foreign Wars.

In 1941 the Academy of Motion Picture Arts and Sciences awarded Hope a special plaque for "unselfish services to the motion picture industry"; in that same year he was *Motion Picture Daily's* "Champion of Champions," *Radio Daily's* "No. 1 Entertainer"; in 1940 he earned a special "Oscar" for an "achievement in humanity," in recognition of the large number of benefit performances which he gave. He calls it his consolation prize (Bing Crosby has a real Oscar).

BOB HOPE

He was one of the ten best money-making stars in the *Motion Picture Herald* Fame Poll for 1941-1947 and 1949-1951, and has received the George Foster Peabody Award for radio. Hope has written a daily syndicated newspaper column, and is the author of three books.

The fifth of six sons of a stonemason, Leslie Townes Hope was born in Eltham, England, on May 29, 1903. His father brought the family to Cleveland, Ohio, when young Hope was four, and the boy received his education there, at the Fairmont Grammar School and High School. He had a good soprano voice when a child and was given singing lessons by his mother, Agnes (Townes) Hope, who had been a Welsh concert singer. According to legend, the future entertainer, who has said he never wanted to do anything but be a comedian, discovered the delight in making people laugh when his voice cracked one day while he was singing *The End of a Perfect Day* at a family gathering.

During his schooldays he earned money selling papers, working in a shoe store, a drug store, and in his older brother's meat market. He was also a golf caddy. A good athlete, he won extra money in Cleveland racing events; he also won prizes for Charlie Chaplin imitations. He learned tap dancing in high school, and when the instructor left for Hollywood, he took over the classes for a time.

After graduating from high school, he spent a brief period as a clerk for the Chandler Motor Company. Under the name "Packy East" he tried boxing, entering the Ohio Novice Championships, but gave it up after being defeated in the semi-finals.

Hope entered show business when he learned that several acts were needed to fill out the bill of a Cleveland theatre where Fatty Arbuckle was to make a personal appearance. He acquired a partner named George Byrne, and together they worked out a dance routine, call-

HOPE, BOB—*Continued*

ing themselves "Two Diamonds in the Rough," and obtained the job. The two then joined a road show musical comedy in which they danced, did a blackface act, and Hope sang in the quartet and played the saxophone. They also helped to move the scenery.

After the show closed the team embarked on a vaudeville tour, playing at theatres in Detroit, Pittsburgh and New York, where they appeared on a bill with Daisy and Violet Hilton, the Siamese twins. Hope and Byrne's manager arranged an audition for them and among the judges were Eddie Dowling, Kate Smith and Ruby Keeler, who chose them for a number in *The Sidewalks of New York*, a Broadway production, in 1927. This was followed by *Smiles* in 1928. After this experience, Hope and his partner created a new act for Chicago. They were booked for a performance in Newcastle, Indiana, to break the jump from New York to Chicago, and it was in this appearance that Hope emerged as a monologist. In announcing a coming performance at the theatre he burlesqued the announcement and told Scotch jokes with such success that he decided to be a solo performer, using the name Bob Hope.

After perfecting his routine in night club and small theatre bookings in Ohio, Bob Hope headed for Chicago. Here he experienced a long jobless period, in which he did a good deal of want-ad searching.

"Before long," Hope said, "I was $4,000 in debt. I had holes in my shoes. I was eating doughnuts and coffee, and when I met a friend one day who bought me a luncheon featuring beefsteak, I had forgotten whether you cut steak with a knife or drank it out of a spoon." The friend took him to an agent who booked him for an engagement in a small Chicago theatre. He moved on to the Stratford Theatre where a scheduled three-day stay extended into six months.

During these early vaudeville days, Hope "developed an uncanny instinct for comedy—the expert emphasis on certain lines, the split-second parries, the correct distribution of key words that produce laughs" (*American Magazine, January,* 1942). At the end of the run at the Stratford Theatre he formed his own company, which included Edgar Bergen and Charlie McCarthy. Successful vaudeville tours followed and Hope, out of debt, decided to try Broadway again. Scoffing at offers from small theatres in the city, he eventually received an offer to play at the Eighty-sixth Street Theatre and signed a three-year contract with the RKO circuit as a headliner.

Ballyhoo gave Hope his first real chance in a Broadway musical in 1932, and the following year, after another tour in vaudeville, he starred as Huckleberry Haines in *Roberta* with Fay Templeton and Sydney Greenstreet. In 1934 he appeared with Harry Richman in *Say When*, in 1935 in the *Ziegfeld Follies* with Fanny Brice, and in 1936 in *Red, Hot and Blue* with Ethel Merman and Jimmy Durante.

Bob Hope's first radio appearance was in 1935 when he was signed for the *Atlantic Family*; he next appeared on the *Rippling Rhythm*

Revue," and invented the stooge called "Honeychile" Wilder.

His own radio program, sponsored by Pepsodent over NBC, was introduced in the fall of 1938. Paramount studios called Hope to Hollywood to appear with other radio performers in *The Big Broadcast of 1938* and, instead of utilizing his comic talents, assigned him the song *Thanks for the Memory* which he sang with Shirley Ross. His performance, however, was a hit, and he made five more movies in that year: *College Swing, Give Me a Sailor, Thanks for the Memory, Never Say Die,* and *Some Like It Hot.* In *The Cat and the Canary* (1939), co-starring Paulette Goddard, he had his most important role to date and emerged as a "comic star and matinee idol combined" (*Life,* October 27, 1941).

Hope and Bing Crosby, who had become friends through their mutual interest in golf, made the *Road to Singapore* with Dorothy Lamour in 1940 and proved a great success as a comedy team. The *Road to Zanzibar,* in which they teamed the following year, was called "some of the most uninhibited, daffy nonsense to hit the U. S. screen since the heyday of Harold Lloyd" (*Time,* April 7, 1941). Other Hope films of 1941, *The Ghost Breakers, Caught in the Draft,* and *Nothing But the Truth* were received with enthusiasm by both critics and the public.

After the United States entered World War II Hope attempted to enlist but was told he could serve better as an entertainer to build morale. With his troupe of entertainers he covered most of the overseas bases, including those in Africa, England, Wales, Ireland, Scotland, Sicily, Alaska, the Aleutians, and the Pacific theatre. John Steinbeck said of his efforts, "It is impossible to see how he can do so much, can cover so much ground, can work so hard and can be so effective." While on a round of shows for Allied troops in England in 1944, Hope visited his 99-year-old grandfather. One of the biggest disappointments in his life is that his parents did not live to enjoy some of the pleasures he could now give them.

In addition to his wartime entertainment schedule, Hope made *Louisiana Purchase, Road to Morocco,* and *My Favorite Blonde* in 1942, and *They Got Me Covered* and *Let's Face It* in 1943. He also began, in 1944, a daily column for the King Features Syndicate entitled "It Says Here." After the war he took his Pepsodent radio program, which had been broadcast from service camps during wartime, to college campuses.

Of his performance in *Monsieur Beaucaire* in 1946 John Mason Brown said, 'the most winning aspect . . . is that he contents himself with being Bob Hope." His other film of that year was *Road to Utopia.* In 1947 he appeared in *My Favorite Brunet* and the following year in *Paleface* and *Road to Rio.* He entertained troops in Europe on Christmas of 1948. *Sorrowful Jones* and *The Great Lover* were Hope productions of 1949 and he made *Fancy Pants* in 1950.

The television show *Star Spangled Revue* presented on Easter Sunday 1950 marked Hope's first appearance on television, and his debut was greeted with mixed critical reaction. "Bob Hope was in rare form," said Jack Gould in the New York *Times,* while John Crosby commented in the New York *Herald-Tribune,* "Hope's pace was, by comparison with the radio Hope, languid." In 1950, in the middle of a ten-year contract with Lever Brothers, the comedian broke with his sponsor and signed a new radio and television contract with NBC. In October of that year he and a troupe of entertainers embarked on a tour of Pacific bases and hospitals in Pearl Harbor, Kwajalein, Guam, Japan, and Korea.

Hope made a vaudeville appearance in England in April 1951 in a two-week engagement at the Prince of Wales Theatre, the proceeds of which were donated to Clubland, a London youth center. He then made a three-month tour of England, France and Germany and returned to the United States to make personal appearances in nine cities. In the fall of 1951 he opened the NBC-TV comedy series *Sound Off* on which he rotated with two other comedians, each appearing once every three weeks. His films of 1951 were *The Lemon Drop Kid* and *My Favorite Spy.*

Hope attended both the Republican and Democratic conventions in July 1952 for NBC, devoting five minutes daily to commentaries. A tour of Europe in the following August and September was climaxed by an appearance at the Palladium in London. On his return to the United States the comedian signed a contract with the General Foods Corporation which provided for his first appearance on daytime radio, a morning show given five days a week and an evening variety program. He appeared in *Son of Paleface* in 1952; his latest movies are *Off Limits* and *Road to Bali.*

Bob Hope's three books are *They've Got Me Covered* (1941), a humorous autobiography; *I Never Left Home* (Simon & Schuster, 1944), which, said Tom O'Reilly in the New York *Times* (June 18, 1944), is an "honest and often touching account of how Mr. Hope and the soldiers reacted to each other"; and *So This Is Peace* (Simon & Schuster, 1946), which dealt with the trials of a postwar world in general and some of the comedian's in particular. Magazine articles which he has written include "Tomorrow Is a New Day," an autobiographical sketch (*American Magazine,* March 1949), "People Are Great" (*Coronet,* June 1950), "It's Great to be a College Man" (*This Week,* December 9, 1951), and "My Old Kentucky Horse" (*Liberty,* May 10, 1941).

The financial aspects of Hope's career are handled by Hope Enterprises, Incorporated, which includes the Hope Corporation, in charge of his publications, and Hope Records, Incorporated. The comedian has various business ventures, having an interest in the Cleveland Indians, the Los Angeles Rams, a soft drink company, the Hope Metal Products Company, a golf driving range, a dairy ranch, an Ohio resort, and a meat-packing firm in Cleveland.

Hope married Dolores Reade, a former popular singer, in 1933 and they have four adopted children, Linda Roberta Theresa, Anthony Reade, Honora Avis Mary, and William Kelly Francis. Their fifteen-room English style "farm house" is located at Toluca Lake in Hollywood. The comedian is an officer of the Hollywood branch of the Friars and was selected president of the American Guild of Variety Artists in 1952. He plays an excellent game of golf and has participated in many benefit matches with Bing Crosby. One of his hobbies is the production of amateur color movies. He is five feet eleven inches tall, weighs 170 pounds, and has brown hair and eyes.

References

Am Mag 147:21+ Mr '49 por
Collier's 122:20 Ag 14 '48
Life 11:102+ O 27 '41 pors; 24:24 Ap 14 '48
N Y Times p11 F 25 '40
N Y World-Telegram Mag p4 F 21 '53
Parents Mag 24:32+ D '49
Sat R Lit 29:22+ O 5 '46
Winchester's Screen Encyclopedia (1948)
Who's Who, 1952
Who's Who in America, 1952-53
Who's Who in the West (1951)
World Biography (1948)

HOPE, CLIFFORD R(AGSDALE) June 9, 1893- United States Representative from Kansas

Address: b. House Office Bldg., Washington 25, D.C.; 323 N. Main St., Garden City, Kan.; h. 1116 Gillespie Pl., Garden City, Kan.

Representative Clifford R Hope, Republican, chairman of the House Agriculture Committee in the Eighty-third Congress, has been a member of the committee since he was first elected to Congress in 1926. He is co-author of the Hope-Aiken price-support law by which farm prices are calculated in relation to the costs of other commodities.

A consistent advocate of soil conservation and a comprehensive long-range farm policy, Hope recommended in 1946 the creation of a National Research Institute to reduce waste of food products. He has served as chairman of the farm division of the Republican National Committee, and was a delegate to the United Nations Food and Agricultural Conference in Copenhagen. The jurisdiction of his committee includes legislation affecting agricultural problems, stabilization of prices, soil conservation, migrant farm-workers, the Commodity Credit Corporation and loan agencies, and also forestry and rural electrification.

Clifford Ragsdale Hope, the son of Harry M. and Olive Armitta (Ragsdale) Hope, was born in Birmingham, Iowa, June 9, 1893. When he was thirteen, he moved with his parents to Kansas. After attending Nebraska Wesleyan University, Hope entered the Washburn School of Law in Topeka, Kansas, where he was president of the Washburn Republican Club in 1916. Receiving his LL.B. degree in 1917, he was admitted to the Kansas bar, and in the same year entered the Officers' Training Camp at Fort Riley, Kansas. Commissioned a second lieutenant in World War I, Hope served in France in the 35th and 85th Divisions.

Wide World Photos

CLIFFORD R. HOPE

Returning from the service in April 1919, Hope established a law office in Garden City, Kansas, where he still maintains residence. While sharing his law practice with William Easton Hutchinson for the next six years, Hope began his political career as a member of the Kansas State Legislature in 1921. He became speaker pro tem two years later and speaker in 1925, in which year he was also made a member of the law firm of Hutchinson, Vance, Hope, and Fleming. In 1928 he was elected to the United States Congress and has been regularly re-elected for successive terms.

In Alfred M. Landon's presidential campaign in 1936, Hope was appointed chairman of the farm division of the Republican National Committee and was regarded as Landon's selection for the post of Secretary of Agriculture. Four years later, Hope served in the same capacity in Wendell L. Willkie's presidential campaign.

On the national scene, Hope opposed the food subsidy plan in effect in 1944 and was quoted by *PM* as saying, "My guess is that some kind of compromise will be effected under which rollback subsidies will not be banned but legalized." The Federal credit agencies received the Kansan's criticism in 1945, when he charged that the agencies were harassing the farmers, although Congress had passed a law to prevent just such "loan-shark methods." During the acute meat shortage in the same year Hope found that "inequitable price ceilings and black-market operations" had caused, in one year, a great change in the pattern of meat distribution.

When the House Agricultural Committee was confronted with the task of working out a postwar farm program in 1946, Hope introduced a bill recommended by the Republican Congressional Food Study Committee to establish a new National Food Research Institute, under a director to be appointed by the President, for a scientific approach to the production, utilization, and distribution of food. In the same year Hope was a delegate to the United Nations Food and Agriculture Conference in Copenhagen, Denmark.

At a meeting of the National Farm Institute in Des Moines in February 1947, Hope, then chairman of his committee, pointed out that his bill, which involved a two-price system in the handling of farm produce, also provided detailed machinery for absorbing farm surpluses. He asserted that a national food research institute would be a great advance toward achieving scientific utilization of maximum farm production and providing an economy of plenty for the nation. Speaking before a meeting of the National Industrial Conference Board in Chicago the following April, Hope called for a national policy with respect to agriculture to relieve the farmer of the uncoordinated, often contradictory programs that had been adopted in recent years. In statements to the press at this time, Hope said, "We need to keep our agriculture geared to developments in other segments of the economy . . . to develop a long-range system of commodity price floors . . . and to generally cushion declines in farm prices and incomes in the event of business recessions."

When Hope began an investigation of the "surplus" food problem which resulted in the destruction of 90,000,000 bushels of potatoes, Marquis Childs in the New York *Post* commented that "by great good fortune, one of the most conscientious and able men in Congress has started a series of hearings to analyze this toughest of all riddles." At about this time, Hope led a revolt against the proposal of an economy-minded Congress to save 32 per cent of the Agriculture Department's budget by slashing the school lunch program, soil conservation program, aids to tenant farmers, and other activities of the Department.

Addressing 2,000 delegates of the American Institute of Cooperation at a meeting held in the Colorado A. and M. College in August 1947, Hope spoke of the place of cooperatives in an extended agricultural program. He said that the two biggest problems that had emerged from his committee's hearings were soil conservation and distribution of farm products. He told the delegates that with good land decreasing and the population increasing, steps must be taken to preserve the soil fertility for future generations. Discussing the problems of marketing and distribution, Hope called the farm cooperative the answer to the individual farmer's lack of bargaining power. He predicted the growth of cooperatives in the future as a necessary part of any long-range agricultural program.

In the fall of 1947 Hope went with the House Agricultural Committee on a "grass roots" tour to acquaint the committee members personally with agricultural problems in different parts of the country, and to hear directly from the working farmers who could not come to Washington to express their views. In a speech made during the tour in Rocky Mount, North Carolina, the Representative de-

HOPE, CLIFFORD R.—*Continued*

clared his support of the Marshall Plan and predicted its adoption.

Hope continued to work for an improved land policy, issuing a warning in 1948 that 5,000,000 acres of cropland were being lost from erosion and improper use, while our population was growing at the rate of two millions annually. In June of that year, the House passed by a voice vote a bill which was primarily the work of Representative Hope, continuing for another two years a Government program for guaranteeing farm prices at specific levels. The measure continued Government price guarantees until June 1950 at 90 per cent of parity on cotton, wheat, milk, hogs, chickens, eggs, potatoes, corn, tobacco and peanuts. In the Senate the bill was modified to point the program toward stabilizing rather than actually subsidizing agriculture, but was defeated. The House and Senate conference on the bill resulted in a House measure extending high wartime supports.

The determination of the Republicans in 1949 to recapture the farm vote led to a program of "educating" the farmer through a detailed explanation and defense of the Aiken-Hope Farm Price Support Act. Although he had been hostile to some features of the measure, Hope gave his approval to the program.

Sweeping new powers to control farm production were requested in the spring of 1949 by Secretary of Agriculture Brannan. As senior Republican member of the House Agriculture Committee Hope denounced the Brannan Plan: it would "make it possible for the Secretary of Agriculture to control all agricultural production and marketing in this country." Addressing the Republican National Committee in Sioux City in September, Hope pointed out that the Brannan Plan had first been outlined at the CIO convention and that while labor organizations were enthusiastic, the farmers were opposed because they "were not consulted before the plan was brought out and haven't been consulted since."

During the House debate, Hope defended the compromise farm bill accepted on October 19 by the House with a vote of 175 to 34, and by the Senate with a vote of 46 to 7. Commenting on the Government's wage-price control order in January 1951, the New York *Times* quoted Hope as approving the measure, but stating that he was "rather dubious" about how price controls would work on some farm products, particularly wheat.

An economy move to cut the soil conservation program was defeated in May 1951, with Hope and other Republicans voting with most Democrats to leave unchanged the $225,000,000 which had been authorized by the House Appropriations Committee for soil conservation in the following year. Hope pointed out that a sizable cut had already been made from the $256,000,000 voted the year before.

At a meeting of representatives of Republican farm groups of eleven Midwestern States in Des Moines in June 1952, Hope branded as

"one of the greatest political lies in history" the assertion which had been made by former President Truman that there was a scarcity of storage space for crops. "If the corn farmers had stopped to think, they'd have known that they never did put their corn in Government warehouses." Hope said, "They usually put it in a crib at home and got a loan on it."

In January 1953 House farm leaders were considering an investigation to determine why declining livestock prices had not resulted in cheaper meat at retail. As the new chairman of the House Agriculture Committee, Hope expressed the belief that his committee should conduct such an investigation, which it did.

In the Eighty-second Congress Hope voted in the affirmative on Immigration, Naturalization and Nationality Revision bill, which was passed over the President's veto on June 26; and on the Agricultural Parity Prices bill, passed on June 30; on the Independent Offices Appropriation for 1952, Phillips motion, limiting public housing to 5,000 units. He also voted in favor of the Social Security Act Amendments bill, passed in June; the Mutual Security Act of 1952, passed in May; the Veterans' Housing Loans bill, passed in February; the Military Pay Increase bill, passed January 15; the Military Construction bill, authorizing expenditures for military and naval public works construction; and the Emergency Powers Extension bill, passed June 11. His vote was against the Supplemental Appropriations bill; against authorizing the construction of the Cheatham Dam Hydro-electric Plant on the Cumberland River, Tennessee; and against the Defense Production Act Amendments bill, passed June 26 (Congressional Quarterly Almanac, 1952).

He was a member of the United States Delegation at the first meeting of the Food and Agricultural Organization (1945) in Quebec; in Copenhagen (1946); in Washington (1949); Rome (1951). Hope was Congressional Advisor to the United States Delegation to the Inter-American Conservation Conference (1948); to the International Wheat Conferences (1948, 1949 and 1952). He was appointed by President Truman in February 1952 as a member of the Missouri Basin Survey Commission.

Hope married Pauline E. Sanders on June 8, 1921. Three children have been born to them, Edward Sanders (deceased), Clifford Ragsdale, and Martha (now Mrs. Frank West). He is a member of the American Legion, the Veterans of Foreign Wars, the Sons of the American Revolution, the Consistory, the Kansas State Historical Society, and the Elks, Odd Fellows, and Masons (Shriner). His religious affiliation is Presbyterian. Hope, who has been described as appearing younger than his years, is said to be of a rather grave manner and smart in dress. His hair is brown, his eyes blue, his height is five feet ten inches, and he weighs 160 pounds.

He received an honorary LL.D. degree from Washburn University in June, 1951 and a Doctor of Civil Law from Sterling College in 1952.

HOPE, CLIFFORD R.—*Continued*

References

N Y Herald Tribune p17 O 24 '48 por
N Y Sun p22 Mr 5 '47
N Y Times p23 Ag 27 '47
Biographical Directory of the American Congress, 1774-1949 (1950)
Congressional Directory (1951)
Who's Who in America, 1952-53
Who's Who in United States Politics (1950)

HOPE, LESLIE TOWNES *See* Hope, B.

HORNEY, KAREN Sept. 16, 1885—Dec. 4, 1952 Psychoanalyst;

started career in 1918 as practicing psychoanalyst in Berlin, later taught at Berlin Psychoanalytic Institute; went to United States in 1932; assistant director and a teacher at Institute for Psychoanalysis in Chicago (1932-34); became a practicing analyst in New York in 1934; lectured at the New School for Social Research; taught at New York Psychoanalytic Institute (1934-41); dean of American Institute for Psychoanalysis since she helped organize it in 1941; author of *Our Inner Conflicts* (1945), *Neurosis and Human Conflict* (1950), and other books. See *Current Biography*, 1941.

Obituary

N Y Times p27 D 5 '52

HORWICH, FRANCES (RAPPAPORT) July 16, 1908- Educator

Address: b. 430 S. Michigan Ave., Chicago, Ill.; h. 1907 Sherman Ave., Evanston, Ill.

The "Miss Frances" of *Ding Dong School*, television's only educational program for the pre-school child, is Dr. Frances Horwich, a widely known specialist in the field of child education. A newcomer to the NBC network, she is at present on leave of absence from her post of professor of education at Chicago's Roosevelt College.

Nearly twenty-five years of classroom experience preceded Dr. Horwich's debut as a television schoolmistress, which she made on October 3, 1952, from the National Broadcasting Company's Chicago affiliate station, WNBQ. The program now has an estimated audience of two million viewers in thirty-six cities. *Life* commented that, "Miss Frances has done what most TV know-it-alls said could never be done: put on educational programs both good and commercially successful" (March 16, 1953).

Ding Dong School won the 1953 children's program award at the thirteenth annual presentation, April 24, 1953, of the George Foster Peabody awards for meritorious public service in radio and television. The program is based on three fundamental conceptions held by the educator: "We must have faith in children; we can't work with children alone, but must work with parents at the same time; and what happens to children up to the age of six is terribly important."

Frances Rappaport was born in Ottawa, Ohio, July 16, 1908, the daughter of Samuel and Rosa (Gratz) Rappaport. She attended the elementary and high schools in Ottawa, then entered the University of Chicago, where she received her Ph.B. in 1929. In the same year she began her teaching career as a first grade instructor in Evanston, Illinois, a position held until 1932. She received the M.A. degree from Teachers' College, Columbia University, in 1933. Returning to Chicago, she became supervisor of nursery schools for the Works Progress Administration there, serving from 1933 to 1935. She was then appointed director of junior kindergartens in Winnetka, Illinois, where she remained until 1938.

The educator's next appointment was that of dean of education in the Pestalozzi Froebel Teachers' College, Chicago in 1938, and from 1941 to 1943 she was counselor of student teachers at Chicago Teachers' College. In 1942 she earned the Ph.D. degree at Northwestern University. She then became director of the Hessian Hills School at Croton-on-Hudson, New York, for two years, and in 1945 began another two-year assignment as visiting professor of education at the University of North Carolina. During this period, in 1946, she also served as a special editor for *Understanding the Child,* a magazine published by the National Committee for Mental Hygiene. From the University of North Carolina, she went to Roosevelt College, Chicago, as professor of education.

The idea of a television nursery school originated with Judith Waller, director of the Office of Public Affairs and Education at NBC's Central Division, and she obtained Mrs. Horwich to conduct it. Whatever technical advice Mrs. Horwich may require she gets from the director-producer, Reinald Werrenrath, Jr., but otherwise the program is hers. Appearing alone on the screen, she demonstrates as she gives instruction, addressing herself directly to the child-viewer and inviting his participation.

The instruction in *Ding Dong School* is varied. It may include finger painting, clay modelling, the use of crayons, or the making of simple and ingenious toys. Into the instruction is unobtrusively blended training in good behavior. The last five-minute period of each program is addressed to the mother, who is given a brief summary of that morning's session which enables her to work out with the child whatever may be unresolved.

When the program was first presented in the Chicago area its appearance was unannounced. The public response, however, was immediate and "virtually unequalled" in Chicago TV history, according to NBC, and within seven weeks *Ding Dong School* was put on the network. It goes on the air every week-day at nine a.m. Central Standard Time for one-half hour. Although at first unsponsored, it is now presented by General Mills, Inc.

The citation for the Peabody award read in part, "The rapid justification of Judith Waller's faith in the television possibilities of straight-forward teaching by child-expert 'Miss Frances' Horwich has not only amazed the in-

Maurice Seymour
FRANCES HORWICH

. . . .Miss Frances's secret is her child-world rhythm of thought and feeling."

Married June 11, 1931, to Harvey L. Horwich, a civilian technical consultant with the United States Air Force, now on temporary assignment in Japan, Dr. Horwich makes her home in Evanston, Illinois. She has no children. The educator is described as "matronly" and possessing "the mysterious alchemy of personality." She has brown eyes and brown hair and is five feet five inches tall.

References

Christian Sci Mon p10 Ap 25 '53 por
Life 34:122+ Mr 16 '53 por
N Y Herald Tribune IV p1 F 1 '53; p22 Ap 24 '53
N Y Times II p11 Ja 4 '53; II p13 Ja 18 '53; p41 Ap 1 '53
Sat R 26:32 Ap 18 '53
Who's Who in America, 1952-53
Leaders in Education (1948)

HORWICH, MRS. HARVEY L. *See* Horwich, F. (R.)

dustry, but has also raised doubts about accepted notions of 'what the public wants.' "

Commenting on the program, Jack Gould of the New York *Times* wrote, "The whole concept of *Ding Dong School* is one for which a good many television parents long have yearned: the use of the screen to stimulate participation by youngsters in what is being shown, not just passive watching of one more video show. Mrs. Horwich achieves this with the greatest success." In a previous comment, the same writer said of Dr. Horwich. "She imbues in the youngsters a sense of friendliness, confidence, and faith that is truly magical television." Dr. Horwich's own explanation for the appeal of *Ding Dong School* is that "little children sometimes feel left out of things. Our little school gives them a sense of belonging. . . .It's this identification with a group that's important."

Active participation in educational affairs has been part of Dr. Horwich's career. In 1943 she was appointed secretary-treasurer for the Association of Nursery Education; she served on the publications committee of the American Education Fellowship from 1943 to 1945, was chairman of the nominating committee in 1945, and national convention chairman in 1947. Dr. Horwich is also a member of the National Education Association and has spoken before numerous educational groups. Her recognized specialties are child development, nursery school education and language arts in the elementary school.

Writing in the *Saturday Review* (April 18, 1953), Robert Lewis Shayon speaks of the "gentle, restful, evocative manner" in which she attempts "to draw the child-viewer to push back the boundaries of his own limitations into everwidening circles of fulfillment." He added, "She seems genuinely to care about [the children's] intelligence, imagination and creativity.

HOWARD, MRS. CHARLES P(AGELSEN) Sept. 30, 1898- United States Government official

Address: b. 1930 Columbia Rd., Washington, D.C.; h. 124 Beacon St., Boston 16, Mass.

Mrs. Katherine G. Howard regards her job as Deputy Federal Civil Defense Administrator as "a crusade against fear of the atomic bomb, which is something we can live with, and recover from." Long active in Republican party fund-raising, Mrs. Howard served during the 1952 presidential campaign as the only woman on General Eisenhower's "strategy and policy" committee. It was largely due to her efforts that the Republican National Finance Committee included four women among its members in 1952.

Katherine Graham was born in Guyton, Georgia, on September 30, 1898, the daughter of Joseph Lewis and Margaret (Nowell) Graham, both native New Englanders. She has one brother, John S. Graham. Her father was a director of R. J. Reynolds Tobacco Company. The family moved to Winston-Salem, North Carolina, and Katherine attended Salem Academy and Salem College.

She first went north to New England to enter Smith College, where she majored in literature and art. She was captain of the college basketball team and vice-president of the student dramatics society, and was graduated with a Bachelor of Arts degree in 1920.

Mrs. Howard began her career in politics as a precinct worker. For eighteen years, from 1924 to 1942, she served as a member of the Republican Town Committee of Reading, Massachusetts, and vice-chairman of this Committee from 1932 to 1942. On the board of directors of the Women's Republican Club of Massachusetts from 1938 to 1940, Mrs. Howard became vice-president of the Club in 1940 and president in 1942. She was a member of the

MRS. CHARLES P. HOWARD

Reading Town Meeting during 1945-48, and was re-elected in 1948.

An alternate delegate at large to the 1944 Republican National Convention, Mrs. Howard became interested in politics on a national level. The following year she became Republican National Committeewoman for Massachusetts. She was also selected in 1945 to be a member of the executive committee of the Republican State Committee. Two years later, during 1947-48, Mrs. Howard organized the women's division of the Massachusetts Republican Finance Committee.

Following recommendations by Governors Thomas E. Dewey of New York and Earl Warren of California, Mrs. Howard was named secretary of the National Republican Committee on June 26, 1948. The second woman to occupy this post in the history of the Republican party, she succeeded Mrs. Dudley C. Hay of Michigan. At the 1948 Republican National Convention, she served as delegate at large and as a member of the arrangements committee, the resolutions committee, and the sub-committee on housing.

Her success in organizing the women's division of the Massachusetts Republican Finance Committee led to her appointment as vice-chairman of this Committee in 1950. Two years later she served as both a delegate at large and secretary to the Republican National Convention which nominated Dwight D. Eisenhower for President.

Announcing her support of his campaign on June 25, 1952, she said "I believe General Eisenhower is the greatest leader to appear in American public life in the present generation, and that he alone can unify the country in this time of world crisis" (New York *Herald-Tribune*).

Mrs. Howard was credited with firm adherence to party rules in her capacity as Republican National Committee secretary. On June 16, 1952 she certified to the National Committee, rather than to the State Committee, and contested Texas convention delegates. Her ruling was made in the face of opposition from other officers of the National Committee, and from supporters of Senator Robert A. Taft, as Republican presidential nominee, who dominated the Texas State Committee.

"My decision was a clear victory over opposition," she stated, "I made a decision and made myself solely responsible for it" (New York *Times,* June 27, 1952). Mrs. Howard added that her action was "impartial in heart and in mind," and resulted from a thorough study of the "legal aspects" of the case. Party rules, she explained, required that the Texas contest go to the National Committee because all the Texas delegates were elected "at large" (New York *Herald Tribune,* June 27, 1952).

General Eisenhower's appointment of Mrs. Howard on August 18, 1952 to be the only woman on his four-member "strategy and policy" committee was in response to complaints of his supporters that his campaign was failing to win votes of independents and Democrats. As explained by Arthur H. Vandenberg, the committee would represent General Eisenhower's personal views in all policies and decision, so that these may be constantly available to the Republican National Committee during the campaign" (New York *Times,* August 20, 1952). Mrs. Howard's particular job on the committee was to coordinate campaign activities among women's groups.

Mrs. Howard was among the "highly qualified" women recommended to President Eisenhower in November 1952 for a high appointment in the Administration by Mrs. Ivy B. Priest, director of women's activities of the Republican National Committee. With a desire to see a more effective program developed in civil defense, President Eisenhower selected Mrs. Howard for the position of assistant to Val Peterson, Administrator of Federal Civil Defense. She took the oath of office on March 13, 1953 and on June 29 she was sworn in as Deputy Administrator.

In case of a war emergency, hers would become one of the most vital jobs held by a woman appointee. Now "going to college" at "the Olney Staff School in Maryland to learn the business" from the top down, Mrs. Howard says her job appeals to her "because it has to do with people and is so closely related to the home" (*Christian Science Monitor,* March 26, 1953).

Active in community health and welfare projects, Mrs. Howard served as a trustee of the Boston State Hospital from 1945 to 1949, as vice-chairman of the ladies visiting committee of the Massachusetts General Hospital in Boston, and vice-president of the Penny Wise Thrift Shop of the House of Mercy. She was also an organizer of the Reading (Massachusetts) Guild Garden Kindergarten, and in 1942 was a staff assistant of the American Red Cross.

Her organization memberships include the Reading League of Women Voters (president 1924), Reading Women's Club (3rd, 2nd, and 1st vice-president), Massachusetts Society of Colonial Dames, Needlework Guild of America, Women's Republican Club of Massachusetts, National Women's Republican Club, American Association of University Women, Cosmopolitan Club of New York, and Chilton Club of Boston. Her religious affiliation is Episcopalian.

Described by Christine Sadler in *McCalls* (April 1953), as slender and soft-spoken, she is five feet seven inches tall, weighs 135 pounds, and has blue eyes and "gray" hair. She married Charles P. Howard on September 15, 1921, and their two children are Margaret and Herbert. Her husband is a lawyer and public official. Mrs. Howard includes gardening, sailing, swimming, and painting among her favorite hobbies.

Security veils much of the preparation for protecting Americans from atomic attacks, but Mrs. Howard recently said that she was "impressed with our state of readiness." Ruth Montgomery in her column "D.C.Wash" in the New York *Daily News,* May 9, 1953, wrote: "Anyone would be impressed with Mrs. Howard's own state of readiness. Besides putting in a five-day week at her crucial job, she commutes [on weekends] between Boston and Washington, and Sunday night boards the 11 P.M. train in Boston—sleeps like a kitten after her weeks of campaign training—and awakens in Washington in time to be at her desk by 8:30 A.M. Monday."

Mrs. Howard announced on August 29, that the Civil Defense Administration had published three pamphlets explaining to individual householders how to build home shelters tested and found to be adequate protection in bombing raids. She urged greatly increased "down-to-earth, home-by-home" civil defense protection through a "family action program" and she called on women's clubs and parent-teacher organizations for cooperation.

References

> Christian Sci Mon p6 Mr 26 '53
> N Y Herald Tribune IX p56 O 26 '52
> N Y Times p23 Ag 28 '52
> Washington (D.C.) Post p23 Ag 28 '52
> Who's Who in America, 1952-53
> Who's Who in United States Politics (1952)

HOWARD, KATHERINE G(RAHAM)
See Howard, Mrs. C. P.

HOWREY, EDWARD F. September 6, 1903- United States Government official; lawyer

Address: b. Federal Trade Commission, Washington 25, D.C.; h. Oak Hill, Burke, Virginia

As head of the Federal Trade Commission, Edward F. Howrey has stressed the importance of the agency in preventing unfair methods of competition as well as punishing those committing deceptive business practices.

Appointed by President Dwight D. Eisenhower on April 1, 1953, as chairman of this

Harris & Ewing
EDWARD F HOWREY

bi-partisan group, Howrey will serve for a term of seven years, succeeding James M. Mead of New York. Since 1937 Howrey has been a partner in the law firm of Sanders, Gravelle, Whitlock and Howrey of Washington, D.C.

Edward F. Howrey was born in Waterloo, Iowa, September 6, 1903, to Ben J. and Ada C. (McStay) Howrey, of English, Scotch and Irish ancestry. His father was a lawyer and banker. Howrey was graduated from the East Waterloo High School and, in 1925, from the University of Iowa, where he majored in political science.

He received his LL.B. degree from George Washington University in 1927, and was associated with the United States Department of Justice from June, 1927, through February, 1929, working on the anti-trust investigation of the Motion Picture industry and the Film Boards of Trade. From February, 1929, to March 1, 1937, he was an associate in the law firm of Sanders, Childs, Bobb & Westcott of Washington, D.C.

Howrey has represented many clients before the Federal Trade Commission; two of them, still under litigation, are: Automatic Canteen Company of America, for whom he argued before the Supreme Court against a decision by the Federal Trade Commission that a buyer is violating the Clayton Act if he accepts discriminatory price discounts; and for the Firestone Tire and Rubber Company, involved in FTC's first attempt to fix the maximum shipment of tires on which a seller can give a quantity discount.

The Federal Trade Commission, which comprises a chairman and four members, administers such laws as the following: the Robinson-Patman Act, passed in 1936, which enlarged the scope of the law against price discrimination; the Wheeler-Lea Act of 1938 which increased its functions in preventing false advertising; the Wool-Products Labelling Act of 1940; the Trade Mark Act of 1946; the McCarran Insurance Act of 1948, which gave the Commission some jurisdiction over insurance; the Anti-Merger Act of 1950; and the 1953 Fur Products Labelling Act. Another function of the Commission is the carrying out of economic studies ordered by the President and Congress.

In testifying before the Senate Committee holding hearings on his nomination, Howrey said that he would disqualify himself before the FTC on any matters pertaining to a former client. Later in the hearing, Howrey spoke of the consumer as "the forgotten man in the trade field" adding, "I do not believe consumers as such are organized or really employ counsel." He stressed that "all the laws committed to the Commission's jurisdiction are good laws and stated he knew of no existing statute that he didn't believe in and would not enforce." In discussing the Robinson-Patman Act, he said he did not think it was a consumer's statute but "a statute that was designed to protect the distribution field, the wholesaler, the jobber, and the retailer. The ultimate objective is to prevent price discrimination."

Howrey favors informal conferences by means of which the Commission gives individual business concerns an oppoortunity to settle cases by agreement without the necessity of formal proceedings. He says that settlements can be as good as court prosecution when both get the same results: compliance with the law.

To offset the charge that many of his former clients were "big business", Howrey submitted a list of the companies which employed his firm to the Senate Committee, and testified, "I think only one could, perhaps, be charged with being 'big business.' By number, we have represented more small companies and small groups, than large." According to U.S. News and World Report, "Howrey is expected to lead the FTC to a more considerate attitude toward business." The Senate Committee approved Howrey's appointment on March 24.

During his legal career he has written for law journals. Among his articles are "Delegated Power in Foreign Affairs Is Constitutionally Tenable" (District of Columbia Journal of Bar Association, May, 1945); "Food Plant Sanitation and Food Drug Cosmetic" (Law Journal, June, 1949); and "Robinson-Patman Act and a Prima Facie Case" (Georgetown Law Journal, May, 1949.)

Edward F. Howrey was married on November 10, 1933, to Jane Pickett Gould. A resident of Oak Hill, Burke, Virginia, and a long-standing Republican, he has actively participated in Republican affairs in Virginia. He is an Episcopalian. His favorite recreation is fox hunting and he is a member of the Fairfax Hunt, Fairfax, Virginia. He is six feet and one inch tall, weighs 182 pounds, and has red hair and blue eyes.

Howrey is a member of the Metropolitan Club and Chevy Chase Club in Washington, D.C., the Academy of Political Science, the English Speaking Union, the American Bar Association, serving on its committee on the FTC, and the District of Columbia Bar Association. He is a member of the Bars of Iowa, Illinois, Virginia and the District of Columbia.

After taking over his new job and surveying the stack of documents waiting to be read, Howrey said he had a nightmare in which he was in a room stacked to the ceiling with files of official documents and couldn't get out until all of them had been read. He said he was going to "ask the Commission's staff to cut down on material the chairman was supposed to read." (Time January 20, 1953).

Since business men have long maintained that a "cease and desist order" and court prosecution for offenders can give a company "a black eye" which they find it hard to live down, even though the Commission may have found the complaints unsupportable, Howrey has emphasized that he favors achieving law observance through voluntary, cooperative action. Firms suspected of violations will be called into conference with members of the Commission and the "alleged infraction thoroughly discussed" (New York Times April 30, 1953).

In an editorial complaining about the vagueness of Federal legislation governing competition, particularly the Robinson-Patman Act, the New York Herald Tribune applauded Howrey's projected plans for the FTC and cited the new chairman's intention to develop more specific standards of compliance with the Act's prohibitions against price discrimination. Noting his decision to investigate the possibility of a standard set of cost accounting procedures aimed at enabling the Commission to measure buying and selling methods more uniformly, the editorial considered his projected innovations "a matter for congratulation," holding that a desirable side effect of Howrey's detailed study might be the exposing of the many weaknesses of the Robinson-Patman Act and a consequent demand for statutory overhaul as well as administrative clarification. (New York Herald Tribune, August 31, 1953).

References

    Bsns W Ap 4 '53
    N Y Times S 5 '52; Mr 25 '53; Mr 29 '53
    N Y World-Telegram Mr 30 '53
    Time Ja 20 '53
    U S News 34:64 Ap 17 '53
    Wash (D C) Post Mr 29 '53
    World Biography (1948)

HULL, JOSEPHINE (SHERWOOD) Jan. 3, 1886- Actress
Address: b. c/o Actors' Equity Association, 45 W. 47th St., New York 19

During her thirty years on Broadway Josephine Hull has probably worked more continuously than any of her contemporaries in the theatre. There have been few seasons when the actress did not fill an engagement, and in many she has appeared in more than one production. Although she has played in an extraordinary number of short-lived plays, she has consistently received favorable reviews for her performances.

She has appeared in three Pulitzer Prize winning plays, *Craig's Wife, You Can't Take It With You* and *Harvey,* and she played in the long-run comedy *Arsenic and Old Lace.* She is the holder of an "Oscar" for her work in the film version of *Harvey,* and is one of the few actresses who has been given an honorary Phi Beta Kappa key. Her extraordinary appeal is indicated by the critical appraisal of her work. Mrs. Hull is "one of our most endearing actresses"; "everybody's favorite actress"; "there are thousands of theatregoers who have been devoted to Mrs. Hull for years." She has become known to the public for her "portrayal of scatter-brain ladies"; "her gallery of hustling, preoccupied matrons"; and her "pixie characters." The critic, Ward Morehouse, has said, "Miss Hull is a vastly skillful trouper who knows what to do with a pause, an inflection, a glance, a jolting utterance—who can nearly always get more out of a line or scene than an author wrote into it."

Her next appearance on Broadway is scheduled for November, in a comedy by George S Kaufman and Howard Teichmann, to be produced by Max Gordon, entitled *The Solid Gold Cadillac.*

Josephine Sherwood was born in Newtonville, Massachusetts, January 3, 1886, the daughter of William Henry Sherwood, an importer, and Mary (Tewksbury) Sherwood, a board of education executive. Josephine attended schools in Newtonville, then went to Radcliffe College in Massachusetts. A leader of the glee club at college, she also participated prominently in school plays.

After finishing school, the young aspirant obtained her mother's permission to join the Castle Square Stock Company in Boston, although at that time, young girls were more apt to encounter parental objection than to sanction a stage career. Josephine studied dramatics under Kate Reignolds, and made her debut in a stock company in 1905. In the first days of her career, she was cast in ingenue roles.

After brief experience with the Castle Square troupe, the young actress toured with George Ober's company in *What Happened to Jones?* and *Why Smith Left Home.* She was a member of the cast with Wilton Lackaye on tour in *The Law and the Man* during 1906. Other early road engagements included parts in *Way Down East, Paid in Full* and *The Bridge.*

Josephine retired from the stage after her marriage to Shelley Vaughn Hull, a well-known actor and elder brother of Henry Hull. Hull was then playing in *The Fortune Hunter*; in 1918 he was co-featured with Effie Shannon in a war play, *Under Orders.* In 1919 he met with an untimely death, and Josephine Hull, after an absence of three years, returned to the theatre as a director for Jessie Bonstelle's stock company in Detroit, Michigan.

"I had decided I was through with acting," Mrs. Hull has said, "but you know what a stock company is. I found myself filling in each week." Mrs. Hull remained with the Detroit stock company for one year. She came to New York in 1923 again in the capacity of director,

JOSEPHINE HULL

this time for the Equity Players, and, "the same thing happened. I found myself playing a bit each week," she recalled.

The Equity Players' production *Roger Bloomer,* which Mrs. Hull directed, opened at the Forty-eighth Street Playhouse in March 1923. In the same year the actress attracted attention in the role of Mrs. Hicks in *Neighbors,* also at the Forty-eighth Street Playhouse. In March, 1924, she was seen in the part of George's mother in the Theatre Guild's presentation of *Fata Morgana.*

The next vehicle in which she appeared was George Kelly's play, *Craig's Wife,* which won the 1926 Pulitzer prize; Mrs. Hull scored a hit in the part of Mrs. Frazier. Kelly wrote a part for her, that of Olly Kipax, in his next play, *Daisy Mayme,* which opened on October 26.

Mrs. Hull's engagement in 1927 was with *The Wild Man of Borneo,* at the Bijou Theatre. The actress played Janet Rodney in *March Hares* at the Little Theatre, and also Hattie in *Hotbed* at the Klaw in 1928. The following year she was at the Maxine Elliot Theatre, playing Cornelia Corbin in *Before You're 25.* She filled two engagements in 1930, appearing in *Those We Love* at the John Golden in February, and in *Midnight* at the Guild in December. In the next season a brief engagement at the Forty-eighth Street in *Unexpected Husband* was followed by a more successful one as Mrs. Piper in *After Tomorrow,* at the John Golden. A motion picture presentation of the latter, made by Fox Films included Mrs. Hull in its cast.

In Mrs. Hull's next New York appearance she was cast as Mrs. Thompson in *A Thousand Summers,* presented at the Selwyn in May, 1932. She was back with the Theatre Guild in *An American Dream* in February of 1933, playing both the parts of Martha Pingres and Mrs. Schuyler Hamilton. As Frau Flastuhl in *Di-*

vine Drudge she appeared at the Royale in October.

Engagements in By Your Leave at the Morosco in January 1934. and in On To Fortune at the Fulton in February 1935, preceded her appearance in the part of Mrs. Quimby in the revival of the George M. Cohan drama, Seven Keys to Baldpate, which opened at the National in May 1935. A third engagement in the same year followed, with Mrs. Hull cast in the role of Lucy Amorest in A Night in the House, which opened at the Booth in November.

In You Can't Take it With You, the 1937 Pulitzer Prize play which had its première at the Booth Theatre in December 1936, Mrs. Hull scored a memorable success as "Penny," Penelope Vanderhof Sycamore, the nitwit authoress-sculptress of the zany Sycamore family. This Moss Hart and George S. Kaufman comedy, featuring Josephine Hull and Henry Travers, enjoyed a run of 103 weeks. The part of "Penny" was a turning point for Mrs. Hull. "I had almost made up my mind to retire and take up writing," she told an interviewer. "For ten years before 'Penny,' I had been busy every year, one or two plays each season, and none of them lasting more than a few weeks. When my agent told me about 'Penny,' I took the part, sight unseen and script unread."

After this success she appeared in a short-lived play, An International Incident at the Ethel Barrymore in April 1940. On January 11, 1941, however, she began another long-run comedy, Arsenic and Old Lace, in which she was co-featured with Effie Shannon as two elderly sisters who administered poison in elderberry wine to lonely boarders.

Presented by Howard Lindsay and Russel Crouse at the Fulton Theatre, this comedy by Joseph Kesselring ran up a total of 1,444 performances. Mrs. Hull was given a temporary leave of absence from the company in order to recreate her role of Abby Brewster in the motion picture version, produced by Warner Brothers, with Cary Grant in the cast.

Her role in Harvey, "the fantasy of the amiable drinking man who kept company with a big rabbit," brought Mrs. Hull's comic genius into greater prominence. Written by Mary Chase, directed by Antoinette Perry, and presented by Brock Pemberton, this play began its four-year run in New York on November 1, 1944, at the Forty-eighth Street Theatre. Sharing honors with Frank Fay, who received an ovation from the press, Mrs. Hull's performance was hailed as a "masterpiece" by Variety: "Her dumpy, comic figure aids her to rouse audience risibilities." The New York Times commented, "Flighty and wide-eyed, Mrs. Hull is a perfect foil for Mr. Fay's casual ease." The review in the Christian Science Monitor was more restrained, "Miss Hull's performance . . . is effective within its vein of near caricature."

The replacement of Frank Fay by James Stewart in 1947 brought in the critics for a second evaluation. The writer for Cue thought, "a tendency to overplay was noticeable even in Josephine Hull," while the reviewer for the World Telegram stated, "Josephine Hull's in-

terpretation of Elwood's distraught sister remains a gem of comedy. With her eyes and hands and panic-stricken moans, she makes Mrs. Simmons an unforgettable joy." Harvey won the Pulitzer Prize in 1945, and was the third winner in which Mrs. Hull had appeared.

The all-time record high of $750,000 for film rights was paid by the Universal-International Studios for Harvey, according to Show Biz. Playing opposite James Stewart, Josephine Hull won the Motion Picture Academy Award (an "Oscar") for the "best supporting actress" in Harvey in 1951.

Fresh critical approval greeted Mrs. Hull's next characterization, that of a Welsh minister's wife in a play written by Richard Hughes (author of A High Wind in Jamaica), although the play itself, Minnie and Mr. Williams, was not favorably received and enjoyed but a short run. Produced by John Gassner and David Dietz and directed by Eddie Dowling, who played opposite Mrs. Hull, the comedy opened at the Morosco in October 1948. Referring to the play as "dismally inept," Variety's reviewer stated, "Eddie Dowling and Josephine Hull put on tours de force. . . .Their performances . . . are real gems of characterization." Describing the play as "thin and artless," Brooks Atkinson, described Mrs. Hull's characterization: "Puffing and flouncing cheerfully around the stage, she plays it with an extraordinary lightness—humorous and motherly, impish and beneficent" (New York Times, October 28, 1948).

Mrs. Hull was starred for the first time in her next vehicle, The Golden State, written by Samuel Spewack especially for her, and presented by Bella Spewack at the Fulton Theatre in November 1950, with Ernest Truex heading the supporting cast. Again, the press comment was favorable to Mrs. Hull, but not to the play, which ran for only twenty-five performances. Wolcott Gibbs of the New Yorker wrote, "It is my sorrowful duty to report that Josephine Hull, who has probably given me more pleasure, pound for pound, than any other actress extant, is now part of a conspiracy to bore even her fondest admirers to tears."

In the summer of 1951 the actress made a summer theatre appearance at Westport, Connecticut, in a trial presentation of a new play, Kin Hubbard, by Lawrence Riley, presented by Lawrence Langner. Again, "the ever-welcome Josephine Hull" was acclaimed but the play was not. This pattern was repeated in Robert Finch's Whistler's Grandmother, in 1952. "What Mrs. Hull needs," the New York Times reviewer asserted, "is a playwright half as sublime as she is" (December 12, 1952).

The actress has made many radio and television appearances. "I'm very happy that I'm frankly a character woman, when I see what the camera does to so many faces on the screen," she says. "I specialize in grandmothers these days and it's fun." TV, she thinks, takes the place of the old stock companies for young actors. "You know, they don't even get much experience in the summer theatres now with the star system."

Her advice to young people who want to act is ". . . get into any little theatre group in your home town. Hold the script, run errands, do anything that's useful; you'll get the feeling of the theatre. Next, go to as good a coach or dramatic school as you can afford and learn to study a part from the inside . . . not the outside."

Mrs. Hull's honorary Phi Beta Kappa key was presented to her by Radcliffe College "for bringing laughter and joy to people." She is five feet two and a half inches tall and weighs 138 pounds. Her eyes "are intensely dark . . . and full of force which is a bit surprising, for her voice is soft, with the wistful overtones that her audiences know so well. . . .She exudes kindness, but she is no flabby sentimentalist" (New York *Herald Tribune,* May 20, 1946).

References

Cue 19 :18 N 18 '50 por
N Y Herald Tribune IV p1 My 20 '46
N Y World-Telegram p7 D 6 '52
Blum, D. C. Great Stars of the American Stage (Greenberg, 1952)

HUMPHREY, GEORGE M(AGOFFIN)
Mar. 8, 1890- Secretary of the Treasury; industrialist; lawyer

Address: b. c/o Department of the Treasury, Washington 25, D.C.; 1300 Leader Bldg., Cleveland 14, Ohio; h. "Holiday Hill Farm," Mentor, Ohio

The selection of George M. Humphrey as Secretary of the Treasury in the Administration of President Dwight D. Eisenhower, who came into office on January 20, 1953, was announced by the President-elect on November 21, 1952. For some twenty-five years a leading figure in the coal, iron, and steel industry and in banking, Humphrey is chairman of the board of the M. A. Hanna Company of Cleveland, which he joined as general counsel in 1918. As

GEORGE M. HUMPHREY

president of the company from 1929 to 1952 he is credited with having initiated many of the mergers and other projects which brought the Hanna Company to prominence among the mining and shipping firms of the nation. Humphrey has served on several governmental advisory committees, including one chosen by Marshall Plan Administrator Paul Hoffman to study German industrial plants and make recommendations in regard to dismantling and reparations.

The son of Watts S. and Caroline (Magoffin) Humphrey, George Magoffin Humphrey was born March 8, 1890, in Cheboygan, Michigan; his ancestry is Scottish and English. He attended public schools in Saginaw, Michigan, where his father practiced law, and finished high school in 1908; as a senior he played football for Saginaw High School, which that year had the State's champion team. Continuing his education at the University of Michigan, Humphrey was first interested in engineering and took several courses in that field; he later decided to study law. At the university he was a member of Psi Upsilon, social fraternity; Phi Delta Phi, law fraternity; the staff of the *Michigan Law Review*; and the Order of Coif, senior law society. He received his LL.B. degree in 1912, the same year in which he was admitted to the Michigan bar.

When he left law school, George Humphrey entered his father's law office in Saginaw, the second Humphrey in Humphrey, Grant and Humphrey. In 1918 he resigned from the family firm to accept the position of general counsel for M. A. Hanna and Company of Cleveland, a firm which had been owned and operated by Ohio Republican Mark Alonzo Hanna until his death in 1904 and which in 1918 was primarily concerned with the shipping of coal and iron on the Great Lakes. After two years as general counsel Humphrey became a partner in the company (1920) and after another two years a vice-president (1922). During his four years (1925-29) as executive vice-president of the M. A. Hanna Company (under which name it was incorporated in 1923), Humphrey succeeded in bringing the firm out of the $2 million deficit it had shown in 1924 and started it on the road to becoming a large business and industrial enterpirse. He unloaded unprofitable properties and undertook new and profitable activities; in addition to hauling iron ore from the Mesabi range and coal from the mines of Pennsylvania, the company began to mine its own ore and to operate its own mills.

Becoming president of the M. A. Hanna Company in 1929, Humphrey continued during the depression years to expand the firm's activities and to show a profit. He merged small companies into big ones within the larger Hanna framework; among the companies thus formed were the National Steel Company (which developed from the Humphrey-organized Great Lakes Steel Corporation in Detroit) and the Pittsburgh Consolidation Coal Company, largest producer of bituminous coal in the United States. (As chairman of the board of Pittsburgh Consolidated, Humphrey played an active part, along with United States Steel's Benjamin

Fairless, in negotiating the coal industry's 1947 contract with John L. Lewis.) When Cleveland banks were undergoing a business decline in the depression, Hanna entered the banking field; and when plastics began to have commercial importance, the company branched out into the plastics industry. The Hanna Coal and Ore Corporation, a subsidiary of the company, is playing an active role in the $225 million enterprise organized in 1950 to exploit Labrador's 400-million ton ore deposit. In 1952 the M. A. Hanna Company had assets totaling more than $120 million, 75 per cent of which is invested in controlled steel, rayon, copper, oil, natural gas, plastics, and two Cleveland banks; the remaining 25 per cent is in mining and shipping. *Time*, giving George Humphrey the major credit for the company's vast expansion, quoted one of his associates as saying, "If you dropped Humphrey in the middle of the Sahara, he'd come out with a newly organized corporation—on a dividend-paying basis."

In 1946 George Humphrey was named chairman of the Business Advisory Council of the Department of Commerce and in December of the following year was appointed by President Harry S. Truman as an industry member of a twelve-man advisory panel set up under the Taft-Hartley labor law. When the Republican-controlled Eightieth Congress ordered the Economic Cooperation Administration to end the dismantling of German plants, Paul Hoffman persuaded Humphrey to head a five-man Reparations Survey Committee to study the industrial situation in Germany and make a report. Technical experts had already started to assemble the relevant data when Humphrey and his fellow committee members went to Paris in October 1948. Of a total of 381 "plants" which were surveyed (the term "plant" was used to designate anything from a single piece of equipment to an entire factory), Humphrey's committee recommended that 167, including 106 complete plants, be removed from the dismantling list. With the committee's report as a basis of their negotiations, British, French, and United States representatives agreed to preserve 159 German industrial units out of the 167 named by the committee. Humphrey, commenting on the agreement, said, "The fact that the negotiations have been carried out to such a successful and prompt conclusion under the able leadership of Messrs. Douglas [Lewis W. Douglas, then American Ambassador to Great Britain], Bevin, and Schuman is another evidence of the unity of purpose in the relationships that exist between the negotiating countries" (New York *Times,* April 14, 1949). Humphrey's committee had also been involved in negotiations which led to the formation in late 1948 of the Ruhr Authority for control of the coal, coke, and steel industries of West Germany. In 1950 Humphrey was elected a trustee of the National Committee for Economic Development.

Less than two weeks after his victory in the 1952 election President-elect Dwight D. Eisenhower, on November 21, announced that George Humphrey, who had the preceding May become chairman of the board of the M. A. Hanna Company, had been designated Secretary of the Treasury in the Republican Cabinet that would come into power after the inauguration on January 20, 1953. Humphrey, who previously had never held political office, had been strong in his support of Robert A. Taft in the 1948 pre-convention campaign but in 1952 had played no conspicuous part in behalf of any candidate. While *Time* and the New York *Times* credited General Lucius Clay with Humphrey's sponsorship for the Treasury post, considered second only to that of Secretary of State, *Business Week* said that Paul Hoffman had instigated the appointment; Humphrey had worked with both Clay and Hoffman when in Europe as chairman of the Reparations Survey Committee in 1948-49. Commenting on Humphrey's qualifications for the position, *Business Week* described his political thinking as "pretty much that of the conservative successful businessman of the midwest—which makes him a stranger to deficit spending. Certainly he is hardheaded on the subject of a balanced budget. Humphrey doesn't have much use for arguments fostering cradle-to-the-grave planning. [His] background points up his ability for organizing to get things done rather than to dream up theories."

During the two months preceding his confirmation by the Senate as Secretary of the Treasury, George Humphrey began to familiarize himself with the responsibilities and problems that would confront him in his new post. In the middle of December he was abroad the U.S.S. *Helena* in the Pacific, participating in private discussions wth Eisenhower and other members of the incoming Cabinet. Quoting Humphrey as "wanting to get his feet on the ground" before specifying the steps he will take when he assumes office, *Newsweek* listed some of the new Treasury Secretary's major long-term objectives: revision of the entire tax structure, with the encouragement of corporate initiative as a guiding principle; reformation of national debt management, with greater emphasis on long-term borrowing as opposed to the short-term loans more frequently favored in recent years; regulation of interest rates by supply and demand rather than by direct controls. "His major jobs," in the view of *Pathfinder,* "will be to make a Republican-promised tax reduction jibe with a national budget based upon tremendous military and domestic demands and to develop sound debt policy." As Treasury Secretary, Humphrey succeeded John W. Snyder, taking his oath of office, following Senate confirmation, on January 21, 1953.

On August 27 Humphrey announced that this country has reached "the essential turning point toward a balanced budget." Economies urged on department heads by President Eisenhower when the 1953 fiscal year ended June 30 made the savings of $2,000,000,000 possible, he asserted.

Before severing all business connections to give full time to his Cabinet office, Humphrey held, besides the chairmanship of the board of the M. A. Hanna Company, the following offices: chairman of the board, Pittsburgh Consolidation Coal Company; chairman of the executive committee of the National Steel Corpora-

HUMPHREY, GEORGE M.—*Continued*
tion and the Industrial Rayon Corporation; and
president of the Iron Ore Company of Canada.
He was also a director of all of these companies and of Phelps Dodge Corporation, the
Jefferson Coal Company, the La Belle Steamship Company, Lake Erie Harbors, Michigan
Steel Corporation, Oak Hill Supply Company,
Renton Investment Company, Tri-County Lands
Company, Virginia Steamship Company, the
National City Bank of Cleveland, and the Canada and Dominion Sugar Company. He maintains membership in the Academy of Political
Science, the Tax Foundation, the American
Iron and Steel Institute, the American Institute of Mining and Metallurgical Engineers,
the Newcomen Society of England, the National Industrial Information Committee, and
the United States Council of the International
Chamber of Commerce.

Chairman of the Joint Committee for the
Advancement of Medical Education and Research of the Western Reserve University
School of Medicine and Affiliated Hospitals,
Humphrey is also a member of the Harvard
University Graduate School of Business Administration Visiting Committee, and of the
Massachusetts Institute of Technology Advisory Council, School of Industrial Management;
a director of the Ford Foundation's Fund for
Adult Education; and chairman of the Rainbow
Hospital Finance Committee. In 1947 the
American Institute of Mining and Metallurgical
Engineers awarded George Humphrey the
Charles F. Rand Medal "for constructive leadership in establishing great enterprises for the
production of iron ore, of steel and coal; for
signal success in administration of large organizations in those basic industries so vital to
the economy of our country." Other honors received by the industrialist are the Saginaw High
School Distinguished Alumnus Award (1948),
honorary Doctor of Laws degree from Western
Reserve University (1950), and honorary Doctor of Engineering Degree from the Case Institute of Technology.

On January 15, 1913 George Humphrey and
his girlhood sweetheart, Pamela Stark, were
married. They have three children, Pamela
(Mrs. Royal Firman, Jr.), Gilbert Watts (who
is a Hanna vice-president), and Caroline (Mrs.
John G. Butler); a second son died. At the
time of his appointment to the Eisenhower
Cabinet, the New York *Times* described Humphrey as "a man of medium build, with an oval
face, receding hair line, strong jaw, large nose,
sharp blue eyes, a quiet voice, quick mind, and
intense concentration." His avoidance of publicity has been frequently noted by the press.
Humphrey's sports interest run mainly to golf,
horses, and hunting; he has his own stables at
Holiday Hill Farm, his 150-acre estate not far
from Cleveland, and is a member of the New
York Jockey Club. His other clubs are Union,
Tavern, Chagrin Valley Hunt, Kirtland County,
and Fifty, in Cleveland; Links in New York;
Duquesne in Pittsburgh; Detroit; Glen Arven
Country in Thomasville, Georgia; and Kitchi
Gammi in Duluth. An Episcopalian, Humphrey

has been a vestryman of St. Hubert's Episcopal Chapel of Kirtland Hills, which is near
his estate.

References

Bsns W p8 Ap 20 '46; p29 N 29 '52
Fortune 35 :90-5+ My '47 por
Life 34 :100+ Ja 19 '53 pors
N Y Herald Tribune p3 N 22 '52
N Y Times p11 N 22 '52
Newsweek 40 :19 D 1 '52; 41 :15 Ja 5 '53
Time 60 :14 D 1 '52; 61 :22+ Ja 22 '53
    pors
U S News 33 :54 N 28 '52
Washington (D.C.) Post p12 N 22 '52
Business Executives of America (1950)
Who's Who in America, 1952-53
Who's Who in Commerce and Industry
    (1951)

HUNTINGTON, MRS. ANNA HYATT
Mar. 10, 1876- Sculptor
Address: Bethel, Conn.

One of America's foremost sculptors and
the first woman creator of heroic statues, Anna
Hyatt Huntington has received from the United
States, France and Spain virtually every honor
possible for her work. Her *Joan of Arc* and
The Cid Campeador rank among the important equestrian statues of the world. She is
said to have done for the work horse in sculpture what Millet did on canvas for the French
peasant. She has modeled groups of farm
horses ploughing, and dray horses pulling
heavy loads up steep and rocky roads.

Mrs. Huntington is a generous patron of the
arts as well as a sculptor. She has enriched
American art with travelling exhibits and donations of her work to schools, galleries and museums throughout the nation. With her husband, Archer M. Huntington, she presented to
the State of South Carolina in 1935 an outdoor museum of 6,635 acres near Charleston,
called Brookgreen Gardens, which represents
the history of American sculpture from the
nineteenth century.

Anna Hyatt was born in Cambridge, Massachusetts, on March 10, 1876, the daughter of
Alpheus and Audella (Beebe) Hyatt. Her
paternal ancestors came from Maryland and
Virginia, and her mother's family was originally from Connecticut. Her father, an eminent
palaeontologist and zoologist, was a pupil of
Louis Agassiz. He was a professor at Harvard
University and a curator of the Boston Society of Natural History.

As the daughter of a naturalist, Anna Hyatt
developed an early interest in animals, and
throughout her childhood studied their anatomy,
movements and attitudes. She liked horses
especially, and before she was school age she
began to model them in clay. When she was a
young girl she broke and trained colts for
neighbors. Anna Hyatt attended private schools
in Cambridge and studied violin for six years
before taking up sculpture seriously at nineteen,
when she began to dream of some day doing
a statue of Joan of Arc.

After studying sculpture with Henry Hudson Kitson of Boston, Anna attended the Art Students League of New York for a few months, receiving instruction from Hermon MacNeil. She sought the criticism of the late Gutzon Borglum, known for his monumental work on Mt. Rushmore in the Black Hills of South Dakota.

Her first work achieved success in Boston, where it was sponsored and bought by Thomas Lawson as fast as she could produce it.

At twenty-four she gave her first one-man show at the Boston Arts Club in 1900. It consisted of forty pieces, large and small animal studies, among them models of lions, tigers and other jungle creatures which she had seen at the Boston and New York Zoological Gardens. One of her small bronzes was acquired by the Metropolitan Museum of Art in 1903. An exhibition was also given in St. Louis in 1904.

Some of Anna Hyatt's most notable early work was done in Europe, where, she states, there is "greater respect for art and the artist, although America is the better proving ground" (Bridgeport *Sunday Post*, December 25, 1949). She lived at Auvers-Sur-Oise, France, in 1907, and created several jaguars that won the praise of international art critics. Going to Naples, Italy, in 1908, she modeled a colossal lion, which was later erected in bronze at Dayton, Ohio. Describing her portrayal of animals, Eleanor M. Mellon writes in *Anna Hyatt Huntington* (W. W. Norton, 1947) that "her knowledge of anatomy and composition enable her to impart to her subjects a sense of vitality and grace which is the result of great physical strength completely controlled."

Deciding in 1909 to start on her equestrian statue of Joan of Arc, she ignored all profitable orders for her work and returned to Paris. On the Impasse du Maine in the Latin Quarter she obtained the ground floor studio built by the French sculptor, Jules Dalou, where it was possible to drive in heavy carts and large animals for models. After considerable search in the stables of Paris, the sculptor found the type of horse she wanted. Working only with the help of a woman assistant, she shut herself up in her studio. She massed a ton of clay and made her own armature for the statue. Besides the physical difficulties she was hampered by what Royal Cortissoz, former art critic of the New York *Herald Tribune*, described as the "distracting shadows" of Dubois' and Freniet's interpretations of Joan of Arc and, he added, "it must have been hard to avoid emulation of the superb medievalism of the former, and the bold picturesqueness of the other." But Cortissoz reported that the finished work triumphed by virtue of the originality which accents its dignity and its grace. *Le Journal* of Quebec (September 2, 1938) termed the statue "a symbol of three nations (France, England and the United States)."

Miss Hyatt exhibited the clay model cast in plaster in 1910 at the Paris *Salon,* the highest international standard for measuring artistic achievement, and won the *Salon's* honorable mention. A replica was cast in bronze for New York City's Riverside Drive at Ninety-third Street. Erected in 1915, it is considered one

Peter A. Juley & Son

ANNA HYATT HUNTINGTON

of the finest statues in the city. This was followed by requests for replicas from San Francisco and San Diego, California; Gloucester, Massachusetts; Quebec, Canada; and Blois, France, which gave the replica one of its best sites, and in 1922 accorded Mrs. Huntington the gift of citizenship.

The French Government in 1915 bestowed upon her the Purple Rosette and in America, she was awarded the Rodin Gold Medal of the Plastic Club of Philadelphia in 1917, and the Saltus Medal for Merit of the National Academy of Design in 1920.

Between 1911 and 1922 she completed a heroic statue of *Diana of the Chase* and a wall sculpture of Joan of Arc. The latter was placed in the Cathedral of St. John the Divine, in New York City. Her *Diana of the Chase,* which has replicas in several universities and museums, is described by Jean Royers as the "deification of beauty in harmony and proportion." This statue won for her the second time the award of the Saltus Gold Medal in 1922. In the same year Anna Hyatt was made a Chevalier of the Legion of Honor in France. In 1923 she married Archer Milton Huntington, poet and philanthropist.

For her equestrian statue of the Cid Campeador, the eleventh century Spanish hero, completed in 1927 and erected in Seville, Mrs. Huntington received from the King of Spain personally in 1929 the Grand Cross of Alfonso XII. She is the only sculptor so honored. This statue was also included in the works which she made for the grounds of the Hispanic Society of America in New York, from 1927 to 1937, which included two flagpole bases, two lions, a red stag, a red doe and fawn, and four animal groups.

A replica of *The Cid Campeador* was placed before the California Palace of the Legion of Honor Museum in San Francisco in 1937, as a companion piece to the *Joan of Arc.* The

HUNTINGTON, ANNA HYATT—*Cont.*

Christian Science Monitor (September 28, 1943) describes the work as the "most arduous piece of sculptural work ever undertaken by a woman."

For her *Bulls Fighting* the artist received the Julia A. Shaw Memorial Prize of the National Academy of Design in 1928, and the Gold Medal of the American Academy of Arts and Letters in 1930, and in 1937 the Widener Gold Medal of the Pennsylvania Academy of Fine Arts for her *Greyhounds Playing*. A retrospective exhibition of her work including 171 pieces, was held at the American Academy of Arts and Letters in 1936.

Anna H. Huntington added a statue of Don Quixote in 1942 and one of Boabdil (last Moorish King of Granada) in 1944 to her work at the Hispanic Society of America. The *Don Quixote,* which she interpreted as a pathetic figure, won the Elizabeth N. Watrous Gold Medal of the National Sculpture Society in 1948.

In her recent works, Mrs. Huntington has chosen to cast in aluminum, which she says has a "vibrant quality." She created twenty aluminum figures from 1948 to 1952 and donated them to museums and schools throughout the United States. Her *Fighting Stallions,* seventeen feet in height and given in 1951 to Southwest Texas State Teachers College, is said to resemble Verochio's *Colleoni* in Venice. To this work Bing Winn, noted Texas muralist, has given an estimated value of at least $100,000 to $150,000. She completed in 1952 a symbolic study of progress which she calls *The Torch.* It is of one man on foot reaching the torch up to another man on horseback, the idea being, Mrs. Huntington said, "that in this age one cannot get very far on foot."

Her sculpture was included in 1950 in a color film "New York's Heritage" released by the New York State Department of Commerce for national distribution. Emile Schaub-Koch, whose book *L'oeuvre d' Anna Hyatt Huntington* (Malfère, 1949) states that "no artist of our day has shown the muscular and nervous structure of the body better than Mrs. Huntington."

Other honors which Anna H. Huntington has received include an honorary Doctor of Fine Arts degree from Syracuse University in 1932, the National Achievement Award in 1948 by Chi Omega society and in 1952 the Allied Arts of America Gold Medal of Honor for her *Nanny and Twins* in aluminum. Mrs. Huntington was elected to the American Academy of Arts and Letters, and a corresponding member of the Spanish Academia de Bellas Artes de San Fernando, an honor never previously given to a woman. She is also an honorary fellow of the National Sculpture Society.

The sculptor is an Episcopalian and a Republican. She is five feet six inches tall, weighs 136 pounds, and has blue eyes and white hair. Her friends call her "level-headed and poised, with charm and a sense of humor, and a great organizer." For recreation, Mrs. Huntington raises Scottish deerhounds.

References

Bridgeport Sunday Post D 25 '49
Christian Science Monitor S 28 '43
N Y Herald Tribune p 13 S 6 '52
Anna Hyatt Huntington (1947)
Who's Who in America, 1952-53
Who's Who in American Art, 1953

HUNTINGTON, MRS. ARCHER MILTON *See* Huntington, A. H.

HUSSEIN, TAHA (hōō″sān′ tä′hä) Nov. 14, 1889- Egyptian educator; author; scholar

Address: b. c/o Journal "Al-Ahram," Cairo, Egypt; h. 3, Al-Baroudi St., Zarnalak, Cairo, Egypt

Free education for the children in Egypt has been accomplished through the efforts of Taha Hussein, who, although blind since the age of three, is one of the most outstanding Islamic scholars. He has devoted his life to achieving academic freedom and the introduction of Western learning in his country.

Having encountered political opposition in trying to apply democratic principles while serving in the Government, Hussein was finally appointed Minister of Education under Farouk I. He is said to have done more for the education of Islamic peoples than any other individual. He is the author of more than forty books, including novels, literary and social studies. His autobiography *Stream of Days* has been translated into fifteen languages.

Taha Hussein was born on November 14, 1889, at Maghagha, a mill town in the province of Minya, Upper Egypt. He was the fifth of the eleven children of Aly Hussein who was an employee in a sugar factory. Taha became blind after an illness when he was three years old. In his first autobiographical work, *An Egyptian Childhood,* translated into English by E. H. Paxton (G. Routledge, London, 1932), he recalls his sadness over the fact that his brothers and sisters were able to do things which were impossible for him. He nevertheless refused to be defeated by his handicap. One of his first accomplishments was to memorize the Koran.

At one time, when young Taha and his family were travelling by train, the elder sons had piled the luggage near the door so that they could unload it quickly. Nothing was forgotten or left behind—except the blind boy. But while waiting at the next station for one of his brothers to come after him, Taha recited passages from the Koran to the fascinated telegraph operators.

In choosing his life work, Hussein relates in his autobiography, *Stream of Days; A Student at the Azhar* (Longmans Green, translated into English by Hilary Wayment, Cairo, 1943; 1948) that for a blind person like himself, who wanted to live a tolerable life, there were only two courses open. He could either study at the theological university, Al-Azhar, in Cairo, until he earned a degree and was assured of a livelihood from the daily allowance of loaves and the monthly pension, or he could make a trade of Koran-reading at funerals and in private houses.

Taha Hussein enrolled at Al-Azhar at the age of thirteen. At the lectures, which constituted the course of training there, he was excited by the controversy between the followers of the Moslem tradition and the disciples of Muhammed 'Abdu, who was attempting to introduce modern subjects. Al-Azhar had been the center of Islamic learning for more than nine centuries. A short while before Hussein entered Al-Azhar in 1899, 'Abdu became Grand Mufti (the official expounder of Mohammedan law) and wanted to reform the Arabic language. He was ousted in 1905, about the third year of Hussein's university study.

Hussein himself wanted to break with tradition. He said that at Al-Azhar it was always "so and so tells us" or "according to so-and-so." The endless tracing of sources seemed pointless to him.

In 1908 a university in the Western tradition, the Egyptian University (nationalized in 1925 and renamed Fuad I University in 1928), was founded in Cairo. Hussein then decided to attend the new university as well. Spending his mornings at Al-Azhar and his afternoons at the Egyptian University, he lived what he felt was a double life. Finally he decided to leave Al-Azhar, but, not daring to tell his father, he purposely neglected to remove his name from the rolls, and was duly certified to have spent the full ten years required for a degree. Meanwhile, he completed the course at the Egyptian University, and was the first to graduate with a doctor's degree from that institution, in 1914. His thesis was on the tenth-century poet, Abul Ala. The university also awarded him a scholarship to the Université de Paris à La Sorbonne, and there he remained for five years, receiving the M.A. degree in 1915.

He married a fellow student, Suzanne Bresseau, in 1917, and obtained his *doctorat-ès-lettres* in 1919. Then, with his wife and their first baby, the year-old Amina, he returned to Cairo to become professor of Arabic literature at the Egyptian University.

At last in a position to carry out some of the techniques he had wished for as a student, he "introduced scientific methods" and "urged that the traditional approach to Arabic culture —in which every bit of folklore was regarded as sacrosanct—be abandoned in favor of an examination of the true facts" (Donald Robinson, *The 100 Most Important People,* Cardinal, 1953).

With the aid of his wife, he began to write. *The Leaders of Knowledge* was published in 1925, followed by *Pre-Islamic Literature* (1927); the latter, doubting the authenticity of much of the Arabic heritage, was so controversial that his life was threatened. In 1930 he became dean of the faculty of arts, but, Ismail Sudky Pasha had established a dictatorship, and Hussein's opposition resulted in his expulsion from the university in 1932. He then experienced four difficult years; much of the time he was hungry, and he was consistently threatened with imprisonment.

Metro Studio, Cairo

TAHA HUSSEIN

With the accession of King Farouk I on April 28, 1936 and the establishment of the Wafdist Cabinet under Moustapha El-Nahas Pasha, Hussein was reinstated at the university. Four years later he was appointed to the Ministry of Education in charge of the cultural program. He became an Under-Secretary of State in that Ministry in 1942, and began to translate his progressive ideas of education into a broad political program. His chief concern was to make it possible for every Arab child to have a free education. He said that education was like fresh air and sunshine, and society should not deny it to anyone who seeks it. In 1942 he founded the Farouk I University in Alexandria and became its first rector. The Ministry of Education in 1943 abolished all fees in primary schools, achieving the first step in the program he had laid out for opening schools to all of Egypt's children.

By this time World War II had broken out and the Germans were advancing toward Alexandria; but Egypt maintained official neutrality. Another temporary eclipse for political reasons occurred in 1945, but Hussein made his contribution to the democratic cause during the war from the studios of the British Broadcasting Company in London, where he spoke almost every day in Arabic "to defend and explain the Allied cause," he has stated.

In January 1950, the victory of the Wafd party resulted in new honors for the blind educator. He was made Minister of Education, and immediately extended his program of free schooling to the secondary schools, bringing the appropriation for education in the Egyptian budget to a level equal to that of the entire national budget less than twenty years earlier (New York *Times,* September 5, 1950).

Hussein opened private schools to the public, with the national treasury paying the expenses. These reforms met with opposition from those

HUSSEIN, TAHA—*Continued*

who were economy-minded, not only in Egypt, but throughout the Arab world, when Hussein proposed to a conference at Alexandria in August, 1950, that all the Arab states follow the Egyptian example.

The New York *Times* stated: "It has been difficult for critics . . . to make headway against the emotional impact of Mr. Hussein's pleading. He is a natural orator with exceptional mastery of his case, and the spectacle of this famous blind man demanding that the masses of Egypt shall be led out of darkness is virtually irresistible."

The Arab Cultural Conference approved Hussein's program in principle. In Egypt, where Hussein was in a position to put some of it in practice, primary school enrollments increased and projects were initiated to translate the cultural heritage of Europe into Arabic, and to allow Egyptians to have the advantages of European study which Hussein himself had enjoyed. He established an Egyptian Institute in Madrid, a chair of Arabic literature at Athens University, and a chair on Mediterranean problems at the Central Universitaire Mediterranéen at Nice, France. He also established an Institute for Desert Questions, and a Ibrahim university. When the Wafdist Government fell in 1952, Hussein's political career was again interrupted. He retired to resume his literary career, continuing as part-time professor at Fuad I University. He also continues to write for *Al-Ahram*, Egypt's oldest newspaper which he describes as "the New York *Times* of the Arab world."

Among his many works are a five-volume study of French drama and translations of the works of Sophocles, Racine, Le Bon and Gide. He is the author of the tracts *The Future of Culture in Egypt* (1937) and *The Dreams of Scheherezade* (1942) and the novels *Lost Love* (1942), *The Tree of Misfortune* (1944), and *Earth's Damned* (1949, a plea for social justice; according to Robinson it was banned in Egypt). He has written studies on the educational problems of modern Egypt.

Since Hussein does not read Braille, he depends on having material read to him. His greatest relaxation is listening to music, particularly that of Bach and Mozart. His daughter Amina is now the wife of Dr. Mohammed al-Zayat, cultural attaché at the Egyptian embassy in Washington, D.C.; his son, Moenis-Claude, born in 1921, is a professor on the faculty of arts at Fuad I University.

Taha Hussein is a slender man, five feet nine inches tall, weighing about 150 pounds, with wiry black hair and "a serene countenance." He has been honored by the governments of France (*grand officier* of the Legion of Honor), Belgium, Lebanon, Greece, Spain, and Iran, and holds honorary degrees from the universities of Oxford, Athens, Madrid, Rome, Montpellier, and Lyon. He is a devout Mohammedan, and a member of the Rotary club.

References

N Y Times p13 S 5 '50
International Who's Who, 1952
Robinson, D. The 100 Most Important People (1953)
Who's Who in Egypt and the Near East, 1952

HYATT, M. ANNA *See* Huntington, Mrs. A. H.

INGE, WILLIAM (MOTTER) (ĭnj) May 3, 1913- Playwright
Address: 1 W. 72nd St., New York 23

Referred to by drama critics in 1950 as "Broadway's most promising new playwright," William Inge has fulfilled that promise in his most recent play, *Picnic*. This was voted the best new American play of the 1952-53 season by the New York Drama Critics' Circle, and also won the 1953 Pulitzer Prize and the Outer Circle award. His first Broadway play, *Come Back, Little Sheba*, received "mixed reviews," but ran for 190 performances, and won the George Jean Nathan award and the Theatre Time award. After a successful nation-wide tour, the play was made into a motion picture in 1952 for which Shirley Booth, the star of both the play and the film, won an Academy award.

Born May 3, 1913, in Independence, Kansas, William Motter Inge is the son of Luther Clayton Inge, a salesman, and Maude Sarah Gibson Inge. He is the youngest of five children. He became interested in acting at the age of seven when he recited a monologue his sister Helene had been memorizing, and was so pleased with audience reaction that he determined to be an actor. Milton Bracker in the New York *Times* (March 22, 1953) wrote that "The third-grade incident revealed him to himself. From the moment he saw the stilled, upturned faces of his classmates he had, in effect, made the theatre his home."

Although Inge was eventually to win his place in the world of the theatre as a playwright, for nearly three decades he spoke the lines of other writers, first as a juvenile monologist, later as an actor in high school and college plays, then as a trouper in stock and in tent shows and on the radio. "I sort of based my life upon the theatre" he said recently.

He attended Montgomery County High School in Independence, and participated in the dramatic activities there. He was also a cheer leader for the school's teams. While in high school he was taken on trips to Kansas City where he saw several plays including *The Barretts of Wimpole Street*, starring Katharine Cornell. He remembers that he was profoundly moved by her performance. His uncle was fond of the theatre and told Inge stories about Edwin Booth, who was a distant relative.

At the University of Kansas, Inge majored in drama and acted in a number of plays including *Androcles and the Lion* and *Juno and the Paycock.* While earning his way through college he acted in the summer theatre sponsored by the Culver Military Academy, and appeared in plays by Rachel Crothers, J. B. Priestley, Sutton Vane and other modern dramatists. He became a member of the National Collegiate Players. He also acted in tent shows and "toby shows" during the depression, and recalls: "we actors considered ourselves fortunate if we earned five dollars a week. Sometimes the farmers of Kansas would bring in flour and meat as barter for admission to Saturday matinees."

Writing of his college experiences in the New York *Herald Tribune* (June 25, 1950), Inge deplored the attitude in many colleges and little theatres which strive only to reproduce Broadway's previous season, offering warmed-over versions of the plays that have become associated in the public consciousness with hits. "When I was a student at the University of Kansas," he recalled, "I studied in a drama department which, I am thankful, did not operate in such a way. Professor Allen Crafton . . . seemed unaware of Broadway and under his direction students got a reliable background in the plays of Shakespeare, Moliere, Shaw and O'Casey."

He believes that probably the most valuable experiences of his own college years were the annual musical comedies—completely original shows—which gave the students a chance to try their own creative talents. "In looking back now, I wonder if there might not have been the same fortunate results if the students had been expected to supply the college with some serious plays."

If this were done, he believes that "our colleges would have something of their own to give audiences and could give up their futile competition with Hollywood and Broadway. And both Hollywood and Broadway would have creative talent to draw from in the future."

After receiving his B.A. degree in 1935, Inge said that he yearned to go to New York to seek work in the theatre there, but since he had no money saved he realized that this would be a rash step. He won a scholarship at George Peabody College for Teachers at Nashville, Tennessee, where he received his Master of Arts degree in 1938. He wrote his thesis on *David Belasco and the Age of Photographic Realism in the American Theatre.*

Despite his dream of becoming a professional actor, he gave it up for what he described as "the security of teaching." He taught English and dramatics in the high school at Columbus, Kansas, for a year, and in 1938 went to Stephens College, Columbia, Missouri, to teach English composition, and later dramatics, until 1943. He had an opportunity to work with Maude Adams in directing some of the students. "I found her to be capable, tireless, charming," he told a *Current Biography* writer recently. "She had a fine descriptive memory of Eleanora Duse and Sarah Bernhardt and other great stars whom she had known during her years as a celebrated actress. Occasionally, she would act

Zinn Arthur—Talbot

WILLIAM INGE

out a role to demonstrate to some student. I remember that she directed *Chanticler* in which she had once appeared."

He obtained a job in 1943 as drama editor of the St. Louis *Star-Times*, where he edited the "entertainment and culture page," wrote criticisms of drama, movies, music, art and books. He held this position until 1946 when the regular critc returned from the war. Inge says that he was quite contented in this work and might never have written a play, but he saw Tennessee Williams' drama, *The Glass Menagerie,* in Chicago, and was so moved by its beauty that he went back to St. Louis and started work on his first play.

It took him about three months to complete it. He called it *Farther Off From Heaven,* and sent it to Tennessee Williams, who showed it to Margo Jones, director of the arena theatre in Dallas. It was produced there in 1947 and Inge recalled that "it came off very nicely, but I realize now that the play had none of the action or plot interest that are minimum essentials in any Broadway production" (*Theatre Arts,* July 1950).

After leaving the *Star-Times,* Inge for the next three years was an instructor in English at Washington University, St. Louis, Missouri. When he finished his play, *Come Back, Little Sheba,* he sent it to his agent, Audrey Wood of Liebling-Wood, and she persuaded the Theater Guild to try it out at the Westport Country Playhouse in the summer of 1949, with Shirley Booth in the role of Lola, the pitiable slattern. The Guild waited to produce it in New York until Shirley Booth was free of other commitments, and it went into rehearsal early in 1950 and opened on February 15.

Writing of the varied reactions to his first Broadway play, Inge described the New York audience "as a sort of schizophrenic wonder.

(Continued next page)

INGE, WILLIAM—*Continued*

Admiration, affection, confusion, dislike, indifference, and warm enthusiasm all have been expressed by reviewers for a play which I expected, perhaps as all writers expect, would have one sure effect on its spectators." *Theatre Arts,* (May 1950). The playwright defended *Come Back, Little Sheba* from the criticism that it was depressing. "I can only answer that I am not aware of its being so. The ending is not hopeless; I think there is cheer in Doc and Lola's sitting together at the kitchen table, coming to a new realization of their need for each other."

He remembers being in a tornado, and compares that experience with the "slow first act of *Come Back, Little Sheba.*" "I wanted," he explained, "the audience to be shocked into incredulity by Doc's outburst in the second act. Like the tornado, it comes like a blast after a morning of unnatural quiet. That is the atmosphere I wanted to create in my play: a slow, slightly suspenseful prelude to the eruption of a man's despair."

Inge stated in the New York *Times* (July 23, 1950) that he was encouraged when the poll of drama critics resulted in his being designated "the most promising new playwright," but he felt that it was being "unfair to a writer if we expect him always to equal our conception of what is his best. Then we set a standard for him and tend to deprive him of his freedom of expression." He regretted "the tendency in our theatre always to expect smash hits . . . until a modest success becomes more and more a thing of the past." In his next play "whether it flops or smashes," he would "like someone to observe, quietly perhaps, the good things in the play, to find some meaning, some enjoyment in them."

His next play, *Picnic,* was produced in February 1953 and received generally favorable reviews, winning both the Drama Critics' Circle Award and the Pulitzer Prize. The Outer Critics' Circle, composed of drama critics on newspapers outside of New York, also voted it the best play of the year. Brooks Atkinson in the New York *Times* (March 1, 1953) called it "an original, honest play with an awareness of people. . . .In three years Mr. Inge has come to full maturity as a dramatic author. The play flows, it has range and depth. . . His people are wholly alive." It is the story of a handsome, irresponsible braggart and the effect of his appearance on a group of lonely women in a small Kansas town.

Henry Hewes in the *Saturday Review (of Literature)* (March 7, 1953) wrote: "Like its predecessor, *Picnic* celebrates the courage with which his characters accept the mistakes they must substitute for life as they had planned it. In it, too, is the same true characterization which makes each person in the story an essence with whom spectators will identify themselves. 'There but for the grace of God go I' was what thousands felt when they saw Shirley Booth as Lola and Sidney Blackmer as Doc. There should be an even larger audience for *Picnic,* because Mr. Inge has stocked his play

with a wider sampling of victims. . . Since the play is descriptive rather than being out to prove a point, its richness consists of its truth, its atmosphere, and its humor."

Although *Picnic* was almost universally admired by drama critics, Eric Bentley in the *New Republic* (March 16, 1953) wrote of Inge, "If he did *not* reach out after ideas, Bright, Literary, and Edifying, he would lose that middle-brow approval without which there can be no rave reviews in the tonier press."

George Jean Nathan commented on *Picnic* in *Theatre Arts,* (May, 1953): "Poor Inge was bombarded by 'hundreds of suggestions' and was prevailed upon to incorporate many of them into his script. . . While there periodically emerges from it clear evidence of Inge's faithful observance of life, sharp appreciation of character and gift for beautifully accurate dialogue, there are many more times when the playwright seems to be shoved into the background by way of allowing the director to make a name for himself . . . everything points to the fact that [*Picnic*] had a quality that was in great part edged out of it in the campaign to Broadwayize it into a financial success."

Described as "quiet, articulate and determined," Inge is now at work on a new play. He expects that it will probably be in the tranquil setting of a small town where he finds "the mysterious quiet" that precedes a Kansas cyclone. He also plans to revive his *Farther Off From Heaven,* which he thinks he can mold into a worthier play. It is described as a domestic comedy-drama dealing with a small-salaried shoe salesman, his ambitious wife and his two maladjusted children. A second project is a musical comedy.

References

N Y Herald Tribune V p4 Je 25 '50
N Y Times II p1 Jl 23 '50; p2 F 15 '53;
   Mr 22 '53
Theatre Arts 34:22 My '50

JACKSON, HENRY M(ARTIN) May 31, 1912- United States Senator from Washington; lawyer

Address: b. 432 Senate Office Bldg., Washington 25, D.C.; h. 3602 Oakes Ave., Everett, Wash.

In one of the only two United States Senate contests in which a Democrat unseated a Republican in the election of November, 1952, Henry M. Jackson of Everett, State of Washington, defeated Harry P. Cain. A member of the House of Representatives since January, 1941, Jackson had been prominent on various committees including Merchant Marine and Fisheries, Appropriations and the Joint Committee on Atomic Energy.

The junior Senator created headlines by resigning from the Senate Permanent Subcommittee on Investigations on July 10, 1953 with two other Democratic members. They objected to giving the subcommittee's chairman, Senator Joseph R. McCarthy, unlimited power to hire and fire subcommittee staff members "without taking a vote."

Henry Martin Jackson is said to have acquired his nickname of "Scoop" during boyhood when he delivered newspapers at Everett, Snohomish County, Washington, where he was born May 31, 1912. Both his parents came to this country from Bodo in Norway. His father, Peter Jackson, was a building contractor; his mother, Marie (Anderson) Jackson, now an octogenarian, still presides over the family home in Everett. "Scoop," who has one brother and two sisters, was educated in local public schools and at the Everett High School, from which he was graduated in 1930. He was a member of the debating, and the manager of the basketball teams. Later he was basketball manager and a member of Delta Chi at the University of Washington, Seattle, Washington, to which he transferred from Stanford University in California. Jackson worked his way through both college and law school and received his LL.B. from the University of Washington Law School in 1935. He was admitted to the State bar in the same year and began to practice law with the firm of Black and Rucker at Everett.

Elected prosecuting attorney of Snohomish County in 1938 he made such a mark that in the summer of 1940 he was nominated by local Democrats as their candidate from Washington's Second Congressional District.

"Jackson has the build of a fullback," Richard L. Neuberger described him in the *Nation* (April 8, 1950). "On the platform he emphasizes points with piston-like fist pounding. He radiates strength and vitality." These attributes, together with his Norwegian ancestry in a district with a large population of fishermen and loggers of Scandinavian extraction, stood him in good stead in his first as well as subsequent Congressional campaigns. He was victorious over his Republican opponent in November 1940. Jackson was not yet twenty-nine when he took his seat in the Seventy-seventh Congress. His assignments were to the committees on Civil Service, Flood Control, and Merchant Marine and Fisheries. He favored such measures as the ship seizure, price control and anti-poll tax bills.

Re-elected by his district in November, 1942, Jackson in January 1943 was designated by Chairman Schuyler Otis Bland of the House Merchant Marine and Fisheries Committee to head a subcommittee to investigate the causes of the recent sinking of the Liberty ship *Schenectady,* which had split in two. Six months later, Jackson reported that in 1,000 ships built under the United States Maritime Commission's war construction program only two had been lost because of structural defects.

As a member of the Select Committee to Investigate and Study Problems of Small Business the Representative attracted notice in July, 1943, by speaking against a "rider" to the War Agencies Appropriation Bill requiring that "all persons who direct the formulation of any price policy . . . shall be qualified by experience in business, industry or commerce" (*PM,* July 7, 1943).

Representative Jackson served with the Army in 1943 and 1944. However, he did not resign

Fabian Bachrach

HENRY M. JACKSON

from Government service and was re-elected to the House in November 1944. When the House replaced the Dies committee in January 1945 with a permanent Committee on Un-American Activities, Jackson opposed this legislation. On the following March 7 he was one of a minority of fifty-four who voted against appropriating to the committee a $50,000 operating fund.

In 1945 and 1946 Jackson was chairman of the Committee on Indian Affairs, and in the first session of the Seventy-ninth Congress pushed through the House a bill to "free the Indians from a tangle of red tape in the Department of the Interior and turn them over to the Commissioner for Indian Affairs" (New York *Sun,* December 4, 1945). He served as adviser in 1945 to the American delegation to the International Maritime Conference at Copenhagen, Denmark, and was appointed by President Truman as United States delegate to its conference held at Seattle in June 1946 at which he was elected president.

Jackson unsuccessfully challenged certain features of a bill establishing a policy of "orderly disposition" to private interests of the Government's wartime merchant fleet as "too generous in setting up methods of fixing sale prices." He declared on July 31, 1946 that conditions under which the Maritime Commission and the War Shipping Administration had agreed to sell its ships "merits an investigation" (New York *Times,* August 1, 1946).

In roll calls during 1946 Jackson voted against passage of the Case Strike Control bill and an amendment which provided that all OPA ceilings reflect current costs of production plus a reasonable profit, and in favor of extending the Selective Service Act of 1942 to 1947 and for the $3,750,000,000 loan to Great Britain. He voted against shelving the Atomic Energy Control Bill.

(Continued next page)

JACKSON, HENRY M.—*Continued*

After the convening of the Eightieth Congress, Representative Jackson introduced on January 20, 1947 a joint resolution authorizing and directing President Truman to establish civilian administrations in Guam, American Samoa, and the Japanese-mandated islands under the jurisdiction of the Department of the Interior. "The native peoples of the former Japanese mandated islands in the Pacific," he declared, "were not belligerent enemies of the United States in the late war. They are a liberated people . . . and not conquered enemies to be ruled . . . under military administration." He added that this would not prevent the President from establishing military reservations on the islands (New York *Times,* January 20, 1947).

During the Eightieth Congress, Jackson opposed limiting the presidency to two terms and the banning of portal-to-portal pay suits, favored Greek-Turkish aid and the Voice of America bill, and voted against overriding President Truman's veto of the Labor Management Act of 1947, the tidelands oil bill and for the displaced persons bill. Jackson became one of the nine House of Representative members of the Joint Congressional Committee on Atomic Energy in 1948. The committee was provided for by the Atomic Energy Act of 1946 to study the activities of the Atomic Energy Commission and problems relating to the development, use and control of atomic energy.

After being selected to serve as Under-Secretary of the Interior, the Representative "reluctantly declined." He stated, "I could better assist resource development in the West, and particularly in the Pacific Northwest, by continuing my service in Congress" (New York *Times,* June 9, 1950). The Congressman voted for extension of the Marshall plan, the long-range housing bill, and the "voluntary compliance" FEPC bill during 1949. Having become a member of the House Appropriations Committee he stated in January, 1951 that President Truman intended to ask the Eighty-second Congress to appropriate $75,000,000 for expanding the Bonneville Power Administration service. Jackson himself introduced the enabling legislation, urging on the following September 27th the immediate construction of eight fuel-burning electric plants in the Northwestern area. Charles E. Wilson, then Defense Mobilizer, stated that the plants were justified as a "straight engineering proposition" (New York *World-Telegram and Sun,* September 27, 1951).

The legislator witnessed an explosion on Eniwetok in May, 1951, and on returning home told newsmen that "we learned that troops can follow up immediately over an area destroyed by an atomic blast with no fear of lingering radiation." Late in August he spoke out against trimming funds for civil defense, and in October urged that the atomic energy budget be increased immediately from $1,000,000,000 a year to between $6,000,000,000 and $10,000,000,000.

In the election of 1952 Jackson opposed Senator Harry P. Cain for the Senate. Jackson defeated the incumbent by 595,675 to 460,884. He was assigned to the Committees on Interior and Insular Affairs and on Government Operations and to the Senate's Permanent Subcommittee on Investigations.

The Senator resigned from that subcommittee with its other Democratic members, Senator Stuart Symington and John L. McClellan, on July 10 when the subcommittee gave to its chairman the power to employ and dismiss members of its staff. The vote on the decision was 4 to 3. The resigning Senators stated that McCarthy's new power "places us in the impossible position of having responsibility without any voice, right, or authority" (New York *Herald Tribune,* July 11, 1953).

The Senator, who is the recipient of an honorary LL.D. degree from the University of Alaska, is a member of the Washington Bar Association, Phi Delta Phi law fraternity, American Legion, Elks, Eagles, and Sons of Norway. He is a Presbyterian and a Mason. Blue-eyed, brown-haired, Jackson, a bachelor, is five feet ten inches tall, weighs 180 pounds, and is of "stocky-build." He enjoys such recreations as skiing, hunting and fishing.

When questioned on a "Youth Wants to Know" radio program on August 2, as to his views on Federal-controlled electric power as opposed to private ownership, Senator Jackson stated that he favored Federal ownership when a dam could "serve a multiple purpose" such as flood control and irrigation as well as for electric power. He declared that Presidents Theodore Roosevelt and Herbert Hoover had supported such types of Government-financed dams, as well as Democratic Presidents.

References

Nation 170:321+ Ap 8 '50
N Y Sun p22 D 4 '45
N Y Times p20 N 6 '52 por; p1 Jl 1 '53
Washington (D.C.) Post p18 N 16 '52
Biographical Directory of the American Congress, 1774-1949 (1950)
Congressional Directory (1953)
Who's Who in America, 1952-53
Who's Who in United States Politics (1952)
Who's Who in the West (1951)

JEFFERS, WILLIAM M(ARTIN) Jan. 2, 1876—Mar. 6, 1953 Railroad official; former United States rubber director; started as office boy with Union Pacific Railroad in 1890; worked as telegrapher, train dispatcher, trainmaster before becoming superintendent in 1915 and advancing through a number of positions to president in 1937 and vice-chairman of the board of directors in 1946; appointed Rubber Director in 1942 by President Roosevelt to create a synthetic rubber industry; resigned after six months. See *Current Biography,* 1942.

Obituary

N Y Times p15 Mr 7 '53

JENKINS, SARA July 20, 1904- Author
Address: b. c/o Thomas Y. Crowell Co., 432
Fourth Ave., New York 16; h. 1558 Sevilla,
Coral Gables, Florida

Reprinted from the *Wilson
Library Bulletin,* June 1953

"I am as southern as cow peas and cornbread," says Sara Jenkins, whose latest novel,
The Happy People (Crowell, 1953), is a People's Book Club selection. This statement is
true of both Miss Jenkins and her books, but
it is just as true that both she and her books
are also spiced with pepper sauce. It is this
element in her nature that keeps her books
from being saccharine and makes her characters not only southern but universal.

Sara Jenkins is, on her father's side, of
French Huguenot and Welsh ancestry; on her
mother's side "mixed British." She was born in
1904 in Guadalajara, Mexico, where her
father, Isaac Cheyney Jenkins, and her mother,
the former Jane Percival Raiford, were in the
mission field. Reared in Florida, she has lived
in all sections of the state. She attended high
school in Gainesville, Florida. In Wesleyan
College, at Macon, Georgia, she majored in
journalism and English and won all the short
fiction prizes. Though her journalism professor
told her, "You may have some talents, but
writing isn't one of them," she kept right on
teaching her how to write. After her graduation Miss Jenkins began teaching in Florida—
English in Brewster; English and journalism
in Lakeland, journalism and creative writing in
Miami.

Her first novel was written at the age of
seven, but was "a complete steal" from *David
Copperfield.* She kept on writing and sold a few
articles. For twenty years her sophisticated
short stories brought only rejection slips. Finally, she changed her type of material. Basing
it on her father's family in Georgia (her father
and his five brothers were Methodist ministers)
she wrote *We Gather Together* (Crowell, 1949),
the story of the Gordon Clan from 1910-1940,
as told by the child Jennie. This book the New
York *Herald Tribune* called "an undistin-
guished, but pleasant and forthright first
novel."

Her next book was *The Lost Lamp* (Crowell,
1950), which tells of the Reverend George Win-
free whose decreasing tact led to increasing de-
motions, until a series of crises make him more
understanding of people. The novel was "highly recommended" by R. P. Tubby in the *Library Journal* and won an immediate success,
being chosen a Family Bookshelf selection. It
was later brought out as a talking book by the
National Foundation for the Blind and was
printed in Braille.

Her third "preacher novel," *Brand New
Parson* (Crowell, 1951), tells of a young Methodist minister's first pastorate in a small southern town in the 1900's, his troubles and his
triumphs. It was a People's Book Club choice.
Her most recent book, *Happy People,* is again
a story about a young Methodist minister who
is torn with the struggle to find personal hap-

SARA JENKINS

piness and at the same time to devote his energies to his duties. The New York *Herald
Tribune* comments: "Planned and resolved with
neat craftsmanship, the story has its own in-
evitability; and, though bordering occasionally
on the sentimental, it is redeemed by a searching insight."

Miss Jenkins has repeatedly tried to write
other types of books besides the "preacher stories." Her *Good Shepherdess* (Bouregy; Mc-
Leod, 1950) and *Crime and Miss Olivia* (1952),
both written under the pseudonym of Joan Sargent, were ignored by the critics. In 1951, she
wrote *Year in Paradise* (Crowell) the story of
a shy young northern school teacher's first year
in a small mining town in central Florida. Of
this, Charlotte Capers of the New York *Times*
said, "Miss Jenkins's wholesome little story
seems destined to enjoy a brisk circulation in
lending libraries." She is at present working
on an historical novel about Florida in 1821.

In 1952, Sara Jenkins married James L. Cunningham, a Miami builder and real estate man.
He built her a new home with a studio just for
writing, but because she was accustomed to
writing on the corners of her time—on buses,
in restaurants—she could not stand the silence
and the lack of pressure. Therefore, she set
up her typewriter in a house her husband was
building, and amid the noise of hammers and
saws she could work.

Miss Jenkins is a short, happy, friendly person with hazel eyes and brown hair. She likes
people, plays, music; she enjoys cooking. Above
all, she likes to travel—on freighters, buses
"where everybody tells you his life story,"
planes, automobiles, and trains. "I think I
would have liked stagecoaches." She has traveled in Central America, Mexico, the Caribbean,
most of Europe. She is a Democrat by inheritance, independent by nature, "Presbyterian
since my marriage in spite of my writing Meth-

JENKINS, SARA—*Continued*

odist, as I no doubt always will." Of course, she likes to read—Dickens and Kenneth Roberts, Pearl Buck and Thorne Smith, Steinbeck and murder stories. Perhaps it is because she is both a reader and a writer that she has been so generous with the young Miami Public Library, to whose Florida Author Collection she has given photographs, manuscripts, and galleys.

Miss Jenkins is that rare person, an admittedly happy one. As she says, 'This is my last year of teaching. I will have finished the twenty-five necessary for retirement, want to write, have a new house, and an almost new husband. I'm quite as contented as these notes [made for this biography] and the books I write sound."

Reference

Miami Sunday News Mag p9 F 25 '51
por

JOHNSON, OSA Mar. 14, 1894—Jan. 7, 1953 Author; explorer; motion picture producer; with her husband, Martin Johnson, made photographic expeditions to South Sea Islands, Borneo, and African jungles; collaborated with Martin Johnson in writing *Cannibal Land, Congorilla,* and other books, some of which were made into films; author of *I Married Adventure, Four Years in Paradise,* and children's books. See *Current Biography,* 1940.

Obituary

N Y Times p30 Ja 8 '53

JOSEPHS, DEVEREUX C(OLT) Oct. 16, 1893- Insurance Company President.
Address: b. New York Life Insurance Co., 51 Madison Ave., New York 10; h. 200 East 66 St., New York 21

Spending most of his business life dealing with investments, Devereux Colt Josephs, president of the New York Life Insurance Company, and former president of the Carnegie Corporation, has also found time to be active in civic affairs. A trustee of the New York Public Library since March, 1952, and chairman of the Greater New York Fund's advisory committee, he now heads the nine-member Temporary State Commission appointed June 4, 1953 by Governor Thomas E. Dewey to study the city manager form of government for New York City.

Josephs became president of the New York Life Insurance company, fourth largest underwriting concern in the United States, in May, 1948 and under his direction the company in 1952 exceeded for the first time the five billion dollar mark in total assets.

Devereux Colt Josephs was born in Newport, Rhode Island, on October 16, 1893, the son of Lyman C. Josephs and Alice Vernon (Wilson) Josephs. The family was originally from Louisiana. Josephs graduated from Groton, in Massachusetts, in 1911, and Harvard University in 1915, completing work for his A.B. degree in three and a half years.

Kaiden-Kazanjian

DEVEREUX C. JOSEPHS

Starting as a messenger in the Philadelphia investment banking firm of Graham, Parsons and Company in 1915, Devereux C. Josephs became successively a securities salesman, a trader, and, in 1923, a partner. He soon achieved national prominence in the investment field. During the first World War he served as a first lieutenant of Field Artillery with the United States Army in France.

He retired from the Philadelphia firm in 1939 and became associated with certain investment enterprises of the Carnegie Corporation. Founded in 1911 by the late Andrew Carnegie, this Corporation provides funds towards the advancement of education.

Josephs' first position in the Carnegie philanthropies was that of investment officer of the Teachers Insurance and Annuity Association, founded by the Corporation to institute retirement plans for college teachers. He also supervised the handling of investments for the Carnegie Foundation for the Advancement of Teaching, the Carnegie Institution of Washington, and the Carnegie Endowment for International Peace. The last was founded in 1910, and supplied ten million dollars for "the speedy abolition of international war."

Josephs was financial vice-president of the Teachers Annuity Association from 1939 to 1943, and was its president from 1943 until 1945. He became a member of the Carnegie Corporation board of trustees in January 1944.

In May 1945 it was announced that Devereux C. Josephs had been elected president of the Carnegie Corporation. He took office June 1, 1945, succeeding Walter A. Jessup, who died in July 1944.

In the annual report for, the fiscal year 1944-45 Josephs stated that the Corporation was seeking proposals from "practical visionaries." He emphasized that the foundation was ambitious to share in creative enterprises, and that it would supply moneys to men or institutions with imagination. In the 1945-46 annual report he declared that "only a decade or so is perhaps left in which to win control over the forces which lead to international conflict." He also noted a change in the Corporation's policy towards the promotion of the humanities and the social sciences, to offset the increasing emphasis on natural sciences.

During the fiscal year 1946 Josephs presided over the administrating of $3,086,385 in Corporation grants for causes including international education, a study of journalism schools, advancement of teaching and foreign relations.

In the 1946-47 fiscal year the income derived from Carnegie Corporation investments totalled $5,232,708, and the book value of the assets of the Corporation was $170,322,715. In this report Josephs expressed his concern over the lack of qualified governmental executive assistants. A small number of grants was made to alleviate this condition, with the expectation that more would follow. Josephs, in a statement of the aims of the Carnegie Corporation and its subsidiary trusts, said that "the officers of the Corporation are guided by the precept that foundation money is the venture capital of philanthropy."

The New York *Sun* on January 7, 1948, commended the training programs for government officials, and predicted that they would produce valuable results. Among investment experts in Wall street, the placements made by the Carnegie Corporation have long been regarded as outstanding examples of investment management.

When George L. Harrison was elected chairman of the board of the New York Life Insurance Company, Devereux Josephs, on May 12, 1948, was elected president and chief administrative officer to succeed him. Josephs had been a director of New York Life since January 15, 1947. Under his presidency the company paid in 1951, $247,969,191 in dividends and policy benefits, on a total income of $597,343,050.

The company also expanded its operations to enter into the personal accident and sickness field and the group insurance business. Discussing the situation in the insurance business, Josephs said: "It is a highly competitive operation which means in the American tradition that the public is the gainer because of the ceaseless efforts to win customers by doing a better job."

He is a director of the J. P. Morgan Company, the Consolidated Edison Company, the American Brake Shoe Company and the American Smelting and Refining Company. He is a trustee of the New York Public Library, the Metropolitan Museum of Art, and of Bennington (Vermont) College. Active in civic and charitable work, he has at various times been a board member of the Federation of Protestant Welfare Agencies, the Welfare Council of New York City and Pomfret School.

In 1952 he served as campaign chairman of the Greater New York Fund, and is now chairman of the Fund's advisory committee. He believes that there is a "direct responsibility on business" for the social well-being of citizens in a community such as New York, where the profits of business and industry are "largely due to the concentration of population."

Josephs was married on June 26, 1922 to Margaret Thayer Graham. They have two children, Devereux C. Josephs Jr, and Margaret G. (Mrs. Peter B. Nalle). He is a member of the Century Association, the Harvard Club of New York (vice-president), and the Links. He is a Republican and an Episcopalian. He weighs one hundred sixty pounds, is five feet seven, and has brown hair and brown eyes.

When Josephs was elected a trustee of the New York Public Library in March, 1952, Morris Hadley, president of the Library board, commented on Josephs' conversance with the philosophy of libraries and the problems of their administration in his nine years with the Carnegie Corporation which has contributed generously to libraries and schools for the training of librarians.

References

N Y Herald Tribune p37 Mr 12 '52
N Y Sun p24 Ja 7 '48
N Y Times D 16 '51 por
Time 60:90 My 24 '48 por
Business Executives of America (1950)
National Cyclopedia for American Biography (1952)
Who's Who in America, 1952-53
Who's Who in Insurance, 1953
Who's Who in New York, 1950

JUNG, CARL GUSTAV (yŏong) July 26, 1875- Medical psychologist; author

Address: 228 Seestrasse, Küsnacht, Zürich, Switzerland

NOTE: This biography supersedes the article which appeared in *Current Biography* in 1943.

Internationally known as the founder of analytical psychology, Dr. Carl Gustav Jung has made many important contributions to modern therapy. Among them are the association method, the theory of complex psychology, the classification of the extrovert and introvert, and the formulation of the collective unconscious and its archetypal images and symbols.

Dr. Jung's books have been published in nine languages. The complete collected edition of his works in English has been undertaken by Routledge and Keegan Paul, Ltd., in England and by the Bollingen Foundation, Inc., through Pantheon Books, Inc., in the United States. Eighteen volumes are in preparation, two of which, *Psychology and Alchemy* and *Two Essays on Analytical Psychology* were published in 1953.

The Swiss psychologist in his own words has worked "for a better . . . understanding of the human psyche," a labor which has led him to the investigation of the psychological basis of such varied manifestations of the human spirit as were to be found in mythology, Taoist texts, beliefs of the yogas of India, Tibetan rituals, alchemy, and the ritual of the Mass.

(Continued next page)

CARL GUSTAV JUNG

Carl Gustav Jung was born on July 26, 1875, in Kesswil, Thurgau, Switzerland, the son of Paul Jung, an Evangelical minister and a philologist, and Emilie (Preiswerk) Jung. Carl Gustav was one of two children. In 1879 the family moved to Basel where Jung attended school. The youth entered the Universität Basel in 1895 obtaining his medical degree in 1900.

In the same year, he began his psychiatric work as a second assistant (interne) at the Burghölzli Mental Hospital in Zürich and at the Psychiatric Clinic of the Universität Zürich. For his doctoral thesis he chose the case of a girl affected by somnambulism and professing to have mediumistic powers. The completed work, *Zur Psychologie und Pathologie Sogennanter Occulter Phänomene* (Druck von O. Mutze, 1902) served as the required publication to qualify him for the position of free lecturer at the Universität Zürich.

For six months (1902-1903) Carl Jung attended the lectures given by Pierre Janet at the Salpétrière in Paris. By 1905 he had advanced to senior staff physician at Burghölzli, and lecturer in psychiatry on the medical faculty of the Universität Zürich. During these years he worked, first as pupil, then as collaborator, with Eugen Bleuler, who headed the "Zürich school", in the research of the new depth psychology. (Dr. Sigmund Freud, the recognized pioneer in this field, headed the "Vienna school.")

He began studying a new system of psychological testing which became known as the "association method." His many published papers on this subject resulted in the recognition of his outstanding contribution in developing the method. In their reliance upon the operation of non-conscious factors in the psyche, the tests which Dr. Jung made were compatible with the work being produced by Freud, whose views he championed at the risk of his own reputation (although from the outset he did not subscribe fully to Freud's theories).

At Jung's invitation, the Vienna and Zürich schools met together in the first Psychoanalytical Congress, held in Salzburg in 1908. This led to the publication, *Jahrbücher für Psychoanalytische und Psychopathologische Forshungen,* with Freud and Bleuler as joint editors; Jung became managing editor in 1909.

In order to devote himself to his increasing work as a physician and psychotherapist, and to scientific research and writing, Jung resigned from the psychiatric clinic in 1909. In that year, Freud and Jung, together with a number of international authorities in psychiatry, psychology and education, were invited to celebrate the twentieth anniversary of Clark University, Worcester, Massachusetts, by a series of lectures and conferences, and to receive honorary degrees. Jung spoke on the "association method."

The International Psychoanalytic Society was founded by Jung in 1911. In the following year a major work, *Wandlungen und Symbole der Libido,* was published, and later in English as *The Psychology of the Unconscious* (Moffat, Yard, 1916). In this work, Jung offered a new psychological interpretation of the mythological elements in dream and fantasy, and presented his discovery of the collective unconscious existing in a deeper stratum than the personal unconscious. The elements of the collective unconscious, Jung asserted, are not a residue of the individual's life but are shared with one's predecessors and race and are characterized by images and symbols. This established Jung as an independent thinker.

Thus, Jung resigned from the International Psychoanalytical Society in 1913 having taken exception not to Freud's basic theories but to Freud's refusal to extend them into new categories and directions. Freud, the discoverer of the symbol-making activities of the human unconscious, regarded such symbols as disguised thoughts. It was Jung who recognized in symbolic language, in dreams and the arts, the communication of truths known to the unconscious mind. In his scheme he replaced psychoanalysis with analytical psychology which begins with the clarification of the frustrative personality and continues into the spontaneous archetypal symbolism that unites all men and offers psychological liberation.

The psychologist in 1913 resigned his instructorship at the Universität Zürich. He participated in the International Medical Congress in London, under whose auspices he lectured at Bedford College in London and in Aberdeen, Scotland. During World War I he was a medical officer in the Swiss Army and was in charge of interned British prisoners of war.

In a major work, *Psychological Types* (K. Paul, Trench, Trubner; Harcourt, Brace, 1923) Jung introduced the conception of extrovert and introvert types and of the four psychological functions of adaptation. Dr. Jung's contribution to the psychology of the conscious mind is largely embodied in this work, and it contains his idea of individuation which is "the centralizing processes in the unconscious that go to form the personality . . ." or the "life-processes which, on account of the numinous character, have from time immemorial provided the strongest incentive to the formation of symbols."

Research into the nature of the collective unconscious led Jung to study primitive psychology. He made his first trip to North Africa in 1921 to observe the natives. A similar study of the Pueblo Indians of Arizona and New Mexico was made in 1924 and 1925. He later conducted seminars at the Eidgenossiche Technische Hochschule (Swiss Federal Institute of Technology) in Zürich where he became a professor in 1935.

The noted psychologist delivered the Terry lectures in 1937 at Yale University, speaking on the relationship of psychology and religion. Dr. Jung's study of the archetypes of the collective unconscious had brought him to the conclusion that what he describes as "a natural religious function" exists in man and that, for his psychic health, it may be imperative for him to take cognizance of this fact. His later writings have been largely devoted to penetrating the deeper implications of the psychology of the religious function.

The analyst and writer, Gerhard Adler, commented, "The task which his awareness of the spiritual obligation of psychology has imposed on Jung has been no easy one. . . .To him, modern man is not the isolated and self-sufficient product of modern times, but the sum total of the history of a European process of individuation. This explains why, starting from modern psychiatry, he has gradually worked his way back into the origins of European psychology, and indeed has gone far beyond Europe itself, in an attempt to discover undertones and hidden trends and urges of this process."

Dr. Jung resigned from the Eidgenössische Technische Hochshule in 1942. The Universität of Basel founded a chair in medical psychology for him in 1944. One of Dr. Jung's interests during these years was alchemy. Having observed alchemical symbolism in the dreams of a number of his patients who did not possess knowledge of this dead "art," he included the subject in his researches, which he discusses in the book, *Psychology and Alchemy*, published in German in 1944 by Rascher Verlag.

In the following year he gave up the chair at the Universität of Basel, and since has concentrated on his researches and writing. In 1948 the C. G. Jung Institute Zürich was opened, a foundation which carries on research in analytical psychology and training of Jungian analysts. In 1950 when Jung's seventy-fifth birthday was celebrated, he was reportedly working simultaneously on the writing of three books.

In *Psychology and Alchemy* Jung writes, "the alchemist's hope of conjuring out of matter the philosophical gold, or the wonderful stone, was only in part an illusion, an effect of projection, for the rest it corresponded to certain psychic facts that are of great importance in the psychology of the unconscious. As is shown . . . by their symbolism, the alchemists projected the processes of individuation into the phenomena of chemical change." According to Jung the processes of individuation are "steeped in mystery; they pose riddles with which the human mind will long wrestle for a solution . . . it is exceedingly doubtful whether reason is a suitable instrument for this purpose. Not for nothing did alchemy style itself an 'art,' feeling . . . that it was concerned with creative processes that can be truly grasped only by experience, though intellect may give them a name."

In Kathleen Raine's review of *Psychology and Alchemy* in the *New Republic*, May 18, 1953, she wrote that many who know of the "bankruptcy of eternal symbols in the present age, . . . see in Jung's insistence on an inner transmutation the best hope of giving new meaning to religion in the west. Thus slowly we are coming to understand truths long ago taken for granted in the religiously civilized world of India and China . . . it is no small thing that a bridge should have been built from the scientific side of the rift in western thought between rational and imaginative knowledge. Jung has been the agent of an irreversible development in western religious thought."

Dr. Jung was elected a fellow of the Royal Society of Medicine and given an honorary D.Sc. by Oxford University, the first psychologist to receive such an honor in England. He was made the honorary president of the Deutsche Arztliche Gesellshaft für Psychotherapie in 1930 and has been president of the International General Medical Society for Psychotherapy, the Schweizerische Gesellshaft für Praktische Psychologie, and is an honorary member of the Swiss Academy of Medicine. He was the recipient of the Literary Prize of the city of Zürich in 1932. He has received honorary degrees from Harvard University, University of Calcutta, the Banaras Hindu University, the University of Allahabad in India, and the University of Geneva.

He is a good classical scholar and is familiar with the literature of many countries; he speaks four languages idiomatically and at least two others fairly well. Amused by American slang he occasionally makes use of it in his seminars.

In 1903 the psychologist married Emma Rauschenbach of Schaffhausen, Switzerland. They have four daughters and a son, who is an architect, nineteen grandchildren and one great grandchild. Mrs. Jung, who has been described as a woman of "unusual character and distinction," has also practiced as an analyst.

Until recent years Dr. Jung's recreations included walking in his native mountains, yachting and swimming in the Lake of Zürich; one of his present recreations is stone carving. Brown-eyed, white-haired, of ruddy coloring, he has been described as "an impressive personality, tall, fine-looking, a man whose depth of scholarship has taken nothing from a genial humanity." Upon the lintel over the door of his home in Küsnacht the words are carved: *Vocatus at que non vocatus deus aderit* (Called or not called, God is present).

(Continued next page)

JUNG, CARL—*Continued*

References

Sat R 32:6+ Jl 30 '49
International Who's Who, 1952
Kunitz, S. J., and Haycraft, H. Twentieth Century Authors
Who's Who, 1952
World Biography (1948)

KAI-SHEK, CHIANG *See* Chiang Kai-shek

KALLEN, HORACE M(EYER) Aug. 11, 1882- Philosopher; educator
Address: b. c/o New School for Social Research, 66 W. 12th St., New York 11

One of the founders of the New School for Social Research in New York City, Dr. Horace M. Kallen has been an outstanding leader in the adult education movement in America. At present a research professor of social philosophy at the New School, he believes that the function of scholarship is to reach out into the vital problems and activities of the community. In this manner he exemplifies one of the most

HORACE M. KALLEN

essential traditions in philosophy, a way of life in a complex world. The author of approximately thirty books and numerous articles in professional journals and popular periodicals, he has expounded the belief that the ideals of democracy are the means whereby man can most adequately adjust to his environment, nurturing his creativity in the spirit of freedom.

Horace Meyer Kallen was born August 11, 1882, in Berenstadt, Silesia, Germany, to Jacob David Kallen, a Hebrew scholar and rabbi, and Esther Rebecca (Glazier) Kallen. The family came to the United States when the boy was

five years old. Kallen attended Harvard University and was graduated in 1903. He then entered Princeton University for post-graduate study and taught English at that university from 1903 to 1905. Originally interested in writing novels and poetry, he discovered that post-graduate courses in philosophy proved more exciting and he soon devoted himself entirely to philosophy and the philosophical implications of the arts and the social sciences. Nevertheless, his writings are enriched with literary quality and beauty of expression. Dr. Kallen has credited George Santayana, William James, Edwin Holt, Canning Schiller, Barrett Wendell, and Solomon Schechter as the "men of paramount influence on the development of my attitude, my point of view and my method. . ."

After studying philosophy at Oxford University and the Université de Paris à La Sorbonne, he returned to Harvard and received the Ph.D. degree in 1908. While an assistant and lecturer in philosophy at the university from 1908 to 1911 he became closely associated with William James and George Santayana who both recognized his outstanding abilities. James left his unfinished book, *Some Problems in Philosophy* for Dr. Kallen to edit. Kallen largely prepared the book which was published in 1912 by Longmans, Green.

After instructing in logic at Clark College in Worcester, Massachusetts in 1910, Kallen received an instructorship in psychology and philosophy at the University of Wisconsin in 1911; he continued in this post until 1918. In that year he lectured at Columbia University in New York. He has also taught during summer sessions at Harvard, Columbia, Wisconsin and Ohio State Universities and at Claremont College, Claremont, California.

Dr. Kallen wrote *The Book of Job as a Greek Tragedy* in 1918 (Moffat, Yard; later Boni and Liveright). He feels that the story of Job indicates the influences of Greek drama and culture upon ancient Hebrew literature. The play was produced with notable success in Milwaukee, at the University of Wisconsin, and by the Menorah Society at Harvard. Proceeds of the play were used for a prize to stimulate the writing and production of plays of Jewish interest in the English language.

Dr. Horace M. Kallen together with James Harvey Robinson, Charles A. Beard, Thorstien Veblen and Robert Bruerre, each of whom wanted to explore new techniques in education, founded the New School of Social Research in New York City in 1919, at 463 West Twenty-third Street. Their purpose was "to seek an unbiased understanding of the existing order, its genesis, growth and present working" (New York *Times*, September 30, 1919). Originally the school confined its instruction almost entirely to economics and maintained a graduate standard for all, although it neither required nor conferred degrees. At present, it offers courses in all the disciplines of social science and the humanities, and awards several degrees. The school has always emphasized adult education. It occupies a modern building on West Twelfth Street designed by Joseph Urban.

The educator has from the outset desired to set before people who attend the school well-elaborated and well-articulated principles of life and conduct. He presented from the beginning two courses, "Beauty and Use" and "Dominant Ideals of Western Civilization." Students who have taken these courses have carried away the notions of universality and oneness that Kallen has found in the philosophies of all times.

Dr. Alvin Johnson, president-emeritus of the New School for Social Research, has written "With the development of the institution, Kallen's position came to express more nearly than any other the real meaning and objectives of the New School . . . no man ever carried his exploration of the newer tendencies with more sympathy, more modesty, and less credulity than Kallen" (*Freedom and Experience,* 1947).

In this period, Kallen was named by Benjamin Paul Blood as his literary executor and in 1920 he edited and introduced Blood's *Pluriverse; An Essay in the Philosophy of Pluralism* (Marshall Jones). He was contributing editor of the *Dial* from 1917 to 1922 and the managing editor of *The Advance* from 1923 to 1925.

Addressing the Summer Cooperative Institute at Massachusetts State College, Professor Kallen stated that the "American people are threatened with political totalitarianism as a result of government invasion of business. Cooperatives are the most likely solution to the problem of economic freedom under the Constitution (New York *Times,* July 15, 1937). In *The Decline and Rise of the Consumer* (Appleton-Century, 1936, Packard and Co., 1946) Dr. Kallen pointed out that "in order to maintain a continuous economy of abundance, the institutions basic to the capitalist system are indispensable." Believing that the National Recovery Administration and the Agricultural Adjustment Administration sought through scarcity to keep prices up, Kallen recommended technological achievement to force prices down. Kallen believes that the basic institutions of capitalism and cooperatives can co-exist as they have in Great Britain and Sweden.

His first and most enduring interest has been aesthetics and in 1942 he published *Art and Freedom* (Duell, Sloan & Pearce) a two-volume work written in the period between the two world wars. It concerns men's ideas of the dynamic relations between beauty and use in the arts from the ancient Greek to the present day. He writes that ". . . there are infinite ways to make man bond, he will struggle to loose himself from all things that he feels bind him till the day he dies." *Use* is the process of this struggle and "art is a new use of nature, or of other art, which liberates the spirit, if for an instant only, from the coercions and constraints which beset it." Thus he refuses to exalt the fine arts over the useful arts, for beauty is "a relation between ourselves and the liberating power."

As to the political attitudes toward art of the totalitarian nations, he asserted, "It would appear that once limits are set to the freedom of thought and expression at any one point, the door is opened wide to every degree of . . . persecution." In Russia he pointed out, the arts are treated "as a class-weapon . . . their beauty is an attribute of 'social significance.' "

Robert Bierstedt wrote that *Art and Freedom* is "brilliantly conceived and beautifully written, profound as well as humane, it is a classic. The book . . . is a defense of the fundamentals and inalienable right of men to be different from one another while living with one another. The artist has a role to play in the enterprise of freedom, for the artist who is true to his being must of necessity be free" (*Saturday Review of Literature,* April 3, 1943).

For two years, 1944 to 1946, Professor Kallen served as the dean of the graduate faculty of political and social science at the New School for Social Research. He has asserted that the problem of education is "a problem of doubt. People believe readily enough and can be taught anything by anybody who knows the technique. What is difficult to teach them is to doubt. Doubt is the beginning of intelligence . . . Indoctrination must be to indoctrinate a faith with which the validity of doctrines can be tested." Such a faith is science.

In *The Education of Free Men* (Farrar, Straus, 1949) the educator has said that there are no confirming instances for assuming that man has reached the limit of his potential. In the search for excellence "the more varied and numerous the sources, the greater the likelihood that it will come." But to Kallen education is not an institution apart. Life to him is whole, education is for the whole life, and the whole life is education.

A volume of essays, *Freedom and Experience,* by twenty-four leading American philosophers in honor of Professor Kallen on the occasion of his sixty-fifth birthday were presented to him at a reception on October 26, 1947 at the New School for Social Research. Among the contributors were John Dewey, Ernest Nagel, Felix Kaufman, John Herman Randall, Jr. and Sidney Hook. In that year the Horace M. Kallen Lectureship was established by pupils and friends of Dr. Kallen. Under it a lecture is given in November of each year on a topic selected from the fields of Dr. Kallen's interests.

In a letter to the editor of the New York *Times* (January 8, 1950) Dr. Kallen, together with John Dewey, John L. Childs, Harry Emerson Fosdick and thirteen other community leaders, urged enactment of Federal aid to education, the appropriation of which should be predicated upon the needs of the individual States. They asserted that, "The bill must contain adequate safeguards against discriminatory treatment of Negroes and other minority groups. . . .The existence of racially segregated schools is itself a blot upon the American public school system. . . .The educational benefits must be limited to tax-supported and publicly controlled education institutions. . . ."

Among his many books are *William James and Henri Bergson* (University of Chicago Press, 1914), *Constitutional Foundations of the New Zion* (Federation of American Zionists, 1918), *The Structure of Lasting Peace* (Marshall Jones, 1918), *Culture and Democracy in the United States* (Boni and Liveright, 1924), *Education, the Machine and the Worker* (New Republic, 1925), *Freedom in the Modern World* (Coward-McCann, 1928), *Indecency and the*

KALLEN, HORACE—*Continued*

Seven Arts (H. Liveright, 1930), *College Prolongs Infancy* (John Day Co., 1932), *Individualism; An American Way of Life* (Liveright, 1933), *The Struggle for Jewish Unity* (Ad Press, 1933), *A Free Society* (R. O. Ballou, 1934), *The Faith of Louis D. Brandeis, Zionist* (Hadassah, the Women's Zionist Organization of America, Inc., 1943), *Consumer Cooperation and the Freedom of Man* (Cooperative League of America, 1944), and *Americanism and Its Makers* (Bureau of Jewish Education, 1945). Dr. Kallen has contributed numerous articles to scholarly journals as well as to popular periodicals.

Professor Kallen has served with the advisory labor committee of the Council of National Defense, as chairman of the American Labor Conference on International Relations (1942 to 1943), the Committee of Inquiry on Terms of Peace (1918 to 1919), unofficially with the United Nations Educational, Scientific and Cultural Organization, the Mayor's Committe on City Planning (New York City) from 1923 to 1937, the Institute of Church and State, the Presidential Commission on Higher Education, and as a member of the executive board of the Institute of Church and State.

He is national vice-president of the American Jewish Congress, chairman of the academic council of the Yiddish Scientific Institute of New York City, a trustee of the Rochdale Institute of New York, and is a member of the American Philosophical Society, Western Philosophical Society, Society for Psychological Research, and the Society of Physical Research.

Dr. Kallen married Rachel Oatman Van Arsdale in 1926. They have two children, Harriet S. and David J. Kallen. The honorary Litt.D. degree was conferred upon Kallen in 1948. His hobbies are painting surrealist pictures and reading detective stories. "To interrogators he is a gentle, witty host, though somewhat digressive if the topic be he. 'Talking about yourself is like chewing gum' he says softly. 'There's no nourishment in it'" (*Saturday Review of Literature*, December 17, 1949).

References

Sat R Lit 32:11 D 17 '49 por

Hook, S. and Konvitz, M. R. Freedom and Experience (1947)
Leaders in American Education (1948)
Who's Who in America, 1952-53
Who's Who in Philosophy (1942)
Who's Who in the East (1948)

KAMAU, JOHNSTONE *See* Kenyatta, J.

KANTER, ALBERT L(EWIS) Apr. 13, 1897- Publisher

Address: b. 101 Fifth Ave., New York 3; h. 314 East 41st St., New York 17

A modern and effective method of arousing young students' interest in classical literature has been devised by Albert L. Kanter, publisher of *Classics, Illustrated*, who began to publish comic-book versions of famous novels in 1940. He is president of the Gilberton Company, Inc., which now publishes and sells over a million copies each month.

In 1950 Kanter added Shakespeare's plays, and since that time over a million comic-strip copies of *Julius Caesar* and half a million of *Hamlet* have been purchased by school children. Each month 25,000 schools receive these "books," and teachers use them as supplementary classroom aids.

Kanter has sold over 250,000,000 copies of his *Classics, Illustrated* comic books. To date, he has published 106 titles; *Mutiny on the Bounty* was the 100th title, and the series included such stories as *Treasure Island, Robinson Crusoe, David Copperfield, Call of the Wild, The Last of the Mohicans, Arabian Nights, The Deerslayer, Crime and Punishment, Two Years Before the Mast* and *The Man Without A Country*.

Albert Lewis Kanter was born in Baranovitchi, Russia, on April 13, 1897, the son of Henry and Ida (Mirsky) Kanter. His parents brought him and his two brothers to the United States in 1904 and settled in Nashua, N.H. Kanter attended the public schools but, as he said, had no college education. Nevertheless, at an early age he became "a serious student of literature, biography and history."

He obtained work at a textbook publishing house and went on the road through the New England States as its sales representative. Later, he became associated with the Elliot Publishing Company in New York City.

The first novel Kanter adapted to the comic-book format and published was *The Three Musketeers*. He printed 200,000 copies which sold so well on the newsstands that he followed it up with *Ivanhoe*. Teachers as well as school children demanded more.

Although some educators at first disliked the idea of condensing the great books and presenting them with "balloons" and garish illustrations, many began to approve of them as, at least, a way of introducing literature to the "un-literary".

Kanter noted during World War II that GI's liked comic books, and found a market for over forty million copies of his comic-book versions of outstanding literature through Army post exchanges and the American Red Cross. Thus classics were introduced to many soldiers who had never read the full-length originals.

However, he became worried that school children, soldiers, and others who read comic books would never experience the pleasure of reading the full-length novels on which the abbreviated (but unexpurgated and unsimplified) comic versions were based, so he printed this injunction at the end of each "story": "Now that you have read the *Classics, Illustrated* edition, don't miss the added enjoyment of reading the original, obtainable at your school or public library." "I was pleased to note in letters from readers that many had followed this advice," he said, recently.

Adapting a classic to comic book formula is a full-time publishing venture for Albert Kanter. "Ordinary comic books are turned out in a couple of weeks," he explained, "but it takes anywhere from eight to fifteen months to prepare one classic. The editorial board—which has its share of professors—meets four times a year to plan new books. They assign a writer to adapt the story—that is, edit it to a point where it can be illustrated in about 350 pictures.

"The editorial board adheres strictly to the original text when preparing a *Classics* version," Kanter said. "A well-organized story continuity or narrative explains the plot, but the characters speak only the words of the author, be he Shakespeare, Dickens or Dostoyevsky." Artists with knowledge of the historical backgrounds and authentic costumes are selected to produce the over 300 colored action drawings for each book.

Acts of violence showing torture, or sadistic treatment, are omitted. If this has occurred in the original plot, it is mentioned in the narration, but is not illustrated. Asked why it was necessary to print the dialogue in balloon type, he explained that he was purposely imitating the comic book style, and if he were to make it more literary, it would defeat its purpose of "wooing youngsters to great books." He also includes a short biography of the author in each issue.

Kanter became an American citizen in 1907 through his father's naturalization papers, and because he is proud of belonging to his adopted country, he includes in the back pages of each issue of *Classics, Illustrated* informative and educational articles "stressing Americana and democracy at work." He also includes opera librettos, biographies of pioneers in science, stories about American rivers, Indians, and other historical topics.

Many teachers have written to Kanter stating that slow readers obtain help from the pictures with words, the explanations and definitions of foreign or difficult words, and the quizzes on famous literary characters, all designed to arouse their desire to read the original works. As soon as a new edition of *Classics, Illustrated* appears, librarians report that "there is a run on the original title".

This experiment in publishing proved so successful in the United States that now *"Classics, Illustrated"* are translated in twelve foreign languages. Despite paper shortages and rising costs of production, he has managed to keep the price for each issue at ten cents, and fifteen cents abroad.

When Kanter's version of *Julius Caesar* appeared in 1950, after months of research in cooperation with New York University, there was considerable editorial comment in the nation's press. The Newark (N.J.) *Evening News* commented: "A 20-man editorial staff has been at work on *Julius Caesar* . . . in comic book form. This concept of ministering on a high plane to youthful desire for action pictures . . . deserves to succeed."

The New York *Times* (March 9, 1950) multicolored books, the tragedies of William stated, "Via the 'balloons' of a new series of Shakespeare will begin an ascension to the level of 'must' reading for millions of comic book fans in this country and abroad. . . .Selections

ALBERT L. KANTER

from the Great Bard's classic verse in *Julius Caesar* will be matched with 320 brightly colored action drawings. According to Albert L. Kanter, president of the Gilberton Company, which publishes the books, this is the first time that anyone has tried to put Shakespeare into the popular juvenile form." The *Chrisian Science Monitor* (March 13, 1950) commented: "Et tu, comic books? Yes, the comics have caught up with Shakespeare. A comic publisher offers a 10-cent illustrated version of *Julius Caesar*."

The St. Paul, (Minn.) *Dispatch* commented on the *Julius Caesar* comic book: "This may be at last the sort of adventure story the grade school pupil will no longer have to hide behind his geography book." The *Julius Caesar* book was translated into French, Spanish, Portuguese, Italian, Chinese, Afrikaans, Hebrew, Hindustani and Tagalog, the language of a large part of the Philippines. As in the case of other literary classics that his concern has published since 1940, Kanter printed *Julius Caesar* abroad in those areas where currency restrictions prevent dollar imports. The printing is done by means of "mats" which are sent from the United States by airmail.

The Parkersburg, West Virginia, *News* commented editorially on November 6, 1951, on *Classics, Illustrated:* "We were gratified recently to find on sale in the five-and-ten stores here a veritable library of the classics—done in true comic book style, with plenty of color and pictures. For this inestimable boon to childhood, you have to thank the ingenuity and enterprise of the Gilberton Company. . . . While we believe all lovers of good books might prefer the standard book issues, which, however, might cost as much as $1 or $2 or even $3 each—beyond the reach of many families—nevertheless the comic book classics, we believe, will fill a long-felt want. Children who otherwise might never know of these classics

KANTER, ALBERT L.—*Continued*

will get an opportunity to delve into this treasure house of the great masters of literature."

Following the success of *Julius Caesar,* Kanter published *A Midsummer Night's Dream,* Homer's *Odyssey* and Shakespeare's *Hamlet,* each of which sold half a million copies.

The publisher was married on December 17, 1917, to Rose Ehrenrich, and they have two sons, Hal and William, and one daughter, Saralee Emerson. Among his clubs are the Knights of Pythias, Masons and Scottish Rite. Kanter has also been an active worker in behalf of the United Jewish Appeal and the Israel Bond Drive. His political affiliation is Republican. He has blue eyes and brown hair, is six feet tall, and weighs 190 pounds. His hobbies are golf and horseback riding.

Seventy-five per cent of the countries of the world buy American comic books, declared Kanter, but Russia and Iron Curtain Countries are not among these. Sixty per cent of *Classics, Illustrated* are purchased by boys; the average age is thirteen. The most popular in the series have been *The Three Musketeers* and *Julius Caesar.*

The stories selected for comic-book versions in 1953 include *Bring 'Em Back Alive* by Frank Buck; *From the Earth to the Moon* by Jules Verne; *Knights of the Round Table; Pitcairn Island* by Nordhoff and Hall; *A Study in Scarlet* by Sir A. Conan Doyle; *The Talisman* by Sir Walter Scott; *Kit Carson* based on biographical and historical records; *The Forty-Five Guardsmen* by Alexandre Dumas, and *The Red Rover* by James Fenimore Cooper.

References

    Christian Sci Mon Mr 13 '50
    N Y Herald Tribune Mr 12 '50
    N Y Times Mr 9 '50

KAUFMAN, IRVING R(OBERT) June 24, 1910- Judge; lawyer·

Address: b. United States Courthouse, Foley Sq., New York 7; h. 1185 Park Ave., New York 28

Internationally famous since April 1951, when he pronounced on Julius and Ethel Rosenberg the first peacetime death sentences for espionage in the history of the United States, Irving R. Kaufman is Judge of the United States District Court for the Southern District of New York. When he was named to that bench in October 1949, Judge Kaufman was said to be the country's youngest Federal jurist. A year earlier he had organized for the Attorney General a new Justice Department section on lobbying and from 1936 to 1940, as Assistant United States District Attorney in New York, had taken part in the prosecution of several important cases, especially in the field of fraud.

A resident of New York City since his birth on June 24, 1910, Irving Robert Kaufman is one of five children (three boys and two girls) of Herman Kaufman, a manufacturer of tobacco humidifying equipment, and Rose (Spielberg) Kaufman. He has spoken of the "under-

standing, love and wise guidance" he received from his parents, now deceased, as the strongest influence on his life. Kaufman attended Public Schools 79 and 10 and DeWitt Clinton High School in New York, from which he was graduated in 1926. Having entered Fordham University at the age of sixteen, he was awarded his LL.B. degree by the university's Law School in 1931. He was a dean's list honor student and the youngest member of the graduating class.

After his admission to the New York bar in June 1932, Kaufman worked in the New York City law office of Louis Rosenberg, who later became his father-in-law, and for two and a half years handled cases in the New York State and Appellate courts. His first official connection with the Justice Department came in 1935, when he was made a special assistant to the United States Attorney for the Southern District of New York, in which position he took part in a number of publicized prosecutions, including that of Noel Scaffa, a private detective charged with perjury in connection with an investigation of interstate transportation of stolen jewels. In June 1936 Kaufman received a permanent appointment as Assistant United States Attorney for the Southern District of New York. That year he participated in the prosecution of Leonard Weisman, who was convicted of swindling and sentenced to fifteen years imprisonment, in a case which, Kaufman has said, "established novel principles of law."

The "boy prosecutor," as the press called Kaufman at this time, was twenty-seven when in the following year (1937) he handled the insurance disability fraud cases, in which he played an important part in breaking up a ring charged with defrauding life insurance companies of millions of dollars annually.

He prosecuted the mutineers on board the S.S. *Pennsylvania* of the United States Lines. A notable trial during his four years (1936-40) as assistant United States attorney was the case involving McKesson & Robbins, Inc., wholesale drug concern (1938). Through Kaufman's insistence on finger-printing F. Donald Coster, head of the firm, Coster was identified as Philip Musica, an ex-convict, and among seven officials of the company convicted of fraud were three other Musica brothers, who had also assumed aliases.

After the completion in June 1940 of his fourth year as Assistant District Attorney, Kaufman returned to private practice in New York City as a partner in the firm of Simpson, Brady, Noonan and Kaufman (later Noonan, Kaufman and Eagan). When the Selective Service Act was passed in 1948, Kaufman was made a Government appeal agent, and through his work in that capacity he is now entitled to wear the Selective Service Medal. Active in the Bar Association of the City of New York, Kaufman has also been a member of the city court committee, the committee on criminal courts and procedure, and the committee on courts of superior jurisdiction. He was chairman of a bar association subcommittee which made recommendations on proposed new Federal criminal rules to the Justice Department and Congress, and was named by the association to assist Harold R. Medina in proceedings to investigate charges that a city magistrate was associated with gambler Frank Costello. Early in October 1947 Attorney General Tom C. Clark announced that Kaufman had been appointed his assistant to "handle special legal matters," the nature of which was not revealed until later in the year, when it was disclosed that Kaufman had been called in to set up and head an investigation of lobbying under the Federal Regulations and Lobbying Act, and to establish a permanent section in the Department of Justice to deal with lobbying. The New York Times reported that Kaufman's work resulted in increases in registrations and in the indictment of four persons and three organizations for alleged willful failure to register, and that prominent organizations which had not previously filed papers did so after the inquiry.

When this special assignment was finished, Kaufman returned to private practice for a year, until nominated on October 15, 1949 by President Harry S. Truman to become a Judge of the United States District Court for the Southern District of New York. Recommended for the post by all the New York City bar associations and by the State, Federal, and American bar associations, Kaufman, at the age of thirty-nine, became the youngest Federal judge in the country. After he was sworn in as an interim appointee in November, his first major judicial decision was to deny a motion made by the eleven Communist leaders sentenced by Judge Medina to "enlarge the jurisdiction of their bail" pending appeal of their conviction. Several months later, in the espionage trial of Abraham Brothman and Miriam Moskowitz, Judge Kaufman imposed the maximum punishment on the defendants, who were found guilty.

A more renowned espionage case was brought to trial in Judge Kaufman's court on March 6, 1951, when Julius Rosenberg, an electrical engineer, his wife Ethel, her brother David Greenglass, and Morton Sobell, an electronics expert, were charged with having conspired to convey atomic and other secrets to Soviet Russia in 1944 and 1945. Greenglass, who had been an Army sergeant stationed at Los Alamos, New Mexico, confessed his complicity, became a witness for the Government, and admitted that he had repeatedly delivered secret data to the Rosenbergs for transmisson to the U.S.S.R. On March 29 a jury found the Rosenbergs and Sobell guilty of wartime espionage, a verdict of which the judge stated his approval. About a week later Kaufman pronounced on the Rosenberg couple the sentence of death, adding the statement, "Plain, deliberate murder is dwarfed in magnitude by comparison with the crime you have committed." Because of his "lesser degree of implication," Sobell received a sentence of thirty years imprisonment, while the testimony given by Greenglass for the State reduced his penalty to fifteen years.

The Rosenbergs' attorney made three unsuccessful appeals for a new trial to the United States Court of Appeals and two appeals to the United States Supreme Court, which rejected jurisdiction on the ground that no con-

JUDGE IRVING R. KAUFMAN

stitutional issues were involved. Then, "having virtually exhausted every avenue of judicial review," the Rosenbergs' attorney entreated Kaufman himself to reduce their death sentence. This petition was denied by the judge who, in a twenty-three page "opinion" made public on January 3, 1953, nine days before the scheduled date of execution, stated that the Rosenbergs "were on the top rung" of the conspiracy and had chosen "the part of traitors." In order that an appeal for clemency might be made to the Chief Executive of the United States, Judge Kaufman postponed the date of execution. President Truman left the decision to his successor, President Eisenhower, who rejected the appeal, finding no "mitigating circumstances which would justify altering this decision," and on February 16 Judge Kaufman set the week of March 8 as the new time for the execution of the Rosenbergs. The date was later again changed to allow further review and appeals of the case.

However, after Judge Kaufman's sentence, the Rosenberg case was merely begun. It became, according to the Saturday Evening Post (August 8, 1953) "the most-appealed Federal trial in recent history. The Rosenbergs' pleas were repeatedly heard, considered and rejected: sixteen times by the Southern District Court of New York, seven times by the Second Circuit Court of Appeals, seven times by the Supreme Court of the United States, which made its final ruling on the day of execution. Beyond the Supreme Court, the Rosenbergs' appeals for executive clemency were passed up by President Truman and twice flatly rejected by President Eisenhower."

The Rosenbergs were executed in the electric chair at Sing Sing on June 19, 1953.

A member of the Tau Epsilon Phi fraternity, Kaufman was chosen that fraternity's "Man of the Year" in October 1951. In March 1952 he

KAUFMAN, IRVING R.—*Continued*

received the B'nai B'rith Virginia State award of merit and in the following October the Certificate of Honor of the Jewish War Veterans of the United States "for exercise of high judicial office in a manner to reflect the utmost credit on American jurisprudence." Kaufman is an officer of the Fordham Law School Alumni, a member of city, State, and national bar associations, a patron of the International Bar Associations, a trustee of Riverdale Country School, and a director of the Anti-Defamation League of B'nai B'rith. He is a seminary associate of the Jewish Theological Seminary of America and a member of the Congregation of the Park Avenue Synagogue. Mrs. Kaufman, the former Helen Ruth Rosenberg, was a volunteer social worker before her marriage on June 23, 1936; the couple has three sons, Robert Howard, James Michael, and Richard Kenneth. The brown-eyed, black-haired jurist is five feet six and a half inches in height and 155 pounds in weight. For recreation he likes golfing at the City Athletic Club, playing the piano, and reading, particularly historical novels.

References

N Y Post Mag p59 N 21 '47 por
N Y Times p18 Je 14 '40; p8 O 8 '47;
   p5 Ag 9 '48 por; p10 Ap 6 '51
Sat Eve Post 226:20+ por
Who's Who in America, 1952-53
Who's Who in New York, 1952

KAYE, NORA 1920- Ballerina

Address: b. c/o New York City Center of Music and Drama, Inc., 130 W. 56th St., New York 19; h. 21 W. 58th St., New York 19

Nora Kaye is regarded by many critics both in the United States and abroad as "the foremost dramatic ballerina dancing today." American by birth and training, she joined the Ballet Theatre at its inception in 1940 and attained the rank of prima ballerina two years later. Since 1951 she has been a member of the New York City Ballet and in December 1952 appeared as the principal dancer in the Broadway revue, *Two's Company*. Among the modern ballets with which Miss Kaye has been closely identified are *Pillar of Fire, Lilac Garden, Facsimile, Fall River Legend,* and *The Cage;* she has also achieved distinction in such classics as *Giselle, Swan Lake,* and *Princess Aurora.*

Of Russian parentage, Nora Kaye was born Nora Koreff in New York City in 1920. (She was named Nora after the heroine of Ibsen's *A Doll's House,* and early in her career changed her surname because she thought "an American dancer ought to have an American name.") Her father, Gregory Koreff, was a former Moscow Art Theatre actor "in the Stanislavsky tradition"; while a young child Nora began practicing the "Stanislavsky method." In keeping with the wishes of her mother, who wanted her to become a dancer, at the age of four she was taken to her first dancing lesson. When Nora was eight, she entered

Margaret Curtis' class at the Metropolitan Opera Ballet School, where she studied for the next seven years. During that time she occasionally had a chance to appear in the operas— as a cupid in *Tannhäuser,* a gnome in *The Sunken Bell,* or a minor Nibelung in *Das Rheingold.* By the time she was fifteen, she had graduated into the Metropolitan Opera's corps de ballet, and she later joined George Balanchine's American Ballet when it became the resident ballet company of the Metropolitan in the fall of 1935. Meanwhile, she took two lessons a week with the celebrated choreographer, Michel Fokine, and rehearsed in a number of his most famous ballets. Nora Kaye has also studied under Vilzak-Shollar and Margaret Craske.

For several years Miss Kaye abandoned the ballet for Broadway. She felt at the time that ballet was "something dragged up from three hundred years ago that didn't make any sense and wasn't going any place" (quoted by *Time* May 2, 1949) and the theater seemed to her a more important and exciting medium. Among the musical comedies in which she danced were *Virginia* (1937), *Great Lady* (1938), and *Stars in Your Eyes* (1939). During this period, she was also a member of the Radio City Music Hall Corps de Ballet for nine months; had a job dancing at the International Casino; and, together with a friend, tried to sell a night club act called *Blue Moon,* which was rejected as "too classical."

When the Ballet Theatre was being organized in the fall of 1939, Miss Kaye went along to the auditions with her roommate and was accepted as a member of the corps de ballet. "I joined only because most of my friends were joining," she has explained. The experience of working under Antony Tudor, one of the company's choreographers and teachers, changed her "whole opinion of ballet" and revealed to her its possibilities as an expressive, dramatic art. During Ballet Theatre's first New York season early in 1940, she danced in the chorus of Tudor's *Dark Elegies* and as one of the guests in his *Lilac Garden.* Bit parts in *Les Sylphides* and *Swan Lake* followed. Then Tudor offered Miss Kaye her first important character role—that of the haughty Russian ballerina in his *Gala Performance,* which had its American première in February 1941. The New York *Times's* dance critic, John Martin, commented on her "fine technique" and "most ingratiating comedy sense." That same year she was also cast as the Bird in *Peter and the Wolf,* the Woman in His Past in *Lilac Garden,* Grisi in *Pas de Quatre,* the Queen of the Willis in *Giselle,* and as one of Florestan's sisters in *Princess Aurora.* It was her portrayal of Hagar in *Pillar of Fire,* Tudor's psychological ballet on the theme of frustrated love, that overnight raised Miss Kaye to the rank of prima ballerina. This part had been composed especially for her by Tudor, who rehearsed with the dancer for months so that each gesture and movement would clearly project the inner conflict of the tortured heroine. In the opinion of Martin, the world première of *Pillar of Fire,* on April

8, 1942, was the most distinguished event in Ballet Theatre's history, and he rated Miss Kaye's characterization as among "the great examples of tragic acting of its generation."

Subsequently entrusted with a wide variety of important assignments, Miss Kaye during the 1942 fall season danced as one of the principals in *Dark Elegies* and was seen as the Princess in *Bluebeard*. The following spring she appeared for the first time as Polyhymnia in *Apollo*, the Gypsy Girl in *Capriccio Espagnol*, the Bride-to-Be in *Lilac Garden*, and in the title role of *Princess Aurora*. Reviewing her performances in the latter two ballets for *Dance News*, Anatole Chujoy said she danced Princess Aurora "with great style and fine eloquence," and showed a deeper understanding of Tudor's intentions than any of her predecessors in the leading feminine part in *Lilac Garden*. In the summer of 1943 Miss Kaye made her debut as the Swan Queen in *Swan Lake* and, according to Edwin Denby (*Herald Tribune*), gave "a careful, serious, and accurate interpretation." That fall (which one reviewer designated as "a distinctly Nora Kaye season") she starred in the world premières of Tudor's *Dim Lustre* and Leonide Massine's *Mademoiselle Angot*. When Alicia Markova was forced to withdraw because of illness, Miss Kaye substituted for her as Juliet in *Romeo and Juliet* and as Zemphira in *Aleko* and received plaudits from the critics for her individual interpretations of these roles.

In 1944 the ballerina danced in the initial production of Balanchine's *Waltz Academy,* and in the spring of 1945 she alternated with Tamara Toumanova as the lead in *Harvest Time.*

During one of her busiest seasons, in the fall of 1945, Miss Kaye created the roles of the Princess in Michael Kidd's *On Stage!* and Della in Simon Semenoff's *Gift of the Magi* and danced one of the principal parts in John Taras' *Graziana*—three ballets that received their world premières. She also assumed the title role in *Firebird* and appeared as Odile in the *Black Swan Pas de Deux*. *Newsweek* reported that when the company paid its first visit to London in the summer of 1946, the opening-night ovation went to Miss Kaye for her performance in this pas de deux, which the *Times'* critic said "excelled anything" seen there "for years." By the time Ballet Theatre returned for its fall season in New York, Miss Kaye had established herself as the organization's most popular star. Denby found her dancing with "rich brilliance" as one of the "three insecure people" in the world première of Jerome Robbins' *Facsimile*. That same season she headed the cast in *Les Patineurs,* and in 1947 she took over the role of the Italian ballerina in *Gala Performance.*

In the spring of 1948 Miss Kaye scored a great success as the Accused in *Fall River Legend,* a ballet based on the story of Lizzie Borden. Illness prevented her from dancing in the world première of this work, which had been devised especially for her by Agnes de Mille, but she assumed the role later in the engagement. This season also marked her first

Helen Merrill

NORA KAYE

appearance as the Ballerina in *Petrouchka*. A year later she added the principal part in *Theme and Variations* to her repertory and made her New York debut in the title role of *Giselle*. Although Martin believed her characterization of Giselle was "still not fully developed," he thought her approach was "profoundly and basically classic," and he praised the dramatic scenes as "not only beautifully played but fabulously danced." (She subsequently starred in the first televised production of *Giselle* in the United States.) For its tenth anniversary season in the spring of 1950, Ballet Theatre presented Tudor's *Nimbus* and William Dollar's version of *Jeux*, with Miss Kaye interpreting the leading roles in both of these novelties. When the company toured Great Britain and the Continent during the remainder of that year, the critic of *Dancing Times* hailed her as "the greatest actress of the dance today."

Early in February 1951 Miss Kaye left Ballet Theatre to join the New York City Ballet. In her debut with the company on February 16 in *Symphony in C,* she took the "enormous technical difficulties of the part in her stride," according to Chujoy, and brought to it "a radiant personal style." Later in the engagement she danced prominent roles in *Pas de Trois, Bourrée Fantasque,* and *The Guests.* When the troupe presented its next season in June, she won acclaim in *The Cage,* a controversial ballet choreographed for her by Robbins, in which she played the Novice of a species of female insect or animal that considers the male as hereditary prey. Her performance was described as "frighteningly inhuman, provocative and glittering" (*Herald Tribune*). She also appeared in *Mother Goose Suite* and *The Age of Anxiety*, and that fall resumed her celebrated role in *Lilac Garden*. In February 1952 Tudor created *La Gloire,* a new ballet for Miss Kaye based on the theme

KAYE, NORA—*Continued*

of an aging tragedienne and her most famous roles. *Newsweek's* critic felt the work was too fragmentary and failed to give Miss Kaye's "great dramatic talents sufficient outlet." During the company's European tour in the spring and summer of 1952, it was reported that her performance in *The Cage* made "a particularly strong impression." On her return in September, she accepted the principal dancing assignment in the Bette Davis revue, *Two's Company,* for which Robbins staged the dances. Before the show opened in December she appeared several times with the New York City Ballet. Reviews of *Two's Company* commented on the deserved ovations given the dancer. "Miss Kaye," noted William Hawkins of the New York *World-Telegram,* "is downright brilliant in *Haunted Hotspot,* haunting in *Roundabout,* and bright as a button in her comedy."

"The whole point of view of the ballerina has changed," Miss Kaye wrote in *Theatre Arts* (September 1950). "In the past she was concerned with the technical aspects of ballet, whereas now she thinks primarily of portrayal." Miss Kaye believes this applies not only to contemporary ballets, but also to the classics. "As an American ballerina . . . I never take anything for granted. I question each tradition, each interpretation, each movement. The answers I have found, sometimes right and sometimes wrong, constitute my contribution to the young American dancer of ballet: not to accept until you understand (at least to your own satisfaction), and not to dance any role, ancient or new, until you do understand. This urge to question and to discover is, I think, the trademark of American ballet." In his article on Miss Kaye for Cyril Swinson's *Dancers and Critics,* Walter Terry called her a dancer "who is concerned with discovering and projecting the content of a movement." Whether dancing in dramatic roles, comedy assignments, or studies in pure dance, she "serves the choreographer by extending rather than simply mirroring his creative process. . . . In this sense, she is an adventurer, and her audience, therefore, partakes of the excitement of adventure."

The ballerina's first marriage, to Michael Van Buren, took place on January 2, 1943. She was married for a second time, on November 10, 1948, to the noted violinist, Isaac Stern. This marriage was subsequently dissolved. The "sad-eyed and mobile-faced" dancer stands five feet four inches tall and weighs 112 pounds. "I'm not exactly an outdoor girl," she told one interviewer. "Dancing is about all the exercise I need to keep physically fit." She is fond of the theater and would like to act in a play on Broadway; enjoys good music and reading; and goes to the movies for relaxation. "Unless you feel that ballet is a religion with you," *Cue* has quoted Miss Kaye as saying, "nothing could compensate for the enormous amount of time and work put in it."

References

Christian Sci Mon p5 F 19 '44
Cue 20:15 N 3 '51 por
Dance 19:4 Ja '45 pors
N Y Herald Tribune p17 Ag 27 '52
N Y World-Telegram p26 D 11 '47
Newsweek 19:64 Ap 2 '42; 22:86 N 8 '43 pors
P.M p22 O 7 '43 por
Time 53:51 My 2 '49

Chujoy, A. (ed) Dance Encyclopedia (1949)
Haskell, A. Ballet Vignettes (1949)

KENNELLY, ARDYTH (kĕn-ĕl′-ĭ) April 15, 1912- Author

Address: b. c/o Houghton Mifflin Co., 2 Park St., Boston, Mass.; h. 2475 N.W. Northrup St., Portland, Ore.

Reprinted from the *Wilson Library Bulletin,* October 1953

With an aunt who insisted that all writers and bookworms eventually go insane—"their families hush it up so it don't get in the papers"—it is perhaps a wonder that Ardyth Kennelly ever dared become a writer. Despite the fact that she is also a bookworm, novelist Kennelly has stood up well—well enough, in fact, to turn out the current best-seller, *Good Morning, Young Lady,* and two other novels since 1949.

Miss Kennelly, in private life Mrs. Egon Victor Ullman, has an interesting family background. Her paternal grandfather, an Ohioan of Irish and French descent, prospected for gold and silver in Utah and Nevada. At forty, he married nineteen-year-old Innocent Clotide Rogers, of English and Dutch ancestry. Miss Kennelly's father, James Daniel Thomas Aquinas Kennelly, was their first child. Her maternal grandmother, Dr. Anna M. Olsen, chiropractor, who was born in Sweden to Later Day Saint converts, arrived in Salt Lake City at sixteen. She did housework in the home of Brigham Young's brother and, at twenty-one, married a Norwegian-born tailor who already had a wife and two children. Their daughter, Lulu Amanda Olsen, was Miss Kennelly's mother.

One of four children, Ardyth Kennelly was born in the tiny coastal Oregon town of Glenada the night the *Titanic* sank—nine years before her father, a lineman for the Utah Power and Light Company, was electrocuted at work. The family lived successively in Glenada, North Albany (Oregon), Salt Lake City, and North Albany again. Her mother later was married to a farmer, Hiram Parker, "a gentleman and a scholar if ever there was one," and the person to whom Miss Kennelly credits a number of her attitudes: "He was a broadminded man, believing in God but not belonging to any church (I'm the same), and a good Democrat (I am too)."

Ardyth Kennelly went to city school in Salt Lake City, country school in Oregon's Benton County, and graduated in 1929 from Albany

High School. She says she was influenced in
the choice of her later work by all her English
teachers, both in high school and at Oregon
State College, where, intent on becoming an
English teacher, she studied vocational education for three years.

Her first writing experience came at the age
of nine: poetry—"a small copybook full, highly
praised by relatives, the elevator man, and
neighbors." She has sold six or seven short
stories in her life, beginning in the early 1930's,
and "hated to write them as much as I love to
write novels."

Perhaps the fact that she was "often sick,
often confined to bed, learned to be quiet, be
alone, think, and read" had something to do
with Ardyth Kennelly's development as a writer of novels. Her first, *The Peaceable Kingdom* (Houghton Mifflin, 1949), portrayed life
among the Mormons during the years after
Brigham Young's death. Critical reaction to it
was generally favorable, including the comments of D. L. Morgan, who wrote in the
Saturday Review, "No one who reads [*The
Peaceable Kingdom*] can resist the temptation
of reading aloud some of the passages that are
sheer delight and go on quoting themselves in
your mind whether or not you are able to pass
them on. . . . Miss Kennelly, this is an extraordinarily fine job."

The Spur, which was published by Messner
in 1951, was based on the last six days of the
life of Lincoln's assassin, John Wilkes Booth.
It was greeted by the critics with mixed, although predominantly favorable comment. Virginia Kirkus remarked that although "the writing is overlush at times. . .Miss Kennelly has
done a challenging piece of research." The
Chicago Sunday *Tribune* reviewer, Paul Engle,
wrote enthusiastically that "The story which
the author makes of this pathetic life is a
fascinating one . . . an excellent job of presenting the facts and inventing dialog."

The current best-seller, *Good Morning, Young
Lady,* published by Houghton Mifflin in June
(1953), is the love story of an imaginative
young girl living in Salt Lake City. Like *The
Peaceable Kingdom,* it is a Literary Guild
selection. Hal Borland commented in the *New
York Times Book Review* that "We've been a
long time waiting for a really good novel dealing with the material that wove itself into
Western balladry, but here is one at last." Virginia Sorensen in the *Book Review* of the
New York *Herald Tribune* agreed on the
novel's merit: "Both tale and style often have
a dreamlike quality along with a certain stark
sense of reality, the combination producing an
effect that this reviewer has never before encountered in fiction." In addition to her published novels, Miss Kennelly has written "Up
Home," an unpublished sequel to *The Peaceable
Kingdom,* and is at work on a novel tentatively
entitled "All Made for Each Other."

Married at twenty-two and divorced five
years later, Ardyth Kennelly was shortly afterward married to her present husband, who, she
says, has influenced her more than any other
person in her adult life. The recreations and

ARDYTH KENNELLY

hobbies of the author, who is tall (five feet
nine inches) and blonde, include Mozart,
antiques, movies, western Americana, fortune
telling, extra sensory perception, "and sending
away for things." Her favorite books include
most of the important authors in English and
American literature. At the moment they are
Shakespeare and Boswell.

KENNY, ELIZABETH Sept. 20, 1886—
Nov. 30, 1952 Australian nurse (called Sister
Kenny) famed for her methods of treatment
of infantile paralysis; successfully treated first
polio case in 1910; during World War I served
with Australian Nurse Corps overseas; returned to development of her then unconventional methods of polio treatment in Australia;
went to United States to demonstrate methods
(1940-50); City of Minneapolis opened an
Elizabeth Kenny Institute for treatment and
training (1942), while other clinics opened in
a number of United States cities; saw her
methods widely accepted during her lifetime as
part of physical therapy technique to prevent
deformities that accompany polio. See *Current
Biography,* 1942.

Obituary

N Y Times p1+ N 30 '52

KENYATTA, JOMO 1893?- African anthropologist; educator; association leader

A trial which may be significant to the
future of Afro-European relations was that
of Jomo Kenyatta and five of his colleagues
who were charged with managing or assisting in the management of the Mau Mau, anti-
white terrorist cult of Kikuyu tribesmen. In

United Press

JOMO KENYATTA

April 1953 they were convicted and sentenced to seven years imprisonment.

However, this sentence was reversed by the Kenya Supreme Court because the court did not have jurisdiction and a new trial was ordered. The East African Appeals Court on August 22 upheld the prison term, but Kenyatta's attorney announced that he would appeal to the Privy Council in London, the highest court in the British Commonwealth, since his client was not guilty of violence.

A Kikuyu tribesman, Kenyatta is the author of an anthropological study of Africa, *Facing Mount Kenya* (Secker and Warburg, 1938, 1953). The late Bronislaw Malinowski, professor of anthropology, University of London, stated in the introduction, "The book is one of the first really competent and instructive contributions to African ethnography by a scholar of African parentage . . . an invaluable document in the principles underlying culture-contact and change." Jomo Kenyatta has also been a leader of a native educational movement since 1929, and was the president of the recently proscribed Kenya African Union founded in 1947.

Early in the trial the deputy prosecutor testified that "Johnston, or John, or Jomo Kenyatta was born, as far as the Crown knew, in 1893" (London *Times,* December 4, 1952). The place is not identified, but was presumably some thatched-hut village in the Kikuyu tribal area near what is now the city of Nairobi. According to the novelist, Richard Llewellyn, Kenyatta remembers that "at eight or nine he carried a bow and arrow to protect his father's cattle from lions and leopards" (*Saturday Evening Post,* May 23, 1953). This would be at about the time (1896 to 1903) when the railway from Mombasa to Victoria Nyanza was being built. The discovery by the builders of the salubrious

highlands near Nairobi led to the settlement of Britons there.

His grandfather was a seer and a magician and Jomo travelled about the Kikuyu territory with him. "The skinny kid with the big smile," Llewellyn continues, was enrolled in the missionary school. "He found that the Lord God of the Old Testament had a lot in common with En-Gai his tribal god." Thus he was able to accept the Christian faith (he was baptized, states *Time,* December 3, 1952, under the name of Johnstone Kamau) and still go through the rites which made him a full Kikuyu tribesman. His native name is "Burning Spear." After attending a Scottish Presbyterian mission school, Kenyatta was employed as a clerk for the Nairobi municipality.

With the formation of the Kikuyu Central Association in 1922, Kenyatta became its general secretary and started the first Kikuyu journal, *Muigwithania.* The purpose was to recover the Kikuyu's lands which were lost when the Crown Colony of Kenya was formed in July 1920 out of the former British East Africa Protectorate. By the Crown Land Ordinance of 1915 and Order in Council of 1921 the Africans became "tenants-at-will" of the Crown. Leaseholds of land were restricted to white settlers, and native "reservations" were established. Gikonyo Wa Kiana, a Kikuyu post-graduate student at Stanford University, wrote, "It seemed only fair that the land of Kenya, which was quite sparsely occupied by a people whose agriculture was purely on a subsistence level, should be handed over to the more efficient white farmers" (*Saturday Review,* May 2, 1953). Harold Ingram, a British Colonial Officer, asserts that the Kikuyu Central Association soon became subversive and went underground, working up hate against the Government and Europeans" (*Saturday Review,* May 2, 1953).

In 1921, after the missionaries denounced certain Kikuyu tribal rites, the Kikuyu Independent Schools Association was established. "Kenyatta was associated with the religious breakaway from the beginning" (London *Times,* November 15, 1952).

Interested in land reform, Kenyatta represented the Kikuyu on several Royal commissions, the Hilton Young Commission in 1928 and 1929, and the Joint Committee on the Closer Union of East Africa in 1931 and 1932. Before the joint committee he presented a memorandum on behalf of the Kenya Central Association. In London he attended the Morris Carter Kenya Land Commission in 1932. Kenyatta was delegated to present the Kikuyu position on land tenure to the Secretary of State for the Colonies on several occasions.

Kenyatta traveled widely in Europe, and spent two of these years as a "student guest" at the University of Moscow. He also studied under Professor Bronislaw Malinowski at the London School of Economics and Political Science of the University of London and "extended the study of anthropology . . . to include both the African religion and the African doctrine of Government and the good life" (New York *Times,* July 1, 1953).

These studies resulted in Kenyatta's *Facing Mount Kenya* which *Time* called "a first rate study of his people." The book relates that the family group is the unifying factor in native life and that "kinship is the root of the Kikuyu ideas of good and evil." He also wrote *My People of Kenya* (Lutterworth, 1942) and a pamphlet, *Kenya: Land of Conflict* which was published at Manchester in 1944.

The population of Kenya is composed of 30,000 whites, 5,500,000 Africans and 91,000 Indians, and when Kenyatta returned in 1946 to his native land the racial problem had become aggravated. The Kikuyu Central Association had been declared illegal in 1939, and in the following year other native political associations were outlawed. An effort to establish a policy of moving all natives to "reserves" made considerable headway in 1943. The following year an African was appointed by the Crown to represent the native interests in the Kenya Legislative Council.

The Kikuyu Independent Schools Association was, however, permitted to continue. Kenyatta extended its scope and became the principal of the Githunguri College. Here teachers were trained and indoctrinated with the notion that "the African . . . has a worthier essential way of life than the European." The Githunguri-trained teachers taught their pupils the following creed, "I believe in God, the Father Almighty, in the holy sacrifice of Gikuyunu Mumbi (i.e., the leadership of Kenyatta) and the righteous complaints and unity of the Kikuyu" (London *Times*, November 15, 1952).

The Kenya African Union was formed with Kenyatta as president in 1947. The proclaimed purpose was "Negro advancement." In the following year, the name of the secret society, Mau Mau, began to be widely whispered, as its "oath takers" began to circulate among the Kikuyu, the largest tribe of Kenya. The Mau Mau had been preceded by two other societies, Dini ya Msanbwa and Watu wa Mungu, whose members were sworn to drive the white men from Kenya.

Kenyatta publicly campaigned for the abolition of the color line, higher wages for Africans, equality of representation in the Government, more and better African housing and redistribution of land, particularly the 16,000 square miles of fertile highland country.

The Colonial Government of Kenya announced on May 24, 1953 that it would investigate the problem of underpaid natives. This study will accompany that of the Royal Land and Population Commission looking into the land hunger of the natives of Kenya. "Britain has contributed financially to a Ten Year Plan" to teach the African natives new agricultural methods but the Mau Mau leaders have "stirred up opposition to better agriculture going so far as to incite people to destroy contour terraces and other improvements" (*Saturday Review*, May 2, 1953).

In June, July and August of 1952 several Kikuyus who had refused to take the oath were murdered. Sir Evelyn Baring, the Governor of Kenya, outlawed the Mau Mau on August 12, 1952. Its membership at that time was believed to be 200,000. During September about forty-three Europeans were killed and nearly 150 head of cattle slaughtered and crops burned on the property of white farmers.

The Governor of Kenya declared a "state of emergency" on October 21, and the cruiser *Kenya* and a battalion of the Lancashire Fusiliers were hurried to the colony to restore order. On the same day Kenyatta and five of his associates were arrested and held in custody at Kapanguria, a small town in the Rift Valley Province. A little over three weeks later the Governor announced that he had "proscribed" the Kikuyu Independent Schools Association because of "connection with Mau Mau" and on November 18 charges against Kenyatta and his fellow prisoners were filed.

The trial opened six days later with Mr. Ransley N. Thacker, a magistrate of the Northern Frontier District, presiding. Denis N. Pritt, Q.C., who had successfully defended Gerhart Eisler in 1949, came from England to undertake the defense but much of the subsequent work of the defense was carried on by Harold Davies. On April 8, an all-white jury found the defendants guilty as charged, and each was sentenced to seven years with hard labor for managing and assisting in the management of Mau Mau and three years for being a member of a proscribed cult" (*Reader's Digest*, June 1953).

There has been speculation on the possibility of the Mau Mau uprising having been inspired by the Kremlin. Robert Ruark stated that he has "a copy of a letter . . . that describes the Mau Mau as the 'Africans Communist Unit.'" The London *Times* declared that "there has been some outside help in the form of advice and assistance by Indians and Europeans, both in Kenya and beyond . . . there is no evidence whatsoever of 'Moscow intervention'."

Continuation of the atrocities brought about the formal outlawing of the Kenya African Union on June 8. An appeal from the April 8 convictions had meanwhile been made by Pritt, and on July 1 the case of the six Kikuyu leaders was reopened at Kitale before the Kenya Supreme Court.

"Whatever the court decides," wrote Albion Ross of the New York *Times*, "the established order finds itself in an almost impossible predicament. . . .Independent of what happens in the courtroom it is the jailed Kenyatta and his doctrine of the essential superiority of the African way of life that is gaining in stature through the publicity. . . ." (July 1, 1953).

At the reopened proceedings, Pritt again appeared for the defense and was assisted by A. P. Kapila, a Hindu lawyer from Nairobi. This lent support to the belief that funds for the defense came largely from Indian sources. On July 15 the Kenya Supreme Court ruled that Magistrate Thacker had no jurisdiction in the Rift Valley Province. He invalidated the sentences imposed on the six defendants and remanded them for a new trial.

At the subsequent trial "The sentence on the bearded Kenyatta, whom thousands of

KENYATTA, JOMO—*Continued*

natives revere," was followed by "millions of surrender leaflets turned out by Government printing presses, ready to be scattered over Mau Mau territory. . . .The terrorists will have the opportunity of surrendering without prosecution unless they prove to be murderers or to have committed atrocities," according to a Reuters dispatch in the New York *Times* (August 23, 1953).

Kenyatta's belief in the superiority of the African approach to life stems from his contention that the African's feeling for family unity is the key to a deeper understanding of life than the European's "exaggerated" individualism. His doctrines have influenced native Africans to feel more self-confidence in themselves, their tribes, and their religion (New York *Times*, July 1, 1953).

During his sojourn in England Jomo Kenyatta married a Sussex schoolmistress and has a son by their union. He is a fine orator and has been described as "a burly, bearded figure who with his open-necked coloured shirts and elephant-headed stick appeared part mountebank, part Hampstead intellectual" .(London *Times,* November 13, 1952).

Robert Ruark in his article, "Your Guns Go With You" (*Life,* February 16, 1953) wrote: "I am convinced that Mau Mau's prime exponent, Jomo Kenyatta, now on trial with five of his associates, is by no means his own man. He was educated abroad, boasts of spending several years in Moscow . . . and is highly intelligent."

The Washington *Post* commented editorially on Kenyatta's trial (July 19, 1953): "Though the British regulars may succeed in destroying the Mau Maus, they can hardly be expected to solve the African problem. The solution, if a solution is possible, is one that will demand the very highest order of statesmanship and historical insight."

In the May 2, 1953 issue of the *Saturday Review* devoted to the discussion of Africa, a Kenya-African, Gikonyo Wa Kiano, stated: "African mistrust of the white man is now widespread. The discrepancy between the white man's professed democracy and religion and his behavior toward Africans has become so glaringly evident that practically anything proposed by any white man is, *a priori,* subject to suspicion and mistrust. Only such remarkable white men in Africa as Albert Schweitzer, Michael Scott, or the late Archdeacon Owen of Kenya can win African confidence. They are very few in number."

References

    Christian Sci Mon p4 Jl 1 '53
    Life 34:132+ F 16 '53 por; 34:150 My
        4 '53 por
    N Y Sunday News p68+ Jl 12 '53 por
    N Y Times Mag p16+ 17 D 7 '52;
    N Y Times p4 Jl 1 '53 por
    Read Digest 62:8+ Je '53
    Sat Eve Post 225:32+ My 23 '53 por
    Time 60:25 S 1 '52 por; 60:36 N 3 '52;
        61:26 Ja 12 '53
    Times (London) p7 N 13 '52; p8
        D 4 '52

KERR, WALTER F(RANCIS) July 8, 1913- Drama critic; playwright
Address: b. New York Herald Tribune, 230 West 41st St., New York 36; h. Davenport Neck, New Rochelle, N.Y.

The drama critic of the New York *Herald Tribune* since October 1951, Walter F. Kerr has built such a strong following of readers not only from the theatrical profession but also from theatre-goers that he is now regarded as a highly influential member of the critical profession.

Previously, he had written 'a musical revue, *Touch and Go,* in collaboration with his wife, Jean, which was a sellout for five months in the 1949-1950 Broadway season, and his *Sing Out, Sweet Land* ran for 101 performances in 1944 and 1945. He had also been a member of the faculty of the drama department of the Catholic University of America at Washington, D.C., for eleven years. In that capacity he directed student productions of the classics, original plays and adaptations. He has lectured at Harvard, Johns Hopkins, Williams and other universities and colleges on playwriting and directing.

Walter F(rancis) Kerr was born in Evanston, Illinois, on July 8, 1913, the son of Walter Sylvester Kerr, a construction foreman, and Esther (Daugherty) Kerr, who were also parents of another son, George, and a daughter, Jean. Walter was first gainfully employed in his present occupation at the age of thirteen, when he began reviewing films for the junior section of the weekly Evanston *Review*; he also edited the section for two years. While a student at St. George High School, in Evanston, he was promoted to regular movie critic and later transferred to the Evanston *News-Index,* a daily, in the same capacity.

He also found time to be editor of the school newspaper and yearbook, a librarian, a member of the dramatic club, and a contributor to the sports pages of several newspapers. He won a four-year scholarship to De Paul University in Chicago, which he attended from 1931 to 1933. At the height of the depression, however, he found it necessary to take a full-time job as a booking clerk for the Fox Film Company.

When he returned to school, in 1935, he chose Northwestern University in his home town, largely because of its excellent drama department. Here he was editor of the fine arts page of the *Daily Northwestern,* contributor to the humor magazine the *Purple Parrot,* assistant editor of the *Drama Magazine,* author of two musicals and publicity director of the university theatre. He obtained the B.S. degree in speech in 1937 and the M.A. degree the following year. He stated that he was considerably influenced by the teachings of Hubert Heffner, John Baird, Lee Mitchell, and Theodore Fuchs, all distinguished in the drama educational field.

Kerr then joined the year-old drama department of the Catholic University of America. He wrote that the drama faculty "started from nothing and in three years built the University's ultimate seven annual theatre productions to a $50,000 a year subscription list, three-week runs and the attendance of all of Washington's first-string theatre reviewers at each show." Student enrollment which was originally twenty-five later expanded to 200.

In Kerr's eleven years of association with the department, he directed about fifty of the plays, wrote several shows that were not only produced on the campus but found their way to Broadway, adapted various classics, such as Molière's *Miser* and Aristophanes' *The Birds,* for modern staging, and lectured on playwrighting, directing and the history of the theatre.

Kerr's first directing chore, and the third production of the campus theatre, was Shakespeare's *Coriolanus* in modern dress in the spring of 1939. His *Christopher Over Chaos,* a "cockeyed farce," was announced as one of the 1939 winners of the Maxwell Anderson play contest at Stanford University (New York *Times,* September 21, 1939). In collaboration with Leo Brady, he wrote *Yankee Doodle Boy,* a "musical biography" of George M. Cohan which was successfully produced at Catholic University with Cohan's presence and blessing in the fall of 1939, and again the next spring. Kerr and Brady originated this type of musical biography, later utilized in Hollywood films about George Gershwin and other composers.

The collaborators wrote *Cook Book,* a musical treatment of the life and vaudeville acts of the comic, Joe Cook, which was successfully produced at the University in May 1941. *God's Stage,* a dramatic anthology tracing the presence of divinity in great drama from Aeschylus to Eugene O'Neill, was assembled by Kerr and performed at the university, in the spring of 1941 and later taken on an extensive tour of university and college theatres.

Kerr and Brady adapted Graham Greene's novel, *Brighton Rock,* which ran at Catholic University in February 1942. Their revue, *Count Me In,* had such a successful campus presentation that producers Lee and J. J. Shubert brought it to Broadway with Charles Butterworth in the principal role. Louis Kronenberger wrote in *PM* the day after the revue opened, "Less a review than a warning." A solo effort of Kerr's, *Stardust,* a play about the students at a drama school, was optioned for Broadway by Michael Myerberg, but closed in 1943 after its Baltimore tryout. It is still quite successful in the amateur theatre market, however.

While in Scranton, Pennsylvania, in 1941, witnessing a production of *Romeo and Juliet,* Kerr met the show's stage manager, Jean Collins, a nineteen-year-old undergraduate at Scranton's Marywood College. Subsequently after studying at Catholic University for three summers and graduating from Marywood, she was married to Kerr on August 16, 1943.

In 1944 the husband and wife team adapted Franz Werfel's *Song of Bernadette,* for the amateur market. Victor Payne-Jennings and Frank McCoy, producers, presented it at the Belasco Theatre in New York on March 27, 1946. Although Howard Barnes wrote in the New York *Herald Tribune,* March 28, 1946 that "it has moments of rare exaltation," the

Warman, N.Y. Herald Tribune
WALTER F. KERR

play received generally adverse notices and closed after three performances.

Kerr then wrote *Sing Out, Sweet Land,* "a musical biography of American song," which was produced at Catholic University May 24 to June 4, 1944; in December it was offered by the Theatre Guild starring Alfred Drake and partly staged by the author. Robert Coleman (New York *Mirror,* December 28, 1944) commented "Walter Kerr's salute to American folk and popular music . . . [scored] a big hit with the first nighters. . . .Kerr has assembled once well-known but today little-known . . . folk music of the country and turned it into a cavalcade of America." Although it received four "rave" notices from the critics it ran in New York for only four months, for 101 performances; its subsequent road tour was successful.

The Kerrs wrote the sketches and lyrics, and Jay Gorney the music, for a revue presented at the university under the title, *Thank You, Just Looking.* George Abbott, producer-director of many Broadway comedy hits, sponsored its New York arrival at the Broadhurst Theatre, on October 13, 1949, after a Philadelphia tryout, under a new name, *Touch and Go.* It was hailed by Brooks Atkinson as "the most enjoyable new show of this season. Apart from being funny, it is intelligent—in an inoffensive way, of course. The Kerrs have a point of view. . . .Mr. Kerr's light touch in the director's stand is exactly right" (New York *Times,* October 30, 1949). A press agent for the show was quoted as saying that it made sport of "many of the current lunacies and hysterias, the vapors of Hollywood bigwigs, the profound trend in modern musical shows, the literary bent of our men in arms and the violently realistic school of direction" (New York *Times,* October 13, 1949). The revue received generally favorable notices and played to full houses until the pre-Christmas slump. It closed

KERR, WALTER F.—*Continued*

on March 18, 1950 after a five month run, and later in the same year ran for six months in London.

At the end of the spring semester, 1949, Kerr took a leave of absence from Catholic University, where he had become associate professor, and with his wife, moved to New York. The New York *Daily News* said that "Catholic University has been cited by *Time* as harboring 'the finest non-professional theatre in the country' (which) is chiefly due to the enthusiasm of the Kerrs."

Kerr became drama critic for *Commonweal*, a weekly Catholic magazine, and it was soon obvious that a new critical power had arrived in New York. In his articles he discussed the Broadway offerings in the dynamic manner of a popular lecturer and with the authority of a scholar. He reiterated his conviction that great theatre is popular theatre, that the purpose of art is to entertain and that art and overt didactic messages do not mix. He exhibited an authoritative knowledge of play structure and of directing.

When Howard Barnes resigned as drama critic for the New York *Herald Tribune* in October 1951, Kerr was offered the position on a temporary basis and in December his appointment became permanent. Kerr has written articles concerning films for *Theatre Arts* and *Harper's Bazaar*. While still at Catholic University several articles by Kerr in the New York *Times* had attracted national attention. In one, he pointed out that the critic, the whipping-post of disgruntled playwrights and producers, had gained his power to close a play or call a hit from the audience themselves, so often disappointed in the past by shoddy attractions billed as masterpieces. "In looking at Shakespeare's theatre we must not make the mistake of concentrating on the absence of critics. We must concentrate on what was present, whatever was in the theatre itself that drew audiences to it, and made critics unnecessary" (November 7, 1948).

In another article, on the tributary theatres, (July 6, 1947) Kerr indicated that it was Broadway which took the gamble on new plays whereas the tributary theatres, which accuse Broadway of commercialism and lack of artistic integrity, present only the tried-and-true shows. If the tributary theatres had a special function, he asserted, it was to present classics and to build up sound repertory experience and acting and to develop audience taste. In "Theatre in the Red" (August 12, 1951), he stated that there was nothing wrong with Broadway costs and production that a good play could not cure every time. "The only thing that really matters to the health of an entertainment enterprise is whether or not audiences like what is presented to them."

He has finished part of a book dealing with the best stage techniques for great plays, but has interrupted the writing of this to complete a book for would-be playwrights, *Don't Write That Play!*, which Simon and Schuster plan to publish. His wife is contributing several revue sketches for John Murray Anderson's pro-jected *Almanac* (*Variety*, July 1, 1953). She is now the mother of four sons, Christopher, Colin and John, who are twins, and Gilbert Alan. She continues to be an avid theatre-goer and is present with her husband at all play-openings.

During the last year Kerr has spoken over twenty-five times at women's clubs and universities. He is five feet eight inches tall, weighs 170 pounds, has gray eyes and brown hair. He speaks rapidly and with great assurance. He is a Roman Catholic and a Democrat and is a member of the National Theatre Conference and of the American Educational Theatre Association. His hobby remains silent movies, on which subject he stands prepared to discourse with any foe or adherent for any length of time.

References

> N Y Sunday N p30 D 4 '49
> N Y Times II p1, N 6 '49

KESTNBAUM, MEYER Oct. 31, 1896- Organization official; business executive

Address: c/o Committee for Economic Development, 444 Madison Ave., New York 22; h. 1218 Madison Park, Chicago 6, Ill.

On January 11, 1953, Meyer Kestnbaum was elected the fourth chairman of the Committee for Economic Development, a private non-profit economic research and education organization, incorporated in 1942. Succeeding Marion B. Folsom, present Under Secretary of the United States Treasury, Kestnbaum is completing the unexpired two-year term of his predecessor, dating from May, 1952. No newcomer to leadership of CED, Kestnbaum was previously vice-chairman of the board of trustees, chairman of its research and policy committee and since 1948 a member of its research group. He is president of Hart Schaffner & Marx, men's clothing manufacturers in Chicago, a position he has held since 1941, having previously served in other executive capacities.

Meyer Kestnbaum was born in New York City on October 31, 1896, the son of Benjamin and Julia (Weintraub) Kestnbaum. After completing secondary school, he entered Harvard College which awarded him a B.S. degree in 1918. He served during 1918-19 as a lieutenant in the 111th Infantry Division of the AEF. After the war he began graduate studies at Harvard University and in 1921 received the M.B.A. degree from the Harvard Graduate School of Business Administration.

Kestnbaum began his business career in the labor relations department of Hart Schaffner & Marx in 1921, serving successively in the credit department, as director, treasurer, vice-president and executive vice-president (1940) before his election as president in 1941.

Kestnbaum predicted in 1941 that increased emphasis on perfecting nylon substitutes would result in the permanent loss of a large part of the silk market by the Japanese. He pointed out that the enforcement of the Wool Labeling Act "had the effect of deterring the use of wool substitutes in clothing lines" (New York *Times*,

August 25, 1941). In spite of Government buying, he indicated that wool inventories of clothing manufacturers in 1941 were fairly adequate, because the "British were pushing wool exports to the fullest possible extent."

On February 18, 1941, as quoted by the New York *Times,* Kestnbaum spoke in favor of the $175 million appropriation approved by the late President Roosevelt for an "off-season" buying program by the Army. He stated it helped clothing manufacturers by relieving the "lag in mill deliveries." The following month, he attributed the need for an advancement of from "$2.50 to $5.00 at retail" of men's clothing to a 10 per cent wage-increase agreement reached by the Amalgamated Clothing Workers of America (New York *Times,* March 3, 1941). In May he described as a fallacy the fear that the draft would greatly reduce the sales of younger men's clothing. "While the number of men in uniform was steadily increasing," he declared, "the improvement in employment and earnings of men already employed offset the loss of this portion of the market" (New York *Times,* May 24, 1941).

He served in World War II as arbitrator and public panel member for the National War Labor Board and for the Regional Board and was also an adviser to the Office of the Quartermaster General of the United States. On February 6, 1943, he stated that "if the worst comes, Americans will have enough wool garments to remain comfortable and healthy, and there is no indication that rationing of clothing will have to take place" (New York *Times*). He said that American consumers were at "a very high standard" with respect to clothing when the war started.

He was elected to membership on the board of trustees of the Committee for Economic Development in 1948, an organization made up of 150 leading businessmen and educators. Supported by voluntary contributions from business, industry and foundations, the Committee endeavors "to get the facts on broad problems of national economic policy . . . to study them . . . and to make recommendations directed toward benefiting the economy as a whole." Kestnbaum became a member of the Committee's principal working group—its research and policy committee. This group studies such national problems as monetary management and the public debt, Government policies on taxation, international economic relations, national security and individual freedom, and small business. The CED supported in 1948 extension of the Reciprocal Trade Agreements Act, and cooperated with New York University workshop on teaching economics in secondary schools.

At a National Conference on Social Work, held June 12, 1949, Kestnbaum criticized social workers for their "tendency to intellectualize and over-verbalize problems" and "to overemphasize the planning function." He affirmed that "planning is useful, but is a means to an end, not an end in itself" (New York *Times,* June 16, 1949). In 1949, the CED condemned the "undue secrecy" in the Government's security program, and urged that the National Security Council be the principal agency for

MEYER KESTNBAUM

formulating and reviewing security policies (New York *Times,* December 15, 1949).

Kestnbaum was elected chairman of the research and policy committee of the CED in 1950 which on May 19 approved a "broadening and deepening" of its research and educational program (New York *Times*). It also welcomed Dwight D. Eisenhower, then president of Columbia University, as a new member.

The State Department named Kestnbaum to the general business committee of the United States Advisory Commission on Information on March 8, 1951 comprising eleven business executives helping the Federal Government carry on its world-wide information program through the *Voice of America* and other projects. Its responsibility was to consider "ways and means whereby American private business . . . can complement and augment the Government's program . . . to win the confidence and understanding of people in other lands" (New York *Times,* March 8, 1951).

Efforts of the CED during 1951, which Kestnbaum shared as a trustee, were of national and international scope. The Committee urged more United States aid to Western Europe in order to increase production and suggested that Great Britain and the Commonwealth nations set $1 billion credit with the European Payments Union (E.P.U.). On the domestic front, it recommended bank credit reforms, including an extension of Federal Reserve regulatory powers, and affirmed that controls needed to be supported by a reduction in bank credit and Government spending.

Kestnbaum was elected vice-chairman of the board of trustees of the CED on May 20, 1952. The following month, the Committee recommended an extension of price-wage controls only until December 31, 1952, and a clause providing for a "90-day freeze of prices and wages in sudden inflation" (New York *Times,* June 4, 1952). Earlier in 1952, it had urged a sales

KESTNBAUM, MEYER—*Continued*

tax, if necessary, on items "other than food, housing, and those already taxed" (New York *Times*, April 22, 1952). In November 1952 CED set up at Brown University one of its several college-community economic research projects, with the aid of faculty and local business leaders. From Ford Foundation it received a grant for ten new college-community research centers.

In October 1952, Kestnbaum was present at Milan at the establishment by European business leaders of the Committee for European Economic and Social Progress, modelled upon and inspired by the Committee for Economic Development in the United States. Not affiliated with or sponsored by the United States group, however, it regarded this Committee "a formulator of progressive and liberal business viewpoints on public problems" (New York *Times*, November 1, 1952).

Kestnbaum was elected chairman of the CED on January 11, 1953 and he led a group of members from the Committee who met with President-elect Eisenhower and presented him with "a favorable report on the immediate economic future" (New York *Times*, January 15, 1953). On March 1, 1953, the CED stated in a report that "continued financial aid to Great Britain was the alternative to collapse of the Anglo-American alliance, and diplomatic and economic isolation for the United States" (New York *Times*). It pointed out that "continuing aid on the present basis would be self-defeating" and recommended a "new approach," based on greater productivity in British export industries, with more effort to penetrate world markets. The Committee also recommended that the United States liberalize trade policies and enlarge its share of the rearmament costs of the North Atlantic Treaty Organization.

Commenting on Kestnbaum's appointment *Business Week* wrote (January 24, 1953) "The continuity of management by CED by the businessmen who belong to it is a big reason why CED has risen to high esteem and influence in national policy making since 1942 . . . there's a marked similarity between CED and the new Administration: both represent the views of a particular type of forward-looking businessman, a sort of progressive conservatism." The new chairman of CED believes that "business can thrive only in a healthy economy."

In 1949, Kestnbaum was awarded an honorary degree of Doctor of Laws by Ripon College in Wisconsin. For his war injuries he received the Purple Heart. He is a director of the Chicago and North Western Railway Company, of the Community Fund of Metropolitan Chicago, and of the Council on Foreign Relations, of which he is past president. He has also been a director and president of the Community Fund, of International House, and Council of Social Agencies all of Chicago as well as a trustee of La Rabida Sanitarium. Other organization memberships include the Harvard Alumni Association (vice-president), and Chicago Symphony Orchestral Association. His clubs comprise the Harvard (past president), Tavern, Mid-day, Cliff Dwellers, Literary, and Gaxton, of Chicago, the Lake Shore Country Club of

Glencoe, and the Grolier Club of New York. The business executive is of Jewish faith, and a Republican. His hobby is book-collecting.

On June 2, 1925, Meyer Kestnbaum married Gertrude Dana. Their children are Ruth Louise and Robert Dana.

References

> N Y Herald Tribune p22 Ja 12 '53
> N Y Times p27 Ja 1 '41
> Who's Who in America, 1952-53
> Who's Who in Commerce and Industry (1951)
> Who's Who in the Midwest (1952)

KIEWIET, CORNELIS W(ILLIEM) DE
See de Kiewiet, C. W.

KING, SAMUEL WILDER Dec. 17, 1886-
Governor of Hawaii
Address: b. Iolani Palace, P.O. Box 2840, Zone 3, Honolulu, Hawaii; h. Washington Pl., Zone 13, Honolulu, Hawaii.

A leader in Hawaii's fight for statehood for almost thirty years, Samuel Wilder King is the first Republican Governor of the Territory in twenty years, and its first of part-Hawaiian ancestry. His nomination by President Dwight D. Eisenhower on February 16, 1953, on recommendation of the late Senator Robert A. Taft, was approved unanimously by the Senate Interior Committee on February 19.

King was named a member, and later chairman, of the Hawaii Statehood Commission when it was formed in 1947, and was president of the Constitutional Convention in 1950 which drafted the document for presentation to the United States Congress that year.

From 1934 to 1942 King served four successive terms as a delegate to the United States Congress, and has never been defeated at the polls. He has been a member of the Hawaiian delegation to all Republican Conventions in the United States since 1936, except at the one held in 1944, at which time he was in the Navy. He was chairman of the 1940 and 1952 delegations. A former Navy officer, he retired from active service with the rank of captain after serving in both World Wars.

Samuel Wilder King was born in Honolulu, December 17, 1886. His father was Captain James A. King, who went to Hawaii in the 1860's, pioneered in the inter-island shipping industry, and from 1893 to 1898 was Minister of the Interior in the period when Hawaii was an independent republic. His mother, Charlotte Holmes (Davis) King, was the great-granddaughter of Oliver Holmes, who went to Honolulu in 1793 from Plymouth, Massachusetts, married Mahi, the daughter of a high chief of the island of Oahu, and served as Governor of that island under King Kamehameha I.

Samuel King attended Honolulu High School (now McKinley High School), graduating in 1905. He was appointed in that year to the United States Naval Academy by Delegate Jonah Kuhio Kalanianaole, and was graduated in 1910.

In the United States Navy Sam King first served as a junior watch officer for two years with the Pacific Fleet, then from 1912 to 1916 with the Asiatic fleet as watch officer, executive officer, and commanding officer of gunboats on the Yangtze River Patrol. During World War I, he was a department head on the *USS St. Louis,* on escort duty in the North Atlantic, convoying troops and cargoes to France and England. At the end of the war he was in command of an armed yacht, the *USS Harvard,* in European waters, and during the armistice negotiations he commanded the *USS Aphrodite,* near British and German shores.

After the war King returned to the Fourteenth Naval District, Pearl Harbor, as intelligence and morale officer. During 1923 and 1924 he was in command of the expedition conducted by the Navy to explore the islands in the South Seas northwest of Hawaii from Hihoa to Midway, to Wake Island, and the islands southwest from Palmyra to Jarvis. He resigned his regular Navy commission in 1924, with the rank of lieutenant commander. In the following year, when the United States Fleet made its first visit to Hawaii, King was executive secretary of the Territorial Entertainment Committee.

One of King's chief interests has been statehood for Hawaii. He entered politics at the precinct club level when he returned from World War I and, in addition to his real estate and insurance business, was an active worker for the Republican Party. He was named to the Territorial Tax Commission which reorganized the tax system and established the taxation maps bureau to simplify identification of real property. In April 1932 he filled a vacancy on the Board of Supervisors of the City-County of Honolulu and in 1932 was elected for the next two-year term, being one of two Republican members to survive the Democratic landslide in that election.

He was named in 1933 one of the three Home Rule Commissioners who were sent to Washington to oppose the proposed Rankin Bill, which would have removed residential requirements for appointment of the Territorial Governor and other officials. The Commission's work was successful, and the bill was withdrawn from consideration.

In the Republican party up to this time King had served as chairman of the Republican Territorial Central Committee, and on several occasions as chairman of convention resolutions and platform committees. In 1934, he ran for delegate to the United States Congress against the Democratic incumbent, and won the election. He was re-elected in 1936, 1938, and 1940.

In the primary election for delegate to Congress in 1942 he received three and one-half votes to one for his Democratic opponent, but decided to withdraw from the campaign and serve in the war.

Re-entering the Navy in his former rank of lieutenant commander, he served on the staff of the Commanding General, Samoan Defense Area, and participated in the attack on Eni-

SAMUEL WILDER KING

wetok Atoll where he remained for a period as Port Director; later he was in command of the Port Director's unit in the attack on Saipan, and remained there to become Commander of the Naval Base under Major General Jarman, the Island Commander.

For his services at Saipan he was awarded the Legion of Merit and promoted from commander to captain in the Naval Reserve. He remained on active duty voluntarily as Port Director of Wakanoura, Japan, the port of debarkation of the United States Sixth Army, until December 1945, when he returned to Honolulu.

Soon after his return to civilian life, King was made a member of the Governor's Emergency Housing Committee and again led the campaign for Hawaii's admission to the Union. At the Constitutional Convention in 1950, which King considered to be the most important political event in Hawaii's history, he was elected president unanimously, and the Constitution was drafted under his leadership. The Majority Report of the Senate Committee on Interior and Insular affairs read: "The Committee feels that this Constitution speaks for itself . . . as an example of the political maturity of the people of Hawaii."

After the Constitution had been ratified by the people of Hawaii, the fight for passage of the enabling act by Congress began. The Eisenhower Administration gave priority on the legislative calendar to the bill for Hawaiian statehood. The proposed legislation was passed by the House of Representatives 274 to 138 in March 1953, but in May the Senate Interior Committee voted to include statehood for Alaska in the same bill, and ordered hearings on statehood for both territories.

Since Alaska usually votes Democratic, the move was regarded as a setback for approval of Hawaiian statehood this year. On June 2 the statehood bill was dropped for the 1953

KING, SAMUEL WILDER—*Continued*
session of Congress. It had generally been felt
that Hawaiian aspirations for statehood were
reaching a climax, and Governor King has
said (*This Week,* March 29, 1953): "If we
don't get it this time, we must seek a different
status."

At the time of his appointment in February,
King was en route to Hawaii from Washington,
where he had been spearheading the campaign
for statehood. The announcement of his nomination was "greeted with relief in political
circles" in the islands, and outgoing Governor
Oren E. Long, a Democrat, said: (New York
Times, February 17, 1953) "In every way the
appointment of Sam King is desirable. He has
had a great career in service to Hawaii and the
nation."

In June 1953 Governor King was awarded
an honorary LL.D. degree by the University
of Hawaii. His membership in the Veterans of
Foreign Wars dates back thirty years, and he
is a charter member of his American Legion
post. He is a member and past president of
the Honolulu Realty Board, the Hawaiian Civic
Club, and the Hawaiian Historical Society, and
also belongs to Alii Chapter of Hui Kamehameha, a Hawaiian fraternal organization. He
attends the Episcopal Church. King married
Pauline Nawahineokalai Evans, a member of
an old part-Hawaiian family, on March 18,
1912. They have two daughters and three sons.

References

Christian Sci Mon p6 Mr 5 '53
N Y Times p15 F 17 '53
This Week p8 Mr 29 '53
Pan-Pacific Who's Who, 1940-41

KNATHS, (OTTO) KARL Oct. 21, 1891-
Artist
Address: 8 Commercial St., Provincetown,
Mass.

Karl Knaths is a modern painter of the
cubist school who achieved high recognition in
American art in the midst of much hostility
toward cubism in painting. While cubist art
is semi-abstract and boldly geometric, Knaths
gives something more than disguised reality to
his canvases, variously described as poetry, harmony of final relationships, and subtlety and
surprise of color.

Knaths, who has lived thirty-four years in
Provincetown, climaxed a long career with two
of the nation's top prizes in painting, awarded
after he was fifty-five years of age. One came
in 1946 when he received the Carnegie Institute's
First Prize with a cash award of $1000. The
other prize was won in the Metropolitan Museum of Art competition, "American Painting
Today" in 1950. Over 6,000 artists competed
for this prize, which was accompanied by a
cash award of $3500.

Otto Karl Knaths was born in Eau Claire,
Wisconsin, October 21, 1891, the son of Otto
Julius Knaths, an immigrant from Leipzig,
Germany, and Maria Theresa (Dietrich), a

descendant of early Wisconsin settlers from
Austria.

Soon after his graduation from Portage High
School in 1910, he was introduced to Dudley
Kraft Watson, director of the Milwaukee Art
Institute, by Zona Gale, a resident of Portage.
He studied at the Milwaukee Art Institute until,
at the suggestion of Watson, he transferred to
the Art Institute of Chicago. He studied there
from 1913 to 1918, working at odd jobs—as
bus boy and as janitor's helper—to support
himself.

Another fortunate acquaintance was Laura
Case Sherry, founder of the Wisconsin Players,
who for five years gave him work painting
scenery for the group.

By 1918 his formal art training was concluded and after a year of painting box cars
and railroad switches, he left the Middle West
and settled in Provincetown. There he met
Agnes Weinrich, a modernist painter who had
studied in Paris, Oliver Chaffee, Ambrose
Webster, Blanche Lazzell and other abstract
painters from the schools of Paris. They gave
young Knaths his first personal insight into the
new modes of painting.

A modest man, Knaths found a haven for
his shy and retiring nature in Provincetown.
He lived poorly, first in a fish house, later in a
Cape Cod hut built mostly by himself of old
lumber and castaway windows and doors. He
also obtained jobs as a carpenter. His house
has now become larger and graceful but it is
still modest.

Knaths rises at five in the morning and paints
until noon. In the afternoon he has hours set
aside for reading, chiefly in philosophy. In
art he reads the works of Klee, Kandinsky and
Mondrian, and is translating Mondrian's *Gestal-
tung* (*The New Creation*).

The history of Knaths as a painter begins in
1919 and his span of painting starts after the
peak of cubism, futurism and expressionism in
the United States, when even disillusionment
had set in and driven many artists back to more
conservative style. His paintings show that the
roots of the artist penetrate deeply into the
painting of the last century in France, and that
he has enriched himself with the experience
and outlook of the storm generated by modern
art, but has retained his individualism. In his
judgment, his work is non-representational, a
statement made by some critics as well.

Many classify Knaths as a cubist, although
the classification at times is obscured by the
subtleties and subdivisions of the bewildering
isms of modern art. Others refer to his work
as cubistic with representational elements. Edward Alden Jewell, the New York *Times* art
critic, said of the winning picture of the 1946
Carnegie Institute award, "While abstract in
feeling and far removed in treatment from
picturesque naturalism, the painting calls into
play, throughout, aspects of the representational," (New York *Times,* Oct. 10, 1946). He
has also been classified as an expressionist. One
writer called him a "cubist, American style"
and Thomas Hess, (*Art News Annual,* 1950)
says, "Today in the hands of a Karl Knaths
. . . cubism still has something vital to say

and is as purely American as the Cajuns of Louisiana."

E. M. Benson writes that he evolved a fresh geometry of forms not without benefit of Picasso, Braque, Klee, Marin, Kandinsky, Arp and Mondrian. Hiss in his book *Abstract Painting*, declares "The space and color of cubism, the evocative calligraphy of Klee, Matisse's swiftly meditative forms and European culture as such are absorbed and metamorphosed in the art of Karl Knaths."

Knaths' exhibitions in New York include showings at the Daniel Gallery in 1930, Downtown Gallery in 1931, Buchholz Gallery in 1942, New York Art Circle in 1944 and 1945 and the Whitney Museum. Beginning with 1946 he has exhibited annually at the Paul Rosenberg Gallery. Outside of New York he exhibited at the Milwaukee Journal's gallery in 1930, the Art Institute of Chicago in 1942, the Baltimore Museum and the Detroit Museum in 1944, and the Buffalo Museum of Fine Arts.

Knaths first exhibited at the Duncan Phillips Memorial Gallery in Washington, D.C., in 1929. Duncan Phillips was first attracted to his works in 1924 and has been his friend and patron for many years. Knaths has exhibited at the Phillips Memorial Gallery on a number of occasions and the Gallery has over forty of his paintings in its permanent collections. He is represented in the Gallery of Living Art, New York University, Philadelphia Museum of Art, Detroit Museum, Art Institute of Chicago, Whitney Museum (New York), Museum of Modern Art (New York), Wustum Museum of Art (Wisconsin), Worcester Museum (Worcester, Massachusetts), Buffalo Museum of Fine Arts. His works are also included in many private collections.

Other awards Knaths has received are the Norman Wait Harris silver medal of the Art Institute of Chicago in 1928 with a cash award of $500, the Art Institute of Chicago's gold medal and the Boston Tercentenary Fine Arts Medal in 1930.

Some three hundred paintings were chosen in the Metropolitan Museum of Art competition of which only seventy were of the advanced or modern school. Knaths' selection as winner of the first prize was all the more striking because the reception for modern art was deemed so uncertain that the competition was boycotted by a group of modern artists who felt that their work would be received with hostility.

Knaths was awarded the honorary degree of Doctor of Fine Arts by the Chicago Art Institute in 1951. He has membership in the Federation of Modern Painters and Sculptors, and the American Abstract Artists.

Each year Knaths emerges from seclusion briefly in February to go to the art galleries in New York and visit friends, and in March to teach a course in pictorial construction at the Phillips Memorial Gallery in Washington, D.C. He also taught at Bennington College, Vermont from 1944 to 1946. On several occasions he has lectured at Yale Summer School, Skowhegan School of Painting and Sculpture (Maine) and the American University in Washington, D.C.

Courtesy, Metropolitan Museum of Art

KARL KNATHS

He has written several articles among which are "Art and the Primary Picture" in the *College Art Journal*, number one (1950) and "Notes and Color" in the *American Abstract Artist*.

Knaths' home is in the west end of Provincetown, near the broad flats stretching to the tip of Cape Cod. He lives there with his wife, Helen Wilhelmina Weinrich, a pianist, whom he married in 1922. The artist, who is politically and religiously unaffiliated, has blue eyes and graying black hair. He is five feet eleven inches in height and weighs 180 pounds.

References

Art N 48:36+ N '49 por
Baltimore Mus N 12:6 Mr '49
Milwaukee J D 6 '50 por
Nation 166:51 Ja 10 '48
Who's Who in America, 1952-53
Who's Who in American Art, 1953
Wight, F. S. Milestones of American Painting in our Century (1949)
World Biography (1948)

KNUTSON, HAROLD Oct. 20, 1880—Aug. 21, 1953 Former Republican Congressman from Minnesota; born in Skien, Norway; brought to United States by parents in 1886; first elected to United States House of Representatives in 1916; voted against declaring war on Germany; became chairman of Immigration and Naturalization Committee in 1924, and opposed relaxing immigration restrictions; became member of House Ways and Means Committee in 1933; was vice-chairman of National Committee to Keep America Out of War (World War II); opposed aid to Allies, but voted for war after Pearl Harbor; became chairman of House Ways and Means Committee in 1946; led fight for income tax reduction voted by Eightieth Congress; New Deal critic. See *Current Biography*, 1947.

Obituary

N Y Times p15 Ag 22 '53

KOCH, FRED(ERICK HENRY) JR.
(kŏch) Sept. 15, 1911- University professor
Address: b. c/o Ring Theatre, University of
Miami, Coral Gables, Fla.

When the trustees of the University of Miami
of Coral Gables, Florida, decided to establish a
department of drama in 1939, they selected
Fred Koch, Jr. as its chairman. Koch brought
the attention of the theatre world to the new
department, for through his efforts and encouragement the university built a $125,000
structure which has been called "America's
Most Flexible Theatre."

Known in the southeastern United States and
neighboring Latin American Republics for opening new and exciting horizons in live theatre,
"The Ring" attracts New York drama critics,
students from numerous colleges and as many
as 40,000 visitors annually from all over the
United States, Havana, Caracas, Mexico City,

Ray Fisher

FRED KOCH, JR.

Rio de Janeiro, and elsewhere. Its unique construction followed Professor Koch's basic plans
in theatrical design. It was the first theatre in
America built for any type of staging, namely,
arena, horseshoe, proscenium, Elizabethan, and
Greek.

Fred Koch has developed a university department which includes classroom instruction,
workshop, and stage productions, and has provided Miami with its only permanent legitimate
theatre and one which serves as a community
center as well. Since "The Ring" opened it has
welcomed participation in its productions by
qualified residents of the greater Miami area.

Frederick Henry Koch, Jr. was born September 15, 1911 to Frederick Henry and Jean
(Hanigan) Koch in Grand Forks, North Dakota. He was inspired in his theatrical interests by his father who was the founder and
director of the Carolina Playmakers at the Uni-

versity of North Carolina in Chapel Hill where
he was professor of dramatic art. He had also
held a similar position at the University of
North Dakota.

Fred Koch, Jr. attended high school in Chapel
Hill, graduating in 1929. Entering the University of North Carolina, he majored in drama
and sociology, a combination which was later
helpful in creating his own characters on the
stage and in his dramatic writings. He won a
Rockefeller Scholarship, was elected to Phi
Beta Kappa and was president of its chapter
at his college. The youth joined Sigma Chi
fraternity, played in a dance orchestra, published two original one-act plays, and was
active in the Carolina Playmakers.

After graduation in 1933, Fred began his
career as a social case worker and statistician
for the Tennessee Valley Authority in the Great
Smoky Mountains of western North Carolina,
a position he left in 1935 to enter the theatrical
field by way of a dental health propaganda
puppet show which he took on the road through
the New England States, North Carolina and
as far south as Louisiana.

By 1937 Fred had developed his own puppet
show. He had married Edna Bryant who had
done play directing and together they toured the
country with "Koch Puppets." They wrote
their own shows, made their puppets to represent animals and demonstrated their construction as a feature of the entertainment. He interrupted the puppet tours in 1938 to return to
the University of North Carolina to work for
the M.A. degree in dramatic arts. His thesis,
a full length play, was entitled *Smoky Mountain Road*. It won top rating for comedy at the
Dock Street Theatre contest and had three
productions at the University of North Carolina, the University of Virginia, and the University of Miami.

Professor Koch began teaching drama in the
summer school of the University of Virginia,
at Charlottesville. He directed summer theatre
there, too, for two seasons, 1939 and 1940. During 1940, he also taught a summer session at
the University of North Carolina. In the fall
of 1939 he was invited to join the faculty of
the University of Miami. Equipped with young
enthusiasm, a scholarly background, experience,
and fresh ideas, he began to build a drama department and a theatre.

"The Ring" was organized in 1946 and held in
the rotund tower of the north campus of the
University of Miami, the old turreted, three-
story hotel which had originally housed the
university classrooms after the hurricane of
1926 had destroyed other buildings on the campus. This area is still in use today. Its tower
offered a circular space for theatre-in-the-round
productions. Calling it "The Ring," Koch later
moved the productions to a mammoth circular
tent on the main campus.

By 1950 sufficient funds had been raised to
begin work on the $125,000 permanent structure
in which architects Robert M. Little and Marion
I. Manley incorporated such features as a revolving stage and moveable riser units (key to
the theatre's flexibility) which seat 400 people.
Eight pie-shaped and four rectangular sections
can be jacked up and rolled into any desired

pattern within the wide area of the circular auditorium which is entirely free of interior posts.

The audience is never more than eight rows from the stage, creating an intimacy bordering on apparent audience participation. This was the first theatre the architects had ever designed but, under Professor Koch's supervision, they adapted its construction to the requirements of a flexible theatre, to lighting its multi-stages, and to the semi-tropical climate of Miami. The entire theatre is enclosed in adjustable screened aluminum jalousies to provide maximum ventilation and to direct the steady Florida breezes inside so that no artificial air-conditioning is required.

The first production in "The Ring" was in February 1951 with a performance of Mary Coyle Chase's play, *Harvey*. Since then, each year, besides its regular repertoire, the University of Miami pays tribute to "the greatest flexible playwright" with a Shakespeare Festival. For the Festival, Fred Koch enlists the cooperation of nearly every department of the university.

The extensive program includes concerts of Elizabethan music and dances, a Shakespeare conference attended by scholars of other universities and colleges, television and radio appearances by distinguished New York drama critics and literary celebrities, theatre exhibits, symposiums, and the dramas themselves staged with meticulous detail. Sam Hirsch, Koch's assistant director and business manager, directs the Shakesperean plays on a stage which is a reproduction of the famous Globe theatre of Elizabethan London. He also has experimented with a successful in-the-round presentation of *Hamlet*.

There are five instructors on the staff of the drama department, including Koch. Over 100 students at the university are drama majors, and as many as 600 participate in some capacity in the performance during a school year. They make use not only of "The Ring" but also of "The Box," the university's theatre with its conventional proscenium stage. More than 40,000 persons attend the two theatres in a single season.

Koch is especially proud of the productions of twelve one-act plays which are written, produced, directed and acted entirely by students each year. Some of his students are members of Equity, a status they achieve by working in summer stock. Several graduates of his department are doing well in Hollywood. Koch's "troupers" played in Havana, Cuba under the auspices of the *Patronata del Teatre*, presenting Moss Hart's play, *Light Up the Sky*, in English before houses packed with Spanish-speaking audiences.

Although there are numerous well known and lesser known theatres-in-the-round in the United States, they all differ from "The Ring" in that none has its flexibility. "The Ring" has won architectural prizes, being cited for its "clean, clear, well-proportioned [design]; it is both a handsome structure and functionally expressive of its architectural intention." The University of Miami and Professor Koch take pride in the fact that "The Ring" attracted, in April 1953, the First National Arena Theatre Conference. Fourteen such theatres were represented, four of them by women directors, and the activities of the conference went on for a full week. These included lectures, round-table discussions, demonstrations, and stage productions. A second conference is scheduled for 1954 in Miami.

Fred and Edna Koch have three young sons, Ricky, Tommy, and Christopher. The professor's hobbies are swimming, hiking, camping, playing chess, and home carpentry. He uses an exquisite Balanese puppet as a wall decoration.

His memberships include Iron Arrow, Rotary, National Theatre Conference, Florida Speech Teachers, Southeastern Theatre Conference, American Educational Theatre Association, and American National Theatre and Academy.

References

N Y Times My 6 '51
Theatre Arts 35:47 My '51

KOHLER, WALTER J(ODOK), JR., Apr. 4, 1904- Governor of Wisconsin; manufacturer

Address: b. State Capitol, Madison 2, Wis.; c/o Vollrath Co., 1236 N. 18th St., Sheboygan, Wis.; h. Windway, Kohler, Wis.

Two years after he had entered politics as a delegate-at-large to the 1948 Republican National Convention, Walter J. Kohler, Jr., in November 1950, was elected to a two-year term as Governor of Wisconsin, to which office he won re-election in November 1952. Since 1949 he has been chairman of the Wisconsin Committee on the reorganization of the Federal Government. From 1925 until 1947 he was associated in various capacities with the Kohler Company, a plumbing appliances plant in Kohler, Wisconsin, and since 1947 has been president of another manufacturing firm, the Vollrath Company in Sheboygan, Wisconsin. During World War II he saw twenty-seven months' sea duty in the southern and western Pacific in the United States Navy, chiefly as an intelligence officer.

Walter Jodok Kohler, Jr., was born April 4, 1904, in Sheboygan, Wisconsin, the second of the four sons of Walter Jodok and Charlotte Henrietta (Schroeder) Kohler. (His brothers are named John Michael, Carl James, and Robert Eugene Kohler.) The Kohler family has been prominent in Wisconsin industry and politics since the early part of the century. As reported by Alfred Steinberg in *Collier's* (November 24, 1951), Kohler's great-grandfather "in a huff when the government would not let him dam a river to erect a mill. Grandfather John Kohler deserted Chicago right after the great fire" and settled in Sheboygan, where he became a leader in local manufacturing and politics. In Kohler, Wisconsin, a town named after this family, John Kohler in 1873 founded the Kohler Company, manufacturer of plumbing equipment and appliances. Walter J. Koh-

Rogers Crocker Studio

WALTER J. KOHLER, JR.

ler, the present Governor's father, was a Presidential elector in 1916, Governor of Wisconsin in 1929 and 1930, and president of the board of regents of the University of Wisconsin. Young Kohler received his elementary education in the public schools of Sheboygan, afterward, in 1917, entering Phillips Academy at Andover, Massachusetts. Upon completing college preparatory training in 1921, he enrolled at Yale University, majored in political science, history, and English, and graduated with the degree of Ph.B. in 1925.

From the age of fourteen Kohler had spent his summer vacations working in the Kohler Company factory, each summer in a different part of the plant. After graduation from college he began employment there on a full-time basis: from 1925 until 1927 he was engaged in engineering and standardizing and for the next three years was occupied with research in ceramics. When his father was elected Governor of Wisconsin in 1929 (Steinberg related), "Walter was shipped East to the Trenton, New Jersey, plant for a year and then to the Philadelphia office of the company." Promoted in 1930 into selling and advertising work, he continued in various phases of sales operations until 1941, meanwhile becoming a director of the company in 1936 and secretary in 1937. In 1940 he was made a director of the Vollrath Company of Sheboygan; this firm, which manufactures stainless steel equipment for restaurants and hospitals, was founded by his great-grandfather.

The day after the Japanese attack on Pearl Harbor Kohler volunteered for service in the armed forces, was commissioned a lieutenant in the United States Naval Reserve in April 1942, and was called to active duty in August of that year. In January 1943 he sailed for overseas duty in the Pacific, to serve on the staff of the Commander, Air Force, Pacific.

As Air Combat Intelligence Officer at the Tulagi Naval seaplane base in the Solomon Islands, beginning in April 1943 he participated in many flights to rescue American pilots and plane crews shot down behind enemy lines. After several months (from October 1943 to January 1944) in the post of officer-in-charge of a joint Army-Navy Technical Air Intelligence Unit based at Munda in the Central Solomons, he was assigned to the aircraft carrier U.S.S. *Hancock* as Air Combat Intelligence Officer. In this capacity he served with the celebrated Fast Carrier Task Force under Admirals Halsey and Mitscher in operations against the Japanese in the Leyte, Mindoro, and Luzon invasions, the Battle for Leyte Gulf, raids against the coast of French Indo-China and the China Coast, support of landing operations at Iwo Jima and Okinawa, and in many carrier raids against Tokyo and other targets in the Japanese home islands. "Five times kamikaze planes exploded in the *Hancock*" (in Steinberg's words), "but each time Kohler escaped unharmed. It was after the costliest explosion that Kohler made up his mind to go into politics, if he got out alive. 'I decided then,' he says, 'that if I got back safely, I had a big debt to pay—especially since America had been better to me than to most.'" He was promoted to lieutenant commander in October 1944 and discharged from active duty a year later. Among other military decorations he is entitled to wear the Asiatic Theater ribbon with five battle stars, the Philippine Liberation ribbon with two battle stars, and the Bronze Star Medal with combat insignia "for distinguishing himself by meritorious achievement in connection with operations against the enemy."

On his return to civilian life, Kohler resumed his position with the Kohler Company, but he gave up active interest in the firm in April 1947 to accept the presidency of the Vollrath Company, of which he had maintained his directorship and in which he purchased a minority interest. His entry into active politics was made in 1948, when he was elected a delegate-at-large to the Republican National Convention at Philadelphia, receiving the largest number of votes of any delegate, and subsequently became chairman of the Wisconsin delegation. In 1949 he was named chairman of the Wisconsin Citizens Committee on the Hoover Commission Findings, a non-partisan group formed to promote adoption of the Federal reorganization recommendations. Nominated for the Governorship in 1950 to succeed Governor Oscar Rennebohm, Republican, he concentrated his efforts on winning the independent vote, and was elected in the following November by a substantial majority vote over the Democratic candidate, Carl W. Thompson. In the first year of his term he worked successfully for the passage of measures providing for higher salaries for State employees, an extensive dairy-cattle disease-eradication program, better care for the aged and mentally ill, and the transfer of corporation dividends to a higher tax bracket.

During the course of a three-week tour of Western Europe, in which he made his own appraisal of the North Atlantic Treaty Organization, Kohler in September 1951 had what he described as a "frank" forty-five minute conversation with General Dwight D. Eisenhower. At the forty-third annual Governors Conference, held at Gatlinburg, Tennessee, later that month, Kohler announced his support of Eisenhower as the Republican Presidential nominee. At the same time he indicated that he might run against Senator Joseph R. McCarthy in the Wisconsin Republican primary election in September 1952, but that he would take three or four months to decide. The possibility that the Governor might oppose McCarthy in the race for the United States Senate provoked considerable speculation both locally and nationally. The prevailing opinion in Wisconsin, according to a survey made by Luther Huston, was that only Kohler stood a chance of winning McCarthy's Senate seat away from him. "Governor Kohler is popular," Huston wrote in the New York *Times*, "and is credited with a good record as Governor. His administration has reduced the State income tax." On January 30, 1952, Kohler announced that he would not run against McCarthy, but would seek renomination as Governor because he wanted to follow through on his State program and present new measures to the Legislature. By a vote of 988,739 to 588,601 Kohler defeated his Democratic opponent, William Proxmire, in the election of November 4, 1952.

As a member of a committee appointed by the Governors' Conference in October 1951, Kohler appeared before Congressional committees the following March to propose an investigation of the relationships between Federal, State, and local governments with a view toward recommending a possible realignment of governmental functions and revenue sources. The Wisconsin Governor, who in 1947 and 1950 was State campaign chairman of the American Cancer Society, has since been president of the society's Wisconsin division, a national director of the organization, and a member of its national executive committee; in October 1952, at the close of the annual meeting of the American Cancer Society, he was named chairman of the board. Before and after World War II he had a prominent part in Community Fund and Young Men's Christian Association campaigns in Sheboygan. Kohler belongs to the Elks, Eagles, Veterans of Foreign Wars, American Legion, AMVETS and Military Order of the World Wars. He is also a member of the Yale Club of New York; the University Club of Milwaukee; and the University Club, the Tavern Club, and the Saddle and Cycle Club of Chicago. He has been a director of the Security National Bank of Sheboygan since 1947 and a director of E. J. McAleer and Company of Philadelphia since 1949. Besides the military decorations cited, he was awarded the American Theater ribbon, the Navy Unit Citation ribbon, and the Victory ribbon. In 1951 Beloit College (Wisconsin) conferred an honorary LL.D. degree upon him.

By his marriage to Celeste McVoy on November 14, 1932, Kohler is the father of two children, Terry Jodak and Charlotte Nicolette. The marriage ended in divorce in 1946. On November 8, 1948, Kohler married Charlotte McAleer. The Governor is five feet ten and a half inches tall, weighs 172 pounds, has blue eyes and black, graying hair. Steinberg has described him as "heavy-browed, square-shouldered, handsome . . . an urbane man . . . with a roundish photogenic face . . . an open friendly smile and natural charm." An occasional game of golf has replaced flying, wrestling, and boxing as Kohler's recreation. His faith is the Protestant.

References
Collier's 128:26-7 N 24 '51 por
New Repub 125:15-16 D 3 '51
Washington (D.C.) Post p3B O 14 '51
Who's Who in America, 1952-53
Who's Who in United States Politics (1950)

KOMAROVSKY, MIRRA (Kŏm'är-äv-skê) Feb. 4, 1906- University professor; sociologist *Address*: b. c/o Barnard College, New York 27; h. 340 Riverside Dr., New York 25

Chairman of the department of sociology at Barnard College, Dr. Mirra Komarovsky has studied the sociological framework in which people function both as an observer of her students for twenty-five years, and as a professional sociologist who has written three books and numerous articles. She has made significant contributions to the sociological study of leisure time, unemployment, suburban life, and women's changing attitudes. In her latest book, *Women in the Modern World* (Little, Brown, 1953) she discusses their education and their roles in the home and in the professional world.

Of her contribution toward the furtherance of the technique of research and evaluation of society, Dr. Paul F. Lazarsfeld has written concerning one of her studies, "The two ideas of making repeated interviews and of selecting case studies within a broader statistical framework are . . . valuable research devices which have developed as a result of the intensive concern of the present study" (Introduction to *The Unemployed Man and His Family*).

Born in Russia on February 4, 1906 to Mendel Komarovsky, a banker and writer, and Anna (Steinberg) Komarovsky, Mirra Komarovsky, the elder of two daughters, came to the United States with her family in 1921. Five years after her arrival she obtained her Bachelor of Arts degree at Barnard College and thereupon became a Caroline Duror Fellow. After earning her M.A. degree, she received an assistant professorship at Skidmore College.

Miss Komarovsky worked in the capacity of research assistant at the Institute of Human Relations, Yale University, from 1930 to 1931. She continued these investigations at Columbia University's Council for Research in the Social Sciences from 1931 to 1935 where she held the position of research associate. In 1938 she became an instructor at Barnard College, then assistant professor and finally associate professor of sociology, becoming chairman of the department in 1947. It was during this period

Stone Studio

MIRRA KOMAROVSKY

at Barnard College that Miss Komarovsky obtained the Ph.D. degree.

The sociologist has spent much of her professional life interrogating people in order to discern their ideals, aspirations and attitudes. In 1932, together with several associates, a survey of the use of leisure hours by inhabitants of Westchester County was undertaken by Dr. Komarovsky under a grant of the Council for Research in the Social Sciences of Columbia University, with the assistance of the American Association for Adult Education and the Westchester County Recreation Commission. Resulting from this survey was a book entitled *Leisure, A Suburban Study* (Columbia University Press, 1934) by Mirra Komarovsky, George A. Lundberg and Alice McInerny.

Recognizing the close relation between observation and intuition, the authors point out, "Science can discover the facts that condition realization and furnish instrumentalities for carrying plan and purpose into effect. Science without dreams is sterile. Dreams without research and science are empty."

With this view forming a major assumption under which the work progresses, the authors perceived that the leisure time which we enjoy is becoming more and more disassociated from our job situation and that "specialization is increasing, with the result that work is more and more ministering to less and less of the personality."

They found that ". . . despite the inroads which clubs, sports, commercial amusements . . . and the bridge game have made, the affectional and leisure function of the family remain."

Commenting upon the contribution of this study to the social sciences, Dr. Robert S. Lynd asserted, "From the scientific point of view the book is noteworthy for its contribution to opening up of two largely neglected social science areas: leisure time behavior, and

the habits of the increasingly numerous share of our population who live in the suburbs of . . . metropolitan areas" (New York *Herald Tribune Books,* September 30, 1934).

Another commentator stated, "The idea is admirable and the choice of field was inspired . . . but for the chart, graph, and questionnaire methods of research which are bringing the social sciences nearer to absurdity. . . .Dr. Lundberg and his associates frequently give the impression of using a steam shovel to unearth a gnat or exploding a depth charge to bring up a periwinkle" (*Saturday Review of Literature,* October 20, 1934).

In 1940 Dr. Komarovsky, continuing a project undertaken by the International Institute of Social Research, presented a study of the relation between man's role as breadwinner and his position of authority within the family, *The Unemployed Man and His Family* (Dryden, 1940). This book surveyed the effect of unemployment upon the status of the man in fifty-nine families and was one step toward the fuller development of the interviewing technique. Reports of the various interviewers, while not susceptible of precise quantitative measurement, resulted in a careful analysis of those matters which are often left to common sense. Recognizing that there is a complex interrelationship of the many social factors in the unemployment situation, Miss Komarovsky indicates that the status of the male may have originated in his original role as provider, but habits of respect and deference may continue long after this function has failed. Furthermore, the patterns of authority in the home have an important influence on our political and social beliefs.

In the *American Journal of Sociology,* the reviewer asserted, "This is an important monograph, both substantively and methodologically. The reviewer believes it constitutes a milestone of sound sociological research" (November, 1941).

The *American Sociological Review* stated "The book has considerable interest for sociologists as an exercise in method. The results probably are not worth much as a basis for generalization, but they suggest many problems for further research" (June 1941).

In a speech delivered at the New York Times Hall before the Advertising Women of New York, Inc., on March 19, 1944, Miss Komarovsky indicated the extent to which statements made by college girls on their future plans reflected the confusion of modern society over the status of women. She termed the present-day standards towards women as a "veritable crazy quilt of contradiction." She made clear that the question of whether a young lady should seek marriage or a career, or both, is a personal question. "The right thing to do," she told the group, "is to give these young women freedom to follow the pattern they regard as best for them." She believes that, "it is the girl with a 'middle-of-the-road personality' who is most happily adjusted to the present historical moment. She is not a perfect incarnation of either role (e.g. homemaker or career woman) but is flexible enough to play both" (*American Journal of Sociology,* November, 1946).

Although she is intimately involved in the endeavor to create an improved environment for women, Dr. Komarovsky takes no part in the great debate over which is the stronger of the species, male or female. "I am trying to get away from the endless debate on which sex is inferior," she says, "Social changes have disturbed one type of equilibrium without as yet replacing it with another. Men as well as women are victims of the confusion" (New York *World-Telegram and Sun,* June 15, 1953).

At a meeting sponsored by the National Federation of Business and Professional Women's Clubs, Daughters of the American Revolution, and other clubs, Professor Komarovsky called upon the women to use constructive imagination in order to remove tensions in specific areas of activity. Some methods of accomplishing this objective, she asserted, are the use of social agencies, the education of public opinion and the encouragement of legislation. Mrs. Eleanor Roosevelt also spoke at this memorable meeting commemorating 100 years of progress by American women since Susan B. Anthony in 1848 at Senaca Falls, New York, drew up a "Declaration of Sentiments" to give women new freedoms.

As a member of the panel of speakers on family research at the forty-fourth annual session of the American Sociological Society meeting at Manhattan Center on December 28, 1949, Professor Komarovsky suggested that the more sheltered is the upbringing of the girl as compared to the boy, the greater will be the girl's handicap in marriage. Such protected upbringing, she indicated, creates ties to the parental family, and marriage requires primary loyalty to a family of her own.

In her latest book, *Women in the Modern World,* the author writes that by clarifying the ends of women's education, the obstacles barring the pursuit of the good life can be cleared away. On the question of career training versus education purely for the homemaker, she states, "To disagree with the antifeminist does not necessarily make one a feminist . . . we can reject the antifeminist program without having to embrace the old-fashioned feminism with its militant hostility towards and its disparagement of the homemaker."

Taking the position that colleges should offer a course on marriage and the family, she believes that in the social sciences there is an opportunity to rationalize human problems, thereby increasing the possibility of enjoying good social relations. The responsibility of the colleges is twofold: to enhance family life by greater emphasis on the principles upon which family life are predicated, and to develop the individual woman student's intellectual, artistic and professional potentialities.

The sociologist has written many articles for *Social Forces,* the *American Sociological Review, Harper's Magazine,* the *Journal of Social Hygiene,* and the *American Journal of Sociology.* She is a member of the American Association of University Professors, the American Sociological Society and the Eastern Sociological Society.

Dr. Komarovsky married Marcus A. Heyman, a businessman, in 1940. She has brown hair, brown eyes, and is five feet, five inches in height and weighs 127 pounds. The sociologist's religious faith is the Hebrew.

References

Ind Woman 32:260 Jl '53
Directory of American Scholars (1951)

KONSTANTINU, MRS. ILIAS *See* Clark, E.

KÖPRÜLÜ, (MEHMET) FUAT (kû'prü-lü mā'mĕd foō-ăt') Nov. 22, 1890- Turkish Foreign Minister; educator; author

Address: b. Hariciye Köşkü (Foreign Minister's Residence), Ankara, Turkey; h. Çankaya Caddesi 311, Yeni, Şehir, Ankara, Turkey

The appointment of Fuat Köprülü as Minister of Foreign Affairs in the first Democratic party Government of Turkey in May 1950 came as a result of his active role in the formation of that party in 1946 and his subsequent efforts in its behalf. Before attaining cabinet status he had served for fifteen years as deputy in the Grand National Assembly, Turkey's major legislative-executive body, and had earned an international reputation as Turkey's leading scholar and author.

His first three years as Foreign Minister have been marked by a vigorous continuation of Turkey's pro-Western policy, notably by his country's entry into the North Atlantic Treaty Organization. As Foreign Minister, he recently signed a tripartite Balkan trade agreement and pact of friendship with Greece and Yugoslavia. In a strong plea for "collective security," Köprülü urged that the Middle East "labor with all the means at our disposal for an organization of defense" (New York *Times,* April 24, 1953).

Mehmet Fuat Köprülü was born in Istanbul on November 22, 1890, to Ismail Faiz Bey, chief secretary of the criminal court in the Beyoglu district of that city, and his wife Hatice. His lineage is traced to an Albanian, Mohammed Kuprili (as the name is frequently spelled) who in the mid-seventeenth century became grand vizier to the Sultan Mohammed IV, the first of five members of the Kuprili family to hold that exalted station; they are credited by historians with the temporary revival of the waning Ottoman Empire.

Young Fuat, who was known as Koprulüzâde Mehmed Fuad Bey until the simplified form of nomenclature was adopted throughout Turkey in 1935, attended the Ayasofya School and the Mercen Lycée in Istanbul, was tutored privately, and at the age of seventeen entered the Istanbul Law School. During his three years there (1907-1910) his first writings on Turkish history and literature were published in a collection, *The Intellectual Life* (1909). Deciding upon an academic career, he taught at various *lycées* (college preparatory schools) until in 1913, at the age of twenty-three, he occupied the chair of the history of Turkish literature at the University of Istanbul. He remained on the university's faculty for thirty years, and was

FUAT KÖPRÜLÜ

several times elected dean of the Faculty of Letters.

Köprülü's years at the university were marked by prolific literary activity, including a volume of verse, *Nasreddin Hoca* (1918), *History of Turkey* (1923) and *History of Turkish Literature* (1928). By the time his four-volume work, *Anatolian Folk Poets* (1929-1930), and *Les Origines de l'Empire Ottoman* (in French, 1935) had appeared, Köprülü was already a distinguished scholar. His international prestige is attested by Sir Edward Denison Ross in the *Encyclopaedia Britannica*: "Literary criticism in Turkey is notably represented by Köprülü Zadé Mehmed Fuad Bey . . . an ardent scholar who is engaged in compiling a new history of the Ottoman literature."

In 1924 Köprülü founded the Institute of Turkish Studies, and became Undersecretary to the Minister of Education in the cabinet of the first president of the Turkish Republic, Mustafa Kemal Pasha (Atatürk). Three years later he was chosen president of the Turkish Historical Society. He taught political history at the School of Political Science and was professor of history of civilization at the Academy of Fine Arts. In the period between 1923 and 1934 he attended many international conferences on oriental culture and civilization.

Entering the field of politics in 1935, he was representative from Kars to the Grand National Assembly. At that time, during Atatürk's presidency, the Republican People's party governed the country without opposition; the same conditions prevailed in the early years of the administration of Ismet Inönü, and Köprülü continued to serve as a Republican deputy while holding his professorship at Istanbul and, after 1935, at Ankara. He was a member of the Assembly while Turkey maintained her non-belligerent status until the last months of World War II, and participated in the unanimous declaration of war against Germany and Japan on February 23, 1945.

Later that year a surge toward reform, culminating in the partial breaking up of large landholdings, presaged a re-organization of Turkish internal policy. Although the one-party control, usually designated a dictatorship, appeared incompatible with the trend toward democratization and a degree of private participation in the nation's industrial economy, many who favored reform hoped to achieve it within the framework of the People's Republican party.

Bernard Lewis described in *International Affairs* (July 1951) how Köprülü, "a distinguished scholar and historian and the outstanding figure in the intellectual life of Turkey," pleaded that his nation's participation in the United Nations required internal adjustments "so as effectively to ensure within Turkey those democratic liberties to which the Turkish Government was giving its theoretical approval in the international field." Such views, appearing in the Istanbul newspaper *Vatan,* resulted in the expulsion of Köprülü and Adnan Menderes (now Prime Minister) from the party; they were voluntarily joined by Celâl Bayar (now President of Turkey), and formed the nucleus of an opposition which emerged in January 1946 as the Democratic party.

Although President Inönü did not place formal obstacles in the path of the new party, claims were made that the elections of 1946 were rigged in favor of the People's Republicans. Köprülü who was elected on the Democratic ticket as deputy from Istanbul, was among the most outspoken critics of the election procedures. It had become evident that Turkey had outgrown its one-party system, and the existence of a second party is credited with hastening reforms. The most dramatic of these was the modernization of the electoral laws which permitted a sweeping victory for the Democratic party on May 14, 1950. In this upset Celâl Bayar became Turkey's third president, and among the Democratic stalwarts chosen for the new Cabinet was Fuat Köprülü as Foreign Minister (May 22, 1950).

The foreign policy of the new administration under Köprülü's leadership continued that of his predecessor, Necmeddin Sadak. Turkey's anti-communist, Western orientation was marked by a series of events: Russia's denunciation of her non-aggression treaty with Turkey and her demand for the return of Kars province (1945); American grants of aid under the Marshall Plan (1947); Turkey's active participation in the European Recovery Program, and pacts with Great Britain and Greece (1948) and Italy (March 1950). Five months after Köprülü had taken office Turkey was elected to succeed Egypt as the 1951-1952 temporary member of the United Nations Security Council.

Köprülü immediately sought to secure Turkey's role as the easternmost bastion of western democracy by applying for full membership in the North Atlantic Treaty Organization, a bid which he described as "an acid test of United States interest in Turkey." The support given by his political opponent, Sadak, to this campaign proved that in Turkey politics ended at the frontier. Turkey's unhesitating contribution of military forces to the United Nations action in Korea made a favorable impression, and the United States indicated approval of a place for Turkey in NATO as early as May 1951. The opposition began to lessen as Great Britain acceded in July, and in September the Atlantic Pact Council at Ottawa decided unanimously that Turkey should be invited to join the North Atlantic Treaty Organization.

With the attainment of NATO membership, a campaign for the regional security of the Balkans was next on Köprülü's agenda. In May 1951 David Ingber and M. Benjenk had observed in *Fortnightly*: "There is . . . considerable support for a possible 'Balkan Entente' of Ankara-Athens-Belgrade as an adjunct to the Atlantic pact proper. Whether such an alliance will be formed remains to be seen." The Foreign Minister acted with dispatch. Two months after Turkey's NATO debut at Lisbon (February 1952) Premier Menderes and Foreign Minister Köprülü paid a goodwill visit to Athens.

By the year's end C. L. Sulzberger reported in the New York *Times* that the Turks were "working hard" on their Balkan program. Turkish and Greek foreign ministers were meeting in Athens while a Turkish military mission was paying a friendly visit to Belgrade. In January 1953, in anticipation of Köprülü's arrival in Belgrade, Yugoslavia announced its acceptance of the idea of a formal pact, a decision which, according to Jack Raymond of the New York *Times*, "came as a result of urging by Greece and Turkey, particularly the Turks." Finally the tripartite treaty was initialed in Athens on February 25, a Turkish-Yugoslav trade agreement was signed at Ankara the following day, and on February 28 at the Crystal Palace in Ankara, Greece's Stephanopoulos, Yugoslavia's Popovic, and Turkey's Köprülü signed a five-year treaty of friendship and collaboration; and Köprülü hinted at future policy by telling a reporter that the door was open for Italy.

Fuat Köprülü appears to be equally at home in an academic or a diplomatic environment. According to *World Today* (July 1950), he "has widespread prestige, but is popular mainly amongst intellectuals." His astuteness is demonstrated by his answer when Charles Foltz, Jr., an editor of *U.S. News & World Report* asked him, "In Cyprus some of the Turks are worried that the island might be transferred from British rule to Greece. What is Turkey's position on that question?" Köprülü replied: "At a time when Turkey and Greece are entering NATO together, and when all the countries of this region ought to be collaborating in the defense of the Middle East, such questions are not, and should not be, raised."

The Foreign Minister is of medium height, slender, with dark hair and mustache. He married Ayse Behice in 1928; they have two children, a daughter, Beyhan, and a son, Orhan, who is an assistant at the University of Istan-

bul. Köprülü's academic honors include honorary degrees from the universities of Heidelberg, Athens, and Paris, and membership in learned societies in Hungary, Czechoslovakia, and Germany; his honorary membership in the Soviet Academy of Sciences, conferred in 1925, was rescinded in 1948. A bibliography of his writings compiled by Şerif Hulûsi Sayman (Istanbul, 1935) does not include such later publications as his *History of Islamic Civilization* (1940) and *Turkish Folk Poets* (1940-41).

The Foreign Minister in reporting to the Grand National Assembly on December 19, 1951 asserted that his policies are based upon "the preservation of peace and security, respect by all nations for the rights, independence, and territorial integrity of other peoples . . . and a firm, courageous, and prepared attitude towards those of ill-will."

References

Encyclopédie biographique de Turquie (1930-32)
International Who's Who, 1952
World Biography (1948)

KRAFT, OLE BJÖRN (ō'lě byûrn) Dec. 17, 1893- Danish Minister of Foreign Affairs
Address: b. c/o Ministry of Foreign Affairs, Copenhagen, Denmark; h. Vengersgade 28, Copenhagen K., Denmark

In the Danish Coalition Government of the Moderate Liberal party and the Conservative party which was formed in late October 1950, Ole Björn Kraft, long a leader of the Conservatives and a member of the Folketing (lower house of Parliament) since 1926, was appointed Minister of Foreign Affairs. Kraft, a former journalist and editor of Conservative papers, had held the post of Minister of Defense in the Government following Denmark's liberation from Germany in 1945 and before becoming Foreign Minister was prominent in the Council of Europe, meeting in Strasbourg. An exponent of collective security, he is chairman of the Danish delegation to the United Nations General Assembly and president of the North Atlantic Treaty Organization Council.

Kraft was one of the main sponsors of a new Constitution for Denmark, having served on the Constitution Commission in 1937 and on subsequent ones after World War II. On June 5, 1953, King Frederick IX signed the new Constitution, approved by popular referendum. Among the changes it allows women to succeed to the throne, thus making thirteen-year old Princess Margrethe the heir apparent. It also paves the way for more international cooperation.

Ole Björn Kraft was born December 17, 1893, in Copenhagen, Denmark, the son of Alexander Kraft, an official of the Horsens state prison, and Karen Margrethe (Christiansen) Kraft. Of old Jutland ancestry, he is a direct descendant of L. N. Hvidt, a minister in the first Government under Denmark's liberal Constitution of 1849. While attending school in

(Continued next page)

OLE BJÖRN KRAFT

Copenhagen, Ole Kraft is said to have participated eagerly in debates on Denmark's defense.

At the University of Copenhagen, where Kraft matriculated in 1912, he became a candidate for the doctor of philosophy degree in 1913, choosing political science as his major subject. In 1916 in protest against the sale of the Virgin Islands to the United States, he organized a campaign which developed into the Young Denmark Movement, with the motto "God, Nation, People." As one of the leaders, Kraft tried to rally the youth of Denmark on a Christian basis for a stronger defense of the nation. The movement stressed a more active policy in external affairs, greater attention to Greenland and the Faroes, and a domestic program for improved social conditions. Turning to journalism upon leaving the university, Kraft contributed in 1919 to the Conservative newspaper *Aarhuus Stiftstidende* and that same year became editor of a daily paper called *Svendborg Amts Dagblad,* an editorship he held until 1922. He contributed to *De Ferslewske Blade,* a chain of Copenhagen papers in 1922, while also editing the Danish daily, *Dagbladet Faedrelandet* in 1922-23. From 1924 to 1931 he was a member of the editorial staff in Copenhagen of *Aarhuus Stiftstidende.*

A candidate of the Conservative party, Kraft in 1926 was elected from the north Jutland city of Aalborg to the Folketing, the lower house of the Danish Parliament, to which he has since been uninterruptedly re-elected by the same constituency. In 1932 he became a member of the Danish Parliamentary foreign affairs committee, on which he was to continue until 1950. For the next four years, from 1933 to 1937, he served as a member of the Danish delegation to the League of Nations.

He joined the Conservative party Parliamentary group in 1932 and having become a member of the party's executive council in 1935,

Kraft pressed for a modern and active Conservative party, free from dependence on the Moderate Liberal party and from the influence of old Right party, which had stood for privileged electoral law in the constitutional framework. He represented a small group within his party who desired a reform of the Landsting, the upper house of Parliament in the 1930's (Poul Hansen, *Contemporary Danish Politicians,* 1949).

For two years (1940-42) in the early phase of World War II Kraft was a contributor to and editor of the largest Danish newspaper, *Berlingske Tidende.* During the wartime occupation of his country by German forces, he was Parliamentary leader of the Conservative party, advancing from vice-chairman in 1940 to hold the chairmanship until 1945. While working for a breach with the occupying power in Denmark and as a member of a political group having contact with the Resistance Movement, he coedited an underground paper entitled *Danske Tidende.* On December 30, 1943, Kraft, awaiting the arrival of an underground courier, was surprised in his home in Copenhagen and wounded by a German assassin. A second attempt was made on his life by the Germans when they sought underground leaders in the headquarters of the Conservative party.

In the Government set up in Denmark immediately after its liberation from Germany, Kraft filled the post of Minister of Defense from May until November 1945, during which period he planned for the rebuilding of the army, navy, and air forces that the Germans had almost destroyed. A member in 1946 of the Danish delegation to the first meetings of the United Nations General Assembly, in London and New York, he made available to the United Nations the Danish forces that took part in the occupation of Germany, as means of combating possible aggression there. From 1946 to 1950 Kraft was a member of the Defense Commission in Denmark simultaneously serving during the greater part of this period again as chairman of the Conservative party Parliamentary group (1947-50).

Because of his interest in international affairs, he was elected in 1949 one of the vice-presidents of the Council of Europe.

When a Coalition Government of the Moderate Liberal party and the Conservative Peoples party came into power in late October 1950, Kraft was named on October 30 as Minister of Foreign Affairs in the Cabinet of Prime Minister Erik Eriksen. In that year he was also a member of the committee of ministers and the joint committee of the Council of Europe. Meanwhile, Denmark had on April 4, 1949, joined the North Atlantic Treaty Organization, an occasion which, Kraft pointed out in *Danmarksposten* (January 1952), marked a break, in principle, with a foreign policy held by Denmark since 1814—that of abstaining from alliances. NATO, he further noted, "constitutes not only a military defense agreement, but the first realistic attempt to create a true community of nations." Kraft signed a treaty between the United States and Denmark on the defense of Greenland on April 27, 1951, replacing a former treaty of April 1941 that gave the United States the right to establish military bases on Greenland. In the new agreement, within the framework of the North Atlantic Treaty Organization, the defense of the area becomes a common concern, and provision was made for access of NATO to Greenland's defense installations.

Opening a three-day debate on foreign policy in the Folketing on October 16, 1951, Kraft said that American published criticism of Denmark's defense efforts were ill founded. As quoted by the New York *Times* (October 17, 1951), he stated that reported criticism given to the United States Appropriations Committee of the House of Representatives claiming "the will to renounce a high living standard was lacking in Denmark" indicated "due consideration for Denmark had not been given. . . .We feel ourselves deeply indebted to America for all her grand help, but we have a right to expect that when judgment is made on Danish defense efforts . . . one must study closely and consider the existing realities and conditions to reach a true picture." At the Paris session of the United Nations General Assembly in November 1951, which he attended as chairman of the Danish delegation, Kraft began his appeal to Russia to consider the Western proposals for disarmament by asking that the Kremlin recognize the American-French-British provisions for disarmament as "an adequate basis for work" (New York *Herald Tribune*). He stated that "Denmark has not forgotten the Soviet Union's share in the liberation of Denmark from German occupation" and appealed to the Soviet Union "to find a new starting point" (*United Nations Bulletin*). On May 7, 1952, Kraft presented a bill to the Danish Parliament which would establish a permanent Scandinavian parliamentary council for discussion of problems of mutual interest among representatives of Governments of Denmark, Iceland, Norway, and Sweden. Such a council was previously proposed at an Inter-Scandinavian parliamentary conference in Stockholm in 1951.

In the absence of Erik Eriksen, Kraft was in July 1952 the acting Prime Minister of Denmark. On arriving in New York in the fall of 1952 to head the Danish delegation to the United Nations General Assembly, Kraft stated that the United Nations truce proposals made to the North Korean and Chinese Communists were "humanitarian" and "reasonable" (New York *Times*). He later denied any knowledge of an alleged Danish-American agreement allowing the United States to establish new air bases in Greenland, saying the United States already has "sufficient" bases there (New York *Herald Tribune*). Among the concepts Kraft expressed in his speech to U.N. correspondents in New York was the belief that Germany is the central European question of today. "We regard a reunification of Germany as the right and just solution," he explained, "in the interest of Germany herself as well as that of her neighbors. . . .Whether or not Germany is to be armed must in the final analysis depend on the wishes of the German people." He noted that Denmark, in her election to the Security Council from January 1953, also became a member of the Disarmament Council. "Our representatives," he said, "will do their utmost" to contribute to resolving the question of disarmament, "which is a condition for creating security in the world." Succeeding Lester Pearson of Canada, Kraft assumed the presidency of NATO for the year 1952-53. Emphasis in the fall meeting of the organization in Paris was on the development of phases of the Atlantic Treaty which provide for fostering international peace by nonmilitary means.

Kraft was the joint founder of the periodical *Den Ny Tid* (The New Time), first published in 1918, and its editor in 1918-19. From 1928 to 1932 and again from 1934 to 1938 he was publisher and editor of *Det Nye Danmark* (The New Denmark). Books he has written are *Danmark Udslettes* (Destruction of Denmark), 1916, and *Fascismen* (Fascism), 1932. Decorations received by the Danish statesman are the Order of Islandic Knights, the British Empire Order, the Swedish Vasa Order, the Order of the French Legion of Honor, and St. Olav's Order of Norway. He is president of the board of directors of the Carnegie Award fund for heroism and is a member of the administrative board of the association Norden, which works for cooperation among Scandinavian countries. He was vice-president of the board of directors of the Federation of Journalists (1938-40) and a member of the Co-operative Press Council of Denmark (1928-32).

On May 3, 1919, Kraft married Gerda Winge, of Aarhuus, Denmark, the daughter of a physician. Their daughter, Gunvor, is a swimming star who took part in the Olympic games in London in 1948. A director of the Danish Olympic Committee from 1938 to 1950, Kraft finds recreation in sports and athletics. The Danish Foreign Minister has been characterized by a Parliamentary colleague as "friendly, plain, and outspoken, level-headed, and appreciative of the point of view of others" (*Contemporary Danish Politicians*, 1949). When he appears on the rostrum of the Folketing, the description continues, he expresses himself in "strong and graphic words, liberally interspersed with superlatives, and spoken with fire and pathos and all the vigour that comes of a passionate faith in high ideals."

References

Hansen, P. Contemporary Danish Politicians (1949)
International Who's Who (1952)
Kraks Blaa Bog (1952)
Who's Who in the United Nations (1951)

KRISHNA MENON, V(EN-GALIL) K(RISHNAN) May 3, 1897- Indian delegate to the United Nations; lawyer

Address: b. c/o India Delegation to the United Nations, 3 E. 64th St., New York 21; c/o Ministry of External Affairs, New Delhi, India; c/o The India League, 47, Strand, London, W.C. 2, England

International attention was focused on V. K. Krishna Menon, India's delegate to the United Nations General Assembly, first in the fall of

V. K. KRISHNA MENON

political scientist, Harold Laski, subsequently chairman of the executive board of the Parliamentary Labor party. During the next three years Krishna Menon attended University College, London, preparing for the M.A. degree, which he took with honors in 1930. His dissertation was entitled *An Experimental Study of the Mental Processes Involved in Reasoning.*

It was in 1928, while Krishna Menon was working for his master's degree that a league was reactivated from an older organization for supporting India's claim to independence. The older organization was founded by Annie Besant in 1912 as the Home Rule for India League and beginning in 1921 was known as the Commonwealth of India League, which Krishna Menon made in 1930 the India League. In 1929 he accepted the unpaid post of secretary of the League in London, a position which he was to retain until 1947, when its aims approached achievement through the granting of dominion status to India. He acquired his M.Sc. degree in political science in 1934 at the London School of Economics for research in English political thought in the seventeenth century. Also in the year 1934 Krishna Menon was admitted to the English bar at the Middle Temple in London. The co-author of the work *Conditions in India, 1932-33* and of many pamphlets issued by the India League, Menon also contributed the articles "The Condition of India" and "Progress and Reaction in India" to the London *New Statesman and Nation* in 1933, and "Labor Militancy Spreads in India" to the New York *Nation* in September of the following year. In 1934 he undertook the editorship of the *Twentieth Century Library*, a series of new books on topics selected by the editor in the context of a "changing civilization," and later became creator and first editor of Pelican Books, the non-fiction division of Penguin. A member of the Labor party, Menon was elected to the Borough Council of St. Pancras, London, during the same year, becoming chairman of that body's arts council and public library committee. He served continuously as a borough councillor until the Indian Independence Act went into effect in August 1947.

At the thirty-fourth annual conference of the National Labor party at Southport, Lancashire, in October 1934, Krishna Menon submitted a resolution "expressing the conviction that it is imperative that the principle of self-determination for the establishment of full self-government for India should be implemented forthwith." About two years afterward (September 1936) he represented the Indian National Congress at the Brussels World Peace Conference. The India League meanwhile grew steadily in influence—at one time it included over one hundred members of Parliament—and for a three-year period beginning 1938 Krishna Menon was the prospective Labor candidate for the House of Commons chosen by the Scottish manufacturing city of Dundee. After World War II broke out, Krishna Menon set forth the Indian position in the India League pamphlet "Why India Must Fight" (1940) and edited the collection of Nehru's writings between 1937 and 1940 which was published under

1952 when he presented a plan for resolving the deadlock in the Korean armistice negotiations created by the question of the repatriation of prisoners, and again in August 1953 when the admission of India to the Far East political conference was debated.

Prior to the creation of the Dominion of India in August 1947, Krishna Menon, who had been a resident in England since 1924, was for eighteen years secretary in Great Britain of the India League. Afterward, from 1947 to 1952, he held the post in London of India's first High Commissioner in the United Kingdom.

Born to Komath Krishna Kurup, a lawyer, and Vengalil Lakshmi Kutty Amma on May 3, 1897, Vengalil Krishnan Krishna Menon is a native of Calicut in Malabar, a district on the west coast of what was then the Madras Presidency of British India. He was brought up with his four sisters until he was seventeen years old. As a boy he attended village and municipal schools and Brennen College at Tellicherry in northern Malabar, the Ganpat High School in his native city, and Zamorins College at Calicut before transferring in 1915 to Presidency College, Madras, where he received his B.A. degree in the following year. Subsequently he studied also at the Madras Law College and in 1918-19 lectured on Indian and English history at National University, Aydar. He also served for six years (1918-24) as Boy Scout Commissioner in Madras and Cochin State.

For a period of ten years Krishna Menon undertook advanced study in economics, politics, psychology, and law in London, England. He taught for a year at St. Christopher's, a modern co-educational school at Letchworth in Hertfordshire, qualified for a London teacher's diploma in 1925, and two years later (1927) received with first class honors in political science his Bachelor of Science degree at the London School of Economics, a subdivision of the University of London. Here he studied under the

the title of *The Unity of India* (1942). Menon further contributed a number of articles on India to the *Labour Monthly*, and in October 1942, acting on a message received from Nehru in the previous April that an appeal be made to the Western Allies to "acknowledge the independence of India," launched an India League drive to persuade President Roosevelt, Marshal Stalin, and Generalissimo Chiang Kai-shek to urge such acknowledgment on Britain. During the war also, the India League secretary served as a civil defense worker for the Borough of St. Pancras, where three important rail terminals attracted unusually heavy enemy bombings, and was one of the three members of the wartime municipal authority in that area.

Named by Jawaharlal Nehru in September 1946 as his "personal representative," Krishna Menon conferred for two hours in Paris on the 28th of the month with Soviet Foreign Minister Viacheslav Mikhailovich Molotov over what an Indian spokesman described as "highly secret matters" involving Russo-Indian relations. Sometime later, when answering questions put to him in the Central Legislative Assembly at Delhi, Nehru explained that he had sent Shri Menon to Paris to convey to Molotov "the interim government's greetings and also its request for food supplies from Russia" and to negotiate an exchange of diplomatic representatives. In October the India League secretary went to the United States as an alternate delegate to the United Nations General Assembly at Lake Success, where (stated a New York *Herald Tribune* dispatch) he proved in trusteeship meetings "one of the most militant champions of colonial people" before his recall to London at the end of November to join Nehru "in Hindu-Moslem conferences with the British Government." While in the United States he had made an address to the New York *Herald Tribune* Forum on what he called "the last lap of India's struggle for emancipation"— namely the working out of an Indian Constitution. As special representative of the Government of India, Krishna Menon visited a number of European countries to arrange for the establishment of diplomatic relations after the implementation of the British Government's plan to divide the former Indian Empire into the two dominions of India and Pakistan. This division, achieved through the India Independence Act, became effective August 15, 1947. When the Union of India on that date became a self-governing member of the British Commonwealth of Nations, it "automatically took over the charter membership that India under British rule had held in the United Nations" (*World Almanac*). At the same time Krishna Menon assumed office in London as High Commissioner for India in the United Kingdom (with functions equivalent to those of an ambassador) ; and in April 1949, was appointed in addition the Indian Minister to Ireland. (He is now a barrister-at-law, *honoris causa*, of Kings Inn, Dublin.)

Krishna Menon was High Commissioner in London until July 1952, his withdrawal from that post being preliminary to his designation as a full member of, and spokesman for, the Indian delegation to the autumn meetings in New York of the United Nations General Assembly. He was (stated A. M. Rosenthal of the New York *Times*) "sent here by Prime Minister Jawaharlal Nehru to deal with the Korean case," a previous effort by Arab and Asiatic nations (including India) to provide a compromise basis for a peace agreement having ended in failure.

An agreement was reached on various aspects of the Korean truce except for the sixty-third article involving the repatriation of prisoners. The two-year deadlock on this article was broken by a United Nations resolution which had been framed and guided by the Indian Delegation under the leadership of Krishna Menon. This resolution said that no force should be used by either side to affect or prevent the repatriation of any prisoner of war. It provided for a Neutral Nations Repatriation Commission which would take custody of any prisoner who insisted on not being repatriated.

When in the custody of this Commission authorities of either side would have the right to speak to the prisoners of war to try to persuade them to return home. If the prisoners of war still insisted on non-repatriation after this process, they would become civilians with the right to go to any country of their choice.

This resolution was distributed by Krishna Menon on November 17, 1952, to members of the Political and Security Committee of the Assembly. The text of the resolution called for repatriation of all prisoners of war after the conclusion of an armistice by a special commission consisting of Poland, Czechoslovakia, Sweden, and Switzerland, which would by agreement appoint an "umpire." In the event of a deadlock the question of the umpire would be referred to the General Assembly.

The resolution concluded that "at the end of ninety days the disposition of any prisoners of war whose return to their homelands has not been effected in accordance with the procedure set out above shall be referred by the Repatriation Commission" to the political conference.

The Foreign Minister of Great Britain, Anthony Eden, pronounced the Indian plan, which was formally submitted by its author on November 19, to be "timely and constructive" but required certain modifications. The Soviet group did not raise any objections to the Indian proposal until on November 24 Foreign Minister Andrei Y. Vishinsky rejected it. Minor revisions of the Indian text made subsequent to its introduction were in conformity with the explanations and clarifications of the Indian delegate when he had presented the proposal. The resolution as it was revised was passed by the Political and Security· Committee on December 1 and was afterward passed by the General Assembly by a vote of 53 to 5, with a minor Danish amendment. The Indian delegate, who did not accept this amendment, abstained from voting on it, with thirteen other delegates.

"The United Nations will not soon forget V. K. Krishna Menon," remarked Joseph P. Lash in the New York *Post* on December 21, 1952, the day before the General Assembly recessed until February 24.

KRISHNA MENON, V. K.—*Continued*

All eyes were turned toward the tall, gray-haired Indian delegate to the United Nations as he spoke to members of the Political and Security Committee of the General Assembly on August 25, 1953. The admission of India to the Korean political conference was the subject of his speech, and he expressed understanding of, but opposition to the United States view that only the belligerents in the Korean war should participate in such a conference. "The position of India," he declared, "is that she will serve if she is useful . . . India is not a candidate, but a prospective invitee or draftee to this conference."

However, on August 27, the participation of India in the Far East political conference was defeated in the Political and Security Committee of the United Nations General Assembly. Krishna Menon withdrew his country's name from participation in the proposed Far East political conference when it became evident that India would not get the two-thirds majority vote required in the General Assembly. The United States informed him, as the chief delegate to the Seventh Special Session held in August, 1953, that it would support the candidacy of Mme. Vijaya Pandit (sister of India's Prime Minister Jawaharlal Nehru) for President of the Assembly convening in September.

Krishna Menon belongs to the India Club, London, and the London School of Economics Society.

He was elected to the upper House in the Indian Parliament in May, 1953, and he was the chief delegate at the Special Section of the Seventh Session of the United Nations.

References

N Y Herald Tribune p8 N 3 '46 por
N Y Post Mag p2 D 21 '52 pors
Time 60:20 D 1 '52 por
Wichita (Kansas) Beacon p1 D 14 '52 por

Indian and Pakistan Year Book and Who's Who, 1951'
International Who's Who, 1952
Who's Who, 1952

KUNIYOSHI, YASUO September 1, 1893—May 14, 1953 Japanese-born artist, came to United States in 1906; studied at National Academy, Henri School, Art Students League; first living painter in the United States to be awarded a one-man show at the Whitney Museum of American Art; founder and first president of Artists' Equity Association; prizes include Guggenheim fellowship, Temple Gold Medal of the Pennsylvania Academy of Fine Arts, Carnegie Institute awards; represented in Metropolitan Museum of Art, Museum of Modern Art and Whitney Museum. New York: Carnegie Art Institute, Cranbrook Academy, Albright and Addison Phillips; taught at Art Students League and the New School for Social Research. See *Current Biography*, 1941.

Obituary

N Y Times p23 My 15 '53

LA FARGE, OLIVER (HAZARD PERRY) Dec. 19, 1901- Author; anthropologist; organization official

Address: b. c/o Houghton Mifflin Company, 2 Park St., Boston 7, Mass.; c/o Association on American Indian Affairs, Inc., 48 E. 86th St., New York 28; h. 647 College St., Santa Fe, N.Mex.

Prominent as an author since the publication in 1929 of his Pulitzer Prize-winning novel, *Laughing Boy*, Oliver La Farge has also become known as an anthropologist and champion of the rights of the American Indian. Studying and working with Indians for more than three decades, La Farge served as president of the National Association on Indian Affairs from 1933 to 1937 and as president of the Association on American Indian Affairs, Inc., from 1937 to 1942 and from 1948 to the present. He joined the Army Air Transport Command in 1942 as its chief historical officer, by the end of the war becoming a lieutenant colonel and writing a history of this branch of service which appeared as *The Eagle in the Egg* (1949). Besides his scientific publications, he has written novels, numerous articles for popular magazines, and an autobiography, *Raw Material* (1945).

Born in New York City on December 19, 1901, Oliver Hazard Perry La Farge is the son of Christopher Grant La Farge, a nationally known architect and lecturer on architecture, and of Florence Bayard (Lockwood) La Farge, an active worker for several nurses' training schools in New York City. A descendant of Benjamin Franklin, Oliver La Farge had other noted forebears, among them his grandfather John La Farge, a painter and an artist in stained glass. One of his two brothers (he also has a sister) is the poet Christopher La Farge. The boy spent most of his childhood in the family home at Saunderstown, Narraganset Bay, in Rhode Island, where with his brothers, he learned to sail, ride, and hunt. His father, an ardent outdoors man, knew the wilderness and the Indians from eastern Canada to Arizona and admired their culture and their proximity to nature. Desiring to emulate him, Oliver called himself "Indian man."

After attending St. Bernard's School in New York City, La Farge completed his college preparatory training at Groton, from which he was graduated in 1920. At Groton, he won a number of athletic and other prizes, received his "letter" in rowing and football, was chosen vice-captain of the school crew, excelled in high jumping, and was editor of the school magazine. The conformity Groton demanded of the "ideal Groton boy," as La Farge has related in *Raw Material*, was in conflict with the liberal atmosphere the youth had enjoyed at home, and he later described his years at Groton as unhappy ones. It was here, at the age of fifteen, that his interest in anthropology was aroused by reading a review of a book entitled *Men of the Old Stone Age*. During his sophomore year (1921-22) at Harvard University, La Farge went to Arizona as an assistant on an archeological expedition sponsored by the Peabody Museum of Archeology and

Ethnology at Harvard. While he had by this time decided to become a writer, he continued his anthropological work to help support himself and win scholarships to finish his Harvard education. Writing continued to be his spare-time occupation for what he has called "eight discouraging years." At Harvard he was editor of the *Lampoon* and president of the *Advocate*, the college literary magazine. In the academic year 1923-24 he again went as an assistant on the Peabody Museum's expedition to Arizona, making the Navajo Indians and their culture his special interest.

When he received his B.A. degree from Harvard in 1924, La Farge remained at the university as a Hemmenway fellow at the Peabody Museum, taking part that same year in his third archeological expedition to Arizona, this time as the director. In 1925 he was assistant, in charge of ethnology and linguistics, to Frans Blom on a Tulane University anthropological expedition to Guatemala and southern Mexico, where after six months they reported the discovery of three centers of Mayan culture. Studying the Mayan Indians, La Farge adopted Spanish as his second language. In 1927, on his second expedition for Tulane University, he spent five months in Guatemala, where he studied Mayan religion among the Jacalteco Indians in the Cuchumantán Highlands. For five months during the academic year 1927-28 La Farge, who had become an assistant in ethnology at Tulane in 1926, worked on a part-time schedule in order to have more opportunity for writing. Earlier in 1927 he had sold a short story about Indians to the *Dial*.

In 1928 La Farge returned to Harvard to do research on linguistics in the Mayan language and the following year took his M.A. degree at this university. When asked by Ferris Greenslet, an editor for Houghton Mifflin Company, if he had anything in book length similar to his short story which had appeared in the *Dial*, La Farge went back to New Orleans to spend his full time finishing his book, *Laughing Boy*. This first novel, a Navajo Indian romance, received the Pulitzer Prize for fiction in 1929 and was described as "revealing an ability considerably out of the ordinary. . . . His novel is one of the most pleasurable that have come from the pen of a young American for some time" (New York *Evening Post*). The critic for *Bookmark* called it "an almost perfect specimen of the sustained and tempered, the lyrical, romantic idyl." Selling the story to a motion picture producer in 1931 and enjoying the proceeds from the book sales, La Farge was able to travel and to visit in the Southwest at his pleasure. He was also free to work on his second novel, *Sparks Fly Upward* (1931), the story of a Spanish Indian in Central America in the middle of the nineteenth century. In his review in the New York *Herald Tribune*, E. S. Sergeant wrote: "The new book is less a poem, more a work of fiction than *Laughing Boy*. . . .It has, I think, a deepened psychological insight into a maturing masculine mind, but it does not seem to be, like the last, the same

Tyler Dingee

OLIVER LA FARGE

product of spontaneous combustion." The critic for the Boston *Transcript* found it "a fine, stirring story, told vividly, and with sympathy." Also in the 1930's La Farge began selling his short stories in increasing numbers, often for as much as $1,000 each, to popular magazines like the *Saturday Evening Post*.

From 1930 to 1932 La Farge held the directorship of the Eastern Association on Indian Affairs and supervised its Inter-tribal Exhibition of Indian Arts in 1931. For two years, beginning in 1931, he was a research associate in anthropology at Columbia University and in this capacity lead the institution's anthropological expedition to Guatemala for six months in 1932. Studying the ethnology and linguistics of the Chuj, Jacalteca, and Kanhobal Indians, he discovered the survival in unusually full form of the ancient Mayan calendar and ritual. In 1933 La Farge was elected president of the National Association on Indian Affairs and served as such until this organization was merged in 1937 with the American Indian Defense Association to become the American Association on Indian Affairs, Inc. He was president of the newly formed association from its inception until he joined the armed services in 1942. The purposes of the A.A.I.A. are "to promote the continuing study of Indian conditions and needs today, and to educate the public to the facts; to support programs and policies that will correct substandard Indian economy and health, with their attendant poverty, disease and death; to defend Indian civil, social and Constitutional rights, wherever attacked; and to help the Indians defend themselves against unjust treatment, prejudice, and discrimination."

Continuing to be occupied with work relating to Indian affairs, La Farge was appointed in 1936 field representative of the United States

LA FARGE, OLIVER—*Continued*

Indian Service, in charge of drafting a constitution for the Hopi tribe, and in 1940 he saw publication of his book, *An Alphabet for Writing the Navajo Language*, written with John P. Harrington, which has been used in Navajo schools. The following year he presided at the Institute of the Future of the American Indian in New York. La Farge meanwhile continued his interest in writing: from 1936 to 1941 he taught a course on the technique of the novel at Columbia University; during 1940-41 he was employed as an editorial adviser to the Alliance Book Corporation; and for the next year (1941-42) he won a Guggenheim fellowship in writing.

Upon joining the armed forces in 1942, La Farge was assigned as a special consultant in the Army Air Transport Command. Promoted to the rank of captain in 1943, to major in 1944, and to lieutenant colonel in 1945, La Farge during this time served as head of the historical section, responsible for assembling a complete secret history of all the Command's activities and the policies underlying them. It was from this work that he drew material for his book, *The Eagle in the Egg* (1949), a history and evaluation of the Air Transport Command. Calling it "a good war book; worth the time and worth the money," J. G. Cozzens in the New York *Times* found that the result was "a narrative of authority, of often gifted expression, of exact eyewitness reporting, of unobtrusive but copious documentation." During the war Houghton Mifflin announced that it would publish a book to be called *The Long Wait* by La Farge, an account of the rescue from an ice cap of the crew of a Flying Fortress. This story, however, was not published alone but was incorporated with some others by Colonel Bernt Balchen and Major Corey Ford in *War Below Zero* (1944), the story of the secret war waged in the Arctic Circle to rid Greenland of the Nazis.

The next year, in 1945, came the publication of La Farge's autobiography, *Raw Material*, which he had completed before the war, but had revised during the war years. About this book Richardson Wright in the New York *Herald Tribune* said: "Here in full measure are the details of each phase of his life told skilfully and with fascination." The *Christian Science Monitor* reviewer wrote: "There is an engaging candor about the disclosures of Oliver La Farge, boy and man, by himself . . . for the most part it is a privilege and an education to be admitted into the presence of this author's thinking. He writes with clarity and intelligence."

After the war, in May 1948, La Farge was again elected president of the Association on American Indian Affairs, Inc., a post he still holds. Early the following year Secretary of the Interior J. A. Krug named La Farge as a member of a ten-man advisory committee to the Government on Indian affairs. That same year, on October 9, 1949, La Farge wrote to President Truman asking that he veto a $88 million Navajo-Hopi rehabilitation bill passed

by Congress because, he said, two of its amendments destroyed Indian rights and jeopardized Indian property. After being reworked, the project, as authorized by Congress in April 1950, provided for a ten-year expenditure of $88 million to relieve poverty, illiteracy, and the high disease rate among 65,000 Navajo and 4,000 Hopi Indians. On July 10, 1952, President Truman signed the Department of Interior bill authorizing $17.5 million for the Bureau of Indian Affairs' reclamation programs, of which about $10 million was scheduled for the Navajo-Hopi project that year. In August 1952 the bureau was allocated about $21 million for medical, public health, and hospital services among the Indians. Again in behalf of the Indians La Farge in 1951 opposed proposals by the Indian Bureau to control lawyers representing Indian tribes. Stating that the Association on American Indian Affairs would take the matter to the courts if these regulations were not modified, La Farge contended that by impeding the discretion of the tribes to choose their own lawyers, who often had to oppose the Indian Bureau's decisions, the regulations would reverse the "march of the Indians toward self-rule" and would reduce them to "second-class citizenship" (New York *Times*, November 12, 1951).

After President Eisenhower signed into law the bills designed to improve the status of America's Indians, Oliver La Farge, declared: "The President . . . seems to show that he is standing by his campaign promise to give the Indians themselves a voice in such important decisions . . . the Indians will be happy that the President remembers" (New York *Times*, August 17, 1953).

Anthropological books of which La Farge is the author include *Tribes and Temples* (with Frans Blom, 1927), *The Year Bearer's People* (with Douglas S. Byers, 1931), and *Santa Eulalia; the Religion of a Cuchumatán Indian Town* (1947). Outside the field of anthropology he has written *Long Pennant* (1933); *All the Young Men* (1935), a collection of short stories; *The Enemy Gods* (1937); *As Long As the Grass Shall Grow* (1940); and *The Copper Pot* (1942). Besides writing short stories which have appeared in the *New Yorker*, the *Atlantic Monthly*, *Collier's*, the *Saturday Evening Post*, the *Ladies' Home Journal*, and other popular magazines, he edited *The Changing Indian* (1942) and has contributed articles on Indian conditions and culture, including "American Indian's Revenge" (*Current History*, May 1934); "Navajos, Most Hopeful Tribe of All" (*Natural History*, October 1948); and "Not an Indian, But a White-Man Problem" (*New York Times Magazine*, April 30, 1950). Expressing his current view of the Indian situation in the last-named article, La Farge stressed the need for less Government paternalism and more guidance for the Indians. "The benevolence has sapped the Indians' strength," he wrote. "More responsibility and authority must be turned over to the Indians themselves, leading them on until they can take their own future entirely in their own hands."

For his short story "Haunted Ground," which first appeared in the *Ladies' Home Journal* in August 1930, La Farge was awarded the O'Henry Memorial Prize in 1931. He holds an honorary degree from Brown University, conferred in 1932. In recognition of his services in World War II he was awarded the Legion of Merit and the Commendation Ribbon for services in military intelligence.

Since the year 1946 La Farge has been a member of the advisory board of the Laboratory of Anthropology at Santa Fe, New Mexico, a membership which he earlier held from 1935 to 1941. He is a fellow of the American Association for Advancement of Science, a member of the American Anthropological Association, and of the committee on Indian Arts and Crafts of the United States Department of the Interior. In 1941 he was vice-chairman of the Institute on Future of the American Indian, and from 1932 to 1934 a trustee for the W.E.B. DuBois prize for Negro literature. He is a member of the Committee of Awards of the Opportunity Fellowships of the John Hay Whitney Foundation. His clubs are Century, Coffee House, P.E.N., and the Authors' League of New York City.

On September 28, 1929, La Farge married Wanden E. Mathews, daughter of a New York stockbroker; their daughter is Povy La Farge and their son is Oliver Albee La Farge. The marriage was terminated by a divorce in 1937. On October 14, 1939, La Farge married Concuelo Otille O.C. de Baca, a literary agent whose father was lieutenant governor of New Mexico. By this marriage La Farge is the father of John Pendaries. The tall and slim author has black hair. His hobbies are riding, hunting, sailing, camping, and archery.

References

> International Dictionary of Anthropologists (1950)
> La Farge, O. Raw Material (1945)
> National Cyclopædia of American Biography Current vol F, 1939-42
> Twentieth Century Authors (1942)
> Who's Who in America, 1952-53

LA FOLLETTE, ROBERT M(ARION, JR.) Feb. 6, 1895—Feb. 24, 1953

Former United States Senator from Wisconsin; served as secretary to his father, Robert M. La Follette (1919-25); elected to fill unexpired Senate term on elder La Follette's death (1925-28); re-elected for full terms in 1928, 1934, 1940; chairman of Senate Civil Liberties Committee (1936); author of Congressional reorganization act passed in 1947; defeated in 1946 Republican primary election for Senator by Joseph R. McCarthy; member board of directors of Sears, Roebuck & Company and vice-president of Sears Foundation. See *Current Biography*, 1944.

Obituary

N Y Times p1 F 25 '53

LAHEY, FRANK H(OWARD) June 1, 1880—June 27, 1953

Surgeon; president of American Medical Association 1941 and 1942; founder of Lahey Clinic in Boston; noted for contributions to the surgery of thyroid gland and of cancer; served during World War II as chairman of the War Manpower Commission's medical procurement and assignment service. See *Current Biography*, 1941.

Obituary

N Y Times p60 Je 28 '53

LANCASTER, BURT(ON STEPHEN) Nov. 2, 1913-

Motion picture actor; producer

Address: b. c/o Norma Productions, United Artists Corporation, Hollywood, Calif.; h. Bel Air, Calif.

Achieving stardom with his first screen appearance, as Swede in *The Killers* (1946), Burt Lancaster has won praise for his unusual versatility portraying "hard guy" roles in gangster films, swashbuckling parts in the Douglas Fairbanks, Sr. tradition, and serious roles in such pictures as *All My Sons* and *Come Back Little Sheiba*. His most recent role of First Sergeant Milton Warden in the film *From Here To Eternity* (August, 1953) based on James Jones' novel, earned for the actor additional acclaim.

In addition to acting for other producers, he is also head of his own company, Norma Productions. His stage experience was limited to a performance in *A Sound of Hunting*, which was presented on Broadway in 1945. Earlier, he had been a vaudeville and circus acrobat. During World War II he spent 26 months in North Africa, Italy and Austria with the United States Fifth Army, Special Services.

Born in the East Harlem section of New York City on November 2, 1913, Burton Stephen Lancaster is a member of a family that traces its ancestry to the royal English house of Lancaster. His father, James Lancaster, was a postoffice employee. His brother, James Jr., is a member of New York's Police Department; his sister, Jane, teaches public school in New York.

He received his early education at PS 83. Lancaster recalls that "the kids on my block used to carry knives", and he might have become a juvenile delinquent in that environment on 106th Street between Second and Third Avenues except that he discovered the neighborhood public library and the Union Settlement house. He became, according to reports, "a scholarly teen-ager for all his brawn and muscle". Until he was fifteen he sang soprano in church. He graduated from De Witt Clinton High School and, at the age of sixteen, having been awarded an athletic scholarship, he entered New York· University as a physical education major. He played on the basketball team and took part in boxing, baseball, track and gymnastics.

After two years he decided to leave college and develop a career as an acrobat. With Nick Cravat, a boyhood friend, he formed the team "Lang and Cravat" and obtained a job with the

BURT LANCASTER

Kay Brothers Circus presenting a horizontal-bar act. At a salary of $3 per week, with board, for each, they worked for thirty weeks, then ioined another circus.

From 1932 until 1939 "Lang and Cravat" presented their act in vaudeville, in carnivals, and in circuses. They performed for the Gorman Brothers and Barnett Brothers circuses, and were featured for a time with Ringling Brothers. Once during this period Lancaster gave up acrobatics, depressed over the fact that after all his experience as an entertainer he was still only a "dumb actor," that is, a performer who never has to speak.

He was employed in a WPA Theater Project, but soon returned to acrobatic work with Cravat. In 1939 he suffered a badly infected finger and was warned that unless he gave up acrobatics amputation would be necessary. He tried a variety of jobs during the next three years, as a floor walker in the lingerie department of Marshall Field's store in Chicago, a salesman in the haberdashery department, a fireman and engineer for a Chicago meat-packing plant. Returning to New York in 1942, he was offered a position by the Columbia Concerts Bureau of the Columbia Broadcasting System, but before he could assume his new duties, he received notice of his impending induction into the Army.

He spent three years in the Army, most of the time overseas with the Special Services of the Fifth Army. Of his military service he said to Irene Thirer, "I had a wonderful time touring Europe as page-turner for a soldier pianist" (New York *Post,* October 10, 1948).

While in Italy, Lancaster met Norma Anderson, a USO entertainer who later became his wife. In 1945 she was working for a producer, and Lancaster, in New York on a 45-day discharge furlough, was in the elevator one afternoon on his way up to see her when he became aware of a fellow passenger staring at him. When he got off, the stranger followed, introduced himself as an associate of Irving Jacobs, the stage producer, and invited him to read for the part of a tough sergeant in *A Sound of Hunting.* Although the position with the Columbia Concerts Bureau was still available, Lancaster decided to try out for the role, and won it. The play lasted only five weeks, but during its run Lancaster received seven screen offers. He accepted a contract from Hal Wallis calling for two pictures a year. On his arrival in Hollywood he found that the script of Wallis' *Desert Fury* was not yet ready.

The late Mark Hellinger saw Lancaster's screen test and signed him for *The Killers* on a long-term picture-a-year contract. Otis Guernsey Jr., motion picture critic for the New York *Herald Tribune,* wrote that Lancaster had made "a most promising screen debut." Bosley Crowther wrote in the New York *Times* that Lancaster gave "a lanky and wistful imitation of a nice guy who's wooed to his ruin." Eileen Creelman, in the New York *Sun,* described Lancaster as a "sound actor, with a strong, likable face. He is here just one of a number of good actors, but his is the central role, a well-written, forcefully acted role."

After appearing in *Desert Fury* (1947), Lancaster was seen in another Hellinger film, *Brute Force,* a study of prison life and prison methods which gave him, according to *Variety,* "added marquee stature." His next performance, a distinct change from the "hard guy" roles he had been playing until then, was as Chris Keller, the upright son of a war profiteer, in Chester Erskine's production of *All My Sons* (1948), adapted from Arthur Miller's play.

A number of critics praised his work highly. By the end of 1948, according to Thomas Pryor in the New York *Times Magazine,* October 1, Lancaster was "at the top of the Hollywood heap. His name on a theatre marquee is said to be worth at least $1,000,000 and it is estimated that his earnings for 1948 will exceed $200,000." Even in a profession where "spectacular ascents" were more or less routine, Pryor added, "the rise of Burt Lancaster is regarded as something extraordinary."

Earlier in 1948 Lancaster had become a producer in his own right by establishing Norma Productions (named after his wife) with his business manager, Harold Hecht. His first production for his own company was *Kiss the Blood Off My Hands* (1948), "an intensely moody melodrama," in *Variety*'s words, "with sufficient emotional kick to make it a good b.o. bet." In 1948 he appeared also in the Hal Wallis production of *Sorry, Wrong Number,* a film version of the half-hour radio monologue. This role marked "a departure from his usual characterizations of hard-hitting hero and tough guy," according to Frank Daugherty.

Two pictures starring Lancaster were shown in 1949—*Criss Cross,* a Universal-International release described by *Variety* as "a Burt Lancaster thriller in the same brash, exciting vein as its predecessors, *Brute Force* and *The Killers,* and *Rope of Sand,* a Wallis melodrama of revenge and greed.

In March 1949 Lancaster concluded an agreement with Warner Brothers, under which he would make three pictures for the studio within the next three years, while his own company would make three pictures for Warners release in partnership with the studio. In April Lancaster began a four-week appearance as an acrobat with the Cole Brothers Circus. *Time* noted that "there was a careful salary adjustment" involved in Lancaster's return to his "first love"—"from the old $3 a week to $11,000."

Lancaster's first independent production under his arrangement with Warner Brothers was *The Flame and the Arrow*, (1950) characterized by Guernsey as a "delightfully outrageous summer extravaganza," in which for the first time on the screen the actor capitalized on his acrobatic skill. Playing the role of a blacksmith, the hero's closest friend, was Nick Cravat, Lancaster's former circus partner.

"Not since Douglas Fairbanks was leaping from castle walls and vaulting over the rooftops of ancient story-book towns," wrote Bosley Crowther in the New York *Times* "has the screen had such a reckless and acrobatic young man to display these same inclinations as it has in Mr. L." According to *Cue*, Lancaster used no stunt men nor doubles during the filming of *The Flame and the Arrow*. Asked why he risked his neck in the dangerous aerial stunts, Lancaster said, "I've got a couple of thousand bucks in that picture. What's a neck?" Upon completion of the picture, Lancaster embarked on an extensive personal appearance tour and, to convince the skeptics, performed the same stunts which he had done in the film.

The exploitation of his athletic prowess in pictures, Lancaster remarked to an interviewer, "opened a whole new facet of my career." This new facet was further shown in *Jim Thorpe—All American* (1951), *Ten Tall Men* (1951), and *The Crimson Pirate* (1952). Lancaster was chosen to portray Jim Thorpe, the late Sac and Fox Indian athlete whose achievements won for him an enduring place in the history of sport. In the opinion of the New York *Times* reviewer, "Warner Brothers could not have assigned a better man . . . than Burt Lancaster. He is equipped physically and, what is more important, professionally, for the job of depicting the storied athlete. Mr. Lancaster . . . is solidly convincing as the man whose pride would not let him accept handouts and who found joy and sadness in competition."

Ten Tall Men, a Foreign Legion melodrama, was produced by Norma Productions for release by Columbia Pictures. *The Crimson Pirate*, another Warner Brothers release filmed partly in Italy and England, was a good-natured parody of swashbuckling sea stories in which Lancaster proved himself "one of our most amiable and strenuous comedians," in the words of Alton Cook. Early in 1952 Lancaster won the coveted role of Doc opposite Shirley Booth in the film version of *Come Back, Little Sheba*. He explained his interest in the role to Erskine Johnson in these words: "I'll go on making swashbucklers for my own company. But in my outside pictures, I want to do things that

will help me as an actor against the time when I have to give up all this jumping around." During 1952 Lancaster spent four months on Viti Levu in the Fiji Islands working in *His Majesty O'Keefe*, a Norma Productions picture released by Warner Brothers.

The actor-producer married Norma Anderson on December 28, 1946. The Lancasters have four children—James Steven, William Henry, Susan Elizabeth, and Joanne Mari. Standing six feet two inches tall, Lancaster weighs 180 pounds; he has light-brown hair and blue eyes. When not engaged on a picture, he works out daily with Cravat in the Warner Brothers studio gymnasium. His favorite hobby is reading.

His 1953 pictures are *South Sea Woman*, released by Warner Brothers June 27; *His Majesty, O'Keefe, The Marines Have a Word For It, The Big Top* and *From Here To Eternity*. The latter was an outstanding box-office success.

References

Collier's p52 N 6 '48 pors
Cue 19:12+ Jl 8 '50 por
Liberty 26:34+ Ja '49
Sat Eve Post 221:38 S 11 '48 pors
This Week p12+ Jl 22 '51 por

LAND, EDWIN H(ERBERT) May 7, 1909- Business executive; inventor; physicist
Address: b. c/o Polaroid Corp., 730 Main St., Cambridge, Mass.; h. 163 Brattle St., Cambridge, Mass.

Polaroid, a trade-mark applied to light-polarizing material, was invented by Edwin H. Land while he was a student at Harvard University. Now president, chairman of the board and director of research of the Polaroid Corporation, he has developed the plastic substance so that it is widely used for such products as sunglasses, lamps, camera filters, variable-density windows and military instruments. Recently, Polaroid production has been enormously expanded to meet the demand for glasses used for viewing three-dimensional motion pictures.

Land is also the inventor of "one-step photography," a camera which produces a completely developed and finished picture one minute after the exposure has been made. In 1948 he and his research team demonstrated a process using ultra-violet light which makes it possible to see living cells in natural color, regarded as an important aid in the study of cancer and other types of diseased cells.

The son of Harry M. and Martha F. Land, Edwin Herbert Land was born in Bridgeport, Connecticut, on May 7, 1909. He attended Norwich Academy, in Connecticut, and Harvard University. While in college he became interested in the problem of light polarization, and after he had developed his first polarizer, Harvard assigned him a laboratory in which to continue his experiments. It had been known for many years that certain crystals would absorb some of the vibration of light rays, but

EDWIN H. LAND

the crystals could not be used for practical purposes because they crumbled easily.

Land succeeded in aligning iodine-plastic molecules uniformly in a sheet plastic called polyvinalcohol by dipping it in an iodine solution. Polaroid, as the substance was called, allows the light which passes through it to vibrate in only one plane and permits objects to be seen clearly while eliminating glare. The discovery was announced at a Harvard colloquium in 1932.

Interested in the potentialities of polaroid, George Wheelwright III, a physics instructor at Harvard, left the university when Land did and together in 1932 they established in a cellar in Boston the Land-Wheelwright Laboratories, a general laboratory consultant service in physics. They were not exclusively concerned with Land's polarizer at the outset, but when the Eastman Kodak Company became interested in the use of Polaroid in camera filters to eliminate reflections, they began, in 1935, to manufacture the filters. The use of Polaroid in sunglasses, one of the most popular applications of the material, was first started in 1936 by the American Optical Company, which also used Polaroid in other ophthalmic devices.

The Polaroid Corporation was established in 1937 in Cambridge, Massachusetts, to take care of the laboratory's expanding enterprises. After some initial difficulties concerning related patents, Land obtained general patents on the polarizing sheet and the manufacturing process because of acknowledged improvements, and in 1938 the patent holders of similar processes sold their interests to the Polaroid Corporation.

In 1941 Land developed a film for three-dimensional pictures. On this film two exposures could be made, and, by means of a process controlling the swaying motions of light rays, making them go in one direction, the two exposures produce a three-dimensional effect when viewed with special glasses made for that purpose. The two images which go on the film are photographed with a camera using two lenses spaced to approximate the position of human eyes.

Land headed research teams during World War II which invented and developed new weapons and materials. Among the devices and techniques perfected by the groups were plastic optical elements used in infra-red night vision instruments, a processing method for vectographs, light-weight stereoscopic range-finders, infra-red search light filters, infinity optical ring sights for anti-aircraft guns, bazookas and other weapons, and a mechanism for training anti-aircraft gunners' tracer fire. The scientist also directed the development and manufacture of a guided missile and served as consultant to Division Five of the National Defense Research Council on guided missiles and to Division Two of the same organization.

During the war the Polaroid Corporation was converted to war production, manufacturing filters for military goggles, gun sights, periscopes, range finders, aerial cameras, and the Norden bombsight. Variety-density goggles enabled air force gunners to look directly into the sun while aiming, and other types were used to eliminate glare on submarine patrol, to adapt the eyes of bomber crews to the dark, and to transform reconnaissance photographs into three dimensions. Land received many Army, Navy, and Ordnance "E's", with stars, and other awards for his war service.

A new "one-step" photographic process was demonstrated by Land on February 21, 1947 at the winter meeting of the Optical Society of America. Called by the society's program "a new kind of photography as revolutionary as the transition from wet plates to day-light-loading film" (New York *Times,* February 22, 1947), the process enables the photographer to produce finished pictures within a minute of the exposure by simply pulling them out of the camera.

One type of camera which uses this method is loaded with a special paper and ordinary film which are pressed together by rollers by turning a knob after the photograph is taken. The pressure breaks a small container attached to the paper and a developing solution spreads between film and paper, producing the negative and positive print simultaneously. The film and paper can be separated immediately and the finished print inspected, thus allowing retakes after unsatisfactory results.

The Land process, it was announced, could be adapted to all varieties of cameras, including X-ray and other technical types. Motion pictures and color photography can also be produced by this method. The first commercial production was announced in December 1948, and Land cameras have since been widely used in commercial, military, and medical photography as well as by amateurs.

Land and his associates developed a technique under contract with the Office of Naval Research that makes it possible to observe living cells in their natural color. Disclosed at the dedication of the Sloan-Kettering Institute for

Cancer Research in New York on April 16, 1948, it is a method which uses a color translation technique to change ultra-violet light to visible light, bringing out the hitherto unseen color of microscopic cells.

This development, it was hoped, would make it possible to differentiate between diseased cells and normal ones. The study of living tissue made possible by the discovery would, it was felt by scientists at the dedication, advance cancer research considerably. Photographs of living cells taken by the color translation method were shown. Development of a color translation microscope, announced at this meeting was subsequently perfected at the Polaroid Corporation.

A device called the self-developing photographic dosimeter which measures the amount of exposure to atomic radiation had been developed by the Polaroid Corporation, it was announced in November 1950. Embodying the principle of the Land camera, it consists of a small metal case containing sensitized film and a pod of developing solution; exposure to gamma rays turns the center of the film light and comparison with a graded scale on the film shows the amount of radiation absorbed. The film is developed by pulling it from the case, thereby spreading the developing materials over its surface, as in the Polaroid camera.

The immense success of three-dimensional motion pictures has provided a vast new market for Polaroid in the manufacture of viewing glasses. The lenses of the glasses are set with the molecular lines at right angles to each other; two pictures taken of the same scene from slightly different angles are thrown on the screen by projectors using lenses set in the same way, and the glasses permit each eye to see only one of the projected images, thus giving an illusion of depth. As production of the glasses reached six million pairs a week in May 1953 with orders for seventy million more, the Polaroid Corporation announced plans to establish factories and distribution points all over the world.

The inventor holds 164 patents in the fields of light polarization, photography, optical systems, plastics, and plastic optics, among others. He is the author of a number of scientific articles dealing with his research and discoveries, including "Polaroid and the Headlight Problem" in the *Journal of the Franklin Institute*, September 1937; "A New One-Step Photographic Process" in the *Journal of the Optical Society of America*, 1947; and "A Color Translating Ultraviolet Microscope" in *Science*, 1949.

Awards given to Land include the Hood Medal of the Royal Photographic Society; the Cresson Medal of the Franklin Institute; the John Scott Medal and Award; the National Modern Pioneer Award of the National Association of Manufacturers; the Rumford Medal of the American Academy of Arts and Sciences; the Holley Medal of the American Society of Mechanical Engineers; and the Duddell Medal of the Physical Society of Great. Britain. The scientist has received honorary Doctor of Science degrees from Tufts College and the Polytechnic Institute of Brooklyn and an honorary LL.D from Bates College.

Organizations of which Land is a member include the Optical Society of America, the Photographic Society of America, the National Academy of Sciences, the Harvard Board of Overseers Committee to visit the Departments of Physics, Astronomy, Chemistry, Biology and Bussey Institution, and the American Academy of Arts and Sciences, of which he is president. He also belongs to the Harvard Clubs of Boston and New York, the St. Botolph Club, the Faculty Clubs of Harvard and the Massachusetts Institute of Technology, and Sigma Xi. He married the former Helen Maislen in 1929 and they have two daughters, Jennifer and Valerie.

References

Fortune 18:74+ S '38
Nature 163:866 Je 4 '49
American Men of Science (1949)
Who Knows—and What (1949)
Who's Who in America, 1952-53

LATOURETTE, KENNETH S(COTT)
Aug. 9, 1884- Theologian; educator; author
Address: h. 409 Prospect St., New Haven 11, Conn.

Author of over thirty books dealing with Christianity and comparative religions, Professor Kenneth Scott Latourette has been director of graduate studies in the department of religion at Yale University since 1946. His most recent book, *A History of Christianity* was published by Harper & Brothers in 1953. He has been president of the Japan International Christian University Foundation since 1951. In the spring of 1953 he retired as Sterling Professor of Missions and Oriental History at Yale, where he has taught since 1921. He was compiler and editor of Chinese terms for a revised edition of Webster's New International Dictionary.

The holder of seventeen academic degrees, thirteen of them honorary, Professor Latourette has made an acknowledged contribution to both Christian leadership and Far Eastern understanding. On his election on February 7, 1951 to the presidency of the Japan International Christian University Foundation, an editorial in the New York *Times* (Feb. 9, 1951) hailed the choice as "a fortunate one." "Dr. Latourette," said the *Times*, is "eminent in the field of scholarship and of Christian education. He is, in addition, a profound student of the Far East and a qualified interpreter of its peoples. He brings to this important task [of creating a social and philosophical revolution in the new Japan] unusual skills and a rich background."

Dr. Latourette's optimistic views on the strength of Christianity in the modern world have been widely quoted. "Never has Jesus been so potent in the affairs of men as in the past fourteen decades. The years from Anno Domini 1800 to Annum Domini 1940 have been the period in which He has moulded mankind as never before." This thesis, first stated in

C. T. Alburtus

KENNETH S. LATOURETTE

1940 in his book *Anno Domini: Jesus, History, and God,* was elaborated in his monumental seven volume work, *A History of the Expansion of Christianity,* (Harper) completed in 1945. According to Dr. Latourette, Christianity, far from showing symptoms of senility, "in the past 150 years . . . has had its greatest geographical extension and its widest influence. . . .From every major period of decline there came resurgence which made Christianity more potent . . . than ever before."

Kenneth Scott Latourette was born on August 9, 1884 in Oregon City, Oregon, the son of De Witt Clinton and Rhoda Ellen (Scott) Latourette. He was graduated from Oregon City High School in 1900. At Linfield College, from which he received a B.S. in chemistry in 1904, he was a member of the debating team and the glee club, was president of the YMCA, and was class valedictorian.

While at Linfield, through the student YMCA and the Student Volunteer Movement, as he stated, he was led to decide against his earlier choice, the law, and to prepare for foreign missionary work. Traveling east to study at Yale University, he took a B.A. with honors in history in 1906, was elected to Phi Beta Kappa, and obtained his M.A. degree in 1907. He received a Ph.D. degree in 1909, having written his thesis on *The History of Early Relations between the U.S. and China, 1784-1844.* He was a Foote Fellow from 1906 to 1909.

After a year (from 1909 to 1910) as traveling secretary for the Student Volunteer Movement for Foreign Missions, Dr. Latourette became a member of the faculty of Yale in China at Changsha, China in 1910. Returning to the United States after 1912, he became a lecturer in history (1914 to 1915) and then associate professor of history (1915 to 1916) at Reed College; associate professor (1916 to 1917), professor (1917 to 1921), and also chaplain (1918 to 1921) at Denison University. He was ordained a Baptist minister in 1918.

Named D. Willis James Professor of Missions at Yale in 1921, Dr. Latourette became in 1925 professor of missions and oriental history. In 1938 he was named chairman of the department of religion, in 1946 director of graduate studies of the department of religion, and in 1949 Sterling Professor of Missions and Oriental History. Since 1944 he has also been a Fellow of Berkeley College at Yale.

In addition to his academic posts, Dr. Latourette has served as honorary pastor in the Calvary Baptist Church in New Haven since 1944. He has held lectureships at many theological seminaries and mission schools: Southern Baptist Theological Seminary (1930, 1936); Princeton Theological Seminary (1935); Canadian School of Missions (1938-1947, 1950); Chicago Theological Seminary (1942); And-over-Newton Theological Seminary (1946, 1950); University of Birmingham (1947); S. W. Baptist Theological Seminary (1947); San Francisco Theological Seminary (1947); Rice Institute (1948); University of Oregon (1949); Drew University (1950); Presbyterian Theological Seminary (1950); Columbia Theological Seminary (1952).

Dr. Latourette was elected president of the American Historical Association on December 28, 1947. In June 1951 he was unanimously elected president of the American Baptist Convention whose membership is about 1,600,000. In that capacity, he stated that the atomic age was "a great and thrilling age, offering great opportunities to the church." In a joint statement with the Southern Baptist Convention, the Joint Committee on Public Affairs, and the religious freedom commission of the Baptist World Alliance, he urged American Baptists to reaffirm their traditional belief in the principle of the separation of church and state and "to begin immediately to crusade for peace and freedom." The statement protested against the "growth of unfounded accusations against men, instigated under the name of national security, which increasingly restrain innocent people from speaking out openly on the great issues of the day and deter them from associating themselves with others in dedicated effort to uphold principles of social justice and world peace." In May, 1952, he told delegates to the Southern Baptist Convention in Miami, Florida, that "we are living in one of the greatest days of the church."

Dr. Latourette received the Order of Jade from the Chinese Government in 1938. He holds the following honorary degrees: D.D., Linfield, 1925; LL.D., Denison, 1942; Litt.D., Baylor, 1945; Litt.D., Princeton, 1947; D.D., McMaster, 1946; D.D., Colgate, 1947; D.D., Oxford, 1947; S.T.D., Glasgow (Scotland), 1947; Litt.D., William Jewell, 1948; Litt.D., Shurtleff, 1952; Litt.D., Kalamazoo, 1952; D.Sc. Rel., Warburg (Germany), 1952; Litt.D., Boston University, 1953. He has been active in many civic and religious organizations, including the Board of Christian Colleges in China, Royal Asiatic Society, American Oriental Society, Society for Japanese Studies, American Catholic Historical Association, American Association for the Advancement of Science, Council on Foreign Relations, American Council of the Institute of Pacific Relations, and Alpha Chi Ro. He has also held committee positions and board memberships in the American Baptist Foreign Mission Society, the World's Student Christian Federation, the Baptist Board of Education, Foreign Missions Conference of North America, the American Society of Church History, the International Missionary Council, the Committee on Promotion of Chinese Studies of the American Council of Learned Societies, Yale in China Board of Trustees, Yale Hope Mission, China Medical Board, the International Board of the YMCA, and the World Council of Churches.

"Precise, energetic," Dr. Latourette has been described as following a rigid "daily timetable" which has allowed him to write so many volumes. These include: *The Development of China* (1917. 6th ed., 1946); *The Development of Japan* (1918. 4th edition, 1938); *The Christian Basis of World Democracy* (1919); *A History of Christian Missions in China* (1929); *The Chinese, Their History and Culture* (2 vols., 1934. 3rd ed., 1946); *Missions Tomorrow* (1936, translated into Chinese, 1937); *A History of the Expansion of Christianity* (7 volumes, 1937-1945); *Toward a World Christian Fellowship* (1938); *Anno Domini* (1940); *The Unquenchable Light* (1941); *The History of Japan* (1947); *A Short History of the Far East* (1946); *The U.S. Moves Across the Pacific* (1946); *The Christian Outlook* (1948); editor, *The Gospel, the Church and the World* (1947, with W. R. Hogg); *Tomorrow is Here* (1948); *The Emergency of a World Christian Community* (1949); *The China That Is to Be* (1949); *A History of Our World* (1949) (with K. M. Gould and J. Mayer); *Missions and the American Mind* (1949); *These Sought a Country* (1950); *The History of the Ecumenical Movement* (with others, 1952); *The American Record in the Far East 1945-1951* (1952); and *A History of Christianity* (1953). In addition, Dr. Latourette has contributed many articles to various journals and magazines.

Dr. Latourette, who is unmarried, has hazel colored eyes and white hair; he is 5' 10" and weighs 177 pounds. His religious affiliation is Baptist and politically he is Republican. His favorite hobbies are walking, gardening, mountain climbing and reading. He is a member of the American Academy of Arts and Sciences and the Connecticut Academy of Arts and Sciences. He belongs to the following clubs: Graduates (New Haven), Yale (New York), Century (New York), and Authors' (London).

References

N Y Times p24 F 9 '51
Time 36:75 N 4 '40; 47:49 Ap 22 '46
Directory of American Scholars (1951)
International Who's Who, 1952
Who's Who in America, 1952-53
World Biography (1948)

LAUREL, JOSÉ P(ACIANO) Mar. 9, 1891- Philippine senator; political leader; educator.

Address: b. c/o Philippine Senate, Quezon City, P.I.

Formerly president of the puppet Republic during the Japanese occupation, Senator José Laurel now heads the Philippine's Nacionalista Party, and is regarded as one of the most controversial figures in the independent Republic.

Wide World Photos

JOSÉ P. LAUREL

"A deeply religious man, Laurel has a name that seems to be magic to the Filipinos," according to *Time*'s Far East correspondent. "They refuse to take seriously the charges of anti-Americanism and collaborationism."

José Paciano Laurel was born March 9, 1891, in Tanauan in Batangas, a province in southern Luzon. His parents, Sotero and Jacoba (García) Laurel, were peasants. By all accounts, young José was recognized early as a brilliant student. Like most ambitious young men in his country, he entered the civil service, starting as a temporary messenger clerk and part-time laborer in the Bureau of Forestry in 1909, when he was eighteen. He worked as a clerk of the Code Committee while studying law at the University of the Philippines. Laurel received his LL.B. in 1915, and the following year was appointed law clerk in the Executive Bureau, and was soon promoted to chief clerk, a post he held until 1921. At the same time he took graduate courses at the University.

Laurel is said to have earned more degrees than any other Filipino—B.A., LL.B., LL.M., D.C.L., Ph.D., and LL.D. In addition, he has received several honorary degrees. In 1919 he received the *Licenciado en Ciencias Juridicas* from the Spanish-language Escuela de Derecho

LAUREL, JOSÉ P.—*Continued*
de Manila, and the following year he went to
the United States for a postgraduate law course
at Yale University.

Back in Manila, Dr. Laurel was promoted
to chief of the Executive Bureau. In 1922 he
was appointed Under-Secretary of the Interior,
and the following year Governor General
Leonard Wood named him Secretary of the
Interior, at the age of thirty-two. What is
called "the Conley incident" occurred shortly
thereafter, putting a stop to Laurel's career in
the Government service. Conley, the American
chief of the Manila vice squad, came under
the authority of Laurel who made unsuccessful
efforts to oust him from his position. Laurel
brought charges of bribery against Conley, and
testified at the court trial. The charges were
dismissed, and Governor General Wood ordered Laurel to reinstate him, but Laurel, after
an unsuccessful appeal to President Coolidge,
resigned rather than to do so, and persuaded
Cabinet members to resign with him.

All the officials who resigned, except Laurel,
were later appointed to other Government positions, and many rose to higher offices. "Inevitably," writes David Bernstein, former adviser
to Presidents Quezon and Osmeña, Laurel
"blamed the Americans for the thwarting of his
political aspirations. . . ."

Devoting his energies to his law practice,
which included many Japanese clients, Laurel
became very fond of things Japanese. He sent
several of his sons to Japan to study, and he
became an expert in *bushido*, the Japanese nobility's intricate code of honor and Emperor-
worship. Repeatedly he called for the Philippines to turn from the West to the Orient, to
their "historic destiny as Asiatics." Laurel is
said to be the first foreigner to be awarded an
honorary LL.D. by Tokyo Imperial University
(in 1938).

Elected Senator from the fifth district, Dr.
Laurel served as floor leader during his 1925-31
term of office. He continued his advanced
studies, and received his Ph.D. from the University of Santo Tomás in 1936. Laurel taught
comparative constitutional law and law reform
there, and has taught law courses also at the
Philippine Law School, Lacson College, Far
Eastern University, Ateneo de Manila, and
National Law College. He served on the chancellory of the National Teachers College, and
was connected with the University of the Philippines as a member of its College of Law
faculty, and as "professorial lecturer on municipal government and municipal problems" at its
College of Liberal Arts in the political science
department.

As a delegate from Batangas to the Philippine Constitutional Convention of 1934, Dr.
Laurel served as temporary chairman and
helped in drafting the important provisions,
especially the Bill of Rights. In 1936 he was
appointed Associate Justice of the Supreme
Court. Five years later, when the constitu-
tionality of the sweeping powers granted to
President Quezon came before the court early
in 1941, Justice Laurel said in a long opinion

that a "constitutional dictatorship" was in keeping with a worldwide trend toward "totalitarianism gradually supplanting democracy," and mentioned with approval the "constitutional and
benevolent dictatorship of Japan."

In a collection of excerpts from Laurel's writings, a passage on "constitutional dictatorship"
states that a "mild despotism" is often necessary
in times of crisis "with enough physical power
behind it to guide the people through a turbulent
and critical period of transition to the goal of
responsible popular government which must
long be vitalized by political education" (*Gems
of Thought*, 1949).

After the attack on Pearl Harbor, when
President Quezon and Vice-President Osmeña
retreated to Bataan and escaped from there to
the United States, José Laurel became acting
Secretary of Justice and Chief Justice of the
Supreme Court. Shortly after the Japanese
occupied Manila on January 2, 1942, he offered
them his services. After the war, Laurel maintained that he did so under orders from Quezon
(who died early in 1944) for the purpose of
mitigating the lot of the Filipinos under occupation.

Laurel was made Commissioner of Justice
and of the Interior in Jorge B. Vargas' Philippines Executive Commission by the Japanese
occupation in 1942. As chief of a "pacification
commission," Laurel was responsible for drives
against Filipino and American guerrillas, and
during a wave of anti-collaborationist assassina-
tions in 1943, he was shot twice while golfing.
A dozen young Filipinos were executed for the
offense, although the would-be assassin was
never identified. Under hospital care, Laurel
slowly recovered his health, and from that time
on was provided with a 600-man Japanese armed
guard.

Appointed chairman of the "Preparatory Commission for Philippine Independence," Laurel
drafted a constitution for the puppet Republic
to be set up within the Japanese "co-prosperity
sphere." He was chosen President-elect by an
assembly mainly of members of the Kalabapi,
described as a totalitarian party and a national
service organization set up to control the population, handle rationing, and eliminate all traces
of Western influence.

After a visit to Tokyo by Laurel, the "Philippine Republic" was proclaimed on October 14,
1943, with Tagalog, the dialect of Luzon, replacing English and Spanish as the official
language. The first act of the new State was
unanimous ratification of an alliance with Japan.

President Laurel, shortly after taking office,
amnestied guerrilla bands. That December he
declared Pearl Harbor Day an "official special
holiday." In his reorganized Cabinet, he took
the Home Affairs and Education portfolios. In
February 1944, the puppet Assembly gave him
dictatorial powers to "take and adopt any measure that may be necessary," including the seizure
of farm lands and businesses to increase or
maintain production. In March Laurel authorized a 20,000,000-pesos issue of twenty-year
bonds; and in September, with the Philippines
under heavy attack by Allied forces, he declared

war on the United States and Great Britain and put the Philippines under martial law. Laurel refused to order conscription, however, a move which his admirers say rendered the declaration meaningless, while satisfying the Japanese. In February 1945 Laurel's Government moved to northern Luzon and in March they were flown to Tokyo. Six months later, Laurel was captured by American forces in Nara, Japan, and imprisoned pending trial.

Accompanied by his son and aide, José Laurel 3d, the puppet President was returned to Manila in July 1946 to stand trial on 132 counts of treason. Soon after arrival, he brought *habeas corpus* proceedings on the ground that the new Republic could not prosecute him for acts against the former Commonwealth Government. Although this move failed, he was freed on $25,000 bail to prepare his defense, after hearings in which he charged that the United States was responsible for his collaboration because its military unpreparedness for World War II had caused the surrender. As it happened, Laurel was never brought to trial. Manuel Roxas, who had served in the Laurel regime, had been received by General MacArthur, and subsequently elected the first President of the independent Philippine Republic in April 1946. Roxas' last important act before his death in April 1948 was to sign a general amnesty for the 5000 accused traitors, of whom Laurel was chief.

Since Roxas' death, Laurel has been a bitter critic of the Quirino Administration's inefficiency and corruption, as well as what he terms American back-seat driving. He led the campaign against the military bases agreement, the Japanese peace treaty, and the Trade Agreement of 1946, which gave American investors equal rights with Filipino investors.

Running for President against Quirino and Avelino in 1949, Laurel scored a 2-1 victory in Manila but lost to him in the provinces. In 1951, when Defense Secretary Ramón Magsaysay policed the elections, Laurel and his slate won eight of the nine Senate seats; Laurel's total of 682,681 votes was the highest. As this result left the Senate split 12-12 between Quirino's Liberals and Laurel's Nacionalistas, a thirty-five day deadlock ensued until one Nacionalista broke ranks to cast the deciding vote for Quintin Paredes, rather than Laurel, as Speaker.

Predicting violence in the 1953 elections, Laurel proposed that, to forestall it, both he and Quirino should renounce their ambitions in favor of Magsaysay. On March 1st, Magsaysay resigned from the Liberal Party, on the ground that it was "either unable or unwilling to honor the standards of public service which its members and citizens of the nation have a right to expect," and ten days later he formally joined Laurel's party. In announcing that he would endorse Magsaysay for President of the Philippines, Dr. Laurel said, "I wasn't looking for a wise man or a sage. I was looking for an honest man with guts." "Perhaps Magsaysay hasn't much cultural background, but the country needs his moral character" (*Life,* April 20, 1953).

Dr. Laurel said recently that his ambitions were to continue his work as a lawyer and Senator, to establish a university, and to improve his family's economic situation. He and Paciencia Hidalgo, married in 1912, are the parents of nine children. A member of many legal societies, he served in pre-war years as president of the Lawyers League of the Philippines and as a director of the Philippine Academy of Social Sciences. He is described as a fiery orator, witty and erudite, capable of winning elections on personality alone. Among his honors is the Order of the Rising Sun, which he received from the hands of Emperor Hirohito.

Among the books written by Dr. Laurel are: *The Election Law* (1922); *Cases on Municipal Corporations* (1924); *Social Government in the Philippine Islands* (1926), and *Forces That Make a Nation Great* (1944).

Despite his advocacy of "constitutional dictatorship" in a period of crisis, Laurel's writings contain many statements in favor of a republican form of government. In an essay on "Social Responsibility," Laurel wrote that "the prime obligation of citizenship is the development of a feeling of responsibility that will compel us to think and to act in civic matters." "The Essence of Republicanism," he wrote in another essay, is "representation, renovation, and popular control." He added that this must be accompanied by State power to act "to enhance the well-being and economic security of the people" through socialization measures (*Gems of Thought*).

References

Harper's 197:82 O '48
N Y Times IV p2 Jl 27 '47; p26 N 7 '49
Nation 169:415 O 29 '49
U S News 27:24 N 18 '49

Bernstein, D. The Philippine Story (1947)
Castillo y Tuazon, T. del and J. del, The Saga of Jose P. Laurel, his brothers' keeper por (1949)
Laus, E. L. Brief Biographies of the 10 Most Outstanding Filipino National Leaders (1951)
Pan-Pacific Who's Who 1940-41
World Biography (1948)

LAWRENCE, MRS. CLARENCE A. *See* Lawrence, M.

LAWRENCE, MILDRED Nov. 10, 1907
Author

Address: b. c/o Harcourt, Brace and Co., 383 Madison Ave., New York 17; h. 1044 Terrace Blvd., Orlando, Fla.

Reprinted from the *Wilson Library Bulletin,* May 1953

There must be more than a trace of printers' ink in Mildred Lawrence's blood, for besides being the author of six books for girls and many stories and magazine articles, she has helped her husband, Clarence Anthony Lawrence, to run various weekly newspapers. Al-

MILDRED LAWRENCE

though at times trying other projects, they are "essentially newspaper people . . . always airing ourselves out with something new and then returning to the newspaper business."

The fresh air and new horizons gained by the forays into other fields also provided inspiration for Mrs. Lawrence's books. Thus, *Peachtree Island* gets its authentic background from an interim spent cultivating a peach orchard on an island in Lake Erie; and while helping to run a motor court in Pennsylvania, she learned about farm life in that state, which serves as setting for *Homemade Year.*

Mildred Elwood was born November 10, 1907 in Charleston, Illinois—a typical small county seat—where her father, De Witt Elwood, was for years superintendent of schools. Among his forebears was Thomas El(l)wood, Quaker, who, it is said, suggested to his friend John Milton that he follow *Paradise Lost* with *Paradise Regained.* Her mother, Gertrude Imogene Jefferson, was a descendant of Anthony Comstock, Boston book censor. Her ancestors on both sides fought in the Revolution.

Mildred's talent for writing first manifested itself when she won a school essay prize at the age of ten. Immediately after World War I, when she was eleven, the family moved to Flint, Michigan, a growing city where her father became an abstractor. Here she attended Central High School, playing in the school orchestra, working on the school paper, and graduating in 1924. She took her B.A. degree in 1928 at her parents' alma mater—Lawrence College in Appleton, Wisconsin. Majoring in English, she won the Tichenor prize in English literature, the Hicks prize in poetry, and a prize for a Spanish play. She served on the staff of the *Laurentian,* took an active part in athletics and student organizations, and was a Senior freshman advisor, yet still found time for writing poetry and had fifty pieces published—although all free. She also belonged

to the Alpha Delta Pi (social), Theta Sigma Phi (journalism) and Phi Beta Kappa. Later post-graduate study at Yale University led, in 1931, to the degree of M.A. in English literature.

Upon leaving Lawrence College she had intended to go into college teaching, and she credits the 1929 depression with sending her back to the Flint *Journal* as society editor, going on to general reporting, feature writing, reviewing books, music and art, and doing historical pieces about Flint.

It was after her marriage, in 1936, that her writing success came. She began doing children's stories, first for Sunday School magazines and later for *Story Parade, Wee Wisdom, Children's Activities, Jack and Jill,* and the *Scholastic* group. Mrs. Lawrence has one child, Leora Mary, now eleven. Writing books for children came next with *Susan's Bears* (1945).

Peachtree Island (1948) was praised by Harriet Morrison in *Library Journal* as a "heartwarming story of a little orphan. . . .Her heroic and successful effort to convince her uncle that she is just as good as a boy [in helping with his peach orchard] makes enjoyable and, at times, humorous reading." This was followed, in 1949, by *Sand in Her Shoes,* which shares with her readers the writer's ups and downs during her first year in Florida, where she and her husband ran a small-town weekly. Says the New York *Times,* "The story is as bright and lively as its several characters. The 8-to-12 year olds will enjoy all they learn." Included are experiences in a hurricane, and a minor mystery.

Homemade Year (1950), tells how the young visting heroine Vicky, with help from neighbors, restored the deserted 200-year-old buildings of a Pennsylvania German communal society, giving a fresh twist to the "saving-from-foreclosure" plot.

Polly Goodwin, writing in the Chicago *Sunday Tribune* approves it as "a story of humor, good sense, and fine characterization." Another Pennsylvania story is *Tallie* (1951), which has a very amusing account of a foxhunt and the thrill of finding a treasure. The *Saturday Review of Literature* says, "Humor is instinctive in every word . . . as . . . in all of Mildred Lawrence's books. In this one . . . she has drawn her most memorable character. Tallie is a unique and lovable young person."

Crissy at the Wheel (1952) tells the story of the change from carriages to automobiles. The New York *Herald Tribune* describes it thus: "Girls under 12 will be amused at the maneuvers of motherless Crissy and her salesman father . . . putting over the first sales of automobiles in a little town in Michigan."

Mrs. Lawrence has also written some adult short stories, and is soon to have an article in *House Beautiful.* She has just finished another children's book and is "mulling over the next one."

A brown-eyed, gray-haired person of medium height and weight, she busies herself with work for the P.T.A. and the American Association of University Women, rings doorbells for Red

Cross and Community Funds, and attends the Methodist Church. Her politics are "varied."

She enjoys sewing and reading, and is especially fond of travel in America and Europe. She reads all kinds of things, adult and juvenile, preferring fiction to nonfiction.

LEAN, DAVID (lēn) Mar. 25, 1908- Motion picture director, producer, writer
Address: b. c/o London Film Productions, Ltd., 146 Piccadilly, W. 1, London, England

The name of David Lean is frequently bracketed with that of Carol Reed as the two foremost directors to have emerged from the renaissance of British feature film production since World War II. Entering the motion picture industry at the age of nineteen, Lean rose through the ranks to become one of Britain's leading film editors. In 1942 he helped Noel Coward direct *In Which We Serve,* and then on his own he directed three films based on Coward's plays, including *Brief Encounter,* which received international acclaim. Lean followed this with two notable screen interpretations of Dickens' novels, *Great Expectations* and *Oliver Twist.* More recently, he conceived, directed, and produced *Breaking Through the Sound Barrier,* which won the British Film Academy's award as the most distinguished picture of 1952.

David Lean was born in Croydon, England, on March 25, 1908, the son of Francis William le Blount and Helena Annie (Tangye) Lean. His younger brother, Edward Tangye Lean, has been comptroller of the British Broadcasting Company's European Services since 1949. Raised in a strict Quaker atmosphere, young David was educated at Leighton Park School, a Quaker institution in Reading. He proved an indifferent scholar, however, and left school in his teens to become an apprentice in the office of his father, a chartered public accountant. Miserable at this work, he sought refuge every evening by going to see the latest efforts of D. W. Griffith, Cecil B. de Mille, Mary Pickford, or Douglas Fairbanks at the neighborhood cinema. "I was fascinated by films," he has since recalled. "But it took me a long time to realize that one could actually work in them." It was in 1928, when he was nineteen years old, that a sympathetic aunt suggested he try and get a job doing what he enjoyed. The following day he went to Gaumont Studios and was taken on for a month's probation without pay. At the end of the month, he was hired to hold out number boards before each sequence was filmed.

Subsequently, Lean was promoted to camera assistant, and he also served for a time as third assistant director, a routine job that included fetching tea for the director and calling the players to the set, but it gave Lean an opportunity to learn more about film-making. He decided that the focal point of the studio was in the cutting rooms where the film is assembled and edited, and ne resolved to become a cutter, or editor. At about this time the British studios were switching to sound, and Gaumont planned to make *The Night Porter* as a talking picture, to be directed by the late

Leslie H. Baker

DAVID LEAN

Sewell Collins. The directors usually did their own cutting in silent films, but with the advent of sound it was necessary to have a technician show them the mechanics of synchronizing the sound track with the visual film. Lean asked Sewell if he might watch the cutting of the picture and Sewell agreed. Young Lean was quick to comprehend the process and in 1930 was put in charge of cutting Gaumont Sound News (for which he also wrote and spoke the commentary). He later transferred to British Movietone News.

In the mid-1930's Lean returned to the field of feature film production and soon became "the highest paid cutter in Britain." After working on a number of "quickies," he edited three notable pictures directed by Paul Czinner and starring Elizabeth Bergner: *Escape Me Never* (1935), *As You Like It* (1936), and *Dreaming Lips* (1937).

In 1938 he was editor of the Gabriel Pascal production of Shaw's *Pygmalion,* which was co-directed by Anthony Asquith and its star, Leslie Howard. The following year Lean edited another Asquith assignment, *French Without Tears,* and then he worked on Pascal's second Shaw film *Major Barbara* (1941). While directing the screen tests for Pascal, David Lean first met the picture's cameraman, Ronald Neame. "We both believed that the camera could force attention where you wanted to force it," Neame has explained. "We used the language common to both cutter and cameraman." Later Lean edited two pictures directed by Michael Powell and written by Emeric Pressburger: *The Invaders* (1941; British title, *49 Parallel*) and *One of Our Aircraft Is Missing* (1942).

It was during this period that Filippo Del Giudice, a producer at Two Cities Films, approached Noel Coward to make a picture. The playwright agreed to write an original script, but only on the condition that he have complete

LEAN, DAVID—*Continued*

control over the story, casting, and production. Realizing that he would need expert help, Coward asked for Neame as his cameraman. Associate-producer Havelock-Allan suggested that Coward invite Lean, whom he described as "the best technical man in the business," to assist him in directing the picture. Thus Lean became both co-director and editor of *In Which We Serve* (1942), the story of a British destroyer and its crew during the early years of World War II. The cast was headed by Noel Coward, Bernard Miles, Celia Johnson, and John Mills. According to an article by Lawrence Earl, Lean not only directed all the action and battle scenes, but also advised Coward about the script. Lean once told an interviewer, "I owe a tremendous lot to Coward. He taught me more about directing actors than anyone else." The picture won several awards. Both the New York Film Critics' Circle and the National Board of Review selected *In Which We Serve* as the outstanding motion picture of 1942. The London *Spectator's* film critic, Edgar Anstey, called it "the greatest of all films about Britain at war."

Coward was so pleased with *In Which We Serve* that he gave Lean permission to film any of his plays. Lean, Neame, and Havelock-Allan thereupon formed their own production company which they called Cineguild. The first Coward play they brought to the screen (in Technicolor) was *This Happy Breed* (1944), which chronicled the life of a lower middle-class London family between two world wars. The cast included Celia Johnson, Robert Newton, and John Mills. Reviewing the picture for *Hollywood Quarterly*, Irving Pichel praised Lean's "imaginative and sensitive perception of character" and his "acute use of the screen medium" and congratulated the Cineguild team on having "realized fully in screen terms the content of the story as extraordinarily vivid and believable extensions of human experience." The trio then collaborated on *Blithe Spirit* (1945,) a Technicolor version of Coward's farcical fantasy about a medium and spiritualism, in which Rex Harrison, Constance Cummings, Kay Hammond, and Margaret Rutherford appeared. A number of critics thought the picture adhered too closely to the limitations of its stage prototype, but the film's special photographic effects won an Academy Award. The film version of *Brief Encounter*, in which Celia Johnson played the lead opposite Trevor Howard, was praised in the *Penguin Film Review* as "a landmark among British films." It was voted the finest British production of 1945 at the International Film Festival in Cannes.

After completing *Brief Encounter*, the Cineguild trio felt it was time to prove themselves apart from Coward. Lean, in particular, was anxious to try his hand at a picture that was not derived from a stage play. They decided to translate Dickens' famous novel *Great Expectations* to the screen, and Lean and Neame (now listed as the producers) collaborated on the adaptation. The leading roles were played by John Mills, Alec Guiness, Jean Simmons, Bernard Miles, Martita Hunt, and Valerie Hobson. After the film's première in December 1946,

Richard Winnington hailed it as "the first great challenge to the world" on behalf of the British cinema. "Here is one of Dickens' best novels brought to film life with such absolute fidelity to character, setting, mood, and dialogue that its equal has never before been approached" wrote Archer Winsten in the New York *Post*. The picture won three "Oscars" in 1947—for art direction, interior direction, and cinematography. Lean and Stanley Haynes subsequently prepared a screen treatment of another Dickens' classic, *Oliver Twist*, in which John Howard Davies, Robert Newton, and Alec Guiness appeared. Bosley Crowther (*Times*) considered it "an eloquent picturization of the social injustices that existed in Dickens' day." The release of *Oliver Twist* in the United States was held up three years because of some objections to the alleged anti-Semitism of the characterization of Fagin.

Lean's next two films for Cineguild were accorded a cool reception by both the critics and the public. The first was *One Woman's Story* (1949) starring Ann Todd, Claude Rains and Trevor Howard, and was based on H. G. Wells' novel *The Passionate Friends*. A reviewer in *Time* (May 30, 1949) found the picture "an expensive warning to all non-Hollywood moviemakers: leave the filming of stylishly dressed romantic triangles to California's old masters of the art." The New York *Times* (May 18, 1949) commented: "Withal, Mr. Lean is a director who makes his actors perform and who uses his sensitive camera with clever mobility."

Lean's second film was *Madeleine* (1950), starring Ann Todd, and the story was based on the actual case history of a Glasgow girl who was brought to trial for murdering her lover in 1857. According to James S. Barstow, Jr. (*Herald Tribune*), Lean had crowded the screen with "too many little vignettes of persons and places," so that there was little conviction."

By 1950, the three partners of Cineguild had agreed to go their own separate ways. Lean left the J. Arthur Rank Organization (which had been sponsoring Cineguild's productions) and shortly afterwards accepted an offer to join Sir Alexander Korda's London Films. In the opinion of Richard Griffith (*The Film Till Now*), Lean had established himself as "a brilliant technician, sensitive and serious about the cinema, probably the most skillful of all the young British directors, obviously waiting for real material of contemporary importance to come into his hands."

Lean got the idea for his next picture from a newspaper account of a jet plane which disintegrated in flight without known reason, except for the speculation that it had something to do with what happens when a moving object outpaces the speed of sound. Attracted by the movie possibilities of the problem of supersonic flight, Lean spent three months visiting aircraft factories and talking with test pilots, designers, and scientists; then he wrote a 20,000-word summary of what he had learned. He passed this on to playwright Terence Rattigan, who devised a plot from the material.

By the time Lean was ready to begin shooting, the script was an accurate blueprint of every word, action, and scene in the picture. A London Films presentation, *Breaking Through the Sound Barrier* (1952; called simply *The Sound Barrier* in Britain) starred Ann Todd, Sir Ralph Richardson, and Nigel Patrick, and listed Lean as the director-producer. "With this film Lean breaks through the thin but definite line that divides exceptionally good directors from great ones," was the verdict of Henry Hart (*Films in Review*). The British Film Academy selected *The Sound Barrier* as the year's best picture from any source and judged Richardson's performance as the finest male acting of 1952. Lean has begun work on a screen version of Harold Brighouse's comedy, *Hobson's Choice*, first staged on Broadway in 1915.

The British film-maker was nominated as the year's best director by the American Academy of Motion Picture Arts and Sciences for *Brief Encounter* in 1947 and for *Great Expectations* in 1948. In 1940 he married Kay (Kathleen) Walsh, the actress who played in *In Which We Serve*, *This Happy Breed*, and *Oliver Twist*. This marriage was terminated in March 1949, and later that year he married actress Ann Todd.

Described as "angularly handsome," the director-producer who has black hair, is five feet eleven and a half inches tall and weighs slightly less than 150 pounds. According to Ronald Neame, Lean is "difficult to get to know," has "no small talk at any time." His greatest asset is "a furious concentration" and while engaged on a picture he "lives at a high pitch of intensity" and concentrates on his work "to the exclusion of everything else." Once asked at what point in making a film he thought he gave his greatest creative contribution, he replied, "Before I've shot any of it." His hobbies are gardening and amateur photography.

References

N Y Sunday News II p2 S 28 '52 por
N Y Times II p5 Je 15 '47 por; II p5 N 9 '52
International Motion Picture Almanac, 1950-51
International Who's Who, 1952
Miller, M. ed. Winchester's Screen Encyclopedia (1948)
Who's Who, 1952
Who's Who in America, 1952-53

LE CLERCQ, TANAQUIL   October 2, 1929-   Ballet dancer

Address: b. New York City Center, 130 W. 56th St., New York 19; h. 41 E. 75th St., New York

Twenty-four-year-old Tanaquil LeClercq has had leading roles in the New York City Ballet Company since it was founded in 1948 by choreographer George Balanchine and Lincoln Kirstein. In the current season she appeared as the Nymph in the première of Jerome Robbins' new version of *Afternoon of a Faun,* a role in which she received much favorable comment in the press.

TANAQUIL LE CLERCQ

During the company's highly successful appearances at the New York City Center, and on its tours throughout the United States, England and Europe, Tanaquil LeClercq has developed her own personal following among balletomanes. In a group noted for its many talented ballerinas, including Maria Tallchief, Nora Kaye, Patricia Wilde and Janet Reed, Miss LeClercq has been singled out by critics here and abroad for her fine technique, her ability to create romantic, tragic or comic roles, and her unusual physical equipment—her legs have been called the longest on the dance stage.

The ballerina's father, Jacques Georges Clemenceau LeClercq, a native of Austria and a naturalized American citizen, was in Paris on a Guggenheim Fellowship in creative writing with his wife, Edith (Whittemore) LeClercq of St. Louis, when their only child was born on October 2, 1929.

Now a professor of Romance Languages at Queens College in New York City, LeClercq wrote poetry and short stories in his youth under the name Paul Tanaquil. He gave his daughter the name Tanaquil, after the wife of the Tarquin, the legendary Roman ruler, and from then on discarded the pseudonym and used his real name for his writings and translations.

"Tanny," as she is called by her associates, was reared in New York City, and received all her training there. Since her talent for dancing was recognized at the King-Coit School in New York when she was four years old, her life has centered on her ballet studies. At seven, she became the pupil of Michael Mordkin, then "the most distinguished teacher in America," according to a writer in *Cosmopolitan* (February 1953).

The young dancer was offered an eight-year Hollywood contract when she was nine years old, but her mother refused it, preferring to keep the child concentrated solely on her ballet training. Although Tanaquil attended the *Lycée*

LE CLERCQ, TANAQUIL—*Continued*

Francais de New York for three years, she dropped out at the age of twelve, and thereafter studied with private tutors so that she could spend most of the day studying dancing.

In 1940 she won a scholarship to the School of American Ballet in New York City, which had been founded by Balanchine and Kirstein. Her first professional appearance took place in August 1945, when she performed two solos at the annual Jacob's Pillow Dance Festival near Lee, Massachusetts.

When Balanchine and Kirstein formed Ballet Society in 1946 for the presentation of new works—rather than the standard classics of the ballet repertoire—Tanaquil LeClercq became prima ballerina of the group. She danced the role of Ariadne in Balanchine's *Triumph of Bacchus and Ariadne,* and also appeared in *Four Temperaments* and *Orpheus.*

Ballet Society became the New York City Ballet during the 1948-49 season, and Miss LeClercq became one of its principal female dancers. The policy again was to avoid old or wornout classics, and to present works especially created for the group. A number of Balanchine's own ballets were revived.

B. H. Haggin of the *Nation,* described her performance of the bride in *Baiser de la Fée* as "its exquisite deployment of bodily configuration, its amazing range of expressiveness, its power of presence and projection that gives an extra animation and radiance to her quietest movement," and in another discussion of her work stated that although the other members of the company danced well, her "distinction and force created . . . the only moments of the 'amplitude of meaning' that art—and dancing like any other art—can give."

Other ballets in the company's repertoire in which she appears are *La Valse, Apollo, Symphony in C, Pied Piper, Bourrée Fantasque,* and *Age of Anxiety,* in which she dances for twenty-five minutes without a break. In February 1952, she danced the leading role in *Swan Lake* for the first time, replacing prima ballerina Maria Tallchief. John Martin wrote in the New York *Times* (February 28, 1952) that she had passed the initiation ceremony "from dancer to ballerina." She later told a reporter that she had wept with terror through that whole performance, pouring tears over her partner, André Eglevsky.

When she danced the role again the following November, Martin praised the "slightly coltish gaucheness . . . unfamiliar youth and helplessness" she brought to the character of the Swan Queen, and predicted that her interpretation of the part would develop further in the future (New York *Times,* November 24, 1952).

She is a favorite with English audiences. On her first London appearance with the New York City Ballet at Covent Garden in 1948, the London *Daily Mail* reported that the young ballerina "is a remarkable dancer, particularly with her arms and hands," and went so far as to compare her "fluttering quality" to that of Pavlova, remarking that she "very rightly received most applause" at the New York company's début.

The ballerina essayed a dramatic role on television in February 1952, in a Studio One production, *A Candle for St. Jude.* She played the part of a young ballet student, and performed in a dance especially created by Ruthanna Boris of the New York City Ballet. Her other appearances on television include a performance on the General Motors 1952 Christmas Show.

She was married on December 31, 1952 to George Balanchine, artistic director of the company. She is unaffiliated with any church or political organization.

The dancer's chief hobby is photography, and in February 1952 some of her pictures were exhibited at the Fifty-eighth Street Branch of the New York Public Library under the title "A Ballerina's View of the New York City Ballet." She takes, develops, prints and enlarges her own pictures. Her subjects are chiefly the other members of the company, rehearsing, resting, or performing onstage, and she has set up a dark room at the City Center. A critic of her photographs wrote that she does well at creating a mood and telling a story, but on the technical side she has to "match her skill in interpretation with greater skill in printing."

The ballerina's other hobbies include seeing movies, crossword puzzles, "resting," "Coney Island," and swimming. Her eyes are gray-blue and her hair is light brown. She is five feet six inches tall in her ballet slippers, and weighs 112 pounds. She dances every day, including Sundays, and appears in two or three ballets six nights a week. "It's like training a racehorse and being a racehorse at the same time," she told a reporter.

The New York *Post* critic said of Tanaquil LeClercq on November 22, 1950 that "she has developed into a unique personality among ballerinas. Her long limbs, her endless extensions, her cocksureness and sense of humor give her a peculiarly individual style. You may or may not be fascinated by it, but you will be constantly aware of her."

References

Cosmopolitan p46 F '53 pors
People Today 1:12 Ag 28 '50 pors

LEE, CLARK (GOULD) Jan. 31, 1907— Feb. 15, 1953 Foreign correspondent; joined Associated Press Bureau in Newark (1929); chief of A.P. bureau in Mexico City (1933) and in Honolulu (1936); covered Japanese war on China (1939-41); in World War II wrote eyewitness accounts of battles in Pacific theater, including the Philippine campaign and the defense of Bataan; author of *They Call It Pacific* (1943); roving correspondent for Hearst's International News Service (1943); covered American occupation of Japan; testified in the treason trial of "Tokyo Rose" (1949). See *Current Biography,* 1943.

Obituary

N Y Times p21 F 16 '53

LÉGER, PAUL-ÉMILE, CARDINAL Apr. 26, 1904- Catholic prelate
Address: b. c/o Roman Catholic Archdiocese of Montreal, 1071 Cathedral St., Montreal 3, Quebec, Canada

When His Eminence Paul-Émile Cardinal Léger was elevated to the Roman Catholic Sacred College of Cardinals on January 12, 1953 in a consistory of the Vatican in Rome, he became the first Cardinal in the See of Montreal and the sixth in Canada. Enthroned as Archbishop of Montreal in May, 1950, Léger won renown as an outstanding theologian, an able administrator and a brilliant speaker. From 1947 to 1950 he was rector of the Canadian College in Rome and from 1940 to 1947 he was vicar-general of the Diocese of Valleyfield in Canada.

The son of Ernest and Alda (Beauvais) Léger, Paul-Émile Léger was born on April 26, 1904, in Valleyfield, Province of Quebec, Canada. He was reared in the predominantly French village of St. Anicet on Lake St. Francis, where his father owned a general store. Although Paul-Émile enjoyed swimming skating and sailing, his devout and studious nature soon asserted itself and led him to an early decision to enter the priesthood. He was encouraged in this ambition by Cardinal Rouleau.

He received his early tutoring in Latin from the Most Reverend Percival Caza, Auxiliary Bishop of Valleyfield, whose house he called his "second home," Léger began his classical studies at Ste. Thérèse Seminary, Province of Quebec and in 1924 was awarded a B.A. degree. He then undertook postgraduate studies, majoring in theology, at the Grand Séminaire de Montréal, where he was considered "a regular fellow, leader, and brilliant student" (The Montreal *Ensign,* January 24, 1953). After receiving his B.D.C. (Bachelor of Canon Law) degree from the Séminaire on May 25, 1929, Léger was ordained to the priesthood by Bishop Georges Gauthier, auxiliary-bishop of Montreal.

Father Léger left Canada in the fall of 1929 to study and teach for three years in Paris. He studied at the Institut Catholique de Paris and in 1930 at La Solitude de Paris in Issy-les-Moulineaux, he became a Gentleman of St. Sulpice, an order that helped to found Montreal. During 1930-31, he taught at the Séminaire de Philosophie in Paris, and in 1931-32 at the Séminaire de Théologie in that city. The following year, he served as assistant master of novices at the Noviciate of the Sulpician Fathers in Paris.

Léger went to Japan in 1933 under the auspices of the Sulpician Order to found the Seminary of Fukuoka, where he remained as superior for six years. He learned to speak Japanese in six months and to give retreats in that language. He was recalled in 1939 from this missionary work to teach in the Séminaire de Philosophie at Montreal. In the following year he was made vicar-general of the Diocese of Valleyfield and curé of the Cathedral, where he remained until 1947.

Monsignor Léger went to Rome in 1947 to become rector of the Canadian College there.

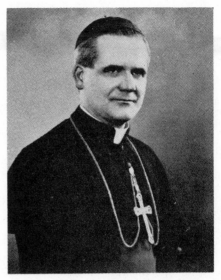

PAUL-EMILE CARDINAL LÉGER

In this post he made the name "Canada" synonymous with "charity" through his efforts to obtain food, clothing and medicine from parishes in Canada for the needy of Rome, Europe and the Near East. During the Holy Year of 1950 he served as a helpful "ambassador" to the many Canadian pilgrims who visited the Vatican.

On March 25, 1950, Léger was elected Archbishop of Montreal succeeding Archbishop Charbonneau as head of the largest ecclesiastical province in the British Commonwealth, including Montreal, St. Hyacinthe, Valleyfield, Joliette, and St. Jean. He was consecrated to this office in Rome by His Eminence Cardinal Piazza on April 26, 1950, and on May 17 of that year was enthroned in Montreal. During the next two years he increased his reputation as an administrator and as an eloquent speaker.

Archbishop Léger took a firm stand against games of chance, euthanasia, materialism, birth control, loose liquor laws, and obscene literature. His efforts contributed largely to the passing of a bylaw by the Montreal City Council which required retail liquor stores not only to remain closed on Sundays, but on all holy days of obligation as well.

In a pastoral letter dated August 22, 1950 on education, Léger stated that for educators the wide range of their mission is "the same as that of the Church" (*Relations,* October 1950). His letter attacked "materialism" and an "absence of spiritual climate in the home, and even more in society." He condemned "those men for whom their profession, title, or rank, is only a springboard to obtain wealth, power, or honors, by any means possible, without caring about honesty or social service." He also declared that "education is a sacred cause," and added that, "under certain circumstances, whoever betrays his task as a minister of education, or corrupts by intrigue the purity of this min-

LÉGER, PAUL-ÉMILE, CARDINAL—
Continued

istry, commits, in the strongest sense of the word, a crime of treason."

On September 20, 1950, the officials of the City of Montreal, in what is described as a "brilliant ceremony," testified to their willingness to cooperate with Léger in his efforts to carry out the responsibilities of his office. In recognizing their support, the Archbishop replied: "The Christian and the citizen do not constitute two distinct realities. It is the same man who serves his Creator and his fellowmen" (*Relations,* October 1950).

Léger endeavored to help solve a local conflict in August 1951, between the Catholic lay teachers and the Montreal Catholic School Commission. In explaining his intervention, he said: "I know that in principle the Church does not go into the technical details of a social question. . . .But when interests such as those of morality or education are concerned . . . then it intervenes." He added that the Church, in recommending syndicates, does not exclude lay teachers. "A syndicate of teachers," he explained, "like all other professional associations, ought to be catholic, faithful to its ends, solid, free, and democratic" (*Relations,* August 1951).

Named by Pope Pius XII to the Roman Catholic Sacred College of Cardinals on November 29, 1952, Léger became the sixth Canadian to receive this honor, and the first Cardinal appointed to the See of Montreal. In his speech of acceptance at the Canadian College in Rome, where he received official notice of his elevation from a papal messenger, Léger stated that "not only Canada as a whole, but particularly the old Province of Quebec, rejoices that a great tradition has been continued and a solid bond unites it to the See of Peter" (the Montreal *Ensign,* January 24, 1953). To a group of Canadian priests, students, and friends at the College, he said that "the Church in Canada is above nationalism," and added that different cultures "can bring to a people a great national wealth."

At the Vatican in Rome on January 12, 1953, Léger was elevated to the Sacred College of Cardinals and received the Red Hat from the Pope in a traditional ceremony before the papal throne in St. Peter's Basilica. His elevation, together with that of twenty-three other prelates, brought the membership of the College of Cardinals to its maximum of seventy. Léger's coat-of-arms bears the motto: *With His aid, you shall not tire.* He was also assigned by the Pope to serve on the Congregation of the Discipline of the Sacraments, the Congregation of the Sacred Rites, and the Congregation of the Fabric of St. Peter's, three of the Vatican's twelve congregations for the transaction of headquarters business of the Church.

Pope Pius XII told a special audience of Canadian pilgrims that they should find leadership in Cardinal Léger in preparing for "the rapid evolution of conditions of life" in Canada. He cited the Cardinal's founding in Montreal of the Foyer de la Charité, and his concern for "the little people, the humble, the sick, and the workers." During a radio broadcast from the Vatican to the people of Canada, Léger, shortly after his elevation, stated that the fostering of "justice, love, and peace on earth" was the desire of Pope Pius XII in creating twenty-four new Cardinals.

In the administration of the Archdiocese of Montreal, Léger is responsible for the spiritual guidance of nearly a million Catholic laymen, 1,927 priests, 197 parishes, 691 schools and convents, 61 hospitals, orphanages, and homes for the aged, 43 scholasticates, 22 juniorates and novitiates, 12 classical colleges, an equal number of public chapels, five normal schools, and the University of Montreal among other institutions of higher learning.

When Léger returned to Canada from Rome on January 29, 1953, he received a joyful reception in Montreal from city dignitaries and citizens representing many nationalities. Bells of churches and chapels were rung, and his greeting was televised and carried over radio stations. In honor of his appointment as the first Cardinal of Montreal, the local newspaper, The Montreal *Ensign,* devoted an issue to him.

Pope Pius XII also conferred upon Léger the honor of titular leadership of the Basilica of St. Mary of the Angels, one of the largest and most well-known basilicas in Rome. In receiving this honor, he has an office formerly held by Rodrique Cardinal Villeneuve of Quebec, whom Léger characterized as one of the three men having "profound influence" on his life (the Montreal *Ensign,* January 24, 1953) in guiding his steps toward Rome.

His Eminence Cardinal Léger is five feet eleven inches tall and weighs 180 pounds. Although the second youngest man to be elevated to the Roman Catholic Sacred College of Cardinals, he states that his hair is "graying." In an editorial in *Relations* (April 1950), Léger is described as combining the qualities of "l'honnête homme" (cultured man) with "zeal for the house of God."

References

Keesing's Contemp Archives p12612 Ja '53
Montreal Ensign p1+ Ja 24 '53
Relations 10:89 Ap '50; 10:283-4; 285-6
Sat Night 68:6 D 20 '52
O '50; 11:197-8 Ag '51 por
Who's Who, 1952

LEIBOWITZ, SAMUEL S(IMON) Aug. 14, 1893- Judge; lawyer
Address: b. c/o Kings County Court, 120 Schermerhorn St., Brooklyn 2, N.Y.; h. 102 Coleridge St., Brooklyn 29, N.Y.

As a judge of the Kings County Court in Brooklyn, Samuel S. Leibowitz presides over the highest criminal court in the State of New York, the same tribunal before which he had practiced for a quarter of a century as "one of the most successful criminal lawyers of all time" (New York *Times*). During those twenty-five years he served as the defense attorney at many famous murder trials, saving all but one of his 140 defendants from the electric chair. He gained international recognition for winning the release of nine Negro defendants from the death sentence in the Scottsboro case, which marked the end of systematic exclusion of Negroes from Southern juries. Since beginning his fourteen-year term as an elected judge of the Kings County Court in January 1941, he has tried to give juvenile and first offenders sentences which provide for rehabilitation. He was the presiding judge from December 1949 through 1953 of the Brooklyn Grand Jury investigation into charges of alleged payments of protection money by gamblers to city policemen.

Although selected in July 1953 by the Fusion party as its candidate for Mayor of the City of New York, Judge Leibowitz decided on August 1 to withdraw from the mayoralty race,

Samuel Simon Leibowitz, born on August 14, 1893, is the son of Isaac and Bina Lebeau. Leaving his dry goods store in the Romanian city of Jassy to avoid the anti-Semitism there, Isaac Lebeau took his family to the United States, changed his name to Leibowitz, and settled first in the tenement section of the Lower East Side of Manhattan. Samuel was at that time four years old. Later the family moved to the East New York district of Brooklyn where Isaac Leibowitz operated a successful store, and his son received elementary and secondary schooling. As a student at Jamaica High School, from which he was graduated, Leibowitz enjoyed debating and elocution and delighted in his superior ability to memorize. Undecided as to what profession he should pursue, Samuel was urged by his father to study law. By working at odd jobs to pay his expenses, Leibowitz attended Cornell University Law School, where he became a champion debater, a member of the dramatics club, an enthusiastic baseball player, and a member of the track team.

In 1915 Leibowitz received his LL.B. degree from Cornell College of Law and in 1917 was admitted to practice. When Leibowitz had told the Dean of the law school that he wanted to become a criminal lawyer, the older man, as related in a *New Yorker* profile by Alva Johnston, was shocked that a Cornell graduate would think of any career except one in civil law. The young attorney, therefore, took a position as a clerk in a civil law firm, in time accepting employment in the office of Michael F. McGoldrick, at a salary of $35 a week. Still eager to practice in the criminal court, he offered his services to penniless defendants there. His first such case, involving the theft of $7 from the cash register of a saloon, came a few days after he had made his offer. By questioning whether a skeleton key—the prosecution's single evidence—could open the saloon's locked door, he persuaded the jury to find the man not guilty (Quentin Reynolds in *Courtroom*). Other such successful defenses of pauper clients followed and while he did not earn any money, Leibowitz gained a reputation for revealing the loopholes in the prosecution's cases, mostly by casting doubt on the "confessions" made during police examinations and by destroying the circumstantial evidence on which the prosecutors often based their charges.

Wide World Photos

SAMUEL S. LEIBOWITZ

With each successful defense, Leibowitz, who opened his own office in May 1919, added to his reputation for destroying the prosecutor's case and for winning the understanding and sympathy of juries. Eight years after his first criminal trial, he was retained by Al Capone and on four separate occasions won the freedom of the underworld leader and his associates on writs of *habeas corpus*. Speaking later of such clients, Leibowitz said: "I never consorted with them in the first place, they never slapped me on the back and called me 'Sam'. . . .I looked upon them as a doctor would a case. I have defended men who on the surface looked guilty . . . men on the doorstep of the deathhouse, who were proved later to be absolutely innocent. Under our system of jurisprudence, a man is given his day in court and he is innocent until proved guilty—that applies to Al Capone, or the president of a national bank" (New York *Herald Tribune*, November 10, 1950).

Having defended dozens of men and women accused of first degree murder, only one of whom was sentenced to death, Leibowitz was by 1929, according to Quentin Reynolds, "the most spectacular criminal lawyer in New York City."

In the widely discussed Hoffman case Leibowitz (acting without fee) was able to free the defendant, previously sentenced to life imprisonment for the murder of .a woman, by picking to pieces the circumstantial evidence which had brought the conviction of Hoffman, by proving erroneous the testimony of the State's ballistic expert, and by revealing that the defendant's own fear had created guilt behavior (*Courtroom*).

A factor that helped Leibowitz win favorable decisions was his serious study of all the issues in a case. A *New Yorker* writer once pointed out: "He is a plodding worker in the preparation of cases. By digesting a library

LEIBOWITZ, SAMUEL—Continued

on the subject of ballistics, he was able to shake the testimony of revolver experts. . . . He studied medicine and surgery for weeks before defending an alleged malpractitioner." While the lawyer represented many known individuals from the underworld, he often refused to defend others. He rejected an offer from "Lucky" Luciano to represent him on a compulsory prostitution charge, for which Luciano was later successfully prosecuted by District Attorney Thomas E. Dewey. Leibowitz also turned down a $250,000 offer from seven of the Murder, Inc., members and in 1935 refused to represent Bruno Richard Hauptmann at his trial for the kidnapping of Charles A. Lindbergh, Jr.

Leibowitz gained international attention through the Scottsboro case in which, from 1933 to 1937, he served, without fee, as chief defense counsel for nine Negro youths accused in an Alabama court of having assaulted two girls. After the youths had been tried, convicted, and sentenced to death, there was much agitation that the case against them had remained unproved and had been the result of racial feeling in the South. Then "in 1935 the United States Supreme Court handed down the momentous decision that the case must be retried on the grounds that Negroes had been denied (by custom and practice, not by law) the right to serve on juries in the State of Alabama" (Columbia Encyclopedia). Subsequently the Alabama Governor ordered jury panels opened to qualified Negroes; thus this case marked the end of systemic exclusion of Negroes from Southern juries. Eventually all nine defendants were freed from the original death sentence, four were released from prison sentences and the other five were later paroled.

At the peak of his success in 1940, Leibowitz decided to give up his law practice to become the Democratic nominee for the fourteen-year term as judge of the Kings County Court in Brooklyn, the highest criminal court in New York State. By that time, of some 140 persons charged with murder whom he had defended, only one had received the death penalty. After his election to the judgeship, Leibowitz stated that he considered his election "a great opportunity to serve the people of Kings County . . . to keep this community free of the professional criminal and racketeer" (New York Times, December 22, 1940). The New York Post (November 7, 1940) reported that the new judge felt that his major problem would be handling first offenders or the casual offender who had committed a crime of passion. He explained that unlike the professional criminal, for whom a judge could simply look up the penalty in the criminal code, the non-habitual criminal had to be given specialized and personal treatment. "The majority of such cases," he noted, "can be rehabilitated, and that's the kind of work I'm going to do!" Subsequently he has been active in programs to reduce gang warfare and delinquency among youths in the slum areas of Brooklyn.

Nine years after his election Leibowitz served as the presiding judge at the Brooklyn Grand Jury investigation of charges of alleged payments of protection money by gamblers to members of the New York City police force and racketeering on the Brooklyn waterfront. From December 1949 through 1951 in the course of the hearings, some 500 witnesses were questioned, many of them members of the Police Department, and, reported the New York Times (March 22, 1951), the investigation "established a close link between policemen and gamblers." Leibowitz, in concurring with the Grand Jury's report and recommendations, placed the major responsibility for eliminating graft on the elected city officials. Later, in an interview with the Christian Science Monitor (October 13, 1950), he emphasized that organized crime and rackets "flourish only when the powers that be are crooked or incompetent. . . .We will only get the right men in public office when the people stand upon their hind legs and fight for good government." In March 1951 he testified before the Senate Crime Investigating Committee in Washington, D.C., charging that gamblers pay between $20,000,000 and $25,000,000 a year to policemen of the New York vice squad. As a means of stamping out organized crime he has recommended the establishment of three bodies: an investigating Grand Jury in each county—not "beholden to" anyone in public office—which would concern itself exclusively with rackets and city departments that become venal; a staff of investigators in each of the District Attorney's offices to check on the workings of various city departments; an independent citizens' crime commission to keep the spotlight turned on the acts of public officials.

While Leibowitz was presiding over the trial of the twenty-one retired or suspended policemen charged with participating in gambling rackets, an article in the New York Times Magazine (June 17, 1951) advised the defendants: "If you've really been framed, pray that Judge Leibowitz hears your case. If you're guilty, pray that he doesn't." The next November (1951) the judge ordered the holdover December 1949 Grand Jury, which had exposed the graft in the police department, to investigate the alleged organized racketeering on Brooklyn's waterfront. On December 12, 1952, he extended the term of the hold-over Grand Jury, referred to the "shocking" revelations brought out at the New York State Crime Commission hearings, and urged the jury to "start the ball a-rolling at the very next session" in investigating crime on the waterfront.

Leibowitz is a member of the New York State and American bar associations and has been affiliated with United Jewish Appeal, Red Cross, Zionists movements, Child Guidance Institute, and the Salvation Army. In 1919 he married Belle Munves; they have twin sons, Robert and Lawrence, both of whom studied at Princeton University, and a daughter, Marjorie. The New Yorker profile described Judge Leibowitz as "a solidly built man with thinning hair," a "forensic complexion," and a "voice of extraordinary timbre which starts sympathetic vibrations in the very bones of jurymen." His interests outside the court room are the theatre, and the study of people.

References

N Y Times p28 D 22 '40
N Y Times Mag p25 Je 17 '51
New Yorker p21+ Je 4 '32; p18+ Je 11 '32
PM p11 Jl 25 '40
Reynolds, Q. Courtroom (1950)
Who's Who in Law, 1937

LEONARD, LUCILLE P(UTNAM) *See* Leonard, Mrs. N. P.

LEONARD, MRS. NEWTON P(ECK-HAM) June 22, 1895- Organization president

Address: b. c/o National Congress of Parents and Teachers, 600 S. Michigan Blvd., Chicago, Ill; h. 341 Sharon St., Providence, R.I.

At the annual meeting of the National Congress of Parents and Teachers, meeting in Indianapolis, Indiana, in May 1952, Mrs. Newton P. Leonard was elected to succeed Mrs. John E. Hayes as president of the organization for a three-year term (1952-55). Mrs. Leonard, a former schoolteacher and welfare worker who has long been prominent in both her local and State parent-teacher organizations, is also active in a number of other State, municipal, and community organizations.

The daughter of Willard and Myra Lavinia (Tenney) Putnam, Lucille Putnam was born June 22, 1895, in New Salem, Massachusetts. Living here until she entered college, she attended the nine primary grades in the local one-room school house before entering the New Salem Academy, the township's public high school, from which she was graduated in 1912. At that period, mathematics and science were her preferred studies.

As a student at Mount Holyoke College, she completed work for the Bachelor of Arts degree, which she received in 1916, in the dual major subjects of history and chemistry. "I majored in history because I felt that I needed the background of knowledge," she has observed, "also because it was a difficult subject and I had been brought up to choose the 'harder' task. Chemistry was very interesting to me. As part of my chemistry major I took a course in zoology and became so interested that I really had a third major in that field." For further professional training after her graduation from Mount Holyoke, Miss Putnam spent a year (1917) at Simmons College, taking the course in institutional management, in which she continued to develop her scientific interests, particularly in the fields of dietetics and bacteriology. By doing volunteer social work in the Italian district of Boston, she came to the conclusion that she wanted to work "with and for people."

MRS. NEWTON P. LEONARD

Upon completing her work at Simmons, Miss Putnam obtained a position as director of "baby diets" at a summer camp for mothers and children operated by New York Associated Charities at Coney Island. The following fall she joined the staff of the New Jersey Reformatory for Girls and Women, where she was matron of the receiving dormitory and dietician of the officers' dining room and three of the dormitories. "The following winter the personnel of the institution completely changed because of political shake-up," she has related. "I resigned as I felt I could not continue under the proposed change of attitude toward the inmates." Shortly after, an occasion arose which enabled Miss Putnam to teach in a Martha's Vineyard (Massachusetts) high school. "To my surprise, I found that I greatly enjoyed teaching, a profession I had severely shunned in college as I was determined not to be a teacher." At a later period, she studied at the Rhode Island College of Education in Providence.

On October 5, 1918, Miss Putnam was married to Newton Peckham Leonard, then a chemical supervisor with E. I. DuPont DeNemours & Company and afterward a teacher of chemistry. (In 1953 he is a vocational counselor in the Providence public school system.) When their elder daughter entered school in 1926, Mrs. Leonard joined the Parent-Teacher Association of the Cranston (Rhode Island) Eden Park School. During that period, Mrs. Leonard has remarked, "Usually my husband and I belonged to several P.T.A.'s at the same time as our two daughters were in different schools and we were teaching in others." Serving at first only on P.T.A. program or hospitality committees, Mrs. Leonard subsequently was elected first vice-president of the branch at the Roger Williams Junior High School in Providence. The branch to which she belongs in 1953 is that at Providence's Nelson Street School. Sent by her local branch as representative to the State

LEONARD, MRS. NEWTON—*Continued*

P.T.A. branch, Mrs. Leonard held a number of positions in that group: chairman of standing committees, treasurer, and vice-president. In behalf of the State branch, she served on the joint committee of the Rhode Island Congress, the Rhode Island Institute of Instruction, the Women's Joint Legislative Committee of Rhode Island, and the Consumers' Conference of Rhode Island. From 1940 to 1943 she was president of the Rhode Island Congress of Parents and Teachers.

Advancing to the national level of the organization, Mrs. Leonard became trustee of the National Endowment Fund and national vice-president from Region I. For three years (1949-52) she held the first vice-presidency of the National Congress of Parents and Teachers. During this same period, in 1950, she was elected a director of *National Parent-Teacher*, the P.T.A. magazine. On May 20, 1952, at the annual convention of the congress in Indianapolis, Indiana, she was elected as unopposed candidate to the presidency of the national Congress of Parents and Teachers, to serve for a three-year term in succession to Mrs. John E. Hayes. "Children and youth," Mrs. Leonard has stated, "need the steady, purposeful support of adults to help them become alert, intelligent citizens ready to face the future. Home, the most important factor in every child's life, must be prepared to make him feel loved and wanted; to care for his physical needs; to teach him through text and example, good citizenship; to give him an active, positive spiritual faith; to enable him to have belief in and respect for his fellowmen. The school, the partner of the home, will further these basic teachings and will train and guide him to the fullest use of his abilities and aptitudes." In November 1952 Mrs. Leonard urged the more than 6,000,000 members of the National Congress of Parents and Teachers to mark the opening of American Education Week by a program calling for closer relations between school and home and more cooperation between school and health agencies, among other aims.

In 1945 Mrs. Leonard wrote an article, "Together We Build Good Citizenship," for *National Parent-Teacher*. She is a member of the Rhode Island Committee for Children and Youth, which grew out of the Governor's Commission of One Hundred for the Midcentury White House Conference on Children and Youth of 1950. Another gubernatorial commission on which she had served was the one formed in 1940 to study public welfare institutions in Rhode Island. In Providence, she has belonged to the mayor's advisory committee on recreation. Another of her services to that city is as member of the Coordinating Curriculum Council of the Providence public schools. Her other contributions to community welfare are made through the Community Relations Committee and through the Commission on Community Organizations of the National Conference of Christians and Jews. She is a member of the Girl Scouts of America.

The Leonards occupy a red brick Colonial house in the Mount Pleasant section of Provi-

dence, where their daughters, Lucille (Mrs. Malcolm L. Jewell) and Nina (Mrs. Calvin C. Sloan) come visiting with the five grandchildren. Mrs. Leonard attends the Westminster Unitarian Church. The gray-haired, brown-eyed P.T.A. president is five feet five inches in height and 150 pounds in weight. Her favorate pastimes are centered in the home—playing cards, knitting, sewing, gardening, hooking rugs, and "cook-outs." Mrs. Leonard, who likes both high school and professional baseball, as well as occasional games of football, calls herself a Red Sox fan.

LEY, WILLY (lā) Oct. 2, 1906- Author; rocket scientist; lecturer

Address: 37-26 77th St., Jackson Heights 72, N.Y.

> NOTE: This biography supersedes the article which appeared in *Current Biography* in 1941.

A well-known author in the field of paleontology and in space travel, Willy Ley is a research rocket engineer with practical experience spanning a quarter of a century and a world authority on rockets and rocket ships. He has written what is called "the first authoritative work for the layman that approaches the question of space travel with cold, unemotional, and unimaginative facts," a prize-winning book entitled *Conquest of Space* (1949). Since 1947 Ley has been a consultant to the office of technical services of the United States Department of Commerce and from 1944 to 1948 he was a research engineer for the Washington Institute of Technology at College Park, Maryland. During the greater part of World War II (1940-44) he was science editor for the New York newspaper *PM*. He is a popular science lecturer with both professional and lay audiences.

On October 2, 1906, Willy Ley was born in Berlin, Germany, one of two children (a boy and a girl) of Julius Otto Ley, a wine merchant, and Frida (May) Ley. His mother was the daughter of an official in the German Lutheran Church; his paternal grandfather was a blacksmith. Willy was reared largely in Berlin, where he attended the public schools. In high school he developed a lifelong interest in all aspects of scientific fact and history.

At intervals between 1920 and 1926 Ley studied at the University of Berlin and the University of Königsberg in East Prussia, specializing in paleontology, astronomy, and physics. His college education was interrupted during the period of inflation which followed World War I in Germany. When Ley in 1926 read a book by Hermann Oberth on space travel, one of the first scientific treatments of the subject, he gave up his plans of making his career in geology and became an enthusiast of the concept of travel beyond the stratosphere, an idea that was making progress in Germany in the early 1920's. After receiving a small check for a scientific correction he sent to a German newspaper, Ley was encouraged to begin his writing career, regularly submitting articles on scientific subjects to a number of German magazines.

In 1926 he published his first book in Germany, *Trip Into Space,* which was concerned with rocket ships. His prime interest became the development of the rocket theory, and for support of his cause he communicated with Hermann Oberth, with whom he won the interest of a group of young German scientists in forming a pioneering rocket research organization called the Verein für Raumschiffahrt (Society for Space Travel) in 1927. In cooperation with other experimentors in the group, Ley helped to build instruments and to launch them—a task that took the lives of several rocket pioneers in the society, including Reinhold Tiling, inventor of the winged rocket. Ley introduced to the organization Wernher von Braun, who headed the project that created the German V-2 rocket. Ley was his first tutor in rocket research.

As vice-president of the Verein für Raumschiffahrt from 1928 to 1933, Ley built the organization membership from a small number of people to an aggregate of more than 1,000 individuals, operating a proving field on the outskirts of Berlin and employing a full-time staff of six engineers and mechanics. Able to speak and write English, French, Latin, Dutch, Russian, and Italian, as well as German, Ley maintained a correspondence with rocket pioneers throughout Europe and America so that the German society served as the world center for news and information on rockets. For financial support, Ley depended upon his employment in a German industrial firm and upon small money grants offered to the group. He was responsible for some of the basic ideas that produced the liquid-fuel rocket that his society sent one mile up in the air in 1931.

In 1928 Ley edited a book in his native Germany entitled *Die Moglichkeit der Weltraumfahrt,* a collection of lectures by authorities on space ship problems and in 1930 he wrote *Konrad Gesner, Leben und Werk.* He then began work on *Grundriss einer Geschichte der Rakete* (1931), a history of rockets, tracing their origin from the ancient Chinese and Greeks, through the fireworks makers of Italy, to the English William Congreve, down to 1931. With the ascension of Hitler and the Nazis to power in Germany in 1933, journals, books, and papers were seized from the Raketenflugplatz (rocket proving grounds) of the Verin für Raumschiffahrt by the Gestapo, and the German press was forbidden to mention the word "Rakete" (rocket). Some of the members of the dissolved society for space travel followed the request of the Nazi regime to staff the laboratories at Peenemünde, where the V-2 was later developed. From a peaceful objective of getting to the moon, held by the original rocket pioneers, the purpose of rocket research became the development of a war weapon. Ley left Germany for what he described as an "extended vacation" in England in 1935 and on February 21 of that year arrived in New York City on the White Star Liner *Olympic,* having accepted an invitation of the American Rocket Society to visit the United States.

In America, Ley in 1935 found the public and the newspapers unsympathetic to rocket theory.

Olga Ley

WILLY LEY

As quoted by *This Week* (November 16, 1952), he said: "No one had the slightest interest in the subject except science-fiction magazines." He made what he calls "a precarious living" writing articles in the field of zoology and other branches of science for such magazines as *Coronet, Esquire, Fauna, Zoo,* and *Natural History.* In early November 1935 Ley was put in charge of a mail rocket test in which a rocket airplane was scheduled to be sent from Greenwood Lake, New York, to Hewitt, New Jersey, an airplane distance of about six miles. Propelled by liquid oxygen and gasolene, the rocket was similar to the famous V-7 that traveled one and three-quarters miles in Austria in 1931.

While employed as science editor of the newly founded New York newspaper *PM* from 1940 to 1944, Ley was responsible for the paper's "New Weapons" page and was the publication's rocket expert. His knowledge and experience relating to explosives, in addition to his newspaper work on weapons, led in 1941 to his writing especially for the members of the National Civilian Defense a book entitled *Bombs and Bombing: What Every Civilian Should Know.* In this book he described bombs of all types, how they are made and used and how they behave, pointing out that any attack could be met with an equally well-prepared defense. Foster Gleason, book reviewer for *Western Flying* (February 1942), said: "Mr. Ley considers the greatest dangers of air bombardment ignorance, misinformation, and panic."

Outside the field of weapons and explosives, Ley wrote a book called *The Lungfish and the Unicorn; An Excursion into Romantic Zoology* (1941), which was the May 1941 choice of the Scientific Book Club. The club's review specified that the author spent thirteen years collecting material for the book, which included a condensed version of articles written for American magazines. To the New York *Times*

LEY, WILLY—*Continued*

reviewer, the publication was "a good book all through," while the book critic for the New York *Herald Tribune* referred to it as "a volume of encyclopedic quality that will remain at the head of its particular category for a long time." Ley, who divided his book into three parts—treating so-called mythological animals, extinct animals, and living fossils—expressed a belief that animal myths are based on facts, suggesting that Scylla of the *Odyssey* and the mythical Medusa are kraken, or giant octopuses that only seldom rise to the sea surface.

In *Days of Creation* (1941), Ley presented a philosophy that "the record of the past is on the whole most decidedly in favor of the continued survival of the human race under any circumstances" (quoted in *Sky and Telescope,* April 1942). Of this book, which reveals in a popular style conclusions of science in regard to the origins and history of life, Howard Zahniser, book critic of *Sky and Telescope,* wrote that it has interest "mainly because its prospective readers are concerned with knowing just what their place is in the whole scheme of Nature." He added that "the same eloquence that made *The Lungfish and The Unicorn* such a welcome collection of wildlife, myth, legend, and lore, makes *Days of Creation* another welcome popularization of the conclusions of science regarding the origins and history of life."

In part a compilation of material first published in the *Coast Artillery Journal* (May-June 1941), Ley's *Shells and Shooting* (1942) traces the development of modern arms from "the first crude tubular device of the Dark Ages" (*Astronautics,* February 1943). "Worth reading by persons interested in mechanics and techniques of warfare," was the comment of the *Springfield Republican* reviewer on this volume on bullets, shells, grenades, mortars, cannon, rockets, and their uses. With emphasis upon early Russian and later German developments of rockets, Ley produced *Rockets; the Future of Travel Beyond the Stratosphere,* in which he dealt with the meteorological rocket, the rocket in cosmic space, and the space ship. "The book is not pedantic," noted the critic for *Book Week* (May 14, 1944), "although it abounds with facts. Ley has a vivid imagination and his writing is exciting, yet he keeps his feet on the ground."

Occasionally during World War II the United States Government called upon Ley for consultation. The day the first V-2 rocket struck London, in November 1944, Ley suddenly found newspapers in the United States willing to print material on rockets and referring to him for information. "It was like a stag hunt," he said, as quoted by *This Week;* "suddenly I was surrounded by baying hounds."

In 1944 Ley was appointed director of engineering at the Burke Aircraft Corporation in Atlanta, Georgia, which was later to become part of the Washington Institute of Technology at College Park, Maryland. While in this position, which he retained until 1948, he prepared in 1947 a revised edition of *Rockets,* entitled *Rockets and Space Travel; the Future of Flight Beyond the Stratosphere,* including a chapter on Hitler's rocket airplane experiments that resulted in the V-2 rocket at Peenemünde, and discussions on atomic energy, radar, submarine and mail rockets. The year 1947 also marked the beginning of Ley's contributions as consultant to the office of technical services of the United States Department of Commerce.

The Lungfish, The Dodo, and The Unicorn (1948), a revision of the earlier *The Lungfish and The Unicorn,* is reportedly considered by Ley to be his most successful book. In the opinion of the reviewer for *Frontiers* (December 1948), it is "a book for the permanent shelf; the age level is indefinite—it can be read and enjoyed by the middle-teen agers and octogenarians." Joseph Krutch of the *Nation* (November 13, 1948) observed, "Mr. Ley writes very clear, direct exposition . . . and digs into history with what is traditionally called German thoroughness." The following year Ley won the nonfiction section prize of the First International Fantasy Fiction Award for *Conquest of Space* (1949), a book described in the New York *Times* as "the latest and in many respects the most fascinating popular account of rocket travel and what people may see when they reach various landing places in the solar system."

Speaking at the first annual Symposium on Space Travel at the Hayden Planetarium on October 12, 1951, Ley told his audience that an unmanned rocket, such as the one that ascended in two stages to 250 miles from the New Mexico proving grounds, might be "practical anywhere from 350 to 22,300 miles" (New York *Times,* October 13, 1951). He explained that he preferred having the establishment of a station in space (artificial planet) precede the sending of an unmanned rocket to the moon, since such a station, if it could be manned, would serve as a fuel supply depot for space ships en route to the moon or interplanetary journeys. In an article appearing in *Science Digest* (December 1951) entitled "First Spaceship by 1970," Ley expressed his belief that "the year of the first spaceship probably will be 1965 or 1970" and discussed the engineering problem of applying atomic energy to rocket propulsion. The rocket expert agreed in 1952 to act as technical adviser to the television program *Tom Corbett, Space Cadet,* whose writers feel free to ask him questions any time; he also gave facts and answers questions during Sunday night talks for the American Broadcasting Company program *Looking into Space.* In October 1952 Ley was coordinator of the second annual Symposium on Space Travel at the Hayden Planetarium.

Articles Ley has written in the field of natural science include "Two-Thumbed Teddy Bear" (*Natural History,* September 1948) and "Roc of Ages" (*Nature,* December 1935). As adviser to *Collier's* in 1952, he helped in the preparation of a project on space travel, to which he was one of the article contributors: his articles are "Station in Space" (March 22, 1952), "Inside the Moon Ship" (October 18, 1952), and "Inside the Lunar Base" (October 25, 1952). Ley is also author of the books *Dragons in Amber; Further Adventures of a Romantic Naturalist* (1951), a description of the early ancestry of unusual plants and animals; *Rockets, Missiles, and Space Travel* (1951), a revision of *Rockets and Space Travel*; and *Lands Beyond* (in collaboration with Lyon Sprague de Camp, 1952), fact and fiction about Lost Atlantis and cities of gold.

Organizations with which Ley is associated are the new German Rocket Society, reconstituted in Western Germany after World War II (honorary member) and the British Interplanetary Society (fellow); he is a member of the American Rocket Society, the Institute of Aeronautical Science, the Society of American Military Engineers, the American Association for the Advancement of Science, the Royal Astronomical Society of Canada, and the Poets, Playwrights, Editors, Essayists, and Novelists. Ley's church affiliation is Lutheran. In 1944 he became a naturalized United States citizen, having taken out his first citizenship papers in 1937.

On December 24, 1941, Ley married Russian-born Olga Feldman, ballet dancer, beauty expert, and artist. They have two daughters, Sandra and Xenia. Ley is five feet ten inches in height and weighs 190 pounds, has greenish-gray eyes, a serious, intellectual face, and dark, graying hair. His hobbies are collecting stamps and making a "topical collection" of objects dealing with science, literature, and music. He likes to fly and his foremost wish is to "live to rise to the moon."

References

This Week p13 N 16 '52
Newsweek 23:80 My 22 '44
Who Knows—and What (1949)
Who's Who in Engineering, 1948

LIEBMAN, MAX Aug. 5, 1902- Stage and television writer, producer, director
Address: b. 130 W. 56th St., New York 19; h. 898 Park Ave., New York 21

Max Liebman, owner, director, and producer of the National Broadcasting Company's weekly television program, *Your Show of Shows*, has been the recipient in 1951, 1952, and 1953 of *Look* magazine's annual TV award for his achievement in that field of entertainment. A former sketch writer and summer hotel social director, Liebman is noted as a "play-doctor" for Broadway musical shows, and has contributed songs and skits to a number of stage and motion picture revues, including *Let's Face It*, *Make Mine Manhattan*, *Up In Arms*, and *Kid From Brooklyn*. He has brought many stars, including Danny Kaye, Sid Caesar, Betty Garrett, Imogene Coca, and Jules Munshin, from the summer hotel circuit to Broadway.

One of the three children of Harry and Sarah (Glazer) Liebman, Max Liebman was born in Vienna, Austria, on August 5, 1902. Having been brought to the United States in his infancy, he was reared in New York City, where his father entered the fur business. At Boys' High School in Brooklyn, Liebman was a member of the drama club and the debating society; he also conducted the humor column of

Zinn Arthur

MAX LIEBMAN

the school magazine before becoming the magazine's editor and wrote class shows in collaboration with Arthur Schwartz. Graduating in 1917, the youth left New York for Texas, where he worked in the oil fields and also acted for a short time as "front man" for a magician.

Back in New York City in 1920, Max Liebman began his career as a sketch writer and for the next five years wrote, produced, and directed vaudeville acts. In the summer of 1925 he was engaged as a social director at the summer camp Log Tavern in Pennsylvania. Seven years later Liebman began his long association with the Hotel Tamiment in Pennsylvania's Pocono Mountains, where he worked as social director for fifteen summer seasons. Every week he produced and directed a completely new musical revue, using the same stock company idea he now employs on television. The *Straw Hat Revue*, a musical that Liebman presented on Broadway in 1939, was first tested at the Tamiment Playhouse and introduced the stars Danny Kaye, Imogene Coca, and Anita Alvarez. Other celebrities whom Liebman brought to Broadway from the Poconos are Betty Garrett, Jules Munshin, Sid Caesar, the dance team of Mata and Hari, and the choreographers Jerome Robbins and Lee Sherman.

An "additional dialogue writer" for motion pictures, Liebman spent several years traveling back and forth across the country to theatres, film studios, and night clubs. "Always I was in with just one foot," he has said of this period (New York *Times*, November 19, 1950). In April 1942 he produced the short-lived suspense play *Autumn Hill*. His chief work having become that of "play-doctor" to faltering musical shows, Liebman lent his hand to such revues as *Up In Arms* (March 1944), *Let's Face It* (May 1944), *Tars and Spars* (February 1945), *The Kid From Brooklyn* (April

LIEBMAN, MAX—*Continued*

1946), *Make Mine Manhattan* (January 1948), *Along Fifth Avenue* (January 1949), and *Tickets, Please* (August 1950). For two of Danny Kaye's motion pictures, Liebman and Sylvia Fine were "literary partners" composing material exclusively for the star. In *Up in Arms* (1944) Kaye sang three song specialties by this team, among them the popular "Melody in 4F," which he had previously introduced in *Let's Face It*. In *The Kid from Brooklyn* (1946) Kaye delivered their monologue "Pavlova," a fast talking routine in which through words, gibberish, and pantomime he satirizes modern ballet. In World War II Liebman was a civilian director and sketch writer for USO camp shows, producing and directing *Tars and Spars* for the United States Coast Guard in 1945. After touring the country during the war, the show was bought by Columbia Pictures and brought to the screen in 1946. The following year Liebman was in Boston, where he produced *Shooting Star*, a musical based on the story of Billy the Kid.

In January 1949 Liebman made his television debut as the producer of the program *Your Show of Shows*, a ninety-minute revue televised by the National Broadcasting Company every Saturday night and said to be "the most diversified and most professional program of its type on the channels—a mixture of comedy, popular music, ballet, opera, and the modern dance" (*Cue*, February 17, 1951). Liebman, who has been called the "Ziegfeld of TV," has done much to develop his program since its inception, when "dancers practiced in a bare room off Broadway, skits were worked out in cubbyhole offices, and . . . the show went on the air without a camera rehearsal" (*Time*). Three seasons after the show's introduction, Liebman was employing an eighty-man staff occupying five floors of a New York building, and twelve arrangers, orchestrators, and copyists who turn out the scores for one week's show. Among the regular performers on the program are Sid Caesar, Imogene Coca, Marguerite Piazza, and Mata and Hari.

Reviewing the opening performance of the 1952 season, Jack Gould wrote in the New York *Times*, "*Your Show of Shows* remains an island of engaging literacy in TV's sea of vaudeville mediocrity. . . .The production as a whole does not vary materially from a year ago; it is lavish rather than imaginative." For its thirty-nine-week season in 1952-53, *Variety* reported (February 18, 1953), *Your Show of Shows* brought gross returns to the network of $7 million. Other TV programs that Liebman has produced was the one on which Bob Hope made his television debut in 1950 and the giant Elgin-American Thanksgiving Day show of the same year, which starred Milton Berle, George Jessel, and the Ritz Brothers. All Liebman's television shows were treated as Broadway productions, with the cameras kept off the stage, and the stagehands hidden from the studio audience.

Liebman, who is much interested in technical advances in television, disclosed in January 1952 his idea for putting his television studio audience "in swivel chairs . . . so that they will be able to see the action on three stages". With three stages, Liebman explained, effects and props used briefly on the show would not clutter up the main stage. In June 1952 Liebman left for Europe on a six-week trip to secure foreign films for American television, planning to buy the reels under the name Max Liebman Productions, a venture independent of NBC. During this trip he visited Madrid, Rome, Paris, London, and Vienna. Unable to find enough good films abroad that were suitable for American television (*Variety*, August 13, 1952), Liebman launched a new plan, a wide-scale purchase of top-budgeted American pictures. The films, which would be "long past their theatrical distribution prime," would not be cut to fit TV programming schedules, but would be run for two evenings, with editing and insertions to give them continuity. Comparing television in Britain and the rest of Europe, Liebman found, "British TV is of course much more advanced, though the programming is still pretty inadequate" (*Variety*). The producer is author of several articles on television which have appeared in *Esquire, Hollywood Reporter, Variety,* and other publications.

The recipient in 1953 of the *Look* television awards for the "individual who best organized and most creatively presented a TV series; for the individual who most effectively utilized the skills of actors and technicians in TV presentations," Liebman had in 1951 and 1952 also won an annual *Look* award for his production of *Your Show of Shows*. He was given the Michaels Award of the Television Academy of Arts and Sciences of 1952, in recognition of the year's best musical show program, and a personal NBC award for the "courage and discernment he had exhibited in bringing new talents and original methods to the field of television." Liebman has also received the *Motion Picture Daily* Award, and the Sylvania Award to the best producer on TV, and the *Variety* Award for 1950. Liebman feels these scrolls "justify the fight he made to bring his own ideas to television against pressure that he model his show after others."

In the fall of 1953 Liebman announced that he had devised a new format for *Your Show of Shows,* and major stage and screen stars will make guest appearances. The show's weekly budget, according to the New York *Times*, September 6, 1953, "has been increased by $10,000; it will now cost the sponsors $80,000 a week—as much as it takes to put on a major Broadway play."

Liebman belongs to the Authors' League and the American Society of Composers, Authors, and Publishers. On March 8, 1931, he married Sonia Glazer, a former opera singer. Described as a "small, slight man," Liebman is five feet six and one-half inches tall and weighs 142 pounds; he has brown hair and brown eyes. He lists as his hobbies horseback riding, photography, and collecting antiques and paintings.

References

Cue 20:15+ F 17 '51 por
N Y Times II p11 N 19 '50 por
Motion Picture and Televison Almanac, 1952-53

LIMÓN, JOSÉ Jan. 12, 1908- Dancer; choreographer

Address: b. c/o Musical Artists, 119 W. 57th St., New York 19; h. Laurelton Hotel, 7th Ave. and 57th St., New York 19

Most dance critics agree with John Martin of the New York *Times* that the "finest male dancer of his time" is José Limón. Born in Mexico, Limón has lived since childhood in the United States, where he received his training and made his reputation as a dancer. In the summer of 1950 he took his company to Mexico City and was welcomed as a native son and a major artist. He was offered an unlimited subsidy by the Mexican Government to set up a modern dance center.

The dancer has toured with his company throughout the United States, and has given major recitals in New York City which have brought him great ovations from audiences and critics. He started his study of the dance at the age of twenty in the Doris Humphrey-Charles Weidman School in New York City, and Miss Humphrey has since choreographed many of his major works.

Limón believes that traditional ballet is unsuited to the expression of contemporary themes. He regards the modern dance not only as an art, but as a way to "affirm man's sanity," *The Dance Has Many Faces* (1951). He feels that women have dominated the dance too long, and he seeks in his own work to make it again a "virile pre-occupation."

José Limón was born January 12, 1908, at Culiacan in the State of Sinaloa, Mexico. His father was a musician whose early interests included painting and music. Although "dancing was part of the scenery," José had no interest in it as a child. When he was seven, his family moved to Arizona. Later, they settled in Los Angeles, where the boy attended high school and spent part of a year at the University of California at Los Angeles. At the age of twenty, Limón decided to become a painter and journeyed east to study at the New York School of Design.

He soon discovered that his mystical, intense manner of painting, influenced by El Greco, was completely out of fashion in the art world of 1928, in which only work in the style of the modern French painters received recognition. Margaret Lloyd quotes Limón as fearing that he might spend the rest of his life "either trying to paint like El Greco, or trying not to paint like El Greco."

He gave away his brushes and went into what John Martin called "a major emotional decline" (New York *Times Magazine*, April 12, 1953). Hoping to arouse his interest in something, friends took him to a modern dance recital by Harald Kreutzberg and Yvonne Georgi. It was the first such performance Limón had ever attended, and he was so impressed with the "substance and serious intent" of this kind of dancing that he immediately enrolled for classes in the Humphrey-Weidman school.

As a dance student, Limón was not an immediate success. He was too big and inelastic,

Arnold Eagle

JOSÉ LIMÓN

with little sense of balance or direction, but he stuck with it because, Margaret Lloyd wrote, "he had found what he wanted." In 1930, he appeared in the Humphrey-Weidman dances in Norman Bel Geddes' Broadway production of *Lysistrata*. Thereafter, he danced in several other Broadway shows, including *Americana* and *As Thousands Cheer*, and then in *Roberta*, for which he staged the dances. During this period, he also composed trios and duets which he danced with Letitia Ide, Pauline Chellis and others on tour. He received a fellowship at the Bennington School of the Dance in Vermont in 1937 and began to do choreography for group dances.

While at Bennington, he developed some dances with Spanish and Mexican flavor, with which he toured the Pacific Coast with May O'Donnell as his partner. He returned to New York in 1942 to perform *El Salón México*, to the music of Aaron Copland, along with other works choreographed by either Miss Humphrey or himself. In 1943, he was inducted into the Army and although he danced in camp shows, he did no serious dancing until after his discharge in 1945.

After spending two years working to perfect his dances, Limón resumed his touring, this time with Beatrice Seckler and Dorothy Bird as his partners. In 1947, he re-formed his company under Doris Humphrey's direction and gave New York recitals at the Belasco Theatre and the New York City Center. These programs included the highly successful dance on the death of a bullfighter—*Lament for Ignacio Sanchez Mejías*, based on a poem by García Lorca, which has become a classic of the modern repertoire. Despite lavish critical praise, *Newsweek* (January 5, 1948) reported Limón's company suffered financial deficits and he had to continue to support himself by teaching.

LIMÓN, JOSÉ—Continued

Limón was quoted as saying of the dance, "Nobody believes in it but us."

Limón has taught at Mills College, Sarah Lawrence College, Temple University, University of California and University of Pittsburgh, as well as Bennington. He has also taught classes at the Dance Players' Studio and the Katherine Dunham School in New York City.

In his native Mexico, Limón has had an even greater success than in the United States. The Mexican Government has an official department of the dance and fine arts, which invited Limón in 1950 to take charge of "a general rehabilitation of the dance in Mexico along modern lines, with an ample subsidy and on a basis of permanence" (New York *Times*, December 24, 1950). He felt, however, that he was not ready to assume so great a responsibility, and instead made a compromise whereby he returns to Mexico for several months each year, but continues his performances in the United States. On Limón's first trip to Mexico with his company in the late summer of 1950, the dancer received an overwhelming reception from the press and public, and became at once a figure of national eminence.

Since the characters Limón portrays are always dependent on the feelings of others, he rarely does a dramatic solo. "He is often a sufferer, sometimes a sufferer who acquires tragic stature, never a hostile or destructive person. . . .Even as a bull fighter he is unaggressive, a man who is great in defeat rather than in triumph." *Theatre Arts* (November 1951).

He made his only European appearance in 1951 in Paris with the Page-Stone Ballet. Limón himself was well received, but the whole venture was handicapped by a combination of adverse circumstances, reported Beatrice Gottlieb in the *Kenyon Review* (Winter, 1951). However, the Paris experience did nothing to dim Limón's reputation in the United States. Analyzing his success, Miss Gottlieb described his talent for characterization and acting: "He takes possession of one set of our emotions by satisfying a desire for a display of skill, and he also gets hold of us by appealing to the more reflective side of our natures, the side that responds to the pathos and terror of human situations."

A reviewer in *Musical America* (January 1, 1950) called Limón "one of the most accomplished dancers to be seen today. He can delineate character and emotion with expressive body and face, and he commands a muscular control that enables him to achieve any degree of mobility or rest. The mind that directs this motion is selective, sensitive, and imaginative."

Doris Humphrey, Limón's first teacher and choreographer of many of his dances, has had a strong influence on his career. "He has never got over his love for the baroque and the romantic in his choreography and his dancing," John Martin asserted in the New York Times Magazine, "but the cool and critical hand of Miss Humphrey is always there to restrain him."

In April 1953, Limón and his company, which included Pauline Koner and Lucas Hoving, participated in the festival of "American Dance" sponsored in New York by the B. de Rothschild Foundation, sharing programs with Martha Graham and other leaders of the modern dance. In addition to repeating such established successes as *The Moor's Pavane*, based on *Othello*, and *The Visitation*, based on a Biblical theme, he introduced *Deep Rhythm*, with choreography by Miss Humphrey. The critics had no wish to change the earlier verdict of John Martin (New York *Times*, April 10, 1949) that ". . . there is no other male dancer within even comparing distance of him."

"Without this great and noble dancer, wrote Winthrop Palmer in *Dance News Annual* (1953), modern dance in the United States would have been the affair of women and children." Limón himself has stressed his feelings of the importance of the male dancer in modern dance, as distinct from ballet. In *The Dance Has Many Faces* (1951), edited by Walter Sorrell, he has written that he feels women have too long dominated the dance, while because of economic factors, men dancers have done their work mostly in musical comedy and films which do not encourage creative effort. In regard to traditional ballet, *Time* (March 3, 1947) quoted him as saying, "The ballet is such a sophisticated vocabulary. It's perfect for the experience of lords and ladies. But those of us who want to talk about our environment here find it inadequate."

Winthrop Palmer described the dancer as "tall, with wide shoulders, a long waist, and long, muscular legs. His head is well-shaped, his neck strong and sinewy. His arms and hands have eloquence. . . His eyes and hair are dark . . . his open features warm and alive." Since 1942, Limón has been married to Pauline Lawrence, a former member of the Humphrey-Weidman company, who has designed the costumes for many of his dances. His semi-annual tours take him to forty-five American cities, and he spends summers on a farm near Stockton, New Jersey, where he and his wife are converting a barn into a studio. His principal spare-time interest remains the piano, on which he particularly enjoys playing Bach.

Dance critic John Martin wrote that Limón is "large, healthy, comfortably and casually dressed, without a hint of personal vanity. He laughs easily, is witty and hearty, and he eats with that unromantic appetite common to dancers. . . With his Mexican heritage and his *norteamericano* training, Limón has 'one foot on either side of the border.'"

A two-week season of modern dance entitled *American Dance* was given at the Alvin Theatre, New York City in April 1953 which featured "the two reigning monarchs of the modern dance—Martha Graham and José Limón—major dancer-choreographers" (*Time*, April 27, 1953).

References

N Y Times Mag p19+ Ap 12 '53 por
Dance Encyclopedia (1949)
Dance News Annual 1953 por

LINCOLN, MURRAY D(ANFORTH)

Apr. 18, 1892- Insurance executive; cooperative organization official

Address: b. c/o Farm Bureau Insurance Companies, 246 N. High St., Columbus 16, Ohio; c/o CARE, 660 First Ave., New York 16; h. 5099 Sunbury Rd., Gahanna, Ohio

For nearly thirty-five years a leader of the farmers' cooperative movement, Murray D. Lincoln has been president of the Cooperative League of the United States since 1941 and is a vice-president and executive committeeman of the International Cooperative Alliance. He has been president, also, of the Cooperative for American Remittance for Europe, the nonprofit food distributing agency popularly known as CARE, since it was started in November 1945. Lincoln was executive secretary of the Ohio Farm Bureau Federation from 1920 to 1948, when he resigned to devote full time to the Farm Bureau Mutual Automobile, Fire, and Life Insurance companies, which he had been largely instrumental in founding.

In August, 1953, it was announced that Lincoln Village, a ten-year-old dream of Murray Lincoln's, had become a reality. When completed, the "village," a $30,000,000 project, will have 10,000 residents, a 20-acre center, apartments, houses priced from $9,000 to $16,000, a school, library, churches and shopping center.

Murray Danforth Lincoln was brought up on the farm at Raynham, near Brockton, Massachusetts, where he was born on April 18, 1892; his parents, Minot J. and Helen S. (Andrews) Lincoln, were hopeful that their son would become a schoolteacher, but the boy preferred farming as his lifework. Thus when he finished high school he chose to attend Massachusetts Agricultural College (now the University of Massachusetts) at Amherst, Massachusetts, where "one of his instructors interested him in the idea of conveying agricultural research to farmers" (Loy Warwick in the New York *Post*, May 20, 1943). Graduated with the B.S. degree in 1914, Lincoln went to New London, Connecticut, as the first county agricultural agent in that State and one of the first in the entire New England area.

The following year in Brockton, Lincoln was engaged as agricultural agent by the Plymouth County Trust Company and in 1916 organized one of the first cooperative milk distributing plants in New England. This venture, which is still in operation, aroused the interest of the late Myron T. Herrick, former Governor of Ohio and twice the United States Ambassador to France, who in 1917 chose the young New Englander to be the agricultural agent for his Society for Savings Bank at Cleveland. In this capacity Lincoln noted that because of high interest rates the farmers had to pay a large part of their profits into the bank. When "in 1919 a small group of farmers decided that a voluntary cooperative effort was a mechanism that might be applied to solve some of the economic and social problems confronting agriculture," he was in agreement. The words quoted are to be found in a paper by Lincoln entitled "Cooperative Insurance and Finance," which was published in the *Annals of the American*

MURRAY D. LINCOLN

Academy of Political and Social Science for May 1937. These farmers formed the Ohio Farm Bureau Federation, a federated group of county farm bureau organizations of which Lincoln became executive secretary in 1920, after resigning his position with the Cleveland bank. Subsequently he helped Dr. James P. Warbusse to organize the now influential Cooperative League of the United States of America, using his own room in a Columbus, Ohio, hotel as the league's first headquarters.

"After seven years of cooperative purchasing and marketing of agricultural supplies and products," Lincoln wrote in the paper on cooperative finance already quoted, "the members (of the Ohio Farm Bureau Federation) began to question what they believed were excessive rates for automobile insurance." The result was the organization of the Farm Bureau Mutual Automobile Insurance Company, $10,000 capital for which was appropriated from dues of the Farm Bureau Federation for 1925. A success from the start, the Farm Bureau Mutual Auto Insurance Company in the first ten years of its existence increased its assets from $114,100 in 1926 to $5,232,000 in 1936; by 1937 it had grown to be the country's eighth largest mutual casualty company and was credited with having "cut insurance rates in Ohio by 40 per cent" (*Scholastic*). The Ohio Farm Bureau Federation also provided capital for the Ohio Farm Bureau Corporation, which in turn invested in two cooperative service organizations, the Farm Bureau Agricultural Credit Corporation and the Farm Bureau Cooperative Association, the latter a buying and selling organization. Two other insurance companies, the Farm Bureau Mutual Fire Insurance Company and the Farm Bureau Life Insurance Company, were formed in 1934 and 1936 respectively, and of these as well as of the automobile insurance company, Murray Lincoln has been president and general manager since their inception.

LINCOLN, MURRAY—*Continued*

(Other subsidiaries of the Ohio Farm Bureau were acquired after World War II, a refinery and pipe line company in 1945 and a radio station in 1946.)

Supplementing his executive work for the Ohio Farm Bureau organization and its insurance subsidiaries and for the Cooperative League, Murray Lincoln became a director and executive committee member of the American Farm Bureau Federation and chairman of its Rural Credits Committee. A frequent contributor to *Consumers Cooperative* and other periodicals, he was also widely known as a speaker on farm problems. For a time he was opposed to the New Deal policy of crop controls. "Stop asking the Government to do things for farmers," he advised the Maryland Cooperative Institute in an address. "The blunt truth is that the Federal aid program is not working for anyone." This was in August 1940, about seven months before his election, in Chicago on March 18, 1941, as president of the Cooperative League of the United States of America. Conversion of the country to an outright war economy after the Pearl Harbor attack somewhat modified Lincoln's views; he became known as "the militant leader in the liberal bloc" of the Farm Bureau Federation, and as a witness at a Senate committee hearing in October 1942 urged the creation of an overall manpower mobilization agency and draft deferment for laborers on the smaller farms. Loy Warwick has observed that Lincoln's "testimony in behalf of the Farm Security Administration was largely responsible for keeping that agency alive. . . . His stand on the FSA split the ranks of the Farm Bureau wide open, and left the way clear for the Administration to continue its efforts on behalf of the small farmer."

As a "lay representative" of American agriculture, Lincoln in the spring of 1943 served on the five-member United States delegation to the United Nations Conference on Food and Agriculture which met in Hot Springs, Virginia. A little more than two years afterward (July 1945) he was named with Howard Cowden of Kansas City to represent the Cooperative League of the United States at the forthcoming meeting in London of the International Cooperative Alliance, the first such assembly since the outbreak of World War II. At the opening of the conference on September 10, Lincoln spoke for Cowden as well as himself in expressing the opinion that "expansion of trade on cooperative lines is the perfect answer to the growing tendency for the intrusion of governments into the regulation of foreign commerce." Lincoln is now a member of the central committee and vice-president of the International Cooperative Alliance and represents that organization as permanent consultant to the United Nations Economic and Social Council.

When the Cooperative for American Remittances for Europe (CARE), was formed by twenty-two member agencies of the American Council of Voluntary Agencies for Foreign Service in November 1945, Murray Lincoln was elected its president. (Donald M. Nelson, former chief of the War Production Board, was the executive director.) The original an-

nounced purpose of CARE, a nonprofit organization working closely with the United Nations Relief and Rehabilitation Administration, was to "attempt to supplement UNRRA relief" through purchase from the Army of 3,800,000 surplus "ten-in-one" food packages.

CARE thereupon undertook to deliver such packages to any individuals in Europe whom the purchaser designated, on receipt of ten dollars for cost of contents and transportation. Later, CARE made up its own packages with contents varying according to national, local, and religious requirements, and within two years had supplied 75 million pounds of food to 3,500,000 European families. Murray Lincoln was re-elected to the presidency of CARE for his eighth consecutive term in November 1952. Another postwar position held by Lincoln was member of President Truman's 1946 Commission of Higher Education. He has also served on Presidential advisory committees on rural electrification and farm tenancy, and in August 1950 was named a representative of agriculture on the National Security Board's committee on mobilization policy.

By 1948 the three mutual insurance companies had collective assets of some $51 million and were serving more than one million policy holders. Thus in February of that year Lincoln resigned his executive secretaryship in the parent Ohio Farm Bureau Federation to devote more time to the insurance organizations. *Business Week* reported in May 1951 that the celebration of the twenty-fifth anniversary of the automobile insurance company was attended by "2,500 home office employees, 1,400 branch office workers from other States, and 3,000 field representatives." The automobile insurance is the largest of the three cooperatives, with over a million policy holders, while the fire insurance company has as many as 250,000. Total number of policy holders in the twelve States in which the three companies are licensed to operate has been more recently estimated as about two million.

In politico-economic views, Lincoln after World War II continued to move towards Fair-Dealism, and while remaining a registered Republican, joined and became a director of Americans for Democratic Action. At the CIO convention in Cleveland in November 1949, Lincoln in a speech described by a New York *Herald Tribune* writer as "sprinkled with homely humor" called for "farmer-labor cooperation and a drive to lift the living standards of people all over the world." Labor leaders including the late Philip Murray began to regard him as a possible candidate to oppose the late Robert A. Taft for re-election to the United States Senate in 1950. On January 18, Lincoln announced that he was "not a candidate," at the same time stating that he was registering as a member of the Democratic party and would do all he could "to advance the interests of the people it represents."

Lincoln is a former director of Antioch College; his fraternity is the Lambda Chi Alpha. In October 1915 he married Anne S. Hurst. He has been described by Loy Warwick in the New York *Post* as "a tall, bald Yankee, lithe and lean. . ."

With agriculture his avocation as well as his vocation, Lincoln operates a 200-acre dairy farm just north of Columbus. One of his hobbies is collecting Currier and Ives prints. In religious affiliation he is a Unitarian.

References

    Ann Am Acad 191:130 My '37
    Antioch R 4:319 Je '44
    Christian Sci Mon p11 Ag 6 '49; p9 Ja 22 '53
    N Y Herald Tribune II p1 N 27 '49 por
    N Y Post Mag p41 My 20 '43 por; p39 D 22 '48
    Newsweek 33:15 Je 27 '49
    Scholastic 31:275 O 16 '37 por
    Washington (D.C.) Post p5B N 27 '49
    Who's Who in America, 1952-53

LINKLETTER, ART(HUR GORDON)

July 17, 1912-   Television and radio broadcaster; producer

Address: b. Taft Bldg., Hollywood 28, Calif.; h. Holmby Hills, Calif.

ART LINKLETTER

Master of ceremonies and ad-libber extraordinary, Art Linkletter estimates that he has talked with some 30,000 persons in his sixteen years on radio and television programs. His three shows, *People Are Funny* and *House Party* (CBS), and *Life With Linkletter* (ABC-TV) which claim a listening audience of 20,000,000, help to provide for his $400,000 yearly income before taxes.

He has announced almost every known type of sports with the exception of bull fights, and he is an expert on special events. He has broadcast from airplanes, dirigibles, battleships and submarines. During one event he was hoisted up and down the front of a skyscraper in a bosun's chair interviewing people on each floor. He has broadcast descriptions of bathing beauty contests, baby shows and cattle shows.

Arthur Gordon Linkletter was born A. G. Kelley in Moose Jaw, Saskatchewan, July 17, 1912. At the age of one month, he was adopted by Fulton John and Mary Metzler Linkletter. The boy was three years old when the family moved to California and decided to settle there. The elder Linkletter after various attempts to earn a livelihood became an itinerant evangelist. Young Art's first contact with audiences was when he attended his foster father's revival meetings on street corners in San Diego.

After he was graduated from high school, Art set out to see the world, often thumbing his way, sometimes riding freights—and visiting almost every state in the union. He held down such jobs as busboy in Chicago, stevedore on New Orleans' docks, meat packer in Minneapolis and coupon clerk on Wall Street during the historic days of the 1929 crash. In New York, he signed on a ship and worked his way to Buenos Aires and back.

Upon his return home, Linkletter enrolled in San Diego State College, where he studied to be a teacher of voice and dramatics. He earned his college expenses by working as a switch-board operator, lifeguard, artist's model, clerk, busboy, bouncer, waiter and ranch hand. He also found time to be captain of the championship basketball team, play in the AAU National Handball Championships and to hold the Southern California 50-yard back-stroke swimming title for a year.

A college classmate who remembers Linkletter's talkativeness, says, "He was the long-playing record of his day, and you could get him started without a needle."

This ability to talk extemporaneously led to his being hired as an announcer in his junior year for station KGB San Diego. When he was graduated in 1934, with an A.B. degree and an A-average, he rejected a teaching position, since it paid $5 less a month, and remained at KGB, where he became the chief announcer.

In 1935 he was appointed program director of the California International Exposition in San Diego and the following year, radio director of the Texas Centennial Exposition in Dallas. In 1937, he became radio director for the San Francisco World's Fair, where he wrote two theme spectacles, *Cavalcade of the Golden West* and *Cavalcade of a Nation*. He left two years later to become a free lance radio announcer and master of ceremonies. During the next six years, Linkletter took part in over 9,000 separate radio programs (*Collier's*, May 28, 1949).

Linkletter moved to Hollywood in 1942 where he met and formed a partnership with John Guedel and inaugurated the zany *People Are Funny* program.

The format of his three programs depends upon audience participation. Thus, *People Are Funny* is built around four stunts involving contestants, and *House Party* has a weekly contest, musical auditions and questions and answers, all requiring volunteers. It also presents Linkletter interviewing five children daily

(Continued next page)

LINKLETTER, ART—*Continued*

from Los Angeles schools. *Life with Linkletter* uses both adults and children.

His staple program elements over the years have been chats with the youngest grandmother in the audience, the oldest father and a search for the woman with the longest hair. He has interviewed persons who have suddenly become front page copy for the newspapers. He has presented "mystery singers" who turn out to be promising unknowns. He has introduced a "Personal Pronoun" quiz, in which he asks visitors such questions as "What my husband likes about me," "What I like about myself" and "What I don't like about myself."

Much of the fun of his programs is slapstick, although Linkletter also prefers situation gags. Thus, a *People Are Funny* contestant was given $20,000 to play the stock market for a month, testing the popular belief that anybody with enough capital can make money in Wall Street. The man was to keep his winnings. The show promised to make good his losses. At the end of the month, the contestant, a truck-driver for a cleaning establishment, had made $1100.

While *House Party* is an extemporaneous show, both *People Are Funny* and *Life with Linkletter* have scripts. Scripts, of course, are not followed too closely, for Linkletter's skill is ad-libbing and framing double entendre questions. He usually extricates himself from situations and provides the audience with numerous unrestrained laughs. Eddie Cantor, known as a top off-the-cuff artist himself, claims that Linkletter is the "best ad-libber in radio."

Linkletter's capers attract an assortment of gifts as expressions of his fans' admiration. Among the gifts have been a Brahman bull, a pair of hamsters, collections of foreign coins, hand-painted neckties and hundreds of pounds of food. One fan keeps him supplied with argyle socks. His children are plied with toys, most of which are sent to charitable institutions, and when his last child was born, 453 pairs of bootees found·their way to the Linkletter household.

Art Linkletter has appeared in two movies— *People Are Funny*, with Jack Haley and Rudy Vallee, and *Champagne for Caesar*, with Ronald Colman, Vincent Price and Celeste Holm. In 1947, he also wrote a book, *People Are Funny* (Doubleday), which gave a backstage view of his radio shows and their master of ceremonies.

In his introduction to the book, Bing Crosby wrote, "It must be said in all fairness that he suffers from astigmatism of the skull. This malicious malady distorts his brain, twists his reflexes and gives him more notions than a five-and-ten-cent store."

The six feet one inch, 210 pound Linkletter has become not only successful in his radio and television endeavors but also as a business man. He owns nine oil wells, lead mines in Colorado, manufacturing plants in Long Beach, Los Angeles and Mexico, in which are produced wiring systems, hand tools and magnesium aluminum products. He also owns restaurants, a bowling alley, a skating rink, warehouses, a construction materials-business, a company that puts on trade shows, an interest in the Dollar Steamship Line and a Hollywood Charm School.

He is chairman of the board of the Great Eastern Mines; a member of the board of directors of the Roller Enterprises, Inc.; Powr-Torker, Inc.; Touch-Plate, Inc. and Amusement Enterprises. He is vice-president of Inland Properties, Inc. and of Caroline Leonetti, Ltd.

In 1936 he married Lois Foerster, then a college student. The Linkletters have five children, Jack, age sixteen; Dawn, thirteen; Robert, eight; Sharon, six, and Diane, four.

Together with Dick Powell, Harold Lloyd and Edgar Bergen he belongs to the Hollywood Stereo Club, which specializes in three-dimensional photography. Linkletter has won several prizes for this type of camera work.

Linkletter is a member of the Hollywood YMCA board of management and of the executive committee of the Southwestern Area of the YMCA.

References

American Magazine 145:36 My '48 por
Collier's 123:26-7+ My 28 '49 il pors
Look 17:18+, Je 2, '53 il pors
McCalls 80:46-7+ My '53 il pors
Newsweek 30:53 O 6, '47 il pors
N Y Times p27 S 25, '47
Sat Eve Post 224:26-7+ My 17 '52 pors
Who's Who in America, 1952-53

LITCHFIELD, EDWARD H(AROLD)
Apr. 12, 1914- University professor; organization official

Address: b. c/o Cornell University, Ithaca, N.Y.; h. Cayuga Heights Rd., Ithaca, N.Y.

Appointed dean of Cornell University's School of Business and Public Administration in March 1953 in his thirty-ninth year Edward H. Litchfield has served as director of Civil Affairs for the United States Military Government in Germany and taken an active part in drafting the plan for the reconstruction of the occupied country.

Beginning his career as a participant in the reforming of civil service laws in Michigan, Litchfield subsequently taught political science at Brown University and at the University of Michigan. In 1949 he was made president of the Governmental Affairs Institute in Washington, D. C., and in 1950, became the first executive director of the American Political Science Association formed that year in Washington; he still holds both positions.

In May 1953, Litchfield announced a plan which the Association had drawn up for educating the American people on the affairs of Congress. Under this non-partisan plan, the Association would give scholarships each year to five outstanding young political scientists, whose services would be available free of charge to members of Congress. Litchfield said that when these political scientists "return to their local communities . . . they will spread the knowledge they have gained to others."

Edward Harold Litchfield was born in Detroit, Michigan, on April 12, 1914, the son of Adelbert Leigh Litchfield and Ethel (McKim) Litchfield. He was graduated from Detroit Northwestern High School in 1932, and three years later received his A.B. degree in political science from the University of Michigan. While in college he was editor of the yearbook, and he was on the debating and track teams. He won the William Jennings Bryan Award and was a Carl Braun Fellow.

In 1937 he became executive secretary of the Michigan Merit System Association, a post he held until 1938. This association was formed in April 1936 by a group of citizens to reform civil service conditions in Michigan. In 1937 it succeeded in having a bill passed by the State Legislature providing, among other things, for a three-man civil service commission whose director would be appointed by the Governor.

When Governor Murphy, a Democrat and a champion of civil service reform, was not renominated, the Merit System Association failed to get enough support to carry out its program. Although Litchfield has no political affiliations, he wrote several magazine articles attacking the Republican administration in Michigan for the "ripper laws" it passed; he claimed they destroy the progress that had been made in civil service reform during Murphy's term of office.

Upon receiving his Ph.D. degree in political science from the University of Michigan in 1940, Litchfield became a political science instructor at Brown University for the academic year 1940-1941. After serving for a brief period as a training specialist in the Panama Canal Zone, he returned to his home state, where, from 1942 to 1945, he was a lecturer in public administration at the University of Michigan and was Deputy Director of the Michigan State Civil Service Commission.

Litchfield's first assignment in the Department of State was as special assistant to the United States Chief of Mission to Germany in November 1945. Less than a year later he returned to Germany as deputy director of the Civil Administration Division, Office of the Military Government. In March 1947, he succeeded Henry Parkmann as director of that Division. At the time he received this appointment he was in Moscow as a member of the United States delegation attending a conference of foreign ministers.

In July 1947, he was again appointed a United States delegate to an international meeting, the seventh International Congress of Administrative Sciences held at Berne, Switzerland.

The responsibilities of Litchfield's Division were supervision over civil service, administrative courts, elections and political parties, drafting of state constitutions and state legislation, and the compilation of statistics on the German government.

The New York Times wrote (December 5, 1947) that Litchfield enjoyed "a greater measure of General Lucius D. Clay's confidence

Cristof Studio

EDWARD H. LITCHFIELD

[United States Military Governor in Germany] than almost any other Military Government official."

In November 1947, Litchfield gave the first speech in *Operation Backtalk*, a series of broadcasts called *Freedom versus Totalitarianism*, which the American Military Government sponsored as part of its propaganda counteroffensive against verbal Soviet attacks on the United States.

Delbert Clark in the New York *Times* (November 20, 1937) reported that Litchfield "had prepared a 'fighting' speech comparing democracy and sovietism, and had included many concrete examples, such as forced labor in the Soviet zone uranium mines. All these were eliminated in three writings and the speech emerged as a generalized comparison of practice under democracy and under sovietism. . . General Clay's position now is that Military Government officials must not throw mud but must stick to generalities. . . . In this connection it was learned that General Clay softened the policy on anti-Soviet radio talks by his subordinate as a result of imperative cables from Washington. According to these reports it was Dr. Edwin H. Litchfield, director of the Civil Administration Diivsion, who persuaded General Clay to 'take off the kid gloves.' "

Litchfield's Civil Administration Division emerged with new powers in a reorganization of the Military Government in February 1948. In addition to its former functions, it took over the work of the Prisoner of War and Displaced Persons Division; the public health, public welfare, and public safety branches of the Internal Affairs and Communications Division, and all quadripartite duties formerly exercised by that division.

(Continued next page)

LITCHFIELD, EDWARD H.—*Continued*

Litchfield drafted a plan with a time-scheme for the political reconstruction of West Germany. His program provided for the establishment of a provisional German government in Frankfort by July 1948. This would be followed by a redrawing of the boundaries of the German states in order to distribute wealth and electoral strength more evenly among them; the election of a German Constituent Assembly in November; the preparation of a German constitution by the beginning of 1949; and the election of a German Parliament in either February or March, 1949. It was substantially Litchfield's plan, (with both the time-scheme and the proposal for establishing a provisional German government, omitted) that General Clay presented to a six-nation conference that met in London April 1948, to decide the political structure of West Germany.

Throughout his stay in Germany, Litchfield worked to promote the American Military Government's objectives for democratizing Germany and making it a self-governing nation. In December 1948, he announced a plan for the United States and Germany to exchange visits of Government officials, health and welfare workers, university professors, and students, hoping, to "plant the seeds of democratic political action in Germany." He sought the admission of Germany into the Council of Europe, a move which he thought would help to curb the rising tide of German Nationalism.

"In the fourth year of the occupation," Litchfield said, "many Germans remain politically confused and a potential prey for a new dictator" (New York *Times*, December 31, 1948.

Litchfield wrote an article for the New York *Times* magazine section of May 14, 1950, in which he pointed out that German nationalism, as well as the Soviet Union, was a threat to United States' interests in Germany. In the article he listed thirteen minimum requirements which the United States must exact before consenting to political unification of the German nation. Among these were the dissolution of "front" organizations, disbanding the People's Police, and the dismissal of civil service employees and teachers who were critical of the Allied Governments. He also pointed out the urgency of building up West Germany before unification took place.

Litchfield returned to the United States in the fall of 1949, when he became a consultant to the Under Secretary of the Army and president of the Governmental Affairs Institute in Washington, D.C. His duties in the latter position have included such functions as planning professional programs for political leaders who come to America from all over the world.

After the American Political Science Association opened its offices in Washington, D.C., in October 1950, Litchfield, as executive director, announced the primary functions which he thought his office should undertake: 1) a personnel service for those political scientists seeking employment in Government service or the teaching profession; 2) assistance in research; 3) a reference service for members of the Association; and 4) service to Federal agencies. According to a resolution passed by the Association's Council, the "primary concern of the Association at all times shall be to be of assistance to individual and institutional research."

He first became associated with Cornell University in 1950 as a visiting professor of public administration. He was appointed director of special programs in the School of Business and Public Administration there n August 1952, and within a year became dean of the School.

Litchfield is five feet eleven inches tall, weighs 180 pounds, and has brown hair and blue eyes. He married Anne Muïr Macïntyre an historian, on September 11, 1940. They have three children, Peter M., Janet M., and Roberta M.

He is a co-author of *The State Administrative Board in* Michigan (1938), and author of *Voting Behaviour in a Metropolitan Community* (1940) and *Governing Postwar Germany* (1953). He has also published numerous articles in professional journals.

Organizations to which he belongs are the American Political Science Association, the American Association of University Professors, and the American Society for Public Administration. He has no political or church affiliations.

References

Fortune 47:53 My 53 por
Litchfield, E. (and associates) Governing Postwar Germany (Cornell University Press 1953)
Who's Who in America, 1952-53

LOEWY, RAYMOND (FERNAND) Nov. 5, 1893- Industrial designer

Address: b. Raymond Loewy Associates, 488 Madison Ave., New York 22; h. 41 W 58th St., New York 19

NOTE: This biography supersedes the article which appeared in *Current Biography,* 1941.

Refrigerators, toothbrushes, automobiles, locomotives, ball point pens, ocean-going liners, airplanes, and many other products of American and foreign manufacturers have been designed by Raymond Loewy. The French-born designer came to America in 1919 and began his career as a fashion illustrator. Today, he is recognized as the "biggest industrial designer in the United States and head of the largest industrial design firm in the world" (*Time*, October 31, 1949). His artistic creed is: "Good design keeps the user happy, the manufacturer in the black, and the esthete unoffended."

Loewy was one of a small group of innovators in 1927 who began to apply the techniques of functional design to industrial products. Since then, Loewy and his staff of approximately 200 designers and engineers have designed for an average of 125 clients. "One rough estimate sets the total retail sales of all Loewy-styled products last year at $3 billion"

(*Life*, May 2, 1949). "Loewy has probably affected the daily life of more Americans than any other man of his time" (*Cosmopolitan*, August, 1950).

Raymond Fernand Loewy was born in Paris on November 5, 1893, the third son of Maximilian and Marie (Labalme) Loewy. His father was a Viennese journalist; his mother, a French woman, was determined that her sons should have successful careers and often prodded them with the maxim: "It is better to be envied than pitied." While still a boy, Loewy showed a talent for sketching, using his school hours at Chaptal College in Paris as well as his leisure time to draw locomotives and automobiles.

Graduating in 1905, he entered Paris University, where he studied electrical engineering. He designed a model airplane which won the J. Gordon Bennett medal in 1906. Obtaining his degree in 1910, he enrolled as a student in advanced engineering at the École de Laneau. His studies were interrupted by World War I, in which Loewy served as a member of the corps of engineers of France's Fifth Army. Entering the war as a private, he left as a captain. In the last few months of his service he acted as a liaison officer to the American Expeditionary Forces. Loewy was chosen an officer in the Legion of Honor and was awarded the Croix de Guerre with four citations and also the Interallied Medal.

After completing his engineering degree. Loewy found himself at twenty-six without a job and without funds. His brother Georges, a research scientist living in the United States, suggested that he look for work in New York City. During the voyage Loewy was asked to contribute to a charitable cause, but since he had nothing of value to offer, he made a sketch of one of the young women passengers and permitted it to be auctioned off.

It was purchased by Sir Harry Armstrong, the British Consul General of New York who, impressed with Loewy's ability, gave him an introduction to Condé Nast, publisher of *Vogue*. This resulted in a job as a member of the magazine's art staff and the beginning of a career as fashion illustrator for a number of American periodicals. He was later a freelance designer of window displays for such New York stores as Saks-Fifth Avenue and Macy's.

Loewy launched his own organization for industrial design in 1927 and became art director for Westinghouse Electric Company in 1929. He completed a successful design for a duplicating machine for Gestetner, Ltd., Hupmobiles, and by 1932 had become identified with the new movement to bring functional styling to the products of industry. According to this concept, every object, no matter how simple or how complex, has an ideal form which can express its function with economy and grace.

At the outset, Loewy's firm had difficulty convincing manufacturers of the value of the new functionalism, but in 1934 he achieved his first major success—a refrigerator for Sears, Roebuck and Company which used non-rusting aluminum shelves for the first time. The first year's sales were 140,000; the next year they

RAYMOND LOEWY

had increased to 275,000. In 1937 the refrigerator design won first prize at the Paris International Exposition, and Loewy's importance in the field of industrial designing was recognized.

Thereafter he became consultant to approximately 100 American and foreign companies and in 1945 he formed the Raymond Loewy Associates, with five partners. The firm expanded to a staff of 200, and now has offices in New York, London, Chicago, Los Angeles, South Bend, and São Paulo, Brazil. It has designed lipsticks, electric shavers, radios, soft drink dispensing machines, automatic pencils, and labels and packaging for soap, toothpaste and antiseptics.

In cooperation with the various engineering departments concerned, Loewy designed automobiles for Studebaker Corporation, locomotives and passenger cars for the Pennsylvania Railroad, buses for the Greyhound lines, trucks for International Harvester Company, sleeper planes for Trans-World Airlines, airplane interiors for Glenn L. Martin and Lockheed, modern, fire-proof passenger liners for Matson, Panama and America-President Lines. The interior design of Gimbel's department store in New York City, a prototype supermarket in California, a 650-acre community at Pernambuco, Brazil, were also his projects.

Among the large stores designed by Loewy are Foley Bros., in Houston, Texas; Lord & Taylor in Manhasset, L.I., Westchester, N.Y., Hartford, Conn. and Millburn, N.J.; Beverly-Robinson in Beverly Hills, California; and the Shopping Center at Fairview Village, Ohio.

In 1952 Raymond Loewy Associates had responsibility for designing and executing the interiors of the famous glass and metal office building of the Lever Brothers firm in New York City. Offices in the building have desks which are adjustable in height and have rounded corners. A basic color of grayish beige was

LOEWY, RAYMOND—*Continued*

chosen but each floor was given a different color scheme in the spectrum. Commenting on the interior, Lewis Mumford wrote in the *New Yorker*: "I don't know any other building in the city in which so much color has been used with such skill and charm over such a large area. Both our school architects and our equally timid hospital architects have something to learn from this." The same critic found the executives' floor, with its plushy ornamentation, a denial of "the clean logic of the whole building." Another 1952 design of Loewy's, the Studebaker automobiles, was favorably reviewed by *Business Week,* which liked the way in which the styling combined "European function with United States luxury," and emphasized that "the scarcity of eye-catching chrome trim gives it a clean look, a sure sign that the basic design is good."

At the beginning of 1953 Loewy created a moderately-priced line of tables, chairs, cabinets, benches and day beds for the Mengel furniture company which he called the "Spectrum" group because of the use of woods stained in color. For Arvin Industries he designed metal dinette sets using a decorator-quality type of plastic fabric upholstery. He is now working on two major packaging and study programs for National Biscuit Company and National Dairy Company.

Loewy introduced one of the first sets of dishes made of fine German porcelain china in modern design for the American market in the medium-price range in the Spring of 1953. He also worked on a series of upholstered furniture pieces for the Kroehler furniture company, and inflatable plastic toys for Vanguard.

When the industrial designer's autobiography, *Never Leave Well Enough Alone* was published in 1951 the *New Yorker* critic described it as "instructive, brash, cocksure, occasionally funny, sometimes vulgar, and always honest." Peter Blake in the New York *Times* paid tribute more to the designer than to the author, describing Loewy as "a man without whose perseverance this country would be an uglier place to live in." The book has been translated into French (1953) with the title *Le Laideur se vend mal* ("Ugliness Sells Badly").

His quarter-of-a-century career has brought him countless awards. In 1937 he was elected Royal Designer to Industry by the British Royal Society of Arts, the first of three Americans to be so honored and later a Fellow of the Society. The first Lord and Taylor American Design Award went to Loewy for his Coldspot refrigerator designed for Sears, Roebuck, and he received the gold medal in the transportation field at the Paris Fair in 1937 for his design of a GG-1 electric locomotive for the Pennsylvania Railroad Company.

The professional associations to which he belongs include the Society for Automotive Engineers, Society of Industrial Designers of which he is a founder and a past-president, and the American Society of Mechanical Engineers. He is an associate member of the Society of Naval Architects and Marine Engineers, a member of the New York City Board of Education's vocational advisory board, and the industrial

design committee of the University of Southern California's College of Architecture.

The designer was married in 1931 to Jean Thomson, who is still a partner of Raymond Loewy Associates. They were divorced in 1945, and each re-married, Loewy to Viola Erickson in 1948. They have a daughter, Laurence, born in 1953. *Time* describes Loewy's voice as "subdued, at the same time apologetic and compelling. His face is reposed, gentle, sad and . . . inscrutable."

Loewy became a citizen of the United States in 1938. He has a midtown apartment in New York City which "reflects its owner's special delight in elegance coupled with a neat, packaged sense" (*House and Garden,* July 1949). He also has homes on the French Riviera (a red-tiled villa overlooking the Côte d'Azur at Saint-Tropez), a sixteeenth-century chateau at Rochefort-en-Yzellines near Paris, and a modern dwelling at Palm Springs, California.

References

Time 52 :68 Ag 23 '48 ; 54 :68-74 O 31 '49
Loewy, R. Never Leave Well Enough Alone (1951)
Who's Who in America, 1952-53
Who's Who in Engineering (1948)
Who's Who in New York (1952)

LONDON, GEORGE May 30, 1921- Singer
Address : b. c/o Constance Hope, 200 W. 57th St., New York 19

The revival of Moussorgsky's *Boris Godunov* at the Metropolitan Opera House in New York in March, 1953, offered three innovations : the opera was given for the first time in America in the form created by its composer ; it featured a new English translation, and it starred a young American bass-baritone—George London. At the end of the highly successful performance, the audience demanded eleven curtain calls for the thirty-one-year-old singer whose brilliant and meteoric career has made opera history.

Beginning as a concert singer during World War II, London appeared in his first operatic roles in Europe during 1949 and 1950, returning to the United States to make his debut at the Metropolitan in 1951. Since then he has sung at a number of European music festivals, including the Wagnerian festival at Bayreuth. He has also been a guest soloist on radio and television programs and has made a number of recordings.

Although born in Montreal on May 30, 1921, George London is an American citizen. His parents, Louis and Bertha (Broad) Burnson, were Russian immigrants who had become naturalized citizens of the United States before moving to the Canadian city where London's father operated a small hat manufacturing and distributing firm. When the boy was fifteen his family moved to Los Angeles where he was graduated from Hollywood High School. While singing in the school's glee club, he first realized that his voice, which had just settled into a baritone, was unusual, although he recalls that it was "deep, woolly, and unmanageable."

By the time he entered the Los Angeles City College he had decided that a career in opera was his goal, and he joined the school's opera group as well as its chorus. To earn money, he sang in night clubs, synagogues and churches, and his voice was "dubbed" into movie sound tracks. Before he was twenty, he was chosen by the English composer-conductor, Albert Coates, to sing in the première of his opera, *Gainsborough*, which was presented in concert form in the Hollywood Bowl in 1941. Other engagements followed, with the American Music Theatre, the Los Angeles and San Francisco Light Opera companies, and, in 1943 with the San Francisco Opera, where he made his debut as Monterone in *Rigoletto.*

After three more years on the West Coast as a featured concert and opera singer, London came to New York with a touring company of *The Desert Song.* Soon after his arrival in 1946 he was selected to sing in the première of Paul Hindemith's *Requiem*, based on a poem by Walt Whitman, which was presented at the New York City Center. On this first visit to New York George Burnson changed his stage name to George London.

In 1947 he joined the Bel Canto Trio, of which Mario Lanza was the tenor and Frances Yeend the soprano. During the two years he performed with this musical group, he also appeared as soloist with the Boston Symphony, the Buffalo Philharmonic, and the Grant Park Symphony in Chicago. At this point in his career, London decided to go to Europe, for reasons he later explained in an article he wrote for the New York *Times* (February 1, 1950): "My concert tour was over. I had some money in my pocket, and I had never been to Europe. . . In this country I have had a wonderful opportunity to establish a concert career but little chance to build up a serious stage career. There was the possibility of a Metropolitan audition, but even if I had the good luck to be accepted, it would still be premature. . . . And so I decided to go abroad, on what you might call artistic speculation."

In the summer of 1949 London was granted an audition by Karl Boehm, conductor of the Vienna State Opera who was then on tour in Brussels. Boehm's high opinion of the baritone's ability was confirmed by Joseph Krips and Egon Hilbert of the Austrian State Theatre, and London was engaged for the four-month 1949 season at the Vienna State Opera. After making his debut in the role of Amonasro in *Aida,* London sang the parts of Mephistopheles in *Faust*, Escamillo in *Carmen*, Prince Galitsky in *Prince Igor,* and the four baritone roles in *Tales of Hoffman.*

In addition, he was the first American to sing the title role in *Boris Godunov* in Russian, the libretto for which he had learned from a Russian teacher. His diction was so clear that Russians in the audience thought that he was well-acquainted with the language, but the only words he knew were those he had memorized to sing in the opera. Audiences and critics

GEORGE LONDON

alike joined in applauding the singing and acting ability of the American who was called by *Time* "the operatic find of the year."

The Vienna reporter for *Musical America* wrote that London had "a genuine gift for the stage and a sense of the dramatic possibilities of each character, in addition to a naturally beautiful voice, well placed and well schooled." Vienna's senior music critic, Heinrich Kralik, commented, "He is not yet Chaliapin, but he's very remarkable."

After his operatic assignment London made a concert tour of Europe, and during the summer of 1950 sang with the Glyndebourne Opera at the Edinburgh Music Festival, creating the role of the Count in Mozart's *The Marriage of Figaro*. He remained in Europe until October 1951, appearing for two more seasons at the Vienna Opera, and singing at music festivals in Wiesbaden, Brussels, Bayreuth, Salzburg and Munich.

London's debut at the Metropolitan Opera on November 13, 1951 brought him acclaim from American audiences and critics. Of his performance as Amonasro in *Aida,* Cecil Smith in *Musical America* wrote that it was "of such complete musical and tonal beauty and such penetrating understanding . . . that I am willing to say I have never encountered a better Amonasro. A really important artist has suddenly risen above the horizon." Virgil Thomson in the New York *Herald Tribune* called London "a great baritone star in the grand manner. . . Last night he took his place among the greatest singing actors we have any of us known or remembered."

Following his Metropolitan debut, London went to Milan to appear for the first time with the La Scala Opera Company, where he took the role of Pizarro in Beethoven's *Fidelio.* Since then London has made two coast-to-coast concert tours in the United States and Canada,

L

LONDON, GEORGE—*Continued*

participated in a number of European music festivals, and has sung several new roles at the Metropolitan, including the hero of Mozart's *Don Giovanni,* Escamillo in *Carmen,* and Scarpia in *Tosca.* In the first of these roles, the *New Republic* critic found London "perfect for the part . . . . an unbelievably gifted and accomplished man."

The most notable creation of London's 1952-1953 season with the Metropolitan was his performance in the English version of *Boris Godunov* on March 6, 1953. He had sung the role in a concert version given by the New York Philharmonic Symphony Orchestra on October 16, 1952. Commenting on the performance at the Metropolitan, Virgil Thomson observed, "So fine a bass voice, handled with such art, so great a gift for drama and so subtle a care for diction have not been met up with by this observer since. . . Chaliapin." London received eleven curtain calls. The critics found his voice a little light for the role, but agreed on the dramatic skill with which he projected the personality of the mad Czar. Thomson reported that "his dramatic skill and temperament are far above current operatic standards," and Louis Biancolli of the New York *World-Telegram-Sun* wrote that London's "voice is warm and rich, the style commanding, the acting forceful." During the 1952-1953 musical season London also appeared on radio and television programs, and completed a number of recordings.

The baritone, who received his first stage training under the late George Huston when he was with the American Music Theater, is particularly interested in vitalizing his operatic roles with dramatic depth. In the Boris role, for instance, he wants to achieve a rounded, living character that will reveal the "brooding and unhappy Russian soul."

London is six feet, two inches in height, weighs 200 pounds, keeps in trim by exercising with weights and dumb-bells. He enjoys dancing, likes jazz, reads a wide variety of books and periodicals, dislikes arrogant opera singers and bullying conductors, and lists bouillabaisse and apple strudel as his favorite foods. His humor has been called "explosive" and his manner "agreeable, and down-to-earth."

References

> Newsweek 41:58 Mr 16 '53
> N Y Herald Tribune IV p1 Mr 1 '53
> N Y World-Telegram p23 Mr 6 '53
> Theatre Arts 36:16 O '52
> Time 55:58+ Ja 9 '50 por; 61:54 Mr 16 '53

LOUDON, ALEXANDER June 5, 1892—

Feb. 4, 1953 Secretary General of the Permanent Court of Arbitration; former Dutch Ambassador to the United States; entered diplomatic service in 1916 and was a member for the next seventeen years of the Netherlands missions in Sofia, Constantinople, London, Buenos Aires, Washington, D.C., Mexico City, and Madrid; Minister in Lisbon (1933-37); became Minister in Berne, Switzerland, and delegate to the League of Nations (1937); Ambassador to the United States (1942-47); was named Secretary General of the Permanent Court of Arbitration in 1951. See *Current Biography,* 1942.

Obituary

> N Y Times p23 F 5 '53

LUBIN, ISADOR (lū'bĭn) June 9, 1896—

Former United Nations official; economist; statistician

Address: h. 730 Park Ave., New York 27

> NOTE: This biography supersedes the article which appeared in *Current Biography* in 1941.

An economist and statistician for more than thirty-five years, half of them spent in the service of the United States Government, Isador Lubin in June of 1950 was named by President Harry S. Truman as the United States representative on the Economic and Social Council of the United Nations, a unit of the world organization second only in importance to the Security Council. In the four years immediately preceding this appointment, Lubin had been a member of a commission of ECOSOC concerned primarily with questions of wages and prices, to which he was assigned after serving from 1933 to 1946 as the United States Commissioner of Labor Statistics. The economist, recognized as a "progressive" who shared the broad philosophy of the New Deal, was during World War II the special statistical assistant to President Roosevelt. At the end of the conflict he became the United States representative to the Allied Reparations Commission, with the rank of United States Minister. He had previously taught economics at the universities of Michigan and Missouri.

On March 30, 1953 President Eisenhower accepted the resignation of Isador Lubin as United States representative on the United Nations Economic and Social Council. His resignation from the Advisory Committee to the Agent General of the United Nations Reconstruction Agency was also accepted.

Isador Lubin, born in Worcester, Massachusetts, on June 9, 1896, is the son of Harris and Hinda (Francke) Lubin, Lithuanian-Jewish immigrants. His father, who had arrived in Boston in the late nineteenth century at the age of thirteen, set up a business of selling kitchenware to housewives throughout New England and before long gained enough capital to open a credit clothing store in Worcester. Here Isador Lubin grew up, attending the local grade school and high school. While in his teens he began to earn money as a collector of installment payments, an occupation he continued when in 1912 he became a student at Clark College in Worcester. Having completed his undergraduate studies with a B.A. degree in 1916, Lubin enrolled at the University of Missouri, where the eminent economist Thorstein Veblen was then teaching. After a year of graduate study at the university, he became in 1917 an instructor in economics. In the summer of 1918 Lubin, who had joined Herbert Hoover's United States Food Administration as a statistician, made a survey with Veblen of farm production in the Midwest. During part of the year 1918-19 he was employed by the United States War Industries Board as a special expert, serving under Bernard Baruch.

In 1919 Lubin left civil service for a year of study at the University of Michigan, where in 1920 he became an assistant professor of economics, remaining as such until 1922. Upon the establishment of the Brookings Institution in Washington, D.C., in 1922, Lubin was one of the first young economists to be invited to join the staff. During his eleven years as a member of the research organization, Lubin from 1923 to 1926 was on the faculty of the Robert Brookings Graduate School, an advanced school for graduate economists closely associated with the Brookings Institution, and from this school also received his Ph.D. degree in 1926. Meanwhile, in 1924, Lubin had taught at the University of Missouri, where he held the rank of associate professor of economics. While employed by the Brookings Institution Lubin became in 1928 an economic adviser to the Senate Committee on Education and Labor, which was investigating unemployment, and in 1931 he acted in the same capacity for the Committee on Manufacturers investigating economic planning. With his known prolabor stand and his expert knowledge of relations of wages, prices, and employment, he was appointed in 1933 United States Commissioner of Labor Statistics in the Department of Labor.

As the director of the Bureau of Labor Statistics, established in 1913, Lubin was responsible for collecting and diffusing useful and comprehensive information on subjects directly connected with labor, particularly those relating to hours, wages, and capital earnings. Thus, the bureau compiled statistical and interpretative data on employment, labor turnover, wage and hour rates, cost of living, prices, industrial accidents and agreements, and living conditions among the labor forces of the United States. These findings for the most part were reported in the *Monthly Labor Review*, the bureau's official publication, and during the years of World War II were used as a basis for formulating economic controls. When Lubin left this post in 1946, President Truman, in accepting his resignation, wrote: "You built up the Bureau of Labor Statistics into an institution that has commanded the respect of all recognized leaders in the field of economics and statistical science, as well as of labor and management throughout the country." The *Nation*, on the same occasion, commented: "Few men have served the government of this country so long and ably as Dr. Lubin."

This editorial praise referred also to the contributions Lubin had made to the other Government agencies in which he served during the years from 1933 to 1946. The first of these was the Federal Emergency Administration of Public Works, for which he was chairman of the Labor Advisory Board from 1933

United Nations

ISADOR LUBIN

to 1939. For part of this time (1933-36) he was a member of an advisory committee to the Federal Co-ordinator of Railroads. In 1933 he was also named vice-chairman of the United States Central Statistics Board, serving until 1938. Other memberships in this period were on the technical board of the President's Economic Security Committee (1934) and on the Cabinet subcommittee on the economic status of the cotton textile industry (1935). Appointed the first United States representative on the governing body of the International Labor Organization in Geneva, Switzerland, Lubin took part in the work of this world group from 1935 to 1937 and again in 1941 and 1945. From 1937 to 1943 he was a member of the industrial resources committee of the National Resources Board, while from 1938 to 1941 he helped conduct an investigation made by the Temporary National Economic Committee of the internal economic and financial structure of industry, and from 1940 to 1941 he was deputy director of the labor division of the Office of Production Management. Lubin formulated in 1941 the first over-all, zone-wide agreement of its kind between shipbuilders and unions on the West Coast.

With his appointment in 1941 as a special assistant to President Roosevelt, Lubin was made responsible for assembling and interpreting statistics on the nation's war programs. According to *Newsweek*, Lubin's "single-page digests of voluminous statistics often decided where American farm crops and production should go." Also during the war he and British Paymaster General Lord Cherwell, "arranged to co-ordinate British and American statistical terms in order to simplify war communications between the British and American executives and military commanders" (*National Cyclopædia of American Biography*).

Lubin's next significant task came in March 1945 when he was appointed by President

LUBIN, ISADOR—*Continued*

Roosevelt (he was later reappointed by President Truman) as the United States associate representative on the Allied Reparations Commission at Moscow, with the rank of United States Minister. At the time of the appointment Lubin was already in Europe on a special mission to study economic conditions in the liberated and conquered areas. In Moscow his responsibility in reaching decisions on the extent and kind of reparations that Germany would have to make to the Allies was described by the *Saturday Evening Post* as "the most important postwar task undertaken by an American." Shortly after his return to the United States, Lubin in 1946 resigned from the Bureau of Labor Statistics and subsequently accepted an appointment as United States representative to the Economic and Employment Commission of the Economic and Social Council of the United Nations. Here his work involved international studies of wages and prices. In June of 1950 Lubin, who in 1949-50 was special assistant to the Assistant Secretary of State, was selected for the position of United States representative with rank of Minister on ECOSOC itself, a post he resigned in 1953.

The Economic and Social Council of the United Nations, which is composed of eighteen member-states elected by the General Assembly, meets three times a year and in a special session when necessary. Each member, having one representative, is responsible for initiating studies and reports on international economic, social, cultural, educational, health, and related programs. ECOSOC has the power to make recommendations that will promote "respect for and observance of human rights and fundamental freedoms" and may prepare "drafts of international conventions for submission to the General Assembly." International conferences to study the fields within its realm may also be called by the council. There are several functional commissions and subcommissions within the organization of the council.

As a member of ECOSOC, Lubin has been concerned with matters relating to agriculture, cartels, and economic aids to underdeveloped nations. On the first of these subjects he introduced a resolution in September of 1951 recommending sweeping governmental measures to improve the position of the world's farmers. These measures, according to a report in the New York *Times* (September 4, 1951), would prevent "insecure tenants" and "rootless laborers" from being persuaded by "false leaders." Such reforms would involve dividing much of the land into farms of efficient size which could be owned by those who till the soil and would establish equitable tenure conditions. After reporting at the same session the existence of at least nineteen international cartels which threaten to nullify efforts to reduce trade barriers and improve standards of living in the poorer countries, Lubin introduced a resolution, which was approved by the Council, calling for United Nations control of such cartels by the application of existing United

States antitrust regulations. On the issue of aid to underdeveloped countries, Lubin in October of 1952 presented to the Economic and Financial Committee of the United Nations General Assembly a detailed report on the recovery achieved thus far in the poorer countries through direct investments by private United States investors and enterprises. Almost a billion dollars, Lubin stated, have been invested by private American groups in the eighteen-month period ending June 30, 1952, and the work of existing governmental agencies has achieved "dramatic results" in the underdeveloped countries. While the report was made to demonstrate the unwillingness on the part of the United States Government to undertake additional financial aid programs, the economist emphasized the determination of Americans to continue to win "the war against want and misery."

From time to time in the United Nations Lubin has also discussed American economy, on one notable occasion defending it against charges made by the Soviet Union delegates. In a lengthy memorandum circulated among the members of ECOSOC he refuted Soviet figures on housing, income, agricultural conditions, unemployment, and industrial profits and in a review of the United States economic condition, made before the council and reprinted in the United States Department of State *Bulletin* (August 20, 1951), he noted that we "have continued to expand output without inflation." Lubin is the author of a number of books on wages, prices, and unemployment described by *Collier's* as "factually sound and unprejudiced." *Government Control of Prices During the War*, written with Stella Stewart and Paul Garrett, was published in 1919; and *Miners' Wages and the Cost of Coal* appeared in 1924. In collaboration with Helen Everett and with the aid of the council and staff of the American Institute of Economics, he wrote *The British Coal Dilemma* (1927). In the words of the *New Republic* critic, "The book is an admirable piece of work, which may be recommended with confidence to all who desire to understand the most serious of the industrial problems confronting Great Britain at the present moment." Other studies made by Lubin are *The Absorption of the Unemployed by American Industry* (1929) and *The British Attack on Unemployment* (1934, with A. C. C. Hill, Jr.). He has also contributed papers on economic subjects to learned journals and periodicals.

A member of the board of directors of the New School for Social Research, Lubin is also on the board of trustees of Brandeis University. The economist has been affiliated with the Intercollegiate Menorah Society (president, 1920-22), the National Child Research Center (chairman of the board, 1930-35), the American Statistical Association (vice-president, 1937; president, 1946), International Association of Governmental Labor Officials (secretary, 1933-46), the International Institute of Statistics (fellow), and the American Economic Association (member). He is vice-chairman of the executive committee of the Franklin D. Roosevelt Memorial Foundation. In 1941 Lubin received an honorary LL.D. degree from

Clark College. He belongs to the Cosmos Club. His faith is the Jewish, and his political party is the Democratic.

Lubin on September 15, 1923, married Alice E. Berliner, of Washington, D.C.; by this marriage, which was terminated by divorce in 1928, he is the father of a daughter, Alice. On February 29, 1932, he married Ann Shumaker, who died in 1935, shortly after the birth of their daughter, Ann Harriet. The economist married Carol Riegelman on January 30, 1952. He enjoys camping trips and deep-sea fishing and takes pride in the gardens on his small farm, located on the shore of the South River near Chesapeake Bay.

References

Collier's 115:17 Je 2 '45
Newsweek 25:56 Mr 26 '45
Sat Eve Post 217:17 Je 16 '45
U N Bul 10:171 F 15 '51
U S News p41 Je 13 '41

Directory of American Scholars (1951)
International Who's Who, 1952
National Cyclopædia of American Biography Current vol G, 1943-46
Who's Who in America, 1952-53
Who's Who in American Education, 1951-52
Who's Who in Commerce and Industry (1951)
World Biography (1948)

LUCE, CLARE BOOTHE Apr. 10, 1903- Ambassador to Italy; writer

Address: b. c/o United States Embassy, Rome, Italy; Time & Life Bldg., 9 Rockefeller Plaza, New York 20; h. "Sugar Hill," Ridgefield, Conn.

> NOTE: This biography supersedes the article which appeared in *Current Biography* in 1942.

With her nomination by President Dwight D. Eisenhower on February 7, 1953, as United States Ambassador to Italy, Mrs. Clare Boothe Luce became the second woman Ambassador in American history and the first assigned to a major world power. To her diplomatic post, in which she was confirmed by the Senate on March 2, 1953, Mrs. Luce brings more than ten years of experience in United States politics, having served in the House of Representatives as a member from Connecticut in the Seventy-eighth and Seventy-ninth Congresses, from 1943 to 1947, and worked actively in the Republican Presidential campaigns of 1940, 1944, and 1952. She also brings, in the words of Anne O'Hare McCormick of the New York *Times*, "a large fund of shrewd ability leavened by charm." Before entering politics, Mrs. Luce had become known as a playwright, particularly for the successful comedy *The Women*, an editor and journalist. In a recent Gallup poll she was listed fourth among the world's "most admired women," after Mrs. Eleanor Roosevelt, Queen Elizabeth II, and Mrs. Dwight D. Eisenhower.

Phillipe Halsman
CLARE BOOTHE LUCE

Ann Clare Boothe was born in New York City on April 10, 1903, to William F. Boothe, a businessman and amateur violinist who was a descendant of a pre-Revolutionary War family, and Ann Clare Snyder Boothe, who had been a dancer before her marriage. Her childhood was spent in Memphis and Chicago, and after her parents were separated, she and her mother lived for a year in France. Educated in private schools, she spent two years, from 1915 to 1917, at St. Mary's in Garden City, New York, and the following two years at Miss Mason's School, "The Castle," in Tarrytown-on-the-Hudson, New York, from which she was graduated in 1919. Meanwhile her parents had been divorced and her mother married to Dr. Albert E. Austin, who later represented in Congress the Fourth Connecticut District for which Clare Boothe herself became Representative in 1943.

After a short period in which young Clare Boothe left home to work in New York City, she entered Clare Tree Major's School of the Theatre. As a child she had been understudy to Mary Pickford in David Belasco's production of *A Good Little Devil* and had played a bit role in a motion picture. (While she has often been confused with actress Claire Luce, she has appeared on the stage only once, in a summer stock production of *Candida* in Connecticut, when she replaced the star who had become ill.) Her plans for a career in the theater were interrupted by a trip to Europe with her parents in 1919, on which she met Mrs. O. H. P. Belmont, through whom she became active in the women's suffrage movement. Also through Mrs. Belmont she met George Tuttle Brokaw, New York clothing manufacturer, whom she married in 1923.

When her marriage to Brokaw was terminated in 1929 (he died in May, 1935) she resumed her former name, and as Clare Boothe, she joined the staff of *Vogue* as an editorial

LUCE, CLARE BOOTHE—*Continued*

assistant in 1930. She became associate editor of *Vanity Fair* a year later and managing editor in 1933. Her satirical sketches for *Vanity Fair* were collected in a book under the title *Stuffed Shirts* (1931). On resigning from the staff of *Vanity Fair* in 1934, Miss Boothe wrote a newspaper column, "This World of Ours," which ran for only a few weeks. During this period her chief interest was in writing for the theater. Her first play to be produced on Broadway (and the fifth she had written), *Abide With Me,* a somber psychological drama which opened in November 1935, was not well received by the critics.

On November 21, 1935, Miss Boothe married Henry Robinson Luce, then president of Time, Inc., and now editor-in-chief of *Time, Life,* and *Fortune.* A year later she achieved theatrical success when her play *The Women* opened in New York in December 1936. This satire on idle rich women, which the critics described as "brittle" and "superficial," won wide popularity: it ran for 657 performances, toured the United States and eighteen foreign countries, and was made into a motion picture. Mrs. Luce reportedly had written the first draft of *The Women* in longhand in three days and rewrote it during rehearsals.

Her next play, *Kiss the Boys Goodbye* (1938), was a comedy suggested by the highly publicized search for an actress to take the role of Scarlett O'Hara in the Hollywood version of *Gone With the Wind.* In her preface to the printed edition of the play in 1939 Mrs. Luce announced that it was "a political allegory about fascism in America," but it was accepted by most audiences merely as "thumping good theater," to use the phrase of the reviewer of the Boston *Transcript. Margin for Error* (1940), a comedy-melodrama, was less oblique in its political references, with a plot concerning the murder of a Nazi agent in the United States. Both plays were later made into motion pictures.

Soon after the outbreak of World War II, Mrs. Luce in 1940 travelled to Europe as a journalist under contract to *Life.* When she returned, she found that she had enough material for a book, which she prepared in six weeks. *Europe in the Spring* (1940) is a lively account of her travels through Italy, France, the Low Countries, and England in the tense days of the great German offensive in the spring of 1940. While some reviewers found the book superficial and inaccurate in details, many of Mrs. Luce's observations were considered shrewd and penetrating. Janet Flanner commented in the New York *Herald Tribune* that "Miss Boothe with a brilliantly accurate eye sees herself in that whole fatal European spring tableau as what she must have been—an attractive, intelligent, observing, hard-boiled, surprisingly soft-hearted, and specially privileged New York woman."

Mrs. Luce entered politics actively in the Presidential campaign of 1940 when she worked for the election of Republican candidate Wendell Willkie. At a rally in New York on October 16, 1940, she criticized the Roosevelt Administration for having failed to prepare the country for the war which then threatened the United States, and launched a feud with newspaper columnist Dorothy Thompson, who supported President Roosevelt. The controversy between the two continued throughout the campaign, but two years later. when Mrs. Luce was a candidate for Congress, Miss Thompson endorsed her candidacy in paid advertisements. Touring China with her husband in 1941 to study war conditions there, Mrs. Luce reported for *Life* the devastation caused by the Japanese invasion, the changes in China's social and economic structure, and the need for a better understanding of that country. In February 1942 she visited Africa, India, and China, and landed in Burma a day after it had been bombed by the Japanese. She interviewed Generalissimo and Madam Chiang Kai-shek, Prime Minister Nehru, Generals Alexander and Stillwell, and other prominent figures, and visited the front lines wherever possible.

In the summer of 1942 Mrs. Luce's name was listed as a candidate for the Republican nomination for Representative from the Fourth Connecticut Congressional District, which includes Fairfield County. Early in August she sent a letter to the Republican State chairman declining the nomination because of her lack of knowledge of the local problems of the district. According to the New York *Times,* the letter was regarded by many "as only a tentative withdrawal of her bonnet from the political ring," and one month later she accepted the nomination, saying that in view of her travels and observations of the war, she "was more qualified by experience to deal with it than any candidate who has so far presented himself in Fairfield County." She achieved the nomination by winning over six opponents, one of whom was the industrialist Miss Vivien Kellems, and swept the nominating convention by a vote of 84 to 2. Using the slogan "Let's fight a hard war instead of a soft war," she campaigned vigorously against her Democratic opponent, LeRoy D. Downs, especially in the industrial Bridgeport district, where she sought the heavy labor vote, and scored a plurality of 6,745 over Downs.

While a freshman Congresswoman, Mrs. Luce, who was appointed to the important House Military Affairs Committee, attracted more newspaper publicity than many senior statesmen. In her maiden speech in Congress, "America and the Postwar Air World," she commented on Vice-President Henry A. Wallace's proposal for freedom of the air to insure international peace: "But much of what Mr. Wallace calls his global thinking, no matter how you slice it, is still globaloney." She went on to say that America's best interest lay in "postwar civilian, as well as military, control of the air." Norman Cousins criticized the speech, which was hailed by isolationists and condemned by their opponents, as "a disservice to the nation, a curious and unforgivable insult to Americans who happen to be fighting and dying in a global war" (*Saturday Review of Literature*). Mrs. Luce replied that her speech had been misinterpreted and that she was not advocating American control over world air lanes, but reciprocal arrangements that would insure each nation's sovereignty over its own skies. Again demonstrating her flair for phrase-coining, she spoke in her keynote address to the Republican National Convention (June 27, 1944) of "G.I. Joe" and "G.I. Jim": the American soldier who had given his life in battle and the other who would return to a civilian world which needed the Republican party to correct the "dictatorial bumbledom" of the Democratic Administration.

For a second time successful when her party's candidate for President, Thomas E. Dewey, was defeated in 1944 Mrs. Luce was re-elected to her seat in the House of Representatives. She spent Christmas 1944 with the American troops in Italy and on her return urged extended aid for Italian victims of the war. During her two terms in Congress, Mrs. Luce's voting record was generally in support of the Administration's foreign policy, while she criticized it from the House floor and in her many public speeches and radio talks. In 1945 she warned against a soft policy toward communism and in the same year proposed as a solution to the problem of communism in China a Chinese federal union with a representative government. As a member of the Joint Committee on Atomic Energy, she spoke in favor of a bill to establish civilian control of the atom under the Atomic Energy Commission.

Some of the bills introduced into Congress by Mrs. Luce were H.R. 110, to acknowledge the national responsibility of the United States for the Yalta surrender of Poland to the Soviet Union; two bills to authorize the admission and naturalization of East Indians and Chinese on the same quota percentage as nationals of other countries, which were passed by the House; a bill to authorize a study of the refugee problem; a bill to establish a bureau in the Department of Labor to insure workers equal pay for equal work, regardless of race, color, or creed; a resolution authorizing a study of profit-sharing in industry; and a resolution "favoring the creation of appropriate international machinery within the framework of the United Nations Organization for international control and reduction of armaments and weapons, especially those involving atomic power."

When Mrs. Luce's second term of office expired in 1946, she announced that she would not seek nomination as the Republican candidate for Senator from Connecticut. One of the reasons given for her withdrawal from politics was her conversion to the Roman Catholic faith in that year, when she was received into the Church by Bishop Fulton J. Sheen. She also wished to have more time for writing, and in 1947 she contributed a series of articles to *McCall's*, describing her conversion. She also wrote many other articles for both religious and secular journals. In 1949 her film story *Come to the Stable* was nominated for the Motion Picture Academy of Arts and Sciences Award. In the same year she wrote the essay *Twilight of God* and lectured widely on such topics as "Christianity in the Atomic Age" and "The Quality of Greatness." A play *Child of the Morning*, starring Eddie Dowling and Margaret O'Brien, was tried out "on the road" but has not yet had a Broadway production. In

1952 Mrs. Luce was the editor of a volume of essays by American and British authors called *Saints for Now*, which included contributions by Evelyn Waugh, Rebecca West, and Whittaker Chambers.

Several months before General Dwight D. Eisenhower received the Republican nomination for President, Mrs. Luce returned to the political scene to work for his nomination. She also sought unsuccessfully to win for herself the Republican nomination for United States Senator from Connecticut. During the Eisenhower campaign she delivered forty-seven radio and television speeches in his behalf, and when he was elected her name was mentioned for an important Government appointment. Reaction to Mrs. Luce's nomination as Ambassador to Italy, which was announced on February 7, 1953, was for the most part favorable both in the United States and in Italy. The only Italian opposition came from the conservative Naples newspaper *Il Mattino*, which objected to the appointment of a woman to so responsible an office, and from communist sources which emphasized her conversion to Catholicism and described her as "a friend of the Pope." In the United States the appointment was questioned by Glenn L. Archer, executive director of Protestants and Other Americans United for Separation of Church and State, who asked if the new Ambassador would also have diplomatic relations with the Vatican. Mr. Archer referred to the controversy which was aroused in 1951 over President Truman's projected appointment of General Mark Clark as Ambassador to the Vatican. In answer to this, Mrs. Luce testified before a closed hearing of the Senate Foreign Relations Committee on February 17, 1953, that she supported "the American tradition of separation of church and state" and would have no relations, "formal or informal, open or secret," with the Vatican in her new post. Confirmed in her diplomatic assignment by the Senate on March 2, 1953, Mrs. Luce, accompanied by her husband, left in April for Rome, where she presented her credentials.

Mrs. Luce in a September interview urged that the United States Government liberalize its trade and immigration policies. "If Italy could trade on more favorable terms in the United States markets . . . it would naturally help her economy," the Ambassador stated. In referring to the problem of overpopulation as one of the main reasons for the large Communist vote in Italy, she expressed the hope that America would not only "take its fair share of people" but would even contribute a "reasonable share to the financing . . . of a world-wide program . . . for moving people to places where they can be economically productive" (*U.S. News & World Report*, September 25, 1953).

Mrs. Luce is a member of the Daughters of the American Revolution. She has received honorary degrees from Colby College and Creighton University, and in 1951 she received the Cardinal Newman Award from the federation of college Newman clubs. The Luces have lived in New York City, on their plantation in South Carolina, in Greenwich, Connecti-

LUCE, CLARE BOOTHE—*Continued*

cut, and in Ridgefield, Connecticut. Mrs. Luce's only child, Ann Clare Brokaw, was killed in an automobile accident in Palo Alto, California, in 1944. Mrs. Luce, who has "white-gold" hair, blue eyes, and a fair complexion, is said to possess "a delicate, fragile beauty."

References

> Collier's 111:20+ Mr 27 '43
> New Repub 109:72-4 Jl 19 '43
> Newsweek 41:30 F 16 '53
> N Y Herald Tribune p1+ F 8 '53
> N Y Times p1+ F 8 '53
> New Yorker 16:21+ Ja 4 '41; 16:24+ Ja 11 '41
> Time 40:18-19 S 1 '42; 48:19-20 Ag 26 '46; 61:19 F 16 '53
> Washington (D.C.) Post p6M F 8 '53; p11S Mr 8 '53
> Biographical Directory of the American Congress, 1774-1949 (1950)
> Hoehn, M. Catholic Authors (1943)
> Kunitz, S. J., and Haycraft, H. Twentieth Century Authors (1942)
> Who's Who in America, 1952-53
> Who's Who in United States Politics (1950)

LUDINGTON, FLORA B(ELLE) Nov. 12, 1898- Librarian; library association official

Address: c/o Mount Holyoke College, South Hadley, Mass.

Having completed a year's tenure as first vice-president and president-elect of the American Library Association, Flora B. Ludington, librarian of Mount Holyoke College, automatically assumed the office of president of the association for 1953-54 at its annual conference, in Los Angeles in June 1953.

Before her appointment to her present position at Mount Holyoke, Miss Ludington was associated for a number of years with Mills College in California as reference librarian, assistant professor, and associate librarian. Distinguished also for her work in library service abroad, she spent two years (1944-46) in Bombay, India, as director of the United States Information Service there.

Flora Belle Ludington, who was born in Huron County, Michigan, on November 12, 1898, is the daughter of Bertram Winslow and Ella Elizabeth (Winterbottom) Ludington. In Michigan, also the birthplace of her parents, her mother had been a school teacher before marriage and her father was a farmer until 1900. When Flora Ludington was about two years old, the family moved to Bonners Ferry, Idaho, where her father became a merchant. He later engaged in the same occupation in Wenatchee, Washington.

At the Carnegie Public Library, established in Wenatchee in 1911, Flora Ludington, whose love of reading had its beginning in childhood, was given her first access to a large supply of books. She began library work as a volunteer library assistant at the age of fourteen while a student at the local public school. For a

year after her graduation from high school in 1916, she attended Whitman College in Walla Walla, Washington, later entering the University of Washington in Seattle to take her B.A. degree in librarianship in 1920. Debating was her chief extracurricular interest during her undergraduate years.

Later studies brought Miss Ludington an M.A. degree in history from Mills College, Oakland, California, and a B.L.S. degree from New York State Library School, both conferred in 1925. In that year, also, her *Newspapers of Oregon, 1846-1870* was published.

Employed as assistant in the circulation department of the library, Miss Ludington remained for another year (1920-21) at the University of Washington before becoming reference librarian at Mills College. She was later named assistant professor of bibliography and then associate librarian. In 1936 she accepted appointment to the position she has since held, librarian at Mount Holyoke College in South Hadley, Massachusetts. She has also taught in summer sessions at the University of Texas (1930), San Jose (California) State Teachers College (1931), and the Columbia University School of Library Science (1936, 1938, 1939, 1941, 1942, and 1943).

On leave of absence from Mount Holyoke College from 1944 to 1946, Miss Ludington held the post of first director of the Office of War Information's United States Information Library in Bombay, India. The following year in May she was present at the thirteenth meeting of the International Library Committee, convening in Oslo, Norway. In Japan from August to November in 1948 she served as visiting expert on information libraries for SCAP (Supreme Command for the Allied Powers).

As librarian of Mount Holyoke College, Miss Ludington was instrumental in establishing the Hampshire Inter-Library Center to serve Amherst, Smith, and Mount Holyoke colleges as a center for scholarly books and periodicals not in frequent demand in the three colleges. In an article appearing in the *American Library Association Bulletin* (January 1952), Miss Ludington pointed out: "No institution is an island sufficient unto itself, especially a library. It is rather a reservoir, continuously fed from many streams but differing from other reservoirs in that the substance of which it is composed is not expended."

Since academic libraries have doubled in size during the past fifteen to twenty years, she explained, universities and colleges are "seeking ways to control bulk and cost through cooperation." The Hampshire Inter-Library Center, which at present is located at Mount Holyoke, is the outgrowth of cooperation among the libraries of member colleges.

Miss Ludington, a long-time member of the American Library Association and former chairman of its board on international relations, was chosen first vice-president and president-elect of the association at its annual conference, in New York City in July 1952. In the closing general session of the seventy-second conference in Los Angeles in June 1953 she was inaugurated as A.L.A. president for the year 1953-54, succeeding Robert B. Downs. In an address on June 26 devoted primarily to a review of the A.L.A.'s hundred-year development, Miss Ludington spoke of some of the continuing values in library service. "A public library," she said, "is the community's embodiment of an urge for knowledge that is basic in human nature. . . . In an age of mass communication by means of the motion picture, radio and television the book may well offer a unique opportunity for one mind to meet another mind. . . .The freer the society, the greater is the responsibility of the individual to be informed on the issues of the day."

"A well-selected library," she continued, "offers the opportunity to gain the information needed to understand diverging points of view on local, national and international affairs. A library does not take an official position of its own on disputed questions and refrains from doing so in the public interest. It imposes no thought control but rather encourages an appreciation of the past and an understanding of the present."

During the course of the Los Angeles conference, attended by some 3,200 of A.L.A.'s 21,000 members, the library association in concert with the American Book Publishers Council endorsed a declaration entitled "On Freedom to Read," described by a New York *Times* editorial (June 27, 1953) as "a document that seems today to belong, civilian and unofficial though it is, with America's outstanding state papers."

In this statement of principles, the librarians supported the cause of complete freedom in the circulation of books and denounced "encroachments on the people's freedom to read by individuals or groups seeking to impose their own standards or tastes upon the community at large" (New York *Times*, June 26, 1953). The association also issued a resolution on United States overseas libraries, proposing full literary freedom as the basis of continued A.L.A. co-operation in the foreign program.

Contributing frequently to library and educational periodicals, Miss Ludington has written a number of articles on problems concerning college libraries. Among them are "Consideration of a College Library Book List" (*A.L.A. Bulletin.* March 1936), "Glance at Salaries in College and University Libraries" (*A.L.A. Bulletin,* February 1940), "New Code and the College Library" (*College and Research Libraries,* March 1942), and "Toward a Better College Library" (*Stechert-Hafner Book News,* March 1950).

Her papers on other subjects include "Public Opinion and Postwar Planning: the Library's Part" (*Library Journal,* May 1943) and "Strengthening the Forces for Peace" (*Massachusetts Library Association Bulletin,* July 1951). Miss Ludington is an adviser on the *United States Quarterly Book Review,* sponsored by the Library of Congress.

The library association president holds an honorary LL.D. degree from Mills College, awarded in June 1953; she is also the recipient of a certificate of achievement conferred upon her in 1948 by the Civil Information and Education Section of SCAP. Miss Ludington's

Blackstone Studios

FLORA B. LUDINGTON

church affiliation is the Presbyterian. She belongs to the Bibliographical Society of America, the Massachusetts Library Association, the American Association of University Professors, the American Association of University Women, the Association of College and Reference Libraries, and Town Hall Club, New York. The brown-eyed, graying black-haired librarian names as her recreations travel and reading.

References

A.L.A. Bul 46:217 Jl '52 por
Pub W 162:133 Jl 12 '52 por

Who's Who in America, 1952-53
Who's Who in Library Service (1943)
Who's Who in Massachusetts, 1942-43
Who's Who in the East (1951)
World Biography (1948)

LYNN, DIANA Oct. 7, 1926- Actress
Address: c/o Actors' Equity, 45 W. 47 St., New York 19

Signed by Paramount Pictures when she was thirteen, Diana Lynn at twenty-seven has attained stardom in many fields of entertainment. A popular screen personality, she also appears frequently on radio and television programs, has recorded both popular and classical music, and has received favorable reviews for her stage performances in both New York and London.

Her latest film, *Plunder of the Sun*, opened at the Paramount Theatre in New York City on August 26, 1953. She achieved a personal triumph in F. Hugh Herbert's play, *The Moon Is Blue*, which opened at the Duke of York's Theatre in London in July, 1953, in which she is still playing the principal feminine role.

Diana Lynn, whose real name is Delores Loehr, was born on October 7, 1926, in Los

DIANA LYNN

Angeles, California. She is the only daughter of Mr. and Mrs. Louis Loehr, of that city. Her father is an executive of an oil-supply concern, while her mother is an accomplished pianist. "Dolly," as she is known, studied the piano from early childhood, and it was this training that was responsible for her start in motion pictures.

Miss Lynn did not attend high school but received her formal education from instructors on the Paramount lot. She had been taken to the studios as accompanist for a child violinist who was auditioning for a part in *There's Magic in Music*. Although the violinist did not get the part, Miss Lynn was signed, as a pianist, for the film which was about Michigan's Interlochen Music Camp.

As she was only thirteen at the time, it was somewhat difficult to find suitable parts for her. As Miss Lynn said, "By the time they had decided on one [a role] I had grown up a little more and was too tall for it." Finally she was given a supporting part in a film starring Ginger Rogers and Ray Milland, called *The Major and the Minor*, which was released in 1942.

Receiving some favorable attention as a result of this film, in which she played a brattish kid sister, Diana Lynn was next cast in the Preston Sturges picture *The Miracle of Morgan's Creek,* in which she portrayed the part of a young sister to Betty Hutton. This film, which was well received generally, was another minor triumph for Miss Lynn of whom Alton Cook, writing in the New York *World-Telegram* said: "That promising ingenue, Diana Lynn, fulfills all the promise with the saucy charm this picture brings out."

It was her success in this role which typecast Miss Lynn as the "kid sister" on the Paramount lot. She appeared in several of the Henry Aldrich series films, probably the best remembered of which was *Henry Aldrich Plays Cupid.*

The pattern of teen-age roles was first broken in *Out Of This World*, in which Diana Lynn portrayed a band leader opposite Eddie Bracken. The reviewer in *PM* commented: "The hit of the film for me was Diana Lynn herself, who it turns out is something of a whizz-bang as a pianist and also something of a songstress. One of her stunts is playing Chopin's *Minute Waltz* in one minute flat by a time-clock."

Diana Lynn's first starring picture was *Our Hearts Were Young And Gay*, a dramatization of the best-selling Cornelia Otis Skinner-Emily Kimbrough book of the same title, released in New York City on October 11, 1944.

In this film Miss Lynn played the role of Emily, the lighter-veined of the two young women who took a tour of Europe, unchaperoned. "That was one thing about *Our Hearts Were Young and Gay,*" said Miss Lynn, "I was nobody's sister." For her portrayal of Emily Kimbrough she won considerable praise. Said *Variety*: "The ever-breathless, slightly madcap Miss Lynn is capital in everything she does."

Her rise to stardom was completed just before her eighteenth birthday, a date she ardently looked forward to, according to an interview with Eileen Creelman in the New York *Sun*. . . "I won't have to have a teacher follow me everywhere in the studio, even into make-up and hair-dressing. I was fond of my teacher. But it's not a pleasant feeling not to be allowed to be alone. That's the law. They have to watch you every minute. But I'll be eighteen next month."

The next production for Diana Lynn was a sequel to her first starring vehicle, entitled *Our Hearts Were Growing Up*. This film, which opened in New York City on August 11, 1946, was not very well received although more fault was found with the script than with the acting of the young star. As Archer Winsten succinctly stated in the New York *Post*: "*Our Hearts Were Growing Up*, sequel to *Our Hearts Were Young And Gay,* completely overlooks the fact that minds usually keep growing with the hearts."

During the making of these films Diana Lynn had been keeping up with her music lessons, and made her concert debut in Los Angeles in 1943. In October 1946 Capitol records announced a three-disk album featuring Diana as piano soloist in such works as Mozart's *Rondo, Laura, Body and Soul*, and *Slaughter on Tenth Avenue*. During the war years Miss Lynn played at numerous benefit concerts. She has also made personal appearance tours around the country, at which she invariably plays the piano, since she admits to not telling anecdotes well.

The next pictures in which Diana Lynn appeared were *Ruthless,* a melodrama with Zachary Scott and Sydney Greenstreet, and *Every Girl Should Be Married*, a light comedy piece, both of which were released in 1948. After these came the first of the *My Friend Irma* pictures, which were based on the successful radio program of the same name starring Marie Wilson. In these films Miss Lynn played the part of Jane Stacy, a young friend of Irma.

Although the two *Irma* films were made by Hal Wallis for Paramount Pictures, Miss Lynn worked in them on a free-lance basis, having decided not to renew her contract with Paramount. Thus she was free to accept radio and television offers. She appeared on such radio shows as *Frank Sinatra Sings, Supper Club,* in addition to being the youngest entertainer to appear on the quiz show *Information Please.*

When she turned to television *Life* magazine commented (May 5, 1952): "Diana Lynn is a television rarity—a major Hollywood player who has also made herself a TV star... In TV she has not only had a happy variety of romantic and comedy parts . . . but has played an entire concerto composed for her."

Her guest appearances on television have been with Jack Carter, Ken Murray, Milton Berle, and Ed Wynn. She recently signed an exclusive television contract with the *Schlitz Playhouse,* at a reported fee of $3,000 per show. She finds the work stimulating, and observes that "More cab drivers recognize me now that I'm in TV than they ever did when I was only in movies."

The young actress has appeared on the legitimate stage in summer stock productions of *Dear Ruth,* and in a number of plays with the La Jolla (California) Players, including *Voice of the Turtle* and *Ring Around the Moon.* Her appearance in the West Coast company production of *The Moon Is Blue* led to her current engagement in the London version of this play. In 1952 she played at the New York City Center opposite Maurice Evans in Henrik Ibsen's *The Wild Duck,* and early in 1953 in *Horses in Midstream* opposite Sir Cedric Hardwicke.

She appeared in *Bedtime for Bonzo,* a film about the problems of bringing up a chimpanzee, for Universal-International in 1951, as well as in *The People Against O'Hara* starring Spencer Tracy, for Metro-Goldwyn-Mayer.

The young star's latest film, *Plunder Of The Sun,* opened at the Paramount theater in New York on August 26, 1953, and was described as "a routine romantic adventure." Miss Lynn plays an alcohol-loving girl in this film.

Diana Lynn was married on December 18, 1948 to John C. Lindsay, an architect. They separated January 5, 1953 and Miss Lynn sued for divorce on May 26, 1953, in Santa Monica, California. The actress prefers to wear feminine clothes, enjoys watching football games and likes dining out, parties and travelling. She is five feet six inches tall, weighs 115 pounds, has honey blonde hair and blue eyes. She is the recipient of an award from the National Secretaries Association for her portrayals of secretaries as diligent businesswomen.

References

Life Mag 32:143 My 5 '52
N Y Herald Tribune p12 Ag 27 '53
N Y Times p3-II O 1 '44
Motion Picture and Television Almanac, 1952-3

LYTTELTON, OLIVER 1893- British Cabinet member; business executive

Address: b. c/o Colonial Office, The Church House, Great Smith St., S.W. 1, London, England; h. 14 Upper Belgrave St., London, England; Trafalgar House, Downton, Wiltshire, England

> NOTE: This biography supersedes the article which appeared in *Current Biography* in 1941.

With the return of the Conservatives to power in Great Britain in October 1951, the Right Honorable Oliver Lyttelton became Secretary of State for the Colonies in the Cabinet of Prime Minister Winston Churchill. A World War I hero, Lyttelton was later known as a highly successful businessman, both before and after his entrance into national political service as Comptroller of Non-Ferrous Metals at the beginning of World War II. From this office he moved into the wartime Churchill

British Inf. Services
OLIVER LYTTELTON

Cabinet, holding successively the post of President of the Board of Trade, Minister of State for the Middle East, and Minister of Production. Since 1940 he has continuously been returned as a Conservative to his seat in the House of Commons, representing the Aldershot Division of Hampshire. In the business world he has served as managing director of the British Metal Corporation and was chairman of the Associated Electrical Industries from October 1945 until October 1951.

Born in 1893, Oliver Lyttelton is the only son of the Right Honorable Alfred Lyttelton, whose father was the fourth Lord Lyttelton and whose aunt was the wife of the famous Liberal leader William Ewart Gladstone. A few years after his son's birth, Alfred Lyttelton

LYTTELTON, OLIVER—*Continued*

from 1903 to 1905 occupied the office of Colonial Secretary in the Conservative Government headed by Arthur James Balfour. Oliver's mother, the former Edith Balfour, daughter of Archibald Balfour, was a writer of distinction and a Dame Grand Cross of the Order of the British Empire before her death in 1948. Oliver Lyttelton was educated at Eton and then at Trinity College, Cambridge, where he became an adept cricketer and also a member of the golf team in 1913.

Leaving Cambridge soon after World War I began, Lyttelton was one of the earliest volunteers for a commission and was gazetted to the Grenadier Guards in December 1914. From 1915 until hostilities ended in 1918, he served in heavy fighting in France; there he three times gained mention in dispatches, won both the Companion of the Distinguished Service Order (1916) and the Military Cross, and on one occasion brought forty German prisoners back to headquarters. He was successively made adjutant of the 3d Guards Battalion (October 1915), brigade major of the 4th Guards Brigade (February 1918), brigade major of the 2d Guards Brigade (September 1918), and a captain upon his discharge.

During the years between the two World Wars Oliver Lyttelton was engaged in business in London, where he joined the British Metal Corporation, Ltd., in 1920, became its managing director, and as such was credited with having "fathered the world tin cartel" (*Time*). Lyttelton was an acknowledged force in British Empire trade when World War II was started in September 1939. Because of his knowledge of the complicated economic ramifications in the nonferrous metal industry, he was named Controller of Non-Ferrous Metals under Prime Minister Neville Chamberlain. Lyttelton bought up for Britain enough nonferrous metal for a three years' war, all before prices had begun to skyrocket. On May 10, 1940, Neville Chamberlain was succeeded as Prime Minister by Winston Churchill, who had known Lyttelton from boyhood and had admired his business achievements and enterprise. When on October 3, 1940, Churchill promoted Sir Andrew Rae Duncan from the Presidency of the Board of Trade to the newly created position of Minister of Supply, Lyttelton was named President of the Board of Trade (equivalent to Secretary of Commerce in the United States), attained Cabinet rank for the first time, and automatically became a Privy Councillor (member of the King's advisory committee).

Since British Cabinet ministers must be in a position to answer questions in Parliament, it was necessary that a seat be found in the House of Commons for the new President of the Board of Trade. Consequently, when Viscount Wolmer, the member for the military town of Aldershot, Division of Hampshire, moved up to the House of Lords, Lyttelton was duly named by local Conservatives as their candidate to succeed Wolmer and was returned unopposed in the by-election of November 26, 1940. (Lyttelton has been returned by Alder-

shot in all three subsequent general elections.) Under the Emergency Powers Defense Act, passed in May 1940 to extend the powers of the President of the Board of Trade, Lyttelton was "enabled to take over industry for defense purposes and to shift and reallocate labor to any tasks he deemed necessary" (Lemuel F. Parton in the New York *Sun,* June 3, 1941). He introduced clothes rationing in wartime Britain and largely succeeded in convincing the populace that shabby clothes were in vogue. In a radio broadcast he declared: "People admire the soldier whose uniform bears the marks of battle or the fireman whose uniform is stained. It is also honorable for us to be seen in clothes that are not so smart because we are bearing as civilians yet another share if our clothes are battle-stained." Lyttelton also sought to plug holes in the War Goods Act by "wider and more inflexible price control on consumer goods and a more thorough control of middleman profits" (Craig Thompson in the New York *Times,* June 20, 1941).

A member of Prime Minister Churchill's War Cabinet, Lyttelton left the Board of Trade at the end of June 1941 to become Minister of State in the Middle East with the responsibilities of serving as administrator of conquered territories, of seeking to unravel political snarls that had hitherto burdened the military, and of relieving the military High Command of "all extraneous burdens." Lyttelton was stationed in Cairo, Egypt, this marking the first time in Britain's history that a full ranking Cabinet Minister was assigned to overseas headquarters. In this post he held talks with Trans-Jordan leaders which resulted in Anglo-Arabian accord. Lyttelton left the Middle East in February 1942, when Churchill appointed him to succeed Lord Beaverbrook as Minister of Production, a post he held until July 1945. Simultaneously during the period from 1942 to 1945 he was co-head with Donald Nelson of the new combined Production and Resources Board aimed at pooling production of the United States and Britain.

As director of his country's World War II production effort, Lyttelton in 1944 was awarded the Order of Suvorov, First Class, for his able organization of Britain's supply of munitions to the embattled Soviet Union. His relations with Washington were highly cordial except for an incident in the summer of 1944 when as the guest of honor at a luncheon given by the London branch of the United States Chamber of Commerce, Lyttelton was urged by the chairman to include in his prepared speech on American-British co-operation some reference to the war in the Pacific. Lyttelton's extemporaneous statement that "Japan was provoked into attacking the Americans at Pearl Harbor" (as quoted by *Time,* July 3, 1944), was reported to have caused considerable indignation in Washington. Later expressing his regrets in Commons, Lyttelton said: "Any misunderstanding is entirely my own fault. . . . The fault was one of expression, and not of intention."

In May 1945, after the end of the war in Europe, Lyttelton again became President of the Board of Trade, while retaining his post as Minister of Production, and held both portfolios until the defeat of the Conservatives in the election two months later. With his party out of power, he re-entered business to hold the chairmanship of the powerful Associated Electrical Industries, Ltd., from 1945 to 1951. He was also a director of the Alliance Assurance, Ltd., and from 1946 to 1949 served as president of the Advertising Association. Retaining his Aldershot seat in the House of Commons, Lyttelton became an Opposition "front bencher." In September 1950 he led the Conservatives in criticizing the exportation of machine tools to Poland and Russia. The following November he resumed the Conservative campaign against the Government's bid for permanent economic control powers by censuring the Laborites for failure to check the inflationary trend, which, he said, could be stopped by cutting Government expenditures. In January 1951 he voiced industry's concern over the Attlee Government's hesitation to plan and to place new orders for arms under its rearmament program.

When the Conservative party regained power in the October 1951 election, Oliver Lyttelton was named Secretary of State for Colonies in the new Churchill Cabinet. In one of his earliest speeches (November 21) in his new capacity he told members of the House of Commons that the new Tory Government was "convinced of the urgent necessity" for a federation of the three British territories in Central Africa, Northern and Southern Rhodesia, and Nyasaland. A conference of representatives from these territories was called for July 1952 in London, but was boycotted by African Negro delegates who opposed the plan that would establish self-government for the white inhabitants, with certain safeguards for Negroes. The meeting was postponed until January 1953, at which time a plan for a Central African federation was perfecetd, but which required endorsement by the three territories and the British Parliament.

In late November 1951 Colonial Secretary Lyttelton flew to Malaya to investigate ways of intensifying the British campaign against the two-and-a-half-year-old Communist rebellion that was threatening British rule and sapping the economy of the territory. Under heavy guard he made a thirteen-day tour of areas to discuss conditions with officials, British rubber planters, Chinese business and political heads, Indian labor leaders, Malayan sultans, and villagers. After a brief visit to Hong Kong, during which he told the inhabitants that Britain was "determined to stay here on the doorstep of Red China," he eased one grievance by ruling that knowledge of the English language would no longer be a prerequisite for British citizenship, thus removing the citizenship ban for about 200,000 Singapore Chinese. Back in London in December, Lyttelton expressed the belief that the Malayan situation "may well get worse before it gets better." Seven months later in a warning against pushing democratization too quickly, he told the House of Commons: "If you were to set up full self-government in Malaya tomorrow, in six months the country would be plunged into such racial strife, conflict and confusion as they have not yet seen."

Another serious problem confronted the Colonial Office in the fall of 1952 when news came from the East African colony of Kenya that a reign of terror had been instituted by the Mau Mau ("Hidden Ones"), a secret organization whose membership has been variously estimated between 100,000 and 300,000 of the Kikuyu tribe. They are pledged by blood oath to drive the white Britishers out of Kenya, particularly from the fertile grounds in the highlands which the whites "monopolize" (New York *Times,* October 21, 1952). When the natives began their raids in which at least forty-three persons were murdered, crops and homes burned, and cattle slaughtered, a state of emergency was announced, a battalion of Lancashire Fusiliers was flown in, and the cruiser *Kenya* was dispatched to the area.

Lyttelton himself flew to Kenya at the end of October to make a seven-day fact-finding tour of the hinterland. Later he told correspondents that it was "quite wrong to link the Mau Mau society directly with economic grievances and added that the Mau Mau was anti-European and anti-Christian "on quite a different model" (New York *Times,* November 3, 1952). He agreed that the Government measures to cut down the rebellion contained certain dangers of turning the whole tribe against its white rulers, but he said he saw no alternative to putting down the rebellion "as ruthlessly as is necessary, but no more ruthlessly than crimes against law and order." The next month the Government announced that a commission to study land and population problems would be dispatched to Kenya.

When Great Britain suspended the Constitution of British Guiana, Oliver Lyttelton, the Colonial Secretary, commented: "Great Britain is not willing to allow a Communist state to be organized within the British Commonwealth. Our friends can take that as a definite statement, and our enemies can attach to it all the importance that I think they should" (New York *Times,* October 11, 1953).

On January 30, 1920, Oliver Lyttelton married Lady Moira Godolphin Osborne, fourth daughter of the tenth Duke of Leeds; they became the parents of three sons (one of whom was killed in action in World War II) and one daughter. An impressive six feet four inches in height, the Colonial Secretary weighs 225 pounds. He has been described as "tall and tweedy, reddish of hair, face, and mustache, and a success in war, business, and Government" (*Newsweek*); and has been called one of England's best-dressed men. Lyttelton is a communicant of the Church of England; and a member of the Buck's, St. James's, Turf, Grillions, and Carlton clubs. He likes to read classical literature; in sports he enjoys golf, cricket, and shooting.

(Continued next page)

LYTTELTON, OLIVER—*Continued*

Time 28:21 Jl 14 '41 por; 40:28 Jl 27
'42 por; 44:20 Jl 3 '44 por; 58:33 N 5
'51 por
U S News 28:41 F 17 '50
International Who's Who, 1951
Kelly's Handbook to the Titled, Landed
and Official Classes, 1952
Ten Eventful Years (1947)
Who's Who, 1952
Who's Who in America, 1952-53
Who's Who in Commerce and Industry
(1951)
World Biography (1948)

MA CHI-CHUANG (mä chē-chōŏăng) Oct.
17, 1911- Commander-in-Chief of the Chinese
Nationalist Navy

Address: c/o Chinese Naval Headquarters,
Tsoyin, Taiwan, China

Commander-in-Chief and Vice-Admiral of the
Chinese Nationalist Navy since April 1952,
forty-two-year old Ma Chi-Chuang is considered one of Nationalist China's most prominent military leaders. His major efforts have
been exerted into improving and training the
Chinese Nationalist Navy with technical assistance from the Naval Section, Military Advisory Assistance Group, American military
mission, in Formosa.

While on a visit with a group of his military
aides to the United States in February 1953,
he asserted in an address before 300 Chinese
community leaders in New York City that the
Chinese Nationalist Army in Formosa numbered 600,000 soldiers, and 40,000 sailors, well-
equipped and trained, who were "continuously
preparing for the offensive against the mainland." While at the United States naval base

Wide World Photos
VICE-ADM. MA CHI-CHUANG

in Norfolk, Virginia, he stated on February
9th, 1953 that "his ships and men were ready to
take the offensive after several years of serving
primarily as a defense force." His recent American mission, including a week's inspection of
naval installations in California and a week in
Washington, D.C., was "to discuss plans for
further aid" from the United States for the
expansion of the Chinese Nationalist Navy so
that its ships, through blockade operations,
could harass the Communist-held mainland.

The Chinese Navy "now consists of approximately forty small vessels, the largest a 1,400-
ton overage destroyer, and a few old destroyer
escorts. It is very probable that a number of
overage U.S. vessels will be promised to Nationalist China under the Mutual Security program" (*U.S. News and World Report,* February
20, 1953).

It was reported in the New York *Times* on
August 19 that "a responsible Government
source confirmed the existence of a secret
understanding with the Chinese Nationalist
Government under which its troops based on
Formosa would not undertake intensified military operations against the Chinese Communists
without prior consultation with United States
military authorities who are still responsible
for the defense of the island."

Born October 17, 1911, and reared in Nan-
Kung in Hopeh, a province in China, Ma Chi-
Chuang pursued general studies in the Nan-
Kung High School. After a two-year course
in mechanical engineering, he received a diploma
from the Hopeh College of Technology in 1930.
On July 1st of that year, he was commissioned
an ensign in the Chinese Navy and entered the
Tsingtao Naval Academy from which he was
graduated in 1934.

He began his active naval service as assistant
navigator in 1934 on the light cruiser, CN *Hai
Chi.* His career was marked by rapid advancement from navigator, gunnery officer, executive officer, squadron commander to chief
of staff.

From 1935 to 1936 he was assistant gunnery
officer (LTJG) on CN *Chu Yu.* After a year
(1936 to 1937) as a navigator on CN *Cheng
Hai,* he became staff officer on the River Defense Command from 1937 to 1943. During the
years of World War II this involved serving
as a unit commander of the coast artillery force
defending the forts along the Yangtze River.

While attached as a staff officer to the Generalissimo's Administrative Office, Ma left for
the United States in 1944 for two years of
naval training at Miami, Florida, and later at
Guantánamo Bay, Cuba. On his return to China
in 1946, he was made executive officer and the
next year commanding officer of CN *Yung
Shun,* and later (1947 to 1948) of CN *Tai
Kang.*

At this time the Chinese Communists revolted against the Central Government. Because of Ma's outstanding performance in
combat actions, he was made First Squadron
Commander in 1948. His squadron succeeded
in many battles in defeating or checking the
Communist advance along the North China
coast.

In April 1949 he was promoted from the rank of commodore to that of rear admiral. At this time his squadron took part in the battle of the defense of Shanghai, inflicting great losses upon the Chinese Communists and successively covering the withdrawal of the garrison forces of Shanghai.

Rear Admiral Ma served between May 1949 and April 1950 as assistant chief of staff, Chinese Naval Headquarters and chief of its Bureau of Operations (Third Bureau). Then followed a brief period of service (April to July of 1950) as deputy commander-in-chief of the Chinese Nationalist Navy.

One of Admiral Ma's best-known military feats was his helping to direct the withdrawal of over 200,000 troops from the Chu Shan archipelago under the Communists' gun sights without the loss of a single life.

His career was climaxed on April 6, 1952 when he was appointed commander-in-chief to succeed vice-admiral Kwai Young-ching. This was followed on April 13th by his promotion to the rank of vice-admiral.

Admiral Ma has eleven military citations. He is also the recipient of the Yun Hui Medal (Class 6, 5, 4, 3), the Pao Ting Medal (Class 4), the Chung Yung Medal, and the Army, Navy, Air Force Medal (Class A, Grade 2). According to the *China Handbook*, he prefers to use G. John Ma, the anglicized version of his name.

References

N Y Times p2 F 9 '53
China Handbook, 1952-53

MA, G. JOHN *See* Ma Chi-chuang

MCCARTHY, KENNETH C(ECIL) 1902-
Physician; veterans' organization official
Address: b. 2228 Ashland Ave., Toledo 10, O.
h. 3637 River Rd., Toledo 14, Ohio

The Medical Veterans' Association, a national organization of physicians who served in World War II, was formed in Ohio in November 1952 and Dr. Kenneth C. McCarthy of Toledo was elected its first president. Its membership, which totalled over 12,000 by March 1953, has been concerned with policies related to the drafting of medical men for the armed forces.

Before the United States' entry into World War II, from 1940 to 1941, Dr. McCarthy served in England with the American Hospital in Britain, a volunteer group associated with the British War Relief Society. He was a member of the Medical Corps of the United States Army from 1942 to 1946, acting as Chief of the Section Anesthesia and Operating Room of Nichols General Hospital at Louisville, giving courses of instruction in anesthesia. He has written a number of books and articles on anesthesiology.

Born in Niagara Falls, Ontario, Canada in 1902, Kenneth Cecil McCarthy is the son of George Arnold and Jennie (Moffatt) McCarthy.

LaSalle & Koch Co.
DR. KENNETH C. MCCARTHY

His father was a civil engineer whose work kept him on the move with his family a large part of the time, both in the United States and Canada. Young McCarthy received his high school education at Malvern Collegiate Institute in Toronto, Canada, graduating in 1919.

He then entered the University of Toronto to study medicine and was awarded his Bachelor of Medicine degree by that institution in 1925. While a student in college he was elected president of his class and of the university dramatic society. He also served as editor of *Epistaxis,* an undergraduate humor magazine and became a member of Phi Rho Sigma.

After receiving his first university degree, McCarthy served for one year until 1926 as the house physician of the Toronto Western Hospital. He received his Doctor of Medicine degree from the University of Toronto in 1928. A three year period between 1926 and 1929 was spent in Maumee, Ohio in general medical practice. In 1929 the physician moved to Toledo, Ohio and became a United States citizen.

Upon moving to Toledo, he began to work in anesthesiology, the specialized branch of medicine which he has pursued since 1929. Hospitals with which he has been connected in the capacity of anesthetist include the Lucas County Hospital, the Toledo Dental Dispensary, the Toledo Hospital, Mercy Hospital, and the Toledo State Hospital. In addition to serving as anesthetist he also acted as the secretary-treasurer of the staff for the Flower Hospital. He was certified as an anesthetist by the American Board of Anesthesiology in 1939.

Dr. McCarthy became a member of the American Hospital in Britain, an organization affiliated with the British War Relief Society and composed of volunteer workers, and served in England with this group from 1940 to 1941. Returning to the United States when war was declared by this country, he joined the Medical

MCCARTHY, KENNETH C.—*Continued*

Corps of the United States Army and attained the rank of lieutenant colonel.

As a member of the Medical Corps he served as the Chief of the Section Anesthesia and Operating Room of Nichols General Hospital in Louisville, Kentucky until 1946. During this time the physician also instructed medical officers and nurses in anesthesia and acted as a consultant in anesthesia to the Fifth Service Command. He was awarded the Army Commendation Ribbon for his war services.

Prominent in the founding and organization of the Medical Veterans' Association, which came into existence in November 1952, McCarthy became the group's first president. The association was originated in Ohio by a number of that State's physicians who had seen war service. It is a nationwide organization whose membership is open to medical men who are veterans of World War II. By March 1953 there were 12,000 members and 4,000 other doctors had signed a petition circulated to staff members of hospitals throughout the country which approved the idea of the veterans' organization.

The Medical Veterans' Association strives for a voice in the drafting of legislation dealing with the recruiting of physicians for the armed forces. In line with that objective a meeting was held in Chicago with representatives of the Defense Department and the American Medical Association to study a new bill to replace the doctor and dentist draft law which expired on June 30, 1953. One result of the conferences was that the American Medical Association agreed to support the maintenance of the maximum draft age at fifty-one years for physicians and surgeons rather than lowering the ceiling to thirty-six years as had previously been suggested.

The A.M.A. further agreed to request uniform standards for deferment of essential physicians; the armed forces agreed to set low standards in physical examinations of doctors. The Medical Veterans' Association, according to Dr. David T. Curtis, secretary of the organization, suggested that any physician having served twenty months or more in the armed forces be exempted from further duty until all doctors who have not served have been called up. The standards of medicine would thus be maintained at a high level, he said, as both experienced physicians and young doctors who have recently been graduated from medical school would become members of the armed forces.

Dr. McCarthy belongs to a number of organizations concerned with his specialized field of medicine: he is a Fellow of the American College of Anesthesiologists and a member of the American Society of Anesthetists, of which he served as director from 1946 to 1952, a member of the International Anesthesia Research Society, a member of the Associated Anesthetists of the United States and Canada, of which he was the vice-president in 1939, and a member of the International College of Anesthetists. He also belongs to the American Medical Association. He has written forty or fifty articles for medical journals.

Dr. McCarthy and the former Shirley Caswell, a nurse, have been married since 1940. They have four children: Brian, Kathleen, Patricia and Terence. McCarthy's political affiliation is Republican and he is a Methodist. He lists his favorite sport as sailing. He has gray eyes and brown hair, weighs 175 pounds, and is five feet eleven inches tall.

Reference

Directory of Medical Specialists (1946)

MCCARTY, DAN(IEL THOMAS, JR.)

Jan. 18, 1912- Governor of Florida; citrus grower; cattleman

Address: b. Executive Office, Capitol Bldg., Tallahassee, Fla.; h. Executive Mansion, Tallahassee, Fla.

Bulletin: Governor Dan McCarty died on September 28, 1953.

From July 1953 issue:

Florida's thirty-first Governor, Dan McCarty, Democrat, took office on January 6, 1953, and in his inaugural address called for "honesty, efficiency, loyalty, and courtesy" as primary requisites in public service, and announced his intention of "immediate dismissal of any official found incompetent, lazy, or dishonest." His early experience in citrus production and cattle raising has given him an understanding of Florida's economic problems, and his legislative career has given him a knowledge of the State's requirements.

Television is credited as an important factor in his victory over Brailey Odham for the Democratic gubernatorial nomination. The majority of Florida voters chose "tall, handsome, forty-year-old Dan McCarty" as their new Governor.

He was three times elected to the Legislature representing St. Lucie County in 1937, 1939, and 1941. In the 1941 session, at the age of only twenty-nine, he was elected Speaker of the House, the youngest in Florida's history. In the May 1952 primary he built up the largest primary vote ever achieved in the State.

As a legislator, McCarty worked for the improvement of Florida's public school system and the establishment of farmers' markets in various production areas. He championed the abolition of slot machines, and assisted in the expansion of unemployment insurance and workmen's compensation.

Daniel Thomas McCarty, Jr., was born on January 18, 1912 in Fort Pierce, Florida. His father was a citrus grower, and so was his grandfather who staked his claim on high hammock land in St. Lucie County in the 1890's. Although McCarty's grandfather was an attorney by profession he became a citrus authority and was engaged by the Governor of the Bahamas in 1895 to train growers. In Florida, he developed the famous Indian River citrus fruit and pineapples. A grapefruit was named for him, the "McCarty grapefruit."

Dan was the oldest of the five McCarty children. When he was ten years old his father, Daniel Thomas McCarty, Sr., died. His mother, the former Frances Lardner Moore, carried on her husband's business and managed to give all of her children a college education, a sound religious training in the Episcopal faith, and developed their consciousness of community welfare.

Dan attended the public schools of Fort Pierce. He captained the football, baseball, and basketball teams, and edited the school yearbook at Fort Pierce High School from which he graduated in 1930. He was awarded a B.S. degree in agriculture and honors from the University of Florida in Gainesville in 1934.

On the campus, he showed leadership abilities by winning the presidency of his class during his junior year. He became a member of Alpha Zeta and Sigma Phi Epsilon fraternities, the Florida Blue Key, the Sabers, vice president of the student body, and cadet colonel of the ROTC Brigade.

On leaving college, Dan returned to Fort Pierce to engage in the citrus business. He became manager of the Somerset Plantations, a grove operation, and in 1937 organized the Indian River Citrus Associates, a cooperative packing and marketing venture which assured better returns to the grower. As secretary-treasurer and general manager, he remained with the organization from 1937 to 1945, and in 1949 sold out his interest entirely.

He was a director of the East Coast Supply and Lumber Company. Active in the Junior Chamber of Commerce in Florida, he served as its president in 1937 and 1938 and as chairman of its legislative committee.

McCarty acquired the Rainbow Groves, citrus groves in St. Lucie County, and the Somerset Groves in 1946. From them, he derives the major source of his income. This wide experience has made him recognize the importance of prosperity for the citrus grower as a primary requisite for a prosperous economy in Florida.

About the same time that he acquired the Rainbow Groves, he became active in the cattle business as president of the Circle M Ranch, an interest still very much alive today and one which has given him his sympathetic appreciation of the value of improved pastures and stock in this rapidly growing Florida industry.

Dan McCarty's marriage to Olie Brown took place on September 21, 1940. She was the daughter of Arthur B. Brown, former editor of the Fort Pierce *News,* secretary of the Florida Press Association, and the Fort Pierce Postmaster. Before her marriage to Governor McCarty Olie was employed as a secretary but now she devotes her time to their three children, Danny (Daniel Thomas McCarty III), who is ten, Mike (Michael Samuel), five years old, and Frances Lela, age four.

When Dan McCarty was called to active duty with the Seventy-fourth Field Artillery Brigade in 1941, Mrs. McCarty assisted in successfully managing his business. McCarty

Goleman Studio

DAN MCCARTY

served fifty-four months in World War II in Africa, Italy, France, Germany, and Austria. At the end of the war he was a full Colonel, decorated with the Legion of Merit, Bronze Star, Purple Heart, and Croix de Guerre for his distinguished service.

Two of Governor McCarty's major activities have been in the fields of public schools and public health. In his recent message to the Legislature, he proposed a $300 annual pay raise for school teachers from State funds and asked every county to bring its own contributions in line. Dan fought for a County Health Unit, helped erect the Fort Pierce Memorial Hospital and in 1949 and 1950 headed the State campaign for the American Cancer Society.

As Governor, he is continuing to promote such governmental reforms as a Constitution revision, which would give Florida a workable instrument uncluttered with eighty-odd amendments, a tightening of auditing and budgeting procedures, reorganization and consolidation of State agencies, thereby lowering government costs and improving efficiency, and substantial and far-reaching reforms in State employment.

In Governor McCarty's opening message to the legislature when it convened on April 6, 1953, he took a firm stand on several issues of vital importance to Floridians. Citing the three chief sources of income to the State as tourists, agriculture and industry, he declared the objective of his administration is to foster, promote, and develop these basic phases of Florida's economy.

Of equal importance to Florida natives and citizens of the United States is his partisanship of Everglades National Park, the vast area of southern Florida encompassing 1,258,361 acres of land and water, the only subtropical region in the United States which guarantees the protection of its wildlife. The Governor spoke firmly against the proposed exploitation of the

MCCARTY, DAN—*Continued*

Park by oil speculators, insuring its safety for the next four years.

He is determined to conserve the State's natural treasures as essential to agriculture, tourism and industry. Even the great salt water fishing resources have been neglected in the past. In appointing Charles William Bevis to his "little cabinet" to head the Conservation Department, the Governor selected a man he knew possessed "the ability and knowledge to make the conservation program genuinely effective."

Recognizing racing as big business in Florida, Governor McCarty has aimed his new tax at the legalized dog tracks. He told the new Legislature that the dog tracks "are not now paying a fair share of the cost of government." He recommended that the additional income from this tax source be used for the construction and operation of urgently needed State mental institutions.

As his primary project, McCarty has pledged to expand to four lanes the United States Highway (#1) which is located along Florida's east coast. This is a highly controversial issue and one destined to affect every tourist if the highway expansion is effected through the "toll turnpike" proposal.

His memberships include the Masons, the Elks, the Shrine, Mahi Temple, Order of Eastern Star, Independent Order of Odd Fellows, Rotary, Woodsmen of the World, Loyal Order of Moose, American Legion, and Veterans of Foreign Wars.

References

Miami Herald N 21 '52; Ag 8 '53
N Y Times p13 My 29 '52
America's Young Men, 1938-39

MCCORMACK, EMMET J. Sept. 2, 1880-
Shipping executive

Address: b. c/o Moore-McCormack Lines, Inc., 5 Broadway, New York 4; h. 9201 Shore Rd., Brooklyn, N.Y.

An executive with nearly fifty years of experience in the maritime industry, Emmet J. McCormack is chairman of the board of directors of Moore-McCormack Lines, Inc., and an honorary deputy commissioner of the Department of Commerce of New York City.

For his efforts to promote trade and travel between the United States and South America, McCormack in 1950 was made a Commander of the Order of the Southern Cross, the highest honor bestowed by the Brazilian Government to foreign persons. His interest in the advancement of the American Merchant Marine brought him the American Legion's Distinguished Service Medal in 1952.

The Moore-McCormack Lines, Inc. provides a major cargo-passenger service to South American and Scandinavian ports, and is the third largest steamship corporation in the United States in tonnage operated.

Emmet J. McCormack was born in Brooklyn, New York, on September 2, 1880, the son of

Joseph and Mary Teresa (O'Rourke) McCormack. His father was an engineer. Young Emmet received his education in local public schools, and in his early teens, began his shipping career as a marine clerk.

At the age of twenty-five he had saved from his small weekly earnings enough money to purchase an interest in two coastwise tugboats. He used these for salvage purposes, as well as other towboat tasks, and because of his initiative, frequently beat more experienced salvage men to a job.

He recalls that one of his first big assignments was ferrying a prize race horse owned by August Belmont from a pier to a ship in New York harbor. "After this job," he states, "I felt I was started as a shipowner . . . it seemed so much more important than towing coal barges and pushing garbage scows" (*Christian Science Monitor,* May 31, 1950).

In addition to his tugboat interests, McCormack gradually accumulated a small fleet of harbor craft and operated his own coal business, specializing in bunkering. He became president of the Commercial Coal Company in 1905, and five years later was vice-president of the Commercial Steamship Lines.

McCormack started the first Staten Island-Brooklyn-New York ferry service with an old side-wheeler in 1912, and he organized the Brooklyn and Richmond Ferry Company.

McCormack and Albert V. Moore formed the shipping firm, Moore and McCormack Company, Inc., in 1913, McCormack assuming the office of treasurer. The partners' first contract entailed hauling dynamite from Wilmington, Delaware to Brazil, and their freighter *Montara* was the first American flagship on the route to Rio de Janeiro.

When World War I curtailed the shipping services of Germany and England to South America, the young partners were provided an opportunity to develop leadership in South American ship traffic, and McCormack established American steamship service to the East Coast of South America in 1915. Following the entry of the United States into World War I, he served as a major.

The shipping executive became one of the operators for the United States Mail Steamship Company in 1919. That same year he established the first American steamship lines to Ireland. His firm included both passenger and freight business in its services. He founded an American steamship line to the Baltic nations in 1924 and the following year he established an Atlantic and Gulf coastwise service.

During the 1920's, McCormack converted several ships of World War I into cargo-passenger vessels for operation to Scandinavian ports. They were called "country clubs of the sea" by a Norwegian news reporter (*Christian Science Monitor,* May 31, 1950).

McCormack became president of the Maritime Association of the Port of New York in 1932. In September of that year he requested in a letter to the Secretary of War that twenty acres of Fort Schuyler grounds in New York be turned over to the State's Merchant Marine Academy as a site for a ground base. He also announced plans for development of a maritime training school for young men from all parts of the United States with graduate courses for Merchant Marine officers.

Returning from a business trip to Norway and Sweden in February 1933, McCormack affirmed that shipping men in foreign countries were awaiting the Roosevelt administration in the expectation that it would help revive international trade "through a new attitude toward foreign trade . . . rather than through settlement of the war debts problem" (New York *Times*, February 18, 1933). The following year he instituted the first American passenger service to the Windward and Leeward Islands of the West Indies and to the Virgin Islands.

McCormack was made chairman of the board of directors of the American Steamship Owners Association (now the American Merchant Marine Institute, Inc.) in 1937. Two years later, returning from South America, he announced that the American Republics Line, recently acquired by his company from the United States Maritime Commission, was being hailed as a new means of promoting friendship between the Americas. He added a sister service from the West Coast of the United States to South America in 1940, when his company took over the Pacific Republics Line from the Maritime Commission. This service, he stated, made "another important link in the United States Government's efforts to cement relationships between the American nations" (New York *Times*, July 28, 1940).

In 1941 McCormack helped promote an $80,000,000 replacement program for Moore-McCormack Lines, which became one of the few shipping concerns offering common and preferred stock for public sale.

The shipping executive was named chairman of the shipowners and operators division of the United Seaman's Service campaign for a $6,000,000 welfare fund in 1942 to found a world-wide system of clubs and rest homes for men of the Merchant Marine. He also served as chairman of the 1944 campaign of the maritime industry which raised $285,000 to modernize the Seamen's Church Institute of New York's building at 25 South Street, shore home for thousands of active merchant seamen of every nationality.

In postwar planning, McCormack specified at the American Merchant Marine Conference in October 1943 the need for tremendous reconversion after World War II and "setting ourselves on the right road to become a real postwar maritime power" (New York *Times*, October 16, 1943).

At the annual meeting of the Propeller Club of the United States in New York City in October 1944, he disagreed with the proposal of the Ship Disposal Bill (under consideration by the United States House of Representatives Committee on Merchant Marine and Fisheries) for the sale of vessels to American and foreign operators on the basis of prewar costs, less depreciation of 5 per cent a year and an allowance of 2½ per cent for extraordinary war use depreciation.

Karsh, Ottawa

EMMET J. MCCORMACK

"Ocean shipping now offers very little chance for the small-business man or the adventurous entrepreneur," McCormack said recently. "This is the age of ship specialization. The 'tramp ship' which roamed the seas picking up cargo is all but a thing of the past."

The shipping executive was named manager of a syndicate of ship operators and financiers in December 1946, bidding close to $9,000,000 for the American President Lines which had been taken over before World War II by the United States Maritime Commission. From 1943 to 1952 he served on the business executive advisory committee of the Department of Commerce of New York City.

He is chairman of the board of directors of the Kingsboro National Bank, director of the New York Dock Company, and one of the board of visitors of the New York State Merchant Marine Academy. His organization memberships include the Society of Naval Architects and Marine Engineers, the Marine Society of the City of New York, and the Boston Marine Society. Among his clubs are the Manhattan, the Lawyers, the Whitehall, Foreign Commerce, the Crescent Athletic, and St. Georges Golf and Country.

McCormack married Elizabeth G. O'Donnell, an educational administrator, on June 26, 1935. He is a member of the Democratic party and his religious affiliation is Roman Catholic. The shipping executive is five feet eight inches tall, weighs 165 pounds, and has blue eyes and grey hair. His favorite recreation is golf.

References

Christian Sci Mon p3 My 31 '50
Fortune 47:60 Mr '53
N Y Times p59 My 17 '50
Who's Who in America, 1952-53
Who's Who in Commerce and Industry, (1947)

MCCORMICK, EDWARD J(AMES) Sept. 25, 1891- Surgeon; medical association officer

Address: b. c/o American Medical Association, 535 N. Dearborn St., Chicago 10, Ill.; 510-14 Ohio Bldg., Toledo 4, Ohio; h. 3715 Sulphur Springs Rd., Ottawa Hills, Toledo, Ohio

At the largest gathering of physicians in the history of the medical profession, in New York City on June 2, 1953, Dr. Edward J. McCormick was inaugurated president of the American

Garrison Studio

DR. EDWARD J. MCCORMICK

Medical Association for the year 1953-54. An Ohio surgeon, Dr. McCormick has maintained a private practice in Toledo since the end of World War I and for many years has been associated with St. Vincent's Hospital and Maumee Valley Hospital in that city.

A prominent figure in a large number of professional, civic, and fraternal organizations, he has held among other positions of national importance that of Grand Exalted Ruler of the Elks (1938-39).

A native of Michigan, as were his parents, Edward James McCormick was one of three children (two boys and one girl) of Michael James McCormick, whose forebears had come from County Cork, Ireland, and of Mary Ellen (Dailey) McCormick, who was of English descent. He was born in Alger in the eastern part of the State on September 25, 1891. The elder McCormick, who operated a general store in Alger, later moved his family to Bradner, Ohio, where he had moderate success in drilling for oil on leased land. Settling afterward in Toledo, Ohio, he managed the Grand Hotel and became interested in automobile association work. His son was educated in Toledo schools until 1903 when he studied for a year at Assumption College in Sandwich, Ontario, Canada.

At St. John's Academy in Toledo, which Edward McCormick attended from 1904 to 1908, his main extrascholastic interests were football, baseball, and basketball. He became active in dramatics as well while taking a premedical course at St. John's University, Toledo. For one summer he worked as a piano salesman, an experience about which he has said, "I sold none, but had a lot of fun."

After having been granted his B.A. degree from St. John's University in 1911 and his M.A. degree in 1913, he entered St. Louis University in Missouri, and received his M.D. degree in 1915. He later undertook graduate study in Chicago, New York City, and Europe.

When he had completed his year's internship (1915-16) at St. Vincent's Hospital in Toledo, Dr. McCormick continued work there as house surgeon. During 1916-17 he was also professor of biology at St. John's University. Having enlisted in early 1917 in the United States Army Medical Corps Reserve, the young physician in August, soon after he had entered private practice, was sent overseas on assignment to the British Expeditionary Force in France.

In the rank of major, to which he had been advanced from lieutenant in 1917, he served throughout World War I with the 47th North Midland British Division, the force that is credited with breaking the Hindenburg line. He was awarded the British Military Cross in 1918. Before his discharge in 1919, Dr. McCormick was stationed for several months at the Walter Reed Hospital in Washington, D.C. From 1923 to 1930 he held the rank of lieutenant commander in the United States Naval Reserve.

Resuming private practice in Toledo in 1919, he was associated for a year with Mercy Hospital as attending surgeon. He rejoined the staff of St. Vincent's Hospital in 1920 as surgeon, served for ten years (1939-49) as chief of staff, and since 1947 has been president of that hospital's advisory board. Meanwhile, he was also engaged as surgeon to Maumee Valley Hospital, beginning in 1924, and from 1934 to 1950 was director of surgery and member of the executive committee and board of trustees. He has been visiting surgeon to Toledo Hospital (1933), surgeon to St. Anthony's Orphanage, and since 1949 surgeon for the Wheeling & Lake Erie Railroad (now Nickel Plate Railway Company).

Dr. McCormick's concentrated participation in the activities of the American Medical Association dates from 1943, when he became a member of that organization's house of delegates and the council of medical service, of which he was chairman in 1945 and 1946. Among other positions that he held were trustee (1946-51), chairman of the council on scientific exhibit (1947-50), and member of the co-ordinating committee (1949-51). At the 101st annual convention of the 140,000-member A.M.A., held in June 1952 in Chicago, Dr. McCormick was chosen president-elect of the association, to take office the following year upon expiration of the twelve-month tenure of Dr. Louis H. Bauer.

In his inaugural address in June 1953 in New York City, during the five-day meeting of the largest medical convention ever held, (attended by some 14,000 members) Dr. McCormick called on county medical societies to expel from their ranks the "small minority" of physicians "who are unethical, dishonest, and unfair." "Let us do this job in an orderly fashion," the new A.M.A. president urged, "making speedy, effective use of the disciplinary machinery already available in our medical societies. By eliminating the wrongdoers in this way we will restore the public faith in the 95 per cent of ethical practitioners whose reputations have been tarnished by irresponsible, generalized accusations" (New York *Times,* June 3, 1953).

He also reviewed progress made in medical science during 1952 and spoke briefly on the issue of socialized medicine, noting that the A.M.A. has encouraged voluntary prepaid health insurance programs.

Expressing his views on earlier occasions toward socialized medicine, Dr. McCormick is quoted as stating, "It is unfortunate that much of [A.M.A.'s] effort must be devoted to a fight against socialism. In this battle we are not especially concerned with the doctor's individual welfare, but we are concerned with the preservation of American tradition and the American way of life. I am proud that we have led the battle to preserve American Democracy."

He has also been outspoken in deploring the use of Veterans Administration personnel and facilities in treatment of illness not incurred in military service.

On the invitation of General Douglas MacArthur, Dr. McCormick was a member of the 1949 medical mission which made a survey of Japan's health needs. The following year he attended the third Assembly of the United Nations World Health Organization in Geneva, Switzerland, as a United States delegate. The Toledo surgeon's report on the assembly appears in the *Journal of the American Medical Association,* October 7, 1950.

Medical papers by Dr. McCormick on cancer and intestinal obstruction have also been published in the A.M.A. *Journal* and in other medical periodicals. He has also written less specialized articles on medical problems, including "American Democracy and American Medicine" (*Ohio State Medical Journal,* November 1946); "Pertinent Facts on Medical Economics" (*Rocky Mountain Medical Journal,* June 1947); "Democracy, Medical Progress and the American Medical Association" (*Rhode Island Medical Journal,* July 1951).

Among the many professional organizations with which Dr. McCormick has been affiliated are the American College of Surgeons (fellow), American Association for the Advancement of Science, Ohio State Medical Association (president 1942), Tri-State Medical Association, Japan Medical Society (honorary member), Medical Alumni Association of St. Louis

University (president, 1948-50), World Medical Association, and American Association of Railway Surgeons. In 1944 he was senior surgeon of the United States Public Hospital Reserve Unit and is currently senior surgeon of the United States Public Health Service Reserve.

A leader in Toledo civic affairs, Dr. McCormick, as member of the board of directors (1935) and president (1936) of the Toledo City Manager League, was in a large part responsible for securing a city manager form of government. During his term of office as president (1926) and trustee (1926-31) of the Academy of Medicine of Toledo and Lucas County, he had a prominent role in taking politics out of local public medical care centers.

He was also a member of Lucas County Charter Commission (1934-35), the budget committee of the Toledo Community Chest (1941), Toledo Chamber of Commerce (trustee, 1942-43; chairman of the committee on public health, 1947-48), president of the Toledo Board of Health (1940-43), and trustee of the Toledo Boys Club (since 1939). The surgeon, who believes that "every citizen must sacrifice some of his recreations and give some of his money to aid in the teaching of American fundamentals," has filled a number of executive positions in the Toledo Area Council of the Boy Scouts of America.

Dr. McCormick won national distinction in 1938 with his election to the rank of Grand Exalted Ruler of the Benevolent and Protective Order of the Elks, an organization in which he was later secretary of the war commission (1940-48) and member of the board of trustees of the national foundation (1948). He also became honorary president of the Elks' cerebral palsy treatment center in Canton, Ohio.

He served as president of the Toledo Lions Club in 1937, was named a Key Member in 1949, and was given his twenty-year Old Monarch certificate in 1951. McCormick's Greek-letter societies are Phi Beta Phi, Delta Phi Lamda, and Alpha Omega Alpha, and he belongs to the American Legion (past commander of Frank Ferneau Post), Forty and Eight, Military Order of the World Wars, and the Inverness Country Club and the Toledo Club. He holds an honorary LL.D. degree from Xavier University, conferred in June 1953. His political affiliation is with the Democratic party.

Married on June 5, 1920, to the former Josephine C. Beck, then a school teacher, McCormick is the father of six children: Edward J., Jr. (an attorney), Richard A. (a priest), Carol Jeanne, Kathleen Ann, Mary Josephine, and Michael J., 2d (a premedical student). The A.M.A. president, a Catholic and a fourth degree Knight of Columbus, is a friend of Samuel Cardinal Stritch, who once said of him, "I found him to be always genial, personable, and gifted with fine qualities of leadership."

The black-haired surgeon stands five feet seven and a half inches tall, with a weight of 160 pounds. He enjoys watching sports pro-

MCCORMICK, EDWARD J.—*Continued*

grams on television and reading detective stories; he is also said to be a "fancier of ties." A characteristic statement of Dr. McCormick's attitude toward his profession is quoted in *Today's Health* (June 1953), "Although medical science has produced many drugs of near-miracle effectiveness in the last decade, I find that among the most potent of all medicines is still the human touch."

References

J Am Med Assn 149:764-5 Je 21 '52 por
Lion 35:26 Je '53 por
N Y World-Telegram p6 Je 2 '53 por
Today's Health 31:28+ Je '53 por
Directory of Medical Specialists (1953)
Who's Important in Medicine (1952)
Who's Who in America, 1952-53
World Biography (1948)

MCCRARY, JINX (FALKENBURG) *See* McCrary, T. and J. (F.)

MCCRARY, JOHN REAGAN, JR. *See* McCrary, T. and J. (F.)

MCCRARY, MRS. JOHN REAGAN, JR. *See* McCrary, T. and J. (F.)

MCCRARY, TEX Oct. 13, 1910- Radio and television commentator; producer

MCCRARY, JINX (FALKENBURG) Jan. 21, 1919- Radio and television commentator; producer

Address: b. National Broadcasting Company, 30 Rockefeller Pl., New York 20; h. 1100 Northern Blvd., Manhasset, N.Y.

Known to a wide audience on radio and television, Jinx Falkenburg and John Reagan (Tex) McCrary, husband-and-wife team, made their debut in 1946 in *Hi Jinx,* an early morning breakfast show in which they achieved notable success. A year later a television program *At Home* launched the couple in the new visual medium. Before her marriage to McCrary Miss Falkenburg was a photographer's model, magazine cover girl, motion picture actress, and tennis and swimming champion. Previous to his radio and television career, McCrary had been a newspaper reporter, columnist and chief editorial writer for the New York *Daily Mirror.* Jointly, Miss Falkenburg and McCrary wrote a column *New York Close-up,* published for two years in the New York *Herald-Tribune* and widely syndicated.

Currently, Jinx and McCrary have an hour-long radio breakfast program, known as *The Tex and Jinx Show,* broadcast five week-day mornings over NBC. Jinx also conducts her own TV program called *Jinx McCrary* thirty-five minutes each day in the afternoon.

Eugenia Lincoln Falkenburg was born in Barcelona, Spain, January 21, 1919, the daughter of a mining engineer, Eugene Falkenburg, and Marguerite (Crooks) Falkenburg. Her father defied superstition and nick-named his daughter Jinx, saying it would be a fortunate name.

Soon after Jinx was born, the Falkenburgs moved to Chile, and then, in haste, during one of Chile's revolutions, returned to the United States, their native country.

In New York City, Jinx Falkenburg soon demonstrated that her nick-name was no handicap. At the age of eighteen months, taught by her athletically-inclined parents, she swam a backstroke in a Y.W.C.A. swimming pool.

On a return sojourn in South America, with alternate stays in Chile and Brazil, the Falkenburg family, increased by two boys, Tom and Bob, further distinguished themselves in athletics. Mrs. Falkenburg won the women's tennis championship in Brazil, and Jinx at thirteen became junior swimming champion of Chile. In addition, young Miss Falkenburg and her two brothers were junior tennis champions.

When Jinx was fourteen, another Chilean revolution caused the family to leave South America without their possessions.

Seeking a permanent home in the United States, the family went to Los Angeles, where her father found employment as an engineer for the Metropolitan Water District. Jinx attended Hollywood High School, and was graduated in 1935.

Her movie career began when she was sixteen. While playing tennis one day, she attracted the attention of a talent scout from Warner Bros., and having learned to speak Spanish well, was hired to play in Spanish language pictures for Warner's and, subsequently, for Samuel Goldwyn Productions and Metro-Goldwyn-Mayer.

While at MGM she met Paul Hesse, a photographer for *American Magazine,* who found Miss Falkenburg a highly photogenic subject. Her picture on the cover of August 1937 *American Magazine* resulted in many offers, and pictures of Jinx appeared on the covers of more than sixty magazines.

An accident in Honolulu resulted in her meeting Al Jolson. She was convalescing in a Los Angeles hospital in a room near the one in which Jolson was recovering from a serious illness. Jolson became curious about the many people who passed his door to visit Miss Falkenburg, was introduced to her, and offered her a part in his musical comedy *Hold On To Your Hats.*

Miss Falkenburg's appearance in this show, which opened in 1940 at the Shubert Theater in New York City, led to the formation of a Jinx Falkenburg Fan Club which grew until the name Jinx Falkenburg began to have strong news value. She met Tex McCrary when he was sent by the *Daily Mirror* to interview her.

In 1941 Jinx Falkenburg was the first Miss Rheingold. When *Hold On To Your Hats* closed, she was the highest paid model in the United States and was called the "No. One Magazine Cover Glamour Girl." Paul Hesse said of her, "She is the most charming, the most vital personality I have ever had the pleasure to photograph."

A film contract with Columbia Pictures recalled her to Hollywood, and by 1943 she had appeared in Columbia's *Sing For Your Supper, Sweetheart of the Fleet, Lucky Legs, Laugh Your Blues Away, She Has What It Takes, Two Senoritas from Chicago* and *Cover Girl.*

During World War II Miss Falkenburg joined the United Service Organization and travelled approximately 86,000 miles entertaining troops. On these tours Miss Falkenburg's path three times crossed that of Tex McCrary, who was serving in the Army Air Force. The couple became engaged in 1942, and on June 10, 1945 they were married in New York City while McCrary was enroute from the Mediterranean area to the Far East, and Jinx was on her way from Hollywood to Italy with a USO troupe.

In December 1945 Miss Falkenburg received the Asiatic Pacific Campaign Service Ribbon for meritorious service in the entertainment of American Armed Forces in the China-Burma India theater of war.

Tex McCrary was born John Reagan McCrary on October 13, 1910 in Calvert, Texas, the son of John Reagan and Margaret (Duggins Adoue) McCrary. His grandfather was the late John H. Reagan, United States Senator and first chairman of the Texas State Railway Commission.

In his youth McCrary, whose father owned a cotton plantation, lived an outdoor life; one of his pastimes was riding and taming horses. When he reached high school age he went North to attend Phillips Exeter Academy, from which he was graduated in 1928. At that time, McCrary's ambition was to be an architect, and he entered Yale University, receiving a degree in architecture in 1932.

On his return to Texas, he met a newspaper editor who influenced him to change from architecture to journalism. He went to New York and obtained his first newspaper job on the New York *World-Telegram* as a copy boy, advancing soon afterward to cub reporter.

Moving to the New York *Mirror,* he became a full-fledged reporter, working under the guidance of the editor, Arthur Brisbane. In 1936 McCrary became editor of the *Literary Digest,* and when that magazine ceased publication, he returned to the *Mirror* as Brisbane's assistant. After the death of Brisbane, McCrary became chief editorial writer.

McCrary married Arthur Brisbane's daughter, Sara, in 1935. They were divorced in 1939. He has a son, Michael Brisbane, by this marriage.

In 1942 McCrary joined the Army Air Force. As photographer and chief public relations officer in the Mediterranean area, one of his assignments was that of arousing opinion to back the Air Force campaign for more pinpoint bombings. To get photographs of the bombings, McCrary flew more than fifty missions and made sixteen parachute jumps, including three in battle, one with American troops in the invasion of southern France, and two with British forces in Greece and Italy.

Discharged at the end of the war as a lieutenant colonel McCrary returned to civilian

TEX AND JINX MCCRARY

life as editor of the *American Mercury* magazine.

In April 1946 McCrary and his wife, Jinx, began their daily early morning radio broadcasts over WEAF. The program, *Hi Jinx,* not only became popular but gained distinction by including serious discussions of controversial problems. Lacking a journalistic background, Jinx started as her husband's pupil and became "leg man" to learn reporting and interviewing. Seymour Peck in *PM* reported, "*Hi Jinx* operates on a slightly higher level than its rivals." In her New York *World-Telegram* column Harriet Van Horne observed, "Tex refuses to sidestep a controversial issue, and he has put together some admirable programs on the atom bomb, venereal disease and the United Nations."

It was McCrary's conviction that serious discussions had their place on *Hi Jinx.* "My newspaper experience," he said, "convinced me that the radio 'execs' were all wrong when they said that people, particularly women, didn't want serious stuff in the morning. I believed that minds are fresh, open to the consideration of serious subjects in the morning."

In one broadcast McCrary took issue with the Hearst newspapers, particularly a *Journal-American* editorial urging Government censorship of motion pictures. McCrary stated that Government censorship was not the answer, but, rather, "courageous critics and enlightened customers."

Another feature of *Hi Jinx* was the appearance of guests on the program, interviewed by Mr. and Mrs. McCrary. Sometimes these appearances were highly provocative. When a group of rival Congressional candidates was invited on *Hi Jinx* to debate face-to-face, this move was called by *Variety* "a milestone in radio."

Hi Jinx, introduced on a sustaining basis (without sponsorship), after eight months ac-

MCCRARY, TEX and JINX—*Continued*

quired sponsors, and within a year of its debut was on a substantial financial basis.

Tex and Jinx made their debut before the television cameras in March 1947 on a Sunday night program *At Home* over NBC-TV. The program integrated the use of film and 'live' production, the 'live' portion showing Jinx and McCrary in a domestic scene interviewing their guests.

Following their initiation into night-time television, the couple started their first commercial daytime television studio program, the Swift *Home Service Club,* a combination of guest interviews and household hint demonstrations.

For both television programs, Tex and Jinx were their own producers and incorporated their own company under the name of Tex and Jinx Productions. Their wish to pioneer in television was expressed by McCrary. "You're always on the edge of discovering the right thing. We have enough capital in reserve now, so that we can lose everything except *Hi Jinx* and get along six months. . . .So we can gamble . . . gamble on our own money . . . our own ideas."

The husband-and-wife team persuaded the National Broadcasting Company, long opposed to the policy of transcribed programs for radio, to transcribe their night-time television program entirely on film for the summer.

A new night-time radio program, *Meet Tex and Jinx,* was added in 1947 as a summer replacement for *Duffy's Tavern.* Commenting on the debut in which Billy Rose and Mary Martin were included as guests, Harriet Van Horne wrote, " *Meet Tex and Jinx* stands up as one of the best summer shows we've had in some time." Again in the summer of 1948 Jinx and McCrary were summer replacements for *Duffy's Tavern,* and comparing them to other husband-and-wife teams, Miss Van Horne commented in her column, "Considering what their colleagues are up to, Tex McCrary and Jinx Falkenburg are a gust of clean mountain air. They're natural, unaffected, and intelligent."

In March 1949 Tex and Jinx introduced a television program titled *Preview,* presented over CBS-TV. The program, which McCrary called a "living television magazine," set its two stars in the roles of magazine editors in the process of preparing stories that covered a week's news in divergent fields that included the theatre, books, motion pictures, sports, and fashions. The general critical opinion of the first viewing was that *Preview* was too ambitious, its staging that demanded split-second cuts and film inserts "too complicated." Of following *Preview* shows John Crosby in the *Herald Tribune* observed, "It's been improving steadily, and the potentialities are unlimited." However, *Preview* did not endure; its last show was on September 5, 1949.

Under the title, "New York Close-Up," Tex and Jinx began a daily column in the New York *Herald Tribune* in September 1949, which featured New York personalities, the lesser known as well as celebrities. In addition, the couple wrote a column in *Variety* called

"Radio Activity" which dealt primarily with the radio and television industry.

They also introduced a *New York Close-Up* program on television, broadcast each weekday evening over NBC-TV. It acquired the sponsorship of the Curtis Publishing Company, reported to be the first time a publishing company entered the television field with a regularly-scheduled program. In April 1949 the Department of the Air Force bestowed on McCrary the exceptional civilian award, with the accompanying citation that McCrary had "inspired young men of the highest caliber to find careers in the Air Force."

Early in 1952, McCrary made it clear that he was staunchly supporting Dwight D. Eisenhower as Republican candidate for President. One of his first moves in launching the Eisenhower-for-President campaign was taking the chairmanship of a rally held in Madison Square Garden, New York City, in February 1952 attended by a reported 18,000 persons. Jinx participated by introducing some of the guest entertainers, who included Ethel Merman and Irving Berlin, and by batting autographed tennis balls around the arena.

The telecast of the rally and its tremendous fan-fare was reviewed with a tone of derision by several New York critics, who thought that the meeting failed to combine television showmanship in good proportion with politics. In February 1952 NBC granted Tex McCrary a leave of absence to devote his full time to campaigning for Eisenhower, while Jinx continued their radio and television programs alone.

The *Daily Mirror* sent McCrary in 1953 on a tour of Korea, Formosa, and other areas in the Far East. Before leaving, McCrary, with his wife, visited President Eisenhower "for guidance." Eisenhower's observation that Korea is a lieutenant's war—a war of patrol action—served as the theme of McCrary's first report, comprising interviews with lieutenants in battle. His tape-recorded conversations with officers and GI's were used on their morning radio programs, and relatives of these men were notified to listen in.

McCrary and Jinx are both authors of a book. *First of the Many,* written by McCrary during his service in the Air Force, was published in 1944 and recounts the exploits of the men and officers of the Eighth Air Force, based in England.

Of *Jinx,* an autobiography by Miss Falkenburg (published in 1951), Bernard Baruch wrote in the foreword: "It has given me two evenings of charming, interesting and wholesome reading."

Miss Falkenburg is 5 feet 7 inches in height and weighs 130 pounds. McCrary is 6 feet tall, and weighs 165 pounds. Each has brown hair. McCrary's eyes are brown, his wife's hazel.

Their morning breakfast shows are broadcast from the McCrary 10-room Colonial style home in Manhasset, Long Island, with recorded interviews of their guests. The birth of a son, John Reagan McCrary III, (Paddy) scarcely altered Jinx's busy schedule in 1946. She conducted the daily radio show with her husband, appeared at benefits and dinners, played tennis, and missed only one broadcast—the day Paddy

was born. The following program she broadcast from her hospital bed. Paddy has a younger brother, Kevin Jock, born in 1948, and Mr.
and Mrs. McCrary manage to be with their two
children as much as possible. "Our family life
is very close," said Jinx. "We're going to keep
it that way."

References

Collier's 106:11+ O 12 '40
Daily Mirror Mag D 29 '46
Life 10:35+ Ja 27 '41 por
Look 12:56 S 12 '48
N Y Post Mag p3 My 11 '46
Newsweek 30:52+ Ag 25 '47
International Motion Picture Almanac,
1946-47
International Motion Picture and Tele-
vision Almanac, 1951-52
Who's Who in America, 1952-53

MCDONALD, DAVID J(OHN) Nov. 22,
1902- Labor leader

Address: b. 1500 Commonwealth Bldg., Pittsburgh 22, Pa.; h. 820 Ridgeview Dr., Pittsburgh
28, Pa.

The second largest union in the Congress of
Industrial Organizations is the United Steel-
Workers of America, headed by David J. Mc-
Donald, who was elected on March 11, 1953 to
succeed the late Philip Murray as its president.
As Murray's "second-in-command," he had
helped to organize the steel industry's employees
into the United Steel Workers, with a membership of more than one million. He also participated in the formation of the International
Confederation of Trade Unions, and urged
members of the CIO to "help the people of
Europe to get the things that we have here
through bonafide trade unionism, so that communism will not have a chance."

In August, 1953, McDonald was named by
President Eisenhower to the seventeen-man
Commission on Foreign Economic Policy which
will review the United States' foreign economic
policies and will submit recommendations to
Congress. He is the first Congress of Industrial Organizations official to be appointed to
an important post in the Eisenhower Administration.

Said to be a "conservative" labor leader,
McDonald takes "the traditional point of view
of regarding economic issues as the major concern of trade unions" (*Fortune*, June 1949). He
rose to union prominence through thirty years'
work in the CIO, beginning as secretary to
Murray in 1923.

The son of Welsh-born David McDonald
and the former Mary Agnes Kelly, David John
McDonald was born in Pittsburgh on November
22, 1902, with, as he once phrased it, "a union
spoon in my mouth." On that day the senior
McDonald, secretary of a local of the Amalga-
mated Association of Iron, Steel and Tin
Workers (since supplanted by the United
Steelworkers), was out on strike. Also a
steelworker and ardent unionist was the boy's
maternal grandfather, Patrick Kelly, who immi-

DAVID J. MCDONALD

grated from Ireland during the Civil War, and
became secretary of a Sons of Vulcan Lodge
in Sharon, Pennsylvania. Young David was
thus reared in a union atmosphere; he remembers that his father once "raised Cain because
I had a date with the daughter of a man who
had scabbed twenty years before" (*Business
Week*, January 10, 1953).

At Holy Cross High School in Pittsburgh
young McDonald began a commercial course,
but left at 15 to work as a stock boy for the
Jones and Laughlin Steel Company. He was
later a steelworker in the polishing mill, and
from 1918 to 1923 a machinist's helper. Meanwhile, he continued his education by attending
night classes at Duquesne University, and later
the drama school of the Carnegie Institute of
Technology, hoping eventually to enter the
theatre.

By the time he had earned his certificate of
graduation from the Carnegie Drama department in 1932, he had written several one-act
plays, and rejected an offer to go to Hollywood
as an assistant director. Other events had
turned his interests from the theatre to labor
union work. In 1923 he had taken a job as
clerk in the sales office of the Wheeling Steel
Products Company at a salary of $80 a month.
In September of the same year he learned that
Philip Murray, then vice-president of the United
Mine Workers of America, was looking for a
private secretary, and applied for the post.
Not quite twenty-one years old, he was hired
for the job at a salary of $225 a month.

In the thirteen years that followed (1923-
1936) McDonald, according to *Time* (January
5, 1953), learned "the union ropes in the tough

MCDONALD, DAVID J.—*Continued*
Appalachian coal district." As Murray's aide, he also worked closely with John L. Lewis, president of the United Mine Workers, and other leaders who were building the miners' union. McDonald participated in important conferences in connection with nation-wide coal strikes, and in 1933 served as assistant secretary of several Appalachian coal conferences. When Murray became a member of the Board of the National Recovery Adminstration, McDonald served as his assistant. He was secretary to the Bituminous Coal Industry Wage Differential Commission from 1934 to 1936.

Shortly after the formation of the CIO, Lewis named Murray chairman of the Steel Workers Organization Committee (SWOC), created to organize the steel industry of the United States and Canada. Murray, in turn, on June 11, 1936, named McDonald secretary-treasurer of the committee. McDonald participated in all the steel organizing drives that followed. When Murray suffered a heart attack in 1941, McDonald took over his duties as head of SWOC, completed the organization of Little Steel, and headed contract negotiations with the Bethlehem, Republic, Youngstown and Inland managements. These campaigns culminated in the formation of the United Steelworkers of America, with Murray as president. McDonald was elected International secretary-treasurer of the new union in 1942, and was thereafter re-elected regularly without opposition.

His new post gave McDonald responsibilities in administration, organizing and collective bargaining and negotiations with steel management. In addition, *Fortune* reported (June 1949), McDonald's job was "to keep track of detail, detail of men and detail of money." He kept "careful check on union funds," publishing "double-bonded, thoroughly audited union financial statements every six months." He also walked on picket lines, and organized conventions. *Business Week* commented that the 1944 Cleveland convention of the United Steelworkers of America "ran so well" because of McDonald's work behind the scenes.

During these years as secretary-treasurer of the United Steelworkers, McDonald "drew up the blueprint for an organizing drive in the South, sat on committees dealing with social security, traveled abroad as a union representative, plugged the Good Neighbor line in Latin America, sat in the United Nation's International Labor Organization" (*Time*, January 5, 1953).

A member of the International and Latin American Affairs Committee of the CIO, McDonald attended many conferences in Europe and South America. As one of the three-man labor delegation under the sponsorship of the Office of Coordinator of Inter-American Affairs in August 1943, he studied labor conditions in Chile, Colombia, Panama, Cuba and Mexico, and later urged "democratic infiltration" of Latin America to offset Nazi, fascist and communist propaganda. McDonald also participated in the 1945 and 1948 meetings of the World Federation of Trade Unions. As Murray's

representative he served in many Government agencies during World War II, and after the war with national health and welfare organizations.

Business Week reported on January 22, 1949 that McDonald was among the CIO "diplomats" who led the move to break up the World Federation of Trade Unions on the grounds that it was impossible to work with the communist unions in the group. The CIO, the British Trade Union Congress, and the Dutch Federation of Labor withdrew after a controversy over the Marshall Plan, which the communist unions had labeled "imperialistic." In December of the same year McDonald served as secretary of the CIO delegation to the London conference which resulted in the formation of the International Confederation of Trade Unions in 1949. On his return to the United States, he spoke at a CIO meeting, and urged that American unions teach the labor organizations of France and Italy the American idea of trade unionism and thus prevent communism.

McDonald became, on May 29, 1951, special assistant to Eric Johnston, director of the Economic Stabilization Administration. The steel union official represented the United Labor Policy Committee, composed of most of the big unions, which had requested that union men be placed in key posts in the defense agencies. Serving the Government without compensation, McDonald divided his time between his two positions.

Early in 1952, the various steel union negotiations with management for a new contract were stalemated and a strike was scheduled for April 8. To avert the walkout of 600,000 steelworkers, President Harry S. Truman seized the steel industry. At the sixth convention of the United Steelworkers of America on May 13, 1952 McDonald urged greater political activity, particularly in connection with the fall elections, as a way to keep the union strong. Although he was a delegate to the Democratic National Convention in July 1952 from the Thirty-first Congressional District in Pennsylvania, McDonald was unable to attend on the opening day because of a union meeting in connection with the steel strike.

After Philip Murray's death November 9, 1952, the executive board of the United Steelworkers of America designated McDonald as acting president of the union (November 15, 1952) until elections could be held in February. Nominated without opposition, McDonald was elected to succeed Murray, with whom he had been closely associated for thirty years. On March 11, 1953 McDonald was installed for a four year term as the second president of the 1,127,000 member union at a reported salary of $40,000 a year, as compared with the $25,000 he had received as secretary-treasurer. McDonald favors a guaranteed annual wage for steelworkers, a demand which is expected to be made in future contract negotiations. He believes in industry councils composed of representatives of government, labor and management with advisory and consultive functions. They should not have any actual control over business or labor organizations.

MCDONALD, DAVID J.—*Continued*

It is predicted that McDonald, in his new post, will follow the "conservative but militant trade unionism of his able predecessor" (*Time,* January 5, 1953). *Business Week* also classified him a conservative, "much in the way that Murray was a conservative in labor," and pointed out that he was a Democrat with "no strain of socialism," who believes British labor people made a mistake when they nationalized the steel industry, because workers fared better in bargaining with private management (January 10, 1953).

McDonald is secretary-treasurer of the CIO Political Action Committee, secretary of its Southern Organizing Committee, and serves on its Executive Board and its International and Latin American Affairs Committee. He is also a member of the General Council of the International Confederation of Free Trade Unions, and the General Council of the Western Hemisphere division of the same group. His activities in charitable and civic organizations include work with the National Conference of Christians and Jews, the National Community Fund, the American Cancer Society, the American Heart Association, the American Arbitration Association, the American Red Cross, and the Community Chest.

"Democratic capitalism, combined with industrial democracy, is unquestionably the best way of life for mankind," he declared when he was sworn in as union president. It is the key to the type of unionism, based on freedom of the individual, which is his fundamental philosophy.

A six-footer, frequently described as "handsome" McDonald weighs 195 pounds, has blue eyes and gray hair. His wife is the former Rosemary McHugh, who was a private secretary before her marriage; he has a son, David, Jr., by a former marriage. He lists his political affiliation as Democratic, his church as the Roman Catholic. His hobbies are golf, baseball, boxing and photography; he pilots his own plane. He is co-author of a book, *Coal and Unionism* with Edward A. Lynch (Lynald Books 1939).

References

Bsns W p93 My 20 '44; p121+ Ja 10 '53
Fortune 29:166 F '44 por; 39:182 Je '49; 47:92+ Ap '53
N Y Herald Tribune p2 N 16 '52 por
N Y Times p46 N 16 '52 por; p8 D 24 '52 por; p10 Mr 12 '53
Time 61:12 Ja 5 '53 por
U S News p36 F 7 '48; 33:77 N 28 '52; 34:84 Ja 2 '53
American Catholic Who's Who, 1952-53
Who's Who in America, 1952-53
Who's Who in Labor (1946)
Who's Who in the East (1951)

MACDONALD, JOHN ROSS. See Millar, K.

MCGRAW, CURTIS W(HITTLESEY)

Oct. 13, 1895—Sept. 10, 1953 Publisher; president and chairman of the board of McGraw-Hill Publishing Company since February 1950; his undergraduate years at Princeton were interrupted by service in the infantry of the United States Army, from which he was discharged with the rank of major in 1919; after graduation from Princeton in 1920 he was assistant coach of his alma mater's football teams of 1920, 1921, and 1922; in 1920 he began his association with the publishing company; of which his father James H. McGraw, Sr. had been co-founder; from a job in the shipping and production departments of the McGraw-Hill Book Company, a subsidiary of the larger firm, he rose to vice president and treasurer, and chairman of the board of directors; in 1930 he became a director of the parent organization, serving from 1943 to 1948 as vice-president and treasurer; from 1948 to February 1950 as vice-chairman of the board, and in 1950 he succeeded his brother, James H. McGraw as president; McGraw also was president of Princeton Hospital, a director of the First National Bank of Princeton, a member of the Book Publishing Advisory Committee of the War Production Board; a director of the Magazine Publishers Association and was recently named by President Eisenhower to the Advisory board of the Post Office Department. *See Current Biography,* 1950

Obituary

N Y Times p21 S 11 '53

MCINTYRE, JAMES FRANCIS (ALOYSIUS), CARDINAL

June 25, 1886- Roman Catholic prelate
Address: b. c/o Roman Catholic Archdiocese of Los Angeles, 714 West Olympic Blvd., Los Angeles 15, Calif.

The first prelate in Western United States to be elevated to the Roman Catholic Sacred College of Cardinals is His Eminence James Francis Cardinal McIntyre, Archbishop of Los Angeles and San Diego, who in January 1953 became the fourth cardinal in the United States. McIntyre had begun his ecclesiastical career at the age of thirty-five, after being employed for several years in a Wall Street firm. Before assuming his duties in Los Angeles in 1948, he had risen to titular Archbishop of Paltus and Coadjutor Archbishop of Francis Cardinal Spellman in the New York Archdiocese.

The son of James F. and Mary (Pelley) McIntyre, James Francis Aloysius McIntyre was born June 25, 1886, in New York's east midtown, where he was to live throughout his first sixty-two years. At an early age he was attracted to the vocation of priesthood and as a boy he assisted at the altar of St. Stephen's and St. Ignatius Loyola churches in New York. His mother having died when he was ten, he was reared by his cousin Mary (Mrs. Robert F. Conley). "A serious-minded, shy boy,"

(Continued next page)

Wide World Photos

JAMES FRANCIS CARDINAL MCINTYRE

Newsweek has said of him, "he . . . in every way was a model son to Mrs. Conley."

In 1899, after his graduation from Public School 70, the thirteen-year-old boy in order to support his invalid father went to work as a runner at the New York Curb Exchange, then the loosely organized, informal brokers' meeting place that its name suggests. From 1902 to 1915 McIntyre worked for the Wall Street firm of H. L. Horton Company (later absorbed by Fahnestock and Company), in positions of increasing responsibility. In the evenings he attended Harlem Evening High School and City College, and also took some courses at Columbia University. When his father died in 1915, McIntyre was office manager of the Horton firm, with the prospect of being taken into partnership. Freed of the necessity of supporting another, thirty-year-old Frank McIntyre left the business world to prepare himself for the priesthood. After his graduation in 1917 from Cathedral College of the New York Archdiocese, he attended St. Joseph's Seminary at Dunwoodie, New York, and was ordained a priest by Archbishop (later Cardinal) Hayes in St. Patrick's Cathedral on May 21, 1921. Father McIntyre's first ecclesiastical post was as curate of St. Gabriel's Church, where his father had gone to school in the 1860's. Very soon, because of his financial experience, the curate was asked to help at the chancery (the Archbishop's business office), and in 1923 he was appointed assistant chancellor and assistant diocesan secretary. As a member of the Archbishop's household, McIntyre thereafter lived at the official residence on Madison Avenue.

Advancing rapidly in the government of his Church, Father McIntyre was appointed in 1934 by Cardinal Hayes to be chancellor of the New York diocese, and the same year Pope Pius XI gave him the title of Papal Chamberlain (he was addressed as Very Reverend Monsignor).

In 1936 he became a Right Reverend Monsignor, when the Pope made him a domestic prelate. Three years later the new Archbishop of New York, Francis Spellman, named Monsignor McIntyre to the Diocesan Board of Consultors, and in November 1940 Pope Pius XII appointed him titular Bishop of Cyrene (a discontinued bishopric in Libya) and Auxiliary Bishop of New York, to assist Archbishop Spellman and his other auxiliary with diocesan duties. For his consecration as bishop on January 8, 1941, Spellman gave McIntyre the ring, pectoral cross, and chain of Cardinal Hayes.

Four years later, in 1945, Cardinal Spellman made McIntyre one of two Vicars-General of the diocese, giving him still wider responsibility for its affairs. The Bishop's first personal contact with the Vatican came in that year, when he flew to Italy for Vatican conferences regarding rehabilitation problems in liberated countries. The following April Bishop McIntyre was named a Knight of the Grand Cross of the Papal Order of the Holy Sepulchre and three months later was elevated to coadjutor (assistant) Archbishop, without right of succession. As all Catholic bishops are supposed to have sees of their own, he was made titular Archbishop of Paltus by the Pope. At a solemn pontifical mass, Cardinal Spellman praised McIntyre as "a bishop who is unsurpassed . . . in the hierarchy of the Church for his priestly qualifications, his administrative experience, and his combination of qualites required in a bishop."

The administrative work of the diocese with which Bishop McIntyre was occupied until 1948, included the management of the many properties of the wealthiest Catholic see in the world, the supervision of parish finances, the management of the parochial school system, a variety of charitable institutions, and the Catholic share of USO work. Among other chancery duties was the preparation of briefs on questions of church law. When time permitted, Bishop McIntyre exercised his more specifically priestly functions. "As a priest and confessor," *Newsweek* noted, "he believes in strict discipline, but the long lines that used to wait for him when he had time to hear confessions at St. Patrick's know he is understanding." Among his speeches at communion breakfasts which drew newspaper attention was one in April 1946, at a time when the United Nations Security Committee was discussing Spain as a possible threat to world peace. In the course of defending the Franco regime, and attacking Soviet Russia, the bishop stated that the Spanish revolution was inspired by "leftist groups," among which he included Communists, Nazis, and Fascists. In other speeches, Bishop McIntyre pressed for the right of parochial school children to share Federal benefits equally with public school children. In opposing the State Austin-Mahoney bill to end the discriminatory quota system in education, he stated that an error "greater than discrimination" was the designation of education as a function of the State, which he termed an infringement of the rights of parents.

Appointed by the Pope in February 1948 to his first post outside what he has called his "native and dearly beloved New York," McIntyre became Archbishop of Los Angeles and San Diego, an Archdiocese which had two auxiliary bishops and 688 priests to serve a Catholic population then in excess of 600,000 (in 1952 the number was given as 835,000). Upon McIntyre's departure in March 1948, Cardinal Spellman said, "In the nine precious years that we have lived and worked and prayed together, he has been to me all things that one man can be to another. . . .Like Joseph, he has fostered close to his holy heart the little people of this archdiocese." By the end of 1952, and after less than five years in Los Angeles, the Archbishop had formed twenty new parishes and had built ten major schools and eighty-two parochial schools. According to the Los Angeles County Assessor's office, the assessed valuation of Catholic parochial schools there was $9 million in 1951. The Archbishop presented to the county board of supervisors a detailed report showing that the schools had saved the taxpayers $20 million a year, with the result that the supervisors cut the assessment by about 62 per cent. Following a campaign for the exemption of the schools from all taxes, the legislature in the spring of 1951 passed such an act, which was approved by a referendum in the 1952 elections.

In January 1951, during nation-wide discussion of the recent Papal decree against priests belonging to, or attending meetings of, Rotary clubs, the Archbishop occasioned some comment by giving the invocation at a meeting of the Los Angeles Rotary Club, at which a young priest was the principal speaker. Two days later he also attracted national attention when he stated that the Government was "devoid of principle," a situation for which he blamed "whimsical evaluations of justice and equity . . . based on a purely social concept" by Supreme Court Justices Oliver Wendell Holmes and Felix Frankfurter (New York *Times*, January 29, 1951). The following December the prelate again aroused controversy by questioning the fitness of Mrs. Franklin D. Roosevelt to be chairman of the United Nations Human Rights Commission because she had expressed uncertainty as to the exact form which personal immortality might take.

When Pope Pius XII named James Francis McIntyre to the sacred purple of the College of Cardinals in November 1952, the Los Angeles *Daily News* commented, "he has in this comparatively short period won the esteem and affection of the entire community for his effective leadership in many civic and social welfare projects. . . .He has more than doubled the archdiocesan school and church facilities and greatly expanded its welfare work and related activities." The prelate was the first cardinal to be named from the West Coast and was the only one from the United States on the list of twenty-four new Princes of the Church, which restored the college to its authorized strength of seventy. At a secret consistory in the Vatican on January 12, 1953, the Pope "created and published" the twenty-four cardinals, who later in the week received the red biretta, symbol of the rank of cardinal.

As a member of the Sacred College of Cardinals, McIntyre is a permanent adviser to the Holy See and has among other duties and privileges the right to chose a new Pope upon the death of the present Pope. His titular church in Rome is St. Anastasia. While in Rome to attend the investment ceremony, the new cardinal was guest of honor at a reception given at the American Embassy. Other cardinals of the United States are Francis Cardinal Spellman of New York; Samuel Cardinal Stritch, of Chicago; and Edward Cardinal Mooney of Detroit.

His Eminence Cardinal McIntyre is a ruddy, six-foot man of stately carriage and cheerful manner. *Newsweek* has termed him "extraordinarily modest and self-effacing" and reported, "A habitual doodler of the geometric-pattern school, he always has a scratch pad handy as he discusses anything from dispensations to Gregorian chants."

References

Cath World 107:83 Ap '48
Los Angeles Daily N p19 D 1 '52
Los Angeles Sunday N p3 N 30 '52 por
N Y Herald Tribune p16 N 20 '40 por; p33 N 30 '52
N Y Post p12 N 19 '40 por
N Y Sun p1 N 19 '40 por; p6 F 13 '48 por
N Y Times p23 N 20 '40 por; p3 Ja 9 '41 por; p14 Jl 23 '46 por; p43 N 30 '52
N Y World-Telegram p1 Ja 8 '41 por; p21 Jl 23 '46 por; p2 N 29 '52
Newsweek 28:78 Ag 5 '46 por; 31:74 F 23 '48
Time 51:73 F 23 '48; 60:53 D 8 '52 por
American Catholic Who's Who, 1952-53
Who's Who in America, 1952-53
World Biography (1948)

MACIVER, LOREN (NEWMAN) Feb. 2, 1909- painter
Address: 61 Perry St., New York 14

Unique qualities of romanticism and symbolism fused with lyricism and a child-like imagination characterize the work of Loren MacIver, who ranks as one of America's outstanding women painters. A retrospective two-woman show with another artist, Irene Rice Pereira, which opened at the Whitney Museum of Art in New York in January, 1953, exhibited fifty-nine of MacIver's paintings beginning with *Sleep* (1929) and included her most recent canvas, *New York*. The exhibition marked a high moment in contemporary art and recognition for two original artists.

Loren MacIver's marriage in 1929, at the age of twenty, to the poet, Lloyd Frankenberg, set the stage for a life of art and poetry which has been lived with depth and singleness of purpose and devotion. In the depression-thirties she worked on the New York Works Project Administration's Federal Art Project during the winters and in the summers lived in a shack in North Truro, Cape Cod which was

LOREN MACIVER

built by her husband. Her first museum purchase was *The Shack,* acquired by the Museum of Modern Art in 1935. Painting for the love of painting since a child, and with only a little formal art instruction, she proved her originality by her inclusion in the 1946 exhibit at the Museum of Modern Art called *Fourteen Americans.*

During the forties MacIver executed important commissions for magazines and murals for steamship companies. Her paintings were purchased by many private collectors as well as by museums and galleries exhibited her work in five one-man shows. In reviewing her 1953 show at the Whitney, the art critic of the New York *Times* spoke of MacIver's twenty years of creative work and reflected that she was "still young and still developing and it is quite possible that her best and most significant work lies ahead of her."

MacIver was born in New York City on February 2, 1909, the daughter of Charles Augustus Paul Newman and Julia MacIver Newman. Her mother, of Scotch-Irish descent, preferred using her maiden name, which Loren also adopted. As far back as she can remember MacIver painted. When she was ten, her parents permitted her to enter the Saturday classes at the Art Students League in New York—the only formal art instruction she ever had, and this lasted only one year. Through high school she continued to paint and also showed a great love for the theatre. After their marriage in 1929 the young couple lived in Greenwich Village, and although moving often, they have always lived in that section of New York "where MacIver's slim figure in faded blue jeans, looking a good deal like a small cowboy's, is a familiar sight."

Winter Dunes was one of her first Cape Cod paintings and *Tern Eggs* followed in 1933.

However in *Strunsky House* (1935) she began to experiment with soft color areas that blend into one another. In all her work she portrays what is significant to her imagination and blurs out the inconsequential. This gives to her work the air of mystery for which she is noted. In this same painting the artist for the first time devised symbols to show the viewer a deeper meaning to her work.

In the catalogue to the Whitney show, curator John I. H. Baur comments: "Such clues are necessary because MacIver's paintings are never solely abstract or solely pictorial in conception. They always have a poetic motivation which depends as much on subject as on esthetic content. The artist prefers the formal arrangement to speak first, impressing the eye with the sheer beauty of color and design. For this reason the objects must not be recognized too easily. But they must be read eventually or the painting achieves only half its meaning. Her cryptic symbols are one means to this end." Her method is to portray a familiar object such as a lamp without modeling, in a few lines to indicate a home, or a bottle indicating a studio, and other shapes. One of the first of her paintings to use these symbols was *Strunsky House* (1935) on Macdougal Street with its rhythm of rectangles suggesting "the multiple relations of life in a city, the mystery of all the strange rooms surrounding the one brightly lit studio."

Her paintings were first hung in group shows by Emily Francis of Contemporary Arts Gallery. The Museum of Modern Art purchased *The Shack* in 1935 and in 1938 she had her first one-man exhibition at Marian Willard's East River Gallery.

She delighted the art world with her *Portrait of Jimmy Savo* in 1944 and the circus clown, *Emmett Kelly* in 1947. In each of these MacIver painted them because they appealed to her and because she loved the color and artistry of their clown characters. Emily Genauer in *Best in Art* says, "In *Portrait of Jimmy Savo,* MacIver says that pantomime is the expression of idea and emotion solely by means of significant gesture. Her admiration of Jimmy Savo's mastery of pantomime springs from many years of watching him performing and observing the wonderfully eloquent way in which he uses his hands, his great wide eyes, his quizzical lifting of his brows, all the small, seemingly spontaneous yet carefully devised movements which create so winning a picture of pathos. Miss MacIver therefore had to accept within her own medium what Savo did with his; to underscore what is significant by underplaying what is irrelevant. . . ." *Portrait of Jimmy Savo* was the natural consequence not only of affection but of affinity between the heart of the painter and her subject."

Two mural commissions, one for the Moore McCormack Lines' ship, *Argentina,* in 1947 and the other for four panels for American Export Line ships in 1948 gave the artist a larger scope for her many-hued and luminous colors. The S.S. *Argentina* mural, nine by eighteen feet in size, brings sea colors inside the lounge.

Against this background pastel butterflies and fish gently float through colorful areas of sky and water, competing with the real ocean visible through the large windows. During this same period MacIver illustrated covers for magazines, such as *Fortune* and *Town and Country*, and book jackets.

She painted the cover for Robert Frost's collection *Steeple Bush* (1947), illustrated Tennessee Williams' story, *The Malediction* (*Town and Country,* December 1945), and the jacket for *Fourteen Americans* (Museum of Modern Art, 1946).

In July 1948 Loren MacIver made her first trip to Europe, visiting France, Italy, England, Ireland and Scotland. Among her paintings resulting from this experience are *Venice* (1949) now in the Whitney Museum of American Art; *Dublin and Environs* (1950) and *Paris* (1949) the latter was acquired by the Metropolitan Museum of Art. The Museum of Modern Art owns *Key West Arrangement,* (1939) inspired by a visit to the nation's southernmost city.

Robert Coates, art critic of the *New Yorker,* refers to MacIver as "a romantic, a symbolic abstractionist" and praises her for her original talent, adding, "But it has its dangers, for it depends for its expression on the fleetingest of impressions and airiest of fancies, both exactly rendered and the surest tread is required to walk such a fine emotional tightrope without falling into bathos."

Other critics have seen influences of Paul Klee, Edgar Degas, and even Georgia O'Keefe in her work but MacIver denies that any one artist has exerted an important influence on her art.

Included in the 1953 Whitney show was one of MacIver's major works, *Hopscotch* owned by the Museum of Modern Art, which, according to James Thrall Soby, its director, "emphasized the unassertive phenomena of daily existence." In his review of this retrospective show he reflected, "MacIver is the artist who has poked into the ashcan of the American "Ashcan" school rejecting the latter's exuberant proclamation of external reality in favor of a wry and memorable offstage whisper. For the truth about MacIver, her attention wanders. No one can predict from one moment to the next what will catch her attention as a painting. We can be certain only that it will be something everyone else overlooked."

In her statement of faith, written for the catalogue *Fourteen Americans* (Museum of Modern Art) MacIver writes: "Quite simple things lead to discovery. This is what I would like to do with painting; starting with simple things, to lead the eye by various manipulations of colors, objects and tensions toward a transformation and reward.

"An ashcan suggests the phoenix; its relics begin a new life, like a tree in spring. Votive lights, flickering and vanishing, become symbols of constancy. In the catalyzing air of an evening a city and its traffic merge; it is as if all the events of wills and people cobbling it,

had left upon the avenue of their passing a stain of circumstance.

"My wish is to make something permanent out of the transitory by means at once dramatic and colloquial, certain moments for the gift of revealing the past and foretelling the future. It is these moments I hope to catch."

Her indifference to established art styles and movements is evident in her two most recent canvases, *New York* which shows shadowy skyscrapers surrounding the kiosk of the Christopher Street subway station, illuminated by a pale yellow glow and showing what John I.H. Baur calls her "characteristic symbols: a leaf, a key, a neon lobster sign, a shoe and hat, and *Les Baux,* a romantic reconstruction of the wild village of that name cut into the bauxite cliffs near Nimes in southern France . . . an abstract image of fantastic crystalline forms. Except for its luminous opulence it marks a departure from anything she has yet attempted."

References

Art Digest 27:7+ Ja 15 '53
Art News 45:24 O '46
New Yorker 28:53-4 Ja 17 '53
N Y Herald Tribune p6 IV Ja 11 '53
N Y Times p11 II Ja 11 '53
Sat R 36:50-1 F 7 '53
Time 61:69 Ja 26 '53
Baur, J.I.H. MacIver and Pereira (1953)
Genauer, E. Best of Art (1950)
Miller, D. Fourteen Americans (1953)
Who's Who in American Art (1953)
Who's Who in the East (1951)

MACK, NILA (?)—Jan. 20, 1953 Radio writer, director, producer of children's program, *Let's Pretend* (1930-53); made first professional appearance at the age of sixteen with a Western repertory company; was a member of Alla Nazimova's theatrical company for six years; played in vaudeville and wrote scenarios for movie shorts before becoming a radio actress for Columbia Broadcasting System; in 1930 took over direction of children's program which became known as *Let's Pretend*; wrote magazine stories and two books for children. See *Current Biography,* 1952.

Obituary

N Y Times p31 Ja 21 '53

MCLINTOCK, (GEORGE) GORDON Feb. 10, 1903- Merchant Marine officer, educator
Address: b. & h. United States Merchant Marine Academy, Kings Point, N.Y.

The superintendent of the United States Merchant Marine Academy, one of the four Federal Academies for officer training, is Rear Admiral Gordon McLintock. Observing its tenth anniversary in 1953, this academy has been called the "Annapolis of the Merchant Marine", and like the Naval Academy, it offers a four year course leading to a Bachelor of Science degree to qualified male citizens of the United States

Chase News Photo.

REAR ADM. GORDON MCLINTOCK

between the ages of sixteen and a half and twenty-one.

The Academy's graduates, according to a December 1951 report in the New York *Herald Tribune,* have been "proving a bulwark of Merchant Marine power in one of the most critical peacetime shortages of crewmen in maritime history." Currently in training as officers are 800 cadets, 200 of whom are on board oceangoing vessels, and 600 of whom are students on the 65-acre campus on the North Shore of Long Island. Over 9,000 have been graduated since its founding.

Beginning as a cadet in the British Merchant Navy in 1918, McLintock saw continuous sea service until 1930, rising to master of an American tanker when he was twenty-four. He left the sea to serve twelve years with the Bureau of Marine Inspection of the United States Department of Commerce, first as steamship inspector, then as head of the License Examination Division, and finally as chief of the Casualty Investigation Review Division. Called to active duty with the United States Navy in 1942, McLintock spent the next six years as Chief Inspection Officer of all the training units for Merchant Marine Officers. In 1948 he took over his present post.

Born February 10, 1903, in Sunderland, Great Britain, into a family of British shipowners, shipbuilders and master mariners, George Gordon McLintock first went to sea at the age of three—aboard his father's ship. His parents were Beatrice Reevel (Maddison) and William McLintock, who was chief engineer of a passenger liner before retiring. His maternal grandfather, A. J. W. Maddison, owned a fleet of sailing vessels, largely in Mediterranean trade; his other grandfather, Alexander McLintock, was managing director of one of the largest shipyards in the world.

Young Gordon's first school was Cowan Terrace, in Sunderland, where his extracurricular interest was football. Graduated in 1914, he enrolled at the Sevenoaks School, (founded 1432) in Sevenoaks, England. The story is told that he disliked the school's emphasis on classics and had the family lawyer write to the headmaster explaining why he needed more mathematics and less Latin and Greek. The headmaster was unmoved, however, and young McLintock, well schooled in the classics, relieved by sports activities, was graduated third in his class in 1918, when he was fifteen. He was then indentured as a cadet in the British Merchant Navy, with corollary wartime status as a midshipman in the Royal Naval Reserve. This service (1918-1920) was with the Dalgliesh Steamship Company, and took him to New York and to ports in South Africa, Australia and the Dutch East Indies.

Meanwhile young McLintock's father had retired from the sea to become a marine superintendent in New York City and there settled with his family in 1920. His cadetship completed in 1920, when he was seventeen, McLintock was named quartermaster on the *Lewis Luckenbach,* at that time the largest cargo vessel in the world. He became a naturalized citizen in 1921.

His next post (he was nineteen) was as third officer on a tanker of the Pan American Petroleum and Transport Company. He remained with Pan American for ten years (1920-1930), rising successively from third officer (1922-23) to second officer (1924-1925) to chief officer (1925-27), and, at the age of twenty-four, to master (1927-1930). He was probably the youngest master in the American Merchant Marine when in 1927 he was put in command of an ocean-going vessel.

Two years later McLintock passed the national competitive examinations for entrance into the United States Steamship Inspection Service, and became, in 1930, perhaps the youngest man ever appointed Steamship Inspector in the Bureau of Marine Inspection of the United States Department of Commerce. His duties for the next seven years included inspecting ships, including nearly all the largest vessels in the world, to determine seaworthiness and compliance with laws; inspecting and testing hulls during building, and preparing specifications for hull construction and alteration; conducting examinations for licenses and certificates for officers and seamen; investigating marine casualties, and other related work.

In 1936 a new post was established in the Bureau of Marine Inspection in order to centralize in Washington, D. C., the examining and licensing of Merchant Marine officers, then being conducting independently by the forty-nine more or less autonomous marine inspection ports, as well as to raise the standards of officers and seamen by standardizing and modernizing license examinations and experience requirements. To this new position—nautical expert and head of the license examinations division—McLintock was appointed, to supervise a staff of 101. The new syllabus which McLintock and his staff developed is still in use

MCLINTOCK, GORDON—*Continued*

today and sets the pattern for studies at the United States Merchant Marine Academy. McLintock also wrote some seventy-five articles on the training and professional standards of Merchant Marine officers, published by the Department of Commerce and in professional and trade journals in the United States, Canada, Great Britain and Australia.

While in this position, too, McLintock introduced competitive signalling exercises among United States Navy and merchant vessels; proficiency reports were published and achievement was thus encouraged. According to an article in *Polaris*, a publication of the United States Merchant Marine Cadet Corps, McLintock's interest in signalling dated back to an experience in 1924 when as second officer of the *Harwood* he helped to rescue the crew of a sinking Danish freighter during a hurricane. Because the foundering ship's radio batteries were under water McLintock, the only officer who knew semaphore signalling, had to use a flashlight to communicate with the vessel in distress.

In 1940 McLintock was appointed Senior Nautical Scientist, and head of the Bureau of Marine Inspection's Casualty Investigation Review Division. This Division, with a staff of 112, reviewed the findings of boards set up to investigate and determine responsibility for marine casualties and to try marine officers and seamen accused of misconduct or incompetency. It also studied unusual conditions in connection with the casualties and drafted suggestions for remedial legislation where this seemed necessary.

After the United States had entered World War II the Division also studied ship torpedoings, procedures for the abandonment of ships, and the improvement of life boat and life raft equipment. While heading the Division (1940-1942) McLintock wrote a series of thirty articles for the monthly Bureau Bulletins entitled "Lessons from Casualties." He was frequently called upon to make final decisions in important cases, such as the stranding and loss of the *S.S. President Hoover*. In March 1942 he was the official observer of the Department of Commerce at the Navy Department investigation of the burning of the *Normandie*.

Holding a commission in the United States Naval Reserve for over a dozen years, McLintock asked for sea duty with the Navy in 1939 but could not obtain his release from the Department of Commerce. In 1942, however, he was called to active duty, and named chief inspection officer of the Bureau of Maritime Services with the War Shipping Administration, as well as special assistant to the chief of the parallel Bureau in the United States Maritime Commission. His duties were to inspect the training units of the United States Merchant Marine Cadet Corps, the State Maritime Academies and the training stations of the Maritime Service. This post he held until March, 1948, when he was named Superintendent of the United States Merchant Marine Academy at Kings Point, and promoted from Commodore, USMS, to Rear Admiral. He succeeded Rear

Admiral Richard Robert McNulty, becoming the fourth Superintendent of the academy.

The institution Admiral McLintock now heads was established by the Federal Government in 1943 to train deck and engine officers for the American Merchant Marine. It is located on the former Walter P. Chrysler estate at Great Neck, Long Island. Students, chosen on the basis of nationwide competitive examinations, become Cadets in the United States Merchant Marine Cadet Corps and Midshipmen in the United States Naval Reserve. The four-year course includes a professional maritime curriculum as well as liberal arts and social sciences; students spend the sophomore year on merchant ships for on-the-job training.

Admiral McLintock places emphasis on the graduate's practical training, but also believes "there is no reason why a skillful merchant officer should not also be a cultured man." Graduates are awarded licenses as third mates or third assistant engineers, commissions as ensigns in the United States Maritime Service and/or the United States Naval Reserve. (The Academy was formally accredited as a four-year college in November, 1949, and Admiral McLintock conferred Bachelor of Science degrees for the first time on the class of June, 1950.)

Admiral McLintock has represented the United States at several international conferences. In 1946 he attended the Conference on Radio Aids to Marine Navigation in London and the International Labor Organization Conference in Seattle, Washington. He represented the U.S., too, at the Special Administrative Conference for the North East Atlantic on Loran, in Geneva, Switzerland, January, 1949.

He is also the United States representative on the International Liaison Committee for the American, British and Danish Institutes of Navigation, and was president of the American Institute of Navigation in 1947, 1948 and 1949. The object of the Institutes is to co-ordinate the knowledge of marine and air navigators, scientists, and those associated with the production of navigational equipment. Great Britain is represented by Sir Robert Watson-Watt, "father of radar", and Denmark by the Astronomer Royal of that country.

Among the professional groups with which the Rear Admiral is associated are the Radio Technical Commission for Maritime Services, the Society of Naval Architects and Marine Engineers, the Naval Institute, the Propeller Club, and the National Education Association. He is a trustee of the United Seamen's Service and of the American Seamen's Friend Society, and holds honorary membership in both the British Institute of Navigation and the British Merchant Navy Club. He is also a member of the Hague Post of the American Legion and vice-president of the St. Andrews Society of Washington, D. C. His church is the Presbyterian. In politics he lists himself as a Republican.

Of medium height (5 feet, nine inches) the Rear Admiral weighs 165 pounds, has blue eyes, brown hair. His wife, the former Wini-

MCLINTOCK, GORDON—*Continued*

fred Russell Kidner, was a domestic science teacher before their marriage on August 8, 1929. Admiral McLintock notes as his favorite recreations "electronics and navigation."

References

Polaris 7:7 Apr '48
American Men in Government (1949)
Who's Who in America, 1952-1953

MCSWIGAN, MARIE (mc-swĭg'an) May 22, 1907- Author

Address: b. c/o E. P. Dutton and Co., 300 Fourth Ave., New York 10; h. 217 Tennyson Ave., Pittsburgh, Penn.

Reprinted from the *Wilson Library Bulletin,* Oct. 1953

That a "nose for news" is an asset to any writer—even to a writer of juveniles—is evidenced by the success of Marie McSwigan's stories. She can detect, in a small newspaper item, the material upon which to build a book

MARIE MCSWIGAN

enchanting to young readers. From childhood, her fingers itched for a pencil. "I wowed my first grade," she confesses, "with a treatise on our doll show"—the news angle even then, rather than the usual tale of fairies and princesses. "And I filled composition books with my early efforts, some of which landed in the famous *St. Nicholas* league." With this early talent for winning a youthful audience, it is not surprising she has become a popular juvenile writer.

Marie McSwigan was born in Pittsburgh, Pennsylvania, May 22, 1907. Her father, Andrew Stephen McSwigan, was one of the reporters who covered the Johnstown flood, and he later became city editor of the old Pittsburgh *Post.* He and her mother, the former

Genevieve Brady, "may have stinted on other things but . . . had the best library they knew how to assemble." One sister, Genevieve, is a writer on the Pittsburgh *Post-Gazette.*

A Carnegie library borrower since she was six, Marie was always a student. After finishing high school she took her B.A. at the University of Pittsburgh, majoring in English. She was active on all three student publications, was chapter president of Pi Beta Phi and of Alpha Lambda Nu, honorary activities fraternity (later Mortar Board). She began her newspaper work as reporter and feature writer, first, on the Pittsburgh *Press* (1927-1932) and later with the Pittsburgh *Sun Telegraph* (1936-1937). She then became assistant publicist for Carnegie Institute, Fine Arts Department, during two International Arts Exhibitions, and handled public relations for the University of Pittsburgh. She also helped to publicize Kennywood Park.

As relief from these more prosaic pursuits, Marie McSwigan began to follow her childhood bent for storytelling. Her first book, *Weather House People,* appeared in 1940, but it was with the publication of her second, *Snow Treasure,* in 1942, that she won national recognition. This account of Norwegian children loading gold bullion on their sleds and coasting down with it, under Nazi noses, to hide it under their snow men, has become a junior classic. Grown-ups transferred the $9,000,000 treasure to a freighter, which landed it in Baltimore in June 1940. The book, which relates the part played in this feat by a twelve-year-old boy, won the Junior Scholastic Gold Seal Award in 1942 and was Young Readers' Choice, American Library Association 1943. F. B. Sloan wrote in *Books:* "If a little group of . . . children can so rise to the occasion . . . the backbone of any child straightens to read about it." The *New Yorker* described it as "intense reading for any child from nine to twelve."

In a lighter vein was *Five on a Merry-Go-Round* (1943), in which a family goes south seeking work and a home, finds an abandoned carrousel in Alabama, and converts it into living quarters. Ellen Lewis Buell of the New York *Times* praised it as "a flavor of fantastic adventure to enthrall readers of ten to fifteen. . . .A portrait of a plucky American family making the best out of very little."

In 1946 came *Hi, Barney!*—the story of a young British lad who spends the war years in America. Of this: "The tale flows fast, smoothly, humorously. Boys and girls of Barney's age should find fun and suspense in it," commented Latrobe Carroll, in the New York *Times. Juan of Manila* (1947) was based on a true incident of the resistance movement—how a Filipino boy broadcast encouraging messages despite Japanese threats. As Virginia Kirkus pointed out, "Humble details of daily life make this of value. . . .Boy scouts and radio fans will like it especially."

A favorite with all children is *Our Town Has a Circus* (1949) with a thrilling rescue of a clown recluse from an icebound island for good measure. Lucille Pannell, in the Chicago *Sunday Tribune,* remarked, "There's a lot of good circus lore tucked into this exciting story."

Binnie Latches On (1950) and *The News Is Good* (1952) follow the fortunes of an "odd one"in her family. In the first she edits the school paper. In the sequel she bends her energies to finding shoes for Indian children. "Binnie's youthful problems make a lively, modern story, one which girls of all dispositions will enjoy." So commented the New York *Times*.

Dutton has published all Miss McSwigan's books. Her latest, *Three's a Crowd* (1953), tells of twins, college juniors, who fall in love with the same man.

Marie McSwigan also contributed the story "Rousing Welcome" to the American Book Company's anthology, *Coonskin for a General* (1951), and has written articles for magazines and book reviews for the New York *Herald Tribune*. With more work in progress, she still finds time to serve as director of St. Rosella's Foundling and Maternity Hospital, and on the executive committee of the Irish Room, University of Pittsburgh. She belongs to the Woman's Press Club, Authors' Club, and Catholic Business and Professional Woman's Club, all of Pittsburgh.

Blue-eyed and gray-haired, Miss McSwigan, who stands 5 feet, 4 inches tall and weighs 120 pounds, loves to swim and to travel. She has made four trips to Europe, three to the Caribbean, two to California, and has taken a river cruise from Cincinnati to New Orleans. Most of all she enjoys seeing the Pennsylvania Dutch country. She is a Catholic and a Democrat.

Reference

Who's Who in the East (1951)

MADDEN, RAY J(OHN) Feb. 25, 1892-
United States Representative from Indiana;
lawyer
Address: b. House Office Bldg., Washington 25, D.C.; h. Hotel Gary, Gary, Ind.

In the November 1952 election Ray J. Madden, United States Representative from Indiana since 1943, was one of the 206 Democrats to be chosen for the Eighty-third Congress. Before becoming a member of Congress Madden was for four years Treasurer of Lake County, Indiana, and earlier, from 1935 to 1938, city comptroller for Gary, Indiana. A lawyer by profession, he was for a short period before World War I a municipal judge of Omaha, Nebraska. In the House, Madden has supported the Roosevelt and Truman administrations and as a representative of the strongly unionized city of Gary has cast a prolabor vote. In 1952 Madden headed the House committee investigating the death of Polish army officials and intellectuals at Katyn Forest during the winter of 1939-40. He has also been a member of the House Rules Committee.

The son of John and Elizabeth (Burne) Madden, John Ray Madden was born February 25, 1892, in Waseca, Minnesota. After attending the local public schools and the Sacred Heart

Wide World Photos
RAY J. MADDEN

Academy, from which he was graduated in 1910, Madden went to Omaha, Nebraska, to study law at Creighton University. He received his LL.B. degree in 1913 and in that same year, having been admitted to the Nebraska bar, he began his career as an attorney in Omaha. In 1916 he was elected a municipal judge of the city, but after serving a year of his term he resigned to join the United States Navy. When he returned to civilian life at the end of World War I, he opened a law practice in Gary, Indiana.

In the steel city of Gary, Madden in 1935 was elected on the Democratic ticket as city comptroller, and in 1938 he became treasurer of Lake County, which includes the city of Gary. Four years later, in 1942, he was elected to the Seventy-eighth Congress as United States Representative from the First District of Indiana, which comprises Lake County and which has a total population of 366,113. He has been subsequently re-elected to each succeeding Congress, and when in the November 1952 election the Republican party took numerical control of the House of Representatives from the Democrats, Madden kept the support of the voters in his district.

During his ten years in Congress Madden has gained the reputation of being a "liberal" Democrat, supporting the broad administration policies of Presidents Roosevelt and Truman. In 1944 when Roosevelt appointed Henry Wallace as Secretary of Commerce to replace Jesse Jones, Madden spoke in the House for Wallace, and opposed Jones. While serving as a member of the House Rules Committee which recommends bills for floor consideration, Madden, particularly when President Truman proposed his "Fair Deal" legislative program, fought to get the individual Administration measures before the House. At the time of the struggle with "Fair Deal" foes in the commit-

MADDEN, RAY J.—*Continued*

tee for control, the *U.S. News & World Report* citing the fact that Madden was from Gary and "speaks for that strongly unionized steel workers' community,"named him as one of the three committee members out of twelve on whom the Administration could depend.

Representative Madden's voting record during the first year of his freshman term in Congress shows him against the Ruml tax collection plan (March), the Hobbs anti-racketeering bill (April), and against a bill providing prison sentences and fines for persons instigating strikes in Government-operated plants (June); while he favored extending the reciprocal trade act for two years (May) and the Fulbright resolution on postwar collaboration (September). The following year he opposed the ban on food subsidies (February), the compromise soldier vote bill (March), and the motion to freeze the social security tax at 1 per cent (December). In 1945 he supported extending the trade agreements act (May), the Bretton Woods agreement (June), the anti-poll tax legislation (June), and the employment-production bill (December). He voted against those bills deemed "antilabor," such as the labor racketeering restriction, the war manpower control bill (March), and the tax adjustment proposal which would have raised exemptions in the excess profits tax. That year he also opposed a measure for a permanent Un-American Activities Committee (January). In the second session of the Seventy-ninth Congress (1946) he cast his vote for the school lunch program (February), the cancer research authorization, and the loan to Great Britain (July). While supporting the right of the Federal Government to prohibit strikes in essential industries seized by the Government (May) he was against the establishment of a board which would assume the strike-settling functions of the Labor Department and apply the antitrust laws to union activities.

On foreign affairs measures in 1947 Madden favored the Administration's policy calling for financial aid to Greece and Turkey and economic supports to other European nations, and that year opposed the Taft-Hartley act (April) and the vote to override the President's veto (June). In 1948 he voted "yea" on the European Recovery Program (March), the repeal of the oleomargarine tax (April), and the measures to aid displaced persons (June); and "nay" on a bill requiring Communists to register their party affiliation and on a proposal exempting railroad rates from antitrust laws. During the Eighty-first Congress the Representative from Indiana, in August 1949, opposed a bill which would have exempted independent gas producers from Federal jurisdiction and a 50 per cent cut in European arms aid and, in August 1950, the bill to strike our commodity speculation controls. Among the measures to which he gave his support were rent control extension (March 1949), a long-range housing bill (June 1949), Korea-Formosa economic aid (February 1950), and a $2 billion increase in farm price supports (June 1950).

With the convening of the Eighty-second Congress in January 1951, Madden, a member of the House Rules Committee, voted against a measure to give that committee tighter controls over what legislature was to be considered.

Other proposals that he opposed that year were a $10 million cut in reclamation funds (May) and the tidelands oil bill (July). During 1952 such key Administration issues as the mutual security bill (June), giving aid to the democratic countries (May), and the economic controls bill (June) were supported by Madden. In line with Administration policies, he voted against the lease of tidelands for exploitation of their oil resources and against the McCarran act, which President Truman vetoed but which was passed over his veto. He also opposed the amendment to the price control act suspending ceilings on any material which has sold below ceiling for three months. During the steel strike of that year, Madden voted against the proposed amendment to the Defense Production Act which would have enjoined the President to invoke the Taft-Hartley law as a measure for forcing the steel workers to return to the mills.

Madden came to wide attention when in 1951 he began an investigation of the so-called "Katyn Forest Massacre," in which some 15,000 Polish army officers and intellectuals were killed during the winter of 1939-40, just after Poland had been divided between the German and Russian occupying forces. In 1943 the Germans had made the original disclosure of the massacre, blaming the Russians. In turn, the Russians had accused the German occupying forces which had held the territory during the fall of 1941. Madden in 1951 introduced a bill in the House to create a special committee to investigate the charges and countercharges. When the bill was passed, Madden was chosen chairman of the committee, and in the course of the investigation traveled through Europe to take sworn testimony from some 400 persons. On the basis of this testimony, together with some 200 other pertinent documents, Madden's committee placed the time of the massacre not later than the spring of 1940, when the Soviet forces were occupying the territory, and recommended that the evidence be presented to the United Nations General Assembly for possible action by the International Court of Justice. Commenting on its findings, the committee compared the Soviet tactics in this case with its position in regard to the missing 8,000 United States personnel and 60,000 South Koreans lost since the beginning of the Korean conflict. An editorial in the New York *Herald Tribune* (December 25, 1952) stated that the "Congressional investigators have performed a very real service."

The Representative from Indiana is a member of the American Legion, of the Elks, and the Moose. His religion is Roman Catholic.

References

Biographical Directory of the American Congress, 1774-1949 (1950)
Congressional Directory (1952)
Who's Who in America, 1952-53
Who's Who in United States Politics (1950)
World Biography (1948)

MAGLIE, SAL(VATORE ANTHONY)

Apr. 26, 1917- Baseball player

Address: b. c/o New York Giants Baseball Club, 100 W. 42nd St., New York 18; h. 2727 Pierce Ave., Niagara Falls, N.Y.

When the usual official statistics were released at the conclusion of the 1952 baseball season, it was revealed that Sal Maglie, right-handed curve-ball and control pitcher with the New York Giants, had the best life-time moundsman's average of any player currently active in either the National or the American League. He had won 64 games and lost only 22 since his major league debut in the summer of 1945. In the 1950 season Maglie, who is nicknamed "The Barber," won 11 games in a row for the Giants, pitching 43⅓ consecutive scoreless innings, the second longest such stretch in the history of the National League. The 23 games won by Maglie in 1951 were a major factor in bringing the Giants their first pennant in 14 years.

Salvatore Anthony Maglie was born at Niagara Falls, New York, on April 26, 1917. His father, who came from Italy, was a pipe-fitter, and later became the proprietor of a grocery store. Sal went to grade school in Niagara Falls, and played the usual outdoor games but in baseball he was considered "not even good enough to pitch for his . . . sand-lot team," he told Stanley Frank (*Saturday Evening Post*, May 5, 1951). However, he succeeded in "making" the Niagara Falls High School baseball team, and developed such proficiency that by his senior year he was pitching two or three times a week for semi-professional clubs at five to ten dollars a game. His principal reputation at high school was, however, as a basketball player, and when he was graduated in 1936, his speed, skill and build brought him an offer of an athletic scholarship from Niagara University, which he rejected in order to work in his father's grocery store.

After holding a job in the shipping department of the Electro Metallurgical Company for a time, Sal had a tryout with the Rochester baseball club of the International League in 1937. During the following summer, he was signed to a $275 a month contract by the former major league catcher Steve O'Neill, then in the first of three years as manager of the Buffalo (New York) Bisons of the International League. Sal made his debut as a professional minor league player in August 1938 in relief against Newark. "Maglie was so nervous his knees shook," W. J. Charlesworth has recalled. "He hit 2 batters, walked a couple, and after a couple of homers, O'Neill took him out." In all, Maglie appeared in 5 games for the Bison in 1938, pitched 12 innings and yielded an earned run average of 3.75. "I thought sure I'd be farmed out to a lower league next season," he states in the article in *Sport*, "but they kept me around all year and I didn't get very much work. Maglie won 3 and lost 7 for Buffalo in 1939, his earned run, average mounting to 4.99. He was even more conspicuously ineffective in 1940 when he lost 7 games straight and was tagged with a very poor earned run average of 7.17.

Wide World Photos

SAL MAGLIE

Permitted to pitch only 54 innings in 1940 as against 101 in 1939, Maglie attributed his poor showing chiefly to lack of steady work. "I had good stuff for 4 or 5 innings. . . .I'd weaken after that and give away the game," he recalls. At his own request late in the 1940 season, Sal was demoted to the Jamestown, New York, club of the Pony League, where he brought his earned run average down to a gratifying 2.73.

The following year (1941) Maglie was advanced to the Elmira, New York, club of the Eastern League, and was given steady work at last, pitching 270 innings, and winning 20 games while losing 15, for an earned run average of 2.67. Maglie was "drafted" from Elmira by the New York Giants that winter, and was sent to Jersey City, New Jersey (the Giants' International League "farm"), where he was used chiefly as a relief moundsman in 1942, winning 9 games and losing 6 for an earned run average of 2.78. "I was becoming a better pitcher," Sal has declared, "but with the war effort growing, I decided to . . . take a job in a defense plant." Thus he was placed on organized baseball's "voluntary retired list" through 1943 and 1944, when he worked as a pipefitter at Niagara Falls, and was in contact with baseball only through managing and pitching for Canadian amateur teams at Niagara Falls, Ontario, and Welland, Ontario.

Maglie returned to "Triple A" baseball in the beginning of the 1945 season, and pitched 118 innings, chiefly in relief, during the next spring and summer, but won only 6 games and lost 7. "I felt stronger and my control was much better," Maglie has stated, "but I just wasn't getting the hitters out at the right time." Late that season, Mel Ott, who was then manager of the New York National League team, was having considerable trouble with his pitching at the Polo Grounds. He gave Maglie "two good jobs" in relief, and then a starting assignment, something with which he had not

MAGLIE, SAL—*Continued*

been entrusted since his days at Elmira. "I appreciated Mel's confidence in me," Sal declared, "and I worked hard each time. I started about 10 or 11 times and 3 of my first 6 games were shutouts." His achievement was far better than a 5 won, 4 lost record would suggest, because he "walked" only 22 batters in 84 innings and his earned run average was 2.36, the best in his entire playing career.

In February 1946 Maglie made the decision which had the surprising consequence of interrupting his major league career for 4 full years while at the same time developing him into one of the most reliable "control" moundsmen of his time. After the regular 1945 season Maglie had gone to Cuba to play "winter" ball for the Giants' coach and former "ace" relief pitcher, Adolfo Luque, manager of the Cienfuegos team. Both Luque and Maglie were approached by the brothers Bernardo and Jorge Pasquel to "jump" to the Mexican League which was then being formed. They agreed, along with numerous other major leaguers including 9 more Giants. "I went into the deal with my eyes open," stated Sal, who received from the Pasquels about double the salary he had drawn at the Polo Grounds.

In Mexico, Maglie was assigned to the Puebla team, of which Luque was appointed manager. When Maglie was hit freely in early appearances on the mound, the manager decided that the chief difficulty was that the Niagara Falls pitcher's chief stock-in-trade, his curve ball, was failing to "break" effectively in the high altitude. "Just *show* them the curve," Luque advised. "Don't make it too good. And then go to the fast ball. . . .Move the ball around. Pitch to spots, never throw the same thing twice, vary your delivery" (*Baseball Stars, 1952*). Sal, who has often stated that Luque's tutelage was "the best thing that ever happened" to him, heeded this counsel and won 20 games in 1946 and another 20 in 1947. He would doubtless have equalled this record in 1948, but the Pasquels tried to cut salaries and most of the players from north of the Rio Grande rebelled. A few, including Maglie, organized as a barnstorming team under pitcher Max Lanier, and were dubbed the "Mexican jumping beans" by sports writers. They were penalized by Commissioner A. B. ("Happy") Chandler, who suspended them from organized baseball for five years, and closed all regular ball parks in the United States to them, even for exhibition purposes. Their tour ended in a heavy financial loss.

Maglie bought an interest in a Niagara Falls gasoline station late in 1948 but sold out within a few months, and in 1949 supported his wife and himself chiefly by pitching for the Drummondville, Quebec, club of the "outlaw" Provincial League of Canada. He was about to leave for Venezuela for the winter season when on November 10, 1949 he was "reinstated" by Commissioner Chandler who, doubtful perhaps of the outcome of a number of pending damage suits against organized baseball, suddenly decided in June to end the 5 years ineligibility of the former Mexican League Players.

Having rejoined the Giants at their Arizona camp for 1950 spring training, Maglie showed well in exhibition games, but during the first 2 months of the regular season was relegated to the "bullpen" by Leo Durocher, who had succeeded Mel Ott as manager. Sal yielded 5 runs in 33 innings of "relief" before he received on June 25 his first start since his reinstatement. This was against the Cincinnati Reds, who hit 3 home runs off his delivery and sent him down to a 9 to 7 defeat. As a consequence, Sal was not called on to start another game until July 24, when the Giants had lost 9 straight games and Durocher was ready to gamble on any change in his pitching rotation. Maglie proceeded to defeat the St. Louis Cardinals by 5 to 4, after which he surprised Durocher by winning 11 straight games, the last 4 of them "shutouts." This tied a National League record, and on his next appearance on the mound Maglie came within 4 "outs" of topping Carl Hubbell's National League record of 43⅓ scoreless innings racked up in 1933. (In the American League, Walter Johnson of Washington had pitched 56 consecutive scoreless innings in 1913). The snapping of Maglie's streak came at the Polo Grounds on September 13, when Gus Bell of the Pittsburgh Pirates touched him for a home run which hugged the foul line and barely reached the stands. Altogether, Maglie won 18 games for the Giants in 1950, while losing only 4, and his winning percentage of 8.18 was the best in the league. His ERA. was 2.71.

"My formula for pitching winning ball," stated Maglie, "is simply this: pitch 'em high inside and low outside. . . .Pitch him tight inside and he can't get set on you." The "high inside" pitch forces the batter to back away from the plate, or to duck, to avoid being hit. Maglie's admitted use of this strategy offers a convincing explanation of his nickname "The Barber," or one who gives close shaves. Stanley Frank on the other hand, tells us that "in baseball parlance a barber is a guy who talks the ear off a brass monkey," and believes that Durocher applied the term to Sal in ironic allusion to the pitcher's sullen manner and taciturnity. Maglie's new-found success could not, however, be solely attributed to his use of the ethically debatable "duster," for, as Arthur Daley of the New York *Times* observed on May 25, 1952, "the experts will tell you that Maglie has the best curve ball in the big leagues" and "now knows what to do with it and how to control it."

No "flash in the pan" performer, in 1951 he won 23 games (the greatest number in the National League), lost only 6, and pitched the exceptional total of 298 innings. He had a new winning streak of 10 straight victories going when he was defeated by the St. Louis Cardinals in mid-June. The "Barber" was the winning pitcher for the National League in the All Star Game of July 10, and his final victory of the regular season, by 3-0 over the Boston Braves on September 29, was a major factor in bringing the Giants their first pennant since 1937. Tired like the rest of his teammates at the time of the World Series against the New York Yankees, Maglie lost (to Allie

Reynolds) on October 8, his only decision by a score of 6 to 2. "I couldn't get loose," he explained, on being relieved after yielding 8 hits and 4 runs in 5 innings.

In 1952 Maglie won 18 games and lost 8, pitching 216 innings for a 2.91 earned run average. When statistics for the season were released in December it was found that Maglie had the highest lifetime winning average for any pitcher currently active in either major league, with 64 victories and 22 losses and a percentage of .744. In his first regular season mound appearance in 1953 on April 17, Maglie went 6⅔ innings against the Brooklyn Dodgers without giving up a hit. However, due to an injury in the early season. Maglie's record was considerably less than anticipated.

Kathleen Pileggi, a Niagara Falls girl whom the pitcher had known since their schooldays, became Mrs. Salvatore Maglie on May 31, 1941. Her husband has said that she "knows baseball like her own name." Maglie is six feet two inches tall, weighs about 185 pounds, and has brown eyes and hair. Basketball and golf are his favorite forms of recreation.

References

Complete Baseball 3:53 Fall '51 por; 4:30-2 S '52 pors
Look 16:54+ Jl 29 '52 pors
N Y Herald Tribune p21 Je 23 '52
N Y Times V p2 My 25 '52 por
N Y World-Telegram p22 S 12 '52 por
Newsweek 39:97-8 My 19 '52
Sat Eve Post 223:29+ My 5 '51 por
Scholastic 57:26 O 11 '50 por
Sport 11:14+ S '51 pors
Time 56:59-60 S 25 '50 por
Baseball Register (1953)
Reichler, J. Inside the Majors (1952)
Turkin, H. and Thompson, S. C. Official Encyclopedia of Baseball (1950)
Who's Who in Baseball (1953)

MAKINS, SIR ROGER (MELLOR) Feb. 3, 1904- British Ambassador to the United States

Address: b. c/o British Embassy, 3100 Massachusetts Ave., N.W., Washington, D.C.; h. Sherfield Court, Sherfield-on-Loddon, Basingstoke, Hants, England

The new Ambassador from Great Britain to the United States, appointed in October 1952 to succeed Sir Oliver Franks, is Sir Roger Makins, regarded as one of his country's ablest economists, an expert on British atomic policy and "a brilliant career diplomat." A member of Britain's foreign service for twenty-five years, he has since 1948 served as the Deputy Under Secretary of State in the British London Foreign Office. Sir Roger's links with the United States are close; he had two previous regular diplomatic assignments in Washington—from 1931 to 1934 as second secretary of the British Embassy and from 1945 to 1947 as minister in charge of economic affairs. In recent years he was an adviser during three separate sets of discussions in Washington be-

British Inf. Services
SIR ROGER MAKINS

tween high-ranking British and United States officials (1949, 1950, 1952).

Roger Mellor Makins, the eldest son of Brigadier General Sir Ernest Makins and Florence (Mellor) Makins, was born in London on February 3, 1904. A hero of the Boer War, his father, now retired, represented the Knutsford Division of Cheshire in the House of Commons for many years after ending his active service with the army. Roger from 1917 to 1922 attended Winchester School in Hampshire, and then studied at Christ Church College, Oxford, where he took first class honors in history in 1925. That same year he became a fellow at All Soul's College, Oxford; he then read law in London, and was called to the bar by the Inner Temple in 1927. After a brief practice as a barrister, he joined the diplomatic service in 1928 as third secretary in the Foreign Office, London, where he remained until being sent to Washington in 1931 as second secretary of the British Embassy. He was recalled to the London Foreign Office in the late spring of 1934, went briefly on a diplomatic mission to Oslo, Norway, as chargé d'affaires, and returned to the Foreign Office for an eight-year stay. Appointed assistant adviser on League of Nations Affairs in 1937, Makins in the following year was named secretary of the British delegation to the Evian Conference on Refugees from Germany and later in 1938 was made Secretary of the Intergovernmental Committee on Refugees from Germany, a position he held until 1939.

In the post of acting first secretary of the Foreign Office in 1939, he was serving that year as the Foreign Office's principal adviser on League of Nations affairs when World War II began. The next year he was named acting counsellor of the Foreign Office and in 1941 he revisited the United States as adviser to the British delegation to the International Labor

MAKINS, SIR ROGER—*Continued*
Conference in New York City. After being loaned in 1942 to the Treasury to serve on the staff of the Resident Minister in West Africa, Makins in 1943 became assistant to Harold Macmillan, the British Resident Minister (political adviser) at Allied Forces Headquarters, Mediterranean Command, stationed first in Algiers and later in Italy. During the war Makins traveled extensively in West, Central, and East Africa, served as a member of the Advisory Council on Italy, and was made a Companion of the Order of St. Michael and St. George in 1944.

The second of his three regular diplomatic appointments to the British Embassy in Washington came in 1945, when Makins began his two-year assignment there as Minister in charge of economic relations. As such he was named Great Britain's representative on the United Nations Interim Commission for Food and Agriculture, and was adviser to the United Kingdom delegation to the first Conference of the Food and Agriculture Organization meeting in Quebec in late 1945. The following year he was appointed alternate delegate to the fifth session of the Council of the United Nations Relief and Rehabilitation Administration held in Atlantic City, New Jersey, and that December was named British head of the Anglo-American Economic Committee for Germany (he has also served as British chairman of the Anglo-French, Anglo-Italian, and Anglo-Norwegian economic committees). In April 1947 Makins was recalled from his Washington post to become Assistant Under Secretary of State for various economic departments in the London Foreign Office and a year later was promoted to Deputy Under Secretary of State. Through elevation to the rank of Knight Commander of the Order of St. Michael and St. George, he became Sir Roger Makins in 1949.

Having returned briefly to Washington in the fall of 1949, Sir Roger acted as adviser to Chancellor of the Exchequer Sir Stafford Cripps and Foreign Secretary Ernest Bevin in their discussions with American officials preceding Britain's devaluation of the pound. That year he also assumed the chairmanship of the council of ten appointed to guide the British Government on major issues of atomic policy. In January 1950 Makins attended the Conference of Commonwealth Foreign Ministers in Colombo, Ceylon, where the so-called "Colombo Plan" was launched; and later in 1950 he took part in the discussions among Prime Minister Clement Attlee, Ernest Bevin, and the French statesmen René Pleven and Robert Schuman which preceded Attlee's departure for the United States for talks with President Truman.

Sir Roger accompanied the Prime Minister to Washington in December 1950 and that same month took over supervision of the United States Section of the London Foreign Office, retaining this post when the Conservatives under Winston Churchill were returned to power in October 1951. With Prime Minister Churchill and Foreign Secretary Anthony Eden, Makins returned to Washington in January 1952, this time to explore with members of the Atomic Energy Commission the possibility of future Anglo-American exchange of atomic data. (The Atomic Energy Act of 1946 had forbidden the United States to release secret information even to friendly foreign powers.) Also during the early part of 1952 Sir Roger was sent by his Government to Kuwait to investigate the oil situation, which had become a major concern of Churchill's Government after the expropriation of the property of the Anglo-Iranian Oil Company by Iran.

At the time of the announcement on October 3, 1952, of the appointment of Sir Roger Makins to succeed Sir Oliver Franks as British Ambassador to the United States, an Associated Press dispatch characterized the new envoy as a "top-flight economist" and as "one of the brightest stars in Britain's diplomatic service," who is "expected one day to become the permanent head of the British Foreign Office." This choice was interpreted as reflecting the Churchill Government's continued emphasis on economic matters in relations between the two countries. "Sir Roger will be welcomed as an old friend . . . whose experience in many fields of diplomatic activity will be useful in cementing the partnership of Great Britain and the United States," stated a New York *Herald Tribune* editorial. The article went on to say: "It is significant that the backgrounds of both Sir Roger Makins and Sir Oliver Franks contain a strong emphasis on economic matters. . . .Such factors as international trade, the balance of payments and the like are now fully recognized as the strongest potential links between states—as well as the most fruitful subjects of discord—and they demand experts in the top levels of diplomacy."

President Truman accepted Makins' credentials as Ambassador on January 7, 1953. "There is some thought that talks looking toward a new plan for exchanging detailed secret data may be one of the first objectives of Sir Roger . . ." reported Jay Walz in the New York *Times*.

Shortly after Sir Roger's appointment Great Britain exploded its first atomic weapon off the coast of Australia. "Britain," suggested Walz, "wanted to use the demonstrations as an incentive to a renewal of exchange of information on nuclear research and atomic explosion with United States scientists and atomic energy officials."

Speaking in October, 1953 about modern economic problems, Makins stated that it is on American world trade policy that "the future of the western association depends far more than on the sort of arguments we have been having recently about what countries should come to a political conference. . . ." (*Christian Science Monitor,* October 13, 1953).

Sir Roger's permanent home is a 500-acre farm, Sherfield Court, near Basingstoke, in Hampshire, England. American-born Lady Makins, described in the Washington *Post* as a "simple and lovely mother, with six children," is the former Alice Brooks Davis, eldest daughter of the late Colonel Dwight F. Davis of St. Louis, one-time Governor General of the Philippines, Secretary of War under President Calvin Coolidge, and donor of the international tennis trophy, the Davis Cup. The Makins were married in Tallahassee, Florida, on April 30, 1934; their six children are Mary and Cynthia (twins), Virginia, Christopher, James, and Patricia. Sir Roger's London Clubs are the Marylebone Cricket, the Travellers', Brooks', and Pratts'. The British diplomat is six feet four inches in height and has brown eyes; he has been characterized as "affable" and "witty."

References

Christian Sci Mon p2 O 4 '52
Manchester Guardian p5 O 4 '52
N Y Herald Tribune p1 O 4 '52 por;
  II p1 O 5 '52; II p4 O 5 '52
N Y Times p14 Ap 9 '34; p1 O 4 '52 por
Newsweek 40 :42-3 O 13 '52
Time 60 :37 O 13 '52 por
Washington (D.C.) Post p1 O 4 '52
  por; p10 O 5 '52
Debrett's Peerage, Baronetage, Knight-
  age and Companionage (1951)
International Who's Who, 1950
Kelly's Handbook to the Titled, Landed
  and Official Classes, 1949
Who's Who, 1952
Who's Who in America, 1952-53
World Diplomatic Directory (1951)

MICKEY MANTLE

MANTLE, MICKEY (CHARLES) Oct. 20, 1931- Baseball player

Address: b. c/o New York Yankees, 745 Fifth Ave., New York; h. Commerce, Okla.

Early in the 1953 season Mickey Mantle, center-fielder of the New York Yankees, made baseball history by becoming the first player ever to hit a home run over the left-field wall of Washington's Griffith Stadium. Batting right-handed, he struck the ball a distance estimated at 565 feet, one of the longest home runs ever hit in the major leagues. At an exhibition about a week earlier, standing at the other side of home plate, he had hit what was described as the "most spectacular drive" in the 44-year history of Pittsburgh's Forbes Field.

Now playing his third season of major league baseball, Mantle made an unusual leap from a Class C "bush league" team directly to the Yankees in 1951. His speed and power in spring training that year made so strong an impression that he was soon being called "the infant prodigy," "the most talked about young ballplayer in the country," and "the most imagination-stirring youngster to come up with the world champions since Joe DiMaggio." DiMaggio himself said that Mantle was the greatest "rookie" he had ever seen.

Although one of the youngest players in the game, Mickey Mantle is regarded by manager Marty Marion of the St. Louis Browns as the greatest player in organized baseball.

Mickey Charles Mantle (Mickey is his real first name) was born on October 20, 1931 in Spavinaw, Oklahoma, the eldest of the five children of Elvin Clark and Lovell (Richardson) Mantle. (Mantle has two brothers who are twins, Roy and Ray, a third brother named Larry, a sister, Barbara, and a half-brother, Theodore, his mother's son by a former marriage). When he was four, the family moved to Commerce, Oklahoma.

The elder Mantle, who worked in the lead and zinc mines in northern Oklahoma, was a right-handed semi-professional baseball pitcher. Mickey's grandfather, Charles Mantle, a left-hander, had pitched for a mining company team. "I was born and bred to be a big-league baseball player," Mantle has said. The two men trained the boy to be a "switch-hitter" (one who bats with equal ability from either side of the plate), teaching him to bat right-handed against his father's pitching and left-handed against his grandfather's.

Long before Mickey had reached his teens, according to Arch Murray, "he was playing ball from 12 to 14 hours a day, one day after another." He was educated at Central Grade School and at Commerce High School, where he played on the football, basketball and baseball teams. During a football practice session in 1946, he was kicked in the left shin, an accident which caused osteomyelitis (chronic bone infection) and necessitated five operations before the condition was arrested.

In addition to playing on his high school baseball team, Mantle also played for the Whiz Kids, a Ban Johnson League team for youngsters under 21 years of age. An umpire who saw him play in 1949 suggested that he go to the Yankee farm club in Joplin, Missouri, and ask for a tryout. "I walked into the Joplin ball park one day in May, 1949," Mantle has related, "and asked manager Johnny Sturm . . . to give me a chance. Three weeks later, a week after I graduated from high school, Tom Greenwade, the Yankee scout, signed me. I got $1,000. I did not ask for any bonus."

Mantle's initial professional experience was with the Independence team in the Class D Kansas-Oklahoma-Missouri League; his salary was $140 a month. During his first season

MANTLE, MICKEY—*Continued*

(1949) he achieved a batting average of .313 and hit seven home runs.

Invited to try out at Yankee farm school in Phoenix, Arizona, in January 1950, Mantle made a strong impression on "Casey" Stengel, manager of the Yankees. "Hitting right-handed in his first squad game," *Life* reported, "he slammed a home run over the right-field fence. Next time he stepped nonchalantly to the other side of the plate and, as a 'lefty,' whanged out a homer into left field." Stengel afterwards declared: "I believe that Mantle is our biggest prize, and that he is the No. One kid ball player in the professional game."

The following season he was promoted to Joplin, a Class C team in the Western Association, where he played shortstop at a salary of $250 a month. That year his batting average soared to .383 and he struck 26 homers. His fielding, however, was weak; according to his own statement, he made 55 errors. In December 1950 he was classified 4-F by his local draft board because of his osteomyelitis.

Training with the Yankees in the spring of 1951, Mantle batted .402 and led the team with 9 homers. Originally the Yankee management had intended to send him to Binghamton for further seasoning, but "so sensational was the kid," in the words of Arthur Daley, "that the only doubt was whether he'd skip one grade to Kansas City or two grades to the Big Time itself." Mantle's performance soon settled the doubt: he skipped two grades, and won a contract with the Yankees at a salary of about $5400.

His designation as a Yankee regular was without precedent, Dan Daniel pointed out, since the Yankees "started to win pennants in 1921 Never before had a youngster jumped all the way from a Class C club into the ranks of the Bombers." His disqualification for military service was reaffirmed in April 1951.

With only about twenty games as an outfielder to his credit, he opened the 1951 season as a Yankee playing right field. He has expressed special gratitude to Joe DiMaggio and Tommy Henrich, then a Yankee coach, for teaching him to play an unfamiliar position.

At the beginning of the season Mantle continued to impress observers with his speed on the base-paths and occasional displays of exceptional power at bat (his first major league home run, a 450-foot drive, was one of the longest in the 42-year history of Chicago's Comiskey Park), but he was generally ineffective against big league pitching.

On July 15 he was sent to Kansas City on option, subject to recall at 24 hours' notice, to make room on the Yankee roster for Art Shallock, a pitcher bought from Hollywood for $50,000. At the time of Mantle's departure for Kansas City, Stengel said: "Mantle has to learn not to strike out so often. He has to get to bunt better. When he does, there will be none finer." In 40 games at Kansas City, Mantle hit .361, struck 11 home runs and drove in 50 runs.

Rated 4-F a third time by Army doctors at Ft. Sill, Oklahoma, on August 23, he was recalled by the Yankees the next day. His record

in 96 games with the Yankees at the end of the 1951 season was a .267 batting average, 13 home runs, 11 doubles, 5 triples, and 65 runs driven in. He was also, Joe Trimble remarked, "the most-fanned Yankee in history. Mickey went down on strikes 111 times, a figure which . . . surpassed the previous Yankee high of 105 in a season set by shortstop Frank Crosetti in 1937.

In the second game of the 1951 World Series Mantle sprained his right knee while chasing a fly ball; he spent the remainder of the Series in the hospital and for the next few months had to wear a special brace and a weighted boot. This injury was responsible for his fourth rejection for military service in November 1952.

For the 1952 season Mantle's salary was raised to an estimated $8,000. He proved himself to be a greatly improved player, compiling a batting average of .311, the third highest in the American League, hitting 23 home runs, 7 triples and 37 doubles, and driving in 87 runs.

At the age of 21, *Newsweek* observed, Mantle was "already rated by some experts as the strongest lefty-righty hitter in history. . . In 1952 other Yankees still had to scold him for not holding up his head like a Yankee whenever he came off the field . . . but he was now a full-fledged Yankee star, successor to the great Joe DiMaggio in center field and a key man in the club's pennant and World Series triumphs." Mantle was one of the outstanding performers of the 1952 World Series with a batting average of .345; his 10 hits included 2 home runs, a triple and a double.

On February 24, 1953 Mantle signed a contract for the coming season calling for an estimated $18,000. Elevated to the "clean-up" position in the Yankee line-up, he ended the exhibition season with a batting average of .412. On April 17, soon after the opening of the regular season, he caused a sensation by hitting a home run described as "the longest ball ever hit by anyone except Babe Ruth in the history of major league baseball." The ball, which travelled 460 feet on the fly, cleared the 55-foot-high left-field wall of Griffith Stadium in Washington, D.C., bounced off a 60-foot sign, and finally came to rest in the backyard of a house some 565 feet away from home plate. Within the next few days arrangements were made to house Mickey's bat and ball in the Baseball Hall of Fame at Cooperstown, New York. About a week later, Mantle hit a 400-foot home run against the Boston Red Sox, and on April 28, a 484-foot homer against the St. Louis Browns. "Within the next five years," Trimble predicted in the *Saturday Evening Post*, "Mickey should establish himself as the game's top star and reach the $100,000-salary class."

Although Mantle's batting average in the 1953 World Series was only 208, he hit two home runs, one of them with the bases loaded ("a grand slam"), a feat which has been accomplished by only three other players in World Series history.

The young star married the former Merlyn Louise Johnson, his high-school sweetheart, on December 23, 1951. The Mantles have a baby son, Mickey Elvin, born on April 12, 1953. The Yankee center-fielder is five feet eleven inches tall and weighs 185 pounds; he has blue eyes and blond hair. "His physical appearance," according to Gilbert Millstein, "serves to evoke the image, traditional and dear to Americans, of the clean-living country boy grappling, at great odds but ultimately in triumph, with the big city and its perils." A crack shot, he enjoys hunting ducks, rabbits, and quail; he is also a Western movie "fan."

References

Collier's 127:24+ Je 2 '51 pors
Life 30:105+ Ap 30 '51; 33:71+ S 15 '52
Look 16:61+ Ag 12 '52 pors
N Y Post Mag p14 Ap 29 '51 por
N Y Times V p2 Ap 8 '51 por; Mag p23+ Je 3 '51 pors
N Y World-Telegram p35 Ap 17 '51; p37 My 22 '51 pors; p31 My 25 '51; p18 My 26 '51; Mag p11 Ja 17 '53 pors
Newsweek 41:77 Ap 6 '53
Pathfinder 60:32+ My '53 pors
Sat Eve Post 225:31+ Ap 18 '53 pors
Sport Life 5:38+ Ag '52 pors
Sports 4:20+ N '52 pors
Sport Stars 4:67+ N '51 pors; 5:15+ Mr '53 pors
Time 61:64+ Je 15 '53
Baseball Register (1953)

British Inf. Services

PRINCESS MARGARET

MARGARET (ROSE) PRINCESS OF GREAT BRITAIN Aug. 21, 1930-

Address: Clarence House, London, S.W., England

The younger daughter of the late King George VI and Elizabeth, the Queen Mother, of Great Britain, Her Royal Highness the Princess Margaret Rose is today the third in the line of succession to the throne of the United Kingdom of Great Britain and the leadership of the British Commonwealth of Nations. She is preceded only by her nephew Prince Charles and her niece Princess Anne, the children of her sister Queen Elizabeth II and the latter's consort, Philip, Duke of Edinburgh.

Her Royal Highness the Princess Margaret Rose was born at Glamis (pronounced Glahms) Castle, in the Angus County, Scotland August 21, 1930. Announcement of her arrival was greeted with joyous celebration accompanied by bagpiping, for the infant princess was the first child of the blood royal to be born in Scotland since the birth of King Charles I at Dunfermline in 1601. She was the second and last child to be born to Prince Albert Frederick Arthur George, then Duke of York and later King George VI, and the former Lady Elizabeth Angela Marguerite Bowes-Lyon, the third and youngest daughter of the fourteenth Earl of Strathmore and Kingshorne.

Princess Margaret spent her earliest days at Glamis, a medieval stronghold and the hereditary seat of the Earls of Strathmore. This castle is famous in legend and drama as the scene of Macbeth's murder of Duncan. Her childhood was divided, until the time of her father's accession to the throne, between the

Royal Lodge on the grounds of Windsor Castle and the Duke of York's official London residence, 145 Piccadilly.

When she began her lessons, her governess, Marion Crawford, was prompt to note the quickness of her mind. Her studies included arithmetic, readings in the Bible, history, grammar, composition, geography, literature, and poetry. These exercises were continued regularly until her late teens.

Musically talented, Princess Margaret could sing all the tunes from the *Merry Widow* before her second birthday. At the age of seven she began piano lessons under the tutelage of Mabel Lander and attended a singing class at the home of the Countess of Cavan. She soon played and sang duets with her sister.

•For playmates at Red Indians or hop-scotch, the little girls were usually dependent on their governess or their father. They enjoyed few opportunities to make friends in their own age group, even among the children of the nobility. For pets they had several ponies, two Welsh Corgies, two collies, and fifteen blue budgereegahs. When taken to the zoo or the horse show, they were always accompanied by detectives.

Elizabeth and Margaret Rose were respectively eleven and six years old when in December, 1936, their uncle King Edward VIII (now the Duke of Windsor) abdicated, and their father ascended the throne as King George VI. The family then moved to Buckingham Palace.

It was at the coronation of their father on May 21, 1937 that the public at large first saw the sisters in the procession and at the Westminster Abbey ceremony as they stood side by side wearing robes of royal purple, trimmed with ermine and coronets.

In order to bring the princesses in contact with other children of their age, a palace unit

MARGARET, PRINCESS—*Continued*

of the Girl Guides was organized and Princess Margaret became one of the two Brownies attached to her sister's unit. As a Brownie, Margaret competed with such zeal that she soon won an assortment of merit badges. Having learned to swim, at the age of eight she was awarded the Children's Challenge Cup at the Bath Club in London. Her very considerable theatrical talent was manifest in an amateur pantomime given at Windsor in February 1942 in aid of wartime charities, and in which she appeared as Cinderella to her sister's portrayal of Prince Charming. The Princesses spent five years during the war at Windsor Castle with their governess whom they called "Crawfie" and their nurse, Mrs. Clara Knight.

World War II ended approximately one year before Princess Margaret celebrated her sixteenth birthday at Balmoral Castle in Scotland. During this period she fulfilled her first public engagement when she visited the Edinburgh Shelter of the Scottish Children's League of Pity. She became honorary president of the league, and later lent her patronage and name to other charities and public institutions.

She is today the patroness of the Princess Margaret Rose Hospital in Edinburgh, and of the Union of Girls' Schools for Social Service; vice patron of the Royal Albert School; commandant-in-chief of the St. John Ambulance Brigade and a Dame of Justice in the Order of St. John of Jerusalem; and president of the chain of orphanages known as Dr. Barnardo's Homes, the Young Contingent of the Victoria League, and the Sadler's Wells Foundation.

The young princess is also honorary colonel-in-chief of the Highland Light Infantry and certain other regiments. Princess Margaret was created Lady of the Imperial Order of the Crown of India in 1947, and was decorated with the Grand Cross of the Order of the Netherlands when she represented the British royal family at the coronation of Queen Juliana on September 6, 1948. About a year later (April-June, 1949) what was originally intended to be a mere Continental vacation and shopping expedition for the young princess was so played up by the newspapers that it turned into an approximation of a royal goodwill tour of France and Italy, in the course of which Her Royal Highness was received in private audience by Pope Pius. This meeting was objected to by the Protestant Truth Society and the National Union of Protestants in Northern Ireland.

According to *Newsweek* of August 18, 1952, it was widely whispered that some of Princess Margaret's dresses were "too daring," that "she was seen too often and too late in West End night clubs." However, since the death of her father, Princess Margaret has been particularly circumspect.

When she attained the age of twenty-one in August 1951 Princess Margaret received from Parliament an income of her own of $16,800 a year. Upon marriage, this will be increased to $42,000. Legacies which passed to her control have made her independently wealthy.

Princess Margaret's name has been romantically linked by the press with that of the young Marquess of Blandford, the Earl of Dalkeith and Group Captain Peter Woolridge Townsend, son of the late Colonel A. E. Townsend. As an officer of the Royal Air Force, Captain Townsend had won the Distinguished Service Cross in 1941, then in 1944 was transferred to the royal household as an equerry. He had married in July, 1941, and is the father of two sons, the younger a godson of the late King George VI.

The fact that Captain Townsend was divorced (even though the innocent party, according to *Newsweek,* July 27, 1953) would raise a problem if a marriage were considered. The British Monarch is "Defender of the Faith" and technically the head of the Church of England, which has never given formal approval to the remarriage of divorced persons.

Soon after the coronation of her sister, Princess Margaret and the Queen Mother, toured Southern Rhodesia. During their absence, Captain Townsend was reassigned to the British Embassy at Brussels as air attaché, this transfer having been made (it was announced) at his own request. After Princess Margaret's return to London in July, *The Times* of London stated editorially that the belief that Princess Margaret wished to marry Captain Townsend was "based on the flimsiest structure of supposition."

A poll conducted by the London newspaper, *Daily Mirror* had revealed that 96 per cent of 70,000 readers believed that the Princess and Captain Townsend should be permitted to marry if they wished to do so.

The intention of Queen Elizabeth and her consort, the Duke of Edinburgh, to begin a tour of the Commonwealth late in November 1953 had meanwhile raised anew the question of the provisions of the Regency Act of 1937. This Act, which "makes provision for the functions of the Crown to be performed in the absence or incapacity of the monarch" entrusts exercise of the royal authority to a Council of State consisting of "the sovereign's consort and the four adults next in succession" to the throne (New York *Times* July 23, 1953). It does not mention the consort in connection with the formal regency which would become necessary in the event of the Queen's death and the accession to the throne of her heir, Prince Charles, before the age of eighteen.

Thus on July 22, Chairman of the Cabinet R. A. Butler, speaking on behalf of the absent Prime Minister Winston Churchill, announced that the Government would sponsor in the autumn session of Parliament a bill to amend the act of 1937 by not only providing for the inclusion of the Queen Mother in the Council of State but also to designate the Duke of Edinburgh as regent presumptive for his son, in place of the Princess Margaret. (The proposed amendment would in no way affect Princess Margaret's third-place position in the line of succession).

On Princess Margaret's twenty-third birthday, celebrated at Balmoral Castle on August 21, a United Press dispatch mentioned among her dancing partners Lord Carnegie, her twenty-four-year-old cousin; Lord Plunkett; Robert McEwen, and James MacDonald.

Personal data, such as measurements, about the British royal family are never officially released, but it became known through a Parisian dressmaker that Princess Margaret is five feet one to two inches in height, and has a twenty-three inch waistline and weighs about 100 pounds; is petite, brown-haired, blue-eyed and animated. She likes to visit the galleries of the Houses of Parliament, listening to the debates. Charles Hussey in the New York *Times* Magazine, August 2, 1953, commented on Princess Margaret's interest in people. "Like many clever women with strong social gifts," he wrote, "she prefers learning from first-rate minds rather than from books; and there may come a day when she will preside over a literary salon." She reads current fiction, "knows her Jane Austen and her Brontës", likes T. S. Eliot's and Christopher Fry's plays, and enjoys meeting editors and political philosophers and "ready-tongued" writers and dons such as Lord David Cecil, Fellow of New College, Oxford, and author of numerous books of biography and criticism.

Since the accession of her sister to the throne, Princess Margaret has been living with her mother at Clarence House. She has, states Hussey, "a rich girl's collection of records from Bach to jazz."

References

Christian Sci Mon p5 Ap 21 '46 por
Collier's 122:16 Jl 17 '48 por; 128:7 D 29 '51 pors
Coronet 30:57 Jl '51
Ladies Home J 67:35+ Ja '50; 67:40+ F '50; 67:43+ Mr '50; 67:42+ Ap '50; 67:42+ My '50; 67:40+ Je '50; 67: 42+ Jl '50; 67:42+ Ag '50
Life 27:96+ O 31 '49 pors
Look 16:25+ D 2 '52 pors; 16:77+ D 16 '52 pors
N Y Times Mag p14+ Ag 21 '49 pors; p24+ D 10 '50 pors; p13+ Ag 2 '53 por
N Y World-Telegram II p13 Jl 30 '51 por; II p15 Jl 31 '51 por; p21 Ag 1 '51 por; p17 Ag 2 '51 pors; p13 Ag 3 '51 pors
Newsweek 36:39 S 11 '50 por; 38:34+ S 3 '51 por; 40:38+ Ag 18 '52 pors; 42:36 Jl 27 '53 pors
Pathfinder 58:23 Ag 22 '51 pors
Read Digest 56:36+ Je 13 '49; 56:37+ Ja '50
This Week p24+ D 3 '50 pors
Time 52:24 Ag 30 '48 por; 53:26+ Je 13 '49 pors; 62:24+ Jl 20 '53 por
Asquith, C. The King's Daughters (1938)
Crawford, M. The Little Princesses (1950)
Davies, P. Her Royal Highness Princess Margaret Comes of Age (1951)
Robyns, G. Her Royal Highness the Princess Margaret 21st Birthday Album (1952)

MARIN, JOHN (măr'ĭn) Dec. 23, 1872— Oct. 1, 1953 American artist; noted for his animated watercolors and symbolical treatment of the sea; studied at Stevens Institute of Technology, Pennsylvania Academy of Fine Arts, Art Students League of New York, and in Paris; debut as an exhibitor made at Alfred Stieglitz' "291" Gallery in New York City in 1909; one-man show at the Museum of Modern Art in 1936; recipient of Fine Arts Medal of American Institute of Architects in 1948; represented in Metropolitan Museum of Art, Museum of Modern Art, Phillips Memorial Gallery (Washington, D.C.), Fogg Art Museum (Cambridge, Mass), San Francisco Museum of Art, Columbus (Ohio) Gallery of Fine Arts, many European galleries. See *Current Biography,* 1949.

Obituary

N Y Times p21 O 2 '53

MARSHALL, S(AMUEL) L(YMAN) A(TWOOD) July 18, 1900 Editorial writer; military critic

Address: b. c/o The Detroit News, Detroit, Mich.; h. 16861 Gilchrist, Detroit 27, Mich.

A military specialist and reporter during World War II, Brigadier General S. L. A. Marshall was also infantry operations analyst with the Eighth Army in Korea during the Chinese Communist breakthrough of November 1950. His book describing this breakthrough, *The River and The Gauntlet,* (William Morrow & Co., 1953) was acclaimed as "superb reporting on the Korean War" by a New York *Herald Tribune* book critic (June 7, 1953). Marshall began his career as a newspaper man after service in World War I, and became a leading editorial writer and military critic on the Detroit *News* in 1927.

Samuel Lyman Atwood Marshall was born of July 18, 1900 in Catskill, New York, the son of Caleb Carey and Alice Medora (Beeman) Marshall. His father, who was British-born, "was a brickmaker and a good one," Marshall recalls, and his mother was a member of an early American family that dates to Revolutionary times.

Marshall was reared in El Paso, Texas, where he attended El Paso High School and Texas College of Mines (now Texas Western) in that city. While in college he was a member of the football, baseball and basketball teams, and majored in mining. He did not take a degree, however, as he left college to enlist in the United States Army on June 11, 1917.

Promoted to officer-rank at eighteen, Marshall became the youngest second lieutenant in the United States Army during World War I. He participated in the Soissons, St. Mihiel, Meuse-

S. L. A. MARSHALL

Argonne and Ypres-Lys campaigns, and also served as instructor in grenades, gas warfare, bayonets, demolitions and minor tactics.

After serving overseas two years, he was commissioned a first lieutenant in 1921. He resigned this commission, and began his career on November 11, 1922 as a reporter on the El Paso *Herald*. He continued with the *Herald* until September 30, 1927, after service as sports editor and city editor. He also served as a private in the Texas National Guard, from 1922 to 1927.

The young newspaperman became associated with the Detroit *News* on September 30, 1927 as editorial writer and military critic, and worked as foreign correspondent in Latin America for both the Detroit *News* and the North American Newspaper Alliance from 1927 to 1935. When the Spanish Civil War broke out, Marshall went to that country as a war correspondent, covering hostilities from 1936 to 1937.

In June, 1942 Marshall was made expert consultant to the Secretary of War, and on September 28 of that year he formally re-entered military service, was commissioned a major of infantry, and was assigned as Chief of Orientation in the United States Army. While holding this position, Marshall established the Army News Service, and wrote the basic national policy concerning Americans of Japanese blood.

In addition to his duties as Chief of Orientation, he developed the plan for indoctrination of enemy prisoners of war. On August 1, 1943, Marshall was made a lieutenant colonel and transferred to the new Historical Division of the War Department General Staff, where his first task was to make a definitive analysis for the Army, Navy and Air Force of the First Tokyo Raid.

His next assignment, in October 1943, was to the Central Pacific Area, where his duties included the pioneering and development of the tactical and weapons research methods now used in all theaters of war. As Chief Combat Historian, Central Pacific, Marshall served with the Twenty-Seventh Division during the invasion of the Gilbert Islands, and with the Seventh Division during the Marshall Islands invasion.

Transferred to Europe just before the Normandy invasion, Marshall personally covered all airborne operations in that theater. Upon receiving the rank of Colonel, on December 1 1944, he was made Deputy Theater Historian and on April 1 1945 he was named Chief Historian, European Theater of Operations, serving on the staff of the Supreme Commander. He was credited with formulating a procedure of systematized research among captured enemy staff and command officers, which became standard operating procedure in the European Theater.

While in Europe Marshall participated in the Normandy and Brittany campaigns, the Siege of Brest, the Airborne Invasion of Holland, the Ruhr Encirclement and battles in Eastern Germany. He continued on the staff of the Supreme Commander until his return to the United States on January 1, 1946.

Among Marshall's books dealing with these experiences are *Blitzkrieg* and *Armies on Wheels*. Of these the author has said: "In my writing in the military sphere, I started mainly as a disciple of Major General J. F. C. Fuller, the British armored tactician and writer. My early work on armor was a dilation of his ideas and theories, though I often disagreed with him radically."

Marshall left the Army on May 8, 1946, but was recalled to active duty for March through July 1948, to write preliminary staff studies looking to the formation of the North Atlantic Alliance. On November 1, 1950 he was assigned to Korea where he served with the Operations Research Office with G3 and with the Eighth Army as an Infantry operations analyst. In the first year of the Korean war he initiated the Korean Service Corps, and wrote the doctrine on illumination of the battlefield.

When the Chinese Communists intervened in the Korean struggle in October-November of 1950, Marshall was acting as Operations Analyst for the Eighth Army, which was then at the Yalu River, northern boundary of the Korean state. In his book *The River and the Gauntlet*, Marshall tells of the retreat of the Eighth Army before the Chinese Communist forces at the Battle of the Chongchon River. In telling the story Marshall makes use of interviews with participants in the battle, from infantry squad members to generals. His unique method of battle reporting builds up a detailed picture of military action.

In a review of the book in the New York *Herald Tribune* on June 7, 1953 Marguerite Higgins, herself a well-known war correspondent, wrote: "His real triumph is that he has maintained suspense and narrative progression. It is a story of great drama and the impact is all the greater because you know that the death or miraculous escape or grievous wound that claims each character is real. This is how it happened."

Miss Higgins takes issue with General Marshall's attempt to evaluate high policy. ". . . What happened to the Eighth Army at the Yalu River cannot, at least in the opinion of many military experts, be fixed on the Korean Command or General [Douglas] MacArthur, as General Marshall suggests but reverts back to the Communists' maddening ability to mask their intentions."

Marshall's book "has given the best answer of our time to the question, 'What is war with the Reds really like?'" wrote Miss Higgins; its great effectiveness comes from its factual description of "both the mean and the noble."

The author was able, by the use of actual names, to portray a vivid and grim picture of the Korean hand to hand fighting, for example: "Corp. Tracy Young threw his carbine at a Chinese, missed him, then grabbed for the pistol in the enemy's hand, only to find that it was tied to his belt. They grappled and went down. Corp. James White shot the Chinese as he lay on the ground, with Young holding him. Corp. Raymond McDaniles, finding his carbine frozen, used it as a club and felled two of the enemy in his same foxhole."

Marshall was commissioned a Brigadier General on August 1, 1951. Among his other books are *Island Victory*; *Bastogne: The First Eight Days*; *The Load of War*; *Hill 440*, and *Critique of Infantry Weapons and Tactics in Korea*. His articles, chiefly technical studies in professional papers, have appeared in *Combat Forces Journal, Marine Corps Gazette, Military Quarterly* and other periodicals serving the military profession. He also contributes to the *Reporter*, New York *Times Book Review, Collier's* and *Harper's* magazines, as well as lecturing at the National War College, Air University, Armed Service Information School, the Infantry School and the Armored School. He is a member of the Historical Advisory Commission and the Public Relations Commission, Department of Army and is Chairman of the Michigan Military Commission.

His medals and decorations include: Legion of Merit, Bronze Star with Cluster, Citation Ribbon with Clusters, German Occupation WW I, German Occupation WW II, Pacific Theater, Africa-Europe Theater, Korea (USA); Croix de Guerre with Palm, Ordre d'Armee (France), Italian War Cross, Ordre de Leopold with Palm, Croix de Guerre with Palm (Belgium).

Formerly interested in polo and in horse show judging, General Marshall now lists his hobbies as music and the collection of porcelains.

He married Edith Ives Westervelt, of Detroit, and has one son, Sam L. Marshall, Jr. He is a widower. Five feet, five and a half inches tall, Marshall has brown hair and eyes, and weighs one hundred fifty-eight pounds. He has no political affiliation, belongs to the American Legion, the Veterans of Foreign Wars, and is a member of the Episcopal church.

Reference

N Y Herald Tribune Book R p5 Je 7 '53

MARTIN, A(RCHER) J(OHN) P(ORTER) Mar. 1, 1910- Biochemist
Address: b. Physical Chemistry Division, National Institute for Medical Research, Mill Hill, London, N.W. 7; h. Curdworth, Theobald St., Boreham Wood, Hertfordshire, England

One of Great Britain's most noted biochemists and a 1952 Nobel Prize winner in chemistry, A. J. P. Martin is chief of the physical chemistry division of the National Institute for Medical Research at Mill Hill, London, England. He recently devised a gas liquid chromatographic technique for fractionating mixtures and compounds weighing only a hundredth of a gram, which may revolutionize basic research in organic chemistry.

With R. L. Millington Synge, Dr. Martin shared the Nobel Prize for chemistry in 1952 for developing a partition chromatography process capable of separating minute quantities of substances in subtle mixtures. This relatively new field of chromatography, according to H. H. Strain, Carnegie Institution, Washington, D.C., is "destined to influence the life of man and beast the world over."

Archer John Porter Martin was born in London, England, on March 1, 1910, the son of William Archer Porter and Lilian Kate (Brown) Martin. His father was a physician in North London and his mother a nurse. Young Archer was reared in London with three older sisters. He attended high school at the Bedford School in Bedford, graduating in 1929. With the intention of becoming a chemical engineer, he entered Peterhouse, Cambridge University, winning the Exhibition at Peterhouse scholarship. His early majors in college included chemistry, physics, mathematics and minerology.

As a part of his university life, Martin attended Sunday tea parties held by Professor T. B. S. Haldane. In talking with the professor, Martin discovered that his real interest lay in biochemistry, and he changed his major to this field. As an extracurricular activity at college, he joined the Jiu-Jitsu Club. Cambridge University awarded him a B.A. degree in 1932. The following year, from 1932-33, he was a researcher in the physical chemistry laboratory of the university. In an article published in *Nature* (April 16, 1932) and written in collaboration with Nora Wooster, he describes the "Preparation and Mounting of Deliquescent Substances," materials which absorb moisture from the air and gradually become liquid.

Martin began his research in chromatography with R. L. Millington Synge while they were associated at Cambridge University in the early 1930's. Together they searched for a means of isolating the constituents of such mixed compounds as carotene, a ruby-red hydrocarbon found in various plants and a precursor of Vitamin A. They found that the compounds could be "zoned" in a tube packed with porous solids, like starch or cellulose, or silica gel.

The young scientist worked as a researcher in the nutritional laboratory of Cambridge University from 1933 to 1938. He held the Grocers' scholarship for original medical research from 1934 to 1936. For two years, while carrying

Wide World Photos

DR. A. J. P. MARTIN

on his nutrition studies, he worked under Sir Charles Martin, whom he states had the greatest influence on his choice of a career. Describing the "Absorption Spectrum of Vitamin E" in *Nature* (August 11, 1934), with several of his collaborators in the nutritional laboratory, Martin depicts "a sharp, if relatively weak" absorption band in a Vitamin E concentrate of wheat germ oil, first submitted to chromatographic analyses by adsorption on alumina.

The biochemist received his M.A. degree from the University of Cambridge in 1935, and his Ph.D. degree in 1936. Two years later he accepted a position as biochemist at the Wool Industries Research Association laboratories at Torridon, Headingley, Leeds, where he remained until 1946. His work involved studies of felting and amino acid analysis and the composition of wool. In his research, he was again associated with R. L. Millington Synge. Together in a joint article entitled "Volatile Aldehydes Liberated by Periodic Acid from Protein Hydrolysates" (*Nature*, October 12, 1940), the scientists stated that "periodic acid in an aqueous solution of sodium bicarbonate rapidly liberates acetaldehyde from threonine."

During World War II, the technique of Drs. Martin and Synge for isolating constituents of mixtures by "zoning" compounds in a tube packed with porous solids allowed scientists to separate several watersoluble compounds, such as carbohydrates and amino acids. These provided a number of starvation correctives. At the 224th meeting of the Biochemical Society at the Imperial College of Science and Technology, South Kensington, London, on November 7, 1942, Martin reported that "the success of chromatography over simple adsorption is parallel to that of fractionating columns over simple distillation." He advised that to separate very similar substances some magnifi-

cation of the differences in their physical properties is necessary, and that where the properties "involve distribution between two phases, counter-current fractionation achieves this magnification."

In collaboration with Dr. Synge, during studies at the Wool Industries Research Association in 1944, Martin devised paper partition chromatography, in which separations of minute quantities of substances from a mixture are effected on strips or sheets of paper instead of on an absorbent in a glass tube. The new mehod has the advantages of simplicity, rapidity, and high resolving power, and makes possible significant advances in bacteriological and biological research. For their discovery of this technique, Drs. Martin and Synge shared the Nobel Prize in 1952.

For two years, from 1946 to 1948, Martin worked in the research department of the Boots Pure Drug Company, Nottingham, England. With R. Consden and A. H. Gordon he describes in an article entitled "Identification of Lower Peptides in Complex Mixtures" (*Biochemical Journal*, February 1947) the use of "ionophoresis followed by partition chromatography on paper" to distinguish lower peptides in protein partial hydrolysates. He also discusses the apparatus used to remove salts from solutions of amino acids and peptides.

Joining the staff of the Medical Research Council at Lister Institute, Chelsea, London, in 1948, Martin remained with this unit until 1950. His work, among other studies, concerned separation of fatty acids by partition chromatography. He found that the more water present, the more slowly the acid travels down the column. In a joint article with G. A. Howard called "Separation of the C_{12}-C_{18} Fatty Acids by Reversed-phase Partition Chromatography," published in the May 1950 issue of the *Biochemical Journal*, the scientist states "long-chain fatty acids . . . saturated acids having 12-18 carbon atoms have been separated, and mixtures of saturated, unsaturated and substituted acids have been analysed."

Martin accepted a post as a biochemist in the National Institute for Medical Research, Mill Hill, London, in 1950, and is currently head of the physical chemistry division. In the *Annual Review of Biochemistry* (1952), he presents a statement of the various applications of partition chromatography. He reveals its use "for routine control of the medium for diphtheria toxin production and for checking the purity of synthetic peptides."

Paper chromatograms, he affirms, have been used to study sugars in urine and legumes, polysaccharides of cell walls and of soil bacteria. Most amino acids, Martin finds, can be resolved on a single starch column, and paper partition chromatography can be applied to vitamins, hormones, and enzymes. He describes the chromatography of Vitamin B_{12}, the growth factor, on columns of silica and starch, and discusses the identification of Riboflavin, of the Vitamin B complex, in earthworms. "The time seems to be approaching," Martin advises "when a complete inorganic analysis scheme based on paper chromatography can be devised."

The New York *Times* (November 5, 1952), attributes to the development of chromatography by Martin and his co-worker "major advances in the 'sterols.'" These substances include such vital materials in the life processes of animals and plants as cortisone, Vitamin D, sex hormones, bile acids, cholesterol, and plant sterols. The *Times* also states that the new chromatography techniques have led to "the discovery of new antibiotics and amino acids in bacteria" as well as to the "solving of a great variety of other chemical problems."

Carrying his studies to "gas liquid chromatographs," in 1953 Dr. Martin disclosed a method of separating minute quantities of volatile substances by blowing them down a long tube with the light pressure of an inert gas (nitrogen). This technique, he states, can be used to fractionate mixtures and compounds weighing only a hundredth of a gram (New York *Times,* July 23, 1953). It is designed to supersede analytical distillation of the components of a substance at their individual boiling points, which does not permit smaller amounts than a gram of a substance to be used. The gas liquid chromatograph is an adaptation of the paper chromatography technique for which the biochemist received the Nobel Prize, and is based on the stratification of mixed substances into their specific color-reaction groups. The horizontal columns of fine bore glass tubes through which the volatile substances are propelled are heated with a vapor jacket and are packed with celite, a fine claylike material.

Dr. Martin has written a number of articles on chromatography for professional journals. In *Biochemical Journal,* August 1951, he gives an illustration of the application of automatic fraction collector and a conductivity recorder to the analysis of a mixture of penicillin in an article called "Automatic Fraction Collectors and a Conductivity Recorder" which he wrote with A. T. James and S. S. Randall. In this same Journal in July 1951, in collaboration with R. R. Porter, he presents evidence of the existence of Ribonuclease in beef pancreas in two distinct forms in an article called "Chromatographic Fractionization of Ribonuclease."

The biochemist was elected a Fellow of the Royal Society in 1950, and the following year was awarded the Berzelius Gold Medal of the Svenska Läkaresällskapet, the Swedish medical society. With Dr. R. L. Millington Synge, he shared the Nobel Prize for chemistry in 1952, (amounting to 171,134 Swedish crowns—about $32,000), receiving a leather fold containing his diploma, an 8-ounce gold medal, and the prize check from King Gustav VI of Sweden, followed by homage from over 1,000 students of Stockholm University.

A. J. P. Martin married Judith Bagenal, a teacher, on January 9, 1943. Their children are Catherine Vanessa, Paul Archer Nicholas, and Anne Elizabeth. The biochemist has dark hair and blue-grey eyes, stands five feet nine inches tall, and weighs 182 pounds. In politics he professes to be "Liberal to Conservative." Al-

though he states he has no current hobbies, in the past he has enjoyed "Jiu Jitsu, gliding, and mountaineering."

References

N Y Herald Tribune p36 N 7 '52
N Y Times p29 N 5 '52
The Americana (1953)
Who's Who (1952)

MARTIN, WILLIAM C(LYDE), BISHOP

July 28, 1893- Clergyman; organization official
Address: b. 1910 Main St., Dallas, Tex.; h. 4223 University Blvd., Dallas, Tex.

The president of the National Council of Churches of Christ in the U.S.A., Bishop William C. Martin, who was elected to that office in December 1952, was advanced in April 1953 from vice-president to president of the Methodist Council of Bishops, the highest position in his denomination. For seventeen years after his ordination as a minister in the Methodist Episcopal Church (South) in 1921, Martin was a pastor for various congregations in Texas, Arkansas, and Alabama. In 1938 he was made a bishop, presiding over the Pacific Area, the Kansas-Nebraska Area, and, since 1948, the Dallas-Fort Worth Area. A supporter of interdenominational cooperation, he was a delegate to the organizing assembly of the World Council of Churches in Amsterdam in 1948.

William Clyde Martin was born in Randolph, Tennessee, on July 28, 1893, one of three sons of John Harmon Martin, a woods foreman for a lumbering company, and Leila (Ballard) Martin. William, whose brothers died in infancy and whose mother passed away when he was a young boy, spent most of his early years on his grandfather's farm in western Tennessee. Upon graduation in 1913 from high school in Prescott, Arkansas, where he had been a football player and debater, Martin studied for a year at the University of Arkansas. He then attended Hendrix College in Conway, Arkansas; here he chose Latin as his major subject, became a member of the debating society and tennis team, and received his B.A. degree in 1918. During World War I he served in France as a sergeant first class in the United States Army Hospital Corps.

Through his study in 1919 at the University of Aberdeen in Scotland, under Professors David S. Cairns and James Stalker, Martin first became interested in ecumenical Christianity. He returned to the United States to attend Southern Methodist University in Dallas, from which he received his Bachelor of Divinity degree in 1921. That same year he was ordained a minister in the Methodist Episcopal Church (South) and became the pastor of Grace Methodist Church in Houston, Texas. In 1925 he was sent to the First Methodist Church in Port Arthur, Texas, and in 1928 to the First Methodist Church in Little Rock, Arkansas. During this period of pastoral ministry, Martin was chiefly occupied with evangelism.

After seven years as pastor for the 4,000 members of Dallas' First Methodist Church,

BISHOP WILLIAM C. MARTIN

Martin became at the age of forty-four one of the youngest men ever to be made a bishop by the former Methodist Episcopal Church (South). Elected and consecrated on May 3, 1938, by the final General Conference of the Church in Birmingham, Alabama, he left his Dallas congregation to become bishop for the next year (1938-39) of the Pacific Coast Area, which comprised Arizona, the Northwest, Pacific, Western Mexican, and Pacific Oriental Conferences. In 1939 the Uniting Conferences of the newly formed Methodist Church made him bishop of the Kansas-Nebraska Area, with headquarters in Topeka. During this residency he served as chairman of his denomination's first nation-wide Conference on Town and Country, held in 1947 at the University of Nebraska, being chosen for this post because he had long been concerned with the problems of rural churches, and had devoted much time to encouraging small and isolated congregations.

Since 1948 when he was transferred as resident bishop to Dallas, Texas, a stronghold of American Methodism, Bishop Martin has administered the 1,200 Methodist churches in the Dallas-Fort Worth Area. That same year he was one of five Methodist bishops to represent his denomination at the formation of the World Council of Churches in Amsterdam, the Netherlands. He also became chairman of The Advance for Christ and His Church, a Methodist movement which during the last four years has raised $12,000,000 from individual congregations for specific missionary and philanthropic projects not provided for in the denomination's regular budget.

Bishop Martin was a key figure at the Southwestern Convocation of the National Council of Churches of Christ in the U.S.A. in the spring of 1952, and when the council formally opened its second biennial meeting in Denver the next December, Martin's election to the presidency, as reported by the New York

Times, "appeared a certainty." On December 12, 1952, Martin was unanimously elected by the 600 delegates as president of the National Council of Churches for two years, succeeding the Right Reverend Henry Knox Sherrill of Greenwich, Connecticut, Presiding Bishop of the Protestant Episcopal Church. Advocating extension of ecumenical cooperation from the top level to the grass roots, Martin told the assembly, "I am concerned in bringing the services of the council into closer relationship with the local community. . . . This overhead fellowship is delightful and enriching, but there should be elimination of the sense of futility that grows out of the overlapping and duplication of denominational programs on the local parish level" (*Time,* December 22, 1952). Martin also expressed hope that the only two major Protestant denominations not now affiliated, the Southern Baptists and the Missouri Synod Lutherans, would eventually join the National Council.

As President of the National Council of Churches, Martin heads the nation's largest religious organization, representing more than thirty-four million churchgoers, including nearly 70 per cent of Protestants. It was established in 1950 in "an effort to bring under one centralized agency the work of twenty-five Protestant and four Eastern Orthodox bodies in such fields as evangelism, social research, missions, education, and charity" (*Newsweek,* December 22, 1952). In what has been called an "unprecedented move in the history of American Protestantism," the national council continued the work of the former Federal Council of Churches as well as ten other interdenominational agencies. During its first two years the council's program included resettlement of displaced persons, shipment of food and clothing to the needy overseas, sending preachers to college campuses and military bases, working to get the churches' message into motion pictures and on radio, voicing opposition to the appointment of a United States representative to the Vatican, and sponsoring publication of the Revised Standard Version of the Holy Bible.

When the National Council at the 1952 meeting issued a "Letter to the Christian People of America," it was the first time such a broad cross-section of Christian churches had joined in a comprehensive declaration. This message sought to present a Christian answer to questions on schools, government, foreign policy, racial equality, and other matters. The council also set up three goals: to increase church unity at all levels; to deepen "spiritual life" through prayer, Bible study, and teaching; and to enlarge participation of laymen in the church's work. Denouncing certain methods used by Congressional committees in their investigation of communism, the general board of the National Council on March 11, 1953, requested Bishop Martin to appoint a "watchdog" committee to protect American freedom against Communist infiltration and against undesirable methods of combating that infiltration.

President of the Methodist Council of Bishops, since April 1953, Martin also heads the Methodist commission on Promotion and Cultivation, and is a member of his denomination's joint committee on family life and of its board of evangelism, he himself having conducted more than eighty preaching missions during his ministry. Bishop Martin gave the Wilson lectures at McMurry College, published in book form as *To Fulfill This Ministry*. He is a trustee of Southern Methodist and Southwestern Universities, McMurry College, and the Methodist Hospital in Dallas. He belongs to Chi Alpha, Theta Phi, and is a 32d degree Mason and a Democrat. He received his first Doctor of Divinity degree (*honoris causa*) in 1929 from Hendrix College, and since then has received another D.D. degree from Central College, Fayette, Missouri (1947), and the LL.D. degree from Nebraska Wesleyan University, Lincoln, Nebraska (1940), and from Baker University, Baldwin City, Kansas (1944).

Martin married Sallie Katherine Beene on July 1, 1918; they have three children, Donald Hankey, Mary Catherine, and John Lee, and four grandchildren. Bishop Martin is six feet tall, weighs 200 pounds, has dark brown eyes, and graying black hair. A member of the Dallas Athletic Club, Martin was once an energetic hunter and fisherman; now his chief form of exercise is taking brisk walks outdoors for about a half-hour daily. He also enjoys reading, especially biography.

References

Newsweek 40:68 D 22 '52
Time 60:50 D 22 '52
Who's Who in America, 1952-53
Who's Who in Methodism (1952)
World Biography (1948)

MARZOTTO, GAETANO, COUNT Oct. 11, 1894- Agriculturist; industrialist

Address: Valdagno, Italy

In an experiment which has been called "planned capitalism," Count Gaetano Marzotto of Valdagno and Castelvecchio, Italy, has successfully combined management of his inherited century-and-a-half old textile mills with planning for the worker as both a farmer and a factory hand. He has invested millions of dollars to "wed" farm and factory in continuous cycles of production so as to end seasonal unemployment, raise living standards, and thwart the drift toward collectivism.

He has developed over six thousand acres adjacent to his factories in the town of Valdagno in the foothills of the Alps. Here he set up modern farms and settled his workers and their families, spending additional millions for housing and social welfare. When the worker is through in the fields and the harvest is in, he goes to work in the factory.

In May, 1953, the latest in Marzotto's chain of thirty-five "Jolly Hotels" was completed at Avellino, and he has thirty-five more under construction in various parts of Italy. These hotels offer tourists clean, modern accommodations at $2 a night, or $6 including three meals. Among his other projects are a sugar factory,

COUNT GAETANO MARZOTTO

a marble quarry and plant, and a model estate. He is known "as one of Italy's few wealthy men to file a correct tax return. . . .His total income for 1951 is said to be 462 million lire ($704,000) of which the government took 60 per cent" (*Time,* June 1, 1953).

Gaetano Marzotto was born October 11, 1894, in Valdagno, Italy, the only son of Count Vittorio Emanuele and Maria Italia Garbin. His father took an active interest in public affairs and served several terms in the Chamber of Deputies around the turn of the century. Gaetano Marzotto was named after his grandfather (1820-1910), who was the son of Luigi Marzotto, the founder of the textile mills in 1836 in Italy.

The Count's experiment at Valdagno has offered a possible solution to the two major problems of Italy: unemployment and communism. Italian industrialists are watching these unorthodox investments closely, not a little skeptical that they can be made to pay.

Valdagno, set picturesquely against the rising mountains, with every improvement from modern farms to company-owned super-markets, is a town of 14,000 reminiscent of the Villages of Unity of the Robert Owenites of England, and New Harmony, Indiana and Hershey, Pennsylvania. The town has its textile mills, modern housing units, a nursery for pre-school age children of working mothers, a pre-natal clinic, a maternity hospital, an industrial training school, a workers' club, a home for the aged, swimming pools, a two-thousand seat theatre, a stadium and a music school.

Next to Valdagno, on the Marzotto acres of modern farms, an entire new village has gone up, which Marzotto has called Villanova. The village is a colony of double houses with modern plumbing, a good-size plot for each house for vegetables and flowers, and a central barn to house all live stock. The farms have tractors in place of oxen, and the sickle and flail

MARZOTTO, GAETANO—*Continued*

have given way to threshing machines and mechanical mowers.

At vacation time, the 13,200 workers of Valdagno go to company resorts, one in the mountains and another on the sea north of Venice, with their families to spend three weeks of vacation with pay at a cost of sixty cents a day per person. These resorts reportedly cost Marzotto $3,000,000.

However, while all this is conceived on sound social lines, the similarity to the Owenites and the Owenite Utopian Socialism ends here. Marzotto declared in the *Rotarian,* February 1951, "All my industrial and agricultural schemes have a strictly economic basis, the only new thing about them is their social aspect—but each must pay."

Marzotto does not believe in the 40-hour work week, or 2080 hours—the theoretical work capacity for 52 weeks, but rather a total working year of 1800 hours, a figure arrived at empirically as the time a worker actually puts in after allowing for illness and other absence. In all the Marzotto establishments a worker may work eight or more hours a day, plus a 35 per cent incentive bonus for increased output, but his basic work year remains 1800 hours, or 35 hours a week.

He has said (*Washington Post,* August 28, 1949), "A worker should have the maximum possible time for self-betterment, vacation and medical attention. He cannot have it on the 40-hour week basis. If production is carefully planned on the 1800-hour system, overtime is obviated, more jobs are created and labor, able to take more time off without loss of income in slack times, becomes more efficient."

While textile factories comprise his major holdings, he also has a sugar mill in Villanova and encourages farmers to grow beets. Likewise, the farmers added flax to their products as raw materials for a new linen mill and a new source of income.

For the growing population of Valdagno there is a Marzotto milk and cheese industry and a dairy capable of processing the output of Marzotto's herd of 2000 cattle, from prize breeding stock which were flown from Canada. The retail prices are reasonable and the investment is paying.

Another ambitious project involves the reclamation of 750 acres of marshland requiring an investment of five million dollars. Marzotto has acquired surplus landing barges ready to transport his herds to the several islands which will be formed in the swampland.

Production in Valdagno and in his factories in Pisa and Manerbio is at a peak of 50,000 yards of cloth a day. With dollars earned by exports to the United States, he imports Texas cotton to work a new cotton mill in nearby Concordia and absorb surplus labor.

The origin of Marzotto's farm-factory scheme as an economic remedy goes back nearly twenty years. In 1934 he left on a two-year cruise of the world and while travelling in strange lands formulated in his mind the outline of his unique project. On his return he acquired the land of the countryside of Valdagno but took no further action. In 1943, with the

Nazis in pursuit, he lived in hiding with peasants who fed him. He realized then, he said, what a peasant's life is like. At the end of the war he began his new enterprises.

He despises communism as much as idleness and inefficiency. Communism, he says, can be beaten by preventing unemployment and poverty and by providing workers with the things essential to their social and physical welfare. Italy's Communist labor leader and head of the General Confederation of Labor has seized upon this theme to declare (*Washington Post*) to industrialists and landowners, "You, too, should do what Marzotto has done and it is your obligation to invest your capital and use it for the welfare of society. Then if you should refuse, we would be obliged to do it ourselves."

In the general election of 1948 the Communists of Valdagno polled only 8 per cent of the vote compared to 50 per cent in a nearby industrial community of the same size.

Marzotto has pursued a tradition in his family of keen interest in public affairs. He is the author of two books: *Panorama della Ricostruzione* and *Problemi Economici e Pacificazione Sociale* (French edition (1948) *Relévement dans la Liberté*). These writings show a highly constructive and very critical approach to the policies of the Italian government in the economic and administrative field. In them he also shows he is a student of the American and British economies.

The Count's decorations include Cavaliere della Gran Croce and Cavaliere del Lavoro. He is a Knight of Malta, an executive officer of the Italian Manufacturers' Association, and charter member of the Rotary Club for his native province. Marzotto is the father of five sons.

The Count may not be the richest man of Italy but is counted among the top ten. In 1951 he filed the highest tax return in Italy under the United States income tax system adopted that year. He believes the tax on income is too hard to apply and claims the old system of a tax on appraisal of income and assessment thereon is preferable as it would penalize other rich men who allow their funds to be idle or who leave the country.

"They call us paternalistic," Marzotto was quoted in *Time* (June 1, 1953) as saying. "It is an ugly word. But we are proud of our paternalism. . . .It's good business, for one thing. But then, too, when I die I want it said of me that I did some good on this earth. Besides, I want to show those numskulls down in Rome—and the skeptics abroad—that some Italians are efficient. I want to make democracy work. That's the only real way to beat the Communists."

References

Rotarian 78:17+ F '51
Annuario d'Italia (1937)
Chi è? (1948)
Dizionario Enciclopedico Labor (1950)
Italia e gli Italiano di Oggi (1947)

MASTERS, KELLY RAY *See* Ball, Z.

MATISSE, HENRI (EMILE BENOIT)
(mȧ-tēs', äN-rē') Dec. 31, 1869- Artist
Address: b. c/o Pierre Matisse Gallery, 41 E.
57th St., New York 22, N.Y; h. 132 Blvd.
du Montparnasse, Paris; Excelsior Hôtel Ré-
gina, 1 Place Charles Felix, A. M., Nice,
France

NOTE: This biography supersedes
the article which appeared in
Current Biography in 1943.

Once the highly controversial leader of a
group of painters castigated under the title,
"wild beasts," Henri Matisse, now in his eighty-
fourth year, is still at work, and is an acknowledged master of modern French art.

Although Matisse actually started to paint
in 1890, it was not until 1905, while with
the fauve group, that he won recognition. Since
that time his reputation as a colorist and decorative easel and mural painter has spread
throughout the world, and he has also made
significant contributions as a sculptor, graphic
artist, illustrator of books, and designer for the
ballet. As the culminating achievement of his
career, he completed in 1951, at the age of
eighty-one, the design and decorations for the
now famous Dominican chapel in Vence, France.
It has been estimated that Matisse has painted
over 2,000 canvases.

Henri Emile Benoît Matisse was born in
Le Cateau-Cambrésis, a small town in the north
of France, on December 31, 1869. His father
was a fairly successful grain merchant; his
mother was artistically inclined, and painted
china. After attending the *lycée* in nearby St.
Quentin, young Henri was sent to Paris in
1887 to study law. Two years later he returned
to work as a clerk in a St. Quentin law office.
Shortly thereafter he began taking a course in
drawing at the École Quentin de La Tour, and
it was while convalescing from an illness in
June 1890 that he attempted his first oil painting, *Nature morte aux livres*.

Despite his father's objections, Matisse eventually decided to abandon a law career, and in
the winter of 1891-92 set out for Paris to study
art. He worked briefly in the class of Bougue-
reau and Gabriel Ferrier at the Académie
Julian, then entered the studio of the more liberal Gustave Moreau at the École des Beaux-
Arts and remained his pupil for five years
(1892-97).

During this period the young artist spent
much time making copies of the old masters in
the Louvre; several were purchased by the
French Government for provincial museums.
His original work drew inspiration from Char-
din and consisted mostly of conventional still
lifes and interiors painted in dark tones. In the
spring of 1896 Matisse exhibited for the first
time at the Salon de la Nationale and won sufficient attention to be nominated a member of
this conservative group.

Matisse soon turned his back on the promising career of an academic painter and began
to explore the more advanced art of his own
time. During the summers of 1896 and 1897
he painted in Brittany and adopted the brighter
palette of the impressionists. His first major

Wide World Photos
HENRI MATISSE

work, *La desserte,* was an impressionist canvas that offended the conservatives at the Salon
de la Nationale of 1897.

In January 1898, Matisse married Amélie
Payrayre, and they spent the rest of the year
in Corsica and the south of France. On his return, he worked from the models at the Académie Carrière. Early in 1899 he tried his hand
at the pointillist technique of Seurat and the
neo-impressionists, but from then on the influence of Cézanne was dominant. The vigorous
drawing and bold color of his work between
1899 and 1901 anticipates his later experiments.

This phase was followed by the so-called
"dark" period (1901-03), when he reverted to
a more somber, disciplined, and realistic manner. He sold few canvases, and his wife had
to open a hat shop to help support the family.
Matisse began exhibiting regularly at the jury-
free Salon des Indépendants in 1901. The next
year he participated in a group show at Berthe
Weill's gallery, and in 1903 sent paintings to
the newly founded Salon d'Automne. His first
one-man show was held at Ambroise Vollard's
in June 1904 but without conspicuous success.

During the summer of 1904, Matisse suc-
cumbed to the pointillist technique for a second
time and returned to a high-keyed palette. His
most celebrated canvas in this style is *Luxe,
Calme, et Volupté*. Within a year, however,
he renounced pointillism, and in the summer of
1905 began building his pictures with broad
planes of pure color applied with greater
variety and freedom in relation to natural appearance than ever before.

At the historic Salon d'Automne of 1905
he exhibited these new canvases along with
those of a group of younger painters who
looked to him as their leader. The group eventually included Georges Rouault and Albert
Marquet (who had been Matisse's fellow students in Gustave Moreau's atelier), André

MATISSE, HENRI—*Continued*

Derain, Maurice de Vlaminck, Raoul Dufy, Othon Friesz, Kees van Dongen, and Georges Braque. Dispensing with perspective, the rendering of volumes, and illusionist chiaroscuro, the group employed strident colors straight from the tubes, used a bold and carefree brush technique, and made willful distortions and simplifications of forms. Their work outraged the public, and prompted one critic to call them "Les Fauves," or the wild beasts.

Although denounced as "the Apostle of the Ugly," Matisse managed to sell one of his new paintings, *Femme au chapeau*, to the Stein family (Gertrude, Leo, Michael and his wife Sarah), who became his first important patrons. Later, the Steins bought *Bonheur de Vivre* (1905-06), which is generally regarded as Matisse's fauve masterpiece and one of the landmarks in the development of modern painting. Among his most celebrated fauve canvases are *Portrait a la raie verte, Le jeune marin I* and *II, Portrait de l'artiste, Le nu bleu, Nature morte bleue,* and *Le luxe I* and *II*.

By 1908, the cubists, under the leadership of Picasso and Braque, had supplanted the fauves as the most *avant-garde* group of painters in Paris. Matisse went his own way, developing new concepts from fauvism and perfecting his flat decorative style. In January, 1907 he opened an art school, which attracted many foreign students during the three years he taught there. The first exhibitions of his work in New York, London, Moscow, and Berlin were held in 1908.

His reputation grew steadily, and within the next five years he became internationally famous as one of the two leaders of the modern movement in painting. His style during this postfauve period (1908-13) alternated between excessive elaboration and extreme simplification. The tendency to all-over decorative patterning is typified by works like *Harmonie rouge* (1908-09) and *Nature morte aux aubergines*.

In contrast, he painted a series of compositions in which simplified, unmodelled nude figures were set against a monochrome background. What is probably his most famous work, *La danse* (1910), was painted in this simplified style and depicts a circle of red dancers against a blue background. This "overpowering climax of luminosity" and its pendant *La Musique* (1910) had been commissioned for the palace of Sergei Shchukin, a Moscow businessman who replaced the Steins as Matisse's foremost patron at that time.

During these years, Matisse visited Algeria (1906), Italy (1907), and made three trips to Germany (1908-10). The winter of 1910-11 he lived in Spain and the latter half of 1911 he journeyed to Moscow. But the experiences which had the most stimulating effect on his art, and inspired new form and color in his painting, came during the two winters (1911-12 and 1912-13) he spent in Morocco. There he painted the gardens, figures in native costume, and the most admired of his Moroccan pictures, *Café Maure*. Although Matisse showed an interest in Japanese prints, Negro sculpture, and the work of the Sienese primitives, it was Near Eastern art, with its flat patterns, brilliant col-

ors, and profusion of ornament, that exerted a stronger influence on him.

Describing the effect of Matisse's trips to North Africa on his works, Janet Flanner commented, "Matisse is a complex mixture of hot and cold—a mélange of his dominant stabilizing intelligence and the flaming, luminous sensibilities of his genius as a colorist—and the quasi-Orientalisms of Tangier and Marrakech gave his brain and eyes what he needed for his balanced excess. His mastery of this controlled extravagance became his typical style" (*New Yorker,* December 22, 1951).

The period from 1913 to 1917 represents a new phase in Matisse's development, during which he produced works severe in style, somber in color, and austere in spirit (*Femme au tabouret, Mlle. Yvonne Landsberg*). Stimulated by the cubists to a renewed study of the architectonics of painting, Matisse experimented with abstract design, vertical construction, and quasi-geometrical forms, but he never completely adopted the cubists' technique. In the opinion of some critics, the monumental canvases of 1916-17 (*Les Marocains, La leçon de piano,* and *Jeunes filles au bain*) are "perhaps the greatest of Matisse's career as a painter."

At the end of 1916 Matisse left Paris to live for the greater part of each subsequent year in Nice. The gradual softening of his style which begins to take place at this time is evident in *Les trois soeurs* and *La leçon de musique*. During this so-called "Nice period" (1917-29), he turned to an intimate, decorative, and more conventionally realistic style.

Among his major achievements are *Intérieur au violin* (1917-18) and *Le thé* (1919), but more representative are *Les plumes blanches* and the popular series of odalisques. In the summer of 1920 and 1921 Matisse painted at Etretat on the Normandy coast. The Luxembourg Museum purchased one of his paintings, *Odalisque,* in 1921. Four years later he was made a chevalier (later a commander) of the Legion of Honor.

Matisse's *Compotier et fleurs* received the first prize at the 1927 Carnegie International Exhibition in Pittsburgh. A short period of renewed experiment (1926-27) resulted in such vigorous works as *Odalisque au tambourin* and *Figure décorative sur fond ornemental*. He visited the United States in 1930 and served on the jury of the Carnegie Exhibition of that year.

Also in 1930, Matisse traveled to the South Seas and spent three months in Tahiti. Later that same year, Dr. Albert C. Barnes, the foremost American collector of Matisse's paintings, commissioned him to do a mural decoration for the private museum of the Barnes Foundation in Merion, Pennsylvania. Choosing the dance as his subject, he painted eight stylized figures in three flat colors on an area covering fifty-three square yards. After *The Dance* was completed in 1932, it was discovered that an error in measurement had been made. Matisse then began all over again on a new design that was finished and installed the following year.

A commission of almost equal importance was to provide the illustrations for a new edition of Mallarmé's *Poésies* (1932). Between

1929 and 1934, Matisse did little easel painting, but during the latter half of the decade he produced a series of flat, decorative rather abstract figure paintings (*Nu rose, Grande robe bleue—fond noir, La Musique*), executed in very bright and gay colors, and displaying elegance and even a certain *chic.*"

After the German occupation of France in 1940, Matisse remained in Nice for three years, then retired to the nearby town of Vence, settling in Nice again in 1949.

Confined to his bed since undergoing a serious operation in 1941, Matisse works continually, "driven by the feeling that there is little time for all the work he still wants to do," reported Janet Flanner in the *New Yorker* (December 29, 1951). When he wishes to work on very large designs, he stands up or sits in a wheelchair, using a ten-foot bamboo pole that has a crayon attached to its tip, manipulating this giant pencil across paper tacked on the wall. Describing his manner of working, the writer said "It is a heroic performance."

The painter has also been making experiments with abstract compositions formed by cutting and pasting brightly colored papers. In the past twelve years Matisse has not only enjoyed a "brilliant late flowering of his art" but has captured the esteem of the younger generation of French painters. Critics have ranked his 1948 canvases, *Intérieur au rideau egyptien, L'ananas* and *Le grand intérieur rouge,* among his most audacious creations.

However, the work that Matisse considers his masterpiece is La Chapelle du Rosaire, in Vence (1947-51). The artist's participation in this undertaking has been attributed to the nurse who had cared for him during his illness. Shortly thereafter she became a Dominican nun, and when her order planned to build a new chapel in Vence she consulted Matisse about the designs for the stained glass windows. He became interested in the project and eventually took over the design and decoration of the entire chapel, in every detail. The ambitious project offered Matisse the opportunity to preserve his art in a form more permanent than canvas, and the Church the opportunity to use contemporary art as it had in earlier times for its buildings. The result is a gay white-and-black modern chapel in which the stained glass windows in blue, yellow and green display typical Matisse patterns.

At the 25th Venice Biennale Art Exhibition in June 1950, Matisse was awarded the million-lire first prize for painting.

The three largest collections of his over 2,000 canvases belong to the Museum of Modern Western Art, in Moscow; the Statens Museum for Kunst, in Copenhagen; and the Albert C. Barnes Foundation in the United States.

Other collectors of Matisse's paintings are Mme. Paul Guillaume; Paul Rosenberg; Pierre Matisse; the Musée d' Art Moderne (Paris); and others. The Museum of Modern Art in New York owns eight oils by Matisse, ten sculptures and six drawings.

In the opinion of the noted critic Roger Fry, Matisse's outstanding gifts are "an astonishing sense of linear rhythm," "an impeccable sense of color harmony," and his "almost uncanny" control of color in pictorial depth. Of the French critics, all those who originally condemned Matisse's paintings at the fauves exhibition now admire his work, with the exception of Camille Mauclair. Some critics hail his genius as a colorist, and as a draftsman, but feel that the plastic limitations of his decorative, two-dimensional work prevents him from achieving the highest rank as an artist.

As part of his general preoccupation with problems of form and structure, Matisse has frequently turned his attention to sculpture. Under the influence of Bayre and Rodin, he created his first works in 1899. The following year he worked at night at the École de la Ville de Paris and studied briefly with Bourdelle. The majority of his fifty or so pieces of sculpture date from the period 1900-1912 or the late 1920's. Among his best known works are *Le serf, Nu couché, La Serpentine, Nu assis,* the five studies of the head of *Jeannette,* and the three versions of *Nu de dos.*

Throughout his career, Matisse has produced thousands of drawings and his mastery of draftsmanship is said to be unequalled by any other artist of his generation. The scope of his graphic art ranges from etchings and dry points to lithographs, monotypes, and woodcuts. Books which he has illustrated include Joyce's *Ulysses* (1935); de Montherlant's *Pasiphaé* (1944); Reverdy's *Visages* (1946); Alcaforado's *Les lettres portugaises* (1946); Rouveyre's *Repli* (1947); *Florilège des Amours de Ronsard* (1948); and *Poèmes de Charles d'Orléans* (1950). Matisse was responsible for the sets and costumes for Stravinsky's *Le Chant du Rossignol* for the Diaghilev Ballet in 1920, and for the Ballet Russe de Monte Carlo production of *Rouge et Noir* in 1939. He has also made designs for tapestries, linen hangings, glass, rugs, and ceramics.

Jean Cassou, curator of the Musée d'Art Moderne in Paris, has written, "Matisse never ceases to make his art live and palpitate, guiding it along difficult paths, continually and mercilessly criticizing himself . . . knowing how to keep his work flourishing, fertile, charming and luminous."

In "Notes d'un Peintre," an article published in 1908, Matisse stated: "What I dream of is an art of balance, of purity and serenity devoid of troubling or depressing subject matter, an art which might be for every mental worker, be he businessman or writer, like an appeasing influence, like a mental soother, something like a good armchair in which to rest from physical fatigue."

Matisse has confined himself to a limited range of subject matter—most often figure compositions of young women, clothed or nude; studio interiors; still lifes; and less frequently, portraits and landscapes—but treated "every time with new and daring plastic variations" (Alexander Room).

The artist has three children: Jean, a sculptor; Pierre, the New York art dealer; and Marguerite, who is married to the art critic, Georges Duthuit, and is herself a painter. A heavy-set man who looks more like a professor than an

MATISSE, HENRI—*Continued*

artist, Matisse has blue-gray eyes, a short clipped white beard, and wears thick-lensed glasses. His personality has been described as strong-willed, serious, and reserved. Although he can be up and about for only a few hours each day, he paints and draws while in bed and is thus able to maintain his lifelong habit of working from morning to night. His hobbies used to be playing the violin, rowing, and horse-back riding.

In *Matisse, His Art and His Public* (1951) published by the Museum of Modern Art, A. H. Barr, has written: "In a world grown dark with fear and muddy with lies, Matisse has sought truth and serenity by transforming his delight in the visible world into works vigorous in form, joyous in color."

References

> Art N 47:16-31 Ap '48; 50:34-81 Ann 21:40+ N '51 pors
> New Yorker 27:30-2 D 22, 26·8 D 29 '51
> Barnes, A. C. and de Mazia, V. The Art of Henri Matisse (1933)
> Barr, A. H., Jr. Matisse: His Art and His Public (1951)
> Diehl, G. Matisse (1951)
> Dictionnaire Biographique Français Contemporain (1950)
> Fry, R. Henri Matisse (1930)
> International Who's Who (1952)
> World Biography (1948)

MEDINA ANGARITA, ISAíAS July 6, 1897—Sept. 15, 1953 Former President of Venezuela; elected President of Venezuela in April, 1941 and ousted in an Army revolt in October, 1945; born at San Cristóbal, the son of Gen. José Rosendo Angarita de Medina; rose rapidly in the Venezuelan Army, made Chief of Staff in 1935; appointed Minister of War and Navy in the Government of President Eleazar López Contreras; resigned in 1941 from the Cabinet to campaign successfully for the Presidency; elected to serve for a five year term and elevated to Division General, the second highest rank in the Army; instituted democratic reforms; cooperated with the Allies in World War II; overthrown by military revolution in October, 1945 and exiled for seven years, but returned to Venezuela in 1952. See *Current Biography*, 1942.

Obituary

N Y Times p33 S 16 '53

MENDELSOHN, ERIC Mar. 21, 1887-
Architect

Address: b. 627 Commercial St., San Francisco 11, Calif.; h. 2423 Leavenworth St., San Francisco 11, Calif.

> *Bulletin:* Eric Mendelsohn died on September 15, 1953.

Since the construction of the famed Einstein Tower at Potsdam in 1920, Eric Mendelsohn has had one of the most important places in the modern movement in architecture. His work has been described as grandiose and monumental in style but in the modern idiom, and his buildings show an imagination of concept so that, although functional, they avoid the severity of some functionalism.

Eric Mendelsohn was commissioned, with sculptor, Ivan Mestrovic, to design a memorial in New York City to the 6,000,000 Jewish martyrs slain in Europe. The design had been approved by the City Art Commission and the foundation stone was laid for the monument on Riverside Drive at 83rd Street in October, 1947.

The architect's first designs were executed in his native Germany, where he was considered a member of the German expressionist movement; his most notable work of this period consisted of plans for industrial plants and department stores. In 1933 he left Germany and for the next seven years worked in England and Palestine, producing in the latter country designs highly praised for their expression of the national character. He came to the United States in 1941, set up his office in San Francisco in 1945, and has designed a number of important buildings in that city. Among these are the Maimonides Health Center, a typical example of the simplification and lightening of Mendelsohn's designs which occurred in his later years. In addition to the Health Center, whose tiers of white iron balustrade have been described as floating in air, is the impressive Russell residence, also in San Francisco. In recent years, too, Mendelsohn has given lectures in architecture at the University of California at Berkeley.

Born in Allenstein, East Prussia, Germany on March 21, 1887, Eric Mendelsohn is the son of David and Esther (Jaruslawsky) Mendelsohn. His father was a merchant and also took a leading part in public life, and his mother was a milliner and a musician. As a boy he was interested in architecture, art, politics, and Greek, particularly Plato, and was the organizer and critic of a "Beethoven Circle", a club to which admittance was granted only on the playing from memory of one of Beethoven's last sonatas.

Mendelsohn began his college education at Munich in 1907 but he soon changed to architecture and received the degree of Master of Arts by the University of Munich in 1911. Among his friends he numbered the Russian and German expressionist painters Wassily Kandinsky, Franz Marc, Paul Klee, and Hugo Ball, and he was active in an expressionist theatre. In the spring of 1914 he began a series of sketches which he continued throughout his war service and which showed interest in the architectural use of steel and reinforced concrete. His early drawings, stated the *New Yorker* (January 3, 1942), were done in "a sort of cyclopean baroque style patterned on the actual forms of machines themselves."

During World War I Mendelsohn served with the Corps of Engineers of the German army at the French and Russian fronts. He set up his office as an architect in Berlin on November 7, 1918. His first design to be constructed was for a hat factory owned by Hermann and Company at Luckenwalde. The Einstein Tower at Potsdam, completed in 1920, was his second commission and is one of the best-known modern structures in the world. The building, which was used as an observatory and astro-physical laboratory for experiments connected with Dr. Albert Einstein's theory of relativity, displays the sweeping curves which identify much of Mendelsohn's work.

The Administration building of the Berliner Tageblatt, twin residences at Charlottenberg, a silk store at Gleiwitz, Silesia, and a power station at Wuestegiersdorf, Silesia were among Mendelsohn's commissions in 1921 and 1922. In 1923 he went to Palestine in connection with the Ruthenberg electrification project and won first prize in competition for a design for a business center at Haifa.

A journey to the United States in 1924 provided an opportunity for Mendelsohn to study the architecture of skycrapers, and he made many sketches embodying his theories of the manner in which the form of these buildings should express their function. In the period following, an important part of the architect's time was devoted to department store design, using cantilevered facades and with a strong horizontal emphasis. Another feature was the use of curved glass stairhalls. His designs were used for the Schocken Department Stores at Nuremberg, Stuttgart, and Chemnitz, the Herpich Fur Store of Berlin, the Petersdorff Department Stors of Breslau, and the Epstein Department Store at Duisburg.

Other Mendelsohn constructions of the 1920's were a "Three Patriarchs" Lodge at Tilsit, East Prussia, a textile factory in Leningrad, a cemetery at Koenigsberg, the "Deukon House" at Berlin, a power station for the Berliner Tageblatt, the Mosse Pavilion for the Presse Exhibition at Cologne, the Universum Cinema of Berlin, a block of flats in Berlin, and the Metalworkers Union Administration Building in Berlin.

Town plans for Lindenstreet and Alexanderplatz were two of the many projects designed by Mendelsohn in the 1920's and 1930's which give evidence of his interest in city planning. The Columbus House in Berlin, the Youth Center at Essen, and Mendelsohn's own house, "Am Ruperhorn", at Charlottenberg, were completed in the 1929-1930 period. At this time the architect also won first prize for a design for the Cathedral Square at Magdeburg and he travelled in France, Spain and Greece.

In the early nineteen-thirties Mendelsohn designed a General Electric power station and a zinc factory in Germany, and two department stores in Ostrowa, Czechoslovakia and in Oslo, Norway. He also won first prize for his design of the Berlin Passenger Transport Company's Administration Building.

Mendelsohn left Germany for Holland the day that Hitler came into power in 1933. Reaching England, he worked in London for a time with Serge Chermaveff. Buildings of this period are the Nimmo residence at Chalfont St. Giles, the Dennis Cohen residence in

ERIC MENDELSOHN

Chelsea, and the De La Warr Pavilion at Bexhill on the Sea, the design for which took first place in competition.

Mendelsohn also designed various buildings for construction in Palestine and went to live in that country in 1937; many consider his most important work to exist there. "Mendelsohn's triumph [in Palestine]," says the *Architectural Review* of February 1940, "is that he has designed *monumental* buildings, incorporating all the up-to-date European building techniques . . . but native in spirit at the same time."

His work expressed the national atmosphere and cultural traditions of Palestine in modern terms without resorting to eclecticism. Another feature of his designs is their close relationship to the natural environment, a quality well illustrated by the University Medical Center on Mount Scopus, which is "balanced in composition, powerful in its sweeping horizontals, a dramatic conception beautifully adapted to the irregular site." (*Architectural Forum*, December 1936).

In his three years in Palestine Mendelsohn also designed Chaim Weizman's residence at Rehoboth, the house and library of Salman Schocken, the Hadassah-Rothschild University Medical Center, the Anglo-Palestine Bank in Jerusalem, the Trade School at Yaguri, the Hebrew University Agricultural College and the Daniel Wolff Pharmaceutical Institute at Rehoboth, and the British Government Hospital at Haifa.

After immigrating to the United States in 1941, Mendelsohn settled in New York and until 1945 lectured at Columbia, Yale, Harvard, and the University of Michigan. He served as consultant to the War Department in Washington, D.C. from 1942 to 1944. In 1945 he moved his residence to San Francisco, California where he became associated with

MENDELSOHN, ERIC—*Continued*
John Dinwiddie and Albert H. Hill. He became an American citizen in 1946.

His executed designs of this period include synagogue-community centers for St. Louis, Cleveland, Baltimore, Grand Rapids, St. Paul, and Dallas. He also designed the electronic plant for Palo Alto, the radiation laboratories for the University of California at Berkeley, and the Maimonides Health Center in San Francisco.

In summing up Mendelsohn's work, an article in the *New Yorker* (January 3, 1942) states, "He has assimilated the innovations and avoided the extravagances of his contemporaries; what is even more important, he has exercised his own fantasy with restraint, with self-discipline, with respect for the conditions of construction and the needs and purposes of his clients." Aldous Huxley (in *Creative Art*, March 1930) praised Mendelsohn for his architectural romanticism, his grandiosity of concept, and his ability to design houses which, because of their warmth, are more than mere "machines for living." According to *Architectural Forum*, Mendelsohn, as an admirer of Henry van der Velde, agreed with his thesis that buildings should have flow and dynamic quality rather than pure intellectual functionalism.

Mendelsohn first conceives a structure as a whole as seen from the outside, as a "highly integrated sculptural composition," then considers the individual parts. Of the architect's creative process, Mendelsohn himself says, "To the architect who thrives on his creative and inventive faculty, visions are the vitamins necessary to his artistic functions. Though the nature of the problems with which he is occupied and which he attempts to solve are mostly practical, the organization of space, its structural support and final appearance demand the constant presence of knowledge and research, incessant control, the will power to coordinate facts and figures, means and desires." (*Magazine of Art*, December 1945).

Four books written by Mendelsohn have been published in Europe: *America—Architect's Picture-book* (1926); *Russia, Europe, America —an Architectural Cross-section* (1928); *The Creative Spirit of the World Crisis* (1930); and *New House, New World* (1931). A fifth, *Three Lectures on Architecture,* was published in this country in 1942. Published works dealing with Mendelsohn's architecture are *Wendingen; Buildings and Sketches; Wright, Dudok, Mendelsohn—an International Evolution; Sinkentiku; The Work of Eric Mendelsohn; L'Architecture Vivante; Eric Mendelsohn,* a biography by Arnold Whittick; and *Il Contributo di Mendelsohn alla evoluzione dell' architettura moderna* by Mario Roggero.

One-man exhibitions of Mendelsohn's works have been held in Berlin in 1919 and 1928, in New York City in 1929 and 1941, in London in 1931, in Milan in 1932, in Chicago, and, most recently, at the Museum of Art in San Francisco in 1941. The architect is a member of the Academy of Arts of Berlin and the American Institute of Architects, an honorary member of the International League of Modern Architecture of Tokio and the Arts Club of London, a fellow of the Royal Institute of British Architects and an honorary fellow of the Mexican Institute of Architects. He held a Guggenheim fellowship in New York City in 1943. He and the former Louise Maas were married on October 5, 1915, and they have one daughter, Esther (Mrs. Peter Joseph).

References

Whittick, A. Eric Mendelsohn (1937)
Who's Who on the Pacific Coast (1951)

MENON, V. K. KRISHNA *See* Krishna Menon, V. K.

MERCER, SAMUEL A(LFRED) B(ROWNE), REV. May 10, 1880- Linguist; Egyptologist; university professor

Address: b. c/o Longmans, Green & Company, 55 5th Ave., New York 3; h. 5 Massachusetts Ave., Worcester, Mass.

Among the works of research and scholarship which appeared during the final months of 1952, few presumably will prove of more enduring importance than *The Pyramid Texts in Translation and Commentary* by the Reverend Dr. Samuel A. B. Mercer, Professor Emeritus of Semitic Languages and Egyptology in the University of Toronto. Dr. Mercer, who taught at Trinity College, Toronto, from 1924 to 1946, has in the four volumes of *The Pyramid Texts* made the first complete translation into any language of what is believed to be the oldest body of religious literature in the world— namely the inscriptions made in the five small pyramids at Sakkâren in the Nile Valley between 2350 and 2175 B.C. He is also the author of some eighteen other archeological books including the two-volume *Tell el-Amara Tablets* (1939) and *The Religion of Ancient Egypt* (1949).

The son of Samuel and Elizabeth (Browne) Mercer, Samuel Alfred Browne Mercer was born in Bristol, England on May 10, 1880 (the year of the discovery by the French archeologist Gaston Maspero of the inscriptions in the five Sakkâreh pyramids previously unearthed by his elder colleague, Auguste Mariette). At an early age Samuel Mercer was taken to North America, where he passed most of his boyhood and youth in Newfoundland, receiving his secondary education at the Bay Roberts Academy. Graduated with the B.S. degree from the Bishop Field College, and Central Training School at St. John's, Newfoundland, in 1900, he came to the United States and entered Nashotah House, an Episcopalian seminary in Wisconsin, to prepare for the Bachelor of Divinity degree, which he received in 1904, and for his ordination as a deacon and priest of the Protestant Episcopal Church in the same year. In the course of his theological studies at Nashotah House he became interested in Hebrew and later took advantage of every opportunity to become fluent in ancient as well as modern languages. On leaving Nashotah House he enrolled at the University of Wisconsin, where he devoted further study to the Semitic languages and prepared to fit himself for practical field work in archeology by taking courses in surveying and engineering, and acquired a degree in civil engineering in 1905. Because of his work at the University of Wisconsin he was given an opportunity to take his first trip to Egypt, by a German scholar who wanted a survey made that required engineering knowledge.

During the three years beginning in 1905 the Reverend Samuel Mercer studied education, law, and general subjects at Harvard University. On receiving his B.A. degree in 1908 he went to Europe for two years of intensive postgraduate work in the Semitic and Egyptian languages and literature. At the University of Göttingen in Germany he pursued advanced studies in Hebrew under the renowned Julius Wellhausen, while at Heidelberg his professors included Ernst Otto Adalbert Merx, then in his final year of teaching, and the philologist and cuneiform authority Karl Bezold, who assigned the subject of his Ph.D. dissertation. This was *The Oath in Babylonian and Assyrian Literature*, completed in 1910 at the University of Munich under the guidance of Fritz Hommel and his colleague, Freiherr Friedrich Wilhelm von Bissing. In Europe, Dr. Mercer has also studied at the Sorbonne in Paris under Gaston Maspero, the discoverer of the Sakkâreh inscriptions, and in Berlin under Kurt Sethe, who had made the first full publication in hieroglyphics of the Pyramid Texts during the period from 1908 to 1910.

After taking his doctorate at Munich in 1910, Dr. Mercer returned to the United States to become professor of Hebrew and Old Testament literature at Western Theological Seminary in Chicago, Illinois, a position which he was to occupy for the next twelve years. At Munich in the summer of 1911 he made at the suggestion of von Bissing some revisions in his thesis, which was first published in Paris in 1912. (This work, which among other theories established that raising of the right hand in the taking of an oath dates back to the Babylon of 2000 B.C., is also to be found in 1913-14 numbers of the *American Journal of Semitic Languages* under the title "The Oath in Cuneiform Inscriptions.") Mercer's *Extra-Biblical Sources for Hebrew and Jewish History* appeared in 1913 and was followed two years later by *The Ethiopic Liturgy*, a work based on his Hale Lectures at Western Theological Seminary, and in 1915 his *Egyptian Grammar*. In 1916 Professor Mercer began sixteen years of service as editor of the *Journal of the Society of Oriental Research* and two years later helped to found the *Anglican Theological Review*, of which he became co-editor with L. C. Lewis. He received his Doctor of Divinity degree from Nashotah House in 1917.

In the year 1918 were published Dr. Mercer's *Sumero-Babylonian Sign List* and his only book outside the archeological field, namely *Allied and American Peace Terms as Seen by a*

REV. DR. SAMUEL A. B. MERCER

Linguist, in the preface of which the author wrote that "his linguistic training has led him to emphasize the part which language . . . must play in the development of internationalism." This short work speculated on the future of Belgium, Luxembourg, Alsace-Lorraine, and the Balkan countries and on the prospects of the League of Nations. During the ensuing year Mercer contributed the articles "The Church in the Future" and "Meditation in Religious Thought" to the *Constructive Quarterly*, and initiated and became general editor of the *Biblical and Oriental Series*, published at Milwaukee and devoted to scholarly monographs, including his own *Growth of Religious and Moral Ideas in Egypt* and *Religious and Moral Ideas in Babylonia and Assyria*, both issued in 1919. His *Ethiopic Grammar*, completed in the same year, was published in England in 1920 and was followed by his *Life and Growth of Israel* and his *Assyrian Grammar* during 1921.

Dr. Mercer gave up his chair at Western Theological Seminary in 1922 to become Dean of Bexley Hall, the divinity school of Kenyon College at Gambier, Ohio, affiliated with the Protestant Episcopal Church. One year later he added to his list of books *Tutankhamen and Egyptology*, which a critic for the London *Times Literary Supplement* judged "an excellent short account of the recent excavations in Egypt . . . with accounts of Tutankhamen and of the inscriptions bearing upon him, of contemporary biblical events, and other cognate matters." In the same year (1923) Mercer left Bexley Hall to become Dean of Divinity at Trinity College, Toronto, Canada, founded in 1851 by the Right Reverend John Strachan, first Episcopalian bishop of the Ontario city, and federated with the University of Toronto since 1904. The following year (1924) Mercer was named Professor of Semitic Languages and Egyptology in Trinity College, a position

MERCER, SAMUEL—*Continued*

he occupied for twenty-two years, until his retirement from teaching in 1946.

After the appearance in 1925 of his short work on excavation and on Mesopotamia and Egypt, *The Recovery of Forgotten Empires,* Professor Mercer wrote a number of articles on Semitic war gods and Babylonian and Egyptian water gods for John Hastings' *Encyclopaedia of Religion and Ethics* (1927). His *Études sur les Origines de la Religion de l'Égypte* appeared in Paris in 1929, and in 1931, after having passed what have been described as "exciting, pleasant, but sometimes dangerous seasons among the monasteries, churches, and palaces of modern Ethiopia," he was in a position to have published his *Ethiopic Text of the Book of Ecclesiastes,* thus helping to complete the seventeenth century *Biblia Polygotta* of Brian Walton. Professor Mercer became editor of *Egyptian Religion* in 1933 and was consultant on Egyptology for the second edition (1934) of *Webster's New International Dictionary.* (He has also contributed to Sneath's *Evolution of Ethics* and Haupt's *Festschrift.*) The two-volume *Tell el-Amara Tablets,* edited by Professor Mercer with the assistance of Professor Frank Hudson Halleck and published at Toronto in 1939, presented with commentary the first English rendition of what has been called "man's earliest large diplomatic correspondence, that between the pharaohs of Egypt and the kings of Mesopotamia." This work was followed by *Horus, Royal God of Egypt* (1942), *The Supremacy of Israel* (1945), and *Sumero-Babylonian Year Formulae* (1946).

On his retirement from teaching in 1946, the Reverend Samuel Mercer was named Professor Emeritus by the University of Toronto. His definitive *The Religion of Ancient Egypt* appeared in London in 1949; the next year he contributed a sixteen-page essay on the same subject to V. T. A. Ferm's *Forgotten Religions.* Most of his time between 1946 and 1952 was devoted to the four-volume *The Pyramid Texts in Translation and Commentary,* published in October of the latter year. This work, a climax of over thirty years of interest in the hieroglyphics of Sakkâreh and of eleven seasons of research in the Nile Valley and the Near East, cost $20,000 to complete and was made possible by what Dr. Mercer has described as a generous grant" from the Zion Research Foundation of Brookline, Massachusetts. (This foundation established in 1920 by Mr. and Mrs. John Munro Longyear "to facilitate and advance research into the origin of the Hebrew religion" is nonsectarian, the term "Hebrew religion" having been used by the donors "to cover the religion founded by the Hebrews in the Old Testament and developed by the Christian church.") It completes the unfinished work of Kurt Sethe, who, in addition to preparing a scientific facsimile of the Sakkâreh inscriptions, had translated about one third of them into German before his death in 1934. The hieroglyphic texts which adorn the tombs of five pharaohs were "collected and inscribed" between 2350 and 2175 B.C., though actually some

of them "predate the Dynastic period of 3000 B.C.," and have been characterized as "a vast literature containing myths and legends, historical references and astronomical lore, geography and cosmolology, religion and rituals, systems of theology, festivals, magic and morals." About three weeks after the publication of *The Pyramid Texts,* Mercer started on his twelfth visit to the Nile Valley.

For his contributions to scholarship Dr. Mercer holds the titles of lauréat of the French Academy and Officier de l'Instruction Publique, and has been decorated by Ethiopia with the Abyssinian Order of the Trinity. He is a member of the American Oriental Society, the German Orient-Gesellschaft, and the Royal Asiatic Society; is vice-president of the International Society of the Apocrypha; and is a fellow of the Royal Geographical Society. He is the recipient of a number of honorary degrees: the LL.D. (1932) from Nashotah House; the Th.D. (1938) from the Sorbonne; and the Doctor of Sacred Literature (1939) from Kenyon College. Among his objectives, he told a New York *Times* reporter, was to see how his "archeological friends from the University of Chicago are getting on with the excavations at Luxor" and to study the *Book of the Dead* and the *Coffin Texts* at Luxor, which, he says, are "religious poetry, something like our psalms." He has stated that he does "not intend to publish anything on the *Coffin Texts* or the *Book of the Dead.*"

Mrs. Mercer is the former Genevieve Magee, of Massachusetts; the couple were married August 15, 1910, and have one daughter, Harriet Martha. The Mercers now make their permanent home in Worcester, Massachusetts, where Dr. Mercer finds outdoor enjoyment in gardening and walking. He is five feet eight inches in height and 145 pounds in weight. Mercer, who has long been a United States citizen, at election time usually votes the Republican ticket.

References

N Y Herald Tribune p16 O 24 '52 por
N Y Times p27 N 16 '52
Time 60:66 N 3 '52 por

Author's and Writer's Who's Who (1948-49)
Canadian Who's Who, 1949-51
Crockford's Clerical Directory, 1951-52
Directory of American Scholars (1951)
Who Knows—and What (1949)
Who's Who, 1952
Who's Who Among North American Authors (1939)
Who's Who in America, 1952-53
Who's Who in Canada, 1949-50
Who's Who in New England (1949)
Who's Who in the East (1951)
World Biography (1948)

MERRIAM, CHARLES E(DWARD) Nov. 15, 1874—Jan. 8, 1953 Political scientist; university professor; joined the faculty of the University of Chicago in 1900, became professor of political science in 1911; chairman of the department from 1923 until his retirement in

1940; was active in local politics and served on a number of Government committees, including various planning boards set up during the Roosevelt Administration. Author of a number of works on government and politics. See *Current Biography,* 1947.

Obituary
N Y Times p21 Ja 9 '53

KENNETH MILLAR

MILLAR, KENNETH Dec. 13, 1915-
Author

Addres: b. c/o Alfred A. Knopf, Inc., 501 Madison Ave., New York 22; h. 2136 Cliff Drive, Santa Barbara, Calif.

Reprinted from the *Wilson Library Bulletin,* Dec. 1953.

Readers of John Ross Macdonald—who has most often been compared to Raymond Chandler and Dashiell Hammett—have been neatly baffled in their efforts to discover what their author looks like. On the jacket of his stories about Lew Archer, his "private eye," he appears in ful-length silhouette. *Meet Me at the Morgue* (1953) offers an X-ray photograph of the writer's skull, made by his sister-in-law.

It is, however, an open secret that Macdonald is really Kenneth Millar, signer of his own name to several thrillers notable for force, style, and excitement. His wife, Margaret Millar (see *Current Biography* 1946), is also the author of a dozen successful mysteries, novels of suspense, and what James McBride has called 'the psychic thriller, or spook sonata played pianissimo." Mrs. Millar says modestly that "there has geen a great deal of cross-influence" in their writing. Mr. Miliar writes enthusiastically that "her example showed me the potentialities of the mystery form," which he believes are comparable with English tragedy of the 1580's (Kyd or Marlowe). "Its social and psychological range is already immense, and I believe that this convention could support a full-scale philosophic assault on the problem of evil." "Experience With Evil" was the title of the *Cosmopolitan* serial version of *Meet Me at the Morgue,* about a kidnapping.

Born December 13, 1915, in California, which he regards as endlessly interesting and largely unexplored, in spite of Harte and Twain, Norris and Hammett and Steinbeck, Kenneth Millar, of Scotch and Pennsylvania-Dutch stock, spent his early life in Canada, where he met his wife, then Margaret Ellen Sturm. His father, John Millar, was a newspaperman and sometime ship captain out of Vancouver, and his mother, Anne Moyer, was a nurse before her marriage. The Millars lived in Manitoba; in Alberta, where Kenneth attended Medicine Hat High School; in British Columbia; and for a longer time in Kitchener, a middle-sized industrial city near Toronto, where he entered the Kitchener-Waterloo Collegiate Institute, graduating in 1932. After a year's travel in Western Europe, especially Nazi Germany, he graduated from the University of Western On-

tario, London, as an honor B.A. in 1938; spent the next year at the University of Toronto; taught English and history at Kitchener-Waterloo from 1939 to 1941; and received his Ph.D. from the University of Michigan in 1951 for a thesis titled "The Inward Eye: a Study of Coleridge's Psychological Criticism." (*The Ancient Mariner, Oliver Twist,* and *Crime and Punishment* were among the "great events" of the writer's adolescence.) He was communications officer in the United States Naval Reserve from 1944 to 1946.

Millar's first printed story was "a parody of Sherlock Holmes, intended to be funny"; from 1939 he published stories, verse, and book reviews in the Toronto *Saturday Night. The Dark Tunnel* (1944), his first full-length novel, was praised by *Book Week* for "anti-reactionary ironies" and called "a humdinger—and well written to boot" by the *New Republic. Trouble Follows Me* (1946) seemed "very grim stuff," "literate and exciting." *Blue City* (1947), serialized in *Esquire,* was called by the *New Yorker* "very, very tough, and a little silly too." Anthony Boucher, writing the first of several enthusiastic reviews of Millar-Macdonald, said that "Mr. Millar is to be congratulated on his sharp prose, his absorbing tempo, and above all on his ability to create a hardboiled hero, who is not a storm trooper." A chorus of praise greeted *The Three Roads* (1948), Virginia Kirkus leading off with "a psycho-thriller that is well plotted, well explained," while James Sandoe thought it contrived, but absorbing and even rereadable.

Partly because there were so many K. and M. Millar titles on the market, the transformation into John Ross Macdonald now began. The *New Yorker* found in *The Drowning Pool* (1950) "the same quality of irrational excitement and depthless depravity" as in the

MILLAR, KENNETH—*Continued*

early Hammett. *The Way Some People Die* (1951), nominated in John Hutchens' *Herald Tribune* book column as the best novel to throw at an umpire, was described by Boucher as "probably Mr. Macdonald's best to date—and thereby automatically the top hardboiled novel of the year." Kathleen Sproul called it a "subtle hard-boiled gem."

The Millars live on Cliff Drive in Santa Barbara, California, with Linda Jane, their fourteen-year-old daughter, who finds the life of a writer too lonely and intends to be a doctor. Mr. Millar is a blue-eyed, black-haired six-footer. He enjoys spectator sports such as baseball and boxing, and likes the work of Farrell, Faulkner, and Fitzgerald; Nelson Algren, Hemingway, and Dreiser; Flaubert, France, Yeats, and Wilkie Collins. He is a Democrat, and a member of the Authors League and Mystery Writers of America. A writer, he believes, should establish a firm home base, get to know himself and his neighbors, govern himself by the rules of his community while rejecting its provincialities and prejudices, and in general try to live down the Byronic-Bohemian tradition.

References

Santa Barbara News-Press p10 Mr 30 '52 por

Warfel, . R. American Novelists of Today (1951)

MARSHALL E. MILLER

MILLER, MARSHALL E(VANS) Oct. 20, 1914- Veterans organization official; lawyer

Address: b. c/o Amvets, National Headquarters, 724 9th St., N.W., Washington, D.C.; 223 N. Neil St., Champaign, Ill.; h. 604 W. Hill St., Champaign, Ill.

The eighth national commander of the American Veterans of World War II (Amvets) is Marshall E. Miller, who represents more than 250,000 members. Elected for the 1952-1953 term at the annual convention in August, 1952, he has since been devoting his efforts to obtaining improved medical care and other benefits for veterans.

Marshall has been a member of the veterans' organization since February 1946 and has held a variety of executive positions, including those of judge advocate of the Champaign, Illinois post, district representative of Illinois and chairman of the national service committee. He was the Amvets' delegate to the World Veterans Federation conference in Belgrade, Yugoslavia, in 1951 and in London, England, in 1952. He is a lawyer by profession.

Marshall Evans Miller was born in East St. Louis, Illinois, on October 20, 1914, the son of Clyde D. and Golde (Evans) Miller. He entered the University of Illinois in 1931 and was elected to Phi Beta Kappa in 1934. After receiving his A.B. degree in 1935 he studied law at the university and obtained the LL.B. degree in 1937. He was then admitted to the American and Illinois bar associations, and from 1937 to

1941 held the position of law book editor with Callaghan and Company. In 1941 he established his own law practice in Champaign, Illinois.

Two years after establishing his practice Miller enlisted in the United States Naval Reserve and served until 1945 as a yeoman. Shortly after leaving the Navy he became interested in the American Veterans of World War II and joined the Champaign Post Three in February 1946. He served as judge advocate of the post and district representative of Illinois in 1917, and the following year was made judge advocate of the Illinois department, housing chairman, and a member of the Illinois service council. He was the State legislative director for the Amvets in 1949 and the national fourth district vice-commander in 1950.

The national executive committee named Miller the Number Two Amvet in 1950 at the national convention held in Cleveland, Ohio. In addition, he was chairman of the national service committee, which established the Amvets national service council to handle the claims of disabled veterans. In 1951 he served as the head of the national peace and preparedness committee, which is concerned with international problems, and from 1951 to 1952 was a member of the board of trustees of the National Service Foundation. He was elected as a delegate from the veterans' group to the World Veterans Federation conference in Belgrade, Yugoslavia, in 1951, and the following year he attended the session held in London, England.

Endorsed as a candidate for the post of national commander of Amvets by the Illinois department, Miller was elected unanimously by the 800 delegates of the 1952 national convention after the withdrawal of Prentice G. Smith, the only other announced candidate. He succeeded John L. Smith of Barberton, Ohio.

The following October, Miller wrote identical letters to presidential candidates Adlai E.

Stevenson and Dwight D. Eisenhower requesting their views on medical care for veterans and on controlling inflation. The letters charged "'critical deterioration' of the Veterans Administration medical program" (New York *Times,* November 4, 1952), and emphasized the special care needed by veterans requiring neuropsychiatric treatment. In his reply Eisenhower told Miller that the veterans' medical program and other VA controversies would be a matter of "primary concern" to him if elected, and that his method of inflation-control would consist of controlling money and credit (New York *Times,* October 31, and November 4, 1952). Stevenson promised "'the best medical care which a grateful nation can give' to the war disabled and a 'positive, vigorous program to control prices' and maintain living standards" (New York *Times,* November 4, 1952).

The American Veterans of World War II was formed in December 1944 by a group headed by Elmo Keel, former Air Force master sergeant, and was composed of some twenty smaller veterans' organizations. On July 17, 1947 the Amvets became the first World War II veterans' organization to have a perpetual charter approved by Congress. The national executive committee voted on July 18, 1950 to allow veterans of the Korean War and of any future wars to join the Amvets. The organization, which by 1951 numbered 250,000 members, has established a number of awards, among them the Harold Russell Award (named for the film star and former commander of the Amvets), the Community Service Award, the Raymond Sawyer Award, the Americanism Award, and the Woman-of-the-Year Award.

Resolutions adopted at the 1952 convention called for abolition of the electoral college and election of the President of the United States by direct vote of the people; also advocating lowering the voting age to eighteen, and stopstopping irregularities in the loan provisions of the ping irregularities in the loan provisions of the G. I. Bill of Rights.

The Amvets convention urged the United Nations to declare that further aggression by Russia or Russian satellites be regarded as an "act of war" to be met by all force "necessary to neutralize and terminate the aggression"; it also urged the United States to invoke "the strongest economic sanctions" against Czechoslovakia until Associated Press correspondent William N. Oatis, was released.

At the Amvets' convention on September 6, 1953 Marshall Miller was succeeded by Henry J. Mahady as national commander.

Miller married Helen K. Blatti, on December 22, 1943; their two children are Jane Allen and Briant Scott. This marriage was terminated. On September 2, 1950 the lawyer married Gloria Coe. He is a member of the Champaign County, Illinois, and American Bar Associations, the National Lawyers Guild, the American Legion, the Moose; Lions; Urbana Youth Committee.

References

N Y Herald Tribune p9 S 1 '52
Who's Who in the Midwest, 1952

MILLETT, JOHN D(AVID) (mĭl-lĕt')
Mar. 14, 1912-   Educator
Address: b. c/o Miami University, Oxford, Ohio

As executive director of the Commission on Financing Higher Education, John D. Millett was responsible for conducting what the New York *Times* has described as "the most comprehensive survey of higher education yet attempted in this country." The commission, which began its work in 1949 and issued a final report in November 1952, was sponsored by the Association of American Universities and financed by the Rockefeller Foundation and the Carnegie Corporation of New York. Since 1948 Millett has served as professor of public administration at Columbia University, where he also became director of the Center of Administrative Studies in the fall of 1952.

On March 28, 1953 it was announced that Dr. Millett had been elected president of Miami University in Oxford, Ohio to succeed Dr. Ernest H. Hahne who died. The new president is the sixteenth to head the 144-year-old southwestern Ohio state university which has an enrollment of over 5,000.

John David Millett was born in Indianapolis, Indiana, March 14, 1912, the son of Grover Allan and Helen Elizabeth (Welch) Millett. Both of his parents came from southern Indiana. One of his grandfathers was a country doctor, the other a road contractor and local politician. Young John grew up in Indianapolis, where his father was engaged in business. After graduating from Shortridge High School in 1929, he entered DePauw University, in Greencastle, Indiana, and majored in political science. As an undergraduate, he held membership on the debating team and in the student senate; served as editor of the student newspaper and as president of the Student Union; and was a Rector scholar and member of Phi Beta Kappa. He received his B.A. degree in 1933. Persuaded by his adviser at DePauw to continue with his studies, Millett attended Columbia University, where Dr. Arthur W. Macmahon, then professor of government, took a particular interest in his career. Columbia granted Millett the M.A. degree in 1935 and the Ph.D. degree three years later. The subject of his published dissertation was *The Works Progress Administration in New York City* (1938).

Meanwhile, in 1935, Millett began his career as both an instructor in government at Columbia and a lecturer at Rutgers University. Three years later he became a postdoctoral fellow of the Social Science Research Council and from 1939 to 1941 was assistant secretary of the council's committee on public administration. He went to Washington, D.C., in the latter year as special assistant to the director of the National Resources Planning Board. After the United States entered World War II, he was commissioned a major in the Army in 1942. Promoted to lieutenant colonel the following year and to colonel in 1945, he served on the staff of General Brehon B. Somervell, commanding the Army Service Forces. Millett received the Legion of Merit in 1945, retired from the Army, and joined the faculty of Columbia as an associate professor of public administration. Recalled to active duty in 1947, he was assigned to the headquarters of the European Command, in Germany, where he remained from May to October. Since 1948 he has held the rank of full professor at Columbia.

It was disclosed on November 6, 1949, that Columbia had given Millett a three-year leave of absence to serve as executive director of the Commission on Financing Higher Education. "The finances of both public and private institutions of higher learning are now in a state of crisis," he pointed out at that time. "The objective of this new commission will be to get the facts and make recommendations not only for developing adequate support for these institutions but also for making savings in their costs by coordination and cooperation in their educational services to the nation." The origin of the commission dates back to the fall of 1947, when, acting upon the advice of a group of college administrators, the Rockefeller Foundation appointed an exploratory committee on financing higher education and research. In its report to the foundation the following August, the committee recommended the creation of a special commission to make a comprehensive survey of the financial conditions and requirements of higher education in the United States. The foundation appropriated $400,000 for the study in April 1949, and the Carnegie Corporation of New York joined with a participating grant of an additional $50,000. Sponsorship of the survey by the Association of American Universities was obtained, and the association's president named five persons to membership on the commission. Subsequently, the commission enlarged its number to twelve—eight educators and four laymen—under the chairmanship of Dr. Frank D. Fackenthal, former acting president of Columbia University.

The Commission on Financing Higher Education held its first meeting on July 11, 1949, at which time Millett was elected executive director, to be responsible·for all activities of the research staff. He assumed his new duties at the beginning of the next month. The exploratory committee had proposed in its report that desirable research studies should be undertaken under two major topics—"research in the nature of American higher education" and "research in the financing of higher education"—and outlined thirteen different areas of inquiry under these two headings. "My major responsibility," Millett has explained, "was to translate this outline into research projects as rapidly as possible." Altogether the staff of senior researchers and research consultants undertook seventeen different major research projects (according to *Time*, the subjects studied ranged from "student fees and Federal aid" to "the size of campus coal bills"), in addition to its statistical analysis and visits to individual colleges and universities. The commission set up offices in Washington, at the Universities of Chicago and Illinois, and at Columbia. Following Millett's suggestion, the commission agreed to issue two different documents as a final report of the three-year survey: *Nature and Needs of Higher Education*, in which the com-

JOHN D. MILLETT

mission as a group would present its own conclusions in brief compass; and *Financing Higher Education in the United States*, written by Millett, which would present in detail the results of the staff research work that provided the factual background for the commission's discussions and decisions. These two volumes were published on November 19, 1952.

The report of the Commission on Financing Higher Education stressed the fact that the rising costs of higher education have far outstripped its income. In 1952 the commission felt that 1,500 colleges, universities, professional schools, and junior colleges needed an additional $250 million to operate successfully. The commission made a strong plea for business and industry to help support America's system of higher education and also urged that labor unions, church groups, foundations, alumni, service clubs, and local groups extend further aid to colleges and universities. Unless the general public comes to the support of higher education to a greater extent than it has done in the past, the commission warned, the Federal Government may be forced to expand the scope of its support. In 1950 the Government provided close to $500 million, or 28 per cent of the entire educational income received in that year. The commission expressed the fear that this was a dangerous trend which may lead to dominance of the independent college by the Federal Government.

On November 17, 1952, it was announced that Millett had been appointed director of the newly established Center of Administrative Studies at Columbia University. This Center is designed to undertake research dealing with administrative problems of government agencies and large nonprofit institutions. According to Millett, the Center will conduct its research program while acting as a consultant service on administrative problems to large-scale public organizations. It will seek to assist graduate research students in the area of public administration by offering them concrete employment experience on administrative problems and by making available to them research data necessary in the preparation of dissertations. As an example of the type of work to be undertaken by the Center, Millett at that time cited two current activities: a study of administrative policies and procedures used in connection with government research contracts to universities; and a study of administrative procedures and organization for a public health program, undertaken for the New York State Department of Health.

While still studying for his degree at Columbia, Millett had served in 1936 as a junior professional assistant on the staff of the President's Committee on Administrative Management, in Washington, D.C. From 1948 to 1949 he was on the staff of the (Hoover) Commission on Organization of the Executive Branch of the Government, first as a member of the task force assigned to examine the problem of the Office of the President and then as an assistant to the Commission's executive director, Sidney A. Mitchell. When the Commission sent to Congress in February 1949 the first of its formal reports pointing the way to administrative reforms for greater efficiency and economy in the Federal Government, the New York *Times* stated that the recommendations were "framed on the basis of the exhaustive research undertaken by a special task force" co-directed by Millett and H. Struve Hensel, former Assistant Secretary of the Navy.

In addition to the books mentioned above, Millett is the author of *The British Unemployment Assistance Board: A Case Study in Administrative Autonomy* (1940) and *The Process and Organization of Government Planning* (1947). Reviewing the latter volume for the *American Political Science Review,* Avery Leiserman commented: "A vigorous style reflects the forthright personality of the author. Although Professor Millett explicitly announces that the book does not follow the method of recounting personal experiences, this reader could not escape the enjoyable impression of a highly personalized, though none the less expert, analysis."

Together with Dr. Macmahon, Millett has written *Federal Administrators: A Biographical Approach to the Problem of Departmental Management* (1939) and *The Administration of Federal Work Relief* (1941). Among the nine supplementary studies issued by the Commission on Financing Higher Education was *An Atlas of Higher Education in the United States* (1952), which Millett edited. He is a frequent contributor to the *American Political Science Review, Public Administration Review, Political Science Quarterly,* and other periodicals.

The public administration authority was one of the United States delegates who attended the seventh International Congress of Administrative Sciences, at Berne, Switzerland, in July 1947. Three years later an honorary LL.D.

degree was bestowed upon him by DePauw University. In Leonia, New Jersey, where he now resides, he has been a member of the Board of Education since 1951. Organizations in which he holds membership include the American Political Science Association (executive council, 1950), American Society of Public Administration, and the Academy of Political Science. His clubs are the Cosmos in Washington and the Century in New York. On September 2, 1934, he married Catherine Letsinger; they have three sons, Allan Reed, David Phillips, and Stephen Malcolm. The educator, who stands six feet tall and weighs 185 pounds, has blue eyes and brown hair. He names his political affiliations as independent and his church as the Methodist. For recreation he watches baseball and football games.

References

N Y Times p7 N 7 '49 por

Directory of American Political Science
    Association (1948)
Directory of American Scholars (1951)
Who's Who in America, 1952-53
Who's Who in the East (1951)

MINER, TONY *See* Miner, W. C.

MINER, WORTHINGTON (C.) Nov. 13, 1900- Television producer
Address: b. c/o National Broadcasting Company Television Network, 50 W. 49th St., New York 20; h. 1 W. 72d St., New York 23

After twelve years as television producer for the Columbia Broadcasting System and ten as manager of that network's television department, Worthington Miner, originator and producer of the award-winning dramatic program *Studio One,* joined the staff of the National Broadcasting Company in April 1952. One of the pioneers of television drama, Miner plans to produce several programs for NBC. In the past he has been an actor and a director in the legitimate theater, directing *Reunion in Vienna* (1931) and *Both Your Houses* (1933), among other successful Broadway productions.

Born in Buffalo, New York, on November 13, 1900, Worthington C. Miner is the son of a lawyer of that city. His mother operated a dress-making establishment. After attending the Kent School in Connecticut, Miner studied at Yale University until he joined the Army to serve in World War I for nineteen months with the 16th Field Artillery, 4th Division, participating in the Chateau Thierry, St. Mihiel, and Argonne offensives. From November 1918 to September 1919 he saw duty with the Army of occupation in Germany.

Leaving the Army, Miner resumed his courses at Yale, from which he was graduated with a Phi Beta Kappa key in 1922. He then went to England for two years (1922-24) of postgraduate study at Cambridge University, before joining the Yale faculty as an instructor in the English department. In England during his vacation, he renewed his association with a

WORTHINGTON MINER

friend who had become a theatrical producer in London and was at that time engaged in rehearsals for a Christmas pantomime. When Miner, having become interested in the details of stage production, was asked to fill in for a prompter who had fallen ill, he readily accepted. It was not long before he had risen to the position of stage manager and later of assistant director, for the English company. By then Miner had resigned his position at Yale and in the fall of 1924 returned to the United States to make his way on the New York stage.

Since there were no openings for an assistant director on Broadway at that time, Miner became an actor, making his debut as a "spear-carrier" in the Walter Hampden road company of *Cyrano de Bergerac* in October 1925. Later, more important roles followed, in *Fallen Angels* and in *The Green Hat*. While employed as stage manager for *The Green Hat*, Miner was recommended by Katherine Cornell, star of the play, to Broadway producer Guthrie McClintic, then looking for an assistant. Miner worked with McClintic on the productions of *Shanghai Gesture* and *Saturday's Children*. Producer Jed Harris then engaged him as his personal assistant for productions of *The Front Page* and Chekhov's *Uncle Vanya*.

For the next ten years, beginning in 1929, Miner directed more than twenty-seven plays, often in association with topflight stage designer Jo Mielzener. His first success, *Up Pops the Devil* (1929), was followed by *Five Star Final* (1930), which was also well received. One of his outstanding achievements as a director was the Theater Guild production of the Robert E. Sherwood play *Reunion in Vienna*, with Alfred Lunt and Lynn Fontanne, in 1931; Brooks Atkinson, the New York *Times* critic, praised Miner's "splendid direction." Among other plays directed by Miner were *I Loved You Wednesday* (1932), *Her Master's Voice* (1933), the Pulitzer prize-winning Maxwell

Anderson play *Both Your Houses* (1933), *Let Freedom Ring* and *Blind Alley* (1935), the Ray Bolger musical *On Your Toes* (1936), and *Father Malachy's Miracle* (1937). He also directed the production of *Jane Eyre* starring Katherine Hepburn, and in 1938 was co-director of Irwin Shaw's controversial anti-war play *Bury the Dead*. Occasionally Miner returned to acting, in his own productions, as he did in *For Love or Money* (1934). In the summers of 1933 and 1934 Miner rounded out his theatrical experience by working as a writer and director for RKO Radio Pictures productions, collaborating on two films with the late Robert Benchley.

As one of Broadway's foremost directors, Miner was named to the executive board of the Theater Guild in 1938. At a panel discussion of the Williamstown (Massachusetts) Institute of Human Relations in the following year, he expressed his dissatisfaction with the state of the theater in America, observing that the theater was reaching far too small an audience: "It is for the rich in the richest city in this country." It was true, he acknowledged, that this select audience did allow theater artists an almost unlimited intellectual freedom, but he hoped that some way could be found to create a national audience for the drama without lowering its artistic standards. A new entertainment medium was to provide Miner with an opportunity to realize that objective. In 1939 he became director-in-chief and then manager of program development for the Columbia Broadcasting System's television network, advancing by June 1942 to manager of the entire television department at CBS. There he worked out his theory of television as a completely new medium, requiring a fresh approach to writing, acting, direction, and production. In an article in the trade publication *Telescreen* in 1944, Miner emphasized that "the primary obligation upon the producers of television programs is to recognize that television is itself a unique and individual form. It cannot be made to fit into preconceived patterns of radio, of motion pictures, or of theater. . . .Television offers, however, a superlative opportunity to absorb every type of experiment in all the other entertainment media. There is no limit to the scope of its coverage."

At CBS Miner developed and produced four major programs: the television version of *The Goldbergs*; the early *Toast of the Town* broadcasts; the children's show, *Mr. I. Magination*; and the dramatic program *Studio One*, which soon gained a reputation as the "bellwether" of television drama. In 1949, when Miner had brought *Studio One* over to television from radio, he laid down three conditions which the new program would have to meet. Above all else it had to tell an interesting story on each show; it had to present adult, provocative productions; and it had to be the showplace of a variety of dramatic forms. As the program developed, Miner reserved ten or fifteen out of the forty-four shows presented each year for experimental productions. While producing *Studio One* Miner brought many classics of literature to the television screen: Nathaniel Hawthorne's *Scarlet Letter*, Charlotte Brontë's

Jane Eyre (which he once directed on the stage), W. Somerset Maugham's *Of Human Bondage,* Gian-Carlo Menotti's opera *The Medium,* and three plays of Shakespeare, *Coriolanus, Macbeth,* and *Julius Caesar.* To Miner, Shakespeare is "the only complete master of good style and good form in television. He needs nothing but cutting."

Studio One was also Miner's principal technical laboratory; it was in his experimental programs that the producer demonstrated his understanding of the new, all-inclusive dramatic values of the television medium. *Time* magazine hailed Miner as an innovator of the first rank: "'Tony' Miner has pioneered in TV with such effective techniques as the use of recordings for unspoken thoughts, the blending of film and live acting, and the combination of close-ups and long-shots to get depth on the screen." A 1949 production of *Julius Caesar* in modern dress was described by Jack Gould in the New York *Times* as "the most exciting television yet seen on the home screen . . . with inspired disregard for the supposed limitations of video, [Miner] imbued the Shakesperean tragedy with a visual power and vitality that lifted television to the status of a glorious art. *Julius Caesar* had the fluidity of the films and the actuality of the stage, which made it pure television."

It is Miner's belief that programs of the type presented on *Studio One* have come close to solving the problem of reconciling the two goals of a mass audience and artistic integrity. *Studio One's* audience was estimated in 1951 to be about ten million. Entertainment experts had always maintained that "serious" or "experimental" drama could be presented only to an audience drawn from the "cultivated" minority, while Miner believes that plays dealing with adult problems in a serious and straightforward manner—"we don't get chichi or phony about them"—are preferred by his huge audiences. In 1950 CBS, testing eight *Studio One* programs for audience response, found that light fare such as *June Moon* and *Boy Meets Girl,* enormously popular as stage plays, when presented on television rated far below difficult and tragic productions like Ivan Turgenev's *Smoke* and Ansky's *The Dybbuk.* This reaction is to be explained, Miner has said, by the individualistic nature of the television audience.

As a member of a group audience, the viewer" in a legitimate or motion picture theater is, in Miner's view, highly susceptible to "mass suggestion." The "viewer" of television is in quite another position; in the privacy of his own home, he relies on his individual tastes and faculties to judge what goes on before his eyes (John Crosby, New York *Herald Tribune,* January 10, 1950). "The only real compensation for being in television," Miner has been quoted as saying, "is in being able to reach so many people with good plays."

With his acceptance of a contract with the National Broadcasting Company, to which he moved on April 1, 1952, Miner began a new phase in his television career. During the summer of 1952 he produced for this network a different kind of dramatic show, *Curtain Call,* which presented a single dramatic incident rather than a fully developed story. *Variety* found the plots too far-fetched and the presentations too light in this first program of several which Miner produced for NBC television.

Miner wrote the section on directing in the book *Producing the Play* by John Gassner, and has also written a number of articles on television for trade papers and magazines. Representative articles are "Television Programs of the Future" (*Telescreen,* Spring 1944) and a discussion of camera-work in relation to television production, "The Pen in the Other Hand" (*Variety,* January). The producer stands five feet eight inches tall; his eyes are brown. Miner relaxes at tennis, hockey, and oil painting. Also interested in carpentry and building, he built his own summer home at South Kent, Connecticut. Worthington Miner's wife is stage actress Frances Fuller, a niece of Governor James F. Byrnes of South Carolina. Their son, Peter, made his debut in Paul Osborn's *On Borrowed Time* in 1938. There are also two daughters in the Miner family, Margaret and Mary Elizabeth.

References

N Y Sun Mr 4 '33

N Y Times II p11 F 11 '51

International Motion Picture Almanac, 1952-53

MINOR, ROBERT July 15, 1884—Nov. 26, 1952 Communist leader; once well known as a newspaper cartoonist, drew for St. Louis *Post-Dispatch,* New York *World,* and other papers; was elected to the Central Executive Committee (now the National Committee) of the Communist party; edited the *Liberator* and later the *Daily Worker* (1920's); during the 1930's was Communist candidate for Mayor of New York City and for Governor of New York State; acting general-secretary of the Communist Party of the United States (1941-42). See *Current Biography,* 1941.

Obituary

N Y Times p25 N 28 '52

MORENO, MARIO *See* Cantinflas

MOULTON, F(OREST) R(AY) Apr. 29, 1872—Dec. 7, 1952 Astronomer; educator; author; member of the department of astronomy at University of Chicago (1896-1926); research associate of Carnegie Institution (1908-23); a director of Utilities Power and Light Corporation (1925-38); was permanent secretary of American Association for Advancement of Science (1936-48); credited with inventing mechanism that led to flickerless projection of motion pictures. See *Current Biography,* 1946.

Obituary

N Y Times p33 D 9 '52

MOWERY, EDWARD J(OSEPH) Mar. 8, 1906- Reporter

Address: b. c/o New York World-Telegram & Sun, 125 Barclay St., New York 7; h. 45 Ingram St., Forest Hills, N.Y.

The winner of many awards and citations for his work in journalism, Edward J. Mowery is a staff writer for the New York *World-Telegram & Sun.* His talent for pursuing the story behind the story brought him the 1953 Pulitzer Award for local reporting—after a seven-year investigation which resulted in the vindication of a man falsely convicted of murder.

Mowery gave the twenty-fourth annual Don R. Mellett Memorial Lecture in September, 1953, at Texas Christian University, Fort Worth. His subject was "Presumption of Innocence—A Myth." He suggested stringent procedural changes in America's judiciary system to assure each man his Constitutional right to be presumed innocent until proved guilty, and to halt the disturbing increase in the miscarriage of justice.

The reporter received earlier awards for presenting facts which led to the exoneration of a man falsely convicted of forgery, and for his writings which exposed and helped to eliminate the narcotic drug traffic among American youth. Mowery began his newspaper career in Columbus, Ohio, and worked in Lancaster, Ohio, before going to New York in 1937 as a staff writer for King Features Syndicate. Before joining the *World-Telegram* in 1943, he worked on several other papers in the New York area.

Edward Joseph Mowery was born in Lancaster, Ohio, March 8, 1906, the son of Arlow Francis and Nellie Cecilia (O'Connor) Mowery. He attended St. Mary's grade school, was graduated from St. Mary's High School in 1923 and attended Ohio State University and Notre Dame University, where he majored in architectural design. His father had been an architect-builder

The early thirties were bad years for a young architect and in 1932, Mowery started a weekly suburban newspaper—the *Eastern News*—in Columbus, Ohio. This, he has said, "sold at a profit in three years," and determined his future in the newspaper field. After a job as managing editor of the *Catholic Columbian,* he became city editor of the Lancaster *Daily Eagle,* staff writer for the Associated Press, feature writer for the Columbus *Sunday Dispatch* and later editor of the Lancaster *Daily Eagle* and *Eagle-Gazette.* At this time *Editor & Publisher* described him as the "youngest editor of a daily newspaper."

As *Eagle* editor, Mowery attracted the attention of the wire services in 1936 by relegating the romance of King Edward VIII and Wallis Simpson to clipped paragraphs on the back pages, declaring that guesses and wishful thinking were not news.

Soon after this, in 1937, Mowery went to New York as staff writer for King Features Syndicate, and shortly thereafter transferred to the New Brunswick (N.J.) *Home News,* as editorial writer. Then he became financial edi-

Walter Albertin, N.Y. World-
Telegram & Sun

EDWARD J. MOWERY

tor of the Newark *Star-Ledger* and staff writer on the New York *Post.* For the past ten years, he has been with the New York *World-Telegram & Sun.*

Mowery's specialty, Charles A. Wyer wrote (New York *World-Telegram & Sun,* May 5, 1953), has been following obscure news tips and developing stories of wide significance. He played an important part in organizing a drive in 1945 to win for the late Bertram M. Campbell a special pardon and an $115,000 award from the State for false imprisonment. Campbell, a Wall Street broker, had been convicted of forgery. On a routine reportorial assignment Mowery, along with several other newsmen, heard the broker's insistence that he had been convicted as a result of mistaken identity. Although most of the other reporters turned away—there was no definitive documentation—Mowery believed Campbell's story. It was his series of articles in the *World-Telegram,* demonstrating his faith in Campbell's innocence, which spurred a drive for re-investigation of the case. For his work toward the freeing of Campbell, Mowery received the Pall Mall Distinguished Service "Big Story" Award in 1947.

Early in 1950, Mowery's stories on the internal revenue scandal in New York's Third District office were the first to point to widespread evidence of shady operations in the Bureau. The chief of the revenue squad and four deputy collectors were later sent to prison.

Mowery next attracted attention with a front page story (*World-Telegram & Sun*) on April 17, 1950 in which he reported that Mayor O'Dwyer had given the "brush-off" to the Medical Society of New York County when that organization had tried to warn the Mayor in 1946 of the rise in drug addiction cases and the marijuana peril. The Society had been active since 1944 in fighting the evil, but was hampered by lack of police cooperation.

The Narcotic Squad of the Police Department, which had been strong after World War I, had successfully cut the drug traffic to a minimum and then reduced its staff. The Society had urged the Mayor to restore the Squad to full strength, but this was not done and by 1950, the city was "reaping the whirlwind of that official apathy toward narcotics addiction. . . ."

In a page one story, (*World-Telegram & Sun,* April 20, 1950) Mowery related that Dr. Lester C. Spier, Chairman of the County Medical Society's narcotic committee, urged that the City Narcotic Squad be increased to 100 men and stressed the need for a city hospital expressly for the cure of addicts.

These stories were the first of many by Mowery which were credited with alerting Federal officials, increasing the help of private agencies and forcing the city to take action. Mowery also contributed articles on the dope traffic to *Story of Our Time, Look,* the *American Legion Magazine* and the *Columbia Magazine.*

For his efforts in exposing the narcotics evil among teen agers, Mowery received the American Legion Citation for Patriotism from both the New York and Brooklyn Chapters in 1951. These were followed on November 11, 1951 by the Silurian Society Annual Award for "exposing and eliminating" narcotic drug traffic among American youth. On February 2, 1952, the National Commander of the American Legion presented Mowery with the Inter-Faith Gold Medal for "fostering inter-faith and inter-racial understanding throughout the world."

Meanwhile, Mowery was working on an investigation that involved another man who had continued to declare his innocence after being convicted of a crime. The plea of Louis J. Hoffner reached Mowery after he had helped free Bertram M. Campbell in 1945, and had caught his interest because Hoffner claimed that a patrolman and a former Assistant District Attorney believed in his innocence. Hoffner, a dime store clerk, had been sentenced to life in prison for the murder of a Queens, New York, tavern keeper during a holdup.

Mowery was called by *Time* (November 24, 1952) "'the single-minded' reporter . . . who never lets go of a story once he gets it." His seven-year pursuit of the case was described as follows:

Mowery" tracked down members of the jury, found that they were so confused by the judge's charge that a majority first voted to free Hoffner, then re-interpreted the charge and voted to convict him. Mowery also found that a cab driver who testified . . . that he had seen Hoffner in Brooklyn eleven miles away at the time of the murder had been threatened by detectives with losing his license. Another witness who saw Hoffner in Brooklyn was never called to testify. . . .Mowery tried to get into Dannemora . . . to see Hoffner himself, but prison officials . . . refused him. So

Mowery got in by tagging along with the assistant D.A. and posing as his aide."

A Hoffner Committee was organized by Mowery to collect signatures on petitions asking that Hoffner be given a new trial. Finally, he enlisted the aid of a newly elected D.A., T. Vincent Quinn of Queens. This was after Mowery had cracked the testimony of a waiter, the sole witness who had identified Hoffner as the killer. The waiter failed, according to *Time,* "to pick Hoffner out of the line-up. . . . Pressed by defense lawyers to explain why . . . the witness said he had not seen him [Hoffner] in profile, as he had viewed the killer. But Mowery checked into the line-up record . . . and proved the witness had seen Hoffner's profile and even so had not identified him at first."

Queens County Judge Peter T. Farrell directed on November 27, 1952 that the indictment against Hoffner be dismissed and the prisoner discharged. He had served twelve years.

Mowery's work on the Hoffner case brought him further honors. In ceremonies broadcast on May 6, 1953 over the NBC radio and television networks, he received a second Pall Mall Distinguished Service "Big Story" Award. The New York Criminal-Civil Courts Bar Association presented him with its 1952 award for "Outstanding Service rendered to the Public Service in the Cause of Justice," an award previously given only to judges, prosecutors and lawyers. In 1953 Mowery also won the Polk Memorial Award given by Long Island University, and the Columbia University Frommer Award.

"I'm overwhelmed," the convalescing Mowery confessed when the news that he had won the 1953 Pulitzer Prize for local reporting reached him in Columbus, Ohio on May 5, 1953. After an initial "I've made it," he paid tribute to the men and women on the Hoffner Committee, saluting "their inherent sense of fair play" (New York *World-Telegram & Sun,* May 5, 1953).

Mowery is a member of the Society of Silurians and of the Notre Dame Alumni Association, and is a Roman Catholic. He is five feet ten and a half inches tall, slender, with brown hair and gray eyes. As a spectator, he is interested in football and boxing. Politically, he is an independent.

He was married to Margaret Josephine Ryan of Columbus, Ohio, on February 26, 1938. Mrs. Mowery was a harpist before her marriage. The couple have two sons, Michael Francis and William Patrick and a daughter; Margaret Eileen.

References

N Y Times p24 My 5 '53 por
N Y World-Telegram p23 N 13 '51 por; p3 My 5 '53 por
Scripps-Howard News p3 S '51; p2 Feb '53 por
Time 60:65+ N 24 '52 por
American Catholic Who's Who (1952-53)

MUIR, MALCOLM (mūr) July 19, 1885-
Publisher

Address: b. Newsweek Bldg., Broadway and
42d St., New York 18; h. 1081 Redding Rd.,
Fairfield, Conn.

Malcolm Muir, president and chairman of the
editorial board of *Newsweek*, began his association with the weekly news magazine in 1937,
after thirty years with the McGraw-Hill Publishing Company, of which he was president for
nine years. A pioneer in the field of business
and technical journalism, he promoted the application of engineering principles to market study
and was largely responsible in 1929 for the
creation of McGraw-Hill's *Business Week*,
which reports and interprets news events in
terms of their significance for business. When
Muir became publisher and president of *Newsweek*, he changed the editorial formula from
a straight reviewing of the week's news to the
magazine's present emphasis on "background
and significance" and "signed opinion" articles
in addition to news reporting.

Of Scottish ancestry, Malcolm Muir was
born in Glen Ridge, New Jersey, July 19, 1885,
to James and Susan (Brown) Muir. He attended private and public schools, including
Montclair High School in New Jersey, and at
the age of twenty went to work as a file clerk
on *The Street Railway Journal* (later the *Transit Journal*), one of a group of trade papers
in the electrical and transportation industries
published by James H. McGraw. By 1916,
eleven years later, he had become vice-president
of the company. An article in *Advertising and
Selling* (March 26, 1936) attributed Muir's
success to his salesmanship—he is said to have
sold 562 pages of advertising for a single issue
of one of the magazines—and to his skill in
directing sales activities. At the death of John
A. Hill, who had been building a similar group
of magazines for the mechanical and engineering industries, the companies were consolidated
in 1917 into the McGraw-Hill Publishing Company, and twenty-eight-year-old Muir was
named general manager of three of McGraw-
Hill's most important periodicals, *Coal Age,
The Engineering and Mining Journal*, and
Chemical and Metallurgical Engineering. He
later also managed the *American Telephone
Journal*.

Under Muir, McGraw-Hill fully developed its
successful circulation policy which stressed "se-
lectivity" as opposed to "mass sales." The "selected" subscribers for each magazine were the
key engineers and executives in a particular
industry, and advertising and news matter were
slanted for the businessman or technician to
whom they were addressed. While vice-president of McGraw-Hill and also president of
Associated Business Papers, Inc., a nonprofit
organization for trade publications, Muir encouraged a movement within industry to apply
engineering principles to market research. By
analysis of buying habits, he believed, the "waste
of guesswork" in advertising and selling would
be eliminated. At a meeting of the New York
Advertising Club in New York in 1928, he
urged the union of research and advertising.

MALCOLM MUIR

When James McGraw became chairman of
the board of the McGraw-Hill Publishing Company in 1928, Muir succeeded him as president.
The firm, then publishing twenty-four national
magazines serving engineers and business executives in ten major industries, with a half
million subscribers and 4,500 industrial adver-
tisers, was also the largest publisher in the
world of scientific and technical books through
its subsidiary, the McGraw-Hill Book Company. At the time that he assumed the presidency, *Coal Age* referred to Muir as an "outstanding leader in the evolution of business
journalism" and remarked also on his "contribution to the improvement of the marketing
philosophy of industry." Muir was chiefly responsible for bringing into existence in 1929
Business Week, a weekly news magazine which
interprets, in terms of their "significance to
business," national and international events, as
well as news of production, finance, labor and
management, and marketing.

For six months, from July 1933 to January
1934, Muir served in Washington with the National Recovery Administration under Hugh S.
Johnson, NRA Administrator. NRA organization planning having been completed in
October 1933, Muir was named a Divisional
Administrator, one of the "Big Four" under
Johnson who had been with the NRA from
its inception. The four administrators also
formed the nucleus of a planning board to co-
ordinate Government and industry in the fight
against the economic depression, with Muir's
division covering heavy goods—construction materials, machinery, transportation, metal products and tools, electrical goods and machinery,
lumber, railway supplies, and furniture. Muir
built an organization of 500 persons and divided "heavy goods" into 150 classifications,
putting through NRA codes for ninety classifications before he returned to McGraw-Hill.

On his departure his work was divided among three administrators.

In 1937 Muir left McGraw-Hill when invited by Vincent Astor and W. Averell Harriman to join Weekly Publications, Inc., which published a magazine called *News-Week*. Astor resigned from the presidency to become chairman of the board and Harriman continued as a board member, while Muir became president and publisher in June of the news magazine. A little over four years old at this time, *News-Week* had been started on February 17, 1933, by Thomas John Cardell Martyn as a weekly newspaper and had been merged with the magazine *Today* in February 1937. Muir remodeled the magazine's editorial formula to place emphasis on interpretation. The name was changed to *Newsweek*, with the subtitle "The Magazine of News Significance." "The tumult of communications, bewildering to the average man and woman, has created a need for a magazine which will report events in their proper perspective and also interpret this changing world," Muir said in announcing the plans for change.

Besides covering the news, Muir stated, *Newsweek* would feature "internationally known commentators" who would interpret news and trends in signed columns. The magazine's circulation listing in Ayer's *Directory of Newspapers and Periodicals* rose from 162,968 in 1937 to 851,036 in 1953. Since February 1949, when Theodore F. Mueller, vice-president and general manager, became publisher of *Newsweek*, Muir has been president and chairman of the editorial board.

Through Muir's direction *Newsweek* expanded greatly during World War II, with a network of foreign correspondents set up to cover war fronts. *Newsweek*'s "Battle Baby," a condensed version of the regular edition without advertising, was called by the publisher "the first miniature magazine to be published exclusively for the armed forces." In 1952 the magazine initiated international editions printed in Tokyo and Paris from photographs of the news pages flown from Dayton, where the regular edition is produced. *Newsweek*, which maintains news bureaus in Paris, London, Bonn, and Tokyo, has about thirty foreign correspondents, 100 domestic correspondents, and New York and Washington staffs of more than 300 persons.

Muir himself took the role of foreign correspondent in December 1942, reporting on the subject "How industry helped to hold the sagging British line in the blitz" in a seven-page special section in *Newsweek*, after an eight weeks' visit to Great Britain as representative of the magazine and chairman of the war committee of the National Association of Manufacturers. Muir had earlier written "Breaking Down Sales Resistance in Industrial Selling," published in the *Annals of the American Academy* in September 1924, and two of his public addresses have appeared in *Vital Speeches*, "Shadows of State Socialism" (October 1, 1941) and "National Dangers of the Thirty-hour Week" (February 1, 1935).

Organizations to which Muir belongs are the National Industrial Conference Board, the New York Chamber of Commerce, the Council of Foreign Relations, and the Economic Club of New York. He is on the board of directors of the American Arbitration Association and the Foreign Policy Association and is a member of the board of trustees of the Committee of Economic Development, United States Council of the International Chamber of Commerce, and the committee of sponsors of the First International Conference of Manufacturers. He has also been a member of the Burns Society, the St. Andrew's Society, and the Pilgrims of the United States. His clubs are Racquet and Tennis, Links, Tuxedo, River, Leash, and Travelers (Paris); he is past president of the Morris County Golf and Country Club. Muir has received the Cross of Chevalier of the French Legion of Honor.

Married to Lida Kelly on May 14, 1914, Muir is the father of Malcolm, Jr., and Eleanor Warfield (Mrs. Collister Johnson). This marriage was terminated by divorce in 1942. On August 19, 1943, the magazine executive married Frances Tener Brown. Muir's church is the Episcopal.

References

    Adv & Sell 26:31-2+ Mr 26 '36
    Coal Age 33:705 N '28
    Who's Who in America, 1952-53
    Who's Who in Commerce and Industry (1951)
    Who's Who in Journalism, 1925

MUNN, BIGGIE *See* Munn, C. L.

MUNN, CLARENCE L(ESTER) Sept. 11, 1908- Football coach
Address: b. c/o Michigan State College, East Lansing, Mich.

Voted the coach of the year 1952 by his fellow members of the American Football Coaches Association, Clarence L. (Biggie) Munn is head coach of Michigan State College, whose squad went undefeated for twenty-four games. An All-America guard in his undergraduate days at the University of Minnesota, he was named captain of the 1931 All-America team. Munn, who has been coaching ever since his graduation, is noted for the variety of his offense tactics and for his unorthodox ideas about football.

Born September 11, 1908, Clarence Lester Munn spent his earliest years on a farm near the Mississippi River in Minnesota. "His father died when he was eight there was hard going for the family of five children thereafter," according to sports writer Bill Wallace (New York *World-Telegram & Sun*, Dec. 10, 1952). "Ever since I was a kid, there have been a lot of things to work for," is the way Munn himself puts it.

In Minneapolis, where the family moved, "Biggie" attended Jordan and North high schools. At the age of fifteen he joined the track team, although he was working at three jobs and had virtually no time for practice. His first track meet took place after he had

MUNN, CLARENCE—*Continued*

worked till 3 a.m. parking cars. The boy fell asleep in the coach's car on the way to the meet, where he was entered in six events. In the words of a *Collier's* article by Bill Fay, "Drowsy but unperturbed, Biggie threw a javelin 174 feet 8 inches, tossed a 12-pound shot 47 feet 2 inches, ran 100 yards in 10 seconds, broad-jumped 20 feet 6 inches, whirled a discus 128 feet 4 inches, and ran anchor leg in the mile relay," winning three first places (in the javelin, shot and relay), six medals, and a gold watch. While at North High he scored 104¼ points in five meets, a record which still stands in 1953. Besides captaining the track team, young Munn was chosen the all-city high school fullback.

At the University of Minnesota, Biggie Munn was to win the Western Conference (Big Ten) award for outstanding proficiency in both athletics and scholarship. Playing football under Coach Bernie Bierman, who is said to be his personal hero, the short, speedy lineman won an All-America rating as a guard for two successive years and was selected as captain of that purely theoretical all-star team in his senior year, 1931. One of the most versatile of football players, he once made a 66-yard punt out of bounds against Northwestern, and carried a ball 18 yards to a touchdown for the Gophers against Wisconsin.

Continuing his track career, Biggie won the Western Conference and Penn Relays shot-put records. His heave in the latter was 48 feet 7⅝ inches. By plotting the graph of his practice throws over several years, Munn found that he hurled the cannonball farthest on the thirteenth through fifteenth tries. From that time on, he always took a dozen practice throws before each meet, so that he started at his peak.

The day of Munn's graduation, he started work as a line coach under Bernie Bierman, leaving after three years to become director of athletics at Albright College in Reading, Pennsylvania. He spent 1937 as assistant coach to Ossie Solem at Syracuse, then headed for Ann Arbor to coach the University of Michigan linemen under Fritz Crisler. Referring to coaches Bierman and Crisler, Joe Williams has said, "Studying defense under them was like studying burglary under Raffles" (New York *World-Telegram & Sun*, December 10, 1952). During Munn's seven-year stay, the Wolverines won 56 games, tied 2, and lost 14.

Munn was called back to Syracuse in 1946 as head coach, but after hard but futile efforts to awaken alumni interest he cancelled his three-year contract when he found that his team had to make all-day trips in buses and day coaches. "I can stand it," he said, "but the boys deserve something better."

The fact that the University of Chicago withdrew from the Big Ten (Western intercollegiate athletic conference) in 1946 is not unconnected with Biggie Munn's appointment as head coach at Michigan State College, beginning that December. M.S.C. president John A. Hannah had been "taking dead aim" at Chicago's membership ever since that university dropped intercollegiate football in 1939.

CLARENCE L. MUNN

With President Hannah taking care of the political maneuvering and Coach Munn handling the football, the "cow college" in East Lansing was elected to Big Ten membership on May 20, 1949. In that year, its football budget was $120,000 and its football receipts, after taxes, were $409,207.14. In order to win the conference seat, which adds an estimated $250,000 a year to the football receipts of its members, M.S.C. had in February suspended the 125 Jenison and Gunston athletic scholarships which had brought M.S.C. most of its outstanding performers, according to Stanley Frank (*Saturday Evening Post*, October 14, 1950). That the college continued to recruit football talent in large numbers, despite the attractions of the rival University of Michigan, is due partly to Coach Munn's wide popularity and persuasiveness as an after-dinner speaker.

The first game of Biggie's tenure at M.S.C. was a 55-to-0 loss to Michigan. The older Wolverine linemen, who had been coached by Munn himself in past years, showed off for their old teacher. Joe Soboleski, for instance, tossed a Spartan line-backer at Munn's feet and called to him, "How'm I doing, Coach?" (*Colliers*, Sept. 27, 1952). Not until 1950 did Munn's Spartans start winning from Michigan. However, they won 7 games and lost 2 that season; won 6, tied 2, lost 2 in 1948; won 6 and lost 3 in 1949; won 8 and lost 1 in 1950; and won all 9 games of the 1951 and 1952 seasons, making a total of 45 wins, 8 losses, and 2 ties.

Although Munn's teams have not included any great stars of the gridiron, a dozen of the players on his six teams, 1947-52, were voted all-America first team positions, these being backs Sonny Grandelius, Lynn Chandnois, Don McAuliffe, Al Dorow, and Jim Ellis, ends Bob Carey and Dorne Dibble, and linesmen Don Coleman, Ed Bagdon, Don Mason, Dick Tamburo, and Frank Kush. About twice as many received second team or honorable mention ratings. Five of Biggie's assistants during those six years are now head coaches: Forest Evashevski at Iowa, Al Kircher at Washington State, Kip Taylor at Oregon State, Red Dawson at Pittsburgh, and Frank Brogger at St. Ambrose (Iowa).

Although Munn's thoroughness is often remarked upon, he puts his team through much less scrimmage than is usual. "Football," he has said (quoted by Bill Fay in *Collier's*), "should be fun, not drudgery. Practice sessions should be short—never more than ninety minutes—and contact work should be limited to one brisk scrimmage a week. And when your players are really keyed up, you can even omit the scrimmage."

He puts emphasis on physical conditioning, on mastering the techniques of blocking and tackling, and on a versatile offense. Instead of adopting a particular formation, such as the T, split T, single or double wing, he teaches his squad sixty-six basic plays which among them inclde all varieties of formation. Munn believes that this is the only major college team which does not permit the players to record their plays in a notebook—"Anybody who can't remember sixty-six plays is too dumb to play football," he has said.

Another of Munn's characteristics is his insistence on freshness and his willingness to go to lengths to obtain it. The week before the important Notre Dame game in 1951, he scheduled no scrimmage at all and would not even allow players to work out against tackling dummies. In the first scrimmage play, his line opened the way for an eighty-eight-yard touchdown run, · the beginning of a 35-0 victory. · Again, when Ohio State was leading 20-10 in the fourth quarter, Munn sent in three untried sophomore substitutes. One of them, Tom Yewcic, promptly scored with what Munn calls a "transcontinental pass," this being the first pass he had ever thrown in a college game and the first time he had ever gotten into a game on offense. Against Syracuse in 1952 Munn used his entire sixty-one squad. Equally unorthodox, Munn selects tall ends and centers and short, fast linemen (his own type of build). Large size and heavy weight are usually regarded as necessary in linemen, but Munn wants his men to move fast enough to stay in front of the ball carrier, and most of them are well under 200 pounds.

Munn took a stand on the controversial limited substitution rule of the NCAA in the fall of 1953. "I think the new rule sets football back a generation," he told a sports writer (*Collier's*, Sept. 4, 1953). "It definitely will make for an inferior game." Noting that men who have never played defense before will be forced to learn how, the veteran coach predicted that "they'll make more mistakes than a defensive specialist working in the two-platoon system and cheap touchdowns will result." He said, too, that an important factor will be injuries—MSC had twenty injuries on its squad during spring training, many more than in seasons past.

In 1950, as in 1951 and 1952, C. L. Munn was named Coach of the Year by the Detroit *Times* Quarterbacks' Club. In the summer of 1951, at the request of the Army, he spent several weeks in Germany, coaching American GI's (Munn has presided over many football summer coaching schools and clinics, including two consecutive summers in Honolulu). Picked as coach of the East team for the benefit Shriner game in 1952, he saw his squad win an unexpected 15-14 victory over a highly favored West team, and repeated the same feat in 1953 for a 21-20 score.

In 1951, the 500 voting members of the Football Coaches Association put him in third place in the balloting for Coach of the Year, behind Chuck Taylor of Stanford and Bob Neyland of Tennessee. The next year, Munn emerged 40 votes ahead of the next highest man, Bobby Dodd of Georgia Tech, an unusually large margin. Since football schedules are set four years in advance, Munn's team played as an independent and not in Big Ten competition until the fall of 1953.

By the middle of October, 1953, Michigan State had won its first four games, thereby making the team undefeated for twenty-eight consecutive games.

To quote Bill Wallace (*World-Telegram & Sun*, Dec. 10, 1952) "Biggie is heavy-set and powerfully built. He has laugh wrinkles around the eyes . . . and worry wrinkles on his brow. Today he weighs 225 pounds, just seven over his old playing weight, and as an outdoor man keeps trim with a rugged fishing trip into Ontario each summer." On his trips he uses what his wife calls "two mink coats' worth" of photographic equipment, taking 16-mm. color movies which he shows on the banquet and lecture tours that take him to nearly every community in Michigan. (Mrs. Munn is Vera Jean Wattles, a Minnesota graduate, and their children are Michael and Jane.) The coach has not slackened his pace. "Even with the pressure of a winning streak," Munn says, "we have had a lot of fun. Without some laughs, the game isn't worth playing."

References

Collier's 130:26 S 27 '53 pors
N Y World-Tel-Sun p42 D 10 '52 por

MUNN, FRANK 1895—Oct. 1, 1953 Former radio singer, "The Golden Voice of Radio"; began working as a shuttle boy in an embroidery factory; started singing in amateur concerts; through efforts of Gustave Haenschen he made his radio debut on the "Brunswick Hour of Music" in 1923; his radio work thereafter included numerous appearances on the 'Palmolive Hour", the "American Album of the Air", and "Waltz Time"; he retired in 1946. See *Current Biography*, 1944.

Obituary

N Y Times p21 Oct 2 '53

MUÑOZ MARÍN, LUIS (mü′ñyōs märēn′)
Feb. 18, 1898- Governor of Puerto Rico
Address: La Fortaleza, San Juan, Puerto Rico

> NOTE: This biography supersedes
> the article which appeared in
> *Current Biography* in 1942.

Now serving his second term as the first elected Governor of Puerto Rico, Luis Muñoz Marín has played a leading role in the island's struggle for economic improvement and self-government under the American flag. Although he began as an ardent advocate of complete independence and as a socialist, he is now a firm believer in gradually increasing autonomy and combining public and private enterprise. "Operation Bootstrap" was devised by Governor Muñoz Marín as a way of improving the island's economy, and it is a free translation of his slogan, *Jalda arriba*, meaning an up-hill climb.

He has divided his life between the United States and Puerto Rico as poet, editor, pamphleteer and politician. After splitting with the Puerto Rican Liberal Party in 1937, which, as a member of the Senate, he had led since 1932, he founded the Popular Democrat Party, and as chairman of the landless *jíbaros* (peasants) he has become the most popular politician in Puerto Rican history.

Among the reforms Muñoz Marín has instituted are the raising of slums in San Juan and replacing them with new low-cost housing such as the Llorens Torres development where some 2,600 rental units are being built at a cost of $70,000,000 to house 10,000 persons.

Puerto Rico was discovered by Columbus, and Ponce de León conquered it for Spain in 1509. With a population of over 2,200,000 and an area of 3,435 square miles, the island is located at the northeast head of the Caribbean Sea. It is one of the most densely populated sections in the world. Its principal crops are sugar, citrus fruits, coffee, and it produces rum and makes cigars. The ninety-five mile long island was taken over by the United States in 1898 in the Spanish-American War, but in July 1952 it became a wholly autonomous community in all matters regarding its local Government, and is voluntarily associated with the United States.

Luis Muñoz Marín was born in San Juan on February 18, 1898, five months before American occupation forces landed in Puerto Rico. He was the only son of Luis Muñoz Rivera and Amalia Marín de Muñoz Rivera. Muñoz Rivera, known as "the George Washington of Puerto Rico," had won from Spain the island's first measure of autonomy. The Spanish-American War having changed that, Muñoz Rivera learned English, became Resident Commissioner in Washington and is credited with getting Congress to grant the islanders United States citizenship and their own elected Legislature.

Young Muñoz. Marín, living mostly in New York and Washington, studied at Georgetown Preparatory School and Georgetown University. While still a student, he contributed articles to

LUIS MUNOZ MARIN

the *Baltimore Sun* and various national magazines.

When his father died, Muñoz left Georgetown law school and went to New York to write. Although legend has labeled him a Greenwich Village bohemian, he actually lived in the Village only a few months. With his Mississippi-born wife, Muna Lee, a poetess, whom he married in 1919, he lived mostly in the suburbs and on West 97th Street.

As free-lance writer and translator, he contributed to *Smart Set*, the *Nation*, the *New Republic* and *American Mercury* and translated Walt Whitman, Edwin Markham and Carl Sandburg into Spanish. In 1917, he published two books, *Borrones* and *Madre Haraposa*, and in 1925 he wrote the section on Puerto Rico in the symposium, *These United States*. He was also editor of *La Revísta de Indias*, a magazine devoted to Latin American culture, and was active in movements for Latin American labor and unity.

In politics, he served as secretary to the Puerto Rican representative to the U.S. Congress from 1916 to 1918, and then, despite his father's opposition, as a member of the Socialist Party. In 1924, he campaigned for Robert La Follette in the United States Presidential race, but was not active in island politics until 1926, when he joined the new Liberal Party. As editor and publisher of *La Democracia*, he urged complete independence for Puerto Rico and renounced his father's conservatism. According to John Lear (*Saturday Evening Post*, December 11, 1943), he has generally spoken of his father formally and impersonally and criticized him for being unaware of the needs of the *jíbaros*.

When Muñoz was elected Senator in the Puerto Rican Legislature in 1932, the island was deep in the depression. Through his connections in Washington and his talks with

President Franklin D. Roosevelt, he worked to get New Deal money for the island.

His announcement that millions of dollars to help the unemployed would come from the United States increased his popularity. The opposition was confounded when the New Deal announced its huge spending plans for Puerto Rico during Muñoz' next trip to Washington. Other spurs to his popularity were his successful drive to have the unpopular Governor Gore removed and his succesful efforts at pushing through the Legislature, against the opposition of the Socialist-Republican Coalition, a bill that, by enforcing the long-dormant 500-acre law, would break up large sugar holdings and redistribute the land among the *jibaros.*

Convinced that the Liberals were not truly representing the cause of the *jibaros,* Muñoz split with them in 1937. He battled not only the sugar growers, who were lobbying in Congress for a curtailment of economic reconstruction, but opposed even a friendly gesture from Democratic Senator Millard Tydings, who had offered up a bill for island independence in response to threatening Nationalist unrest in 1936.

Muñoz fought this bill because he believed the island could not survive political freedom without continued aid from the United States. To help the islanders prepare themselves for the economic responsibilities of eventual independence or statehood, he organized the Popular Democratic Party in 1938 and began campaigning in the hills.

Under the slogan, "Bread, Land and Liberty," he spoke on roadside stumps and in the smallest villages against the customary practice of selling votes. "I know $2 is worth something," *Time* (May 2, 1949) quoted him as saying, "But if you don't sell your vote, you can use it to get justice for your family. So remember: justice or $2. But you can't have both."

Visiting more than 500 of the 786 election districts, Muñoz sent recordings of his speeches to be broadcast over loudspeakers elsewhere. Once, he had to wade a mile along the shore of the Caribbean to appear at a labor meeting on a sugar plantation which had been especially fenced to bar him. If things didn't get better, he told voters everywhere, they should be ready to turn him and his party out at the next election. Party candidates had to swear publicly that they would push enforcement of the 500-acre law, set minimum wages, encourage new industry, expand rural electrification and regulate the sugar industry.

Although Muñoz received the heaviest vote of any candidate in the 1940 election, his Popular Party won control of the Senate by only one vote, failed to control the House by two votes, but managed to elect the Speaker of the House with the aid of independent votes. Elected President of the Senate, and with the backing of Rexford G. Tugwell, who had been appointed Governor in 1941, Muñoz set up industrial- and farm-development corporations and the Land Authority, to buy up and redistribute excessive land holdings.

By 1948, 70,000 acres had been redistributed as "proportional profit farms"—one-acre plots rented to *jibaros* and worked on a profit-sharing basis. Co-operatives were organized for cheap power, water and transportation. Each small landowner contributed to the crop and shared the profits. To meet the island's housing needs, both public and private projects totaling some 28,000 units were built or under way by 1949. An Insular Power Authority was created to buy and operate privately owned utilities.

In the inevitable opposition among Congressmen and Coalition legislators to "socialistic experiments," it was Tugwell, a New Dealer, who caught most of the attacks. The mass popularity of Muñoz impressed even such conservatives as Senator Robert A. Taft, according to John Lear (*Saturday Evening Post*, December 11, 1943), with the need for Government-supported industry in the island.

In 1944, Muñoz and his party polled twice as many votes as all other parties combined, took all but two of the thirty-nine House seats and all but two of the seventeen Senate seats.

Writing in *Inter-American* (June 1946) on industrialization and autonomy, Muñoz noted that with the population of two and one quarter million expected to grow to three million by 1960, the island would be less able than ever to support itself agriculturally. Population growth might be controlled, he wrote, by raising the average annual income above $800 a year, since above that level, Puerto Rican families tended to be smaller. Industrialization was the quickest way to raise that income. If the United States would give the island political authority over its own resources, full production could eventually be achieved. As he had said in a 1943 plea for autonomy, what Puerto Rico needed was "more vitamins and less aspirin."

After World War II, the Puerto Rico Industrial Development Corporation was organized and "Operation Bootstrap" began. It offered a twelve-year tax exemption and general assistance on labor problems and plant construction to new industries. By 1950, according to *Fortune* (May 1950), over sixty plants had been opened by mainland investors.

As of April, 1953, *Scholastic* (April 10, 1953) reported more than 200 plants were employing over 15,000 workers—more industrial workers than ever before employed in the island outside the sugar industry. Among the new products were rayon, nylon, shoes, optical lens and electronic components. PRIDC also promoted such old industries as rum and tourism. Muñoz reported that the island income had grown from $228,000,000 in 1940 to $647,-000,000 in 1950, while unemployment had dropped from 90,000 to 82,000 despite the large increase in the population. It has been accompanied by steps in increased autonomy. In August 1947, Congress granted Puerto Rico the right to elect its own Governor. Muñoz was elected the following year and re-elected in 1952. In July 1950, Congress gave the island the chance to write its own Constitution and to approve it by popular referendum.

(Continued next page)

MUÑOZ MARÍN, LUIS—Continued

Despite some opposition to Muñoz as an alleged dictator, Congress approved the new Constitution and Puerto Rico became a Commonwealth on July 25, 1952, with its own flag and the right to make its internal laws and elect its own officials without Federal approval. Because of his party's overwhelming power in the Legislature, Muñoz himself put into the Constitution provisions to curtail the Governor's power and insure that minority parties have at least a third of the legislative votes.

In 1923, according to *Time* (November 29, 1948), Muñoz had described himself as "God's pamphleteer, [going] with the mobs of hungry men and women towards the great awakening." Once belittled as a heavy-drinking, heavy-eating dilettante playing at revolution, (*Time* May 2, 1949) he has become Puerto Rico's hero. He is a husky, stooped man with sad-angry eyes who, as *Time* has described him, thinks in both English and Spanish and can explain his ideas "in either language with literary dignity or colloquial directness . . . that can go straight to the heart and mind of the humblest and least educated hearer." When in November 1950, the Nationalists, still demanding immediate independence, tried to assassinate President Truman and seize the Puerto Rican Government, Muñoz himself was one of their targets.

Muñoz's marriage to Muna Lee was terminated in 1940. He has a grown son, Luiz, and daughter by his first marriage, and two daughters, Victoria and Vivian, by his second marriage to Inés Maria Mendoza. He says he feels uncomfortable in the Spanish colonial atmosphere of La Fortaleza and prefers the Governor's summer home at Jajome in the hills.

Presiding over a gala celebration in honor of the first anniversary of the Puerto Rican "commonwealth" Constitution in July, 1953, Governor Muñoz Marín received messages of congratulation and good wishes from President Dwight D. Eisenhower and New York's Mayor Vincent Impelliteri. "We are at war to destroy poverty," he told a huge radio audience. (New York *Times*, July 26, 1953).

Speaking from a platform on which the red, white, and blue flag of Puerto Rico was paired with the Stars and Stripes, the Governor reviewed Puerto Rico's accomplishments in the fields of industry, business, health, and civil rights and promised cooperation with the United States in the field of defense and diplomatic relations. Noting the unity of the two Governments, the message from President Eisenhower said the United States shared the Puerto Ricans' pride in their achievements.

References

Christian Sci Mon My 3 '52 por
N Y Times p56 Mr 25 '48 por
N Y World-Telegram p13 Mr 1 '52 por
Time 37:15-16 Mr 31 '41 por; 52:40 N
   29 '48 por; 53:33+ My 2 '49 pors
Sat Eve Post 216:12+ D 11 '53
Torregrosa, A. M. Luis Muñoz Marín,
   su vida y su patriotica obra (1944)
Who's Who in America, 1952-53
Who's Who in Latin America, 1940

MUNRO, LESLIE KNOX   Feb. 26, 1901-
Ambassador of New Zealand to the United States; United Nations delegate; editor; lawyer

Address: b. c/o New Zealand Embassy, 19 Observatory Circle, Washington 8, D.C.; c/o United Nations, New York 17; h. 27 Observatory Circle, Washington 8, D.C.; 258 Kepa Rd., Mission Bay, N.Z.

The Ambassador of New Zealand to the United States and the head of its delegation to the United Nations, as well as President of the U.N. Trusteeship Council, is His Excellency Leslie Knox Munro. A successful Auckland (New Zealand) barrister and solicitor from 1924 to 1941 and a lecturer on law, he was the editor of the Auckland morning paper, the *New Zealand Herald*, from 1942 to 1951. Named to his present diplomatic posts late in 1951, he succeeded Sir Carl August Berendsen.

Leslie Knox Munro, who is one of five brothers, was born at Auckland, New Zealand, on February 26, 1901; both his parents, Colin Robert and Marie Caroline (Knox) Munro, had also been born in New Zealand, where the former became a headmaster and later on inspector of schools. From the Remuera primary school young Munro went on to Auckland Grammar School (equivalent of high school), where he was a leader in scholarship and athletics, and head prefect in his final year.

Having won a university entrance scholarship, he studied at Auckland University College, a constituent of the University of New Zealand. Although he majored in languages he decided to become a barrister, and was graduated as a Master of Laws in 1923. Besides receiving awards for his year in English and Latin, he was Senior Scholar in Roman Law, and was recommended by the English examiners for First Class Honors in the Law of Contract and Roman Law. Munro also holds the M.A. degree from Auckland University College.

Munro served as a lecturer in jurisprudence, Roman law, and constitutional law and history at Auckland University College from 1923 to 1938. At the same time, his private practice—as both solicitor and barrister—at Auckland, begun in 1924, reflected mounting success. Among other activities he wrote for the *New Zealand Law Reports*.

His success continued to be so striking that in 1936 he was elected to both the presidency of the Auckland Law Society and the Council of the New Zealand Law Society, for two and three year terms respectively. (At thirty-five Munro was the youngest advocate ever to attain the Auckland Law Society presidency). Also in 1936 he began a series of fortnightly radio talks on international affairs over the New Zealand National Broadcasting System.

Two years later Munro was named dean of the Faculty of Law at Auckland University College, but relinquished this position when he was nominated to the Auckland University College Council in 1939. Munro's regular broadcasts on international matters ceased with the outbreak of World War II; but in 1939 he began contributing to the *Weekly News* a series of articles on world affairs which he

LESLIE KNOX MUNRO

continued until his appointment as Ambassador to the United States twelve years later.

In 1940 Munro began two years of service on the executive committee of the Opposition party in the New Zealand Parliament, the National Party. That same year, the Hon. Sidney G. Holland, who in 1949 became Prime Minister, assumed the Leadership of the Opposition. (Founded in 1931 as a result of a merger of the conservative and liberal parties, the National Party, according to the *Political Handbook of the World,* "stands for free enterprise and is opposed to state socialism.")

It was during this period of political activity that Munro left his law practice to accept (1941) the associate editorship of the *New Zealand Herald,* an influential morning paper published at Auckland since 1863, with an editorial policy latterly favoring the Nationalists. A year later (August, 1942) Munro was made editor and may well have had an influence on the outcome of the elections of 1943 and 1946, in which the Nationalists, though not securing a clear majority in the House of Representatives, nevertheless made substantial gains.

Selected as one of the delegates of New Zealand to the Imperial Press Conference at London in 1946, Munro during that summer not only travelled extensively in England and Scotland, but toured Europe and the World War II battlefields as the guest of the British War Office and the French Government. In the following year he was named to the Senate of the University of New Zealand as a representative of Auckland University College, and in 1948 he became Vice-chairman of Auckland Grammar School Board (whose jurisdiction in secondary education includes five large New Zealand schools).

The influence of the *New Zealand Herald* on Dominion political, economic and international thinking continued to grow, especially after the election of November 30, 1949, in which the National Party won 46 of the 80 seats in the New Zealand House of Representatives, thereby ending the Labor Government which had lasted for fourteen years. Sidney Holland thereupon became Prime Minister and Minister of Finance and increased his majority over Labor by a 50-30 ratio in a subsequent election held in September, 1951. At that time the daily circulation of the *New Zealand Herald* was 150,000, 50,000 more than that of the second-largest paper in the Dominion, the Auckland *Star,* whose evening circulation reaches 100,000. Munro continued to direct the *Herald* until November, 1951, when he turned over the editorship to H. G. Bell.

Prior to the September, 1951 election, Munro spent four months in the United States as guest of the State Department under the terms of the Smith-Mundt Act, met leading personalities in both government and law and spent time studying American politics, foreign policy, and university education.

On December 2, 1951, Prime Minister Holland announced the appointment of Munro as Ambassador of New Zealand to the United States and head of the New Zealand delegation to the United Nations to succeed the greatly honored and respected Sir Carl Berendson (who had been appointed to the former post by Labor Party Premier Peter Fraser in December, 1948, and to the latter in 1944).

Ambassador Munro took up his new duties in Washington in January, 1952, and presented his credentials as chief New Zealand delegate to the United Natons to Secretary General Trygve Lie on February 29 of the same year. (New Zealand, as the administering power for Western Samoa and the Union or Tokelau Islands holds a seat on the United Nations Trusteeship Council).

During the first week of August, 1952, the Ambassador accompanied the Hon. Thomas Clifton Webb, New Zealand's Minister of External Affairs, to Honolulu for conferences with Secretary of State Dean Acheson of the United States, and with the Australian Minister of External Affairs, Richard Gardiner Casey, on ways and means to implement the Tripartite Security Treaty. This Treaty had been signed by the three countries at San Francisco on September 1, 1951, and pledged the signatory powers to "meet the common danger" in the event of "an armed attack in the Pacific Area on any one of the ·parties."

Later in the same week Munro was designated by Foreign Minister Webb as his deputy in the Pacific (ANZUS) Council, to serve with David K. E. Bruce of the United States and Sir Percy C. Spender of Australia in carrying on at Washington "the consultative work of the Council between the annual meetings that will be attended by the top officials themselves" (New York *Times* August 6, 1952).

Ambassador Munro, who had hailed the ANZUS Treaty as "a guarantee of peace in the Pacific," was in the Washington news of March 13, 1953, when he formally protested to the United States Department of State on

MUNRO, LESLIE KNOX—*Continued*
quotas, admitedly mandatory, imposed by the Department of Agriculture, on New Zealand dairy products under the so-called "cheese amendment" to the Defense Production Act. The New Zealand envoy not only pointed out that these quotas deprived his country of purchasing power in the American market but charged that they represented a "clear breach" of the General Agreement on Tariffs.

Speaking in the United Nations General Assembly on March 28, Ambassador Munro was one of those who, while conceding that outgoing Secretay General Trygve Lie was within his rights in moving to dismiss all "subversives" from the U.N. Staff, nevertheless feared that such action might severely impair morale.

"The international Secretariat, in which both staff members and Governments have taken pride," he said, "could quicky disintegrate into a diplomatic corps of national groups each playing for its own hand. . ."

Munro was elected president of the United Nations Trusteeship Council on June 16. In a statement reviewing the achievements of the Council as it adjourned its twelfth session in July, the new president characterized as the major accomplishment of the annual meetings the rapid improvement in recent months in the administration of Somaliland by the Italian Government. According to Munro both the detailed interrogation by council members of spokesmen for the administering nations and the reports submitted by visiting missions were responsible for "slow but gradual improvement in various fields" (New York *Times,* July 22, 1953). He was elected chairman of the Credentials Committee of the UN Assembly in September.

Munro appeared, in July, at the annual Colgate University Conference on American Foreign Policy. A principal speaker, he told the nearly 300 participants·and delegates that his nation, like the rest of the Commonwealth, was ready to explore any peace feelers no matter what their origin. Suggesting that his tendency was to side with those who felt that the Chinese Communist regime was at least partly sovereign, he said that "we should address ourselves to the Chinese and their rulers and let them know that no benefit to themselves can come from Korea no matter what benefits might accrue to the Soviet Government" (New York *Times,* July 13, 1953).

Since his diplomatic appointment Ambassador Munro has severed all formal political affiliations; his church is the Presbyterian and his social clubs are the Northern, Auckland and Rotary in New Zealand and the Metropolitan in Washington. He was married to Christine Mary Priestley in October, 1927, and they were the parents of one daughter, Ann Christine. Mrs. Munro died in 1929. On November 9, 1931 Munro married Muriel Olga Sturt, by whom he has a second daughter, Esme Sturt Munro. New Zealand's envoy is six feet two inches tall

and weighs 210 pounds, has hazel eyes and dark hair "greying". He lists tennis and reading as his favorite recreations.

References

Washington Post p58 F 17 '52 por
International Who's Who (1952)
Who's Who in New Zealand (1951)

MURROW, EDWARD R(OSCOE) April 25, 1908- Radio and television news reporter
Address: b. c/o Columbia Broadcasting System, 485 Madison Ave., New York 22

NOTE: This biography supersedes the article which appeared in *Current Biography* in 1942.

Long familiar to the radio audience as a news analyst, Edward R. Murrow became a prominent television personality in 1951 with the program *See It Now,* a weekly Columbia Broadcasting System news feature which he narrates and produces. The program's format was suggested by Murrow's radio program, *Hear It Now,* which originated a year earlier and which in turn stemmed from *I Can Hear It Now,* a three-volume series of recorded historical events narrated by the newsman and issued by Columbia Records.

Murrow first became known as a radio voice when he broadcast from London for the CBS before and during World War II and built up the reputation for accuracy and objectivity which he has since maintained. "I try to be a reporter," he says. "A commentator is a kind of oracle, and I am never so sure I'm right." A CBS vice-president from the end of the war until 1947, he resigned at that time to resume broadcasting the news over that network.

One of the top radio news reporters without newspaper training, he has written articles for educational journals as well as prefaces and introductions to several other volumes. A selection of his London broadcasts, *So This Is London,* appeared in book form in 1941 (Simon & Schuster). A new Murrow television presentation, *Person to Person,* offered on the CBS network in October 1953, features "live pickups" and uses no film whatever.

The reporter, born April 25, 1908 in Greensboro, North Carolina, was christened Egbert Roscoe but changed his name to Edward Roscoe Murrow in his sophomore year at college. His parents, Roscoe C. and Ethel (Lamb) Murrow, and two brothers moved to Skagit County, Washington when the boy was six, and his father, who had been a farmer in North Carolina, became a railroad engineer for a logging company.

To earn money for college, Murrow worked for two years as a compassman and topographer for timber cruisers in northwest Washington. He attended Leland Stanford University, the University of Washington, and Washington State College, graduating from the latter in 1930 with a degree of Bachelor of Arts in history and speech and a Phi Beta Kappa key. While at college he worked as a houseboy for

EDWARD R. MURROW

a sorority, served as president of the junior class and in his senior year, as student-body president. He was a top cadet in ROTC, and was noted for his effective drill voice, an asset that he continued to develop as a debater and actor.

Murrow became president of the National Student Federation after his graduation and in this capacity visited three hundred American colleges, travelled in Europe, set up a student travel bureau, and arranged international debates between American and European universities. In 1932 he left this position to serve as assistant director of the Institute of International Education, which is financed jointly by the Carnegie and Rockefeller Foundations. His work with this organization entailed supervising personnel, finances, publications, and foreign offices in London, Paris, Geneva, and Vienna. For two years, beginning in 1933, he was secretary of the Emergency Commission for the Aid of Displaced German Scholars and was instrumental in bringing almost three hundred of these to safety.

Resigning from the Institute of International Education, he joined CBS in 1935 and has been with the broadcasting company ever since that time. He spent the first two years as director of Talks and Education, and in May, 1937 he was sent to London to take charge of CBS' European Bureau. His work consisted largely of arranging speeches and cultural programs, but events soon made Murrow's job a vital one.

While he was on his way to Poland in 1938 to organize a broadcast for the CBS *School of the Air* the Nazis entered Austria, and the newsman chartered a plane and got to Vienna in time to describe on the radio the German march into the city. To cover the fast-breaking news events of that time he hired a European staff which included William L. Shirer for the Berlin post. Late in 1938 he lectured

in the United States for a brief period before returning to London.

During World War II Murrow personally handled most of the broadcasts from London; his opening phrase, "This is London", became familiar to millions in the United States. He returned to this country in November 1941 and was honored on his arrival at a banquet given at the Waldorf-Astoria by William S. Paley, president of CBS. After a few months of rest (and of a nationwide lecture tour) he returned to his London post. He covered many of the important pre-war and wartime events: the fall of Czechoslovakia, Munich, Churchill's declaration of war, the campaign in North Africa, the invasions in France, V-E day, etc. The London blitz provided him with personal encounters with bombs, the CBS offices being bombed twice and the BBC studios from which he was broadcasting at the time was bombed.

Murrow broadcast an eyewitness account of an air raid from a rooftop and a description of his voyage aboard a mine-sweeper (which CBS had firmly forbidden because of the danger). In addition to maintaining his news schedule he served as a fire warden.

A selection of Murrow's radio broadcasts from August 28, 1939 to December 31, 1940 (with an introduction by Elmer Davis) was published in 1941 under the title *This Is London.* "This book," said the New York *Times* (April 13, 1941), "is in the full sense the stuff of history", and a review in *Books* (April 13, 1941) stated, "Mr. Murrow's broadcasts read well, because the language of good spoken speech is good language, and so good prose." Because "he is the best known and most influential American commentator on World War II", according to the publisher of *Bloody But Unbowed*, Murrow was chosen to write the preface for that pictorial record of England under bombing, published in 1941.

Murrow returned to the United States at the end of the war and in December 1945 was made a CBS vice-president in charge of all news, education, and discussion programs. In resigning from the post in 1947 he said, "I'm not the executive type. Budgets throw me for a loop . . . and I can't get myself to fire anybody." He resumed his news broadcasts on September 29, 1947 on a five-a-week basis. Murrow was elected a director of CBS on April 31, 1949.

Fred W. Friendly and Murrow in 1948 decided to produce an album of records presenting history through an aural medium. The first album, *I Can Hear It Now,* was issued by Columbia Records and was the product of many hours of research spent in selecting and editing excerpts of speeches and other recorded events of the previous thirteen years. Narrated by Murrow, the collection was so well received that two subsequent volumes have been issued since 1948.

In August 1950 Murrow journeyed to Korea to do some first-hand reporting on the war. *Hear It Now,* an hour-long weekly digest of the news presented through recordings of events as they happened, was inspired by the previously produced Murrow-Friendly albums. Another radio feature of Murrow's is a five-minute pro-

MURROW, EDWARD R.—*Continued*

gram, *This I Believe*, in which personalities, famous and otherwise, expound their philosophies of life. Selections from this program have been issued in book form with an introduction by Murrow. The newsman also conducts the annual CBS year-end show on radio and television.

See It Now, inaugurated in November 1951, represents a translation of *Hear It Now* to the visual medium of television and is co-produced by the now famous team of Murrow and Friendly. The program reaches three million homes, according to the Neilsen rating, and through his appearance on the screen as narrator Murrow has achieved even greater popularity and recognition. *See It Now* scored a "first" only two months after its inception by presenting the first television broadcast from a submerged submarine, the U.S.S. *Sablefish*. In March 1952 the program became the first regularly scheduled foreign feature carried by the French national network. The joint Air Force-Civil Defense mock air raid staged in July 1952 to determine if an enemy plane could penetrate America's air defense system was filmed for presentation on *See It Now*; Murrow rode in one of the F-94 jets which attempted to intercept the "enemy" bomber. For presenting the picture of our air defense requirements to the nation on this program Murrow received the Arts and Letters Award for 1952 of the Air Force Association from Lieutenant General Jimmy Doolittle.

The most discussed and praised presentation of *See It Now*, "This is Korea . . . Christmas 1952", was given on December 28, 1952. Murrow and several crews of cameramen and reporters flew to Korea in December "to try to portray the face of the war and the faces of the men who are fighting it". The cameras concentrated on individual soldiers and their reactions to life in Korea rather than on large-scale military operations; soldiers of all nations told why they thought the war was being fought, sent messages to the "folks at home", and were shown in their various celebrations of Christmas. "One of the most impressive presentations in television's short life," commented Philip Hamburger in the *New Yorker* (January 10, 1953) and went on to say, "Mr. Murrow and his associates . . . pictured for us a tragic living legend of our own time and did so with great piety and understanding."

Proving that a legislative body at work can be televised, Murrow took the *See It Now* cameras into a session of the Arkansas General Assembly on February 15, 1953. Murrow sought to demonstrate that television viewers could be shown the workings of Congress.

Despite his success in television, Murrow is said to prefer radio as a more flexible medium; there are many current news happenings which he does not feel lend themselves to visual presentation. He is known as a perfectionist who "bleeds" over the copy he writes; "the more experienced I get, the slower I get", he said in a biographical article in *Cue* on February 21,

1953. He has been called "the social philosopher of radio correspondents", and *Variety* (April 15, 1953) says of him "He brings to his work intellectual integrity, taste and restraint, and a sensitive awareness of human values."

Honored many times for his reporting, Murrow has received the Overseas Press Club Award several times, two George Foster Peabody awards, the Dupont Annual Award, the Headliners Award, the One World Award, the L. S. Weiss Memorial Award, and two George Polk Memorial Awards. He has been given awards by the Southwest Journalism Forum, the Syracuse University School of Journalism, Ohio State University, and the Poor Richard Club.

See It Now was called the "Program of the Year" by the National Association for Better Radio and Television in 1952, and received an "Emmy" award from the Academy of Television Arts and Sciences, a Look-TV award, a Sylvania Television Award, and a Variety Showmanship Award. A member of Kappa Sigma, Murrow was named "Man of the Year" for 1941 by the fraternity for his London reporting.

Five colleges have given Murrow honorary degrees: he has received LL.D.s from Washington State College, the University of North Carolina, and Muhlenberg College, the degree of Doctor of Humanities from Rollins College, and of Doctor of Journalism from Temple University. He is a reserve first lieutenant in the United States Army, a trustee of the Institute of International Education, a director of the National Institute of Foreign Affairs, a member of the Council on Foreign Relations, and a trustee of the Carnegie Endowment for International Peace. He was elected president of the Association of American Correspondents in London in 1944. His clubs are the Savile, the Century, and the Lambs.

Much in demand for his lectures on international relations, Murrow has spoken to groups at Yale, Columbia, Oxford, and the Royal Institute of International Affairs in London. His magazine articles include "Radio in a Democracy" (reprinted from a broadcast) in *Scholastic*, March 18, 1946; "The Schoolroom and the Ballot Box" in the *National Education Association Journal*, November 1950, and "A Problem in Equality" in the *Saturday Review of Literature*, April 21, 1951.

Murrow and Janet Huntington Brewster were married in 1934 and have one son, Charles Casey. Mrs. Murrow made occasional broadcasts from London during the war and served as London head of Bundles for Britain. The Murrows spend their weekends at their eight-room "log cabin" near Pawling, New York, where the newsman hunts, fishes, and golfs. Other hobbies are darts and conversation. He is 6'1" tall, weighs 170 pounds, has dark hair, and has been called "handsome enough to play a movie war correspondent" (*Cue*, February 21, 1953). Edith Behrens in the *Christian Science Monitor Magazine* (December 11, 1948) describes him as "a tall, lanky man with a luminous grin and a dark, intense face."

References (Murrow, Edward R.)

Christian Sci Mon p5 D 11 '48
Cue 10:34 D 27 '41 por; 22:10 F 21 '53 pors
Newsweek 41:40 Mr 9 '53 pors
Scribners M 104:7-11 D '38 por
Who's Who, 1952
Who's Who in America, 1952-53
World Biography (1948)

NASON, JOHN W(ILLIAM) Feb. 9, 1905-
Educator
Address: b. The Foreign Policy Association, 345 E. 46th St., New York 17

When Dr. John W. Nason assumed the presidency of the Foreign Policy Association in 1952 at the age of forty-seven he kept pace with his own record as a young man in high administrative positions. At the age of thirty-five he had been made president of Swarthmore College in Swarthmore, Pennsylvania. He was the youngest professor on the faculty when chosen, and had already established a reputation as a scholar and an educator.

John William Nason was born in St. Paul, Minnesota, February 9, 1905, the son of Albert John and Mary (Eaton) Nason. On his paternal side, he is a descendant of New England Puritans, and on his maternal side, mid-Westerners. An ancestor, Richard Nason, came to America in 1638 from Stratford-on-Avon. His descendants were clergymen and Army officers. John Nason's grandfather was a Congregational minister. His father was a business man, who started work in Pennsylvania and later settled in Wisconsin and then in Minnesota.

Nason attended St. Paul public school until his family moved to Chicago in 1918 where he entered Chicago Latin School. After graduation he returned to St. Paul and got a job as a bank messenger. His first business venture started earlier, however, when he built and sold bird houses for 25 cents.

After two years at Phillips Exeter Academy, New Hampshire, he returned to Minnesota and entered Carleton College. He received his B.A. degree *summa cum laude,* in 1925. From Carleton he went to Yale Divinity School where he was elected Fellow of the National Council on Religion in Higher Education. He studied at Harvard University for his M.A. degree, which he obtained in 1928. He was then sent to Oriel College in Oxford, England, as a Rhode's scholar from Minnesota.

After his marriage in 1935 to Bertha Dean White, a Quaker, Dr. Nason became a member of the sect. Swarthmore was founded by Quakers during the Civil War. Discussing Quaker ideals in an article in the New York *Times* in 1940, Dr. Nason wrote: "The Quakers have always emphasized the spiritual quality of life— not life on Sunday, but daily life. Little interested in creeds and ritual, they have kept a deep concern for the religious character of daily living."

He became president of Swarthmore in 1940. Regarding Swarthmore's Quaker heritage, he

Photo-Crafters

JOHN W. NASON

wrote "Character cannot be handed over in lecture courses, nor can a religious spirit be forcibly instilled. They come, if at all, by contagion, by slow growth, by what Quakers themselves call the inward working of the spirit." He pointed out that the Friends have always been individualists, which led them to seek education for women at a time when the idea "was considered a dangerously radical doctrine."

As a Quaker, however, Dr. Nason did not shirk the implications of national defense during World War II. He discussed the conflict in his first annual report presented in 1941 entitled "What stand Swarthmore takes as a co-educational college with two traditions in regard to national defense." He wrote, "To be consistent both with the Quaker's testimony against war and with their respect for individual conscience, the College should neither institute military training nor yet set obstacles in the way of students (or faculty) who may wish to enlist."

Being an educator in the "investigating '50's" imposes upon a college president the necessity of stating his position. Dr. Nason in The New York *Times* of February 24, 1952, warned against the dangers inherent in bowing before attack: "If the schools are to fulfill their function, they must oppose the censorship of textbooks, the futile and disgraceful imposition of teachers' oaths, the submission to the economic and political prejudices of any one group."

Nason is active in many civic and educational organizations. He has served as chairman of the Philadelphia Committee for Federal Union and the National Japanese-American Student Relocation Council, and president of the United Nations Council of Philadelphia and the World Affairs Council of Philadelphia. He has been a member of the board of directors of the National Council of Christians and Jews in

NASON, JOHN W.—*Continued*

Philadelphia, and of Vassar College; of the board of the Philadelphia Branch of the United States Committee for the Care of European Children; of the editorial board of *The American Scholar*; of the executive committee of the Friends Civilian Public Service; and of the Commission to Study the Organization of Peace. He is also a trustee of Phillips Exeter Academy.

Dr. Nason believes that "teaching is an art" and that "for effective teaching there must be genuine communication—a contagion struck from the impact of mind on mind, an idea planted, a stimulus to thought and understanding" *Journal of Higher Education* (November 1950). He also believes that "passion for knowledge and personal humility are virtues our education should encourage. One teaches not so much what one knows, as what one is."

He favors the honors system for college students. "At the undergraduate level, there is no better method of developing individual initiative, independence of judgment and disciplined intelligence," he told a New York *Herald Tribune* reporter (March 14, 1948). He stated that Swarthmore had succeeded in this experiment begun in 1923, and "the fact that 'honors' has survived the war years demonstrates the soundness of the method and its importance in today's quest for the best in education." Juniors and seniors at Swarthmore who "read for honors" do not attend regular classes but meet in small seminars once a week with various instructors.

"With students and instructors working together like a coach and his team," Dr. Nason asserted, the honors system "constitutes a perfect device for bringing faculty members and students together. In a period when mass education is taking another great leap and educators are talking of three or four million college students, it is the special and particular responsibility of the small independent college to stand for quality."

In accepting his new office, Dr. Nason stated, "There is no more important work to be done today than to present the facts and point up the issues relating to world events and thereby to provide the American people with the means of making their decisions about American foreign policy."

The Foreign Policy Association, established in 1918, is a non-partisan, non-profit group organized for the purpose of supplying unbiased facts about news behind the headlines through its two publications, its community programs in many cities and discussion aids. Under a reorganization plan the national office will become a service center for world affairs councils, forums and study groups.

Grants from the Fund for Adult Education, an independent agency established by the Ford Foundation, will be spent over a period of three years for the expanded program. The Association moved in June 1953 to the Carnegie building, which is part of the United Nations group in the East Forties, New York City.

The New York *Herald Tribune* in an editorial on December 7, 1952, welcoming Dr.

Nason to his new office, wrote, "As a brilliantly successful teacher, elevated to a college presidency at thirty-five . . . a distinguished philosopher and man of affairs, Dr. Nason is an excellent choice to carry out his own precepts and to fulfill the ideals of the Foreign Policy Association."

Dr. Nason has been described as a "tall, genial mid-Westerner with the frankness and sincerity of a natural leader."

References

N Y Herald Tribune II p4 D 7 '52
N Y Times p35 O 27 '40; II Ja 5 '41
PM Mag p3 O 31 '43
Time 35:46 Jl 24 '40

Adventure in Education (1941)
Who's Who in America, 1951-52

NAVARRE, HENRI (EUGÈNE) July 31, 1898- French Army officer
Address: Saigon, Viet Nam, Indo-China

The appointment of General Henri Navarre as Commander in Chief of the French Union troops in Indo-China on May 8, 1953, focused attention on an area that is becoming increasingly important in respect to Asian politics and the delicate international balance of power. Although he has inherited a stalemated seven-year war from his predecessor, General Raoul Salan, Navarre comes to his post well-equipped to discharge his duties.

Until his appointment to this command, he was Chief of Staff to Marshal Juin, Central European commander of Supreme Headquarters, Allied Powers Europe (SHAPE), and before that had held several top echelon commands with the French Occupation Army in Germany, including that of Inspector General, Chief of the Plans and Operations Division and Deputy Commander in Chief. He has been an Army career man since his graduation from St. Cyr in 1918, and has seen service in Syria, Morocco and Algeria.

Since his appointment, General Navarre, according to *Time* magazine, August 10, 1953, has been "revalorizing" the French Union Army by converting it from static offense to fluid offense. He demonstrated his ideas in August by attacking by sea, land, and air "in the face of tremendous odds" (high winds and rain). The battle pointed up "the basic difficulty of valorizing the war in Indo-China: the Viet Minh are everywhere and nowhere; they wage war by sabotage, terror, propaganda and guerrilla action."

Henry (Eugène) Navarre was born on July 31, 1898, at Villefranche de Rouergue, in southwestern France. During the First World War he joined the infantry, in July 1916, and a year later was admitted to St. Cyr, the French West Point. He won a cavalry commission as sublieutenant of the Second Regiment of Hussars on the battlefield, during the last great Allied offensive in November, 1918.

Following the war, he served with the Army in Syria (made a French protectorate by the Treaty of Versailles), in French Morocco, and with French occupation forces along the Rhine in Germany. He came to be regarded as one of the foremost French Army specialists in German language and culture.

While studying at the Cavalry School at Saumur, Navarre became convinced that the decisive role in future warfare would be played by the mechanized divisions and transferred to the armored forces. He then served for several months in the mountainous Rif region of Spanish Morocco when the French and Spanish conducted a joint campaign against the Arab leader, Abd-el-Krim (1925-26) and received the Legion of Honor with three palms. In 1928 he entered the Ecole Superieure de Guerre (War College) where, after studying for two years, he received the brevet (honorary) rank of Military Attaché.

When Hitler came into power, in March 1933, Captain Navarre was called to direct the German Section of the Second Bureau of the Army (equivalent to G-2, or Intelligence Division, of the American General Staff), and remained in charge of this highly-important desk until September, 1939. He was then promoted to Chef d'Escadrons (Major) and, in December of that year became Intelligence Chief for General Maxime Weygand who, in May 1940, as France was falling before the German attack, replaced General Gamelin as supreme commander of the Allied forces.

Navarre accompanied General Weygand to Algiers that November in the same capacity, when the General was made a delegate to North Africa for the Vichy Government. The same year he aided in organizing the underground intelligence service in Occupied France. In January 1942, as a Lieutenant Colonel, he took command of the Twelfth Regiment of Cuirassiers (heavy cavalry) under General Juin. The Germans, however, had made every effort to have him removed from the staff of General Weygand and, later, of Juin. When they occupied the southern part of France, in November 1942, they insisted that Navarre not be one of the 100,000 man army permitted France under the Armistice terms, and Admiral Darlan returned him to France.

There he entered the Organization of Army Resistance (O. R. A.), in January 1943, and became Chief of the underground Service Renseignement (Intelligence Service), which played a decisive role in the liberation of France the next year. When the Allied forces landed in Southern France (August 15, 1944), Navarre joined them, was promoted to Colonel, and fought along with them in the liberation of the Rhone Valley.

After a brief period with the Direction Général des Études Recherches (French Intelligence Office), he joined the staff of Marshal de Lattre de Tassigny's *Rhin et Danube* army, and on Jan. 19, 1945, was named Commander of the Third Regiment of mounted Moroccan Spahis. He participated in the liberation of Colmar, the opening of the Rhineland and the capture of Karlsruhe and Siegmaringen.

Navarre's brilliant work in the Resistance movement and his thorough knowledge of Germany earned him the office of Chief of

French Embassy Press & Inf. Div.

GEN. HENRI NAVARRE

Staff to the French Commander in Chief in Germany, in March 1945. He was promoted to Brigadier General that October. He then became Inspector General of the French occupation Army in March 1946 and subsequently, that September, Chief of the Plans and Operations Division in Germany. In January 1948 he took command of the Constantine Division.

After having attended the Institute of Advanced Studies for the National Defense in 1949, he was elevated to the rank of Major General, on March 2, 1950, and given charge of the Fifth Armored Division, then stationed in Germany. Two years later, in March 1952, he was appointed deputy commander in chief of the French Occupation forces and made a Lieutenant-General the next April twenty-third. Last September he succeeded General de Lassus Saint-Genies as Chief of Staff to NATO's Marshal Juin, at Fontainbleau.

On May eighth of this year the French Cabinet named General Navarre as Commander in Chief of French Union Forces in Indo-China, succeeding General Raoul Salan, who has been Indo-Chinese commander since Marshal de Lattre's death in January 1952. Navarre replaced Salan ostensibly, according to the New York *Times* (May 9, 1953), because General Salan's tour of duty in the Far East was up, but also because "the seemingly easy invasion of Laos by the Communist-led Viet Minh (in April) has unleashed a strong attack here on the French high command for having done little on its own to halt it."

The Cabinet announcement emphasized that Navarre's close association with Marshal Juin was a strong factor in his selection to unravel "what could be mildly described as an unenviable situation." Navarre and Juin are both determined advocates of "counter-guerilla tactics" against the Viet Minh instead of the less

NAVARRE, HENRI—*Continued*

immobile, "Maginot line tactics" waged by his predecessors.

Upon reaching his headquarters at Hanoi on May 20, the General revised his top command immediately, placing Generals Jean Giles and René Cogny in command of all French Union forces in Laos and northwest Viet Nam respectively; Major General Louis Bodet was assigned as Deputy Commander.

While flying in an American-built, two-engine Dakota transport over Mocchau, eighty miles west of Hanoi, on May twenty-second, Navarre and his senior officers narrowly escaped death when very heavy anti-aircraft fire smashed one of the plane's engines and forced an emergency landing at Nasan, a French garrison town, in the Thai hills.

In accordance with Navarre's plan to free French forces for a more mobile warfare, the French defense post at Yenvi in the southern delta region of Northern Viet Nam was evacuated, thus releasing three to four battalions of infantry and relatively large artillery and air forces for duty elsewhere (New York *Times,* May 28, 1953). On June third, the new commander flew to Pnompenh, the capital of Cambodia, for conferences with French officers in that area. A month later, after further inspections of his new command, he flew to Paris to present recommendations for stepping up the seven-year war. While favoring wider independence, Navarre is understood to believe that the French must receive certain rights from the native states in order to carry on the war. He would not receive the nomination of Commissioner General for Indo-China, as he wished, said the New York *Times* (July 3, 1953), since it was decided that the Commissioner, who would play a leading role in the desired political negotiations, should be a civilian. That same day the Laniel Government proposed simultaneous but separate negotiations with Cambodia, Viet Nam and Laos to revise existing agreements with them in order to broaden their independence.

Navarre is said to have discussed with the French Cabinet a new strategy for operations after the rainy season ends and the mobilization of 20,000 additional French troops and 108 native Indo-Chinese battalions. Although the conscription of more French troops is now forbidden by a 1950 law, and although the war is politically unpopular in France, Georges Bidault, continuing as Foreign Minister in the Laniel Cabinet, is said to favor Navarre's proposals, contending that independence promises to the Indo-Chinese states commit France to defend them (New York *Times,* July 9, 1953).

Meeting with Secretary of State Dulles in Washington, D.C. on July 12, Bidault presented General Navarre's counter-offensive plans, which will cost an estimated additional $285,000,000, to Dulles, who "was reported to have expressed his 'very great satisfaction' with the plan's aggressive features." Bidault emphasized "that the 'Navarre plan' for regaining the initiative in Indo-China was still under study by the French Supreme Council" (New York *Herald Tribune,* July 13, 1953).

He did not indicate how much of the anticipated extra cost would have to be supplied by the United States.

On July 17 the General told reporters in Paris that if he receives the desired increase in troops and material, if full independence is granted the three Indo-Chinese states, and if China does not increase its aid to Viet Minh forces, he believed the war could be ended in eighteen months. He warned, however, that the eight Communist divisions had never been stronger, and that, "as soon as autumn starts we must be prepared for an extremely hard blow."

He said it would be necessary to change the whole morale and habits of the French and Indo-Chinese troops by that time. Once independence is granted, he stated, the Indo-Chinese would find it only "normal" to continue their military, political and economic ties within the French Union. (New York *Herald Tribune,* July 17, 1953).

The first large-scale example of the mobile warfare advocated by Navarre was given the same day (July 17, 1953), when more than 3,000 parachuters and supporting troops destroyed Langson, ten miles from the Chinese frontier, the main Viet Minh center for supplies from China and withdrew sixty miles back to their base, in a raid that cost the lives of two French troops. The raid was held to have been a severe blow to the Viet Minh supply position, costing their forces over 5,000 tons of matériel, and also to have been proof of the accuracy of French intelligence about Communist-held areas.

Meanwhile, the French Government was seeking a way to give Navarre French reinforcements without changing the 1950 law which forbade sending further conscripts to Indo-China. On July 19 General Navarre and Marshal Juin met with French Cabinet ministers to overcome differences between the compromise policy of Vice-Premier Paul Reynaud and the pro-Navarre forces of M. Bidault.

Speaking editorially on July 18, 1953, the New York *Times* said that "General Navarre is no defeatist. He opposes strongly the group in France that would favor getting out of Indo-China altogether by any available means. In that position he is defending the best interests of the Indo-Chinese, since their liberty is dependent on the French. He is also defending the interests of the United States, and indeed, of the whole free world."

General Navarre, who is a Commander of the Legion of Honor, also holds the Croix de Guerre with seven citations for bravery (three from the last war and three from the Moroccan campaign 1925-26, and one from World War I, "Order of the Brigade"). He also wears the Resistance Medal with rosette, the Distinguished Service Cross and the Virtuti Militari (Poland), and is a Grand Officer of Ouissam Alaouite. He has a younger brother, Jacques, recently made a lieutenant colonel, who now commands a battalion in Indo-China. He is described by *Newsweek* (June 1, 1953) as being "short, handsome and silver-haired" and by *Time* (May 18, 1953) as "thin" and "elegant." *Time* also says that "while lacking the dash of the late Marshal de Lattre de Tassigny, General Navarre has an advantage over old-line French officers: he was a Resistance fighter and has himself practiced underground tactics." Assessing the new Indo-Chinese commander, the French *Climats* (May 21-27, 1953) said, "very young in appearance, elegant . . . considered as one of the Intelligence aces, and being, besides, recognized as an outstanding organizer, both during the Resistance and while serving with Allied staffs, he is better qualified than anyone else to handle a situation which is at best confused, being entangled in both political and strategic difficulties. From this point of view the Government's choice seems excellent." He is married and has a son, Jacques, age 27.

References

Newsweek 41:46 Je 1 '53
Time 61:31 My 18 '53; 62:21 S 28 '53
por

NEVILLE, SIR ROBERT A(RTHUR) R(OSS) Dec. 12, 1896- Governor of the Bahamas

Address: b. Government House, Nassau, Bahamas; h. Uplands Park, Brook, Surrey, England

Sir Robert A. R. Neville has been the Governor of the Bahama Islands since December 1950, when he retired from the Royal Marines with the rank of Major General. Between the two world wars Major General Neville served as an aide in the island possessions of Great Britain, and during the second war he served in the Admiralty as assistant director of Naval Intelligence.

The islands which Sir Robert governs are known as the Bahamas, a far-flung archipelago of nearly 800 units, stretching from a point off the south-east coast of Florida to the northeastern end of Cuba. Nassau, on the little island New Providence (20 square miles), is the capital. Once the islands belonged to Spain, then became a rendezvous for pirates, and in 1627 were taken by Great Britain. The first Governor was Captain Woodes Rogers, and the Duke of Windsor governed the islands from 1940 to 1945. There are 29 large islands, including the popular tourist resorts, Nassau and Hog Island (on which Paradise Beach is located) and 661 Out Islands, connected by plane and ship service. One of the islands in the group is Watling, or San Salvador, where Christopher Columbus is believed to have made his first landing in the New World. Recently developed islands for the tourist trade include Bimini, Eleuthera, Harbor, and Andros. Many cruise ships make Nassau a port of call, and daily planes carry American tourists from Miami. A Royal Air Force unit is stationed in the archipelago.

A British Crown Colony since 1717, its Constitution provides for a nominated Legislative Council and a popularly elected Assembly. The Governor is advised by an Executive Council. About 87 per cent of the population of the Bahamas is Negro.

SIR ROBERT A. R. NEVILLE

Major General Sir Robert Arthur Ross Neville was born on December 17, 1896 in England, the son of Colonel William C. Neville, Distinguished Service Order, and Amy (Ross) Neville. His father was a colonel in the Cheshire Regiment, and his mother was born in Scotland. His great-great grandfather, Hercules Ross, was an associate of Admiral Lord Nelson, whom he met in Jamaica where he owned a considerable interest in shipping.

Robert Neville attended preparatory school at Twyford, near Winchester, pursuing his studies there from 1907 until 1911. He enrolled in Cheltenham College, Cheltenham, England, remaining there from 1911 to 1914. Just before the start of World War I Neville joined the Royal Marines and was accepted as a second lieutenant on August 2, 1914.

The coming of war curtailed the training of all young officers in England, and early in 1915 Robert Neville was assigned to His Majesty's battleship *King Edward VII*. He remained on board the *King Edward* until January, 1916, when his ship was sunk by a mine in the North Sea. Subsequently, Neville was appointed to another ship, H. M. S. *Royal Oak*, in which he fought at the battle of Jutland.

Neville volunteered for shore duty and in July 1917 joined the Royal Naval Division as an infantry soldier. He fought at Arras, Paschendale, Cambrai and on through the victorious allied advance until the Armistice of November 1918, when he returned to England.

The twenty-two year old officer next served as aide-de-camp to the Governor of Hong-Kong from 1921 until 1925. He was private secretary to the Governor of Ceylon from 1926 to 1927.

Neville was then assigned as aide to the British Governor at Bombay, India, a post which he held from 1927 to 1928. While in India Neville served as staff officer on the

NEVILLE, SIR ROBERT—*Continued*

Indian Statutory Commission, a body which, under the leadership of Sir John Simon, was appointed to consider Indian demands for revision of the existing governmental system so that opportunity for more native participation in the Colonial government might be provided. Another member of this all-party commission was Clement Attlee.

After service in His Majesty's ships in China, Ceylon, India, and the Mediterranean, Neville returned to his studies, attending the Royal Naval College, Greenwich, England, where he passed the Naval staff course in 1935. He then returned to the West Indies as Naval Intelligence officer on the staff of the Admiral commanding the West Indies and the South American Station. At the beginning of World War II Neville, a major in the Royal Marines, was Naval Intelligence officer in Shanghai. A promotion to lieutenant colonel in 1940 resulted in his being transferred, and thereby escaping the incarceration by the Japanese which was the fate of his successor at Shanghai.

During the rest of World War II, Neville served in London as assistant director of Naval Intelligence, and later in Admiral Mountbatten's Combined Operations organization. He also served on Admiral Sir John Cunningham's staff in the Mediterranean theater. He was promoted to the rank of colonel in 1945, and served as aide-de-camp to His Majesty the King from 1946 to 1948.

At the end of World War II, Neville returned to England from the Mediterranean theater and was assigned to the Royal Marine Headquarters at Plymouth, as Commandant of the Royal Naval School of Music. He was promoted to major general in 1948, at which time he was named commander of the Eastern Group of Royal Marines, a post which he held until his retirement from military service in 1950. He was created a Knight Commander Saint Michael and Saint George in 1952.

Upon his installation as Governor of the Bahamas, Sir Robert, according to a dispatch of December 23, 1950, cautioned Americans not to believe Communist propaganda aimed at dividing the United States and Western Europe. He was quoted by the New York *Times* as saying: "Communists are putting out a lot of propaganda, trying to divide Americans from Western Europeans and particularly the British. I believe absolutely implicitly that the only hope we have is for the British and Americans to hook together."

During Sir Robert's term as Governor of the Bahamas, an expected deficit of £611,000 was avoided. A boom in tourist trade and in building was predicted by Sir Robert in a speech of November 22, 1951, and a revenue increase for the year of £2,000,000, thus permitting a surplus of £175,000. The Bahamas' chief exports include lumber, tomatoes, citrus fruits, sisal, sponges and lobsters, in value about £1,020,000 annually. The island imports about £7,650,000 worth of goods.

Sir Robert Ross Neville was married to the former Doris Marie Collen on September 27, 1943, just before his departure for the Med-

iterranean theater. They have two children, Emma, born in 1944, and Colin Ross, born in 1947. The Governor has blue eyes, dark hair, and is five feet eleven inches tall. He weighs one hundred and sixty-five pounds. He is a member of the Church of England. He belongs to White's Club and to the United Service Clubs, both in London.

His chief hobby was formerly polo, which he frequently played for the Navy. He is also fond of water sports, such as spearfishing and water skiing, in addition to enjoying golf and tennis.

A dispatch from the Bahamas in the New York *Times* of August 30, 1953 reported that Sir Robert, whose term as Governor expires in December, will be replaced by Thomas Daniel Knox, sixth Earl of Ranfurly.

References

N Y Times p20 D 23 '50
Who's Who in Great Britain, 1951

NEWBY, P(ERCY) H(OWARD) June 25, 1918- Author

Address: b. c/o Alfred A. Knopf, 501 Madison Ave., New York 22; Broadcasting House, London, W.1.; h. Cherry Tree Cottage, Blackpond Lane, Farnham Royal, Buckingshamshire, England

Reprinted from the *Wilson Library Bulletin*, March 1953

With the publication in the United States since the end of World War II of the works of Henry Green, William Sansom, V. S. Pritchett, Ivy Compton-Burnett, and P. H. Newby, American readers are discovering a new dignity, freshness, and artistic seriousness in the novel. P. H. Newby, is the youngest of this group. Anthony West of *The New Yorker* calls him "the only English writer with anything approaching genius to be produced by his generation so far." *John O'London's Weekly* writes: "Not since the death of Virginia Woolf has the art of the novel been practiced by so deliberate an artist as P. H. Newby." And the London *Times Literary Supplement,* though qualifying its praise with reservations over "the dubious marshes of allegory" in his work, sums up: ". . . it is a tribute to the quality of Mr. Newby's writing that a new book by him is always opened with eager expectancy."

Percy Howard Newby, son of Percy and Isobel Bryant Newby, was born in Crowborough, Sussex, June 25, 1918. Raised in the Midlands and in South Wales, Newby's earliest memories are "of contrast between green fields and the industrial darkness of the mining valleys." He is, he says, "the first male member of the family to earn a living and wear a collar and tie at the same time." His father was a tradesman, "with an itch to keep moving," so the boy and his family wandered all over the country. But Worcestershire, where his paternal grandfather ran a market garden and did chimney sweeping (like the grandfather of the boy Philip in *The Young May Moon*) is that part of England to which he claims allegiance. Newby attended the Hanley Castle Grammar School in Worcester, and from 1936 to 1938 St. Paul's College in Cheltenham.

In 1939 Newby entered the British Army. He served first in France from 1939 to June 1940, then from 1941 to 1942 in Egypt. On receiving his military discharge in 1942 he remained in Egypt, teaching English at Fouad I University. Newby feels that living in Egypt, "outside Europe and the Christian tradition was . . . the best thing that has happened to me." Certainly it has given his novels something of their curious mixture of the familar and the foreign —the quiet English countryside setting and the exotic Greek heroine of *A Season in England,* for example, or the hazy Mediterranean scene of *Agents and Witnesses.*

From the beginning, with the publication of his first novel, *Journey Into the Interior* (1945), Newby caught the attention of readers with his singular ability to evoke atmosphere and his sensitive observation of character. Similarly in *Agents and Witnesses* (1947) *The New Yorker* found: "A deceptively light novel with a deep undercurrent of emotional tension, in which Mr. Newby examines penetratingly, if inconclusively, the tragic quality in the lives of a number of unheroic, even trivial, people."

The characters of Newby's *The Young May Moon* (1950) may be equally "unheroic" and "trivial" in the larger social and moral sense, but they are vivid, drawn lovingly, "with fraternal warmth and no condescension," in the words of *Time*'s reviewer. In this story of an adolescent boy adjusting to the loss of his stepmother and coming to a new and richer understanding of his father and of himself, Newby has apparently drawn heavily on his own memories: the descriptions of a shabby English suburb, the quiet Welsh town, the craftsmanship of the boy's uncle who is a baker, and most of all, the mystery and wonder of a boy's coming of age.

With *A Season in England* (1951), Newby received lively, if not always favorable, criticism from the reviewers. There are elements of the mystery story in the plot—a young man returns to England from Egypt to meet the parents of his dead friend. When his friend's beautiful widow also appears, there is an inevitable crisis and a flareup of melodrama. Critics found the plot weak and implausible, but many of them were delighted with Newby's style and characterization. A reviewer for *Commonweal* felt that he measured up well against Evelyn Waugh and Graham Greene. Even more striking is the suggestion of E. M. Forster that one finds in Newby's novels mystery (not in the detective story sense), sudden and seemingly irrational outbursts of violence, understatement, and restraint. To a lesser degree, he has something of Forster's humor, if so far none of his brilliant wit.

Newby has also written two stories for children, *The Spirit of Jem* (1948) and *The Loot Runners* (1949), and a critical study of the early nineteenth century Irish novelist, Maria Edgeworth. His first publication was a poem which appeared in *The National Review* when he was eighteen, but he has written no poetry

P. H. NEWBY

since then. His latest novel, "The Retreat," will be published next month.

Since 1949 Newby has been a producer in the Talks Department of the B.B.C. In the autumn of 1952 he visited the United States under the auspices of the Smith-Mundt Leader Scheme and traveled all over the country. He has been married since 1945 to Joan Thompson and they have a daughter, Sarah Jane. The Newbys live in Buckinghamshire in a house called "Cherry Tree Cottage." There the novelist does what he likes best to do: "writing and digging the garden."

NICHOLS, WILLIAM T(HOMAS) Dec. 26, 1901 Organization official, engineer

Address: b. American Institute of Chemical Engineers, 120 E. 41st St., New York 17; c/o Monsanto Chemical Co., 1700 S. 2nd St., St. Louis 4, Mo.; h. 618 N. Woodlawn Ave., Kirkwood 22, Mo.

The election of William T. Nichols as president of the American Institute of Chemical Engineers for the 1953 term culminated many years of participation in that organization's activities. Since he became a member in 1940, he has held posts in the Institute including chairmanship of both the South Charleston, West Virginia, section and of the national committee on professional guidance.

Since 1949 Nichols has been the director of the general engineering department of Monsanto Chemical Company, in St. Louis, Missouri. He is a chemical engineer whose experiences have been executive as well as professional, including work in research engineering, sales of products, organization of new plants and laboratories and administration. Nichols has developed patented processes involving alkalis and the halogens, a chemical

WILLIAM T. NICHOLS

family of fluorine, chlorine, bromine, iodine, and chlorinated hydrocarbons, adding chlorine to such organic compounds as methane and ethyl.

William Thomas Nichols was born in Allegheny (now Pittsburgh), Pennsylvania, December 26, 1901, the son of William Walter and Myra Jane (Harris) Nichols. He received his primary and secondary education in Pittsburgh, and he entered the University of Pittsburgh, graduating in 1922. He was a member of the Alpha Chi Sigma fraternity.

Upon graduation, he won a research fellowship in chemical engineering at the Mellon Institute of Industrial Research in Pittsburgh, where he remained until 1926. In that year, he became research engineer in the Columbian Rope Company of Auburn, New York. Nichols joined the Westvaco Chloride Products Corporation in 1930 as a research engineer and became its divisional director of research and development in South Charleston, West Virginia, in 1935. From 1943 he served as technical assistant to the executive vice-president until he was appointed technical sales director in 1946 of the South Charleston division.

When the Westvaco corporation built the first commercial elemental phosphorus plant based on Idaho phosphates, and the first commercial soda ash operation based on the Wyoming trona mines, Nichols had the responsibility of selecting sites and of choosing processing methods of extracting elemental phosphorous and soda ash from ores. His most difficult task was to convince the local Chambers of Commerce, townspeople, newspaper editors, and officials that the presence of a chemical plant in their town would not pollute the countryside, and that it would benefit the town economically.

In 1949, Nichols was appointed director of the general engineering department of the Monsanto Chemical Company, which was expanding at that time. This provided Nichols with an opportunity to utilize his experience in organization and planning. His present project is the company's new central headquarters, being built in the St. Louis, Missouri, suburbs, which will house the main research and service departments and have direct communication to the executive department.

Nichols has devoted thirteen years of service to the Institute of Chemical Engineers. The Institute provides means for the publication and exchange of technical information in its field and of maintaining a professional standard of conduct; it is also concerned with means of promoting a wider recognition of chemical engineering as a profession, which will be effective in improving the professional and economic status of chemical engineers. Nichols has been a member of its committees on professional legislation and admissions, chairman of the committee on professional guidance from 1941 to 1943, chairman of the Charleston section from 1943 to 1944, chairman of the committee on the future of the Institute from 1951 to 1952, and vice-president in 1952.

Nichols regards himself as an "utility infielder," directing and co-ordinating the phases of chemical engineering and research and unifying them into efficient and profitable channels. A man whose broad experiences have given him a clear comprehension of his field, he deplores the modern trend toward specialization. He argues that engineers graduating from colleges today are so specialized that they are incapable of solving problems outside their field without the help of other specialists.

The engineer married Elizabeth Margaret Austen in Aspinwall, Pennsylvania, June 1, 1927. They have two children, Caroline Jane and William Austen. Nichols is a member of the American Chemical Society and was chairman of the Kanawha valley section in 1940. His clubs are the Chemists in New York, Greenbriar Hills Country and Missouri Athletic. For relaxation he enjoys painting and cabinet making.

References

Chem Eng 59:308 D '52 por
Chemical Who's Who, 1951
Who's Who in Engineering, 1948

NKRUMAH, KWAME (qua'mĕ ncrōō'mà)
1909- Prime Minister of the Gold Coast, West Africa

Address: Accra, Gold Coast, West Africa

After an absence of twelve years from his native land, Kwame Nkrumah returned to the Gold Coast of British West Africa and became the first African-born Prime Minister under the Constitution granted by Great Britain. Added to this dramatic front-page news was the fact that Nkrumah was in jail for sedition at the time of his election, held in February, 1951, in which most of the native Africans who voted for the first time were illiterate.

Upon being released by Sir Charles Noble Arden-Clarke, Governor of the Gold Coast, Nkrumah was carried in triumph through the streets of Accra. Later, as Prime Minister, he formed the first African government in history.

Since Nkrumah took office the Gold Coast has made great progress on the road to self-government, cooperating fully with Britain in her new colonial policy of "creative abdication." *The Nation* magazine hopes "responsibility will soften militant nationalism." With both friend and foe watching, the Gold Coast has so far proven the validity of self-government but world opinion differs as to what will be the outcome of Nhrumah's government and its influence on the rest of Africa.

Nkrumah was born in 1909 in the remote village of Nkroful in British West Africa. His father, a Twi tribesman, was a goldsmith. As a boy he was educated at a Roman Catholic mission at Essima and Sekondi. He was sent to Achimota, the unique Gold Coast College. After graduating in 1931 he became a school master and developed a taste and talent for public speaking. Through the financial help of his uncle, a diamond prospector, he furthered his education in the United States and in England.

He entered Lincoln University, a college for Negroes in Oxford, Pennsylvania, in 1935, where he majored in sociology. *Time* lists comments by his teachers at Lincoln about Nkrumah: "Biology: strongly individualistic; history and philosophy: ace boy; German: loved controversy; Physics: noticeable but not spectacular." His classmates voted him "most interesting" and in the college yearbook, wrote: "Africa is the beloved of his dreams; philosopher, thinker, with forceful schemes."

He was graduated from Lincoln in 1939 with a Bachelor of Divinity degree, and later instructed there while attending the University of Pennsylvania. He showed his talent for leadership when he became president of the African Students' Association of America and Canada. Here he met left-wing Negro leaders and by 1942 was making speeches condemning Britain's colonial rule.

After ten years in the United States he returned to England in 1945 and attended the London School of Economics where he became increasingly interested in politics. With little to live on, he trained himself in London's hard school of labor organization and agitation. Patrick Donovan, writing in *The Rotarian* noted, "It is a life that many politically conscious Africans know who have chosen voluntary exile and it doesn't make them more tolerant." While in England he published a magazine called *The New African* which was barred from the Gold Coast.

He return to the Gold Coast on December 16, 1947, on the invitation of Dr. James B. Danquah, to become general secretary of the United Gold Coast Convention, the popular nationalist party. Nkrumah soon differed with the older men who ran the party and by June, 1949 he had started his own Convention People's Party.

The time was ripe for political unrest, as only the year before riots over cocoa prices broke out in Accra and spread to other centers. The British Government sent a commission headed by Aiken Watson to study conditions

British Inf. Services

KWAME NKRUMAH

in the Gold Coast. In *The Christian Science Monitor*, Carlyle Morgan commented, "The Watson commission exceeded its terms of reference and recommended a Constitution which would give the Gold Coast at least the beginnings of real self-government," adding "There is still much argument as to whether, since the riots were caused by shortages of goods and high prices, they required so sweeping a political answer. But the Watson report which included a draft Constitution fanned the desires of Gold Coast Africans for self-government. An all-African committee under Sir James Henley Coussey was appointed in 1949 to draw up a Constitution and self-government began at the top" (October 24, 1952).

Nkrumah as leader of the Convention People's Party, spoke against the new Constitution and demanded "positive action", and was jailed for violating the then existing law against political agitation. In a short time he became a martyr and gave his followers the party slogan, "Freedom." To this the Convention People's Party added a salute, the raised forearm with all five fingers outspread to denote five freedoms and a vision of Utopia. The British sent out sound trucks to instruct the Gold Coasters how to vote. The election was orderly and demonstrated that an illiterate people, which comprises ninety per cent of the Gold Coast's population, can vote. Both vindication and power were Nkrumah's when the election returns came in. When the Governor on his own initiative released Nkrumah from jail the Colonial Office approved.

In his first speech after the election Nkrumah asserted, "I am a friend of Britain", and spoke of his desire for the Gold Coast to acquire the status of a dominion within the Commonwealth. The British, however, reserved three of the Cabinet posts for themselves, the ministries of Defense, Finance and Foreign Affairs. The eight other posts are held by Africans. The

NKRUMAH, KWAME—Continued

Legislature is overwhelmingly composed of elected African representatives.

William S. White, in a special report to the New York *Times* (May 16, 1952) wrote of the British making themselves expendable and added, "In their hearts, the British hope they can stay on for perhaps twenty years more. Mr. Nkrumah's plans for them, however, are different. He would like to get rid of them tomorrow and his highly nationalistic followers consistently press him toward such a cause."

Minister Daniel Malan of South Africa called the Gold Coast experiment "a disastrous step in Africa. . . .If the other African native territories demand with the same success what the Negroes in the Gold Coast have been granted, it means the expulsion of the white man from everywhere between South Africa and the Sahara" (*Time*, February 9, 1953).

Nkrumah told a correspondent of the New York *Herald Tribune* that he took a dim view of Malan's victory. "It shows us how necessary it is for Africans to unite against the danger. Here on the West Coast some of us are working for a federation of West African countries." In the same interview Nkrumah told the correspondent that he believes, once a few African countries gain their independence, there will be no stopping an African upsurge.

It has never been proved that Nkrumah was a member of the Communist party. One group of whites in Accra thinks that he is; another group thinks that he was, but has had "a change of heart and has met good will with good will" (*Saturday Evening Post*, March 7, 1953). The second opinion is "the official line."

Many of the tribal chiefs of the Gold Coast call Nkrumah a "city slicker out for his own ends" and some extremists at home accuse him of selling out to the British. One of his most unpopular duties since assuming office was convincing the African farmers that they must comply with measures begun by the British to control the virus disease that threatens the cocoa farms. This means a temporary loss to many of the rich farmers but assures the Gold Coast of continuous production of cocoa, of which they grow one-third of the world's supply.

Nkrumah has also tackled the problem of illiteracy and is strongly behind a program of education. At present he is studying the British proposal to dam the Volta River at a cost of $400,000,000.

"I think I have the confidence of the masses", Nkrumah has said, "but about self-government, they must not make me go too fast—and I must not go too slow. If I tried to stop their urge to be free, they would turn on me. My job is to keep things level and steady. . . ."

His appeal is said to lie in his ability to convince Africans of their own dignity. With his background, "charm, and slightly sullen good looks", he gives his 4,500,000 people hope and courage. He holds two graduate degrees, a Master of Arts and a Doctor of Law.

References (Nkrumah, Kwame)
   Life 34:61 My 4 '53
   Nation 172:193 Mr 3 '51
   New Republic 124:9 Ag 16 '51
   New Statesm & Nation Mr 22 '52
   New Yorker 28:74+ D 20 '52
   Sat Eve Post 225:30+ Mr 7 '53
   Sat R 36:21 My 2 '53
   Scholastic 59:18 O 17 '51 por
   Time 59:29 Mr 17 '52 por; 60:32 D 8 '52
      por; 61:22 F 9 '53 por

NOVAES (PINTO), GUIOMAR (gē′ō-mär nō′vī-ŭs) Feb. 28, 1895- Pianist

Address: b. c/o National Concert and Artists Corporation, 711 Fifth Ave., New York 2, N.Y.; h. Rua Ceará 457, São Paulo, Brazil.

The eminent Brazilian pianist, Madame Guiomar Novaes, has been judged "one of the towering pianists of our century," a "flawless technician and a searching musician." Since her debut in Paris, when she was sixteen years old, and her subsequent New York City debut in 1915, Madame Novaes has played in all the leading concert halls of Europe, North and South America, and with every major orchestral group. She has made twenty-three tours of the United States and Canada, and in this country alone has given over 500 concerts and recitals. She makes appearances in twenty to twenty-five cities on each annual tour, at private schools, colleges, women's clubs, and often with civic symphony orchestras.

Madame Novaes was one of the nineteen children of Manoel da Cruz and Anna (De Menezes) Novaes. She was born on February 28, 1895 in the village of São Joao da Boa Vista, in the district of Parana, Brazil, near the metropolis São Paulo. Her musical career began when at the age of four she was able to play marches on the piano by ear for her companions in kindergarten. When she was six her parents, then living in São Paulo, arranged regular piano lessons for her with an Italian teacher, Luigi Chiafarelli. A year later, she was ready for her first public appearance as a skilled musician, and soon after she made her first concert tour of her native State. The young girl continued her lessons with Professor Chiafarelli until 1909. During this period she also attended school in São Paulo, getting a well rounded education in languages, history, literature, and mathematics, but music was her strongest interest. Because of her remarkable talents in that field the Brazilian government in 1909 sent her to study in France. In a contest for a scholarship at the Paris Conservatoire, competing with 388 entrants and judged by the leading French exponents of the piano—Fauré, Debussy, and Moszkowski—the youthful Brazilian was chosen one of the twelve winners. The works she had chosen to play were Chopin's *Ballade in A Flat* and Schumann's *Carnaval*, both of which continue to appear on her recital programs.

Madame Novaes studied at the Paris Conservatoire with Isidor Philipp for two years. Upon graduation in 1911 she was awarded the

Premier Prix. She made her Paris concert debut shortly after at the age of sixteen and the success of this concert led to a tour of the musical auditoriums of England, France, Germany, Italy, and Switzerland.

After two years in Europe, the young pianist returned to Brazil. Two years later, November 15, 1915, she gave her first concert in New York City. Here her performance made a deep impression, "less through her transcendent technique," wrote one critic, "than through maturity of conception far beyond her years." The New York *Times* reported that "not every generation hears a Guiomar Novaes." The Brazilian musician remained in the United States for the next four years, taking advanced coaching from Sigismond Stojowski in New York City and appearing with symphony orchestras in the major American cities. She also began her annual tours of the South American countries, particularly Brazil where, under the auspices of the government, she made an extensive tour of all the small villages and cities of that country. Her efforts resulted in the formation of "Culturas Artisticas," an organization which fosters concerts of all kinds in every community in Brazil.

Sponsored in her career by the Brazilian government when she was only twelve years old, Madame Novaes has always shown particular interest in the music of her native country, performing its folk music as well as that of its modern composers, and assisting young Brazilians to further their musical studies.

She is particularly admired by her fellow countrymen, who consider her their special cultural ambassadress. Plaques in her honor have been placed in many of the theatres and concert halls of Brazilian cities. On the entrance to Rio de Janeiro's Teatro Municipal, Brazil's largest theatre, there is a bronze plaque which reads: "In this theatre Guiomer Novaes has played."

Critics have mentioned "the intense individuality" of her playing; her "controlled vigor and enthusiasm," "the fineness of shading and marked contrasts," her "impeccable technique," "brilliant artistry" and "great personal charm," all of which have combined to make Madame Novaes "one of the most beloved musical artists of our time," and have placed her in a special niche among contemporary keyboard artists.

Subsequent concerts have resulted in similar praise. In 1950, when the sudden death of her husband caused Madame Novaes to cancel her commitments in the United States, she did fulfil her engagement with the New York Philharmonic Orchestra by playing Chopin's *F Minor Piano Concerto*. Louis Biancolli of the New York *World-Telegram* wrote: "It was the most beautiful rendering of the Chopin classic heard in New York in years." The critic for the New York *Times* called her "the romantic pianist par excellence. . . .Her playing has the quality that the old heroic pianists used to bring to their Chopin—marvelous detail [and] a large-scale, over-all sweep."

Returning to the United States in the fall of 1951, she gave a Town Hall recital and two weeks later appeared as soloist with the New York Philharmonic-Symphony under the di-

Yvonne Le Roux

GUIOMAR NOVAES

rection of George Szell before a capacity audience as well as a radio audience estimated at twelve million. Every year she also fulfills numerous engagements in Europe and gives a regular series of recitals in Latin American countries.

Honors which the musician has won include the decoration of a Chevalier of the Legion d'Honneur and an honorary professorship at the Rio de Janeiro Institute of Music. She is a member of Mu Phi Epsilon, and an honorary member of Centro de Ciências, Letras e Artes de Campinas, and of the Hispanic Society of America. In 1941 she established the Guiomar Novaes Award which pays for the expenses of two young pianists, one Brazilian and one American, to study and give concerts in each other's country. Until 1951 Madame Novaes recorded for Columbia; since then she has been an exclusive artist for Vox, for whom she has made a number of recordings—Beethoven's *Piano Concerto Number Four,* Schumann's *Piano Concerto in A Minor,* and *Carnaval,* and several works of Chopin's, including the *Preludes, Fantasies,* and *Sonatas.* Her recordings of Chopin's music were praised by the critic for the *Saturday Review* who placed her among "the foremost recording pianists. . . ."

The pianist was married on December 8, 1922, to Octavio Ribiero Pinto, a Brazilian architectural engineer and composer, whom she had met at the farewell concert she gave in Brazil on the eve of her departure for Paris at the age of twelve. The architect was then a young man of nineteen who followed her career with interest and admiration. After their marriage, he often accompanied her on her American and European tours. He died in 1950. She frequently plays her husband's compositions at her recitals.

Madame Novaes and her two children, Anna Maria, a vocalist, and Luiz Octavio, an engineer, have a permanent home in São Paulo, Brazil.

(Continued next page)

NOVAES, GUIOMAR—*Continued*

In appearance the pianist is small, with black eyes and black hair. She enjoys reading, writing, going to the opera and the theatre. She is especially fond of New York City.

To those who wish to make music a career she lists three indispensables: a true talent, a general background, and the best teacher obtainable. Music has always been a natural and sustaining interest for Madame Novaes and of it she has said: "It never seems like work to me."

> *References*
>
> Christian Sci Mon p4 Ja 22 '47
> Baker's Biographical Dictionary of Musicians (1940)
> International Cyclopedia of Music and Musicians (1939)
> International Who's Who in Music (1951)
> Who's Who in Latin America, Part VI (1948)

O'HARA, MAUREEN Aug 17, 1921- Motion picture actress

Address: b. c/o Twentieth-Century Fox Film Corporation, 10201 Pico St., Los Angeles, Calif.

Irish-born Maureen O'Hara, popular Hollywood motion picture star, received early dramatic training in Dublin's famed Abbey Theatre School and has been an actress most of her life. After a successful screen performance with Charles Laughton in the British-made film, *Jamaica Inn* (1939), Miss O'Hara moved to the United States, where, among other notable Hollywood films, she appeared in *How Green Was My Valley* (1941), *Miracle of 34th Street* (1946), and *The Quiet Man* (1952). Her unusual beauty has won for her the title of "Queen of Technicolor."

Born Maureen FitzSimons on August 17, 1921, at Milltown, near Dublin, Ireland, Maureen O'Hara is the daughter of Charles FitzSimons, who is in the clothing business, and Marguerite (Lilburn) FitzSimons, formerly an Abbey player and singer who has performed on the Dublin stage. Of her three sisters and two brothers, all have appeared on the British or American screen except the oldest girl, who became a Sister of Charity and is now head of a convent. In early childhood Maureen began acting in the back yard of her Dublin home, starring in plays that she made up for the neighborhood children. At the age of five she gave her first stage performance when she read a short poem between acts of a school play. In the same year she entered Burke's School of Elocution, which she attended regularly until she left Dublin twelve years later.

With her appearance on a radio program twelve-year-old Maureen O'Hara earned her first money as a professional entertainer. Continuing her dramatic activities, she took part in neighborhood plays, pageants, festivals, and choruses; studied music and dancing; served

six semi-annual sessions in the volunteer ballet chorus of the Dublin Operatic Society; and was graduated from "spear-carrying" to small roles in the famous Abbey Theatre. By the time she was fourteen she was enrolled in the Abbey Theatre School and had received numerous awards and medals bestowed in Ireland's frequent play festivals and dramatic contests. At seventeen she had been playing Shakespearean roles for two years and had won the All-Ireland Cup for her portrayal of Portia in *The Merchant of Venice*.

Maureen O'Hara took her final examinations at Trinity College at the age of fifteen, the youngest student to complete the Guildhall School of Music's drama course. Within six months she received a degree and an associateship from the London College of Music. With the degree she was also awarded a medal as honor student for the entire British Isles. When she finished the Abbey Theatre School course in her eighteenth year, she was also given the unusual offer of a leading role with the Abbey Players themselves. (Miss O'Hara holds a certificate from the Abbey Players to qualify as a teacher of elocution.) At the same time she received from an English film company a letter at the suggestion of Harry Richman, inviting her to go to London immediately for a screen test. Miss O'Hara accepted the latter offer and played a minor part in a picture that was never produced. A brief cut from her scene, however, came to the attention of Charles Laughton and Erich Pommer, who chose her for the feminine lead in *Jamaica Inn* (1939). Since her film experience was negligible, they first gave her a very small part in a minor picture as training for the important role. Believing that London would be her home for some time, she took a seven-year lease on a house in Hyde Park, but had lived there only six weeks when her success in *Jamaica Inn* won her the offer of the leading feminine role in *The Hunchback of Notre Dame*, again playing opposite Laughton.

Under contract to Mayflower Pictures, the company name of the Laughton-Pommer production partnership, Miss O'Hara sailed for America, arriving on June 19, 1939. Her mother, who had accompanied her to England, also came to the United States, but soon after the beginning of the war, returned to Ireland to be with her family. *The Hunchback of Notre Dame* (1939) was followed by *A Bill of Divorcement* (1940) and *Dance, Girls, Dance* (1940), again with Miss O'Hara in leading roles. After her performance in *They Met in Argentina*, she played in *How Green Was My Valley* (1941), winner of six Academy Awards, which was directed by John Ford. He has subsequently starred Maureen in other successful films and, according to the New York *World-Telegram* writer Erskine Johnson, considers her Hollywood's best actress. Miss O'Hara's 1942 films were *To the Shores of Tripoli, Ten Gentlemen From West Point,* and a romantic tale of adventure, *The Black Swan,* in which she co-starred with Tyrone Power. The next year she acted in a film again with Charles Laughton, in *This Land Is Mine*. She appeared also in 1943 in *Immortal Sergeant* and in the spy melodrama *The Fallen Sparrow*.

For some years Miss O'Hara had been working under a contract by which she shared her film commitments equally with Twentieth-Century Fox and RKO Radio Pictures. In accordance with a contract signed March 7, 1944, she agreed to play primarily for the former with one picture each year delegated to RKO. In her next film, the Technicolor Western *Buffalo Bill* (1944), costarring Joel McCrea, Miss O'Hara took the part of Buffalo Bill's wife. In 1945 she was cast as a Spanish noblewoman in the pirate tale, *The Spanish Main*, and in 1946 played the role of a staid college dean transformed into a glamorous woman in *Do You Love Me?* In 1947 she played in *Sinbad the Sailor,* opposite Douglas Fairbanks, Jr., recently returned from the Navy to appear in this Technicolor story of ninth-century Persia.

During 1946 Miss O'Hara traveled to Ireland for her first visit home in seven years. Upon her return she worked in New York on the scene-shooting for her next picture, *Miracle of 34th Street*. This was followed in 1947 by *Homestretch*, on which *Variety* commented, "Miss O'Hara, with a beautiful wardrobe which amply sets off her looks, shows signs of increasing thespian ability." After appearing in *Foxes of Harrow* (1947), with Rex Harrison, she was seen in *Sitting Pretty* (1948), a comedy featuring Clifton Webb as a baby-sitter, and in *A Woman's Secret* (1949). Her performance in *Forbidden Street*, based on a Margery Sharp novel, drew varying criticism from reviewers: Howard Barnes of the New York *Herald Tribune* found her "superb" in a number of sequences; while Eileen Creelman in the New York *Sun* commented, "Maureen O'Hara, still enormously pretty, still quite unbelievable as an actress, is the confused, impetuous Adelaide." For her role as Princess Marjan in *Bagdad* (1949), a Technicolor tale of romantic adventure, Miss O'Hara had the opportunity to prove her ability in singing and dancing. In late 1949 she also worked on the *Sons of the Musketeers,* an RKO Technicolor production costarring Cornel Wilde, which appeared, with revisions, in 1952 under the title *At Sword's Point.* In a performance which "for the most part captures the flavor of the period," *Variety* noted, "Miss O'Hara shows surprising skill with a rapier, and her visual charms stand up well in the romance department."

Working under John Ford's direction in 1950, Maureen O'Hara had the feminine lead in the Argosy production *Rio Grande*, a tale of Indian warfare and emotional conflict. "Miss O'Hara plays with feeling and a delicate sense of pantomime," was Howard Barnes's comment on her performance. The following year she went to Ireland to be filmed in John Ford's Argosy picture *The Quiet Man,* which costarred John Wayne and boasted an almost all-Irish cast, including Miss O'Hara's two brothers, Charles and James. "Miss O'Hara is perfect as the Irish maid," *Variety* wrote, "complimenting the Technicolor hues and doing well on the performance end by displaying a fitting vitality."

MAUREEN O'HARA

After *The Quiet Man*, she starred in *Flame of Araby* (1951), depicting love and battle on a desert; *Against All Flags* (1951), with Errol Flynn; *Kangaroo* (1952), which was filmed in Australia; and the Western Technicolor *The Redhead From Wyoming* (1952). In June of 1951 Maureen O'Hara, L. B. Merman, Will Price, and John Payne announced the formation of Price-Merman productions to make seven Technicolor films in the ensuing three years. According to their plan, the first of these will be *Jamaica*, a romantic action picture to be produced in Jamaica.

Generally acknowledged to be one of the most beautiful actresses in Hollywood, auburn-haired Maureen O'Hara has been described as having a "perfect Technicolor complexion" and has been given the title of "Queen of Technicolor." Motion picture critics have frequently pointed out that her many appearances as the heroine in elaborate Technicolor spectacles, in which she has been praised as "decorative" and "ornamental," have limited her opportunities to display her acting ability. "Almost every letter I receive," the actress herself was quoted in 1945 as saying, "asks why Hollywood doesn't take me out of those silly Technicolor pictures and give me dramatic pictures. It's nice to have some one on your side" (New York *World-Telegram*, May 28, 1945).

Maureen O'Hara was married in 1939 to George Hanley Brown, a British film director whom she met while playing in *Jamaica Inn*; the marriage ended in divorce in 1941. On December 29, 1941, she married Will Price, a film director who worked on some of the pictures in which she appeared. A daughter, named Bronwyn Bridget after Maureen's oldest sister, was born to them on June 30, 1944. When the marriage terminated in divorce on August 4, 1952, Miss O'Hara was given custody of the child. She had filed her first citizenship papers

O'HARA, MAUREEN—*Continued*

in November of 1941 and on January 25, 1946, became a United States citizen. The actress is five feet seven and a half inches tall and weighs 122 pounds. She enjoys taking long walks, painting in water colors, composing poetry, singing and accompanying herself on the piano. Interested in clothes, she and a nonprofessional friend, Sue Daley, for a time operated a dress shop in San Fernando Valley. Miss O'Hara writes and speaks Gaelic and has deep respect for the folklore of her native land.

References

Christian Sci Mon p13 Ap 10 '40
Collier's 104:11+ O 7 '39
N Y Herald Tribune IX p7 D 6 '42;
    VI p3 My 30 '43
N Y Post Mag p9 Jl 11 '42
International Motion Picture Almanac,
    1952-53
Who's Who in America, 1952-53

OLLENHAUER, ERICH Mar. 27, 1901-
German political leader
Address: b. c/o Social Democratic Party of Germany, Friedrich-Ebert-Allee 170, Bonn, Germany; h. Bonner Talweg 194, Bonn, Germany

Following the death of the German Socialist leader Dr. Kurt Schumacher on August 20, 1952, Erich Ollenhauer became chairman of the Social Democratic party (SPD), West Germany's second largest political party. In his present post Ollenhauer, who has spent all his adult life as an active worker for the German Socialist party, carries on the work of Schumacher to unify Germany and affirm its independence from the Western powers. Ollenhauer has been a member of the Bundestag (parliament) of the Federal Republic of Germany since 1949. In the September, 1953 West German elections, Erich Ollenhauer led the Social Democratic party in an unsuccessful campaign against Chancellor Konrad Adenauer's Christian Democratic party.

Erich Ollenhauer was born on March 27, 1901, in Magdeburg, Germany, one of four children (two girls and two boys) of Wilhelm Ollenhauer, a bricklayer, and Marie (Seger) Ollenhauer. He was educated in the elementary and commercial schools in Magdeburg and at the age of fourteen (in 1915) entered the Social Democratic party by way of the Socialist Youth Federation of Germany, later in 1918, joining the party itself. After working for a time in 1919 as a reporter on *Volksstimme*, a Madgeburg newspaper, Ollenhauer went to Berlin in 1920 to become editor of *Arbeiterjugend*, organ of the Socialist Youth Federation. For the next eight years he was also national secretary of the youth movement. The SPD, which was founded in 1863, "derives from Marxist roots but may in practice be compared to the British Labor party" (*Political Handbook of the World*, 1951).

As secretary-general of the Socialist Youth International, to which he was elected in 1921,

Ollenhauer was occupied during the following twenty-five years (until 1946) with matters relating to the organization and administration of youth movements all over Europe. Meanwhile, in the last years of the German Republic, from 1928 to 1933, he held the chairmanship of the Socialist Youth Federation of Germany. Ollenhauer was elected to the executive committee of the Social Democratic Party in 1933, and, as Nazism became more powerful, in the spring of that year went into exile in Prague, where he engaged in propaganda work against the Nazis. As a result, in 1935 he was deprived of German citizenship. When Nazism spread to Czechoslovakia in 1938, Ollenhauer fled to Paris, remaining there until the fall of France to the German armies in 1941. He spent the last years of the war in London.

On his return to Germany in February 1946, Ollenhauer joined forces with anti-Nazi groups to work for the re-establishment of a new German government and to repel Communist infiltration into the German labor movement. A few months later he was named deputy to Dr. Kurt Schumacher, chairman of the SPD. In 1949 he became a member of the constituent Parliamentary Council and in August 1949 was elected to the Bundestag, in which he has been a member of the foreign policy committee. Schumacher, as spokesman for the Social Democratic Party, represented the strongest opposition element in the Bonn Government headed by Dr. Konrad Adenauer. An ardent proponent of the reunification of Germany, he resisted any measure that would delay or discourage the restoration of German national unity; he opposed the use of German troops in a Western army, Europeanization of the Saar, the Schuman Plan, the incorporation of Germany into a United States of Europe—always on the grounds that these measures would retard the cause of unification. Since Schumacher was a semi-invalid, Ollenhauer, as vice-chairman of the party, frequently represented him in political meetings and beginning in early 1952 served unofficially as the acting leader of the Social Democrats. Described as less fiery but as uncompromising as Schumacher, Ollenhauer is committed to the same policies.

The importance of the Social Democratic Party as an opposition party was demonstrated in January 1952 in the appeal made by Adenauer to the party for co-operation in a bipartisan foreign policy. At that time Adenauer was seeking the opposition's support to a German conscription plan to provide soldiers for a European army under the North Atlantic Treaty Organization. His appeal was answered by Ollenhauer, speaking in the illness of Schumacher, who replied, according to Russell Hill of the New York *Herald Tribune*, "the co-operation suggested by the Chancellor would be possible only after joint talks to review the basis of German foreign policy." Two days later the United Press reported from Bonn that the Social Democrats had declared absolute opposition to the conscription plan. Ollenhauer and Karl Schmidt (the party's foreign policy expert) were expected to continue to meet for talks with Chancellor Adenauer.

In the debate in the Bundestag on European defense, which opened in February 1952, Adenauer defended the conception of a European army to withstand possible Soviet aggression. Opposing this view, Ollenhauer objected that Germany was not given political equality by the Western Allies and further criticized the Adenauer Government for committing itself to Western defense without first receiving satisfaction on this and other issues. On the threat of Soviet aggression, Ollenhauer said that "even if there was an increased danger, German rearmament would not help any to prevent it at this moment." In a radio address on March 28, when Allied plans were under way for a West German peace treaty, Ollenhauer expressed his belief that the Western powers wanted to dictate the policy of a reunited Germany. He reiterated the fundamental premise of his party that the most urgent task was "the restoration of the national unity of the people on a democratic basis."

While the Western powers bid for West German co-operation, unification offers were also made to the Bonn Government by the Soviet Union. Ollenhauer voiced his party's stand on the Soviet offer by commenting that "no moment can be early enough to start talks with the Soviet Union"; that German unification must precede any West German commitment to join a Western defense bloc; and that the Saar must be returned to Germany. Foreign correspondents have pointed out that Ollenhauer's apparent interest in the Soviet offer does not reflect pro-Soviet sympathies so much as it represents an opportunity to force the Adenauer Government to adhere to Socialist policies and to fight for immediate unification. Ernest S. Pisco reported in the *Christian Science Monitor* that the "anti-Communist attitude [of the Social Democrat leaders] has stood repeated tests." Anne O'Hare McCormick stated in the New York *Times* that Ollenhauer was not for acceptance of the Soviet offer but favored a complete renegotiation of the agreement between the Federal Government and the Western powers. The basis for her statement was a speech to the Foreign Press Association early in May 1952 in which Ollenhauer proposed that if the Bundestag failed to approve the present agreement, new negotiations, based on suggestions by the Bundestag, should be opened. Two months later at the Socialist International which met at Frankfort, Germany, the attitude of Ollenhauer and the SPD toward Soviet relations was further clarified. The group, of which Ollenhauer was elected a deputy chairman, endorsed United States policy in Korea and adopted a resolution expressing regret that the policies of the Cominform had forced the free democratic countries to build up armies and military defense.

A few weeks after the death of Schumacher on August 20, 1952, Ollenhauer was elected chairman of the Social Democratic party at the Dortmund convention on September 24. In the meantime, on August 24, Don Cook had reported in the New York *Herald Tribune* that the election of Ollenhauer was certain and commented that "the Social Democrats will be more

Schafgans-DGL-Bonn

ERICH OLLENHAUER

temperate and moderate in their opposition in the months ahead, particularly where foreign affairs are concerned." *Business Week* described Ollenhauer as "more moderate and more pro-Western" than Schumacher. At the funeral services for Schumacher, Ollenhauer pledged himself to continue the former leader's fight "for a democratic and unified Germany." The hopes of some Western commentators that Ollenhauer would moderate Schumacher's opposition to co-operation with the Western powers—especially on the issues of the Schuman Plan and the Europeanization of the Saar—were at least partly dampened by a speech Ollenhauer delivered at the Social Democratic party's congress at Dortmund, in which he reiterated the party's previous stand on these issues.

On September 13 West European delegates to the European Coal and Steel Community Assembly approved a proposal to accept the task of federation offered by the Schuman Plan. German Socialist delegates threatened to boycott the special assembly to draft plans for the federation, while Ollenhauer continued and intensified his criticism of the Adenauer Government. Drew Middleton wrote in the New York *Times* that the Social Democratic Party and the German Trade Union Federation, "two of the most powerful political forces in Germany," had formed an alliance "to fight for the political leadership of West Germany." Drifting still further away from the pro-Western Adenauer policies, Ollenhauer welcomed the proposal made at the Second Congress of the Socialist International, of which he is vice-president, that the United States, Britain, France, and the Soviet Union discuss the unification of Germany. He was quoted as saying, "If after a reasonable period of negotiations [with the Soviet] no concrete results are achieved, we would admit that a new situation had been created and therefore revise our atti-

OLLENHAUER, ERICH—*Continued*

tude toward the rearmament of Germany and all connected problems."

The problem of the re-unification of Germany received further attention in the summer of 1953 when an attempted revolt in East Germany and the pending September elections in West Germany caused the Soviet Union to suggest again that a conference be called to draw up a German peace treaty and to propose that a provisional government for a united Germany be formed. Although the Socialist party policy still stood for the priority of the unification of Germany over closer alliance with the Western powers, Ollenhauer showed more skepticism towards these Soviet suggestions than he had towards the Soviet unification offer in 1952, and termed the central features of the proposal "unsuitable".

In the September 1953 election, the West German voters substantially rejected the policies of the Socialist party, which gained only 150 seats in the Bundestag in comparison to the 244 seats of the Christian Democrats. Ollenhauer was returned to the Bundestag as he won 51 per cent of the vote in his constituency, Hamburg.

After the elections were over, Ollenhauer declared that his party still objected to the proposed European Defense Community and the proposed "Europeanization of the Saar", and still believed that East and West Germany should be re-united before any closer ties with the Western or European powers were considered.

By his marriage on May 27, 1922, to Martha Müller, a former clerical worker, Ollenhauer is the father of two sons, Peter and Hermann. The blue-eyed, gray-haired statesman has been described as "stocky", "comfortable, businesslike and considerate." Outside the political field his interests are skat playing, reading, and family life.

References

Bsns W p80 Ag 30 '52
Time 60:38 O 6 '52
International Who's Who, 1952
Wer Ist Wer? (1951)

ORLANDO, VITTORIO EMANUELE

May 19, 1860—Dec. 1, 1952 Italian statesman; lawyer; began his career as a professor of law (1882); entered political life as a representative in the Chamber of Deputies (1897); during early 1900's served as Minister of Education, Minister of Justice, Minister of the Interior; as Italy's World War I Premier (1917-19), represented his nation at the Versailles Peace Conference, becoming one of the "Big Four" (with Woodrow Wilson, Georges Clemenceau, David Lloyd George); elected president of the Chamber of Deputies (1919), later named its honorary president; after overthrow of fascism, became member of the Constituent Assembly and later of the Senate. ·See *Current Biography*, 1944.

Obituary

N Y Times p31 D 2 '52

OVERHOLSER, WINFRED (o'ver hŏl ser) Apr. 21, 1892- Hospital administrator; psychiatrist

Address: c/o St. Elizabeth's Hospital, Washington 20, D.C.

The recipient of the 1952 Isaac Ray Award of the American Psychiatric Association, given annually to that individual who "is most worthy by reason of his contribution to the improvement of Law and Psychiatry," was Dr. Winfred Overholser. Since 1937 he has been the superintendent of the Federal Security Agency's St. Elizabeth Hospital in Washington, D.C. and for over three decades has been recognized as one of the leading psychiatrists in the country.

During fifteen years of notable service in the Massachusetts State hospital system, Dr. Overholser advanced from assistant superintendent of Gardner State Hospital, (1920-21) to commissioner of the Department of Mental Diseases (1934-36). For five years the psychiatrist has been closely identified with Massachusetts' progressive socio-criminological legislation, in particular, the Briggs Law. He served as president of the American Psychiatric Association in 1947 and 1948, and since 1938 has been professor of psychiatry at George Washington University School of Medicine.

Winfred Overholser was born on April 21, 1892, in Worcester, Massachusetts, the son of Edwin Moses and Mary Jane (Walker) Overholser. His childhood and early youth were spent in Wellesley Hills, Massachusetts, where he received his primary and secondary school education. He has one brother and one sister. From his father, who was a surgical supply manufacturer's representative, young Winfred acquired an early acquaintance with one field of medicine.

Following graduation from Wellesley High School in 1909, Overholser entered Harvard College. He majored in economics, and won the Russell Scholarship in his second college year. Harvard University awarded him in A.B. degree *cum laude* in 1912. Interested in postgraduate study, both in law and medicine, he attended Boston University, from which he received an M.B. degree in 1915. Turning his full attention to medicine, he obtained an M.D. degree from this University in 1916.

He began his medical career as a resident doctor in Evans Memorial Hospital, Boston, Massachusetts, in 1916. The following year he became assistant physician at Westborough State Hospital, Massachusetts, which cares for mentally disturbed patients. During World War I, he received military leave from February 1918 to June 1919 to serve as first lieutenant of the neuropsychiatric section in the Medical Corps of the United States Army.

Offered the position of assistant superintendent at Gardner State Hospital, Massachusetts, for the mentally ill, Winfred Overholser accepted in 1920. A year later, he became assistant superintendent at Medfield State Hospital. His administrative ability and progressive ideas resulted in his promotion in 1924 to assistant to the commissioner of the Massachusetts Department of Mental Diseases. Dr. Overholser attributed to parole boards a "backwardness about availing themselves of psychiatric advice, even when reports of competent psychiatrists were readily available" (*Mental Hygiene,* April 1927).

Interested in the advancement of legislation which would recognize the value of a routine psychiatric examination of defendants in criminal courts, Overholser aided in the administration of the "far-sighted" Briggs Law of Massachusetts (*Mental Hygiene,* October 1937). This law, according to Dr. Overholser in his book, *The Psychiatrist and the Law,* "has pointed the way to a new approach in the matter of the mental state of persons accused of crime." Briefly, the law provides for the examination by neutral, impartial psychiatric experts of all persons indicted for a capital offense or known to have been previously convicted of a felony. The law, applying essentially to criminal cases, has been upheld by the Supreme Judicial Court of the Commonwealth of Massachusetts against attackers. "The significant thing about the Briggs Law is that . . . it has provided for the prompt recognition of defendants who should be in hospitals, thus preventing trial of mentally ill persons," Dr. Overholser has written, noting that it has been emulated by the States of Michigan and Kentucky.

In addition to his work in the Massachusetts State hospital system, from 1925 to 1930 Dr. Overholser was also director of the division for examination of prisoners. He served, too, as instructor in psychiatry at Boston University in 1925 and 1926, advancing to the rank of assistant professor in 1926. The psychiatrist lectured in Boston University School of Law from 1929 until 1937.

The Massachusetts Department of Mental Diseases promoted Dr. Overholser to the status of assistant commissioner in 1930. In his teaching post at Boston University, he advanced to associate professor of psychiatry in 1932, and to full professor in February 1934. He relinquished this position in September 1934, when he was made commissioner of the Department of Mental Diseases in Massachusetts. His efficiency and forward-looking views in State hospital service brought him national distinction.

Winfred Overholser was one of three top ranking psychiatrists recommended to former Secretary Harold Ickes, of the United States Department of the Interior, and to President Franklin D. Roosevelt by officials of the National Committee for Mental Hygiene and the American Psychiatric Association to head St. Elizabeth's Hospital in Washington, D.C. The selection was made on September 21, 1937 "on the basis of professional merit and fitness" to fill the vacancy left by the death of Dr. William A. White in the Government's chief hospital for the mentally ill (*Mental Hygiene,* October 1937). Overholser was also named director of the division of mental hospital research in the National Committee for Mental Hygiene.

Beginning in 1938, the hospital administrator was also professor of psychiatry at the George Washington University School of Medicine,

Harris & Ewing

DR. WINFRED OVERHOLSER

Washington, D.C. He was elected a director of the Research Council on Problems of Alcohol at the Council's annual meeting on October 15, 1940, which was attended by leaders in the fields of medicine and psychiatry and representatives of business, civic, and social groups.

Addressing the symposium of the American Association for the Advancement of Science held in Philadelphia on December 27, 1940, Overholser called alcoholism "the greatest public health problem which is not being scientifically attacked" (New York *Times,* December 28, 1940). He added that there had been "much emotionalism and loose thinking" on the subject.

Expressing a deep concern with the problems of the aged and the mental disorders common to the older age group, Dr. Overholser declared on June 4, 1941 at the National Conference of Social Work in Atlantic City that "industry must be expected to use wiser methods in employment and retirement of workers with reference to age" (New York *Times,* June 5, 1941). He said that old-age pensions would probably be "one of the most important developments in the prevention of mental breakdowns in later life."

At a symposium of the American Philosophical Society, Dr. Overholser declared on April 18, 1946, that "it should be no more difficult, legally or in any other way, for a patient to receive care for a mental disorder than for any other sort of disability." He urged that the laws of the several States reduce to a minimum the formal requirements for such care.

Speaking as president of the American Psychiatric Association on May 17, 1948, Dr. Overholser advised the psychiatric profession to give the public "material which is sound, truthful, and progressive" (New York *Times,*

OVERHOLSER, WINFRED—*Continued*

May 18, 1948). He served as chairman of the United States Delegation to the International Congress on Mental Health held in London, England, in 1948. On April 13, 1949, he told about 130 hospital superintendents and officials at the American Psychiatric Association's institute that the "most notorious hospitals for neglect of mental patients" were those where staff appointments were made "on the basis of partisan politics instead of on professional qualifications" (New York *Times,* April 14, 1949).

He was chosen vice-president of the First World Congress on Psychiatry held in Paris in 1950. Selected to deliver the Charter Day Lecture observing the ninety-third anniversary of New York Medical College, Flower and Fifth Avenue Hospitals, New York City, on April 13, 1953, the psychiatrist urged greater cooperation between the psychiatrist and the general practitioner. He declared "the psychiatrist can . contribute greatly to the general practitioner's understanding of problem patients" (New York *Times,* April 14, 1953).

Author of many articles in professional and lay magazines on psychiatry and law, Dr. Overholser has written two books. His *Handbook of Psychiatry* (1947), in collaboration with W. V. Richmond, is called a "well-written, clear . . . good review of psychiatry for the practitioner" (*American Journal of Public Health,* March 1948). *The Psychiatrist and the Law* (1953), which discusses the various State laws governing the mentally ill and the role of the psychiatrist in the courtroom, is a collection of the lectures delivered by Dr. Overholser at Harvard in November, 1952 as first recipient of the Isaac Ray Award of the American Psychiatric Association. In the book's preface the author expresses the hope that "the comments presented in the following pages may prove a small contribution to a close understanding and co-operation between the practioners of the law and of psychiatry."

The psychiatrist received an honorary Doctor of Science degree from Boston University in 1940. He was awarded the United States Selective Service Medal, and in 1948 Ecuador gave him the Al Merito award. France made him a Legion of Honor Chevalier in 1951 and awarded him a Medal of Liberation in 1952. He is a fellow of the American Medical Association and of the American Psychiatric Association, serving the latter as president from 1947 to 1948 and secretary-treasurer from 1941 to 1946.

Dr. Overholser is a diplomate of the American Board of Psychiatry and Neurology and is president of the board of managers of the Washington Institute of Mental Hygiene. He is a past post commander and member of the American Legion, is president of the board of directors of the Committee for Study of Suicide, Inc., is on the executive board of the American League to Abolish Capital Punishment and is a moderator of the American Unitarian Association.

He was married to Dorothy Stebbins on June 4, 1919. Their children are Dorothy, Jane, and Winfred, Jr. The psychiatrist stands six feet one inch tall, weighs 200 pounds, and has hair of "mixed" color and hazel eyes. His clubs are Cosmos and Literary Society, Washington, D.C., and his fraternities include Alpha Sigma Phi and Sigma XI. The physician enjoys "travel, photography, music, and book-collecting." He is described as having "a slight Harvard accent and a sharp wit" (New York *Post,* January 28, 1951).

References

Mental Hygiene p682-3 O '37
N Y Post p2 Ja '51
American Men of Science (1949)
Who's Who in America, 1952-53
World Biography (1948)

PAGE, GERALDINE   Nov. 22, 1924-
Actress

Address: b. c/o Warner Bros. Pictures, Inc., 321 W. 44th St., New York 18; h. 21 E. 11th St., New York 3

The triumph of Geraldine Page, an unknown actress, has the gratifying excitement of the theatre's best Cinderella story. She was not an understudy who stepped into the star's part, but reached stardom in her own highly dramatic way by making such a success of her role in an off-Broadway production of Tennessee Williams' play, *Summer and Smoke,* that drama critics beat a path to the door of the Circle-in-the-Square in New York City's Greenwich Village.

She went on to play a leading role in Vina Delmar's drama, *Mid-Summer,* on Broadway, and received a glowing set of notices and a seven-year Hollywood contract which permits her to act in Broadway plays in between pictures. In her first film, *Hondo,* (Warner Brothers) she plays opposite John Wayne. The actress has been variously described as a "young Laurette Taylor," a "young Lillian Gish," a "young Helen Hayes."

Geraldine Page was born in Kirksville, Missouri on November 22, 1924, the daughter of Dr. Leon Elwin Page and Mrs. Pearl Maize Page. She has a younger brother, Donald, who served in the Army in Korea. Her father is an osteopathic physician who encouraged her in her ambition to be an actress.

"My father is responsible for all this," said Miss Page recently. "He always wanted to write. He did write some—a book on the relationship between osteopathy and medicine—and he hoped I'd inherit his enthusiasm. But I didn't. I wanted to act." (New York *Journal-American,* March 15, 1953).

She continued, "I think this was a disappointment to him until after he saw me in a play put on by the Young People's Society at our church. When I got home we had a long talk and I believe I convinced him it was maybe just as important to interpret what people write as to have done the writing. Anyway, he's been in my corner ever since."

Miss Page told the *New Yorker* reporter (February 7, 1953) that she had originally wanted to be a pianist. "The family couldn't afford to give me piano lessons," she said. "So I tried painting. When I found that painting wasn't going to be the thing, I tried acting. I was seventeen when I played in *Excuse My Dust,* put on by a group of amateurs. Afterward, people came up and said I'd made them cry. That seemed absolutely marvelous to me."

Because Dr. Page was pleased with his daughter's performance as Jo in *Little Women* (even though he thought she was more suited to the role of Beth) he kept his promise to send her to the Goodman Theatre Dramatic School in Chicago where the family had moved After high school she had enrolled at the University of Chicago but after three weeks she left, having determined to be an actress. "I knew I wouldn't make money at first," she recalled, "so I very carefully kept my taste down to peanut butter" (*Time,* February 2, 1953).

Upon graduation from the Goodman Theater Dramatic School, she asked the dean where she could get acting experience and he advised her to organize her own company. "A group of us did just that," Miss Page told Emory Lewis of *Cue* (February 14, 1953). "At Lake Zurich, thirty-five miles out of Chicago, I played alternate leads there for four summers, while wintering and starving in New York. I also did leads at Woodstock, Illinois, for two years. In New York I have taken every kind of job: hat-check girl, theatre usher, book salesman. When I went into *Summer and Smoke* I was doubling as a clerk and negligee model in a dress shop."

While Miss Page was acting with the Lake Zurich group, Claudia Cassidy of the Chicago *Tribune* saw her playing the role of Bela Manningham in *Angel Street* and gave the young actress her first great "rave" notice.

She worked in New York for the International Thread Company wrapping thread cones, and studied Shakespearean roles. She said that four cold and undernourished winters in New York almost banished her "delusions of grandeur." She stopped going to producers' offices because she "had a special talent for not being noticed" and worked intermittently in small theatrical groups and off-Broadway companies.

The young actress acted in off-Broadway shows for four winters, in the Blackfriars' Guild Shows, with a group at the Hotel Des Artistes (where she played the title role in Oscar Wilde's *Lady Windermere's Fan*), and the Rat Wife in Henrik Ibsen's *Little Eyolf.* Jose Quintero, director of the Loft Players in the Circle-in-the-Square, located in the old Greenwich Village Inn near Sheridan Square, gave her the role of an old pagan crone who lived in the hills with her fourteen children in Federico Garcia Lorca's *Yerma.* For this she received $10 a week and lived on peanut butter sandwiches and milk, but was very contented.

Quintero recognized her talent and gave her the leading part in Tennessee Williams' play *Summer and Smoke.* Playing the lovelorn Alma Winemiller, she caught the critics' startled eyes and sent them back to their typewriters to write paeans of praise about their

GERALDINE PAGE

"discovery", calling her performance "great," "astounding", "sheer magic."

Skeptical producers and directors journeyed downtown to see her, and went away filled with enthusiasm. Hollywood agents were equally enthusiastic and offered to give her screen tests. But she refused their offers "even though powerfully tempted by that kind of money," she admits, because she wanted a Broadway play first.

She continued to play this role for ten months in 1952, receiving such comments as: "To the complex role of Alma Winemiller Miss Page brought maturity of technique, charm of person, and—the rarest quality in modern acting—intellect" (*Theatre Arts,* July, 1952).

Her first Broadway role was in Vina Delmar's play, *Mid-Summer,* which opened at the Vanderbilt Theatre on January 21, 1953, and which ran for 109 performances. Producer Paul Crabtree and Frank Hale had given her the part of Lily, the idealistic heroine without education married to a school teacher, after they had seen her performance in *Summer and Smoke.* Wolcott Gibbs wrote in the *New Yorker* that the heroine "may be the noblest woman put on the stage in my generation . . . who might be completely insufferable if the role were in any other hands than those of Geraldine Page, an actress of great charm and pathos and almost matchless technique."

"When the reviews of *Mid-Summer* appeared the critics had already made Miss Page a star by acclamation, though she was technically co-featured with Mark Stevens, a movie actor also making his Broadway debut, and with veteran actress Vicki Cummings. Miss Page ran away with the notices . . . the play got at best mild approval and at worst was written off as sentimental claptrap. . . .The producers accepted the critics' and the public's view of the situation and elevated Miss

PAGE, GERALDINE—*Continued*

Page to stardom . . . co-starred with Mr. Stevens, and her name was raised above that of the play on the theatre marquee" (*Theatre Arts*, April, 1953).

Ward Morehouse, drama critic of the New York *World-Telegram and Sun*, commented May 8, 1953: "There's the matter of the best performance given by an actress, featured or starred, in a straight play since the season's parade began as of last September. My vote goes unhesitatingly to that actress new to the Broadway scene, Geraldine Page, for her inspired playing in Vina Delmar's *Mid-Summer* . . . Miss Page's work was so honest, so sharp, so true, she is selected above two other brilliant female performers of the season now ending— Kim Hunter in *The Children's Hour* and Shirley Booth in *The Time of the Cuckoo*."

When interviewed after her initial and successful venture on Broadway, Miss Page told Norton Mockridge in the New York *World Telegram and Sun*, April 4, 1953, that her life was very different. "I think the greatest change that has come into my life," she said, "is the complete lack of time. I have no time any more. I never realized—before—what luxury I had. Time to read, time to rest, time to think. You know, I used to read a great deal. I'd rather read a good book than eat a meal. Devour some essays by Shaw, for instance, and you feel you're full. But now I haven't time to sleep, and I crawl on the stage practically exhausted."

Miss Page has been working in Uta Hagen's acting classes. "I've learned a lot," she said. "Things like this: when a character in a play is talking, she doesn't know all the words she's going to say. Sometimes she'll hesitate till she finds them. It's the same with listening. You don't know what the other person is going to tell you. These are some of the ways to keep your part feeling new and fresh to you" (Helen Ormsbee in the New York *Herald Tribune*, February 22, 1953).

While still playing in *Summer and Smoke* she was signed for seven years to act in Hollywood films for Charles K. Feldman, independent producer. Her contract permits her to appear in Broadway plays in between pictures, and she is scheduled to appear in late 1953 in producer Billy Rose's production of *The Immoralist,* an adaptation of the late André Gide's novel.

Her first Hollywood role is in *Hondo,* a three-dimension motion picture in Warner Color, a Wayne-Fellows production released by Warner Brothers. The picture was made near the village of Camargo in the State of Chihuahua, Mexico. Miss Page is starred opposite John Wayne in a story about U.S. Cavalrymen and Apaches in the southwest in the year 1874. She plays the part of a frontierswoman during an Apache uprising.

Actually, *Hondo* is not her first motion picture. After the word had spread about her superlative acting in *Summer and Smoke* she won a bit-part ("I had 21st billing", she recalls) in a New York-made film called *Taxi.* "With *Mid-Summer,* her first Broadway show,

her salary jumped from *Summer and Smoke's* $40 to more than $300 a week" (*Time,* February 2, 1953). Her next picture will be in a dramatization of John Steinbeck's story, *The Wayward Bus.* "My part is a doozer, a perfect doozer", Miss Page commented happily. (*New Yorker,* February 7, 1953)

In addition to her theatre and film work, Miss Page has appeared on the radio for the Theatre Guild of the Air in Ferenc Molnar's *Liliom* and in Tennessee Williams' *The Glass Menagerie* and *Summer and Smoke.*

The young actress is five feet seven inches tall, weighs 120 pounds, has blonde hair and gray eyes. She has a lively sense of humor, a profound interest in the theatre, an irresistible smile. She is not much interested in clothes, can't drive an automobile. Reading is her chief recreation. She is devoted to her father and mother who look upon her success with benevolence and to her brother Donald, just out of Korean service. Her family and friends call her "Gerry". She enjoys oil painting and listening to classical music.

"I do a lot of walking," Miss Page said, "and for years I walked around in the Village and got lost and always ended up on Varick Street" (*New Yorker,* February 7, 1953). "I knew the Village before I'd seen it . . . and all the good things and the bad things. I've lived them over a hundred times, but I'm not one—bit—bored with them."

She admits that the parts she wants most to play are Ibsen's Hedda Gabler, and Roxane, the heroine of Rostand's *Cyrano de Bergerac.*

References

Cue 22:12 F 14 '53
Life 33:107-8+ S 8 '52 pors; 34:67-68
  Mr 2 '53 pors
Look 17:20 Mr 24 '53
N Y Herald Tribune IV p3 F 22 '53 por
N Y Journal-American p28L Mr 15 '53
  por; Pictorial p4 Mr 1 '53 pors
N Y Times Ja 22 '53
N Y World-Telegram p11 Ap 4 '53 por;
  p40 N 19 '52
Newsweek Ja 29 '53
New Yorker 28:24 F 7 '53
Theatre Arts 37:18 Ap '53 pors
Time 61:48 F 2 '53
Vogue 121:136-7 Mr '53

PARSONS, HARRIET (OETTINGER)
(ĕt'ĭn-ger) Motion picture producer; writer
Address: b. c/o RKO-Radio Studios, 780 N. Gower St., Los Angeles 38, Calif.; h. 815 Malcolm Ave., West Los Angeles 24, Calif.

One of the very few women producers active in Hollywood today, Harriet Parsons has been associated with the screen industry since 1928— in the early part of her career as a writer for magazines, as a radio commentator on activities in the film capital, and as a newspaper columnist. She entered the field of motion picture production in 1933 with *Screen Snapshots,* a series of short subjects for Columbia Pictures, and later produced for Republic Studios a similar series called *Meet the Stars.* Among her productions for RKO-Radio Pictures, which she joined as a writer-producer in 1943, are *The Enchanted Cottage* (1945), *I Remember Mama* (1948), and *Clash By Night* (1952). Harriet Parson's mother is the well-known motion picture columnist Louella O. Parsons.

The only child of John Dement and Louella Rose (Oettinger) Parsons, Harriet Parsons was born in Burlington, Iowa. Her father, who was in the real estate business, died in 1919 as he was returning from active duty with the United States Army in France. (Her great-great-grandfather on her father's side, Colonel Henry Dodge, and his son, Augustus Caesar, had served six years in the United States Senate at the same time—reportedly the only instance of a father and son serving simultaneously as United States Senators.) When Harriet was four years old, she was taken to Chicago by her mother, who first got a job in the syndicate department of the Chicago *Tribune* and later became a story editor and scenario writer for the old Essanay Studios in that city. At the age of six, Harriet appeared as "Baby Parsons" in two Essanay pictures—*Margaret's Awakening* and *The Magic Wand*—for which her mother had written the scripts.

In 1914 Louella Parsons started her first motion picture news column for the Chicago *Record-Herald,* remaining with that paper until 1918, when she and her daughter moved to New York City. There she obtained a position as editor of the movie section of the old *Morning Telegraph*; in 1922 she joined the Hearst syndicate with which she has since been associated. Harriet, meanwhile, attended Horace Mann School for Girls, in New York, where she served as editor in chief of the school paper during her junior year and as president of the student government organization during her senior year.

Graduating from Horace Mann in 1924, Miss Parsons entered Wellesley College (Massachusetts) and majored in literature. As an undergraduate, she staged plays for Zeta Alpha, the dramatic society, contributed poetry to *The Twig,* wrote lyrics for the class and crew songs and won a letter in basketball as a member of the varsity team. During her sophomore year in order to make some extra spending money, she covered film exchanges in Boston at space rates for the New York *Morning Telegraph,* but abandoned this project when she discovered that her trips into Boston were costing her more than she earned. For a brief period she also reviewed art exhibitions in Boston for *Art News.* After receiving her B.A. degree from Wellesley in 1928, she departed for Europe on a student tour.

Upon her return later that year, Miss Parsons took a position on the scenario staff of Metro-Goldwyn-Mayer Studios, in Hollywood, but soon resigned from this post, because, according to *Pic,* she felt that she had been hired solely on the strength of her mother's name. Going back to New York in 1929, she was employed by *Photoplay Magazine* to write advice to the lovelorn and to operate the office switchboard in her spare moments. She was soon promoted to staff interviewer and then to associate editor, and in 1930 was transferred to the

Ernest Bachrach

HARRIET PARSONS

magazine's West Coast office as a staff writer. For the next three years (1930-33) she did free-lance writing for such fan magazines as *Modern Screen, Movie Mirror,* and *Silver Screen,* and also conducted a column for *Liberty.* In 1931 she joined Hearst's Universal Service (which later merged with International News Service) as a columnist and feature writer, and created the "Keyhole Portrait" type of stylized biographical and character sketch of the film stars—a form that has since been much imitated. Four years later she assumed additional work as a member of the motion picture staff of the Los Angeles *Examiner,* holding this and the INS post simultaneously until 1943. During 1938 she conducted a weekly sponsored radio program of news from the film capital, *Harriet Parsons' Hollywood Highlights,* for the National Broadcasting Company. That same year she originated the "Hollywood in Review" department for *Woman's Day,* and edited this magazine feature until 1940. When her mother was ill or on vacation, Miss Parsons often wrote her daily syndicated column on films and the stars.

In 1933 Harry Cohn, president of Columbia Pictures, offered Louella Parsons the opportunity to produce *Screen Snapshots,* a Hollywood newsreel showing the stars in their homes, at play, and in off-duty moments on the lot. When she was unable to accept, her daughter was asked to take over the series in December of that year. "I didn't know an iota about film production," Miss Parsons told a New York *Post* interviewer, "but, believe me, in the years that followed I gave my heart and soul and mind and disposition to the cause!" With the production unit for *Screen Snapshots* consisting of the cameraman and Miss Parsons, she served not only as producer, but also as writer, director, narrator, editorial supervisor, location manager, casting director, and idea man, even

PARSONS, HARRIET—Continued

acting in the pictures occasionally. Her stay at Columbia lasted six and a half years (1933-40), during which time she made over a hundred of these monthly short subjects. In 1940 she went to Republic Studios to write, direct, and produce, a similar series of short subjects called *Meet the Stars*. At Republic, she got her first chance at a full-length, feature production, *Joan of Ozark* (1942), starring Judy Canova and Joe E. Brown, with Miss Parsons listed as the associate producer. A *Film Daily* reviewer commented that the film provided "generous helpings" of slapstick comedy and that it would "make the grade nicely as family entertainment."

Leaving Republic in 1943, Miss Parsons in August of that year signed a seven-year contract as a RKO-Radio Pictures writer-producer, the position she still holds. Her first production on that lot was *The Enchanted Cottage* (1945), directed by John Cromwell and starring Dorothy McGuire, Robert Young, and Herbert Marshall. This picture was adapted from a play about a disfigured war veteran, written by Sir Arthur Wing Pinero in 1921 to build up the morale of soldiers who had returned from World War I. When Miss Parsons came across the story in the studio files, she realized its applicability to World War II. With the locale changed from England to New England and other details brought up to date, she secured approval of the script from the War Department because its central character was a returned American Army flier. On its release, the picture received varying reviews. The *PM* critic called it "rather hugely over-produced". *Time* commented, "With genteel taste and loving care, RKO has turned it into the best sentimental picture of the season." *Variety* rated the film "an artistic production which will catch both critical praise and plenty of audience attention," and added that Miss Parsons had "turned in a most able job" as the producer. *The Enchanted Cottage*, which cost $950,000, made a gross profit of more than $3,000,000. She was next assigned to produce *Night Song* (1947), also directed by Cromwell. While some critics praised the performances of Dana Andrews, Merle Oberon, and Ethel Barrymore, they generally agreed that this story of a blind pianist-composer and his rich and beautiful patroness was too hackneyed and sentimental.

Soon after she joined RKO, Miss Parsons read—and saw the screen possibilities in—*Mama's Bank Account*, Kathryn Forbes' novel about a Norwegian immigrant family in San Francisco during the early 1900's. She brought the story to the attention of the studio, which acquired the screen rights that same year (1943) and assigned her to produce a modest film adaptation. However, in 1944 John van Druten dramatized the novel, and his stage play, entitled *I Remember Mama*, was presented on Broadway from October 1944 to June 1946. Consequently the screen version became a major enterprise at RKO and was budgeted at about $2,300,000. The studio and Miss Parsons, to whom the film had been reassigned, decided to use both the book and the play as the basis for the scenario. Since Miss Parsons was eager to have George Stevens direct the picture and since he had already attained the status of producer-director, she agreed to be credited as the film's producer while he was listed as the executive producer and director. Starring Irene Dunne in the title role, *I Remember Mama* (1948) received unanimous praise from the critics. Typical comments were: "a picture glowing with affection" (New York *Sun*); "highly agreeable film entertainment" (New York *Post*); "virtuoso work in all departments" (New York *World-Telegram*); "genuine and fine and moving" (*PM*); and "the production comes through with tremendous cinematic and emotional power . . . a photoplay to restore one's faith in Hollywood" (New York *Herald Tribune*).

Two years later Miss Parsons produced *Never a Dull Moment* (1950), starring Irene Dunne and Fred MacMurray. In the opinion of Otis L. Guernsey, Jr. (New York *Herald Tribune*), this story of a sophisticated lady songwriter who marries a rodeo cowboy skirted "the edges of an amusing, if unoriginal, idea," but he thought its potential satire was "almost wholly dissipated in the gimmick and the pratt-fall." Miss Parsons subsequently became the only producer under contract to the Jerry Wald-Norman Krasna independent producing unit at RKO, for which she made her next picture, *Clash By Night* (1952). Adapted from Clifford Odets' play, directed by Fritz Lang, and starring Barbara Stanwyck, Paul Douglas, and Robert Ryan, this movie, Miss Parsons has said, presented her with a very difficult problem—how to handle the delicate subject material without risk of offending younger theater goers. Alton Cook in the New York *World-Telegram* thought the production was enhanced by a strong cast and understanding direction. The reviewer of the Los Angeles *Times,* expressed the opinion that the film, which was a notable commercial success, "possesses the slashing power of a real drama in raw. It is contrived excellently and played with high efficiency by its cast nine-tenths of the way."

Miss Parsons told Irene Thirer of the New York *Post* that there is a good future for women producers in Hollywood and that no real resentment against them exists. "It's the women themselves who, for the most part, prefer other jobs in the industry," she has explained. "They're scared of the headaches involved: budget trouble, cast difficulties, wardrobe, sets, properties, and a thousand and one other responsibilities." But if the picture plays well, Miss Parsons finds it "the most gratifying experience in the world—worth every single sleepless night of splitting headaches and aspirins." She feels that if more women were producers, pictures would take on new and desirable qualities. "The combination of a masculine director and a feminine producer is often very successful. It tends to result in an all-round presentation of human nature, which should exist in all good pictures. Any motion picture should mirror something that has touched every spectator's life, either in reality or imagination, at some point. This is a value I strive for" (*Christian Science Monitor,* March 21, 1952).

The producer holds membership in the Academy of Motion Picture Arts and Sciences and the Wellesley Alumnae Association. She is the only woman member of the Screen Producers' Guild, and serves on its public relations and grievance committees and as studio captain at RKO. She was one of a panel of speakers chosen from the guild members to lecture at the University of Southern California in 1952. During World War II she was on the board of directors and entertainment committee of the Hollywood Canteen, where she had charge of the show presented every Monday night. She belongs to the Westside Tennis Club and the Hollywood Women's Press Club, of which she is a member of the board of directors and former vice-president. On September 28, 1939, she married King Kennedy, a writer and publicist; they were divorced in April 1946. Miss Parsons, who has blue eyes and brown hair, stands five feet one inch tall, and weighs 108 pounds, has been described as "petite and ultra feminine in appearance," with a "softly curled light-brown bob, deep-set pensive eyes, trim figure" (*New York Post*). Comments on her personality emphasize her "almost fanatical honesty," business acumen, and independence. Her political party is the Republican. Tennis and swimming are her favorite sports; she also enjoys reading, gardening, and photography, and is said to be fond of any pet that can be tamed.

References

Christian Sci Mon p5 Mr 21 '52
N Y Post p13 My 12 '45 por
N Y Sun p30 My 11 '45; Mr 18 '48
N Y Sunday News II p2 Je 8 '52 por
Pic p15-17 Mr 13 '45 pors
International Motion Picture Almanac, 1950-51
Parsons, L. The Gay Illiterate (1944)

PASTORE, JOHN O(RLANDO) Mar. 17, 1907- United States Senator from Rhode Island

Address: b. Senate Office Bldg., Washington 25, D.C.; h. The Dorchester, Washington, D.C.

Rhode Island's junior Senator, John O. Pastore, Democrat, was first elected to Congress in November 1950 to fill the unexpired term of J. Howard McGrath, who had become United States Attorney General, and was re-elected on November 4, 1952, for a full term. While a freshman Senator, he was made chairman of the Civil Service Committee. Pastore, who had earlier held a number of political offices in the State government, was Governor of Rhode Island from 1945 to 1950.

John Orlando Pastore, the second of five children of Italian-born Michele and Erminia (Asprinio) Pastore, was born March 17, 1907, in the Federal Hill district of Providence, Rhode Island. His father, a tailor who had moved to the United States in 1899, died when John was nine. For the next three years, while his mother and older brother worked to support the family, the schoolboy helped with the housework and cooking and cared for the babies. "When he cleaned house," his mother has recalled, "he moved every stick of furniture. He never did anything by halves" (quoted by Delos W. Lovelace, New York *Sun*, October 12, 1945). Mrs. Pastore set high standards for the family; she saw to it that they were better dressed and better behaved than the neighbors' children (Samuel Lubell in the *Saturday Evening Post*, November 12, 1947). Upon the mother's marriage to her late husband's brother, Pasquale, she resumed the homemaking tasks. John Pastore then spent his after-school hours delivering coats and suits for his stepfather, who, like his father, had a tailor shop in the home. During summer vacations John worked as an errand boy, as office boy in a law office, and as a foot-press operator in a jewelry factory. A former employer, quoted by Lubell, described Pastore as the best office boy he ever had, well-behaved, likable, and conscientious. In 1925 young Pastore was graduated with honors from Classical High School in Providence.

With his mother's encouragement, Pastore, who upon leaving high school had taken a fifteen-dollar-a-week job as a claims adjuster for the Narragansett Electric Company, in 1927 enrolled in an evening law course given by Northeastern University at the Providence Young Men's Christian Association, and received his LL.B. in 1931. Admitted to the bar in 1932, Pastore set up his law office in the basement of the family home, but when clients were lacking, he turned to the possibility of using his oratorical skill in politics. One Sunday in 1933, as Lubell has related, John Pastore accosted Tommy Testa, a local political figure whom he had never met, and told him, "I'd like to go into politics." Favorably impressed by Pastore's manner, Testa helped him to get the Democratic nomination for the State House of Representatives in 1934, and the twenty-seven-year-old lawyer won the election in a district considered "strongly Republican." Re-elected in 1936, he became chairman of the House Corporations Committee.

In 1937 Pastore accepted an appointment as fifth assistant to the State attorney-general. After losing that position as a result of the Republican election victory of 1938, the attorney served in 1939-40 on the Providence Charter Revision Committee. With the return to a Democratic State administration in 1940, he was appointed assistant attorney-general in charge of the criminal calendar. Pastore has described himself as "a tough prosecutor." When Rhode Island's Governor J. Howard McGrath resigned to become President Truman's Solicitor-General, Pastore, who had been elected lieutenant governor in 1944, succeeded to the Governorship on October 6, 1945.

During his campaign for election to a full term in 1936, many rich Italian-Americans who were lifelong Republicans contributed more than $60,000 to his Democratic fund. Pastore, who won that election by 22,000 votes and the next by 73,706, has said, "I'm the only Governor who

JOHN O. PASTORE

ever went from the smallest to the largest plurality in one election" (*Saturday Evening Post*).

As Governor, Pastore refused to follow the suggestion that he build up his own political organization by appointing Italian-Americans to office whenever possible. Thus he avoided a struggle over patronage with the predominantly Irish-American leadership of his party in the State. He preferred, in his words (as quoted by Lubell), to build "a record, not an organization." Measures sponsored by Governor Pastore included a State antipollution authority, a direct primary, and a fair employment practices law. As the first postwar Governor, he had to raise $13 million in additional revenue (half again as much as the prewar State budget) to pay for increased salaries and for highways and public works that could not be built during the war. The Democrats, who controlled one house of the legislature, recommended that the money be raised by a corporate income tax, while the Republicans, who controlled the other chamber, pressed for a sales tax. The governor's compromise combined a 1 per cent sales tax with a 4 per cent corporate levy.

In keeping his official house in order, Pastore did not initiate investigations, but acted promptly when questionable situations were brought to his attention. Upon hearing in January 1947 that a number of elderly women patients of the State mental hospital had died of influenza within twelve days, Pastore appointed two hospital superintendents and a past president of the State Congress of Parents and Teachers to study the situation. According to Lubell, "These investigating committees seemed to serve Pastore as a buffer against his own party bosses," should they seek to protect those involved. The size of Pastore's plurality in the 1948 election indicated that he must have drawn many Republican votes, as well as the full Democratic

strength. After election, he canceled the traditional inaugural ball, explaining that since he had already been given one such ball in 1946, the expenses of another were unnecessary.

Shortly thereafter, Pastore was chosen chairman of the six-man New England Governors' Conference. He called for a uniform nationwide unemployment insurance tax, either through "federalization of the program or some form of Federal reinsurance." With financial groups, he tried to help overcome the situation in which high taxes, wages, and power prices were causing industrial plants to leave the State. In January 1950, following the example of Governor Sherman Adams of Vermont, he warned that he would veto any new taxes. Two years earlier, the Governor had proposed pay increases for all State employees—except the Governor—and had not allowed any Democrat to propose a salary increase for him (a Republican introduced the eventual bill raising the Governor's salary from $8,000 to $15,000). Later in 1950 Pastore testified in Congress for the extension of Federal rent controls. In November of that year he ran for the United States Senate to fill the unexpired term of J. Howard McGrath, who had given up his seat in Congress in 1949 to take his appointment as United States Attorney General.

By his election to the Senate with 184,530 votes to 114,890, Pastore proved himself, to quote an Associated Press report, "the biggest vote-getter in the history of the nation's smallest State." One of the youngest Senators at forty-three, he was named to the committees on Labor and Public Welfare and on Post Office and Civil Service, as well as to the Committee on the District of Columbia. Senator Pastore has been described in the Washington *Post* as "one of the best and most effective Congressional friends of Federal employees." As chairman of the Civil Service subcommittee, he held hearings on, and introduced, bills relating to cost-of-living increases and annual leave. In October 1951 Pastore was floor manager for a bill authorizing the use of Federal funds to improve private nonprofit Washington hospitals. While it is rare for local District of Columbia issues to be debated on the floor, this measure was fully debated, as it involved the larger issues of national hospital needs and the question of public funds for denominational institutions.

Senator Pastore's voting record in the Eighty-second Congress indicated he favored authorizing grants for local public health units, against limiting the troops which the President might send to Europe, against requiring India to repay in strategic materials an emergency loan of American grain, against a cut in public housing units, and against cutting funds for public health, hospitals, medical care, and medical research. He went on record for authority to roll back excessive prices, for allowing OPS to set slaughter quotas, against legalizing the basing-point method of private price-fixing, against limiting the airline subsidy to regularly scheduled carriers of air mail, for two proposals intended to raise the corporate and personal income taxes in the higher brackets, and against killing the bill for economic aid to friendly countries. In March 1951 Pastore joined several Republicans in denouncing the treaty limitations on Italy's armed forces, which would weaken her as a member of the Atlantic Pact countries. The next year he was one of the principal speakers against the 302-page McCarran immigration bill (which was later passed over President Truman's veto). After the death of Senator Brien McMahon, he was appointed in August 1952 to fill the vacancy on the Joint Senate-House Committee on Atomic Energy. During the 1952 campaign he directed the Democratic Presidential and Congressional campaigns among Americans of Italian ancestry. Successful in his own race for office, Pastore was re-elected Senator from Rhode Island on November 4, 1952.

The recipient of honorary degrees from five Rhode Island colleges, Pastore holds the LL.D. degree from Providence College and Rhode Island State College, the Ed.D. degree from Rhode Island College of Education, and the Sc.D. degree from Rhode Island College of Pharmacy and Bryant College. The Senator is general chairman of an American committee formed to work with a group of Italian experts for the establishment of "boys' towns" in southern Italy. Pastore and Elena Elizabeth (Caito) Pastore, married on July 12, 1941, are the parents of John, Jr., Frances Elizabeth, and Louisa Marie. He is five feet four inches tall, weighs 150 pounds, and is noted for his careful grooming. Anecdotes about Pastore deal with his powerful voice, his explosive sensitivity to small annoyances and elations combined with his "icy calm" under trying conditions.

References

Sat Eve Post 222:31 N 12 '49 pors
Time 56:21 N 20 '50 por
American Catholic Who's Who, 1952-53
Congressional Directory (1951)
Who's Who in America, 1952-53
Who's Who in United States Politics (1952)
World Biography (1948)

PASVOLSKY, LEO Aug. 22, 1893—May 5, 1953 Economist; came to United States at age of 12 from Russia; attended College of the City of New York, Columbia University, University of Geneva, received Ph.D. degree from Brookings Institution 1937; economist in United States Bureau of Foreign and Domestic Commerce, 1934; special assistant to Secretary of State, 1934-46; participated in Bretton Woods and Dumbarton Oaks conferences, 1944; prepared final draft of United Nations Charter, 1945; Director of International Studies at Brookings Institution, 1946-53; author of many books on monetary problems. See *Current Biography,* 1945

Obituary

N Y Times p31 My 7 '53

PAULDING, MRS. C. GOUVERNEUR
See Peterson, V.

PAZ ESTENSSORO, VÍCTOR (ĕs"tĕn-sō'rō vēk'tôr) Oct. 2, 1907- President of Bolivia

Address: Palacio Presidencial, La Paz, Bolivia

Bolivia's President is Víctor Paz Estenssoro, former attorney and professor of economics. As leader of the country's powerful Movimiento Nacionalista Revolucionario party, he directed a revolution which placed his party at the head of the Bolivian government in 1943; three years later, deposed by a counter-revolution, he went into a six-year exile in Argentina. After an election in 1951 in which he received a plurality but not a majority of the votes, he returned from exile in April 1952, to be inaugurated as President following Bolivia's 179th (and most violent) revolution.

In August 1953, President Paz Estenssoro signed his Government's promised land-reform decree, which will expropriate large estates (half of them owned by absentee landlords), and will pay for them in 25-year Government bonds. "Land reform may prove harder to bring off than nationalization of Bolivian tin," commented *Time,* August 17, 1953. "Aside from the danger of violence between landlords and peasants, there is an admitted risk that the Indians, once they own the land, will grow just enough for their needs, leaving Bolivia (which spends 35 per cent of its national income for imported food) hungrier than over."

Víctor Paz Estenssoro was born on October 2, 1907, at Tarija, Bolivia. He was the son of Domingo Paz Rojas and Carlota Estenssoro de Pa, and is said to be related to the Argentine family of Paz de Cordoba. His early education was at the Colegio Nacional Bolívar, Oruro. He studied economics and law at the University of San Andrés at La Paz, and in 1927 began his career as an attorney. The following year he entered governmental administrative work as secretary of the Directorate of Financial Statistics. In 1931-32 he was attorney for the Permanent Fiscal Commission, and in 1932 and again in 1936-1937 he served as superior officer of the Department of Finance. He was made president of the Banco Minero de Bolivia in 1939.

Paz Estenssoro's first entry into the legislative department of Bolivia's government was in 1938, when he was convention deputy for a year for his native town of Tarija. In 1940 he was elected to the National Congress as deputy from Tarija, and for the years 1940 and 1941 served as Vice-President of the Chamber of Deputies. He was appointed Minister of Economy in 1941.

In the late 1930's a new political party was established in Bolivia—the Movimiento Nacionalista Revolucionario, or M.N.R.—composed chiefly of young military officers and civilians. The party has been characterized as being both pro-Nazi and pro-leftist; it is admittedly strongly nationalist. Paz has been described as "the head and brains of the M.N.A., whose members call him *el jife* (the boss)." He has said of the M.N.R., "Our party is of the masses . . . we not only have the tin workers in our ranks but the destitute peasants, the

VICTOR PAZ ESTENSSORO

middle-class and the university students—it is
a national party." As spokesman for the party,
Paz opposed Congressional approval of the
Atlantic Charter and led members of the
M.N.R. out of the House of Deputies when
that body approved the Charter. He opposed
the exclusive sale of Bolivian quinine, rubber,
tin and other minerals to the United States, and
in October 1942 spoke against Bolivian acceptance of a loan from the United States.

Since becoming an independent state in 1825,
Bolivia has had difficulty in solving its economic
and social problems. Ninety per cent of the
food supply has to be imported, and for many
years the ownership of the single large product,
tin (which provides 80 per cent of the country's
foreign exchange), lay outside of Bolivia. In
its 127 years of existence, the small, land-locked
nation has suffered four wars and 179 revolutions.

In 1941 Paz was accused of taking part in a
revolutionary plot by the M.N.R. to seize the
government. The projected coup was alleged
to have German support. Paz, who claimed
parliamentary immunity to arrest, denied the
charges and was absolved. In 1943 a group of
M.N.R. leaders, including Paz Estenssoro,
visited Buenos Aires, where they were reported
to have conferred with Argentinian nationalists.
During the visit, Paz was guest of honor at a
banquet given by the newspaper *El Pampero*,
and spoke over the Prieto radio. Reports were
later published that he had at that time received
"some millions of Argentine pesos" to finance
a revolution.

On December 20, 1943, the anniversary of the
"Catavi massacre" in which nineteen striking
tin miners had been killed by government
troops, a revolution placed the M.N.R. in control of the Bolivian Government. Paz Estenssoro, acknowledged leader of the coup, became
Finance Minister of the new regime, and Major

Gualberto Villarroel was named President. The
program of the new government was described
in a dispatch to the New York *Herald Tribune*
(December 22, 1943) as "a mixture of anti-
imperialism, anti-Semitism, nationalism, socialism, and chauvinism." Paz himself declared the
regime would favor "collaboration with the
United States and the United Nations" and
would "try to better the workers' conditions and
those of the middle class and to take advantage
. . . of the richness that is to be found in
Bolivia." Only Argentina among the Latin-
American governments recognized the new
state, and recognition by the United States was
refused with a State Department statement
calling the revolution "but one act committed
by a generally subversive movement . . . hostile
to the Allied cause." In July 1946 a counter-
revolution overthrew the administration. President Villarroel was assassinated, and most of
the M.N.R. leaders were killed or fled into
exile. Paz Estenssoro spent six years in exile
in Argentina, working in the banking system
of that country.

During these years the government accused
the M.N.R. of several attempts to gain power.
In the fall of 1949 the party partially succeeded in a revolutionary attempt which was
defeated after three weeks. A presidential election was held on May 6, 1951. Still in exile,
Paz Estenssoro, as the M.N.R. candidate, received 54,129 of the 126,125 votes cast, a plurality of five-to-three over his nearest opponent,
but failing of a simple majority. Under Bolivian
law, such an election is decided by a vote of
Congress. Since the strongest support for Paz
came from miners, peasants and laborers unable
to vote because of literacy requirements, his
popularity as a candidate clearly exceeded his
vote. It was thought that the administration-
dominated Congress was likely to elect the administration's presidential candidate. Using this
situation, a military junta seized the government
before the Congressional vote could take place.

The junta offered to allow Paz Estenssoro to
return to Bolivia in August; the M.N.R. leader
was quoted as replying that he would return at
a time of his own choosing. He returned trium-
phantly on April 15, 1952 after a three-day
revolution in which about 450 Bolivians were
killed. He was sworn in as President the
following day, declaring the new regime "a
revolutionary return to legality," and he promised a better standard of living to Bolivian
workers (New York *Times*, April 10, 1952).

The principal point in the new government's
program, Paz Estenssoro announced, would be
nationalization of the tin mines. Because of a
price dispute, United States imports of tin from
Bolivia had virtually ceased several months
before the April revolution. On June 1 Bolivia
released shipments of tin to the United States,
and at the same time Paz Estenssoro announced
the formation of a commission to work out the
nationalization procedure. On June 2 the United
States granted diplomatic recognition to the Paz
Estenssoro government, issuing a statement that
"our action does not imply any judgment of
Bolivian domestic affairs."

On November 1, 1952, Paz Estenssoro announced the nationalization of the three principal companies—the Patino Mines and Enterprises Consolidated, the Compagnie Aramayo de Mines en Bolivie, and the Hochschild Mines—which produce about 72 per cent of the country's tin. This was called "the most important act of nationalization in Latin America since Mexico seized the foreign oil companies in 1938." The government offered some reparation ($21,750,000) to the owners of the three mines, but in return asked payment of $520,000,-000 charged against them for income tax evasion and other government claims. Various discussions leading to a peaceful cash settlement are under way.

President Paz has insisted that "lawful compensation must be paid," and is quoted in *Time* (November 10, 1952) as offering engineers and other foreign employees of the three companies "security of tenure, salary and other contract benefits if they will keep on working for the government's newly constituted Bolivian Mining Corporation." President Paz hopes to make a peaceful settlement with the owners of the three mines, Patino, Hochschild and Aramayo, with some cash compensation for their shareholders including the United States citizens who own 26 per cent of stock. A long-term contract was signed in February 1953 with the British for the output of the Patino mines which represent about half of Bolivia's tin production.

Another aim of his government enunciated by Paz Estenssoro is agrarian reform and agricultural improvement. Despite the nationalization of the large mining companies, the Bolivian President has expressed the nation's need for foreign capital and has offered "attractive" return on investments. He has said that small independent companies would remain in private hands, but "we cannot have companies that are greater than the state."

Because of the falling prices of tin during 1953, Paz Estenssoro wrote to President Eisenhower that the financial situation of Bolivia "has deteriorated dangerously." Eisenhower then announced on October 14, 1953 that the United States would help Bolivia with a four-point assistance program of $5,000,000 worth of agricultural products and $4,000,000 for other essential products (New York *Times,* October 15, 1953).

President Paz was formerly a member of the faculty of the Universidad Mayor de San Andrés, as professor of the History of Economic Doctrines. He is co-author with Jorge Palenque of *Esquima of the Political, Economic and Administrative Organization of Bolivia* (1929), and author of *Aspects of the Bolivian Economy* (1940) and *Development of Economic Thought in Bolivia.* In November 1936 he was married to Carmela Cerruto; they have two children. Among Paz Estenssoro's decorations are the Merito Militar, and war medal for service in the Chaco War.

Reference

Who's Who in Latin America pt 4 (1947)

World Biography (1948)

PEARSON, JAY F(REDERICK) W(ES-LEY) May 7, 1901- University president; marine zoologist

Address: b. c/o University of Miami, Coral Gables, Fla; h. 2475 So. Bayshore Drive, Miami

On May 7, 1953, the University of Miami installed as its second president, Jay Frederick Wesley Pearson. The event made national news headlines, for what was once dubbed "the cardboard college" now has an enrollment of nearly 8,000 students and a campus of streamlined, modern buildings to replace those demolished in the disastrous hurricane of 1926, when the university was one year old. It celebrated, too, Dr. Pearson's fifty-second birthday and his twenty-seventh year as a member of the faculty.

Succeeding Dr. Bowman Foster Ashe, founder of the university, who died in December, 1952, Dr. Pearson stepped from the post of executive vice-president, in which he carried much of the responsibility of developing the university, into the presidency. His promotion was marked by considerable fanfare. Ten college presidents, representatives from 318 universities, a faculty of 500, and an audience of more than 3,000 witnessed the impressive inaugural ceremonies in an outdoor arena, and heard the laudatory address of Chancellor Rufus K. Fitzgerald of the University of Pittsburgh, Pearson's former alma mater.

Twenty-seven years ago, Jay F. W. Pearson was called to the University of Miami as an instructor of zoology. The university, but a year old at the time, was endowed with $15,000,000 and had plans for the quick development of a big campus with expensive Spanish-type buildings. Pearson was already on a train en route South when newspaper headlines which he read in a railroad station startled him: Miami was in ruins. The hurricane of 1926 had struck. Arriving in Miami, Pearson discovered that what buildings there had been on the young university's campus had literally been blown down.

With the campus a shambles, the handsome endowment become a $500,000 debt and the anticipated enrollment of 5000 dwindled to 275 students, the university made shift in an abandoned, uncompleted three-story hotel. Jay Pearson knocked together his own laboratory tables, painted floors and taught classes behind movable wallboard partitions. Deriders dubbed the shaky institution "cardboard college", and thus it was known throughout the United States. But those makeshift partitions later became a planned feature of educational buildings and proved to be the first of the university's educational innovations in many of which Pearson had a directing hand.

The "cardboard college", a pioneer in startling contemporary architectural design, has grown to be unique, "best looking" and certainly the most modern in the country, with its hurricane-proof buildings of steel, concrete and glass, its breezeways, walkways and sheltered galleries. The marine biology department

Ray Fisher

JAY F. W. PEARSON

founded by young Jay Pearson has developed over the years into one of the foremost of its kind in the country.

Dr. Pearson did not plan originally on being a scientist nor even on an educator's career. When he entered college in 1921 his objective was to major in foreign banking. He had already worked for three banks and his ambition was to become branch manager for one of them, preferably in South America. His father, Charles Albert Lane, was an examiner in the Patent Office in Washington. His grandfather had been a judge and a United States Congressman from Monroe County in Ohio.

Jay Frederick Wesley Pearson was born in Woodsfield, Ohio, May 7, 1901, but the grandfather's appointment to Congress caused the family to move to Washington. His mother's family—she was Sarah Evaline Hays—were merchants and farmers. Jay's father died at the age of thirty-four, when Jay was only four years old, and his mother learned typing and shorthand, working for years as a secretary in Washington while Jay's grandmother raised him. Young Pearson was only fifteen and a freshman in high school when his Sunday school teacher, a cashier in the Grove City, Pennsylvania, National Bank, offered him his first job. All through high school he worked in the bank after classes and on Saturdays. Nevertheless, he finished high school as valedictorian of his class.

For three years after graduation he worked at the Columbia National Bank, then back at the Grove City bank, and finally during his freshman year at college in the Pittsburgh branch of the Federal Reserve Bank of Cleveland. Scholarships and his own initiative took him through the University of Pittsburgh. In his first year there, to fulfill his science requirement, Pearson took a course in zoology,

largely because the chemistry classes were crowded. It was not long until he found himself neglecting his business studies to work in the zoology laboratory. By his junior year, science had completely won his interest and he decided to major in zoology. At the end of that year, the head of the zoology department recommended him to William Beebe to accompany the scientist on an expedition to British Guiana. The trip determined his final specialties —tropical zoology, ecology, and entomology.

Again, in his senior year when Beebe asked that a student be recommended, Pearson was the department's choice and he joined the Arcturus Expedition to the Sargasso Sea and the Galapagos Islands as assistant in the study of jellyfish, crustaceans, and other macroplanktonic organisms.

The University of Pittsburgh graduated him in absentia, *magna cum laude* in 1925. On this trip, he became interested in octopi and squids and decided to continue at Pittsburgh for his Master's degree in invertebrate zoology. During that year, he took a class to British Guiana and was given his Master of Science degree in absentia, in 1926. The subject of his Master's thesis was "Cephalopodes of the Arcturus Expedition".

Pearson's extracurricular college activities were curtailed somewhat by the teaching duties he assumed during his undergraduate days. He served as undergraduate assistant to three instructors in three different departments. In the department of zoology, he kept the financial records, as well. Summers and Christmas vacations, he worked in the bank. He was, however, a member of the Student Senate and the Pitt Glee Club, the first college glee club ever to sing over the radio.

It was during his freshman year at the University of Pittsburgh that he first met Bowman Ashe. Ashe was the dean of freshmen and his counselor. In the summer of 1926, when Ashe was looking for someone to initiate a zoology department in his year-old University of Miami, he cabled Pearson in British Guiana offering him the job.

For three years he was instructor and assistant at the University of Miami. Then he studied at the University of Chicago for his Ph.D. degree, and worked as a graduate assistant on leave of absence from the University of Miami. He received his Doctorate in 1932. The subject of his thesis was on Taxonomy and Ecology of Native Bees in the Chicago area. The University of Chicago recommended that Dr. Pearson be put in charge of biological exhibits for the Century of Progress World's Fair and Dr. Ashe extended Pearson's leave.

Shortly after his return to Miami in 1933, Dr. Pearson was encouraged by President Ashe to devote more time to administrative work. He was secretary to the university from 1933 to 1942, dean of administration from 1939 to 1941 and dean of faculty from 1944 to 1946. The University was far from affluent and Pearson's banking training came brilliantly into play. As administrator he had three problems, he states, "to build the student body, to get paying students, and to expand and develop the

478

faculty by convincing people they should work with us and would get paid." With increasing enrollment, he cautiously and ingeniously began extending the campus.

By the late 1930's the university, so near the rocks in preceding years, had become one of the best rounded educational institutions in the country. Dr. Ashe and Dr. Pearson had gathered to themselves a young and eager faculty, all working as a team. Before World War II, the peak of enrollment was 1370 day students, and in 1941 Dr. Pearson had achieved an important goal: the university was accredited by the Southern Association of Colleges and Secondary Schools.

Between 1938 and 1939, Dr. Pearson had taken another leave of absence to take charge of the biological and medical exhibits for the Golden Gate Exposition in San Francisco. On his return to Miami, he was selected to assist the Air Corps in setting up their academic program for air cadets. He rapidly became Major Pearson and tackled what he considers the greatest educational job ever attempted. He developed the plan for the "12-week West Point" which was the Officer Candidate School at Miami Beach, where "men were taught in twelve weeks how to keep themselves alive and take care of the men in their command—a complete new way of living." He was transferred as Director of Training to Boca Raton, Florida, and finished his military career as commanding officer of the Officer Candidate School at San Antonio, Texas.

Out of the Army in 1944, Dr. Pearson returned to his administrative duties at the University of Miami which had greatly expanded. The housing and teaching of the Air Force had contributed largely to its development. Now, the campus grew spectacularly under his hands. War-time barracks made way for handsome, modern, streamlined buildings. Enrollment climbed to over the 10,000 mark; (the 1953 enrollment is 7,755). Dr. Pearson was appointed executive vice-president in 1947.

President Pearson's future plans for the university call for continued expansion in faculty, student body, and building program—a Medical school, where the study of tropical diseases will be developed, a School of Music to replace the present barracks quarters, a Law School, a School of Tropical Agriculture, and a Beaux Arts Pavillion.

Through the years, Dr. Pearson has found time for both civic interests and home interests. He married Hazel Manning Heinrich, a student in his first zoology class, making a quick trip from Chicago in February, 1931, for the wedding. Their two boys are Jay Jr., age ten, and Michael six. He has served on the board of directors of the Dade County Community Chest, as a lay member of the Miami Heart Association, president and treasurer of the Florida Academy of Science, president of the Florida Association of Colleges, and Universities, and has been a member of the Higher Commission on Colleges and Universities of the Southern Association of Colleges and Secondary Schools for six years.

His organization and club memberships include Sigma Xi, Sigma Chi, Omicron Delta Kappa, a Fellow in A.A.A.S., the Committee of One Hundred, a Miami organization, Cosmos Club, Century Club, Flamingo Dinner Club, The Miami Club, and the Coral Gables Country Club. The Dominican Republic decorated him *Caballero de Orden del Merito Juan Pablo Duarte.* Pearson is a Protestant and a Democrat, and has served his State on the Basic Science Board.

References

Miami Daily N My 7, '53; Ag 28 '53
Miami Herald Ja 18 '53; My 3 '53; My 5 '53; My 8 '53
Miami Hurricane Ja 16 '53
Nat Geog Mag 98:561 N '50
Newsweek 38:94 N 19 '51
Sat Eve Post 222:26 N 19 '49
Time 61:50 My 18 '53 por

PELLA, GIUSEPPE (pělla jo͞o-zĕp′på) April 18, 1902- Premier of Italy; economist *Address:* b. Palazzo Viminale, Rome, Italy; h. Via Fratelli, Ruspoli 10/6, Rome.

As a result of the downfall of Premier Alcide de Gasperi's Government in July 1953, the Republic of Italy was without responsible leadership for nineteen days. To end this crisis, Giuseppe Pella, former Budget, Treasury and Finance Minister, successfuly undertook in August the formation of a "stop-gap" Government designed primarily to see his country through the financial impasse threatened by the expiration of the budget at the end of the month.

In a Government which subsequently won votes of confidence in both houses of the Italian Parliament, Signor Pella succeeded de Gasperi as both Premier and Foreign Minister, and retained the portfolio of Minister of the Budget, which he has held since 1948. Pella, who has been characterized as the "architect of the nation's post-war financial recovery," is the proponent of stable currency and eventual balancing of the budget, as well as firm adherence to NATO.

Giuseppe Pella was born April 18, 1902 at Valdengo, near Vercelli in the Italian province of Piedmont, to Luigi and Viglielma (Bona) Pella. "His parents were modest sharecroppers who went to work in a spinning mill to pay his way through college," the New York *Times* correspondent Arnaldo Cortesi has stated. At the University of Turin Pella majored in political economy, making a special study of financial, monetary and domestic industrial problems; his record has been described as "brilliant" and, after taking his doctor's degree (*Laurea*), he was made a professor of banking and industrial science.

"In a comparatively few years," said Cortesi, "he had made a name for himself as a consultant to the wool industry in the Biella region, and by age thirty he already commanded large fees." During 1932 Pella was chosen to represent the Italian textile interests at that

Fotostudio Cantera, Rome

GIUSEPPE PELLA

year's International Wool Conference, and in the same capacity attended all subsequent conferences until 1939.

After the Allied invasion of his native land Pella became known as "a prominent organizer of Catholic Youth, who during the Partisans' fighting in northern Italy raised funds for the Garibaldi brigades" (New York *Times,* June 4, 1947).

Although a figure of local prominence in the Catholic Action movement by the time the war was over, Pella had expressed no ambition to enter the political arena. However, in the summer of 1946, following the June 2 plebiscite which determined that the Italian monarchy should be supplanted by a republic, he ran for the interim parliament as deputy for Biella and became a delegate to the Constituent Assembly as the Christian Democrat (Catholic Party) representative for the Turin-Novara-Vencelli area. ("His original refusal to enter public life was overridden by the urgent appeals of others in his home town," stated Walter Lucas in the *Christian Science Monitor* of August 25, 1951. "If he did not stand, they said, the Communists would sweep . . . the industrial district of Biella").

Elected by an "overwhelming majority," Pella, as secretary of the Parliamentary Commission for Finance and the Treasury, not only helped to draft the new Italian Constitution, but in October 1946 accepted the post of Under-Secretary of Finance in the Christian Democrat-Socialist-Communist coalition Government of the Christian-Democrat leader Alcide de Gasperi, who had become Premier on December 10, 1945.

During Pella's first tenure of governmental office, he served under the famous and deeply respected Liberal economist Luigi Einaudi, who became Minister of Finance and "who was, in a certain sense, his discoverer" (New York *Times,* August 30, 1953).

In June 1947, de Gasperi dissolved his coalition Government, and formed a new Cabinet in which the Communists were not represented, and in which Einaudi, as Minister of the Budget, appointed Pella Minister of Finance. He became identified with the "sound money policy" which Einaudi inaugurated through a flexible devaluation of the lira, cutting the lending power of the banks, raising taxes, and establishing the Fondo Industrie Meccaniche to make loans to small business.

In addition, $150,000,000 was borrowed from the International Monetary Fund and $100,-000,000 from the Import-Export Bank, while it was estimated at the time that Italy would receive $1,000,000,000 in Economic Recovery (Marshall Plan) funds. "Defense against the specter of inflation is today the basic problem," Pella declared in the Chamber of Deputies. "Let us remember that prices go up by the elevator, while salaries walk up by the stairs" (*Christian Science Monitor,* August 25, 1951).

The new Italian Constitution became effective on January 1, 1948; and on the following April 18 the first general election held under its provisions resulted in a Chamber of Deputies consisting of 306 Christian Democrats, 183 members of the Popular Front coalition of Communists and Socialists, 33 right wing Socialists and 52 representatives of minor parties. On May 11 the Deputies and the Senate, meeting in joint assembly, elected Luigi Einaudi to a seven-year term as the first President of the Republic of Italy; the new President promptly reappointed de Gasperi as Premier, and on June 3 Pella took over Einaudi's former portfolio of Minister of the Budget in addition to that of Treasury Minister.

Submitting his first budget to the Parliament towards the end of the month, Pella reported that the national income was already up to 80 per cent of the pre-war level, and painted a "moderately optimistic picture of the future," while stressing that he "pinned much of his hope" on the Economic Recovery Program (New York *Times,* June 19, 1948). On April 8, 1949, in submitting his second budget to the Senate, he was again "optimistic," pointing out that revenues for the current year had exceeded estimates.

Meanwhile, Pella had become the vice-president of the Italian E R P Committee, and in a report to the Senate on June 1 on Italy's progress toward internal and external financial stability under E R P he not only forecast the liquidation of the Fondo Industrie Meccaniche as having outlived its need, but announced that the Government would "seek to consolidate the large floating short-term debt into medium long-term securities." ("This seemingly technical operation," explained Michael Hoffman in the New York *Times,* June 2, 1949, "represents an attainment of fiscal strength unseen in Italy for a generation, according to the U.S. financial experts. . . .Signor Pella is the first Minister of the Treasury since the founding of a united Italy who has been able to point to Government bonds selling above par").

In connection with the concluding, on March 26, 1949, of a treaty providing for a customs union with France, the Italian Budget and Finance Minister came forward with the so-called "Pella Plan" for "progressive reduction of tariffs on a preferential basis" (*Americana Annual*, 1952). One objective was, however, to eliminate "dumping," and at the second post-war tariff conference held at Annecy in the summer of 1949, Italy was "in the position of defending one of the highest schedules of customs duties in Europe".

In September, 1949, Pella visited the United States as head of an Italian mission on world currency; a year later, for discussions prior to the third tariff conference to be held at Torquay in England, he met at Paris with other governors of the International Monetary Fund.

The de Gasperi Government having been accused by the Economic Cooperation (Marshall Plan) Administration of "following a too deflationary policy," Pella made what he described as "a fundamental modification of our previous approach" by advocating low tariff protection for industry. He pointed with a certain pride to the fact that Italian industrial output had reached 120 per cent of that of 1938, but at the same time stressed his country's lack of natural resources and heavy unemployment. Italy, he asserted, was "doing her utmost to use her resources in conformity with the defense program of the North Atlantic coalition and with the European integration aims of the Marshall Plan Council" (New York *Times*).

During the ensuing year the effectiveness of the customs union was much impaired in both France and Italy by opposition from farmers as well as many industrialists, and the "Pella Plan" gradually faded from the picture. Unemployment in Italy stood at about 2,000,000 in a population of 46,600,000 and there was much popular resentment at the cost of the Italian armament under NATO, despite the fact that ECA aid reached a $3,000,000,000 total.

A rift occurred within the Christian-Democratic party itself over what the New York *Herald Tribune* characterized editorially as "Pella's cautious fiscal policies," which were blamed for the disappointing pace of industrial recovery and the slow progress of social reform. The Pella issue was thus the direct cause of de Gasperi's dissolution of his sixth Government in July, 1951. However, the resulting concern of wage earners and small merchants temporarily stilled the anti-Pella faction, and in the seventh de Gasperi Government Pella was again chosen the Minister of the Budget.

On February 1, 1952 he became Treasury Minister as well, on an interim basis. Buying power among the people nevertheless continued to decline, and at the end of October, in anticipation of the coming NATO meeting at Paris, Pella warned that his country could not "assume new financial burdens . . . in the new year (New York *Herald Tribune,* October 29, 1952).

Neither the $200,000,000 a year special rearmament effort nor the $160,000,000 a year emergency social welfare program would be increased, he announced.

Although (as Ernest O. Hauser stated in the *Saturday Evening Post* of August 8, 1953), "the lira was among the most stable currencies in Europe" when the Italian Republic's second general election was held on June 7 and 8, 1953, a combination of factors made the outcome touch-and-go for de Gasperi. Neo-Fascist and Monarchist resurgence split the right-wing support while anti-clericals viewed the Christian Democrats as the tools of Catholic action and the Vatican. The Socialists, led by Pietro Nenni, had been bound in a working agreement with the Communists since 1946 and were said to be Communist-controlled.

The Government's *Atlantic extremism* (Nenni's phrase) was the object of attack. Thus when the votes were counted "the Christian Democrats were down from 12,711,305 in 1948 to 10,834,466, and their three center party allies [the Social Democrats, Liberals and Republicans] among them had lost more than 1,000,000 votes." "On the other side of the ledger," according to Ernest Hauser, "the Communists and Socialists, together, were up from 8,136,637 to 9,561,723—while the Monarchists and Neo-Fascists had cannon-balled from 1,255,960 to 3,434,730." The "intricacies of the proportional system" nevertheless gave the four center parties a majority of sixteen in the Chamber of Deputies, and de Gasperi formed a new Government. It lasted only thirteen days, falling on July 28, 1953 after a vote of no confidence, in which the three center parties sided with the Left.

Italy was without a Government for the ensuing nineteen days. During this interim, President Einaudi invited Attilio Piccioni, the former Deputy Premier and the second-ranking Christian Democrat, to take the helm, but Piccioni's proposed Government was rejected by Parliament when the moderate socialists refused to approve de Gasperi as Foreign Minister. The country was meanwhile operating on a temporary budget which would expire on August 31.

On August 13 Pella undertook, at the request of Einaudi, to form a temporary "business government" composed largely of "technicians" and which, being primarily non-political would have a good chance of pushing through a new budget. On August 15 Pella offered a Cabinet in which he himself took over the portfolio of Foreign Minister as well as the premiership and the budget ministry. Having won the endorsement of Parliament, he was sworn into office on August 17.

Two days later in his first address as Premier, Pella told the Parliament that his "stop gap" Government intended "to remain unswervingly faithful to the North Atlantic Treaty Organization" as well as "firm in the defense of Italian interests in Trieste" (Arnaldo Cortesi in the New York *Times*). The Pella Government won a 140 to 86 vote of confidence in the Senate on August 22, and

PELLA, GIUSEPPE—_Continued_

the backing of the Chamber of Deputies by 315 to 215 three days later.

His budget submitted to the Senate on August 25, and in which about $774,000,000 was earmarked for defense, was the largest in Italian history, amounting in all to around $3,444,600,000. Even so, there was a huge deficit which, Pella warned, would have to disappear entirely within the next few years. "In the long run," he stated, "financial stability cannot hold out against an unbalanced budget."

The new Italian Premier and Foreign Minister was quickly faced with an international problem involving the status of the former Austrian port of Trieste, which in the period between the two world wars had been unofficially seized by Italians led by the poet and playwright Gabriele d'Annunzio.

A clause in the Italian Peace Treaty of 1947 provided for the creation of a "Free Territory" of Trieste under United Nations trusteeship, and the appointment by the Security Council of .a Governor General, pending which the northern half of the territory was to be occupied by American and British, and the southern half by Yugoslav troops. The western and Soviet blocs were unable to agree on a governor, and in 1948, admittedly with a view to encouraging Italian support of the prowestern de Gasperi in the election of that year, Great Britain, France and the United States came out with a "declaration . . . in favor of giving the entire territory to Italy" (New York _Times_).

In the following year, however, when Marshal Tito of Yugoslavia split with the Kremlin, the Big Three (states the same newspaper) soft-pedalled, though never actually withdrew, the 1948 declaration and urged Italy and Yugoslavia to work out the Trieste problem by direct negotiations." These negotiations came to nothing; and on August 28, 1953, less than one month after the Pella Government had been formed, a Yugoslav press agency stated that Marshal Tito's Government was "seriously reconsidering its policy" regarding Trieste. Pella responded by rushing troops to the Yugoslav border and fleet units to the northern Adriatic, and in an official note warned Yugoslavia against "such an ill-considered and irresponsible act" as the annexation of Trieste. Yugoslavia countered by demanding the withdrawal of the Italian border re-enforcements and threatened to send troops into Trieste, if Italy occupied the zone under British and American administration (Zone A) which had been again promised to Italy on October 8.

Pella announced on October 17 that his Government would resign if the foreign ministers of the United States, Great Britain and France, who were then meeting in London, reversed their intention of returning Zone A to Italian Administration. He also stated that Italy would participate in a conference concerning these matters only if she were first put on an equal basis with Yugoslavia, namely, permitted to occupy Zone A, or if Yugoslavia no longer controlled Zone B.

Giuseppe Pella and Ines Cardolle were married in 1935 and are the parents of one daughter, Wanda. In the New York _Herald-Tribune_ (August 23, 1953) the new Premier has been described as "six feet tall . . . heavy" and "professorial in manner, fond of quoting classics." Arnaldo Cortesi in the New York _Times_ has written that "Pella's manner is cordial and friendly," and that he is "quick and often witty in repartee."

References

Christian Sci Mon II p10 Ag 25 '51
N Y Herald Tribune II p1 Ag 23 '53 por
N Y Times p14 Je 4 '47; p5 Ag 14 '53; IV p6 Ag 30 '53
Chi è? (1948)
Codignola, A., comp. L'Italia e gli Italiani di Oggi (1947)
International Year Book and Statesmen's Who Who, 1953

PENNEY, SIR WILLIAM GEORGE
June 24, 1909- Atomic physicist

Address: b. c/o Atomic Research Station, Harwell, England; h. Edmiston Rd., W. Norwood, London, S.E. 27, England

The chief superintendent of armament research in the British Ministry of Supply, which has the responsibility for atomic energy development, is Sir William George Penney, England's leading authority on atomic weapons and one of the world's foremost authorities on nuclear fission. In 1952 he directed the technical aspects of the atom-weapon test in Australia, which gave Britain her first atomic bomb. During the last year of World War II (1944-45), Penney worked with United States scientists at Los Alamos atomic laboratories in New Mexico, where he helped to produce the first atom bombs. He was the only British observer of the atomic bombing of Nagasaki, Japan, in 1945 and at Bikini the following year was reported to have contributed to some of the most practical results of the American atomic experiment.

William George Penney was born June 24, 1909, in Gibraltar, the son of W. A. Penney, a native of Sheerness, Kent, who was stationed as a sergeant in the Royal Ordnance Corps at Britain's Mediterranean fortress. From 1922 to 1927 Penney attended the Junior Technical School in Sheerness, England. Until he was fifteen years old, his principal interest was in football, which he played on a team that produced four professional players and one international contestant. At eighteen, he won a scholarship to the Imperial College of Science and Technology of the University of London, where in 1929, he took his B.S. degree, qualifying in two years for a degree that usually requires four years. He was also awarded the Governor's Prize in Mathematics and First Class Honors in Mathematics and was made an associate of the Royal College of Science, a division of the Imperial College of Science and Technology.

For the next three years (1929-31) Penney engaged in research at the Royal College of Science and at the University of Groningen, the Netherlands. After submitting a thesis on the structure of metals, he received the Ph.D. degree in 1931 from the Imperial College of Science and Technology and a Commonwealth Fund Fellowship for postgraduate study at the University of Wisconsin in the United States, where he specialized in paramagnetism, the study of the magnetic properties of crystals. In 1932 he prepared an article titled "Effect of Nuclear Spin on the Radiation Excited by Electron Impact," which appeared in the March issue of the *National Academy of Science Proceedings*. His extrascholastic interests in the United States included playing soccer on a local non-university team.

With the M.A. degree in physics from the University of Wisconsin, Penney returned to England in 1933. Awarded a fellowship as Senior Student of the Royal Commission for Exhibition of 1851 (an annual award given to five selected students of proven ability for not less than two years of advanced scientific study) at Trinity College, Cambridge University, he continued his research into the structure of molecules. In 1934 he was joint author with John Hasbrouck Van Vleck of a paper presented at the Ann Arbor (Michigan) meeting of the American Physical Society and entitled "Magnetic Dipole and Atmospheric Absorption Bands of Oxygen." Cambridge University awarded Penney the Ph.D. degree in 1935 for a paper, "The Theory of Molecular Structure." The same year, he received a Doctor of Science degree from the University of London. In the July 1935 issue of the London publication, *Nature*, appeared a paper by Penney and G. B. B. M. Sutherland on the shape of the NO_2 molecule, which stressed that "an extensive and careful re-examination of the contours of dent of the Italian E.R.P. Committee, and the infra-red bands" would be necessary before they could be used as a reliable guide to the shape of the molecule.

The recipient in 1936 of a Stokes Student fellowship at Pembroke College, Oxford University, Penney was also appointed that year an assistant professor of mathematics in the Imperial College of Science and Technology, a position he retained until 1945. In 1940 the scientist was loaned by the college to the British Ministry of Home Security (until 1943) and later to the Admiralty (for the year 1943-44). Penney was asked to undertake research which would reveal what damage might be expected from German bombs dropped on London. As quoted by Peter Barttelot in the New York *Times* (September 21, 1952), the scientist found that the most interesting fact he discovered in this research was that "the human body resists the shock wave of explosions far better than bricks and mortar. The body flattens and bounces back into shape again, but rigid surfaces, with no give, just disintegrate."

Late in World War II (1944-45) Penney was the principal scientific officer leading a team of British scientists sent to the United States to help develop the world's first atomic

British Inf. Services

SIR WILLIAM GEORGE PENNEY

bomb in the Department of Scientific and Industrial Research at Los Alamos, New Mexico. In accordance with a decision made by Winston Churchill and Franklin D. Roosevelt in 1943, all Anglo-American atom bomb research and the extensive equipment necessary was centered in the United States. As reported by *United States News* (November 7, 1952), Penney "produced many ingenious ideas as the experimentation progressed." With his staff, he laid the foundation for later setting up Britain's own atomic research projects. He was present when the first atomic bomb was exploded in the New Mexican desert in July 1945, and he flew with the American project team to the Mariana Islands to help assemble the atom bomb dropped on Hiroshima, Japan. Flying in an accompanying plane, he was "the only British atomic scientist" permitted to observe the United States' atomic bombing of Nagasaki, also in 1945 (*Christian Science Monitor*, October 24, 1952).

After World War II Dr. Penney was invited to participate in postwar development of the atom bomb in the United States. His work in this project was cut short by his appointment as scientific adviser to Sir Alexander Cadogan, Britain's delegate to the United Nations Atomic Energy Commission, which was endeavoring to effect international control of atomic weapons. In the summer of 1946 Penney attended the two American atomic bomb tests at Bikini, one of the main objects of which "was to learn more about the behavior of the shock wave that turned concrete into dust in Hiroshima" (New York *Times*, September 21, 1952). It was at this time that the British scientist built his reputation for "sagacity on a shoestring," by measuring the shock wave in its effect on 1,000 gasoline tins filled with sea

PENNEY, SIR WILLIAM GEORGE—
Continued

water and sealed with cardboard flaps (*Time*, October 13, 1952). "We were able to tabulate the displacement of water in each case accurately," he has stated, "and this gave me enough data to draw 500 points on a fairly interesting curve. Then I did a bit of a sum and was able to tell everybody something about the blast" (New York *Times*, September 21, 1952). Meanwhile, many of the American recording instruments had either failed to register the shock wave or had been destroyed, as Penney had previously predicted.

Returning to the United States in August 1946 from the Bikini atom bomb tests, Penney represented the United Kingdom in the United Nations Atomic Energy Commission. He said that he believed neither the Russian nor the American plan for international control of atomic energy would be acceptable, but he added, "I think it's clear that we simply have to find the solution or perish" (New York *Times*, August 22, 1946). He warned that while the Bikini bombs did not destroy the whole fleet, the power of the atom bomb against ships or against cities should not be underestimated: "If ever used again, atomic bombs will be used against cities." In 1946 Penney was appointed chief superintendent of armament research in the British Ministry of Supply, in charge of atomic weapons development. The world's first electron synchrotron was being built at Harwell, England. As head of the British atomic project, Penney favored atomic partnership between the United States and Britain. Under the McMahon Act, sponsored by Brien McMahon of the United States Senate Special Atomic Committee and enacted by Congress in 1946, Anglo-American atomic energy cooperation was ended, on the grounds of security. Often approached with offers from the United States to work in atomic research in that country, Penney expressed a preference for his annual salary of $8,400, as chief of Britain's armaments research, to a reported $42,000 a year in America (New York *Times*, May 15, 1952).

On October 3, 1952, Dr. Penney directed from the British aircraft carrier *Campania* the test that resulted in the explosion, about fifty miles off the northwest coast of Australia, in the Monte Bello Islands, of Britain's first atomic weapon, the development of which is estimated to have cost over $280 million. The test was an interservice operation, in which Britain's Royal Navy, Army, and Air Force cooperated with the Royal Australian Navy and Air Force (no American observers were permitted). Penney reported in a radio broadcast by the British Broadcasting Corporation on November 7, 1952, that "the experiment went according to plan, and the scientific records were complete" (New York *Times*, November 8, 1952). The first atomic bombing carried out by Britain was the thirty-sixth known to have taken place in the world. According to the London *Evening News* (October 2, 1952), the British weapon was "far ahead of anything America has produced," and Penney had greatly reduced the size of the

atomic weapon by decreasing the critical mass of uranium needed for the explosion. The *Manchester Guardian* (October 4, 1952) reinforced the belief that Britain may have produced a new type of atomic weapon with the statement that the color of the flash at the time of the explosion "seemed much deeper than indicated by descriptions of American atomic blasts," and for half an hour after the explosion "an area of a mile in diameter was still hot enough to send up a dense cloud of smoke." The test was conducted in secrecy in an area of about 23,500 square miles, patrolled by naval squadrons, after Britain had rejected an invitation from the United States to use American testing grounds for the experiment.

The ship from which the atomic weapon was fired, Penney stated, was completely vaporized and was fitted out as a transmitting station to send out "a vast number of measurements" before its equipment was destroyed. Some 300 different electronic devices were used to record the explosion, including a camera capable of taking 100,000 pictures a second. "A cloud of mud, water, vapor, and smoke more than two miles high was shot by the atomic bomb into the sky—twice as high as that sent up by the American atomic explosion at Bikini," Penney was quoted as saying by the *Christian Science Monitor* (November 8, 1952). Penney was the scientist in charge of the second British atom bomb test which took place in Australia on October 15, 1953. The weapon was described as much "less powerful" and "smaller" than the first British atomic weapon which was exploded last year in Australia (New York *Times*, October 15, 1953).

In 1946 the Most Excellent Order of the British Empire, with the rank of officer, was conferred by King George VI upon William George Penney and five other atomic energy research scientists for their war services. Penney was made a Fellow of the Royal Society in 1946. For his contribution to the atom bomb experiments at Bikini in 1946, he was awarded the United States Medal of Freedom (Silver Palm). On October 25, 1952, it was announced by Winston Churchill that Queen Elizabeth II had made the scientist a Knight Commander of the British Empire.

Among articles Penney has written for scientific journals are "Absorption Spectra Evidence of the Decomposition of the Ground Term of $Nd+++$ Ion Due to Crystalline Fields" (with G. J. Kynch, *Nature*, July 17, 1937) and "Energy of Dissociation of Carbon Monoxide" (with A. G. Gaydon, *Nature*, October 3, 1942). He is the author of a book entitled *The Quantum Theory of Valency* (1935), a collection of monographs on chemical subjects. Penney's expertness in atomic arithmetic was called by Peter Barttelot in the New York *Times* (September 21, 1952) "the trump card" of British Prime Minister Churchill who hopes that the United States will agree to a full exchange of atomic energy information with Great Britain. "Penney," Barttelot remarked, "is Britain's most valuable human asset in the international race for atomic supremacy."

In 1935 William George Penney married Adele Minnie Elms, now deceased; in 1945 he married Eleanor Joan Quennell. He has two sons. Britain's atomic scientist has been described as "a placid, soft-voiced man, weighing 200 pounds, and given to rumpled clothing and comfortable conversation" (*United States News*). Sir William studies insects as a hobby and finds recreation in making wool rugs by hand and playing golf.

References

    N Y Times Mag p52 S 21 '52
    Time 60:33 O 13 '52
    U S News 33:52 N 7 '52
    Commonwealth Fund Directory of British Fellows (1925-50)
    Who's Who, 1952

PEREIRA, I(RENE) RICE August 5, 1907- Painter
Address: 121 West 15th Street, New York 11

Experimenting with texture and rarely used materials in painting, as well as with light and luminosity, I. Rice Pereira has achieved a unique position in abstract art, creating a completely new art form that is hers alone. Although this artist never painted until she was seventeen, her first one-man show was given in New York in 1933 when she was twenty-six. In the last twenty years, culminating with the retrospective show of sixty of her paintings at the Whitney Museum in New York, with those of Loren MacIver, opening January, 1953, she has had twenty-two one-man shows in New York, Chicago, San Francisco, Washington, D.C., Baltimore, Memphis, and other cities.

She was born in Chelsea, Massachusetts, a suburb of Boston on August 5, 1907, the daughter of Emanuel and Hilda Vanderbilt Rice. Her mother was of American and German ancestry and her father was Polish, having come to the United States as a child. When she was about five the family moved to Great Barrington, Massachusetts where Irene recalls happy memories of a big house on a hill surrounded by fields. A few years later her father moved the family to Brooklyn, New York, where she attended the public schools.

When she was fifteen her father died and the family was left in dire financial straits. Immediately she changed from her high school academic course to the commercial and finished three years' work in six months. This led to a job as stenographer and to her becoming the wage-earner for her family. Later her younger sister helped, but it was many years before Irene was free of financial responsibility. During these years she dreamed of writing and spent many hours in the Brooklyn public libraries, later taking literature courses at New York University and a course in fashion designing at the Traphagen School.

Acting upon the advice of one of her teachers to try painting or stage design, she entered her first art class at the Washington Irving High School, "and a new world opened its portals." She fell in love with art and found an emotional outlet that she never knew existed for her. In October, 1927 she enrolled in night

I. RICE PEREIRA

classes at the Art Students League, where her teachers were Richard Lahey and Jan Matulka. In 1929 she married Humberto Pereira, a commercial painter, but marriage did not bring release from financial pressure. She continued to work during the day and paint at night.

After a trip to Europe she returned to New York in 1932 and was now able to paint full time. Her paintings at this time were bold and not the least feminine. In her first-man show held the next year at the American Contemporary Art Gallery (New York), she exhibited *Anchor,* a painting, of which Pereira said, "It seemed very necessary to me. I needed to establish my own balance and feel anchored. With each stroke I felt more and more secure." From this motif she went on to paint boats, wharfs and objects connected with the sea but in a few years she made another change, painting various concepts of the machine age.

Her ultimate turn toward abstract painting was partially due to her association with the Design Laboratory founded by the WPA Federal Art Project begun in 1935. Later it was taken over by the Federation of Architects, Engineers, Chemists and Technicians. Here Mrs. Pereira taught painting, composition and design synthesis and soon became absorbed in textural studies which were reflected in her work. In 1937 she painted her first pure abstractions of which *White Rectangle No. 1* was a turning point in her career. In this work she realized that her textures were affecting light vibrations and that her colors, without the job of representing objects, could produce pure luminosity. Despite personal problems—she was divorced in 1938—she had found her direction, and from then on painted only the abstract.

Speaking in 1940 at a symposium arranged by United American Artists, she gave three definitions of abstraction. The first was "representational," meaning that it broke down objects in nature; the second was "intuitional," or shapes drawn from the subconscious; and

PEREIRA, I. RICE—*Continued*

the third, her own kind of abstract, was "the pure scientific or geometric system of esthetics which seeks to find plastic equivalents for the revolutionary discoveries in mathematics, physics, biochemistry and radioactivity."

In the Whitney Museum Catalogue of her 1953 show, John I. H. Baur, wrote of her development: "Throughout her mature career Pereira has pursued two major objectives—form and light. At first the formal search seems to have been, by a narrow margin, the more important. It has led her through a number of stylistic changes, which do not follow a consistent line of development but are rather experiments in different directions. From each of these she has learned lessons and gained new qualities which enrich her subsequent work in a kind of cumulative process."

Reviewing the *Fourteen Americans* show at the Museum of Modern Art in 1946, Aline B. Loucheim (art critic, New York *Times*) referred to the painters in this show as the "Favored Few" and spoke of "the precise geometrics of Pereira" with an unfavorable criticism, remarking "Pereria's expert investigations into constructed space and planes and into varied textures and the daring juxtapositions of color are too often 'sound and fury signifying nothing.'"

On the other hand, the *Art Digest* reviewer of the 1953 Whitney show observed that to understand a Pereira painting is to understand the structure of the universe, and "as the universe is sustained by energy so these geometric arrangements of lines and color planes are sustained by light that flows in and out of them. Her paintings might also be called a 'house of light' for this painter is very much an architect and like a modern architect she displays great ingenuity in her use of the new materials." She was given a $500 award from the Pepsi-Cola-sponsored "Portrait of America" exhibit and $100 award from the La Tausca Art Competition of 1947.

On September 9, 1950 she married the poet, George Reavey, and they first lived in Manchester, England, returning to this country in May, 1951. That summer she taught art classes at Ball State Teachers College, Muncie, Indiana and returned to New York where she and her husband now reside.

Many magazine articles and books about art have dealt with the work of Pereira not only because of her well-earned position in the art world but because of her unique and original contribution. In a book by Ray Bethers, *Pictures, Painters and You,* the artist explains *White Lines,* painted in 1942, "*In White Lines* I endeavored to explore the formal and design possibilities of painting with special emphasis on constructional ways of expressing space on a two dimensional surface, and experimenting with new materials and mediums. I have also tried to develop a working process using pigment itself to produce textural effects, vibrancy, luminosity, transparency, density of painting, the effect of light on incised and relief surfaces. *White Lines* employs actual textures as well as implied visual external effects. The

composition is held together with a network of white lines in semi-relief."

In reviewing the joint show of MacIver and Pereira at the Whitney, *Time* commented: "Both are considered abstractionists but the term covers a lot of ground and their paintings are as different as cumulus and calculus."

Irene Pereira has dark brown hair, is gray-eyed, five feet, two inches tall and looks like one of America's best dressed women. She has a great love for poetry and philosophy and often gives lectures on abstract art. From her early days as a creative artist she has been influenced by C. Howard Hinton's *The Fourth Dimension* which gave her new concepts of matter, energy, and space.

An innovator and a pioneer, Pereira sums up her painting experience: "I employ the abstract idiom in painting rather than the more traditional forms of expression because it offers me a wider range of experimentation. The paintings on glass are executed in a number of planes in spatial opposition. In these I have tried to produce an integrated picture with actual light as part of the painting. I have tried to achieve results by developing a working process with the medium itself rather than by creating an illusionistic interpretation."

References

Art Digest 27:7+ Ja 15 '53
Art News 51:34-7+ S '52
Life 34:72+ Ja 26 '53
New Yorker 28:53+ Ja 17 '53
Sat R 36:50-51 F 7 '53
Time 56:64-69 Ja 26 '53

Who's Who in American Art (1953)
Who's Who in New York (1952)

PERSONS, WILTON B(URTON) Jan. 19, 1896- Former United States Army officer; Deputy Assistant to President of the United States

Address: White House Office, Washington, D.C.

Major General Wilton B. Persons (retired) was appointed on January 20, 1953, special assistant to President Dwight D. Eisenhower, to be in charge of liaison with Congress. An expert on military legislation for over a decade, General Persons often represented the Army and the Defense Department at Congressional committees. When General Eisenhower was supreme commander of NATO forces in Europe in 1951-52, General Persons was a member of his personal staff at the Supreme Headquarters, Allied Powers, Europe in Paris.

He also served as assistant to Arthur E. Summerfield, chairman of the Republican National Committee during Eisenhower's political campaign. From 1948-49, he was director of legislative liaison in the Office of Secretary of Defense, and for ten years (1939-49) served as United States Army legislative representative in Congress.

On September 5, 1953 it was announced that President Eisenhower had created the new office of Deputy Assistant to the President for Major General Wilton B. Persons, U.S.A., retired. General Persons thus became the right-hand man to Sherman Adams, who as the Assistant to the President, functions in the role of Chief of Staff.

Wilton Burton Persons was born in Montgomery, Alabama, on January 19, 1896, the son of Frank Stanford and Kate (Abrams) Persons. He was educated in his native State, and graduated from the Alabama Polytechnic Institute with a B.S. degree in electrical engineering in 1916. He was assigned to the Seventh Provisional Training Regiment at Fort McPherson, Georgia, and on August 5, 1917, was commissioned a second lieutenant in the Coast Artillery Reserve and given active duty.

He received his commission as a second lieutenant in the Coast Artillery Corps of the Regular Army, and on the same date (October 26, 1917) was promoted to the rank of first lieutenant. An assignment to the Coast Defense of Baltimore followed, when the young officer was stationed at Fort Howard, Maryland. His promotion to status of temporary captain came on July 27, 1918.

Persons went to France with the 58th Coast Artillery in 1918 and served in the Second Army, which became part of the Meuse-Argonne drive in October of that year. Returning to the United States in June 1919, he joined the 31st Artillery Brigade at Fort Winfield Scott, California. He was transferred to the Eighth Signal Battalion at Camp Dodge, Iowa, and in June 1920 to the Fourth Signal Company at Camp Lewis, Washington, and in July was promoted to the permanent rank of captain.

Assigned to the maintenance of the Alaskan Military Submarine Cable in 1921, Persons was stationed at Seattle, Washington, and in 1923 was transferred to the Signal Corps which operated a communication network that extended to Honolulu, San Juan, Panama, Alaska and Manila. Persons was sent to Springfield, Ohio, in June 1924 to supervise the development and manufacture of new communication apparatus for the Alaskan Submarine Cable. After completing this work, Persons became a professor of Military Science and Tactics at the University of Minnesota, where he remained until 1929.

In order to prepare himself for administrative work, Persons entered the Graduate School of Business Administration at Harvard University in September 1929 and was awarded a Master of Business Administration degree, *magna cum laude*, in 1931. He was then assigned to the Office of the Chief Signal Officer in Washington, D.C., which advises the Secretary of the Army and Chief of Staff on all matters concerning Signal Corps communications and operations, and is in charge of the Corps' agencies, installations and activities. While Persons was stationed in Washington, D.C., as a junior officer he first met Dwight D. Eisenhower, at that time a junior officer in the Army. The two men became friends.

In August 1933 Persons was transferred to the Office of Assistant Secretary of War, where he served as liaison officer with the military affairs committee of the United States House of Representatives until 1937. He was given the permanent rank of major on August 1,

U. S. Army
MAJ. GEN. WILTON B. PERSONS

1935. Two years later he entered the Command and General Staff School at Fort Leavenworth, Kansas, from which he was graduated in June 1938.

He was sent to the Air Corps Tactical School at Maxfield, Alabama, where he was graduated in June 1939. The Army assigned him as signal officer of the First Division at Fort Hamilton, New York, then transferred him in July 1939 to the Office of the Chief of Staff. Here Persons directed liaison between the War Department General Staff and United States Congress. He received the permanent rank of lieutenant colonel on August 18, 1940.

Persons became chief of the liaison branch of the Office of the Deputy Chief of Staff of the Army in December 1941, receiving a promotion to the temporary rank of colonel. In March 1942 the three divisions—including the liaison branch, the legislative branch, and the budget and legislative planning branch—were combined into the legislative and liaison division of the Office of the Chief of Staff, and Persons was made head of this new organization. He received the temporary rank of brigadier general on June 24, 1942.

When General Dwight D. Eisenhower, as European commander, asked for the services of Persons, the Chief of Staff of the Army, General George C. Marshall, requested that Brigadier General Persons remain at the Pentagon for important work on Congressional liaison. In November 1944 Persons was promoted to the temporary rank of major general. He received the rank of permanent brigadier general on August 1, 1947.

During 1947-48 the Army's legislative program considered by the 80th United States Congress was extensive, and Person's responsibilities as chief of the legislative and liaison division were increased. The Army, like other military services, was reorganizing to meet a combination of peacetime and "cold war" needs.

(Continued next page)

PERSONS, WILTON—*Continued*

Important legislative measures included unification of the armed forces, inactive-duty training pay for reserves, and a uniform code of military justice. On January 24, 1948, Persons was advanced to the grade of permanent major general, with date of rank retroactive from August 18, 1944.

The Army's legislative program was coordinated with those of the Navy and Air Forces under the Office of the Secretary of Defense in the fall of 1948. General Persons was appointed director of the new Office of Legislative Liaison in August 1948. His office formulated the legislative program for the entire Department of Defense: important measures presented to the 81st United States Congress included the Mutual Defense Assistance Program, providing military equipment to members of NATO and other countries (enacted into law October 6, 1949), the Unification Act to effect the unification of military services (enacted into law August 10, 1949), and legislation to promote housing facilities near military installations (enacted into law August 8, 1949).

When the announcement of General Persons' retirement was made in April 1949 "for reasons of health," Louis Johnson, Secretary of Defense, stated that "he had persuaded General Persons to remain as director of legislative liaison through the period of pressing legislation affecting the National Military Establishment." Upon completing this work, General Persons retired from the Army on June 30, 1949. He later became superintendent of Staunton Military Academy in Virginia, where he remained for a year and half.

He was recalled to active duty with the Army in January 1951 and assigned to the Supreme Headquarters, Allied Powers, Europe. On June 2, 1951, he left for France to become a special adviser to General Eisenhower. His task was to direct four sections of SHAPE concerned with specialized problems, including troop indoctrination, psychological warfare, legislative liaison, and public relations, in connection with the twelve-nation army organization (NATO). A function of the legislative liaison section was to provide the French National Assembly, the British Parliament, and the governments of the other treaty nations with periodic reports as they might request them. In the area of troop indoctrination, efforts were directed "along the lines of the troop information and education division in the American armed forces" (New York *Times,* February 20, 1951).

Returning to the United States in August 1951, Persons resumed his retired status with the Army. He joined the Republican National Committee as assistant to chairman Arthur E. Summerfield, and travelled with the presidential candidate Dwight D. Eisenhower during his campaign. Part of his task was to greet, entertain, and brief the Representatives and Senators and other political leaders wanting to confer with the prospective President. He was considered "devotedly loyal" to Eisenhower, whom he referred to as "boss" not "Ike" (*U.S. News & World Report,* June 6, 1952). On July 18,

1952, this publication stated that, if elected, "Eisenhower will need an aide thoroughly familiar with the ways of Congress" and predicted that "Major General Wilton B. Persons is most likely to occupy that role."

On November 27, 1952, President-elect Dwight D. Eisenhower appointed Persons to the White House staff as his special assistant and legislative liaison representative to Congress. Three days after the President's inauguration on January 20, 1953, General Persons called on Senator Leverett Saltonstall of the Armed Services Committee regarding the confirmation of Charles E. Wilson, the President's appointee to the post of Secretary of Defense. As President Eisenhower's representative to Congress, he is required to "sit in" on the weekly conferences which the President holds with Congressional leaders, "a group larger than the 'Big Four' that regularly met with former President Truman" (New York *Times,* January 24, 1953).

General Persons was awarded the Distinguished Service Medal and Legion of Merit. His foreign decorations include the Ecuadorian Order of Abdon Calderon, and the Brazilian Medal of War and Grand Officer of the Cross of the Sun. He is a member of Phi Delta Theta. Said to be on a first-name basis with more than half the members of the United States Congress, Persons is described by *U.S. News & World Report* (June 6, 1952) as "a slender, well-groomed, and jovial Alabamian."

References

Fortune 48:76 Jl '53 por
Newsweek 40:33 O 6 '52
U S News 32:47-8 Je 6 '52; 33:19 Jl 18 '52; 33:44 D 5 '52; 34:24 Ja 23 '53 por
Washington (D.C.) Post p20 Ja 20 '53
Who's Who in America (1952-53)
Who's Who in the Army (1948)
Who's Who in the South and Southwest (1952)

PETERSON, VIRGILIA May 16, 1904-
Lecturer; writer; television moderator

Address: c/o WABD Dumont Television Station, 515 Madison Ave., New York 22; h. 163 E. 81st St., New York 28

The moderator of the nationwide television program, *The Author Meets the Critics,* is Virgilia Peterson who brings to the show her experiences as a lecturer, book reviewer and critic. An author of several books, Miss Peterson wrote the best seller, *Polish Profile* in which she described her life in Poland during the troubled years between the two World Wars.

The younger of two daughters of the late Dr. Frederick Peterson, eminent psychiatrist and one-time president of the American Neurological Association, Virgilia Peterson was born in New York City on May 16, 1904. Her father came to the United States from Sweden as a child; her mother, the former Antoinette Rotan, was born in Waco, Texas. She was named Virgilia for the gentle wife of Coriolanus in Shakespeare's play of that name.

. Virgilia's school years were spent at private academies (Charlton, Brearley, MacIver's) in the New York area and at the Westover School in Middlebury, Connecticut, where her extracurricular activities included the glee club, basketball and writing verse for the school magazine. After her graduation in 1921 she spent two years at Vassar College, at Poughkeepsie, New York majoring in modern languages.

In her twentieth year she went to France and attended the University of Grenoble in Provence. There she became engaged to Prince Paul Sapieha of Poland, but their respective families objected to their marrying. Before her next meeting with the Prince nine years later, she had recovered from a polio attack, had become Mrs. Malcolm Ross, and had published a number of short stories (in such magazines as *Scribner's* and *Harper's*), articles, poems and book reviews in the New York *Herald Tribune*.

In 1932 she decided to revisit Vienna to write a novel. There Prince Paul resumed his courtship. Virgilia Ross obtained a divorce, and in 1933, in London, became Princess Sapieha.

Her life on the estate near Lwow (Lemberg) and in Warsaw, during the years when Poland wavered between infatuation for Nazism and fear of it, was a round of lavish entertainments, boar hunts concerts at Salzburg, trips to Paris, Vienna Berlin, London, and America, and all the obligations of semi-feudal aristocracy and modern business connected with her husband's interests; for he was not only manager of his own huge estates, but also at various times partner in chemical and mining enterprises, shareholder in a Warsaw newspaper and secretary of the Conservative Party. His uncle was the Archbishop (later Cardinal) Sapieha who officiated at Dictator Pilsudski's funeral service and two years later aroused Poland by ordering the decaying remains removed from the cathedral crypt. The Sapiehas met important, indeed, often notorious people at parties and dances. At one luncheon party, for example, the Princess found herself talking with Frau General Goering about her pet lions.

In 1934 the couple's daughter Krysia (Christine) was born in a Vienna hospital, and three years later their son Nicholas was born in Warsaw. The illness of their daughter was responsible for the family's trip to Vienna for a medical consultation just as the Nazis took over the city. And, as World War II inundated Poland in September, 1939, the Princess and her children fled from Silesia through Rumania and managed to reach America.

Princess Sapieha's account of her adventures, *Polish Profile* (1940), became a bestseller. The reviewer in the New York *Times* called it "a strangely naive book," adding that "its simplicity . . appears to spring from a genuine directness of mind on the part of the author." Mildred Adams in *The Nation* observed: "Gilly Peterson has learned many things besides the ways of Poland in these last six years."

The successful book was followed by a series of articles in 1940 and 1941 on Poland, of

VIRGILIA PETERSON

which "Word From Poland", first appearing in the *New Yorker* (July 27, 1940) and reprinted (September, 1940) in *Reader's Digest* is representative. These efforts to help support her stranded family were accompanied by numerous war activities, including speaking tours on behalf of the Treasury's bond-selling campaigns and, in 1942-43, leaflet writing for the Office of War Information.

In 1942 Lippincott published Princess Sapieha's first novel, *Beyond This Shore*. Its characters were a Polish politician and his American wife, its locale was Poland and Austria in the prewar years. E. H. Walton in his New York *Times* review described it as "clearly in part autobiographical," commenting that "because she is so good a writer, one hopes that the Princess, in her next book, will break new ground." She is completing another novel to be called *The Small Voice*.

Following the war the Princess resumed the name Virgilia Peterson, and continued her professional career. An article in *Commonweal* (August 29, 1947), titled "Home on the Range," deplored the stampeding of independent thought by self-appointed intellectual arbiters whom she termed "the gray eminences of American opinion." The name Sapieha reappeared briefly on the title-page of *Eminent Women: Recipients of the National Achievement Award*, a series of biographical sketches in which Virgilia Peterson had collaborated several years previously with Ruth Neely and Mary Love Collins, published by Banta in 1948. She was divorced from Prince Sapieha in 1950.

Miss Peterson worked as the director of publicity for the New York publishing house of Appleton-Century-Crofts, a post she held from April, 1947, until October, 1948. From 1949 to 1951 she was assistant to the director of special events for Radio Free Europe.

She then devoted herself to translating French books into English. Her first translation

PETERSON, VIRGILIA—*Continued*

was of *The Mesh,* a novel by Lucie Marchal, and appeared early in 1950. It was followed by a translation of a newly discovered and previously unpublished record of a cure observed in 1903 by Dr. Alexis Carrel, called *Voyage to Lourdes,* for which Charles Lindbergh wrote the preface.

In 1952 Miss Peterson translated a parable entitled *Golden Goat,* by a Dominican priest, Father Raymond Leopold Bruckberger. During these years she continued to review books and to lecture; she believes she has become a "better speaker than writer, unfortunately, by force of circumstances." She was acclaimed for her speech on the topic, "Does Our Literature Mirror American Life?" which she gave at the Middle Atlantic Regional Library Conference on October 17, 1953.

She appeared on several occasions on *Author Meets the Critics* programs, opposing or defending various books. In September 1952 she relinquished the critic's chair to become moderator of one of television's most difficult panels, including celebrities from left, center and right, with an unpredictable variety of boiling points. The writer in *Cue* observes: "Like any good referee, she serves the double function of keeping the fight interesting and preventing any undue bloodshed. [Television audiences] are amazed that she is able to listen to an obviously unfair statement by a panelist without flying off the handle."

In June 1950 she married C. Gouverneur Paulding, who is an associate editor of *Reporter* magazine. Her children, Christine and Nicholas Sapieha, whose father is now a major in the United States Army serving in Korea, live with the Pauldings. Virgilia Peterson has hazel eyes and brown hair. She is five feet nine and three-quarters inches tall, and weighs 131 pounds. Her favorite relaxations are swimming, sunbathing, and working double acrostics. She is a Democrat. She belongs to the Cosmopolitan Club in New York City.

References

Cue 22:14 Ap 18 '53 pors
TV Guide VI 11:19 Mr 13 '53 por
Sapieha, V. Polish Profile (1940)

PETITPIERRE, MAX Feb. 26, 1899- Federal Councilor of Switzerland; Minister of the Political Department; lawyer

Address: b. c/o Palais Fédéral, Berne, Switzerland; h. 45 Junkerngasse, Berne, Switzerland

A member of the Federal Council, the executive branch of the Swiss Government, Dr. Max Petitpierre has been elected three times to this office. He is the head of the Political Department (Foreign Office), one of the seven executive departments which the members of the Federal Council direct. He served, in 1950, as the President of the Confederation, an office which is rotated among the seven Federal Councilors.

Petitpierre is an expert on private international law and comparative civil law, and has

taught law at the Université de Neuchâtel. He is a strong proponent of Swiss neutrality in world affairs, nevertheless he believes that this neutrality should be one of armed preparation and international cooperation rather than isolationism.

Max Petitpierre was born on February 26, 1899, in Neuchâtel, Switzerland, the son of Edouard and Mathilde (Vuithier) Petitpierre. After studying law at universities in Neuchâtel, Zürich and Munich, he received his Licentiate in law from the Université de Neuchâtel in 1921 and the next year became an attorney-at-law, when he earned his LL.B. degree. He received his doctorate in law from the Université de Neuchâtel, in 1924, upon presentation of his thesis, *The Recognition and Execution of Foreign Civil Judgments in Switzerland* (Librairie Générale de droit et de jurisprudence, Paris, 1925).

At the age of twenty-seven, already recognized as a specialist in his field, Dr. Petitpierre received an appointment as professor of private international law and comparative civil law at the Université de Neuchâtel and held that chair until 1931 and again from 1938 to 1944. In addition to his private practice and his lecturing, he wrote several technical treatises, among which were *Les conventions conclues par la Suisse avec l'Allemagne, l'Autriche et la Tchécoslovaquie concernant la reconnaissance et l'exécution des jugements civils* (Orell-Füssli, 1933); and *Le droit applicable à la succession des étrangers domiciliés en Suisse.*

Dr. Petitpierre was president of the Swiss Chamber of Watch Industries in 1943 and 1944. He was also active in politics as a member of the Radical Liberal party. Elected, in 1937, a member of the Great Council of the Canton of Neuchâtel, he was sent in 1942 as one of its two deputies to the Council of States. He served as the president of the Council of States, one of the two bodies of the Federal Assembly (Swiss national legislature), until December, 1944, when he was elected to the Federal Council.

The Federal Council, the executive arm of the Government, consists of seven members, each elected for a four-year term; one of their number is annually chosen by the Federal Assembly as President of the Confederation. Each member also assumed the function of a Cabinet head. Since his first appointment to the Federal Council, Dr. Petitpierre has been in charge of the Political Department. He was voted Vice-President of the Confederation for 1949, and President, for 1950, on December 15, 1949, by an overwhelming majority of votes. He was supported by all political parties except the Communists.

In accordance with Swiss procedure, Dr. Petitpierre, during his one-year presidential tenure, retained his functions as a Federal Councilor and as head of the Political Department; as President he had only diplomatic and social duties. Petitpierre was re-elected to the Federal Council in 1948 and again in 1952.

As the head of the Political Department, he regarded the re-establishment of partly-ruptured relations with foreign countries, including diplomatic exchange with Russia with whom relations had been nonexistent for many years, as his first duty after the war. He told a congress of the Radical Liberal party that Switzerland would fight only in a war of self-defense (New York *Times,* May 22, 1950).

In a report in that year, he warned that "today we must more than ever be convinced of the fact that the first condition for the independence of a nation in a world dominated by force is the will to take weapons in hand and defend ourselves in case of aggression, whatever the circumstances and the military power of the aggressor may be." He stated his Government's awareness of the political and economic implications of the Korean war, which was persuading Switzerland to modify its traditional neutrality enough "to take part in those activities and organs of the United Nations which have as [their] aim to improve the fate of humanity."

The *Christian Science Monitor* (October 4, 1950) postulated that Swiss neutrality was being altered because of a growing realization that a Europe controlled by Russia would not enable Switzerland to carry on peaceable trade relations as it had with the Nazis in the last war, nor would the Communists even permit the Swiss to remain an independent capitalist State. Beach Conger reported in the New York *Herald Tribune,* October 8, 1950, that President Petitpierre's Government was quietly proceeding with defense preparations by doubling its rearmament budget, stock-piling food and strategic materials in the Alps and in tanks beneath Swiss lakes, and rooting out Communists and fellow travelers from the Government.

Speaking to Parliament on the legality of the United States Treasury practice of arbitrarily blocking Swiss dollar balances in America, Petitpierre said that "the American measures were based on American war legislation. . . .That alone would not justify the blocking of Swiss dollar balances. Swiss banks concerned were reproached with having done business with China or North Korea. The banks assert that they never served Chinese or North Korean interests. The American measures are incompatible with international usage."

"Beyond doubt," he continued, "these American measures affect unfavorably the existing good relations between the two countries. The United States should discontinue this incorrect practice. Americans seem indeed to have recognized the unfairness of their actions as the greater part of the Swiss assets have been unblocked" (New York *Times,* June 23, 1952). A month later Dr. Petitpierre warned United States Minister Richard C. Patterson that the Swiss-American Trade Agreement of 1936 would be "robbed of its substance" if America increased import duties on Swiss watches.

In an important declaration on Swiss foreign policy, Dr. Petitpierre stressed that the Government would never accept any commitment that would cause Switzerland to deviate from strict military and political neutrality. Although the old European balance-of-power conflicts which protected Switzerland do not have, any longer, substantial world force, there are

MAX PETITPIERRE

at present, he continued, growing signs of a desire for a European or world integration, in which the Swiss would be interested.

After citing the many regional and global ideological wars now prevailing, he stated that Switzerland recognized its cultural kinship with the West while it strove to maintain good relations with all countries. The present world struggle was not so much for a political or economic doctrine as it was for the very structure and form of human society. He warned that Switzerland must defend its nonisolationist neutrality and accept the tangible risks involved in such a policy (*Christian Science Monitor,* April 18, 1953).

Last June 16th, India's Prime Minister Nehru met with Dr. Petitpierre in Berne for talks on the role of neutral nations at such a time as a Korean truce would be signed. They were reported to be in close agreement on the subject. Switzerland had been reluctant to serve as a neutral observer unless assured that while an armistice was in operation South Korean troops would be internationally controlled by the United Nations and not directly by their Government.

On receiving this assurance the Swiss Government had therefore agreed to act as a neutral observer in case of a truce. Dr. Petitpierre was defending participation of Switzerland under such an understanding to the Federal Assembly when news of the freeing of prisoners by South Korean troops, under President Rhee's orders, reached him. He told Parliament that this action "considerably modifies the situation and threatens to have consequences both for the conclusion of the armistice and for the activities of the commission of five neutral states."

However, when President Syngman Rhee assured the United States and the world in mid-July that South Korea would not obstruct an armistice in Korea for at least six months,

PETITPIERRE, MAX—*Continued*

Switzerland agreed to serve on the Neutral Nations Supervisory Commission, composed of one representative from Sweden, Switzerland, Poland, and Czechoslovakia, and on the Neutral Nations Repatriation Commission, composed of an Indian delegate (chairman) and one delegate each from Sweden, Switzerland, Poland, and Czechoslovakia.

In a major foreign policy address to the Swiss Parliament in Berne on March 20, 1953, Dr. Petitpierre declared: "We will persevere in the way we have chosen and that our history lays down for us with the conviction that our neutrality is not a sin against Europe and that collaboration, as we [Swiss] conceive and practice it with respect to all countries with which it is possible, is not a sin against neutrality." The Swiss diplomat's speech drew this comment in the New York *Times*: "It will surprise many Europeans and it should please Washington that in this speech of the most neutral of the neutrals, there was absolutely no trace of the neutralism voiced in some Atlantic pact nations." Dr. Petitpierre emphasized that the "drive for expansion in the centers of Communist power is one of the obstacles to the re-establishment of peace."

Dr. Petitpierre married Antoinette de Rougemont, sister of the noted Swiss writer, Denis de Rougemont, on April 5, 1928. They have four children. In appearance he bears a certain resemblance to the Irish actor, Barry Fitzgerald. He has always shown a keen interest in social welfare. He is a member of the French-speaking third of Switzerland's population.

References

International Who's Who, 1952
Who's Who in Switzerland, 1950-51
World Biography (1948)

PHILBRICK, HERBERT A(RTHUR)

May 11, 1915- Advertising salesman; writer
Address: b. c/o New York Herald Tribune, Inc., 230 W. 41st St., New York 36

Herbert A. Philbrick, who spent nine years as a counterspy in the American Communist party, is the author of the 1952 best-selling *I Led Three Lives*, an account of his activities as an underground agent for the Federal Bureau of Investigation. The testimony given by Philbrick in 1949 as to the conspiratorial nature of the party has been spoken of as the turning point in the trial of the eleven Communist party leaders for conspiracy against the United States Government. In early 1952 he became an advertising salesman for the New York *Herald Tribune*; he is also coauthor of the paper's weekly column *The Red Underground*.

A descendant of farmers, seamen, and fishermen and the son of a railroad trainman, Herbert Arthur Philbrick was born May 11, 1915 and was reared in New England. After spending his early years in Rye Beach, New Hampshire, he attended school in Somerville, Massachusetts, where he decided to become a civil engineer. As related in *I Led Three Lives,* he earned money for college by selling papers and magazines; and while taking courses in the Lincoln Technical Institute of Northeastern University in Boston at night, he held a variety of jobs during the day, such as soap salesman, plumber's assistant, interior decorator's helper, construction worker, and chauffeur. He spent much of his spare time in Baptist Church activities: the orchestra, the dramatic group, and the newspaper, *The Tattler,* which the Church sponsored. Through his interest in the newspaper he obtained in 1934 some work with an advertising agency. In 1938, having graduated from the university, he attempted to find a position as an engineer, but since at that time there were no openings in that field, he turned again to advertising and salesmanship, studying these subjects at Harvard University and the Advertising Club of Boston.

As a salesman for the Holmes Direct Mail Service in Cambridge, Philbrick in the spring of 1940 made a call at the office of the Massachusetts Youth Council. Upon expressing an interest in the council's antiwar pamphlets, he was told by a woman in the office that the possibility of setting up a youth council in Cambridge, where he was living, had been considered. The young salesman, who had then helped establish the Cambridge Youth Council, found that while he was the nominal head of the new group, the people to whom he had been referred were doing most of the organizing and making most of the decisions in the council. By comparing the policies of the small controlling body with the Communist literature which some of the members had given him, he began to realize that the council was being used as a Communist front and propaganda machine.

When Philbrick told the Federal Bureau of Investigation about his suspicions, he was advised to remain with the Cambridge group and to turn over any information to the FBI. Philbrick hid his aversion to the Communist party line and convinced his associates that he was coming to agree with their views. With Hitler's attack on Russia in June 1941 and the subsequent change in the Communist party's attitude toward war, the Cambridge Youth Council and other Communist-dominated pacifist organizations collapsed. In March 1942 Philbrick found a position as assistant advertising director with the M. & P. Theaters Company of Boston of the Paramount Theaters Division of New England. His Communist associates, reasoning that he could begin party work completely incognito in a new community, asked him to join the Young Communist League. After an indoctrination period in which he learned in cell discussions the Marxist theory and practice, he was given such assignments as circulating petitions and collecting funds.

In Wakefield, a suburb of Boston, to which he moved, Philbrick was assigned by the league to re-establish the disintegrated cell in that town. He was also ordered to continue his accustomed activity in the Baptist Church, thus establishing a completely respectable reputation, and to utilize the connection to further Communist aims. The salesman was advanced in position in the party and was kept occupied in many front organization activities. Following the dissolution of the Young Communist League in 1943, Philbrick became a member of the American Youth for Democracy as a Baptist youth leader. In February 1944 he joined the Communist party itself, which soon afterward, under the influence of Browderism, became the Communist Political Association. When the Communist party was reinstated, Philbrick got nearer to the core of the group. He was picked to attend classes for future teachers of Communist doctrine in which the necessity for revolution as opposed to peaceful change was inculcated. Shortly thereafter the party tried to use him as a counterspy to ferret out traitors in the ranks; after he had turned in a noncommital report on one member he was relieved of this responsibility.

Other important activities during these years, as Philbrick has told in *I Led Three Lives*, included his attending a meeting in February 1947 in which the "colonizing" (infiltration) of Communists in key industries was discussed and planned for the apparent purpose of subsequent sabotage. Some months later he became a member of the publicity committee of what was to become the Progressive party (he later rewrote a speech for Henry Wallace). He was thereafter informed of another change in assignment: he was to become a member of Pro-4, a cell of the Professional Group of the Communist party. The work of this group included such tasks as directing strategy in a labor drive, raising funds, and securing secret information about industrial firms as well as exerting intellectual influence on behalf of party doctrine.

After the Federal Grand Jury in New York had indicted twelve Communist leaders on July 20, 1948, on the grounds of conspiracy against the United States Government, Philbrick was asked by an FBI contact man to testify in the trial. Conferences with FBI men in New York were held to secure information from him, and on April 5, 1949, he received word that he was to be called as a surprise witness. Taking the stand the next day, he testified that the Communist party had been re-established with the aim of revolution in mind and described the literature and teaching he had received that were devoted to that aim. The defense tried to discredit Philbrick in various ways, such as by implying that he had received large sums of money for his FBI work (the FBI paid only expenses incurred in his work as their agent), but was unsuccessful; the defendants were convicted.

Following his testimony Philbrick returned to Boston, where he worked for a period as the advertising manager for the Maintain Store Engineering Service. At that time he refused a number of newspaper offers for his story, but in 1951 Ogden Reid of the New York *Herald Tribune* persuaded him to write the account of his work and assured him that he could tell the story "straight," without sensationalization of the facts. His story was serialized in seventeen installments in the paper and then expanded into the book *I Led Three Lives*, which was published in February 1952. Reviews characterized *I Led Three Lives* as an important revelation of Communist activity in the United States. "One of the most absorbing and im-

HERBERT A. PHILBRICK

portant books in recent anti-Communist literature," commented Harrison Smith in the Washington *Post*. The *Atlantic* critic wrote, "He tells (his story) without sensationalism and without hate—in an artless manner that carries the stamp of a thoroughly decent personality." In the opinion of the New York *Times* reviewer Harold B. Hinton, "It is a dour tale, and the pedestrian, unrelieved style in which it is written is appropriate. There are no bright moments in a Communist's existence, the reader would judge, so that no brightness can be employed in writing about it." On completion of his book Philbrick accepted a position with the New York *Herald Tribune* as an advertising salesman and the writer of a bi-weekly Sunday column appearing in that paper, *The Red Underground*, which deals with Communist subversive activities in the United States. In 1952 he addressed the Book and Author Luncheon in New York City and the National Exchange Club in Atlantic City, among other groups.

A television dramatization of the book, *I Led Three Lives,* on film, with Richard Carlson portraying Philbrick, is shown on Sunday evenings over the NBC-TV network.

Married on September 3, 1939, Herbert and Eva (Luscombe) Philbrick have five daughters: Connie, Sandra, Dale, Brenda, and Leslie. For relaxation Philbrick enjoys golf and hunting. In the 1952 election he supported Dwight D. Eisenhower. He is described by the New York *Herald Tribune* as a "mild, curly-haired, bright-eyed young fellow . . . as typical a young American as you could find."

References

Christian Sci Mon p4 Mr 24 '52
N Y Herald Tribune Book R p2 F 10 '52
New Yorker 28:27 Ap 5 '52
Philbrick, Herbert A. I Led Three Lives (1952)

PIÑERO JESÚS T(ORIBIO) Apr. 16, 1897—Nov. 19, 1952 Former Governor of Puerto Rico; agriculturist and engineer for ten years before entering politics in 1928; chairman of the municipal assembly of Carolina, P.R., (1928-33) ; was named president of the Puerto Rico Sugar Cane Farmers Association (1933) ; one of the founders in 1938 of the Popular Democratic party, dominant in local politics since 1940; member of the Puerto Rican House of Representatives (1940-44) ; resident commissioner of Puerto Rico with headquarters in Washington, D.C. (1944-46) ; appointed by President Truman in 1946 as the first native Puerto Rican to become the island's Governor (1946-48). See *Current Biography,* 1946.

Obituary

N Y Times p31 N 20 '52

PINZA, EZIO (pēn'tsä ĕts'ē-ō) May 18, 1892- Singer; actor

Address: b. c/o National Concert and Artist Group, 711 Fifth Ave., New York 22, N.Y.; h. 11100 Chalon Rd., Los Angeles 49, Calif.

NOTE: This biography supersedes the article which appeared in *Current Biography* in 1941.

A member of the Metropolitan Opera Company for twenty-two seasons (1926 to 1948) Ezio Pinza won laurels in the title roles of *Don Giovanni* and *Boris Godunov,* and as Mephistopheles in *Faust,* and also sang a repertory of seventy-six standard bass roles in opera. His voice, which possesses unusual range and richness, is usually classified as *basso cantante,* although some baritone roles are well within his range. In 1949 Pinza created the memorable role of Emile de Becque in the

EZIO PINZA

Broadway musical play *South Pacific,* and has since made numerous appearances in films and television, as well as on radio.

On September 12, 1953 he began a new National Broadcasting Company television weekly series, *Bonino,* in which he plays the role of an opera star who is a widower with eight children. Critic Harriet Van Horne commented on his initial appearance: "It's a role right in TV's most eroded rut. Mr. Pinza brings it off by the sheer force of his charm. And what a magnificent charm it is . . . he is pleased with the show and greatly enjoys working with the children" (New York *World-Telegram and Sun,* September 15, 1953).

The boy destined to win fame as Ezio Pinza was born in Rome, Italy on May 18, 1892; his parents wished him to be called Ezio, after a family friend, but a priest objected to the name of a pagan Roman general for a Christian child, and he was baptized Fortunio. The seventh of the nine children of Cesare and Clelia (Bulgarelli) Pinza, he was the first to live beyond infancy; his younger brother and sister have also survived and are, respectively, a salesman and a dressmaker.

His father, a carpenter, moved the family to his native city of Ravenna when his eldest surviving child was only two, and started a lumber business; the enterprise failed, and from the age of twelve onward Ezio (as he was called in the home circle) helped support himself by part-time work in his father's carpentry workshop and, also, as delivery boy for a local baker. He enjoyed attending, with his parents, the week-end performances of opera but showed no desire for a musical career; indeed his early ambition was to be a civil engineer and at one period in his youth he had a year of technical schooling at Ravenna.

At eighteen Pinza decided, against his father's wishes, to become a professional bicycle rider and to compete in both indoor and cross-country races. ("Although I did not know it at the time" Pinza has stated in the *American Magazine* for October, 1949, "I was developing the lung power which now makes people hear my voice even in the top row of the peanut gallery."). He won no prizes, however, and after about two years his father urged him to seek musical instruction. ("Since all you are good for as an athlete is singing in the shower," his son has quoted him as saying, "you might as well learn to sing right.")

Auditioned by Vezzani, the director of the Rossini Conservatory at Bologna, Pinza was rejected as having "no voice," but was accepted by another teacher, Maestro Ruzza. After Ruzza's death, Pinza again presented himself to Vezzani, and this time was accepted for the Bologna Conservatory. "They gave him a scholarship with six dollars a month living expenses on the side," Winthrop Sargent has stated in *Life,* December 1, 1947. "He filled out his income between lessons as a carpenter and handyman."

Having spent two years at Bologna (his only formal musical education) Pinza joined a small opera company in 1914 at Soncini, near Milan; he made his professional debut as a Druid priest in Bellini's *Norma* and sang other roles with the Soncini company prior to Italy's declaration of war on Austria-Hungary in May, 1915. Enlisting in the Italian army as a private, he spent most of World War I with an artillery regiment high in the Alps; he became a captain, but was not demobilized until 1919, being held in service for riot-prevention duty at Naples.

He worked briefly as a railroad brakeman before being engaged later in 1919 by the Teatro Reale dell'Opera at Rome, where his first appearance was as King Mark in *Tristan and Isolde*. His two years with the Rome company were followed by engagements at Turin, Naples and his home city of Ravenna, where he is said to have sung Mephistophiles in *Faust* at twenty consecutive performances (*New Yorker*, May 7, 1949). Three years under Maestro Arturo Toscanini, then director of La Scala at Milan, followed, during which time Pinza was assigned a principal role in Arrigo Boito's spectacular opera *Nerone*, given its world première at La Scala in 1924.

Giulo Gatti-Casazza then general manager of the Metropolitan Opera Company, heard Pinza at La Scala and engaged him for New York; the *basso* made his first appearance at the "Met" on November 1, 1926 as the Pontifex Maximus in Spontini's *La Vestale*, and scored an instantaneous success. ("A majestic figure on the stage, a basso of superb sonority and impressiveness," Olin Downes wrote of Pinza in the New York *Times* while another critic hailed the advent of a "young Chaliapin").

A Metropolitan première in which Pinza appeared in his third season was that of Respighi's *La Campana Sommersa* ("The Sunken Bell") on November 24, 1928 and at which he sang the role of the Pastor. He was the Podesta in Pizzetti's *Fra Gherarde* when that work was heard at the Metropolitan on March 2, 1929, and later in 1929 (November 29) when Moussorgsky's *The Fair at Sorochinsky* was added to the repertory he sang the role of Cherevik "with vocal sonority and unctious comedy" (Olin Downes).

In the same year Pinza sang for the first time at the "Met" the title role of Mozart's *Don Giovanni* (a work in which he has since been seen and heard some 200 times) (Bruno Walter six years later chose Pinza for the 1935 revival of *Don Giovanni* at the Salzburg Festival). Pinza's growing reputation as one of the Metropolitan's most versatile and accomplished actors since the day of Antonio Scotti was sustained by his performances during 1932 as Jacopo Fiesco in Verdi's *Simon Boccanegra* and as "the strutting and roaring" Gaudenzo in Rossini's one-act musical farce *Il Signor Bruschine*.

He also sang many standard roles (including Mephistophiles in *Faust*) and in 1937 (when he was again engaged for the Salzburg Festival, this time in Mozart's *The Marriage of Figaro*) he made an extended concert tour of Europe, the United States and Australia. In 1939 Pinza became the Metropolitan's Boris Godunov, succeeding Chaliapin, who had died the preceding year. Prior to the outbreak of

World War II, Pinza also made appearances in San Francisco, Chicago, London, Paris, Vienna, and certain South American cities.

The Metropolitan's leading *basso* took out first United States citizenship papers in 1938.

He was voted one of the ten most "glamorous men" in the *Harper's Bazaar* poll of 1944. He officially celebrated on March 20 1946 the twentieth anniversary of his engagement by the "Met" by appearing as Don Giovanni. (Olin Downes in his review of this gala performance, noted that Pinza both "sings magnificently" and "acts not only with gesture and facial expression, but with his voice"). Pinza continued with the "Met" through the 1947-1948 season.

Among the roles in his repertory other than those previously mentioned are Ramfis in *Aida*, Raimundo in *Lucia di Lammer-Moor*, Doctor Dulcamara in *L'Elisir d'Amore*, Furst in *William Tell*, Alviso in *La Gioconda*, the music teacher, Don Basilio, in *Il Barbiere di Siviglia*, the Marquis in *La Forza del Destino*, the blind Archibalde in *L'Amore del Tre Re*, the marriage broker in *The Bartered Bride*, Golaud in *Pélléas et Méllsande*, Colline in *La Bohème*, the father in *Louise*, King Dodon in *Coq d'Or*, the Indian priest Nilakantha in *Lakmé*, and the Landgrave in *Tannhäuser*. Of his many operatic recordings, his renditions of "To Sol Quest' Anima" (*Aida*) "Deh Vieni Alla Finestra" (*Don Giovanni*) and "Le Veau d'Or" (*Faust*) are among the most popular.

In the course of his operatic career Pinza made a study of the art of make-up while his carefully devised analyses of character rendered "each of his roles an integrated conception" (*Living Musicians*). His histrionic ability led to success in media other than grand opera and concert. In the fall of 1948, accordingly, Pinza left the "Met" to accept a contract with the Broadway producing firm of Rodgers and Hammerstein to play the role of the French planter Emil de Becque, opposite Mary Martin in the musical comedy, *South Pacific*. At the New York première at the Majestic Theatre on April 7, 1949, Pinza's dignity and presence in an extremely difficult role were generally hailed, while (according to one critic) he made "the hit number, 'Some Enchanted Evening,' sound worthy of a Massenet." (His recording of this song has since become the most widely distributed of his discs).

He continued in *South Pacific* until May 31, 1950, when he left for Hollywood to make the films *Mr. Imperium* and *Strictly Dishonorable*. Both of these pictures were disappointing, but for reasons unconnected with Pinza himself.

In a subsequent film *Tonight We Sing*, based on the life of Sol Hurok and released in 1953, Pinza was "shrewdly cast as Chaliapin" and offered some of his "best singing . . . in a long time" (*Musical America*).

Successful in concert as well as opera (his first New York recital took place as far back as January 27, 1936) Pinza is a frequent guest singer at the Lewisohn Stadium

PINZA, EZIO—*Continued*

Philharmonic Concerts and on such radio musical programs as the *Telephone Hour.*

Another phase in his diversified career began on September 8, 1951 when he made his first TV appearance as master of ceremonies for the National Broadcasting Company's *All Star Revue.* (The New York *World-Telegram and Sun* critic Harriet van Horne thought him "even more attractive in television than in the theatre"). A fortnight later he appeared on the *Colgate Comedy Hour,* and then on November 23 introduced his own RCA-Victor-TV program, *The Ezio Pinza Show,* playing alternate Friday evenings.

In March, 1953 the *basso* and his twelve-year-old daughter Clelia launched the Saturday morning NBC radio program *Ezio Pinza's Radio Show,* which, in the words of *Variety* was "conceived as a music appreciation course without getting heavy-handed" (Records appealing to juvenile listeners were interspersed with stories and anecdotes).

He made his first appearance in a play without music late in June, 1953, when he began a tour of the New England summer playhouses in a revival of Ferenc Molnar's comedy *The Play's the Thing,* acting the role created in New York by the late Holbrook Blinn.

Ezio Pinza has married twice. By his first wife, the former Augusta Cassinelli, he has one daughter Claudia, a lyric soprano with whom he co-starred in *Faust* in a San Francisco opera production in 1947.

After his first marriage was terminated by divorce, Ezio Pinza married, on November 28, 1940, the former Doris Leak (one-time member of the Metropolitan Opera *corps de ballet* and the daughter of a Larchmont, New York dentist). He has three children, Clelia, Pietro and Gloria, by this second marriage. Six feet tall and around 200 pounds in weight, Pinza is athletically built; his eyes have been described as "dark and intense." He "dresses smartly, and has a preference for vivid colors." The *basso's* enthusiasms include good food (he is himself an excellent cook of Italian dishes) and all kinds of sports (especially cycling).

References

Am Mag 144:107 N '47 por; 148+ por
Christian Sci Mon Mag p7 Mr 3 '45 por
Collier's, 124:16+ D 31 '49 pors
Life 23:130-2+ D 1 '47 pors; 27:94-6+ D 19 '49 pors; 29:159-60+ S 18 '50 pors
N Y Herald Tribune p1 Je 5 '42 por; IV p1 Je 4 '50 por; p23 Mr 20 '51; IV p1 O 28 '51 por
N Y Times p19 Je 5 '42; II p1 My 1 '49
New Yorker 25:26-7 My 7 '49
Newsweek 18:8 D 9 '40 por; 27:86 Ap 1 '46; 33:85-6 Ap 11 '49 pors
Read Digest 56:23-6 Mr '50 por

Theatre Arts 22:138-44 F '38 pors; 34:42-3 Ja '50 por
Time 41:70+ Je 25 '43 por
Baker, T. ed. Biographical Dictionary of Musicians (1940)
Ewen, D. ed. Men and Women Who Make Music, rev. ed. (1949)
Hughes, R. and Taylor, D. eds. Biographical Dictionary of Musicians (1940)
Thompson, O. ed. International Cyclopedia of Music and Musicians (1949)
Who's Who in America, 1952-53
Wier, A. E. ed. Macmillan Encyclopedia of Music and Musicians (1938)
World Biography (1948)

PITKIN, WALTER B(OUGHTON) Feb. 6, 1878—Jan. 25, 1953 Educator; psychologist; author; lecturer in psychology at Columbia University (1905-09) and professor of journalism (1912-43); on editorial staff of New York *Tribune* (1907-08), *Evening Post* (1909-10), *Parents' Magazine* (1927-30), *Farm Journal* (1935-38); *Encyclopaedia Britannica* (1927-28); story supervisor for Universal Pictures in 1929; wrote more than fifty inspirational and self-help books, including *Life Begins at Forty* (1932). See *Current Biography,* 1941.

Obituary

N Y Times p19 Ja 26 '53

PLACZEK, MRS. A. K. *See* Struther, J.

PLASTIRAS, NICHOLAS 1883—July 26, 1953 Former Premier of Greece; born in Thessaly and entered army in youth; led revolutionary movements against King George II in 1930's and Gen. George Metaxas, who set up a dictatorship in 1941; after World War II formed Cabinet, then resigned; became Premier in March 1950 as leader of Progressives and formed Coalition Government with Liberals; was designated as Premier last time by King Paul in September 1951; was succeeded in November 1952. See *Current Biography,* 1950

Obituary

N Y Times p19 Jl 27 '53

PLESMAN, ALBERT Sept. 7, 1889- Netherlands airlines official

Address: b. c/o K.L.M.—Royal Dutch Airlines, Badhuisweg 260, The Hague, the Netherlands; h. Tapijtweg 5, The Hague, the Netherlands.

President of K.L.M.—Royal Dutch Airlines (Koninklijke Luchtvaart Maatschappij), the world's oldest existing airline, Albert Plesman is credited with having established Holland as one of the four leading nations in civil aviation. K.L.M., with a fleet of seventy-two modern aircraft, maintains regular services to Indonesia,

Australia, Japan, North America, South America, South Africa, and numerous cities in Europe and the Near East, and operates its own network of air routes in the West Indies. During his association with K.L.M., since its founding in 1919, Plesman has extended his interest in air commerce beyond his own country. He was instrumental in forming the International Air Traffic Association, of which he was president in 1949-50, an organization that helps seventy international airlines to maintain global standards of quality and service in air transportation.

Albert Plesman was born in The Hague, the Netherlands, on September 7, 1889, the seventh child of Johan Cornelis Plesman, a baker, and Hendrika Wilhelmina (van Wessel) Plesman. After attending high school in The Hague, the Cadet School at Alkmaar, and the Royal Military Academy at Breda, he was commissioned as second lieutenant in the Netherlands Army in August 1911. He was posted to the 5th Infantry Regiment at Amersfoort and in the spring of 1914 attained a first lieutenancy. Following a six-month period (April 1915 to October 1915) in the cyclist regiment in Gouda, Plesman, who had some years earlier become interested in aviation, was transferred to the Dutch air force as an observer officer. At the end of another six months he returned to the cyclist regiment, this time in Roosendaal, to serve for a year before being sent in April 1917 to Soesterberg for training as a pilot. He received his military flying license in November 1918.

From February 1 to October 1, 1919, after two years as a flying officer, Lieutenant Plesman organized and enlisted financial support for the First International Aviation Exhibition (E.L.T.A.) in Amsterdam; he also acted as chairman of its executive committee. As related by Ernest O. Hauser in an article in the *Saturday Evening Post* (April 15, 1951), Plesman had persuaded an Amsterdam shipping man to help in sponsoring the exhibit: "We've been a seafaring people for centuries," the lieutenant told him. "Now we should go in for airfaring before others beat us to the draw." The air show was so successful that its backers, a group of influential Amsterdam businessmen, decided to follow Plesman's advice and go further into "the air age." They invited the young air officer to become manager of the newly formed K.L.M.—Royal Dutch Airlines (Koninklijke Luchtvaart Maatschappij) at a salary equivalent to three hundred dollars a month. In May 1920 K.L.M.'s first Amsterdam-London flight was made. Plesman soon became the company's managing director and later its president. In 1928 he founded the Royal Netherlands East Indies Airlines (K.N.I.L.M.) and two years later instituted fortnightly flights to Batavia (now Jakarta), a trip of 8,700 miles, then the longest aerial route in the world. He was the managing director of K.N.I.L.M. until its merger with K.L.M. in November 1945.

During the first twenty-one years of K.L.M.'s existence Plesman succeeded in building up a large network of air routes which brought prestige and air power to his country. When the Germans occupied the Netherlands in World

ALBERT PLESMAN

War II, they seized most of K.L.M.'s planes, and eight months later imprisoned Plesman in Scheveningen; he was later released and ordered to live under Nazi surveillance in the woods of East Holland, at Twenthe, where he remained from April 16, 1942 to April 2, 1945. Immediately after the liberation of the Netherlands, he went to London. In 1945 Plesman began the task of rebuilding K.L.M. With the aid of United States surplus planes, K.L.M. reopened its flights to the Indies six months after Holland was freed from German occupation. A year after V-E Day (May 1946) Atlantic flights were in operation and the prewar network of air routes was restored, with the exception of certain services which could not be re-established because of special circumstances, such as airfields not cleared of mines. By 1948, with the help of $26 million of the $400 million allotted by the United States Economic Cooperation Administration for Holland, K.L.M. had developed a world-wide network of air routes far exceeding its prewar size— 120,000 miles of air routes linking ninety-seven cities in sixty-five countries. In reconstructing his airline, Plesman did more than rebuild K.L.M. As Gill Robb Wilson expressed it (New York *Herald Tribune*, October 1, 1948), "he lit a light down the middle of the road for a broken-hearted and despoiled nation." The airport at Schipol is said to have been regarded as a symbol of faith and courage to the peoples of Western Europe.

K.L.M. is in 1953 housed in a $5 million administration building, which has been called the world's finest airline building, and has a staff of over 12,000 employees scattered about its far-flung branches and a fleet of seventy-two modern aircraft. Announcing plans for expansion, Plesman disclosed on March 23, 1952, that K.L.M. would open new services to Naples, Salzburg, Barcelona, Helsinki, and Bogota and would extend its flying distance from

PLESMAN, ALBERT—*Continued*

153,000,000 to 190,000,000 kilometers by summer. He has predicted that K.L.M. might have one or two atomic-powered planes by 1967 (New York *Times,* October 8, 1952).

K.L.M faces growing competition from other national airlines. Since international air transport privileges are based on reciprocity, K.L.M., with the small nation of Holland as its operating base, has little to offer the United States or other large nations in exchange for the privilege, for example, of picking up passengers between New York and the West Indies (*Saturday Evening Post*). To remedy the situation, Dr. Plesman is interested in eliminating national politics from air agreements. On September 13, 1949, as president of the International Air Traffic Association for the year 1949-50, he asked for multilateral traffic pacts to replace bilateral systems and scored excess government controls. In October 1950, in an article in *United Nations World,* he stated that "long-distance international air services can only be operated on a remunerative basis if the aircraft are allowed complete freedom to land and pick up passengers, mail and freight in other countries along the route."

Dr. Plesman is the recipient of several Dutch and foreign decorations. He was made Knight in the Order of Orange Nassau in 1924 on the occasion of the first flight from Amsterdam to Jakarta and was promoted in 1931 to Officer in the Order of Orange Nassau on the opening of the weekly air service between the two cities. He is also a Knight in the Order of Dannebrog (Denmark), Knight in the Order of the Netherlands Lion, Commander in the Order of the White Lion (Czechoslovakia), Grand Officer in the Order of the Royal Phoenix (Greece), Commander in the Order of Nicham-Iftikbar (Tunis), Commander in the Order of the Crown (Belgium), Commander in the Syrian Order of Merit; and Grand Officer of the Cedars (Lebanon), Commander in the Order of Leopold II (Belgium), and Commander in the Order of Vasa (Sweden). Other honors bestowed upon him are the Gold Medal of the Royal Netherlands Aero Club, Taylor Medal of the Royal Aeronautical Society, Gold Medal of the Royal Netherlands East and West Association, and Commemorative Medal of the Netherlands Post Office.

A member of the general committee of the Royal Dutch Society for Aviation, Plesman is also associated with the Royal Institute for Engineers and the Netherlands Society for Trade and Industry in Haarlem, and serves on the general committee of the Dutch Boy Scouts. He led the way to the foundation of the Netherlands Training Institute for functions abroad and is in 1953 a member of its board. On January 8, 1947, he received the honorary degree of Doctor of Technical Science from the Technical University of Delft. Plesman is author of "World Aviation Means World Peace," an article which appeared in *United Nations World,* October 1950. Other of his writings are "Plan for International Cooperation", "Our Historic Duty," and, in 1952, "Het Wereldverkeer in Vogelvlucht" (A Bird's Eye View on World Transport). At a London conference on world government in September 1951, he presented a plan for international cooperation which called for the establishment, by the eighteen countries now cooperating through the Marshall Plan, of a thirty-year institute to further international understanding and teamwork. Among the areas of cooperation he suggested were large-scale migration from overpopulated countries, land reclamation, and the construction of transportation facilities and giant power plants.

Dr. Plesman and Suzanne Jacoba van Eyk were married on December 27, 1917. Two of their sons were killed during World War II; the third, Albert, is manager of the K.L.M. office at Milan, Italy. Their daughter, Pia, is the wife of a K.L.M. official. Heavy-set and erect, blue-eyed, gray-haired Dr. Plesman is a familiar and popular figure on the streets of The Hague. His religious affiliation is Protestant. He maintains his earlier interest in sports and reading among other hobbies

References

Sat Eve Post 222:46-7 Ap 15 '50 pors
UN World 4:80 O '50
International Who's Who, 1952
Who's Who in Commerce and Industry (1951)
Wie is Dat? 1948
World Biography (1948)

POLLARD, WILLIAM G(ROSVENOR), REV. Apr. 6, 1911- Physicist; educator; clergyman

Address: b. c/o Oak Ridge Institute of Nuclear Studies, Inc., P.O. Box 117, Oak Ridge, Tenn.; h. 191 Outer Dr., Oak Ridge, Tenn.

With his re-election in October 1952 to the post of executive director of the Oak Ridge Institute of Nuclear Studies, Dr. William G. Pollard undertook his second five-year term as head of the agency which has made the research facilities of the Atomic Energy Commission available to students and faculty of American universities. Pollard, who was a wartime research scientist in nuclear energy and former professor at the University of Tennessee, combines in 1953 his administrative work at the institute with duties in assisting the rector of the Oak Ridge St. Stephen's Church, having been ordained into the ministry of the Protestant Episcopal Church in December 1952.

One of three children (two boys and a girl) of Arthur Lewis and Ethel Mae (Hickox) Pollard, William Grosvenor Pollard was born in Batavia, New York, on April 6, 1911. His parents, both of English descent, were born in western New York State; to them Pollard has attributed his interest in the humanities and the sciences. Throughout his business career the elder Pollard maintained an active interest in both the social and natural sciences and from 1947 to 1952 was a lecturer in bacteriology and chemical engineering at the University of Tennessee. The family lived in Batavia until William was twelve years old, when his father, a mining engineer, moved to Knoxville, Tennessee, as a manufacturer's representative. While attending the Knoxville High School, from which he was graduated in 1928, William Pollard was engaged in part-time employment in an iron foundry.

At the University of Tennessee in Knoxville, which he entered in 1928, Pollard became a member of the Phi Kappa Phi, honor fraternity, and the Beta Alpha Omega, social fraternity, and took his B.A. degree in 1932. "Although physics was the field that appealed to me most," he has said, "I took a broad undergraduate curriculum in both the sciences and humanities. My major work was in philosophy, and most of my undergraduate physics was taken in noncredit courses." On graduation he obtained a two-year fellowship at Rice Institute in Houston, Texas, for postgraduate study in theoretical physics and received his master's degree in 1934. After a year as an assistant in physics at Rice, he qualified for his Ph.D. degree and was elected to the Phi Beta Kappa and Sigma Xi fraternities. His thesis, *On the Fermi Theory of the Beta Ray Type of Radioactive Disintegration*, was published in the *Philosophical Magazine* supplement for November 1936.

At the end of the second academic year (1935-36) of his assistantship at Rice Institute, Pollard joined the faculty of the University of Tennessee as assistant professor of physics. During the years that followed he was engaged in research work in his chosen field of beta ray spectra and energy distribution in cosmic rays, and in electrostatic control of small particles, the kinetic theory of gas flow, and the theory of diffraction of neutrons by crystals. Dr. Pollard became an associate professor in 1941 and in 1942 was appointed consulting physicist for the Chicopee Manufacturing Company of Springfield, Massachusetts. The *Mathematical Monthly* published in November 1942 a paper he wrote on the evaluation of surface integrals by electrical images.

"Early in 1942 Dr. Pollard had tried to join one of the research laboratories where he felt that his talents could best be used in the prosecution of the war," stated an article on Pollard in the Nashville *Tennessean* of December 26, 1948. "The need of the university was great, however, and he stayed . . . working up schedules for 1200 frisky air cadets." He became a professor at the University of Tennessee in 1943. The next year at the request of Dr. Francis Slack of Vanderbilt University, one of the pioneers of the venture, he joined the SAM (Substitute Alloy Material) Laboratories at Columbia University, New York City, for what proved to be about a year of outstanding research in theoretical physics. "This project," Dr. Pollard has explained, "was charged with perfecting the gaseous diffusion method of separating Uranium-235, a fissionable isotope, from normal Uranium-238. About one atom out of 140 is of Uranium-235." Dr. Pollard is co-author with R. D. Present of the scientific article "On Gaseous Self-Diffusion through Long Capillary Tubes," which was published in the *Physical Review*, and is also the author of a book, still "classified," on this subject.

With the end of the war, Professor Pollard returned to the University of Tennessee. Shortly afterward at a reunion party for faculty

REV. WILLIAM G. POLLARD

members, one of his colleagues pointed out that the Government's K-25 atomic plant at Oak Ridge, Tennessee, had many facilities that United States universities lacked (*Time*, January 27, 1952). The suggestion that these research facilities be made into a permanent educational institution greatly interested Professor Pollard, who in October was freed of his teaching duties so that he might devote his time to promotion of the project. President Frank P. Graham of the University of North Carolina and vice-president Paul Magnus Gross of Duke University were also enthusiastic in support, as were Deans E. W. Goodpasture of Vanderbilt and George B. Pegram of Columbia, and by December 1945 organization work for the Oak Ridge Institute for Nuclear Studies had begun. Pollard, then granted formal leave of absence from the University of Tennessee, served as a member of the executive committee and "carried a crusade to every important campus in the South, preaching the simple doctrine that Oak Ridge will be just a Federal island within the South, unless we can add its research potential to our educational system" (*Time*). Pollard, who became a consultant to the Carbide and Carbon Chemical Corporation and Monsanto Chemical Company plants at Oak Ridge in 1945 and 1946 respectively, was named acting executive director of the new educational and research center in February 1946. The Oak Ridge Institute for Nuclear Studies was formally chartered under the laws of Tennessee on October 15, 1946, by fourteen southern universities which are charter members. It now has twenty-nine members. Dr. Pollard was also a member of the board of directors until his appointment as permanent executive director on November 7, 1947, at which time he resigned from the University of Tennessee.

The Oak Ridge Institute is managed by a central council and board of directors representing the member institutions and, reported

POLLARD, WILLIAM G.—*Continued*

Time, "in its five short years under Executive Director William Pollard . . . has become a major mecca, not only for physicists, but for scientists of every sort." Many of its students are professors and graduate students working for advanced degrees in fields which "cover everything from agriculture to biology, chemistry to cancer." There were in 1952 ten different training programs. *Time* further observed that the influence of the institute extends far beyond the South itself: "It is under contract to the United States Atomic Energy Commission, and the AEC fellowships it administers are open to students from any university. In the past six years more than 800 scientists from 45 States and twelve foreign countries have taken its special course in using radioisotopes (so-called 'tracer atoms'). For such students the institute offers . . . the use of the largest of the national atomic energy laboratories, the biggest gaseous diffusion plant."

In November 1950 Pollard was admitted as a postulant for Holy Orders in the Tennessee Diocese of the Protestant Episcopal Church and as a candidate for Holy Orders one year later. "My decision to enter the Episcopal ministry was no sudden aberration," he has stated. "I have been a lifelong member of the Church and an active participant in its worship and activities. Like many other scientists who worked on the atomic energy project, I was deeply disturbed over this elemental new force of destruction. Although these feelings were not decisive at the time, the period since has resulted in a gradual deepening of religious faith and a growing conviction in the deeper validities and profound truth of the revelation of God in Christ." He said that the ministry of the Reverend R. F. McGregor, rector of St. Stephen's Church at Oak Ridge, where he has been a vestryman, "has given powerful stimulus to this emergence." Dr. Pollard, who explained that he carried out much of his study for Holy Orders while traveling between lecture engagements and visits to universities, was ordained a Deacon at the Oak Ridge church on December 17, 1952. "My present plans," he made known, "are to carry out my ministry on a part time basis as assistant to the Reverend R. F. McGregor. . . .While serving the Church in Holy Orders, I plan to continue my association with the Oak Ridge Institute of Nuclear Studies in my present capacity." Dr. Pollard was re-elected executive director in October 1952, for a new five-year term. For his accomplishment as executive director of the Institute, the scientist was given the Distinguished Service Award of the Southern Association of Science and Industry in 1950, and was nominated by *Dixie Business* as "Man of the South" in the following year. He was the recipient of an honorary Sc.D. degree from Ripon College, Wisconsin, in November 1951 and from the University of the South in Sewanee, Tennessee, in June 1952.

A fellow of the American Physical Society, Dr. Pollard was vice-chairman of its southeastern section in 1951 and chairman in 1952. He is a member of the American Association for the Advancement of Science, the Commission on Graduate Programs of the Southern Regional Education Board, the Mathematics Association of America, the Tennessee Academy of Science, and the board of trustees of the Southern Association of Science and Industry.

Mrs. Pollard is the former Marcella Hamilton of Nashville; the couple were married December 27, 1932, and are the parents of four boys, William Grosvenor 3d, Arthur Lewis 2d, James Hamilton, and Frank Hall Pollard. The physicist is five feet nine inches in height and 165 pounds in weight; he has brown hair and blue eyes. He enjoys hiking in the Great Smoky Mountains.

References

Nashville (Tenn.) Tennessean Mag p5+ D 26 '48 pors
Time 57:89 Je 18 '51; 59:59-61 Ja 7 '52 por
American Men of Science (1949)
Chemical Who's Who, 1951
Who's Who in America, 1952-53

PROKOFIEV, SERGE (SERGEYEVICH) Apr. 23, 1891—Mar. 4, 1953 Composer; pianist; conductor; studied at St. Petersburg Conservatory (1910-14); composer of many works for orchestra, concertos, chamber and piano music, songs, choral works, operas, music for ballet and films; associated with Diaghilev, Koussevitzky, Eisenstein; after Russian revolution, lived in Paris until 1934, when he returned to the Soviet Union; made many trips to United States to conduct his own works with the Philharmonic, Boston, and Chicago symphony orchestras; in 1948 was rebuked by the Communist party, along with other noted Soviet composers, for "bourgeois formalism" in his music, and recanted; best known in United States for *Peter and the Wolf* (1936) and *Classical Symphony* (1916). See *Current Biography*, 1941.

Obituary

N Y Times p90 Mr 8 '53

PUGMIRE, ERNEST I(VISON) Mar. 4, 1888—June 24, 1953 National Commander of the Salvation Army since 1944; served as officer for forty-six years in the United States, Canada, China and Japan. See *Current Biography*, 1945.

Obituary

N Y Times p27 Je 25 '53

PUSEY, NATHAN M(ARSH) (pūzē) Apr. 4, 1907- University president

Address: b. Office of the President, Harvard University, Cambridge 38, Mass.; h. The President's House, 17 Quincy St., Cambridge 38, Mass.

The twenty-fourth president of Harvard University is Dr. Nathan M. Pusey, who was elected in the summer of 1953 to succeed Dr. James Bryant Conant, now president-emeritus and United States High Commissioner in Germany. Formerly the president of Lawrence College in Appleton, Wisconsin, since 1944, Dr. Pusey was a *magna cum laude* member of the Harvard Class of 1928, and was a professor of Greek and ancient history in several colleges.

As president of Harvard, Dr. Pusey heads America's oldest educational institution (Harvard College was founded in 1636) as well as the most richly endowed of American universities. Harvard University, which includes the law, medical, business and other graduate schools as well as the College, had in 1952-1953 an enrollment of 10,239 and a faculty of 3,041.

Nathan Marsh Pusey, the youngest of the three children of John Marsh and Rosa (Drake) Pusey, was born at Council Bluffs, Iowa, on April 4, 1907. He is the brother of Major John Pusey, an artist who has seen service with the United States forces in both World War II and Korea, and of Mrs. Esther Pusey Briggs of the Army Quartermaster's Office. Their father died when Nathan Pusey was a small child, but their mother, who had been principal of a school in Wisconsin before her marriage, had the satisfaction of seeing her youngest son become a college president three years before her death in 1947.

Brought up in the city of his birth, Nathan Pusey is a graduate (1924) of the Abraham Lincoln High School in Council Bluffs, where he made practically a "straight A" record, was editor of the school paper, president of the Philomathian Literary Society, and prominent in both debating and basketball.

During summer vacations, Pusey worked at a variety of jobs including that of messenger for a local savings bank. His subsequent enrollment at Harvard College, Cambridge, Massachusetts, was made possible only by the winning of one of two $450 a year scholarships established by Mrs. Charles Elliott Perkins.

These scholarships could be renewed only if the recipients were on the "Dean's List," and to assure the necessary high grades the young Iowan (said to have been the first to hold a Perkins' scholarship through all four years of college) developed methodical work habits and placed a strict limit on extracurricular activity. Basketball was the only college sport in which Pusey participated, and this only as a substitute in his freshman year. In his senior year he took first place in a Harvard-Yale competitive examination in English literature given to teams from each university.

Having majored in English and comparative literature, studying especially under the late Irving Babbitt, he received his A.B. degree, *magna cum laude*, in June, 1928 and was elected to Phi Beta Kappa. He spent a year in Europe, returning to the United States in 1929. After trying in vain to find an opening in a publishing house he joined the faculty of the Riverdale Country School on the outskirts of New York City. "During the [next two] years," he has stated, "I . . . discovered that I had an aptitude for teaching, and perhaps as a result soon began to be seriously interested in education."

In the fall of 1931, accordingly, he returned to Harvard to prepare for the M.A. degree.

Walter R. Fleischer,
Harvard Univ. News

NATHAN M. PUSEY

To qualify for admission to one of Professor William Scott Ferguson's courses, he devoted the summer of 1931 to learning Greek, with the consequence that he "shifted" his "major academic interest from English to Greek and ancient history." Pusey, who made a special study of Athenian civilization under Ferguson's guidance, took the M.A. degree (with highest honors) in 1932.

He worked at Harvard as a part time assistant from 1933 to 1934 when the award of an Archibald Cary Coolidge Fellowship enabled him to continue research in his specialty at the American School of Classical Study in Athens. His essay entitled "The Political Theory of Demosthenes" (written under the pseudonym of "Pseudo Politicus. Gent.") brought him one of the Bowdoin Prizes in 1934.

He was still in Greece when in the summer of 1935 President Henry M. Wriston cabled him an invitation to come to Lawrence College as a "sophomore tutor." The college was experimenting with a tutorial system. Pusey accepted and began to interest his students in the classics ("This man's crazy," one professor is reported to have told Wriston. "He's got sophomores reading Aristotle's *Aesthetics*"). (Dr. Wriston, now president of Brown University, has considered Pusey "without question the most brilliant young teacher" he has ever known).

Pusey received his Ph.D. degree at Harvard in 1937. (His thesis was written in Greek on a typewriter with Greek letters.) The typescript in the Harvard University Library is catalogued in Greek, and is described as "a collection of laws from the Attic orators together with an account of the Athenian legislature."

In 1938, the educator went to Claremont, California, to take up the assistant professorship in history and literature which he held at Scripps College for the next two years. He

PUSEY, NATHAN—*Continued*

moved to Middletown, Connecticut, in 1940, to become an assistant professor of classics at Wesleyan University. He remained at Wesleyan for four years, being advanced to associate professor in 1943. Here he "developed new liberal arts courses for freshmen and sophomores" and "during World War II . . . taught physics courses for Navy V-5" (New York *Times,* June 2, 1953).

Elected the eleventh president of Lawrence College at Appleton, Wisconsin on May 20, 1944, Dr. Pusey succeeded Thomas N. Barrows, who had resigned on account of ill health. Dr. Pusey proved an effective administrator of Lawrence College which in 1952 had an enrollment of 799 students and a faculty of seventy-one. In his nine years as president he "more than doubled Lawrence's endowment (to $2,-500,000), raised faculty salaries, put up a new science building, arts building and student union" (*Time,* June 8, 1953).

One innovation introduced by Pusey at Lawrence was the establishment of what Edwin R. Bayley has called "a sort of great books course, with the student being required to read, discuss and write about widely varied branches of learning." This course was made obligatory for freshmen. Another innovation was the policy of conferring honorary degrees "only on persons who have never received a similar honor from any other institution," and never in the expectation of publicity or financial contributions.

He also served on the Wisconsin Governor's Commission on Human Rights and as chairman of both the Midwest President's Conference and the commission on liberal education of the Association of American Colleges.

In 1952 he made what is said to have been his "only venture into the world of politics" by becoming one of seventy-one other Wisconsin citizen-sponsors of a small book *The McCarthy Record,* opposing the re-election of Wisconsin's junior United States Senator, Joseph R. McCarthy.

The announcement on June 1, 1953 (just before the twenty-fifth anniversary reunion of his Harvard class) that Pusey was the choice of the Harvard Corporation evoked favorable comment in the press which noted that he is the first non-New Englander to become president of Harvard. It was also observed that his field of distinction lay in the liberal arts and in the training of undergraduates, while the emphasis at Harvard during Conant's administration had been on the graduate schools, the sciences and research. His gifts "will be recognized as somewhat different from those which Mr. Conant contributed," declared the New York *Herald Tribune* in an editorial. The New York *Times* on the other hand did not "believe that Harvard will be conscious of any abrupt change when Dr. Pusey takes over". The election of the new president was confirmed by the Board of Overseers, and thereby made official, on June 10.

Addressing the Divinity School of Harvard on September 30, 1953, Pusey asserted that "faith is the consciousness that moral values

. . . have a sacred character. It is more of this consciousness that we most desperately need, and, difficult as it may seem epistemologically, that we must learn again to know by faith with thanksgiving." For the scholar, "it is necessary to recognize that truth can be lost in a formless and uninformed faith. . . .We need to know, but also to believe, and what we want especially to do is to believe knowingly and with conviction" (*Christian Century,* October 13, 1953).

On taking office in October, Dr. Pusey told of his plans to redevelop the Divinity School and to strengthen the Graduate School of Education. He stated that instead of criticizing public educators the university must help them find a new philosophy. Emphasizing that "young people growing up should have liberating intellectual experiences," he declared that the liberal arts college is "essentially, or rightfully, a teaching community. It is the place where young people make the transition from the family to political society . . . where they acquire a good deal of knowledge, but even more importantly where they learn a method of living."

President Pusey has been the recipient of three honorary degrees, an LL.D. from Wesleyan University in 1944, an LL.D. from Ripon College in Wisconsin in 1945, and an L.H.D. from Coe College in Iowa in 1948. Nathan Marsh Pusey and the former Anne Woodward of Council Bluffs were married June 10, 1936 and are the parents of two sons, Nathan Marsh, Jr. and James Reeve, and one daughter, Rosemary. The new president of Harvard is about six feet tall, weighs around 180 pounds, and is variously described as "affable," "soft-spoken" and "handsome." In his autobiographical sketch in the Harvard '28 anniversary report he wrote "I have become increasingly interested in religion, am a member of the Protestant Episcopal Church. . . . I consider myself to be a member of the Republican party—though definitely more to the 'eastern' than 'midwestern' persuasion."

References

Boston Globe p1 May 21 '53 por
Christian Sci Mon p4 Je 4 '53; p2 Je 12 '53 por
Life 34:53 Je 15 '53
N Y Herald Tribune II p1 Je 7 '53 por; p1 Je 11 '53 por; p26 S 14 '53
N Y Post Mag p2 Je 14 '53 por
N Y Times p8 My 21 '44; p31 Je 11 '53
N Y Times Mag p11+ S 27 '53 por
N Y World-Telegram p5 Je 1 '53
New Yorker 29:17 Je 20 '53
Newsweek 41:60 Je 8 '53; 41:49 Je 22 '53
Time 61:79+ Je 8 '53 por
Washington (D.C.) Post p4 Je 2 '53 por; p14 Je 3 '53; p3B Je 14 '53 por
Directory of American Scholars (1951)
Leaders in Education (1948)
Presidents of American Colleges and Universities, 1952-53
Who's Who in America, 1952-53
Who's Who in the Midwest (1949)
World Biography (1948)

QUILL, MICHAEL J(OSEPH) Sept. 18, 1905- Labor union official

Address: b. c/o Transport Workers Union of America, 153 W. 64th St., New York 23

NOTE: This biography supersedes the article which appeared in *Current Biography* in 1941.

While working in a New York City subway change booth, Michael J. Quill, with six other transit employees, in April 1934 first made plans to organize the Transport Workers' Union of America. Less than two years later he became its president and in 1937 was named International President, after the union had become affiliated with the Congress of Industrial Organizations. He has been re-elected to that post biennially, most recently at Philadelphia on December 13, 1952. The Irish-born trade union leader, who has also served as a New York City councilman both as a member of the American Labor Party and as an independent, has been a vice-president of the Congress of Industrial Organizations since August 1950. In an effort to win a forty-hour week for New York City bus drivers, Quill on January 1, 1953, called a strike against eight bus companies.

A native of southwestern Ireland's mountainous County Kerry, Michael Joseph Quill was born September 18, 1905, in Gourtloughera, about three miles from Kilgarvan, the second youngest of the eight children (five sons and three daughters) of John Daniel Quill, a potato farmer, and Margaret (Lynch) Quill. He was brought up in Kerry and attended national (free) schools there between 1910 and 1916, the year of the famous Easter Rebellion. Quill has been quoted as stating that his "entire family was active in the Sinn Fein movement," and according to many accounts the boy was only fourteen when he first fought as a rifleman with the 3rd Battalion, Kerry No. 2 Brigade in the revolutionary forces. Quill's own testimony to a Congressional committee was that he was fifteen when "transferred from the Boy Scouts to the Irish Republican Army."

After immigrating to the United States in 1926 (he landed on March 17—St. Patrick's Day), Quill worked for a time in the boiler room of a large hotel and at other jobs before entering the employ of the Interborough Rapid Transit Company as a gateman in a subway station. "Two years later," reported A. H. Raskin in the New York *Times*, "he was promoted to change maker at 33 cents an hour. He worked twelve hours a night, seven nights a week, in the change booth at the Jackson Avenue station in Long Island City."

In 1929 Quill sold Roman Catholic religious art in the mining and smelting districts of western Pennsylvania; by the spring of 1930 he had returned to work in an IRT change booth and was thus employed when he became a naturalized United States citizen in December 1931.

In the spring of 1932 Quill took a leave of absence from his subway job to undergo in Vienna an operation on his faulty hip joint by the celebrated Dr. Adolf Lorenz. When Quill

MICHAEL J. QUILL

returned from Austria he was informed that the IRT company union had agreed to accept a 10 per cent decrease in wages to help the company, which had gone into receivership. He talked with some of his fellow employees about the possibility of starting an independent union, but while "he found them ripe for organization . . . the movement did not get off the ground until the Communist party sent an emissary to him in March 1934, and invited him to join forces with the Communist-controlled Trade Union Unity League" (A. H. Raskin in the New York *Times*). A month later (April 12, 1934) Quill and six of his coworkers met to plan what was later named the Transport Workers Union of America. The new union, which enjoyed a steady growth, was by 1935 strong enough to require a full-time organizer. Quill thereupon left his IRT job and was elected TWU president, effective at the beginning of 1936. The union, as yet unaffiliated, formed a brief connection with the International Association of Machinists. No permanent attachment was made until April 1937 when, largely at the instance of President John L. Lewis, the Congress of Industrial Organizations granted the TWUA an international charter. Within six months the membership of TWUA had increased to about 44,000, and closed shop contracts were swiftly concluded with the IRT, BMT, and IND subway systems in New York, and with the principal street car and omnibus companies of the city. In September Quill was elected first International President of TWUA and became a member of the CIO's National Executive Board. Later, the CIO-affiliated union organized transportation and taxi workers in a number of other cities, including Akron, Philadelphia, Chicago, San Francisco, Omaha, Flint, and Columbus.

As the American Labor party representative from the Bronx, in November 1937 Quill was elected to the first New York City Council

QUILL, MICHAEL J.—*Continued*

(successor to the Board of Alderman) and during the next two years championed slum clearance, public low-cost housing, free municipal distribution of milk for infants, and other social welfare projects. Before the 1939 election he was repudiated by the American Labor Party for refusal to endorse a resolution which supported President Roosevelt's foreign policy and condemned the Russo-German peace pact concluded just prior to the outbreak of World War II. In his campaign for his council seat as an independent, he was defeated. While he denounced the war in Europe as designed "to keep the masses at home and the colonies in subjection" before the German invasion of Russia, he shortly afterward appealed to Irish-Americans "to call on their brothers and sisters in Ireland . . . to give all practical assistance" to the Allies (Frederick Woltman in the New York *World-Telegram*, December 14, 1951).

Since 1937 Quill has threatened on a number of occasions to call a major subway strike in New York and a major strike on private bus lines, reported Frederick Woltman in 1951, adding, "Only once . . . did Mr. Quill actually come through with a legitimate trade union strike, duly authorized by the TWU to gain union demands." This was in March 1941, when a strike of 3,500 employees of the New York City Omnibus Corporation was called to back demands for a work week of 48 instead of 54 hours, pay increases, and other benefits. In other disputes with private operators, Quill invariably "based his demands . . . on the company's earnings" (*Time*), and in most instances the threat of a strike was sufficient to win at least part of his objectives. In his dealings with the city, which had become operator of New York's subway and elevated system, the union leader had an effective weapon in the fear of the municipal authorities of being blamed by the public for the inconvenience caused by a transportation walk-out. Quill threatened a subway tie-up in December 1942 and again in January 1943.

When, in November 1943, Quill again ran for the City Council as an independent, he was elected with a plurality of 8,000 over any other candidate. Two years later Quill returned to the American Labor party, and in the first postwar election as councilman (November 1945) was returned to his Bronx seat on the ALP ticket. The Transport Workers Union meanwhile continued to grow, its membership rising to around 110,000 by early in the year following, partly as a result of its penetration into the air transportation industry. In its 1945 contract with Pan American World Airways the union won a forty-hour week for maintenance employees, and organization was subsequently extended to workers of American Airlines, Transworld, United, Royal Dutch, and other airlines, and maintenance and service corporations. The TWUA international president's prestige as a labor leader was strengthened in early 1946 when John L. Lewis, who had taken his United Mine Workers back into the American Federation of Labor, failed in an attempt "to raid Quill's union" with his catch-all "District 50" even though he "invited the AFL Federation of Municipal Transit Workers . . . to join forces against Quill" (*Newsweek*).

One of the original members of the Greater New York City CIO Council, Quill was for several years its vice-president and (reported a TWUA release) "assisted in the organization of the Mine, Mill and Smelters Union, the Department Store Employees Union, Communications Workers Union, and sundry white collar and professional groups." He was elected president of the CIO New York Council in 1947, from which he resigned in March 1948. In the following month he withdrew also from his vice-chairmanship in the American Labor Party, which he charged was dominated by Communist "merchants of confusion."

At the TWUA's sixth biennial convention held at Chicago in December, Quill was re-elected International President despite the strenuous efforts of a leftist opposition to unseat him. Subsequently, stated Frederick Woltman, he "pushed through a constitutional amendment barring not only Communists but their supporters from office," after having "booted out" some fifteen members of the TWU executive council and sixteen of the union's thirty national organizers. Quill, who was re-elected International President of the TWUA again in 1950 and 1952, was elected President of the reorganized New York City CIO Council on April 25, 1949, and has since been re-elected annually. Also in 1949 he was a member of the CIO delegation to the first International Conference of Free Trade Unions in London; named Vice-President of the CIO at Chicago in 1950, he was a CIO delegate to the second I.C.F.T.U. Conference at Milan, Italy, in 1951 and the chairman of its committee on resolutions and standing orders in Berlin, Germany, in 1952.

"The achievement of the 40-hour work week for transit workers has been one of Quill's major goals as a trade unionist," stated a TWUA biographical release. "The 40-hour work week has now become a reality in such widely separated cities as Houston and San Francisco." An important stride towards this end in New York City was taken by Quill in the summer of 1950. "He won an 11-cent-an-hour increase for 36,000 city transit workers, signed an unprecedented memorandum of agreement with the Board of Transportation recognizing in principle the desirability of a forty-hour week for those workers," wrote Stanley Levey in the New York *Times* of September 9, 1951. At the same time Quill pledged himself not to call a strike until July 1, 1952, but by the use of the "slowdown" and other harassing tactics (it has been stated), he was able to persuade Mayor Vincent R. Impellitteri to appoint a fact-finding board which on July 1, 1951, provided a "formula for instituting the five-day, forty-hour week" (New York *Times*), publication of which was accompanied by an extension of the no-strike agreement through 1953.

Meanwhile (March 1950) Quill had extended his operations to Puerto Rico, where San Juan's bus, streetcar, and taxi drivers became TWUA Local 600. In February of the following year he launched a campaign to unionize New York

City's police force, a movement which made little headway after August 1951, when Police Commissioner Monaghan issued an order prohibiting members of the New York police force from becoming a member of any labor union. A strike, affecting 3,500,000 daily riders, called for January 1, 1953, against eight privately owned bus companies in New York City ended after twenty-seven days when the strikers voted by 4,256 to 895 on January 28 to submit to arbitration their demands for a forty-hour week. TWUA membership in the United States is estimated by the union at 110,000. "More impartial observers," noted the New York *Sunday News*, "put the figure at about 65,000."

In his home in the Bronx, where, with his wife and his son, John Daniel, Quill occupies a four-and-a-half room apartment in the Kingsbridge section, he participates in many nonpolitical civic activities. He has been at one time or another the chairman of the Bronx Conference for Racial and Religious Unity, and a member of the Bronx Committee of the American Red Cross, of the Coordinating Committee on Child Care, and of the Kerrymen's Protective and Benevolent Association. Mrs. Quill is the former Maria Theresa O'Neill; the couple were married in Ireland on December 26, 1937. The blue-eyed labor union executive has brown balding hair; with a weight of 200 pounds, he stands five feet eight inches tall. "He dresses conservatively, usually in blue serge," noted Raskin. "His only extravagance is in his speech. A masterful raconteur, he manages to give the impression of the utmost ingenuousness in telling outlandish stories about his own life and experiences." Collecting union buttons and mountain-climbing have been mentioned as among Quill's hobbies. He also enjoys horseback riding, swimming, photography, reading history and biography, and listening to Irish and American folk songs.

References

Bsns W p106-110 D 18 '48 pors
Cue 10:16 Je 28 '41 por
Fortune 44:58+ S '51 por
Harper 197:49-56 N '48
Life 27:38 Jl 25 '49 por
N Y Herald Tribune p25 F 28 '50 por
N Y Sunday News p72+ Ja 11 '53 por
N Y Times Mag p11+ Mr 5 '50 pors; p17+ S 9 '51 por
N Y World-Telegram p14 Mr 11 '41 por; p1+ Je 16 '41; p21 D 10 '51 por; p29 D 11 '51 pors; p27 D 12 '51 pors; p27 D 13 '51 pors; p29 D 14 '51 por; p13 D 15 '51 pors
Newsweek 27:66 Mr 4 '46 por; 32:20-3 S 27 '48 por
PM p14 Mr 13 '41
Read Digest 54:51-5 Ja '49
Time 37:18 Mr 24 '41 por; 47:22 F 4 '46 por
Washington (D.C.) Post p2M Mr 28 '48 por
International World Who's Who, 1948-49
Who's Who in America, 1952-53
Who's Who in Labor (1946)

RAMSEY, DEWITT C(LINTON) Oct. 2, 1888- Former Naval officer; aircraft association president
Address: b. c/o Aircraft Industries Association of America, Inc., Shoreham Bldg., Washington 5, D.C.; h. 3661 Upton St., Washington, D.C.

Admiral DeWitt C. Ramsey (retired), a pioneer naval aviation officer, served with the United States Navy for more than forty years before his retirement on May 1, 1949. Active during both World Wars, he became distinguished in the second war for his achievements as commanding officer of the *Saratoga* in the Solomons Campaign, as Chief of the Navy's Bureau of Aeronautics, and as Chief of Staff of the United States Fifth Fleet. After the war, Ramsey was successively appointed Vice-Chief of Naval Operations (1946), Commander in Chief of the Pacific Fleet (1948), and High Commissioner of the Trust Territory of the Pacific Islands (1948). Following his retirement from active duty, he was elected president of the Aircraft Industries Association, a position he has filled since July 1, 1949.

The son of Captain Frank DeWitt and Lillian Carlotta (Zulick) Ramsey, DeWitt Clinton Ramsey was born on October 2, 1888, at Whipple Barracks, Arizona, where his father, a West Point graduate, was on duty with the United States Army. His maternal grandfather served as Governor of Arizona during one of Grover Cleveland's Presidential administrations. After spending his early childhood in Albany, New York, Ramsey attended DeWitt Clinton High School in New York City. While a midshipman at the United States Naval Academy in Annapolis, Maryland, to which he was appointed in 1908, he won his letter in track, numerals in baseball, basketball, and football, and as a first classman was president of his class and president of the Midshipmen's Athletic Association. In June 1912 he received his B.S. degree from the Naval Academy and was commissioned an ensign.

From 1912 until 1915 Ramsey served consecutively on the U.S.S. *New Jersey*, the U.S.S. *Montana*, the U.S.S. *Nashville*, and the U.S.S. *Tingey*. In 1916 he reported to the Naval Air Station, Pensacola, Florida, for flight training and on May 31, 1917, was designated Naval Aviator Number 45. The United States having meanwhile entered World War II, he was sent to France as inspection officer for the United States Naval Air Stations in France and became a member of the commission which planned the routing of seaplanes across the mid-section of France. A member of the Inter-Allied Armistice Commission, Ramsey made two trips into Germany during the Armistice.

After the war he was on duty in London, England, until 1921, serving as a member of the Board of Claims and as assistant Naval Attache for Air. Upon his return to the United States in 1921, Ramsey was appointed fleet aviation officer on the staff of the Commander in Chief, United States Fleet. In this capacity he saw duty on the flagships *Pennsylvania, Columbia, Maryland,* and *Seattle,* and was a member of the American delegation to Brazil in 1922 upon the celebration of the anniversary of Brazilian

U. S. Navy

ADM. DEWITT C. RAMSEY

Independence. The following year he was sent again to the Pensacola Air Station, where, after a refresher course in 1924, he became superintendent of flight training and aide to the commandant. During 1926 he was on duty aboard the U.S.S. *Wright*, one of the earliest aircraft carriers, with Torpedo Bomber Squadron Number 1. In 1927 he was assigned to San Diego, California, as navigator on the aircraft carrier, U.S.S. *Langley*, with the responsibility of training pilots in deck take-offs and landings.

For the next two years (from the fall of 1927 until the fall of 1929) Ramsey occupied the position of fleet aviation officer on the staff of Commander in Chief, United States Fleet, U.S.S. *Texas* flagship. He was then given a three-year assignment at the Naval Academy in Annapolis, where he commanded the Training Squadron VN8D5, serving at the same time as a member of the Maryland State Aviation Commission. Following two years' duty (1932-34) as the executive officer of the *Wright*, he was stationed until 1936 with the Navy Department, Washington, D.C., in charge of the Aviation Section, Ships' Movements Division, Office of the Chief of Naval Operations. In June of 1937, upon completion of the course offered by the Naval War College at Newport, Rhode Island, Ramsey was assigned to duty as fleet aviation officer on the staff of Commander in Chief, United States Fleet, U.S.S. *Pennsylvania* flagship. The following year he was transferred to similar duty on the staff of Commander, Battle Force, U.S.S. *California* flagship, and in June 1938 joined the U.S.S. *Saratoga* as executive officer of that aircraft carrier. In Washington, D.C., he was head of the plans division of the Navy's Bureau of Aeronautics, Washington, D.C., from April 1939 to July 1941 and Assistant Chief of the bureau from July 1941 to May 1942.

In command of the aircraft carrier *Saratoga,* Ramsey from May 12 until October 27, 1942, participated in the first real offensive against the Solomon Islands, when in August planes from the *Saratoga* with those of the *Enterprise* and *Wasp* gave air support to the landings on Guadalcanal and Tulagi. After the occupation of Guadalcanal—United States carriers having been assigned the mission of guarding supply lines between New Caledonia, the New Hebrides, and the Solomons—the *Saratoga*, in conjunction with the *Enterprise*, was victorious in major action against a Japanese carrier task force. Following detachment from command of the *Saratoga*, Ramsey reported to the Commander in Chief, Pacific Fleet, for staff duty and from November 1942 until August 1943 commanded a task force which included the *Victorious*, the first British aircraft carrier to operate with the United States fleet. On October 6, 1942, he had been promoted to the rank of Rear Admiral and on October 15 had been awarded the Navy Cross "for extraordinary heroism and distinguished service during the occupation of Guadalcanal, Tulagi, and the Battle of the Solomons."

As Chief of the Bureau of Aeronautics, Navy Department, Washington, D.C., to which he was named on August 6, 1943, Ramsey was responsible for maintaining United States superiority over the enemy in aircraft and equipment. While holding this post, he gave repeated warnings against underestimating Japanese strength, stating at a press conference on August 20, 1943, that Japanese air power was probably greater than we realize and on other occasions predicting a long and hard war. At the same time he directed attention to increasing United States air strength. Speaking in Boston at a dinner given in honor of his wife on January 23, 1944, he noted that the aircraft carrier had replaced the battleship as backbone of the fleet; at the annual dinner of the Wings Club held on March 20, 1945, in New York, he said that the war of naval aviation was in its final phase in the Pacific as a result of the policy of carrier building and carrier fighting. In December 1944 he presented to the House Naval Affairs Committee an advanced picture of naval aviation in which jet-propelled fighter planes would operate at speeds above 700 miles an hour, and on May 14, 1945, told the Senate Appropriations Committee that the Navy is planning planes which may revolutionize aviation.

For his services in the office of Chief of the Bureau of Aeronautics (terminating in June 1945), Ramsey was awarded the Legion of Merit, which was withdrawn in favor of the Distinguished Service Medal. Following detachment from the Bureau of Aeronautics, he was appointed Chief of Staff to Admiral Spruance, Commander of the United States Fifth Fleet in the Pacific. Soon after assuming his new position on July 13, 1945, he estimated at his first press conference that Japan's military and naval air power at the time amounted to about 9,000 planes, most of which were probably being conserved for defense against invasion. Later in the month he stated in a broadcast from Guam that the invasion of

Japan would be made "by the most overwhelming forces ever concentrated in military history." When Admiral Spruance was assigned to the command of the Pacific Fleet in November 1945, Ramsey, with the rank of Vice-Admiral, succeeded him in the position of Deputy Commander in Chief, Pacific Fleet and Pacific Ocean Areas.

On January 15, 1946, with the rank of Admiral, Ramsey assumed duty as Vice-Chief of Naval Operations, Navy Department, Washington, D.C. The following June he testified in favor of a Congressional bill providing for military advice and assistance to China. Late in the summer of the same year he was for a time Acting Chief of Naval Operations in the absence from Washington of Admiral Nimitz. Upon being relieved of duty as Vice-Chief of Naval Operations on January 3, 1948, Ramsey was awarded a Gold Star in lieu of a second Distinguished Service Medal for "exceptionally meritorious service" in that capacity. He took up his new duties as Commander in Chief of the Pacific and United States Pacific Fleet on January 12, 1948, at ceremonies aboard the aircraft carrier, Valley Forge, stationed at Pearl Harbor. On April 17 of the same year he received the additional appointment to the position of High Commissioner of the Trust Territory of the Pacific Islands, and on July 13, 1948, he expressed his opinion, in reply to Congressional leaders favoring civilian control of the Trust Territory, that no other agency of the Federal Government was so well equipped as the Navy to handle the administration of these islands. Ramsey served in his two Pacific assignments until May 1, 1949, when he was relieved of all active duty and transferred to the retired list of the Navy.

Two months later, July 1, 1949, Ramsey succeeded Major General Oliver P. Echols in the presidency of the Aircraft Industries Association of America, Inc., an organization composed of ranking executives of the leading manufacturers of aircraft. At the close of the year he reported an increase in war planes but decrease in civilian planes produced during 1949 as compared with the preceding year. At this time he predicted a corresponding military rise and civilian decline for 1950. In his forward to the *Aircraft Year Book* for 1949, Ramsey pointed out that the aircraft industry, an insignificant factor in our national economy in the 1930's, had become a major employer in at least eight States. With the outbreak of the Korean war in the summer of 1950, military aircraft production was further increased. On December 28, 1950, Ramsey reported that warplane production had risen about one-fifth and dollar sales volume one-third that year over 1949. At the end of August, 1953, Ramsey said that the United States' annual output of military planes had risen from 3,000 in 1950 to 12,000 but that Russia had a greater number (New York *Times,* August 29, 1953).

Ramsey was married to Juanita Gabriel Holmes on August 25, 1926. Besides the Navy Cross and Distinguished Service Medal with Gold Star, he holds the Mexican Service Medal, the Victory Medal, and is entitled to the American Defense Service Medal, the American Area Campaign Medal, the Asiatic-Pacific Area Campaign Medal, and the World War II Victory Medal. He was made honorary Commander of the Military Division of the Order of the British Empire, and the Decoration and Diploma, Commandeur del Ordre Grand Bucae de la Couronne de Chene, was presented to him by the Government of Luxembourg. He is an honorary member of the Institute of Aeronautical Sciences and a member of the United States Naval Institute. Ramsey belongs to the Army and Navy Club and enjoys gardening for recreation. His religious affiliation is Protestant. He has brown hair and brown eyes, is five foot ten and one-half inches tall, and weighs 175 pounds.

References

Aviation W 50:13 Ap 4 '49
N Y Sun p18 D 10 '44
N Y Times p11 Mr 31 '49
Who's Who in America, 1952-53

RANCE, SIR HUBERT ELVIN July 17, 1898- Governor and Commander in Chief of Trinidad and Tobago, British West Indies

Address: b. Government House, Port-of-Spain, Trinidad, British West Indies; h. Oakhurst, Gordon Ave., Camberley, Surrey, England

The Governor and Commander in Chief of the British colony of Trinidad and Tobago since 1950 is Major General Sir Hubert Elvin Rance who was chairman of the committee which formulated the plans for the proposed British Caribbean Federation. For his work as chief civil-affairs officer in Burma during the British military occupation (1945-1946), Rance was knighted and later served as Governor of Burma. He had fought in both world wars and occupied important posts in the Military Training Branch of the British War Office before his retirement from the Army with the rank of major general in 1946.

Hubert Elvin Rance was born July 17, 1898 of English West Country stock. His father was the late Frederick Hubert Rance, an engineer. Young Rance graduated from Wimbledon College and entered the Royal Military College, Sandhurst in 1915. When only eighteen, he joined the Worcestershire Regiment, saw action in France and in Belgium and was twice decorated.

After World War I, he remained with the regiment and served in many places including Singapore and India. He was transferred, in 1926, to the Royal Corps of Signals and was adjutant in the Second Division Signals from 1927 to 1930. He served in Malaya from 1932 to 1935.

After a course at Army Staff College, he was made a captain in 1936 and an instructor of amphibious attack in the training directorate of the War Office. Under his direction, a combined operations exercise to attack the Isle of Wight was carried out and for the first time, Staff College students acted out their parts in the maneuvers as privates.

Rance was sent to France in 1939 as a major on the staff of the signal-officer-in-chief of the

SIR HUBERT ELVIN RANCE

British Expeditionary Forces and in April 1940 was given command of the Fourth Divisional Signals. He was mentioned in dispatches and created an Officer of the Order of the British Empire.

Evacuated at Dunkirk, June 1, 1940, he continued in command of the Fourth Signals Division until ordered to the Military Training Branch of the War Office to help in producing the new type of Army then urgently needed. The importance of his work in building up mechanized forces was recognized in September 1942, when he was made director of technical training, responsible for the doctrine being taught newly formed corps in the Military College of Science.

The Observer (London), August 18, 1946, reported that when Rance was assigned in May 1943 as chief of staff·to General Edmund Schreiber, of the Western Command, he began giving "lectures on his own on world affairs to Army audiences. . . .He had a talent for imparting his wide interests to others. . . .As a result of this unofficial but successful enterprise, General Schreiber recommended a course at the Civil Affairs College in London."

Two years later, in April 1945, Rance was sent to Burma as Admiral Mountbatten's chief civil affairs officer. According to *The Observer,* "General Rance was the most enthusiastic exponent of Mountbatten's policy of reconciliation, the keynote of which was to move with the rising tide of Asiatic nationalism. In Burma, this meant for Rance the delicate task of implementing the 'Kandy Agreement' between Mountbatten and the Burmese resistance leader Aung San, head of the Anti-Fascist People's League, which became the biggest political organization in Burma after Japanese occupation. During this period, Rance applied himself with great diligence to the economic and socal problems of the people. Instead of remaining rooted in Rangoon, he moved about

the country and insisted upon his junior officers doing the same."

Civil government was restored to Burma in January 1946, by the return of the Governor, Sir Reginald Dorman-Smith. Rance had made an excellent impression as a sympathetic but forceful administrator. Upon his return to England in 1946, he was made a Knight of the Grand Cross Order of the British Empire and a Companion of the Bath.

When the Governor of Burma resigned because of ill-health, Sir Hubert, just retired from the Royal Corps of Signals, was appointed to succeed him, and took office in August 1946. This post was described by *The Observer* (London) (August 18, 1946), as "the most important Governorship in the British Empire," adding that Sir Hubert's task would be to restore "coherence and hope, wealth and good order to a war-ravaged country." His patience, persistence and self-discipline in negotiations were compared to Lord Wavell's handling of affairs in India.

By September, Sir Hubert had succeeded in forming a coalition Executive Council representative of all the political parties in Burma. In a radio speech, he announced that the Council would have all the authority and power held by the ministry that had governed Burma before the war.

As an expert on colonial affairs, Sir Hubert attended a conference held at Montego Bay, Jamaica, in 1947. The following year, he was appointed chairman of the Standing Closer Association Committee, British West Indies, and British co-chairman of the Caribbean Commission. He left Burma then to devote full time to drafting a federation plan for the British West Indies. It was at this time that he was created a Knight of the Grand Cross of St. Michael and St. George.

The plan for British West Indian federation, submitted by Sir Hubert in 1949, would dissolve the separate administrations of Barbados, British Guiana, British Honduras, Jamaica, the Leeward Islands, Trinidad and Tobago and four of the Windward Islands—Dominica, Grenada, Saint Lucia and Saint Vincent—and put them all under a single Governor General and Council of State. This would give them increased self-government, but not Dominion status.

The plan also provides for a single system of currency, customs regulations and immigration. It was accepted by the British Government in 1950 and is known unofficially as the Rance plan. Sir Hubert's appointment as Governor of Trinidad and Tobago followed soon afterward, in March 1950.

There has been considerable opposition to the federation plan in the West Indies colonies. British Guiana, on the mainland of South America, and British Honduras apparently fear the dropping of immigration bars. Both of these colonies are sparsely settled, whereas the other British islands, particularly Barbados and Jamaica, are over-crowded. Trinidad, the only colony in the group that has never required aid from the Crown, because of income from its oil refineries and its "Pitch Lake" asphalt industry, fears possible financial burdens. Jamaica hesitates because the island seems to feel it might lose its individuality and importance under federation.

When interviewed for the New York *Times* (January 19, 1953) Sir Hubert said that the federation plan appeared to be the logical conclusion of a process already occurring. He stated, however, that although certain cooperation in the currency and tariff systems exists among the colonies, their life is still unnecessarily complicated by these monetary, customs and administrative differences.

At the London conference of April 1953, attended by Colonial Secretary Oliver Lyttelton and representatives of the Caribbean colonies, some amendments were made to the Rance plan and five of the colonies—Jamaica, Trinidad and Tobago, Barbados, and the Windward and Leeward Islands—signed a proposal for a federal union with its capital on Grenada, one of the Windward group. The Legislatures of each colony must ratify the draft constitution before further progress can be made, and this first step is expected to take at least another year.

It is more than thirty years since the first plan for such a federation was drawn up. The London conference which closed April 30, 1953 is regarded by the British Government as the most encouraging to date. Much of the credit for this progress goes to Sir Hubert.

At the opening session of Trinidad's Legislative Council on October 23, 1953, Sir Hubert warned of the spread of Russian communism in the colony, and cited British Guiana's recent crisis in which its constitution was suspended as "a lesson for Trinidad."

Sir Hubert is six feet, two inches tall, weighs 205 pounds, and has blue eyes and brown hair. He enjoys cricket, tennis and shooting as recreational activities and belongs to the Army and Navy Club.

He was married on January 27, 1927 to Mary Noël Guy, daughter of the late C. A. Guy of St. Helens, Hastings, England. A daughter, Elizabeth Monica, was born in 1931 and a son, David Elvin, in 1935.

References

Observer (London) Ag 18 '46 por
Who's Who, 1953
International Who's Who, 1953

RAND, WILLIAM M(CNEAR) Apr. 7, 1886- Government official; retired business executive

Address: b c/o Mutual Security Agency, Washington 25, D.C.; h. R.F.D., South Lincoln, Mass.

With his confirmation on March 10, 1953, as Deputy Director of the Mutual Security Agency, William M. Rand, retired president of the Monsanto Chemical Company since 1951, re-entered public life. According to MSA chief Harold E. Stassen, Rand is devoting special attention to the development of overseas sources for raw materials, an activity designed not only to provide materials needed for American defense but also to supply dollar earnings to for-

eign countries. Earlier, in November, 1950, while still president of Monsanto, Mr. Rand had declined the government post of director of Price Stabilization in the Economic Stabilization Agency.

William McNear Rand, one of two sons of William Dwight and Emily (McNear) Rand, was born April 7, 1886, in Watertown, Massachusetts. His father's family came from England to the United States in 1640; on his mother's side he is descended from Captain John McNear, who emigrated from Scotland in 1701. His boyhood was spent on the farm of his maternal grandfather, a retired sea captain and ship owner. After attending Chauncey Hall and public schools in Boston and Cambridge, Rand was graduated from Phillips Exeter Academy in 1905. At Harvard University, from which he received his B.A. degree in 1909, he was captain of the track team in his senior year, when it won the intercollegiate championship of the United States. Representing his country at the Olympic Games in 1908 in London, England, Rand took fourth place as hurdler. Thirty-nine years later, in 1947, Rand placed a notice in the London *Times* seeking to locate members of the 1908 British team for a reunion, and three of the original ten turned up for a luncheon at Claridge's (New York *Herald Tribune*, September 26, 1947).

Rand's first job on graduation from Harvard was as a messenger for the Mutual National Bank in Boston, where he was soon promoted successively to assistant bookkeeper, discount clerk, and teller. In 1913 he took the post of treasurer of the City Fuel Company, a Boston coal firm, which he held for six years.

Commissioned as an ensign in the Navy in 1917, Rand saw several months of sea duty, and then was assigned to Washington as an aide to Admiral William S. Benson, Chief of Naval Operations. When discharged in February 1919, he was lieutenant, senior grade.

Rand's first association with the chemical industry came in 1919, when he was appointed treasurer of the Russell Company which managed the Merrimac Chemical Company, manufacturers of heavy chemicals in Everett, Massachusetts, of which he became sales vice-president in 1921. Monsanto Chemical Company bought the stock of Merrimac in 1929, and two years later Rand became a member of Monsanto's Board of Directors. After becoming president of its Merrimac division in 1935, Rand was named vice-president of Monsanto and general manager of its Merrimac Division. Transferred to St. Louis in November 1943, he served on Monsanto's four-member executive committee as vice-president and became president of the company on October 1, 1945, a position he held until his retirement on May 1, 1951. In 1950 he was also director of the company's subsidiaries in Australia and India.

During Rand's long association with Monsanto the company participated in the dramatic expansion of the entire chemical industry. Founded more than fifty years ago in St. Louis, the firm now holds fifth place among the nation's chemical producers, reported *Business*

WILLIAM M. RAND

Week, and has grown to four times its prewar size, more than doubling its capital investments between 1946 and 1948. Among the new products introduced by the company is a fire-resistant hydraulic fluid known commercially as Skydrol, brought out in 1948 for use in aircraft hydraulic systems to reduce fire hazards, a major advance in the safe operation of modern airliners and combat planes. A further important development was the company's expansion in September 1950 into the production of acrylonitrile, a primary ingredient in several new wool-like synthetic fibres which involved a $30,000,000 investment in new facilities at Monsanto's Texas City, Texas, plant.

Rand has served as president of the Associated Industries of Massachusetts (1937-39), and holds a directorship in the following corporations: the Liberty Mutual Insurance Company, the John Hancock Mutual Life Insurance Company, Monsanto Chemical Company, the Chemstrand Corporation, St. Louis Union Trust Company, and the First National Bank of St. Louis. He has also been chairman of the board of the Manufacturing Chemists Association.

During World War II Rand acted as adviser to the Chief of Chemical Warfare Service. As one of management's eighteen principal representatives for the President's Labor-Management Conference in Washington in the fall of 1945, he served as a member of the Management Executive Committee. In 1946 he received an honorary LL.D. degree from Northeastern University. Awarded the Seventeenth Chemical Industry Medal of the American section of the Society of Chemical Industry in November 1950 in recognition of his "conspicuous service to applied chemistry, to education, to human welfare, and to industrial progress," Rand stressed in his acceptance speech the need for public understanding of the chemical industry and its contributions to agriculture, medicine, and other areas of public welfare.

Rand is an overseer of Harvard University, a member of the Corporation of Northeastern University, a member of the executive committee of the St. Louis Crime Commission, vice-chairman of the Civil Defense Committee of St. Louis, an advisory committee member and former president of the Phillips Exeter Alumni Association of New England, a director of the St. Louis Chamber of Commerce, and director and president of the St. Louis Community Chest (1951). He is a member of the Automobile Association and a past vice-president of the National Association of Manufacturers. His professional and social organizations include the Chemists' Club, Cruising Club of America, Harvard Club (of Boston and St. Louis), Noonday Club of St. Louis, Deer Creek Club and Racquet Club of St. Louis, Round Table Club of St. Louis, St. Louis Country Club, Links Club of New York, and Newcomen Society. He is also the author of articles for chemical papers.

A blue-eyed "big, silver-haired New Englander," Mr. Rand is said to possess along with that region's traditional virtues of conscience and industriousness a sense of humor. He is a Republican and a member of the Unitarian Church. On September 17, 1914, he married Lucy Kimball Robbins, also of New England. Their five children are Emily L. (Herman), William M., Jr., Lucy R (Abbot), John R. and Peter W. His hobbies include fishing, hunting, sailing, farming, and skiing. As an expert photographer, he has taken hundreds of feet of motion picture film of his many outings in Maine.

References

Chem & Eng N 28:2264 Jl 3 '50 por
Oil Paint & Drug Rep 158:4 N 18 '50
Business Executives of America (1950)
Who's Who in America, 1952-53

RASMUSSEN, GUSTAV Aug. 10, 1895—Sept 13, 1953 Former Danish Foreign Minister; Ambassador to Italy; in foreign service since 1917; graduated in law from University of Copenhagen 1921; was secretary of Danish delegation in Petrograd (1917); was secretary and chargé d'affaires at Berne, Switzerland, 1927-1931; in 1934-35 was counselor to Danish delegation to League of Nations; represented Denmark in London in World War II as a member of the Danish Council and Military Mission; chosen Foreign Minister, 1945; from 1946 to 1949 served as head of Danish delegations to United Nations General Assemblies in London, Paris and New York; was chairman of Committee of Ministers of the Council of Europe, 1949-50. See *Current Biography,* 1947.

Obituary

N Y Times p27 S 14 '53 por

REAVEY, MRS. GEORGE *See* Pereira, I. R.

REDFIELD, ROBERT Dec. 4, 1897- Anthropologist

Address: b. University of Chicago, Chicago 37, Ill.; h. Box 2421, R. 1, Des Plaines, Ill.

Originally a lawyer, Robert Redfield turned to anthropology in his early twenties and eventually became a recognized authority on Middle American folk culture. His field trips sponsored by the Carnegie Institution of Washington (D.C.) as well as by the University of Chicago where he is the Robert Maynard Hutchins Distinguished Service professor, have taken him inside native villages in Yucatan, Southern Mexico and Guatemala.

Granted leave from the university in 1951 in order to head the $75,000 Ford Foundation project to study world-wide intercultural relations, Professor Redfield has been working on the premise that the major requirement for peace is a better understanding of the world's races and peoples.

Robert Redfield was born in Chicago, Illinois, December 4, 1897. His father, Robert Redfield, was a successful attorney and his mother, Bertha (Dreier) Redfield, was the daughter of the Danish consul in Chicago. Redfield's grandfather, John A. Kennicott, had settled in Northfield Township in 1823, where Professor Redfield still maintains a home.

After attending the University High School in Chicago, and graduating in 1915, Redfield entered the University of Chicago, majoring in law. His education was interrupted during World War I when he volunteered as an ambulance driver in the American Field Service. Resuming his university studies, he was elected to Phi Beta Kappa and Sigma Xi, and was University Marshal. Graduating *cum laude* with a Ph.B. degree in 1920, he continued at the university for another year, receiving a Doctor of Jurisprudence degree in 1921.

Robert Redfield became associated with the Chicago law firm of Tolman, Sexton and Chandler, but while studying at the university, he was influenced by sociology professor Robert A. Park to leave the law profession. He accepted an instructorship in sociology at the University of Colorado, in 1925. Within one year he became a fellow in the Social Science Research Council.

Redfield returned to the University of Chicago in 1927 as an instructor in anthropology and received a Ph.D. there in 1928. In the same year, he became an assistant professor, and two years later an associate professor. He was promoted to a full professorship and made dean of the division of social sciences in 1934.

In 1926 Redfield took his first field trip under the auspices of the Social Science Research Council. His studies of Mexican folkways in Tepoztlan, Mexico, laid the ground work for his later field studies. The immediate result was the book, *Tepoztlan, A Mexican Village* (1930), and a growing interest in Yucatan.

The Album

ROBERT REDFIELD

As Redfield later remarked, the Yucatan natives' physical features were so strongly Mayan in physical cast that they looked like living archaeological statues dug out of prehistoric Mayan ruins. Secluded from the rest of Mexico, these Yucatan villages appeared to offer a splendid chance to study a purely native culture.

In 1930, Robert Redfield obtained a leave of absence from the University of Chicago to undertake ethnological and sociological studies in Yucatan for the Carnegie Institution of Washington which had appointed him research associate in charge of social field work in Yucatan and Guatemala. Spending five months in the town of Chan Kom, he befriended Alfonso Villa R., in charge of the Chan Kom school, who was an excellent guide to native folklore.

Although the people of Yucatan were living in relative isolation, he found the culture of Chan Kom was not purely Mayan although Indian characteristics predominated. Spanish and other European elements had been integrated into the social structure.

Later, during the field trips of 1931 to 1933, he perceived a similar cultural diffusion in the Quintana Roo district of the Yucatan Peninsula, which borders the Caribbean Sea on one side, and the countries of British Honduras and Guatemala on the other.

From this direct research Redfield wrote, in conjunction with Alfonso Villa R., *Chan Kom, A Maya Village* which was published by the Carnegie Institution of Washington in 1934. This was followed by a more comprehensive report, *The Folk Culture of Yucatan* (1941). Of *Chan Kom, A Maya Village,* Stuart Chase wrote, "It is hard to praise sufficiently the scope, the scholarly detail, the magnificent presentation, with charts, maps and tables, of this study" (*New Republic*, February 20, 1935).

(Continued next page)

REDFIELD, ROBERT—*Continued*

The Folk Culture of Yucatan examines the culture of four communities in Yucatan and prevailing concepts of the nature of society in this section of Central America.

During World War II, Redfield served as an adviser to the War Relocation Authority. Afterwards, he attended the initial conferences of the United Nations Educational, Scientific and Cultural Organization in Europe. He became the chairman of the department of anthropology at the University of Chicago in 1948.

In that year, upon revisiting Yucatan with his wife, Margaret Park Redfield, an authority on Yucatan folklore, he discovered that these Indian villages had progressively adopted other foreign habits. Some towns became pueblos with Protestant chapels which displaced the Catholic cathedrals, and socialist ideals were becoming more predominant in the intellectual climate than the ancient Mayan values and beliefs.

He found that technology had annihilated the isolation of Yucatan, and that Chan Kom, and other Yucatan villages had developed more modern and more uniform cultures. His book, *A Village That Chose Progress* (1950), describes the cultural changes in Chan Kom.

The Yucatan trip was followed by a visit to Nationalist China in 1948, when he was visiting professor to National Tsing Hua University in Peiping. He became director of the American Council on Race Relations in 1948.

In 1951 the Ford Foundation allocated $75,000 for the study of the relation of international race relations and world peace, and Dr. Redfield was chosen to direct the project. Upon completing the research, he went to the University of Paris as an exchange professor in 1952.

In 1953, Professor Redfield reached the highest scholastic standing in the University of Chicago when he was made Robert Maynard Hutchins Distinguished Service professor. His most recent book is on folk anthropology, *The Primitive World and Its Transformation* (Cornell University Press, 1953).

In a panel on ethics and politics in the Bicentennial Convocation held in Aspen, Colorado, July 1949, Professor Redfield said that the issue was one of competence and altruism peculiar to the educational profession. An individual is a single moral being in both public and private life and therefore his actions during his working hours could not be separated from his behavior at other times. "The competence of teacher, scientist or scholar is part technical, part moral. A man who lies, deceives and changes his view in response to a political order or in response to personal advantage is not competent to teach or do research" (New York *Times,* July 11, 1949).

In an article, "Does America Need a Hearing Aid?" (*Saturday Review,* September 26, 1953) Professor Redfield suggests that we can help other peoples of the world understand us better if we, in turn, attempt to understand them. "We know how great is the distinction between allegiance won blindly and that won understandingly. . . .Our country . . . needs all the strength that reason can give to our powers of understanding. To indulge hateful passion for political advantage is to drive ourselves downward toward that dark reliance on force which today is Russia's. At home and abroad to talk and then to listen, to listen with the help of reason and then reasonably to talk, is to strengthen us just where we can be so much stronger than the Soviets. It is to build the community of free minds, 'the civilization of the dialogue.' "

Included in the books written by Professor Redfield are *Notes on the Ethnography of Tzeltal Communities of Chiapas* (1939) with Alfonso Villa R. and *Disease and Its Treatment in Dzitas, Yucatan* (1940) with Margaret Park Redfield.

Robert Redfield is five feet and ten inches in height with blue eyes and brown hair. His weight is 150 pounds. He and Margaret Lucy Park were married June 17, 1920. They have three children, Lisa Redfield Peattie, Joanna Redfield Gutman and James Michael Redfield.

He is a trustee of the Social Science Foundation, a fellow of the American Association for the Advancement of Science and the American Philosophical Society. Dr. Redfield is a member of the American Academy of Arts and Sciences, the American Anthropological Association, the Research Association, the Folklore Association, the Sociological Society, a member of the board of directors of the American Council of Learned Societies since 1952, and of the Scientific and Cultural History of Mankind, of the United Nations Educational, Scientific and Cultural Organization. He is a member of Phi Gamma Delta. Fisk University conferred upon him the honorary Doctor of Humanities degree in 1947. Dr. Redfield's hobby is gardening.

References

American Men of Science (1949)
Directory of American Scholars (1951)
International Who's Who, 1952
Leaders in Education (1948)
Who's Who in America, 1952-53
Who's Who in American Education, 1947-48
World Biography (1948)

REED, DANIEL A(LDEN) Sept. 15, 1875- Representative from New York
Address: b. House Office Bldg., Washington 25, D.C.; h. 761 Central Ave., Dunkirk, N.Y.

In the Eighty-third Congress, the chairman of the House of Representatives Ways and Means Committee is Representative Daniel A. Reed of the Forty-third New York District. A long-time advocate of reduced taxation and an opponent of increased Federal expenditures under both the New and Fair Deals, Chairman Reed is one of the senior Republicans in the national Legislature.

A lawyer by profession, he was first elected to the Sixty-sixth Congress in November 1918 and is now serving his eighteenth consecutive term. For some years he was chairman of the House Committee on Education, and was co-author in 1928 with the late Senator Charles

Curtis of Kansas of a bill to create a United States Department of Education.

Daniel Alden Reed was born to Anson William and Alfreda Reed on September 15, 1875, in Sheridan, New York, where he attended a grade school and Silver Lake High School in Chautauqua County. A student at Cornell University from 1896 to 1899, the future Congressman qualified for his LL.B. degree there in 1898. He was admitted to practice before the Appellate Division of the Supreme Court of the State of New York in 1900.

Reed first hung out his lawyer's shingle at Silver Lake, later moved to Dunkirk, Chautauqua County's second city in population and his present legal place of residence. For a period of about six years beginning in 1903 he was an attorney for the New York State Excise Department. He then served nine years as football coach for Cornell. ("I never let my football team play dirty and I don't myself," *Time* reported his saying when, in the Eighty-third Congress, it was suggested that he could use his House Ways and Means Committee chairmanship to force Administration assent to his own legislative ideas.) A Chautauqua lecturer on civic and commercial subjects, "Dan" Reed was an experienced public speaker by the time of his election, on November 5, 1918, to the Sixty-sixth Congress, as the Republican representative of the Forty-third New York District which covers Allegany, Cattaraugus and Chautauqua counties—in the southwestern part of the State.

The new Representative of the Forty-third New York District, who was sent by the United States Government on a special mission to France in 1918-19, came into Congress on a Republican tidal wave and for a while was a minor figure in party affairs. He sponsored his first important legislative proposal in January 1922, a bill to authorize, as an alternative to the projected St. Lawrence-Great Lakes Waterway, an "all-American" ship canal to link Lake Erie at Buffalo with the Hudson River just south of Albany, to be privately financed by Millard F. Bowen and associates of Buffalo.

Reed was also greatly interested in educational matters and was early assigned to the House Committee on Education. He helped to promote a bill sponsored by Representative Horace Mann Towner to create a Federal Department of Education whose Secretary would be a member of the Cabinet. When Towner was named Governor of Puerto Rico, Reed succeeded him as the Committee's chairman. The education bill became an issue in the 1924 election, when Reed received a substantially increased majority in his own normally Republican district; and his margin of victory was even greater in November 1926, when he was returned to the Seventieth Congress. The new education bill, introduced during that Congress was sponsored in the House by Representative Reed and in the Senate by Charles Curtis of Kansas, who later became Vice-President of the United States. Reed has also served as chairman of a Committee on Industrial Arts and Expositions.

Wide World Photos

DANIEL A. REED

The defeat of many Republican legislators with high seniority in the election of November 1932 brought better committee assignments to those G.O.P. members who survived the Democratic landslide. Reed, as a member of the House Ways and Means Committee, commanded in the Seventy-fourth and subsequent Congresses wide attention not only as a champion of sound money and thrift in Federal expenditure but also as a critic of the Franklin D. Roosevelt Administration. Reed, as "an old party wheelhorse who seldom has had trouble finding at least a little flaw in a Democratic argument" (Delos W. Lovelace in the New York *Sun*), was in January 1935 bitterly critical of the Doughton Federal Securities Bill; in July, after abandonment of the gold standard. he assailed as a "dishonorable legislative proposal" a bill to bar individuals from suing the Government for damages incurred through abrogation of the gold clause.

Reed attempted to amend the lobbying bill in March 1936 by a clause forbidding government officials from visiting the Capitol except by request, and in 1937 he tried to put social security on a pay-as-you-go basis through an amendment to the Social Security Act. Having assailed both President Roosevelt's tax message of March 1936 and Secretary of the Treasury Henry Morgenthau's 1937 budget, Reed proposed in March 1938, an amendment to the tax revision bill to "allow tax deductions for revocable trusts made to endow colleges and universities." (Representative—later Chief Justice—Fred Vinson called this "the first attempt to strike at the revenues of this bill," and the amendment was defeated by 82 to 23.)

Samuel A. Carlson, the popular former mayor of Jamestown, New York, announced in August 1938 his intention of running against Reed in the coming Congressional election as "an independent candidate to represent the progressive

REED, DANIEL A.—*Continued*

rather than the reactionary viewpoint," and at the primaries later in the same month secured the Democratic nomination. ("Mr. Carlson," stated Reed on hearing this news, "enters the field as a candidate of the New Deal in an effort to broaden the purge to include me.") The incumbent nevertheless won the election, and early in the Seventy-sixth Congress Reed was named by minority leader Joseph W. Martin to head a Republican committee to examine a forthcoming Administration proposal to raise the limit on the national debt to $50,000,000. Reed was also named in 1939 as a United States delegate to the last meeting of the Interparliamentary Union before the outbreak of World War II. He sponsored the Reed Bill to extend the benefits of the municipal bankruptcy act, a measure signed by President Roosevelt on March 5, 1940. A month later Reed attracted nation-wide attention when he challenged' the right of the Census Bureau to include questions regarding the income of individuals. "To answer such question would be a violation of my oath of office," he declared, and returned a blank questionnaire to the bureau.

"Before we got into the war," wrote Delos W. Lovelace in the New York *Sun* on March 16, 1944, "opponents called Reed an isolationist, but his own story is rather that he opposed the New Deal's foreign policies. 'Way back in 1938 he insisted that the Administration was laying the foundation of a face-saving war to hide its domestic failures. Two years later he protested that, far from preparing the country for defense, the arms production program of the New Deal had developed into just another boondoggle." He attacked the Hull reciprocal trade agreements with Canada and Venezuela in 1940 and the United States-Argentina trade pact in 1941.

In domestic matters the New York Congressman was a supporter of the 1943 Beardsley Ruml Plan for "pay-as-you-go" income tax collection. He successfully moved (October 1943) that the House Ways and Means Committee reject a Treasury recommendation of a substantially increased tax scale on incomes over $2,000. He was named in March 1944 to the chairmanship of a twenty-five-member Republican Post-War Tax Study Committee. (This committee announced two months later that a 50 per cent reduction in Federal taxes would be a party aim, and in October that it would give "serious consideration" to a program devised by R. V. Fletcher of the Association of American Railroads for "retiring the national debt at a rate of one per cent annually over a period of 100 years.")

On April 19, 1944, Reed joined the minority of 21 (as against a majority of 334) members of the House who voted against extension of the lend-lease act, and in June 1945 he was the only member of the New York delegation to oppose taking the anti-poll tax bill out of the Rules Committee for debate on the floor of the House. Reed declared that he would support either a constitutional amendment abolishing the poll tax, or individual action to that

end by the seven States concerned, but held' that a mere act of Congress would be unconstitutional.

In the Republican-controlled Eightieth Congress, Representative Reed became the ranking member of his party on the House Ways and Means Committee and the chairman of that committee's subcommittee on social security. He sponsored legislation to freeze the social security payroll tax for two years at the existing one per cent rate, which legislation passed the House on June 18, 1947, without a dissenting vote. Later in the same month he served as chairman of a House-Senate conference committee which became deadlocked over the same legislation.

Reed voted during the 1947 session in favor of a two-term limit on the presidency, and supported the Taft-Hartley law; he opposed Greek-Turkish aid and was paired against the *Voice of America* bill. In the 1948 session he was recorded in favor of the tidelands oil bill and the Mundt-Nixon subversive activities control bill and against six billion dollars in Marshall Plan aid; he also authored a bill extending social security coverage to 3,500,000 new persons which passed the House on June 14, 1948, but later "died" in the Senate Finance Committee. As chairman of the Republican Conference Committee on International Economic Problems, Reed was a United States delegate to the Interparliamentary Union meeting at Rome, Italy, late in 1948. In September of the following year he was a delegate to the meeting at Stockholm, Sweden, and is a vice-president of the Interparliamentary Union.

During the Democratic-controlled Eighty-first and Eighty-second Congresses, Representative Robert L. Doughton of North Carolina was again the chairman of the Ways and Means Committee, with Reed as the ranking Republican. As such he was the author in January 1950 of a bill which he described as "a Republican answer to . . . President Truman" and which would not only have raised personal income tax exemptions to $700 but would have reduced most excise taxes by 10 to 20 per cent, while putting a 50 per cent tax ceiling on all incomes. He was also consistently critical of the Truman Administration's tariff policies and opposed renewal of the reciprocal trade agreements as well as Korean-Formosa economic aid and extension of the Marshall Plan. Reed further viewed with disfavor the legislation proposed in July 1950 to create a Federal Department of Health, as well as the universal military training bill of April 1951.

As early as July 1952 Reed stated in a campaign speech that should General Dwight D. Eisenhower be elected in the coming November along with a Republican Congress, and "barring all-out war," the savings under a G.O.P. administration of "billions of dollars in government spending" would "provide the climate for a tax cut-back." On December 1, 1952, after the election was over and his elevation, by virtue of seniority, to the chairmanship of the Ways and Means committee in the Eighty-third Congress was assured, he announced that he would introduce into the House on January

3, a bill to cut individual income taxes an average of nearly 5½ per cent in 1953 and another 5 per cent in 1954. Reed announced at the same time that he favored permitting the excess profits tax to expire on June 30, 1953.

Without apparently consulting the new President, who made it clear in his State of the Union message that he believed reduction of revenue should wait on balancing of the budget, Reed introduced almost with the opening of Congress a measure (H.R.1) to repeal on June 30 an already authorized 11 per cent income tax increase, and at the end of January declared that the House itself would delay passage of his bill "only over my dead body." On February 16, "without even bothering to hold hearings" (*Time*), the Ways and Means Committee approved the Reed bill by a vote of 21 to 4. Nevertheless (wrote John D. Morris of the New York *Times*), the measure "faced a possible ten-week delay in the Rules Committee and an uncertain fate in the Senate."

Although the excess profits tax was continued in 1953 despite his position against it, Reed is carrying on his battle against high taxes. He warned, in the fall of 1953, that any proposal for a general sales tax would meet opposition in the House of Representatives and predicted that Congress would not approve such a tax (New York *Times,* September 13, 1953). In August 1953, Reed was appointed to serve on the seventeen-man Commission on Foreign Economic Policy which will study and make a report on American tariff and trade policies.

A member of the bar of the State of New York, Federal district Court, United States Court of Appeals and the United States Supreme Court, Congressman Reed is also a member of the Society of American Arts and Letters, the Council of Cornell University, Delta Chi fraternity and the Quill and Dagger. He is a 32d degree Mason, a Knight of Pythias, and a Kiwanian. Mrs. Reed, the former Georgia E. Ticknor, is the parliamentarian of the Congressional Club. The Reeds have one son, William Ticknor; their only daughter, Ruth Alden, died in 1947.

For recreation Reed enjoys physical exercise and reportedly often walks the four miles to his place of work on Capitol Hill (*Washington Post,* October 4, 1953).

References

N Y Sun p18 Mr 16 '44
N Y Times Mag p9+ Jl 5 '53 por
N Y World-Telegram Mag Mr 14 '53
U S News 34:50+ F 27 '53 por; 34: 64+ My 29 '53
Biographical Directory of the American Congress, 1774-1949 (1950)
Congressional Directory (1952)
Who's Who in America, 1952-53
Who's Who in Law, 1937
Who's Who in the Nation's Capital, 1938-39
Who's Who in United States Politics (1952)

REINARTZ, F(REDERICK) EPPLING, REV. DR. June 21, 1901- Clergyman; church organization official
Address: b. 231 Madison Avenue, New York 16; h. 254 Boulevard, New Rochelle, New York

Representing nearly 2,000,000 members and over 4,000 churches, the Reverend Dr. F. Eppling Reinartz has been general secretary of the United Lutheran Church in America since January 1, 1947. Previous to his election when

Fabian Bachrach

REV. DR. F. EPPLING REINARTZ

he succeeded Dr. Walton H. Greever, he served the organization, which is the largest Lutheran body in the United States, as first secretary for promotion from 1938-45. During 1945-46, he was pastor of the Evangelical Lutheran Church of the Holy Trinity in New York City. His earlier pastoral experience included service from 1930-38 as minister of St. John's Evangelical Lutheran Church in East Liverpool, Ohio, where he succeeded his father, who had been the pastor for forty-four years.

Frederick Eppling Reinartz was born in East Liverpool, Ohio, on June 21, 1901, the son of John Godfrey and Sarah Julia Pauline (Eppling) Reinartz, and one of seven children. Church leadership was a tradition in his family. He is the great-nephew of Johannes Huppertz, the first Lutheran missionary to Borneo, and the great-nephew of Sister Elizabeth Huppertz, who in 1849 helped found Passavant Hospital in Pittsburgh, Pennsylvania, the first general Protestant hospital in America.

Reared in his native town of East Liverpool, Ohio, F. Eppling Reinartz attended the local schools. In high school, he was captain of the track team, made dramatics one of his activities, and was editor of the year book.

In 1919 he entered Gettysburg College in Pennsylvania, where he majored in philosophy. His extracurricular activities included hold-

REINARTZ, F. EPPLING—*Continued*

ing the offices of president of his class and president of the student council. He was also captain of the college track team and debating team. He joined the dramatics club, and wrote the Alma Mater song of the college. To add to his financial income, he worked as a shipping clerk for the Electrical Power Installation Company, and as a warehouseman for a pottery concern. In 1924, Reinartz received a B.A. degree, with general final honors, from the college. As an undergraduate, he was elected to Phi Beta Kappa, Tau Kappa Alpha (honorary debate), Pen and Sword (honorary athletic), and was a member of Alpha Tau Omego fraternity.

During 1924-25, Reinartz attended the Divinity School of Harvard University; 1926-29 the Lutheran Theological Seminary in Philadelphia, Pennsylvania. During 1929-30, he was a graduate fellow and an instructor in New Testament Greek at the Seminary. On June 5, 1929, he was ordained by the Evangelical Lutheran Ministerium of Pennsylvania. He became in 1930 the pastor of St. John's Evangelical Lutheran Church, East Liverpool, Ohio, where he succeeded his father and remained until 1938.

Reinartz received the Bachelor of Divinity degree from Lutheran Theological Seminary in 1932, and was awarded a Master of Sacred Theology degree by this institution in 1934. Four years later he was appointed first secretary for promotion in the United Lutheran Church in America, with headquarters in Philadelphia. In 1942, he was appointed chairman of the organization's commission to the Federal Council of Churches of Christ in America, a position he retained until 1950.

Between World Wars I and II, Reinartz served as a corporal in the Reserve Officers Training Corps at Gettysburg College. In July, 1945, he was called to the pastorate of the Evangelical Lutheran Church of the Holy Trinity in New York City to succeed Dr. Paul E. Scherer. He preached his first sermon there as pastor in October of that year. One year later, in October 1946, he was elected general secretary of the United Lutheran Church in America, effective January 1, 1947. He functions as administrator, evangelist and counselor.

Dr. Reinartz was a signer for the United Lutheran Church in America of the Constitution of the National Council of Churches of Christ in U.S.A., established at Cleveland, Ohio, in November 1950. The new National Council, with 32,000,000 members in 30 national Protestant and Eastern Orthodox communions, merged several interdenominational agencies, including the Federal Council of Churches of Christ in America, into one comprehensive agency. It reflected a marked trend in 1950 among Lutherans in America to bring about closer unity among their own churches and fuller cooperation with other Protestant churches.

In August 1952, Dr. Reinartz was a delegate and chief of protocol to the Lutheran World Federation assembly in Hanover, Germany. As quoted by the New York *Times* (August 5, 1952), it was stated at this assembly that around "6,000,000 Lutherans" had had to flee

from their homes as war refugees. Plans were made to aid these displaced persons. In a sermon delivered at his former parish, the Evangelical Lutheran Church of the Holy Trinity in New York City, on January 11, 1953, Dr. Reinartz paid tribute to the many churchmen who opposed the persecution by the Nazi regime. He recognized four ideologies as warring for supremacy, namely "atheistic communism, national socialism (nazism), power politics, and Christianity" (New York *Times,* January 12, 1952). Christianity, he declared, is "man's largest fellowship."

From 1939 to 1945, Dr. Reinartz was a member of the staff of *The Lutheran,* a publication of the United Lutheran Church in America. From 1938-46, he was editor of the *Pastor's Plan Book* appearing annually. He edited a handbook entitled *Forth!* (1943), dealing with the study and promotion of Foreign Missions. In 1947, he became editor of the Year Book of the United Lutheran Church in America, a position he currently maintains. During 1948, Reverend Dr. Reinartz was co-editor of the Lutheran Youth Hymnal.

Dr. Reinartz is a member of the executive committee of the National Lutheran Council, the agency which functions for most Lutherans in America, carrying on public relations, services to military personnel and displaced persons, orphan missions, and ministry to college students. He is also a member of the U.S.A. Committee for the Lutheran World Federation, which in August 1949 voted to discontinue aid to the Hungarian church unless specified requirements were met. Since 1946, he has been a director of Wagner Memorial College, Staten Island, New York, which conferred on him a Doctor of Divinity degree in 1943. Gettysburg College also gave him this degree.

During 1944-50, Dr. Reinartz was a member of the advisory and executive committees of the Federal Council of Churches of Christ in America. From 1946-49, he served as a member of the promotion division of the Church World Service, an organization then comprising the Federal Council of Churches of Christ in America, the American Committee for the World Council of Churches, and the Foreign Missions Conference of North America. The clergyman was secretary of the committee of executive secretaries of the United Lutheran Church in America from 1939-45. During 1935-45, he served as a director of Lutheran Theological Seminary, and from 1936-42 was a member of the Board of Foreign Missions of the United Lutheran Church in America and secretary in 1943. In 1931-38, he was president of the Commission on Religious Ethics of East Liverpool, Ohio. His political affiliation is Republican.

As described by G. Paul Butler in *Best Sermons, 1949-50,* Dr. Reinartz is "a warm-hearted individual . . . with a good deal of the poet in him, and is a sharp observer of life." The editor adds that the sermon selected shows the churchman's "penetrating analysis, excellent word choice, spiritual insight, and vision."

On June 27, 1930, Reverend Dr. F. Eppling Reinartz married Isabella Lang Martin, a high school teacher and a graduate of Gettysburg College. Their children are Sara Jeannette, Carolyn Angela, and Frederick Eppling, II. The clergyman, who is five feet and eleven inches tall and weighs 180 pounds, has gray-green eyes and "graying" hair. He states his hobbies are watching baseball (he favors the Dodgers), reading biographies, writing musical improvisations, and swimming. He considers his work "a creatve Christian opportunity."

References

Butler, G. P. ed. Best Sermons, 1949-50
Religious Leaders of America, 1941-42
Who's Who in America, 1952-53
Who's Who in the East (1951)
Who's Who in New York, 1947

REINER, FRITZ Dec. 19, 1888-
Conductor

Address: b. c/o Chicago Symphony Orchestra, 220 S. Michigan Ave., Chicago 4, Ill.; h. Westport, Conn.

NOTE: This biography supersedes the article which appeared in *Current Biography* in 1941.

During a professional career of over forty years, Fritz Reiner has become recognized as an outstanding and versatile conductor. He has conducted opera, serious and comic; and the symphonic repertoire, classical, romantic and modern, in Europe, the United States and South America. Critics consider him an authoritative interpreter of the music of Richard Strauss. In addition, he has taught such prominent young American musicians as Leonard Bernstein and Lukas Foss.

Since 1948 Reiner has been one of the most popular conductors at the Metropolitan Opera House in New York. In the spring of 1953 it was announced that he would become the musical director and conductor of the Chicago Symphony Orchestra. Rudolf Bing, manager of the Metropolitan Opera, told the press: "I hope it will be possible for him to return as a guest conductor." For video audiences, Reiner is conducting the Chicago Symphony Orchestra on Wednesday nights over the DuMont television network for twenty-six weekly concerts.

Fritz Reiner was born in Budapest, Hungary on December 19, 1888. His father, Ignatz Reiner, hoped Fritz would become a lawyer. His mother, Vilma (Pollak) Reiner, was a good amateur musician and encouraged her son's interest in music. At his own request, he began to study the piano when he was six years old. Three years later, he was able to play the overture to Wagner's *Tannhäuser* from memory. "There is one person," he told Mary Braggiotti (New York *Post,* December 8, 1948), "to whom I owe more gratitude than to anyone else: Leo Weiner, the composer. I was eleven and he was twelve when he recognized that I should be a conductor. That's when I decided to go into music." When Reiner was thirteen years old, he made his

Bender

FRITZ REINER

debut as a conductor at the annual student concert of his high school.

The young musician entered the Royal Academy of Music in Budapest. Among his teachers were Béla Bártok, Hans Kössler and Stefan Thomán. He also continued his academic studies and, to please his father, studied law at the University of Budapest.

Upon being graduated from the Royal Academy of Music in 1908, Reiner was hired as singing coach of the Opéra Comique in Budapest. One evening when Bizet's *Carmen* was scheduled, the regular conductor became ill. In desperation, the manager turned to the nineteen-year-old Reiner and put him into the pit. "Nothing will ever again be so difficult," Reiner has recalled. When he became a teacher, he repeatedly told his students: "Be ready for an emergency. When an emergency comes, that is your opportunity."

Reiner then acquired invaluable experience in both operatic and symphonic conducting at the Landestheater in Laibach (1910) and in his native Budapest at the Volksoper (1911-1914). He married Berta Gardini and two daughters, Tussy and Eva, were born of this marriage. In Budapest he conducted one of the first European performances of Wagner's *Parsifal* outside of Bayreuth.

Early in 1914 Reiner was offered the conductorship of the Royal Opera House in Dresden. The appointment was extraordinary not only because of his youth but also because he was not a German. On arrival, he was asked to conduct all of the operas in Wagner's "Ring" cycle without rehearsal. He did this, successfully, and during the ensuing eight years achieved international prominence as conductor of one of the most important musical posts in Europe.

While at Dresden, he became the protégé of Artur Nikisch, the famous conductor. Cesar

REINER, FRITZ—Continued

Saerchinger wrote in the Saturday Review, May 31, 1952 that there is a " 'tamed Nikisch' in Reiner's persistent right-hand beat, the somewhat languid gestures of his left, and quasi-hypnotic use of the eyes."

He was also influenced by the "ascetic classicism" of Karl Muck and Gustav Mahler. Another important influence in Dresden was Richard Strauss, with whom Reiner studied the production of Salomé and the other Strauss operas. While conducting at Dresden, Reiner also had guest-conducting engagements in Hamburg, Berlin and Vienna.

Amid the unsettled conditions of post-war Germany, Reiner became dissatisfied with his position in Dresden. During 1921 and 1922, he acted as guest-conductor in Rome and Barcelona. In 1922, he was invited to become the musical director and conductor of the Cincinnati Symphony Orchestra. "I arrived in this blessed country," he recalls, "on September 26, 1922."

Reiner remained with the Cincinnati orchestra from 1922 until 1931. He made four visits to Europe where he was guest conductor of the La Scala Symphony Orchestra in Milan at Arturo Toscanini's invitation (1926-1930). In addition, he appeared at Budapest, Vienna, Stockholm, Venice, Turin, Rome, Naples and Buenos Aires. He became a United States citizen in 1928.

He resigned, in 1931, from the Cincinnati Symphony Orchestra to become head of the orchestra and opera departments and teacher of conducting at the Curtis Institute of Music in Philadelphia. Later he stated, "when students have completed a course under my direction, anyone of them can stand up before an orchestra they have never seen before and conduct correctly a new piece at first sight, without verbal explanation and by means of only manual technic."

In an article in Etude of October 1951, Reiner also declared that "each conductor develops (gestures and special signals) out of his physical and suggestive power. . . .The best conducting technic is that which achieves the maximum of musical result with the minimum of (physical) effort. . . .The conductor must have a stimulating personality . . . and a thorough musical, artistic, literary, historical background . . . [it is indispensable] to study and restudy scores. . . .I do not believe a conductor can be accomplished under fifty."

While teaching at the Curtis Institute, Reiner organized a new opera company combining the Philadelphia Symphony Orchestra and the Philadelphia Grand Opera under the management of the Philadelphia Orchestral Association. Reiner has said of opera that it "is easier to absorb than symphonic music, because it is a show. It is a gate to the musical world. You learn history from it, ethnology, geography. That's why opera is such a worthy art—and why . . . it manages to survive" (New York Post, December 8, 1948).

During this period, Reiner also conducted opera in London during the coronation season of 1936, and in San Francisco (1936, 1937 and 1938) and has conducted the New York Philharmonic-Symphony, the Philadelphia Symphony and other leading orchestras. He made numerous radio appearances on the Ford Sunday Evening Hour and for the British Broadcasting Company (BBC) in England.

Dr. Reiner became, in 1938, the musical director of the Pittsburgh Symphony orchestra, a post he held for the next ten years. Under his direction the orchestra became one of the leading symphony groups in the country. He continued his work at the Curtis Institute of Music until May 1941.

The conductor resigned his position in Pittsburgh in 1948 because the orchestra's directors wanted to meet a deficit by decreasing the number of players and the length of the season. He told Newsweek (March 8, 1948) that "I agreed to let them reduce my salary if they would not reduce the number of men or the length of the season." In the fall of that year, he became a regular conductor at the Metropolitan Opera.

He experienced some of his greatest triumphs in conducting the operas of Mozart, Wagner, Richard Strauss, and Bizet's Carmen. Richard Strauss wrote to him in 1948 when Strauss heard that Reiner would conduct his Salomé: "That is good news. . . .Opera needs men like you." Virgil Thomson said of the Salomé: "One of the great music-dramatic performances of our century."

After the announcement of Reiner's engagement with the Chicago Symphony, the Metropolitan's Opera News of April 6, 1953 published a eulogy of Reiner echoing Rudolph Bing's hope that the conductor would return. Discussing his Chicago plans with Jay S. Harrison in the New York Herald-Tribune of March 22, 1953, Reiner announced that he was planning to emphasize contemporary American music. For his first season, he has chosen works by Aaron Copland, Samuel Barber, Walter Piston, Alvin Etler and Virgil Thomson.

The conductor was decorated an Officer of the Crown of Italy in 1930. He also received honorary music degrees from the University of Pennsylvania in 1940 and from the University of Pittsburgh in 1941.

Reiner's favorite composer is Mozart and his favorite among his own recordings include the six Brandenburg concertos of Bach and Beethoven's Symphony No. 2. A review of the Reiner recording of Bartók's Concerto for Orchestra in the Saturday Review of Literature of December 25, 1948, stated that Reiner "clarified the composer's purpose with a magnificent sense of contrast and balance."

Reiner has encouraged conductors to include modern music on their concert programs. He was the first conductor to play Paul Hindemith's compositions in the United States, and has played five of Sergei Prokofiev's symphonies, three symphonies of Dmitri Shostakovich, and many works of Igor Stravinsky and Béla Bartók. He has also conducted first performances by such contemporary American composers as Leonard Bernstein, Walter Piston and Morton Gould. Included among the conductor's compositions are a string quartet and several songs.

When not conducting, Reiner tries to spend as much time as possible at his home in Westport, Connecticut with his wife, Carlotta Irwin (whom he married in 1930). His hobbies are photography (his pictures have appeared in *Country Life* and *Arts & Decorations*), reading and languages.

References

Etude 68:16+ N '50; 69:16+ O '51
Mus Am 72:3 D 15 '52
Newsweek 31:78 Mr 8 '48; 33:74 F 14 '49
N Y Herald Tribune IV p6 Mr 22 '53
Opera N 17:5 Ap 6 '53
Sat R 35:42+ My 31 '52
Time 53:77 F 14 '49
Baker, T. ed. Biographical Dictionary of Musicians (1940)
Ewen, D. Dictators of the Baton (1943)
Gramophone Shop Encyclopedia of Recorded Music (1948)
Saleski, G. Famous Musicians of Jewish Origin (1949)
Thompson, O. ed. International Cyclopedia of Music and Musicians (1949)
Thomson, V. The Art of Judging Music (1948)
Who's Who in America, 1952-53

RENAUD, MADELEINE *See* Barrault, J., and Renaud, M.

REUTER, ERNST July 29, 1889—Sept. 29, 1953 Mayor of the Western Sector of Berlin; joined the German Social Democratic party before World War I; served for three months in 1921 as secretary-general of the German Communist party but returned thereafter to the Social Democrats; entered Berlin politics and as chief of the transport and utilities department developed the city's subway system; elected as Reichstag member (1930) and as Mayor of Magdeburg (1931); after three imprisonments by the Nazis, he spent World War II in Turkey as a specialist in economics and as a professor; returned to Berlin to become its Lord Mayor in 1948; rallied West Berliners against Communist influence; was a strong advocate of German friendship with the West. See *Current Biography,* 1949.

Obituary

N Y Times p1 S 30 '53

REUTHER, VICTOR (GEORGE) (rōōth'ẽr) Jan. 1, 1912- Labor leader
Address: b. c/o Congress of Industrial Organization, 718 Jackson Pl., N.W., Washington, D.C.; h. 11304 Mark Twain St., Detroit 27, Mich.

As part of its activities in the fight to repel communism, the Congress of Industrial Organizations established in March, 1951, a European office and placed in charge of it as its special representative, Victor Reuther, the youngest of three brothers who have become important figures in the American labor movement. Previous to his appointment, Reuther was educational director of the 1,400,000 member United Automobile, Aircraft and Agricultural Implement Workers Union (U.A.W.) of which one brother, Walter, is president and another Roy, is coordinator of political activity.

Under Victor Reuther the U.A.W. developed one of the outstanding workers' educational programs in the country, spending nearly half a million dollars a year for this purpose. He helped to establish labor institutes, radio stations, moving picture producting units, drama groups, and summer schools.

On September 30, 1953 it was announced that Reuther would be succeeded as CIO representative in Europe by Michael Ross. Reuther will be assigned to national CIO headquarters as administrative assistant to his brother.

Victor George Reuther was born in Wheeling, West Virginia, on January 1, 1912, the son of Valentine and Anna (Stocker) Reuther. The father, president at twenty-three of the Ohio Valley Trades and Labor Assembly, taught his sons the first principles of unionism and helped them to develop as public speakers.

Following his graduation from the local high school, Victor Reuther studied economics and sociology at West Virginia University and later at Wayne University in Detroit. While attending Wayne, he roomed with his brother, Walter, at that time a foreman in the Ford Company plant. The brothers decided to pool some $800 in savings and take a trip abroad.

Starting out in January 1933, the Reuthers landed in England. They bicycled through England, Belgium, Holland, Scandinavia and France. The brothers also visited Italy and Germany and saw fascism in power. Proceeding to Russia, they worked for sixteen months as machinists in the Gorki auto plant. They frequently noticed the disappearance of fellow workers, but Communist control of all the avenues of information, permitted the Reuthers to obtain only hints of what was occurring. Leaving Russia, they traveled across Siberia, India and Japan where they obtained jobs on a ship bound for the United States.

Returning to Detroit in the latter part of 1935, Victor Reuther went to work for the Kelsey-Hayes Wheel Company. When auto union organizers came to Detroit, Victor joined the union and helped launch West Detroit local 174. He was a leader of the first sit-down strike in the Detroit area in 1936 which resulted in winning union recognition and a wage increase at the Kelsey-Hayes Wheel Company. Through the impetus of this victory, local 174's membership which was originally seventy-eight jumped to 30,000 in the next few months.

Afterwards, Reuther's activities were transferred to Flint, Michigan, where a crucial struggle between the U.A.W. and the General Motors Corporation broke out in December, 1936. Reuther assisted in mapping the strategy for the 50,000 Flint strikers. General Motors signed a union agreement with the U.A.W. on February 11, 1937. For the next four years Reuther played important parts in a series of organiz-

Wide World Photos

VICTOR REUTHER

ing drives which culminated with the unionization of the Ford Company.

During the war, Reuther served as a labor member on the War Manpower Commission. He was also co-director of the war policy division of the UAW, helping to increase the production of essential goods by emphasizing the peaceful settlement of labor disputes.

From the beginning, the U.A.W. has been marked by internal disputes between the Communist wing and their left-wing supporters, and the anti-communist wing led by Walter Reuther.

This factional dispute was climaxed at the U.A.W. convention held in March 1946 where the anti-communists elected Walter Reuther president of the union. Although they failed to win control of the UAW executive committee, they were able to make Victor Reuther educational director. He removed the Communists who had been using that office as a key post in the battle for control. He then gathered together a group of anti-communists and gave them intensive training in public speaking and parliamentary law. By the next UAW convention in November 1947 this training resulted in the election of a complete slate of anti-communists.

Through union literature, films, speeches, and the U.A.W. monthly, *Ammunition*, members learned the aims of their union and the techniques for making it most effective. Reuther believes that strong unions are part of a system of checks and balances which is essential for the peaceful solution of labor-management problems. But beyond that, Reuther believes, "unionism is also one of the institutions through which men are seeking to satisfy a thirst for community life" (New York *Times*, September 28, 1947). Union members are, therefore, constantly being encouraged and helped to im-

prove local education, start consumer cooperatives and participate in politics.

The unionist served as fraternal delegate of the CIO at the London meetings in 1948 of the Trade Union Advisory Committee of the European Recovery Program and as the representative of American labor and co-chairman of the Anglo-American Committee on Productivity for ECA. After a study of British industry, he made a number of suggestions to increase its efficiency. In this connection, however, he insists that raising industrial productivity does not automatically improve workers' standards. He believes that workers must win for themselves, through trade union action, higher wages, shorter hours and better working conditions.

On his return from Europe in the spring of 1949, Reuther and his wife were sitting one night in the living room of their home, reading. Suddenly a shotgun was fired through the window, almost exactly as it had been at his brother Walter thirteen months before. One bullet pierced Reuther's right eye. Six others struck him in the face and neck. He was rushed to the hospital. The murderous assault, still unsolved, meant only a temporary halt to Reuther's activities. Less than two months later he was able to speak at the U.A.W. convention in July, 1949.

Reuther was one of a committee of three sent by the CIO to study the trade union and economic conditions of Europe in 1951. Among the committee's recommendations were that American labor help European workers to build strong trade unions as a means of resisting communism. This advice led to the establishment of the CIO European office and to the appointment of Victor Reuther as its representative.

Traveling widely over free Europe, Reuther worked closely with the anti-communist International Confederation of Free Trade Unions. One of their joint projects is to improve the housing facilities of European workers. In his periodic reports to American labor Reuther has stressed the need of supporting European unions in their efforts "for a better and more secure world."

With his new assignment at CIO headquarters in Washington, Victor Reuther will be his brother Walter's "eyes, ears, and voice on CIO work". He will also represent the CIO at conferences with representatives of the Administration.

The labor leader married Sophia Good on July 18, 1936. At that time and for some years later, she was an organizer for the U.A.W. The couple have three children: Carole Luise, Eric Val and John Stocker. Reuther's hobbies are swimming, cycling, tennis, ping pong, woodworking, and gardening.

References

Am Mercury 76:3+ My '53
Bsns W p166 O 10 '53
Newsweek 33:19+ Je 6 '49 por
Time 53:24+ Je 6 '49
Who's Who in Labor (1946)
Howe, I. UAW and Walter Reuther (1949)

REYNOLDS, R(ICHARD) S(AMUEL)
Aug. 15, 1881- Business executive

Address: b. c/o Reynolds Metals Company, Richmond 19, Va.; h.° 300 Old Lock Lane, Richmond, Va.

Now second only to the Aluminum Company of America in aluminum production, the Reynolds Metals Company, founded by R. S. Reynolds, entered into competition with Alcoa eleven years ago. Before setting up his own company in 1912, Reynolds was employed by his uncle, the late R. J. Reynolds, and had attained the rank of vice-president in the latter's tobacco business at the time of his resignation. Reynolds' company, known as the United States Foil Company before it became the Reynolds Metals Company in 1928, specialized in the fabrication of metal foils until 1941, when it added ingot aluminum to its production. President of the organization until 1948, Reynolds resigned at that time and became chairman of the board.

One of seven children of Abram David and Senah (Hoge) Reynolds, Richard Samuel Reynolds was born in Bristol, Tennessee, on August 15, 1881. His father, who had been a major in the Civil War, was engaged in the tobacco business. When Richard had completed his studies at King College in Bristol, Tennessee, the University of Virginia at Charlottesville, and Columbia University in New York City, where he majored in law, he accepted employment in 1903 with the R. J. Reynolds Tobacco Company. His beginning salary with the organization, which had been founded by three of his uncles, was, reported *Reader's Digest* (June 1944), fifty dollars a month. Within four years of his joining the company, the same publication further stated, its income had been doubled by one of his inventions, a tin tobacco container which replaced the cheesecloth bags formerly used. Another improvement which he instituted was the mixing of burley tobacco with stronger types to produce a milder cigarette. As sales manager and vice-president of the tobacco company, he introduced Prince Albert Smoking Tobacco.

In 1912 Reynolds resigned from the R. J. Reynolds Company to found a business of his own, with the intention of exploiting the natural resources of lands in eastern Tennessee and western North Carolina. During World War I the organization turned to production of war materials and developed an inexpensive waterproof paper container for powder to replace steel containers. The United States Foil Company was organized by Reynolds in 1918 in Louisville, Kentucky, and was the first to produce metal foil wrappers for such articles as candy, cigarettes, chewing gum, and bottles. The foil was fabricated from lead, tin, and aluminum, the latter material becoming the predominant one of the three. The company, of which Reynolds was president and director, soon grew from one plant to a number scattered along the Eastern seaboard and bought a controlling interest in railroads and mines and in the Eskimo Pie Corporation. In 1928 the United States Foil Company transferred its

R. S. REYNOLDS

manufacturing function to the subsidiary Reynolds Metals Company and became a holding company. Partly because of the large variety of products which it manufactured, the organization was able to withstand the depression and continued to find new applications for foil in many fields. In 1938 the company began the manufacture of sheet aluminum, rod, and extrusion.

Before the United States entered World War II, Reynolds, since his company was a large consumer of aluminum, urged the board chairman of the Aluminum Company of America, Arthur V. Davis, to expand the production capacity of Alcoa (*Time*, May 26, 1941). Foreseeing the huge demand for aluminum which would be created by defense production of aircraft, he suggested that Davis ask for government funds to finance expansion. At this time government agencies and Alcoa were agreed that the present productive capacity would be sufficient. Convinced that his view was sound, Reynolds in 1940 borrowed $20 million from the Reconstruction Finance Corporation, using as security mortgages on the twenty-eight plants then owned by Reynolds Metals to finance the building of aluminum reduction plants. Long a customer of Alcoa, from which it bought the basic metal for fabrication, the Reynolds company was the first in over fifty years to enter into competition with it in the production of virgin aluminum. Since all existing bauxite mines were owned by Alcoa, Reynolds opened up new mines in Arkansas to supply his plants with the raw ore from which aluminum is made. The first reduction plant, at Listerhill, Alabama, near Muscle Shoals, began operation only six months after construction was begun (coincidentally with this, in March 1941, the government acknowledged the accuracy of Reynolds' prediction by proclaiming that an emergency existed in aluminum), and a second was completed soon afterward at Longview, Wash-

REYNOLDS, R. S.—*Continued*

ington. Reynolds Metals also built other defense plants for the Navy and the Defense Plant Corporation, and produced such needed material as laminated foil-lined wrappers for ammunition.

Testifying before a Senate committee in 1944, Reynolds stressed that aluminum could and should play a large part in the American postwar economy. He detailed uses to which the metal could be put, such as combining it with soft woods to provide a building material. He went on to warn of the possible consequences if basic aluminum production were allowed to return to the control of one company, stating that the many industries which could use the metal would be wary of becoming dependent on a commodity so controlled. The executive repeated this warning on February 28, 1945, in testimony given before the Senate Committee on Small Business. Criticizing the policies of the War Department, the Reconstruction Finance Corporation, and the Aluminum Company of America, he reviewed the difficulties which had attended the entry of Reynolds Metals into the aluminum producing field, and urged government support in developing competition in the postwar light metals industry. As reported by *Fortune* (May 1946), the Reynolds company produced 7 per cent of the aluminum supply during the war and lost money on ingot production, making up for this loss by the profit on fabrication.

"The postwar possibilities of the aluminum industry," Reynolds told his company's stockholders, "are almost unlimited. It is a definite part of your company's policy to cooperate with other industries and achieve a use of its metal in combination with other materials such as steel, wood, paper and plastics" (quoted by the New York *Times*, April 9, 1945). Expressing his belief in the possibility of great expansion in aluminum production Reynolds emphasized new purposes to which aluminum could be put in home construction and furnishings. Reynolds Metals first leased and later purchased many of the government-owned aluminum plants which were disposed of at the war's end. In April 1948, the industrialist warned of a possible aluminum shortage which would impede the rearmament program, stating that the stockpile existing at the end of the war had been absorbed by greater demand for the metal. As a solution he suggested that plants with a yearly capacity of a million tons be constructed.

When Reynolds resigned in August 1948 as president of Reynolds Metals Company to become chairman of the board, he was succeeded by his son, R. S. Reynolds, Jr. (Reynolds' three other sons also hold important positions in his company.) At the time of Reynolds' resignation, the organization's productive capacity exceeded the entire output of aluminum in the United States before his company entered that field. Expansion of the Reynolds Metals plants at Listerhill was announced in October 1949 and further increases in capacity have been made since then to accommodate defense needs. Reynolds, his son J. Louis Reynolds (vice-president of Reynolds Metals), and Governor Arthur B. Langlie of Washington spoke at a ceremony in Longview, Washington, on August 29, 1952, on the completion of additional production facilities in the Reynolds plant at that location. Previously, on January 8, 1952, the Reynolds company announced progress on plans for the construction of a $42 million aluminum plant in San Patricio County, Texas, to process bauxite shipped from Reynolds' rich bauxite deposits in Jamaica.

According to a report issued October 21, 1953 the Reynolds Metal Company established new records for sales and earnings in the first nine months of 1953. The consolidated net profit amounted to $15,704,253, an increase of 68.8 per cent over the $9,304,914 earned in the first nine months of 1952.

Reynolds holds the chairmanship of the board of Reynolds Research Corporation, Reynolds Mining Corporation, Eskimo Pie Corporation, Robertshaw Fulton Controls Company, Richmond Radiation Company, Charter Oak Stove and Range Company, and Reynolds Internacional de Mexico. He is a director of Frozen Products, Inc., Plantation Yacht Harbor, Inc., Reynolds Aluminum Company, and the United States Sanitary Manufacturing Company; the president and a director of the United States Foil Company, the Reynolds Alloys Company, and Arlette, Inc.; and is associated with other Reynolds subsidiaries. In June 1949 he was awarded the honorary degree of Doctor of Laws by Hampden Sydney College at Hampden Sydney, Virginia. Known as the "poet-industrialist" (New York *Sun*), Reynolds has written two books, *War Enthroned and Other Poems* and *Crucible; Poems* (published in 1950). "Credo," a poem, appeared in the *North American Review* in December 1936. To encourage both poetry and home building, he arranged a meeting of writers in September 1937 to compose a collective poem on homes.

By his marriage to Julia Louise Parham on December 23, 1905, Reynolds is the father of four sons: Richard S., J. Louis, William G., and David Parham. Besides writing poetry for relaxation, the executive enjoys reading and playing bridge and canasta. His clubs are the Metropolitan in New York City, the New York Yacht (Nassau County, Long Island), the Surf and the Indian Creek Country Club (Miami Beach, Florida), the Country Club of Virginia and the Commonwealth (Richmond, Virginia), the Pendennis Club and the Louisville Country Club (Louisville, Kentucky), and the Country Club (Bristol, Virginia). He is a member of the Presbyterian church. He has gray-blue eyes, gray hair, is five feet four and one-half inches tall, and weighs 160 pounds. Lemuel F. Parton in the New York *Sun* (June 4, 1941) describes him as "a quiet, soft-spoken man, round-faced and stocky in figure."

References

N Y Sun p21 Je 4 '41
Read Digest 44:81-4 Je '44

Business Executives of America (1950)
Who's Who in America, 1952-53
Who's Who in the South and Southwest (1950)

RHOADS, C(ORNELIUS) P(ACKARD)
June 20, 1898- Physician; pathologist
Address: b. c/o Memorial Center for Cancer and Allied Diseases, 444 E. 68th St., New York 21

As director of Memorial Center for Cancer and Allied Diseases, Dr. C. P. Rhoads, noted physician and authority on malignant growths, heads the world's largest concentrated program for the study, treatment, and ultimate elimination of cancer. This program, instituted in 1950, sprang from a co-operative merger of Memorial Hospital, James Ewing Municipal Hospital, Sloan-Kettering Institute for Cancer Research, and Sloan-Kettering Division of Cornell University Medical College. Prior to the integration of the facilities of these four major medical institutions,. Dr. Rhoads had directed Memorial Center and Sloan-Kettering Institute for Cancer Research in their separate functions. In World War II as colonel in the Army Medical Corps he served as chief of the medical division of Chemical Warfare Services, and in the postwar period has accepted a number of appointments in Federal organizations, among them the post of consultant at the Brookhaven National Laboratories of the Atomic Energy Commission (1947-49). Rhoads, who is Professor of Pathology, Department of Biology and Growth, Sloan-Kettering Division of Cornell University Medical School, has written many articles for medical periodicals on cancer and allied subjects.

Cornelius Packard Rhoads was born in Springfield, Massachusetts, on June 20, 1898, to George Holmes Rhoads, an ophthalmologist, and Harriet E. (Barney) Rhoads. Having completed college preparatory courses at Central High School in his native city, he enrolled for his premedical training at Bowdoin College, Maine, from which he received his B.A. degree in 1920. He later attended Harvard Medical School, where he became president of his class and was graduated *cum laude* in 1924 with the M.D. degree.

After serving a year's internship (1924-25) in surgery at Peter Bent Brigham Hospital in Boston, Massachusetts, Dr. Rhoads was appointed a Trudeau fellow at Trudeau Sanitorium, New York, for 1925-26. The following fall he returned to Massachusetts as an instructor in pathology at Harvard Medical School and an assistant pathologist at Boston City Hospital. For the next eleven years Rhoads was on the staff of the Rockefeller Institute for Medical Research in New York: from 1928 to 1933 as an associate, from 1931 to 1939 as a pathologist in the hospital of the institute, and from 1933 to 1939 as an associate member in charge of service for the study of hematologic disorders.

In 1940 when Dr. Rhoads became director of New York's Memorial Hospital for Cancer and Allied Diseases, in succession to Dr. James Ewing, the hospital, which had been founded in 1884, was described by *Time* as the "largest cancer institution in the world." The New York *Times* in 1943 reported that it had a 213-bed capacity and a research program costing $170,000 annually. By mid-1950 the cancer center headed by Rhoads, having combined the resources of four major medical institutions, had some 600 beds at its disposal and a yearly research program of $1,800,000—in 1952, according to the New York *Times*, Memorial's research program amounted to over $2,500,000 a year. Expansion and integration of facilities was begun in 1945 when plans were made by New York City to build a municipal cancer hospital, the James Ewing Hospital, which would cooperate closely with Memorial. At about this time $4 million was provided by the Alfred P. Sloan Foundation to construct for the cancer center a research division, to be known as the Sloan-Kettering Institute for Cancer Research. The Strang Cancer Prevention Clinic also joined the Memorial project. In the fall of 1947 Rhoads, who emphasized the importance of a university for the study of cancer, pointed out that in the space of five years Memorial had grown from a simple hospital to a scientific and educational institution concerned with all phases of neoplastic disease. In a step described by Rhoads as "the first large-scale recognition by a university of the semi-independent position of a program for cancer treatment and research in the United States" (quoted by the New York *Herald Tribune*), Cornell in June 1950 signed an agreement to set up a graduate division in its medical college, the Sloan-Kettering Division of Cornell University Medical College, as part of the unified effort against cancer. The Society of New York Hospital also agreed to make available to Memorial its clinical and research facilities.

With a staff of several hundred technicians, chemists, librarians, statisticians, laboratory assistants, and leading scientists from all parts of the world, Dr. Rhoads, who had become Professor of Pathology at Cornell Medical College (1940) and director of Sloan-Kettering Institute (1945), was chosen to head this complex organization for the study, diagnosis, treatment, and elimination of cancer. At the Sloan-Kettering Institute "more than 10,000 chemicals, molds, hormones, and viruses have been tested for their ability to destroy cancer in animals and in test tubes," according to an article in *Collier's* (October 4, 1952). "Altogether 200 substances have been uncovered that restrain the growth of experimental cancer." Among a large number of reports made by Rhoads on the work of the cancer center was his address in October 1946 before the New York Herald Tribune Forum on Current Events, in which he explained the limited use of atomic energy thus far in cancer treatment. In October 1950 he told an assembly of the District of Columbia Medical Society about new hormone treatments which were expected to show promise in cancer therapy.

In December 1951 Dr. Rhoads disclosed at a meeting of the American Academy of Dermatology and Syphilology that virus organisms were being bred to attack cancer and suggested that this technique had opened a new field of research in treatment of the disease. At the time of the dedication in October 1952 of the $1,440,000 Physiology Laboratory and Beta-

RHOADS, CORNELIUS—*Continued*

tron Unit of Memorial Center, a New York *Times* editorial pointed out, "It will give Memorial's cancer specialists what they want— that is, a machine which will deluge a malignant tumor with a deadly dose of X-rays yet virtually spare surrounding healthy tissues."

Additionally occupied during World War II as a colonel in the medical corps of the United States Army, Rhoads served from 1943 to 1945 as chief of the medical division of the Chemical Warfare Service. In this capacity he directed the establishment of the Toxicological Research Laboratory at Edgewood Arsenal, Maryland, and the Medical Research Laboratory at the Dugway Proving Ground, Tooele, Utah; he also set up medical testing stations at Bushnell, Florida, and San Jose Island, Canal Zone. For his contributions toward advances in chemical warfare he was awarded in May 1945 the Legion of Merit, his citation reading in part: "He developed new methods of diagnosis and treatment for the relief of injuries due to toxic chemicals and perfected a compound to counteract the effects of blister gas. . . .He also developed equipment for detecting the presence of war gases in air, food, and water." Also during the war years Rhoads was chairman of the blood procurement program and vice-chairman of the committee on treatment of gas casualties for the National Research Council. He was later associated with the council as chairman of the committee on growth (1945-48), member of the committee on atomic casualties (1946-47), chairman of the executive committee of the committee on growth (1946-47), member of the advisory committee of the chemical-biological coordination center (1946-47), and member-at-large of the division of medical sciences (1946-47).

Other postwar appointments to Federal organizations held by Dr. Rhoads are special consultant to the national advisory cancer council of the United States Public Health Service (beginning in 1947), consultant at the Brookhaven National Laboratories of the Atomic Energy Commission (1947-49), and consultant to the medical division of the chemical corps of the Army Chemical Center in Maryland (beginning in 1948). In July 1952 the cancer specialist accepted a twelve-month assignment as consultant in oncology at the United States Naval Hospital in St. Albans, New York. A prominent member of the American Cancer Society, Rhoads also belongs to more than thirty professional organizations, among them the New York Academy of Medicine, the American Association for the Advancement of Science, the American Geriatrics Society, the American Society of Tropical Medicine, the Society of Medical Jurisprudence, the Blood Transfusion Association, and the American Radium Society. He is currently a trustee of the Charles F. Kettering Foundation, which contributes financially to Memorial Center.

An authority in several branches of medicine, Dr. Rhoads has written on poliomyelitis, renal physiology, anaemia, deficiency disease, diet in experimental cancer, clinical biochemistry of gastric and other cancers, steroid metastasis in cancer, chemotherapy of cancer, and related subjects. A complete list of his publications since 1926 comprises over one hundred articles. The most recent include "Kreboizen" (*Science*, September 14, 1951); "Cancer Chemotherapy" (*Review Gastroenterol*, March 1952); "Cancer Early Diagnosis" (*Americana Annual*, 1952); "Fundamental Concepts Relating to Pathogenesis of Cancer" (*New York State Journal of Medicine*, July 1952). He edited, and prepared the introduction to, "Viruses as Causative Agents in Cancer," published in *Annals of the New York Academy of Science*, July 10, 1952. Rhoads holds honorary D.Sc. degrees from Bowdoin College (conferred on June 24, 1944) and from Williams College (conferred on June 16, 1952). Another honor received by Memorial's director was the Clement Cleveland award for outstanding work in cancer control during 1947, an award made annually by the New York Cancer Committee.

Dr. Rhoads is a member of the Army and Navy Club, the Century Association, Harvard Club of Boston, Harvard Medical Alumni Association, the Museum of the Marine Historical Association, and the University Club, and is a former member of the Harvard Club of New York City. On September 9, 1936, he married Katherine Southwick Bolman. His recreations are sailing, reading, and collecting Civil War trophies. Standing five feet eleven inches tall, he weighs 190 pounds; he has blue eyes and gray hair. Observers of his work have commented on his energy, initiative, and tenacity in the face of great challenges.

References

    Colliers 130:25+ O 4 '52 por
    N Y Herald Tribune p36 N 3 '46
    Read Digest 55:13+ S '49
    Time 53:66+ Je 27 '49 por

    American Men of Science (1951)
    International Who's Who, 1952
    New York State Medical Directory (1952)
    Who Knows—And What (1951)
    Who's Important in Medicine, 1951
    Who's Who in America, 1952-53
    Who's Who in The East (1951)
    World Biography (1948)

RICHARDSON, SETH (WHITLEY) Feb. 4, 1880—Mar. 17, 1953 Lawyer; United States Government official; Republican; assistant State's attorney for Cass County, North Dakota (1904-08); special assistant to the North Dakota State's attorney (1919-20); United States District Attorney for North Dakota (1923); Assistant Attorney General of the United States (1929) assigned to head Public Lands and Indian Affairs Division of the Department of Justice; chief counsel for the Congressional committee investigating the Pearl Harbor bombing; chairman Loyalty Review Board (1947-50); headed Subversive Activities Control Board (1950-51). *See Current Biography*, 1948.

Obituary

    N Y Times p31 Mr 18 '53

RICKOVER, HYMAN G(EORGE) Jan. 27, 1900- United States Navy officer
Address: h. 4801 Connecticut Ave., N.W., Washington, D.C.

In charge of the United States Navy project which produced the atomic-powered submarine SSN-571 *Nautilus* from its conception in 1947, Captain Hyman George Rickover received from former Secretary of the Navy Dan Kimball the following commendation: "Captain Rickover more than any other individual is responsible for the rapid development of the nuclear ship program. . . .He has accomplished the most important piece of development in the history of the Navy" (*Look*, March 10, 1953). Rickover was also in charge of planning and building the power plants for a second atomic submarine (with a different heat exchange system) and an atomic-powered aircraft carrier. A graduate of the United States Naval Academy at Annapolis, during World War II he headed the Electrical Section of the Bureau of Ships and received the Legion of Merit for his work there.

Advanced to Rear Admiral by a Navy Selection board in July, 1953, Rickover was selected in October to supervise the new program for the construction of the United States' first full-scale atomic energy plant for peacetime use.

Born in Russia on January 27, 1900, Hyman George Rickover is the son of Abraham and Rachel (Unger) Rickover. His parents immigrated to the United States and settled in Chicago, Illinois, where his father was a tailor. Young Rickover attended John Marshall High School and after his graduation was appointed to the United States Naval Academy and commissioned an ensign in 1922.

Having served five years aboard the U.S.S. *Lavallette* and the U.S.S. *Nevada,* he returned to Annapolis to study electrical engineering in the postgraduate school. He continued his work in this subject at Columbia University to earn the degree of Master of Science in electrical engineering in December 1929. Further study in submarine training followed, from January to June of 1930, at the Submarine Base in New London, Connecticut, and he next spent three years in the U.S.S. S-9 and the U.S.S. S-48. From July 1933 until April 1935 Rickover was attached to the Office of the Inspector of Naval Material in Philadelphia, Pennsylvania. He returned to sea duty aboard the U.S.S. *New Mexico* and in the fall of 1937 assumed command of the U.S.S. *Finch,* later that year reporting for duty at the Navy Yard at Cavite, Philippine Islands. At this time he also became an E.D.O. (engineering duty only) officer.

In June 1939 Rickover returned to the United States for assignment to the Bureau of Ships of the Navy Department at Washington, D.C., and throughout the war served as head of the Electrical Section. He received the Legion of Merit in recognition of his effectiveness in procuring men and equipment to produce the Navy's electric power and lighting equipment. After a term of temporary duty from April to July 1945 on the staff of the Commander Service Force of the U.S. Pacific Fleet, he was made Industrial Manager at Okinawa and Com-

Wide World Photos
REAR ADM. HYMAN G. RICKOVER

manding Officer of the Naval Repair Base on that island.

The following December he became Inspector General of the Nineteenth Fleet, with headquarters at San Francisco. He left this post for an assignment at the Atomic Energy Commission's Manhattan Project at Oak Ridge, Tennessee, where he remained from June to December 1946. For his work as Assistant Director of Operations of the Manhattan District at Oak Ridge he received a Letter of Commendation from the War Department in recognition of his service in connection with the development of the atomic bomb.

On the completion of his Oak Ridge assignment, Rickover and four other officers who had been with him at the Manhattan Project toured atomic research installations and, convinced that an atomic submarine was possible, prepared and submitted plans for its construction to the Navy. The report was shelved, but Rickover, whose principal interest has long been submarines, continued to push the idea and by the end of 1947 had persuaded Admiral Chester Nimitz, Chief of Naval Operations, to write a letter in which he declared that "the atomic submarine is militarily desirable." Rickover obtained from the Atomic Energy Commission a definite statement that an atomic-powered engine was practical and got himself assigned to the AEC as head of the Naval Reactors Branch while retaining the Navy post as head of the Nuclear Power Division, thereby being able to supervise the work of both organizations.

The AEC proceeded with the design and construction of the reactors for the submarine while Rickover and his staff began planning the hull of the vessel. This staff is composed of both naval officers and civilians, the status within the group being determined not by Navy rank but by ability, with the result that a commander may take orders from a lieutenant.

(Continued next page)

RICKOVER, HYMAN—Continued

To get together his working force for the tremendous task of completing the *Nautilus* in the short time he demanded, Rickover recruited top men from industry, universities, and research organizations, offering them little but long hours and hard work. The New York *Times* (October 26, 1952) has stated, "His guiding principle is to enlist loyalty, encourage individualism . . . and give people all the responsibility they can possibly handle. An associate says of him: 'He seldom looks at the present—always at the future. And he helps others to think that way.' "

It is reported that "the devotion of the team of nuclear-power specialists to Rickover is almost fanatic. . . .He gets the last ounce of work out of his team, and nobody on his staff works harder than its chief. Their great enemy is time" (*Look*, March 10, 1953).

While the work on the submarine went on, Rickover established an atomic-sub school at the Massachusetts Institute of Technology and recruited officers from the submarine fleet for the three-year course. In order to save years in the construction of the *Nautilus* he had the atomic reactor, which was made in Arco, Idaho, by Westinghouse working with the AEC, built to the submarine's specifications. Ordinarily the reactor would have been tested first and then redesigned to fit into the vessel. The construction of the engine went on simultaneously with some of the preliminary research.

In 1950 it was decided to submit a report of progress to the Joint Chiefs of Staff and the go-ahead for the completion of the submarine was given when $40,000,000 of the Navy budget was assigned for its construction. The contract was awarded to the Electric Boat Company of Groton, Connecticut.

At the keel-laying of the *Nautilus* in June 1952 President Truman said, "The day that the propellers of this new submarine first bite into the water . . . will be the most momentous day in . . . atomic science since that first flash . . . in the desert seven years ago" (*Look,* Mar 10, 1953). The submarine, powered by a steam plant which turns the propulsion turbines connected with the propeller shaft, the steam being produced by a controlled atomic pile, can travel around the world without refueling. Able to stay beneath the surface for most of the time, and to dive deeper and travel at a greater speed than present submarines, the atomic sub can strike with deadly efficiency at enemy submarines, surface vessels, or targets far inland. "Anything a conventional submarine can do," says Rear Admiral Homer N. Wallin, Chief of the Bureau of Ships, "an atomic-powered submarine should do better" (*Collier's,* December 20, 1952).

Rickover began work on a submarine intermediate reactor to power a second sub while the first engine was still in construction. By 1949 he had completed sketches for an atomic reactor suitable for an aircraft carrier, and in 1952 initiated a third project, whose nature is still undisclosed.

Although Rickover's advancement from captain to rear admiral was supported by former Secretary of the Navy Dan Kimball (*Christian Science Monitor,* March 10, 1953), the Navy selection boards which determined promotions passed over the Captain twice, in July 1951 and 1952. *Look* reported that the selection boards found Rickover's experience too specialized for promotion to the post of rear admiral, which according to Navy precedent requires a background of all-around duty. As a result, Rickover was headed by Navy rule for mandatory retirement in June 1953. After the Senate Armed Services Committee took up the case, the Washington *Post* reported that Secretary of the Navy Robert Anderson agreed to appoint new selection boards to consider Rickover's retention and advancement "under precepts as favorable to him as the law permits" (March 10, 1953). The regular selection board, which met in July, was directed to promote one engineering officer "experienced and qualified in the field of atomic propulsive machinery for ships." In the interim, President Eisenhower approved a recommendation on March 27 that Captain Rickover be kept on active duty for another year (New York *Times,* March 28, 1953). Captain Rickover was promoted to Rear Admiral by the selection board.

Appointed in October, 1953 by Dr. Lawrence R. Hafstad who is director of the Atomic Energy Commission's reactor development division, Rickover will be responsible for the supervision of the new atomic industrial power project which will produce a minimum of 60,000 kilowatts of electrical energy—"capable of supplying a city of 60,000 to 100,000 population" (New York *Times,* October 23, 1953).

Admiral Rickover has worked on a new type of underwater craft powered by nuclear fission and an atomic-powered aircraft carrier. He was largely responsible for the shockproofing of electrical equipment on ships, noise reduction in submarines and the developments of infra-red signaling, an underwater detector and a magnetic mine sweeper.

Honors awarded Rickover include the Legion of Merit, the Commendation Ribbon with Oak Leaf Cluster, the World War I Victory Medal, the China Service Medal (1937), the American Defense Service Medal, the Asiatic-Pacific Campaign Medal, the American Campaign Medal, and the World War II Victory Medal. In 1948 he received the Order of the British Empire with the rank of Honorary Commander from the British Government for service during World War II in electrical research.

Rickover and his wife, the former Ruth Dorothy Masters, have one son, Robert. The naval officer's only hobby is reading: technical material, biography, history, and philosophy. The New York *Times* (October 26, 1952) has described him as "small—short and spare, gray, rather tired looking, not smiling often but actually having much humor and gentleness in him."

Admiral Rickover sums up his own philosophy in one sentence: "The more you sweat in peace the less you bleed in war."

References

Life 31:18 S 3 '51 por
Look 17:23 Mr 10 '53 por
N Y Times p14 O 26 '53 por

RILEY, SUSAN B. May 1, 1896- Educator; women's organization official
Address: b. c/o American Association of University Women, 1634 I St., N.W., Washington 6, D.C.; Department of English, George Peabody College for Teachers, Nashville, Tenn.; h. 1602 18th Ave., Nashville 4, Tenn.

Meeting in Atlantic City at the biennial convention in 1951, more than 1,000 delegates of the American Association of University Women unanimously elected Susan B. Riley, an educator, as association president for a four-year term. Dr. Riley, who began her teaching career in 1914, has been an officer of the A.A.U.W. almost continuously since 1934, first as president of the Nashville branch of the association, then as chairman of the education committee of the Tennessee division, and afterward in offices on a national level. Since 1928 she has been on the faculty of George Peabody College for Teachers in Nashville, where in 1947 she became professor of English.

Both parents of Susan B. Riley, who was born on May 1, 1896, in Brookhaven, Mississippi, were educators: her father, George Washington Riley, a Baptist minister, held the presidency of a number of denominational colleges; her mother, Lily (Waller) Riley, was for forty years teacher and dean of women in Baptist colleges in Mississippi. After spending her early childhood in Kentucky (her mother's native State), Texas, and Mississippi, Susan Riley attended high school in Jackson, Mississippi, to complete after three years the required number of college entrance units and proceed to college without graduating. From 1911 to 1914 she studied at Blue Mountain College for girls in Mississippi, where she took part in musical activities—voice, piano, and organ—and in the programs and dramatic productions of the Eunomian Literary Society. Before completing her undergraduate training, she began her career as a teacher, at the age of eighteen, in a public school in Houston, Mississippi. At the end of three years in Houston she taught for a year (1917-18) in Plano, Texas. In 1918 she returned to Blue Mountain College as an instructor and continued teaching on the college level for several years: at Blue Mountain until 1920 and at Hillman Junior College in Clinton, Mississippi, from 1920 to 1924.

While teaching at Hillman Junior College, Susan Riley resumed her own education, studying at George Peabody College for Teachers in Nashville, Tennessee, for her B.S. degree, which she received in 1923. After a year (1924-25) as teacher in a Sherman, Texas, public school, she returned to George Peabody College to take her M.A. degree in 1927. For the school year 1927-28 she taught at Western Kentucky State Teachers College in Bowling Green before joining the faculty of George Peabody College for Teachers. Since 1947 she has been a professor of English at Peabody and for some years was chairman of the English department. In the meantime, Susan Riley continued her own studies while teaching others: she was awarded her Ph.D. degree from George Peabody College in 1934, submitting for her

SUSAN B. RILEY

doctoral dissertation *The Life and Works of Albert Pike*, and took graduate courses at Vanderbilt and Columbia universities. Her study at Columbia, in 1930-31, was facilitated by a General Education Board fellowship, and in 1949 she was the recipient of a Carnegie grant-in-aid for research on nineteenth century American periodicals.

Dr. Riley's leadership in the American Association for University Women began nearly twenty years ago on a local level when, in 1934, she was elected president of the association's Nashville branch. After holding this office for two years, she became chairman for a six-year term of the education committee of the Tennessee State division. In 1945 she was elected to membership on the A.A.U.W. board of directors as vice-president from the Southern Central Region. At the association's national convention in 1947 Dr. Riley was one of the principal speakers; her address, "Education the Tool of Society," so impressed the delegates that many requested publication of the full text, which subsequently appeared in the June 1947 issue of the association's *Journal*. Becoming a member of the national education committee in 1949, Dr. Riley served with this group until her election to the presidency of the association two years later.

When more than 1,000 delegates of the American Association of University Women met at the 1951 convention in April in Atlantic City, they unanimously elected Dr. Riley to be their president for the next four years in succession to Dr. Althea K. Hottel, dean of women at the University of Pennsylvania. The A.A.U.W. comprises over 1,200 local branches with a membership of some 122,000 women from about 280 colleges and universities in the forty-eight States, Alaska, and Hawaii. Founded in 1882, the association has long worked for higher standards in education and for the more in-

RILEY, SUSAN B.—*Continued*

telligent participation of college women in civic and international affairs: it provides yearly fellowships to both American women and women from foreign countries; and sponsors projects in local branches for improved public schools, greater school-community cooperation, better motion picture, radio, and television programs. Also on a local level the A.A.U.W. through study groups, radio broadcasts, public meetings and other media helps to develop popular knowledge of American foreign policy, a fuller understanding of other countries, and an awareness of the United Nations and its work. The association has been active in sponsorship of the arts and in support of local and national legislation related to its program.

In a message published in the bulletins of various State divisions of the A.A.U.W. during the first year of her presidency, Susan Riley wrote: "As educated women there are certain specific responsibilities which we have in these critical times. We can combat the widespread criticism of public education which would weaken the very basis of a democratic form of society. We can oppose those tendencies which would level down our culture to the mediocre. We can give no credence to the loose and unsubstantial attacks on the integrity of both individuals and organizations." Giving the commencement address at Greensboro College (North Carolina) in May 1951, Dr. Riley had also stressed her sense of the obligation of the college graduate to society: "An educated person is better than an uneducated one only in so far as he matches his unusual privileges by meeting his responsibilities. . . .The untutored and inexperienced have aesthetically become the court of last appeal. . . .Reduction to uniformity, response to the sensational, the acceptance of goals which are personal and immediate rather than social and distant, passivity in accepting culturally what is foisted on us commercially . . . all this leveling down of our art connotes a loss of faith in the goodness and worth of people. . . .Educated individuals should not be ashamed to fight against the vulgarizing tendencies now thriving like weeds in a garden. . . . As persistently as we are being subjected to mediocre standards and cynicism, should we expose ourselves to habits of high standards and faith in human integrity."

Dr. Riley has frequently addressed other educational groups. She has also written articles for various professional journals as well as bibliographies and study guides on Southern literature. In 1939 she began contributing to the *Peabody Journal of Education* and several of her articles have appeared in the A.A.U.W. *Journal.* For the *Peabody Journal* she wrote "The English Teacher and the Reading Program", "Knowing the South Through Books," "Goodly Company", "No Defense Needed," and "The Art of Survival." "Apollo and the Muses" appeared in the *Madison Quarterly,* and the A.A.U.W. *Journal* published, among other articles, "College Women in the Current Crisis Through Community Service." From 1949 to 1951 Dr. Riley was a consulting editor

in connection with L. W. Singer's prose and poetry series.

In an article in the *Nashville Tennessean Magazine,* Louise Davis has said of Dr. Riley: "American literature is her special field of study, but with her customary eagerness to get at a problem from every direction, she has broadened her courses—most of them on the graduate level—to include study of regional economy, sociology, art, crafts. . . .The thing that fascinates her students above all else is that she builds no wall around her field; it extends into all areas of knowledge." Among the nonacademic fields into which Dr. Riley's knowledge extends are cooking and singing. The "tall, gracious" educator has sung leading roles in several choral programs and on one occasion took part in an amateur production of *The Marriage of Figaro* in a Nashville theater. Susan Riley is a member of the National Council of Teachers of English; the College English Association; the American Council of Education; and the Tennessee Folklore Society (president 1942-44). She also belongs to Kappa Delta Pi, honorary education fraternity. She is a Baptist in religious affiliation, a Democrat in politics.

References

> Journal of American Association of University Women 44:237+ Summer '51 por
>
> Nashville Tennessean Mag p5+ My 13 '51 por
>
> Who's Who in America, 1952-53

RITNER, ANN (GILLILAND) June 21, 1906- Author

Address: b. c/o J. B. Lippincott Co., East Washington Square, Philadelphia 5, Pa.; h. 3719 N. Campbell Ave., Route 5, Box 103, Tucson, Arizona

> Reprinted from the *Wilson Library Bulletin,* Dec. 1953

When Ann Ritner's *Keepsake* was published, her son wrote that it was "the sixth book purchased out of the little time left for concentration when a house must be scrubbed, a family put together, and meals prepared." Mrs. Ritner herself sums up her three-sided career neatly—"Housewife, Mother, Writer." Her husband, her son, and a wide reading public will testify to her success in all three fields.

Born in Clearfield, Pennsylvania, June 21, 1906, to John Lawrence Gilliland and Sophia Catherine (Fisher) Gilliland, she was christened Anna. She dropped the final "a" when she was six and has been Ann ever since to everyone except her many aunts. Her mother was of German descent and her father a mixture of German and Scotch Irish. Both were teachers in their earlier years, her mother abandoning the career for marriage at twenty, and her father also turning from pedagogy later to become a banker.

The family moved to La Junta, Colorado, when Ann was seven. Her mother died six years later, leaving five children, two older and two younger than Ann. Young Ann graduated from the La Junta High School in 1923 and lists her extracurricular activities as "basketball, boys, and attempts to write." She attended Colorado College in Colorado Springs and Pennsylvania State College, majoring in journalism. But she forsook the pursuit of a degree in 1926 to marry Fred Vincent Ritner, a fellow student at Penn State. Because her husband is an engineer they have moved about a great deal—Texas, New York, Colorado, New Jersey, Utah—but she says they have settled down now in Tucson, Arizona. Their only son, Peter Vaughan Ritner, is at present assistant production editor of *Saturday Review*.

Concerning her inheritance of a love for writing Mrs. Ritner says, "Possibly my mother influenced me most. She had always wanted to write and told stories with a great love for the magic of words. My paternal grandfather went to sea at seventeen and kept a magnificent record of his adventure." Ann Ritner's writing career began when she was nine and won second prize (a copy of *Black Beauty*) in a *Continent* contest. Her successful story was titled "When Danny's Dream Came True." In 1939 her first novel, *And Some Had Wine,* was published. The *New Yorker's* reviewer called this an "unpretentious but extremely amusing story of an irresponsible family. . . .A good family to drop in on some evening."

Elizabeth, My Daughter in 1940 and *Shelter Without Walls,* two years later, were both praised mildly by reviewers for the author's ability to make her characters warm and human. And both fell into the pattern of family living and youthful romance which librarians sometimes designate as suitable for "the hammock brigade."

Face of Things (1944), a story of a woman who loses her husband and learns to make a new life for herself, drew mixed reviews. The New York *Times* reviewer felt that it "meets with only moderate success." The New York *Herald Tribune Book Review* said of it "The author handles her theme with considerable insight, and without allowing the narrative to bog down in psychopathic mire."

Both *The Green Bough* (1950) and *Keepsake* (1952) were selected by Sears People's Book Club. In a Pennsylvania small town setting, *The Green Bough* is a family story of the pre-World War I period in which each character claims a share in the reader's interest though the central theme is the development and maturing of the love story of eighteen-year-old Ella May and the "problem" boy next door.

Keepsake, with an Arizona setting, goes back to the Spanish-American War period and tells the story of Cathy Brett, sheltered daughter of a wealthy industrialist and a gentle, beautiful mother. Cathy is seventeen and relates the story. A. F. Wolfe in the New York *Times* said, "The story focuses with competent cinematic directness on typical scenes and episodes of a semi-raw frontier society."

Besides her novels she has had short stories published in *Woman's Home Companion;*

ANN RITNER

Woman's Illustrated (London, England); and *Ladies' Home Journal. The Green Bough* appeared in the latter magazine prior to its publication in book form and Samuel French also made a play from it. Mrs. Ritner is currently working on another novel, and between times she works on short stories though not because she considers them easier to do.

Her reading tastes range widely—Austen, Tarkington, Dickens, Trollope, and Cather. Other favored forms of recreation include traveling, bridge, dancing, concerts, and plays, "and the kind of informal parties featuring good talk and good food which life in Tucson seems to engender."

Blue-eyed, light-brown-haired, Ann Ritner, who is five feet six inches tall and weighs 130 pounds, has been described by her son as "a small graceful woman with keen, sparkling eyes." She is a Democrat in politics and Presbyterian in church affiliation. As for her working habits, once a story is started she works at it regularly four or five hours every morning, preferably wearing blue jeans and pigtail braids.

ROBERTS, C(HARLES) WESLEY Dec. 14, 1903- Public relations counsel; former political party leader
Address: h. Holton, Kan.

As successor to Arthur E. Summerfield, who in January 1953 resigned to accept the office of Postmaster General, C. Wesley Roberts was unanimously chosen by the executive committee for chairman of the Republican National Committee. Roberts himself resigned the chairmanship on March 27, 1953, and was succeeded by lawyer Leonard W. Hall of New York.

Since 1936 Roberts was active in the Republican party in Kansas, where earlier he was a

Chase Photo.

C. WESLEY ROBERTS

reporter and editor for a chain of Kansas newspapers, and has held the post of secretary to the Republican Governor Payne Ratner, chairman of the Kansas Republican State Committee, and vice-chairman of the Republican Midwest State Chairmen's Association. During the first part of 1952 Roberts was executive director of the Eisenhower National Headquarters until, with the Republican nomination of General Dwight D. Eisenhower for President, he became organization director of the National Committee and had the special task of coordinating the activities of the National Committee with those of the Independent Citizens for Eisenhower.

Charles Wesley Roberts, who was born on December 14, 1903, in Oskaloosa, Kansas, is the youngest of four sons of Frank H. and Daisy (Needham) Roberts. A member of the Roberts family which since 1860 has been engaged in newspaper publishing in Kansas, his father is the editor and publisher of a chain of weekly newspapers in Kansas. Young Roberts attended the public schools of Oskaloosa and then studied at Kansas State College in Manhattan, Kansas, where he majored in journalism. While at college he also played football and basketball and met some of his college expenses by selling news stories to his father's weekly publications. He left college before receiving a degree in order to take a job as reporter on the family papers, writing both news and sports stories. At about this time he also refereed football games of the Jefferson County Conference High School matches. By 1926 Roberts was listed as coeditor and copublisher of the Oskaloosa *Independent*, the Meriden *Message*, and the McLouth *Times*, all weekly papers which he owned and managed with his father and his brother, J. W. Roberts. Of these the *Independent* is the oldest weekly in Kansas, having been published

continuously by the Roberts family since 1860 when the political leader's grandfather, J. W. Roberts, established it six months before Kansas was admitted to the Union.

After working for ten years, from 1926 to 1936, as a journalist, Roberts entered politics as campaign manager for the Kansas Republican gubernatorial candidate, Will G. West. Although his candidate was defeated by the Democratic landslide of 1936, Roberts continued in Republican party affairs, serving for the subsequent two years as executive secretary of the Kansas State Republican Committee and earning what some have called "the major share of the credit" for rebuilding the Republican organization, which after the 1936 defeat has not lost an election in Kansas. During the 1938 gubernatorial election Roberts was occupied as assistant to the Kansas State Republican chairman and in 1939 became secretary to the newly elected Republican Governor, Payne Ratner, a position that Roberts held for two successive terms. At the end of that period, in 1943, he joined the United States Marine Corps, in which he was commissioned a captain and assigned as intelligence and operations officer to the 4th Marine Air Wing Bomber Squadron. Roberts saw action on Tinian, Guam, Iwo Jima, and Okinawa, before his discharge in February 1946 in the rank of major.

On his return to civilian life, Roberts changed his residence from Topeka to Holton, where he established his own public relations and publicity firm, with the Kansas State Highway Commission as one of his major clients. He continued his interest in Republican party programs, serving from 1947 to 1950 as chairman of the Kansas Republican State Committee and simultaneously as vice-chairman of the Republican Midwest State Chairmen's Association, a group which comprises representatives from nineteen States. In 1950 Roberts managed the successful campaign of Frank Carlson for election to the United States Senate. When, in January 1951, Senator Carlson became director of the Eisenhower National Headquarters in Washington, D.C., Roberts moved to the nation's capital as executive director of the group which worked toward the nomination of General Eisenhower at the Republican National Convention in July of 1952. At this convention, Roberts assisted Herbert Brownell, Jr., Eisenhower's campaign manager. With Eisenhower chosen the Republican nominee, Roberts became organization director of the Republican National Committee, working directly with Arthur E. Summerfield, then chairman of the group.

Later, Roberts was given the special task of coordinating the operations of the National Committee with that of groups not normally associated with the Republican party, particularly the independent National Citizens for Eisenhower-Nixon. It was during this preelection time that Roberts won his reputation for settling disputes among various political factions. In January 1953, when Summerfield resigned from his chairmanship of the National Committee to accept the Presidential appointment as Postmaster General, Roberts was the unanimous choice of the nineteen-member executive committee for the vacated post. It was

ROBERTS, C. WESLEY—*Continued*

reported that President Eisenhower approved of the selection and that Republicans throughout the country welcomed Roberts as national chairman because of his connection with the Midwest branch of the party, thus reducing criticism of the new administration as being dominated by the "Dewey-Brownell East Coast faction." The forces which had supported the Presidential nomination of Senator Robert A. Taft also gave their approval to the selection of Roberts.

Roberts' major task, made complex because the Republicans have been out of national office for twenty years, was to supervise, in cooperation with the President and his department chiefs, the distribution of Federal patronage. By March 1953 about 12,000 applications had been received in Roberts' office for several hundred thousand Federal positions that are available for appointment by the new Republican administration. The procedure of classifying these applications and recommending applicants to the proper departments and agencies, Roberts told newspapermen, would be worked out "as a team" by the National Committee, the local State governments, and the Congressional representation. At an interview on the television program *Meet the Press*, Roberts reported that Democrats who had supported the Eisenhower campaign in the Southern States would have a voice in job appointments. He also stated that his committee would not attempt to remove postmasterships from among the positions filled by the Civil Service Commission, where the Truman Administration had placed them. Roberts' other tasks included developing a "practical political program," as he phrased it in his acceptance speech, which would result in the election of more Republican Senators and Representatives in the 1954 contest. He was also expected to try to build a strong party by taking advantage of the break made in the 1952 elections in the "Solid South."

Shortly after accepting his new position, Roberts was questioned about an $11,000 fee he received from a Kansas insurance company in connection with the sale of a hospital owned by the company to the State of Kansas. He denied any lobbying, and explained that when he assisted the insurance company he received his fee as a public relations counsel, and not as a lobbyist, that he held no political position at the time, and that he did not approach any legislators in an effort to get the appropriation bill passed. After he was questioned, Roberts resigned as chairman of the Republican National Committee on March 27, 1953, since he felt that his usefulness to the party had been impaired. However, on August 7, 1953 Harold R. Fatzer, Attorney General of Kansas stated that "Roberts' conduct did not violate our statute as it is now written." After the issuance of the Fatzer report, Roberts was quoted in the *Christian Science Monitor* (August 10, 1953) as saying: "It is gratifying that after an exhaustive investigation of over four months' duration, my original word has been made good and grounds for complaint do not exist."

The public relations counselor has gray eyes and gray hair, weighs 160 pounds, and is five feet eleven inches in height. In religious affiliation he is a Methodist and is said to recall that he used to pump the hand-organ of the Methodist Church his family attended when he was a boy. Since November 29, 1929, Roberts has been married to the former Ruth Patrick, a high school companion of his and a schoolteacher before marriage. The couple has a son, Patrick. A profile by Peter Edson in the New York *World-Telegram* has described Roberts as "a wiry, quarterback type of man. . . .He is extremely quiet. . . .He gets things done without friction or fireworks." Edson believed Roberts' success as a politician stemmed from his application of the grass-roots, precinct-level technique to every campaign.

References

Christian Sci Mon p3 Ja 16 '53
Newsweek 41:35 Ja 26 '53
N Y Herald Tribune p1 Ja 17 '53
N Y Times p9 Ja 17 '53
N Y World-Telegram Mag p2 F 14 '53

ROBERTS, ROBIN (EVAN) Sept. 30, 1926- Baseball player

Address: b. Connie Mack Stadium, 21st St. and Lehigh Ave., Philadelphia, Pa; h. 1345 Robinhood Rd., Meadowbrook, Pa.

Effective control of a superior fast ball, capacity for hard work, and assiduous study of the weaknesses of opposing batters have all helped to establish Robin Roberts, right-handed pitcher with the Philadelphia National League Club, as one of baseball's outstanding players. Roberts, whose apprenticeship in organized minor league baseball was limited to about two months, has been on the roster of his only major league team for less than five full seasons, but in that time he has won slightly over one hundred games for the "Phillies."

In 1952 he was credited with 28 victories and only 7 defeats, completing 30 of the games he started and pitching no fewer than 330 innings. He won his one hundredth game in the major leagues on June 6, 1953 and four days later became the first pitcher in either the National or the American League to be credited with ten victories. At the season's end he had pitched 22 winning games.

Robin Evan Roberts, the fifth of the six children of Thomas and Sarah Roberts, was born September 30, 1926 on the outskirts of Springfield, Ilinois. He is of Welsh descent on his father's side and English on his mother's. The elder Roberts, for the past eighteen years a night foreman with the Sangamo Electric Company at Springfield, had worked in the Lancashire coal mines before emigrating with his wife to the United States in 1921.

Robin or Robbie (as he is known in baseball circles, though nearly all his relatives and close friends call him Evan) began his education at the East Pleasant Hill Grade School, where he won prizes for speech and mathematics. One of his two teachers, C. B. Lindsay, "put in considerable time organizing the few available boys into athletic teams, and did much to get Robbie started on sports" (Harry T. Paxton

ROBIN ROBERTS

in the *Saturday Evening Post,* January 10, 1953).

Robbie's father was a baseball fan, and whenever possible took his sons to watch the St. Louis (National League) Cardinals in their home games. Despite this initiation, however, Robbie made little impression in athletics when he attended Springfield High School. It was not until he transferred to the Lanphier High School (also in Springfield) for his junior and senior years that he became interested in a variety of scholastic sports.

In basketball (states Harry Paxton) he became "a marvelously slick and deceptive ball handler" and in football was "a very alert end." (To develop his muscles he worked during the summers as a loader at the Pillsbury flour mills). He also played baseball, but was more often used in fielding positions than on the mound.

During his senior year at Lanphier High School Roberts qualified as an Army Air Force cadet and, one month after his graduation in June, 1944, was sent by the Air Force to the Student Training Reserve Unit at Michigan State College, East Lansing, Michigan. Here he played basketball for an Air Force team and so impressed the college officials that he was offered, and accepted, an athletic scholarship. He remained at East Lansing until his transfer from reserve to active status in March, 1945.

In November, after having undergone basic and specialized training at Sheppard Field, Texas and at Chanute Field, Illinois, he received his military discharge. Returning to Michigan State College, he completed work for his B.S. degree and won the Detroit *Free Press* trophy for "Michigan's outstanding collegiate basketball player" of 1946.

In the spring of 1946 Roberts tried out for the first base posiiton on Michigan's baseball team. "Our pitchers were in pretty good shape

by then and Robin didn't hit very well in the batting cage," Coach John Kobs recalled in *Sport,* June 1952. "I told him why, and he said, 'well, he also pitched in high school and he would just as soon try that'." Roberts lost to Western Michigan by 9 to 1 in his first starting assignment, but when he next took the mound, Roberts pitched a no-hit, no-run game against the formidable Great Lakes Naval Training Station.

This, and other feats aroused the interest of Ray Fisher, the baseball coach at the University of Michigan, who invited Roberts to play under his management at Montpelier, Vermont, in the 1946 season in the independent, non-professional, college-boy Northern League. Roberts accepted this offer, and won eleven and lost eight games. By 1947, however, he had begun to acquire pitching know-how and, with Ray Fisher's help, developed a real curve ball to go with his fast one. He won 18 games and lost only three.

Jack Rossiter, then a part-time "scout" for the Philadelphia National League Club, had reported favorably on Roberts as early as 1946, but at that time the Phillies failed to act on his recommendation. Roberts worked out for the St. Louis Browns after the 1947 Northern League season ended, and was scheduled to "show his stuff to some other clubs, when Scout Chuck Ward, of the Phillies, came along and offered him $25,000."

After signing for this bonus, Roberts returned to Michigan State to finish his studies. Receiving his B.S. in physical education in March, 1948, he reported to the Phillies' organization and was assigned to the Wilmington, Delaware, "farm" in the Class B Interstate League. (In the only two months he ever spent in professional minor league baseball, Roberts won nine games for Wilmington while losing only one, struck out 121 batters and had an earned run average of only 2.06).

Hurriedly summoned on June 17, 1948 to join the parent Phillies at Shibe Park (now Connie Mack Stadium) in Philadelphia, Roberts made his major league début the following night, and although he lost to Elmer Riddle of the Pittsburgh Pirates by 2 to 0, he was considered to have made an impressive showing. Four days later, Roberts won his first major league victory by 3 to 2 over the Cincinnati Reds.

The Phillies' pitching coach, George Earnshaw, in particular liked what he saw of the newcomer. "If you line up all the bonus kids in a row," he declared shortly after Roberts joined the club, "and talked to them one at a time, you could tell that Roberts is the one most likely to make good. He has a education, background and an elusive quality known as poise" (Jack Newcombe in *Sport,* June, 1952).

Having finished the 1948 season with a 7-9 won-and-lost record and a respectable earned run average of 3.18, Roberts appeared in thirty-four games in 1949, winning fifteen and losing fifteen. (Several of his losses were directly due to hurrying his pitch, a fault which Coach Benny Bengough is credited with correcting).

Roberts was meanwhile keeping a detailed "book" on the idiosyncracies of opposing batters, and in 1950 really struck his stride along with the younger of his teammates, the celebrated "Whiz Kids" of that year. By midseason he had amassed an impressive record and was chosen for the National League's mound staff in that year's All-Star Game, in which he pitched the regulation three innings, allowing three hits and one run.

Before the regular season was over, Roberts had taken the mound in 304 innings, winning twenty and losing eleven of the forty games in which he participated, and recording 146 strikeouts as against only 77 "walks." It was Roberts who clinched the pennant for the Phillies on the last day of the season, settling down the Brooklyn Dodgers by 4-1 in a ten inning game in which he allowed only five hits.

In the ensuing World Series with the New York Yankees, Roberts appeared in two games, pitching eleven innings and allowing eleven hits. He was charged with the loss of the second game of the series, in which the score was 2 to 1; the decisive moment came in the tenth inning, when Joe DiMaggio hit a home run for the New York Yankees. Roberts has called his final 1950 victory over the Dodgers the "greatest thrill" of his career, and the loss of his first world series game his "greatest disappointment."

The Phillies failed to repeat in 1951, partly because their best left-handed pitcher, Curt Simmons, had been called into military service; an added burden was accordingly placed on Roberts, who in that year again led the National League in total number of innings pitched (315). He won twenty-one games while losing fifteen, and his earned run average of 3.03 suggests that many of his losses were due to a lack of good "clutch" hitting by his teammates.

In 1952 (during which the Phillies' manager Eddie Sawyer was replaced by Steve O'Neill) Roberts pitched a record-breaking 330 innings, and won twenty-eight games while losing seven. (His was the greatest number of victories recorded in a single season by a National League pitcher since Dizzy Dean won thirty games for St. Louis in 1934).

Roberts struck out 148 batters in 1952 while allowing only 45 bases on balls; his earned run average was a 2.59, and the twenty-third of his twenty-eight victories was a seventeen-inning contest with the Boston (now the Milwaukee) Braves, in which he "went the distance."

In the balloting for the National League's "most valuable player" of 1952, Roberts was runner-up to Hank Sauer of the Chicago Cubs.

In the 1953 season he won his one hundredth game of his major league career on June 6 when he defeated the Milwaukee Braves by 6-2 at Philadelphia; and on June 10 he became the first pitcher in either of the major leagues to record ten triumphs in 1953. On August 12, in Pittsburgh, "the Phillies' ace right-hander," according to the New York *Times* (Aug. 13, 1953), "batted across three

runs with an infield out and a triple in beating the Pirates, 8-4, . . . for his twentieth victory of the campaign." This victory moved him into the twenty-game winning group for his fourth straight season. For the third successive year he was named to the twenty-five man National League all-star team by manager Charlie Dressen.

Called the "best pitcher in baseball" by Stephen O'Neill, the manager of the Phillies, Roberts has said: "I suppose it sounds funny for me to say it, but baseball is fun for me. Maybe that is why I've been so lucky. I hope I can stay lucky for ten more years" (Washington *Post,* August 10, 1953).

Good sportsmanship, clean playing and clean living are qualities universally associated with the name of Robin Roberts; even the most contentious of opposing managers and players never charge him with throwing a "duster", and it is rarely that he disputes an umpire's call. Like his fellow moundsman Curt Simmons, who is his room-mate on the road and next-door neighbor in the suburb of Philadelphia where he makes his home, Roberts never smokes, drinks or gambles. He was married on December 26, 1949 to the former Mary Kolnes of McFarland, Wisconsin, whom he met while she was teaching history in one of the Springfield schools. They are now the parents of two sons, Robin Evan, Jr. and Don Stephen. Roberts is six feet one inch in height, weighs 190 pounds, and has blue eyes and brown hair. He is a Presbyterian

Roberts' fast ball, his excellent control, his intelligence and his stamina, remain his principal pitching assets. He rarely uses a trick delivery and, according to Harry Paxton, "still lacks a bona-fide change-of-pace" (*Saturday Evening Post,* January 10, 1953.

References

   Baseball Annual 1953 1:61+ por
   Baseball M 90:14-15+ Spring '53 pors
   N Y Times p41 Mr 26 '53 por
   Newsweek 41:60-1 Ap 13 '53 por
   Sat Eve Post 225:25+ Ja 10 '53 pors
   Sport 12:33+ Je '52 por
   Sport Stars 5:43 Mr '53 por
   Baseball Register (1952)
   Reichler, J. Inside the Majors (1952)
   Turkin, H. and Thompson, S. C. Official Encyclopedia of Baseball, Jubilee Editions (1950)
   Who's Who in Baseball (1953)

ROBERTSON, WALTER S(PENCER)
Dec. 7, 1893- United States Government official; business executive
Address: b. c/o Department of State, Washington 25, D.C.; h. "Milburne", Windsor Farms, Richmond 21, Va.

The Assistant Secretary of State for Far Eastern affairs, Walter S. Robertson, headed a mission to Korea in June 1953 in an attempt to end the opposition of Dr. Syngman Rhee, South Korean President, to a Korean armistice. Since 1943, Robertson has held a number of important diplomatic posts in China. He was

Wide World Photos

WALTER S. ROBERTSON

formerly an investment banker and has been active in the civic affairs of Richmond, Virginia.

The son of William Henry Robertson, a tobacconist, and Anne M. (Robinson) Robertson, Walter Spencer Robertson was born in Nottoway County, Virginia, on December 7, 1893. Reared in Southern Virginia, he studied at the Hoge Military Academy and in 1910 enrolled at the College of William and Mary. The following year he attended Davidson College, but left in 1912 in order to enter the banking business.

His career was interrupted during World War I, when he served with the United States Air Corps as a pursuit pilot with the rank of second lieutenant. After the war Robertson resumed his banking career with the Richmond investment banking firm of Scott and String-fellow, becoming a partner in 1925. From 1922 to 1925, he was also vice-president of the State and City (now the State-Planters) Bank and Trust Company in Richmond.

His first diplomatic assignment came in 1943, when the late Edward R. Stettinius, Jr., the Lend-Lease administrator, appointed him chief of the United States Lend-Lease Mission to Australia. According to reports, Robertson entered foreign affairs because he was "too old to fight in World War II." "I considered my service solely as war work," said Robertson (New York *Times*, March 22, 1953). He held this post until September 1944.

In the following year he became economic adviser to the Department of State, serving until 1946 as minister and counselor on economic affairs at the American Embassy in Chungking. For the period September 1945 to July 1946, Robertson acted as chargé d'affaires in the Chinese capital. His assignment there was to supervise American economic activities and to coordinate the work of United States civilian war agencies in China.

Regarded as a "specialist on Far Eastern economic problems" (New York *Times*, March 22, 1953) Robertson was in 1946, United States Commissioner at the Peiping Executive Headquarters. A member of General George C. Marshall's Truce Commission, he acted as neutral chairman of the three-man team trying to enforce a truce between the Chinese Nationalists and Communists. Although the team which became known as the "Robertson Commission" failed in its attempt to end hostilities, for his "exceptionally meritorious service" during this assignment, Marshall awarded Robertson the Medal for Merit on October 12, 1946. Robertson, who had formally resigned from the foreign service in late September 1946, returned to the United States the following month. In 1948 Robrtson was one of five men serving on an advisory committee under Paul G. Hoffman for the Economic Cooperation Administration's China Aid Program.

President Eisenhower designated Robertson as Assistant Secretary of State for Far Eastern Affairs on March 19, 1953 and the appointment was approved by the Senate Foreign Relations Committee six days later. Of his new post Robertson said, "I have the greatest confidence in the character, the ability, the selfless patriotism and the purposes of President Eisenhower and Secretary of State Dulles. I feel greatly honored to be selected as a member of their team. It is one to which I can give whole-hearted and unalloyed allegiance" (New York *Times*, March 22, 1953). As personal representative of both President Eisenhower and Secretary of State Dulles, Robertson left for Tokyo and Seoul on June 22, 1953, carrying a secret message to South Korean President Syngman Rhee.

The mission which Robertson headed hoped to settle the crisis which arose when Rhee refused to accept the Korean armistice on terms which both Communist and United Nations delegations at Panmunjom had virtually accepted. To persuade Rhee to reconsider his refusal was Robertson's assignment. Before his departure from the United States, Robertson said, "I will discuss with General Clark and Ambassador Briggs as well as with President Rhee and the other Korean leaders, all aspects of the situation in Korea. . . .In this way my visit should enable us in Washington to have a first hand and up-to-date picture of how things stand in Korea" (New York *Herald Tribune*, June 23, 1953).

The first of the series of Rhee-Robertson meetings was held on June 26, 1953 in Tokyo. The main points of difference between Korea and the United Nations command which Robertson sought to resolve were, Dr. Rhee's rebellion against allied authority, his refusal to accept the armistice terms, and his unilateral release of more than 27,000 North Korean anti-Communist prisoners of war (New York *Herald Tribune*, June 26, 1953). During their talks, Dr. Rhee disclosed to Robertson two points in the armistice terms which were unacceptable to South Korea. Rhee objected first, because the terms did not provide for a unified Korea but instead permitted one million Chinese troops to remain in the territory. Secondly, he complained that armed Indian troops were to guard anti-Communist prisoners while the Communists were permitted to "propagandize and lead them to volunteer for repatriation" (New York *Herald Tribune,* June 26, 1953). "Mr. Robertson has brought good ideas and our mutual understanding has been greatly improved," Dr. Rhee stated after his first meeting with Robertson (New York *Times,* June 27, 1953). After their third meeting, Robertson expressed confidence that the misunderstandings which existed would be cleared up, but the talks continued in Seoul without a settlement in view. As *Time* wrote, "Rhee has thrown up a great smoke screen of words, often accompanied by a studied show of amicability. But his position has not altered in the slightest" (July 6, 1953).

After sixteen days of arguments, debates, and negotiations with Dr. Rhee, Robertson left Seoul, having finally won the South Korean leader's acceptance of a truce and also his word not to obstruct an armistice even though he might not agree to it. In return for Rhee's cooperation, it was reported, some concessions were made to South Korea during Robertson's visit (New York *Times,* July 13, 1953). Dr. Rhee was promised a mutual defense pact, economic and military aid, a pledge that the United States would strive for unification of Korea through peaceful means, and a promise that South Korea would be heard at the Far East political conference (New York *Times,* July 12, 1953).

After returning to the United States, Robertson explained the reason for Korean opposition to an armistice: "They were opposed to it because of a deep fear that [it is] a Communist trick and device to win by negotiation what they have failed to achieve on the battlefield, a deep fear that the United Nations . . . might sacrifice Korea as Koreans feel they have been sacrificed in the past to great power interests" (*Time,* July 27, 1953).

Robertson's mission, which was aimed at convincing Rhee that United States and Korean differences lay not in objectives but in methods to be used for the achievement of a common objective was regarded as a test of his tact, persuasiveness and endurance.

"Few in Korea believed that Mr. Robertson would succeed when he came over here. . . . Because [he] took the trouble to see things Dr. Rhee's way, Dr. Rhee is now able to understand the U.S. position. He understands things which had never been explained to him" (New York *World-Telegram and Sun,* July 13, 1953).

Speaking at the annual Far East Conference held under the auspices of the Far East-America Council of Commerce and Industry, Robertson stated that the United States is ready and willing to help free Asiatic countries with their economic and defense problems if they take the initiative themselves. He stated that the United States has already given extensive aid in the Far East, and that "we expect to aid in the reconstruction of Korea to the extent of about $1,000,000,000." America has already made, Robertson continued, "an invest-

ment beyond all valuation—150,000 American casualties, 25,000 American lives—in addition to 15,000,000,000 American dollars in defense of the independence of the Republic of Korea, and I should add, the independence of the rest of free Asia" (New York *Times,* October 10, 1953).

The diplomat has been a director of the Camp Manufacturing Company, the Robertson Chemical Corporation, a member of the board of governors of the Stock Exchange Firms, and president of the Richmond Stock Exchange. Active in the civic affairs of Richmond, Robertson was a "key leader" in many fund campaigns of the American Red Cross and the local Community Chest. At the beginning of World War II he helped Richmond to exceed its Red Cross war quota months ahead of any other city.

He has served on the board of the English Speaking Union (Virginia) and the British War Relief Society, was president of the Richmond Community Council from 1940 to 1943, president of the Community Memorial Hospital since 1947, and a trustee of the Virginia Historical Society, Virginia Museum of Fine Arts, Community Welfare Foundation, St. Christopher School, and William and Mary Endowment Association. Other organizations in which he holds membership are the Society of Cincinnati and Society of Colonial Wars. Robertson is a member of the honor fraternities Phi Beta Kappa and Kappa Alpha. He was decorated, in 1946, with the Chinese Order of the Cloud and Banner.

Walter S. Robertson and Mary Dade Taylor were married on November 4, 1925. Their children are Walter Spencer, Jr., Catherine Taylor and Jaquelin Taylor. Robertson is a member of the Episcopalian Church and is a Democrat. During the 1952 presidential campaign he was affiliated with the "Democrats for Eisenhower." His clubs are the Metropolitan (Washington), Commonwealth and the Country of Virginia (Richmond).

References

N Y Herald Tribune p6 Mr 19 '53; II p1 Je 28 '53
N Y Times p16 Mr 6 '53; p15 Mr 19 '53
N Y World-Telegram Mag p9 Jl 18 '53
Time 61:17 Mr 30 '53
Who's Who in America, 1952-53

ROBITZEK, EDWARD H(EINRICH)

Dec. 12, 1912-   Physician

Address: b. 100 Central Ave., Staten Island 1, N.Y.; h. 37 Windsor Rd., Staten Island 14, N.Y.

When newspapers reported in February 1952 that Dr. Edward Robitzek and his colleagues at Sea View Hospital, Staten Island, New York, had perfected a new "wonder drug" to combat tuberculosis, the "dedicated young specialist who had labored without pay for years among TB cases" was concerned about the world-wide publicity received. With scientific

ROBITZEK, EDWARD—*Continued*

caution he had simply stated: "We have a drug that is *useful* against tuberculosis."

With his associate, Dr. Irving J. Selikoff, Dr. Robitzek had conducted clinical studies at Sea View Hospital (headed by Dr. George G. Ornstein) on the action of iproniazid and isoniazid, antituberculous drugs, hydrazide derivatives of isonicotinic acid.

Despite the remarkable effect of these drugs on tubercular patients, Dr. Robitzek and his associates are continuing their studies. "We don't intend to stop our investigations and if any better drugs come along, we'll use them," he told an interviewer in the New York *World-Telegram and Sun,* March 14, 1953. "Tuberculosis won't die, however, until we can render it noninfectious."

Dr. Marcus D. Kogel, Commissioner of Hospitals in New York City, declared that the research work on antituberculous drugs by Dr. Robitzek and his colleagues is "of ultimate significance." The New York Foundation provided a grant of $28,000 for continuation of the work.

Edward Heinrich Robitzek was born in New York City on December 12, 1912, the son of Arthur Harrison and Kate (Heinrich) Robitzek. He was reared in his native city, to which his great grandfather came in 1826 from Prague. Robitzek describes himself as of "15/16ths German extraction" with an ancestry of businessmen dealing in fuel, pottery and real estate. He attended Evander Childs High School in the Bronx, New York, making membership in the swimming team his extracurricular activity.

After being graduated from high school in 1930, Robitzek entered Colgate University, and majored in chemistry and biology. His liking for swimming as an outside activity continued, and he joined the college team. He also became a member of the Maroon Key Club. His interest in tuberculosis developed from a history of this disease in his own family. He decided to study medicine and, upon receipt of his B.A. degree from Colgate University in 1934, went to the College of Physicians and Surgeons at Columbia University. This institution awarded him an M.D. degree in 1938.

Robitzek was an interne at Fordham Hospital in New York from 1938 to 1940. During the next four years he was successively resident physician in medicine, resident in roentgenology, and chief medical resident at Sea View Hospital, Staten Island, New York, for tuberculosis patients. He then served as pathologist at this hospital, and also at Richmond Memorial Hospital, Staten Island, from 1944 to 1946.

Robitzek began private practice as a lung specialist in Staten Island in 1946. He became attending pneumonologist at Richmond Memorial Hospital the same year, and attending physician at Sea View Hospital in 1947. Robitzek was chief of the chest clinic at Staten Island Hospital during 1948, and the next year was attending physician at this hospital. He served as assistant director of medicine at Sea View Hospital during 1951 and 1952.

With his colleagues at Sea View Hospital, Robitzek initiated clinical studies in humans in June 1951 on the action of three hydrazide derivatives of isonicotinic acid to discover the therapeutic value and possible toxic effects of these synthetic compounds in the treatment of tuberculosis. For this study, 175 patients were selected, all of whom had extensive, active pulmonary tuberculosis and who were not benefiting from the regular therapy. One of the drugs tested, a glucosyl compound, was soon eliminated as inferior to the other two, iproniazid and isoniazid, which were synthesized from coal tar.

"Evidence so far," declared Robitzek on February 22, 1952, "indicates that the chemicals are bactericidal—that is, germ killers—rather than bacteriostic, or inhibitors of germs" (New York *Times*). He affirmed that no development of "germ resistance" to the drugs in the patients was observed, "nor any toxic effects on hearing, as with streptomycin." Patients treated demonstrated rapid improvement in appetite, weight, energy and general outlook, and there were enthusiastic reports over the new compounds. Dr. Robitzek, however, viewed this optimism with caution and later referred to the publicity as "premature and explosive". Nevertheless, according to *Collier's* (August 7, 1953) "the stampede was on".

Since the disease of tuberculosis is a scourge in Greece, the new drugs were hailed with enthusiasm and the directorate general of the Greek Ministry of Welfare announced in February 1952 a plan to act immediately to import the drugs as soon as they became available. In the United States authorities began predicting that the cost of therapy for each tuberculosis patient might be reduced "to $100 instead of the average cost of $3,500" (New York *Times,* February 22, 1952).

At the annual meeting of the National Tuberculosis Association in Boston in May 1952 opinion on the new antituberculous drugs was divided. The United States Pure Food and Drug Administration released isoniazid for use under close medical supervision and for large-scale production on June 4, 1952, but recommended that it be employed only in streptomycin-resistant cases of tuberculosis.

Robitzek presented a report on the new antituberculous drugs at the annual meeting of the American College of Chest Surgeons in Chicago on June 5, 1952. In a paper read before the Section on Diseases of the Chest of the American Medical Association on June 10, 1952, he pointed out that the use of iproniazid results "in a greater incidence of and more severe toxic side-effects" than that of isoniazid. He described this toxicity as affecting "principally . . . the central nervous system", especially in elderly persons, in persons with unstable or psychic personalities, or in those who were anemic. He stated that the new drugs could be taken by mouth rather than by injection (*Journal of the American Medical Association,* November 8, 1952).

Results with combinations of streptomycin and the new hydrazide compounds in a small group of nine patients, Robitzek advised the

American Medical Association, "give promise of enhanced superiority over each [drug given] independently".

Referring to clinical evidence of the effects of the new antituberculous drugs as therapeutic agents, he stated that monthly X-rays of patients showed improvement in about "60 per cent of cases," that "rapid and significant" reduction in cough and expectoration was achieved, and that conversion to negative sputum was found in "approximately 25 per cent" of the patients.

Addressing the semicentennial meeting of the New York Tuberculosis and Health Association, Robitzek cautioned against assuming any "cure-all" for tuberculosis had been found. "Our more recent studies," he said, "are in conjunction with streptomycin and paraamino-salicylic acid; but further studies are needed to determine whether such combined therapy should be concurrent, consecutive, intermittent, interrupted, or alternating" (New York *Times*, November 22, 1952).

Therapy with the new hydrazide drugs and other antituberculous agents at New York City Health Department clinics are said by Dr. Arthur B. Robins, chief of the tuberculosis bureau, to be reaching sufferers who are "either unable to get into a hospital or unwilling to remain in one" (New York *Times*, March 26, 1953). Before a United States Senate Appropriations subcommittee in Washington on May 13, 1953, Dr. Robert J. Anderson, head of the tuberculosis control division of this country's Public Health Service, said isoniazid had "not come up to the high hopes many once held for it . . . but we can expect other and better . . . drugs" (New York *Times*, May 14, 1953).

Robitzek is the author and co-author of numerous articles on the diagnosis and care of tuberculosis in such professional medical journals as *American Review of Tuberculosis, Diseases of the Chest*, and *American Journal of Pathology*. He is the past editor of the *Quarterly Bulletin of Sea View Hospital*. The lung specialist is a fellow of the American College of Physicians and Surgeons and of the American College of Chest Surgeons. He is also a diplomate of the American Board of Internal Medicine and a member of the executive committees of the New York and the Staten Island Tuberculosis and Health Associations.

His organization memberships include the New York Academy of Sciences, the American Trudeau Society, the American Medical Association, the New York State Medical Society, and the Richmond County Medical Society. His fraternity is Lambda Chi Alpha. In the New York *World-Telegram and Sun* (March 14, 1953), Muriel Fischer describes him as "a mild-mannered man with a world of patience."

Robitzek married Katherine D. Robertson on November 9, 1940, and she died in 1945. Their children are A. Scott and John E. Robitzek. The physician married Christine Baldwin on June 4, 1952. He is six feet one and one-half inches tall, weighs 195 pounds, and has blue eyes and blonde hair. He usually votes Republican and he is a Presbyterian. Robitzek declares that his hobbies are "golf and fishing."

Dr Robitzek is continuing his work on the cure of tuberculosis with isoniazid and isoniazid-stretomycin. Recent work with Dr. Selikoff on eighty-three private TB outpatients show hopeful results although many problems remain from the standpoint of contagion. Dr. Robitzek told a *Current Biography* writer, "Our scientific papers speak for themselves, are conservative. . . .We would not retract a single word." He is currently consulting physician at St. Vincent's Hospital in Staten Island, New York.

References

N Y World-Telegram p7 Mr 14 '53

Directory of Medical Specialists (1951)

Who's Who in New York (1952)

ROCKEFELLER, JOHN D(AVISON), 3d
Mar. 21, 1906- Philanthropist
Address: b. 30 Rockefeller Plaza, New York 20; h. 1 Beekman Pl., New York 22

A third-generation philanthropist is John D. Rockefeller 3d, chairman of the board of trustees of the Rockefeller Foundation, established in 1913 by the oil magnate, John D. Rockefeller, Sr., "to promote the well-being of mankind throughout the world" by advancing public health, medicine, natural and social sciences, and the humanities. In support of programs in these fields, the fund made grants totaling $16,640,355 in 1952. The Rockefeller Foundation has given away $540,856,208 since its formation forty years ago (New York *Herald Tribune*, September 12, 1953).

John D. Rockefeller 3d is also chairman of the Board of trustees of the General Education Board, founded in 1902 by his grandfather John D. Rockefeller to promote education in this country "without distinction of race, sex or creed." In 1940 he became president of the Rockefeller Brothers Fund, established that year by the five third-generation Rockefeller brothers for charitable purposes. He is also a director of other philanthropic and educational organizations.

John Davison Rockefeller 3d was born in New York City on March 21, 1906, the son of John Davison and Abby Greene Aldrich Rockefeller, Jr., and the grandson of John D. Rockefeller, the oil industrialist. His mother, the daughter of United States Senator Nelson W. Aldrich of Rhode Island, encouraged in him a liberal attitude and an interest in the arts, while his father soon aroused his interest in many philanthropic projects.

Reared in New York City and in Tarrytown, New York, John D. Rockefeller 3d attended Browning School in Manhattan, where his father had preceded him. He then entered Loomis School in Windsor, Connecticut, where he was chosen vice-president of the French Club, business manager of the yearbook, member of the student council, and player on the tennis team. During summer vacations he went with his family to Seal Harbor, Maine, or to Pocantico Hills, Tarrytown, where he enjoyed picnics, swimming, boating, and the usual boyhood pursuits. To earn more pocket money

Gábor Éder

JOHN D. ROCKEFELLER 3d

than his parents provided, he and his brothers "raised rabbits, ran errands, hoed the garden, cleaned shoes, and killed flies at ten cents a hundred" *(Saturday Evening Post,* December 30, 1950).

After graduating from Loomis School in 1925, Rockefeller 3d entered Princeton University, where he majored in economics and history. He became interested in international problems and during a summer vacation served as an assistant in the information section of the League of Nations at Geneva. He also taught English to immigrants in the town of Princeton. In extracurricular activities, he was a member of the business board of the *Daily Princetonian,* vice-president of the undergraduate Young Men's Christian Association, and a member of the Cap and Gown Society. In 1929 Princeton University awarded him a B.S. degree and his class voted him the member most likely to succeed.

He was one of four young men selected to be junior secretaries at the 1929 conference sponsored by the Institute of Pacific Relations at Kyoto, Japan. He made a trip around the world with James F. MacDonald, who was later United States Minister to Israel. In all they visited a dozen countries, took the trans-Siberian railroad across Russian territory and came home by way of the Pacific.

"That trip showed me the world," Rockefeller said long afterward. "I felt I had learned the real meaning of the word 'international.' I knew then that only by visiting a country could you understand its problems. It is like the difference between seeing an accident and reading about it in the newspaper. If our country is going to meet its obligations of world leadership, our people will have to get abroad and see the world."

This journey and subsequent visits to the Far East and Africa, as well as to other under-developed or laggard economic areas, did a great deal to influence his later thinking in regard to Rockefeller philanthropic enterprises, according to Joe Alex Morris, author of the biography *Those Rockefeller Brothers* (1953).

He returned to New York to enter philanthropic work in his father's office on a full-time basis. He explains this by saying: "I suppose it's worked out that way because I'm the oldest" *(Saturday Evening Post,* January 6, 1951). Considered financially sagacious and conservative, in 1931 he was given the responsibility of serving as a trustee of the General Education Board and of the Rockefeller Foundation.

At a conference on industrial relations at Princeton University in September 1932, John D. Rockefeller 3d advocated more cooperation between capital and labor for collective dealing in place of collective bargaining. "Industrial leaders," he said, "must avoid confusing the means, that is, the details of organization, with the end, which is the spirit of the men who make up the organization" (New York *Times,* September 20, 1932).

In 1932 he became a director of Rockefeller Center, Inc., a $125,000,000 real estate project in which he shares ownership with his father, brothers, and sisters. In the following year he was elected a trustee of the American Museum of Natural History in Manhattan. In 1934 he became a member of the board of trustees of Colonial Williamsburg, Inc., and a director of Williamsburg Restoration, Inc. In 1939 he was made chairman of both, and served until April 27, 1953, when he was succeeded by his brother, Winthrop Rockefeller. He was appointed a trustee of Princeton University in 1937.

In Rockefeller's view, Williamsburg is not just a place of beauty and tourist interest, but a stage for a deeper spiritual presentation of the inspiring story of early America. "We are thinking increasingly of the broader significance of this community as a reflection of the character and faith of the people of Colonial America by whom it was built. Williamsburg was a vital force in the life and thought of 18th-century America. We hope and intend that it shall be a living force in the 20th century," he told his biographer, Joe Alex Morris.

Almost $30,000,000 has been spent, and an estimated six million visitors have seen the restoration and reconstruction of more than 400 colonial buildings. Additional work planned is said to require a "decade longer and $15,000,000 more" (New York *Times,* January 12, 1953).

From 1930 to 1940 John D. Rockefeller 3d was a director of the Boys' Bureau, a department of the Community Service Society to aid New York City's homeless boys. In 1939 he served as chairman of the delinquency committee of the bureau in a study of the causes and treatment of juvenile delinquency. In an article entitled "Salvaging the Young Criminal" (New York *Times,* November 10, 1940), he stated that the findings of the committee agreed with those of the American Law Institute that proposed each State create a youth correction authority responsible for the organization, administration, and policy-making "of a State-wide system to integrate handling of offenders above juvenile court age but not yet 21." With the American Law Institute, he helped to prepare the Youth Correction Act and to advise States desiring to make the statute a part of their criminal justice systems. To date five States have done so.

John D. Rockefeller 3d was made president and a trustee of the Rockefeller Brothers Fund, which was established in 1940 by the five third-generation Rockefeller brothers for charitable purposes, without territorial limitations. The Fund, which he says helps meet the brothers' "citizenship responsibilities" (*Saturday Evening Post,* January 6, 1951), contributed to the USO drive and to United China Relief in 1941. It is one of three foundations underwriting the initial expenses of Chinese Intellectuals, an organization formed in part to aid refugees. Other recipients include Protestant, Catholic, and Jewish charities.

In 1942 Rockefeller 3d joined the staff of the American Red Cross as assistant to chairman Norman Davis. During World War II he served in the United States Navy from July 1942 to October 1945, leaving with the rank of lieutenant commander. From 1942 to 1943 he was assigned to the Bureau of Personnel; he then was transferred to the Office of the Chief of Naval Operations, Naval Military Government, where he worked mainly with the combined civil affairs committee and the State-War-Navy coordinating committee. With his Navy service, he was concurrently director of the British War Relief Society, from 1940 to 1945, and of the United China Relief, from 1941 to 1946.

Following his discharge from the Navy, John D. Rockefeller 3d traveled widely to obtain first-hand information about world economic and social conditions. During 1946 he studied the postwar situation in England, France, Germany, and Austria. In Mexico he examined agricultural and health problems. The knowledge he secured, as stated by the New York *Times* (August 24, 1946), was "for guidance in making future grants" of the Rockefeller Foundation.

In 1946 he became director of Rockefeller Brothers, Inc., a "limited-partnership company" formed by the five sons and daughter of John D. Rockefeller, Jr., as an outlet for "risk" capital. With the purpose of promoting "social and economic progress," it encourages promising new business enterprises (*Saturday Evening Post*).

In December 1946 John D. Rockefeller 3d agreed, with his father and brothers, to the purchase, for $8,500,000, of property in midtown Manhattan for a gift to the United Nations as a permanent headquarters. In recognition of this gift and outstanding civic service, the Rockefeller family received in 1948 the first Dr. John H. Finley Award conferred by New York City College.

From 1947 to 1951 Rockefeller 3d was president of the American Youth Hostels (of which he had been a director since 1946), an active movement in twenty-five countries to promote international good will through youth cycling and hiking trips. He was made director in 1948 of the American International Association for Economic and Social Development which is a Rockefeller project in Latin America to help undeveloped areas "stand on their own feet in the world economy" (*Saturday Evening Post,* January 13, 1951). In 1947 he visited Japan, China, and Korea, and in 1948 Venezuela and Central and South Africa, and predicted Africa's potential trade development.

As chairman of the Greater New York Fund drive in 1949, Rockefeller 3d urged that labor union leaders have full representation on the Fund's board and committees. Also in 1949 he became a director of the New York Life Insurance Company. Early in 1951 he was consultant for the John Foster Dulles mission to Japan on the peace settlement, and in September of that year was adviser to the United States delegation at the Conference for Conclusion and Signature of the Treaty of Peace with Japan, in San Francisco. He visited Japan as a private citizen in 1951 to explore opportunities for greater cultural interchange between that country and the United States. This resulted in negotiations that two years later brought to the United States at the National Gallery of Art in Washington, D.C., an exhibit of ninety-one works of Japanese painting and sculpture.

In December 1952 John D. Rockefeller 3d was elected chairman of the board of trustees of the Rockefeller Foundation to succeed John Foster Dulles. He was also named president on March 26, 1952, of Japan Society, Inc., a private nonpolitical organization to advance a better understanding between the people of the United States and Japan. This same year he became a director of Phelps Memorial Hospital Association in Tarrytown, New York, working to improve hospital facilities in that area. In February 1952 he established the Rockefeller Public Service Awards for civilian service in the Federal Government, to include education benefits to recipients. During November 1952 he visited Negro colleges in the South in a campaign by industrial leaders to raise $25 million for thirty-two of these institutions.

Rockefeller 3d and his family have sought to preserve the Grand Tetons in Wyoming, and have supplied funds for low-cost tourist facilities on Jackson Lake in the Grand Teton National Park. The total cost is expected to reach $6,000,000 by 1955 when it will be completed. The Foundation made a grant of $400,000 to the Louisville Philharmonic in April, 1953, so that the orchestra may commission 184 more works.

Among articles written by John D. Rockefeller 3d are "Right Handling Can Reduce Youth Crime" (*Life,* October 26, 1942) and "Four Things I Believe" (*The Rotarian,* September, 1950). In the latter article he stated, "I believe we ought to know what we are for, not merely what we are against. . . .I believe that the happiness of men and nations depends upon what they put into life." He is the author of the foreword to *Protecting Our Children from Criminal Careers* (John R. Ellingston, 1948).

On October 18, 1953 Rockefeller preached a Laymen's Sermon at the Reformed Church, Bronxville, New York and proposed a four-point code of conduct for the United States

ROCKEFELLER, JOHN D., 3d—*Cont.*

to follow in its relations with other nations:
1) refrain from a tendency to impose our
ideas or way of life on other peoples; 2) evince
as much willingness to learn from them as to
help them; 3) acquire a knowledge of their
needs, aspirations and accomplishments, and
4) recognize that the success or failure of one
people increasingly affects all and is the responsibility of all.

Rockefeller 3d received the Commendation
Ribbon from the United States Navy in 1945
and in 1947 was given the Order of Auspicious
Star for outstanding service to China by the
Chinese National Government, and the Order
of the British Empire in June 1948. Among
his numerous organization memberships are the
Academy of Political Science of New York,
the American Academy of Political and Social
Sciences, the American Association of Mu-
seums, the Citizens Committee for Reorganization of the Executive Branch of the Govern-
ment, the Council in Foreign Relations, the
Foreign Policy Association, the Historical So-
ciety of the Tarrytowns, the Institute of Pacific
Relations, the Metropolitan Museum of Art,
the Museum of Modern Art, the New York
State Chamber of Commerce, the New York
Zoological Society, and the Westchester County
Conservation Association. His clubs are the
Century, the Metropolitan (Washington, D.C.),
the River, the Sleepy Hollow Country Club,
the University, and the Broad Street. He is a
Republican, and his church affiliation is Baptist.

On November 11, 1932, John D. Rockefeller
3d married Blanchette Ferry Hooker. Their
children are Sandra Ferry, John, Hope Aldrich, and Alida Davison. The philanthropist
stands six feet one inch in height, weighs 175
pounds, and has blue-gray eyes and brown hair.
His hobbies are watching baseball, riding, tennis, and sailing. He recently gave $95,000 to
the American Museum of Natural History to
build the first of a series of museum halls devoted to the study of man.

References

Outlook 153:617+ D 18 '29
Sat Eve Post 223:14+ D 30 '50; 223:
  36+ Ja 6 '51; 223:23+ Ja 13 '51
Business Executives of America (1950)
Morris, J. A. Those Rockefeller Broth-
  ers (1953)
Who's Who in America, 1952-53
Who's Who in Commerce and Industry
  (1951)
Who's Who in New York, 1952
Who's Who in the East (1951)
World Biography (1948)

ROGERS, WILL, JR. Oct. 20, 1911- Publisher; actor

Address: b. and h. 427 No. Canon Dr., Beverly Hills, Calif.

Will Rogers, Jr., son of the late humorist,
has recently added radio acting to a varied
career. For eighteen years he was the editor
and publisher of a southern California newspaper. He supplemented this activity with a
session in Congress, a distinguished record in
World War II, an active role in Democratic
politics in California, and an interest in certain
minority problems.

His acting career began with the motion
picture, *The Story of Will Rogers,* in which
he portrayed his famous father, and has since
broadened to include another motion picture,
a television production, and in 1953 the leading
role in a Columbia Broadcasting System radio
serial entitled *Rogers of the Gazette,* in which
he plays the part of a small town newspaper
editor.

The oldest child of William Penn Adair
and Betty (Blake) Rogers, Will Rogers, Jr.,
was born on October 20, 1911 in New York
City. He has a sister, Mary, and a brother,
James, who is a cattle rancher. The paternal
grandfather, Clem Rogers, was a leading citizen of Oklahoma; of part Indian extraction,
he had been a Cherokee chief, had served as
a member of the Oklahoma State Constitutional
Convention, and founded the bank at Clare-
more in Rogers County, named in his honor.

Will Rogers, Sr., in the words of his son,
"preferred to play the banjo and do rope tricks
rather than work on his father's ranch," which
led to his career as an entertainer in vaudeville,
motion pictures and the theater, and as the
author of a nationally-syndicated column.

At the time of the younger Rogers' birth,
his father was appearing in the Ziegfeld Follies.
During the next few years the family lived on
Long Island, in Oklahoma and in Arkansas.
In 1919 they moved to Beverly Hills, California, where young Will went to school. When
he was thirteen he traveled for two months in
Europe. He was graduated from Beverly Hills
High School, and after a year at the University of Arizona (1932-1933), enrolled at
Leland Stanford University. During his undergraduate days he set a 100-yard backstroke
swimming record, was captain of the university's polo team and a member of the debating
team, and edited the Stanford *Daily* and an
off-campus periodical, *New.* He graduated in
1935 with an A.B. degree in journalism. On
August 15 of that year his father was killed
in a plane crash.

A few months after graduation, Rogers,
with his brother and sister, bought the Beverly Hills *Citizen,* a weekly newspaper. Will
became the active publisher and editor of the
paper, a post he maintained for eighteen years.
Among the editorial campaigns he conducted
were an appeal for a declaration of war on
Germany when France fell in 1940, an attack
on appeasers in 1941 and advocacy of the Marshall Plan in 1947.

In 1942 Rogers entered the primary campaign of the Sixteenth Congressional District
for nomination to Congress, opposing the incumbent, Leland M. Ford. Nominated by the
Democratic party (both candidates ran for
both Democratic and Republican sponsorship),
he was unable to make one campaign speech
before being called into the Army. His wife
and friends conducted a campaign in his behalf which won Rogers a seat in the House
of Representatives. In January 1943, in response to an appeal to Congressmen-elect serv-

ing in the armed forces from Henry L. Stimson, Secretary of War and Sam Rayburn, Speaker of the House, Rogers left Camp Hood, Texas, where he held the rank of second lieutenant in a tank destroyer battalion, and took his place in Congress.

A member of a small liberal bloc in a predominantly anti-administration Congress, Rogers said in August, 1943: "The past six months have been bitter, partisan and have sent crashing down many of the great social gains of the past ten years." The freshman Congressman's first speech in the House attacked Congressman Martin Dies. Rogers voted negatively on extending the life of the Special Committee to Investigate Un-American Activities, an anti-strike bill, and a cut in appropriations to the Office of Price Administration; and he voted for an anti-poll tax bill, UNNRA authorization, and the Administration's soldier vote bill.

He voted against overriding President Roosevelt's vetos of an anti-strike bill, two anti-subsidy bills and a tax bill. He served on the House Foreign Affairs Committee. A column of his observations of the legislature at work, entitled *War Congress,* was published in the Beverly Hills *Citizen* and from time to time in sixteen other papers.

He resigned from Congress on May 24, 1944 and re-entered the Army. Attached to the 814th Tank Destroyer Battalion of the Seventh Armored Division, he fought in most of the major battles of World War II in France, Germany and Belgium. On February 18, 1945 the War Department announced his promotion to first lieutenant and awarded him the Bronze Star for heroism in the Battle of the Belgian Bulge, where "he led a patrol against a German force which threatened to cut off part of the division's withdrawal from St. Vith." He was wounded in the leg during the American drive on Kassel, Germany, on April 9, 1945, and subsequently received the Purple Heart.

Discharged from the Army in November 1945, Rogers returned to the editorship of the Beverly Hills *Citizen.* In November 1946 he ran unsuccessfully for the Senate against William F. Knowland. Earlier in 1946 he had been instrumental in the election of James Roosevelt, son of the late President, as California State chairman of the Democratic Central Committee; the following year he repudiated what he called Roosevelt's "appeasement" of Russia, and anti-Truman sentiments. Rogers was a delegate to the Democratic National Convention in 1948.

Rogers went abroad in 1943 as co-chairman of the Emergency Committee to Save the Jewish People of Europe. In 1947, as co-chairman of the American League for a Free Palestine, he investigated the plight of the Jews made homeless by the Nazis. While in Congress he co-sponsored a bill calling for United States aid for these refugees. Long active on behalf of America's Indian population, he was in 1949 named president of ARROW, Inc. (American Restitution and Righting of Old Wrongs), an affiliate of the National Congress of American Indians.

CBS-Radio

WILL ROGERS, JR.

The motion picture based on his father's life in which Will Rogers, Jr. starred was the culmination of a ten-years project. Mrs. Betty Rogers' book about her husband, *Uncle Clem's Boy,* was purchased in 1941 by Warner Brothers. Several motion picture scripts based on the book were written but were rejected, and many actors were tested for the title role. Will, Jr.'s physical resemblance to his father suggested his portrayal of the part, but he rejected two offers since he was occupied with his Congressional campaign.

It was not until 1951 that he finally agreed to act in the picture which was directed by Michael Curtiz, a family friend who had known the humorist. *The Story of Will Rogers* was described by John Beaufort in the *Christian Science Monitor* as a "mellow, garrulous, entertaining" film which "commemorates richly a memorable American." The younger Rogers' performance was praised chiefly for its fidelity to his father's manner and personality. "I'm not an actor trying to imitate a well-known character," Rogers told interviewers. "I'm just myself, hoping not to let the old man down."

Although he had expected that this would be his only acting chore, he agreed in September, 1952 to make a second film, a Western entitled *The Boy From Oklahoma.* In February, 1953 he sold the Beverly Hills *Citizen,* announcing: "I found to my surprise that . . . you can't make even one movie a year and operate a newspaper too." Upon the completion of his second picture, he said he would like to make another Western, although he minimized his acting ability, saying "so far I've mastered only two expressions—hat on and hat off" (New York *Times,* June 28, 1953).

Rogers, Jr. also started an acting career in radio and television. Following his first film performance he played the leading role in a picture made for television, *Life, Liberty and*

ROGERS, JR., WILL—*Continued*

Orrin Dooley, which John Crosby praised as "full of fresh, sparkling touches of humor and considerably enlivened by Rogers' homespun speeches." The actor has said, however, that he prefers radio to television because "radio is milder, and I just happen to be a mild-mannered fellow." On June 26, 1953 he was the narrator of an hour's radio program, *38th Parallel—USA,* and in July he began the C.B.S. radio-network transcribed series, *Rogers of the Gazette.*

He was married on June 24, 1939 to Collier Connell, who had been a classmate at Leland Stanford University and who had subsequently worked on the San Francisco *Chronicle* and on political campaigns for Upton Sinclair and Franklin D. Roosevelt. Mrs. Rogers has participated actively in her husband's journalistic and political career. They have adopted three Navajo Indians, Randy, Clem and Carl.

Five feet eleven inches tall and weighing 180 pounds, with brown eyes and hair, Rogers, Jr. has been described as having "the same rawboned frame, the twinkling eyes, the large mouth, the infectious grin" as his father. He attends the Methodist Church. In sports he prefers football. His favorite recreations are omniverous reading (preferred authors are Stendhal, Céline and Henry James), and the riding and roping which he learned from his father.

References

N Y Herald Tribune p7+ My 25 '52
N Y Post Mag p3 N 8 '47
N Y Sun p26 Mr 13 '46
Who's Who in America, 1950-51

ROMANOFF, ALEXIS L(AWRENCE)

May 17, 1892- Embryologist; university professor

Address: b. Rice Hall, Cornell University, Ithaca, N.Y.; h. Belleayre Apartments, Ithaca, N.Y.

During his affiliation of nearly thirty years with Cornell University, Alexis L. Romanoff has become an authority on the structure and chemistry of eggs. Professor of chemical embryology since 1948, he is the author of more than 180 scientific and technical publications and popular reviews. With his wife Anastasia J. Romanoff, he completed in 1949 a definitive treatise, *The Avian Egg.* Dr. Romanoff's work has been of economic importance to poultry husbandry and the egg processing industry.

A native of Russia, Alexis Lawrence Romanoff was born in St. Petersburg on May 17, 1892, to Lawrence Mercury Romanoff, a professor, and Daria (Kondratieff) Romanoff. When Alexis, the eldest of seven children (four sons and three daughters), was twelve years old, his father died in the Russo-Japanese War. The boy then left grammar school and was given private tutoring in literature and the arts.

At the end of a two-year preparatory school course that he finished in half the prescribed time, Romanoff in 1910 entered St. Petersburg

Teacher's College where he maintained the highest scholastic ranking in his class. He also attended St. Petersburg Fine Arts Academy (1912-14) and took a course for medical assistants, developing a technical skill which he was able to put to practical use when he later chose a career in embryology.

Since his brothers had died in childhood, Alexis Romanoff, as the only surviving son in his family, was exempt from peacetime military service. However, following the outbreak of World War I, he was sent for military training to Vladimir Commissioned Officers School and the Nicholas Military Engineering Academy in St. Petersburg and to the Officers School of Chemical Warfare at Kazan University.

As a lieutenant in the engineering corps, he commanded a company of engineers until 1919, when he was appointed military commander and technical adviser in the Provisional Government that had been set up in Saratov.

During the next three years, as the Russian revolution advanced, Romanoff took courses in physics and mathematics at Kazan University and at Tomsk University, where he held an assistantship in chemistry, and a course in mechanical engineering at Vladivostok Polytechnic Institute. Leaving Vladivostok in 1920, he crossed the border into China and found employment as a portrait painter. He also worked for about a year as an engineer for the Russian Chinese Eastern Railway Company before "shipping as an oiler on a freighter bound for New York" (*New Yorker,* June 27, 1953).

Shortly after his arrival in the United States in December 1921, Romanoff enrolled at the New York State Institute of Applied Agriculture in Farmingdale, New York, where he soon was employed as manager of the poultry plant. Attracted to Cornell University because of the reputation of its Agricultural College, he went to Ithaca, New York, in September 1923 as a member of the university's freshman class.

The Russian *émigré* secured a research assistantship through the interest of the head of the Poultry Husbandry Department, thus enabling him to study for the next few years. With biochemistry, biophysics, and biology as his major subjects, he was granted his B.S. degree in 1925, his M.S. degree in 1926, and his Ph.D. degree in 1928. For his doctoral thesis he submitted a study on the effect of humidity on the growth and calcium metabolism of chick embryos.

Except for a research fellowship in biology at Harvard University (1939-40), a research fellowship at Yale (1940-41), and a research associateship in physics at the University of Florida (1942), Romanoff's academic association during some thirty years has been entirely with Cornell University. Appointed research instructor in 1928, he was advanced to research assistant professor in 1932 and to associate professor in 1943. Since 1948 he has held the title of professor of chemical embryology. His inquiries and experiments are conducted at Cornell's laboratory of experimental embryology, department of poultry husbandry, agricultural experiment station of the New York State College of Agriculture.

The earliest notable research project undertaken by Romanoff in the laboratory of experimental embryology in the university's Rice Hall was completed in 1924 and concerned the practical testing of eggshell strength. Among his outstanding accomplishments have been the successful use and patenting of the humidity controlling device (1928), disclosure of a need for CO_2 by the early embryo (1930), demonstration of living embryo at all stages of development (1931), development of a method of cultivating the chick embryo outside the shell (1943), and studies of early potentialities of the blastoderm as partial explanation of congenital malformations (1951).

Published papers on these and similar studies have appeared in *Science, Poultry Science, Journal of Experimental Zoology,* and *Food Research.* Romanoff is also the author of a section on eggs for the *Encyclopedia of Chemical Technology* and has illustrated a number of technical publications.

Much of his work has been of economic importance to the poultry industry. He discovered in 1932 the practical usefulness of lowering temperature at hatching time and in 1939 disclosed the embryo's need for higher temperature during early development. After a series of studies on the possibility of determining infertility before incubation, he reported in 1944 that an annual loss of more than 150,000,000 marketable eggs could be prevented.

He has also made investigations into preservation of eggs by flash-heat treatment and preservation of shell eggs by coating with plastics. Another result of research conducted at the experimental station in Ithaca was the development of an electronic method of grading eggs, described by Professor Romanoff as "the first successful attempt to grade eggs mechanically." In listing the advantages of the electronic method, he noted, "it is highly sensitive and can distinguish several quality gradations in fresh eggs; and it can be used to evaluate eggs for marketing, for processing, for cold storage, for hatching, and for identification of good breeding hens" (*Farm Research,* April 1947).

Romanoff, whose work is made possible by funds from private concerns interested in poultry husbandry as well as by Federal and State grants, produced in 1937 in collaboration with E. S. Phillips a motion picture *Where Chick Life Begins,* financed by the Purina Mills Research Laboratory of St. Louis. The first undertaking of its kind, the film shows in natural colors the growth of the chicken egg's embryo. Three different methods were used to photograph this development, as outlined in a review of the picture in *The Cornell Countryman* (January 1938): "through ·the shell by transmitted light, through a hole or 'window' in the blunt end of the egg, and by dissecting the egg in a dish." The *New Yorker* (June 27, 1953) quoted Romanoff as referring to *Where Chick Life Begins* as a "by-product" of his research: "Picture trivial but widely circulated. But if youth, seeing it, is encouraged to become great scientist, my adventure in celluloid becomes important."

Harris & Ewing
ALEXIS L. ROMANOFF

The Avian Egg, written by Romanoff with his wife as junior co-author, was published by John Wiley & Sons in 1949. The 918-page volume deals with laying, external characteristics, structure, and abnormalities of the egg; the chemical and physical properties of the egg; food value, preservation, and industrial uses of the egg. Two outstanding features of the book noted by several critics are Alexis Romanoff's 435 illustrations, including graphs and drawings, and the extensive bibliography covering American, European, and Asiatic literature. Commenting on the broad scope of the treatise, the *United States Quarterly Book List* (June 1949) pointed out that it "should be a most useful volume for anyone working with avian eggs either in the so-called 'pure' fields of biology or in the 'applied' ones of poultry husbandry."

Romanoff is preparing another book, a projected 4,000-page *The Avian Embryo,* which will take him several years to complete. "To bring up to date the known, then plunge with all my heart and soul into the unknown," he has said, "that is my aim" (*New Yorker,* June 27, 1953).

Twice a recipient of the Poultry Science Research honorary mention (1931 and 1935), Professor Romanoff is also winner of the Borden award and Gold Medal from the American Poultry Science Association (1950). His professional memberships include the American Association for the Advancement of Science (fellow), World Poultry Science Association, American Chemical Society, Society for Experimental Biology and Medicine, American Physiological Society, American Society of Zoologists, American Genetics Association, Poultry Science Association, and New York Academy of Science. His fraternity is Sigma Xi and his clubs are the Statler, Cornell University, and the Rotary in Ithaca.

(*Continued next page*)

ROMANOFF, ALEXIS—*Continued*

Alexis Romanoff's Polish-born wife, Anastasia J. (Sayenko) Romanoff, whom he married on September 1, 1928, was formerly a bacteriologist and was recently, for a time, a research associate in the department of geography at the University of Maryland. An article about Cornell's professor of embryology appearing in the *Saturday Evening Post* (November 25, 1950) and a two-part Profile in the *New Yorker* (June 20 and June 27, 1953) picture him as a shy scholar whose interests are limited to the study of the egg. He has blue eyes and blond hair, and with a height of 140 pounds stands five feet five inches in height. In 1927 he became a naturalized citizen of the United States. He attends the Greek Orthodox Church and in politics prefers the Republican party. His hobbies—painting, sketching, and designing of scientific apparatus—have been turned to valuable use in his embryological research.

References

New Yorker 29:32+ Je 20 '53; 29:32+ Je 27 '53
Read Digest 30:106+ F '51
Sat Eve Post 223:20+ N 25 '50 por
American Men of Science (1949)
Who Knows—and What (1949)
Who's Who in America, 1952-53
Who's Who in American Education, 1952
Who's Who in New York, 1952

ROMBAUER, IRMA (VON) S(TARKLOFF) Oct. 30, 1877- Author

Address: h. 5712 Cabanne Ave., St. Louis 12, Mo.

Author of one of America's best selling cookbooks, the *Joy of Cooking* (first published privately in 1931 and then in 1936 by the Bobbs-Merrill Company), Mrs. Irma S. Rombauer says her chief purpose in writing the book was to "lift everyday cooking out of the commonplace." Her many readers attest to the fact that she has succeeded.

Since the *Joy of Cooking* was combined in 1943 with another of the author's books, *Streamlined Cooking* (Bobbs-Merrill, 1939), it grew steadily in popularity and by 1953 had sold over 1,300,000 copies. "Mrs. Rombauer's expert, explicit manner of writing recipes is nearly baffle-proof," commented *Time* (August 16, 1943).

A revised edition, *The New Joy of Cooking*, published in 1951 by Bobbs-Merrill, took into full account new food processing methods, pressure cookers, electric blenders and other modern equipment. Mrs. Rombauer's daughter, Marion Rombauer Becker, collaborated with her mother on this volume, and Ginnie Hofmann did the illustrations. Called by J. H. Jackson of the San Francisco *Chronicle* "one of the classic American volumes on cookery" this edition has gone into many printings. Now a gray-haired energetic and sociable St. Louis grandmother Mrs. Rombauer became the au-

thor of her best seller almost accidentally when she began collecting recipes for her children.

She was born Irma von Starkloff in St. Louis, Missouri, October 30, 1877, the daughter of Dr. H. M. von Starkloff and Clara (Kuhlmann) von Starkloff. Her father, descended from a German family from Stuttgart, was a soldier, physician and American consul in Bremen (Germany). Her mother's antecedents were also German, a family who for generations were in the spice business in Lübeck and were members of an early *hansa*. There was a barony on the father's side, a grandmother who was an Austrian countess and a great-grandfather who was a general under Napoleon. Mrs. Rombauer's mother came to the United States with Susan Blow to found the first kindergarten in St. Louis in 1873.

With this European background, it was natural for young Irma von Starkloff to spend a number of her early years abroad, learning to speak German and French fluently (later to be of help in recipe collecting) and studying at various Swiss boarding schools in Lausanne and Geneva. She recalls, "I was brought up to be a 'young lady'—heaven save the mark! I played the piano poorly, embroidered and sewed, painted on china, and entertained 'callers.' As a family we travelled extensively . . . filled our hours with opera-going, gallery-visiting and letter writing. All utterly delightful and almost useless from a practical standpoint."

Marriage to a young lawyer, Edgar Roderick Rombauer, on October 14, 1899, found her unprepared for domestic duties—"but," recalls Mrs. Rombauer, "few of my contemporaries were better fitted—were not there plenty of maids to be had at ten dollars a month? So my camp-loving husband taught me to cook."

By degrees Mrs. Rombauer took an interest in menu-planning and in cooking. She established high standards for the family table. With increasing prosperity, the Rombauers and their two children entertained more and more and she began to acquire a reputation in St. Louis for her social arts, not the least of which was her cooking.

In 1930, when Mrs. Rombauer was fifty-three, her husband died. After her son and daughter married and set up their own households, they asked her to write them a little cookbook, containing recipes of the good dishes she had taught them to enjoy. She eagerly agreed, glad to have something to occupy her mind. In 1931, she completed this collection of recipes, which she entitled *Joy of Cooking* and paid to have it published. The book sold 3,000 copies. She then rewrote and enlarged the volume and added the step-by-step method of listing the ingredients as the mixing process proceeds which is still a feature of subsequent editions.

The first Bobbs-Merrill edition, published in 1936, sold fairly well but it was not until the 1943 revision that Mrs. Rombauer's cookbook began to take American housewives (and their grateful husbands) by storm. In that year, in her home town, the sales of the *Joy of Cooking* even topped the current best seller, Wendell Willkie's *One World*. The *Joy of Cooking* was the only cookbook to carry a money-back

IRMA ROMBAUER

guarantee. Out of the first million and a quarter copies sold only one was returned. Said Bobb-Merrill's President D. L. Chambers: "The reader didn't follow instructions."

The 1951 revision brought this comment from Valerie Bowers, Chicago Sunday *Tribune*: "An enlarged and vastly improved edition of the book that has become the final authority on food preparation in more than a million homes."

Although her royalties have put Mrs. Rombauer in the comfortable income class, she continues to live very simply in a St. Louis apartment. She visits her son, Edgar Rombauer, in Seattle and her daughter, Marion Rombauer Becker, who is married to a Cincinnati architect, each year. She owns ten acres of wooded land in Pevely, Missouri, on which she has built a hideaway home. She devotes much of her time to her fan mail, answering questions in longhand.

Mrs. Rombauer also wrote *Cookbook for Girls and Boys* published in 1946 by Bobbs-Merrill, and has contributed articles to the St. Louis *Post-Dispatch* and *Ladies' Home Journal*.

Active in civic affairs, she is a past-president of the Wednesday Club of St. Louis and of the St. Louis Symphony Women's Association, and has been a board member of the Children's Lunch Association, Community Music Schools, Audubon Society, People's Art Center, and the St. Louis Opera Guild. She collects antiques, enjoys gardening, and reading biographies. She has brown eyes and gray hair, is five feet three and a half inches tall, and weighs 140 pounds. She states that her political affiliation "varies" and her church is the Unitarian.

References

Chicago Sunday Tribune p5 Ag 12 '51
Coronet p146+ O '50
San Francisco Chronicle p14 Jl 23 '51
Time 42:102 Ag 16 '43
Who's Who in America, 1950-1951

ROOME, MRS. CHARLES O. *See* Goertz, A.

ROSE, WILLIAM C(UMMING) Apr. 4, 1887- University professor; biochemist
Address: b. c/o Noyes Laboratory of Chemistry, University of Illinois, Urbana, Ill.; h. 710 Florida Ave., Urbana, Ill.

Professor of biochemistry at the University of Illinois, William C. Rose is a world authority on nutrition who discovered, isolated, and identified in 1935 the amino acid *threonine*, making it possible to prepare experimental diets in which proteins are replaced by mixtures of purified amino acids. During his thirty years of research and teaching at the University of Illinois, Rose has performed or directed research mainly in the biochemistry of proteins and in the role of amino acids in the metabolism and nutrition of man and other animals, which has led to a number of new commercial products.

William Cumming Rose was born April 4, 1887, in Greenville, South Carolina, the son of John McAden and Mary Evans (Santos) Rose. His father was descended from early American families, largely of Scotch and English origin, who settled in North Carolina; his mother's grandfather was Portuguese consul at the port of Norfolk, Virginia. John McAden Rose, a Presbyterian minister, having moved from South Carolina to North Carolina, young William was reared in Laurinburg and Fayetteville. He attended private school in Laurinburg until he was fourteen years of age, when he prepared for college under the direction of his father. His interest in chemistry was aroused by reading a textbook in elementary chemistry used by his sister in college. "Thereafter," he has said, "I never had any problem concerning my lifework." At Davidson College in North Carolina, he was active in the debating society, the Sigma Alpha Epsilon fraternity, and the Young Men's Christian Association, and during his senior year, he was an assistant in the chemistry department. In 1907 he received his B.S. degree, graduating second in a class of sixty-eight students.

While studying for his doctor's degree in biochemistry, which he took at Yale University in 1911, Rose served (1908-11) as assistant in physiological chemistry to Professor Lafayette B. Mendel of the Yale Sheffield Scientific School. With Mendel he discovered that tryptophan and lysine are indispensable amino acids in food, giving the first proof that certain essential amino acids cannot be synthesized by body cells but must be provided in food. His doctoral thesis was concerned with the metabolism of mucic acid, creatine, and creatinine. In 1911 Rose was appointed instructor in biochemistry at the College of Medicine of the University of Pennsylvania. After several months (from February to August) of postdoctoral study in 1913 at the University of Freiburg, Germany, he became associate professor in biochemistry at the College of Medicine of the University of Texas. The following year he was advanced to professor of biochemistry and head of the chemistry department, positions he retained until 1922, when he went to the University of

WILLIAM C. ROSE

Illinois as a professor of physiological chemistry.

At the annual meeting of the Federation of American Societies for Experimental Biology in April 1935, Rose reported his isolation in pure form and his artificial preparation of a new amino acid, threonine, bringing the total known amino acids to twenty-two. This new amino acid (Amino-Beta-Hydroxybutyric), Rose discovered, was an essential element in food, without which animals, including man, could not grow. As a result of this discovery, it was possible to feed animals a mixture of amino acids in place of proteins, together with other basic essentials of a normal diet, and have them grow. Unlike proteins, he reported, amino acids may be introduced directly into the bloodstream. Another study, "Nutritive Significance of the Amino Acids and Certain Related Compounds," appeared in _Science_ (October 1, 1937).

Appointed professor of biochemistry at the University of Illinois in 1936, Rose was also named acting head of the chemistry department in 1942. Meanwhile, in the summer of 1938 he was a visiting lecturer at the University of Michigan and fourteenth Hektoen lecturer at the Institute of Medicine in Chicago. Of his abilities as a teacher, H. E. Carter, a coworker at the University of Illinois, has said, "Rose instills a special brand of enthusiasm into any discussions he enters. It is an enthusiasm which isn't forced, but simply overflows from an intense personal interest in biochemistry" (_Chemical and Engineering News_, June 2, 1952). Another colleague called him the most polished lecturer in the university. Rose is credited with developing the division of biochemistry at the university into a teaching and research unit "of utmost value—not only to chemistry, but to biology and related departments" (_Chemical and Engineering News_).

In 1942 Rose began concentrating in his research on the amino acid requirements of man, a study which he was to conduct over a period of ten years. He tested the amino acid needs of graduate male student volunteers at the university with carefully controlled diets of purified amino acids, starch, sucrose, butterfat, and vitamins. By these tests Rose ascertained that the lack of any one of eight amino acids in food produced a negative nitrogen balance in man which resulted in a loss in appetite, extreme feeling of fatigue, and increasing nervous irritability. Taking part in a symposium, arranged by the Nutrition Foundation, Inc., in 1946 in New York City, to strengthen research in nutrition, Rose discussed the possibility of administering amino acid mixtures to patients unable to consume food normally. In the same year at a meeting of the American Chemical Society he read a paper, "The Role of Amino Acids in Human Nutrition," in which he reported that the amino acids histidine or arginine, required by the rat and dog, are not essential in man's diet to maintain satisfactory nitrogen balance. The difference between animal and human amino acid requirements, he stated before the New York Academy of Medicine in 1947, was probably due to the "ability of the human body to interchange the acids in the digestive process, or to synthesize the missing ones out of simple materials" (New York _Times_, October 14, 1947).

After discovering the eight essential amino acids required by man in food, Rose was able to determine by continuing experiments on volunteer graduate male students at the University of Illinois, the minimum daily amounts of these acids needed for proper nitrogen balance in the body. These experiments made it possible "to evaluate the nutritive quality of any protein in its ability to meet human needs, provided the protein is known to be digestible" (_Chemical and Engineering News_, June 9, 1952). Rose also found that an amino acid deficiency is likely only in individuals who are diet faddists or who maintain highly limited diets. Mainly interested in the biochemistry of metabolism, Rose has determined many intermediary metabolic processes in the body involving creatinine, purines, mucic acid, creatin, as well as amino acids. In 1952 the biochemist began the investigation of the problem of how amino acids not present in food are manufactured in the body.

In an advisory capacity Rose has served on a number of Government organizations: as civilian chairman of the committee on protein foods and a member of the food and nutrition board of the National Research Council (1940-47), a member of the advisory health council of the National Institute of Health (1944-49), and as consultant to the United States Public Health Service (1945-49). He was a member of the council on pharmacy and chemistry of the American Medical Association (1936-43) and of the advisory board of Wistar Institute (1936-40). Rose—the author of more than one hundred articles on creatine, creatinine, purines, and amino acids—has contributed papers on nutrition and intermediary metabolism and biochemistry of the amino acids to the _Journal of Biological Chemistry_, _Journal of Nutrition_,

Journal of Pharmacology and Experimental Therapeutics, and *American Journal of Physiology,* among others. From 1935 to 1939 he was a member of the editorial board of the *Journal of Nutrition* and from 1936 to 1949 of the *Journal of Biological Chemistry.*

An honorary member of the Harvey Society, Rose also holds membership in the National Academy of Sciences, the American Association for the Advancement of Science, the American Medical Association (associate fellow), the American Chemical Society, the American Society of Biological Chemists (councilor 1931-34, vice-president 1937-39, president 1939-41), the American Institute of Nutrition (vice-president 1944-45, president 1945-46), the Illinois Academy of Science, the Nutrition Foundation, Inc. (science advisory committee 1943), and the Society of Experimental Biology and Medicine. His Greek-letter societies are Phi Beta Kappa, Phi Kappa Phi, Sigma Xi, Phi Lambda Upsilon, Sigma Alpha Epsilon, Phi Beta Pi, and Alpha Chi Sigma; among his clubs are the Chaos Club of Chicago and the University Club of Urbana, Illinois.

Rose holds honorary degrees of Doctor of Science from Davidson College and Yale University, conferred in 1947. Awards received by the biochemist are the Annual Scientific Award of the Grocery Manufacturers of America for his research and discoveries in nutrition (1947); the Osborne-Mendel Award of the American Institute of Nutrition (1949); the Willard Gibbs Medal Award from the American Chemical Society (Chicago Section) "for measurement of the amino acid requirements of animals and man." This award, conferred in 1952, was also in acknowledgment of his many other contributions to nutrition research, and is regarded as one of the highest honors in American chemistry. On June 16, 1952, *Chemical and Engineering News* announced that Rose was one of four men awarded a Guggenheim Fellowship of $15,000 "to be used in any way he sees fit during a three-year period in furtherance of his research."

A colleague observes of Rose in *Chemical and Engineering News* (June 2, 1952) that "uncluttered could be used to describe the desk, the office, the laboratory, the research reports, the mind—in fact, the life of W. C. Rose." His quiet efficiency in research carries over into his administrative duties.

On September 3, 1913, Rose married Zula Franklin Hedrick, formerly a school teacher. The Rose home at Illinois University has been called a "haven for biochemistry graduate students," and the attendance of Rose and his wife at scientific meetings is said to engender a graduate reunion. With a height of five feet seven inches, Rose weighs 135 pounds; he has brown eyes and gray hair. He names gardening, photography, and amateur ornithology as his hobbies. He votes independently, and his church affiliation is Presbyterian.

References

Chem & Eng N 30:2298-9 Je 2 '52
American Men of Science (1949)
Who's Who in America, 1952-53
Who's Who in Chemistry (1951)

ROYEN, JAN HERMAN VAN (van roi′ yen) Apr. 10, 1905- Ambassador from the Netherlands to the United States
Address: The Netherlands Embassy, 1470 Euclid St., N.W., Washington, D. C.

Since his appointment as Ambassador from Holland to the United States in June 1950, Dr. Jan Herman van Royen has endeavored to maintain and strengthen the political and economic ties between Holland and the United States. This appointment followed his Ambas-

Official Netherlands Photo.

JAN HERMAN VAN ROYEN

sadorship to Canada and membership on the United Nations Security Council.

One of his principal achievements was his part in the arrangement to transfer sovereignty of Indonesia from the Dutch Government to the United States of Indonesia in 1949. In the opinion of Stewart Alsop of the New York *Herald Tribune* (June 27, 1949) his activity in these negotiations marked him as a "thoughtful, fair-minded, highly intelligent diplomat."

Jan Herman van Royen was born in Istanbul, Turkey, on April 10, 1905, the son of Jan Herman and American-born Albertina (Winthrop) van Royen. The elder van Royen, who served at that time with the Netherlands Legation at Istanbul, later was the Netherlands Minister to the United States from 1927 to 1933. Jan van Royen studied law in Utrecht, where he received his Ph.D. degree in 1929.

From the beginning his career has been in the Netherlands diplomatic service. In 1930 he was named attaché to the Netherlands Legation in Washington, a post he held until 1933, when he was recalled to the Ministry of Foreign Affairs at The Hague. He was appointed secretary to the Netherlands Legation in Tokyo in 1936, and three years later he was named chief

ROYEN, JAN HERMAN VAN—*Continued*
of the political division of the Netherlands
Ministry of Foreign Affairs.

When the Germans overran Holland in World
War II, Dr. van Royen became active in the
Resistance and was jailed three times by the
Nazis before he made a final escape to Eng-
land in 1944. At the end of the European hos-
tilities, he returned to Holland and in 1945 was
appointed Minister without portfolio in the
Dutch Cabinet. In 1946, from March to July,
Dr. van Royen held the post of Minister of
Foreign Affairs.

In debating the territorial rectification with
Germany after the war, Dr. van Royen emphasized that the Netherlands "did not want
a peace of revenge for Germany but only a
settlement of the German question which will
prevent this potentially dangerous neighbor from
starting again an aggressive war" (*Christian
Science Monitor*, October 31, 1946).

At the United Nations conferences and assemblies in San Francisco, London, New York,
and Paris from 1945 to 1948, Dr. van Royen
served first as an assistant delegate and then as
a delegate; he was appointed Ambassador to
Canada in 1947, and from 1948 until his present
appointment he served simultaneously as the
Netherlands representative on the United Nations Security Council.

At the time of his appointment to the latter
post, Dutch citizens in Indonesia were seeking
protection in the conflict over sovereignty of
the islands. Defending Dutch police action
against terrorists, Dr. van Royen challenged
the United Nations' jurisdiction in the case saying that the Republic of Indonesia had specifically agreed that sovereignty in the whole of
Indonesia was and would remain with the
Netherlands Government until the establishment
of the United States of Indonesia.

In a speech to the Security Council he denied
charges by the United States and other countries that the Netherlands was failing to carry
out the Security Council's orders. He maintained that "the unalterable aim of the Netherlands Government remains the immediate creation of an all-Indonesian federal interim government, followed as soon as possible by free
elections for a representative body with a view
to the establishment of a Netherlands-Indonesian
union and the creation of a United States of
Indonesia, to which sovereignty will be transferred" (*Christian Science Monitor,* Janury 15,
1949).

Opposing the American-sponsored resolution
in the Security Council which established a
timetable for giving full sovereignty to the
United States of Indonesia, Dr. van Royen
told the Security Council that it would be " 'extremely difficult' for his country to accept the
joint resolution on grounds that it required the
Netherlands to surrender an important part of
its sovereignty. . . ."

Dr. van Royen was named chief delegate
from the Netherlands to the preliminary conference at Batavia in June 1949 to lay the
groundwork for the round-table conference to
be held at The Hague. In a speech soon after
his arrival emphasizing his belief that neither
the social soil nor political climate of Indonesia

would permit the development of communism,
he made the statement, "The Western world
will find in Indonesia the first effective resistance to the spread of Russian communism
in this part of the world" (*Christian Science
Monitor,* June 22, 1949). A writer for this
newspaper added that Dr. Van Royen "believes that the Islands offer an almost classic
opportunity for economic values and political
advantages of democracy to prevent both ideological communism and the communism that
springs from hunger."

As vice-chairman of The Hague Conference
in August 1949 Dr. van Royen was given much
credit for the arrangement to transfer sovereignty of Indonesia and to settle all the complex problems that would attend that transfer.
His role in the negotiations was to present a
new Dutch colonial policy which recognized
the nationalist rights and aspirations of native
populations.

Dr. van Royen was appointed Ambassador to
the United States in 1950, succeeding Dr. Eelco
van Kleffins. Feeling that the value of Western
Europe as a defender of the free world is directly related to her economic condition, he
listed three steps necessary to recovery in the
Netherlands: increased home production, lower
world trade barriers and increased exports. The
Ambassador believes that the United States
should share essential raw materials with the
Western Europe in order to reinforce European
productivity. He has sought increased investment of capital in Europe, especially American
capital, assuring Americans that his country has
made liberal provision for the transfer of
profits, dividends and royalties.

Urging Dutch-American industrial cooperation at a speech made before the Milwaukee
Association of Commerce in February 1952, the
diplomat said, "We want to travel on the road
of industrialization together . . . we want
wherever necessary to lean on American industrial wisdom and know-how, and we want,
where feasible, an exchange of knowledge."

An advocate of international cooperation, Dr.
van Royen has championed the United Nations
as a vitally useful and effective instrument. He
has remarked, "They [the United Nations] do
create a forum, they do create a possibility and
an opportunity for the representatives of the
countries of the East and West to meet, to
exchange their ideas and get an inkling of what
the other side is thinking."

Dr. van Royen also supports restricted international endeavors such as the North Atlantic Treaty Organization and the Benelux Union.
He considers the success of the Benelux Union
to be concrete evidence of the value of international cooperation and of the possibility of
even larger and more ambitious European fed-
erations. A major reason for the success of
the Benelux Union is, according to van Royen,
the fact that "all tariffs between Belgium, the
Netherlands and Luxemburg have been abolished and that there is now one common tariff
applied for the three countries in their trade
relations with the outside world." In advocating
the North Atlantic Treaty Organization as a
collective instrument of a united Western
World, he is not content with the merely mili-

tary objectives of NATO. The Ambassador stated "A further almost equally important motive is the desire of the European NATO-countries to be partners with the United States and Canada in a democratic community which has not solely a military character, but which also constitutes a positive step in strengthening the economic, social and cultural relations between its members."

As to the NATO powers' attitude toward the Soviet "peace offensive," he urges that we maintain our common defense effort, make the most of any real possibility offered by the Russians for a genuine Korean peace, and resist efforts to create dissension among NATO countries themselves.

The diplomat was the recipient of the honorary degree of Doctor of Humane Letters from Morningside College, Sioux City, Iowa, in 1951 and the honorary LL.B. degree from Hope College of Holland, Michigan, in 1952, Hofstra College of Hempstead, Long Island, in 1952, and New York University in 1953. He is a commander in the Order of the Netherlands Lion and an honorary commander in the Order of the British Empire. Van Royen married Anne Snouck Hurgronje in 1934. They have four children, Henriette Albertina, Jan Herman, Digna, and Willem. Royen has been described as "slim, patient . . . [and] able."

References

International Who's Who, 1952
International Yearbook and Statesmen's Who's Who, 1953
Wie is dat? (1948)
World Biography (1948)

ROYSTER, VERMONT C(ONNECTICUT) Apr. 30, 1914- Editor; writer

Address: b. c/o Wall Street Journal, 44 Broad St., New York 4; h. Hastings-on-Hudson, N.Y.

"An ability to discern the underlying moral issue, illuminated by a deep faith and confidence in the people of our country," was attributed to Vermont C. Royster in the citation for the Pulitzer Prize which was awarded to him in 1953 for editorial writing. The prize was not given for one specific editorial, but for his work in general, which was credited with "warmth, simplicity and understanding of the basic outlook of the American people." A senior associate editor of the *Wall Street Journal,* Royster's editorials appear in a daily column called "Review and Outlook."

Vermont Connecticut Royster was born April 30, 1914 in Raleigh, North Carolina, the son of Wilbur High and Olivette (Broadway) Royster. His father was a professor of Latin, Greek, and law at the University of North Carolina, and later a lawyer. Royster attended the Webb School, a preparatory school at Bell Buckle, Tennessee, and was graduated in 1931. He entered the University of North Carolina, where he majored in English literature, was editor of the university newspaper, contributed

Maury Garber

VERMONT C. ROYSTER

to the literary magazine, and was elected to Phi Beta Kappa.

Having always wanted to be a newspaper or magazine writer, he went to New York City after he was graduated in 1935 and began his career as a reporter for the New York City News Bureau. Royster joined the staff of the *Wall Street Journal* in 1936 as a correspondent in Washington, D.C., reporting on national affairs. His news beat included the White House, Congress, the Supreme Court, and the Treasury.

Enlisting in the Navy, in 1941, Royster became a line officer and commanded, successively, a subchaser, a patrol ship and a destroyer escort. He participated in operations in the Palau Islands, the Philippine Sea and Okinawa, and was assigned to escort duty in the Atlantic Ocean. He was discharged in 1945 as a lieutenant commander.

Returning to the *Wall Street Journal* after the war, Royster became chief correspondent in charge of the Washington Bureau. In 1948 he was made associate editor, and in 1951 senior associate editor. Royster's experience in political reporting has included the covering of the Democratic and Republican conventions in Philadelphia in 1948 and of both parties again in Chicago in 1952. In economic affairs he covered the United Nations Monetary and Financial Conference on Wilmington Island, near Savannah, Georgia, in 1946, when the International Monetary Fund and the International Bank for Reconstruction and Development, better known as the World Bank, were officially activated.

Royster likes to use quotations in his editorials from Lewis Carroll to illustrate a point satirically. Referring to *Through the Looking Glass* he compared the Federal tax system in 1948 to the Red Queen's demand that Alice must run twice as fast to get some place in her country. In an article entitled "What Can

ROYSTER, VERMONT—*Continued*

We Do About Taxes" (*Saturday Evening Post,* March 30, 1948) he described the wage earners' attempt to "outrun the treadmill," that is, to buy more and show material gain as they advanced in their jobs and earned higher pay.

Comparing Federal taxes before and after World War II, he showed how, in cases of selected average individuals, the income tax had increased at a faster rate than the advancement in salary, leaving the worker with actually less money despite his higher post-war earnings. He emphasized that taxes are "propped up by a big budget and by the fact that the Government no longer levies taxes only to raise revenue. Taxes have become an instrument for carrying out other economic and social policies."

On October 6, 1949 Royster undertook to analyze the Number One enigma of the time, Joseph Stalin. In an editorial (which the *Wall Street Journal* reprinted March 9, 1953, after the announcement of Stalin's death) he wrote "that to judge communism by the personalities of its leaders is to misjudge it tragically." He pointed out that like all revolutionists, this "little band of communists" led by Lenin came to slay inhumanities, but whereas other revolutionists "came to set men free, the communists came to remake the world into a world as they would have it be."

He continued, "When men are snared by the vision to rebuild the world, nothing but evil can ensue. . . .Not only will such men do evil, but in time they come to justify evil to themselves. Compulsion, enslavement, and even murder become the stepping stones up the altar. . . . Stalin appears monstrous because he sees clearly what Lenin or any other of the great leaders must soon have seen, that what must be done must be done. Had he done it less ably, there would have been no enigma."

Royster's conclusion was that "nothing is so corrupting to a man as to believe it his duty to save mankind from men. He comes to evil because he must first usurp the rights of men and finally the prerogatives of God. . . .So the evil that is Stalin is no enigma, whatever his personality be."

One of his editorials, reprinted in the July 1950 *Reader's Digest,* stated that "morality may be valued these days but not as much as a dollar bill. There is," he wrote, "nothing new in the idea of raiding the public treasury. What is novel is its newly acquired respectability. . . .Everybody's doing it. Strangely, everybody is also denouncing it. . . .Businessmen have been in the forefront of those denouncing government extravagance. Yet when the line is formed, there are businessmen seeking subsidies for this or that industry . . . both the big businessman seeking millions and the little businessman seeking a few thousands.

"There, too, is the union man who deplores these handouts to business. All he wants from the Government is a subsidized house, subsidized food, subsidized medical care, subsidized retirement. The farmer thinks he ought to have subsidized tools, subsidized electricity, subsidized irrigation and—to go the others one better—a guaranteed subsidized income. The doc-

tor chips in to fight all these things and merely wants the government to subsidize his training and his laboratories. The professor sadly says this is the way Rome went and suggests that government subsidize his university."

Even young people, Royster said, have come to feel that "the government owes them an education, and the old people that it owes them a rocking chair, and the veterans, young and old, are convinced that the government owes them everything."

Royster's views on foreign policy were expressed in his column on December 26 and 27, 1950. While condoning neither containment of communism, which he said would unintentionally tend to make all forget that it is primarily the responsibility of other peoples to defend themselves, nor the idea that self-defense means retiring to a continental fortress, Royster stated that the policy is to avoid embroilments which debilitate our strength. This would permit the debate which the policy of containment precludes and allow Congress and the Administration to listen to the best military and economic judgments on particular problems. "There is then at least hope that we will move by judgment and not by inspiration."

Observing the way in which some people were studying the Korean truce news in relation to the stock market, Royster said they talked as if war were bullish and peace were bearish. "War itself is a terrible thing," he wrote, "but we find more terrible the fact that there are men walking about who talk of peace as if it were terrible" (*Wall Street Journal,* March 31, 1953).

Royster is an Episcopalian; his clubs are the National Press Club in Washington, D.C., and the University Club in New York City. On June 5, 1937 he married the former Frances Claypoole; they have two daughters, Frances C. and Eleanor. Royster's given names are the same as his grandfather's, whose own father named all his children after States in the Union. He said he was the last descendant to be named this way.

References

N Y Herald Tribune p16 My 5 '53
N Y Times p24 My 5 '53
Reader's Digest July '50

RUNDSTEDT, GERD VON   *See* Rundstedt, K. R. G., von

RUNDSTEDT, KARL (RUDOLF GERD) VON Dec. 12, 1875—Feb. 24, 1953 German army officer; became major in World War I and was appointed to General Staff; in World War II commanded invasions of Poland (1939) and France (1940) and the campaign against Russia; headed German defense units and retreating forces at close of the war; captured by Allies in 1945 and imprisoned in England, but released because of failing health, thus escaping trial as a war criminal. See *Current Biography,* 1941.

Obituary

N Y Times p27 F 25 '53

SABIN, FLORENCE R(ENA) Nov. 9, 1871—Oct. 3, 1953 Anatomist; famed for her discovery of the origin and processes of the lymphatic system, developing a method of studying living cells, and studies in tuberculosis; educated at Smith College and Johns Hopkins Medical School; first woman elected to life membership in the National Academy of Science and first woman member of Rockefeller Institute of Medical Research; awarded the Jane Addams Medal for distinguished service by an American woman, the Lasker Foundation award for public health achievement, and Trudeau Medal of National Tuberculosis Association. See *Current Biography,* 1945.

Obituary

N Y Times p89 O 4 '53

SADAK, NECMEDDIN 1890—Sept. 21, 1953 Former Foreign Minister of Turkey, editor and publisher; born in Isparta, Turkey; educated in Istanbul and at the University of Lyon, France; founded *Aksam,* an Istanbul daily in 1917; elected to the National Assembly in 1929 as a representative of the Republican People's party; in 1932, appointed delegate to the Geneva Disarmament Conference; permanent Turkish delegate to the League of Nations from 1936-1939, "roving envoy" for Turkey during World War II; served as Foreign Minister from 1947-1950; advocate of a Mediterranean agreement to supplement NATO; in 1949 chief of his country's delegation to the General Assembly of the United Nations. See *Current Biography,* 1950.

Obituary

N Y Times p31 S 22 '53

SALEH, ALLAH-YAR May 17, 1897- Former Ambassador from Iran to the United States

Address: Shimran, Iran

At the time of his appointment as Iranian Ambassador to the United States, Allah-Yar Saleh, who presented his credentials in Washington, D.C., on September 24, 1952, was known chiefly for his prominent role in nationalizing British-owned oil properties in Iran in 1951 and in submitting Iran's case in the British-Iranian dispute before the United Nations Security Council and the International Court of Justice. A leading political figure in Premier Mohammed Mossadegh's National Front in the Madjlis (lower house of the Iranian Parliament) in 1950-51, Saleh was a member of the Oil Nationalization Committee of that body and chairman of the Parliamentary Mixed Committee for supervision of the execution of the Oil Nationalization Law.

After Mossadegh was deposed by Iranian mobs in August 1953, and was succeeded by General Fazlollah Zahedi as Premier, Allah-Yar Saleh resigned as Ambassador. He asked permission to name one of the senior officers of the Embassy to take charge and he stated that he planned to return to Iran as soon as possible.

Since 1933 he held important government posts, including Minister of Finance, Minister of Justice, and Minister of the Interior, and had occasionally represented his country on brief missions abroad.

Allah-Yar Saleh was born in Kashan, Iran, on May 17, 1897, one of nine children (eight boys and one girl) of Hassan Saleh, a civil servant, and of Khorsheed (Legha Khanom) Saleh. For his high school education, Saleh went to Tehran, Iran's capital city, to attend the American College, founded by Samuel Martin Jordan of the Presbyterian Board of Foreign Missions in Iran, whom Saleh has spoken of as having had considerable influence on his decision to seek a career in government service. As a student, Saleh, who graduated from the American College in 1918, was chiefly interested in law, philosophy, logic, and religion. After additional training at Alborz College in Tehran and a period of private study in law, he was appointed to the position of investigating judge in Tehran in April 1928.

For the next five years Saleh held a number of posts in the state judicial system of Iran, until in December 1933 he was chosen director of the Iranian Government Monopoly for Opium and Tobacco. Following a year's service as director general of the Iranian Customs Administration (from October 1934 to September 1935), he entered the Ministry of Finance, where in December 1936 he was promoted from director general of the ministry to Deputy Minister of Finance. On his first diplomatic mission, Saleh in March 1938 was a member of the Iranian delegation sent to Moscow to negotiate a commercial agreement with the Soviet Union. As chairman of the Iranian Commercial and Economic Delegation he went to Washington, D.C., in August 1940 in connection with the negotiation of a reciprocal trade agreement between Iran and the United States. The following year in November he attained cabinet rank as Minister of Finance, an office to which he was again named in February 1942. In October of that year he became chairman of the board of directors of the Mortgage Bank of Iran and the next month was sent abroad again as Iranian commercial representative in India. Saleh was made Minister of Justice in May 1944 and reappointed to head the same ministry the following year in May upon his return to Iran from the United Nations Conference held in April in San Francisco, which he attended as a member of the Iranian delegation. Subsequent cabinet posts held by the Iranian statesman were Minister without Portfolio (appointed in November 1945), Minister of the Interior (appointed in December 1945), and Minister of Justice (appointed in August 1946).

Elected to the sixteenth Madjlis (the lower house of the Iranian Parliament) from his native Kashan, Saleh represented that district in 1950-51. It was during his term as a legislator that Saleh joined the "Vatan" group, or National Front, then forming under the leadership of Mohammed Mossadegh, who was to be-

ALLAH-YAR SALEH

come Premier of Iran in April 1951. With this group of deputies Saleh supported the scheme for the nationalization of the properties of the British-owned Anglo-Iranian Oil Company and became a member of the eighteen-man Oil Nationalization Committee of the Majlis, which was instrumental in rejecting the company's proposals for a new royalties agreement and for securing the passage in April 1951 of the Oil Nationalization Act. On May of that year the law creating the Iranian National Oil Company, to take over the properties and function of the Anglo-Iranian Company, became operative under a decree of the Shah. Saleh was made chairman of the Parliamentary Mixed Committee, which supervised the execution of the law. In this capacity, he later told Elizabeth Maguire of the Washington *Post*, he had to "talk with at least fifty newspaper reporters a day, of mixed nationalities."

When the British Government brought its claims for restitution before the United Nations Security Council in New York in November 1951, Saleh was a member of the delegation headed by Premier Mossadegh which presented Iran's case to the council. The Mossadegh mission was able to dissuade the council from taking action, pending a decision by the World Court. Soon after returning to Iran, Saleh, in January 1952, was appointed Minister of the Interior in Mossadegh's Cabinet. The following June he went to the Netherlands to join an Iranian delegation to the International Court of Justice in The Hague, where he took part in presenting Iran's case, the crux of which was a denial of the court's jurisdiction in the British-Iranian oil dispute. The Iranian contention was in part upheld by the court, and the dispute continued unresolved.

It was against this background of international tension over nationalization of Iranian oil that Saleh was appointed Ambassador from his country to the United States. Almost im-

mediately upon his arrival in Washington D.C., in September 1952, he made clear the importance that his government attached to the role of the United States in the British-Iranian controversy. On September 18 he appealed to Secretary of State Dean Acheson to use his "good offices" in promoting a settlement of the oil crisis. When he presented his credentials to President Harry S. Truman on September 23, Saleh advised the chief executive that economic conditions in Iran were becoming "very dangerous." Amplifying his remarks aferward for the press, the new Ambassador maintained that the British "blockade" of Iran (the effort to prevent the export of Iranian oil until the question of ownership was settled to the satisfaction of both parties) was having dangerous economic, social, and political repercussions in his country. He urged that the United States use its influence to bring the blockade to an end and warned that "it is possible that if nothing is done the [communistic] Tudeh party may succeed in their activities" in Iran (New York *Times,* September 25, 1952). As predicted by Saleh in early October, with the refusal of the British to accept Mossadegh's latest proposal for settling the oil dispute, the Iranian Premier announced on October 16 that he intended to sever diplomatic ties with Great Britain. In December 1952 Ambassador Saleh stated, at a news conference, in answer to British threats to take legal action against buyers of Iranian oil that "any respectable court" would uphold the oil purchasers.

After the overthrow of Mossadegh's Government, a spokesman for the Iranian Embassy in Washington, D.C. stated that Ambassador Saleh "believed that Premier Mossadegh symbolized the will of the Iranian people and that he did not see how an opposing Government could be successful in that respect" (New York *Times,* August 21, 1953).

Saleh, who married Saffia Khanom in 1922 is the father of a son, Feridoun, and a daughter, Parvine (three other children are deceased). His faith is the Moslem. The Ambassador has been described in the Washington *Post* as "a direct, forceful, intelligent man . . .an easy conversationalist" who can express himself well on a variety of subjects.

References

Washington (D.C.) Post p3S O 12 '52
World Biography (1948)

SALOTE TUPOU, QUEEN OF TONGA

(sa-lŏ'tĕ tōō'-pōō) Mar. 13, 1900-

Address: The Royal Palace, Nukualofa, Tongatabu

One of the most impressive personages present at the coronation of Queen Elizabeth II in June 1953 was Her Majesty, Queen Salote of the Tonga Islands. Numerous observers spoke with admiration of her striking physical presence, her regal bearing and her kindly manners. The New York *Times* referred to her as "Britain's most popular coronation guest." The London *Daily Telegraph* stated: "Few visitors can ever have endeared themselves so widely and so speedily."

Salote Tupou was born on March 13, 1900, the daughter of the reigning monarch of Tonga, King George Tupou II. The kingdom includes approximately 150 coral and volcanic islands in the South Pacific about 2,000 miles northeast of Australia, comprising about 250 square miles of territory. Its chief exports are copra and bananas. The three principal island groups are Vavau, Haabai and Tonga. Tongatabu, an island in the Tonga group, is the seat of Nukualofa ("Abode of Love"), the capital of the kingdom. At the end of 1951, according to *Whitaker's Almanac*, the population of the islands amounted to almost 50,000—48,460 Tongans (the Tongans are a Polynesian people), 312 other Pacific Islanders, 580 persons of mixed descent, 235 Europeans, and eighty members of other races. The northern islands were discovered by the Dutch in 1616, the rest of the group by Abel Janszoon Tasman, a Dutchman, in 1643. The English navigator James Cook visited the islands in 1773, and again in 1777, and was so well impressed by the hospitality shown him that he named the group the Friendly Islands. In token of his appreciation he presented a tortoise, Tu'i Malila, to a Tongan chief; the tortoise is rumored to be still alive in the grounds of Queen Salote's palace, and receives traditional offerings of food at important ceremonies.

Queen Salote is a scion of the world's oldest ruling dynasty, tracing her ancestry back in an unbroken line to Ahoeitu, the Tui Tonga (supreme ruler) of the islands in the tenth century. The modern kingdom of Tonga came into existence in 1845, when the Queen's great-great-grandfather, King George Tupou I, established himself as the first King of the consolidated State of Tonga. (All Tongan monarchs are named either George or Charlotte, by way of compliment to England's George III and his Queen Consort, Charlotte of Mecklenburg-Strelitz who were the reigning monarchs when a treaty between the two kingdoms was first considered. Salote is the Polynesian form of Charlotte). King George I of the Tongan Islands, who patterned his monarchy on a European model and voluntarily limited his own powers by instituting a constitutional Government, reigned until his death in 1893 at the age of ninety-six. He was succeeded by his great-grandson, George II, the father of the present Queen.

King George II negotiated a Treaty of Friendship with Great Britain in May 1900 which placed the islands under British protection. Under this treaty, a British agent advises the Tongan monarch. Technically, however, Tonga is independent and self-governing; the monarch reigns with the assistance of a prime minister, a privy council and a legislative assembly of twenty-one native members.

Queen Salote was educated at the Diocesan Ladies' College of the Church of England at Auckland, New Zealand, and at the University of Sydney. She was married to Prince Tugi in 1917; the marriage united the two noblest families of Tonga. On April 12, 1918, following the death of her father, Salote ascended

British Inf. Services
SALOTE TUPOU, QUEEN OF TONGA

the throne. Her husband, in accordance with custom, became her Prime Minister. Upon his death in 1941, the office devolved upon his eldest son.

During her reign, the Queen has won a widespread reputation as an enlightened and progressive ruler. As J. C. Furnas wrote in the New York *Times,* "There is no question of the high character of Queen Salote, who is universally respected by her people and everybody else in the Pacific." She has taken special interest in public health and education. Since her accession, education has become compulsory and free; there is virtually no illiteracy in Tonga. Islanders are provided with free medical and dental care. Upon reaching manhood every Tongan youth is entitled to an allotment of land. There is scarcely any crime, and no housing problem. According to the London *Times,* "Tonga has neither dissensions at home nor enemies abroad and must be one of the happiest countries in the world."

Upon the outbreak of World War II, Tonga at once declared war against the Axis. In the course of the war, the Tongan people mustered troops, presented three fighter aircraft to Britain and contributed heavily to various defense funds. When the United States Navy landed troops at the islands, Queen Salote, according to a New York *Times* report on June 19, 1947, "urged her people to go back into the bush, leaving the port and its European-style houses to the [troops]. . . .In that way she protected them from the ills that befell many other island peoples from too close association with an alien civilization."

To celebrate the Queen's fiftieth birthday, in March 1950, group after group of Tongan men, women and children brought gifts of food, drink, bark cloth, and mats to the royal palace from early morning on. They carried whole roasted pigs on wooden platforms and

SALOTE, TUPOU—Continued

brought baskets of fish and vegetables which they laid out on the palace grounds. At the end of a daylong program of festivities, the Queen declared: "I have had much to be grateful for in my life, and I pray for wisdom and grace to enable me to continue to meet problems which may arise in the future."

Memorializing the anniversary of the Treaty of Friendship between Tonga and Great Britain in 1950, the late King George VI sent the Queen greetings which read in part: "Under your wise guidance Tonga enjoys prosperity and peace. I pray wholeheartedly for the continuance of these blessings and for the lasting happiness of yourself and your people." On the same occasion, the Queen asserted: "Britain has right and justice as her heritage. Tongans today acknowledge their debt of gratitude to her, and will hand on the same spirit of goodwill to future generations."

Three years later, Queen Salote attended the coronation of the late King's daughter and was accorded a cordial welcome. *Time* summarized her activities on her first visit to Great Britain in these words: "She turned up at the ballet to see Margot Fonteyn dance *Sleeping Beauty*, at Lord's to watch the cricket, hefted babies at the Chelsea welfare center, inspected Canterbury and Cambridge, saw *Dial M for Murder*, rounded up and gave a tea party for 45 fellow old girls. . ." of the Diocesan Ladies' College in New Zealand. Afterwards, she toured Scotland and Ireland. Upon her departure for Tonga, the queen stated: "I have been touched by the warm welcome I have received in England, Scotland and Ireland. I thank you all most sincerely. I take back with me the most imperishable memory of your generosity and kindness."

Queen Salote was created an Honorary Dame Commander of the Order of the British Empire in 1932; in 1945, she was made an Honorary Grand Commander of the same order. She is head of the Tonga Red Cross. A Methodist, she is also head of the Wesleyan Free Church of Tonga. A writer for the Australian periodical *Missionary Review* noted: "Queen Salote is known throughout the kingdom as a sincere Christian, one who not only believes in the tenets of Christianity, but is most energetic in seeing that her beliefs find practical expression in daily life. . . ."

Two of her three sons survive: Crown Prince Taufaahau Tupoutoa and Prince Jione Gu Manumataogo. Her Majesty is six feet three inches tall and weighs 280 pounds. "A better poised or more dignified figure it would be impossible to imagine . . . [She is] charming, gracious, kind and regal" (London *Spectator*). Joseph Driscoll wrote that she "embodies the friendliness and dignity of her pure Polynesian people" (New York *Herald Tribune*, November 22, 1943).

References

Missionary R of the World 62:366 Jl '39
N Y Herald Tribune N 22 '43
N Y Times p7 My 31 '53 por
Spectator (London) 185:538+ N 24 '50
Time 61:24 Je 29 '53 por

SANTELMANN, WILLIAM F(RED-RICK HENRY) Feb. 24, 1902- Leader of the United States Marine Band

Address: b. Marine Barracks, 8th and Eye Sts., S.E., Washington, D.C.; h. 2907 N. Edison St., Arlington, Va.

The leader of the United States Marine Band since 1940 has been Lieutenant Colonel William F. Santelmann, who joined that organization as a private in 1923 when his father was leading the band. As conductor of the "oldest and most famed" of all United States military bands (*Time*), Colonel Santelmann appears with his scarlet-coated musicians at White House social affairs, in parades, and at receptions for foreign dignitaries visiting in Washington.

Born in Washington, D.C., on February 24, 1902, William Frederick Henry Santelmann is one of six children (three boys and three girls) of Captain William Henry Christian and Clara Marie (Becke) Santelmann. The senior Santelmann was a member of the United States Marine Band for thirty-seven years and its leader from 1898 to 1927, the first Marine Bandmaster to broaden the band's scope to include symphonic works, and the first to attain the rank of a commissioned officer. (The famed leader John Philip Sousa had been an enlisted man.) Having studied the violin at the Conservatory of Leipzig, Germany, the elder Santelmann gave William violin lessons from the time the boy was six years old. While William was a pupil at McKinley Manual Training High School in Washington, D.C., from which he was graduated in 1921, he played the violin in the school orchestra and studied harmony with Arthur Tregina, appearing in 1920 for the first time as guest soloist with the Marine Band. He attended the Washington College of Music and from 1921 to 1923 the New England Conservatory of Music, Boston, Massachusetts. Under such teachers as George Chadwick, Wallace Goodrich, Frederick Shepherd Converse, and Harrison Keller, he studied violin, counterpoint, composition, and all secondary musical subjects, and received orchestral and ensemble training.

While at the conservatory, Santelmann occasionally substituted for absent artists in the Boston Symphony orchestra, and upon graduation, he decided to look for a position as violinist in a symphony orchestra, preferably the Cleveland Symphony. Before applying there he returned on a brief vacation to Washington, where he went to the branch office of the musicians' union to get a card and was told he would have to pay a $50 fine for having played in the nonunionized Boston orchestra. "I was too much of a Dutchman to take anything like that," Santelmann later told Henry F. Pringle (*Saturday Evening Post*, April 14, 1951). "I . . . decided to get in the Marine Band." On his first application, young Santelmann was rejected by his father, then the leader, because he knew only the violin and no band instrument, the rule being that a musician must be proficient on both an orchestral and a band instrument. Having practiced for a few weeks on the euphonium, a small double tuba, he tried again, but his father was dissatisfied with his playing. He then began serious study of the instrument under Peter Hazes and Robert E. Clark, and after months of hard work passed auditions on both the violin and the euphonium. Less successful in the Marine Corps physical examination, he failed because of flat feet, a disqualification later waived by higher authorities on the grounds that musicians work sitting down. Bill Santelmann became on September 5, 1923, a "private, attached to the United States Marine Band."

Appearing during the first concert season as a violin soloist, Santelmann was a musician in the band from 1923 until his promotion in 1925 to concert master. Ten years later when he was appointed assistant leader of the band, he remained concert master. Both positions were relinquished upon his becoming full leader on April 1, 1940, in succession to Captain Taylor Branson, who retired thirteen years after following the senior Santelmann as leader. The younger Santelmann himself had advanced to second class musician in 1924, first class in 1926, principal musician in 1934, and on February 9, 1947, to major. He now holds the rank of lieutenant colonel, the highest ever attained by a Marine musician.

Founded in 1798 and known as "The President's Own," the eighty-five man Marine Band plays "Hail to the Chief" every time the President appears at a large state affair and has played for every President except General Washington. It made its first appearance in a President's house at a reception given by John Adams on New Year's Day 1800 and has played at every inauguration since Thomas Jefferson's day. Under the leadership of John Philip Sousa from 1880 to 1892, the Marine Band became one of the best-known bands in the world. When Sousa left to organize his own group, Francesco Fanciulli led the band for five years; William H. Santelmann was bandmaster for twenty-nine years, Captain Taylor Branson for thirteen years, and William F. Santelmann since 1940. The story is told that during President Roosevelt's occupancy of the White House Santelmann got a call requesting that the full band appear on the south lawn of the Presidential mansion to give a concert honoring British Prime Minister Churchill. Since the day was cloudy, Santelmann brought along the orchestral instruments for use if the party should adjourn to the East Room in case of rain, because the band instruments would be too loud indoors. While the band was playing, the rain began to fall heavily, and Santelmann looked anxiously at the President for a signal to retire, but received none. The band continued its full concert in the pouring rain while the President and Prime Minister seemed oblivious of their drenching. When President Truman and his family moved into the White House, the band played for them frequently, sometimes as often as five times a week. In February 1946 Santelmann led the orchestra at a White House dance given by the President's daughter, Margaret. This marked the first time the Marines had played in the White House since 1941 and Santelmann commented happily: "White House entertaining is getting back to normal" (*Time*, February 18, 1946).

LT. COL. WILLIAM F. SANTELMANN

Besides playing for Presidents, Santelmann has also conducted before visiting royalty. When the King and Queen of England visited the United States in 1939, Santelmann sent to England for the score for the British National Anthem which, while it resembles "My Country 'Tis of Thee," is different enough to make "perfectionist" Santelmann want the official arrangement. After the band's rendition of the British anthem at a state dinner, the King and Queen asked that the leader and bandsmen be presented to them so they might express their appreciation. In 1942 the Marine Band played for three rulers within a period of a few months—King George of Greece, King Peter of Yugoslavia, and Queen Wilhemina of the Netherlands, and on each occasion the royalty personally thanked leader Santelmann. On the subject of playing at Presidential social functions Santelmann once commented: "The effect on the guests is psychological. Something about the tempo of a march makes you feel . . . things have got to move" (*Time*).

Colonel Santelmann, who has conducted all the annual fall tours of the Marine Band since 1939, first began making these tours under the direction of his father in 1924 and has played and conducted in all forty-eight States. For the yearly tours, in which half the band members participate, the other half staying in Washington for White House calls, the itinerary is arranged by a private agent and the concerts are sponsored by Rotary, Kiwanis, Chamber of Commerce, and other organizations. With a collection of some 500,000 musical scores, the band's repertoire ranges from military marches to popular songs, classical numbers, comedy pieces, and many original works composed by its members. Each day Santelmann rehearses his men from 9 A.M. to 12 noon at the old Marine Barracks in Washington.

(Continued next page)

SANTELMANN, WILLIAM—*Continued*

Santelmann is also the musical director of the Gridiron Club and of the Military Order of the Carabao. Having served as vice-president of the American Bandmasters Association, he became president in April 1953. He is also an honorary member of the Iowa State Bandmasters Association, the Pennsylvania State Bandmasters Association, and the musical fraternity, Kappa Kappa Psi.

On May 19, 1925, Santelmann married Margaret Randall of Medina, Ohio, a former music teacher; they have two children, Betsy Jane and William F., Jr. Colonel Santelmann gives his church affiliation as Protestant. His hobbies are carpentry and gardening. He is five feet nine and one-half inches tall, weighs 177 pounds, has blue eyes and graying-brown balding hair. Santelmann has been described as "a bluff and hearty fellow who looks more like a marine combat officer than the fine musician which he really is."

References

Sat Eve Post 223:28-9+ Ap 14 '51
Time 35:46 Ap 8 '40; 47:70 F 18 '46
Who's Who in America, 1952-53
Who's Who in the South and Southwest (1950)

SAYRE, MORRIS Nov. 27, 1885—Mar. 7, 1953 Business executive; manufacturers' association official; progressed from boiler tender (1908) to president (1945) and board vice-chairman (1948) of the Corn Products Refining Company; director of National Association of Manufacturers (1946-53); was elected its president in 1947 and board chairman in 1949. See *Current Biography*, 1948.

Obituary

N Y Times p90 Mr 8 '53

SCELBA, MARIO Sept. 5, 1901- Former Italian Minister of the Interior; lawyer
Address: h. Via Orazio 3, Rome, Italy

Mario Scelba, Minister in various cabinets of the postwar governments of Italy, succeeded under Premier Alcide de Gasperi in 1947 to the post of Minister of the Interior. For the past five years (until the defeat of de Gasperi in the July 1953 election) he controlled the administrative organization of a strong central government in every province of the country, the appointment of prefects (with powers of a mayor) for each province, and particularly, control of the police of the nation. In this office (which the communists sought but never obtained in coalition governments from 1945 to 1947) Scelba built up in one year a weak and demoralized police organization to the size of a small army in constant readiness against the communists in any show of force in public places.

Mario Scelba was born on September 5, 1901, in Caltagirone, a small town in Sicily. He was the son of a peasant sharecropper on land owned by the priest Don Luigi Sturzo. The cleric took an interest in young Mario (who had joined the Catholic Youth Action group) and paid his way through seminary and the University of Rome. Since Sturzo lived much of the year in Rome, Scelba was able to study and also to act as the priest's private secretary. This early association brought him in contact with political leaders who later became powerful in Italy. He completed his undergraduate work and then studied law at the University of Rome, where he received a doctor's degree.

At the outset, his political career was quiet and inconspicuous. It started with the historic Popular party (the prototype of the Christian Democratic movement in other countries of Europe), which was founded in Italy in 1919 by Don Luigi Sturzo. The party was suppressed in 1923 by the Mussolini regime and reconstituted in 1943 under the Allied occupation as the Christian Democratic party under the leadership of de Gasperi, with the guidance of Don Sturzo and Scelba, his protégé.

Scelba joined the Popular party in 1919 in Caltagirone and served as an organizer of the local section. With its suppression, he dropped out of politics and took no active part in the fascist regime either for or against. In 1941 he reappeared to participate in the clandestine re-formation of the Catholic party, becoming a member of the secret central committee. There is no record of active participation in the resistance movement against Mussolini. After the Nazis occupied Italy, Scelba published a newspaper distributed clandestinely for which he was arrested, but he was regarded as of little importance and freed after three days' imprisonment.

In 1945 he was a member of the Consulta, an informal parliament in the government set up during the war by the Allied Control Commission to serve until a parliament was chosen at a general election. The next year Scelba was elected to the Constituent Assembly which drew up the constitution for the new Republic of Italy.

The continuity of Scelba's service as a cabinet Minister since 1945 has been unbroken. Prior to 1947 his presence in the cabinet gave no sign of the determination he later came to show in public affairs, and which now characterizes him in the public mind as "the strong man of Italy"; nor did his presence in Rome in the two decades of the Mussolini regime (during which he practiced law in the nation's capital) indicate his strong-mindedness. With the end of the war and the formation of the Parri government, the first government of Italy under the Allied Control Commission, Scelba unobtrusively became Minister of Post and Communications, a secondary position largely technical in scope. He held this post through two succeeding governments organized by de Gasperi. With the formation of a third de Gasperi government (February 3, 1947) he was named Minister of the Interior and confirmed in the fourth (June 1, 1947) and following cabinets.

Scelba has organized and equipped a formidable police force, armed with tanks, armored cars, jeeps, tear gas bombs and automatic weapons, and numerically larger than any police force in the history of the country. While the figures are not divulged, it is believed that he has raised the police strength from 150,000 to 200,000 and increased the *carabinieri* (militarized police, similar to a National Guard) to treaty strength of 70,000. Rome, the main target of any insurrection, and other key cities are especially policed by the Celere, high speed units of selected police organized and equipped as mobile riot squads, as emergency adjuncts to the reinforced local police. Scelba has also backed his vigilance by obtaining cabinet approval of emergency banning of public assembly and of shop meetings of workers in factories.

As Interior Minister and as a prelude to his future role as the "strong man" of Italy, in 1948 this little-observed leader in the top ranks of the Christian Democratic party declared to the Senate that Italy was faced with the danger of communist revolt and the government was in possession of ample evidence of communist plans to seize the powers of government by force (New York *Times*, August 5, 1948). This was stated after Scelba had been in office one year and had quietly built up the police strength in every town and village with strong cadres of selected officers and men sifted from the military to meet communist force with superior force.

Up to then the communists had executed some bold moves, testing and probing the government's strength in one place after another in Italy. The attempt on the life of Palmiro Togliatti, the leader of the communists in Italy, marked the simultaneous outbreak of violence in key centers of the country in what appeared to be a coordinated plan preceding national insurrection. The communists occupied Genoa, seized the radio station in Venice, took over plants in Milan and Turin, and in the North went to the hills in armed guerilla bands similar to the partisan formations which during the war had fought bloody battles against the Nazi occupation.

Against this background of manifest readiness of forces in the country to defy the authority of the government, Scelba's slow mobilization of the police power of the state proved repeatedly adequate to the challenge of communist defiance. In the same address to the Senate he declared, as reported by the New York *Times,* that it was indispensable that the police be kept at maximum efficiency and remain in constant readiness.

The climax to all this dissension came two years later in the general strike of 1950 called by the Communist-controlled General Confederation of Labor. In one day, March 3, 1950, hundreds were wounded, including many policemen, and 7,000 were arrested. However, nowhere did the police lose control of the situation. The contest was a definitive test of forces and since then the communists have shown no willingness to challenge the government by a show of violence.

Scelba has been much criticised at home and abroad. The New York *Times* in an editorial (January 28, 1950) called him "tough and ruthless" and the Washington *Post* (October 1949)

Wide World Photos

MARIO SCELBA

reported that "liberals fear Italy's new strong man."

The decisive measures with which he successfully fought communist force have been used in minor demonstrations which occasionally occurred in isolated places and on a very small scale. For a time, he also tried to enforce censorship by proscribing two-piece bathing suits and causing nude statues to be covered. For these various reasons the Washington *Post* reported that non-communist elements feared for Italy's democratic future.

However, the Italian Social Movement, a neofascist party, when it took to rowdy public demonstration in 1951, was promptly given the same treatment by Scelba's force as it gave to communist-dominated groups.

Scelba is married and has two daughters. He has been described as 'mild-mannered", "a tough boss" (*Catholic World* April 1951) who "is fighting a winning battle against the Reds." As a "devout democrat" he explains that any party which tries to take the law into its own hands must be suppressed. "The Communists spread fear and panic by threatening violence," he said, in discussing an incident in Capri. "All I did was to show them that I am not afraid. We have beaten the Left by showing them they could not bully the Government."

A law defining and banning fascism in any of its phases is on the books in Italian courts and is known as the Scelba Law.

References

Cath World 173:43-7 Ap '51
Time 51:34 F 16 '48; 53:21 My 30 '49;
    56:39-40 O 9 '50 por
Washington (D.C.) Post p2B O 2 '49
Chi e' (1948)
Enciclopedia Italiano (Trecane) (1948)
Italia e gli Italiano di Oggi (1947)
New International Year Book, 1950

SCHACTER, MRS. JULES *See* Edwards, J.

SCHÄFFER, FRITZ May 12, 1888- German Minister of Finance; lawyer
Address: b. Poppelsdorfer-Allee 42/1, Bonn, Germany; h. Trogerstrasse 36/3, München, Germany

The rapid economic improvement of Western Germany in the period since the Federal (Bonn) Republic began to function on September 20, 1949, is largely credited to Fritz Schäffer, Minister of Finance in the Cabinet of Chancellor Konrad Adenauer. A Bavarian by birth, a Roman Catholic in faith, and a lawyer by profession, Dr. Schäffer was leader of the Bavarian People's party (Catholic-Conservative) from 1929 to 1933 and Bavaria's Finance Min-

FRITZ SCHÄFFER

ister from 1931 to 1933, when he was dismissed by the Nazis. Following a period in which he was interned at the Dachau concentration camp in 1944, he served for a few months in 1945 as Minister-President of Bavaria under the United States occupation.

A descendant of Lower Bavarian farmer folk, Fritz Schäffer was born in Munich, Germany, on May 12, 1888, one of ten children of the postal official Gottfried Schäffer and Amalie (Maier) Schäffer. (Presumably he was baptized Friedrich, as his name appears in this form in almost all news dispatches through 1947.) Part of his boyhood was spent in his native Munich, capital of what was then the kingdom of Bavaria within the German Empire; he later lived in Neuberg on the Danube, where he attended the *Humanistisches Gymnasium* (high school of the humanities) and passed entrance examinations for the University of Munich in 1907. Schäffer, who saw one year (1915-16) of World War I duty with the

Royal Bavarian Infantry Regiment, passed with distinction the state law examinations at the University of Munich Law School in 1916. Entering government service in 1917 as an *Assessor* (counsel) at Kelheim on the Danube, he passed in October 1918 an advanced civil service examination, and for eleven years beginning in 1920 occupied increasingly responsible positions in the Bavarian Ministry of Education and Culture at Munich. Also in 1920 Schäffer was elected for the first time to the lower chamber (Landtag) of the Bavarian Diet. He became president of the Bavarian People's party (Catholic-Conservative) in 1929.

When the Nazis came to power in Germany in 1933, Schäffer was head of the Bavarian Ministry of Finance, having been named to that office in 1931. Dismissed from his post, he was arrested on March 9, 1933, held for one night, and then released. Two months later he was again arrested and held for two weeks at Stadelheim. He was permitted to collect retirement pay as a state councilor and on release was allowed to practice law at Munich. There he represented German convents and Catholic Church organizations until August 28, 1944, when he was interned at the Dachau concentration camp, although (as he later pointed out) he "had been neither tried nor sentenced."

After two months in Dachau, Schäffer was set free on October 28, 1944. He then resumed law practice in Munich through the rest of World War II in Europe and up to May 28, 1945, when the Military Government of the United States Occupation Zone (of which Bavaria was a part) instituted what the New York *Times* characterized as the "most ambitious effort yet made to extend the scope of the American Military Government . . . to the city and county level." On the recommendation, it has been said, of Michael Cardinal von Faulhaber, Schäffer was named "temporary Minister-President of Bavaria and entrusted with the formation of a civil government of limited power. He was warned that failure to carry out orders of United States occupation authorities would make him subject to action by a military tribunal and was charged with removing Nazis and Nazi sympathizers from public office at all levels (New York *Times*). Four of Schäffer's Cabinet appointees, including the Ministers of the Interior and Transportation, who had prior records of affiliation, were subjected to mandatory dismissal early in September. Schäffer tendered his own resignation on the dual ground that the occupation authorities had "lost confidence" in his administration and that the efficiency of his government depended upon the support of such experienced men as he had brought into his cabinet. When Schäffer's resignation as Minister-President was accepted on September 28, Wilhelm Hoegner, described as "a Social-Democrat and anti-Hitlerite for many years" was appointed in his place.

Schäffer then resumed his law business and continued as chairman of the Munich branch of the Christian Social Union until late in April 1946, when the American military government announced that he had been "forbidden to vote, belong to a political party, or run for office" as a "Nazi sympathizer and supporter of mili-

tarism" (New York *Times*, April 26, 1946).
He was formally deprived of his citizen's rights
on May 24, but upon his being brought before
a de-Nazification court on the following November 19, the charges against him were dismissed for lack of evidence. His rights were
restored on February 18, 1947, and the following
year he was re-elected to leadership of the
Upper Bavarian Wing of the Christian Social
Union.

On August 14, 1949, Schäffer was elected to
the first Bundestag (lower chamber) of the
new Federal Republic of Germany (Bonn Republic) as a Christian Socialist deputy from
Munich. Designated Minister of Finance in
the Cabinet of Chancellor Konrad Adenauer, a
Christian Democrat, during the following
month, he took office on September 20, one day
before the Allied High Commission turned over
civil administration of the British, French, and
American zones to the new Republic. Pending
the working out and ratification of a formal
peace treaty, the occupation authorities retained
veto right over legislation by the Bonn Parliament and in April 1950 exercised this right
through "provisional rejection" of an income
tax law largely drafted by Schäffer. This measure reduced taxation in the higher income
brackets with a view to encouraging industrial
investment, but was proposed at a time when
the current budget showed a deficit of nearly
two million dollars. The Allies (and in particular the United States) argued that it "would
increase budgetary deficits" and make the country more dependent upon external assistance.
Schäffer, who was described in a dispatch to
the New York *Times* as "a pillar of the Adenauer Cabinet" and "also a man who stands
up to the Allies whenever he feels he is in the
right," continued to argue for his measure and
threatened to resign if it was not accepted.
During the ensuing conversations an agreement
was reached on April 28 whereby Schäffer assented to the principle of the balanced budget,
promising a series of tax-collecting reforms and
compensatory revenue-raising measures, in exchange for which the Allied commission withdrew its provisional rejection of the income tax
law.

While Schäffer did not balance the budget
in the fiscal year beginning April 1950, he
came very close to success. In the words of
Don Cook in the New York *Herald Tribune*
of June 10, 1951, there was "a lot of government vacillation and uncertainty on the im-
posing of much-needed luxury taxes," yet
"when the tax returns and expenditures for
the year were totalled up . . . revenue amounted
to 11,760,000,000 *Deutschmarks* ($2,798,880,000)
for the year and expenditures to 11,870,000,000
Deutschmarks ($2,825,060,000)." For the in-
coming fiscal year, Dr. Schäffer presented a
preliminary budget which balanced expenditures
and revenues at 13,390,000,000 *Deutschmarks*.
Having proposed this by disregarding part of
the Allied occupation bill, he was in a controversy with the Allies over the amount of occupation costs. (Schäffer had moved unsuccessfully for a reduction of these costs in June
1950.) The progress, in both economy and
morale, made by Western Germany in the space

of one year was in many respects noteworthy.
"Under able Finance Minister Fritz Schäffer,"
wrote correspondent Enno Hobbing in *Time* of
August 5, 1951, "employment is up, luxury
taxes are stiffer. As economic inequality tends
to diminish, a feeling of opportunity grows. On
the streets, fewer Germans glare enviously at
expensive automobiles. . . .Already more Germans own cars than in 1936."

During the nine months of negotiations which
preceded the signing at Bonn on May 26, 1952,
of the peace contract between the Federal Republic of Germany and the Western Allied
powers, Finance Minister Schäffer worked effectively to limit his country's financial responsibilities for mutual defense. By the terms
of the agreement Western Germany is to contribute 850,000,000 *Deutschmarks* (about $200
million) monthly up to June 30, 1953. "During
the first six months," it was stated, "the Germans will contribute an average of 551,000,000
marks (over $130 million) to 'assist in the
support of foreign forces'. . . .In the following three months the monthly average will be
319,000,000 marks (about $76 million). The
balance will be used for the expenses of German units to be created. The idea is that their
expenses will be lower in the initial period"
(Russell Hill in the New York *Herald Tribune*). Not long afterward Germany, along
with Japan and Burma, was elected to membership in the International Bank for Reconstruction and Development and the International
Monetary Fund, and Schäffer attended the joint
conference of both Bank and Fund at Mexico
City between September 3 and 12. En route to
the conference he told reporters, "we have
doubled taxes, which now amount to 40 per cent
of the total national income. Our budget is
balanced, and a further tax increase is impossible." In presenting his 1953-54 budget estimate to the Bundestag on January 28, 1953,
Schäffer advised foreign observers against
adopting an overoptimistic view toward West
Germany's present financial situation, which
finds the country a creditor to the extent of
some 2,500,000,000 *Deutschmarks* ($595,238,000).

After the German elections in September
1953, when Adenauer's party received a majority in the Bundestag, Schäffer was again
appointed Minister of Finance.

Fritz Schäffer and Else Dyroff were married
September 12, 1917, and are the parents of three
children, Gerda, Lili, and Fridrun; a son, Walter, is deceased. West Germany's Finance Minister has been credited (by a *Christian Science
Monitor* correspondent) with "dry humor and
an inexhaustible flow of statistics which generally leave" his critics "gasping." Dr. Schäffer is five feet six inches in height and weighs
about 150 pounds; his eyes are brown and his
hair is gray. Now, sixty-four, Schäffer still
enjoys mountain climbing and skiing.

References

Christian Sci Mon p6 D 6 '50
N Y Times p4 My 29 '45
Newsweek 42:32 N 2 '53

International Who's Who, 1952
Wer Ist Wer? (1948)

SCHRAM, EMIL Nov. 23, 1893- Financier, farmer; philanthropist
Address: b. c/o United Service Organizations, Inc., 500 Fifth Ave., New York 36; h. 784 Park Ave., New York 21

> NOTE: This biography supersedes the article which appeared in *Current Biography* in 1941.

When Emil Schram was appointed president of the New York Stock Exchange in 1941, Wall Street was "suffering its worst trading slump in twenty-three years" (*Time*, September 4, 1950). During his ten years in that office Schram played a large part in re-establishing public confidence in the world's largest securities exchange, of which he is still a consultant. Before coming to the Exchange, Schram was chairman of the Reconstruction Finance Corporation from 1939 to 1941, after serving as a member of its Board of Directors for three years. On his retirement from the Exchange in 1951, Schram returned to operating his farms

David Berns
EMIL SCHRAM

in Peru, Indiana, and Hillview, Illinois. In February 1953 he became president of the United Service Organizations.

Descended from German immigrants, Emil Schram was born on November 23, 1893, in Peru, Indiana, to Emil Alexander and Katharine (Graf) Schram. After attending public schools in his native city, young Emil was graduated from the local high school in 1911. His first job was as a general handyman with the J. O. Cole Company, a lumber and coal concern. After advancing to bookkeeper of the firm, Schram was made manager in 1915 of a project to drain and develop 5,000 acres of swamp land on the Illinois River at Hillview, Illinois. Within a few years the land's annual yield increased from 6,000 to 140,000 bushels of

corn. While acquiring a substantial interest in the project, which became known as the Hartwell Land Trust, Schram at the same time became a member of the board of directors and secretary of the Hartwell Drainage and Levee District. During the same years (1915-33) he served as manager of the Community and the Grand Pass elevators, Hillview's two grain elevators.

As chairman of the board of the National Drainage Association from 1931 to 1933, Schram applied to the Federal government for loans for flood control and reclamation along the Illinois River. After 1933 he left his post as Hartwell manager to move to Washington, D.C., as chief of the drainage, levee, and irrigation division of the Reconstruction Finance Corporation, in charge of loans to needy drainage and irrigation districts. Appointed a member of the Board of Directors of RFC in 1936 by President Roosevelt, Schram was reappointed to the post at the expiration of his term in January 1938. During this period, Schram became president of the board of trustees of the Electric Home and Farm Authority, a TVA subsidiary to finance the sale of electrical appliances, particularly to rural electric cooperatives. He was also named a member of the Board of the Federal National Mortgage Association, a member of the executive committee of the Export-Import Bank of Washington, and in 1938 a member of the Board of the Federal Prison Industries, Inc., representing agriculture.

When Jesse Jones resigned as chairman of the RFC in 1939 to become Federal Loan Administrator, he suggested Schram as his successor. Elected chairman of the board of directors of RFC on July 16, 1939, Schram was described by the New York *Times* as "probably the only man in government whose work is admired equally warmly by Jesse Jones and Thomas Corcoran" and the only one whose career had been "jointly fostered by this ill-assorted pair." The following December, Schram was named a member of the National Power Policy Committee and in 1940 president of the Defense Plant Corporation. During this period he was also appointed assistant priorities administrator in the Office of Production Management to allocate raw materials for defense.

When Schram was suggested in the spring of 1941 as a candidate for the office of President of the New York Stock Exchange, *Forbes Magazine* commented that the appointment "indicates that New York Stock Exchange authorities have lost hope, that they have been so whipped that they have no fight left, that they have abjectly surrendered to Federal bureaucrats" (May 14, 1941). The article went on to say that for the head of the Exchange to be chosen "by Washington" signified that political domination of the investment world had become increasingly "authoritarian, not to say totalitarian." Other observers took the opposite view, and predicted that the selection of Schram for the post would bring about better co-operation between Washington and Wall Street and help to remedy the drop in Stock Exchange trading which had sunk to the lowest levels since the turn of the century. In many quarters the choice of Schram to head the Exchange was considered a "revolutionary move to eliminate friction between the financial district and the Securities and Exchange Commission which may be hampering business" (New York *Sun,* May 6, 1941),

Schram stated in an interview with Peter Edson in the New York *World-Telegram* (May 20, 1941) that he did not want to accept the job if traders thought "they would be getting someone who would act as a fixer with the government, a go-between who, because of his eight years in high government office, might come down and make the Securities and Exchange commission lay off."

Unanimously elected by the Board for a three-year term, Schram accepted on the condition that the Exchange setup would be altered to give more management control to the paid personnel, including the president himself, and less to the board of governors and the membership committees, reforms which had been advocated by the former Exchange president, William McChesney Martin, Jr., who quit the post to enter the Army.

Described by his former boss, Jesse Jones, as "unusually capable and well qualified for this position of great trust," Schram moved from his $10,000 a year job as RFC head to become Exchange president at $48,000 a year on July 1, 1941. The New York *Times* commented that "The new president assumed his duties just as the Exchange completed its smallest six-month business in twenty-seven years" (July 6, 1941). By the following October, *Newsweek* observed that "Since last June Emil Schram has won the respect of those in Wall Street who are allergic to anything connected with Washington by the quiet, unassuming way he has tackled the problems of the harassed institution" (October 6, 1941). When Schram's annual salary was raised to $100,000 four years later, *Fortune* (January 1946) commented: "Today Wall Street is practically unanimous in approval of the administrative and public relations job that Schram has done, and of his raise."

After Schram had held his post for another four years, C. Norman Stabler in the New York *Herald Tribune* (August 25, 1950) paid tribute to "the work he has done in re-educating the public to the place of the investment business in the national and international economy." When Schram took over the presidency, Wall Street was "suffering its worst trading slump in twenty-three years" (*Time,* September 4, 1950), which brokers attributed to federal controls, but which Schram believed originated in the public's recollection of the 1929 crash, and its resulting mistrust of the whole institution. "To help sell the Street, Schram stumped the U.S. His plain, corn-fed manner convinced many a U.S. citizen that the stock market was a good place to invest money" (*Time*). He issued advice which reflected "a sense of responsibility on the part of the Exchange which is wholly desirable and reassuring." After lunching with President Roosevelt, Schram made the statement quoted by *Time* (March 22, 1943): "I told the President I was determined to keep un-informed people out of the market." I am

going to continue to say to people who don't know what they are doing to stay out."

Another major contribution made by Schram during his presidency of the Exchange was his campaign to obtain a more liberal capital-gains tax law to aid the investor. In November 1947 Schram collaborated with Franklin Cole and Company, economic consultants, in a tax study which they said showed that "capital gains taxation and double taxation of dividends are unsatisfactory as they now stand" (New York *Times,* November 2, 1947). In Washington he submitted evidence to the Senate Finance Committee on the "'unhealthy state of the nation's capital markets,' pressing his fight for modification of the tax structure to provide an incentive for the investment of surplus funds, which would result from tax relief" (New York *Herald Tribune,* March 14, 1948).

During his presidency Schram was frequently opposed by old-line brokers, who considered his $500,000-a-year advertising budget unnecessary. In November 1949 several of them tried to give some of the president's authority back to the member committees, but Schram successfully opposed this move by pointing out that it was just this "'old, discredited committee system' which had given Wall Street its bad name" (*Time,* September 4, 1950).

When Schram resigned in September 1950 after suffering a heart attack, C. Norman Stabler wrote that "The departing president can justly point with pride to the changes that have come about in the nation's market place during the decade that he has held the No. 1 spot. . . .The big institution lost $1,500,000 the year before he joined it, and had only about $3,000,000 in its treasury. Now it has some $15,000,000 and an additional $7,000,000 is due over the next year or two on listing fees." Schram went back to operating his farms in Peru, Indiana, and in Green County, Illinois, (total acreage 2,200), while retiring on a ten-year pension of $25,000 a year as a consultant.

Schram was elected president of the United Service Organizations, Inc., on February 4, 1953 to succeed Lindsley F. Kimball, vice-president of the Rockefeller Foundation. As sixth president since the USO was founded in 1941, Schram serves as the volunteer head of the 265 USO centers in the United States and overseas. He announced in August that a new program would extend USO activities into the field of religion in cooperation with clergymen and their congregations adjoining military stations.

Long active in civic affairs, Schram has served as chairman of the 1946 fund raising campaign of the Visiting Nurse Service of New York, the Manhattan financial section of the 1949 Salvation Army Appeal, the Greater New York 1950 March of Dimes drive for the National Foundation for Infantile Paralysis, and as a director of the New York Police Athletic League. He is a director of the Federal Prison Industries, Inc., and the Cities Service Company, and is also a graduate member of the Business Advisory Council. His clubs are the Columbia Country (Chevy Chase, Maryland) the Metropolitan (Washington, D.C.) and the Links (New York). He is a Demo-

SCHRAM, EMIL—*Continued*

crat, a Presbyterian, a Mason, and a member of the Newcomen Society of America. In March 1947 he was named the "oustanding Hoosier of the year" by the Sons of Indiana for his role "in directing attention to the need of broad, free markets in the nation." The following year he was awarded two honorary Doctor of Laws degrees—one from the University of Vermont and the other from New York University.

On December 28, 1914, Schram married Mabel Miller of Anderson, Indiana. They have three sons: Robert Miller, James Edward, and Daniel Conway.

Schram is six feet one inch tall, has blue eyes, and balding sparse blond hair. Watching baseball is his chief hobby. Called "cautious" and "conservative" as exchange president (*Time*, June 14, 1948), he has also been characterized as "rugged" (*Newsweek*, May 19, 1941), "burly" (*Business Week*, May 10, 1941), and as "pleasant-mannered . . . quiet-spoken and reserved" (New York *Sun*, May 6, 1941).

Successful in many fields, Schram told *Time* magazine (September 4, 1950) that he operates on the premise that "All business is essentially the same."

References

N Y Herald Tribune p1+ My 7 '41;
  Ag 25 '50
N Y Post p1+ My 6 '41
N Y Sun My p1+ My 6 '41; p23 My 7
  '41
N Y World-Telegram p24 My 20 '41
Time 56:78+ S 4 '50
Business Executives of America (1950)
Who's Who in America, 1952-53
Who's Who in Commerce and Industry
  (1951)
World Biography (1948)

SCOTT, (GUTHRIE) MICHAEL, REV.
July 30, 1907- Clergyman
Address: c/o The Africa Bureau, 69 Great Peter St., London, S.W.1, England

Since 1947 the Reverend Michael Scott has been gaining international attention through his efforts to present before the United Nations the case of several native tribes of South-West Africa, a territory which the Union of South Africa has held as a mandate since World War I and is now attempting to annex. Scott, who first went to South Africa at the age of nineteen, served as an Anglican clergyman in England and in India before World War II. He returned to South Africa in 1943 and took up the cause of its non-European peoples, becoming a controversial figure in Europe and the United States as well as in South Africa, to which he has been forbidden to return.

The son of the Reverend Percival C. Scott and Ethel Maud (Burn) Scott, Guthrie Michael Scott was born in England on July 30, 1907. His grandfather, father, and brothers were all Anglican clergymen, and the family also had Naval connections. After a "conventional English middle-class education" (*Time*, April 14,

1952), including study at King's College, Taunton, he fell ill at the age of nineteen and was advised by doctors to go to South Africa to recuperate in the warm climate. For a year he worked in a leper colony near Capetown and then began his theological studies at Grahamtown, where he stayed for three years. He returned to England in 1930 to complete his training at Chichester Theological College, and was ordained an Anglican priest. In England he worked in country parishes, in a fashionable London church, and in the slums of the city's East End, before being sent to India, where he became curate to the Anglican Bishop in Bombay and then in Calcutta. He studied Hindu religion and philosophy, and was strongly influenced by the teachings of Mohandas Gandhi, particularly the doctrine of passive resistance.

Having returned home on leave in 1939, Scott was in England when World War II began. He enlisted in the Royal Air Force as an aircraftsman, because he believed he could not urge others to fight if he remained a noncombatant himself. Before he could finish his training, his health failed, and he was discharged from the Air Force. On medical advice, he returned to South Africa in 1943 to settle in Johannesburg, where he became assistant pastor to the African community and chaplain to an orphanage for colored children near Sophiatown, one of Johannesburg's slum areas. Conditions there having roused his sympathies, with the goal of coordinating progressive activity throughout the country he founded the Campaign for Right and Justice, gaining support among Europeans in South Africa as well as the native population. When the campaign began to develop into a new political party, Scott resigned.

In 1946 the South African Parliament passed what was popularly called the "Ghetto Act," which imposed restrictions on South Africa's Indian population. Indians in Durban organized a passive resistance movement, a form of protest urged by Scott. For several nights white mobs attacked the Indian groups, including Indians who were not taking part in the demonstration. After the riots Scott, who had joined the passive resisters, was imprisoned and given a three-month jail sentence (*PM*, November 3, 1947). On his release, he was relieved of his parish in Johannesburg, but the Bishop granted him a general license to preach. Late in 1946 Scott went to live in Tobruk, a shanty town built outside Johannesburg by former African servicemen. Arrested and convicted by the South African Government for living in a segregated native area, he received a suspended sentence. During the next year Scott moved to Bethal, a rich agricultural area in the Eastern Transvaal, where the natives complained of their treatment by the farmers. When the press published stories based on Scott's reports of conditions there, the farmers protested and the government promised an inquiry.

At this time Scott's help was sought by the high chief of the Herero tribe in Bechuanaland, who, with 14,000 of his people, wished to return to their tribal lands in South-West Africa.

They had fled this area because of the racial extermination policies of the German government which held the territory as a colony before World War I. In 1915 the Union of South Africa had taken the territory from the Germans and administered it under a League of Nations mandate and after World War II declared its desire to annex it. At the request of the chief that he investigate living conditions of the Hereros who had remained there, Scott visited South-West Africa and talked with tribal leaders, returning with the report that the natives were living in extreme poverty and in unsanitary conditions under the Union of South Africa's administration. Scott aided the chief in drawing up a petition to the United Nations which disputed South Africa's claim that the majority of South-West Africa's natives wanted incorporation into the Union and asked that the Hereros be allowed to return to their ancestral lands. The petition also requested that South-West Africa be placed under the international trusteeship system, or under the protection of Great Britain or the United States. Since the Herero and other tribal chiefs could not go to the United Nations in person, they asked Scott to be their representative.

Scott's difficulties in obtaining an American visa were overcome with the help of the Indian Embassy in Washington, which arranged that he be admitted to the United States as a member of the passive-resistance delegation to the United Nations. His permit restricted his stay in the United States to the time of the General Assembly's session and to the vicinity of United Nations headquarters, and forbade him "to engage in extracurricular, subversive or propaganda activities or agitation against the United States." The manner of his admission was protested by the American Civil Liberties Union. Because of the delay in getting the visa, Scott arrived too late for most of the United Nations discussion of the South Africa question and was not heard officially.

As Scott was leaving South Africa for the General Assembly's next session, held in 1948 in Paris, he was ordered by the government to surrender his visa, but escaped across the border into Rhodesia. The following year, when the U.N. Assembly again met at Lake Success, the Trusteeship Committee voted 25 to 15 to hear Scott speak for the first time. With the Union of South Africa boycotting the meeting because it considered his appearance illegal, he spoke for more than an hour on November 26, 1949, describing South Africa's land policy in South-West Africa and asking the United Nations to intervene. "The matter has been made urgent now by the passage of the South-West Africa Act claiming to terminate the mandate and in effect absorbing or annexing the territory to South Africa," Scott told the Trusteeship Committee. From Pretoria, South African Prime Minister Daniel Malan challenged the United Nations' right to extend its "interference mania" to his country's administration of South-West Africa, but on December 6 the General Assembly adopted a resolution calling for a ruling by the International Court at The Hague on the territory's

REV. MICHAEL SCOTT

status. When the Court considered the case in the spring of 1950, Scott was not permitted to testify because he lacked legal support for such testimony. In July it ruled that United Nations approval was required before South Africa could change the mandate status of South-West Africa; this did not entail an obligation to change it to a trusteeship, and the *status quo* remained.

When in 1950 Scott again was delayed in securing an American visa, Socialist leader Norman Thomas, Walter White of the National Association for the Advancement of Colored People, and other American leaders spoke in his behalf. As in 1947, only a restricted visa was granted, allowing "transit" through New York to the United Nations. In December of that year the General Assembly voted 45 to 6 to establish a five-nation committee to negotiate with South Africa about carrying out the Court's advisory opinion. While the South African delegate thought that the resolution "practically closed the door" to a "friendly" solution, Scott hailed it as "a great reassurance to Africans everywhere." Eleven months later (November 1951) in Paris, the Trusteeship Committee granted the request of leaders of the Nama, Berg Damara, and Hereros tribes to plead their case in person, but the Union government refused them passports. Scott spoke three times during the United Nations 1951-52 session, primarily recounting the chiefs' efforts to appear and charging that the Union government wanted to expand its control to include the British protectorates of Bechuanaland, Basutoland, and Swaziland. In South Africa, Prime Minister Malan called Scott "a well-known hostile and fanatical foreigner and agitator" and accused the United Nations of having "committed aggression" against his government. Scott was declared a "prohibited inhabitant" of South Africa and

SCOTT, MICHAEL—*Continued*

told that if he tried to return, he would not be admitted. On January 11, 1952, forty states in the Trusteeship Committee voted to express their "admiration and gratitude" to Scott. Tribal leader Hosea Kutato in Windhoek, South-West Africa, told a New York *Herald Tribune* writer, "Our faith in Michael Scott will never slacken so long as he lives and we live."

In December 1952 Scott, who had again obtained a restricted visa to be present at the General Assembly session in New York, appealed in a letter to Gerhardus F. Jooste, chief of the South African delegation, for permission to return to South Africa and face charges which ranged from Communism to treason, and to discuss the question of the tribes of South-West Africa. "I should like to have an opportunity of telling the whole truth about the matter and of submitting myself, humanly speaking, to the judgment of the court, and to clear suspicion, if any, of those against whom there are no grounds for reproach."

Banned from southwest Africa by the union government, Scott went to Nyasaland where he fought against the proposed British plan for central African federation. He was deported on May 28, 1953 by the British colonial au-authorities and went to London. In late October he appeared at the United Nations stating that he had been given a mandate by eighty African chiefs to represent them and to oppose the Central African Federation.

Michael Scott is the author of the pamphlets *Shadow over Africa* and *Civilization in Africa* and coauthor of the book *Attitude to Africa*. Many of his sermons and articles have also been published. Described by *Time* as "tall and strikingly handsome," the Anglican clergyman is six feet two inches in height and has gray eyes and brown hair. A writer for the *Christian Science Monitor,* who found him "no spellbinder or firebrand," has spoken of "the persistent quality of his convictions."

References

Christian Sci Mon p3 Oct 30 '50
N Y Times p12 D 3 '51
Time 59:41 Ap 14 '52

SELYE, HANS (HUGO BRUNO) (sĕ'lyā) Jan. 26, 1907- Endocrinologist; medical researcher; physician

Address: b. c/o Institute of Experimental Medicine and Surgery, University of Montreal, P.O.B. 6128, Montreal, Canada; h. 659 Milton St., Montreal, Canada

An internationally known endocrinologist, Hans Selye has impressed the entire medical world with the epochal discovery that our body has a unified defense against disease, pain, fatigue, and stress, a concept which "promises to take its place with the medical milestones of Pasteur, Koch, Behring, and Ehrlich", (*Look,* March 27, 1951). After 15 years of research he has demonstrated in his experiments that many of our worst diseases, including heart disease, kidney disease, and arthritis, result from an unbalancing of hormones under prolonged stress.

Director of the Institute of Experimental Medicine and Surgery at the University of Montreal, and a professor since 1945, Dr. Selye has a wide background in medical research, as a Rockefeller research fellow at Johns Hopkins University in Baltimore and McGill University in Canada, where he has been a professor in biochemistry and history. Since 1947, Selye has been expert consultant to the Surgeon General of the United States Army. He is a special guest lecturer of the Naval Medical School at Bethesda, Maryland, and at the Royal College of Physicians in Canada.

Hans Hugo Bruno Selye was born on January 26, 1907, in Vienna, Austria, the only child of Hugo and Felicia Maria (Langbank) Selye. His father was a noted doctor, and his grandfather and great-grandfather were physicians. After receiving his early education from a governess, the boy attended high school and college at the College of the Benedictine Fathers in Komarom, Czechoslovakia, from 1916 to 1924, when he entered the German University of Prague as a medical student. The following year he continued his medical studies at the University of Paris, transferring in 1926 to the University of Rome. He returned a year later to complete his studies at the German University of Prague, which awarded him an M.D. degree in 1929, and a Ph.D. degree in chemistry in 1931. During his years as a student his extra-curricular activities included fencing and swimming.

While completing his doctorate Selye began his career in medicine and research as assistant in experimental pathology at the German University of Prague in 1929. He was awarded a Rockefeller research fellowship in 1931 in the department of biochemical hygiene of Johns Hopkins University, in Baltimore, Maryland. The next year he went as a Rockefeller research fellow to the department of biochemistry at McGill University in Canada, where he was appointed a lecturer in biochemistry in 1933, and an assistant professor in 1934.

Selye secured the first evidence for his *stress* theory of disease in 1936 in laboratory tests to discover the effects of ovarian hormones upon the glandular system of rats. He states: "I found that injections of the ovarian hormone stimulated the . . . outer tissue of the adrenal glands of the rats, caused deterioration of the thymus glands, and produced ulcers and other symptoms. . . .The rats died; later I found that any artificial hormone compounds, and stresses, and any kind of damage did the same thing" (Toronto *Star Weekly,* June 16, 1951). He published the result of his experiments in *Nature,* including an article entitled "Syndrome Produced by Nocuous Agents" (July 4, 1936). However, his revolutionary concept received little support or attention from the medical field. He obtained the stimulus to continue his research largely from the encouragement and financial help of Sir Frederick Banting of Toronto, who provided his first grant of $500.

In 1937 Selye was promoted to the rank of assistant professor of histology, in charge of research laboratories. That year he reported that he was able to obtain evidence in his experiments with rats that "appendicitis is caused by histamine," if present in too great quantity in the blood (New York *Times*, May 6, 1937). Continuing his research on the effects of stress on laboratory animals, he reduced the amount of stress—worry, heat, cold, infection, hunger, terror—to the point where it did not kill the animal. He observed what he called a "general adaptation syndrome" (G-A-S), beginning with an "alarm reaction," continuing, if stress remained, to an "adaptive" stage, and leading to an "exhaustion" state that results in death. Selye attributed to the adaptive stage what he terms "adaptation" or "civilized" diseases, such as arthritis, heart disease, kidney disease, and other circulatory disturbances. The common denominator of all these diseases he recognized as "stress", leading to "over-adaptation and over-production of adrenal hormones" (*Magazine Digest,* April 1952). He states that "the apparent cause of illness is often an infection, an intoxication, nervous exhaustion, or merely old age, but actually a breakdown of the hormonal adaptation mechanism seems to be the most common ultimate cause of death in man" (New York *Times*, December 16, 1951).

Selye was advanced to the rank of associate professor of histology at McGill University in 1941 and awarded a D.Sc. degree in medical research in 1942. The next year, Selye published the first four volumes of a six-volume *Encyclopedia of Endocrinology,* a labor to which he refers as "finger exercises" (*Time,* October 9, 1950). Selye left McGill University in 1945 to accept an appointment as director of the Institute of Experimental Medicine and Surgery at the University of Montreal, with a professorship in the Institute. In that year, he also represented Canada at the celebration of the 220th anniversary of the Academy of Sciences of the U.S.S.R. in Moscow and Leningrad. He accepted the post of expert consultant to the Surgeon General of the United States Army in 1947.

At the twenty-ninth annual meeting of the Association for Research in Nervous and Mental Disease held in New York in December 1949, Selye stated he found in animal experiments that, under physical stress, the adrenals produce a large amount of a hormone called desoxycorticosterone (DOCA), as well as the hormone cortisone. He added that when "desoxycorticosterone and cortisone are produced in the right proportions . . . no disease develops" (New York *Times,* December 3, 1949).

At the fourth General Assembly of the World Medical Association in New York in October 1950, Selye advised that experiments on animals and clinical tests had led him to conclude that "the production of disease by many systemic and local irritants depends largely upon the function of the pituitary-adrenal cortex system" (New York *Times,* October 19, 1950). Speaking before the Nassau County (N.Y.) Chapter of the American Academy of General Practice in November 1951 he stated that somatrophin (STH), the so-called "growth hormone" produced by the pituitary gland, suppresses. the action of ACTH, also secreted by that gland, as indicated by his experiments

Ric

DR. HANS SELYE

with rats. It reduced the ability of ACTH to lower the body's resistance to infection, he explained. As described in *Magazine Digest* (April 1952), STH has become a "No 1 project" in the research program of Selye, as its potentialities may contribute to the prevention of infections and may slow down man's aging process.

Selye wrote more than 400 scientific papers, including articles published in the London magazine *Nature,* and several written in German and published abroad, before he came to America. In addition to his six-volume *Encyclopedia of Endocrinology,* the last two volumes of which appeared in 1946, Selye has written the following books: *On the Experimental Morphology* of the Adrenal Cortex (in collaboration with H. Stone, 1950); *Textbook of Endocrinology* (2nd Edition, 1949), called the "most complete account of the subject which has yet appeared . . . a miniature of the much larger *Encyclopedia of Endocrinology*" (*Nature,* June 19, 1948); *Stress* (1950), dedicated "to those who are under the exhausting nervous strain of pursuing their ideal" (*Newsweek,* June 26, 1950); *First Annual Report on Stress* (1951), "a review of 3,000 research papers published in the field" (New York *World-Telegram and Sun,* January 16, 1952); *The Story of the Adaptation Syndrome* (1952); *Endocrinologia* (1952); and the recent *Second Annual Report on Stress* (in collaboration with A. Horava, 1952). Selye plans to publish a yearly report on *Stress,* his first book on the subject having sold around 10,000 copies in 1950. Currently he is on the editorial boards of the *American Journal of Proctology, Experimental Medicine and Surgery, Revue Canadienne de Biologie,* and several European publications.

"One of the most honored men in medicine" (*Coronet,* July 1950), Selye has received the Gordon Wilson Medal by the American Clin-

SELYE, HANS—*Continued*

ical and Climatological Association in 1948; the Casgrain and Charbonneau Prize awarded by McGill University for his original work leading to improvement in the prevention or treatment of disease; the Heberden Research Medal in London, England in 1950; the Medal of the Academia Medico Fisica in Italy; and the title doctor *honoris causa* from the National Universities of Argentina. He is a fellow of the American Association for the Advancement of Science, the New York Academy of Sciences, and the Royal Society of Canada. The scientist is an honorary member of the Aesculapian Society of the University of Ottawa, the American Clinical and Climatological Association, the Essex County Pathological and Anatomical Society, and of numerous medical societies in Europe and South America. His organization memberships include the American Association for Cancer Research, the American Heart Association, the American Society for the Study of Arteriosclerosis, the Canadian Society for the Study of Allergy, the National Society for Medical Research, and a number of biological and endocrinological societies in North America and Europe. As a corresponding member, he participates in several medical associations in Argentina, France, Italy, Portugal, and Spain. His faith is Catholic.

On December 5, 1936, Selye married Frances Rebecca Love, and has one daughter, Catherine, by this marriage. He is the father of three children, Michel, Jean, and Marie by his second marriage, to Gabrielle Grant on February 17, 1949. The endocrinologist, standing five feet ten inches tall and weighing 164 pounds, has gray eyes, and "graying dark blond hair." A pipe-smoking man, lithe and slim, with a lively step, Selye says the best way to meet the stress of modern living is to "roll with the punch" (*Coronet,* July 1950).

Selye "has become the world's outstanding expert on the endocrine glands—although many dispute some aspects of his theories. . . .Dr. Selye hopes that specialists in stress will be able to catch up with—and eventually get ahead of—the stresses of civilization." (*Time,* October 9, 1950).

David Dietz, science editor of Scripps-Howard newspapers, wrote that Dr. Selye's theory of "over-activity of bodily mechanisms" has stirred up controversy in the medical world in much the same way that Dr. Sigmund Freud's theory of psychoanalysis did.

References

Coronet 28:32-37 Jl '50
MacLean's 78:12, 77-78 Je 1 '47; 64:22-23, 35 D 1 '51
Magazine Digest p43-48 Ap '52
Star Weekly (Toronto) p2 Je 16 '51
Time 56:93-4 O 9 '50
American Men of Science (1949)
Canadian Who's Who, 1949-1951
Robinson, D. The 100 Most Important People (1953)
Who's Who Among Physicians and Surgeons, 1938
Who's Who in America, 1952-53
World Biography (1948)

SETON, ANYA 1916(?) Author

Address: b. c/o Houghton, Mifflin Co., 2 Park St., Boston, Mass.; h. Binney Lane, Old Greenwich, Conn.

Reprinted from the *Wilson Library Bulletin,* March, 1953

Anya Seton seems to be one of the few successful American women writers whose father was a famous author. His name familiar to two generations of American boys, was Ernest Thompson Seton, the Scotch-English-American author of such perennial outdoor classics as *Wild Animals I Have Known* and *Two Little Savages.* In 1896 he married a native Californian, Grace Gallatin, herself the author of several books on the Orient and Near East. Their only daughter Ann, was born in New York City late in their marriage, probably during World War I [1916?].

Ann Seton grew up on her father's large estate in Cos Cob and Greenwich, Connecticut, where visiting Indians taught her Indian dances and woodcraft. One Sioux chief called her Anutiha, signifying "cloud gray eyes," a name which the family gradually shortened to Anya. She was educated by governesses and at the Spence School in New York, and then went abroad, first to England, then to France in pursuance of her plan to become a doctor. She studied medicine for a while at L'Hôtel Dieu, a hospital in Paris, but decided not to complete her studies. She later worked as a nurse's aide and secretary of a mental hygiene clinic. She has two children by a first marriage. She is now married to Hamilton Chase, an investment counsel, and they have one daughter. The Chases have recently built a small modern house "practically in the water" on Lond Island Sound at Old Greenwich, Connecticut. Writing as a profession had seemed too familiar to be glamorous when she lived at home, but, she confesses, "the urge suddenly caught up with me in 1938" when she sold a short-short to a newspaper syndicate for five dollars. Attracted by the figure of Theodosia Burr Alston, Aaron Burr's daughter, who was drowned at sea in 1813, she did research in South Carolina for a long historical novel, *My Theodosia* (1941), called "workmanlike and interesting" by the New York *Times,* which also praised its careful period background.

Dragonwyck (1944), the next novel, was a Hudson River Gothic, period 1840, which displayed its author's flair for arresting titles and was a resounding success, serialized in the *Ladies' Home Journal,* a Dollar Book Club selection, translated into nine languages (including Israeli), and made into a good thrilling motion picture. "For all its trappings and devices . . . the novel manages to have life and substance," wrote Harriet Colby in the New York *Herald Tribune Book Review.*

Visits to her father's ranch in Santa Fe, memories of a Scottish grandmother with second sight, and the advice of the late Mary Austin determined the writing of *The Turquoise* (1946), described by the *Weekly Book Review* as "a warm, highly readable book." Edmund Wilson in the *New Yorker,* however,

SHANTZ, BOBBY *See* Shantz, R. C.

SHANTZ, ROBERT CLAYTON Sept. 26, 1925- Baseball player
Address: b. c/o Athletic's Ball Park, 21st St. and Lehigh Ave., Philadelphia, Pa.

The winner of the Baseball Writers Association of America's annually awarded Kenesaw Mountain Landis Memorial Plaque in 1952 for the "most valuable player" in the American League was Robert Clayton (Bobby) Shantz of the Philadelphia Athletics, who won twenty-four games and lost only seven in that year and whose earned run average was the third best in the league. Five feet seven inches in height, Shantz is one of the smallest pitchers in the history of organized baseball and the smallest in the major leagues since the days of "Wee Willie" Sherdel. He throws with his left hand and bats with his right, hits and fields well, and possesses unusual control.

Robert Clayton Shantz, the elder son of Wilmer and Ruth Shantz, was born September 26, 1925, in Pottstown in eastern Pennsylvania, and is of Pennsylvania German descent. Bobby and his brother Bill were brought up in Pottstown, where their father, a template maker, played third base for a neighborhood semiprofessional team and taught his sons the rudiments of baseball at an early age. "When Bobby was eight," Edgar Williams has written in the *Saturday Evening Post* (July 25, 1952), "he formed a team called the Sanatoga Pee Wees. 'I owned the ball,' he recalls, 'so naturally I was the pitcher.'" He also pitched for his elementary school team, was second baseman for the St. James' Lutheran Church team in the Pottstown Sunday School League, which he joined at the age of twelve, and played center field in his four years at Pottstown High School. He also distinguished himself in interscholastic swimming and diving, winning "letters" for ability in all three sports.

Under average height, Bobby Shantz was four feet eleven inches tall and weighed about 110 pounds when he was graduated from Pottstown High School in June 1942. For this reason professional ballplaying, and particularly pitching, seemed out of the question for him. He was rejected by the Army when he reached the age for military service on his eighteenth birthday because he was below minimum stature. In Philadelphia, where the family moved when Wilmer Shantz took a wartime job in the Navy Yard, Bobby worked as a saw glazer at the Disston Saw Works. He and his brother Bill joined the Holmesburg Ramblers, a neighborhood sandlot team, early in 1944. Bobby played his old high school position, center field, until "one day just for kicks" he pitched during batting practice. As Edgar Williams has related, Alton Cuthbertson, the Ramblers' manager, noted Bobby's "natural curve" and, calling him from the hill, made him a pitcher on the spot. Shantz won nine games for the Ramblers and lost only one before being recalled by the Army for a new medical examination. This time he was accepted, having grown to an even five feet and added ten

ANYA SETON

found it "as synthetic, as arbitrary, as basically cold and dead, as a scenario for a film."

The scene of *The Hearth and the Eagle* (1948) was a waterfront inn of that name at Marblehead, Massachusetts, a composite of various old houses. Hesper, the heroine, loves a moody artist, Evan Redlake, who "in some ways resembles one of our famous American painters," says Miss Seton. A Literary Guild selection after serialization in *Woman's Home Companion,* it was called "a substantial and well told story" in the New York *Herald Tribune.*

Foxfire (1950), located in a modern gold-mining camp in Gila, Arizona, had been simmering in Anya Seton's imagination since, as a bride, she visited her father-in-law's mining camp in Colorado. She went down into a mine, violating the universal miners' taboo against women in mines, and stayed in two Apache reservations before writing the novel.

A fictional biography of the fourteenth century Katherine Swynford and her lover, later her husband, John of Gaunt, Duke of Lancaster, is Anya Seton's current work in progress. She did research for the book in England. When not writing, she reads for pleasure six or seven hours a day, a wide variety "but always Jane Austen, Dickens, American and English history, and metaphysics". More active recreations include badminton, swimming, bridge, and travel—she has visited every state in the Union except Washington. Black-haired and hazel-eyed Anya Seton is of medium height and weight, is an Episcopalian and—usually— a Republican. "Perhaps my greatest joy and hobby is research," she writes, "and in consequence I have great affection for libraries and librarians, who are endlessly patient and helpful. Bless them all!"

References

Who's Who in America, 1952-53

ROBERT CLAYTON SHANTZ

pounds to his weight; after basic training he was sent to the Philippines as a private with the 342nd Infantry Regiment, 86th Division. Becoming a member of the regimental baseball team, Shantz received many pointers from the former Chicago White Sox pitcher Gordon Maltzberger, and when in October 1945 his outfit was matched against a visiting team of major league players, Shantz was sent to the mound. He lost to pitchers Ed Head of the Brooklyn Dodgers and Bill Voiselle of the New York Giants by a score of 4 to 2, but held to eight singles an opposition line-up which included Whitey Kurowski of the St. Louis Cardinals and Frank McCormack of the Cincinnati Reds.

Demobilized as a corporal in September 1946, Shantz returned to Philadelphia to rejoin both the Disston Saw Works and the Holmesburg Ramblers. After he had played with the Ramblers for a few weeks at the beginning of the 1947 season, he was signed up by Larry Glick, the new manager for Souderton in the highly rated semiprofessional Eastern Pennsylvania League, who needed fresh pitching talent for his team. Under Glick's guidance, he and his battery-mate Tony Parisse proceeded to score eight straight victories for Souderton and were largely responsible for assuring the team of a meeting in October with Egypt of the Lehigh Valley League for a regional championship. Parisse, who had been catcher for the Philadelphia Athletics during the war, recommended Shantz to that club, but scouts for the major league clubs were agreed that his underpar stature and weight made him a risky prospect, although he now topped five feet six inches and weighed nearly 140 pounds. In his game against Egypt, Shantz was pitted against another southpaw, young Curt Simmons, who had recently been paid a $65,000 bonus to join the Philadelphia National League team. He defeated Simmons by a 4 to 1 score and yielded

only five hits while racking up fourteen strikeouts. This achievement revived the interest of the major league baseball clubs in Shantz, and instead of offering him a Class D contract as previously planned, the Philadelphia Athletics now proposed a Class A agreement at three hundred dollars a month. Bobby Shantz having signed with the Athletics on the condition that his brother, a catcher, would also receive a Class A contract, at the beginning of the following season Bob and Bill Shantz began their careers in professional baseball as members of the Athletics' Lincoln (Nebraska) "farm" in the Class A Western League.

In his single season (1948) with the Lincoln club, Shantz pitched 214 innings in 28 games, winning 18 and losing 7, while striking out 212 opposing batters and issuing 55 bases on balls. Shantz, who trained with the parent Athletics in the spring of 1949, made his major league debut on May 1 of that year, when he was sent to the mound for two-thirds of an inning of relief pitching against the Washington Senators. The Athletics' manager and owner, Connie Mack, decided that Shantz would benefit from further minor league experience and a day later "optioned" him to the Buffalo, New York, club in the Triple A International League. Just after he left Philadelphia's Shibe Park, two of the Athletics' regular starting pitchers developed sore arms, and on his arrival in Buffalo he found orders awaiting him to return to the Athletics for their western trip. Shantz joined the team in Detroit, and on May 6 was called to the mound in the third inning to relieve pitcher Carl Scheib with three runs in, a man on third base, and nobody yet retired. In what the *Baseball Register* has recorded as the outstanding single performance of his career, the southpaw pitched nine consecutive innings of no-hit, no-run baseball, and won the extra-innings game from the Detroit Tigers, while yielding two hits and one run in the thirteenth and final inning. In his next appearance on the mound against the St. Louis Browns five days later, Shantz was beaten by 5 to 4, and he ended the 1949 season with six victories to eight losses. This was the only year in his baseball career that Shantz "walked" more batters than he "fanned." During the 1950 season the Philadelphia team, which finished up in last place, showed weakness almost immediately, and Shantz, called on frequently for relief in addition to regular starting assignments, was seriously overworked. He won only eight games while losing fourteen, and his earned run average of 4.60 was the lowest in his career.

"Shantz is foxier than a Philadelphia lawyer," the magazine *Pathfinder* has commented. "He employs a four pitch repertoire to bamboozle .300 hitters and make them look like .190 bushers. He has an adequate fast ball, a knuckler, a corking curve and a maddening change of pace." The leading batter of modern times, Ted Williams, has been quoted as calling Shantz's curve ball "the best in the [American] league," and the "knuckler," which he "throws off the tips of the three middle fingers" (Edgar Williams) is regarded by all, including Shantz himself, to be his most bewildering delivery. Shantz has stated that he had worked on his knuckle ball over a period of years, but was not permitted to use it in a major league game until the middle of 1951, when Jimmie Dykes took over field management of the Athletics from Connie Mack. At about this same time Shantz acquired a new battery-mate in Joe Astroth, who did much to curb his tendency to be hasty and nervous. When in July he was named by Casey Stengel of the New York Yankees to the American League pitching staff for the 1951 All Star Game, Shantz's morale improved, although he was not called to the mound. He finished the season with a record of 18 games won and 10 games lost, and an earned run average improved from 4.60 to 3.95, and through the first half of 1952 he was considered the outstanding pitcher in either league. After he lost his second game in 1952 to the New York Yankees (April 21) —he himself had singled home the victory-making run in his first (April 17)—he was not again defeated until June 24, when a two-run "homer" by Rosen of the Cleveland Indians snapped his streak. Meanwhile Shantz had held the same team to three hits in one of his other games and on May 30 had struck out eleven Yankees in fourteen innings. On June 8 he became the season's first ten-game winner in either major league.

For the 1952 All Star Game, Shantz pitched one inning (the fifth), striking out Whitey Lockman, Jackie Robinson, and Stanley Musial, the only three National Leaguers to face him. On August 5, he registered over the Boston Red Sox his twentieth victory as against three defeats, his earned run average at this stage in the season being a low 1.55. Much speculation developed as to whether or not Bobby could become the first thirty-game winner in many years, but his early season pace had evidently tired him, for he slipped rapidly after August 10, when the Washington Senators ended his last extended victory streak. On September 19 he displayed a revival of his prowess by "blanking" the Yankees with four hits, but a few days later (September 23) his season's activity was halted by a broken left wrist, an injury which is not expected to have any permanent ill effects. Shantz ended the season with a record of 24 games won to 7 lost, the best pitching percentage (.774) in the American League, an overall earned run average of 2.48 (the third best in the A.L.), and 152 strike-outs to only 63 bases on balls. His margin of victory in the balloting by the Baseball Writers Association of America on November 13 for the annual award of the Kenesaw Mountain Landis Memorial Plaque for the American League's "most valuable player of the year" was decisive. He scored a total of 280 points to 183 for Allie Reynolds of the New York Yankees, who took second place, after receiving sixteen first choice votes on the first ballot to four for Reynolds.

Bobby Shantz and Shirley Vogel of Lincoln, Nebraska, were married January 20, 1950, and make their permanent home in Lincoln. They have a son, born October 8, 1953. In the winters Shantz has been employed at the post office as a parcel post deliveryman, and plans to open a sporting goods store in the Nebraska capital. On the official 1953 roster of the Philadelphia Athletics the height of the blond, blue-eyed pitcher is given as five feet seven inches and his weight as 150 pounds. "Away from the ball park," Edgar Williams has written, "Bobby lives baseball. His reading consists almost entirely of *The Sporting News*, the baseball trade paper, and sports magazines. On days off in Philadelphia, he attends sandlot games." Due to a shoulder injury in the 1953 season, Shantz did not make an outstanding record.

References

American Weekly p11+ S 7 '52 pors
Baseball 1952 1:80+ pors
Baseball Digest 11:73-8 O 8 '52
Christian Sci Mon p15 Jl 18 '52 por; p29 D 6 '52 por
Life 33:49-52 Jl 21 '52 pors
Look 16:94-5 Ag 26 '52 pors
N Y Times p42 S 24 '52 por; p27 N 14 '52 por
Newsweek 40:76-7 Jl 28 '52 por
Pathfinder 59:41 Ag 20 '52 pors
Sat Eve Post 225:25+ Jl 26 '52 por
Sport Life 5:56 O '52 por
Sports 4:12-14 N '52 pors
Time 59:57-8 Je 23 '52 por
Washington (D.C.) Post p21 Ap 12 '50
Baseball Register (1952)
Who's Who in Baseball (1952)

SHIELDS, JAMES P. 1890—June 29, 1953 Grand chief engineer of the Brotherhood of Locomotive Engineers since 1950; joined Division 136 of the union in 1920, and in 1932 was elected general chairman for the Union Pacific's Eastern Division; elected assistant grand chief engineer in 1942. See *Current Biography*, 1951.

Obituary

N Y Times p23 Je 30 '53

SHINN, EVERETT Nov. 7, 1876—May 1, 1953 Artist; painter of New York and Paris life; last one of "Eight Men of Rebellion," who protested against the "old National Academy" output; born in Woodstown, New Jersey; studied industrial design at Spring Garden Institute in Philadelphia; attended Pennsylvania Academy of Fine Arts; elected to National Institute of Arts and Letters, 1951. See *Current Biography*, 1951.

Obituary

N Y Times p89 My 3 '53

SHOCKLEY, WILLIAM Feb. 13, 1910- Physicist

Address: b. c/o Bell Telephone Laboratories, Inc., Murray Hill, N.J.; h. Madison, N.J.

A small paragraph in the radio columns of the New York *Times* on July 1, 1948 introduced to lay readers the word transistor, a thimble-sized device which had been developed under the supervision of Dr. William Shockley at the Bell Telephone Laboratories, Inc. This

WILLIAM SHOCKLEY

transistor may possibly make obsolescent the three-element vacuum tube invented in 1907 by Dr. Lee DeForest.

Although Dr. Shockley did not actually invent the transistor (it is attributed to John Bardeen and Walter H. Brattain, two members of his group at the Bell Laboratories), he fathered it in the same way in which Dr. Albert Einstein fathered the atomic bomb by advancing the hypothesis and pointing the way. The device itself is a semiconductor, which can amplify electrical signals as they are transferred through it from input to output terminals—precisely the same function as the vacuum tube in radio, television, telephones, hearing aids, computing devices, guided missiles, and bomb sights.

William Shockley was born on February 13, 1910 while his parents, William Hillman and May (Bradford) Shockley, were living in London, England. He was brought to the United States at the age of three and was reared in California. His father was a mining engineer. After graduating from Hollywood High School in 1927, and the California Institute of Technology in 1932 with a Bachelor of Science degree, Shockley was appointed to a teaching fellowship at the Massachusetts Institute of Technology, where he concurrently worked for the Ph.D. degree. Upon receiving his doctorate in physics, he joined the Bell Telephone Laboratories as a member of the technical staff in 1936.

The young scientist knew that the freeing of electronics from the inherent weaknesses of the vacuum tube (short life, bulkiness, fragility, and high power consumption) had long been an industrial dream. Scientists had been discouraged from experimenting in this area because of the prohibitive cost of conversion from the vacuum tube. This financial difficulty was somewhat alleviated when it was discovered that vacuum tubes could not rectify the extremely high-frequency radar signals.

Rectifying is the transforming of an alternate current into a direct one and, in early crystal radio sets, had been accomplished by a piece of galena with a "cat whisker" probe—technically a crystal diode. Galena rectifies because it is one of the class of materials known as semiconductors (whose electrical properties are intermediate between those of metals and insulators) but it had early been discarded by the radio and allied industries in favor of the vacuum tube, which could rectify and amplify both. With the realization that in radar, vacuum tubes failed in their primary purpose, semiconductors were revived and Dr. Shockley was among the leading "solid state" physicists who ushered them out of the "scientific doghouse."

Nevertheless, in order to use them again, they had to contain the amplifying qualities of the vacuum tube. Shockley, therefore, began experiments in 1939 toward making a semiconductor amplify as well as rectify. It was an elusive quest and it was interrupted by the war. With many ships being sunk by the Nazis in 1942, he was assigned by the Navy to the Columbia University division of war research as director of research for the anti-submarine warfare operations research group. He was also named to the office of the Secretary of War as an expert consultant in 1942.

The scientist returned to Bell and his semiconductors in 1945, and there, while examining the prevailing theory of electrical conduction in semiconductors, he came to the conclusion that it was possible to control the supply of movable electrons inside a semiconductor by influencing them with an electric field imposed from the outside. This was the genesis of the transistor, although actual experiments were disappointing in that the electrons kept getting tangled up in the surface of the material and generally not behaving as expected.

"We got negligible results," stated Dr. Shockley, "even though we could calculate what results we should get. John Bardeen . . . proposed a theory involving surface states to explain why the device didn't work. You see, we started with a device idea, then got a physics idea. This led to more physics experiments to learn more about surface states" (*Fortune,* March, 1953).

The experiments were conducted by Bardeen, a theoretical physicist, and Brattain, an experimental physicist. The key experiment involved a germanium diode immersed in an electrolyte (a solution that conducts electricity) and connected to a source of direct current. This, as Bardeen and Brattain reported, "led to the concept that a portion of the current was being carried by holes flowing near the surface. Upon replacing the electrolyte with a metal contact, transistor action was discovered."

This was the birth of the transistor, the rugged little device that, without vacuum, grid, plate, or cathode—and requiring only one-fiftieth the space of a vacuum tube and one-millionth the power—can perform most of its functions, and even extend them.

Francis Bello wrote in *Fortune,* March, 1953: "The active bit of solid substance in a transistor is barely visible to the naked eye, yet the transistor and its minute relatives will almost certainly stimulate greater changes in commerce and industry than reaction motors, synthetic fibers, or even, perhaps, atomic energy. Reason: the new solid state devices will provide the reliability, compactness, and low power consumption needed to lift information-handling and computing machines—the nub of the second industrial revolution now upon us—to any imaginable degree of complexity. In the transistor and the new solid state electronics, man may hope to find a brain to match atomic energy's muscle."

The search for a "brain" to match the atom's "brawn" continues with Dr. Shockley and his Bell associates. The original "point contact" transistor has already been supplemented by Dr. J. N. Shine's "photo" transistor (controlled by light rather than electric current) in 1950, by Dr. Shockley's "junction" transistor in 1951 and by R. L. Wallace, Jr.'s "tetrode" transistor in 1952.

The first important use of the transistor by Bell Telephone is a device called the card translator. Its purpose is to rapidly select routes for long-distance phone calls. Inside the card translator are approximately 1,000 metal cards, about five by seven and a half inches, standing like books on a shelf. Each card represents the called exchange and its geographic area, carries a particular code, and changes its position magnetically.

"A light shining through the card stacks emerges at the far end in a pattern dictated by the . . . position of the cards. This pattern, read by a grid of phototransistors and amplified by transistors, provides the key to available intercity circuits. The card translator will select called routes in less than a half second, and Bell expects to install about 150 of them in the next couple of years" (*Fortune,* March, 1953). The transistor has made such phenomenal progress in its infancy that Dr. Shockley and his associates are beginning to feel justified in thinking they have made "an encouraging start" toward realizing its immeasurable potential.

Dr. Shockley is a member of Sigma Xi and of Tau Beta Pi, of the American Physical Society, and of the Scientific Advisory Panel of the Secretary of War. The War Department awarded him the Medal for Merit in 1946 and he received the Certificate of Appreciation from the Department of the Army in 1953. He has also received the Morris Liebmann award of the Institute of Radio Engineers (1952) and the Oliver E. Buckley Solid State Physics Prize (1953) of the American Physical Society.

Dr. Shockley married Jean Bailey, a teacher, in 1933. With his family, which includes a daughter, Alison, and two sons, William and Richard, he lives in Madison, New Jersey. He is five feet eight inches tall, weighs 150 pounds, and has brown hair and gray eyes. Shockley is a Republican.

The physicist whose professional interests include ferromagnetic domains, semiconductors, the plastic properties of metals, the theory of solids, and semiconductor amplifiers of transistors, and who has written a book, *Electrons and Holes in Semiconductors* (Van Nostrand, 1950) likes to relax by climbing mountains. He is a member of the Appalachian Mountain Club.

References

Bell Telephone Mag 32:73 Summer '53
Fortune 47:128 Mr '53
N Y Times Jl 1 '48
Read Digest 62:87 My '53
American Men of Science (1949)

SIMPSON, RICHARD M(URRAY) Aug. 30, 1900- United States Representative from Pennsylvania

Address: b. House Office Bldg., Washington 25, D.C.; h. "Taylor Highlands," Huntingdon, Pa.

Having been first elected to Congress in May 1937 and re-elected to each subsequent Congress, Republican Richard M. Simpson has represented the Eighteenth District of Pennsylvania for sixteen years. During this period he has become known as an authority on taxes and an advocate of protective tariff, and in the Eighty-third Congress is a high-ranking member of the House Ways and Means Committee. As newly appointed chairman of the Republican Congressional Campaign Committee, Representative Simpson is responsible for directing the campaign of Republican candidates for the House in the 1954 election. At the close of the first session of the Eighty-third Congress Congressman Simpson was appointed a member of the seventeen-man Commission on Foreign Economic Policy.

Richard Murray Simpson, the son of Warren Brown and Sue (Miller) Simpson, was born in Huntingdon, Pennsylvania, on August 30, 1900. Following his graduation from the local public high school, he joined the United States Army to become in 1918 a member of the 301 Company, Tank Corps, in Raleigh, North Carolina. He then attended the University of Pittsburgh, where he took his B.S. degree in 1923. Some years later in Washington, D.C., he studied at the Georgetown University Law School for his LL.B. degree, which was granted in 1942.

While engaged in the insurance and guaranty business, which he had entered upon leaving college in 1923, Simpson was elected, in 1935, to the Pennsylvania House of Representatives. After representing Huntingdon County in the State legislature for two terms (until 1937), he won a seat in the Seventy-fifth United States Congress at a special election held on May 11, 1937, to fill a vacancy caused by the death of Representative Benjamin K. Focht. Simpson, who is now the senior Republican Representative from his State, was subsequently returned from Pennsylvania's Eighteenth District to each succeeding Congress, most recently to the Eighty-third Congress in the election of November 4, 1952.

During his first year (1937) in the House of Representatives, Simpson voted in opposition to

Harris & Ewing

RICHARD M. SIMPSON

proposed legislation granting $1,500,000 for relief in 1938 (June), a two-year extension of the "nuisance tax" (June), and to the passage of the Wagner housing bill (July). In the second session (1938) he supported a measure for Naval expansion (March) and the wage-hour bill (May). The following year he voted "nay" on the Townsend old-age pension plan (June) and "yea" on the "pernicious political activities" bill (July).

Other votes cast by Simpson show him against the Trade Agreements Act extension (May 1945) and the $3,750,000,000 loan to Great Britain (July 1946), in favor of the Case strike control bill (February 1946) and extension of the draft to 1947 (April 1946). In the Eightieth Congress he was for rent control extension (May 1947), the Greek-Turkish aid bill (May 1947), the tidelands oil bill (April 1948), and the displaced persons bill (June 1948); while opposing the *Voice of America* bill (June 1947) and the repeal of Federal taxes on oleomargarine (April 1948). He approved extension of the Marshall Plan (April 1949).

On measures regarding Government spending Simpson voted to cut European arms aid by 50 per cent (July 1949) and to reduce Federal expenditures by $600,000,000 (May 1950); he also approved a $10,000,000 cut in reclamation funds (May 1951). In opposition to a bill passed by the House in July 1951 to provide severe penalties for violation of the Federal narcotics laws, Simpson maintained that the penalties might work an injustice on victims of drugs. During June 1952, in the second session of the Eighty-second Congress, he supported a proposal to use the Taft-Hartley labor law to halt the steel strike and also a measure to end Federal rent controls by September of that year. He agreed with a large Republican majority in approving President Dwight D. Eisenhower's plan for reorganizing the Department

of Agriculture, on which the House voted in June 1953.

Representative Simpson's assignments on Congressional joint committees in the Eighty-second Congress were to the Internal Revenue Taxation Committee and the Economic Report Committee. For several years a member of the powerful tax-writing House Ways and Means Committee, in 1953 he ranks third in seniority among its Republicans. In discussing an agreement reached by this committee in November 1950 on a $3,000,000,000 excess profits tax bill, the Pennsylvania Representative, as a spokesman for his party's committeemen, pointed out that the measure afforded no relief provisions for the airplane manufacturing industry or the television industry, both of which would be called upon to expand in the war effort.

The Congressman reported in April of 1951 that a survey which he had carried out in cooperation with the Committee of Americans showed a strong backing by businessmen for a Federal sales tax. Such a tax, he estimated, would make unnecessary an increase in individual and corporate income taxes. In May 1951 he introduced a proposal for a straight 10 per cent increase for all taxpayers, which was rejected by a Democratic majority preferring an increase of 12½ per cent.

At a meeting in October 1951 of the American Tariff League in New York, Simpson described 1951 as a "milestone year for tariff" because Congress for the first time in seventeen years had resumed its traditional control over trade agreements and exercised its power "to protect workers and farmers when imported goods endanger their economic well-being." As reported by the New York *Herald Tribune* (October 25, 1951), he charged in this speech that the war in Korea had "saved the Truman Administration the political embarrassment of having to admit the 'complete failure of their much-touted reciprocal trade program.'"

When the Republican Eighty-third Congress had been in session a few months, Simpson introduced a controversial restrictive tariff bill, to extend the Reciprocal Trade Agreements Act for one year beyond its expiration date on June 12, 1953, and to remove the power of the President to set tariffs below "peril points" established by the United States Tariff Commission. It would also require the commission to find "injury" in instances where American workers become unemployed as a result of import competition, although only a segment of the industry might be harmed.

This measure, in conflict with an Eisenhower Administration appeal for a simple one-year extension of the Trade Agreements Act, was supported by groups such as the independent oil producers, leather processors, the coal industry, the dairy industry, lead and zinc miners, and manufacturers of cotton goods, pottery, glass, and watches. Opposed to the Simpson bill were the United States Chamber of Commerce, the International Chamber of Commerce and the Committee for Economic Development on the ground that it would discourage international trade.

After several weeks of hearings on the Simpson bill in the Ways and Means Committee, its sponsor introduced, in June 1953, a compromise bill endorsed by the Administration which withheld restrictions provided in the original measure. Besides extending the trade agreements law, it set up a bipartisan committee to study the nation's foreign economic policy and it enlarged the Tariff Commission to seven members to allow for a Republican majority. At the same time Simpson presented a second bill embodying the limitations of his earlier proposal.

By a vote of 363 to 35 the House passed on June 15, 1953, Simpson's compromise bill to extend the reciprocal trade programs for one year. In the debate on the Tariff Commission amendment, some Democratic leaders protested that enlargement of membership might destroy the bipartisan character of the commission. Simpson's view was that the amendment would increase "the protection of the American working man and his employer." The additional member, the New York *Herald Tribune* (June 16, 1953) reported him as stating, would bring an end to split decisions and provide "a little more hope" to American industries seeking a tariff raise under the escape clause.

Earlier, in May, Pennsylvania's senior Representative had expressed his attitude toward reciprocal trade before a meeting in New York of the National Association of Wool Manufacturers. " 'Trade, not aid' as a slogan is attractive," he observed. "However, it accepts without reservation that aid is necessary. It contains the assumption that trade can remove the need for foreign aid. If such a position is true, then certainly the trade envisioned must be a healthy trade. If we substitute unhealthy trade for aid abroad, we will have to adopt . . . a policy of 'Dollars for Domestic Aid' to American citizens thrown out of work by foreign competition at home—aid to retrain them and aid to move them" (New York *Times,* May 8, 1953).

The Senate passed by voice vote the one-year extension of the Reciprocal Trade Agreement and the amendment to set up the bipartisan committee on August 3; however, the amendment to add one member to the Tariff Commission was rejected in a committee. The second bill, with the restrictions which were originally proposed, was defeated by a House vote of 242 to 161 on July 23.

Among other legislative matters considered by the Ways and Means Committee in the spring of 1953 was President Eisenhower's request for a six-month extension of the excess profits tax. Simpson had stated in February, "I am confident that the Congress will not extend the excess profits tax nor will it increase the corporate rate. There is no possibility that excises [sales taxes] or individual taxes will be increased (New York *Times,* February 19, 1953). At the time of the hearings before the committee on the excess profits tax extension, in June, Simpson and two other Republican Representatives expressed their opinion that a truce in Korea, reducing the Government's financial burden, would warrant the Treasury's reconsideration of the tax program. (On July 15 the Senate passed the bill to extend the excess profits tax for six months).

A member of the House Republican Policy Committee, Simpson was also elected in March 1953 to succeed former Representative Leonard W. Hall (now chairman of the Republican National Committee) as chairman of the Republican Congressional Campaign Committee. Heading this thirty-eight member group, the Pennsylvania legislator is in charge of campaign plans of the Republican party candidates for seats in the House of Representatives in the 1954 Congressional elections.

Representative Simpson is married to May Josephine (Cox) Simpson. His first wife, Grace (Metz) Simpson, is deceased. He has five children: Susan and Barbara, James, Edward, and Joe Cox. Organizations to which the Congressman belongs are the American Legion, the Odd Fellows and the Patriotic Order of the Sons of America.

References

Biographical Directory of the American Congress, 1774-1949 (1950)
Congressional Directory (1952)
Who's Who in America, 1952-53
Who's Who in United States Politics (1950)

SLIGH, CHARLES R(OBERT), JR. (sli) Jan. 8, 1906- Business executive; organization official

Address: b. c/o National Association of Manufacturers, 14 W. 49th St., New York 20; 1661 Monroe Ave., N.W., Grand Rapids 2, Mich.; h. 1621 So. Shore Rd., Holland, Mich.

Meeting in New York City in December 1952 at the fifty-seventh annual Congress of American Industry, 3,000 industrialists elected Charles R. Sligh, Jr., the 1953 president of the National Association of Manufacturers. NAM's first president from the furniture industry, Sligh established his business in 1933, when many furniture manufacturers were operating at a loss, and is now president of four enterprises, the Charles R. Sligh Company, the Sligh-Lowry Furniture Company, the Grand Rapids Chair Company, and the Sligh Furniture Show Rooms, Inc. To his executive work, Sligh has added extensive participation in community, church, philanthropic, and educational activity.

Charles Robert Sligh, Jr., was born on January 8, 1906, in Grand Rapids, Michigan, to Charles Robert and Edith (Clark) Sligh. His father was president of the Sligh Furniture Company and a director of the National Association of Manufacturers (1925-26), and his mother was a teacher. (There were four girls in the family, one Charles's sister and the other three his half-sisters.) Graduated from the Central High School of Grand Rapids in 1924, Sligh enrolled at Colgate University, from which he withdrew after one year to take a job as a laborer for the building construction firm of Owen-Ames-Kimball. Later in 1925 in Tacoma, Washington, he was employed as a laborer for the Henry Mill & Timber Company and as a blacksmith's helper. Returning to Grand Rapids in 1926 he went to work in

CHARLES R. SLIGH, JR.

his father's furniture manufacturing business, where beginning as a case assembler, he became successively an office clerk, a salesman, and treasurer of the company. Following his father's death in 1927, the business declined and was liquidated in 1933.

In 1933, a year in which the average loss in the furniture industry was 14 per cent, Sligh and a partner, O. W. Lowry, took over an abandoned factory in Holland, Michigan, which had reverted to municipal ownership, the city agreeing to give the new project $1 credit toward the purchase price for every $7 of payroll the factory created. Beginning with a capital of $14,000, the partners employed forty men during the first year, in which their volume of business totaled $140,000. Sligh was president (at a salary of $35 a week) and salesman, while Lowry supervised production for the new firm, which was called the Charles R. Sligh Company. In 1940 the two men bought another idle factory at Zeeland, Michigan, where they established the Sligh-Lowry Furniture Company. Five years later Sligh purchased the Grand Rapids Chair Company, then losing several thousand dollars a month. Under his management, both employment rolls and wages of the firm more than doubled. Recently the Sligh Furniture Show Rooms, Inc., was opened in New York City. Sligh is president of all four enterprises, the gross income of which was estimated as about $4,500,000 in 1952 and which employ about 400 people. Sligh has stated that while none of his plants is unionized he is not opposed to trade unions. At his invitation, in October 1952 officials of the Upholsterers International Union (AFL) addressed the employees of the Grand Rapids Chair Company; following the officials' talk and one by Sligh, a vote resulted in rejection of the union by 70 per cent of the 110 workers. Sligh is also vice-president and treasurer of Ply Curves, Inc., Holland (since 1948) and a

director of Bodart Furniture Company, Sligh Realty Company, Santiam Timber Company, and the Michigan Trust Company.

At the fifty-seventh annual meeting of the National Association of Manufacturers, Sligh, on December 4, 1952, was elected president of the association for 1953, in succession to William J. Grede. Active in the organization for several years, he had been a member of its board of directors since 1949. In 1950-51 he served as chairman of NAM's taxation committee and in 1952 was a regional vice-president, vice-chairman of the Government economy committee and the public relations advisory committee, and a member of the national development advisory committee. As chairman of the association's education and research committee, he was instrumental in establishing a four-year course at the University of Michigan to train furniture executives. Graduate work in this field is now being planned, and similar courses have been instituted at the University of Minnesota and the University of North Carolina. In recognition of his leadership in this project, Sligh was named "Furniture Man of the Year" in 1945.

Founded in 1895, the NAM now represents 19,000 manufacturers, who produce 85 per cent of the manufactured goods of the United States. The organization's stated aims are: "to promote the industrial interests of the United States; to foster domestic and foreign commerce of the United States; to improve relations between labor and management; to protect the individual rights and liberty of employer and employee; to disseminate information with respect to the principles of individual liberty and ownership of property; to support legislation which furthers those principles, and oppose legislation in derogation of them." In a report published in February 1953 the NAM contended that it was impractical to base wage increases on the general increase in productivity in the economy of the country as a whole. The American Federation of Labor had earlier called for a general wage rise on this basis, and the principle was incorporated into a 1952 contract between General Motors and the Automobile Workers Union. Other recent actions of the association were a boycott of the Wage Stabilization Board in December 1952; public criticism of United Nations approval of a measure calling for any country's right to nationalize private property without specifying compensation to owners; and a proposal to reduce the Federal budget for 1953 by $14 billion. On the occasion of his election, Sligh pledged industry's "whole-hearted cooperation" with the Eisenhower Administration and expressed the confidence of business leaders that "with sound national leadership" the United States could "overhaul through production the inflationary tendencies which now beset us." In March 1953 the NAM president testified at a Senate Committee hearing against proposals to establish stand-by controls authority for the President.

The manufacturer was awarded an honorary degree of Doctor of Science in Business Administration by Cleary College at Ypsilanti, Michigan, on January 14, 1953. During World War II he served on the Regional War Labor

Board and was a member of the War Production Board. He is a past president of the National Association of Furniture Manufacturers, the Furniture Manufacturers of Grand Rapids, the Furniture Salesmen's Club, the Holland Chamber of Commerce, and the Ottawa-Allegan Boy Scout Council. Sligh attributes much of his business success to his fulfillment of community responsibilities; he has led a number of philanthropic drives and is a trustee of several Michigan colleges. Club memberships include the Rotary Club of Holland, and the Peninsular Club and Kent Country Club of Grand Rapids. He is chairman of the Kent County Republican Committee.

On January 2, 1926, Sligh married Charlotte Pelton Klumph and is the father of four children, Charles R. 3d, Robert Lewis, Richard C., and Patricia Ann. Sligh is five feet ten and a half inches tall and weighs 168 pounds; his eyes are gray-blue. Associates have been quoted as saying that his main asset as a "voice" of the NAM is his refusal either to "go pompous" or to be "too folksy." A member of the Grace Episcopal Church of Holland, he also is active in several church organizations in the Diocese of Western Michigan. Sligh, who began taking flying lessons in 1928, owns a Cessna 190 plane, has more than 1500 solo hours to his credit, and is a captain in the Michigan Wing of the Civil Air Patrol. He also belongs to the Aircraft Owners and Pilots Association of Washington, D.C., and the Aero Club of Michigan. President of the Water Ski Association, he became interested in water skiing when he visited the New York World's Fair in 1939, invited by President Franklin D. Roosevelt to represent the State of Michigan. After seeing a water-skiing exhibition, he took up the sport and in 1941 won the National Open Water Ski Championship, which he held for five years.

References

Bsns W p180 D 6 '52 por
Look 17:23 F 24 '53 por
N Y Herald Tribune p18 D 5 '52 por
N Y World-Telegram p19 Ag 25 '51 por
Time 60:100 D 15 '52 por

Business Executives of America (1950)
Who's Who in the Midwest (1949)

SMALLWOOD, JOSEPH R(OBERTS)

Dec. 24, 1900- Prime Minister of Newfoundland

Address: b. Canada House, St. John's, Newfoundland, Canada

A few months after the Atlantic island of Newfoundland and its mainland territory of Labrador united with Canada on March 31, 1949, to become that Dominion's tenth province, Joseph R. Smallwood, a native of the island and leader of the forces for confederation with Canada, became the first Prime Minister of the new province. Since his landslide election to the high office, Smallwood has initiated broad industrial programs and projects that are expected to change the previous fishing economy of the province to a diversified one, utilizing

the natural resources of Newfoundland more completely than in the past. Smallwood had earlier been a printer, reporter, and editor in Newfoundland, Canada, and the United States, and had for seven years conducted a radio program from St. John's, capital of the province.

After a period devoted to organizing trade unions and cooperatives in Newfoundland, Smallwood turned to politics in 1946, becoming a member of the first delegation to Ottawa to discuss union with Canada. Subsequently, he organized and directed the Confederation Association, which won the referendum on the issue of union, and formed and headed the Liberal Party, which was chosen to direct the political affairs of Newfoundland. The Prime Minister is also the author of several volumes devoted to the leaders and the history of Newfoundland.

The oldest of thirteen children born to Charles W. and Minnie (Devannah) Smallwood, Joseph Roberts Smallwood was born December 24, 1900, in the village of Gambo, on Bonavista Bay, Newfoundland. His father, like many other Newfoundlanders, was a woodsman in the surrounding forests. Young Joseph left his home to attend school in St. John's, first at British Hall, then at Centenary Hall, and later Bishop Field College, where his best subject was history. At fourteen Smallwood took his first job, as an apprentice in a St. John's printing house, at a beginning salary of five dollars a week. Learning that reporters earned more money than he, Smallwood applied for and received a position as a reporter for the St. John's *Evening Telegram.* Soon after being named editor of the newspaper, at the age of eighteen, the youthful writer left the capital city in order to take an assignment with the Halifax (Nova Scotia) *Herald,* where he remained until he decided to move on to the United States. In Boston he became a reporter for the Boston *Herald-Traveler* and later in New York City he was a free-lance writer and reporter for several newspapers and journals, specializing in articles about Newfoundland. He also attended classes at the Labor Temple and the Rand School.

While residing in New York City, Smallwood became interested in American politics, with the result that in 1924 he campaigned throughout New York State on behalf of Senator Robert LaFollette in that year's Presidential election. He wrote his first book *Coaker of Newfoundland* (1926), a biography of a former Minister of Marine and Fisheries who had worked to improve the condition of the island's fishermen.

Smallwood went to England in 1926 where he campaigned for the Independent Labor Party. In 1927 he returned to St. John's, continued to supply papers in Canada and the United States with news items and feature stories, and took a part in the politics of his native island, in 1928 acting as campaign manager for Sir Richard Squire's Liberal Party. As Newfoundland began to feel the effects of the world-wide depression and as its residents began to be threatened with economic disaster, Smallwood turned to union organizing among the railroad workers of Newfoundland. He also participated in the organization of workers at pulp and paper

JOSEPH R. SMALLWOOD

mills and helped the fishermen of Bonavista Bay form the first cooperative among such workers on the island.

In these years Smallwood accumulated his knowledge of the small fishing villages along the island's 6,000 miles of coastline and of lumber camps in the isolated interior districts. When he was unionizing the railroad section hands, for instance, he is reputed to have walked "clear across the island to persuade railroaders not to accept a pay cut" (*Pathfinder*). During these years he also began to collect the numerous stories and legends that he was later to use on his weekly radio programs.

In 1932, after being defeated as a candidate on the Liberal Party ticket, Smallwood, who had used radio to further his campaign, was employed to broadcast a weekly radio show at a salary of forty-five dollars a week. For the next seven years he was known throughout Newfoundland as "The Barrelman" (in fishing language, the lookout on a sealing boat), who each week wove accounts of news on the island into stories and anecdotes of the people and history of Newfoundland. Meanwhile, he produced the books *The New Newfoundland* (1932), the *Book of Newfoundland* (1937), and *Newfoundland Handbook, Gazeteer and Almanac*, the *Life and Letters of Dr. William Carson*, and *Surrogate Robert Carter*, all four of which were published in 1940. While these works did not sell very well, they made his name prominent in Newfoundland and helped to enrich his already extensive knowledge of his native region.

With the beginning of World War II and the increased demands for food supplies, Smallwood left radio to operate a large farm near Gander Airport, the halfway stop in the United States to Britain bomber route, and to furnish the Allied forces stationed there with pork,

eggs, and poultry. For a while his farm had the largest number of pigs in Newfoundland. At the cessation of hostilities, Smallwood sold his farm and once more entered the political field. In December of 1945 British Prime Minister Clement Atlee requested the people of Newfoundland to elect delegates to a national convention at which a form of self-government could be debated. Smallwood was elected a member of this convention.

Until 1934 a self-governing British dominion (Britain's oldest overseas possession), Newfoundland in that year was forced by financial conditions to apply to the mother country for economic support, thus causing its dominion status to be suspended and its affairs to be directed by a seven-man Anglo-Newfoundland Commission, responsible to the British Minister of Commonwealth Relations. This status, under which economic conditions gradually improved, was generally agreed to be politically unsatisfactory. In June of 1946 a National Convention was elected to recommend possible forms of government to be submitted to the electorate in the form of a referendum. The issues presented to the voters in the June 1948 vote were three: union with Canada, sponsored by the Confederation Association, headed by Smallwood; return to dominion status, proposed by the Responsible Government League, under the leadership of Major Peter J. Cashin, with the help of the Economic Unionists, who favored closer economic relations with the United States; and continuation of the existing commission system. Since no one of the three choices received the required majority and since comparatively few Newfoundlanders voted for the commission form of government, a second referendum was offered on the first questions in July 1948. This election gave a 52 per cent majority to union with Canada, and on March 31, 1949, Newfoundland joined the Dominion of Canada as its tenth province, with Smallwood appointed interim Prime Minister. In June, after an election in which he and his Liberal Party received an overwhelming number of votes, Smallwood became the first Prime Minister and Minister of Economic Development of the Province of Newfoundland. Subsequent provincial elections have continued Smallwood's party in power.

In his campaign for union with Canada and in his subsequent actions as Prime Minister, Smallwood has stressed the need for Newfoundlanders to participate in the Canadian social security benefits and to develop an industrial economy, founded on the potentially valuable natural resources of timber, water power, and minerals. He has favored spending the $29 million cash surplus which Newfoundland had accumulated during its prosperous war years. Soon after becoming Prime Minister, he initiated a series of exhaustive surveys and preliminary inventories of the island's resources which convinced him that more mines, pulp mills, and diversified industries could be established, thus lessening the island's centuries-old dependence on fishing. In his more than two years as political and economic leader of Newfoundland, Smallwood has persuaded numerous foreign firms in England, the Continent, and the United States to establish cotton mills, oil refineries, paper factories, fur-processing and dyeing plants, and to develop lead, iron, zinc, and copper mines in the province. In 1952 he offered British investors the opportunity of tapping the known mineral riches of Labrador, a territory controlled by Newfoundland. His government has also built three sample plants—a cement factory, a gypsum mill, and a birch-veneer mill—to prove to skeptical industrialists Newfoundland's industrial potentials. With more labor in the factories and less on the fishing boats, the cod industry is being modernized and is shifting from salting cod by hand to fresh-frozen fish packing. "Newfoundland's income," reported *Time* in September 1952, "is already up nearly 300 per cent, about the 1939 level."

An article in a Canadian journal, *The Standard* (August 27, 1948), has pointed out that Smallwood, in addition to emphasizing economic development, is interested in advancing social security and labor legislation on the island and has made an effort to encourage the cooperative movement there and to expand the tourist industry. Smallwood has been quoted as saying, "Newfoundland is going to be either a drag on Canada as a whole or will stand on her own feet and become self-supporting. . . . We want to develop our resources and contribute as well to receive benefits and add strength to the union we've joined." Another Canadian journal, *The New Liberty* (July 1951), writes of Smallwood that "Newfoundland has been his life, its full development of its resources his dream."

Smallwood in an article in *Saturday Night*, April 4, 1953, wrote that the union of Newfoundland with Canada has succeeded "brilliantly, for it is one of the happiest marriages of modern times. . . .Newfoundland, a British colony of 152,000 square miles and 370,000 souls, became a nation of millions of square miles and fourteen million people. . . .We travel now to the mainland of Canada at much less cost, and when we do we are still in our own country."

Newfoundland's Prime Minister, who was married in 1924 to Clara Isobel Oates, has two sons, Ramsey and William, and a daughter, Clara. He belongs to the Laurier and the St. John's clubs of Newfoundland and is a member of the United Church of Canada. With a weight of 130 pounds, Smallwood is five feet six inches in height; he has been described by one commentator as "dapper, dynamic" and by another as "colorful, volatile, and aggressive." He is considered a forceful and appealing speaker. The Prime Minister likes meeting people and enjoys reading history.

References

Maclean's Mag Ag 15 '49
New Liberty (Toronto) Jl '51
Pathfinder 56:28 Mr 23 '49
Time 60:40 S 22 '52
Canadian Almanac and Directory for 1952
Canadian Who's Who, 1948
Who's Who in Canada, 1949-50

SMITH, BRUCE May 23, 1892- Police administrator

Address: b. c/o Institute of Public Administration, 684 Park Ave., New York 21; h. 19 Kensington Rd., Garden City, N.Y.

Since beginning his professional study of police administration in 1917, Bruce Smith has become a leading international expert on police organization. He has advised on police matters in many major cities in the United States and has been called upon for consultation by the governments of pre-Hitler Germany, France, Belgium, Great Britain, and Canada. As acting director of the Institute of Public Administration, Smith in 1952 directed a survey which resulted in a critical and controversial report on the New York City Police Department.

Bruce Smith, the son of Clarence B. and Jessie A. (Annin) Smith, was born in Prospect Place, Brooklyn, New York, on May 23, 1892. From Brooklyn's Erasmus Hall High School, he entered Columbia University, where he majored in police science and received his B.S. degree in 1914. Remaining at Columbia for graduate study, Smith was granted in 1916 both the LL.B. degree and the M.Sc. in political science, which he had studied under Charles A. Beard. Upon completion of his graduate work he began his study of police systems and became a staff member of the Institute of Public Administration (then called Bureau of Municipal Research), a national organization with headquarters in New York City.

In the rank of second lieutenant Smith served during World War I in the United States Air Force from 1917 to 1919. After the war he returned to his interests in the improvement of the standards of law enforcement, becoming in 1921 manager of the Institute of Public Administration, a position which he held until 1928. From 1922 through 1923 he acted as counsel for the Joint Legislative Commission on Taxation and Retrenchment of New York State. During the next two years he was associated with a number of State and national organizations: the Missouri Association for Criminal Justice (1925), the National Crime Commission (1925-26), the New York State Crime Commission (1926-27), and the Illinois Association for Criminal Justice (1927). Interested in crime detection, he maintained affiliation with the Scientific Crime Detection Laboratory from 1929 through 1938.

Smith's first book, *The State Police; Organization and Administration* (1925), a study of the organization, administrative methods, and statutory powers of American State police, has been described as "a first-hand investigation of the existing State police systems, as well as a comparative record of their accomplishments" (*Springfield Republican*). As a result of a special committee survey he wrote in collaboration with others *Uniform Crime Reporting,* which was published in 1929. Since methods of reporting and recording crime were not uniform, police in United States cities had long been confronted with the difficulty of being unable to obtain a picture of the crime situation in the country as a whole. In an attempt to overcome this obstacle, a special committee

SMITH, BRUCE—Continued

under Smith's directorship surveyed the situation in the United States, while Smith himself went abroad to study European police administration. The resulting publication called for a national bureau to be located within the Department of Justice, which would receive and tabulate the crime reports that each police department would be required to submit. In his capacity as director of the Committee on Uniform Crime Records of the International Association of Chiefs of Police from 1928 to 1931, Smith served as senior author of the 1929 report and also as editor of the 1940 *Uniform Crime Reports.*

Meanwhile, in 1929, Smith had become engaged in plans for the reorganization of the Chicago Police Department. In late January of that year the presidents of Northwestern University, the University of Chicago, the Chicago Crime Commission, and the American Institute of Criminal Law and Criminology, upon the request of Commissioner Russell of the Chicago Police Department, had appointed a committee of eight to study the conditions then existing in the Chicago Police Department for purposes of proposing solutions to the department's many serious problems. Applying to the Institute of Public Administration, this committee secured Smith's services as director of the survey. After approximately two years of study, in which attention was confined to the administrative function of the police department aside from questions of police corruption, Smith prepared in collaboration with his committee a report that was submitted to the mayor, the City Council, and the citizens of Chicago. On January 1, 1931, adoption of the report was recommended, and later in the year it was published by the University of Chicago Press under the title *Chicago Police Problems.*

After the completion of the report, Smith was retained by the City of Chicago, upon recommendation of the mayor to assist the Police Commissioner in putting into effect the report's recommendations for reorganization. As a member of the Mayor's Advisory Committee from 1931 through 1933, he played an important part in the reorganization of the Chicago Police Department. In 1934 the Institute of Public Administration issued a small, paper-bound volume *Chicago Police Problems; An Approach to Their Solution* by Smith and the Police Survey Staff of which he was director. Simultaneously Smith had also been engaged in the study of police administration in Cincinnati, where his association with the Cincinnati Police Department during 1928 and 1930 had resulted in the 1932 publication by the Institute of Public Administration of another paper-bound volume under his authorship, *A Regional Police Plan for Cincinnati and its Environs.*

Rural Crime Control (1933), an extensive survey of the growth and methods used to combat rural crime in the United States, was based on Smith's direct observations made both in that country and abroad. F. M. Stewart in the *American Political Science Review* (October 1933) commented that "both Mr. Smith and the Bureau of Social Hygiene under whose

auspices the work was done are to be congratulated for contributing a much needed study on a very vital problem." Also concerned with metropolitan crime, Smith had taken part during October of the preceding year in a two-day public conference organized by the faculty of New York University for purposes of examining shortcomings in the urban areas of New York, New Jersey, Connecticut, Pennsylvania, and Delaware. Smith suggested to the conference that, in order to increase police efficiency so that it might move swiftly across county lines and keep up with the complicated movements of crime in metropolitan districts, local police power should be replaced by a State authority.

With his appointment on July 7, 1934, Smith became a member of the New York State Law Revision Commission, which had been newly created as an aid to the Legislature in examining and recommending changes in common law, New York statutes, and judicial decisions. From 1934 through 1936 he served with the Westchester County (New York) Commission on Government and in 1937-38 with the Massachusetts Special Commission on Taxation and Expenditures. In 1937 he had returned to his work as police reorganizer, filling an assignment with the Pittsburgh Police Department in 1937-38, organizing the police mobilization programs of New York, New Jersey, and Virginia during 1940, and from 1940 to 1941 helping to reorganize both the St. Louis (Missouri) and Baltimore (Maryland) police departments. The year 1940 also saw the publication of two more volumes under Smith's authorship, *Mobilizing Police for Emergency Duties,* brought out by the Institute of Public Administration, and *Police Systems in the United States.*

On December 8, 1941, the day after Pearl Harbor, General Henry H. Arnold summoned Smith to Washington to put Air Force operations on a more efficient basis. During the years of World War II he was occupied on the War Department Price Adjustment Board (1942), various Army advisory committees (1942-43), the Westchester County (New York) Park Commission (1943), the Rhode Island Public Expenditure Council (1943-45), the Philadelphia City Planning Commission (1945) and the Providence Police Department (1945). Smith's work as "police doctor" called him to assist the New Orleans Police Department (1946-47) and the Board of Police Commissioners, Springfield, Massachusetts (1949-50), with which he had previously been associated in 1941. As a member of a committee of six appointed by the International Association of Chiefs of Police, Smith took part in a study in early 1952 of the New York City Police Department's new method of compiling crime statistics. Stating on April 21, 1952, that the method developed under Police Commissioner George P. Monaghan gave an accurate picture of crime in the five boroughs, this committee recommended its acceptance by the Federal Bureau of Investigation. In October Smith submitted to the Mayor's Committee on Management Survey a report on the New York City Police Department, advising extensive changes in organization and operation to eliminate serious and long-standing defects. The report, as summarized by the New York *Herald Tribune*, "concluded that the force is neither undermanned nor underpaid, that what is needed is a better system of choosing policemen, better training, a different system of promotion, better discipline, and divorcing the department from politics and from the Civil Service Commission." Approved by a subcommittee of the mayor's committee and endorsed by the latter group with reservations on the part of some, Smith's program nevertheless incurred the opposition of such groups as the police line organizations and the Municipal Civil Service Commission. The report, the product of a fifteen-month survey, was the most extensive study of the department since 1898 and was conducted through an $85,000 city appropriation.

Smith has been a member of the executive board of the American Institute of Criminal Law and Criminology (1930-42), the New York State Commission on the Administration of Justice (1931-39), the Governor's Crime Commission for New York State (1935-36), the executive board of the Governmental Research Association (1935-37, 1941-43, since 1950), the Mayor's Committee on Police Reorganization of San Francisco (1936-37), and the board of directors of the Citizen's Crime Commission of New York (1937-41). He has served as chairman of the committee to revise the New York Code of criminal procedure (1933-39); the boards to select a chief of police for Cincinnati (1935), Los Angeles (1939), Woonsocket (1943), and Connecticut State Police (1943); the New York City board to select a city-wide sheriff (1941); and the committee on police training and merit systems of the American Bar Association (1943-44). In the International Association of Chiefs of Police he has maintained membership as adviser (State and provincial section) and in the Institute of Public Administration as acting director from 1941 through 1946 and again since 1950. His activity on the committee on police training and merit systems of the American Bar Association dates from 1938.

The problem of police-citizenship relationship is not a simple one, in Smith's opinion. "In the good old days," he said, "we knew and liked the cop on the beat . . . but he didn't regulate traffic. . . .From the enforcement of traffic regulations comes much of the ill will between police officer and citizen." He believes that a well planned program can help people to develop confidence in the police force, through personal contact, lost by motorized patrols (*Christian Science Monitor*, September 14, 1953).

The police-work authority has held the position of lecturer at Columbia, Yale, Harvard, Wayne, Chicago, and Northwestern universities, as well as at the United States Army and Navy Schools of Military Government and at the Traffic Institute and National Police Academy of the Federal Bureau of Investigation. He has contributed articles to the *Encyclopaedia Britannica*, the *Encyclopedia of the Social Sciences*, the *Journal of Criminal Law and Criminology*, the *Annals of the American Academy of Political and Social Sciences*, and has been the author of survey reports on police administration in about fifty leading American cities, fifteen States, and the police systems of England, France, Belgium, and Germany. While he has never served as a policeman, Smith has worked in plain clothes for the New York State police, often taking part in raids. On October 23, 1915, he was married at Millers Place, Long Island, to Mary Belle (Rowell) Smith, and is the father of Bruce and Miriam Rowell Smith. He is a member of Delta Tau Delta and of the Century Club (New York). Standing six feet two inches tall, the expert on police matters weighs 190 pounds; he has closely cropped gray hair, bushy black eyebrows, and a gray mustache.

References

N Y Herald Tribune II p12 O 26 '52
Scholastic 61:6 N 10 '52

Who Knows—and What (1949)
Who's Who in America, 1952-53
Who's Who in New York, 1952

SMITH, WALTER BEDELL Oct. 5, 1895-
United States Government official

Address: b. c/o Department of State, Washington 25, D.C.

NOTE: This biography supersedes the article which appeared in *Current Biography* in 1944.

Soon after the Republican Administration of President Dwight D. Eisenhower came into power in January 1953, General Walter Bedell Smith, then Director of the Central Intelligence Agency, was appointed Under Secretary of State to rank second in the Department of State to Secretary John Foster Dulles. Smith, who is not affiliated with any political party, thus gained the distinction of being one of the few high-ranking officials of the Truman Administration to be assigned to an important position under Eisenhower, whom he had served as chief of staff during World War II when Eisenhower was Supreme Commander of the Allied Expeditionary Forces.

An expert in the field of foreign affairs as well as in the military, Smith held the difficult diplomatic post of Ambassador to the U.S.S.R. for three years after the war. In his most recent assignment for the Army, the General commanded the First Army in New York from March 1949 to September 1950, before assuming direction of United States intelligence efforts.

Walter Bedell Smith, the son of William Long Smith, a merchant, and Ida Frances (Bedell) Smith, was born on October 5, 1895, in Indianapolis, Indiana. On his father's side he is descended from the English settler Samuel Stanhope Smith, who made his home in New Jersey in 1781. While attending St. Peter and Paul's School in Indianapolis, young Smith in 1911 became a private in the Indiana National Guard. As related by W. H. Lawrence (New York *Times Magazine*, March 1, 1953), he later enrolled in Butler University in In-

U. S. Army

GEN. WALTER BEDELL SMITH

dianapolis, but because of his father's illness had to leave school shortly thereafter to help support his family.

At the age of eighteen Smith, who had continued his training in the National Guard, became an infantry first sergeant, and a few years later, following an officers' training course, in November 1917 he was commissioned a second lieutenant in the United States Army. After a short period with the 39th Infantry, Fourth Division, at Camp Greene, North Carolina, he was sent to France in April 1918 to fight with the Fourth Division in the Marne and Aisne battles. He was returned to the United States the following September for duty in the Bureau of Military Intelligence in Washington, D.C.

During the next few years he was assigned to a number of stations in the United States, including Camp Sherman, Ohio; Camp Dodge, Iowa; Fort Sheridan, Illinois; Camp Custer, Michigan; and headquarters of the Sixth Corps Area in Chicago, Illinois. He was then ordered to four years' duty, beginning April 1925, as assistant to the chief coordinator of the Bureau of the Budget in Washington and to two years' duty with the 45th Infantry at Fort William McKinley in the Philippine Islands.

Between wars, Smith studied war classics, and "worked hard to make up for lack of West Point or college training" (*Life,* June 12, 1944). Having returned to the United States in March 1931, he entered the Infantry School at Fort Benning, Georgia, where, after completing the course the next year in June, he remained as secretary until August 1933. Later, he was again sent to the Infantry School, as instructor in weapons for a year, following two years of study at the Command and General Staff School in Fort Leavenworth, Kansas. Upon his graduation on June 23, 1937, from the Army War College in Washington, D.C., the most ad-

vanced training school in the United States Army, he was reassigned to the faculty of the Fort Benning Infantry School. Smith, who had held the rank of captain since September 1929, was promoted to major on January 1, 1939.

Again ordered to duty in Washington, Major Smith in October 1939 was named assistant secretary of the General Staff on the War Department General Staff, becoming secretary in September 1941. The following February, soon after his country had entered World War II, he took up the assignment of first United States secretary of the Combined Chiefs of Staff (Anglo-American) in Washington, with additional duties as first secretary of the Joint Board. For his achievements in this post he was given the Distinguished Service Medal in July 1943.

While attending Army schools, Smith had come to the attention of George C. Marshall, who later, as Army Chief of Staff in World War II, recommended him to General Dwight D. Eisenhower. Smith, in the rank of brigadier general (temporary), went to England in September 1942 as Eisenhower's chief of staff of the European theater of operations and later served as chief of staff of the Allied Forces in North Africa and the Mediterranean theater.

In this capacity he was in charge of coordinating the entire planning of the invasions of North Africa and Normandy. The citation that Smith received in July 1943, with an Oak Leaf Cluster to the Distinguished Service Medal, noted: "He has been largely responsible for the fine spirit of integration which exists in Allied Force Headquarters and for the cooperation among British, French, and United States units that made possible the outstanding success of the combined forces. His contribution to the victorious termination of the Tunisian campaign has been a notable one."

When General Eisenhower became commander of the European theater in January 1944, Lieutenant General Smith accompanied him, and two months later he was made chief of staff of the Supreme Headquarters, Allied Expeditionary Forces (SHAEF) and of the European theater. On behalf of Eisenhower, he had signed the Italian surrender document in September 1943, and in May 1945 he headed the Allied group which accepted the unconditional surrender of Germany.

The New York *Times* (January 8, 1953) reported that Eisenhower described Smith as "the general manager of the war," while *United States News & World Report* (July 31, 1953) quoted Eisenhower as saying, "He was a godsend—a master of detail with clear comprehension of main issues."

Smith, relieved of his assignment as chief of staff in December 1945, was appointed the following February by President Harry S. Truman to succeed W. Averell Harriman as United States Ambassador to the U.S.S.R. In his recommendation to Congress, Truman requested legislation permitting Smith, a major general since August 1945, to retain his military status. Ambassador Smith was a member of the United States delegation to the Paris Peace Conference in 1946.

My Three Years in Moscow, which was published by J. B. Lippincott Company in 1950, is General Smith's account of his experiences in Russia. It was serialized in the New York *Times* and also in shorter form in the *Saturday Evening Post.* With his broad knowledge of Russian history, the American diplomat discussed such subjects as Soviet industry and agriculture, slave labor, Russian foreign policy, and the possibility of war.

"We are forced to a continuing struggle for a free way of life that might extend over a period of many years," Smith foretold in his book. "We dare not allow ourselves any false sense of security. We must anticipate that the Soviet tactic will be to attempt to wear us down, to exasperate us, to keep probing for weak spots, and we must cultivate firmness and patience to a degree we have never before required."

Reviewing *My Three Years in Moscow* for the San Francisco *Chronicle* (January 8, 1950), Gordon Pates commented: "'Beetle,' a good example of the military mind at its best, is not a word-waster, and he crams a great deal into his 346 pages of straightforward, soldierly prose." Smith is also the author of "Eisenhower's Six Great Decisions," a series of articles which appeared in the *Saturday Evening Post* (June 8 to July 13, 1946).

Leaving Moscow in March 1949, Smith returned to the United States to assume command of the First Army on Governors Island, New York. He was called from this post in September 1950 by President Truman, who nominated him to be Director of the Central Intelligence Agency. C.I.A., the first permanent intelligence agency to be established by the United States Government in peacetime, has as its function "the coordination of the intelligence activities of the Government departments and agencies in the interest of national security" *(United States Government Organization Manual).*

As C.I.A. Director, Smith, who is said probably to know more about Communists' activities than any other Government official, was responsible for gathering and evaluating information as to the plans and capabilities of potential enemies of the United States. During the 1952 presidential campaign he succeeded in his personal appeal to candidates to avoid making C.I.A. a political issue. "So important is the Agency considered," stated *United States News & World Report* (October 10, 1952), "that General Smith periodically briefs both candidates on what it knows in order to guide their comments."

With the appointment in February 1953 of General Smith as Under Secretary of State in the Republican Administration, a number of political observers commented upon the revival of the "Ike and Beetle" team. The office of the Under Secretary, who assists the Secretary of State in the formulation and implementation of foreign policy, was expected to assume increased importance in view of Smith's close association with the President and the likelihood of Eisenhower's relying heavily on him for advice.

He serves also as Acting Secretary during the absence of Secretary John Foster Dulles, whose duties require him to travel frequently outside the United States. In agreement with Eisenhower and Dulles, Smith has expressed his view that the United States needs more than a program of "containment" or "passive resistance" to combat world-wide communism. He advocates positive action short of military aggression: "It has got to be dynamic," W. H. Lawrence quoted him as saying, "and has got to mean just what is implied by the term 'determined opposition'" (New York *Times Magazine,* March 1, 1953).

Under Secretary Smith testified in May 1953 that passage of a bill to admit 240,000 refugees into the United States during the next two years would be helpful in the fight against communism. Addressing the graduating class of Washington and Jefferson College in June, he warned against the United States' relaxing its guard after a Korean armistice. "Korea is but one flank of a conflict which girdles the world," he told the students. "Danger spots are many; we must remain alert and ready" (New York *Times,* June 9, 1953). Smith reported in August that while the United States continued to support the United Nations' plan for international control of atomic energy, prospects for such control are "dim because of Soviet intransigence."

As a measure to insure better coordination in carrying out the United States security program, President Eisenhower on September 3 created the Operations Coordinating Board, to replace the Psychological Strategy Board, and appointed General Smith chairman of the new agency. Anthony Leviero of the New York *Times* (September 4, 1953) described the O.C.B., which reports directly to the National Security Council, as "designed to have the effect of binding closely together the critical function of conceiving, developing, and implementing high national strategy."

On September 11, 1953 General Smith handed Georgi N. Zarubin, Soviet Ambassador to the United States, a memorandum "demanding the return of the 670 ships supplied to Moscow under the Lend-Lease program of World War II" (New York *Times*).

Besides the military decorations already mentioned, Smith, who received his present rank of general in July 1951, holds a second Oak Leaf Cluster to the Distinguished Service Medal, the Navy Distinguished Service Medal, the Legion of Merit, and the Bronze Star Medal. Among many foreign honors awarded him are Knight Grand Cross Order of the British Empire; Knight Commander, Order of the Bath; Lion of the Netherlands; Crown of Belgium; Croix de Guerre of France; Cavalier of the Order of Kutuzov (Russia); and White Lion (Czechoslovakia). His honorary degrees include the LL.D. from Duquesne University, Hofstra College, Butler University, University of New Hampshire, and the University of South Carolina; the D.Sc Mil from Pennsylvania Military College; and the D.C.L. from Colgate University.

SMITH, WALTER BEDELL—*Continued*

He married Mary Eleanor Cline on July 1, 1917. The General's faith is the Roman Catholic. With fishing as his hobby, he is said to be "a great hand at making fly fishing rods, expertly, tirelessly, and painstakingly working in split bamboo" (New York *Times Magazine,* August 27, 1950). During World War II Prime Minister Winston Churchill gave Smith the nickname of "Bulldog" because of his tenacity in handling problems. Smith himself is so fond of his other nickname, "Beetle," that he has his personal stationery engraved with a small black beetle. General Eisenhower, as quoted by *United States News* (July 31, 1953), described his wartime chief of staff as follows: "Serious, hardworking, and loyal, he proved equally as capable in difficult conference as he was in professional activity. Strong in character and abrupt by instinct, he could achieve harmony without appeasement."

Selected References

> Life 10:94 Je 12 '44 pors
> N Y Sun p14 F 21 '44
> N Y Times p1+ Ja 8 '53 por
> N Y Times Mag p15+ Mr 17 '46; p30
>   Ag 27 '50; p11+ Mr 1 '53
> Time 56:14 Ag 28 '50
> U S News 33:47+ O 10 '52 por; 34:
>   47+ Jl 31 '53 por
> International Who's Who, 1952
> National Cyclopædia of American Biography Current vol G, 1943-46
> Who's Who, 1953
> Who's Who in America, 1952-53
> World Biography (1948)

SOKOLOVSKY, VASSILY D(ANILO-VICH) (sŏ-kŏ-lôv'skĭ vä-sē'lĭ da-nē'lô-vyĭch) July 20, 1897- Russian Army officer
Address: Moscow, U.S.S.R.

The promotion of Marshal Vassily D. Sokolovsky from First Deputy Minister to Chief of Staff of the Soviet Army was announced on February 21, 1953. He had commanded the Red Army troops in World War II which had crossed the Dneiper River, recaptured Smolensk, Russia, and Krakow, Poland, culminating in victories at Breslau in Silesia, and finally in Berlin. Sokolovsky had headed the Soviet Military Government in Berlin from 1946 until 1949, and had maintained an unrelenting policy during the land blockade of the Allied sectors of the German capital. (The blockade was lifted on September 30, 1949 after United States and British aircraft had flown over two million tons of food and coal into Western Berlin.) Sokolovsky was appointed First Deputy Minister of the Soviet Armed Forces in March 1949.

Vassily Danilovich Sokolovsky was born to peasant parents in 1897 in Kosliki, a village in the district of Grodno, Russia. At the outbreak of the Revolution in 1917, he left the seminary where he was studying to become a teacher, joined the young Bolshevik movement, enlisted in the Red Army, and became a company commander. He was sent to the Red Army's military academy.

By 1940 Sokolovsky was a lieutenant-general and for a period served on the staff of Marshal Timoshenko, defender of Moscow. He was later appointed colonel-general. After the successful defense of Stalingrad and the inauguration of the Russian offensive, Sokolovsky was placed in command of the occupation of Vyszma in March 1943. For his participation in a series of Russian victories over the retreating German Army in the summer of 1943 Sokolovsky was awarded the Order of Kutuzov and was promoted to the rank of full general.

In the fall of that year the extensive Russian front was divided into fourteen separate units, with Sokolovsky named commander of the Western front; on September 25, troops under his command recaptured Smolensk, the Russian city which had been occupied by the Germans for two years. The Russian offensive to liberate Southern Poland was also under his command, culminating in victories at Krakow and Breslau. During the winter campaigns of 1943-1944 he was commander in chief of the First Ukrainian Front Troops, serving as chief of staff for Marshal Koneff. The military strategy of the Russian Army during these and subsequent campaigns was described by Sokolovsky as "blitz-grinding," the careful maintenance of strategic reserves which could be thrown into offensive action once the enemy was worn down by unremitting and active defense at all points.

Sokolovsky's troops had penetrated into German Silesia by the early part of 1945 and by March of that year had crossed the Oder River. As commander of three groups of the Red Army, Sokolovsky participated in the entrance into Berlin and the capture of that city in April 1945. In June he was appointed First Deputy of the Soviet military administration of the territories of the Soviet occupation in Germany, under Marshal Zhukoff. He replaced Zhukoff in April 1946, and two months later he was made a marshal of the Soviet Union.

Marshal Sokolovsky served both as commander of the Russian occupation forces in Germany and as the Soviet member of the Allied Control Council from April 1946 until March 1949. Thus, he was directly involved in the four-power controversies which began in the spring of 1948 and culminated in the presentation of the Berlin blockade as an issue for settlement at the October 1948 meetings of the United Nations Security Council. *Time,* on October 4, 1948, described the "Berlin Crisis" as the "gravest issue yet referred to U.N.'s uncertain authority."

Under the principles of the Yalta Declaration, supreme authority in Germany is exercised by the commander in chief of the armed forces of each of the occupying powers in each of the four zones. Matters touching upon Germany as a whole are administered by the Allied Control Council, composed of the commanding officers of each of the four powers—England, United States, Russia, and France. Sokolovsky, as representative of one of the powers, therefore, participated in debates and agreements on such over-all German problems as the level of industrial production, reparation payments, the dissolution of the old State of Prussia, German agriculture, size of occupation forces, and denazification programs.

Writing in the September 7, 1947 issue of the New York *Times*, Delbert Clark concluded that the Control Council, in spite of its frequent and long discussions had "been able to agree on almost nothing of importance." The final break between the East and the West began in March 1948, when at a meeting of the Council, Sokolovsky left abruptly, declaring: "The Control Council no longer exists as an organ of government."

Since that time transportation and commerce into and out of the Russian occupied areas has become increasingly restricted. When the Russians closed Berlin to rail traffic in 1948 the Americans instituted an "air lift" service for the delivery of essential food and fuel supplies into Berlin. The failure to agree on policy was submitted to Stalin by envoys of the Western powers in August, 1948. At the Moscow meetings, Stalin agreed to the lifting of the Berlin blockade if the Russian mark was accepted as Berlin's sole currency. The agreement, however, was subject to the approval of the four military governors.

According to *Time* (October 4, 1948), Sokolovsky overlooked the Moscow agreement, and requested further traffic restrictions and control by the Soviets of all trade between Berlin and the Western zones. As a result, the Western powers submitted the dilemma to the United Nations Security Council on October 4, 1948 on the grounds that the Russian actions were a threat to peace and thus a subject for the authority of the Security Council.

Two days before the problem was presented to the U.N., Marshal Sokolovsky issued an 8,000 word statement to correspondents of the Soviet-licensed press in Berlin (reported in the New York *Times,* October 3, 1948), in which he defended the Russian position, reiterating Russia's willingness to reopen negotiations on the Berlin question, and making it clear that solution of the crisis would be sought by Russia on a four-power basis outside the jurisdiction of the U.N.

He declared that "there was and is no blockade of Berlin," that "in the main," Berlin was being supplied, that "the fundamental" cause of the crisis was the establishment of a Western German State by the English and Americans, and that any attempts to solve the situation in the UN were aimed "merely at continuing the abnormal situation in Berlin."

Late in March, 1949, the Soviet radio announced that Marshal Sokolovsky had been replaced as Soviet commander in Germany by General Vassily I. Chuikov, and had been elevated to First Deputy Minister of the Soviet Armed Forces. "Marshal Sokolovsky's transfer from the role of soldier-diplomat to the Ministry restores him to the sphere in which he made his reputation in World War II as one of the Soviet Union's ablest tacticians," commented the New York *Times* (March 30, 1949). That Marshal Sokolovsky's removal from Berlin constituted a reward and not a rebuke for his hard-hitting policies was clear when,

MARSHAL VASSILY D. SOKOLOVSKY

in May, 1949, *Pravda* published as the first comment on the German situation since the announcement of the agreement to end the Berlin blockade an authoritative statement by the former commander in Germany. In a long article commemorating the fourth anniversary of Germany's defeat, the Marshal attacked the Western Allies in his already familiar aggressive and uncompromising tone.

Marshal Sokolovsky succeeded General Sergei M. Shtemenko as Chief of Staff of the Soviet Armed Forces on February 21, 1953. At that time it was revealed also that he is a full member of the powerful Central Committee of the Communist party elected by the All-Union Congress of the Communist party (highest organ of the party) and charged with electing the executive body (Politburo), the organizational bureau (Orgburo) which manages the party, and the party Secretariat.

Newsweek has described Sokolovsky as a "modest man" who won the friendship of Americans and the nickname of "Sock" (April 22, 1946). He is an "extrovert," "gruff," and "hearty." He prefers vodka to whiskey, is a chain-smoker, takes his work seriously "like most Russians," and seems to enjoy paper work connected with his assignments.

Of the marshal, General Lucius D. Clay, former American member of the Allied Control Council, wrote, "quiet, unassuming, and dignified, he was ready in debate, which he flavored with a delightful sense of humor and the frequent use of Russian proverbs. I learned to respect his ability" (*Decision in Germany,* 1950). Sokolovsky is about six feet tall and weighs approximately 200 pounds. His awards and decorations include four orders of Lenin, two orders of Kutuzov, one of Suvórov, and the American Legion of Merit. He holds a star as a Hero of the Soviet Union and he is Knight Commander of the Order of the Brit-

SOKOLOVSKY, VASSILY—*Continued*

ish Empire, awarded in Berlin in 1945 by Field Marshal Viscount Montgomery.

The Marshal is an avid reader of the master military strategists from Julius Caesar to Eisenhower and Montgomery, but he likes nothing better than to curl up with a good book by that past-mistress of social strategy, Jane Austen (*Washington Post,* October 14, 1948).

References

N Y Herald Tribune p1 F 22 '53
N Y Times p1 F 22 '53
Newsweek 27:51 Ap 22 '46
U S News 34:62 Mr 6 '53
Washington (D.C.) Post p2 O 14 '48
International Who's Who, 1952

SPALDING, ALBERT Aug. 15, 1888—May 26, 1953

Violinist; last appearance June 20, 1950 at Lewisohn Stadium with New York Philharmonic-Symphony Orchestra; made debut in Paris, Theatre Nouveau, 1905; American debut with New York Symphony, 1908; appeared as soloist with Paris Conservatory Orchestra; first American to judge at Paris Conservatory examinations; played in Milan's La Scala Opera House; performed as soloist with every leading orchestra in the United States, and with practically every major orchestra in Europe; educated at Bologna Conservatory, was pupil of Chiti at Florence, Lefort at Paris, and Juan Buitrago, New York; composed violin concertos, sonatas; author of *Rise to Follow;* served in World War I and World War II. See Current Biography, 1944.

Obituary

N Y Times p31 My 27 '53

STALIN, JOSEPH Dec. 21, 1879—Mar. 5, 1953

President of the Council of Ministers of the U.S.S.R.; Generalissimo; General Secretary of the Communist party of the U.S.S.R.; became a Marxist at the age of fifteen while studying at a theological seminary in Tiflis; imprisoned eight times by the Czarist Government (1903-17) and escaped; founded party's paper, *Pravda* (1911); Lenin's aide and military leader against the White armies (1919-20); General Secretary of the Central Committee of the Communist party (1922); Lenin's successor as chairman of the Politburo (1924); exiled Trotsky (1928) and liquidated other opposition in "purge trials" of 1934-38; initiated first (1928) and second (1932) Five-Year Plans for industrialization and collectivization; promulgated new constitution of the U.S.S.R. (1936); military leader of the U.S.S.R. in World War II, becoming marshal (1943) and generalissimo (1945); attended Tehran (1943) and Yalta (1945) conferences with Roosevelt and Churchill, and Potsdam conference (1945); author of many volumes on socialism. See *Current Biography,* 1942.

Obituary

N Y Times p1+ Mr 6 '53

STEACIE, E(DGAR) W(ILLIAM) R(ICHARD) (stā′cĭ) Dec. 25, 1900- President of the National Research Council of Canada; physical chemist

Address: b. c/o National Research Council, National Research Bldg., Sussex St., Ottawa 2, Ontario, Canada; h. 10 Birch Ave., Rockcliffe, Ottawa 2, Ontario, Canada

After two years as vice-president of the National Research Council of Canada, E. W. R. Steacie in April 1952 became president of this organization, which serves the dual purpose of co-ordinating the work of other research groups and of conducting its own research on projects of national interest. Active for sixteen years in teaching and research at McGill University, Steacie left the school in 1939 to become the director of the division of chemistry of the National Research Council; during the following years of World War II he helped organize Canadian research in chemistry for war purposes and served as deputy director of the United Kingdom-Canadian Atomic Energy Project. The scientist has published reports in the fields of photochemistry and gas reactions and has received decorations and awards for his research work.

Edgar William Richard Steacie was born December 25, 1900, in Westmount (near Montreal), Quebec, Canada, the only child of Richard and Alice Kate (McWood) Steacie. His father, a native of Ireland, was secretary-treasurer of Smart Woods, Ltd., of Montreal and during World War I was killed in action at Ypres in 1915. His mother was born in Westmount, where she still lives. Young Steacie attended Bishop's College School in Lennoxville, Quebec, for one year (1911-12) and in 1912 entered the Westmount High School, being graduated in 1916. Two years later he enlisted in the Canadian army, in which he served as a corporal until he entered the Royal Military College in 1919 in Kingston, Ontario, for a year of study. Having won an Imperial Order of the Daughters of the Empire Scholarship, in 1920 he went to McGill University, where in 1923 he received his Bachelor of Science degree in chemical engineering, being graduated with first class honors and the British Association Medal. At college his sports were skiing and golf.

After his graduation, having been influenced by Dr. Otto Maass of McGill University, an internationally known Canadian chemist, Steacie decided to take graduate courses in physical chemistry rather than engineering. From 1923 to 1925 he worked for the university as demonstrator in chemistry and during this time (1924) received his M.Sc. degree in physical chemistry. Continuing his graduate studies at McGill under a National Research Council Studentship (awarded in 1925), he was granted in 1926 the Ph.D. degree in physical chemistry, for which he had submitted the thesis *Solubility of Gases in Metals.* He then held a Sterry Hunt Fellowship from 1926 to 1928 at McGill, in 1928 became a lecturer in chemistry, and two years later was promoted to the post of assistant professor of chemistry.

With a fellowship from the Royal Society of Canada, Steacie took leave from McGill

University in 1934 to work in Leipzig with the German chemist K. F. Bonhoeffer on gas reactions. The next year he spent a short time in Frankfurt and then went to King's College in London to carry on research in photochemistry with Professor A. J. Allmand. Steacie returned in 1935 to his duties at McGill, where two years later he became an associate professor of chemistry.

In 1939 the National Research Council of Canada, with headquarters in Ottawa, appointed Steacie the director of its chemistry division, which in the past thirteen years, under Steacie's administration, has become a laboratory known throughout the world. Maintaining that "a group of scientists doing only applied work lack a great deal of stimulus which comes from having pure researchers around the place," Steacie has created a department devoted to pure research, whereas previously the emphasis had been on applied research (*Saturday Night,* September 6, 1952). He also organized the division so that it would consist in part of recent recipients of Ph.D. degrees working for NRC under fellowships in postdoctoral research, directed by one or two senior scientists. During World War II Steacie was occupied, with Dr. Otto Maass, in organizing Canadian chemistry for war purposes, especially in chemcal warfare and the development of explosives, serving as the chairman of the Associate Committee on Explosives. From 1944 to 1946 Steacie was deputy director of the United Kingdom-Canadian Atomic Energy Project, in which capacity he chose locations for laboratories and equipped them and selected personnel. He was also responsible for the successful operation of the Montreal laboratory of the Atomic Energy Project. In recognition of his war work, Steacie in 1946 was made an officer of the Most Excellent Order of the British Empire.

A fellow of the Royal Society of Canada since 1934 and its honorary secretary from 1940 to 1942, Steacie became president for the year 1947-48 of the society's section 3 (chemical, mathematical, and physical sciences). In 1948 he was elected a fellow of the Royal Society of London for his "important contributions to chemical kinetics and photochemistry." The following year the scientist was awarded the Gold Medal of the Professional Institute of the Public Service of Canada for "the most outstanding contribution to science, pure and applied." He became an honorary member of the Polish Chemical Society in 1949 and also the president for a year of the Chemical Institute of Canada. In April of that year he was chosen to give three special lectures at the University of London.

Upon his appointment on July 24, 1950, to the vice-presidency of the National Research Council, Steacie was made responsible for the co-ordination of all NRC scientific activities. Becoming vice-president of the International Union of Pure and Applied Chemistry in 1951, he spoke that year at the World Chemical Conclave in New York City on the subject of gas-phase decomposition. Then in April 1952 Steacie was named president of the National Research Council, when Dr. C. J. Mackenzie, Canada's "Mr. Atom," left the post to become

Maillet

E. W. R. STEACIE

the head of the Atomic Energy of Canada, Ltd. This new Crown company took over direction of the Chalk River reactor or nuclear furnace, which up to then had been supervised by the NRC. On the new appointment Michael Barkway (*Saturday Night,* September 6, 1952) commented that Steacie had "to assume a triple role to match the job: research chemist, administrator and diplomat. Canada has been lucky to find a second man capable of filling such diverse requirements."

At a time (1916) when very little research was being undertaken in Canada, the National Research Council, now a twenty-man body consisting mainly of specialists from universities with several representatives of labor and industry, was founded to advise the government on research policy. The first step that the council took to further scientific research in that country was to establish grants and scholarships so that students could receive advanced scientific training and instructors could do research while teaching. The NRC ceased being purely an advisory and money-giving body in 1932 when it established laboratories to conduct its own research. Steacie has said: "We are interested in seeing that useful research work is done—research that will benefit all the people of Canada. Sometimes it is most convenient to do it in our own labs. Sometimes it can be done elsewhere, and we are just as happy" (*Saturday Night*). Consequently NRC continues to make grants and many schools for graduate scientific study could not exist without NRC support. Approximately three hundred postgraduate students are now attending universities on NRC scholarships, and grants are being made to some four hundred scientists, who employ seven hundred other workers for "assisted research."

Principally interested in research on chemical kinetics, photochemistry, and atomic and

STEACIE, E. W. R.—*Continued*

free radical reactions, Steacie has written some 170 papers dealing with photochemistry and gas reactions and was the junior author with Dr. Otto Maass of *Introduction to Physical Chemistry*, which was published in 1926. With F. M. G. Johnson he wrote *Viscosities of the Liquid Halogens* (1925) and with Otto Maass, *Attempt to Determine the Osmotic Pressure of Very Dilute Solutions* (1929).

The year 1946 saw publication of Steacie's book, *Atomic and Free Radical Reactions*, which *Chemical and Metallurgical Engineering* (June 1946) called "a fine piece of workmanship and a painstaking assembly of facts, collected by an expert who knows his field well. Dr. Steacie must be congratulated for having rendered such a service to chemistry." The *Journal of the American Chemical Society* (August 1946) commented: "Notwithstanding [some] defects the book can be recommended as a very useful aid to those who wish to obtain up-to-date and exhaustive information in the field covered by the book." An abridged version of the book, entitled *Free Radical Mechanisms*, is now used as a school textbook. Steacie has pointed out that while some publications have called him "a foe of specialization," the reverse is true.

Steacie has received a number of honorary degrees: Doctor of Science degrees from McMaster University, Hamilton, Ontario, in 1946 and from the University of New Brunswick in 1950; and from Laval University in 1952; and LL.D. degrees from both Queen's University and from Dalhousie University, Halifax, Nova Scotia, in 1952.

He holds membership in the American Chemical Society, the Chemical Society of London, the Faraday Society, the Society of Chemical Industry, and the Chemical Institute of Canada. Steacie married Dorothy Catalina Day in 1925; their children are Diana Jeannette (Mrs. W. A. Magill) and John Richard Brian. Mrs. Steacie is active in Red Cross Society affairs. The scientist is five feet ten inches tall, weighs 155 pounds, and has blue eyes and graying brown hair. His hobbies are skiing, sailing, and enjoying his summer home north of Ottawa.

References

> Chem & Eng N 27:1795 Je 20 '49
> Sat Night 67:9 S 6 '52
> American Men of Science (1949)
> Canadian Who's Who, 1949-51
> International Who's Who, 1952
> Who's Who, 1952

STENNIS, JOHN C(ORNELIUS) Aug. 3, 1901- United States Senator from Mississippi; lawyer

Address: b. Senate Office Bldg., Washington 25, D.C.; h. DeKalb, Miss.

In a special election to fill the vacancy created by the death of Theodore G. Bilbo, John C. Stennis on November 4, 1947, became the junior Democratic Senator from Mississippi, an office to which he won re-election in November 1952. While opposing civil rights legislation and favoring a "reasonable and proper segregation," Stennis, unlike his predecessor and several of his political opponents, has not used racialism as a campaign issue. The Mississippi lawyer had been a member of his State's House of Representatives from 1928 to 1932 and a circuit judge from 1937 until his election to the Senate. Interested for many years in farm affairs, he has been president of the State 4-H Advisory Council and has promoted farm youth training programs.

The youngest of the seven children of Hampton Howell and Cornelia (Adams) Stennis, John Cornelius Stennis was born on a small farm in Kemper County, Mississippi, on August 3, 1901. He began his education in a one-room schoolhouse at Kipling crossroads; in 1919 was graduated from the Kemper County Agricultural High School in Scooba. The next four years were spent at Mississippi Agricultural and Mechanical College (now Mississippi State College), from which he received his Bachelor of Science degree. At the University of Virginia, where he attained membership in Phi Beta Kappa, he took his LL.B. degree in 1928. That same year, after he had been admitted to the bar and had begun law practice in DeKalb, he was elected to the Mississippi House of Representatives from Kemper County. In the course of his four-year term, in 1931, he was chosen district attorney for the 16th judicial district and four years later was renamed to that post without opposition. Appointed circuit judge of the district in 1937 to fill a vacancy, he served in that office for twelve years, being elected in 1938 and re-elected in 1942 and 1946.

In the election held November 4, 1947, to choose the successor to the late Senator Theodore G. Bilbo, Stennis was opposed by four other Democratic candidates, two of whom expressed strong "white supremacy" ideas reminiscent of those of Bilbo. Campaigning on an agricultural platform and making no mention of the race question, he received the support of liberals and Negroes (although the latter, reported John N. Popham of the New York *Times,* did not work openly for him fearing that their backing might prejudice his chances of success). He became the new junior Senator from Mississippi with more than 47,000 votes cast in his favor, a victory that was regarded as partly due to the fact that he was widely known in the State through his activity as president of the State College Alumni Association and the State 4-H Advisory Council. In the last days of the Eightieth Congress' first session he cast a negative vote on the Malone amendment to the interim aid bill and voted for the Barkley amendment to the antiinflation bill.

Before returning to Congress in early 1948, Stennis expressed his support of the Marshall Plan as the best method of combating Communism and as the way to rebuild world markets for the United States export trade. He also, he said, wished to further agricultural progress in his State and the nation, wanted a "fair deal for labor and management," and favored the United Nations, for which he thought the United States had failed to supply proper leadership. When the Senate filibuster against the anti-poll tax bill took place in late July 1948, Stennis led off for the Southern opponents of the measure. Speaking with "relative restraint," he put forth the argument that the passage of such a bill by Congress would be unconstitutional and might lead to Federal interference in local elections. He discussed the history of the poll tax and cited many court decisions on its legality. In the second session of the Eightieth Congress the Senator voted in June against abolishing poll tax requirements for members of the armed forces, and in March and April against bills which would have provided that no Federal aid be given to church schools and which would have restricted such aid to a token amount. He favored the Republican tax reduction bill in March and the Vandenberg Foreign Policy Resolution, passed almost unanimously in June. A "nay" vote was recorded for him in May on the bill which would have admitted 200,000 rather than 100,000 displaced persons to the United States.

At the convening of the Eighty-first Congress in January 1949, the conflict over civil rights began with an attempt to change the Senate rules so that a filibuster could be stopped. Stennis lost in his effort to force the hearings on this matter to be held open to all testimony when it was decided to limit the hearings to Senate members. He then announced that he would support several "compromise" rule changes, such as the application of the "gag rule" to foreign affairs and national security measures only and a ban which would require support by 90 per cent of the Senators; he voted for the compromise revision of the Senate cloture rule. With twenty-three other Democrats he helped to defeat the upholding of the Barkley antifilibuster ruling in March and voted "nay" with the majority on a bill to forbid segregation in public housing the next month. In May the Senator opposed an attempt to prevent the commitment of arms to Western Europe by the United States. He voted affirmatively on the bill to provide Federal aid to education and on the coalition revision of the Taft-Hartley Act. On the first vote on the issue of reducing Federal spending 5 to 10 per cent he answered "yea" but reversed his stand on the second vote. Stennis' committee assignments were to the Committee on Rules and Administration and the Committee on Public Works.

Returning from an inspection trip of Europe in December 1949 Stennis announced that a "very substantial" reduction should be made in allotment of funds under the Marshall Plan. He also favored a loan to Spain which would allow that country's purchase of cotton and other commodities from the United States. In the second session of the Eighty-first Congress he reiterated his stand on civil rights by characterizing attempts to secure such a program as "the selling of our people down the river by bartering away our Constitution, bit by bit, to various pressure groups at political conventions," (quoted by the New York *Times*, May 19, 1950). He also filed exhibits purporting to prove that the "fountainspring" for the bill had been provided by the Communists' 1928 platform. On September 3, 1950, Stennis came

Wide World Photos
JOHN C. STENNIS

out in favor of Congressional immunity from libel and damage suits. In debate on Hawaiian and Alaskan Statehood he opposed the admittance of those territories on the grounds that the four new votes thus added to the Senate would influence the decisions on all affairs, domestic and foreign. In December 1950 he joined other Democrats in denouncing the Administration's "lack of leadership" in defense preparations. Other votes cast by Stennis in 1950 show that he favored the passage of the Lodge-Gossett constitutional amendment which would have abolished the electoral college (February), the extension of Federal rent controls (June), the $100 million loan to Spain (August), and the overriding of the Communist control bill veto (September). He again opposed a liberalized displaced persons act in April and voted against allocating $45 million for the Point IV Program in June and against striking out optional draftee segregation in June.

On a "county courthouse" tour, which he made before returning to Congress in 1951, Stennis visited thirty-four counties in his native State to report his views to the people. He became a member of the Armed Services Committee in the first session of the Eighty-second Congress. An investigation of charges that the Mississippi State Democratic Committee was selling Federal jobs and contracts was begun by a Senate subcommittee after these accusations were set forth in speeches made by Stennis and Senator James O. Eastland, also of Mississippi. In April 1951 the Senator voted in opposition to the McClellan amendment which provided that no troops beyond the four divisions planned could be sent to Europe without Congressional approval. In August he voted with the majority for a $250 million cut in economic aid to Europe and cast an affirmative vote on cutting housing units from fifty thousand to five thousand. He voted "nay" on re-

STENNIS, JOHN C.—*Continued*

ducing the river and harbor funds 10 per cent, and on the amendment which would have eliminated provisions for universal military training and service, and on the amendment prohibiting the OPS from restricting livestock slaughtering.

During the second session of the Eighty-second Congress Stennis again indicated his opposition to Alaskan statehood by voting to shelve the measure in February. The following month he favored killing a measure providing for the reorganization of the Bureau of Internal Revenue. He voted in May against cutting foreign aid by $1 billion and for cutting it $200 million. The Senator recorded a negative vote on providing forty-five thousand as opposed to five thousand public housing units in 1953. He opposed giving the President power to seize the steel mills and approved of using the Taft-Hartley Act in the steel strike (both in June). In the same month he voted to shelve the St. Lawrence seaway project and to override the omnibus immigration bill veto. The Senator retained his seat in 1952.

Stennis toured military bases in England, the Mediterranean area and other parts of Western Europe in the fall of 1953 with two other members of the Senate Armed Forces subcommittee. Although the senators did find evidence of money wasted in military construction abroad, they were optimistic about Western defenses in Europe. "A position of formidable strength is being attained—within minutes from our strategic targets," the subcommittee's report to President Eisenhower stated (New York *Times,* October 15, 1953).

Stennis served as president of the Mississippi 4-H Advisory Council in 1947 and is a past president of the Mississippi State College Advisory Association. He is a member of the Mississippi Farm Bureau, the Mississippi Bar Association, and the American Bar Association. Greek letter societies, besides Phi Beta Kappa, to which he belongs are Phi Alpha Delta (a legal fraternity) and Alpha Chi Rho. The Senator is a director of the Bank of DeKalb and the chairman of the board of deacons of the DeKalb Presbyterian Church. He also belongs to the Lions and is a Mason.

In a magazine article, "What You Don't Know About the South," published in *Collier's,* March 26, 1949, Stennis discussed advances in health, education, and other aspects of Southern life as related particularly to the Negro.

Stennis and the former Coy Hines, whom he married December 24, 1929, have two children, John Hampton and Margaret Jane. His wife has served as a county Home Demonstration Agent. The Mississippi Senator has been described in the New York *Times* as "a tall, spare man, with slightly Lincolnesque features . . . a scholarly jurist . . . deliberate of speech."

References

Christian Sci Mon p12 F 13 '51
Biographical Directory of the American Congress, 1774-1949 (1950)
Who's Who in America, 1952-1953
Who's Who in United States Politics (1950)

STEPINAC, ALOJZIJE, CARDINAL

(stĕ-pē'nătz à-loi'zĭ-à) May 8, 1898- Roman Catholic prelate of Yugoslavia

Address: Krašić, Croatia, Yugoslavia

Of the twenty-four high Roman Catholic churchmen designated by Pope Pius XII to become cardinals in January 1953, none has greater world-wide fame than Alojzije Cardinal Stepinac, Archbishop of Zagreb, the Primate of Yugoslavia. Tried for alleged "crimes against the state," including wartime collaboration with the Nazis, by a four-man People's Court in Zagreb in October 1946, he was sentenced to sixteen years imprisonment and loss of civil rights. After five years, during which he was widely regarded as a martyr and a symbol of resistance to Communist antireligious policy, he was released from jail in December 1951 and permitted to return to his native village but not to perform his episcopal duties. Announcement of his designation as a Prince of the Church precipitated the severance of relations with the Vatican by Marshal Tito on December 17, 1952.

Alojzije (in English Aloysius) Stepinac, seventh of the eleven children of Joseph and Barbara (Penic) Stepinac, was born on May 8, 1898, at Krašić in Croatia, which was then a part of the Austro-Hungarian Empire, owing allegiance to the Hungarian crown but enjoying a status of semiautonomy. His father, a farmer, belonged to an old and respected peasant family, and one of his great uncles, Matias Stepinac, was a scientist and a canon of the Roman Catholic Church. For his elementary education young Stepinac attended school in his native village before going on to the Episcopal Minor Seminary in the Croatian provincial capital of Agram (now Zagreb). A little over sixteen years old when World War I began, he was conscripted into the Hungarian Army and, after basic training, served on the Italian front until captured by the enemy, having meanwhile risen to the rank of cadet warrant officer and twice won the Hungarian medal for valor. Later he fought on the Salonika front as a second lieutenant in an Allies-sponsored force of volunteers and was subsequently awarded the highest Yugoslav decoration for heroism.

Alojzije Stepinac was still in uniform when on December 1, 1918, the "Kingdom of the Serbs, Croats and Slovenes" was proclaimed, with King Peter of Serbia as its first monarch. This new state, soon to be known as Yugoslavia, was the outgrowth of the collapse of the Austro-Hungarian Empire, comprising as it did the kingdoms of Serbia and Montenegro and the former Austro-Hungarian provinces (or dependencies) of Croatia-Slovonia, Dalmatia, and Bosnia-Herzegovina. It was harassed from the start by religious as well as racial antagonisms, the majority of Serbs belonging to a branch of the Eastern Orthodox Church, while the Croats were predominantly Roman Catholic. Led by Dr. Stephen Radic, they were soon agitating for autonomy.

For a period following his return to civilian life in 1919 Stepinac worked for the Hungarian

Board of Agriculture (the first constitution of the new Yugoslavia did not go into effect until June 28, 1921). Simultaneously he studied agriculture in the Economics College of the University of Zagreb. With his degree, he returned to his native village to engage in farming, but in 1924 having decided that his vocation was that of a priest, he went to Rome, where he entered the Gregorian University and took his Ph.D. degree in philosophy in 1927. Continuing his studies, he was ordained a priest on October 26, 1930, and acquired his Doctor of Theology degree in the summer following, having been considered during those years a very brilliant scholar (A. H. O'Brien in *Archbishop Stepinac; The Man and His Case*). Within a year after beginning parochial work as a curate in the slums of Zagreb in July 1931, Stepinac was made secretary to Archbishop Ante Bauer of Zagreb. On May 28, 1934, he was named titular Archbishop of Nicope by Pope Pius XI, as well as Coadjutor to his superior, Archbishop Bauer, to become at the age of thirty-six "one of the youngest archbishops in Roman Catholic history" (*New York Herald Tribune*). A factor in the rapid advancement of Stepinac, who succeeded to the see of Zagreb after Archbishop Bauer's death on December 7, 1937, was the friendship, admiration, and interest of the Papal Secretary of State, Eugenio Cardinal Pacelli, who was to become Pope Pius XII in 1939.

It was in 1934, the year in which Stepinac became bishop, that Adolf Hitler first assumed the title of *Führer* of Germany. Four years later the German Reich had been expanded, through the annexation of Austria in September 1938, to the border of Yugoslavia; whereupon Stepinac, by then Archbishop of Zagreb (appointed in 1937) and Roman Catholic Primate of Yugoslavia, "formed a committee to aid . . . Jewish refugees who were now streaming into Croatia from Austria" and other parts of the anti-Semitic Reich. The quoted words are to be found in a letter to the New York *Times* from Stephen Lackovic, who had been for five years a secretary to Stepinac and who continued: "This committee not only supplied material aid to these refugees, it also provided means for them to get out of Europe as the Nazi legions rolled towards them." About the time of the Nazi occupation of Croatia in April 1941, when a puppet administration, the so-called "Ustashi" regime, was set up with Dr. Ante Pavelic as its head, Stepinac issued on April 28, 1941, a pastoral letter urging his clergy to give the Pavelic Government "full support." The Archbishop, further, accepted the post of Supreme Apostolic Vicar to the Ustashi troops and a seat in Pavelic's Council of State. When told by Captain Rapotec (an emissary of the Yugoslav Government-in-Exile who visited him secretly later in the year) that he was being "much criticized abroad for not breaking openly with the Quisling regime," the Archbishop was quoted as replying that "he could easily do that and be forced to retire to a monastery, but he had to take into account thousands of victims who would remain helpless in such a case" (Ilija Jukitch, former

Wide World Photos

ALOJZIJE CARDINAL STEPINAC

Yugoslav Under Secretary of State in Yugoslavia's Ministry of Foreign Affairs, in a letter to the New York *Times*). The Archbishop, it is further stated, offered through Captain Rapotec, to "distribute to the war victims any funds that might be sent to him secretly by the exiled government in London, including all persecuted for their political convictions."

During the 1946 treason trial of Archbishop Stepinac, a former Ustashi leader, Slažko Kvaternik, testified for the prosecution that Pavelic had personally "hated" the Catholic Primate. Stepinac had formally protested against the oppression of Jews, Serbs, and other racial minorities in Croatia in June 1941, and had "used his own episcopal residence and other church buildings to hide persecuted Jews from their Nazi tormentors" (Stephen Lackovic). "The same year, on New Year's Eve, in a sermon in Zagreb Cathedral," former Under Secretary Jukitch had stated, "he condemned in the strongest terms the foundations of Nazism and Ustashism. . . .After that sermon the Ustashis openly threatened to kill him." Some fifteen months later (March 14, 1943), following an Ustashi order that all Jews should be treated according to the Nuremberg decrees, the Primate preached another sermon assailing discrimination against any persons "because their family shrine was not in accord with the theories of Nazism"—a sermon considered of sufficient world significance to be rebroadcast by the Vatican radio in July. Shortly before the entrance of Marshal Tito's Partisans into Zagreb in May 1945, the Archbishop issued a call to rally to the defense of the Croat puppet state and to resist the advancing Allies. A British liaison officer who visited him a number of months later wrote in a letter to the London *News Statesman and Nation* of October 26, 1946, that the Archbishop had told him that "he and his priests had collaborated with

STEPINAC, CARDINAL—*Continued*

the Germans because the issue of the war had been a clear one between Fascism and Communism. He had chosen the former."

On entering Zagreb in May 1945, the Partisans arrested Stepinac, but after about two weeks Marshal Tito personally ordered his release. (A ninety-six-page book, *The Case Against Archbishop Stepinac*, issued by the Yugoslav Embassy at Washington in 1947, explains that the reason charges of "crimes against the people" were not brought against the prelate until well over a year afterward was the "sincere" hope of the new government that a means for coexistence of Catholicism and Communism in Yugoslavia might be worked out.) The Archbishop strongly resisted Communist efforts to discourage religious instruction and in his last pastoral letter before his arrest on September 18, 1946, charged the Tito regime with "attempts to undermine the filially cordial relations between the faithful and their shepherds" and with the hope of hastening a break in relations with Papal Rome which "would mean the liquidation of living Christianity and ruin Catholicism in Yugoslavia." The Archbishop was one of eighteen persons—twelve of them priests—who were accused of collaboration with the Ustashis and of other "crimes against the people" and brought before a three-man court at Zagreb. Stepinac himself was indicted on fourteen counts, including urging his clergy to support the Pavelic regime, provoking racial hatred, approving "forcible conversions" to Catholicism, and influencing priests to organize "Crusader Units" against the Communist state. Stepinac, who pleaded "not guilty," was allowed to call witnesses for the defense and to address the court on his own behalf. The trial was ended on October 11, with the prelate being found guilty on all counts. He was sentenced to sixteen years imprisonment at hard labor, with confiscation of all his property and loss of civil rights for five years.

A New York *Times* editorial two days later called the proceedings "clearly a political trial" and expressed the view that Stepinac's life was spared because "Marshal Tito did not feel quite strong enough to make a new martyr." Earlier the Regent of the Apostolic Nunciature, Bishop Joseph P. Hurley of Florida, had stated at Zagreb that he expected the Vatican to continue to regard Stepinac as head of the Church in Yugoslavia; on October 14 the Sacred Congregation of the Council, through Cardinal Marmaggi, pronounced sentence of excommunication on "all those who have contributed physically or morally" toward the "judicial action" whereby the Archbishop had been "arbitrarily arrested and unjustly sentenced." By the middle of November it was being rumored that Pope Pius XII might make Stepinac a Cardinal at a special Christmas consistory, and while this was without loss of time "categorically denied" in Vatican circles, the rumors themselves reflected a general expectation that Catholics the world over would increasingly recognize the symbolic value of the prelate's incarceration. With the break

between Tito and the Kremlin in the summer of 1948, the opinion of the outside world became a matter of rapidly growing importance to the Yugoslav government and was generally considered to have prompted the Marshal's decision in November 1950 to permit C. L. Sulzberger of the New York *Times* to interview the Primate in Lepoglava Prison. The correspondent found the prisoner in good health and housed in a clean though small room. While he was permitted to receive books, the prelate informed Sulzberger, he "had no access to newspapers." The "hard labor" part of his sentence had not been enforced, and he was allowed, with two other priests, to perform his religious services and to take communion. Some five months later, when interviewed by Alex H. Singleton of the Associated Press, Stepinac expressed the belief that religious affairs in Yugoslavia had "improved within the last three years".

Release of Archbishop Stepinac from prison in December 1951 was generally looked upon as a substantial victory for the Vatican, even though the prelate remained adjudged a traitor by the Yugoslav Government and not allowed to resume his episcopal duties at Zagreb. He was, however, permitted to function as a priest in his native village of Krašić. Such was his situation when on November 29, 1952, he was one of the new Princes of the Church designated by Pope Pius XII, to be invested as Cardinals in the following January. Stepinac told newsmen that he would not go to the Vatican to receive the red hat. "To go to Rome I would have to ask permission," he explained. "This I will not do, because I do not consider myself guilty before the Communists. And if I should go to Rome then I could never come back." A little less than three weeks later (December 17) Tito broke off diplomatic relations with the Vatican, stating that the creation of Stepinac as a Cardinal was a "political move" and that the Archbishop was a "war criminal" who would never be allowed to return to Zagreb. Stepinac did not attend the ceremonies in mid-January 1953 in the Vatican.

In his now celebrated interview C. L. Sulzberger described the Croatian churchman as "a man of pale, but evidently healthy countenance, fine features, thin brown hair, and facial expression that clearly denotes a tremendous inner passion." To Alex Singleton he appeared "a man of medium height, wiry." He speaks Serb, Croat, Italian, French, and German fluently.

References

Commonweal 45:3-4 O 16 '46
Life 31:26-7 D 17 '51 pors
N Y Herald Tribune II p2 O 13 '46
  por; II p1 D 9 '51 por
N Y Times p26 O 9 '46; p20 O 19 '46;
  p1 N 12 '50 pors
Scholastic 59:12 Ja 9 '52
Washington (D.C.) Post p3 Ap 7 '51 por
International Who's Who, 1952
O'Brien, A. H. Archbishop Stepinac;
  The Man and His Case (1947)
Wallace, B. Trial of Dr. Aloysius Stepinac, Archbishop of Zagreb (1947)

STEVENS, ROBERT T(EN BROECK)

July 31, 1899- Secretary of the Army; textile manufacturer

Address: b. Department of the Army, Washington 25, D.C.; h. R. 1, Woodland Ave., South Plainfield, N.J.

Five times called from business into Government service, Robert T. Stevens became Secretary of the Army in February 1953. He had been designated for this post by President Dwight D. Eisenhower and his appointment was confirmed by the United States Senate on February 2. On taking office, he announced that he would fly to Tokyo to obtain first-hand information on the ammunition situation. In Seoul on April 1, he declared that Eighth Army ammunition supplies in Korea, in Japan, and en route were adequate for "any situation that might be faced."

The former textile manufacturer, president of the J. P. Stevens Company, served during the first administration of Franklin D. Roosevelt as a member of the staff of the National Recovery Administration. His second Government appointment came in 1940 when he was named head of the textile section of the National Defense Advisory Commission.

Robert Ten Broeck Stevens, the son of John Peters and Edna (Ten Broeck) Stevens, was born on July 31, 1899, in Fanwood, New Jersey. His birthplace is near his present home at South Plainfield, where he has lived most of his life. He attended Phillips Academy, Andover, Massachusetts, graduating in 1917. In World War I, Stevens served as a second lieutenant in the Field Artillery. Following his service in the Army, he continued his education at Yale, from which he was graduated with a B.A. degree in 1921.

He entered the textile business which had been started in a small woolen mill at North Andover, Massachusetts, in 1813 by his New England ancestor, Nathaniel Stevens. Beginning as a salesman, Stevens continued with the firm, becoming president upon his father's death in 1929. and chairman of the board of directors in 1945, a position he retained until the acceptance of his present post. The firm of J. P. Stevens and Company, Incorporated, with headquarters in New York City is one of the largest concerns in the textile industry, accruing $44,000,000 before taxes in 1951.

In 1933, Stevens served as an administrative representative in the industry section of the National Recovery Administration. He held the post of Class B Director in the Federal Reserve Bank of New York from 1934 to 1942; six years later Stevens was appointed a Class C Director, and chairman of the board. Other business positions he held included: director of the General Electric Company; the General Foods Corporation; the Jackson Mills, Wellford, South Carolina; the Marion Manufacturing Company, North Carolina; the New York Telephone Company; the Alexander Smith and Sons Carpet Company; the Whitney Chain Company of Hartford, Connecticut; the Owens-Corning Fiberglas Corporation of Toledo, Ohio; and the American Cotton Manufacturers Institute, Incorporated. Stevens also

Wide World Photos

ROBERT T. STEVENS

served as a trustee of the Mutual Life Insurance Company of New York, and of the Roosevelt Hospital, New York. Other posts filled by Stevens were the vice-presidency of the Association of Cotton Textile Merchants and chairman of the Business Advisory Council of the Department of Commerce.

In World War II, Stevens received various assignments, including that of district coordinator of Defense Contract Service, Office of Production Management, for the New York Area in 1941. In that year, he attended the Command and General Staff School at Fort Leavenworth, Kansas, and was assigned to the Office of the Quartermaster General, with the rank of colonel; in this post he was director of purchases from 1943 to 1945.

After a conference with Charles E. Wilson, then Secretary-designate for Defense, on December 19, 1952, President-elect Eisenhower appointed Robert Stevens to the post of Secretary of the Army. As reported in the New York *Times* of December 20, Stevens told newsmen that he had accepted the appointment after a fifteen-minute conference at which he had met the President-elect for the first time.

When the nomination of Stevens was sent to the Senate for confirmation, a poll of the fifteen-member Armed Services Committee showed that the majority wanted Stevens to dispose of his stock holdings in companies doing business with the Department of Defense.

Stevens, according to *Time* Magazine, (February 9, 1953) argued that while he was willing to sell other holdings, he should be allowed to keep his $1,400,000 worth of stock in the J. P. Stevens Company. "I am steeped in sentiment and tradition with respect to the company that bears my father's name," he said. Requiring him to give up the stock, he contended, would establish "an important precedent" which would

STEVENS, ROBERT T.—*Continued*

"have a long and serious effect on the willingness of successful executives to serve."

The Committee, however, did not alter its opinion, and on January 29 Stevens agreed to sell the 42,800 shares of stock which he owned in the Stevens Company and in Owens-Corning Fiberglas, and on February 2, 1953 his nomination was confirmed by the Senate.

A special Senate inquiry into alleged shortages of ammunition in Korea brought the comment from Secretary Stevens on March 17, that there was an adequate supply of ammunition at that time. Speaking from Joliet, Illinois, where he was making an inspection tour of the arsenal, the Secretary declared, "Production and supply are increasing rapidly . . . but none of us is completely satisfied. We will bend every effort."

Secretary Stevens visited the Louisiana Ordnance plant near Shreveport, as one of a series of field visits to observe directly ammunition supplies, and on March 27, the Secretary announced that he would fly to the Far East.

He inspected the Eighth Army in Korea and also the Seventh in Europe, and on his return told a group of military and educational leaders who assembled on May 3 at Virginia Military Institute: "Americans have every right to be proud of these two great armies. Especially is this true when we realize that for the first time in our military history, we are mobilizing, fighting a war and demobilizing all at the same time."

Both the Legion of Merit and the Distinguished Service Medal have been awarded to Robert Stevens for his services during World War II. Two honorary degrees, a D.C.S., by New York University and an L.H.D. by Lafayette College, were conferred on him in 1950. Societies and clubs of which he is a member include Psi Upsilon, Wolf's Head Society, the Biltmore, (North Carolina) Forest Country Club, the Downtown Association, Links, Merchants, Union League, and Yale Clubs.

Stevens was married to Dorothy Goodwin Whitney on October 6, 1923. Their five children are Robert Ten Broeck, Jr., Whitney, Joan Peters, William Gallon, and Thomas Estes. Secretary Stevens is a Presbyterian and a Republican. *Time* Magazine has described him as "a trim, grey-haired, ruddy-cheeked, easy-smiling man."

Speaking at Syracuse University on June 1, 1953 when he received an honorary degree, the Secretary said, "the nation faces an enemy whose goal is universal slavery. The enemy is well-trained, his target is the minds of men and women."

The Secretary of the Army told a Senate Appropriations sub-committee on June 2 that the proposed cut of about $1,000,000 below the estimates presented by President Truman before leaving office would not affect adversely the current combat effectiveness of the Army. He said that the revised budget would call for a reduction of 117,000 men in the Army's strength below the Truman-projected level, the new level to be reached by June 30, 1954.

Addressing the National Guard Association convention in San Diego, California on October 22, Secretary Stevens said that the new atomic cannon which is accurate even in darkness "will greatly enhance our defense capabilities . . . the anti-aircraft defenses of our great cities and industrial centers have been materially strengthened in many ways, including the equipping of some battalions with the new electronically controlled Skysweeper (a 75-millimeter gun). The first battalions of Nike—the Army's new anti-aircraft guided missile will soon be in position."

References

N Y Herald Tribune p28 Ja 24 '53
N Y Times p1+ D 20 '52
N Y World-Telegram p8 D 19 '52
Newsweek 40:11 D 29 '52
Time 60:11 D 29 '52 por
U S News 34:90 F 6 '53 por

Business Executives of America (1950)
Who's Who in America, 1952-53
Who's Who in Commerce and Industry (1951)

STOKOWSKI, LEOPOLD (ANTON STANISLAW (stô-kôf'skê)) Apr. 18, 1882- Orchestra conductor; composer

Address: b. c/o Schulhof, 113 W. 57th St., New York 19; h. 10 Gracie Square, New York 28

NOTE: This biography supersedes the article which appeared in *Current Biography* in 1941.

In his book *Music for All of Us* Leopold Stokowski wrote: "Formerly, music was chiefly confined to privileged classes in cultural centers, but today, through radio and records, music has come directly into our homes no matter how far we may live from cultural centers." In the decade since these words were written, Stokowski, acknowledged as one of our greatest conductors, has helped through his study of acoustics and recordings to make it possible for music to be reproduced in the home with greater fidelity of tone and considerably less distortion. He foresaw and has worked for binaural broadcasting with its greater tonal perspective. He has also been concerned with the problem of giving contemporary composers an opportunity to be heard under the most favorable circumstances.

In Carnegie Hall on October 17, 1953 he conducted the first major concert of contemporary Canadian music ever given in the United States, the first of a series under the auspices of the Contemporary Music Society. The programs will be divided between American contemporary music and "seldom heard masterpieces."

Leopold Anton Stanislaw Stokowski was born in London, April 18, 1882 of a Polish father, Josef Boleshaw Kopernicus Stokowski. His mother was Irish. Leopold was named for his grandfather, Leopold Stokowski of Krakow and Lublin.

From his earliest days he was interested in music and learned to play the piano and violin.

Before he could reach the pedals he was playing parts of the organ works of Bach on a four-manual organ. At the Royal College of Music in London he studied harmony, counterpoint and composition under Sir Charles Parry and Sir Edward Elgar. He continued his education at the Paris Conservatoire and in Germany, concentrating upon the fugue and orchestration.

He has subsequently studied different kinds of music during his travels in Arabia, China, India, Java and Bali. He is a Fellow of the Royal College of Music and a Bachelor of Music of Queen's College, Oxford. While a student in London he was organist of St. James' church in Piccadilly.

In 1905 he came to New York to be organist and choirmaster at St. Bartholomew's church. (The story that he was known there as Leo Stokes is wholly legendary.) In 1908 he left the sphere of church music to begin his career as an orchestra conductor in Cincinnati.

This transition from the choir loft to the podium was not as strange as it might seem. The modern pipe organ with its orchestral stops and great variety of color, somewhat approximates a symphony orchestra. Furthermore, familiarity with great organ literature, particularly the works of Bach, provided a sound musical background for the future conductor.

In 1912 Stokowski left Cincinnati to assume the leadership of the Philadelphia Orchestra. Here his innovations and successes made him one of the most controversial figures of the American musical scene.

Virgil Thomson wrote, "He has violated tradition and made tradition. His first violation of tradition was to arrive at the top of the conducting profession by an unorthodox and improbable route. The best conductors have mostly learned their job in the theatre. . . .Mr. Stokowski came from the Royal College of Music to St. Bartholomew's Church as a perfectly good organist in the English style, no more. He went from there to conduct in Cincinnati. . . .He stepped up to Philadelphia and made colossally good" (New York *Herald Tribune,* November 17, 1940).

Stokowski has always had certain fundamental beliefs in his music and in himself. He has also been able blithely to disregard his critics and to pursue his beliefs if need be in open defiance. He was able to transform a somewhat mediocre Philadelphia Orchestra into an instrument of such beauty and fame that he was given the Bok award as "the person who has done the most for Philadelphia." He accomplished this by engaging only the finest players for each section. Then he permitted these players some freedom of expression even as he kept a firm hand on the ensemble.

Charles O'Connell, who was associated with Stokowski for eighteen years, writes in his book *The Other Side of the Record,* "I am told that Stokowski had periods of being a martinet, . . . of being an amiable friend or a remote and Olympian deity. I never have witnessed any of these manifestations during the last eighteen years."

O'Connell continues: "With his men he is pleasant, slightly aloof, impersonal and correct in his rehearsal deportment and quite insistent

Bender

LEOPOLD STOKOWSKI

upon the incompatibility of mercy and justice. He will not for one moment tolerate inattention or stupidity. . . .The superb, the incredible legato of which the Philadelphia Orchestra alone seems capable is the result of Stokowski's insistence on free bowing; that is, the players were not obliged to follow the bowing of the section leader but handled their instruments in the way that was most natural and easy for them in producing the effect the conductor demanded."

Stokowski's years in Philadelphia were far from serene either for him or for his audiences. He was intolerant of late-comers and "train-catchers" and frequently chastised them publicly. His critics have accused him of using these tactics to make the headlines. He had violent disagreements with his board of directors over modern music.

During the depression financial support for the Orchestra fell off appreciably. In 1932 the directors announced that there would be no modern compositon or "debatable music" played that year. When Stokowski, who had been in New Mexico, returned, he called in reporters and gave them a statement. He "would play a modern piece whenever he saw fit to do so and he would play it twice for whoever cared to listen." The press sided with him and another Stokowski victory was won.

It was inevitable that these clashes would one day not resolve themselves. He resigned in 1936 as musical director, continuing to conduct concerts each season until 1941. He had organized the All-American Youth Orchestra in 1940 with which he toured this country, South America and the West Indies.

Again the skeptics were openly scornful of an attempt to play virtuoso symphonic pieces with an orchestra of young musicians who had never before played together. In a very short time Stokowski had welded into shape a remarkably fine organization.

(Continued next page)

STOKOWSKI, LEOPOLD—*Continued*

Glenn Dillard Dunn of the Washington *Times-Herald* wrote: "I can assure Americans of either continent that this is just what Stokowski said it would be: one of the great orchestras of the world." However, since its members were of draft age, it had to be disbanded during World War II.

Stokowski was co-conductor with Toscanini of the newly formed NBC Symphony from 1941 to 1944. He has led the New York City Symphony in 1944 and 1945, the Hollywood Bowl orchestra from 1945 to 1947, the United States Army Band at Fort MacArthur, California, and was co-conductor in 1948 and 1949 of the New York Philharmonic. Having been a guest conductor all over the world, his most recent appearance was with the Saint Cecilia Orchestra of Rome on May 31, 1953.

Stokowski's transcriptions of Bach's organ works have brought the wrath of the purists upon his head. On the other hand, they have brought the music of Bach to thousands who might never have heard it. Of this the conductor himself said "The most free and sublime instrumental expressions of Bach are his greater organ works, and of these the greatest is the *Passacaglia in C minor.* Unfortunately one does not often enough have opportunity to hear it, and so, to bring it nearer to those who love Bach's music, I have made it for orchestra."

The late Lawrence Gilman, reviewing a concert for the New York *Herald Tribune* (April 4, 1937) wrote glowingly of an interpolated number *Mein Jeus, was für Seelenweh befällt dich in Gethsemane* (My Jesu, what befell thee in Gethsemane) "There is no more beautiful and poignant music than this in all of Bach's innumerable utterances of mystical and sacred grief; and Mr. Stokowski's setting for the strings, of magnificent felicity, made it well-nigh insupportable".

Stokowski worked with RCA Victor and with Dr. Harvey Fletcher of the Bell Laboratories to improve radio and recording techniques. Long opposed to· broadcasting from "dead" studios, he struggled consistently to persuade radio technicians to broadcast from acoustically "live" studios. His persistence in this field is largely responsible for the greater realism in reproduced music, now accepted as a matter of course.

Not only did he work closely with the engineers on every broadcast and recording session but he seated his orchestra differently for each composition to be played. Charles O'Connell says of this: "He decided that, given sympathetic cooperation in the recording room, he could accomplish more by manipulation of the orchestra than by revolving a rheostat."

He was first lured to Hollywood to make *The Great Broadcast of 1937.* This was followed by *One Hundred Men and a Girl,* and *Fantasia* (1941) which he made with Walt Disney, featuring Stravinsky's *Le Sacre du Printemps,* and *Carnegie Hall* (1947).

An enthusiast for modern music, Stokowski was the first to conduct in this country Gustav Mahler's *Symphony of a Thousand Voices,* Stravinsky's *Le Sacre du Printemps* and important works of Arnold Schoenberg, Serge Prokofieff and Dmitri Shostakovich.

He also gave the first performance of a number of American compositons including Ernest Schelling's *A Victory Ball,* Aaron Copland's *Dance Symphony,* Walter Piston's *1929 Suite for Orchestra,* Abram Chasins' *Second Concerto in F-Sharp Minor for Piano and Orchestra,* Samuel Barlow's *Babar* and Elie Siegmeister's *Harvest Evening* from the *Prairie Legend.*

In April 1952 Stokowski conducted over CBS a concert from Columbia University as the climax of its Festival of American Music. He was subsequently given the Alice M. Ditson Memorial Fund award as a tribute to the conductor's "adventurousness".

During the season of 1952-1953, under the auspices of the American Composer's Alliance and of Broadcast Music, Incorporated, he presented two concerts at the Museum of Modern Art. Here, under nearly ideal circumstances, several new composers were introduced to the public. An unusual feature of these concerts was the tape-recording of the performances as they took place.

Of this innovation Stokowski said in an introductory speech, "The conventional composer usually has to wait for somebody else to play his music and it might be to his advantage to work, like the painter, directly on the materials of sound—the tape-recorder, for instance."

In September 1953 it was announced that Stokowski would conduct the six Sunday radio concerts sponsored jointly by the Columbia Broadcasting System and the American Composers' Alliance. The program, featuring the CBS radio orchestra, and offering both contemporary and classical music, is entitled *Twentieth Century Concert Hall.*

Stokowski became an American citizen in 1915. In 1911 he married the concert pianist Olga Samaroff; they were divorced in 1923. His marriage to Evangeline Brewster Johnson in 1926 ended in divorce in 1937. On April 21, 1945 he married Gloria Vanderbilt di Cicco. He had a daughter, Sonia, by his first marriage; two daughters, Lyuba and Sadja by the second marriage and two sons by his third marriage.

He has blue eyes and gray hair. Concerning his famous hands which have been the subject of much comment and some derision, O'Connell wrote "the illusion of beauty that they give comes from the instinctive grace with which they are used".

Stokowski is a member of the American Federation of Musicians in Philadelphia and Los Angeles. He has received the Order of Polonia Restitute, Officer of the Crown of Rumania and Chevalier of the Legion of Honor. He holds honorary degrees from the University of Pennsylvania and the University of California.

His book, *Music for All of Us* (1943), has been translated into five languages. He composed *Dithyrambe* for flute, cello and harp which was played in Phiiadelphia on November 15, 1917. Among his other compositions are *Negro Rhapsody, Prelude on Two Ancient Liturgical Melodies,* and *Benedicite Omina Opera* for organ.

On June 14, 1953 Leopold Stokowski conducted the Bergen, Norway Symphony Orchestra at. the World Music Festival which was broadcast to the United States.

References

Mus Am 61:4 Mr 25 '51
N Y Herald Tribune Ap 14 '37
N Y Times Ja 13 '36; O 27 '52
Newsweek 17:60 Mr 24 '41
Times 47:69+ F 18 '46 por
Washington Times Herald Jl 13 '40

Brooks, D. International Gallery of Conductors (1951)
Columbia Encyclopedia (1950)
Ewen, D. Dictators of the Baton (1943)
International Motion Picture Almanac, 1950-51
O'Connell, C. The Other Side of the Record (1947)
Reis, C. Composers in America (1947)
Thompson, Oscar, ed, The International Cyclopedia of Music and Musicians (1949)
Who is Who in Music (1951)

STOLK, WILLIAM C. Aug. 11, 1900-
Business executive

Address: b. c/o American Can Company, 100 Park Ave., New York 17; h. Taylor Rd., Mt. Kisco, N.Y.

As the chief executive officer of the American Can Company, William C. Stolk heads the country's largest producer of metal containers, with a 1952 gross sales of more than $600 million. Stolk, who first was employed by the company as a sixteen-year-old timekeeper, advanced through the ranks in the sales department, where he was responsible for several innovations in can manufacturing. Elected president of Canco in April 1951, he was a year later named to his present position in succession to C. H. Black, chairman of the board.

The son of Cornelius and Dolores Munoz (Tebar) Stolk, William C. Stolk was born August 11, 1900, in Caracas, Venezuela. His father owned a large cocoa plantation in Venezuela and was engaged in the export-import business, with offices in that country and New York. When the boy William was seven years old, the family moved to the United States. In 1916, while he was a student at the Cranford (New Jersey) High School and hoping to attend Yale Medical School in order to become a surgeon, his father told him that he must either return to Venezuela and complete his schooling there or make his own way in the United States. Hearing through a friend of a vacancy in the Manhattan plant of the American Can Company, William Stolk applied for the position and was accepted. His first job was as timekeeper at a wage of seventeen cents an hour. Except for a period of service in the United States Army (sergeant in the tank corps) during and shortly after World War I and a year in South America as salesman for a cotton goods firm, he has been with the American Can Company ever since.

In 1922, two years after Stolk returned to Canco from South America as a solder clerk in the Atlantic branch of the company, an elevator operator told him of an opening in the sales department. His application for the job having been accepted, in this department he moved steadily forward to increasingly important positions: in 1926 he became sales manager in the company's Pittsburgh office and three years later was transferred to Philadelphia in the same capacity. He was sent to New York City in 1932 to fill the position of sales division manager for the Atlantic district, where in 1941 he became general manager of sales. Elected vice-president in charge of sales in 1944, he reorganized the sales department, effecting a consolidation of all sales operations into a single executive organization. Gross sales rose from $242 million in 1945 to $555 million in 1950; in 1952 its volume totaled $621,691,000. From vice-president in charge of sales he was promoted to executive vice-president and a director of the company in 1949. On April 24, 1951, at the annual meeting of stockholders of the American Can Company, Stolk was elected president, to succeed C. H. Black, who became chairman of the board of directors. A year later (April 1952) Stolk became chief executive officer when Black retired after forty-four years with the company.

The leading producer in its field, the American Can Company, incorporated in 1901, was organized through a consolidation of sixty-five manufacturers of metal containers for foods, chemicals, tobacco, paints, and other products. With fifty-eight plants in the United States, Canada, and Hawaii, Canco in 1953 manufactures more than 2,000 different types of metal and fibre containers and a variety of metal ware and sheet metal, as well as machinery and tools for making its products. The company, which also operates the largest research laboratories in the food and container industries, has some 35,000 employees. After World War II, Canco began an expansion and modernization program costing in excess of $250 million. By the fall of 1953 new plants at Lemoyne, Pennsylvania, and Plymouth, Florida, were completed.

William Stolk believes that salesmanship plays a dominant part in the growth of business and industry in the United States. "The salesman who is competing from day to day in the market place," he has said, "has many chances to open new fields, help develop new products, create additional markets, provide greater employment, and contribute to a better standard of living for people far beyond the scope of his own operations." In his own company, salesmen have conceived the ideas for many successful projects, such as canned beer, canned motor oil, and single-trip milk containers. When Stolk himself was a young salesman he was alert to ideas which might come from customer complaints and suggestions, and passed them along to the company's main office. One of his most successful ideas was conceived while he was sales manager in Pittsburgh: the pressurized container which would keep the bounce in tennis balls by equalizing the pressure from within and outside the balls, an idea which was sold to the Pennsylvania Rubber Company. In

Buschke's Studio

WILLIAM C. STOLK

1953 the pressurized can serves many other purposes: blood plasma, for instance, is shipped to Korea in this type of container.

A recent project for which William Stolk is primarily responsible is "Operation Survival," American Can Company's special research program, which has had as its target the development of the "tinless tin can" to meet the tin shortage. This program was a natural answer to the uncertainty of the supply of tin for which the United States is almost wholly dependent on other countries. Ways have been found to manufacture cans of tin-free solders which are suitable for nonfood use; cans of steel plate with side seams sealed by a plastic cement instead of solder are now used by several nonfood packers. The research staff has developed can-lining enamels which require only domestically produced materials, an achievement which should extend the use of tin-free steel plate into the field of food packaging.

William Stolk is a director of United Chromium, Inc., and of the Metal and Thermit Corporation. By his marriage to Fern Gibson on December 29, 1922, he is the father of three daughters, now all married: Shirley (Mrs. Irving S. Fellner, Jr.), Natalie Joan (Mrs. William J. Graham), and Ann (Mrs. Gustavo de la Rosa, Jr.). A golf enthusiast, Stolk is a member of the Mount Kisco Country Club and was at one time its president. His other clubs are Cloud, Union League, Links (New York City) and Pacific Union (San Francisco).

References

Fortune 43:24 Je '51 por; 45:49 Je '52 por
Time 57:89 My 7 '51
Business Executives of America (1950)
Who's Who in America, 1952-53
Who's Who in Commerce and Industry (1951)

STOLZ, MARY SLATTERY March 24, 1920- Author
Address: b. c/o Harper & Brothers, 49 E. 33rd St., New York 16; h. 247 Clinton Ave., New Rochelle, N.Y.

Reprinted from the *Wilson Library Bulletin*, Sept. 1953

With all its other trials and tribulations, the "awkward age" brings that "awkward stage" in reading when the teen-ager is too old for children's books and not quite ready for serious adult reading. The need for "in-between" reading has been met in recent years with a whole body of teen-age fiction, only a small part of which, however, has any real literary merit. The novels of Mary Slattery Stolz, who writes, the *New Yorker* finds, "with proper regard for the dignity of young boys and girls," belong in that small group of really distinctive books. Although she has also written a book for young children, and her first adult novel, *Truth and Consequences,* has just been published, Mrs. Stolz is best known for her warm and sympathetic portrayals of the problems of growing up.

Mrs. Stolz's sensitive memories of her own childhood are the source of much of the charm of her books. "I had a rich childhood (personally) and a poor one (financially). I've always loved, and had, music; have an extraordinary fondness for cats; and believe strongly in familial ties. What you write must be a reflection of all these things that you believe in and love . . . a reflection of yourself, I guess."

She was born Mary Slattery, the daughter of Thomas Francis and Mary (McManus) Slattery, in Boston, Massachusetts, March 24, 1920, of ancestry "heavily weighted on the Irish side." Young Mary, her sister Eileen, and a first cousin Peg ("in our eyes, the third sister") were raised together in New York City. She attended the Birch Wathen School, Teachers College of Columbia University, where she had a scholarship and majored in English, and the Katherine Gibbs School.

Her first jobs were selling books in Macy's and working as secretary to Dr. Thomas Alexander of Teachers College. By then she was, however, a seasoned writer, for writing began for her not long after she had learned to read, at a very early age. "At about the same time that the meaning of words became clear to me, I also made the stirring discovery that you needn't simply read them, it was possible to move them about, choose among them, and all exactly as you pleased. That was a long time ago, but I still remember the sometimes almost unbearably exciting prospect of a sheet of blank paper and an idea."

All through school she wrote verse, essays, stories, biographies. She stopped writing for a while when she met Stanley Burr Stolz, a civil engineer, married him in 1940, and became the mother of a son, William, now ten. The enforced leisure of a long illness set Mrs. Stolz to serious writing again, and since 1950 when her first book was published, she has pro-

MARY SLATTERY STOLZ

ceeded at an astonishingly rapid pace—eight books and three short stories (sold to *Seventeen* and *Ladies' Home Journal*) to date.

The first book was *To Tell Your Love,* which Ellen Lesle Buell called "a wise and sensitive story of first love." The story of a summer in the life of a seventeen-year-old girl, painfully in love, coming gradually into an understanding of the real meaning of mature human relationships, has been told many times before. But Mrs. Stolz told it with fresh insight and, as a reviewer in the Los Angeles *Times* said, "a generous store of wisdom, humor, and tenderness."

The Organdy Cupcakes (1951) was again a familar story—a career book about three student nurses in a New York hospital. But again Mrs. Stolz brought such freshness, humor and depth of characterization to her story that reviewers agreed that it was "by far the best 'career' book of the spring." The *Saturday Review of Literature* found it "both moving and convincing. . . .The characters are real people who are good to know and hard to forget." With *The Sea Gulls Woke Me* (1951), the story of a sheltered sixteen-year-old girl's first summer away from home, Ellen Leslie Buell hailed Mrs. Stolz as "one of the best present-day novelists for older girls." *Horn Book* was even more enthusiastic in its review of *Ready or Not* (1953), a People's Book Club selection, calling her "our most outstanding writer of teen-age novels today." This novel was an honor book in the New York *Herald Tribune* Spring Book Festival and a selection of the People's Book Club. *In a Mirror,* her latest book, was published in the fall of 1953 by Harper and Brothers. This is the fifth of her novels for young people.

Successful as Mrs. Stolz's teen-age novels were, there was one reader who resisted them. For him—her young son Billy—she wrote her first children's book, *The Leftover Elf* (1952),

a charming story of the only elf left in a disbelieving world who wanders through Ireland on a search for someone who will believe in him.

The Stolz family lives a quiet suburban life in New Rochelle, New York, devoted to each other, to reading, to music (a high-fidelity sound system "is spreading around our home like a weed"), and to Mrs. Stolz's cooking. A friend of the family writes: "Once having dined at the Stolz home, one wonders if Molly will take time to write a cookbook in addition to children's books, adult novels, short stories, a play she has in mind, and the libretto of an opera she is planning." Mary Stolz is a strikingly pretty young woman with blue eyes, fair skin, and dark hair. She likes her life, but she is clear-eyed, not starry-eyed about it. "Like everyone else, we are sick with worry over a world which seems to be going to disaster in a handbasket, but we try to think clearly, hope to stand firmly. . . ."

STOREY, ROBERT G(ERALD) Dec. 4, 1893- Attorney

Address: b. c/o Republic Bank Building, Dallas, Texas; h. 7040 Tokalon Drive, Dallas, Texas

President of the American Bar Association for 1952-1953, and representing about 50,000 lawyers, Robert G. Storey is a Dallas, Texas attorney and also is the dean of Southern Methodist University Law School. In his early public career Storey rose from the position of city attorney in Troup to assistant attorney general of Texas, and later became special assistant district attorney in Dallas. As a Colonel in the United States Army Air Forces Intelligence he gained attention as executive trial counsel to Justice Robert H. Jackson in the Nüremberg trial of major war criminals in 1945-1946.

In recent years Storey has been interested in the improvement of legal education, the improvement of the American system of justice, and in what he regards as the world struggle for survival between the American and the Soviet judicial systems. "To maintain and improve our sovereign judicial system is the front-line responsibility of the organized bar," he declared at a Judicial Conference in June, 1953.

Robert Gerald Storey was born in Greenville, Texas on December 4, 1893, the son of Frank Wilson and Mary Edith (Thomson) Storey. He studied at Southern Methodist University and at the University of Texas, receiving his B.A. degree in 1914. Admitted to the Texas bar in 1914, he held the position of city attorney in Troup, Texas, for three years. In 1917 he was appointed assistant county attorney for Smith County, Texas.

The young attorney's career was interrupted by the entry of the United States into World War I; he saw service (1918-1919) as a second lieutenant of heavy artillery. After his return to civilian life, in addition to devoting himself to his private practice, he became active in the American Legion, serving as a member of its

Gittings

ROBERT G. STOREY

National Executive Committee in 1921 and 1922.

Reentering public service in 1921, he was assistant attorney general of Texas in charge of all criminal appeals until 1923. He served in 1924 as special assistant district attorney in Dallas, Texas, where he has since made his home, and where in 1934 he became a senior partner in the law firm of Storey, Armstrong and Steger.

Storey was a delegate to the International Convention on Comparative Law at the Hague in 1932. After the outbreak of World War II, he went to England at the height of the blitz as a representative of the American Bar Association to report on the condition of English solicitors and barristers. On the day of the bombing of Pearl Harbor, according to one report, he was studying home defense in England "for the benefit of the Lone Star State."

Following the entry of the United States into the war, Storey, who had been active in the National Guard, was named in 1942 a Colonel in the Air Corps G-2 section. For his war service he received the Legion of Merit for Combat Intelligence Service in the Mediterranean Theater of Operations, and the Bronze Star for work on war crimes in Bulgaria. After the war Colonel Storey worked on the preliminary negotiations for the Four Power Agreement (signed by Great Britain, France, the United States, and the Union of Soviet Socialist Republics in London, on August 8, 1945) for a charter of the International Military Tribunal that was to try the major Axis war criminals at Nüremberg. The Agreement, later also signed by nineteen other nations, was described by Justice Robert H. Jackson as "a basic charter in the International Law of the future." In a review of the book *The Nüremberg Trial and Aggressive War.* by Sheldon Glueck (Knopf, 1946) Storey wrote: "Having worked

with Dr. Glueck in the early stages of the negotiations of the International Agreement and Charter for the Nüremberg trial, I realized his initial doubts about the waging of aggressive war being a punishable crime. I must confess this was the only question that troubled me—it was new, debatable and uncertain." Storey adds, however, that after analysis of "the convincing evidence from captured documents of the enemy," he, like the rest of Dr. Glueck's staff, became convinced that "the planning and waging of aggressive war in violation of a treaty was a crime for which the guilty could be punished."

Early in November 1945 Colonel Storey was appointed executive trial counsel under Justice Jackson, Chief of Counsel for the United States on the war crimes trial staff. As reported in the New York *Times* (November 7, 1945), Storey would be assisted by a special panel of nine, and charged with various duties designed to expedite the presentation of the prosecution's case. As he later recalled the events of the trial, Storey noted that the "real problem" was "to sort out and use the most outstanding evidence" since the defendants had been "great record keepers." Two thousand documents were introduced, and the Americans alone, he recalled, had forty-five briefs, many running into hundreds of pages.

The trial was completed September 1, 1946, and in October, eleven of the defendants, including Field Marshal Herman Goering and Joachim von Ribbentrop, were sentenced to be executed.

After leaving the Army in 1947 Storey became dean of the law school of Southern Methodist University at the same time continuing with his private practice in Dallas. One of his tasks was to provide leadership in the development of the Southwestern Legal Center, organized on the campus of Southern Methodist University in April 1947 by a group of businessmen, lawyers and educators, and sponsored and financed by the university and the Southwestern Legal Foundation. (Storey was named president of the latter in 1948.) New buildings for the center were to be erected at a cost of $2,000,000.

As Storey conceived of its functions, the center was designed "to modernize legal education" as well as to provide "a 'clearing house' for legal problems." It would stimulate research, conduct institutes, conferences and seminars on subjects of special interest to the southwest—oil and gas law, for example.

In a report of a survey he had made among ninety-six law schools on the development of law centers (*Southwestern Law Journal,* Fall, 1950) Storey argued that modern law centers were a natural nucleus to bring together law schools, practicing lawyers and bar associations, thus providing continuing education for the bar, and improving both the quality of legal education and the administration of justice.

In a description of the operation of the legal aid clinic at the Southwestern Legal Center (*Journal of Legal Education,* Summer, 1951), Storey told how the clinic provided practical training for law students, who, under faculty supervision, cared for cases referred to the clinic. He also offered another argument for such clinics: "The legal profession must guarantee equality of justice. In practical terms that means an adequate system of legal aid offices."

Storey has long been active in Bar Association activities: he was president of the Dallas Bar Association in 1934, chairman of the Section of Legal Education of the American Bar Association from 1938 to 1940, and a delegate to the Assembly of the American Bar Association in 1947-48. He also represented the Inter-American Bar Association in Havana in 1941, and in Lima, Peru, in 1948, and became a member of the Council of the Inter-American Bar Association in 1947.

Elected president of the Texas Bar Association in 1948, at the end of his one-year term, in August 1949, he reported on the "reforms in which our State Bar has participated this year," and urged continuing work along similar lines by the 10,000 lawyers of the Texas State Bar. The five points he stressed were continuing cooperation in a survey of the legal profession, designed not to "whitewash" mistakes but to recommend necessary changes; continuing education of lawyers after graduation; free and low cost legal service along the lines of the Legal Aid Bureaus that had already been established in many Texas cities; criminal law revision (he noted the recent creation of a Texas Criminal Law Commission to rewrite and recodify out-of-date criminal laws); and reforms in judicial selection and tenure of members of higher courts.

From 1949 to 1952 Storey was a member of the Board of Governors of the American Bar Association. In September 1952 the Association elected him president for a year's term. Storey outlined a five-point program for the organization's seventy-fifth year (the ABA was founded in 1878). He urged (1) the development of ABA property in Chicago as the American Bar Center, providing a library and research programs, and a clearing house for research projects in law over the nation, thus preventing duplication of effort.

Arguing that the ABA's 50,000 members, or one-fourth of the lawyers in the United States, were not a sufficiently large body, Storey urged (2) "unit" membership, by which a member accepted by a local association would be billed for local, state and national dues. (3) He advocated that lawyers pay a small sum annually "to provide indemnity for losses of clients' money entrusted to members of our professional organizations," thus providing insurance against the rare lawyer who embezzled his client's funds.

He urged (4) the extension of low cost and free legal assistance to those unable to pay and of low income in programs administered by Bar Associations, without Government subsidies. He emphasized (5) that lawyers must take "an unselfish interest" in local, state and national governments, and the international scene. "Lawyers should asume their obligation of leadership to preserve our constitutional form of Government and improve our independent judiciary and legal profession . . .

[and] lead in the study and interpretation of the principles at issue in the cold and hot war between the free world and the Communists."

At the annual dinner of the New York County Lawyers' Association in December 1952 Storey reviewed some of these points, and also advocated, as he has done at other public meetings, the ABA plan for selection of State judges by a combined appointive and elective system without political campaigning; an increase in salaries of Federal and State judges; maintenance of judicial independence as a check on excesses of administrative power, and better training for lawyers, especially in ideals of public service.

In 1952 also Storey was named a Member of Council of the International Bar Association. His view of the lawyer's responsibilities on the world scene appeared in the legal publication *Dicta* (November, 1952) in an article entitled "Impact of World Conditions on the Legal Profession." After reviewing the modern history of the legal profession he compared the two "remaining dominant legal systems," the Anglo-American and the Soviet. The latter, he pointed out, considered law "a tool of the State," and saw the protection of the right of the individual as subordinate.

"With the worldwide conflict between the free and Soviet worlds, and with the system of justice at issue, we must improve our legal system," he concluded. Reforms which he suggested included more speedy and effective procedures to terminate both civil and criminal litigation, and the establishment of the ABA plan for selection of judges without direct decision by the voters. He also discussed the cold war, based on his recent personal observations in Berlin, Jerusalem and Korea.

In announcing the appointment of Herbert R. O'Connor as chairman of the ABA's Special Commttee on Communist Tactics, Strategy and Objectives in March 1953, Storey noted that the association was "giving major emphasis to the responsibility of lawyers to become informed about the evils of communism and to lead in making them conscious of the threat to our institutions, including the judiciary and legal profession" (New York *Times,* March 9, 1953).

Storey is also director of the Southwestern Bell Telephone Company, Chairman of the Board of the Lakewood State Bank, and director and general counsel of three insurance companies. He was president of the Park Board of the City of Dallas from 1939 to 1942. A member of the Kiwanis Club, he served as president of this group in 1927, and Governor of the Kiwanis Texas-Oklahoma District in 1931. He is also a 32d degree Mason and a Shriner. He is a member of the Christian (Disciples of Christ) Church. Texas Christian University awarded him an LL.D. degree in 1947.

He was married in July 1917 to Frances Hazel Porter. Their two sons, Robert G., Jr., and Charles P. Storey, are both attorneys in the law firm in which their father is a partner. At the 75th Annual Convention in Boston in August, 1953, Storey was succeeded by William

STOREY, ROBERT G.—*Continued*

J. Jameson of Billings, Montana, as president of the American Bar Association for 1954-55.

The high responsibility of lawyers to bring about justice was stressed by Storey as he delivered the opening address which launched the diamond jubilee anniversary of the American Bar Association. "As I have come to know my fellow lawyers in every State of the Union more intimately during the past year," he told the 6,000 delegates, "so have I been reassured that the essential spirituality of the American lawyer is as strong today as it was when the lawyers of colonial America led the nation to its freedom, and drafted the charters of its independence and of its government.

"I have seen," he continued, "that manifestation of spirituality—the selfless service to community, state, and nation—in every region of the land. . . .We have not yet found the key to universal peace, nor have we built a temple of justice ·for all mankind." He concluded: "Let us give of our best efforts, individually and through the legal profession, to establish a society based upon morality, dedicated to justice, and tempered by mercy. Each lawyer must assume his share of the burden in the constant effort to improve the administration of justice" (Christian Science *Monitor,* August 24, 1953).

References

Michigan State Bar Journal 27:9-10 S '48
N Y Sun p26 N 9 '45
N Y Times p10 N 7 '45
Tennessee Law Review 25:188-9 D '46
Who's Who in America, 1952-53
Who's Who in the South and Southwest (1952)

STRATTON, WILLIAM G(RANT) Feb. 26, 1914- Governor of Illinois

Address: b. State Capitol, Springfield, Ill.; h. Executive Mansion, Springfield, Ill.

Elected in November 1952 as Governor of Illinois, Republican William G. Stratton succeeded Adlai E. Stevenson on January 12, 1953. Earlier, in the State government Stratton had been Treasurer for two terms and in the Federal government had twice represented Illinois as Congressman at large in the House of Representatives. In the Eightieth Congress he served on the House Committee on Banking and Currency and sponsored a much-contested bill providing for immigration of 400,000 European displaced persons to the United States.

William Grant Stratton was born in Ingleside, Lake County, Illinois, on February 26, 1914, one of two sons of William J. and Zula (Van Wormer) Stratton. His mother taught school, and his father was prominent in Republican circles in Illinois, having been the first Director of Conservation in the State and later Secretary of State of Illinois. For his early education William attended public schools in Ingleside and later the Gurnee (Illinois) High School, from which he was graduated in

1930. At the University of Arizona in Tucson he majored in political science and was a member of the Arizona National Guard during his last two years. Returning to Ingleside after his graduation in 1934 with the B.A. degree, he worked as a salesman there and in Morris, Illinois, for the next five years.

During these years Stratton was a delegate to several Republican State conventions. Nominated in 1940 by his party for the office of Congressman at large for the State, he campaigned, it is reported, in 95 counties and during the last three months of the contest he made an average of eight speeches a day. He was elected to the Seventy-seventh Congress "by polling more votes than any other Republican in the House," his vote topping that of Presidential candidate Wendell Willkie in Illinois. In the 1941 session the voting record of Stratton, the youngest member of the Congress, included negative votes on lend-lease, on arming merchant ships, on extending military service eighteen months, on the ship seizure bill, and on amendments to the neutrality act. On six key issues chosen by *Editorial Research Reports* as indicative of support of or opposition to the Administration, Stratton's score was two "no records" and four votes against the Democratic Administration. In the second session of the Seventy-seventh Congress (May to October, 1942) he supported a bill proposing a cut in the Works Progress Administration appropriation and opposed continuance of the Civilian Conservation Corps, two New Deal agencies. Other issues which he favored were an emergency anti-inflation bill, an anti-poll tax bill, and a bill authorizing the drafting of teen-agers into the armed forces. His committee assignments during this term were the Civil Service Committee, the Committee for the District of Columbia, and the Flood Control Committee.

As Treasurer of Illinois, to which post he was elected in 1942, he served as chief fiscal officer, handling a billion dollars of State funds during his two-year term. During this time he was also a member of the Illinois Public Aid Commission, which cared for underprivileged citizens. In 1945 he entered the United States Navy with the rank of lieutenant (j.g.) and saw service in the Pacific theater. While he was returning to the United States in April 1946 from a tour of duty abroad, Stratton learned from a radio broadcast that he had again received the Republican nomination for Congressman at large, friends having placed his name on the ballot. His opponent in the November election was Mrs. Emily Taft Douglas, wife of Illinois' Senator Paul Douglas, who in the previous Congressional election (1944) had defeated her Republican opponent, Stephen A. Day, by a plurality greater than the 142,000 plurality the State gave Presidential candidate Franklin D. Roosevelt. Stratton won the 1946 contest by 367,000 votes. At the time it was said he brought "a resolute isolationism and conservatism back into the House" (*United States News & World Report* November 15, 1946).

His record in the Eightieth Congress again one of party allegiance, Stratton voted to override at least six significant Presidential vetos. In 1947 he supported a bill limiting the Presidency to two terms (February), a measure to restore cuts in farm funds (May), a rent control extension bill (May), and opposed the Greek-Turkish aid bill (May). During the second session (1948) he voted "yea" on the Republican tax reduction bill (February), the $6 billion foreign aid authorization (March), the tidelands oil bill (April), the subversive activities control bill (May), and on the displaced persons bill (June). Throughout his term in the Eightieth Congress he was a member of the House Committee on Banking and Currency.

The displaced persons bill that Stratton introduced in 1947 became the center of a heated controversy. There were at that time about a million people who were unable or reluctant, largely for political or religious reasons, to return to their homelands; 850,000 of them were living in UNRRA camps in Germany, Austria, and Italy. The Stratton bill proposed allowing 100,000 of these persons a year, for the following four years, to enter the United States outside of quota regulations, with priority given to relatives of United States citizens and members of the armed forces. The bill, which also called for maintenance of existing protective restrictions of the immigration laws as to health, morals, economic status, and political integrity, was sponsored by the Citizens Committee on Displaced Persons, whose chairman was Earl G. Harrison, Dean of the University of Pennsylvania Law School and former Commissioner of Immigration and Naturalization. After being introduced by Stratton on April 1, 1947, the bill went to a subcommittee of the House Judiciary Committee, which held hearings on it from June 4 to July 18. Shelved by the subcommittee, it never came to the floor of the House for a vote.

Returning to Illinois State government after the expiration of his second term in Congress, Stratton, who had been the successful candidate of Secretary of State of Illinois in 1948, was re-elected State Treasurer in 1951 and the following year announced his candidacy for the Governorship. On November 4, 1952, he won a victory over Sherwood Dixon, Governor Adlai E. Stevenson's lieutenant governor, by at least 175,000 votes (*Time*) in an election in which Republican candidates gained almost all of the State offices in Illinois. At his inauguration on January 12, 1953, when he succeeded Stevenson, the defeated Democratic candidate for the Presidency, Stratton pledged to cut waste in State administration and to prevent an increase in taxes. The new Governor, who had said that if elected he would be available to citizens at all times, began in late February to hold a weekly open house in Springfield to give people an opportunity to speak with him directly about complaints and suggestions relating to State affairs. During the first few months of his administration he was much occupied with patronage, preferring so far as possible to handle personally appointments to 20,000 political offices, than delegate the task to department heads and local party chairmen. Governor Stratton told James K. Sparkman of

Herbert Georg Studio
WILLIAM G. STRATTON

the *Christian Science Monitor* that since government efficiency was the "keynote of his policy" he ranked patronage high in importance in his administration.

The Governor is a Mason and a Shriner and member of the American Legion, the Veterans of Foreign Wars, the Lions, the Eagles, and the Delta Chi fraternity. Stratton and his wife, the former Marion Hook, who were married on September 4, 1934, have two daughters, Sandra Jane and Diana Joy. The Governor's favorite recreations are golf and bowling. His church is the Methodist.

References

American Magazine p82 Je '41
Biographical Directory of the American Congress, 1774-1949 (1950)
Congressional Directory (1948)
Who's Who in America, 1952-53
Who's Who in Chicago and Illinois (1950)
Who's Who in United States Politics (1950)

STRAVINSKY, IGOR (FËDOROVICH)
(strá-vĭn'skĭ) June 17, 1882- Composer; conductor

Address: b. c/o Boosey and Hawkes, 30 W. 57th St., New York 19; h. 1260 N. Wetherly Dr., Hollywood 28, Calif.

NOTE: This biography supersedes the article which appeared in *Current Biography* in 1940.

It has been said of Igor Stravinsky that "no other living composer has made a more notable contribution to the music of our Western world." Born in Russia, he achieved international fame as a musical innovator with *L'Oiseau de Feu,*

Gene Fenn

IGOR STRAVINSKY

Petrouchka, and *Le Sacre du Printemps,* which were written for Diaghilev's Ballets Russes before 1914. During World War I he lived in Switzerland and then in 1920 settled in France. From this time on his music developed increasingly in the direction of classicism. Since 1939 he has made his permanent home in the United States and he is an American citizen. His first full-length opera, *The Rake's Progress,* received its American première at the Metropolitan Opera in February 1953.

Igor Fëdorovich Stravinsky was born on the feast day of St. Igor, June 17, 1882, in Oranienbaum, near St. Petersburg, Russia. His father Fëdor Ignatevich Stravinsky, partly of Polish descent, came from an old and noble family bearing the name of Soulima-Stravinsky; his mother was from Little Russia. Since his father was the leading bass singer at the Imperial Opera in St. Petersburg, young Igor grew up in a musical atmosphere. He started taking piano lessons when he was nine years old and soon developed a taste for improvisation, but his parents had no thought of training him as a professional musician, and at the age of seventeen he was sent to study law at the University of St. Petersburg. It was agreed that he could have harmony lessons on the side, and he began to teach himself counterpoint at this time.

In the summer of 1902 Stravinsky showed some of his early efforts at composition to Nikolai Rimski-Korsakov, who encouraged him to continue his studies in harmony and counterpoint. Upon graduating from the university three years later, he decided to devote himself entirely to music and he received private lessons in composition and orchestration from Rimski-Korsakov until the composer's death in 1908. The first of Stravinsky's compositions of which there is record was an unpublished Piano Sonata (1903-04), but his official Opus 1

was the *Symphony in E Flat* (1905-07), reportedly written in the academic style of Alexander Glazunov. His next two orchestral works, *Scherzo Fantastique* (1907-08) and *Feu d'Artifice* (1908), reflected the influence of the French impressionists. The first performances of these pieces in the winter of 1909 attracted the attention of the noted impresario, Sergei Diaghilev, who commissioned a new work from Stravinsky for a season of Russian ballet he was planning to present in Paris. This marked the beginning of an artistic collaboration that was to last for twenty years, during which time Diaghilev's Ballets Russes produced most of Stravinsky's new works for the stage. The first of these was *L'Oiseau de Feu,* a ballet based on a Russian fairy tale, which had its Paris première on June 25, 1910, and overnight established the unknown young composer as a musical celebrity. Although the score remained within the picturesque descriptive style of the Russian nationalist school, it proved, as one critic remarked, that Stravinsky "could rival, if not excel, his master in brilliance and glamour of orchestration."

The innovations that won for Stravinsky "the incontestable leadership of modern Western music" were first revealed in his score for *Petrouchka.* According to Aaron Copland (*Our New Music*), they included the exploitation of *ostinato* and unusual rhythms, the bold use of unconventional harmonies (including the introduction of bitonality for the first time), and an orchestral timbre in which the tonal values of the various instruments and choirs were clearly distinguishable in the orchestral mass. The "dynamic verve" of this new style represented a revolt against the lush vagueness of late romanticism and impressionism. *Petrouchka,* a ballet about puppets at a Russian carnival, was first performed on June 13, 1911, with Waslaw Nijinsky dancing the title role, and immediately acclaimed as a masterpiece. It is generally agreed, however, that the composer's "most strikingly original" work is *Le Sacre du Printemps,* a ballet representing pagan rites in ancient Russia, for which Nijinsky devised the choreography. At the historic Paris première on May 29, 1913, the music provoked a violent demonstration in the theater and outraged listeners claimed that its pounding rhythms and harsh dissonances represented an attempt by Stravinsky "to destroy music as an art." Now considered "a landmark in the history of music," *Le Sacre* has been called "the most important symphonic creation of the twentieth century." Early in 1914, shortly before visiting Russia for the last time, Stravinsky completed *Le Rossignol,* a three-act opera based on the Andersen fairy tale, which he had begun six years before. The score was later converted into a ballet, *Le Chant du Rossignol,* which was staged in 1920.

The outbreak of World War I found Stravinsky living in Switzerland, where he remained for the next six years. During this period he began to experiment with various chamber orchestra combinations, but vocal music was his chief preoccupation and Russian folk material continued to be his main source of inspiration. Between 1914 and 1918 he worked intermittently on *Les Noces*, a ballet-cantata depicting a Russian village wedding, and another five years elapsed before he decided on the final scoring for voices, four pianos, and seventeen percussions instruments. Rollo Myers has praised "the essential and profound originality of this masterpiece." Another ballet based on Russian folk lore was *Renard* (1916-17), a burlesque tale for dancers or acrobats, vocal soloist, and chamber orchestra. Neither of these works was produced until after the war, but in 1918 Stravinsky collaborated with the Swiss writer C. F. Ramuz on *L'Histoire du Soldat*, a theater work for dancers, actors, a narrator, and seven instrumentalists, which was presented in Lausanne that year. Described by Alexandre Tansman as "one of the most personal and engaging works of our time," *L'Histoire du Soldat* revealed the composer's interest in various popular dances, including ragtime.

At the conclusion of the war, Diaghilev suggested that Stravinsky write a ballet based on some manuscript fragments by the eighteenth century composer, Pergolesi. The result was *Pulcinella* (1919-20), which marks the beginning of the so-called "neoclassical" phase of Stravinsky's musical development. After he settled in France in 1920, he became increasingly preoccupied with the composition of absolute music written in the various classical forms in which the style and spirit was akin to the masters of the baroque period. To this category belong the polyphonic Octet for wind instruments (1922-23), *Piano Concerto* (1923-24), Piano Sonata (1924), and *Sérénade* in A for piano (1925). The last of his works to use both a Russian subject and text was the one-act opera buffa *Mavra* (1921-22), based on a tale by Pushkin. During the early 1920's Stravinsky embarked upon a subsidiary career as a conductor and piano soloist playing his own works, and in 1925 he made his first concert tour of the United States. A significant landmark in the evolution of his neoclassical style was *Oedipus Rex* (1926-27), an opera-oratorio adapted from Sophocles by Jean Cocteau. The French text was then translated into Latin in order to attain "the least temporal and most universal means of expression." This was followed by the ballet *Apollon Musagètes*, which had been commissioned for a festival of chamber music held at the Library of Congress, in Washington, in April 1928. According to Abraham Skulsky (*Musical America*), *Apollon* was the first of Stravinsky's works in which melody was the most important element. That same year saw the première of *Le Baiser de la Fée*, written for the Paris season of the dancer Ida Rubinstein. For this allegorical ballet, "inspired by the Muse of Tchaikovsky," Stravinsky borrowed most of his thematic material from that composer's works.

The 1930's were devoted to a further consolidation of the classical style. Prominent among Stravinsky's works of this decade was the *Symphonie de Psaumes*, composed "for the Glory of God" and dedicated to the Boston Symphony on the occasion of its fiftieth anniversary. Philip Hale judged this choral symphony to be "one of the sincerest expressions of Stravinsky's genius." The composer next wrote the *Violin Concerto* (1931) and *Duo Concertante* (1932) for the violinist Samuel Dushkin, with whom he gave a number of recitals. Then, at the request of Ida Rubinstein, he undertook the composition of *Persephone*, a "melo-drama" for soloist, chorus, and orchestra, spoken recitation, miming, and dancing, set to a poem by André Gide. In his monograph on the composer, Eric White called the work "a pure and lucid example of the classical spirit working with full objective awareness and perfect control." In June 1934, two months after the Paris première of *Persephone*, Stravinsky became a French citizen. He made his second concert tour of the United States early in 1935, and during the remainder of that year completed an important *Concerto for Two Pianos*, without orchestral accompaniment. Two years later, he visited the United States again to conduct the world première at the Metropolitan Opera House of *Jeu de Cartes*, a satirical ballet based on a poker game, which had been commissioned by the American Ballet Company.

The composer returned to the United States to accept the Charles Eliot Norton Chair of Poetry at Harvard University for the academic year of 1939-40. After the fall of France, he settled in Hollywood, becoming an American citizen in December 1945. The critics have discerned in Stravinsky's recent work a tendency "to consolidate all his findings and to restate them in new terms," as well as "a new mellowness appropriate to his maturity." The *Symphony in C* (1939-40), composed for the fiftieth anniversary of the Chicago Symphony Orchestra, is said to present "a synthesis of his earlier classical usages," while the *Symphony in Three Movements* (1942-45) is "a summary of all the main characteristics exhibited in his total output up to that time." Of Stravinsky's score for *Orpheus*, which was given its première by the Ballet Society of New York in 1948, Robert Sabin observed in *Musical America*: "a supremely eloquent melos . . . treated with miraculous economy and purity of design." The *Mass in C* (1948) for male chorus and wind instruments reportedly shows the influence of his present enthusiasm for the Flemish contrapuntalists of the fifteenth century. Among the other works written during this decade are *Danses Concertantes* (1941-42), which the Ballet Russe de Monte Carlo staged in 1944; *Circus Polka* (1942), commissioned by Ringling Brothers for an elephant ballet; *Scènes de Ballet* (1944), written for Billy Rose's Broadway revue, *The Seven Lively Arts*; and *Ebony Concerto* (1945), for Woody Herman's swing band.

At an exhibition in 1947 Stravinsky came across *The Rake's Progress*, a set of engravings by the eighteenth-century English painter, William Hogarth, and the series at once appeared to him as the successive scenes of an opera. He asked the poet W. H. Auden to write an original English libretto using the Hogarth series as a point of departure. The text was completed in the spring of 1948 and the composition of the music occupied Stravinsky for the next three years. *The Rake's Progress* received its world première in Venice

STRAVINSKY, IGOR—*Continued*

on September 11, 1951, and was introduced in the United States by the Metropolitan Opera in February 1953. A moral fable about a young rake's downfall and redemption, the opera returned to the traditional form of arias, duets, ensembles, choruses, concerted numbers, and other set pieces, linked by recitative. To Colin Mason (*Music & Letters*), it seemed "the greatest and most important neoclassic work that has yet been produced," and Nicolas Nabokov wrote in the New York *Herald Tribune* that it was "an unquestionable masterpiece whose Mozartian dimensions and transparent beauty have not been matched by any other work for the lyric theater in the first half of our century." In May 1952, shortly before celebrating his seventieth birthday, Stravinsky made his first public appearance in Paris in thirteen years, at the International Exposition of the Arts of the Twentieth Century, where his return was greeted with "a tremendous ovation." Six months later his second work set to an English text, the *Cantata on Anonymous Elizabethan Songs,* was presented for the first time.

In addition to the works already mentioned, Stravinsky has written: *Symphonies d'Instruments à Vent* (1920); *Capriccio* for piano and orchestra (1929); *Dumbarton Oaks Concerto,* in E Flat, for chamber orchestra (1937-38); *Norwegian Moods* (1942) and *Ode* (1943) for orchestra; Sonata for Two Pianos (1943-44); *Concerto in D* for strings (1946); works for string quartet, songs, and piano pieces. Most of his compositions have been recorded. As a guest conductor, he has led nearly all the major orchestras of Europe and America. He is the author of an autobiographical *Chroniques de ma Vie* (1935), and the text of his Harvard lectures was published in 1942 under the title *Poétique Musicale*. Both of these books have been translated into English.

While critics are in agreement about the originality and importance of Stravinsky's Russian-inspired works, there is considerable difference of opinion over the value of his later output. His detractors maintain that he has "retired into a self-made world of cerebral austerity from whence at certain intervals he offers a displeasing *pastiche*—a synthetic rehash of previously existing formulas" (*The Chesterian*). His champions find beneath the variety of his styles, forms, and techniques "a line of development that has been guided by a unified purpose." In the opinion of Arthur Berger (*Stravinsky in the Theatre*), it is "the restatement of organic principles, rather than the evocation of the past" that provides the real differentia of Stravinsky's classicism. The reason why Stravinsky's works seem "so fresh and new" and why he has become "one of the great reformers of music," according to Henry Boys (*The Score*), lies in "the intensity and persistence with which his genius seeks answers to its problems in the very bases of music."

A member of the National Institute of Arts and Letters, Stravinsky was awarded its Gold Medal for Music in 1951. On January 11, 1906, he married his cousin, Catherine Nossenko, and they had four children: Theodore, a painter; Ludmilla, now deceased; Sviatoslav

(Soulima), a well-known pianist; and Milene. After the death of his first wife, he married Vera de Bossett Sudekine, a former dancer with the Diaghilev troupe, on March 9, 1940. The composer, who has been called "a wiry, intense man," stands about five feet four inches tall and has light brown hair. Descriptions of his personality emphasize his energy and vitality, his sharp wit, and his "love for order and method." His faith is the Russian Orthodox. He always composes at the piano, slowly, in what has been called "a day-to-day exploratory manner." "My only system," he has remarked, "is my ear. I use no other guide."

References

Atlan 184:21-7 N '49
Life 34:151 Mr 23 '53
N Y Times Mag p20 Je 15 '52 por
New Yorker 10:23-8 Ja 5 '35
Tempo No. 8 Summer '48
Time 52:46-51 Jl 26 '48 pors
Armitage, M. ed. Igor Strawinsky (1936)
Baker, T. ed. Biographical Dictionary of Musicians (1940)
Collaer, P. Strawinsky (1930)
Corle, E. ed. Igor Stravinsky (1949)
Dictionnaire Biographique Français Contemporain (1950)
Fleischer, H. Strawinsky (1931)
International Who's Who in Music (1951)
Lederman, M. ed. Stravinsky in the Theatre (1949)
Myers, R. H. Introduction to the Music of Stravinsky (1950)
Onnen, F. Stravinsky (1949)
Ramuz, C. F. Souvenirs sur Igor Strawinsky (1929)
Reis, C. Composers in America (1947)
Schaeffner, A. Strawinsky (1931)
Stravinsky, I. An Autobiography (1936); Poetics of Music (1947)
Tansman, A. Igor Stravinsky (1949)
Thompson, O. ed. International Cyclopedia of Music and Musicians (1946)
Who's Who (1952)
Who's Who in America, 1952-53
White, E. W. Stravinsky's Sacrifice to Apollo (1930); Stravinsky (1948)

STRUTHER, JAN June 6, 1901—July 20, 1953 Author; best known for *Mrs. Miniver*; born Joyce Anstruther in England; wrote poems, articles and short stories for periodicals; created Mrs. Miniver on request of the *Times* of London to do a story about an ordinary woman; gave lectures during war while living in New York; appeared on "Information Please" radio program; also wrote *The Glassblower and Other Poems, A Pocketful of Pebbles, Betsinda Dances and Other Poems, Sycamore Square and Other Verses, Try Anything Twice, Letters from Women of Britain,* and the *Modern Struwwelpeter.* See *Current Biography,* 1941.

Obituary

N Y Times p23 Jl 21 '53

STUMP, FELIX B(UDWELL) Dec. 15, 1894- United States Naval officer

Address: b. c/o Department of the Navy, The Pentagon, Washington 25, D.C.; h. 518 Stanley Ave., Clarksburg, W. Va.

Returning to the Pacific as commander of the entire Pacific Fleet, Vice-Admiral Felix B. Stump succeeded Admiral Arthur W. Radford, on July 10, 1953, to this post. In World War II Admiral Stump had commanded the second aircraft carrier *Lexington* which had one of the most illustrious records in the annals of flat tops. Following the war, he was in command of the Second Fleet with headquarters at Norfolk, Virginia.

Felix B. Stump in September 1952 was the senior officer of the eighty United States ships participating in the North Atlantic Treaty Organization's first naval maneuver, Exercise Mainbrace, involving altogether about 200 ships, 1,000 aircraft, and 80,000 men from nine nations. From the time that he became a naval officer in 1917, Stump has been active in the air wing of the Navy, serving during the years immediately preceding World War II as commander of a scouting squadron and of a seaplane tender.

The son of John Sutton and Lily Ragland (Budwell) Stump, Felix Budwell Stump was born December 15, 1894, in Clarksburg, West Virginia. When he had completed his early studies at the public school in Clarksburg and the Werntz Preparatory School in Annapolis, Maryland, he received an appointment to the United States Naval Academy (Annapolis) in 1913. Four years later he was granted his B.S. degree from Annapolis and at the same time his commission as an ensign in the United States Navy. From the gunboat *Yorktown*, to which he had been first assigned, he was transferred in December 1917 to the U.S.S. *Cincinnati*, then on escort duty, and six months later became its navigator, serving as such through the last months of World War I and until the cruiser was placed out of commission in the spring of 1919. After a brief assignment on the U.S.S. *Alabama*, in September 1919 he began flight training at the Naval Air Station, Pensacola, Florida, which resulted in his designation as Naval Aviator in May 1920. Remaining for two additional months at the Pensacola Station for instruction in the NC seaplanes (the large flying boats of that period), he was in July assigned to duty on the U.S.S. *Harding*, working with the Atlantic NC Plane Division.

From this tour of service he moved in December 1920 to the Naval Air Station Hampton Roads, Virginia, and a year and a half later (June 1922) to the postgraduate school at Annapolis for instruction in aeronautical engineering. He continued his engineering studies at the Massachusetts Institute of Technology in Cambridge, where he took his Master of Science degree in June 1924, and then studied further at the Naval Aircraft Factory in Philadelphia and at the Bureau of Aeronautics in Washington, D.C. He was assigned in December 1924 to Torpedo Squadron Two, an experimental naval project based on the carrier

VICE-ADM. FELIX B. STUMP

Langley, operating with the Aircraft Squadron of the Battle Fleet. From June 1927 to September 1930 Stump served as assembly and repair officer of the Hampton Roads Naval Air Station, afterward being transferred to the command of scouting squadrons on cruisers (1930-32). In the latter assignment he was first with Scouting Squadron Nine and then with Squadron Ten; he also assumed additional duties on the staff of the Commander of Cruisers of the Scouting Force. For two years beginning in April 1932, Stump worked in the maintenance division of the Bureau of Aeronautics in the Navy Department.

When Stump returned to sea duty in June 1934, he began a two-year tour as commanding officer of Scouting Squadron Two, based on the flagship U.S.S. *Saratoga*. In June 1936 he became navigator aboard the U.S.S. *Lexington* and then in 1937 went back to Washington, D.C., to head the maintenance division of the Bureau of Aeronautics until May 1940. During the months preceding America's entrance into World War II, Stump was executive officer of the U.S.S. *Enterprise* (1940-41) and after a brief assignment with the Fleet Air Detachment at the San Diego Naval Air Station in California, he assumed command in September 1941 of the U.S.S. *Langley*, a seaplane tender, which he continued to command until joining the staff of the Commander in Chief of the Asiatic Fleet in January 1942.

He served in command of the Combined Operations and Intelligence Center of the American-British-Dutch-Australian High Command in Java, and left Java for the United States just ahead of the Japanese occupation of the island. From May to November 1942 he was Air Officer of the Western Sea Frontier.

Stump, who had been present at the Bethlehem Steel Company plant at the time that the new U.S.S. *Lexington* was being fitted out,

STUMP, FELIX B.—*Continued*

assumed command in February 1943 of the aircraft carrier upon her commissioning and directed the war service of the ship until, torpedoed by enemy planes in December 1943, it was forced to return to the United States for major repairs. The carrier's first notable military engagement came in September 1943 when it fired on the Japanese-held Gilbert Islands; it then moved to action against Wake Island the next month. In November the U.S.S. *Lexington* became part of a task group operating off the Gilberts to neutralize Japanese air power and to cover operations of the American Fleet and ground units in the Tarawa, Makin, and Apamama area. The carrier moved on with the invasion force which raided the centers of Japanese airpower in the Marshalls. As commander of the *Lexington* Stump was awarded the Silver Star Medal, his citation noting his "conspicuoųs gallantry and intrepidity . . . in sustained offensive operations against the enemy," in which he "boldly fought off persistent aerial attacks for more than two hours before he could retire from the combat area" with his badly damaged ship. In April 1944 the naval officer assumed command of Carrier Division 24, which functioned as the air support group for the capture of the Southern Marianas the following summer. His carrier division then furnished air support to the amphibious attack groups landing troops on the shore of Leyte Gulf in the Philippines. At the end of that year the task unit under his command gave air cover to convoys, battleships, cruisers, and destroyers operating in the occupation of Mindoro, in the Philippine Islands; and in January 1945 he commanded a task unit in the invasion of Luzon. From the latter part of March 1945 until May, Stump was in command of seven support carriers in the capture of Kerama Retto and Okinawa.

During the war Stump had become a Rear-Admiral and the recipient of a number of awards—a Legion of Merit with Combat "V" for "exceptionally meritorious conduct . . . during operations against enemy Japanese forces in the Mariana Islands"; a Navy Cross for "extraordinary heroism as Commander Task Unit . . . during the Battle of Samar Island [in which he] contributed in large measure to the sinking of several hostile ships"; and three Gold Stars (two in lieu of a second and third Legion of Merit and one in lieu of a second Navy Cross) for command of escort carriers engaged in the invasion of the Philippine Islands and Okinawa. At Okinawa he led his carrier task unit as air support for ground forces in almost 4,000 "daring neutralization strikes." Admiral Stump's other awards include a War Department Distinguished Service Medal, the Presidential Unit Citation Ribbon with two stars, the Philippine Liberation Ribbon with two bronze stars, the American Defense Service Medal with Fleet Clasp, the American Campaign Medal, the Asiatic-Pacific Campaign Medal with ten engagement stars, and the World War I and II Victory medals.

Stump returned to the United States in June 1945 to become Chief of Naval Air Technical Training, stationed first in Chicago, then in Pensacola, and later in Memphis, Tennessee. On November 1, 1948, he was promoted to his present rank of Vice-Admiral. The next month he assumed command of the Air Force for the Atlantic Fleet, continuing in this position until April 11, 1951, when he was appointed Commander of the Second Fleet, one of the principal operating forces of the United States Navy. As chief executive officer for the Atlantic Fleet Air Force, Stump spoke in May 1950 at a civilian orientation course at the Norfolk Naval Base in Virginia, where he emphasized the effectiveness of the aircraft-carrier task force as a weapon in war. To achieve the objectives of keeping war from American shores and of keeping communism out of Western Europe, Stump said, the United States must have full control of the seas. He explained that such control could come from the use of the aircraft-carrier force, since it served as a mobile airfield, capable of moving 1,400 miles within 48 hours, striking targets within that period separated by over 2000 miles, safe from atomic bomb total destruction because carriers were usually spaced at least a mile and one-half apart.

In September 1952 Stump was named the senior officer in tactical command afloat of the eighty United States ships participating in the twelve-day North Atlantic Treaty Organization naval maneuver known as Exercise Mainbrace, the largest Allied naval exercise ever held. About 200 ships—aircraft carriers, destroyers, submarines, battleships, and smaller craft—1,000 airplanes, and more than 80,000 men from nine nations took part in operations in the Norwegian and North seas. The exercises, simulating sea and land battles, were designed principally to give the Allies an opportunity for working together and developing common signal codes, gunnery practices, and refueling methods. It was agreed that an important political and psychological by-product of the exercise was to demonstrate that the Baltic Sea would not become a "Soviet Lake" if the Allies could prevent it and that naval forces could give "great assistance" in any future land battles in Europe. It was also reported that joint Allied naval doctrine and technique set forth in the newly published NATO manuals had worked "very well" in their first test.

When Stump took command of the Pacific Fleet in 1953, he also became Commander in Chief of the Pacific. In this latter position, Stump will have "operational control" of the combined Army, Navy and Air Force units in the Pacific Ocean, except for those areas under the Far East and Alaskan commands.

Stump married Myra Morgan on December 22, 1923; they had one son, John Morgan Stump. By his second marriage, to Elizabeth Smith, on August 11, 1937, he is the father of two children, Frances and Felix, Jr. Vice-Admiral Stump is a member of the Army and Navy Club of Washington.

Reference

N Y Times p 16 Jl 5 '53

Who's Who in America, 1952-53

SUGRUE, THOMAS (JOSEPH) May 7, 1907—Jan. 6, 1953 Author; radio commentator; reporter for the New York *Herald Tribune* (1931-34); staff writer for *American Magazine* (1934-38); his writing career handicapped by crippling illness; author of *Such Is the Kingdom* (1940), *Stranger in the Earth* (1948), *A Catholic Speaks His Mind* (1951), among other books, and of numerous book reviews and magazine articles; conducted a radio program over station WINS in New York (1947-48). See *Current Biography*, 1948.

Obituary

N Y Times p31 Ja 7 '53

SULLIVAN, A(LOYSIUS) M(ICHAEL) Aug. 9, 1896- Poet; advertising executive; editor

Address: b. c/o Dun & Bradstreet, Inc., 99 Church St., New York 8; h. R.D., Stanhope, N.J.

A. M. Sullivan's dual interests in the worlds of realism and of the imagination are evident from the fact that he is an associate editor of *Dun's Review,* (published by Dun & Bradstreet), an analyst of current economic trends and early history of trade in the United States, and that he has found time after a crowded day to write ten volumes of poetry.

Called the "bard Jekyll, and businessman Hyde", by Anna Fremantle in *Catholic World* (March 1953), Sullivan has been the president of the Poetry Society of America on five occasions, in 1939, 1940, 1941, and in 1950 and 1951. His poetry has appeared frequently in the *Saturday Review, Spirit* and a score of other magazines. His book of lyrics, *Incident in Silver* (McMullen, 1950), won the Catholic Press Citation in 1951. He conducted *The New Poetry Hour* on WOR from 1932 to 1940, and introduced three hundred poets to radio audiences.

Since 1934 he has been the director of public relations and advertising at Dun & Bradstreet; he wrote and supervised the company's documentary film, *Credit, Man's Confidence in Man,* in 1950. His book, *Opportunities in Retail Trade for Service Men* (Dun & Bradstreet, 1945), has had a printing of 200,000 copies.

Aloysius Michael Sullivan was born in Harrison, New Jersey, on August 9, 1896, the son of William Henry and Mary Elizabeth (Flynn) Sullivan. His ancestry is completely Irish, with roots in Kenmare, County Kerry, Ireland, and in Tipperary. His maternal great-grandfather was a stone mason and bridge builder, who came to America to erect railroad arches, some of which are in northern New Jersey. The poet describes his father as a gifted storyteller, in Irish a *seanachie*. Originally a steelworker, he later developed large areas of real estate in Essex County, New Jersey. The writer's mother had some artistic talent and inscribed many of the deeds of Hunterdon County, New Jersey, in copperplate script.

Sullivan was one of a family of twelve children, and his parents adopted two more. He was reared in Oxford Furnace, New Jersey, a small town in the State's northern hills. After attending local schools, he entered St. Benedict's Preparatory College in Newark, New Jersey, and was graduated in 1913. For the graduation issue of the school magazine he wrote his first poem "Alma Mater," which he describes as "a piece of pious doggerel" and the end of his poetry "for ten years."

At the age of sixteen he went to work for the General Electric Company in Newark, New Jersey, later for the Public Service Corporation, and in 1916 as a salesman for the Knabe Piano Company. A heart condition resulted in his rejection six times for military service during World War I.

Sullivan accepted a position as house organ editor in 1917 with the Submarine Boat Corporation at Port Newark, New Jersey and "watched a hundred and fifty cargo ships slide down the ways." Many night hours were spent writing short stories, including "Wings for an Eagle" which was later made into a radio play. Father John Henry O'Rourke, editor of the *Sacred Heart Messenger* bought one of these stories.

Aroused by the Easter Rebellion in Dublin, Ireland, in 1916, Sullivan began reading extensively in the history and literature of his ancestral country. He studied Gaelic for about four years, which later enabled him to read Gaelic poetry on his radio program.

Joining the staff of J. P. Muller & Co., an advertising agency in New York City, in 1924, for the next ten years he wrote industrial copy covering tugboats, diesel engines, automobile trucks, and airplanes. His serious interest in writing poetry was stimulated by a friend's comment that the Petrarchian sonnet was more difficult to write than the Shakespearean. "I searched back through Father Coppens' textbook of English literature to find the difference," Sullivan recalls, "then, for personal punishment set out to write 100 Petrarchian sonnets." These he produced at the rate of one a day for 100 days, and published in a volume called *Sonnets of a Simpleton* (D. S. Colyer, 1924), his first book. "This," he says, "arises to plague me on the second-hand book shelves."

A short lyric, "Shadows are Black," written during one sitting at the typewriter, brought Sullivan the Edward Coate Pinckney prize of $100 for poetry in 1926. Three years later he published a small brochure called *Progression and Other Poems* (The Chisholm Press, 1929), which contained one long philosophical poem and a few lyrics. Most of the poems had previously appeared in *The Century, Commonweal, The Circle, The Lantern,* and the New York *Herald Tribune.*

Elbows of the Wind (Kingsley Press, 1932), his "first serious volume" of verse, describes "the strident voice of one desiring to be heard above the pandemonium of the hour." Critic Shaemas O'Sheel of *Commonweal* (May 12, 1933) writes: "It is evident Mr. Sullivan carries a poet's quick eye, a poet's endless curiosity, and a poet's capacity for constant excite-

Globe Photos

A. M. SULLIVAN

ment around with him in all his daily voyaging of city streets. . . ."

The poet states he "saw in radio an opportunity to recapture for the bard some of the eloquence lost in cold type." After appearing on a poetry forum over WJZ in 1926 and on other occasions, Sullivan was invited on January 1, 1932, to conduct *The New Poetry Hour* over WOR on Sunday mornings. His original time of fifteen minutes was increased within six weeks to half an hour. He presented to the radio audience such well-known poets as Edgar Lee Masters, Tristram Coffin, Stephen Vincent Benét, and Padraic Colum.

In 1934, Sullivan accepted a position in the advertising and public relations department of Dun & Bradstreet, Inc., where he is now director of the division. He continued until 1940 his radio program over WOR, and later joined the Mutual Network. Sullivan answered more than ten thousand fan mail letters. On November 30, 1934, he wrote in an article "Radio and the Poet" for *Commonweal* that "radio is ushering back the age of the troubadour," and added that "poetry may have a minority audience, but it is a loyal and appreciative one."

By 1940 he had arranged for broadcasts by about three hundred poets. Although WOR gave him the time on the air, he spent more than $3,000 of his own money on his radio program. Many of his broadcasts, including some over NBC, WNYC and other radio stations and those especially written for poetic chorus, were recorded for use in high schools and colleges.

Describing the recordings made from Sullivan's radio broadcasts, another poet, Mark Van Doren, wrote: "The reading is very simple and convincing, entirely audible and intelligible, and altogether entertaining; it is modest but moving" (*Catholic World*, March, 1953). The chorals produced by A. M. Sullivan over

the Mutual Network appear in the poet's volume *Day in Manhattan* (Dutton, 1941). Ruth Lechlitner, critic for the New York *Herald Tribune* (February 15, 1942), writes that "like all good writers for radio, Mr. Sullivan makes use of strong action verbs, and of figures and images with a rich concrete visual texture."

A. M. Sullivan claims a preference for the old ballad meter as a poetic form. He has published two single ballad volumes, *Ballad of a Man Named Smith* (J. A. Decker, 1940) and *The Ballad of John Castner* (Fine Editions Press, 1943), and a collection relating to the American past called *Tim Murphy, Morgan Rifleman, and Other Ballads* (D. X. McMullen Co., 1947). His feeling for locale is represented in a small book *New Jersey Hills*.

The poet's verses interpreting science and industry appeared in a collection, *This Day and Age* (*Dun's Review*, 1943) and *Stars and Atoms Have no Size* (Dutton, 1946). The author states he does not deal in equations but looks upon the machine "as a fruit of man's conquest of nature." Of *Stars and Atoms Have No Size*, Gerald McDonald writes in the *Library Journal* (February 15, 1947) "these poems . . . have a surprising kinship with the work of the great metaphysical poets; they are clear, clean poems of the scientific mind, without metaphor or symbolism."

In his article, "The Poet in Search of His Audience," (*Saturday Review*, July 21, 1951), Sullivan states: "When the poet puts aside the garb of the pundit and the sibyl and becomes a child again to describe the iridescence of a soap bubble he may find his way back to a lost audience." He finds that children "think in images. . . .They are natural poets until they learn idiom and acquire the patterns of daily speech . . . [which often confuse meanings]." The poet thinks that poetry and the theatre are in for "a thorough regeneration through the younger poets with a rekindled faith in the purposes of God and the works of man. The cycle of frustration and denial has spent itself."

Friends of the poet call him "Sully" or "A.M." Sullivan is a member of the New York Folklore Society, the American-Irish Historical Society, New York and New Jersey Historical Societies, and the Advertising Club of New York. He is an independent voter and a Roman Catholic. He was awarded the Poetry Society of America medal in 1941.

A. M. Sullivan married Catherine Veronica McNamee on October 8, 1919. Their children are Catherine Rose and Mary Rose. The poet is five feet eleven inches tall, weighs two hundred pounds and has blue eyes and dark hair. His hobbies include farming on a 100-acre farm he owns near Hackettstown, New Jersey, amateur astronomy, and legerdemain. "To me," he says, "a poem is a group of words, walking on tiptoe to the rhythm of the senses."

References

Scholastic p20E D 17 '38
Hoehn, M. ed. Catholic Authors, 1930-47
Who's Who in America, 1952-53
Who's Who in Commerce and Industry (1951)

SWIRBUL, LEON A. Mar. 18, 1898- Aircraft company executive

Address: b. c/o Grumman Aircraft Engineering Corporation, Bethpage, N.Y.; h. Wood Acres Rd., W., Brookville, N.Y.

The leading manufacturer of fighter planes for the United States Navy since the 1930's and the first recipient of a Navy "E" for excellence in World War II, Grumman Aircraft Engineering Corporation, is headed by Leon A. Swirbul. Since establishing the Grumman company in 1929, with Roy Grumman and William Schwendler, Swirbul served as the vice-president and general manager of the corporation until he became president in 1946. He was responsible for production and also, as head of personnel relations, largely formulated the policies which kept Grumman's rate of labor turnover during World War II at half of the aircraft industry's average rate.

The son of Frederick and Lena (Dannenberg) Swirbul, Leon A. Swirbul was born March 18, 1898, in New York City and spent his boyhood in the Long Island town of Sag Harbor. From high school he entered Cornell University at Ithaca, New York, but left college in 1917 to join the United States Marines, where he first became interested in planes. This interest grew when he became an Army inspector of aircraft. After a period as a professional basketball player, Swirbul joined the Loening Aeronautical Engineering Corporation and became the works manager in 1928. In Loening's merger with Curtiss-Wright in that year, he and Roy Grumman, with whom he had directed production at Loening, were given the positions of subordinate managers in the new organization. Dissatisfied in their new posts, Swirbul, Grumman, and William Schwendler, a designer for the same corporation, decided to form their own company and succeeded in obtaining the Loening brothers' backing for the project.

The Grumman Aircraft Engineering Corporation, with Grumman as president and Swirbul as vice-president and general manager, came into being December 26, 1929, with the first plant located in a garage in Baldwin, Long Island. The chief business for the first year (and the principal reason for the Loening brothers' interest in the company) was the repair of Loening air yachts. Grumman also produced, with C. S. Lyon's Motor Haulage Corporation, truck bodies for use on standard chassis. Another early profit came from his buying for $450 a plane which had crashed into a lake and, after repairing the damage, selling it for $20,000. In 1930 the company made its first transaction with the Navy, in the sale of a monocoque aluminum float with retractable landing gear which converted Navy scout planes to amphibians. Because of the unconventional design of the float, Navy engineers predicted that it would collapse in a test. To prove their faith in the product, Swirbul and Grumman volunteered as passengers in the first trial of the float on a Navy plane and found their faith justified when the plane was successfully catapulted from a battleship. The partners sold eight floats to the Navy and, after redesigning the

Jean Raeburn

LEON A. SWIRBUL

float and adding arresting landing gear so that planes could land in restricted areas such as the decks of aircraft carriers, received orders for fifteen more.

In new quarters in Valley Stream, Long Island, the Grumman company began work in 1931 on a Navy contract for an experimental fighter plane, the XFF-1, which so impressed the Navy with its speed of 206 miles per hour that twenty-seven planes were ordered. With wheels which retracted into the floats, the XFF-1 was also notable as the first military plane with retractable landing gear. After another move to Farmingdale, Long Island, the company continued its production of Navy fighter planes with the F2F-1, the first single-seater, and the F3F-1, the fastest military airplane at that time. Informed in 1936 by an aircraft authority that because of the invulnerability of bombers and the anticipated reliance on antiaircraft artillery for protection, fighter planes would soon become obsolete, Swirbul and Grumman were faced with deciding on their company's future course. They chose to retain production of fighters in an important spot in Grumman's schedule. Besides manufacturing military aircraft, the company during the 1930's fabricated amphibians, beginning in 1934 with the J2F (Duck) and later the G-21 (Gray Goose); the latter, the first commercial Grumman planes, were ordered by wealthy sportsmen like Marshall Field 3d, Colonel Robert McCormick, and Lord Beaverbrook.

When in 1937 the Grumman company ran out of working capital, it was saved from serious financial trouble by a stock issue, much of which was underwritten by Bernard E. Smith. The final relocation of the organization also took place in that year with the construction of Plant Number 1 at Bethpage, Long Island. At the advent of World War II, before the United States had entered the conflict, Grumman pro-

SWIRBUL, LEON A.—*Continued*

duced its single-engine land-or-carrier-based Wildcat fighter, the F4F, first for France and then for Great Britain. A flight to England in August 1941 gave Swirbul the opportunity to observe these planes in action and to discuss them with the British Admiralty, and on his return he was able to suggest valuable improvements in both the Wildcat and in Grumman's experimental torpedo plane. A new plant built by the Navy at Bethpage to expand the airframe company's capacity was opened on December 7, 1941.

With enormously increased Navy orders for Wildcats, after the United States entered World War II, Grumman "exploded" its production capacity by following a plan which Swirbul had observed in England, that of plant dispersal. Small plants were leased all over Long Island and subassembly work carried on, thus maintaining production without delays for new construction. In recognition of Grumman's achievement, the Navy in April 1942 singled out the company as the first airframe manufacturer in the country to win the Navy's "E" for excellence. Swirbul flew to Pearl Harbor in June 1942 to confer with Navy flyers on the Wildcat's performance and the suggestions he received were incorporated into the Hellcat, the F6F fighter, which was first produced in August 1942. Commenting on Grumman's efficiency in expansion, *Time* (September 11, 1944) related, "When a Navy brass hat dropped in to tell Grumman that he should expand to take care of Hellcat production, Swirbul pulled a mess of blueprints from his desk, said: 'We are.' When the officer said he would rush priorities for steel, Swirbul said: 'I've got steel.' And he had it, from Manhattan's razed Second Avenue elevated subway." In the last two years of the war Grumman concentrated on Hellcat production, having turned over to General Motors in 1943 the manufacture of Wildcats and Avengers, the Grumman TBF torpedo plane. Swirbul made a third trip of observation in January 1944, traveling 24,000 miles in the Pacific area and becoming the first civilian, except for war correspondents, to land on captured Japanese territory when he went ashore on Kwajalein Atoll after its bombardment by United States forces.

Grumman's war production performance—which includes the all-time record for the aircraft industry in accelerating production and a world's record for production in March 1945 when it turned out 664 planes in one month—is attributed by Grumman and Swirbul to the high morale of its employees. This in turn was greatly influenced by Swirbul's policy of employee relations which made a Grumman job one of the most prized in the war industries. Known as "Jake" to all employees, even during the war when these numbered 25,000, the executive has carried out his informal approach by leaving the door of his office, which he shares with Roy Grumman, always open to any employee with a complaint. He instituted an emergency service known as the "little green truck" which repairs employees' automobiles and runs various errands for workers. An incentive wage plan, the first in the aircraft industry, was in-

augurated by Swirbul, paying workers a bonus every three months figured on the overall production of the plant. Other methods by which he kept production rate high were insistence on simplified design and manufacturing techniques, cutting Navy red tape, and ignoring unnecessary design and production changes. For the production and excellence in design maintained by Grumman, Swirbul was awarded the Medal for Merit, the highest honor that can be paid a civilian, by President Truman on March 14, 1946.

Roy Grumman having assumed the newly created post of chairman of the board of Grumman Aircraft Engineering Corporation on July 11, 1946, Swirbul was elected to succeed him as president. The new president, who continued to function as general manager of the company, also became a member of the board at that time. With the cutback of Navy orders at the war's end, Grumman turned to production of aluminum truck bodies and canoes to supplement income derived from the manufacture of its commercial amphibians, the Mallard and the Widgeon. The company continued to show a profit, as it has every year since its founding. In the postwar years the corporation also supplied the Navy with Bearcat fighters and F9F carrier-based jet Panthers and did repair work on Navy and foreign airlines planes.

Increased business made it necessary to farm out much of the work in 1951 on subcontracts to avoid overexpansion of the company's plants. In that year Grumman began producing the F9F-6 Cougar and supplied Albatross amphibious hospital planes to the Air Force, the Navy, and the Coast Guard. Work was begun the following year on the XF10F-1 Jaguar, a carrier-based transonic fighter with variable sweep wings, the twin-engine X52F-1, and the S2F-1, a plane which hunts out submarines electronically and destroys them with guided missiles.

Swirbul is chairman of the Long Island Regional Hospital Planning Council and the Long Island Industrial Hospital Commission, vice-chairman of the American Cancer Society, trustee of Hofstra College, and director of Republic Pictures Corporation, Yankee Stadium Club, and Nassau Hospital. He is a member of the Greater Cornell Council, the Aircraft Industry Advisory Committee of the Munitions Board, the Westchester Racing Association, and the United States Trotting Association, and is a commissioner of the New York State Racing Commission. His clubs are the Chevy Chase, Cornell, Garden City Golf, Links, Madison Square Garden, Meadow Brook, Surf, Turf and Field, and Indian Creek Country Clubs. Formerly married, Swirbul is the father of two children, Philip and William. He has blue eyes and brown hair, is five feet and eleven inches tall, and weighs 180 pounds. *Newsweek* (January 17, 1944) has described him as "voluble, dark, and gregarious."

References
Fortune 37:112 Je '48 por
Time 44:79 S 11 '44 por

Grumman at War (1945)
Who's Who in America, 1952-53

SYNGE, RICHARD L(AURENCE) M(ILLINGTON) (sing) Oct. 28, 1914-
Biochemist

Address: b. Rowett Research Institute, Bucksburn, Aberdeenshire, Scotland; h. Craigness, Muchalls by Aberdeen, Scotland

The 1952 Nobel Prize for chemistry was awarded jointly to British biochemists Richard L. M. Synge, head of protein and carbohydrate chemistry at Rowett Research Institute, Scotland, and A. J. P. Martin, for their 1941 invention of partition chromatography. Especially in its later form of paper chromatography, this relatively simple, quick, and precise method of separating substances into their component parts has played a part in major advances in biochemistry.

Richard Laurence Millington Synge has told *Current Biography* that his family is "from Bridgenorth, Shropshire, and before that from Millington near Altringham, Cheshire, England. Some members went to Ireland in the seventeenth century, and it is that branch"— which includes the late poet and playwright John Millington Synge—"that has created the impression that the family is Irish."

Synge himself was born October 28, 1914, in Liverpool, where his father is a stockbroker. The first of three children, and the only son, of Laurence Millington and Katharine Charlotte (Swan) Synge, he was reared in Great Barrow, Chester, Cheshire. The youth attended 566-year-old Winchester College, one of the best-known English private preparatory schools for boys, located in Hampshire, England.

In 1931, two years before his graduation from Winchester, young Synge won an exhibition (scholarship) in classics from Trinity College, Cambridge University. However, he tells us, he "decided to study biochemistry on advice from a medical great-uncle, and particularly in view of F. G. Hopkins' address to the British Association at Leicester, 1933." (Sir Frederick Gowland Hopkins (1861-1947), professor of biochemistry at Cambridge from 1914 to 1943 had shared the 1929 Nobel Prize in physiology and medicine for his pioneer work on vitamins, and made important contributions to the knowledge of carbohydrate metabolism and muscular activity.) Richard Synge took the honors course in biochemistry, and in 1935 was awarded the college's senior scholarship. His graduate study at the Cambridge Biochemical Laboratory in 1936-39 was financed by scholarships from Trinity and from the laboratory.

Among the first of the fifty scientific papers, mostly in the British *Biochemical Journal,* which Synge authored or coauthored, were *Reaction of 4,6 ethylidene-beta-methylglucoside derivatives of 4,6-dimethylglucose* and two subsequent papers by D. J. Bell and R. L. M. Synge. Synge's doctoral research, under the supervision of N. W. Pirie, was in the field of protein analysis—specifically, the separation of acetyl amino acids. The apparatus which A. J. P. Martin had built at Cambridge for the extraction of Vitamin E attracted Synge's interest, but proved unsuitable. Synge and Martin joined

Elliott & Fry, Ltd., London
DR. RICHARD L. M. SYNGE

forces to build a three-unit mechanism for extraction by means of a pair of appropriate solvents. Their collaboration was interrupted when Dr. Martin left Cambridge in 1938 for the Wool Industries Research Laboratories in Leeds, and resumed in 1939 when Synge followed him there on a scholarship from the International Wool Secretariat (where Synge remained after receiving his Ph.D. in 1941 and worked mostly on the chemistry of silk and wool). At Leeds the researchers built a forty-unit mechanism for their extraction work.

Synge's papers report the results of experiments with a number of different methods of separating and analyzing proteins. Among them are a series of four papers under the general title *Amino Acids,* published around 1939. Martin and Synge published a half-dozen papers on the use of periodic acid in this connection, around 1940, before their *Separation of the Higher Monoamino Acids by Countercurrent Liquid-liquid Extraction—Amino Acid Composition of Wool* which was followed the next year by two papers on the use of a kind of chromatography employing two liquid phases in the microdetection of the higher monoamino acids. According to *Chemical and Engineering News,* "their original idea, in which the column was packed with parallel cotton and wool fibers and chloroform was passed downward around the wool and water upward around the cotton, didn't work, but it led to a simplification which did. The water was held stationary with a silica gel packing, and an indicator was added to show the position of the zones."

Basically, the partition chromatography for which Drs. Synge and Martin were to receive the Nobel Prize was a continuation of the work of Russian botanist Michael Tswett, who in 1904 separated the constituents of plant colors by allowing the dissolved pigments to trickle down a tube filled with fine sand or similar

SYNGE, RICHARD L. M.—*Continued*

material; the different components, having different rates of trickle, were thus sorted out into bands of pure substances. Among the problems to be solved in chromatography were the selection of the best solvents and insoluble substrates. When Martin and Synge used butanol as the solvent, silica gel proved an unsatisfactory substrate. Cellulose worked better, and fine filter paper worked best of all. The substance used by the researchers for analysis was albumin.

In 1943, Dr. Synge moved to London to work on the chemistry of antibiotic peptides at the Lister Institute of Preventive Medicine, and Dr. Martin continued the partition chromatographic work with others. They collaborated, however, in proceeding from one-dimensional to two-dimensional work with paper whereby still better and sharper separation was obtained by using two solvent streams flowing at right angles. The first complete two-dimensional chromatogram was made of amino acids from stomach mucin. Dr. Synge used partition chromatography with starch as one means of studying the antibiotic called gramicidin. Around 1945, he published an over-all account of the chemical characteristics and amino-acid composition of gramicidin S.

Among papers not mentioned above are eight by A. H. Gordon with Martin and Synge, dealing with such subjects as cowhide gelatin, amino acid composition of gramicidin, tyrocidin, and silk fibroin, and the use of partition chromatography in studying proteins. Among Synge's more recent papers are *Synthesis of Dipeptides Related to Gramicidin*; *Gramicidin S: The Sequence of Amino-Acid Residues* (by R. A. Consden, Gordon, Martin, and Synge); *Fractionation of Hydrolysis Products of Amylose by Electrokinetic Ultrafiltration in Agar-Agar Jelly*; *Partition Chromatography: VII Applicability of Methods*; and *Chromatographic Methods in Amino-Acid Analysis*.

Dr. Synge spent the winter of 1946-47 in Sweden, studying in Arne Tiselius' new Institute of Biochemistry at the University of Upsala. Tiselius was to receive the 1948 Nobel Prize for his development of electrophoresis and adsorption analysis; Synge was studying mainly the adsorption of amino acids and peptides on charcoal. In 1948, Dr. Synge assumed his present post as head of the department of protein and carbohydrate chemistry at Rowett Research Institute near Aberdeen, Scotland. There his work deals mainly with the nutrition of farm animals with, according to an American Chemical Society publication, "protein digestion in the ruminant animal, the isolation and characterization of natural peptides, and physicochemical methods of fractionating polysaccharides." In recognition of their contributions, Drs. Martin and Synge were elected fellows of the Royal Society in 1950; Dr. Synge is also a member of the editorial board of the *Biochemical Journal* and a fellow of the Royal Institute of Chemistry.

When, in November 1952, the choice of Martin and Synge as co-recipients of the Nobel Prize for chemistry became known, it was pointed out that chromatography had helped produce new antibiotics and had helped solve many other chemical problems. H. H. Strain's remark, "Chromatography has been destined to influence the life of man and beast the world over," was quoted, and Arne Tiselius remarked in a Swedish journal that British scientists "seem to have a special gift for making great discoveries with small resources." The prize award to be divided between Synge and Martin was 171,134 Swedish crowns—11,408 British pounds, or about $32,000.

Six feet two inches tall and weighing 180 pounds, Richard L. M. Synge has blue-gray eyes and what he terms "mouse" colored hair. His professional affiliations include the Biochemical Society, Nutrition Society, Society for General Microbiology, Société de Chimie Biologique. Synge is also a member of the "scientists' labor union," the Association of Scientific Workers. He enjoys gardening. Fond of skiing, travel, foreign languages and literature, he is a member of Den Norske Turistforeningen. His club is the Strathcoma (Bucksburn).

During World War II, Dr. Synge was in a Home Guard anti-aircraft rocket battery. It was during that period, in 1943, that he married Dr. Ann Stephen, physician niece of writer Virginia Woolf, who still practices medicine on a part-time basis. The Synges have five children, Jane, Elizabeth, Thomas Millington, Matthew Millington, and Patrick Millington. The scientist is a member of the Aberdeen and North East Peace Association and vice-president of the British Peace Committee which sponsored the December 1952 People's Congress for Peace, held in occupied Vienna.

References

Aberdeen Press and Journal N 7 '52
Chemical Age 61 :664 N 15 '52
Chemical and Engineering News 31 :155 Ja 12 '53 pors
Dagens Nyheter og Morgentidningen N 7, D 11, D 12 '52
N Y Times p29 N 5 '52
Stockholm Tidningen N 7, D 11, D 12 '52
Svenska Dagbladet N 7, D 11, D 12 '52
Who's Who 1952

TAFT, ROBERT A(LPHONSO) Sept. 8, 1889—July 31, 1953 Republican United States Senator from Ohio since 1938; B.A., Yale (1910), LL.B., Harvard Law School, and admitted to Ohio bar (1913); member of firm of Maxwell and Ramsey; first public office was as assistant counsel (1917 to 1919) for Herbert Hoover's United States Food Administration, and was decorated by Belgium, Poland, and Finland for war relief work; first elected to Ohio House of Representatives in 1921 and served until 1926; was Republican floor leader in 1924 and 1925; served in Ohio Senate during 1931-1932 term; was favorite son from Ohio for presidential nomination in 1936; first ran for United States Senate in 1938 and defeated Democratic opponent; became known as "Mr. Republican"; served on Senate Committees on Appropriations, Banking and Currency, Education, Labor and Finance; opposed America's entry in World War II, but afterwards supported war effort; opposed such measures as selective service, lend-lease, draft extension, revision of the Neutrality Act and public power development; favored balancing budget by reducing expenditures of all kinds, clarification of antitrust laws and aid to farmers; re-elected in 1944 and in Eightieth Congress was named chairman of the Senate Republican Policy Committee and Senate leader on domestic affairs; co-sponsored Taft-Hartley Act; voted against Reciprocal Trade Agreement Act of 1945, and the Atlantic Pact, and proposed instead a Monroe Doctrine for Western Europe and a stronger United Nations; made second bid for presidential nomination in 1948 and third bid in 1952 when he was a strong contender against General Eisenhower; was chosen Floor Leader in the Senate in Eighty-third Congress; thirteenth American to lie in state in the Capitol rotunda; author of book, *A Foreign Policy for Americans,* 1951). See *Current Biography,* 1948.

Obituary

N Y Times p1+, p6 Ag 1 '53

TALBOTT, HAROLD E(LSTNER) Mar. 31, 1888- Secretary of the Air Force; industrialist; financier

Address: b. Department of the Air Force, Washington 25, D.C.; h. 450 E. 52 St., New York 22

Secretary of the Air Force Harold E. Talbott has been actively associated with the aircraft industry since its pioneer days, He was director of aircraft production with the War Production Board during World War II. A fund-raiser for the Republican party for over twenty years, he was active in the presidential campaigns of Wendell Willkie in 1940, of Thomas E. Dewey in 1948, and of Eisenhower in 1952.

Harold Elstner Talbott was born in Dayton, Ohio on March 31, 1888, one of the nine children of Harry Elstner and Katharine H. (Houk) Talbott. He attended the Hill School at Pottstown, Pennsylvania before entering Yale, where he enrolled at the Sheffield Scientific School, graduating in 1910 with a degree in engineering.

The young engineer joined his father's construction firm of H. E. Talbott Company as vice-president and general manager in charge of hydroelectric development and industrial construction. He remained in this capacity until 1915 when he joined the Dayton Metal Products Company. With his father, he formed the Dayton-Wright Airplane Company in 1916 and the Dayton Wright Company in 1919, serving as president of both.

The Talbott family estate is controlled by a holding company, the Talbott Corporation, Dayton, with assets largely in real estate. Talbott, whose interest in the corporation (with that of his children) amounts to one-ninth of the estate, was for several years a director and chairman of the board. In 1924 he moved to New York City and established the H. E. Talbott & Co. to manage his own investments.

Among the positions he held were chairman of the board of Standard Cap and Seal Corporation from 1929, chairman of the board of North American Aviation Company, Incorported, in 1931 and 1932, director and chairman of the finance committee of the Mead Paper Corporation from 1937, director and member of the executive committee of the Commercial National Bank and Trust Company, director and chairman of the finance committee of the Electric Auto-Lite Company, director and member of the finance committee of the Chrysler Corporation. He has been a director of the Russell Manufacturing Company, Madison Square Garden Corporation, James Stewart and Company, Incorporated, and the Mary Chess Company, chairman of the board of the Standard Packaging Company, member of the board of Baldwin-Lima-Hamilton Company, and a partner of the industrial engineering firm of Mulligan and Company.

Since the early thirties Talbott has been active in Republican party affairs. In 1934 he was eastern chairman of the party's finance committee and in 1943 of the finance committee for Metropolitan New York. During the Wendell Willkie campaign for president in 1940, Talbott strongly supported his party's nominee. He headed the national finance committee in 1948 and 1949.

Talbott was one of the "team" of confidential advisers who organized the 1948 presidential campaign of Thomas E. Dewey, Governor of New York. In this "privy council", which included John Foster Dulles, Allen Dulles, J. Russell Sprague and Herbert Brownell, Jr., Talbott's function was the direction of the raising of campaign funds.

The financier again directed fund-raising for the Dwight D. Eisenhower campaign of 1952. *Time* Magazine has reported that before the beginning of the campaign Talbott retained a management consulting firm to prepare an exhaustive fourteen-volume analysis of "every top policy-making job" which would have to be filled by the new administration in the event of a Republican victory.

On December 19, 1952 Talbott was nominated by President-elect Eisenhower for the post of Secretary of the Air Force, one of four civilian service secretaries to serve in the Department of Defense. Among his qualifications for the position were a year's service as a major in the United States Army Air Force in 1918, and directorship of aircraft production with the War Production Board from March, 1942 to January, 1943. News of the appointment reached him on a Florida vacation. In his acceptance he said, "I shall dedicate myself to the best of my ability to the problems of our Air Force and also give full cooperation to the other branches of our armed forces" (New York *Times,* December 20, 1952).

As in the case of other nominees, Talbott was called to appear before the Senate Armed Services Committee for inquiry into his finan-

U. S. Air Force

HAROLD E. TALBOTT

cial holdings in firms doing business with the Department of Defense. The Hughes report of 1918 and a 1951 Congressional committee report of dealings with the Government of two of the companies of which Talbott had been a director were also introduced at the hearings.

Talbott agreed to dispose of stock holdings and to resign from all positions in corporations which might be involved in Department of Defense contracts. On February 4 his nomination was confirmed by the Senate by a vote of 76 to 6. Shortly after his appointment the new Air Secretary made a tour of inspection of the United States Air Force bases in Korea. Upon his return on March 8, 1953 he issued a statement saying that "as far as the Air Force is concerned, there are no worrying conditions in the present situation there" (New York *Times,* March 9, 1953).

Air Force Secretary Talbott assured President Eisenhower that he planned "to go along with the budget despite his distaste for the slash in Air Force funds" (*Time,* June 15, 1953). The $5 billion cut as proposed by Secretary of Defense Charles E. Wilson would delay the building "toward a strength of 143 wings" and leave the country with a "second-best Air Force" according to retiring General Hoyt Vandenberg. A wing is the basic operating unit of the Air Force and contains from thirty to seventy-five planes, depending on the mission. The Administration's plan, as outlined by Secretary Wilson and Secretary Talbott, is to build 110 wings by June 30, 1954, and 120 wings by June 30, 1955.

Secretary Talbott addressed the seventh annual convention of the Air Force Association on August 22, 1953 and admitted that in the face of Soviet air gains the United States "does indeed look vulnerable." "Modern airpower," he stated, "combining the tremendous speeds brought about by the jet engine and enormous power of hydrogen and atomic explosives, overlaps so easily all the traditional barriers that have sheltered us through our history." He spoke of the difficulty of recruiting and maintaining adequate personnel in the Air Force. "The trend of Congress to decrease pay of the military is penny wise and pound foolish," he declared.

He estimated that the Air Force would lose 180,000 airmen next year through failure to re-enlist. The minimum cost of bringing each man into the service and training him was estimated at $14,600, and thus the basic cost of replacing the 180,000 men would be $2,600,000,-000. "Many of these men could be saved for long, useful careers in the Air Force," he said, "if we could just spend a portion of this $2,600,000,000 for improving the pay and fringe benefits of these men" (New York *Times,* August 23, 1953).

When asked what impact Russia's progress with the hydrogen bomb would have on America's defense planning, Talbott replied: "Our present planning is based on nuclear weapons so the change will be one of degree." He said that while the Red Air Force is numerically larger than this country's, "it is in the quality field of both our personnel and equipment that we maintain, and must continue to maintain, our advantage" (*Newsweek,* September 28, 1953).

Talbott was one of this country's leading polo players in the 1930's. A racing enthusiast, he formerly owned a stable of thoroughbred horses. Other favorite sports are big game hunting and baseball. His club memberships include the Dayton Republican Club, Buzfuz, Miami Valley Hunt & Polo, Dayton Country, Racquet and Tennis, Meadow Brook, Turf and Field, The River, Piping Rock, and the Links.

Mrs. Talbott is the former Margaret Thayer of Philadelphia, whose father, a vice-president of the Pennsylvania Railroad, was lost in the sinking of the S.S. *Titanic.* The Talbotts were married on August 11, 1925. The successful head of a knitting business before her marriage, Mrs. Talbott has since directed many fundraising campaigns for the New York Infirmary. Their four children are Mrs. Pauline Talbott Toland, Mrs. Margaret Talbott Noyes, of *Vogue* Magazine, and John Thayer and Harold Elstner Talbott III, twin sons now in school in New York. They have one granddaughter, Alixe Toland. In addition to an apartment in New York City, the Talbotts have a home in the Georgetown section of Washington and an estate at Old Westbury, Long Island; the forty-five room house on the latter property burned down in 1951. The entire Talbott family, consisting of 110 descendants of Harold Talbott's parents, holds a reunion every five years in Dayton.

References

Time 60:11 D 29 '52 por
U S News 34:90 F 6 '53 por
Washington (D.C.) Post p21 Ja 20 '53
Business Executives of America (1950)
International Who's Who, 1952
Who's Who in America, 1952-53

TALLANT, ROBERT April 20, 1909-
Author

Address: b. c/o Harper & Brothers, 49 East
33rd St., New York 16; h. 3324 Carondelet
St., New Orleans, La.

Reprinted from the *Wilson
Library Bulletin,* April 1953

Robert Tallant is a New Orleanian—born
in New Orleans, raised there, living there still,
and taking for the subject matter of his books
the fabulous, glamorous, and all-too-human
material which New Orleans offers a writer.
He has written novels and histories, juveniles
and crime reports, ghost stories and a guide
book: twelve books, altogether, since 1946
when he began serious writing. Yet, Tallant
insists, "I loaf a lot," and he explains, "The
secret is that I've written all my books in one
draft and can turn out a lot of pages on the
days I'm working. This may indicate that
I'm really lazy, but I like to think it is the way
I have to work, and I'm probably right."

A fifth generation American of English,
Scotch, French, Spanish, and Welsh ancestors
long settled in Louisiana, Robert (Magruder)
Tallant was born April 20, 1909, the son of the
late James Robb Tallant, a newsaperman, and
Lucy Texada (Magruder) Tallant. He was
educated in the public schools of New Orleans
and graduated from Warren Easton High
School in 1926. Tallant says that he does not
know why he started writing. He may have
drifted into it from the job of advertising
copywriter, one of many jobs he held, including
bank teller and various kinds of office clerk.
The fact remains that he became a writer. He
met and received encouragement from the late
Lyle Saxon, the famous New Orleans author,
and during the depression he worked as an editor on the Louisiana Writers' Project. The result of the work of this program appeared in
1945 in *Gumba Ya-Ya* a collection of Louisiana
folktales compiled by Lyle Saxon and others.
The final writing of this volume was done by
Tallant.

By the next year Tallant was a full time
writer producing full length books. He had
already written his share of short stories and
articles for magazines—pulps, "little" magazines and slicks—but he says that the short
things were "too hard; books are much easier."
Easy or not, they came rapidly for him. *Voodoo in New Orleans* (1946) was, to quote Virginia Kirkus, "an interesting investigation and
straightforward handling" of the cult of voodoo. It was followed in 1947 by Tallant's
first novel, *Mrs. Candy and Saturday Night,*
a warmly humorous study of life in a rooming
house in a shabby section of New Orleans.
The New York *Times* labelled it "a happy-go-
lucky novel of present-day New Orleans, written with engaging freshness and gusto . . . a
pleasant hammock-special.'

Angel in the Wardrobe (1948), the story of
the inevitable clash between the old and the
new in New Orleans society, received a mixed
but generally favorable reception from the
critics. "The satire isn't deep enough, nor is
the characterization rich enough for a master-

ROBERT TALLANT

work of social comedy," Hubert Creekmore
wrote in the New York *Times.* The *Library
Journal* recommended it with reservations—
"The characters lack vitality and the story
almost bogs down. But the mood of an ante-
bellum New Oreans society, tenacious, yet
crumbling under today's standards, is master-
fully sustained."

The next novel, *Mr. Preen's Salon* (1949),
which dealt lightly with life in the French
Quarter of New Orleans, was found "for the
most part dull reading" by Virginia Kirkus.
But Carl Carmer, reviewing it for the New
York *Times,* found it an interesting "novel of
sophistication" which "might well have been
hailed as a masterpiece a score of years ago."
To Carmer it suggested comparison with Norman Douglas' masterpiece of 1917, *South
Wind.* (Tallant, incidentally, cites *South Wind*
—along with the work of Somerset Maugham,
James Thurber, William March, Carson Mc-
Cullers, the early novels of Evelyn Waugh,
and good science fiction—as one of his favorite
novels.)

Two other novels by Tallant have appeared.
One of these, *A State in Mimosa* (1950), is set
in a small southern town and considers the
issues of prejudice and bigotry toward out-
siders. The other is *Southern Territory* (1951),
a story of a group of traveling salesmen and
their dreary, lonely existence. The New York
Herald Tribune found it "mildly interesting,"
and in the *Saturday Review of Literature* G. F.
Scheer, though praising the realistic evocation
of the drabness of the characters' lives, found
the novel unsatisfying and narrow in scope.

In nonfiction, Tallant's history of voodoo
was followed by *Mardi Gras* (1948), a history
and description of the great New Orleans carnival and its tradition; *The Romantic New
Orleanians* (1950), an anecdotal history of the
city and its famous families; and *Ready to
Hang* (1952), an account of seven famous

TALLANT, ROBERT—*Continued*

New Orleans murders. In 1951 Tallant made his first appearance in the juvenile field with *The Pirate Lafitte and the Battle of New Orleans,* a Landmark Book which won the 1951 award of the Louisiana Library Association. Soon to be published is another juvenile, *The Story of the Louisiana Purchase,* and he is currently at work on still another—a story of the Acadians.

Tallant is unmarried. He has a definite list of likes and dislikes which includes, on the positive side—eating, drinking, reading, sitting, talking, longhair music and jazz, and parties, even big ones—and on the negative, sports, games, parlor games, and hillbilly music.

Reference

Who's Who in the South and Southwest

TAMAYO, RUFINO Aug. 26, 1900- Painter
Address: Malitzin 20, Coyoacan, Mexico D.F.

The Mexican artist Rufino Tamayo, whose work has been described as a successful fusing of ancient Mexican primitive art and modern French art, is regarded as a foremost colorist of the time. Not a member of the Mexican left-wing mural movement which began in the early 1920's and has been prominent in Mexico's artistic development, he has mainly preferred to paint within the smaller scope of the canvas and to work for a "pure" art form. The selection of Tamayo to paint a two-panel mural in Mexico City's Palace of Fine Arts, the first part of which he completed in October 1952, is seen as evidence of a change in the government's attitude toward nonpolitical art.

The only child of Manuel Arellanes and Florentina Tamayo, Rufino Tamayo was born in Oaxaca, Mexico, on August 26, 1900. From the nearby ruins of Mitla and Monte Albán, the boy, of Zapotec Indian blood himself, became familiar with the ancient art of Mexico. His father, a small businessman, and his mother having both died when their son was eight years old, young Tamayo went to live with an aunt in Mexico City. After school he helped his aunt in the small fruit and fuel shop which she owned in La Merced, the market quarter of the city. This early influence has manifested itself throughout the career of the artist, who often uses fruit as a subject for his paintings; some of his most frequently used colors have been likened to fruit stains. From his early childhood he displayed a talent for painting and also in his schooldays was much interested in music. The boy attended evening art classes until his aunt, wishing to prepare him for a career in the fruit business, sent him to a commercial school to learn bookkeeping. Because of his preference for art, he left the bookkeeping course to attend classes at the School of Fine Arts. After a year of study there, finding the teaching too tradition-bound for his taste, he withdrew from school and for the next three years supported himself, while painting in his spare time.

After a visit to José Vasconcelos, who did much to promote free creative activity in Mexico during his term as Minister of Education, Tamayo was appointed in 1921 the head designer of the department of ethnographic drawing in the National Museum of Archeology in Mexico City. Here he was surrounded by many pre-Columbian objects of art which he studied and drew and which subsequently influenced his paintings. At this time he also began to teach art in the primary and open air schools.

Visiting New York City for the first time in 1926, Tamayo showed the paintings which had formed his first Mexico City exhibition that summer. Several years later he became ill and returned to Mexico to recover his health. In 1928 he served there as a professor at the National School of Fine Arts and the following year taught at the Academy of San Carlos, where he had previously studied. The artist acted as a representative on a four-man council for fine arts in the Ministry of Education in 1932 and was for a time in 1933 head of the section of plastic arts in the department of fine arts, which was concerned with primary art teaching. Meanwhile, another exhibition of Tamayo's paintings had been held in New York City in 1930.

Tamayo's first mural, done in the stairway of the National Conservatory of Music in 1933, depicted Indian angels playing various musical instruments and did not follow the Mexican political-artistic trend, which was then at its peak. He showed his pictures in San Francisco in 1935 and the following year returned to New York City as a delegate of the National Association of Artists to the Congress of Revolutionary Artists. In 1937 his work was exhibited at the Valentine Gallery, which has handled most of his production. After the artist began to teach at the Dalton School in New York City in 1937, it became customary for him to return to Mexico each summer and live the rest of the time in New York. The earlier paintings of Tamayo are more obviously Mexican in subject matter, although not in feeling, than his later work, and have a decorative quality which is later subordinated. Many of his first shows contained pictures of women of Tehuantepec "as stately as the carvings of a Greek frieze" (*Art Digest*), and paintings of fruit and fruitsellers. In the early 1940's his work became simpler and more powerful—to some critics and viewers, so powerful that it was almost frightening. A series of animal paintings dating from this time, which includes *Mad Dogs, Lion and Horse, Animals,* and *Dog Howling,* are done with little detail and with flat, strong colors. The dogs, particularly, show the influence of Tarascan clay figurines, although Tamayo's dogs are a much fiercer breed than the ancient ones.

In 1943 Tamayo painted a mural for the Hillyer Library of Smith College at Northampton, Massachusetts. Since the room's layout prevents one from seeing the entire wall on entering, the artist divided the painting into two parts. The larger portion, *Nature and the Artist,* can be viewed as a whole; then, as one approaches the wall, the smaller, *The Work of Art and the Observer*, is seen and becomes a part of the mural. The first section depicts five elements: earth, nature, fire, air, and water, surmounted by a rainbow symbolizing the color the artist uses to express these elements; the artist himself stands before the easel translating the elements into a work of art. *The Work of Art and the Observer* shows a man examining a piece of sculpture with his back turned to the representation of the five elements, to emphasize that the observer must forget the original elements from which the work of art is drawn and consider the work on its own terms. The forms of the mural are geometrical and abstract and the colors are strong and flat.

At one of the Tamayo exhibitions given at the Valentine Gallery in January 1946, a critic for the New York *Herald Tribune* found the work less grotesque than some done previously by the painter and termed several pictures, notably *The Bird's Nest* and *The White Nude*, "gentle and poetic." The Brooklyn Museum instituted a "Tamayo Workshop" in the fall of 1946, a studio course conducted by the artist. An exhibition held shortly thereafter contained many paintings expressing a new interest—astronomy. Constellations, the sun, and the moon were pictured, sometimes as a composition by themselves, sometimes with figures as part of the design. An interest in atomic science was also evinced in *Cataclysm, 1946*. Of the show as a whole the New York *World-Telegram* (February 8, 1947) critic said, "The fiery intensity, the brooding sullenness of his previous paintings of animals and idols has been supplanted by a new feeling of poetic fantasy." The color which dominated the artist's work at this time was blue-black.

The Mexican government sponsored a three-month exhibition of Tamayo's art at the National Institute of Fine Arts in Mexico City in 1948. The painter spent two years, from 1949 to 1951, traveling in Europe and worked for a time in Paris, which he is said to regard as the most beautiful city in the world. One room at the international art show, the Biennale, in Venice in the summer of 1950 was hung with his work, which was received with great enthusiasm by visitors to the gallery. After the success of this showing, the first given of his works in Europe, Tamayo received many requests for exhibitions from various continental countries. The one arranged in Paris received the comment, "Original among the most original" from Jean Cassou, director of the Paris Museum of Modern Art (*Look*). The pictures were then exhibited in Brussels. As a contributor to the survey of Mexican art presented in Paris in the summer of 1952 by the Mexican National Institute of Arts, Tamayo once again scored a European triumph.

The first of two large panels of a mural commissioned by the government of Mexico for the Palace of Fine Arts in Mexico City was completed by Tamayo in October 1952. *The Birth of Mexican Nationality*, as the panel is called, represents in predominant reds and purples and in stylized, semiabstract forms the conquest of the Indians by the Spaniards, the destruction of the native culture and the im-

Wide World Photos
RUFINO TAMAYO

portation of the European, and the new Mexican nationality that arose from a fusion of the two races. "Superbly organized," wrote Emily Genauer (New York *Herald Tribune*), who also discussed the importance of the inclusion of Tamayo in a building that had previously contained only murals by the "Big Three" of Mexican painting, Orozco, Siqueiros, and Rivera. "Instead of employing artists exclusively because the subject matter of their work was also excellent propaganda," the critic stated, "[the government] will now, indications are, pursue the unprecedented course of employing artists solely because their art is good." The second panel entitled *Mexico Today*, which depicts "a nation alive with activity, building a symbolic structure of industry, farming, art and science," was completed in August 1953. A retrospective show of Tamayo's work opened at the Pan American Union in Washington, D.C., in October 1952.

In October 1953 the Dallas Museum of Fine Arts displayed an eighteen by ten foot mural by Rufino Tamayo titled *El Hombre* showing an earth-bound giant reaching toward the stars. "I wanted to show man as a rational being going to higher places," explained the artist.

"My feeling is Mexican, my color is Mexican, my shapes are Mexican, but my thinking is a mixture," Tamayo has said of his own work, disclaiming association with any particular school of painting (*Time*). Critics feel that he has combined elements of modern French art, especially that of Picasso, with his Mexican artistic heritage to produce a uniquely personal product. Braque, the French painter of still-lifes, is named by Tamayo as his own preference among living artists. The painter's oil colors are always thinned with turpentine before being laid on the canvas and have been said to derive from "the raw earth of Mexico—scorched-lava black, poisonous pinks, burnt reds, sulphurous yellows, and the

TAMAYO, RUFINO—*Continued*

mysterious, menacing blues of Mexican mountains" (*Look*). The first lithographs produced by Tamayo were done in Paris several years ago for inclusion in an art book, and a portrait head of his wife Olga done in 1941 is the only piece of sculpture by the artist. Tamayo is represented in many museums in the United States and Europe, among them the Museum of Modern Art in New York City and the Paris Museum of Modern Art. Books consisting principally of reproductions of his work are *Drawings by Tamayo,* introduced by Enrique F. Gaul (1949); *Rufino Tamayo,* by E. F. Gaul (1950); and *Tamayo* (1948).

Tamayo and Olga Flores, a music student, met while the artist was painting the murals in the National Conservatory of Music and were married in 1934. Music is Tamayo's most frequent relaxation. He is an excellent guitarist and likes to sing the songs of his native Mexico. The artist also enjoys the theater; in reading his taste runs to fiction in Spanish or English. Mary Braggiotti of the New York *Post* has described him, "Slightly above middle height, he is lean and broad-shouldered. . . . His manner is taut, self-assured, and smiling."

References

Look 15:107 S 25 '51 por
N Y Post p23 F 3 '47 por
Goldwater, R. J. Rufino Tamayo (1948)
Who's Who in Latin America (1947)

TEBBEL, JOHN (WILLIAM) Nov. 16, 1912- Author

Address: b. c/o New York University, Washington Sq., New York 3; h. 50 West 9th St., New York 11

Reprinted from the *Wilson Library Bulletin,* Nov. 1953

Heredity and environment as well as experience have combined to fit John Tebbel for his dual role of historical novelist and historian of American journalism. (His soon-to-be-published novel, "A Voice in the Streets," combines both aspects, since it deals with a figure resembling James Gordon Bennett of the New York *Herald* and the city as it was in his time.) On his mother's side Mr. Tebbel is a descendant of Henry Schoolcraft, a noted Michigan historian and perhaps the first ethnologist in this country, whose wife, Jane Johnston, was the granddaughter of a Sault Ste. Marie, Michigan, Indian chief; he is also a distant cousin of the late Mary Johnston, author of *To Have and To Hold, Lewis Rand,* and other romantic novels of the colonies and early Republic.

John William Tebbel was born November 16, 1912, at Boyne City, Michigan, the son of William Tebbel, of English-Canadian farming stock, and Edna Mae (Johnston) Tebbel, whose father, George, was a lumberman "in the famous crews of the Upper Peninsula and the Saginaw Valley, which Stewart Holbrook has written about so often." At twelve the boy left the farm for a small town in central Michigan, where he lived five years and attended

JOHN TEBBEL

Shepherd High School, graduating from Mount Pleasant High School in 1931. Mount Pleasant was the county seat which became the oil capital of the state in 1928, doubled in population by an influx of Texans, Oklahomans, and Californians. "For a writer, it was a background to be drawn on endlessly—although so far I've never done it."

At fourteen, young Tebbel was writing for the local weekly, the county seat daily, and by correspondence for several state dailies. At Central Michigan College of Education in Mount Pleasant, where he was graduated with an A.B. degree in 1935, (receiving an honorary Litt.D. in 1948), he continued this work, besides editing *Central State Life,* the college paper, and *Chippewa,* the college yearbook. He also wrote two student musical comedies. Yielding again to the impulse recently, he wrote book, lyrics, and some of the music for *Washington Squared,* a satirical revue presented by the faculty and students of the department of journalism at New York University's School of Commerce (he is vice chairman of the department).

After college graduation young Tebbel was city editor of the Isabella County (Michigan) *Times-News,* but left for New York at the urging of the Methodist minister in Mount Pleasant, who thought he should attend graduate school. He received an M.S. from Columbia University School of Journalism in 1937, and has taught there. Since then he has been a reporter for the Detroit *Free Press,* feature writer and editor for the Providence (Rhode Island) *Journal,* Sunday staff writer for the New York *Times,* writer for *Newsweek,* managing editor of the *American Mercury,* and associate editor of E. P. Dutton and Company.

Mrs. Tebbel (Kathryn Carl), a Wellesley graduate whom he married April 29, 1939, is now a copy editor for Doubleday. As a publisher's editor, Tebbel "learned that the only

·way to write a book is to sit down and keep sitting down until it is finished." This sedentary method (with occasional forays for research) has resulted in the production of ten books in seven years.

An American Dynasty (1947), the first, dealt frankly with the Chicago, New York, and Washington newspaper hierarchy of Medills, Pattersons, and McCormicks, and was called by Turner Catledge in the New York *Times* "a highly readable story and a revealing appraisal." Next in line was *The Marshall Fields* (1948), described by the *New Republic* as "an interesting study of a remarkable American family and of the growth of such enterprises as the Marshall Field store, *PM,* and the Chicago *Sun*"; the *Times* thought it fell short of being a complete and balanced appraisal. *George Horace Lorimer and the Saturday Evening Post* (1948), was written *con amore,* and is the favorite of most Tebbel readers. The New York *Times* praised its "evocative pages"; the New York *Herald Tribune,* called it "an important piece of documentary history"; the *American Historical Review* deemed it "a judicious, accurate and fairly complete portrait of America's greatest popular magazine editor." *The Battle for North America* (1948), a selection from Francis Parkman, was a choice of the History Book Club, while *Your Body: How to Keep it Healthy* (1951), a book on personal hygiene, "is written with a positive attitude and a common sense philosophy of healthy living," according to the Springfield *Republican.* Frank Luther Mott, dean of American historians of journalism, called *The Life and Good Times of William Randolph Hearst* (1952) extremely readable, comprehensive, and the best of the several biographies of Hearst. Tebbel is also co-author with Kenneth N. Stewart of a textbook, *Makers of Modern Journalism* (1952).

Now came the historical novels. *The Conqueror* (1951), a novel about colonial New York, was called by Margaret Widdemer, herself an historical novelist, "a valuable, even though a little one-sided, introduction to a great and almost forgotten Founding Father." It sold nearly half a million copies in all editions. The *Herald Tribune* described *Touched with Fire* (1952), dealing with La Salle's experiences in North America, as "vivid and on the whole satisfactory." It is now available in a pocket edition as well as a full-size edition.

John Tebbel in person has high cheek bones (showing his Indian blood), blue eyes, and light-brown hair; is compactly built, weighing 160 pounds, and five feet, eight inches in height. He likes music and tennis, good food and wine. He lists no political or religious preferences. He is a member of the Players in New York and of Kappa Tau Alpha, the honorary journalistic fraternity. Somerset Maugham is his favorite writer.

Tebbel's friends describe him as invariably cheerful, and a prodigious worker.

References

 Directory of American Scholars (1951)
 Who's Who in America, 1952-1953 (addenda)

TEITGEN, PIERRE-HENRI (tēt'-gĕN pyâr-äN'rē) May 29, 1908- French political leader; lawyer

Address: b. Palais Bourbon, Quai d'Orsay, Paris 7ᵉ, France; h. 14 rue Dominique, Paris, France

An increasingly important political figure in France since the end of World War II, Pierre-Henri Teitgen was elected president on May 24, 1952, of the Popular Republican Movement (M.R.P.), which first came into power under Georges Bidault in 1946 and which strongly supports Western European integration. After the liberation of France in 1944, Teitgen was appointed Minister of Information in the Government of Charles de Gaulle and has since held posts in several French cabinets. He has represented Ille-et-Vilaine on the M.R.P. ticket in both constituent assemblies and in the National Asembly. In the government which was formed by Joseph Laniel at the end of June, 1953, Teitgen was named Vice Premier.

On May 29, 1908, Pierre-Henri Teitgen was born at Rennes, France, in the Department of Ille-et-Vilaine, son of Henri and Madeleine (Goux) Teitgen. He attended the school of St. Sigisbert in Nancy and the University of Nancy. Having passed on January 1, 1935, the competitive examination which grants the rights to a mastership in French lycées or to a lectureship in faculties, he was appointed Professor of Public Law at the University of Nancy, the youngest competitor ever to receive such a promotion. He occupied this position for four years.

Between the years of 1935 and 1939 Teitgen was engaged in research on contemporary social and economic problems, and on several occasions during 1936 he was called on to act as arbitrator in labor disputes. By 1939 he had founded and become editor of the magazine *La Revue de Droit Sociale,* which dealt with legal aspects of labor relations. With the outbreak of World War II, Teitgen became a lieutenant in the 133d infantry regiment of Nancy and was sent to the Maginot line. When, in 1940, the Germans invaded France, Teitgen was captured and imprisoned at Sarrebourg until escaping in August of the same year. Having made his way to the south of France, he obtained a position teaching public law at the University of Montpellier. At this time the French Resistance movement was just beginning; Teitgen and François de Menthon, among its first active participants, formed a group called Liberté, which later fused with similar organizations under the name of Combat. The Vichy Government having become aware of Teitgen's political activities, he was dismissed from his post at Montpellier in 1942 and went into hiding. Under the pseudonym of Tristan, he helped found the first clandestine newspaper of the Resistance. Following a period of underground activity in Lyon, he went to Paris, where he served on the Comité Général and he wrote several articles for the *Cahiers Politique.* He prepared a number of draft bills which were planned to meet France's problems after the war. While acting as the

French Embassy Inf. Div.

PIERRE-HENRI TEITGEN

provisional Commissioner of Information in the Underground, he was recaptured by the Gestapo on June 6, 1944, and deported to Germany. He escaped in transit and joined American forces to take part in the fighting around Montdidier.

After the liberation of France a few months later, a provisional government headed by General Charles de Gaulle was established in Paris. On September 2, 1944, Teitgen arrived in the capital city and shortly thereafter was appointed Minister of Information, a post which he filled until becoming Minister of Justice on May 30, 1945. In subsequent cabinet changes, he retained the latter position through November 1946, at that time under Georges Bidault. Meanwhile, Teitgen had become associated with the Popular Republican Movement, which developed out of the Resistance and was the successor of the Popular Democratic Party, to which he had earlier belonged. Its platform advocates limited nationalization, collective bargaining, full employment, and development of exports; and opposes the two ballot electoral system in use prior to the war. In foreign policy the M.R.P. is a strong supporter of Western European integration. As reported in the *Political Handbook of the World* (1952), the M.R.P. "derives support from some conservatives who see it as a bulwark against Communism, [although] its program has been moderately leftish in character. At the same time the party contains strong Catholic elements. In the recent shift toward the right, it has lost many adherents." In October 1945 Teitgen was elected on the M.R.P. ticket from the Department of the Ille-et-Vilaine to both constituent assemblies and later to the National Assembly, of which he is still a member.

With the formation of a new Cabinet under Premier Paul Ramadier, Teitgen was named Vice-President of the Council, holding this post

from January 22, 1947 to October 22, 1947. During this time as spokesman for the modification of certain M.R.P. policies, he told party members in March 1947 that the "French government and economy were weak because of 'excessive centralization' of power" and made public a trend in his party to retreat from its original platform of nationalization of basic industries to limited nationalization (New York *Herald Tribune*, March 17, 1947). In the ensuing Cabinets of Ramadier and Robert Shuman he held the post of Minister of the Armed Forces (October 22, 1947-July 17, 1948). From July 26, 1948, through August 1948, he was once again Vice-President of the Council, this time under Premier André Marie. He was simultaneously also occupied as professor of law at Rennes, where he had delivered his first lecture, on the 1946 constitution, in May 1948. A representative at the Consultative Assembly of the Council of Europe, Teitgen in July 1949 supported a program of human rights to prevent any other peoples from being sent "on the road to Dachau or Buchenwald." He was mainly responsible with Sir David Maxwell Fyfe for writing the *Magna Charta of Common Man*, which was presented to the assembly.

When Georges Bidault was returned to power, Teitgen on October 28, 1949, took up the portfolio of Minister of State in charge of Information. In exercising his jurisdiction over press, radio and film, he at times aroused Communist antagonism, as happened in November 1949, when he made a decision to ban a program on which Communist Maurice Thorez had planned to appear. A bill presented by Teitgen in January 1950 forbidding anyone to be both a member of Parliament and a newspaper publisher at the same time, was regarded by Communists as a direct blow against the publisher of *L'Humanité* (Communist party organ), who was a deputy in Parliament. He sponsored in June 1950 a bill to censor all films judged to be controlled by any party.

As Minister of State charged with matters of information, Teitgen was spokesman for the French Government on a number of important issues. At the time of the passage of the antisabotage bill in March 1950, he told French workers in a radio broadcast that "the Government will not confuse the provocations and disorders of the Communist party with the just claims of the workers" (quoted by the New York Times, March 11, 1950). During the same month he expressed the French view that Great Britain should take part in all schemes for continental union, since Britain would counterbalance the industrial potential of Germany. On other occasions Teitgen voiced the stand of his party in advocating some supernational European authority to which Germany might become a member, but be closely watched. He was not in favor of Germany's joining the Atlantic Pact and he opposed all measures which threatened France with the danger of becoming an industrial subsidiary to Germany.

On May 24, 1952, Teitgen became President of the Popular Republican Movement in succession to Bidault. A few months later in August, Teitgen was offered the position of French representative in the court of justice of the European Coal and Steel Community (Schuman plan pool) and was urged by Robert Schuman among other M.R.P. members to accept. Teitgen declined the offer, considered a high honor, in order to retain the presidency of his party.

Pierre-Henri Teitgen is married to Jeanne Fonlupt and is the father of five children. The French statesman is an officer of the Legion of Honor and Companion of the Liberation. He is a recipient of the Croix de Guerre 1939-1945, the Medal of the Resistance with rosette, and the Escaped Prisoners Medal.

References

Dictionnaire Biographique Français Contemporain (1950)
International Who's Who, 1952
World Biography (1948)

THOMAS, ELBERT D(UNCAN) June 17, 1883—Feb. 11, 1953 High Commissioner of the United States Trust Territories of the Pacific; Former United States Senator from Utah; Mormon missionary in Japan (1907-12); instructor in Latin and Greek and registrar at the University of Utah, later taught political science there and at the University of California; served eighteen years in the Senate as an advocate of New Deal measures (1932-50); was named chairman of the Committee on Education and Labor and of the Military Affairs Committee, and member of the Foreign Relations Committee; appointed High Commissioner of the Trust Territory of the Pacific Islands in 1951; author of several books, including one in Japanese. See *Current Biography*, 1942.

Obituary

N Y Times p27 F 12 '53

THORNDIKE, DAME SYBIL Oct. 24, 1882 English actress; Commander of the Order of the British Empire
Address: 98 Swan Court, Chelsea, S.W.3, England; Cedar Cottage, Fairseat, Wrotham Hill, Kent, England

With her half-century record of distinguished and sometimes brilliant portrayals of roles in Shakespeare's and Shaw's plays, in Greek tragedy, regional and psychological drama, and in modern "high" comedy, Dame Sybil Thorndike has been called the "most astonishingly versatile" of contemporary British actresses. The late George Bernard Shaw is said to have written his *Saint Joan* with her talent and personality in mind, and since 1924 she has performed the title role in this play more than two thousand times in different parts of the world.

Dame Sybil, who played New York engagements in *The Distaff Side* and *Time and the Conways* in 1935 and 1938 respectively, embarked on the longest "run" of her career in 1951, when she was co-starred with Dame Edith Evans in N. C. Hunter's play *Waters of the Moon*, which continued until late 1953. Her latest appearance is in *A Day By The Sea*, a new play by N. C. Hunter, which stars Dame Sybil and her husband, Sir Lewis Casson, and Sir Ralph Richardson.

Born at Gainsborough in Lincolnshire on October 24, 1882, Sybil Thorndike is the eldest of the four children of a Church of England clergyman, the Reverend Arthur John Webster Thorndike, and the former Agnes Macdonald Bowers. (The actor and novelist Russell Thorndike is her surviving brother; a younger brother, Frank, who also went on the stage, was a casualty of World War I; Eileen Thorndike, now an instructor at the Royal Academy of Dramatic Art, is their sister).

Sybil Thorndike's earliest aspiration was for a musical career, and after attending the High School at Rochester in Kent (where her father became an honorary Canon at the cathedral) she took courses at the Guildhall School of Music in London and made professional appearances as a pianist. Having decided to become an actress, she entered the Ben Greet Academy, and made her first appearance on the stage at Oxford on June 18, 1904 in the farce *My Lord from Town*; her debut in Shakespeare was made in *The Merry Wives of Windsor* in the same city a few days afterwards. During the next four years she toured the United States with the Ben Greet Players, playing roles in Shakespeare and English classic comedy.

She made her debut in London at the Scala Theatre on February 9, 1908 in *The Marquis*. She became in the following summer the wife of the actor Lewis Casson, who had been a member of the Ben Greet company at the time of her Oxford appearances in 1904.

In September, 1908 Sybil Thorndike and her husband joined the stock company established by Miss Annie E. F. Horniman at the Gaiety Theatre in Manchester, England. Here she gained invaluable experience in realistic as well as romantic drama, playing such varied roles as Bessie Carter in *Marriages Are Made in Heaven*, Judith in Bernard Shaw's *The Devil's Disciple*, and the title role in Harold Chapin's *The Marriage of Columbine*. In March, 1910 the Cassons joined the repertory company of the American manager, Charles Frohman, at the Duke of York's Theatre in London. (Roles in which Sybil Thorndike appeared included Emma Huxtable in Granville Barker's *The Madras House*: Romp in *Prunella*, by Barker and Laurence Housman; and Maggie Massey in Elizabeth Baker's *Chains*).

Frohman then engaged the Cassons to play the roles of Fletcher and Emily Chapman in support of John Drew in the American production of W. Somerset Maugham's *Smith*, and they appeared in these roles at the Empire Theatre, New York, beginning September 5, 1910, and on tour. In the summer of 1912 Sybil Thorndike appeared under her husband's direction at the Aldwych and Playhouse in London as the millowner's daughter, Beatrice Farrar, in the most celebrated of the Lancashire regional dramas, Stanley Houghton's *Hindle Wakes*. At the Gaiety, Manchester on April 21, 1913, Miss Thorndike scored a personal acting triumph in the title role of St. John Ervine's *Jane Clegg*, and repeated her characterization at the Court Theatre in Lon-

British Inf. Services

DAME SYBIL THORNDIKE

don on May 19. The following October she achieved another personal success in the leading role of Eden Phillpotts' *The Shadow.*

While her husband served in the British Army during World War I, Sybil Thorndike appeared in Shakespearean productions at the Royal Victoria Hall (the "Old Vic") in London. During the four years beginning in 1914, she played in such roles as Constance in *King John,* the Fool in *King Lear,* also as Lady Macbeth, Portia, Rosalind, Beatrice, and Mistress Ford. She left the old playhouse in June 1918 to appear in a playlet *The Kiddies in the Ruins* which was introduced into the solidly established C. B. Cochran production *The Better 'Ole.* For about three months beginning September 1919, Miss. Thorndike appeared in the Louis N. Parker-George R. Sims melodrama *The Great Day* at the Drury Lane. She returned to the "Old Vic" for one special performance as Hecuba in the Gilbert Murray translation of *The Trojan Women* of Euripides. Her success in this role encouraged her husband, after his discharge from the Army, to join with a fellow actor Bruce Winston in presenting her in a series of matinees at the Holborn Empire from February to April, 1920, and during which she offered a repertory consisting of *The Trojan Women* and the *Medea* of Euripides, and Bernard Shaw's *Candida.*

It was during this Holborn Empire season that Miss Thorndike first won general acclaim as an actress of major stature. (The critic, W. A. Darlington, writing in the London *Daily Telegraph* of April 8, 1920, was amazed at the "exhibition of sheer power" which she gave as Medea, though he thought her characterization "too inhuman"). From May to August 1920, Miss Thorndike was engaged at the St. James' in London in *The Mystery of the Yellow Room.*

In September 1920 the directorship of an English "Grand Guignol" company was undertaken by Lewis Casson at the Little Theatre in the Adelphi, and during the next two years Miss Thorndike appeared there in a series of one-act thrillers and macabre comedies. In 1922 Miss Thorndike played a summer season under her own management at the New Theatre, offering a revival of *Jane Clegg,* a play by the French dramatist Henri Bernstein entitled *The Scandal,* Percy Bysshe Shelley's *The Cenci* (in which she acted Beatrice Cenci) and was again seen as Medea.

In contrast with her Euripides characterizations, Miss Thorndike's Jane Clegg was "quiet, restrained, rounded," observed Hermon Ould in the *English Review.* At the same theatre in September 1923, she revived *Cymbeline,* and in the following month played the maligned elder sister in Henry Arthur Jones's drama *The Lie.*

On March 26, 1924 she first appeared as the Maid of Orleans in Bernard Shaw's *Saint Joan.* (The role, although actually first played in New York by Winifred Lenihan the previous December, had been written with Sybil Thorndike in mind). The play ran at the New Theatre in London for 244 consecutive performances; then after an interval of a few weeks was re-presented at the Regent (January 14, 1925) for 132 additional performances. The actress has since played Saint Joan in London, the British provinces, the colonies and the dominions, and in Europe more than two thousand times.

During the Regent Theatre run of *Saint Joan,* Sybil Thorndike gave one special performance of Susan Glaspell's drama, *The Verge,* achieving (in the words of the critic E. A. Baughan) a "harrowing representation" of a "mind shown hovering on the brink of madness." Later in 1925 she appeared at the Wyndham Theatre in Lennox Robinson's *The Round Table* and a brief revival of *The Lie;* at Christmas time she gave a much admired performance as Katharine of Aragon in *Henry VIII.*

In 1926 she appeared at the Ambassador Theatre in Clemence Dane's *Granite* and at the Princess as Lady Macbeth. When the "Old Vic" company played an engagement at the Lyric Hammersmith Theatre in 1927. the actress won admiration with her Katharina in *The Taming of the Shrew,* Portia in *The Merchant of Venice* and Beatrice in *Much Ado About Nothing.*

In the same year she made her first film, playing Nurse Edith Cavell in *Dawn.* For nine months of 1928 Miss Thorndike toured South Africa in a repertory including *Saint Joan,* returning to London in January 1929 for an appearance in the title role of Shaw's *Major Barbara,* as Lily Cobb in Clemence Dane's *Mariners,* and in a double bill consisting of *Jane Clegg* and *Medea.* During 1930 the versatile actress played in *Phèdre* in French, Mrs. Alving in Ibsen's *Ghosts,* and Emilia in *Othello.*

For her services to the stage the actress was created a Commander of the Order of the British Empire in 1931 and thus became Dame Sybil Thorndike. After touring Egypt, Palestine, Australia, and New Zealand in 1932-33, she returned to London and appeared as Eve in John van Druten's *The Distaff Side*. She repeated this role with much personal acclaim at the Booth Theatre in New York on September 25, 1934. ("Dame Sybil won all our hearts," wrote Brooks Atkinson in the New York *Times*. "The simplicity, quiet force and womanly beauty of her drew the audience close around her"). Her next and only subsequent New York appearance in J. B. Priestley's *Time and the Conways* on January 3, 1938 was, however, less approved, Brooks Atkinson noting that she had "some difficulty in assuming the mask of genteel shrewishness as the Conway mother." (In England meanwhile, she had added to her laurels by appearances in the Grace George role in *Kind Lady* and in Mark Reed's American comedy *Yes, My Darling Daughter*). Later in 1938, at the Duchess Theatre in London, Dame Sybil made another of her outstanding successes in Emlyn Williams' *The Corn Is Green*, creating the character later interpreted in America by Ethel Barrymore.

In May, 1943, when the historical Theatre Royal in Bristol was reopened as Great Britain's first State-owned playhouse and adjunct to the "Old Vic," Dame Sybil spoke the inaugural prologue and played Kate in Goldsmith's *She Stoops to Conquer*. Later in the same month she visited Dublin to play Lady Cecily in Shaw's *Captain Brassbound's Conversion* and Mrs. Alving in *Ghosts* with the Gate Theatre company. The New York critic Richard Watts, Jr., reviewing these performances, thought she played Lady Cecily "with humor, graciousness and charm."

Between 1940 and 1943 Dame Sybil and Lewis Casson made with the "Old Vic" company six tours of World War II camps and bases, and in recognition of this patriotic service Casson received the accolade of knighthood in 1945, thereby becoming Sir Lewis Casson. The Cassons played with the "Old Vic" company at the New Theatre in 1944, and in 1945-6 toured Belgium, Germany, and France.

Having created the character of Mrs. Frazer in Clemence Dane's *Call Home the Heart* at the St. James' in London in the latter year, Dame Sybil was next seen as Mrs. Linden, in the 1947-48 run at the Duchess Theatre, of J. B. Priestley's *The Linden Tree*. In December, 1948 she acted with John Gielgud in a revival of St. John Hankin's *The Return of the Prodigal*.

Her subsequent roles, with the exception of that of Lady Randolph in the 1951 Edinburgh revival of Home's *Douglas,* have all been in the realm of comedy; her recent triumphs in this field, beginning with her Isabel Brocken in Margery Sharp's *The Foolish Gentlewoman* (Duchess, February 2, 1949) have tended to eclipse memories of her earlier work in Greek and Shakespearean tragedy. W. A. Darlington in the New York *Times* of April 3, 1949, wrote of her acting in *The Foolish Gentlewoman*: "As a middle-aged or elderly ditherer she combines an uncanny sense of the ridiculous with absolute character."

Dame Sybil made an equally hilarious impression as Aunt Anna Rose in M. J. Farrell's and John Perry's Irish comedy, *Treasure Hunt*, which ran at the Apollo and St. Martin's theatres in London for 359 performances beginning September 14, 1949. Her most recent comedy trumph was at the Haymarket Theatre, London, beginning on April 19, 1951, in N. C. Hunter's *Waters of the Moon*, in which she shared acting honors with another "great lady" of the British stage, Dame Edith Evans. Dame Sybil's role in this Chekhovian play about the guests at a Devonshire boarding house was that of Mrs. Whyte, an "exceedingly severe lady" who "with a grim countenance broods over the wealth she once had" (Harold Hobson in the *Christian Science Monitor*), and who is cannily contrasted with the vivacious Mrs. Lancaster, played by Dame Edith. ("It is Dame Sybil's triumph that she is funny," wrote W. A. Darlington in comment, ". . . so funny that she gets her first laugh for the expression on her face as she makes her first entrance, and yet never allows us to forget for a moment that Mrs. Whyte is a real and gallant woman").

Illuminating details regarding Dame Sybil's career may be found in her brother Russell Thorndike's book, *Sybil Thorndike*, originally published in London in 1929 by Thornton Butterworth, and revised and reissued in 1950 by Rockliff. Dame Sybil herself is the author of the essay *Religion and the Stage* (Benn, London, 1928) and a contributor to both the biography of Lilian Baylis published in 1938 and the *Essays in Honor of Gilbert Murray* (1936). She has spoken on behalf of the National Theatre movement in Britain, and at meetings of the British Actors' Equity Association has opposed moves to tighten the conditions of admission to membership. Sir Lewis and Dame Sybil have two sons, John and Christopher, and two daughters. Dame Sybil enjoys "the piano and home" and swimming is her favorite exercise.

In the recent motion picture *Melba*, Dame Sybil played the role of Queen Victoria.

References

Bookman 63:278-9 Mr '23 por
Christian Sci Mon p6 Je 26 '43
Graphic (London) 106:810-11 D 2 '22 pors
Theatre Arts 36:67-70 Ja '32
Theatre World 21:192-3 Ap '34
Burke's Peerage, Baronetage and Knightage (1953)
Columbia Encyclopedia (1950)
Encyclopaedia Britannica (1952)
Halliday, F. E. A Shakespeare Companion (1952)
Hartnoll, P. Oxford Companion to the Theatre (1951)
Sobol, B. ed. Theatre Handbook (1940)
Thorndike, R. Sybil Thorndike (1929, 1950)
Thorndike, S. Religion and the Stage (1928)
Who's Who, 1953
World Biography (1948)

THORPE, JIM May 28, 1888—Mar. 28, 1953 Athlete; of Sac and Fox Indian descent; winner of pentathlon and decathlon in Stockholm Olympic Games of 1912; Olympic awards revoked in 1913 for lack of amateur standing; played major league baseball (1913-19) and professional football (1915-29); collaborated on *Jim Thorpe's History of the Olympics* (1932); played bit parts in Hollywood films (1933-37); active in Indian affairs (1937); in 1943 and 1952 legislative groups attempted unsuccessfully to have his Olympic medals restored; joined Merchant Marine (1945); voted greatest football player and greatest male athlete of first half of twentieth century in 1950 Associated Press poll of sports writers; movie of his life, *Jim Thorpe—All American*, released by Warner Brothers (1951). See *Current Biography*, 1950.

Obituary

N. Y Times p92 Mr 29 '53

TOBEY, CHARLES W(ILLIAM) July 22, 1880—July 25, 1953 Republican United States Senator from New Hampshire; elected to New Hampshire House of Representatives in 1915, 1916, 1919, 1920 (as Speaker), 1923 and 1924. In 1925 was elected Senator and in 1929 Governor of New Hampshire; from 1933 served as United States Representative to 1939 when he became United States Senator; introduced Tobey Resolution opposing inquiry into person's income and opposed what he believed to be Government encroachment on individual liberties; was member of Senate Crime Committee in 1951. See *Current Biography*, 1941.

Obituary

N Y Times p1 Jl 25 '53

TOBIN, MAURICE J(OSEPH) May 22, 1901—July 19, 1953 Former Secretary of Labor and Governor of Massachusetts; elected to Massachusetts House of Representatives in 1926, and to the Boston School Committee in 1931; elected mayor of Boston in 1937 and Governor of Massachusetts in 1944; for that state he achieved a fair employment practices act, increased workmen's compensation and unemployment insurance benefits; appointed Secretary of Labor in 1948 by President Truman; was leader in fight to repeal the Taft-Hartley law and the re-enactment of the Wagner Act. See *Current Biography*, 1946.

Obituary

N Y Times p17 Jl 20 '53

TOLSTOY, ALEXANDRA (LVOVNA) July 1, 1884- Writer; lecturer; welfare worker

Address: b. c/o Tolstoy Foundation, Inc., 300 W. 58th St., New York 19; h. "Reed Farm," Valley Cottage, N.Y.

The youngest daughter of Leo Tolstoy, formerly his secretary and the executrix of his estate, Alexandra Tolstoy has devoted much of her life to perpetuating her father's ideas

through welfare work, lectures, and writing. Since 1939 she has been president of the Tolstoy Foundation, which aids anti-Communist Russian refugees and maintains a resettlement center for them in Valley Cottage, New York. In the years following the Russian revolution and before leaving Russia in 1929, she established an educational center on her father's estate and organized a society to prepare a complete edition of his works. Miss Tolstoy, who became an American citizen in 1941, has dropped her inherited title of countess.

Alexandra Lvovna Tolstoy was next to the last of the thirteen children of the famed Russian writer Count Leo Tolstoy and Sophya A. (Bers) Tolstoy. At the time of her birth, on July 1, 1884, at Tolstoy's family estate, Yasnaya Polyana, in Russia, her father had completed his great novels and was devoting his writing and his thoughts to religion. He was also endeavoring to put his theories into practice—against the opposition of his wife and, except for Alexandra, of his children. Alexandra received most of her education at home. As a child, "she was a good deal of a tomboy," according to a *New Yorker* profile (March 15, 1952), and spent much time at Yasnaya Polyana "tree-climbing, horseback riding, ice-skating and the like. Music had an important place in the family's life . . . with special emphasis on Chopin and gypsy songs."

In 1901 Alexandra Tolstoy became her father's secretary, her chief task being to transcribe his manuscripts. She also at this time worked in the village clinic and school and learned something about farming. In *The Tragedy of Tolstoy* she has told of her devotion to her father during the last years of his life and of her refusal to accept offers of marriage because she wanted to remain with him. Tolstoy's death in 1910 is believed to have been caused by pneumonia that he caught in a railroad station while, with his daughter's help, he was trying to get away from his unhappy home life. In accordance with Tolstoy's will, Alexandra, his literary executor, prepared an edition of his unpublished works. Also acting on his wishes, she used the proceeds of the sale to buy back the family estate, which in the will had been divided among Tolstoy's widow and children, to distribute it to the peasants. The four years between her father's death and the outbreak of the First World War were devoted to European travel and to such pastimes as starting a racing stable at an estate that she bought near Yasnaya Polyana.

At the start of World War I Miss Tolstoy took refresher courses in anatomy, pathology, and related subjects, of which she had gained some knowledge while working in the clinic near her father's estate. She became a nurse on a hospital train carrying wounded soldiers, and when in 1915 an epidemic of typhus and typhoid broke out on the Armenian front where the Russians were fighting the Turks, she joined one of the emergency medical detachments which were formed to handle it. For this service, she received the Medal of St. George.

After recovering from a siege of malaria, Miss Tolstoy became an executive in a relief organization which operated, not far behind the lines, emergency schools and dining centers capable of caring for ten thousand children. Her next post was chief of a military medical attachment, with a rank roughly equivalent to colonel, in command of three front-line medical units comprising a personnel of more than four hundred fifty. She received her second Medal of St. George as a result of her service during a gas attack in which she herself was gassed and hospitalized at the end of 1916. Her convalescence lasted through the days of the Russian Revolution of February 1917. When she left the hospital, she returned to her duties with the medical detachments and attempted to repair the disorder into which they had fallen as a result of the revolution; for this, she was recommended for a third Medal of St. George. At the end of 1917 she went first to Moscow and then to Yasnaya Polyana, which, although much of the Tolstoy land was confiscated, was left intact because of the esteem in which the writer was held.

Returning to Moscow in 1918, Miss Tolstoy founded, with government permission, a Society for the Dissemination and Study of Tolstoy's Works. With some of her father's former followers, she worked among the manuscripts at the Rumiantsev Museum to prepare a complete edition of Tolstoy's writings in ninety-one volumes, the publication of which was started by the Soviet Government in 1928, but apparently has not yet been completed. During the course of her years in Russia under the Soviets, she was arrested five times and in 1920 sentenced to three years in prison after a group of White Russians had held clandestine meetings in her house. At the prison camp she started a school, organized a chorus, "and astonished both her jailers and her fellow-prisoners by her ability to get on with a prison camp full of discontented intellectuals and common criminals as easily as if they had been a group of refugee children" (*New Yorker*). After a year, she was released without explanation.

Later in 1921 Miss Tolstoy was appointed curator of Yasnaya Polyana, which was to become a national museum and educational center. During her eight years in that post, she established a hospital, a dispensary, a clinic, four elementary schools, an industrial high school, and an agricultural high school. No politics were taught at the schools until in 1924 the center began to come under attack and was assigned a "political grammar" teacher. Because of her objection to Soviet-instilled antireligious propaganda in the Tolstoy schools, Miss Tolstoy made plans to leave Russia and in October 1929 obtained the government's permission to go to Japan to deliver a series of lectures on her father. For almost two years she lectured in English and Russian in Tokyo, Osaka, Kyoto, and other Japanese cities before embarking for the United States.

Since her arrival in the United States in 1931, Miss Tolstoy has lectured widely in schools, universities, and clubs on Leo Tolstoy and, in recent years, on the dangers of Communism. She was also occupied for a number of years in farming, first in New Square, Pennsylvania (1931-33), and then in Haddam, Connecticut (1933-39)—raising chickens, milking

ALEXANDRA TOLSTOY

cows, and doing other farm work. Meanwhile, in 1933, her book, *Tragedy of Tolstoy*, was published and acclaimed as "an important document" on Tolstoy's life at Yasnaya Polyana and his relationship with his wife and children. Alexander Nazaroff, reviewing the volume for the New York *Times*, commented, "as though having inherited a grain of that genius in which her father was so fantastically rich, Alexandra Lvovna writes remarkably well, with a keen sense of humor, with vividness and with a noteworthy gift of characterization." Her experiences of more than ten years in Russia after the Revolution were recounted in *I Worked for the Soviet* (1934), described as "a stirring and entertaining record, told with fairness and vigor and a minimum of recriminations and complaints" (*Saturday Review of Literature*). Another book, *The Life of Leo Tolstoy—My Father,* was published by Harper and Brothers in August 1953. The New York *Herald Tribune* reviewer wrote: "She has written of her father with extraordinary modesty and tenderness."

On February 6, 1939, with the aid of Russian *émigrés* and influential Americans, the Tolstoy Foundation was organized to help victims of Russian persecution. Miss Tolstoy sold her farm in Connecticut and turned over the proceeds to the foundation, of which she was made president. At first the group operated solely from New York, sending food and clothes to Russian prisoners of war in Finland and Russian refugees in France. At the end of 1940 the foundation acquired Reed Farm in Valley Cottage, New York, where a temporary home has been provided for displaced persons, orphans, and for children whose parents are just establishing themselves in America. In World War II it collected $65,000 to help Russian prisoners of war in Finland. The foundation still maintains offices in New York and assists Russian refugees with immigration problems, money,

TOLSTOY, ALEXANDRA—*Continued*

medical aid, and resettlement problems. It sends assistance as well to displaced persons in camps in Germany, Austria, and Trieste, and food to tuberculosis patients in Austria. Operating with a budget of five hundred thousand dollars a year, it also has branches on the West Coast, in Chicago, Bridgeport, Connecticut, and Washington, D.C. Executive director Blair Taylor heads the organization with Miss Tolstoy, who commutes from Reed Farm to New York. The Foundation has established fifteen offices in Europe to help escapees from Russia.

Alexandra Tolstoy, who would prefer to have no association with politics, has become a strong anti-Communist and has urged unity of groups fighting Soviet aggressions. She is a member of the Russian Orthodox Church. Heavy in build, Miss Tolstoy weighs 175 pounds and stands five feet five inches tall; her eyes and her hair are gray. Whatever spare time she has is spent in reading, fishing, and raising flowers.

References

N Y Herald Tribune II p5 Ag 15 '48
N Y Times Book R p2+ Ap 26 '42
New Yorker 28:34-47 Mr 15 '52; 28:36-59 Mr 22 '52
Yale R 22:264-87 D '32
Tolstoy, A. L. Tragedy of Tolstoy (1933); I Worked for the Soviet (1934)
Who's Who, 1952
World Biography (1948)

TREFFLICH, HENRY (HERBERT FREDERICK) Jan. 9, 1908- Wild animal dealer

Address: b. c/o Trefflich Bird and Animal Company, Inc., 228 Fulton St., New York 7; h. 15 Abbey Pl., Yonkers 3, N.Y.

In the center of the financial district in lower Manhattan, Henry Trefflich operates a $500,000 to $1,000,000 bird and animal business which makes him the largest animal importer in the United States. One of the main functions of his business is to provide monkeys needed for experimentation purposes in medical research. He also supplies zoos, circuses, carnivals, and private buyers with birds and animals which he imports not only from Africa, where in Sierra Leone he maintains a branch of his corporation, but from the great markets of Bombay, Bangkok, Calcutta, Singapore, and from Brazil.

Henry Herbert Frederick Trefflich was born January 9, 1908, in Hamburg, Germany, one of four children (one boy and three girls) of Henry Herbert Frederick and Caroline Jahn Trefflich. His father, who was reared in Thüringen, Germany, as a young man was a captain in the Kaiser's navy. Two years before his son's birth, he became, in 1906, an animal dealer in Hamburg, an occupation which took him, just before World War I, to India on a hunting trip, where he trained police dogs for the British. Following the outbreak of the

war, he was interned by the British when he refused, as a German citizen, to continue training police dogs for the English. In Germany, his zoo was confiscated. Young Henry did not see his father again until he was thirteen years of age.

Reared in Hamburg, Germany, Henry Trefflich attended public schools there until at the age of fourteen, he withdrew from school and signed on a German tramp steamer as a mess boy. After making two trips around the world in one and a half years, he left the tramp ship at Hamburg and sailed on a steamer for America. In the United States he worked about two years in Riggs Restaurant, before going back to Germany temporarily. When Trefflich re-entered the United States six months later, he returned to restaurant work, finding employment in Child's Restaurant in New York City. In 1928 he financed his father's passage to America and later went with him to India to hunt animals. Young Trefflich, who at twenty-one had been bitten by a cobra and clawed by a leopard, sold the animals he obtained to Benson's Animal Farm in New Hampshire, while his father took a shipment back to Germany, where he had reopened a zoo.

Following a second hunting trip in India with his father, in 1929, he returned to New York with his merchandise and peddled it among animal dealers in the city. Later in the same year he again went to India, with an agreement to supply a dealer in the United States with wild animals. When the dealer, unable to remain in business, refused to accept the animals shipped to him or to pay for them, Trefflich, who had himself paid the cost of securing the animals and the shipment, was without funds in India and living "on the beach," as he has said, with natives. In 1930 a sister paid his return passage to the United States. After working at odd jobs for several months and accumulating a small bank account, with the help of friends he was able to open a small business as an animal dealer in the Bronx, New York, in 1931. He specialized in importing monkeys, as he has expressed it, "bit by bit." The following year he moved his business to the financial district in downtown Manhattan.

The "Monkey King of America," as Trefflich came to be called in newspapers, brought eight baby gorillas into the United States in 1939, the first to arrive in this country in twenty years—since those captured by Martin Johnson, the big game hunter. One, Makoko, became famous at the Bronx Zoo in New York, where it survived for ten years. Frightened by its popularity, this gorilla in May 1951 fell into a six-foot moat and drowned, ending the hope of the park director and its original owner, Trefflich, that it would mate to produce the first baby gorilla born in captivity. Since 1939 Trefflich has introduced forty-seven gorillas into the United States (including two that arrived in November 1952); approximately half of this number are still alive. During the 1940's he sent exploring parties into the forests of East Africa and the mountains of the Belgian Congo to obtain the high-priced gorillas, which can be captured alive only as infants and which sell for about $5,000 each. He has also brought about fifty elephants into the United States.

During World War II Trefflich supplied the United States Government and the National Foundation for Infantile Paralysis with monkeys for medical research. He believes he is responsible for bringing to this country most of the rhesus monkeys used in the laboratory research that led to the discovery of the RH factor in pregnant women. People seeking household pets purchase more than a hundred monkeys a month from Trefflich, who has described the rhesus as the most intelligent monkey and a better watchdog than a dog. "Monkeys," he was quoted by E. C. Albright in *Coronet* (December 1950) as saying, "can teach human beings a lot. They rarely fight among themselves in the jungle." He considers them "brighter than people" and has stated that it is impossible to be unhappy in the presence of a monkey (*Parade,* February 11, 1951). Among the chimpanzees imported by Trefflich that have become famous is Cheetah, noted for appearances with Johnny Weissmuller in the Tarzan movies. Psychiatrists studying anxiety states or sleeplessness in human beings purchase chimpanzees for research purposes from Trefflich, as do universities for use in psychological studies. Determining the intelligence of the chimpanzee from the shape of its face, Trefflich looks for a high forehead and high cheekbones as signs of a superior intelligence quota.

A serious threat to Trefflich's occupation as an animal dealer occurred on May 11, 1946, at which time approximately one hundred monkeys escaped from the four-story building he owns into the streets of lower Manhattan. "When I saw thousands of people congregated," he said, "and my monkeys running everywhere, I thought my business was gone." The pack, which for more than five hours ran about the Washington Market area, comprised a shipment of rhesus monkeys from India. Trefflich asked neighborhood store keepers for assistance and was also aided by police, firemen, and agents from the Society for the Prevention of Cruelty to Animals. One monkey remained at large until May 29, after those that had been retrieved were sold. On May 15, 1946, Trefflich was called to Lower Manhattan Summons Court by a police summons for alleged violation of a penal law dealing with failure to safeguard wild animal life and causing injury to the public. He employed a lawyer who invited the magistrate to visit the Trefflich pet shop and "see for himself," an invitation that was not accepted (New York *Times,* May 15, 1946). After an investigation by the Police Department's legal bureau, Trefflich was permitted to continue in his business.

Again in 1947, Trefflich drew public attention because of two monkeys that escaped while being unloaded at the New York City docks. One of these, called The Mugg, resisted captivity for fourteen months, living under the girders of the pier; the other died of pneumonia. Two years later, in 1949, Tref-

HENRY TREFFLICH

flich brought in from Bangkok and Singapore the world's largest airplane shipments of birds, reptiles, and animals in two chartered "Noah's Ark" planes. The shipments were escorted by a young woman animal scout whom Trefflich referred to as "Jungle Jenny." When criticized by competitive dealers for mixing publicity with business, Trefflich replied, "Of course we told the newspapers about it; what do you think we are, smugglers?" (quoted by *Collier's,* September 10, 1949).

At Walston Farm near Accomac, Virginia, Trefflich in 1950 established what he calls a "monkey reconditioning" project, which provides housing units with drinking fountains, feeders, and electrically heated hutches for about 1,000 monkeys. It is expected that the project will have facilities to handle 10,000 to 15,000 monkeys annually. In this reconditioning center, the monkeys, after their trying trip to the United States from their native country, are given an opportunity to become accustomed to a new way of life. Without this interim before being sent to research laboratories, hospitals, zoos, or circuses throughout the country, they frequently develop illness or neurosis. Specimens from the Walston Farm are considered the finest monkeys available for medical experimentation in polio, malaria, and the RH blood factor (Washington *Post,* September 16, 1951).

With the increased demand for wild animals in the United States, Trefflich opened his own supply station in Sierra Leone, Africa, in the early 1950's. Delays in filling orders are frequently due, Trefflich has explained, to "an embargo that may be placed by the United States or a foreign government, or a combination of both" (New York *Sunday News,* September 28, 1952). He has had standing orders for several years for giant pandas, which are scarce and difficult to obtain, since China has made no shipments following the Communist

TREFFLICH, HENRY—*Continued*

regime. Trefflich states there is only one living panda in the United States. For a number of years he has also held requests for large pythons that he cannot secure, partly because the natives of Siam consume those they capture as a delicacy. After his trappers had spent several months finding a suitable specimen, Trefflich recently filled an order for a rhinoceros which had been placed two years ago, in 1950, by Central Park Zoo in New York City.

Trefflich, who takes an active part in all phases of his business, has a loud-speaker communication system in his four-story headquarters—where his staff comprises seventeen assistants—so that he may be reached when he is away from his desk and occupied on another floor. On the first floor of this building he maintains a shop in which he sells such bird and animal accessories as bird seed, bird cages, bird baths, dog biscuits, doghouses, harnesses, leashes, rubber bones and catnip, as well as guppies and Japanese goldfish. At one time he may have on sale or awaiting shipment a variety of birds and animals including canaries, parrots, temus, mynah birds, finches, owls, kangoroos, kittens, white mice, puppies, gibbons, chimpanzees, gorillas, panthers, tigers, and reptiles.

In an article entitled "No Business for Sissies," appearing in *Collier's* (September 10, 1949), E. M. Wylie said of Trefflich: "When it comes to showmanship, Trefflich is without an equal in the business." Organizations to which he belongs are the Liederkrantz Club in New York City and the Amackassin Club in Yonkers. He is an independent voter and his church affiliation is Presbyterian. On June 27, 1942, Trefflich married Alberta Esther Stetin, secretary to the chief veterinarian at the Bronx Zoo. They have four children: Richard, Carol, Arno, and Marlene Trefflich. The animal dealer is five feet nine inches in height, weighs 175 pounds, and has blue eyes and blonde hair. His hobby is collecting hand organs, which he often rents. He has said: "America is the only place in the world where one can develop a business from a nickel. I never gave up."

References

> Collier's 124:30-1+ S 10 '49
> Coronet 29:105-6 D '50

TROOST, LAURENS (trōst)   Mar. 19, 1895- Naval architect; educator

Address: b. c/o Department of Naval Architecture and Marine Engineering, Massachusetts Institute of Technology, Cambridge 39, Mass.; h. 8 Craigie St., Cambridge 38, Mass.

Laurens Troost, an international authority in naval architecture, was appointed in August 1952 as professor and head of the Department of Naval Architecture and Marine Engineering at Massachusetts Institute of Technology. Coming to his position with more than thirty years of experience in designing, building, and testing naval ships, Troost had been a naval constructor in the Royal Netherlands Navy (1919-29)

and later a superintendent of the Netherlands Ship Model Basin in Wageningen, the Netherlands (1929-51). During 1951-52 he was a visiting professor of naval architecture at the Massachusetts Institute of Technology and at the University of California.

Born in Rotterdam, Holland, on March 19, 1895, Laurens Troost is one of two sons of Marius and Willempje Gerarda (Jekel) Troost, both elementary school teachers. Troost grew up in Rotterdam, where in 1906 he entered the second Higher Citizen's School (the equivalent of high school and one year of college in the United States), being graduated from its five-year course in 1911. His interest in ships was aroused early by the surroundings in his native city. "From my earliest youth," he has said, "I overlooked the harbor of Rotterdam through my window and so got interested in ships and shipping as a youngster."

With a government scholarship, Troost in 1911 entered the Institute of Technology in Delft, the Netherlands, where he majored in naval architecture. His extrascholastic interests were playing the violin in chamber music groups and taking part in football and track activities. In 1916 he became a lieutenant in the Netherlands Artillery Service Reserve; three years later (1919) he received the degree of Naval Architect from the Delft institute. He then joined the Royal Netherlands Navy in 1919 as a naval constructor. Here, gaining experience in design, building, and repair of naval vessels, he remained until 1929, when the Foundation of the Netherlands Ship Model Basin asked him to take charge of designing and building a new modern ship model basin in Wageningen, the Netherlands. In this assignment he saw the completion in 1932 of the construction of the basin, which was operated from that time until September 1951 under his supervision.

Introducing many new testing methods and original instruments in the operation of the Wageningen Ship Model Basin, Troost directed its development from a small institute, with a staff of eight people and a testing capacity of ten ship models a year, to a world-famous institute with a staff of seventy-five persons and a testing capacity of 120 self-propelled ship models a year. About half of the commissions now come from the Royal Netherlands Navy, shipowners, and shipbuilders in the Netherlands, while the other half come from foreign shipbuilding interests, including those in Europe and America.

During World War II Troost was a captain in the Netherlands Artillery Service Reserve, having remained in the reserve since joining it in 1916. He left this service in 1945 to become for the next three years a commander in the Netherlands Naval Reserve. After supervising reconstruction of the war damage to the Wageningen Ship Model Basin during 1945-46, Troost went to the United States for the first time, visiting laboratories on a tour planned and organized by the United States Navy. In 1946 he returned to Holland, where, along with his position as head of the ship model basin, he assumed the duties of a part-time professor of

LAURENS TROOST

naval architecture at the Institute of Technology in Delft and was so occupied until the Massachusetts Institute of Technology in 1951 invited him to be an exchange professor in the Department of Naval Architecture and Marine Engineering. With his further stay in the United States sponsored by M.I.T., Troost during 1951 was also a visiting professor of naval architecture at the University of California in Berkeley. On August 30, 1952, he was named a professor and the head of the Department of Naval Architecture and Marine Engineering at Massachusetts Institute of Technology by James R. Killian, Jr., president of the institute. In this position, he succeeded Admiral Edward L. Cochrane, who was appointed Dean of Engineering at M.I.T.

Troost has written a number of papers and articles on ship hydromechanics. He is a co-author of the handbook *Resistance, Propulsion and Steering of Ships* (1948), with W. P. A. Van Lammeren and J. G. Konig. In 1937 the Queen of the Netherlands awarded Troost an officership in the Order of Orange-Nassau, and in 1949 she bestowed upon him the gold De Ruyter Medal for outstanding services in the field of shipping and shipbuilding.

Organizations of which Troost is a member are Sigma Xi, the Society of Naval Architects and Marine Engineers, the Institute of Naval Architects, the North East Coast Institution of Engineers and Shipbuilders, the Association Technique Maritime et Aëronautique, and the Schiffbautechnische Gesellschaft. He was formerly a council member of the Royal Dutch Institute of Engineers and chairman of its section for engineering and naval architecture. In 1933 he organized the first International Conference of Tank Superintendents in The Hague, now an operating international organization; at its sixth Congress, held in Washington, D.C., in September 1951, Troost was a member of the standing committee. In 1947 he founded the Dutch Shipbuilding Research Association, of which he became the first chairman, serving in 1949 as vice-chairman.

By his marriage on March 4, 1926, to Martha Christina Versluys, of Rotterdam, a biologist, Troost is the father of two sons, Marius and Daan, both students at the Massachusetts Institute of Technology. Troost weighs 186 pounds, stands five feet eleven inches in height, and has brown eyes and brown hair. His hobby is violin playing. "I am a strong believer in private enterprise and in the Rotary service principle," he has said. "My strongest hope is that the rapid development of research and technology ultimately will be to the benefit of mankind."

References

N Y Times p17 Ag 31 '52
International Who's Who, 1952
Wie Is Dat? 1948

TWINING, NATHAN F(ARRAGUT) Oct. 11, 1897- United States Air Force officer
Address: c/o Department of Defense, The Pentagon, Washington 25, D.C.

When it was proposed that the Air Force be reduced by mid-1955 to 120 Wings instead of a planned 143, General Nathan F. Twining appeared before a Congressional committee and insisted that a 143-wing force was "essential to the security of the nation" (New York *Times,* May 31, 1953).

The General said that "the F-86 Sabre jet gunsight makes sights of several years ago resemble elementary toys." He pointed out that there are many indications that "the rapid improvement of air weapons by the U.S.S.R. is gradually overtaking the technical superiority we have always counted on. Without that superiority in trained men as well as planes, the United States would have a poor chance against Russia" (Washington *Post,* July 8, 1953).

Warning against building first-class combat planes without enough trained men to keep them flying, General Twining spoke on July 8 at the Mississippi American Legion convention and stressed that the Air Force's most highly skilled men have the lowest re-enlistment rate. The reasons are low pay compared with private industry, and dissatisfaction with housing and living conditions, he said.

Appointed Air Force Chief of Staff to succeed General Hoyt S. Vandenberg on June 30, 1953, General Twining had served as Vice-Chief of Staff for Air since October 1950. A former infantry officer who became a pursuit pilot, he had commanded the Fifteenth Air Force in Italy and the Twentieth Air Force in the Pacific during World War II.

Nathan Farragut Twining, born in Monroe, Wisconsin, October 11, 1897 is a descendant of William Twining who came from England to join the Plymouth colony in 1635. He is one of the four sons of Clarence Walter and Maize (Barber) Twining; two of his brothers are Captain Robert Twining (retired) of the United

GEN. NATHAN F. TWINING

States Navy, and Major General Merrill Twining of the Marine Corps.

The boys' father, who was a banker at Monroe, later moved his family to Portland, Oregon, where Nathan Twining completed his secondary schooling and began military training as a member of the Oregon National Guard.

First called to active duty in June 1916, he served on the Mexican border until the following September as a corporal.

Again mustered into service in March 1917 one month after the United States broke off diplomatic relations with Germany, Twining served in the Oregon National Guard as a sergeant of infantry until June, when his appointment to the United States Military Academy at West Point became effective.

At West Point he was a football end, stood at the middle of his class, and was graduated in November 1918. Commissioned a second lieutenant of infantry, he served three months with the occupation forces in Germany, and made a tour of observation of World War I battle fronts in Belgium, France and Italy.

In September 1919 Lieutenant Twining entered Fort Benning Infantry School and graduated in June 1920. He remained a few months at the fort in the 29th Infantry, served as aide to Brigadier General B. A. Poore at other military posts, and in 1923 entered Primary Flying School at Brooks Field, Texas. After graduation there, he attended the Kelly Field, Texas Advanced Flying School, receiving a pursuit pilot's rating in September 1924.

Lieutenant Twining returned to Brooks Field as a flying instructor, and was formally transferred from the infantry to the Air Service (predecessor of. the Army Air Corps) on November 16, 1926.

From September 1929 to February 1930 Lieutenant Twining was an instructor at March Field, California, after which he served for a little over two years with the 18th Pursuit Group at Schofield Barracks, Hawaii. He was stationed at Fort Crockett, Texas from July, 1932 until March 1935, when he was relieved as adjutant of the Third Attack Group and transferred to Barksdale Field, Louisiana, to become assistant operations officer of the Third Wing.

He was promoted to the rank of captain in August 1935 when he entered the Air Force Tactical School at Maxwell Field, Alabama. Graduating the following year, Captain Twining entered the Command and General Staff School at Fort Leavenworth, Kansas. In June 1937 he was assigned as Air Corps technical supervisor of the San Antonio Air Depot at Duncan Field, Texas.

Advanced in rank to major in August 1940 when he was transferred to the office of the Chief of Air Corps at Washington, D.C., he served first as assistant chief of the Inspection Division and later as chief of the Technical Inspection Section.

Transferred to the Operations Division shortly after the United States entered World War II, he was made assistant executive in the office of the Army Air Forces Chief of Staff in February 1942. He became director of War Organization and Movements in that office in the following May.

Major Twining was sent overseas in August 1942 as chief of staff of the Army Forces (ground and air) in the South Pacific. About six months later he was appointed commanding general of the newly activated 13th Air Force formed to cover the campaign in the Solomon Islands.

Major General Twining and fourteen others were on a combat mission when their B-17 heavy bomber was forced down in the Coral Sea by a tropical storm on January 26, 1943. They were adrift for six days in rubber liferafts before being rescued, and General Twining shot one of the two albatrosses which helped to provide the party with food. After the rescue he made a "memorandum of suggested needs for forced landing" which included smoke smudge for rafts and water-tight watches.

Reassigned on July 25 as commander, Aircraft, Solomon Islands, Major General Twining had "tactical control of all Army, Navy, Marine and Allied Air Forces in the South Pacific." These combined forces destroyed some 700 Japanese planes in the course of the next four months, during which period he directed the air movements supporting the occupation of the Treasury Islands and Bougainville.

It was his force which completely wiped out the effective Japanese air strength on Bougainville," declared Admiral William F. Halsey, Jr. when Twining was relieved by Major General Ralph J. Mitchell in November in the normal process of command rotation.

While on leave in the United States during the following month, Major General Twining was ordered to the Mediterranean theater of operations to take over command of the 15th Air Force from Major General James H. Doolittle, who had been reassigned to head the 8th Air Force based in Britain.

Assuming this new post on January 3, 1944 and in the same month becoming in addition the commander of the Mediterranean Strategic Air Forces, he directed from bases in Italy air attacks on German-held Bologna, targets at Vienna and Linz in Austria, Budapest in Hungary and Regensburg in Bavaria. Most important of all were the attacks beginning April 5, 1944 on the eleven oil refineries at Ploeşti in Rumania, later to be described by Lieutenant General Ira Eaker as "the bloodiest single air battleground of the war." The attacks, made by 221 heavy bombers of the 15th Air Force, practically eliminated Germany's principal European source of petroleum.

Soon after the end of the war in Europe, Twining was returned to the United States for interim duty at Washington, and on July 24 he was appointed to succeed Major General Curtis E. LeMay as commanding general of the 20th Air Force based on the Mariana Islands in the Pacific. B-29 Superfortresses of Twining's command dropped the atom bombs on Hiroshima and Nagasaki, and other 20th Air Force "very heavy" bombers made devastating incendiary and demolition attacks on the Tokyo area.

For various World War II achievements, including feats of personal courage, Twining was awarded the Distinguished Service Medal, the Legion of Merit with one Oak Leaf Cluster, the Distinguished Flying Cross, and the Air Medal with one Oak Leaf Cluster, as well as the Yugoslav Order of Partisan Star and the rank of Companion of the Order of the British Empire.

Returning to the United States after the Japanese surrender, Lieutenant General Twining was assigned to Continental Air Force headquarters at Bolling Field, Washington, D.C., in October 1945. In December he was named commanding general of the Air Material Command, with headquarters at Wright Field, Ohio.

On October 1, 1947 he was appointed commanding general of the Alaskan Department and later in the month became commander-in-chief of the Alaskan Command, continuing as such until May, 1950, when he was recalled to Air Force headquarters at Washington to become acting deputy chief of staff for personnel.

Twining, whose permanent rank dating from February 19, 1948 is that of major general, became a four-star general (temporary) on October 10, 1950, when major changes in the top Air Force command brought him an appointment as Vice-Chief of Staff. At that time the Washington *Post* characterized him as "something of an elder statesman in the Air Force despite his relative youth," since his "unusually rounded command" had made him fully acquainted with "the tactical support as well as the strategic side of the Air Force job."

When Lieutenant General Hoyt S. Vandenberg, the Air Chief of Staff, was hospitalized for an extended period beginning in the summer of 1952, Twining "ran the Air Force in all but name, distinguished himself for even-handedness and loyalty to Vandenberg's policies" (*Time,* May 18, 1953). On May 7, 1953 in consequence of notification by General Vandenberg that he intended to retire on the expiration of his tour of duty on June 30, President Dwight D. Eisenhower announced the appointment of General Twining as Air Chief of Staff.

In an address at Dallas, Texas, his first after the announcement of his appointment, General Twining stressed the feasibility of strategic air bombardment of Soviet Russia rather than possible operations in the Orient.

Discussing Air Force plans before a Congressional committee in July, General Twining said that "the steadily rising Communist strength in the air makes it increasingly necessary that Air Force personnel be on the alert at all times against a sudden and heavy attack."

With other high ranking officers General Twining was present at the formal delivery of America's version of the British Canberra jet bomber to the United States Air Force on August 20, 1953. The B-57 Night Intruder, as the new twin-jet plane is called, was built by the Glenn L. Martin company of Baltimore, modeled after the original Canberra. The General witnessed the first demonstration of the rotary bomb door, which allows the plane to unload its bombs without loss of speed.

Nathan Farragut Twining and Maude McKeever, daughter of a plantation owner, were married at Lihue, Hawaii, on March 9, 1932 and are the parents of two sons, Richard McKeever and Nathan Alexander, and one daughter, Olive Barber. The General numbers fishing among his favorite recreations, is said to possess an "unruffled disposition and good humor" and to be essentially moderate in his viewpoint. *Time* has described him as "handsome, silver-haired."

References

Bsns W p34+ Ag 16 '52 por
N Y Herald Tribune p1 My 8 '53
N Y Times p7 Ja 6 '44; p8 My 8 '45 por; p12 D 12 '45; p13 Ap 29 '53; p1 My 8 '53 por
Time 43:27 Ap 24 '44 por; 46:29 Ag 6 '45 por; 61:25 My 18 '53 por
U S News 32:62+ Mr 14 '52 por
Washington Post p10 O 12 '50
Who's Who in America, 1952-53
Who's Who in Aviation, 1942-43
World Biography (1948)

ULLMAN, MRS. EGON V. *See* Kennelly, A.

UTRILLO, MAURICE (oō-trē'lō) Dec. 26, 1883- Artist
Address: b. c/o Galerie Pétridès, 53 rue La Boétie, Paris 84; h. Villa de La Bonne Lucie, Le Vésinet, Seine-et-Oise, France

Now in his seventieth year, Maurice Utrillo is ranked among the five or six most famous living French artists. He began to paint at the age of nineteen on the advice of his mother, Suzanne Valadon, who was a noted artist, and she gave him his first and only instruction.

His talent was not generally recognized until after World War I, when his work suddenly

MAURICE UTRILLO

received critical acclaim and began to command high prices. Since 1925 his reputation as one of the foremost contemporary landscape painters has been established throughout the world. He is best known for his street scenes of Montmartre and the Paris suburbs.

Maurice Utrillo was born on December 26, 1883, in the Montmartre section of Paris. His mother, Marie-Clémentine Valadon (1865-1938), was a model who posed for such celebrated painters as Renoir, Toulouse-Lautrec and Degas. During the year of Maurice's birth, she first began to draw, and revealed such talent that Lautrec and Degas persuaded her to change her career from that of model to artist, at which time she took the name Suzanne Valadon.

According to A. Tabarant's biography of Utrillo, Maurice's father was a man named Boissy, an untalented amateur painter who earned his living as an actuary with an insurance firm. Maurice's surname was given him by Miguel Utrillo, a Spanish journalist and art critic who formally adopted him when he was eight years old. When Maurice started painting, he signed his canvases "Maurice Valadon," later changed to "Maurice Utrillo-Valadon," and finally settled on the signature "Maurice Utrillo, V."

Throughout his childhood and youth, Utrillo was cared for by his maternal grandmother. His formal education was started at the La Flesselle school in Montmartre in 1892, and continued in a primary school at Montmagny.

In 1896 Suzanne Valadon married Paul Mousis, a wealthy lawyer, who arranged for Maurice to enroll at the Collège Rollin, a preparatory school in Montmartre. Except for some ability in mathematics, he was a poor student, and after three years was taken out of school and put to work as a bookkeeper with the Crédit Foncier. He remained in the employ of this bank only a short while. Because of

Utrillo's continuing ill health, Suzanne Valadon consulted a doctor who advised that her son should take up some form of manual therapy.

Thus, in 1902, Utrillo began to draw and paint, but without enthusiasm. His mother forced him to sit at his easel every day, supplied him with her palette limited to five colors, and gave him rudimentary instructions. He gradually became interested and began to make progress.

At first he painted views from the window of his room; then, as he gained confidence, he moved his easel out of doors and painted directly from nature. His earliest canvases, depicting the countryside around Montmagny, Pierrefitte, and La Butte Pinson, were thick in pigment and dark in tone, but had an intensity of expression. Later Utrillo settled in Paris, where he painted the *quais* and bridges along the Seine and vistas of the city as seen from the heights of Montmartre.

This period of painting directly from nature, 1903 to 1905, was followed by a phase, 1905 to 1907, in which his work was in the manner of the impressionists, seeking to convey the atmospheric effects of light in vibrating tones. By 1908 Utrillo had achieved a style that was distinctly his own, and during the next six years he produced his most celebrated canvases. This is known as his "white period," because he employed a palette dominated by various tones of white in an attempt to capture the look of the white stucco walls of Paris buildings.

His white period was divided into two distinct phases. From 1908 to 1910, he spread his pigment on with a palette knife in heavy impasto and sometimes mixed plaster, sand, and glue with his oils to stimulate the texture of weather-beaten walls; from 1910 to 1914, his low-keyed harmonies became more luminous and radiant, and his brush smoothed over the roughness of surface.

Because of shyness, Utrillo did not like to paint in the city streets, and from 1909 on he started to rely on picture postcards for his landscapes, which he painted in his room, often at night by lamp-light, doing a number of different versions of favorite scenes.

Among his most characteristic pictures were views of the streets, squares, cafés, and landmarks of prewar Montmartre (*La Rue du Mont Cenis, La Place du Tertre, Le Lapin Agile, Le Moulin de la Galette, La Maison de Berlioz*). Almost as familiar were paintings of various Paris suburbs, Stains, Sannois, Grosley, with their endless deserted avenues, flanked by blank façades, under an overcast sky.

At this time he also began his celebrated series of churches: not only the famous churches in and around Paris, Sacré-Cœur, Notre-Dame and Saint-Denis, and the great French cathedrals, Chartres, Rheims, Rouen, and Bayonne, but also obscure provincial churches and humble village chapels.

He began to attract the attention of a few amateurs and collectors in 1909, among them Louis Libaude, a writer and art dealer, who arranged to take most of Utrillo's output and guaranteed the painter a very small monthly income. That same year Utrillo's *Le Pont*

Notre-Dame and two other paintings were accepted at the Salon d'Automne, where they were never noticed, and his application to enroll for study at the Ecole des Beaux-Arts was rejected.

Francis Jourdain, a critic, became interested in Utrillo's work and in 1910 called it to the attention of several well-known collectors, who bought paintings at about fifty francs apiece. Meanwhile, the artist had become an almost legendary figure in Montmartre.

During the summer of 1912, he went to Brittany, where he painted such landscapes as *Le Phare d'Ouessant* and *La Rue au Conquet,* and a year later he and his mother visited Corsica for several months, a sojourn that resulted in *Le Presbytère de Murato, La Rue à Corte,* and other works.

Jourdain invited Utrillo to participate in a group show in 1912 at the Galerie Druet. He exhibited for a second time at the Salon d'Automne that year and made his debut at the Salon des Indépendants in 1913.

When Libaude organized Utrillo's first oneman show, at the Galerie Eugène Blot in May 1913, only two of the thirty-one paintings were sold. Most critics still regarded his work as merchandise suitable only for cafés and *bistros.*

During World War I, Utrillo produced more than 1,000 pictures. In these years he moved towards a mere linear, dry and precise, architectural style. The painter was rejected by the army after a medical examination in 1915. His life began to alternate between intervals of freedom and voluntary confinement in various sanitariums.

At this time he was assisted financially by Zborowski, the Polish poet and dealer who had helped support Utrillo's best friend, the Italian painter, Amedeo Modigliani.

The first solid recognition of Utrillo's talent came in December 1919, when the Galerie Lepoutre held a successful one-man show of forty-six pictures painted between 1910 and 1915.

Utrillo's reputation as a painter grew steadily in the early 1920's. Important exhibitions of his work were held at the Galerie Berthe Weill (1921, 1922, 1923), Paul Guillaume's gallery (1922), and Bernheim-Jeune's (1923, 1924). The latter gallery signed a contract with Utrillo and his mother in 1923 for their future output, giving them a guaranteed joint income of a million francs a year (then about $50,000). Utrillo exhibited in the Salon d'Automne in 1922 and 1923 and in the Salon des Indépendants of 1923.

By 1924 he was one of the most talked about painters in Paris, and dealers were combing Montmartre cafés and *bistros* to find his early canvases. The following year his work was exhibited in Germany, Belgium and the United States. Utrillo's pictures had "skyrocketed" in value: at a 1919 auction one had brought 1,000 francs; in 1926 his *L'Eglise Saint-Séverin* sold for 50,000 francs.

In 1953 a Utrillo painting of the Lapin Agile was sold for 2,010,000 francs (about $5,300) reportedly the largest sum ever paid for one of his works at a public sale.

The painter again spent considerable time in sanitariums between 1921 and 1924. According to R. Coughlan (*The Wine of Genius*), Utrillo's mother and her second husband, the painter André Utter, took him to their newly acquired Château de Saint-Bernard, near Lyon in southeastern France. There his health began to improve, and for the next decade he spent long periods of each year at the château and painted the region along the Rhône.

Official recognition came in 1928 when he was made a chevalier of the Legion of Honor. In the 1920's Utrillo adopted his so-called *manière colorée,* and the tragic element gradually disappeared from his meticulously drawn pictures, which became increasingly animated in line and bright in color.

On April 18, 1935 Utrillo married Mme. Lucie Pauwels, a former actress and the widow of a Belgian banker. In 1937, they bought a villa in the Paris suburb of Le Vésinet, where they have since resided. According to report, Utrillo's wife, who paints under the name of Lucie Valore, has managed the artist's business affairs so ably that he became a wealthy man.

The painter was honored in 1948 by a large retrospective exhibition at the Salon d'Automne. In the opinion of some critics, Utrillo's painting after the 1920's declined into formula, "repeating with increasing facility but preserving only rarely the impact of earlier work." Alfred Werner has called his latest pictures "pretty but flimsy." Other critics, however, have praised the "vitality and heightened mood" of Utrillo's recent work, which has been characterized by a looser, more carefree style and with progressively more brilliant and varied color.

Utrillo occupies a unique position in contemporary painting because of his isolation from the dominant currents of modern art. "Utrillo is in a sense truly a primitive . . . because his transcriptions of his world . . . are suffused with humility and reverence," wrote Robert Allerton Parker.

As is the case with most prolific painters, Utrillo's work is uneven in quality. His range of subject matter is mainly limited to landscapes (he has painted very few figure pieces and only recently turned to still lifes of flowers), and his work is said to be "totally lacking in intellectual conception." Yet as a "colorist of high sensitivity," with "a remarkable instinct for the quality of surfaces" he has produced "indisputable masterpieces." According to Manny Farber in the *New Republic,* Utrillo's best work "has an extraordinary harmoniousness, a solidity of luminous color, and the quality, rare in our time, of being entirely and perfectly completed."

Utrillo's *Consulat d'Auvergne* received second honorable mention at the 1938 Carnegie International Exhibition, in Pittsburgh, and his work is represented in the leading public and private collections of the world. In addition to oils, he has done *gouaches,* water colors, lithographs and drawings. He also designed the scenery and costumes for *Birabeau,* which was produced by Diaghilev's Russian Ballet in 1926, and for the décor for the 1950 revival of Charpenier's *Louise* at the Opéra-Comique.

The artist has written a number of poems and an unpublished autobiography. A recent reviewer found Utrillo "a small husk of a man

UTRILLO, MAURICE—*Continued*

with a tottering walk;" he has blue eyes, thinning dark hair, and "an emaciated look."

His days are divided between his studio, where he works for several hours each afternoon and evening, finishing some dozen pictures a year, and his private chapel, which is filled with images of his favorite saint, Jeanne d'Arc.

References

Life 28:87+ Ja 16 '50 por
Time 29:44+ Ja 18 '37; 33:53 F 20 '39; 52:49 O 25 '48 pors
U N World 7:30+ Ja '53 por
Bernheim de Villers, G. Little Tales of Great Artists (1950)
Carco(F. La Légende ea la Vie d'Utrillo (1928)
Coquiot, G. Maurice Utrillo, V. (1925)
Coughlan, R. The Wine of Genius (1951)
Dictionnaire Biographique Français Contemporain (1950)
Gros, G. J. Maurice Utrillo; Sa Légende (1947)
Raynal, M. History of Modern Painting (1950)
Slocombe, G. Rebels of Art (1939)
Utrillo, M. Utrillo; texte de P. Courthion (1948)
Utrillo, M. Utrillo; texte de F. Jourdain (1948)
Utrillo, M. Maurice Utrillo. Text by A. Werner (1952)
Who's Who, 1952
World Biography (1948)
Zahar, M. Utrillo (1949)

VAN ROYEN, JAN HERMAN. *See* Royen, J. H. van

VAUGHAN WILLIAMS, RALPH Oct. 12, 1872- Composer

Address: h. The White Gates, Dorking, Surrey, England

Among the composers of special music for the coronation of Queen Elizabeth II was eighty-one year old Ralph Vaughan Williams, who has written for the symphony orchestra, chorus, solo voice, chamber music ensemble, the church, the stage, the ballet, and the films. "More remarkable than the total output, which is enormous, are the integrity and high seriousness of the music" (New York *Times,* September 28, 1952). Among his recent compositions are his seventh symphony, *Sinfonia Antarctica,* first played in April, 1953 which was written in his eightieth year and *Pilgrim's Progress,* an opera performed in 1951 at the Royal Opera House, Covent Garden, London.

Ralph Vaughan Williams was born on October 12, 1872 at Down Ampney, Gloucestershire, England, the son of the local rector, the Reverend Arthur Charles Vaughan Williams, and his wife, the former Margaret Jane Wedgwood. On his mother's side he is related to

British Inf. Services
RALPH VAUGHAN WILLIAMS

the family of Josiah Wedgwood, pottery makers.

His first instruction in music was received from an aunt, a Miss Wedgwood. The composers he heard chiefly at home were Handel, Mozart, Haydn, and Beethoven. He attended a preparatory school at Rottingdean, near Brighton, where he was given lessons by C. T. West in the piano. In 1887 he went to Charterhouse School, a well-known English public school, where he joined the school orchestra and played the violin and the viola.

Having determined on a musical career, he entered the Royal College of Music, London, in 1890, where he studied harmony under Dr. Francis E. Gladstone and composition under (Sir) Hubert Parry. Writing in 1950, he recalled that he hated Beethoven. "To this day," he continued, "the Beethoven idiom repels me, but I hope I have at last learnt to see the greatness that lies behind the idiom I dislike, and at the same time to see an occasional weakness behind the Bach idiom which I love."

He entered Trinity College, Cambridge, in 1892, where, in addition to his general education, he studied the organ with Alan Gray and continued lessons in composition under Charles Wood. After receiving the A.B. Mus. degree in 1894 and the B.A. degree in 1895, he enrolled for further study at the Royal College of Music, where fellow students were John Ireland and Gustav Holst (the latter a lifelong friend, with whom he habitually compared notes over a period of forty years).

In his autobiographical notes to Foss' biography, Vaughan Williams quotes this duologue between himself and his teacher, (Sir) Charles Stanford: "Damnably ugly, my boy. Why do you write such things?" "Because I like them." "But you can't like them, they're not music." "I shouldn't write them if I didn't like them."

Vaughan Williams took his first and last organist's post, at the Church of St. Barnabas, South Lambeth, London in 1895. He had first heard Richard Wagner's music during a visit to Munich in 1890; and, in 1896, he visited Bayreuth and met the great composer. In 1897 he decided to study in Berlin, where he worked hard for some months under Max Bruch at the Akademie der Kunst. Bruch warned him against writing *Augenmusik* instead of *Ohrenmusik*. "This warning was wasted on me," writes Vaughan Williams, "as I habitually and unashamedly use the pianoforte when composing. . . ."

On his return to London, Vaughan Williams left his organist's post "and settled down to try and learn how to compose—not by studying, but by doing." Refused by (Sir) Edward Elgar of whom he requested lessons in orchestration, Vaughan Williams wrote later, "Though Elgar would not teach me personally, he could not help teaching me through his music. I spent several hours at the British Museum studying the full scores of the *Enigma Variations* and *Gerontius*. The results are obvious in the opening pages of the finale of my *Sea Symphony*."

Vaughan Williams received the Doctor of Music degree at Cambridge in 1901. He was asked to edit the music for a new hymnbook called "The English Hymnal" in 1904. During this period he became interested in English folk music. H. C. Colles in Grove's *Dictionary of Music and Musicians* writes that it was in this area that Vaughan Williams found "his own musical language, for which he had searched the schools of London and Berlin in vain." One result of this was the "Three Norfolk Rhapsodies" for orchestra (1906).

In 1908, records Vaughan Williams, "I came to the conclusion that I was lumpy and stodgy, had come to a dead-end, and that a little French polish would be of use to me. So I went to Paris, armed with an introduction to Maurice Ravel." With Ravel he practised chiefly orchestration. "He showed me how to orchestrate in points of colour rather than in lines."

At the Leeds Festival of 1907 his first important work for choir and orchestra, *Toward the Unknown Region,* was successfully produced. This brought him recognition as a coming composer, and, according to Colles, *A Sea Symphony,* at the next festival (1910) "declared his arrival." This work, on a theme by Walt Whitman, for baritone, soprano, choir, and orchestra, showed the influences of Purcell and Parry. It was in 1910, too, that he was invited by the Purcell Society to edit the second volume of the "Welcome Songs."

Another famous work of this early period was *Fantasia on a Theme by Thomas Tallis,* for double stringed orchestra and string quartet. It was first performed under the direction of Sir Thomas Beecham at the Queen's Hall, London, in 1909, and was given again at the Gloucester Three Choirs' Festival in 1910. Vaughan Williams worked on a ballad opera, *Hugh the Drover,* with libretto by Harold Child, from 1911 to 1914. This opera is rich in feeling for the country, and has a boxing match as its central episode. It remained unplayed until July 1924, when it was presented at His Majesty's Theatre, London, with (Sir) Malcolm Sargent conducting.

A *London Symphony* was conducted by Geoffrey Toye at the Queen's Hall in March 1914. It was, says Hubert Foss, "in dimensions the largest piece Vaughan Williams had so far conceived. It won him followers who had but faintly admired him before. . . ." Although well received, it was not heard again until 1918, when it was played by the London Symphony Orchestra, with (Sir) Adrian Boult conducting.

At the outbreak of World War I, the composer was forty-two, well over military age. Nevertheless, he joined the territorial branch of the Royal Army Medical Corps as an orderly, and served in Macedonia in 1916 and 1917. He took a heavy gunnery course, was commissioned as a lieutenant in the Royal Garrison Artillery, and served in France during the campaign of 1918.

Discharged from the service shortly after the Armistice, Vaughan Williams was appointed a teacher of composition at the Royal College of Music. He succeeded Sir Hugh Allen as conductor of the London Bach Choir in 1920. The knowledge of his music was spread by the International Society for Contemporary Music, and by performances in foreign countries under such famous conductors as Sir Henry Wood, Sir Adrian Boult and Albert Coates.

His first opera, a "pastoral episode", called *The Shepherds of the Delectable Mountains* was composed in 1922 and was later embodied in *The Pilgrim's Progress. A Pastoral Symphony* was also written in 1922. It is a quiet, contemplative composition and was introduced by the Royal Philharmonic Society, conducted by (Sir) Adrian Boult, at Queen's Hall, London. It was hailed as a major work, and in 1923 Vaughan Williams came by invitation to the United States to conduct it at a Norfolk, Connecticut, festival.

Soon afterward, he completed "Flos Campi," a piece for the viola, with a small chorus intoning a wordless melody, and small orchestra. *Sir John in Love,* an opera whose libretto is based upon Shakespeare's *The Merry Wives of Windsor,* was composed in 1929.

At Bryn Mawr College, the composer gave a course of lectures in 1932 which were later collected into a book, *National Music* (Oxford University Press, 1934). In it he said: "Art for art's sake has never flourished among the English-speaking nations. We are often called inartistic because our art is unconscious. Our drama and our poetry have evolved by accident while we thought we were doing something else, and so it will be without music. The composer must not shut himself up and think about art: he must live with his fellows and make his art an expression of the whole life of the community. If we seek for art we shall not find it."

His work has continued to spring from national roots. His devotion to folk-music has remained constant, and since the death of Cecil Sharp in 1933 he has directed the music of the English Folk-Song and Dance Society.

(Continued next page)

VAUGHAN WILLIAMS, RALPH—*Cont.*

From time to time national honors were offered to him, but he refused them all until, in 1935, he was admitted to the small but distinguished membership of the Order of Merit—probably the highest of all British orders, awarded literally on merit only, and carrying no title but the affix of the letters O.M.

At the outbreak of World War II Vaughan Williams was close to his sixty-seventh birthday and since more active work was ruled out by age, he cheerfully undertook addressing of envelopes and other duties connected with the salvage work. He also composed music for documentary and propaganda films and acted as chairman of a Home Office voluntary committee to advise on the proper release of certain alien musicians who had been interned. His seventieth birthday, in 1942, was celebrated by special B.B.C. broadcasts, by concerts of his music given by provincial music societies, and by concerts in London, some of them at the well-attended lunch-time sessions which had been inaugurated at the National Gallery.

For Vaughan Williams the past decade has been rich in endeavor, during which he wrote three symphonies, the *Fifth, Sixth, Seventh*; and other compositions. Of the *Fifth*, Foss writes: "Here, in fresh invention, is the complete fusion of all Vaughan Williams's symphonic essays—in form, in matter, in manner." Of the *Sixth,* introduced by Sir Adrian Boult conducting the Royal Philharmonic Orchestra at the Albert Hall, London, in April 1948, the New York *Times* says: "It is the quietest and most serene piece of music imaginable. Every instrument that can be is muted. It is as though stillness were made audible, and from these almost motionless sounds Vaughan Williams has created a medium for the expression of his deepest and wisest musical thought." In August 1948 this work had its first American performance, at the Berkshire Festival with the late Serge Koussevitzky conducting the Boston Symphony Orchestra. Speaking of a later performance in New York, Virgil Thomson wrote in the New York *Herald Tribune*: "The piece has power and depth and a very personal, very English beauty."

In April, 1951 the Royal Opera House, Covent Garden, London, staged an opera, or, as the composer called it, "a morality" entitled *The Pilgrim's Progress,* based on John Bunyan's book. Cecil Smith, of *Musical America,* writing as guest critic in the London *Daily Express,* described it as "the noblest new work produced on any of the world's lyric stages since the war."

The composer's eightieth birthday, October 12, 1952, brought many greetings and also a summation of Vaughan Williams' career in the New York *Times Magazine* (October 12, 1952) by Ernest Newman. "An expression that has no rival anywhere in music of what thoughtful Englishmen regard as one of the most precious possessions of their race, the vein of mellow mysticism . . ." is what Vaughan Williams gives us, wrote Newman.

And still one more symphony was to come, the seventh, or *Sinfonia Antarctica,* played in April 1953. It resulted from the search by film musical director Ernest Irving of Ealing Studios, London, for an appropriate musical composition for the film *Scott of the Antarctic* (1951). "Everything in the symphony is on a large scale", commented the *Christian Science Monitor.* "It can only be played by an orchestra of very great size."

At the coronation of Queen Elizabeth II on June 2, 1953 Dr. Vaughan Williams was among the British composers chosen to compose special music for the crowning of the Queen. The music was sung by a massed choir of 400 men and boys and played by sixty of Britain's finest musicians under the baton of Sir Adrian Boult. London Records issued a commemorative coronation release of some dozen disks of famous British compositions which included the *Pastoral Symphony* by Ralph Vaughan Williams, performed by the London Philharmonic.

Hubert Foss writes: "Vaughan Williams is in person a man of big build, of yeoman appearance, countrified by nature and wish, sociable but not social, and uncompromisingly truthful in utterance." Another English critic, Stephen Williams, says in the New York *Times*: "He looks like a farmer. . . .He is a man entirely without self-consciousness: a big, heavy, lumbering figure, usually dressed in rough tweeds, who looks as though he is on his way to judge the shorthorns at an agricultural show." He married Adeline Fisher, who died on May 12, 1951. In 1953, he married the writer, Ursula Wood. Dr. Vaughan Williams is the author of *English Folk Songs* (J. Williams, 1912?). He was made an honorary life-fellow of the Worshipful Company of Musicians in 1934, was the recipient of the Shakespeare Prize at Hamburg in 1938, and has been given honorary degrees by the universities of London, Bristol, Liverpool, Wales, Oxford, and by Trinity College, Dublin.

References

Christian Sci Mon p4 My 29 '48
N Y Times II p7 My 30 '48
Dickinson, A. E. F. An Introduction to the Music of Ralph Vaughan Williams (1928)
Foss, H. Ralph Vaughan Williams (1950)
Grove, G. Dictionary of Music and Musicians (1927-28)
Howes, F. The Dramatic Works of Ralph Vaughan Williams (1937)
Who's Who, 1953

VELDE, HAROLD H(IMMEL) (vĕl-dē') Apr. 1, 1910- United States Representative from Illinois; lawyer

Address: b. House Office Bldg., Washington 25, D.C.; 1119 First National Bank Bldg., Peoria, Ill.; h. 700 S. 9th St., Pekin, Ill.

With the reorganization of the House of Representatives committees under Republican leadership in January 1953, Harold H. Velde, Representative from the Eighteenth District of Illinois, was named chairman of the Committee on Un-American Activities. Velde had been elected to the Eighty-first Congress in 1948 and named to the Un-American Activities Committee during his freshman term; he was re-elected to the House of Representatives in 1950 and again in 1952. Before entering Congress he was county judge in Tazewell County, Illinois, a post to which he was elected in 1946. During World War II he served in the Army Signal Corps and in the sabotage and counter-espionage division of the Federal Bureau of Investigation.

Of East Frisian and German ancestry, Harold Himmel Velde was born in Parkland, Tazewell County, Illinois, on April 1, 1910, one of the three sons of Henry Jacob Velde, a farmer, and Laura Amanda (Himmel) Velde. In 1927 he was graduated from Manito High School, where he had been a member of the basketball and track teams. At Northwestern University, which he entered in 1929 after two years of study at Bradley University, he became a member of the school band and the baseball team. Graduating with his B.A. degree in 1931, he spent the next four years as a teacher and athletic coach at Hillsdale (Illinois) Community High School. In 1937 he was granted the LL.B. degree by the Law School of the University of Illinois, and after being admitted to the Illinois bar, practiced as a member of the law firm of Velde and Prettyman at Pekin, Illinois, until 1942, when he enlisted as a private in the Army Signal Corps.

In 1943, upon being honorably discharged from the service, Velde became a special agent in the FBI's division of sabotage and counter-espionage, serving for a year in the San Francisco area as a wiretap specialist. As reported by *Pathfinder*, an investigator for the Un-American Activities Committee credited Velde's "tenacity and firsthand knowledge of the 'Scientist X' affair (in which a former University of California physicist was accused of passing atomic secrets to Russia) with piling up enough evidence to indict . . . [the physicist]." Velde was employed by the FBI until his election in 1946 as county judge of Tazewell County. His work for the FBI having heightened his interest in the United States Government, he campaigned for a seat in the House of Representatives and was elected on the Republican ticket to the Eighty-first Congress in 1948.

During the first session of the Eighty-first Congress in 1949, Velde voted in favor of extending the trade agreement act (February), opposed extension of the rent control act (March), supported extension of the Marshall Plan (April), voted against a long-range housing bill (June), advocated an anti-poll tax bill (July), and favored a 50 per cent reduction in European arms aid (August). He was named to the House Un-American Activities Committee in January 1949. In May of that year, testifying before a special Federal grand jury investigating subversive activities, he stated, the New York *Times* reported, that "he favored legislation that would extend the time for prosecution or eliminate the time limit in espionage cases." The next month he was one of five members of the Committee who opposed the action of Committee Chairman John S. Wood, of Georgia, in requiring seventy-one

Walden S. Fabry

HAROLD H. VELDE

colleges and the education boards of all the States to submit textbooks to be examined for traces of Communist doctrines. In July he joined Representative Richard M. Nixon in criticizing the conduct of Judge Samuel F. Kaufman during the trial of Alger Hiss, alleging that the record abounded "with unusual rulings favorable to Hiss," but he subsequently commented that Judge Kaufman "must have been under 'terrific pressure' from Hiss sympathizers in the Government" (New York *Times*, January 24, 1950). Following President Truman's announcement in September 1949 of an atomic explosion in Russia, Velde charged that Russia had "undoubtedly gained three to five years in producing the atomic bomb" as a result of a "soft" official attitude toward Communism during the past fifteen years "from the White House down" (New York *Herald Tribune*, September 26, 1949).

Early in the second session of the Eighty-first Congress, on February 27, 1950, Velde charged that efforts to get records for the Un-American Activities Committee were blocked by executive order of President Truman. His voting record in 1950 shows him against a bill extending economic aid to Korea and Formosa (February), in favor of an FEPC bill recommending voluntary compliance, and opposed to a $2.7 billion Marshall Plan extension bill (March). He supported bills to reduce federal spending by $600 million (May) and to appropriate an additional $2 billion for farm price supports (June), favored the Lodge-Gossett constitutional amendment (July), and voted to cancel a cut in postal service (August).

Re-elected to the House of Representatives in November 1950, Velde in April 1951, in connection with the Un-American Activities Committee's investigation of Communism in the entertainment field, stated that he was "certain that Communist propaganda had been put into

VELDE, HAROLD H.—*Continued*

films—perhaps not in an open manner, but in the way the writers think if they are Communists" (New York *Times*, April 16, 1951). In April he opposed the draft-extension—universal military training bill and the next month advocated a $10 million cut in appropriations for reclamation loans and voted to limit public housing in 1952 to 5,000 units. He opposed government building of defense plants, supported the tidelands oil bill (July), and voted for a reduction of $350 million in economic aid to Europe (August) and against the $7.5 billion foreign assistance bill (August). When Speaker Rayburn announced in February 1952 that coverage of Congressional hearings by television, newsreels, and tape recordings would be banned, Velde criticized his action as "political." He added, as the New York *Herald Tribune* reported, that "the House should have the opportunity to vote on the question of the use of television, newsreels, and tape-recordings." During the second session of the Eighty-second Congress he voted to shelve the UMT bill (March 1952), to cut economic aid to Europe by $615 million (May), to end consumer price controls on June 30, 1952, to use the Taft-Hartley law to end the steel strike, to end Federal rent controls on September 30, 1952 (June), and to keep 90 per cent of farm price supports (June).

Upon Velde's re-election to the House in November 1952, the New York *Times* mentioned that he had "frequently urged Congress to investigate the 'entire security set-up' of the Government," and that he had "once introduced a bill to require the Librarian of Congress to list all books that could be regarded as 'subversive' and at another time proposed a loyalty oath as a requirement for voting in national elections." Shortly after his re-election Velde predicted that Communists would make an attempt to infiltrate the Republican party now that it was in power and stated that additional legislation was needed to control the Communist party. In a recorded interview with *United States News*, which appeared in early January 1953, he stated: "I feel that we should look into the field of education. That has been largely left untouched up till now. I realize, of course, that we're going to have a lot of opposition from various educators, particularly from the 'left-wing' educators, but I believe that is a very fertile field for investigation and th..t it should be done. . . .We should go into the field of labor much more than we have—into the Communist penetration of labor unions. . . . In my opinion, any person can think anything he wants to, as long as he doesn't do or perform any overt act which would be considered disloyal, and therefore, as far as freedom of thought is concerned, I think we'll make no inroads on that freedom whatsoever by our investigations." Later that month Velde indicated that the Un-American Activities Committee, of which he became chairman, would need more funds for 1953 than the $285,000 spent in 1952, in order to expand its staff.

Velde is on the official board of the First Methodist Church, a member of the American Legion, chairman of the Tazewell County Chap-

ter of the American Cancer Society, and since 1948 has been president of the Tazewell County Bar Association. He belongs to the alumni clubs of Bradley, Northwestern, and Illinois universities, to the Creve Coeur Council of the Boy Scouts, the Pekin Chamber of Commerce, the Illinois Bar Association, the Illinois County and Probate Judges Association, the Illinois Welfare Association, and the Tazewell County Farm Bureau. The Illinois Representative's fraternities are Lambda Chi Alpha and Phi Alpha Delta; his clubs are the Pekin Sportsmen's the Lions, and the Eagles (Pekin Aerie No. 1869). In 1947 he headed the Salvation Army Drive in Pekin; in 1947 and 1948 he served as chairman of the American Cancer Society campaign. Velde, who married Olive Pfander on June 6, 1931, has two children— Richard W. and Joan. (Mrs. Velde is deceased.) The legislator is six feet two inches tall, weighs 210 pounds, has brown hair and hazel eyes. His favorite forms of recreation are golf and game hunting.

References

N Y Times p6 My 7 '49; p30 N 8 '52
Pathfinder 59:17 D 17 '52 por
Who's Who in America, 1952-53
Who's Who in United States Politics (1952)

VINSON, FRED(ERICK) M(OORE) Jan. 22, 1890—Sept. 8, 1953 Thirteenth Chief Justice of the United States; appointed to the Supreme Court by President Truman in 1946 after a long career in Democratic politics; began law practice in Kentucky in 1911; member of Congress in the House of Representatives from 1923 to 1929 and from 1931 to 1935; associate justice of the United States Court of Appeals for the District of Columbia, 1938-43; chief judge of the United States Emergency Court of Appeals, March 1942 to May, 1943; director of the Office of Economic Stabilization, 1943-45; appointed Federal loan administrator, March 5, 1945; appointed director of the Office of War Mobilization and Reconversion in April 1945; appointed Secretary of the Treasury on July 23, 1945; nominated Chief Justice of the United States and confirmed by the Senate in June 1946. See *Current Biography*, 1943.

Obituary

N Y Times p1+ S 9 '53 por

VOGT, WILLIAM May 15, 1902- Organization official; ecologist; ornithologist

Address: b. c/o Planned Parenthood Federation of America, Inc., 501 Madison Ave., New York 22; h. 36 E. 68th St., New York 21

In May 1951 William Vogt, ecologist and former ornithologist, became national director of the Planned Parenthood Federation of America, Inc., the largest organization in the field of birth control. An authority on conservation and related population problems, Vogt is author of the international best-seller, *Road to Survival* (1948), and former chief of the conservation section of the Pan American Union (1943-50). Among earlier posts held by him are associate director of the division of science and education of the Office of Coordinator of Inter-American Affairs, consulting ecologist to the Government of Peru, and field naturalist and lecturer for the National Association of Audubon Societies.

William Vogt was born in Mineola, New York, on May 15, 1902, the son of William and Frances Belle (Doughty) Vogt, and a descendant of Reverend Francis Doughty, the first Episcopalian rector in New Amsterdam. After an early childhood in Garden City, Long Island, he lived in Brooklyn, New York, where he attended Manual Training High School. At the age of fourteen, while recovering from an attack of infantile paralysis, he is said to have spent considerable time reading such authors as Rousseau, Rostand, Turgenev, Tolstoy, and Shaw. On graduation from high school in 1917, he entered St. Stephens (now Bard) College on a four-year scholarship. Here, while majoring in romance languages, he won the poetry prize and edited the college literary magazine, and in 1925 received his B.A. degree with honors.

Having become interested in ornithology through the books of the famous mammalogist, Ernest Thompson Seton, Vogt after two years as assistant editor at the New York Academy of Sciences (1930-32), spent the next three years as curator for the Jones Beach State Bird Sanctuary. Concurrently, he edited *Bird Lore* magazine and wrote several articles for professional magazines, including "Dovekie Influx of 1932" (with R. C. Murphy) for *Auk* (July 1933) and "Experimental Study of Sex Recognition in Birds (with G. K. Noble) for *Auk* (July 1935). While employed, from 1935 to 1939, as field naturalist and lecturer for the National Association of Audubon Societies, Vogt prepared a pamphlet for the association entitled *Thirst for Land* (1937), which made a plea for water conservation for the benefit of man and wildlife. For *Audubon's Birds of America* (1937), Vogt compiled about 500 Audubon illustrations and wrote a descriptive text for each. His introduction to the volume was praised as "admirable" by *Booklist*. This book was reissued by Macmillan in 1953. At the North American Wildlife Conference in February 1938, Vogt spoke on the problem of mosquito control in relation to natural resources.

For three years, beginning in 1939, Vogt was consulting ornithologist to the Compañía Administradora del Guano at Lima, Peru. In 1942, on a fellowship from the Committee for Inter-American Artistic and Cultural Relations, he studied climatology in Chile. His studies in South America, revealing the decrease in natural resources, first aroused his interest in human populations in relation to their environment and turned his attention from ornithology to ecology. During World War II he served, in 1942, as consultant on South America to the United States War Department and, in 1942-43, as associate director of the division of science and education of the Office of Coordinator of Inter-American Affairs. Chiefly for the use of country school teachers in South America, he

Fabian Bachrach

WILLIAM VOGT

wrote in 1944 *El Hombre y la Tierra* (Man and the Earth). The *Saturday Review of Literature* (August 7, 1948) quoted him as saying he felt there was a need for this book because in matters pertaining to man and his environment "the Spanish are even more indifferent than we."

As chief of the conservation section of the Pan American Union (1943-50), Vogt found "an alarming downward trend" in the natural resources of the Western Hemisphere (New York *World-Telegram*, January 18, 1946). He pointed out that Latin America "is far from being the rich storehouse of untapped resources that is generally supposed," because of overgrazing, increased destruction of forests, soil erosion and floods; and pictured Mexico as largely destroyed within 100 years "unless there is a radical change in land management." The situation seemed to him less serious in North America, which spends "in the neighborhood of a million dollars a year on conservation, whereas Latin America . . . does not spend 5 per cent of this amount." In 1946 Vogt prepared a number of reports for the Pan American Union on population and natural resources in several Latin American countries. He was secretary general of the first Inter-American Conference on Conservation of Renewable Natural Resources at Denver, Colorado, in September 1948, which recommended that the American countries establish agencies to protect and enrich their resources and warned that about 55 per cent of the land in the United States had undergone, or was undergoing, erosion. Representing the Pan American Union, Vogt attended the Conference of the International Union Protection League that met at Fontainebleau in 1948 under the auspices of the United Nations Educational, Scientific and Cultural Organization to promote nature protection. He was also a delegate of the Pan American Union

VOGT, WILLIAM—*Continued*
to a Consultation on Geography held in Rio de Janeiro in 1949.

Vogt's best-selling *Road to Survival* (1948), "germinated" in his article "Hunger at the Peace Table," which had appeared in the *Saturday Evening Post* (May 12, 1945). The book, which was translated into nine languages and read by several million people throughout the world, exposes the discrepancy between increasing populations and the earth's food supply and offers suggestions for meeting this problem. In an introduction to the volume, Bernard M. Baruch comments that "it asks more questions than it answers, as any scientific book must." Bernard De Voto in a New York *Herald Tribune* review found, "*Road to Survival* is by far the best book so far in this literature. It is more basic, more comprehensive, more thorough-going than any of its predecessors . . . and is written with marked brilliance and drama." Answering critics who consider his outlook pessimistic, the ecologist has said: "If I didn't think there was a very good chance of solving our problems, I never would have written *Road to Survival*" (*Saturday Review of Literature*, August 7, 1948). The recipient of combined Fulbright and Guggenheim fellowships in 1950-51, Vogt made a nine-month study of population problems in Denmark, Norway, and Sweden in relation to management of these countries' resources. He examined the way in which many questions posed in *Road to Survival* are being answered by the Scandinavians and is preparing a new publication on the results of his studies.

On his return from Europe, Vogt in May 1951 accepted the position of national director of the Planned Parenthood Federation of America, Inc., which has eleven State leagues and ninety-one local affiliations in the country. Besides providing a network of clinical and other services in the field of birth control, including infertility treatment for the childless, the organization conducts a broad program of education through books, pamphlets, magazines, press, and radio supported by voluntary contributions. It is one of the planned parenthood groups active in twenty-one countries and has taken part in recent world conferences on family planning in Sweden, England, and India. At the Bombay conference in November 1952 Vogt, in replying to an Indian scientist's view that a high level of industrialization might solve India's population problem, contrasted "the relative simplicity of planned parenthood" with the social, economic, and technical problems involved in industrial development (New York *Herald Tribune*). In 1952, when a hospital in New York State requested that seven physicians withdraw from the local Planned Parenthood organization or be removed from the hospital staff, Vogt sent a protest to the State Commission Against Discrimination stating that the demand was an "apparent violation of the law forbidding discrimination against employes . . . on religious grounds" (New York *Times*). In a telegram to the American Medical Association he protested that "the coercion of physicians . . . inflicts grave injustice on doctors and is a dangerous, unethical act against the entire

medical profession" (New York *Times*). (The seven physicians were later re-instated at the hospital).

Speaking to an assembly of students, including several from India and other Asiatic countries, at the New York Academy of Medicine on April 24, 1952, Vogt stated that the Point IV Program of the United States would in all probability add to "the destruction of resources, including forest and soils, in most parts of the world where it is operating" (New York *Times*). The student gathering represented the first forum discussion of planned parenthood provided for college students in the metropolitan area. Earlier, in a *Saturday Evening Post* article (July 23, 1949), "Let's Examine our Santa Claus Complex," Vogt expressed the view that "the greatest danger in trying to carry out President Truman's Point IV Program may well lie in speeding up population increases. . . .Anything that we do to speed up the rate of population increase without assuring a parallel increase in the necessities of life imposes an extremely grave responsibility upon us." Vogt believes that planned parenthood is not a panacea, but is an indispensable factor in the future of mankind.

Vogt has received the field research prize of the Linnaen Society of New York (1938); the Mary Soper Pope Medal from the Cranbrook Institute of Science (1948); the First National Conservation Award of the Izaak Walton League of America (1949); a special Gutenberg Award for *Road to Survival*, as one of the "books most progressively influencing American thought in 1948"; and the Albert and Mary Lasker Foundation award in Planned Parenthood (1951). He is a fellow of the Soil Conservation Society of America and of the New York Zoological Society. Other professional organizations to which he belongs are the American Association for the Advancement of Science, the American Ornithologists Union (chairman of the conservation committee, 1938), the American Geographical Society, the British Ecological Society, the Ecological Society of America, the Society for General Semantics, the Linnaean Society of New York (former president and secretary), the Sociédad Geográfica de Lima, the Sociédad Mexicana de Historia Natural, and the Conservation Foundation. His club is the Cosmos (Washington). He votes independently.

On April 4, 1946, Vogt married Marjorie Wallace, a psychiatric social worker. The ecologist weighs 175 pounds, is five feet ten inches in height, and has blue eyes and bushy gray hair. The *Saturday Review* has observed that Vogt has "a rich, melodious voice for the podium." His friends have found him "patient, sympathetic, and intellectually generous" (New York *Herald Tribune*). For recreation he turns to listening to music, travel, photography and reading—mostly nonfiction.

References
N Y Herald Tribune X p10 O 24 '48
American Men of Science (1949)
Who's Who in America, 1951-53
Who's Who in the East (1951)

VON EINEM, GOTTFRIED See Einem, G. Von

VON RUNDSTEDT, KARL (RUDOLF GERD) *See* Rundstedt, K. R. G. von

WAGNER, ROBERT F(ERDINAND)
June 8, 1877—May 4, 1953 Former Democratic United States Senator from New York; New Dealer; sponsored labor measures initiating collective bargaining; came to United States at age of 8 from Germany; B.S., College of the City of New York (1898), LL.B., New York Law School (1900); elected to New York Assembly 1904; Justice of Supreme Court of New York 1919; United States Senator 1926, re-elected 1932, 1938 and 1944; chairman of National Labor Board, 1933; in 1935 sponsored National Labor Relations Act, Social Security bill, and unsuccessful anti-lynching bill; introduced housing and slum clearance legislation in Wagner-Steagall Act (1937) and Wagner-Taft-Ellender Housing bill, and "cradle to grave" social security legislation in Wagner-Murray-Dingell bill; supported lend-lease, anti-inflation, price control, international stabilization fund; Chairman of American Palestine Committee; retired in 1949. See *Current Biography,* 1941.

Obituary

N Y Times p26 My 5 '53

WAINWRIGHT, JONATHAN M(AY-HEW) Aug. 23, 1883—Sept. 2, 1953 Former Commanding General of the Fourth Army of the United States; graduated from West Point in 1906; promoted through grades to brigadier general in 1938; served in World War II in Bataan campaign; commanded the Philippine Islands garrison; forced to surrender his very meager forces on Corregidor to the Japanese on May 5, 1942; held a prisoner of war until rescued in August 1945; promoted to general September 1945; received Medal of Honor for his "intrepid and determined leadership against greatly superior enemy forces"; after retirement from the Army in August, 1947, was an insurance company executive. See *Current Biography,* 1942.

Obituary

N Y Times, p1+ S 3 '53 por

WALLER, FRED(ERIC) Mar. 10, 1886-
Inventor; motion picture producer; manufacturer

Address: b. c/o Cinerama, Inc., 10 E. 52d St., New York 22; h. 136 Southdown Rd., Huntington, N.Y.

The inventor of Cinerama process, which gives the effect of three-dimensional motion pictures, Fred Waller, has been connected with the film industry for some forty years as a photographer, research technician, and producer. In 1953 chairman of the board of directors of Cinerama, Inc., which is the development and equipment unit for Cinerama process, he is also president of Vitarama Company, where, since 1938, he developed many of the basic patents used in Cinerama. As an inventor, he has more than fifty patents to his credit, including the first photographic printer and timer and the Waller Flexible Gunnery Trainer used in World War II by the United States armed forces and the British Admiralty. From 1924 to 1936, except during 1927-28, Waller was associated with Paramount Pictures Corporation, designing its first optical printer, handling photographic research, and producing many short features.

Frederic Waller was born in Brooklyn, New York, on March 10, 1886, the son of Frederic and Katherine (Stearns) Waller. His maternal grandfather invented the hand winch used on ships and built the first steam derrick boat in the United States. Waller's father was the first commercial photographer in New York City as well as a newspaper reporter and magazine editor. Reared in Brooklyn, young Waller attended school there up to the age of fourteen, when he left Brooklyn Polytechnic Institute to work in his father's photographic studio.

In 1905, five years after Waller joined his father in the commercial photography business, the enterprise was organized as the Fred Waller Company, and Waller was elected vice-president, an office he retained until 1917. He invented a number of photographic machines, the majority of which he did not patent because he did not wish to disclose them, but to use them himself. One that he did patent was the first automatic photographic printer and timer. Waller, who first entered the motion picture field as the creator of lobby displays in 1905, became vice-president in 1917 of the Rotograph Company in New York City. Unable to continue his activities in lobby display because of shortages of photographic display supplies from Europe during World War I, in 1918 Waller opened an illustrating studio, one of the first in New York. He retained his studio until 1923, creating photographic title illustrations for the silent movies and from 1919 to 1922 producing exclusive title illustrations for Famous Players Lasky (now Paramount Pictures Corporation).

With Dwight Deere Wiman and others, Fred Waller in 1922 helped form the Film Guild, Inc., an independent motion picture company, of which he was treasurer in charge of production. The five pictures and three three-reel historical films produced by the Guild were a dramatic success but resulted in a financial loss. From 1924 to 1926 Waller was again employed by Paramount studios as head of the special effects department, where he managed the trick film division and handled photographic research. In 1925 he designed Paramount's first optical printer. When the Eastern feature production studio closed in 1927, Waller became a partner in William H. Young & Company, a New York sales agency for motor boats and boat equipment. Also interested in boats and sailing as a hobby, he invented and patented the first water skis, testing their efficiency himself.

Rejoining Paramount Pictures Corporation in 1929, Waller was put in charge of produc-

FRED WALLER

tion and direction of short subject films. While supervising work on over two hundred one-reel features between the years 1930 and 1936, he also established the film corporation's commercial department, and originated a number of short feature series, including *Paramount Pictorial, Movie Memoires,* and *Screen Souvenirs.* In 1936 he again left Paramount Pictures Corporation to begin work on special features for New York World's Fair (1939-40). During the same year (1936) Waller, with a group of associates, bought the assets of the original Kenyon Instrument Company of Boston. He incorporated the new company as the Kenyon Instrument Company, Inc., located it in Huntington, New York, and undertook the manufacture of nautical instruments. As president of the company (1936-42), Waller expanded its production in 1938 to include aircraft instruments and accessories. He became chairman of the board in 1942.

The Vitarama Company was formed by Waller, with Ralph Walker, in 1938 for the purpose of developing a concave screen process, the forerunner of the Cinerama process. This company, of which Waller became president in 1940, controls all of the patent rights used in the latter process. In 1939-40 Waller produced for the World's Fair Corporation the motion pictures of the figures on the inside of the Perisphere that marched in time to the theme song of the Fair; he also constructed the sound track that recorded, under the direction of André Kostelanetz, sixty-five musicians and twenty singers, as well as the off-stage voice of H. V. Kaltenborn. For Eastman Kodak Company, he planned and executed the Hall of Color demonstration at the Fair. He again demonstrated his projection method for a rounded screen surface in the *Time and Space* show he wrote and produced for the Hayden Plane-

tarium in New York, giving the effect of travel through space.

It was during the period of New York World's Fair that Waller built his first model of the Cinerama process, hoping to sell it to one of the Fair's exhibitors; but his invention was considered too radical. He was convinced that pictures made with a wide-angle lens were surprisingly "three-dimensional" when projected on a concave surface, "duplicating the way light falls on the curved retina of the eye" (New York *Herald Tribune,* September 28, 1952). Making use of the spherical screen and projection method he had developed in his Cinerama model, he created the Waller Gunnery Trainer. He demonstrated this trainer, which used films of moving planes projected on a spherical screen to imitate battle conditions for airplane pilots in combat, to all divisions of the armed forces and to British military representatives. In 1941 he received his first order for trainers from the United States Navy; other orders followed from various branches of the services and from the British Admiralty. According to estimates of the Air Force, Waller's invention prevented "350,000 casualties in training and combat during World War II" (New York *Post,* September 28, 1952). In the year before the war Waller had produced more than three hundred short subjects for juke box use by Minoco Products.

At the end of World War II Waller set up a small research laboratory at Huntington, Long Island, near his home, to continue development of his Cinerama project. Concurrently he designed and built gunnery analysis cameras for the United States Air Force that determined what happened to bullets fired from fast-moving airplanes. He also produced special slide projection equipment for use by *Life* magazine, George Eastman House, and other purchasers. On an estate in Oyster Bay, Long Island, in 1946, Waller began to build the demonstration apparatus of Cinerama process which he was to use in the public theater. An "entire new set of motion picture tools had to be constructed, as none of the existing projection equipment could be used" (New York *Herald Tribune,* September 28, 1952). For the development of stereophonic (all-around sound) to complement the cinerama camera, Waller worked with Hazard Reeves, in 1953 the president of Cinerama, Inc.

In developing test pictures Waller used the principles involved in his gunnery trainer, but employed a camera with three lenses taking pictures on three reels of film for projection on a spherical screen, instead of the five-lens, five-reel film combination used in the trainer. His screen spread over an arc of 146 degrees, closely approaching the eyes' horizontal range of 165 degrees. Vertically, it covered a range of 55 degrees, almost equaling the eyes' vertical vision of 60 degrees. One of his principal problems was the spherical screen, which permitted light to bounce back and forth within its arc, degrading the shadows. To solve this problem, Waller invented, among five others, a screen composed of eleven hundred overlapping strips of perforated plastic ribbon running vertically, like a Venetian blind set on edge. In an indoor tennis court on the estate in Oyster Bay which he made his laboratory, Waller gave his first private demonstration of Cinerama in 1949. Reports of those viewing this and other demonstrations expressed surprise at "the startling reality" of the production (*Variety*, December 28, 1949). Depth perception in Cinerama, Waller has pointed out, "as in life, results partly from the wide angle of vision of the eye. . . .It also depends on imagination and experience. Peripheral vision (clues seen out of the corners of the eye) is duplicated by Cinerama" (New York *Herald Tribune*).

Having gained the interest of Lowell Thomas, well-known broadcaster and film producer, Waller received new impetus for his project. Thomas organized Cinerama Productions Corporation, of which he became vice-chairman and Louis B. Mayer chairman of the board, to bring added financial backing and foresight to the development of Cinerama. In the interest of the improving equipment for the Cinerama project, Cinerama, Inc., was established, with Waller as chairman of the board of directors. On September 30, 1952, an invited capacity audience, attended the opening of *This is Cinerama* at the Broadway Theatre in New York City. "The distinguished gathering was as excited and thrilled by the spectacle presented as if it were seeing motion pictures for the first time," commented Bosley Crowther in the New York *Times*. Most of the scenes were in long shots, and there was little attempt to attain expression and emphasis through cutting and juxtaposition. *Newsweek* quoted playwright Robert E. Sherwood as describing Cinerama as "a tool with which we playwrights can subject the audience to any experience we want to give them." Waller said of his process: "Cinerama was designed as a medium not simply of entertainment but of experience. . . .The Cinerama audience will not merely observe events on the screen but have the sense of actually participating in them" (New York *Post*).

The reaction of the general public to *This Is Cinerama* was enthusiastic: some regarded it as "the movies' answer to television" (*Newsweek*); others "screeched in terror, gasped in awe, and applauded with delight and amazement" (New York *World-Telegram*). The demonstration program, which opened with a realistic ride in a roller coaster car, included a series of short films and travelogues in Europe and America. The innovation in sound (stereophonic sound) reproduced sounds from the portion of the screen where they originated by means of seven microphones recording on seven separate sound tracks and fed to eight loudspeakers scattered throughout the theater. John Molleson in the New York *Herald Tribune* noted that "stereophonic sound contributes to the three-dimensional illusion." By the end of 1953 some fifteen to twenty-five theaters in America have been remodeled and equipped for Cinerama, the first of these in Chicago. Meanwhile, two Cinerama pictures are reportedly being made in Hollywood.

Twelve months after Cinerama was introduced to audiences in New York, Chicago, Detroit and Hollywood, it had grossed $4,300,-000 (New York *Herald Tribune,* September 27, 1953).

When Cinerama was chosen the winner of the United States Camera Achievement Award in 1952, Waller received honorable mention as inventor of the process. He is a fellow of the Society of Motion Picture Television Engineers and holds the rank of Class A cameraman in the International Photographers of the Motion Picture Industry. His club membership includes the Huntington Yacht Club. He is nonsectarian "but religious," and is an independent voter who "believes in good government." Married on October 2, 1905, Fred Waller and Irene Seymour have two children, Muriel and Stuart; the marriage ended in divorce in 1919. On August 12, 1920, the inventor married Grace Fortescue Hubbard, who died in 1941. He married Doris (Barber) Caron, of Canada, on July 21, 1942.

The inventor is firmly convinced that Cinerama has unparalled potentialities for education, giving the learner a direct experience. Waller has said: "I would love to see this process used to civilize mankind and help to create peace in the world."

References

N Y Post p13 S 28 '52

N Y Sunday News II p2 S 21 '52; p90 O '52

New Yorker 27:23 My 5 '51

National Cyclopaedia of American Biography Current vol G, 1943-46

International Motion Picture Almanac, 1951-52

WARREN, LEONARD, Apr. 21, 1911-
Opera singer
Address: b c/o Hurok Attractions, Inc., 711 Fifth Ave., New York 22

For fifteen years Leonard Warren, American baritone, has been a member of the Metropolitan Opera Company, and has given over 400 performances in twenty-two different roles. At the end of the 1952-53 opera season while on tour, he sang the title role in *Rigoletto* for the one hundredth time.

Leonard Warren was born in the Bronx, New York, on April 21, 1911, the son of two Russian immigrants, S. and Sarah Warrenoff. (The family name was later changed to Warren.) Leonard's father was a fur merchant who expected that his son would also pursue this trade. Leonard attended Public School No. 11 in the Bronx, was graduated from the Evander Childs High School, and then enrolled as a night student at Columbia University, where he took courses in commerce and merchandising.

During the day Warren learned the fur brokerage business from his father and in the evenings studied music at the Greenwich House Music School. He soon discovered that as his interest in music increased, his interest in a business career waned. When the depression of the 1930's reduced opportunities in the fur business, he left his father's firm to seek other work. For a year Warren tried a number of

J. Abresch

LEONARD WARREN

jobs, including one as a grease-monkey at a service station. Then a friend arranged an audition for him with the Radio City Music Hall Glee Club. Warren was accepted into the glee club and began then to develop his voice under the tutelage of Sidney Dietch. For three years he continued to sing at the Music Hall.

In 1938 Warren decided to try out for the *Metropolitan Auditions of the Air*, a radio program in which young American singers are given an opportunity to sing before a large audience and compete for a contract with the Metropolitan Opera Company. To prepare for the contest, Warren requested two weeks leave from his Music Hall commitments, but the glee club director instead discharged the young singer.

The story is told that when Warren auditioned at the preliminary hearings for the contest, the Metropolitan conductor and judge of the program, Wilfred Pelletier, had had an exhausting session of listening to seventy-eight singers and had failed to hear any that he considered noteworthy. Warren was the next contestant, and when he began to sing Pelletier thought the sound technicians were playing a recording as a joke. He was assured that the voice he was hearing was that of the young man at the microphone. At the end of the aria, Pelletier simply thanked the singer and Warren went out believing he had failed. Only later that evening did he learn that he was to be among the final competitors.

Subsequently, Warren won first honors over 700 singers and was granted a contract with the Metropolitan for his singing of the aria "Largo al Factotum" from Rossini's *The Barber of Seville*. At this time, he did not know any operatic roles, only a few arias. The late George A. Martin, president of the Sherwin-Williams Company which at that time was sponsoring the auditions, gave Warren a check

for $5,000 so that he could study in Milan and develop a repertoire. The baritone received instruction from Maestro Pais and Ricardo Picozzi and learned seven roles in less than eight months.

On his return to the United States, Warren began singing at the Metropolitan's Sunday evening concerts. On January 13, 1939, he made his operatic debut as Paolo in *Simon Boccanegra*. Although Warren handled this minor assignment well, he was not an immediate favorite of the audience or critics. His development as an operatic artist was so gradual that for a time he was known as "the man most unreviewed at the Metropolitan" (*Newsweek*, December 13, 1948).

He sang the role of the High Priest in the New York première of Gluck's *Alceste* in January 1941 and portrayed Ilo in Gian-Carlo Menotti's *The Island God* on February 20, 1942. However, Warren did not become widely known until December 17, 1943 when he appeared for the first time in a leading role, Renato, in Verdi's *The Masked Ball*. The New York *Times* critic applauded Warren's "robust and sonorously-sung Renato," and described his voice as a "splendid" one, which he used with "marked intelligence and with more than roaring melodrama" (December 18, 1943). The next day, at a matinee performance, Warren was called on to replace the ailing Lawrence Tibbett in the title role of *Rigoletto*, and the critics were impressed by his performance.

In 1944, when he sang the title role in the English version of *Falstaff*, Olin Downes, wrote: "It was a pleasure to observe in this part an artist who made his points without exaggeration or affectation either. . . .The fine quality of his voice was put at the service of significant diction" (New York *Times*, December 12, 1944).

During that season his characterization of Count di Luna in *Il Trovatore* was praised by Virgil Thomson: "Leonard Warren has a beautiful voice, a dependable manner of handling it and a fine musical style. He is in the process of becoming one of the greatest singers in the world of Italian baritone roles" (New York *Herald Tribune*, February 26, 1944).

Each year since his debut in 1939 Warren has added to his repertoire. He has sung the leading baritone parts in *Aida, Il Barbiere di Siviglia, Carmen, Pagliacci, La Forza del Destino, Simon Boccanegra, La Gioconda, Il Trovatore, La Traviata, Falstaff* and *Rigoletto*.

He sang the role of Iago in the 1948 production of *Otello* at the Metropolitan, earning such comments on his performance as "vocally magnificent", "acted the cunning Iago skillfully and convincingly," "the world's finest baritone" (*Newsweek*, December 13, 1948). He played the title role in *Simon Boccanegra* in 1949 and also drew praise from the critics.

In addition to his work with the Metropolitan Opera, Warren has sung with several major symphony orchestras, opera companies in San Francisco, Chicago, Cincinnati, Mexico City, Rio de Janeiro and Buenos Aires, and has given recitals throughout the United States, Canada and South America. From the Municipal Department of Culture of the city of São Paulo,

Brazil, Warren received a citation plaque for his contributions to the 1945 musical season. He has also received citations from the Brazilian Society of Culture and from the National Association of American Composers and Conductors.

Warren has become familiar to both radio and television audiences through his guest appearances on such programs as *The Treasury Hour,* the *Ford Sunday Evening Hour* and the *Voice of Firestone.* His many recordings for RCA Victor include diversified solos comprising operatic arias, sea chanties, and Kipling ballads, and also the complete score of *Rigoletto.*

In September 1952 the baritone established the Leonard Warren Scholarship Fund for gifted young singers. Since he himself was helped by a patron, Warren considers the fund a way of repaying his debt of gratitude. Recipients of the scholarship will be given a minimum of one year's free instruction under Warren's own voice teacher, Sidney Dietch. Warren, who lists Wilfred Pelletier and Giuseppe de Luca, the late Italian baritone and operatic coach, as men who most influenced him in his career, also recalls that it was in a candy store window that he noticed a blotter with the word "Confidence" printed on it. This word inspired him to achieve certainty in each operatic role in order to have complete confidence in his performances. Warren believes that such assurance can only be attained by a study of the character as well as of the musical score. He wrote, "A role isn't just sung—it must be worked out, molded, deepened, given continuity and fluidity. And this is achieved only by research and experience" (*Etude,* March, 1949).

Warren was married on December 27, 1941, to Agatha Leifflen, a graduate of Juilliard School of Music, whom he met while studying in Milan. The singer is dark-complexioned, has brown hair and eyes, is five feet, eleven inches in height, and usually keeps his weight at 200 pounds.

As a change from his musical work, he enjoys building model railroads, driving his motorboat, fishing, gardening and sailing. The baritone also lists the collecting of paintings as one of his absorbing interests.

References

Etude 67:149 Mr '49
Mus Am 71:15 Mr '51
N Y Star Jl 29 '48
Opera News N 23 '42
Who is Who in Music (1951)
Saleski, G. Famous Musicians of Jewish Origin (1949)

WATSON, LUCILE May 27, 1879- Actress
Address: h. 143 E. 63d St., New York 21

Wise dowagers and witty matriarchs have been the type of roles for which actress Lucile Watson is best known. She has played in about fifty productions on Broadway and in a score of motion pictures in Hollywood since 1900.

She has acted in such successful plays as *Yes, My Darling Daughter* (1937), *Watch on the Rhine* (1941), and *Ring Around the Moon* (1950). She appeared in Rosemary Casey's comedy, *Late Love,* in the fall of 1953.

Born in Quebec, Canada, on May 27, 1879, Lucile Watson is the daughter of Thomas Charles and Leila (Morlet) Watson. Her father was a major with the Royal Sherwood Foresters. Lucile was educated privately and in Ursuline Convent. She made her first stage appearance at the Opera House in Ottawa in 1900, playing Mrs. Chillington in *A Morning Call.* Determined upon a career as an actress, she came to the United States at the age of twenty-one and studied at the American Academy of Dramatic Arts, New York City, for two years.

The actress was introduced to the New York stage in February 1902, when she appeared at the Empire Theatre as Mrs. Ralph Wuthering in *The Wisdom of the Wise.* She was quickly in demand for parts in other plays, and found she had no need of a theatrical agent. Regular bookings at Broadway's leading theatres followed. In the next few years she played such roles as Maggie in *The Girl with the Green Eyes* (1902), Mrs. Bowie in *The Dictator* (1904) and Mrs. Stonington in *Captain Jinks* (1907). She played in *Young Fernald* at the Majestic Theatre in Boston in 1906 and during 1908 she toured in *Vera the Medium.*

One of Miss Watson's early successes was the role of Teresa Rand in *The City,* a drama by Clyde Fitch, which was a vehicle for the young actress from December 1909 until 1911. The next year she appeared in three Broadway dramas, *The Truth Wagon, The Point of View* and *Just To Get Married.*

Melodrama was again a successful vehicle for her in 1913, and 1914, when she appeared in *Under Cover* by R. C. Megrue. Her role was that of the alert wife of a millionaire who helped uncover the smuggler of a $200,000 necklace.

Going to the Pacific coast in 1917, Lucile Watson played in Henry Miller's company. She was Mrs. Forsythe in the *Fountain of Youth* (1918), and Mrs. Langley in *Moonlight and Honeysuckle* (1919). For the Theatre Guild in New York in 1920, she portrayed the part of Lady Utterwood in George Bernard Shaw's *Heartbreak House.* The Broadway stage kept her busy the next few years in roles in various comedies.

Her first appearance on the London stage was at Queens Theatre in March 1925, playing Mrs. Zola Massarene in *Dancing Mothers.* In New York the following year, she portrayed Mrs. Alving in Ibsen's *Ghosts,* Lady Bracknell in Wilde's *The Importance of Being Earnest* and Mrs. Wallbridge in *The Zoo* in 1927 in Washington, D.C. She then retired from her acting career for three years.

The first play in which Miss Watson returned to the stage was *That's the Woman* (1930). *Life* (September 26, 1930) commented that one of the most unreal things about the play was the appearance of Lucile Watson, "that excellent comedienne, in a role that re-

LUCILE WATSON

quires her to hand out ignoble advice instead of her accustomed crisp admonitions."

The actress played in productions by the American Women's Club in Paris during 1932, and returned to New York where she appeared at the Booth Theatre in January 1934 in a comedy by A. E. Thomas called *No More Ladies.* Melvyn Douglas was a member of the cast. and Miss Watson played the part of Mrs. Fanny Townsend. The play was included by Burns Mantle in his collection *Best Plays (1933-34).* *Theatre Arts* (April 1934) recognized Miss Watson's contribution by stating: "When she comes on stage, everyone else might as well go off." The reviewer called the "farce pattern perfectly fitted to Lucile Watson's form of acting, which has no nuance or restraint." In Hollywood, she acted in several motion pictures including *Florian, Waterloo Bridge, Mr. and Mrs. Smith,* and *Model Wife.*

A mystery comedy, *Post Road,* engaged Miss Watson on Broadway early in 1935. This was followed by her performance as Mrs. Bennet in *Pride and Prejudice,* a dramatization of Jane Austen's novel by Helen Jerome. The *New Republic* (December 11, 1935) review stated that the Mrs. Bennet of the novel "is not quite so engaging a creature as we see in the play," but concedes this is probably good for the stage.

In 1937 Mark Reed's play, *Yes, My Darling Daughter,* Miss Watson was featured in the role of a modern mother whose daughter tries to justify her rebellion against middle-class conventions by citing her mother's own Bohemian past. Of this comedy, Eva Le Gallienne wrote in *With a Quiet Heart* (1953): "For Lucile Watson's second act alone the play was worth seeing . . . she plays with her brain—but there is heart in her work too—and knowledge and understanding of life and people; a sort of shrewd kindness."

For two seasons, during 1941 through 1943, she played Fanny Farrelly in Lillian Hellman's

prize-winning drama *Watch on the Rhine* at the Martin Beck Theatre in New York. The actress was "witty, sententious, and varied in mood" in her portrayal of the matriarch. Brooks Atkinson stated in the New York *Times* (August 24, 1941) that "with an instinctive sense of right proportions, Miss Watson heaped the surface nonsense on a character of inherent dignity . . . making the silliness, pettiness, courage and contempt all logical parts of a singularly spirited lady."

Miss Watson played the same role in the film version of *Watch on the Rhine,* and the reviewer for *Variety* (July 28, 1943) wrote that "her incisive playing . . . a gem in the original play, is even more striking in the expanded part on the screen." In the same year the actress portrayed the Russian granny in Victor Wolfson's stage adaptation of Nina Fedorova's novel *The Family.* She was described by Howard Barnes in the New York *Herald Tribune* (March 31, 1943) as "holding a group of desperate exiles together with matriarchal dignity." Following this play the actress devoted herself primarily to screen productions for the next seven years.

In *Uncertain Glory* (1944), a psychological melodrama of France under the Nazis, Miss Watson portrayed the role of Madame Maret, the town matriarch. On leave from Warner Brothers, she portrayed the Mother Superior in *Till We Meet Again* (1944), produced by Paramount Pictures. Of her acting, *PM*'s reviewer stated: "Lucile Watson holds the stage superbly as a quite worldly Mother Superior." In 1945, the actress appeared as a "detective's understanding mother" in the mystery film *The Thin Man Goes Home,* produced by Metro-Goldwyn-Mayer.

Miss Watson was a Victorian mother in Warner Brothers' *My Reputation* (1946), a domestic drama. As described by Eileen Creelman in the New York *Sun* (January 26, 1946), the actress brought "to each scene a forcefulness and high comedy sense rare on screen and stage alike." In International Pictures' production of *Tomorrow is Forever* (1946) Miss Watson played Aunt Jessie in an Enoch Arden story.

Among the screen plays on which the comedienne acted supporting roles as grandmother, elderly aristocrat, mother, mother-in-law, or aunt are *Never Say Goodbye* (1946), *The Emperor Waltz* (1946), *Ivy* (1947), *Julia Misbehaves* (1948), *Everybody Does it* (1949), *That Wonderful Urge* (1949), and *Little Women* (1949). In *Let's Dance* (1950), she was a stern Boston great-grandmother "except when she relaxes to dance with Mr. Astaire and turns on the charm" (New York *Times,* November 30, 1950).

Miss Watson was commended as one of "an unusually good supporting cast" in the screen version of George Kelly's *Craig's Wife,* entitled *Helen Craig* (1950). In the film, *My Forbidden Past* (1951) she portrayed the role of a guardian aunt and "patrician schemer."

Returning to the Broadway stage in November 1950 for the role of Madame Desmermortes in the "charade-with-music" translation by Christopher Fry of Jean Anouilh's comedy

Ring Around the Moon, Lucile Watson gave "a royal performance as a witty-minded matriarch" anchored to a wheelchair (*New York Times,* November 24, 1950). "She is one of the most extraordinary comediennes in the theatre, impeccable in timing and delivery, getting her effects with a wonderful economy of gesture and admirable vocal restraint," wrote the *New Yorker* critic, Wolcott Gibbs, on December 2, 1950. She played the role of the intrepid spinster in the revival of Mary Roberts Rinehart's *The Bat,* early in 1953.

The actress remembers John Barrymore as an "awkward youngster" who made his first stage appearance in her third Broadway play. Her hobbies include housekeeping, music and poetry, and she makes a habit of writing letters to critics. She lists her political affiliation as "conservative" and her church as "Anglican." She is a member of the Colony Club in New York. She was married in 1928 to Louis Shipman, editor and playwright; he died in 1933. Miss Watson was described by Gilbert Millstein in the New York *Times,* October 11, 1953, as "a marvel of gentility in toque, veil, fur stole and navy blue." She admitted that she "never had to traipse Broadway, never needed an agent." During her twenties, she said, she played "second women;" during her thirties, she developed what the trade now knows as "Lucile Watson" parts. "They were all high comedy," she observed, "with feeling, with pathos—funny, gay, kind, tart and naughty." She admitted that she had taken the part in *Late Love* because "it fills the evenings."

Brooks Atkinson commented in the New York *Times* (October 14, 1953) on Miss Watson's performance in *Late Love*: "She is giving one of her most delightful performances . . . she has publicly announced that she is going to leave the stage after this performance. But there are countless theatregoers who have not had enough of her crackling mind, her peppery speech, her fluffy hair, her grand manners . . . she sails through [the play's] placid persiflage like a full-rigged ship."

References

N Y Sunday News II p6 D 31 '50
N Y Times II p3 O 11 '53 por
N Y World-Telegram p13 F 26 '41
International Motion Picture Almanac, 1951-52
Who's Who in the Theatre (1952)

WEEKS, SINCLAIR June 15, 1893- United States Secretary of Commerce; industrialist
Address: b. c/o Department of Commerce, Washington 25, D.C.; 1014 Statler Bldg., Boston, Mass.; h. 282 Beacon St., Boston, Mass.

Chosen by President Dwight D. Eisenhower as Secretary of Commerce in the Republican Administration, Sinclair Weeks was sworn into office, following Senate approval, on January 21, 1953. Weeks, a Boston manufacturer and one-time United States Senator by appointment, had been in charge of raising funds for the Eisenhower 1952 Presidential campaign and had

Wide World Photos
SINCLAIR WEEKS

served as chairman of several national and Massachusetts Republican finance committees.

The only child of John Wingate and Martha A. (Sinclair) Weeks, Sinclair Weeks was born on June 15, 1893, in West Newton, Massachusetts, a suburb of Boston. His father, who was a member of the Boston brokerage firm of Hornblower & Weeks, served in the House of Representatives and in the Senate, was a candidate for Presidential nomination in the 1916 Republican National Convention, and later became Secretary of War in the Harding and Coolidge cabinets. From Newton High School, Sinclair Weeks entered Harvard University to take his B.A. degree in 1914.

For two years after he had graduated from college, Weeks was employed at the First National Bank in Boston, as clerk to the assistant cashier, before being called in 1916 to serve in the Massachusetts National Guard on the Mexican border. Entering the Army as a second lieutenant in 1917, he advanced to the rank of captain and commanded the B Battery of the 101st Artillery in the Twenty-sixth Division in France. (During World War II his son, John, was to attain the same command.) After his discharge from the Army in April 1919, he returned to the bank, where by 1923 he attained the position of assistant cashier. In that year he left banking to become a manufacturer of metals. Within five years (1928) he was named vice-president of Reed & Barton Corporation (silversmiths); he was elected president and in January 1945 chairman of the board. Associated also with United-Carr Fastener Corporation (manufacturers of metal fasteners, buckles, zippers, and clips), he became a director of that firm in 1929 and chairman of the board in 1942.

Through his father's activities, Sinclair Weeks acquired an early interest in politics. "When you sit around the breakfast table and hear

WEEKS, SINCLAIR—*Continued*

politics discussed daily," *Time* has quoted him as saying, "you are bound to develop an interest." In 1914 he was one of the founders of the first Young Men's Republican Club in Massachusetts. After the war he combined his early business career with participation in local politics, serving as a member of the Newton board of aldermen (1923-30) and as mayor of that city for six years (1930-36). In the latter office he announced that it was his intention "to run this city as nearly as possible along business lines" (*Time*). At the preprimary Republican State Convention in 1936, Weeks unsuccessfully sought the nomination to the United States Senate in opposition to Henry Cabot Lodge, Jr., "losing the endorsement to Senator Lodge by a few convention votes," wrote Edgar M. Mills in the *Christian Science Monitor*. Shortly afterward he was named chairman of the Republican State Committee and two years later became both chairman of the Republican State finance committee and eastern treasurer for the Republican National Committee. At the 1940 Republican National Convention, Weeks was a strong supporter of Wendell Willkie, who won the nomination. Weeks became chairman of the executive committee of the Republican National Committee in 1940 and from 1941 to February 1944 held the post of treasurer of the national committee.

When Senator Lodge resigned from the Senate to enter the World War II Army in February 1944, Massachusetts Governor Leverett Saltonstall named Weeks to complete Lodge's term. During his eleven months in the Senate (February 8 through December 19, 1944), Weeks voted for cloture on the 1944 anti-poll tax bill discussion and for a measure requiring TVA appropriations to be allocated by Congress: he opposed eliminating an appropriation for FEPC, a proposal to connect the Tennessee and Tombigbee rivers, and the 1944 proposal for the St. Lawrence Seaway. On other issues he supported bills to end all existing food subsidy programs and to permit cotton prices to be raised, an appropriation for UNRRA, and a measure affording State (as opposed to Federal) administration of unemployment benefits. Weeks did not seek to return to the Senate in 1944, and the Republican nomination went to Saltonstall.

In the Presidential election year of 1948 the influence of Weeks in Massachusetts politics was considered very strong. "When and if Massachusetts' thirty-five delegates to the GOP National Convention swing away from favorite-son support to back another nominee," wrote Mills, "the man behind the swing undoubtedly will be Sinclair Weeks of Boston" (*Christian Science Monitor*). Regarded as one of the party's most successful fund raisers, in 1950 he became chairman of the Republican National finance committee, charged with the responsibility for raising and administering funds for the 1950 Republican Congressional campaign. Shortly before the 1952 national convention Weeks told the party that under his direction the committee had raised three times as much money as had been raised in 1948. Having earlier announced himself as a supporter of

General Dwight D. Eisenhower, Weeks in June 1952 called on Senator Robert A. Taft to withdraw as a candidate for the Presidential nomination. After Eisenhower's nomination at the Chicago convention, Weeks was once again named chairman of the Republican National finance committee and as such was credited by *Life* with having raised nearly $6 million for the Eisenhower campaign.

Several weeks after the victory of Eisenhower in the November 1952 election, Sinclair Weeks was designated as the Secretary of Commerce in the new Republican Administration. His nomination confirmed by the Senate, he took office on January 21, 1953. Weeks "has consistently supported the forward-looking elements of the party," commented the New York *Times* in its editorial on Weeks's appointment. "His preconvention declaration for General Eisenhower's cause was one of those sure signs indicating where the political currents were tending. . . .He should not only fill successfully the post of Secretary of Commerce, but make of that position something more creative and significant than has frequently been the case in the past." The functions of the Department of Commerce, which has about 50,000 employees, are "to foster, promote, and develop the foreign and domestic commerce, the mining, manufacturing, shipping, and fishing industries, and the transportation facilities of the United States" (*United States Government Organization Manual*). Besides determining the policies and programs of the department, Weeks is responsible for the operation of the Bureau of Census, Civil Aeronautics Administration, Coast and Geodetic Survey, Bureau of Foreign and Domestic Commerce, Inland Waterways Corporation, Maritime Administration, Bureau of Standards, Weather Bureau, and other offices.

As reported in the press, Weeks in early December 1952 expressed himself on four major points of policy: he believes that the excess profits tax should either be eliminated completely, or, if needed for revenue, cut sharply; that private industry can quickly take up any slack that might be caused by a curtailment in defense production; that, while he is an internationalist, he is not a "free trade man" and believes in adequate tariffs; and that he opposes the use of American funds abroad to develop industries that will compete with American industry and would rather see that money spent to develop backward nations (New York *Herald Tribune*). In a Lincoln Day Dinner address in Boston in 1953, Weeks said that the "Washington mess" was worse than the public thought and that there were many opportunities to save money in the government. He defended Eisenhower's appointment of businessmen to government posts: "Some thumpers and pundits . . . complain because the new Administration no longer gives high priority to the theories of foreign Socialists or to the notions of local egg heads" (quoted in the New York *Times*).

At the time of his appointment to Eisenhower's Cabinet, *United States News* commented that Weeks was "giving up an income that runs into six figures to head the Department of Commerce at $22,500." Besides holding the chairmanship of the two Massachusetts manufacturing concerns previously mentioned, Weeks is director of a number of corporations: Atlay Plywood Company, First National Bank of Boston, Pacific Mills, Gillette Safety Razor Company, Wentworth Institute, Rand-Avery-Gordon-Taylor, Inc., and the Pullman Company. He is also president of the American Enterprises Association and a director of the National Association of Manufacturers. Weeks is a member of the board of overseers of Harvard University and a member of the corporation of Northeastern University. During World War II he was civilian aid in charge of civilian procurement under the Secretary of War.

By his marriage to Beatrice Dowse on December 4, 1915, Weeks had six children—Frances Lee, John Wingate 2d, Martha S., Sinclair, William D., and Beatrice. Mrs. Beatrice Weeks died in July 1945. On January 3, 1948, Weeks was married for a second time, to Jane Tompkins Rankin. In religion he is a Unitarian. He is stocky (five feet ten inches, 183 pounds) and has balding gray hair. The Commerce Secretary, who has been called an "innate woodsman," enjoys the outdoors and has a beef and dairy farm in Lancaster, New Hampshire, where he likes to spend part of each summer.

References

Bsns W p29 D 6 '52 por
Christian Sci Mon Je 14 '48
Life 34:39 F 16 '53 por
N Y Herald Tribune p11 F 9 '44 por
Newsweek 40:21 D 2 '52 por
Time 43:21 F 21 '44 por; 60:21 D 8 '52 por
Biographical Directory of the American Congress, 1774-1949 (1950)
Who's Who in America, 1952-53
Who's Who in Massachusetts, 1940-41
Who's Who in New England (1949)
Who's Who in United States Politics (1950)

WHITE, GILBERT F(OWLER) Nov. 26, 1911- College president; geographer
Address: b. c/o Haverford College, Haverford, Pa.; h. 1 College Circle, Haverford, Pa.

The president of Haverford College, a highly regarded small liberal arts college established by the Society of Friends in 1833, is Dr. Gilbert F. White, who before his appointment in 1946 was an administrator of Quaker relief activities in Europe and Asia. Formerly employed by the United States Government as geographical technician and authority on flood control and water conservation, Dr. White has also served on the Natural Resources Task Force of the Hoover Commission and is the vice-chairman of President Truman's Water Resources Commission. In 1949 he headed a board of sixteen eminent Quakers who recommended ways and means of relaxing tension between the United States and the Soviet Union.

A native of Chicago, Illinois, Gilbert Fowler White was born on November 26, 1911, to Arthur Edward and Mary Louisa (Guthrie)

White. He was graduated from the University of Chicago High School in 1928 and four years later, having majored in geography, received his B.S. degree from the University of Chicago, where he was elected to Phi Beta Kappa. After taking his M.Sc. degree at Chicago in 1934, he was engaged as a research technician for the Mississippi Valley Committee of the Public Works Administration and was employed by the National Resources Board in 1934-35. Specializing in water supply and drought problems, he was appointed secretary of the land and water committee of the National Resources Committee and later the National Resources Planning Board from 1936 to 1940. During this time he directed his committee's administrative and research work, wrote several government pamphlets on flood control and water conservation and contributed articles to scientific journals, and lectured in the graduate school of American University (1938-40). While working for his Ph.D. degree, which he received from the University of Chicago in 1942, White was employed by the Bureau of the Budget as a legislative analyst (1941) "to review and appraise reports and legislation relating to land and water conservation."

In 1942 White, then a member of the faculty of the University of Chicago, went as a delegate of the American Friends Service Committee to unoccupied France for World War II refugee relief and children's aid work. When the Germans took over Vichy from the Pétain Government, he was sent with the American diplomatic staff to Baden-Baden, where he was interned for one year. Released in 1944 through an exchange agreement, he returned home, where he was appointed assistant professor of Geography at the University of Chicago. The following year he became assistant executive secretary of the American Friends Service Committee and went to India and China to administer the American relief program. He returned to Europe early in 1946 as a member of the mission of American Voluntary Agencies to open relief services in Germany.

At the age of thirty-five Dr. White was elected, on July 14, 1946, to succeed Dr. Felix Morley as president of Haverford College, a small liberal arts college founded by the Religious Society of Friends in 1833 near Philadelphia, Pennsylvania. With a student enrollment of 485 and a faculty of 61, Haverford is one of the best-endowed small colleges in the country, having in 1952 an endowment fund of about $8 million. In his inaugural address on November 16, 1946, White warned educators to guard against lowered scholastic standards in the postwar period and pointed out that Haverford was already revising its own curriculum "to strengthen sense of social responsibility." During the war Haverford had conducted a graduate training program in reconstruction and relief work, the graduates of which were later engaged by UNRRA and other organizations. Under Dr. White's administration, Haverford has extended its effort to respond to the government's personnel needs created by the Point IV Program.

In 1951 a postgraduate course was instituted "to train men and women as technicians and ad-

Fabian Bachrach

GILBERT F. WHITE

ministrators of economic and social development programs in distressed parts of the world" (New York *Herald Tribune*). The course, which leads to the M.A. degree in social and technical assistance, was taken in 1951-52 by seven men and thirteen women. "Included in the curriculum for the first year," wrote Mark Sexton in the *Christian Science Monitor*, "has been the study of languages, human relations, economics, fiscal management and administration, cultural anthropology and case studies of projects conducted by the United Nations, by agencies of the United States Government, and by private relief groups."

White looks beyond the large-scale undertakings supported by the U.N. and the Point IV Program to "basic advances . . . at the village level" as a major phase into which technical assistance efforts must move. "Without discounting the importance of the large-scale technical projects," he told a New York *Herald Tribune* Forum audience in October 1952, "it seems likely that the tide of poverty will be turned only by the concurrent development of a vast number of small-scale projects centering upon the patient, simple action of workers in rural communities of Asia, the Middle East and Latin America. . . .If so, all of the programs will need to make large increases in the opportunity for relatively junior workers—both native and foreign—whose assets are good-will and general competence rather than long experience and specialized training." Late in 1950 a three-year grant by the Carnegie Corporation enabled Haverford to introduce what the New York *Times* characterized as "an experimental study program devoted to human values in Western civilization," which includes contemporary American literature as well as ancient Greek works and gives attention also to student writing.

For the year 1948-49 President White added to his executive duties at Haverford membership in the Task Force Committee on Natural Resources of the Hoover Commission. A member also of the United States delegation to the United Nations Scientific Conference on the Conservation and Utilization of Resources held at Lake Success, New York, in 1949, he wrote a lengthy account of the proceedings in the *Geographical Review* of October 1949, describing the conferences as the "first world effort to assess resources." He was appointed vice-chairman of President Truman's Water Resources Policy Commission the following year.

A "working group" of sixteen prominent Quakers headed by Dr. White was detailed in February 1949 by the American Friends Service Committee to study Soviet-American relations. The group, of which Elmore Jackson was secretary and former President Frank Aydelotte of Swarthmore was a prominent member, met in New York, Washington, and Philadelphia, to talk over East-West problems with other Quakers and with State Department officials and Soviet leaders like Deputy Foreign Ministers Andrei A. Gromyko and Jacob A. Malik (New York *Times*). Its twenty-eight page "tentative report," released on July 17, 1949, and sent to Secretary of State Dean Acheson and to Russian Ambassador Alexander S. Panyushkin, maintained that "war between the United States and the Soviet Union is not inevitable," and made specific recommendations for relaxing tension. These included abandonment of the United States embargo policy and the lifting of barriers to normal exports to Russia and Eastern Europe, inclusion of Eastern Europe in the Point IV Program, and promotion through the United Nations of "effective international control of armaments and atomic energy." The report further stated that "United States policy should have as its objective the political and economic unification and the neutralization of Germany."

White, who holds an honorary LL.D. degree from Hamilton College (1951), is a member of the Association of American Geographers, the American Geographical Union, and the Sigma Xi and Phi Beta Kappa fraternities. His clubs are the Cosmos in Washington and the University in New York City. Mrs. White, an economist before her marriage on April 28, 1944, is the former Anne Elizabeth Underwood, of Washington, D.C. The Whites have one son, William Deakins, and one daughter, Mary Bayard. Standing six feet in height, White is 155 pounds in weight; he has blue eyes and brown hair.

References

N Y Herald Tribune IX p8 O 26 '52 por
N Y Sun p18 O 14 '46
N Y Times p16 Jl 15 '46 por
American Men of Science (1949)
America's Young Men, 1938-39
Directory of American Scholars (1951)
Who Knows—and What (1949)
Who's Who in America, 1952-53
Who's Who in the East (1951)
World Biography (1948)

WHITE, WILLIAM Feb. 3, 1897- Railroad president

Address: b. c/o New York Central Railway System, 230 Park Ave., New York 17

In the summer of 1952 William White was elected president of the New York Central System, the nation's second largest railroad, after more than a decade (1941-52) as president of the Delaware, Lackawanna and Western Railroad. Starting his career as a clerk for the Erie Railroad in 1913, for the next twenty-five years he advanced in this line to become general manager of the eastern district in 1938. For three years (1938-41) he was vice-president and general manager of the Virginian Railway in Norfolk.

Often called "a railroader's railroader," William White, who has devoted his entire working life to the rail transportation business, has since childhood been interested in trains. Born in Midland Park, New Jersey, on February 3, 1897, to Garrett White, a master mechanic who came to this country from the Netherlands, and Anna (Amos) White, William was brought up in his native suburban community, where he was graduated from the Midland Park grade school. As a child he "liked the smell of train smoke," stated an article in *Time*. "As he grew up he spent his Sundays sneaking along the Erie tracks, hopping rides. The neighbors were scandalized, but Billy thought of himself as a dedicated railroader."

Thus when he left the Ridgewood (New Jersey) High School (1909-13) at the age of sixteen, he sought a railroad job; and, having had some instruction in bookkeeping, he was engaged as a clerk in the office of the Erie Railroad's auditor of freight accounts in New York City, beginning August 13, 1913. Later the same year White was transferred to Jersey City, New Jersey, as a stenographer and clerk in the office of the superintendent of the New York, Susquehanna and Western Railroad, an Erie subsidiary. He returned to the New York branch in March 1916 to serve in the office of Erie's vice-president, and that December was promoted to be secretary to the vice-president, the position he was holding when the United States entered World War I and operation of the country's railroads was taken over by the government. He was then made secretary to the assistant director of the eastern region and secretary of the New York district conference committee of the United States Railroad Administration. It was also at this time that White met Gustav Metzman, then on leave from the Baltimore and Ohio Railroad, who was to be his immediate predecessor as president of the New York Central System.

During 1918-19 White served in the Army as a sergeant major, stationed at Camp Humphries, Virginia. With the end of the war and the return of the railroads to private control, White upon his discharge from the army asked for a transfer to the operating end of the Erie (the main line of which runs through southern New York and north central Ohio and Indiana to Chicago) because, as he put it, he had "the engine house smoke in his nostrils." His

WILLIAM WHITE

request was granted, and in March 1920 he moved to Youngstown, Ohio, for a three-year period as office manager of the operating department of the Erie's Ohio Region. For a little over three years, beginning in January 1923, White was a trainmaster, first with the Erie's Kent Division in Marion, Ohio, and then with the Marion Division in Huntington, Indiana. In November 1926 White was made assistant superintendent of the Mahoning Division, and in February 1927 was promoted to superintendent. (He had in the middle 1920's, the financial writer Joseph d'Aleo of the New York *World-Telegram* observed, "set a goal . . . of becoming an Erie division superintendent by the time he was thirty. He missed it by twelve days.") Steadily advancing in responsibility, White moved to Cleveland, Ohio, in September 1929 as assistant general manager of Erie's western district, and after a little less than five years (June 1934) was made assistant to the vice-president in charge of operations at Cleveland. His final position with the Erie road was in New York as general manager of the eastern district from April 1936 to January 1938.

With his appointment as general manager of the Virginian Railway, which has offices in Norfolk, Virginia, White left the Erie railroad at the end of January 1938. The Virginian (stated *Railway Age*) was "a relatively new railroad built 'all of a piece' . . . to haul coal from West Virginia fields to tidewater at Norfolk." Controlled by the Kopper-Mellon interests, it had never failed to pay a dividend since its construction shortly before World War I, and its prosperity continued under White, who, in addition to being general manager, assumed the office of vice-president on May 17, 1938. White remained with the Virginian until January 1, 1941, when he became president of the Delaware, Lackawanna and Western Railroad in New York in succession to John Mar-

WHITE, WILLIAM—*Continued*

cus Davis. He was then forty-four years old—
"one of the youngest executives to move to a
top railroading post" (New York *Herald Tribune*, October 2, 1950).

Originally a short line linking the hard coal
fields of north-eastern Pennsylvania with the
Delaware River, the "Road of Anthracite" (as
the D. L. and W. was nicknamed) later came
to control about a thousand miles of track between Hoboken, New Jersey, and Buffalo, New
York. Formerly the line had been very profitable, but its revenues had declined along with
the demand for hard coal; consequently the
Eastern banking interests responsible for
White's election to the presidency were calling
for an overhauling of both fiscal structure and
operating policy. "He tackled the Lackawanna's
finances with what he calls the 'cut and fit
method,'" stated *Time*, "consolidating its eighteen separate companies into one, and by so
doing trimmed its Federal income-tax liability
by 20 per cent." In slightly more than a decade
White brought the Lackawanna $32 million in
profits and gained for the line "a well-earned
reputation for round and economical operating"
(New York *Herald Tribune*). In the early
spring of 1952, shortly before White left the
Lackawanna, it was estimated that the road's
net income for the year might reach $5 million,
even without a rate increase for which application had been filed. Holding the philosophy
that a railroad's "first job is to serve the public well," White did much to improve suburban
passenger service in New Jersey, and even
moved his home to East Orange, on the Lackawanna line. "This way," he was quoted as
saying, "you get to be a commuter and learn
of their problems at first hand" (New York
World-Telegram).

White left the Lackawanna upon his election
at the end of June 1952 as president of the
New York Central System, one of the two largest railroad consolidations operating east of
the Mississippi River. Now the owner of
11,000 miles of track, this system combined
the old New York Central and Hudson River
Railroad with the Michigan Central, the Lake
Shore and Michigan Southern, the West Shore,
the Cleveland, Cincinnati, Chicago and St. Louis,
and several other lines. When White was
elected to succeed Gustav Metzman, who moved
up to become chairman of the board, the new
president commented: "There are no great men.
Somebody quits, somebody dies, or you happen
to be the right age. . . .So much of it is luck"
(quoted by *Time*.) After a month's vacation
(his first in several years) White assumed his
new duties on August 1, just two days before
a strike was scheduled to begin on the New
York Central lines east of Buffalo by three
railroad brotherhoods—the Brotherhood of Locomotive Firemen and Enginemen, the Brotherhood of Locomotive Engineers, and the Order
of Railroad Conductors. The Brotherhood of
Railroad Trainmen was also seeking concessions, but was absent from the strike threat,
having been placed on a year's probation not to
strike by a Federal court in Cleveland because
of its series of "sick strikes" in 1950.

The three unions agreed to postpone the
walkout to give the National Mediation Board
an opportunity to formulate a settlement.
Through negotiation the claims and grievances
on working rules and conditions which were at
the center of the dispute were reduced from
the 324 that existed in 1950 to 58. During the
course of conferences in Washington, D.C.,
White expressed his view (August 19) that
"collective bargaining is an attempt to maintain peace and not create strife" and that "honest men can have honest differences of opinion." On September 19, 1952, an agreement
was reached by the company and the three
unions.

Since White took over as the New York
Central's head, the last of the coal-burning
locomotives have disappeared from the railroad's commuter lines, which carry 50,000
suburbanites to New York City daily. As
president he has made several important
speeches, among them the one at the Railroad
Day luncheon of the Commerce and Industry
Association in New York City. There, on
September 16, 1952, he criticized "government
over-regulation of the railroads" and listed five
"major recommendations . . . for streamlining
national transportation laws." These included
speeding up the action by the Interstate Commerce Commission on rate adjustments, modernizing "the rule of rate making" in relation
to railroad credit, and taking "passenger train
abandonment precedings out of the realm of
State and local politics." Concluding, as quoted
by the New York *Herald Tribune,* he described the railroads as "a captive industry in
a free economy" and added, "We ask only for
the freedom to be enterprising."

In an address the following month before the
seventh annual convention of the National Defense Transportation Association in New York
City, White reiterated his stand that obsolete
regulatory laws were hampering railroad development. "One of the major difficulties," he
said, "is inability to make needed rate adjustments promptly" (New York *Times,* October
29, 1952). "This was but one of a number of
points cited by Mr. White," stated a New York
Times editorial (October 30, 1952), "to emphasize the theme . . . that while the railroads
are one of the most competitive businesses in
the country they are still treated for the purpose of regulation as if their competitive position had not changed since 1890." On December 4, 1952, White became the first rail executive to speak before a National Association
of Manufacturers session in thirty years. Criticizing manufacturers for actively opposing rate
increases for railroads, he urged the NAM to
fight instead for freedom for the railroads to
get their own prices as a step away from socialism.

White has served as a director of the Manufacturers and Traders Trust Company of Buffalo, the National Biscuit Company, the New
York Telephone Company, the Railway Express Agency, Inc., and the Lehigh and Hudson River Railway Company. He is a trustee
of the East River Savings Bank of New York
City and a director of the First National Bank

of New York City. Elected vice-president of the New York State Chamber of Commerce in 1944, he is also a director of the New Jersey State Chamber of Commerce. In Scranton, Pennsylvania, he has served as director of the First National Bank and of the Moses Taylor Hospital. In railroad organizations he is a director of the Association of American Railroads, chairman of the public relations committee of the Eastern Railroad Presidents Conference, and chairman of the railroad panel of the Transportation Association of America. His most recent appointments were as a director of the American Telephone and Telegraph Company (November 1952) and as a trustee of the Community Service Society, a New York City non-sectarian family welfare organization (December 1952).

William White and Margaret Elizabeth Crane were married on April 16, 1918, and have two daughters, Helen Marie (Mrs. Richard W. Freeman) and Doris Margaret (Mrs. Jerome Chester Cuppia, Jr.). About a year after the death of his first wife, White on September 2, 1948, married Ruth S. Dougherty. The railroad executive is a Republican. His clubs are the Railroad-Machinery and Recess (New York), the Buffalo, the Scranton, and the Chicago. With golf as one of his sports (fishing is another), he is a member of the Montclair (New Jersey) Golf Club. He now makes his home in Scarsdale, New York, from which he commutes on the Central to New York City, in keeping with his policy of living "on line."

References

Bsns W p86 Ja 3 '53
Fortune 46:53 Ag '52 por
Newsweek 40:64 Jl 7 '52 por; 40:69 S 29 '52 por
Railway Age 109:870-71 D 7 '40 por; 133:17-18 Jl 7 '52 por
Time 60:74-5 Jl 7 '52 por
Business Executives of America (1950)
National Cyclopædia of American Biography Current vol G, 1943-46
Who's Who in America, 1952-53
Who's Who in Commerce and Industry (1951)
Who's Who in Railroading, 1946
World Biography (1948)

WHITEHEAD, DON(ALD FORD) Apr. 8, 1908- Journalist

Address: b. c/o The Associated Press, 330 Star Bldg., Washington, D.C.; h. 3900 S. 7th St., Arlington, Va.

The highest honor available to newspapermen, the Pulitzer Prize, has been twice conferred upon Don Whitehead of the Associated Press. The first prize, for international reporting, was awarded in 1951 for his stories written in Korea while he accompanied American troops during the fall of Seoul, the retreat of United Nations forces south of the thirty-eighth parallel, and most of the major battles of 1950. The second, for national reporting, was given in 1953 for

his day-to-day log of President Eisenhower's post-election trip to Korea.

He has seen as much ugly front line combat as most soldiers and probably more than any other correspondent. He made five amphibious assault landings in World War II, reporting the war in Africa, Sicily, Italy, France, Belgium, Holland, and Germany.

Donald Ford Whitehead was born in Inman, Virginia, on April 8, 1908. He is the younger son of Harry Ford Whitehead, from Kent County, England, and the former Elizabeth Bond of Virginia. When the boy was five the family left Inman where the father had been a mine superintendent, and moved to Harlan, Kentucky, where the elder Whitehead opened a furniture store. Don attended public schools in Harlan and for extracurricular activities he played basketball, football and baseball and edited the sports section of the high school paper. His English teacher and the example of his elder brother, Kyle, then a journalism student at the State university, helped to guide him into newspaper work.

After his graduation in 1926, Don enrolled at the University of Kentucky where he studied journalism. He also played football, joined Sigma Alpha Epsilon, worked on the student publication, *The Kentucky Kernel,* and visited the Keeneland race track so faithfully that he was nicknamed "Clocker" Whitehead.

During his junior year he left the university to go to work for his brother who was running the *Weekly Press* in La Follette, Tennessee. The paper could not support both brothers, and Don returned to Harlan and became managing editor of the Harlan *American,* then a weekly newspaper owned by J. M. Alverson. Shortly afterward, Alverson combined the *American* with another weekly and established the daily Harlan *Enterprise* with Whitehead as city editor. As local correspondent for the Associated Press, he wrote the story of the battle of Everts, a bloody episode in the Kentucky coal field labor strike.

Whitehead became the night editor on the Memphis bureau of the Associated Press in 1935. Later, he was appointed correspondent from Knoxville, where his reporting earned him a promotion to the Associated Press feature service in New York in 1941. His flair for that type of writing later lent warmth, color and "human interest" to his coverage of two wars.

From the outbreak of World War II in 1939, Whitehead had wanted to be in it, but his chance was delayed until 1942 when the Associated Press assigned him to India. En route, he stopped off in Cairo where his India trip was cancelled as a consequence of the capture by the Germans of an Associated Press correspondent. He was sent, instead, to cover the British Eighth Army at the outset of Montgomery's drive against Rommel. He reported the experiences of the people freed in Tripoli, gave an eye-witness account of the Rommel attack south of the Mareth line and the drive into Tunisia.

Assigned, then, to the American forces, he covered all the major American campaigns, including five amphibious assault landings. One

DON WHITEHEAD

of Whitehead's outstanding accomplishments was his first story out of liberated Paris, a 1600-word article which he pounded out in forty-five minutes. He landed with Allied forces on the Normandy beaches on D-Day—and this, he says, was his worst experience of the war. "So many were being killed, that I finally lost my fear. I was resigned to being killed." He was one of the nineteen correspondents honored with the Army's Medal of Freedom, in 1945.

After the war, he headed the Associated Press bureau in Hawaii, where for two years his only official contact with the military was during the atomic bomb tests at Bikini. He returned to Washington as a member of the Associated Press Senate staff in 1948. When the Korean War began, Whitehead again volunteered for overseas duty and a month later, in July, 1950, filed the first of the series of reports which won him a Pulitzer Prize. For nearly a year he again slept, ate and traveled with American soldiers, setting up his light portable typewriter (which he carried in a haversack on his back) on the seat of a weapons carrier, a stone, a stump, or wherever he could.

He wrote of his direct observations of the American stand to hold the Naktong line against the power drives of the North Korean Reds; he landed on the Inchon beachhead and reported the crossing of the Han river and the capture of Seoul. After the fall of Seoul, he followed the Army north with the first troops into Pyongyang when Americans and South Koreans seized the capital of North Korea. Joining an armored task force, Whitehead with another reporter discovered the infamous massacre of sixty-eight Americans by Communist guards. His stories on the shortage of adequate winter clothing for the troops in Korea resulted in the "airlifting" of warm apparel.

His next assignment was in 1952, as one of a corps of Associated Press correspondents covering both Presidential candidates in the election campaign. Because of his ensuing acquaintance with President Eisenhower and his knowledge of Korea, he was selected as one of the three news-service men who accompanied the President-elect on his secret flight in December, 1952 to Korea. As soon as censorship was lifted, Whitehead filed a spot news report, followed by a story of 4,400 words which won him his second Pulitzer Prize.

Newspapermen agree that Whitehead, a big, soft-spoken, modest man, deserves the rare distinction of two Pulitzer Prizes in three years.

Whitehead was married on December 20, 1928 to Marie Patterson of Pineville, Kentucky, a fellow-student at the University of Kentucky. They have a daughter, Ruth. At his home in Arlington, Virginia, Whitehead, now a grandfather, cultivates his chief interests—golf, fishing and reading—between assignments. An honorary Doctor of Laws degree was conferred upon him in 1948 by the University of Kentucky. In addition, Whitehead is the recipient of the Sigma Delta Chi award for foreign correspondence, the George Polk award, and the Long Island University of New York citation for Korean War reporting. He is a member of the American Newspaper Guild and the National Press Club.

References

Louisville Courier-Journal p4 My 17 '53 por
N Y Herald Tribune p22 My 8 '51
N Y Times p28 My 8 '51; p24 My 6 '53 por

WHITTON, CHARLOTTE (ELIZABETH) Mar. 8, 1896- Mayor of the City of Ottawa, Canada; social worker; journalist; lecturer

Address: b. City Hall, Transportation Bldg., Ottawa; h. 236-C Rideau Terrace, Ottawa, Ontario, Canada

First woman Mayor of a Canadian city, Charlotte Whitton has been chief magistrate of Ottawa, the nation's capital, since October 1951. Elevated to this post by vote of the Council to complete the term of the late Mayor Goodwin after serving nine months of her first term as controller, Miss Whitton in the civic election of 1952 won for herself a two-year term in the mayoral office. She had previous experience in politics as private secretary to the Minister of Trade and Commerce during 1922-25. Deeply interested in welfare work, Miss Whitton for fifteen years (1926-41) was executive director of the Canadian Welfare Council, and represented her country on the League of Nations Social Questions Section, as well as at international social service conferences. She is a well-known consultant, journalist, and lecturer, and author of several studies of welfare conditions, the most extensive of which, *The Dawn of Ampler Life,* was published in 1943.

Charlotte Elizabeth Whitton was born March 8, 1896, in the Ottawa Valley town of Renfrew,

Ontario, to John Edward and Elizabeth (Langin) Whitton. Her father, a third generation Canadian of Yorkshire descent, was employed by the provincial forestry department; her mother, born in Rochester, New York, was of Irish descent. The four Whitton children (two boys and two girls), of whom Charlotte was the eldest, attended the local public school and the Renfrew Collegiate Institute, and then proceeded to take degrees at Queen's University, Kingston, Ontario. On entering Queen's in 1914, Charlotte held scholarships in English, history, Latin, modern languages, mathematics, and science. When she graduated with the M.A. degree in 1917 she won university medals in English and history. (Her thesis was on the relation of the French and English in Lower Canada.) Devoting the following year to a course given by the faculty of education at the same university, she added to her honors the Governor-General's medal in pedagogy. While an undergraduate Miss Whitton distinguished herself by being the first woman editor of the *Queen's Journal*, university semiweekly newspaper, and the first woman elected to the Alma Mater Society, student governing body. She was president of the Levana Society (women's undergraduate association) and made her name as a debater. In sports also she was outstanding, captaining the women's hockey team and winning letters in field hockey and basketball. Her association with Queen's has been maintained since graduation; she is a past president of the Queen's Alumnae Association and was a member of the university's board of trustees from 1928 to 1940.

On leaving the university, Miss Whitton refused a position with the Public Archives, national repository of Canadian historical materials, to become assistant secretary of the Social Service Council of Canada, then in process of formation in Toronto. This post entailed assistant editorship of the organization's magazine *Social Welfare*. In 1920 she assumed in addition the honorary secretaryship of the newly formed Canadian Council on Child Welfare. Six years later, after a three-year interlude on the Ottawa political scene, Miss Whitton became executive director of the child welfare organization, which in the 1930's became the Canadian Welfare Council. During the fifteen years (1926-41) she served the agency in this capacity, Charlotte Whitton traveled from its headquarters in Ottawa to all parts of the country effecting the work of her organization as a liaison body between voluntary welfare groups and government agencies. An article in *Saturday Night* (September 16, 1944) said of her service in this period: "She put the social welfare work of Canada on the basis of a science." The publication *Canadian Welfare* was founded during Miss Whitton's term of office with the council and was edited by her until her resignation in 1941.

On seven trips to Geneva, Switzerland, Miss Whitton represented Canada as delegate to the Social Questions Section of the League of Nations. In Ottawa she served on the Employment Service Council of Canada (1930-40) and the Advisory Council on Immigration of Women and was special consultant of the

Malak, Ottawa

CHARLOTTE WHITTON

National Employment Commission of Canada during 1936-37.

She served on the executive committee of the Canadian Association of Social Workers, was vice-president of the National Conference on Social Work, United States, and represented the Canadian Welfare Council at the 1940 decennial White House Conference. The department of social service of the University of Toronto and the Montreal School of Social Work called her in as a lecturer. With the coming of World War II the federal government named Miss Whitton a special consultant to the Wartime Prices and Trade Board; to the Dependents' Board of Trustees; and on the organization of the movement of British children to Canada.

In December 1941 Charlotte Whitton resigned from the directorship of the Canadian Welfare Council to work as consultant, publicist, and lecturer, with residence in Ottawa. Among the more than fifty pamphlets which ensued were *Canadian Women in the War Effort* (1942), *Security for Canadians* (1943), *Health Services for the Canadian People* (1944), *Welfare Must Be Planned and Paid For* (1945). Articles by Miss Whitton appeared in numerous magazines including *Maclean's Magazine, Saturday Night, Country Guide*, and in time she became a columnist for the Canadian newspapers Ottawa *Citizen*, Halifax *Herald Chronicle*, and the chain of ten dailies owned by Roy Thomson. As a lecturer she addressed many social work conferences in the United States and Canada, as well as groups such as the English-Speaking Union and the Foreign Relations Council of Chicago. Two confidential reports on welfare were prepared for the Minister of Welfare and the Secretary of the Province of Ontario in 1943-44. Her study of the Province of Alberta welfare system, under the auspices of that province's chapter of the Imperial Order of the

WHITTON, CHARLOTTE—*Continued*
Daughters of the Empire, completed in 1947,
led to recommendations by a Royal Commission for improvements in the child welfare
branch of the provincial Ministry of Health.

A study of certain proposals for social insurance and health insurance then before Parliament was undertaken by Miss Whitton in
1943 at the request of John Bracken, then Progressive Conservative party leader. Upon its
publication, the report was called "a careful,
informed study of the whole social security
problem in Canada" (Blair Fraser, Montreal
Gazette). In it Miss Whitton criticized the
proposals as being too costly and ill-adapted to
Canadian conditions, and advocated, according
to an account in *Canadian Business*, "a flexible
system of public assistance or relief rather than
a standardized system of allowances." The social
worker's attitude to the problems of the welfare
state is further evident in her article "Threat
to Liberty Clearly Seen in Central Welfare
Control" (*Saturday Night*, April 12, 1949).
The welfare worker has also urged women to
greater participation in public life. "Everything in life is a partnership and we women
should take the partnership of home into the
community," she has been quoted as stating
(*Maclean's Magazine*, March 1, 1951). To be
effective in politics, women must learn to participate in it at the local level, she maintained
in "It's Time for the Woman Voter to Learn
the Facts of Political Life" (*Saturday Night*,
April 12, 1947).

Miss Whitton's first experience in politics
came in 1922 when she went to Ottawa as private secretary to the Honorable Thomas A.
Low, Minister of Trade and Commerce in the
first Mackenzie King Cabinet. (Although a
Conservative, she served a Liberal Minister.)
She remained in the position until the defeat
of that government in 1925, when she again
gave her full time to social service work. In
1950, assured of the active support of the Ottawa Council of Women, and sponsored by the
city's two newspapers, she entered the capital's
civic elections as candidate for the Board of
Control. (Ottawa, the country's fifth largest
city, with a population of nearly 300,000, has a
governing body of thirty-three members: Mayor, four controllers, twenty-eight aldermen.)
After a campaign described as "the most lively
Ottawa had ever seen" (*Maclean's Magazine*,
March 1, 1951) and a record turn-out at the
polls (60 per cent of the voters' list), Charlotte Whitton was elected Ottawa's first woman
controller, with 38,405 votes, 10,000 more than
the Mayor polled.

Controller Whitton's majority, with the highest vote recorded to that date in Ottawa civic
elections, entitled her to be considered Deputy
Mayor, a prerogative on which she insisted
when the Council showed hesitation in according it in view of the fact that she was a new
member. She was made responsible for the
social utilities department, newly created to include health and hospitalization, social aspects
of housing, child care, the aged and infirm,
charitable institutions, social aid assistance, delinquency, and community agencies. The new

controller was also named to the Civic Hospital Board, the Ottawa Recreation Commission,
and the Board of Health.

Upon the death of Mayor Grenville Goodwin, Charlotte Whitton in August 1951 became
Acting Mayor of Ottawa, by virtue of her
standing as Deputy Mayor, and in October of
that year was unanimously voted Mayor by the
Council. In December 1952 the electorate returned Miss Whitton to the chief magistracy
for a two-year term by the highest vote ever
recorded in the city. She has the distinction
of being the capital's first woman Mayor and
the country's only woman mayor of a community of over 6,000 population. One of Mayor
Whitton's earliest official statements was the
promise of a drive for low-cost housing. As
one of her first duties in office she received the
former Princess Elizabeth and the Duke of
Edinburgh on their visit to the capital in the
course of their 1951 tour of Canada. She
represented Ottawa at the coronation in June
1953 of Queen Elizabeth II.

She may decide to enter federal politics,
a report supported by a February 1953 statement: "It seems that the only way the city can
get its case properly presented is for the Mayor
of Ottawa to stand for Parliament without retiring as Mayor" (Toronto *Globe and Mail*).
The Mayor had reference to disputes of long
standing between the city and the government's
national capital planning committee as to details of a city plan including a site for a new
city hall. Miss Whitton belongs to the Progressive Conservative party.

Charlotte Whitton in 1934 was created a
Commander of the Order of the British Empire and was awarded the Jubilee Medal in
1935 and the Coronation Medal in 1937. At its
centenary celebrations in 1941 Queen's University bestowed on her the honorary degree of
Doctor of Laws, citing her as its "most distinguished woman graduate." Other honors accorded her by educational institutions are:
D.C.L. degree by King's College, Halifax, in
1939 and by Acadia University, Wolfville, Nova
Scotia, in 1948; LL.D. degree by the University of Rochester, New York, in 1952. A
Canadian Press poll of women's page editors
chose her "Woman of the Year" twice in succession (1951 and 1952). Miss Whitton is a
member of the executive committee of the Imperial Order of the Daughters of the Empire
and of the executive committee of the council
for social service of the Church of England
in Canada, the church to which she belongs.
She is a member of the Canadian Women's
Press Club, the Business and Professional
Women's Club, and the University Women's
Club, of which she is a past president. Among
her other clubs are Chelsea (Ottawa); Ladies'
(Toronto); Forum (London, England).

Described as "stocky," Ottawa's Mayor is
five feet one and one-half inches tall and weighs
135 pounds. She wears her black hair in a
close shingle; her eyes are brown. In dress
she is said to prefer tailored suits. *Newsweek*
states that Miss Whitton is known for her
"good-humored pugnacity," she commands an
"adder-sharp tongue, keen satirical wit, terrifying memory, and tremendous knowledge".

Her recreations are swimming and carpentry at her summer cottage at Perkins Mills, Quebec. Her interest in history finds expression in her collection of books on Queen Elizabeth I of England, whom she is said to consider the first modern woman, and in her book on lumbering in the Ottawa Valley, *Twenty Years A-Fellin'*, published in 1943.

References

American City 66:9 D '51
Maclean's Mag 64:10 Mr 1 '51
Newsweek 38:45 O 15 '51
Ottawa Citizen p1 N 18 '51; N 20 '51; N 21 '51
Sat Night S 16 '44; O 20 '51
Survey 76:47 F '40; 78:20 Ja '42; 87: 488 N '51
Canadian Who's Who, 1936-37; 1949-51
Who's Who (1952)
Who's Who in Canada, 1951-52

WIGNER, EUGENE P(AUL) Nov. 17, 1902- Theoretical physicist; university professor

Address: b. Palmer Physical Laboratory, Princeton University, Princeton, N.J.; h. 8 Ober Rd., Princeton, N.J.

One of the world's outstanding theoretical physicists is Eugene P. Wigner, professor of mathematical physics at Princeton University. A member of the general advisory committee of the Atomic Energy Commission, Wigner has been active in nuclear research since 1930, when he left Germany to make his home in the United States. After the discovery of nuclear fission in 1939 by two German scientists, he endeavored with other physicists to convince the United States Government of the need for an atomic bomb project and beginning in 1942 has taken part in atomic research in Chicago, Oak Ridge (Tennessee), and Hanford (Washington).

Eugene Paul Wigner was born in Budapest, Hungary, on November 17, 1902, the son of Anthony and Elizabeth (Einhorn) Wigner. Reared in Hungary and Germany, he received his early schooling in Muegyetem, Budapest, where he was graduated from the Lutheran high school in 1920, and attended the Technische Hochschule in Berlin to take the degree in chemical engineering in 1924 and the doctor's degree in engineering in 1925. Wigner began his professional career in 1926 as an assistant in the physics department of the Technische Hochschule in Berlin and in the following year became an assistant at Göttingen. He returned in 1928 to the Technische Hochschule as an unsalaried lecturer (*privat-docent*), receiving only student fees for his teaching, and remained there until 1930, when he left Germany to reside in the United States.

At Princeton University Wigner served for a year as a lecturer in physics and then, from 1931 until 1937, as a half-time professor in mathematical physics. On leave of absence from the university in 1931 he was scientific guest of the Kaiser Wilhelm Institute in Berlin. In an article in *Scientific Monthly* (in collaboration with R. W. Ladenbury, May 1933), Wigner pointed out that "the problem of modern physics is no longer the constitution of the whole atom. . . .The most urgent question in physics is now: What is the structure of the nucleus?" He presented a paper at the Tercentenary Conference of Arts and Sciences at Harvard University in September 1936 describing the consequences of the symmetry of the nuclear Hamiltonian on the spectroscopy of nuclei" (*Physical Review*, January 15, 1937).

After a year, 1937-38, as professor of physics at the University of Wisconsin, Wigner returned to Princeton to accept the Thomas D. Jones professorship in mathematical physics at the Palmer Physical Laboratories. That summer (1938) Wigner and several of his colleagues, including foreign-born scientists Fermi, Einstein, and Szilard, began their efforts to convince Government authorities of the need to support research on nuclear fission. When in 1939 two German scientists made new discoveries in this field, Wigner has said, he and his associates "began to see that the new discovery might ultimately become the basis of a horrible military weapon. . . .We realized that, should atomic weapons be developed, no two nations would be able to live in peace with each other unless their military forces were controlled by a common higher authority" (*Saturday Review of Literature*, November 17, 1945).

Following the Japanese attack on Pearl Harbor, the United States Government began to support research on the atomic bomb. Working on the plutonium project in the metallurgical laboratory at the University of Chicago (1942-45), Wigner was present at Stagg Field on December 2, 1942, when the first self-sustaining nuclear chain reaction took place under the direction of Enrico Fermi and, as Wigner said, "the Atomic Age arrived." During his first two years at the University of Chicago, Wigner and his associates completed "the part of the job" for which they "felt responsible," and he devoted a large part of the next year to postwar applications of nuclear power. He and his colleagues, as quoted in the *Saturday Review of Literature*, emphasized that "the atomic weapon must not be used without adequate warning, and must be used only after consultation with, and the consent of, the other members of the United Nations."

Testifying before the United States Senate special atomic energy committee, which was considering legislation for atomic energy control, Wigner on December 7, 1945, expressed his view that attempts to maintain secrecy would be both "unsuccessful" and "harmful" (New York *Times*). He further advised that by withholding information on chain reactions, the United States could delay progress in the laboratories of other countries only about nine months and that attempts to keep details of the atomic bomb a secret would retard nuclear fission research in the United States.

Wigner became director of research and development in 1946 at the Clinton Laboratories in Oak Ridge, Tennessee, which operated under a contract given by the War Department Manhattan Engineer District to Monsanto Chemical Company, of St. Louis, and

EUGENE P. WIGNER

which were the only manufacturers of radio-isotopes for outside research. There he was responsible for directing a staff of about four hundred scientists and technical men. By August he presented the first unit of the radio-isotope, Carbon 14, made available by the Clinton Laboratories for research institutions to the Barnard Free Skin and Cancer Hospital of St. Louis. In September of that year he also gave instruction to graduate scientists employed by industrial research organizations and to heads of science departments of universities.

Wigner directed the first bicentennial conference at Princeton University on the future of nuclear science in September 1946, when approximately a hundred of the world's outstanding nuclear physicists assembled to help shape blueprints of new research and scholarship in the field. In his foreword to a published report on the conference titled *Physical Science and Human Values* (1947), Wigner wrote, "After the war, it soon became apparent that the scientist, *as a scientist,* will have to face social responsibilities and human problems to an increasing degree. . . .Most scientists feel these responsibilities deeply." At the centenary meeting of the American Association for the Advancement of Science, held in September 1948 in Washington, D.C., Wigner stated that atomic energy will be genuinely useful for peaceful pursuits only through the discovery of new needs which it is able to satisfy. He pointed out that the present sources of energy, such as coal and gasoline, and the abundant solar energy available, are sufficient for current needs. (*Science*, November 12, 1948). In "Second Thoughts to the Problem of Nuclear Energy," in *Science* (November 26, 1948), Wigner expanded these ideas on atomic energy; he named as the principal advantage of atomic fuel the fact that it has practically no weight, and as its chief disadvantage the "dangerous and very

penetrating radiations" that accompany burning. Because of the need to neutralize radiations, machinery using nuclear fuel has considerable weight and bulk, he explained, and only when this machinery can be made simple, light, and safe will atomic energy have economic importance.

On May 10, 1950, the New York *World-Telegram and Sun* named Wigner as one of the top atomic scientists "probably working on the hydrogen bomb project." In his report on the International Oxford Conference on Nuclear Physics sponsored in September 1950 by the British Ministry of Supply and organized by the British Atomic Energy Research Establishment, Wigner stated that "all realized that important new physical principles are in the course of being formulated." The physicist, who had been a member of the advisory committee of the National Bureau of Standards from 1947 to 1951, was in 1952 given a post on the general advisory committee of the Atomic Energy Commission. When he was asked in December of that year to express his personal feeling about the atomic bomb, he told a New York *World-Telegram* writer, "It has been a very terrible disappointment to me." He and his colleagues originally believed that in their hands "it would force an effective United Nations—a way to permanent world peace," he explained, but "we haven't yet learned to neutralize it."

Wigner's numerous articles for professional journals relating to nuclear physics have appeared in publications in Germany and in the United States. The physicist contributed a chapter called "Roots of the Atomic Age" to *One World or None* (1946), a collection of essays by scientists, including many who worked on the atomic bomb. He is also the author of a book published in Germany entitled *Gruppentheorie und ihre Anwendungen auf die Quantenmechanik der Atomspektren* (The Group Theory and its Application to the Quantum Mechanics of the Atom Spectrum, 1931), which was favorably reviewed in Germany.

Wigner holds the Medal for Merit from the National Academy of Science (1946) and an honorary doctor of science degree from the University of Wisconsin (1949) and from Washington University (1950). On October 18, 1950, he was awarded the Franklin Medal, the highest medal given by the Franklin Institute in Philadelphia at its traditional Medal Day ceremony, for his "important contributions to the field of modern atomic physics." He is a fellow of the American Physical Society, a member of the National Academy of Sciences, the American Academy of Arts and Sciences, the American Association for the Advancement of Science, the American Mathematical Society, and the American Philosophical Society, and a corresponding member of the Akademie der Wissenschaften, Göttingen, Germany. His fraternity is Sigmi Xi.

Wigner's first wife, Amelia Z. (Frank) Wigner, whom he married on December 23, 1936, is deceased. He married Mary Annette Wheeler, a professor of physics at Vassar College, on June 4, 1941, and they have two children,

David Wheeler and Martha Faith. Weighing 138 pounds, Wigner stands five feet eight inches tall; his eyes are gray and his hair is brown. He became a naturalized United States citizen in 1937.

References

N Y World-Telegram p17 D 1 '52
American Men of Science (1949)
International Who's Who, 1952
Who's Who in America, 1952-53
World Biography (1948)

WILLIAMS, RALPH VAUGHAN *See* Vaughan Williams, R.

WOOD, PEGGY Feb. 9, 1892- Actress; author

Address: Columbia Broadcasting System, 485 Madison Ave., New York 22; h. 158 E. 64th St., New York 21

NOTE: This biography supersedes the article which appeared in *Current Biography* in 1942.

CBS-TV

PEGGY WOOD

To the role of Mama Hanson in the popular television show, *Mama,* actress Peggy Wood brings the experience garnered in more than sixty Broadway plays, in some of which she was associated with such stars as the late John Drew and George Arliss. Since her theatrical debut as a member of the chorus of Victor Herbert's *Naughty Marietta* in 1910, Miss Wood has starred in musical comedies, Shakespearean productions and Noel Coward plays. She has also been a USO entertainer and has acted in motion pictures. In the literary field, she has four books to her credit.

For her television interpretation of Mama, she was given the Royal St. Olav Medal by King Haakon of Norway. She took an active part in the formation of the Actors' Equity Association.

Peggy Wood was born to Eugene and Mary (Gardner) Wood on February 9, 1892 in Brooklyn, New York. Her father was a feature writer for the New York *World* and the author of the humorous books, *Back Home* (1905) and *Folks Back Home* (1908), and *Our Town* (1913). While still a child, her father encouraged her talent for singing and later she studied voice under Arthur Van der Linde and Madame Emma Calvé, the opera singer.

At the age of eighteen, Peggy Wood obtained her first theatrical engagement, as a member of the chorus—at twenty dollars a week—in the first New York production of Victor Herbert's *Naughty Marietta,* which opened on November 7, 1910. Her apprenticeship as a chorus girl was brief, for the following season she was assigned the part of Vera Steinway in *The Three Romeos,* and the season after, appeared as Valerie in *The Lady of the Slipper.*

Miss Wood's engagements in the musical comedies, *Mlle. Modiste, The Madcap Duchess, Adele, Hello Broadway, The Girl of My Dreams,* and *Young America,* all preceded her

second appearance, in 1916, in *Naughty Marietta,* this time as the star. Her engagements in *The Fire Fly* and *Love of Mike* followed, and then she had the leading part in Sigmund Romberg's musical romance, *Maytime.* Opening in August, 1917, the presentation became an outstanding success and Miss Wood's portrayal of Ottilie further endeared her to the public, both in New York and on the road.

After two years with *Maytime,* Peggy Wood was seen in *Buddies, Marjolaine* and *The Clinging Vine,* before appearing in a straight comedy, *The Bride,* which had its première in May, 1924. The run of the show, however, was not long, and in the same year Miss Wood returned to musical comedy, first in *The Three Roses,* and later in a touring engagement of *The Clinging Vine.*

The star was not content, however, to remain in musical comedies, and with her appearance in the title role of George Bernard Shaw's *Candida* in 1925, she was won over to dramatic parts.

From Shaw to Shakespeare was the next step taken by Peggy Wood, when she played the role of Lady Percy in a presentation of *Henry IV,* Part One in 1926. Following this, she became a member of the cast of *Trelawney of the Wells,* starring John Drew. During the tour of the play, which was to prove the last for John Drew, Miss Wood kept a diary. Upon his death, she turned the diary to good account by writing of the actor as she had known him. Under the title, "Splendid Gypsy," it was published in the *Saturday Evening Post* and subsequently appeared in book form.

Experience with another outstanding actor of the old tradition came with Miss Wood's portrayal of Portia to the Shylock of George Arliss in *The Merchant of Venice* in 1928. Following this engagement, the actress continued in dramatic roles, appearing in *A Lady*

WOOD, PEGGY—Continued

in *Love* and *A Play Without a Name*. She was lured back into the musical field by an offer from Noel Coward to play the leading part in the London production of *Bitter Sweet* and, in 1929, made her English debut. This play enjoyed a long run, and Miss Wood subsequently appeared before London audiences in *The Cat and the Fiddle* and *Tonight or Never*.

In 1933 Miss Peggy Wood appeared in three New York theatrical productions, *A Saturday Night, Best Sellers,* and *Champagne Sec,* and the next year in *Birthday*. She played Katherine in *The Taming of the Shrew* in Berkeley, California in 1935, and in 1936 was seen in a musical, *The Countess Maritza*.

After a New York run of *Miss Quis* in 1937 (she had collaborated with the critic, Ward Morehouse, in the writing of the play), she returned to the west coast and played Truth in *Everyman* in the Hollywood Bowl.

The star returned to England to appear in another Noel Coward offering, *Operette,* in 1938. She remained in England the next season, playing Fanny Cavendish in *Theatre Royale,* a play known in the United States as *The Royal Family*. Returning to New York in 1940, Miss Wood was first seen in a Players' Club production of *Love for Love,* and later that year in John van Druten's *Old Acquaintance,* with Jane Cowl.

Blithe Spirit opened in November, 1941, and marked Miss Wood's third appearance in a Noel Coward play. She has expressed a deep appreciation for his artistry, voicing the belief that Coward's stature will be "increasingly recognized." It was in *Blithe Spirit* that Miss Wood entered the ranks of USO entertainers, appearing both in England and France.

Work in films preceded Miss Wood's entrance into the medium of television. July 1, 1949, was the date of the première of *Mama,* the TV show based upon the successful play, *I Remember Mama,* which in turn had been dramatized from the book *Mama's Bank Account,* by Kathryn Forbes. Peggy Wood in the title role is the star of the program which on August 5, 1949, acquired the sponsorship of General Foods Corporation. Seen on CBS television, the show deals with the Hanson family of San Francisco, *circa* 1910. Peggy Wood's characterization has been described as "just as warm, wistful, and amusing as an old snapshot album come to life."

It is a tribute to Miss Wood's skill as an actress that no conflicts arise out of the entirely separate personalities of "Mama Hanson" and Peggy Wood. "I've arrived at the point where none of my roles affect me," she has said, "I just don't let 'Mama' rub off on me." Miss Wood terms the idea that an actress must "be" her part ridiculous. "An actress's own personality is the core of what she plays. If you're absolutely the part, you lose your own identity" (*TV Guide,* October 2, 1953).

She wrote *The Flying Prince* (D. Appleton, 1927) with Eugene Wood, *The Splendid Gypsy: John Drew* (E. P. Dutton, 1928), *The Star Wagon* (Farrar and Rinehart, 1936), *How*

Young You Look: memoirs of a middle-sized actress (Farrar and Rinehart, 1941). Miss Wood has also been a frequent contributor to periodicals.

The actress was married to John Van Alstyn Weaver, poet, novelist and playwright, who died in 1938. They had a son, David. Miss Wood, in 1946, married William H. Walling, chairman of the board of a New York printing firm who was, at the time of their marriage, a lieutenant-colonel in the Army.

Miss Wood is blonde, tall and finds recreation in swimming and outdoor sports, although the theatre is the central interest in her life. She is vice-president of the American National Theatre and Academy (ANTA) and of the Episcopal Actors Guild. For a number of years Miss Wood was a member of the council, Actors' Equity Association and currently serves on the national board of the American Federation of Television and Radio Artists.

References

N Y Herald Tribune VI p22 D '40
T V Guide 1:27 O 2 '53

Who's Who in the Theatre (1952)
Wood, P. How Young You Look (1943)

WU, K(UO-)C(HENG) (wōō gwō chŭng)
Oct. 21, 1903- Former Governor of Formosa; Nationalist Chinese Government official

Address: c/o Taiwan Provincial Government, 1 Chung Cheng Rd. East, Taipei, Taiwan (Formosa)

As Governor of Formosa from December 1949 until April 1953, and as Minister without Portfolio in Chiang Kai-shek's Cabinet, K. C. Wu was largely responsible for stabilizing, reforming, and democratizing this single part of China that remains in the hands of the Kuomintang Government. Prior to his appointments in Formosa, Wu, described as "one of the ablest administrators in China," had impressed foreign observers by his handling of the many problems of a beleaguered and divided city as mayor of Shanghai from 1946 to 1949. The American-educated Chinese statesman had earlier been mayor of Hankow (1932-38) and of Chungking (1939-42).

The son born to Wu Ching-Ming and Chu Chih-Yia on October 21, 1903, in Chien-Shih, Hupeh Province, in the mountains of Central China, was named Kuo-Cheng, "Pillar of a Nation." The elder Wu, a peasant's son from Hupeh Province, had attended the Japanese army cadet school and had risen to director of military training for the Imperial Chinese Army. Kuo-Cheng was therefore reared in the Chinese capital, Peking, where one of his classmates was Chou En-lai, who became Premier and Foreign Minister of China's Communist Government. When Wu was ten years old he entered high school, Nankai College in Tientsin, and at seventeen was graduated from a junior college, Tsing-Hua College of Peking, where an American professor advised him to attend a small American college before attempting university training. Kuo-Cheng subsequently went to the United States and enrolled in Grinnell College in Iowa. Here he received A's in every course except municipal government and was elected to Phi Beta Kappa.

Graduated from Grinnell in 1923 with the B.A. degree, Wu was admitted to Princeton University, at which he took his M.A. degree in government in 1924 and his Ph.D. degree in 1926, submitting for the latter the dissertation *Ancient Chinese Political Theories*. Wu, who had an $80-a-month allowance from his Chinese college, also won the Nova Caesaria Scholarship in 1925 and the $1,200 Procter Fellowship for the following year, and was thus enabled to tour thirty-six States and take summer courses at Colorado and Cornell universities.

On his return to China in 1926, Wu attempted to enlist in the Kuomintang revolutionary forces under Chiang Kai-shek, but was reportedly told that he was too highly educated. After teaching for a while at the National Institute of Political Science, in 1927 he became a secretary of the Kuomintang Ministry of Foreign Affairs (1927-28) and served on its treaty revision committee in 1928, the year that the Kuomintang Government received diplomatic recognition and Chiang became the chief of state. K. C. Wu then was named assistant chief of the first division of the ministry at Nanking. While visiting his native Hupeh Province, Dr. Wu wrote a memorandum to the province's war lord and dictator, Hsia Tou-yin, proposing some tax reforms. Receiving no answer, he wrote again in stronger language and was appointed by the war lord as director of the Hupeh tobacco and wine tax bureau (1928-29). "Shortly," wrote William P. Gray in *Life*, July 21, 1947), "the taxes were rolling into Hupeh's provincial coffers."

Wu's success as a tax collector led to his appointment in 1929 as counselor to the special municipal government of Wuhan—the term for the three neighboring river-port cities of Hankow, Hanyang, and Wuchang, with a total population of about 1,500,000. That year the mayor of Hankow appointed K. C. Wu director of the city's land administration bureau. In 1930 he was transferred to the post of Hankow's finance director and within six months had eliminated the city's debt. During 1931-32 as commissioner of finance for the whole Hupeh Province, Wu suffered a setback when the great flood, which swept forty-six of Hupeh's seventy-one districts, destroyed the sources of tax money. After ten months he had to resign.

Soon afterward, Wu was back in Nanking as personal secretary to Generalissimo Chiang, who in 1932 sent Wu to Hankow as the mayor, a post he retained for the next six years. During the 1936 flood, when the swollen Yangtze threatened the city, Mayor Wu conscripted 30,000 coolies to repair a broken dike. For thirteen days and nights be remained atop the dike, directing operations, while the unwilling laborers were kept in line by machine guns

Wide World Photos

K. C. WU

trained on them (*Time* August 7, 1950). Wu left Hankow in October 1938, nine hours before it fell to the Japanese. During 1939 he was director of the Second Department of the Supreme National Defense Council, which retreated from Nanking to Chungking in western China that November. A short time later Generalissimo Chiang appointed Wu mayor of the beleaguered wartime capital of Chungking, whose population had grown from 200,000 to more than a million. During the months when winter fog prevented bombings, Wu directed thousands of laborers in tunneling air raid shelters out of the underlying rock and also organized disaster squads. When the first 1940 raids came, *Life* related, and Wu found all the firemen hiding in the shelters, he politely requested them to emerge and fight fires; they were so ashamed that from that time on they acted with complete disregard of danger. "Dashing from fire to fire, from crisis to crisis," Mayor Wu "became a sort of glorified La Guardia . . . a hero" (*Time*). In June 1941 when 988 persons were crushed or smothered in a panic-stricken mob, Chiang expressed indignation by stripping Wu of the title of mayor, while giving him additional powers. Wu has explained this as "the Chinese way."

Vice-Minister of Foreign Affairs from 1943 to 1945, Wu was the acting Minister for most of the two years, during which Minister T. V. Soong was in Washington. According to Gray (*Life*), he soon learned not to commit himself and became a chain-smoker to give him more time to frame answers to questions; for a time he was nicknamed "Wordless Wu." In August 1945 Wu was appointed Minister of Information, and in May 1946 Chiang made him the mayor of Shanghai, which then was entirely under Chinese control. The largest city in China, the main seaport, and the

WU, K. C.—Continued

classic refuge of the stateless, Shanghai was considered chaotic in the best of times. The New York *Herald Tribune,* January 10, 1950, commented: "As mayor of . . . a modern Tower of Babel [Wu] managed to keep reasonable peace between Chinese and foreigners, between labor and capital, between Left and Right, and between business and officialdom for a length of time that amazed all observers." *Time* magazine's evaluation of his work was: "Wu has not made Shanghai into a model city, but as its tireless mayor he has quashed the rice black market, raised coolie living standards, and, by a combination of cajoling, arguing and policing, kept labor troubles at a minimum."

One of Wu's first problems in Shanghai concerned some 97,000 corpses which had accumulated in the city morgues and funeral parlors awaiting the day when they could be shipped to their ancestral villages for burial; Wu consequently forbade corpses to remain aboveground more than thirty days. Rioting occurred frequently: once Wu was beaten by a mob of students; another time he harangued 3,000 student rioters for eighteen hours and persuaded them to depart peacefully. It has also been reported that in January 1947 Wu averted a textile strike by inviting the union leaders and their wives to tea, where contact with dignitaries gave them so much "face" that they cut their demands from five months' extra pay to forty days'. Between crises, Mayor Wu balanced the city's $25 million budget without subsidy from the National Government.

As the Communist army advanced toward Shanghai, Generalissimo Chiang ordered the seriously ill mayor to go to Formosa, the semitropical island refuge of the Chinese Nationalist Government, less than 100 miles off the Chinese mainland, with a population of about six million augmented by two million mainland refugees. In December 1949, in what many called "a reshuffle plainly designed to . . . win United States support" (New York *Times,* December 16, 1949), the Generalissimo made Wu Governor of Formosa (Taiwan Province), because, in the words of the New York *Herald Tribune,* (January 10, 1950), "during the postwar years as Mayor of Shanghai, Mr. Wu [had] made an outstanding impression on Americans as a whole." Wu also became a member, without portfolio, of Chiang's National Cabinet.

Among the problems facing Wu in Formosa were lack of funds in the provincial treasury, poor relations between the islanders and the mainlanders, widespread smuggling and corruption, and the necessity of improving economic and political conditions. Wu, Finance Commissioner Jen Hsien-chuen, and national Prime Minister Chen Cheng (who had preceded Wu as Governor) jointly took effective action against inflation by striking fictitious soldiers and officials from the payroll, by stopping generals from using the army payroll for blackmarket commodity speculations, by cooperating to stamp out smuggling, and by discharging unnecessary officials "by the carload" (*Time*). Through the sale of former Japanese houses,

floating liberty loans, introducing taxes aimed primarily at the commercial community and the rich refugees, and through American aid, Wu and his Finance Minister succeeded in meeting the Formosa Provincial Government's budget of $1,750,000 monthly. Wu was responsible in 1950 for the first free elections in the island's history. He also attempted to create better relations between the mainlanders and the Formosans, who for fifty years preceding V-J Day had been ruled by the Japanese. In the hope of giving the Formosans "a feeling of being part of the Nationalist Government" (New York *Herald Tribune,* January 27, 1950), Wu appointed large numbers of the islanders to government posts and seventeen of them to his twenty-three man executive committee.

Campaigning for the adoption of Anglo-Saxon justice—"rule by law, limitations on the power of police, and review of cases . . . with due attention paid to the rules of evidence"— in August 1950 Wu announced: "I have started a series of speaking engagements hammering home the fact that real democracy cannot be built save on a foundation of respect for the dignity of the individual." That same month he revealed that the Chinese Nationalist Government would adopt the English trial system under which a person is presumed innocent until proved guilty and would also ban arrests without warrants. He continued the land reforms that Chen Cheng had begun in April 1949, arranging in June 1951 for the sale to tenants of large tracts of Government-owned land on easy credit terms. In August 1952 Wu obtained approval at a Provincial Government conference of a land reform act which the New York *Times* (November 23, 1952) termed "one of the most sweeping 'land reform' programs in Asia." Signed by President Chiang in January 1953 as the Land to the Tiller Act, the plan provides for the compulsory sale by landlords of more than half a million acres to about 240,000 tenant farmer families—more than one third of Formosa's farm population. The Nationalist Government would compensate the landlords and then be paid back by the tenants on easy credit terms. In the spring of 1952 a New York *Times* editorial (May 31, 1952) commented: "The Provincial Government . . . under the brilliant leadership of K. C. Wu, has shown itself to be progressive, socialminded, and receptive to honest help. It is co-operative in the best sense."

On April 10, 1953, the Nationalist Cabinet accepted the resignation of Dr. Wu as Governor of Formosa. It was announced by the Premier that President Chiang Kai-shek had accepted the resignation with reluctance, and that Dr. Wu's offer to resign had been turned down three times during his term as Governor. Retaining his Cabinet rank as Minister without Portfolio, Dr. Wu planned to visit the United States to undergo treatment for asthma.

Of his three-year term as Governor, the New York *Times* remarked editorially on April 13, 1953 that "he has helped to spark the movement toward genuinely popular democratic government and the enlistment of whole-hearted Taiwanese support for it. He has played an important role in the carrying out of the major land reform that is now in its final stage. . . .It is unthinkable that free China should lose the services of such a gifted and devoted patriot."

On April 15, 1931, Wu married Edith T. K. Huang (Huang Cho-Chun), semiprofessional painter, whose father was one of China's few big industrialists. Conversion to his wife's Anglican faith preceded the marriage. Wu writes the interpretive captions for Mrs. Wu's watercolors of classical Chinese subjects. He has often enjoyed games of croquet with her, their daughters, Shiu-Yung and Shiu-Hwei, and their sons, Shiu-Kwang and Shiu-Huang.

References

Life 23:80 Jl 21 '47 pors
Time 48:35 D 2 '46 por; 56:21 Ag 7 '50 por
International Who's Who, 1952
China Handbook (1950)
World Biography (1948)

YANG, YOU CHAN Feb. 3, 1897- Korean Ambassador to the United States; physician
Address: b. c/o Korean Embassy, 2322 Massachusetts Ave., N.W., Washington 8, D.C.; h. 2320 Massachusetts Ave., N.W., Washington 8, D.C.

Dr. You Chan Yang, who was named Ambassador from the Republic of Korea to the United States in March 1951 to succeed John M. Chang, took up his official duties in Washington the following June, about a year after the outbreak of the Korean war. Before entering the field of diplomacy, Yang, who was trained in American medical schools and hospitals, had practised as a physician and surgeon in Honolulu for nearly three decades. For many years he combined his professional interests with activity in the Korean independence movement and was a leader of Korean patriotic and religious groups in Hawaii.

Born in Pusan, Korea, on February 3, 1897, You Chan Yang is the son of Dai Bong and Mary (Kim) Yang. The Yang family having moved to Hawaii in 1903, young You Chan received his early training in Honolulu, where he attended the Kaahumanu School until 1912 and was graduated from McKinley High School four years later. While in high school and later in college, he played shortstop on school baseball teams and was also a short-distance runner (100, 200, and 400 yards). He studied at the University of Hawaii in 1916-17; then, having won a scholarship, he entered Boston University's College of Liberal Arts, which conferred the Bachelor of Science degree on him in 1920. The following year he took his Bachelor of Surgery degree and in 1922 his M.D., both from the Boston University Medical School. In 1923 in Honolulu he opened a private practice, which he maintained until his appointment as Korean Ambassador to the United States in 1951. Meanwhile, in 1929 and 1930 he undertook further training in surgery, gynecology, and obstetrics at the New York Post Graduate Hospital, the New York

Lying-in-Hospital, and the Harvard Medical School.

While active from 1918 to 1922 in the organization of the League of Friends of Korea in the United States, Yang was also prominent in the movement to liberate Korea from Japanese domination. Following the departure of Dr. Syngman Rhee, then President of the Provisional Korean Republic, from Hawaii in 1939, Yang became leader of the Korean community in the island. During World War II he was director of a medical unit under the Office of Civilian Defense. In March 1951, when John M. Chang, then Korean Ambassador to the United States, became Premier of the Republic of Korea, President Rhee named Yang to succeed Chang in the Washington post. Upon presenting his credentials at the White House on June 6, 1951, the Ambassador told President Harry S. Truman that both the people and government of Korea were indebted to the United States. "It was your inspired leadership," he added, "which summoned the United Nations to assist the Republic of Korea in repelling the lawless Communist invader and brought the free world to a consciousness of the danger confronting it" (quoted by the New York *Times*).

Soon after Yang had assumed his diplomatic duties in Washington, the Soviet delegate to the United Nations, Jacob A. Malik, proposed in late June in a radio address in New York that negotiations be started for cease-fire in Korea. Yang relayed a message from President Rhee in which complete reunification of the Korean peninsula was stressed as the basic Korean requirement for ending the war which had been in progress between the United Nations forces and forces of the Korean and Chinese Communists. The Ambassador added in his own behalf that he distrusted the sincerity of the Russians in suggesting cease-fire negotiations and expressed the hope that they were not "merely looking for a breathing spell for the Communists to rearm and regroup so they can wage the bloody war again." The following month Yang submitted to Dean Rusk, Assistant Secretary of State for Far Eastern Affairs, a request for assistance from the United States in rebuilding South Korea's schools and training Korean technicians to help in restoring the war-devastated country. In September 1951 Yang was one of three South Korean representatives attending (without power to sign the treaty) the Japanese peace treaty conference held in San Francisco. The next month he headed a special Korean mission to Tokyo which sought to reach an agreement with post-treaty Japan on the disposition of 800,000 Koreans who faced possible deportation from Japan to Korea. Many of these Koreans, Yang explained in a press interview, "were brought from Korea at the point of a gun as contract or slave workers between 1937 and 1945 when Japan was building up military potential." In an address prepared for delivery before a meeting of the National Conference of Christians and Jews, the Canadian Council of Christians and Jews, and World Brotherhood, Yang said in November 1951 that Koreans had paid "the heaviest price in suffering, devasta-

YOU CHAN YANG

tion, and death that has ever been exacted from any people in history."

On his return from a trip to Korea and to Japan, where he had headed a delegation to arrange a treaty of "peace, amity and commerce" with the Japanese Government, Yang charged that the 7,000,000 Koreans who remained in North Korea were facing "deliberate and . planned mass starvation" by the Communists, who had, he said, "cold-bloodedly determined to wipe out the Korean population" (quoted by the New York *Times*). On another trip to Japan in April 1952, Yang took part in negotiations for a Japanese-Korean peace treaty which went into effect at the end of April. Early in January 1952 Yang had reported after a call at the White House that President Truman had assured him that the United States would continue in its support of Korea, although the President had declined "to promise anything at this moment" concerning Korea's request for a mutual security agreement similar to those the United States holds with Australia, New Zealand, the Philippines, and Japan.

In February 1952 Yang wrote an address for delivery before the University of Rochester's Institute of International Affairs. In it he surveyed the achievements of the Korean Republic in the two years prior to the Communist invasion, citing in particular the adoption of the secret ballot, the extension of the franchise, the granting of legal equality to women, the expansion of educational opportunities, and the development of a program of land reform. In conclusion he declared: "The future of Korea is the future of the democratic way of life. . . .If free men everywhere sense the fact that what is happening now to us is positively vital to their own welfare and security, then we do have a future within the invincible walls of an indomitable democratic alliance."

Among other speeches made during 1952 in which the Korean Ambassador sought to make clear the problems and point of view of his country was his address before a convention of the Korean Student Association in New York in June. He urged the Koreans in his audience to return home at once upon completion of their studies so that the term "student" would not become a "shield" behind which an individual may hide from military and economic problems. At Colgate University's fourth annual Conference on American Foreign Policy in July he defended Syngman Rhee's insistence upon a popular election rather than one by the National Assembly. Speaking in September before a meeting in St. Louis of the National Federation of Republican Women's Clubs, he reiterated an appeal made earlier in a letter to the New York *Times* that greater attention be given by the United States to training and equipping the South Korean soldier. He also proposed an all-Pacific conference "to which all anti-Communistic nations would be invited to join hands in a collective security pact against the common enemy."

The Korean Ambassador is a trustee and board member of the Korean Christian Institute, a trustee of the Korean Christian Student Movement of Hawaii, a member of the advisory board of Dong Ji Hoi, a trustee and executive member of Kokokahi, honoray national chairman of American Relief for Korea, and vice-president of the Pan-Pacific Union. He is a past president and member of the executive council of the Korean University Club and holds memberships in the alumni clubs of McKinley High School, Boston University, and the University of Hawaii. Yang belongs to the Lions Club and the Young Men's Christian Association and also to a number of professional associations: the American Medical Association, Territorial and Honolulu medical societies, the Academy of General Practitioners, the Surgical Society, the Gynecological and Obstetrical Society, and the Honolulu Academy of Sciences. On June 21, 1924, Yang married Rita J. Waldron, now deceased. A daughter born of this marriage is Marguerite Joy (Mrs. Warren Beers). His present wife is the former Pauline Tai, whom he married on February 5, 1938; the Yangs have two children—Sheila and Channing. The brown-eyed, black-haired diplomat is five feet three inches tall and weighs 134 pounds. His church is the Methodist Episcopal.

References

Pan Pacific Who's Who, 1941
Who's Who in America, 1952-53

YEH, GEORGE K(UNG-)C(HAO) (yä jou kŏōng) Sept. 12, 1904- Minister of Foreign Affairs of Nationalist China
Address: b. c/o Ministry of Foreign Affairs, Taipei, Taiwan (Formosa)

The Minister of Foreign Affairs of the Chinese Nationalist Government (in exile on the island of Formosa), George K. C. Yeh, is also chairman of that government's delegation to the U.N. General Assembly. During most of

World War II Yeh directed the Chinese Ministry of Information in London, England, in 1946 entered the Ministry of Foreign Affairs in Chiang Kai-shek's Government in China, and three years later was named Foreign Minister. His major concern since has been to maintain recognition by other nations and by the U.N. of the Nationalist Government as the legitimate ruler of China, as opposed to the Chinese Communist People's Republic which, in fact, holds power on the mainland.

George Kung-Chao Yeh, the son of Yeh Tao-sen and Chao Hua-ting was born in Canton, the capital city of the southern province of Kwangtung in China, on September 12, 1904. Following preparatory training in China, he went to the United States to enter Amherst College in Massachusetts, where he received his B.A. degree in 1922. He continued his study of English literature, in which he had majored as an undergraduate, at Cambridge University in England, which granted him the M.A. degree in 1926.

On his return to China George Yeh entered on a fourteen-year teaching career as professor of English at National Peking University (1926-27). He afterward held the same rank at the National Chinan University (1927-29), Tsing Hua University (1929-35), and again at National Peiping University (1935-39), where he headed the English department. When Peiping fell to Japanese invaders with the outbreak of war in 1937, universities and colleges moved southward, out of Japanese occupied areas, and National Peiping University became part of the National Southwestern Associated University. While Yeh was teaching in the south, his translation of a short story by the Chinese poet Pien Chin Lin appeared in *Life and Letters Today* (October 1939), a British literary periodical, with a comment by the editors that both the poet and Yeh had been introduced to the magazine by William Empson, the noted English critic. Yeh is also the author of a study entitled *Social Forces in English Literature*.

Turning from teaching and literature to political work, Yeh in 1941 took the post of Director of the Malaya Office of the Chinese Ministry of Information. The following year, with Great Britain and the United States both in the war against Japan, he traveled to London as director of the United Kingdom office of the Chinese Ministry of Information and counsellor to the Chinese Embassy. In a talk on India and China before the East India Association in London in 1942, Yeh said that the early philosophies of India and China guided their actions in resistance to aggression in the modern world, and stressed the relative parts played by Buddhism, Taoism, and Confucianism in Chinese culture. Another lecture on religion, "The Confucian Conception of Jên," was published in pamphlet form in London in 1943. Earlier, in a foreword to a series of articles, "China Today and Tomorrow," that appeared in the periodical *Great Britain and the East* (September 1942), Yeh had urged realism in the study of China, opposing both indiscriminate eulogy of her heroism and importance, and emphasis on her remoteness and pictur-

Wide World Photos

GEORGE K. C. YEH

esqueness. "There is no doubt," he wrote, "that [China's] problems are tremendous and that she stands today at the cross-roads between a degenerate farm economy and the necessity of large scale industrialization."

By the time Yeh returned to China in 1946 as director of the European affairs department in the Ministry of Foreign Affairs, the eight-year war between China and Japan had ended, but at the end of the year civil war flared between the Kuomintang and Chinese Communists forces. As Administrative Vice-Minister for Foreign Affairs, Yeh traveled to Burma in the rank of Ambassador Extraordinary on a special mission to claim for China certain areas of North Burma which he held to be within Chinese territorial borders. Meanwhile the Nationalist Chinese had adopted a constitution and in April 1948 elected Chiang Kai-shek, leader of the Kuomintang party, first President of the Republic of China. In 1949 Yeh was named Political Vice-Minister for Foreign Affairs in Chiang's Government and in September of the same year was advanced to Minister for Foreign Affairs in Taiwan, Formosa, 110 miles off the Chinese mainland. The Chinese Communist armies had meanwhile swept southward and by December 1949 the Chinese Nationalist Government was forced to flee to the island of Formosa.

When in February 1950 the Chinese Communists signed a thirty-year pact with the Soviet Union, Foreign Minister Yeh described the agreement as an aggressive military alliance directed against the United States. The following month the Nationalist Government on Formosa was reorganized under Premier Chen Cheng, and Yeh was again named Minister for Foreign Affairs in a cabinet made up of men who have been described as "comparatively liberal and young Kuomintang leaders." In July 1950 Yeh described the plan offered by India's

YEH, GEORGE K. C.—*Continued*

Prime Minister Nehru for ending the Korean war as an "appeasement" because it suggested the seating of Communist China in the United Nations as one of the first steps toward achieving peace. His comment in January 1951 on the rejection of the United Nations cease-fire plan was that perhaps the rejection would bring [the U.N.'s] understanding of China's Communists a step closer to that of ours"; he stated that "the Communist International calls for world revolution and world conquest and not for the promotion of world peace."

As the result of lack of agreement between the United States and Great Britain as to which Chinese government to invite to the September 1951 San Francisco conference for the signing of the Japanese peace treaty, China was excluded from the meeting. Yeh resigned after criticizing Nationalist China's exclusion, but his resignation was rejected by Premier Chen Cheng. In an interview the following September Yeh said his government was "willing to sign a bilateral treaty with Japan," on condition of the recognition by Japan of the Nationalists as the only legitimate government of China. Yeh later warned that China would veto Japan's admission into the U.N. if the Japanese concluded a peace treaty with the Chinese Communist regime. With Yeh as chairman, in February 1952 a Chinese Nationalists delegation met with Japanese representatives in Formosa for treaty negotiations, which were successfully concluded in April 1952 when Yeh signed the treaty for the Chinese Government. The terms of the treaty were restricted to territories "which are now, or which may hereafter be, under the control" of the Chinese Nationalists. Regarding a proposed Pacific alliance in June 1952, Yeh stated that Nationalist China would join such an alliance only on condition that the nations involved first outlaw the Communist party in their countries. At a session of the Chinese Legislative Yuan to discuss ratification of the treaty with Japan Yeh stressed that Nationalist China would consider the treaty invalid if Japan recognized Communist China. When Chinese Communist leader Chou En-lai went to Moscow in August 1952, Yeh warned that the Chinese Communist mission might be seeking military supplies as well as economic backing from the Soviet Union in preparation for possible new aggression in the Far East.

In opposition to the Communist nations, the U.N. General Assembly voted on October 25, 1952, to seat the Nationalist Chinese delegation at its seventh regular session. As chairman of the Nationalist group, Yeh told the Assembly that to admit the Chinese Communists to the U.N. would be "asking us to recognize and accept the fruits of aggression . . . to help in the creation of a Communist world empire." He described the Chinese Communist Government as a "Soviet puppet," which was "the result of many years of Soviet conspiracy and intrigue." In the November debate of the Assembly's Political Committee on the Korean question Yeh warned that the Communists would use an armistice in Korea to "strengthen

their military position," so that in the long run an armistice would be "an obstacle to peace." When India proposed a plan to send Korean war prisoners to a neutral island, Yeh criticized it as "only a delay in forced repatriation" by the Communists. In debate in the General Assembly (November 13, 1952) he held that the history of the truce talks had made it "crystal clear" that the Communists did not want peace in Korea and asked the Assembly to condemn Communism as a threat to world peace, calling it "a new form of colonialism which may perhaps be more accurately described as 'satellitism.'" Appearing on the television program *Meet the Press* in December, Yeh said he believed the United Nations would be better off without the membership of the Soviet Union. Because of pressing duties in Formosa, it was announced in February 1953, Yeh was unable to attend the second half of the seventh General Assembly session opening in late February.

On July 27, 1953, Yeh warned that the Communists might use the truce in Korea to seek "political compensations" from the United Nations or take advantage of it to follow aggressive designs elsewhere.

The Chinese Foreign Minister has been decorated with the Grand Cordon of the Order of the Brilliant Star and is a member of the Royal Asiatic Society of the United Kingdom. He is coauthor with Charles P. Fitzgerald of *Introducing China*, published in England in a school edition in 1948. In 1930 he married Edna Yün-hsi Yuan; their children are Max Wei Yeh and Marian T'ung Yeh.

References

Washington (D.C.) Post p19 N 15 '52
China Handbook, 1950
International Who's Who, 1952
Who's Who in the United Nations (1951)

YOUNG, ALAN Nov. 19, 1919- Comedian; actor.

Address: b. c/o Columbia Broadcasting System, 485 Madison Ave., New York 22; h. North Hollywood, Calif.

Making his debut on an American radio network in 1944, Alan Young won immediate recognition when he appeared as a summer replacement for Eddie Cantor on his National Broadcasting Company program. This appearance launched the young comedian on a career in radio, motion pictures and television.

From April 1950 until June 1953 he appeared in his own television show, the Columbia Broadcasting System's *Time to Smile*, in which he portrayed the character of a young man overwhelmed by the complexities of modern life. The versatile actor's most recent role in pictures was as Androcles in Paramount's *Androcles and the Lion* which had its première in January, 1953.

Alan Young was born in North Shields, Northumberland, England, on November 19, 1919, of Scotch parents who christened him Angus. The family moved four years later to Vancouver, Canada. When Angus's older sister Harriet changed her mind about doing a serious monologue at the Caledonian Society, she asked her thirteen-year-old brother to go on in her place. He made his first stage appearance without hesitation, and gave a parody of the monologue which greatly amused the audience. Following this experience, Alan and Harriet Young teamed up to do radio and vaudeville stints.

By the time he graduated from Vancouver High School he had his own radio program, *Stag Party*, over the Canadian Broadcasting Corporation network. Young wrote his own show, served as announcer, assistant news editor, and when necessary as stenographer. All this netted him the salary of $15 a week, and when he asked for a raise he was fired. Again he teamed up with his sister, the youthful pair going on the road in a variety act in which Angus (who had by this time changed his name to Alan) played the bagpipes, drums and saxaphone, and developed his own brand of wry humor. When his sister's marriage terminated their vaudeville tour, Young returned to radio at a salary of $150 a week as star of a situation type of comedy show originating from station CBL in Toronto.

One September night in 1942 Frank Cooper, an agent in New York, accidentally tuned in CBL, Canada, via short-wave, instead of the *Duffy's Tavern* program he was trying to dial. He heard Alan Young, liked his work, and immediately after the broadcast telephoned him and asked for some transcriptions of some of his best shows. Upon receipt of these, Cooper, convinced that here was a new talent, sent the comedian a contract and a bid to come to New York. The contract was signed, but by the end of 1942 Young was in the Canadian Navy as a sub-lieutenant.

It was not until 1944, after a medical discharge, that he arrived in New York to appear on a nation-wide program. He won approval from both critics and the radio audience which led to his stardom in his own *Alan Young Show*, which made its premiere over the American Broadcasting Company network on October 3, 1944.

Young was chosen by radio editors in January 1945 in a poll by the trade paper *Radio-Daily* as the "male star of tomorrow," and won a similar poll conducted by *Motion Picture Daily*. Simultaneously, he was rated by Crossley as the "top funnyman" of the Blue Network.

That same year motion picture companies were also bidding for the services of the comedian who signed a two-year contract with Twentieth Century-Fox for $35,000 a picture. Moving with his show to the West Coast, Young, within the span of two years, went before the cameras in three pictures in which he played feature roles: *Margie, Chicken Every Sunday,* and *Mr. Belvedere Goes To College.*

Critics' reviews of *Margie*, first shown in March 1946 and starring Jeanne Crain, were for the most part tepid, and Young, cast as a shy high-school lad, won no laurels. After a summer hiatus in 1946, Young returned to the radio in a new show over NBC, but this ended on January 6, 1947 because of lack of good material, according to the critics. Twentieth-Century Fox also lost interest in their comedian who only two years before had been at a high

ALAN YOUNG

peak of success, and failed to renew his contract. Upon recovery from an automobile accident, Young received a bid to co-star with Jimmy Durante on a radio show beginning in October, 1948. Interest in Young's comedy talent was revived and he was again placed in a show of his own which had its first broadcast on NBC from Hollywood January 11, 1949. In its review of the première of *The Alan Young Show,* in which Young portrayed an actor frantically trying to avoid his prospective father-in-law's attempts to push him into the plumbing business, *Variety* reported, "Young himself has distinctive, individual qualities as a comic. He can even vest the role with a warmth and create audience sympathy. . . . But just as he's been bogged down in the past by some lack-lustre material, so too, on . . . his new show, the spark was missing." This opinion was echoed by other reviewers, nor did reviews of the motion pictures *Mr. Belvedere Goes To College* and *Chicken Every Sunday* released that same year, enhance Young's box-office appeal.

While his radio show was nearing its end, Young began work on his own format for a television show, and after months of preparation a half-hour audition script written by David Schwartz, Leo Solomon, and Young was presented to officials at CBS-TV. Alan Young's television show made its debut in April 1950 over CBS and was hailed as an immediate hit. It was the consensus of opinion that his skill in pantomime proved especially suitable to the visual medium.

In one of the sketches of his initial show he portrayed a bewildered passenger taking his first plane trip and unwittingly, in wide-eyed, bungling, and disarming style, harrassing the seasoned traveller who sat beside him. The show maintained its successful pace set in the première, and in 1951 Young was cited by the Academy of Television Arts and Sciences as the best television actor of that year and he re-

YOUNG, ALAN—*Continued*

ceived the Academy's gold-plated statuette, the equivalent of the motion picture industry's Academy-award Oscar. Young's show was also named as the best television variety show of 1950.

Motion pictures once more beckoned to Young. Gabriel Pascal, a producer at RKO studios, signed Young as Androcles in his production of G. B. Shaw's *Androcles and the Lion*. He was also placed under contract by Paramount for two pictures, *Aaron Slick from Punkin Creek* and *The New Sad Sack*.

Early in 1953, the *Alan Young Show* on television underwent changes in format from a variety program to situation comedy and taking the title *Time To Smile*. In this comedy Young plays the hapless, boyish hero who stumbles into a bewildering maze of situations. As described by Harriet Van Horne, "Alan roams through a world bristling with hostility. High moments of the show are the wild, complex bits of business that are the comedian's trade mark" (*N.Y. World-Telegram*, Feb. 16, 1953).

In June 1953 spokesmen for the comedian announced that he would not return to his television program on CBS in the fall but instead would resume his work in pictures in his own Alan Young Productions with Alan Dinehart serving as supervising film director.

In real life Young is described as quiet and modest-mannered. He is 5 ft. 11 inches tall, weighs about 150 pounds, and has blond hair and hazel eyes. He collaborates with his writers on the weekly television script and is considered easy to work with. Young sometimes relates something that happened to him which usually becomes the inspiration for a sparkling show.

In 1948 Young married Virginia McGurdy who had been vocalist with the singing group "Four Chicks and a Chuck." They have a son, Cameron Angus, and a daughter, Wendy. By a former marriage in 1940 to Mary Anne Grimes (which ended in divorce seven years later) Young has a daughter Alana and a son, Alan, Jr. Young's hobbies include furniture-making, sketching and tennis. Proud of his Scottish ancestry, he is entitled to wear the Cameron tartan. He is a descendant of William Wallace of "Scots wha' ha' wi' Wallace bled." The comedian has taken out United States citizenship papers.

References

Am W p13 Ja 3 '51
Christian Sci Mon p9 Jl 29 '52
Collier's 128:26+ O 6 '51
Look 9:49 F 20 '45
N Y Herald Tribune p14 Ja 25 '51
N Y Times II p1 O 15 '50
N Y World-Telegram p12 Jl 3 '44; p25 O 20 '44; p16 N 6 '45; p6 F 17 '51; p20 O 15 '52; p25 F 16 '53
N Y World-Telegram Mag p15 F 14 '53
Newsweek 24:92 N 6 '44; 35:54 Ap 17 '50
Sat Night 67:8+ Ja 26 '52
Motion Picture and Television Almanac, 1952-1953
Treadwell, B. 50 Years of American Comedy (1951)

ZÁPOTOCKY, ANTONÍN (zä'pō-tȧ-tskē')
Dec. 19, 1884- President of Czechoslovakia
Address: h. Srobárovà 137, Prague 12, Czechoslovakia

Twice during the year 1953 Antonín Zápotocký, former Premier of Czechoslovakia, has made headlines: when he succeeded Klement Gottwald to the presidency of Czechoslovakia on March 21, and when he announced on May 15 that his Government had released Associated Press correspondent, William Oatis.

On September 15, 1953 it was announced that a twelve-man governing Presidium of Ministers headed by President Antonín Zápotocký was dissolved, and was replaced by a group of six men, including Zápotocký. The reorganization "along the latest Soviet lines" was said to mean tightening of controls over the police and agriculture. The Prague radio announced the shake-up.

An "orthodox Communist", Zápotocký began his political career as a member of the Social Democratic party, the precursor of the Czechoslovakian Communist party. Although he is regarded as a "relatively reasonable figure among a group of ambitious Communist leaders" by some Western observers, the Czech people "remembering the pressures to which they were subjected under Zápotocký's trade union leadership, did not hail his promotion to the presidency with enthusiasm" (New York *Herald Tribune*, March 22, 1953).

Antonín Zápotocký was born December 19, 1884 in Zákolany, Czechoslovakia, the son of Ladislav and Barbora Zápotocký. His father was a tailor and one of the founders of the Czech Socialist Party. He was educated in the public schools and began his career as a stone mason. His first political job came in 1902 when he served as the head of the Imperial Propaganda Commission of the Social Democratic Youth in Prague.

Joining the trade union movement, he became in 1907 the political secretary of the All-Trade Union of Kladno (a mining town) and in 1911 a member of the Kladno town council. During this period he spent some time in prison for his political activities. During World War I he served as a private in the Austro-Hungarian army, and after being discharged, was chosen the secretary of the Social Democratic movement in Kladno. He was sentenced to two years imprisonment for instigating the general strike of Kladno miners and smelters in 1920. One of the founders of the Czechoslovakian Communist Party, he became its secretary general in 1923 and was elected a member of Parliament two years later. In 1929 he was named the secretary general of the Revolutionary Trade Union Organization of Czechoslovakia.

During the World War II occupation of Czechoslovakia by the Germans, Zápotocký was imprisoned in the Sachsenhausen concentration camp for six years. When peace came in 1945 he was elected chairman of the United Revolutionary Trade Movement of Czechoslovakia and served as a deputy to the Provisional National Assembly. A deputy to the Constituent National Assembly in the following year, he was chosen its chairman. In February 1948, the

Communists seized political control of Czechoslovakia and Zápotocký, who had organized factory "action committees" to support the *coup d'état*, was made a Deputy Prime Minister. On June 14, 1948, he became Premier after Klement Gottwald left this office to assume the presidency upon the resignation of Eduard Benež.

In his first speech to the Czechoslovakian Parliament after becoming Premier, Zápotocký promised that a program would be instituted to eliminate all traces of capitalism and, simultaneously, would protect private enterprise with regard to small businesses and small farms. He asserted that the economic system would be aligned with that of the Soviet Union. In August, the Premier announced that labor discipline courts similar to those in Russia would be introduced to adjudge the cases of workers who did not fulfill production goals.

Three months before Czechoslovakia's two-year plan was to be completed, he claimed that its goal, an increase of ten per cent above the production of 1948, had been realized. Despite this statement, the economic situation was grave, due largely to pre-war dependence upon trade with western nations, and in December Zápotocký headed a delegation to Moscow to discuss his country's problems. The result of the ensuing conferences was a new trade agreement by which Russia granted a loan to Czechoslovakia.

On the anniversary of the Communist revolt in Czechoslovakia Zápotocký said, "Give the workers in the capitalist democracies the weapons and in that very moment, there will be no capitalist democracies." (New York *Times,* February 27, 1949). In June of that year the Premier in a radio address criticized the Catholic hierarchy of Czechoslovakia.

This criticism, the most definite in the church-state controversy, was aimed particularly at Archbishop Josef Beran, whom it accused of spreading untruths about the Government. The following month Zápotocký stated that Czechoslovakia owed allegiance to Joseph Stalin rather than to the Vatican. A rigid set of laws to control the church was passed, and in December 1949 the Catholic Bishops reported receiving a letter from the Premier rejecting their request for modification of the laws which sounded, according to the Bishops, as if it were addressed to "criminals".

Zápotocký in September 1949 declared at the opening of the fiftieth Prague autumn fair that despite differences in political ideologies Czechoslovakia wished to trade with the other nations of the world. Speaking at a workers' meeting in October the Premier disclosed the fate of political prisoners recently arrested; they had been sent to labor camps for re-education to adapt them to life in a Communist country. He also announced the organization of a corps of informers to report on those inimical to the government or indulging in a luxurious life.

He resigned as director of the United Revolutionary Trade Movement on June 30, 1950. In September of 1951, the government and the Communist Party were reorganized. The Political Secretariat and the Praesidium became

Wide World Photos

ANTONÍN ZÁPOTOCKÝ

the preponderant bodies, respectively, and Zápotocký was appointed a member to each.

The deposition of Rudolf Slansky, formerly general secretary of the Czechoslovak Communist Party, brought from Zápotocký the first official intimation of anti-Semitism in Soviet satellites. In speaking of Slansky, who was Jewish, the Premier declared, "we shall not tolerate any foreign influence in our affairs, whether from Washington or London, Rome or Jerusalem." (New York *Times,* December 20, 1951).

Zápotocký has served as the chairman of the Central Council of Trade Unions, the Permanent Committee of Parliament, the Central Committee of National Competition, the Commission for Raising of the Living Standard, and the Society for Economic Reconstruction. He founded the Association of Stone Sculptors (1902) and is the author of two autobiographical novels, which have been staged and filmed, and of *Po Staru Se Žít Nedá* (1948); *Nová Odborová Politika* (1948); *Odborové Hnutí a Budováni Socialismu* (1949); and *Boj o Jednotu Odborů, 1927-1938* (1950). His honors include the Royal Cross of Roumania, the French Cross, and two Czechoslovak medals.

Zápotocký and Marie Sklenivcková were married on September 22, 1910 and have two daughters. His hobby is sculpture. John Gunther described him as "a very shy man, inarticulate in speech. . . .He has tough workman's hands, a nervous manner and very blue eyes." (New York *Herald Tribune,* February 9, 1949).

References

N Y Herald Tribune p8 F 9 '49; II pl Mr 29 '53
N Y Times pl Mr 22 '53
N Y World-Telegram p21 Mr 25 '53
Time 51:31 Je 21 '48
International Who's Who, 1952

ZAROUBIN, GEORGI N(IKOLAE-VICH) (zä-rōō'bǐn gyǐ-ôr'gyû-ǐ nyǐ-kǔ-la'yě-vyǐch) 1900- Soviet Ambassador to the United States

Address: c/o Embassy of the U.S.S.R., 1125 16th St., N.W., Washington, D.C.

In a reorganization of Soviet diplomatic personnel in June 1952, Georgi N. Zaroubin was appointed to succeed Alexander S. Panyushkin as Ambassador to the United States. Zaroubin, who presented his credentials in Washington on September 25 of that year, had earlier been Ambassador to Canada (1944-46) and Ambas-

Wide World Photos
GEORGI N. ZAROUBIN

sador to Great Britain (1946-52). Representing the U.S.S.R. after World War II at four-power meetings of deputy Foreign Ministers that attempted to negotiate an Austrian peace treaty, the Ambassador has also been a delegate to several sessions of the United Nations General Assembly.

Georgi Nikolaevich Zaroubin was born in 1900 near Moscow in Russia. Seventeen years old when the Russian revolution took place, he was educated partially under the Czarist regime and partly under the Communist. After attending the Moscow Textile Institute and the Stalin Industrial Academy, he held various posts in the Soviet engineering industry in the 1920's and early 1930's and served as director of the Industrial Academy from 1933 to 1938.

Zaroubin first visited the United States in an official capacity in 1938 as assistant commissar-general of the Soviet section of the New York World's Fair. When the fair closed in 1940, he was appointed to the People's Commissariat of Foreign Affairs and became head of the Consular Bureau, where he supervised the American Department from 1941 to 1944. On June 8, 1944, Zaroubin took up his duties as the first Soviet Ambassador to Canada, succeeding

Feodor Gusev, who had been Minister. During his two years in Ottawa a series of espionage activities took place which culminated in the Canadian "spy ring" trials of the spring of 1945. The Ambassador was in Moscow on a leave of absence when the Canadian Government disclosed in February 1945 that military secrets had been transmitted to Russia. While members of his Embassy were found guilty of espionage, Zaroubin was absolved of complicity by the Canadian Royal Commission, which found that he had no access to certain rooms at the Embassy; that the Russian intelligence heads had orders to keep Zaroubin ignorant of their activities; and, confirming this latter point, that one spy leader was rebuked for making a "slip" which gave Zaroubin possible knowledge of their work (New York *Herald Tribune,* August 27, 1946).

Designated by the Soviet Government in September 1946 as Ambassador to Great Britain, one of Russia's most important diplomatic assignments, Zaroubin was officially accredited to the post on January 26, 1947, again in succession to Feodor Gusev. Commenting on the significance of Zaroubin's appointment, Walter Kerr said, "On the surface, it would appear as though the Kremlin were engaged in a series of moves designed to strengthen the hand of the 'get-tough-with-the-West group in Soviet political circles'" (New York *Herald Tribune,* August 26, 1946).

While serving as envoy in London, Zaroubin was also occupied in attending the fifth session of the Council of Foreign Ministers in London in 1947 and in representing the Soviet Union at meetings of the Foreign Ministers' deputies of the United States, Great Britain, Russia, and France, dealing with postwar treaties in Europe. In October 1947 when the sessions reached a deadlock in procedural matters over the question of the future of Italian colonies, Zaroubin's attitude was described as "friendly and cheerful, even though unyielding" (New York *Times,* October 9, 1947). The four-power deputies met in London in January 1947 to begin drafting a peace treaty for Austria. At various times progress in negotiations was delayed by the Soviet deputy's charges that Austria had not been denazified or demilitarized, and by mid-December 1950, after 258 meetings, the treaty remained unconcluded. On this occasion, reported the New York *Herald Tribune,* Zaroubin "introduced the lack of agreement on Trieste as an excuse for not proceeding with an agreement on Austria"; the meetings were adjourned until the following March.

In June 1952 Zaroubin figured in a general reorganization of Russian top diplomatic assignments when he was named Ambassador to the United States to replace Alexander Panyushkin, who was sent to represent the U.S.S.R. in Peiping, China. Zaroubin was succeeded in the London post by deputy Foreign Minister Andrei A. Gromyko. At this time the New York *Times* observed that except for Gromyko and Jacob A. Malik, the newly designated Ambassador was the best-equipped Soviet diplomat for the post. "Zaroubin has been one of the most active members of the Soviet foreign service in international conferences," noted *Times* writer Walter H. Waggoner. "Such activity gives credence to the appraisal by observers here that he is one of the more trusted of the Russian officials on the level of practical diplomacy." After Zaroubin's appointment, which came about the same time that George Kennan, United States Ambassador to Russia, arrived in Moscow, *Business Week* magazine expressed its hope that for the first time it might be possible to see the end of the "cold war" and the restoration of the "cool but cordial" relations between Russia and the United States which prevailed in the 1930's. Zaroubin, characterized by the New York *Herald Tribune* as "more direct in his dealings than the usual Soviet diplomat," told President Truman, when he presented his letters of credence on September 25, 1952, that his Government "in pursuing consistently the policy of the strengthening of peace, is striving to maintain friendly political, economic, and cultural relations between the Union of Soviet Socialist Republics and the United States of America."

In an article in *Cosmopolitan,* January, 1953, James E. Brown wrote: "The Soviet robot diplomat never veers in the slightest from the Moscow-dictated policy. He knows that a deviation, no matter how small, will produce grievous consequences—not only to himself but to his family. . . .So the Soviet diplomat reads obediently from his prepared script the strident speeches accusing the United States of employing germ warfare in Korea or insisting on the Soviet Union's desire for 'peace' all in the same monotonously harsh tones used by a Red Army drill sergeant."

At the conference in San Francisco in September 1951 on the Japanese peace treaty, Zaroubin was one of the U.S.S.R.'s three top representatives. He has also been a delegate in 1950, 1951, 1952, and 1953 to sessions of the United Nations General Assembly. During the seventh session of the General Assembly in October 1952 he introduced before the Credentials Committee an unsuccessful resolution calling for the disaccreditation of the Chinese Nationalists. The following month he presented to the Administration and Budgetary Committee proposals for cuts in the operations of U.N. headquarters at Geneva and of the Office of the High Commissioner for Refugees.

He was elected in October 1952 an alternate on the Central Committee of the All-Union Communist Party, one of the four Central Committee spokesmen representing the Soviet Union at the U.N. The Russian diplomat, who was married in 1926 to Elizaveta Kulkova, is the father of one son, Victor. With a weight of 145 pounds, Zaroubin stands five feet six inches tall. *Newsweek* magazine writer found that "he is willing to talk volubly in passable English—as long as the subject is fishing or some other sport"; his other interests include flying and motorcycling.

References

N Y Herald Tribune II p1 Je 15 '52
por; IV p2 S 1 '46
U S News 33:38 Jl 4 '52 por
Who's Who, 1952
Who's Who in the United Nations (1951)

ZATOPEK, EMIL (zä'tō-pĕk ĕ'mĭl)
1923 (?)- Athlete; army officer
Address: Czechoslovakia

Emil Zatopek, triple-threat running star of the Czech Olympic team in December 1952 was named the foremost athlete of today in a poll taken by *World Sport*, official publication of the British Olympic Association. Holder of the Olympic 5,000 meter, 10,000 meter, and marathon titles simultaneously, the Czech distance runner has established six new world records in his eleven years of competition. By profession, he is a major in the Czechoslovakian People's Republic Democratic Army.

The son of a carpenter and descendant of peasant forebears who had settled in Moravia, a south central province of Czechoslavakia, Emil Zatopek was born thirty years ago in Koprinivice, as reported by Milt Marmor in the Washington *Post*. In his youth, Zatopek worked as an apprentice in a shoe factory and saved his wages toward his tuition in a trade school. When he had completed his studies, he went on to earn a further degree in foreign languages and chemistry at the Czechoslovakian equivalent of an American junior college. Because of his scientific interests, reported Allison Danzig of the New York *Times*, Zatopek "decided to make a study of the human body and put himself to a test to determine his strength, and that was the beginning of his training as an athlete."

Adopting a rigid daily schedule, the young Czech student "ran across woods and roads" in all kinds of weather to average about twelve miles, or twenty kilometers, in a style which varied spurting with jogging to diminish the monotony of the practice. Zatopek placed second in his first race, a 1941 Czech provincial competition. At the end of that year he succeeded in obtaining twenty-seventh ranking in the national 1,500-meter ratings, for a best time of four minutes twenty seconds. Within two years he had worked down his time to 1:58.7 for eight hundred meters. During the war his training was impeded by the Nazi invasion of his country, and after the war he was drafted into the Czech army as a private. He continued his practice in his spare time and on leave, sometimes wearing "heavy boots and cumbersome pack equipment" (Bob Allison, *Sport* magazine). In 1946 the twenty-four-year-old soldier emerged as national 5,000-meter champion in the Prague competitions and scored a victory in the 5,000-meter event at Berlin. He had bicycled to Berlin from Prague, only to meet the officials' derision when he sought permission to enter the Allied Occupation troops international competition. "He ran the field into the ground and turned the jeers of the 65,000 present into cheers," observed Danzig. Running at that time under the colors of the Zlin Club (which he represented until the establishment of the Communist Government in Czechoslovakia in June 1948), Zatopek also competed in the European championships at Oslo, to take fifth place. His time had been considerably bettered by 1947, wrote Marmor, for by then the Czech runner could clock the 1,500 meters in 3:52.8, the three thousand meters

EMIL ZATOPEK

in 8:08.8, and the five thousand meters in 14:08.2.

Assigned to the Czech Olympic team in 1948, Zatopek started practicing immediately on his arrival at London's Wembley Stadium, without bothering to change into track clothes. In a record clocking for the 10,000-meter event, he made a time of 29:59.6 to break the previously established count by 11.8 seconds, by coming in 320 yards, almost a full lap, ahead of his nearest contender. For this victory he received an Olympic gold medal, and promotion from second to first lieutenant in the Czech Army. He was not able to duplicate his victory in the 5,000-meter competition, where he ran second behind Belgium's Gaston Reiff by a distance of two yards. Two years later, at the European track and field championships held in Brussels, Zatopek defeated nearest runner Reiff in the 5,000 meter race by a wide margin of 150 meters. In 1950 he clocked 29:02 for 10,000 meters to set a new record, as well as 14:03 for 5,000 meters, the second fastest time ever recorded.

In 1952 Zatopek was again named by his Government to represent his country on an Olympic team sent to the July meet in Helsinki, Finland. Of his showing in the 5,000-meter event, Marmor wrote, "Zatopek made a mockery of the race" by dropping back from the leaders to direct lagging runners, only to place ahead of the whole field and finish first himself in record time. The Czech racer soon added another crown by winning the 10,000-meter event, bettering his own 1948 Olympic record by 42.6 seconds. In an epoch-making third victory, Zatopek took his third 1952 Olympics gold medal by running a full marathon distance of twenty-six miles, 385 yards (his first time to do so) to come in half a mile ahead of the nearest contender in two hours, 23 minutes, and 3.2 seconds—6:16 minutes better than the previous record. "He ran evenly,

sharp elbows protruding sidewise as though he had his hands clasped in prayer," reported Red Smith, at a pace "between eleven and twelve miles an hour after twenty miles."

An invitation extended to the Olympic triple medalist by Dan Ferris of the United States Amateur Athletic Union to perform on American tracks was refused in late July 1952 by Zatopek on the pretext that he was unused to indoor board tracks. In a subsequent statement given in a broadcast over Radio Prague in mid-August, he characterized such offers as "ridiculous, unsportsmanlike" and said, "It was the brutal and harsh play of the United States ice hockey team in the winter Olympics which drove me to my most recent performance."

Sport magazine has commented that "only a man of Zatopek's energy and stamina could bear the strain that his awkward style imposes. His head is thrown back and tilted to one side, his shoulders are hunched and he jerks, twists and strains as he runs. His arms flail across his midriff. . . .Yet this formless madman sets a pace that kills off all effective opposition, and he unleashed an explosive finishing kick." Another writer, Danzig, has found that "there is nothing labored or tortured about Zatopek's leg action. It is rhythmical and straightforward as he pounds along tirelessly with a short stride that carries him away as though he were wearing seven-league boots."

A poll of outstanding sports authorities taken by *World Sport*, official organ of the British Olympic Association, in December 1952 revealed that they considered Zatopek the foremost contemporary athlete. At the 1948 Olympics in London Zatopek met Dana Ingrova, noted Czech javelin thrower, who was also a 1952 Olympic gold medalist, and married her soon afterward. Zatopek is a staff-captain (equivalent to an American major) in the Czech Army, but his military duties are "mere window dressing," according to Bob Allison of *Sport*, "Emil calls his own shots on training time, facilities, traveling expenses, equipment, anything he wants or needs." The runner is a competent linguist, able to converse in five tongues. His consolation for his rare moments of defeat is found in his violin. The Czech athlete is about five feet nine inches tall, weighs 165 pounds, and has blond hair with a "rugged but pleasantly handsome" face.

References

Sport 13:66 Ag '52
Washington (D.C.) Post p43 Ag 3 '52

ZINNEMANN, FRED Apr. 29, 1907- Motion picture director

Address: b. c/o Stanley Kramer Company, Inc., Columbia Pictures Corporation, 1438 N. Gower St., Hollywood 28, Calif; h. Santa Monica Calif.

About twenty years after going to Hollywood from Austria to study sound techniques in film production, Fred Zinnemann first won wide critical attention in 1948 when *The Search*, his motion picture about the displaced children of World War II, brought his special talents into full focus. From 1929 to 1937 Zinnemann had worked principally in the American movie capital as an extra, script clerk, and assistant director, and had then been employed by Metro-Goldwyn-Mayer, directing a series of short subjects and several well-received feature pictures. After his success in *The Search* he directed a number of other notable films, among them *The Men* in 1950, *High Noon,* which received two New York Film Critics awards in 1952, *The Member of the Wedding* and *From Here to Eternity* in 1953.

Born in Vienna, Austria, on April 29, 1907, Fred Zinnemann is the son of Dr. Oskar and Anna Zinnemann. He first thought of music as a career and at an early age began the study of the violin, but when he realized that he could not become a great concert artist, he turned to law, enrolling at the Vienna University. While Zinnemann was a law student, he saw Von Stroheim's *Greed* and King Vidor's *The Big Parade,* which made such an impression on him that he decided to become a motion picture director. He left Austria to take courses for a year at the École Technique de Photographie et de Cinématographie in Paris, where he learned the fundamentals of optics, photochemistry, developing, and printing. After working as an assistant cameraman in Paris and Berlin, in the early part of 1929 he set out for Hollywood to study the new sound techniques being developed there.

In Hollywood, Zinnemann's first job was as an extra in *All Quiet on the Western Front.* By the end of his first year there, he was hired by Berthold Viertel, one of Europe's outstanding directors, then working in the United States, as an assistant cameraman and film cutter. From Viertel he learned some of the basic principles of directing. Having by this time become interested in the documentary film, Zinnemann traveled to Berlin to work with the late Robert Flaherty, a pioneer in the documentary field. Flaherty had gone there to arrange to produce a motion picture about a little-known tribe in Russia, and Zinnemann spent six months designing the projected film with him. Since they were not permitted by the Russian Government to make the kind of production they had in mind, the project was dropped. "They wanted propaganda," Zinnemann, in an interview with the *New Yorker,* recalled, "and we didn't." Of his association with Flaherty, Zinnemann said in the same interview: "Just listening to him talk was a liberal education for me."

Back in Hollywood by 1931, Zinnemann took out his citizenship papers and secured employment as a script clerk. When the Mexican Government contracted with producer Paul Strand to make a picture about Mexico, Strand chose Zinnemann as his director. The crew of the film, *The Wave,* lived for a year on the coast near Vera Cruz, using nonprofessional residents to dramatize the film's theme, which was the attempt of Mexican fishermen to organize their industry and achieve better working conditions. While the picture was later recognized as an artistic and commercial success, the director had to wait for a year and one-half before being offered another assignment. In 1937 Metro-Goldwyn-Mayer hired Zinnemann to di-

FRED ZINNEMANN

rect a series of short subjects. The first was *Friend Indeed,* about seeing-eye dogs; the second, *The Story of Dr. Carver,* concerned the famous Negro scientist; and the third, *That Mothers Might Live,* was a pictorial account of the work of Dr. Ignaz Philipp Semmelweiss, the Hungarian physician who pioneered in the use of antiseptic methods in obstetrics. This last-named work won for Zinnemann the 1938 Award of the Academy of Motion Picture Arts and Sciences for short subjects and a seven-year contract with Metro-Goldwyn-Mayer as a director of feature films.

Kid Glove Killer, released in 1941, was Zinnemann's first major production, a low-budget film which impressed the New York *Times* reviewer as "a little crackerjack of a picture" with an "expert straightforward job of directing." Other feature pictures followed, and in 1944 upon the release of *The Seventh Cross,* Zinnemann again won acclaim, with the New York *Herald Tribune* critic praising this story of the escape of seven prisoners from a German concentration camp for its "vivid sequences and splendid directorial touches." The New York *Times* reviewer also gave credit to the director and his camera man for "much of the crackling tension and hard-packed realism that prevails."

While still with Metro-Goldwyn-Mayer, Zinnemann was invited by the Swiss producer Lazar Wechsler (in 1946) to direct a picture about the displaced children of Europe. Zinnemann then went to Germany and Switzerland to film *The Search,* released in 1948, in which he used only a small number of professionals for the adult roles and relied principally on the children in the several placement camps of the United Nations Relief and Rehabilitation Administration for the dramatic action. Filming the picture in bombed-out German cities, Zinnemann achieved what the critic for the New York *Herald Tribune* called "a wonderful mo-

ZINNEMANN, FRED—*Continued*

tion picture . . . an authentic, sincere semi-documentary about a modern tragedy." Bosley Crowther of the New York *Times* commented: "No film today is better acted or more humanly illuminated than *The Search*," while the reviewer for the New York *World-Telegram* thought that in this film Zinnemann had found "the first outlet for his creative craftsmanship." *The Search*, which established Zinnemann as "one of the top-flight directors," won for him the first award of the Screen Directors Guild as the best director of the year. In 1950 it received the British Film Academy Award as the best film embodying the principles of the United Nations Charter.

Zinnemann completed his contract with Metro-Goldwyn-Mayer with *Act of Violence* (1949), "a routine cat-and-mouse thriller" (New York *Herald Tribune*), which was praised by a number of critics for its direction. In 1950 Zinnemann became an "independent," accepting single-film contracts from individual producers. When producer Stanley Kramer hired him to direct *The Men*, a motion picture about the paraplegic veterans of World War II, which starred Marlon Brando, the director again made as much use as possible of nonprofessional actors, in this case the patients at the Birmingham Veterans Hospital near Los Angeles. Because they had undergone the experience in real life, Zinnemann felt that they were able to give authenticity to the film. Explaining this aspect of his directing to a *New Yorker* reporter, he said: "I wanted people who would be behaving rather than acting. . . .The real paraplegics made jokes about their condition that sounded genuine; they'd have sounded horrible coming from actors." Crowther of the New York *Times* wrote that "nothing yet demonstrated has so fully realized and portrayed . . . the inner torments, the despairs, the loneliness and the possible triumphs of a paraplegic as this picture does. . . .A striking and authentic documentary quality has been imported to the whole film in every detail, attitude and word." The New York *Herald Tribune* critic, who considered Zinnemann's direction designed "to squeeze every ounce of meaning out of the various hospital incidents," thought that occasionally the effort resulted in "overplaying the material." In his 1951 film, *Teresa,* made in Italy and among the tenements of New York City, Zinnemann again used authentic settings as much as possible. To do this, he had to redestroy a church in the little Italian town of Scascoli which had been destroyed during the war and then partially rebuilt. While the New York *Times* called the story of an American soldier and his Italian bride, a "compassionate tale" and one which placed "these two real young people in a world that is equally real," *Variety*'s reviewer commented that Zinnemann's direction was "too consciously documentary."

Zinneman also directed a short documentary, *Benjy,* designed to aid the fund-raising campaign of the Los Angeles Orthopedic Hospital. This film, which was not released commercially, won the 1951 Academy Award as the best documentary of the year.

The second picture which Zinnemann made with Stanley Kramer, *High Noon* (1952), starring Gary Cooper, won the New York Film Critics Award as the best picture of the year and, for Zinnemann, the citation as the best director. On March 19, 1953, three men were awarded "Oscars" by the Academy of Motion Picture Arts and Sciences for their work in *High Noon*: Gary Cooper for the best acting in 1952, Dimitri Tiomkin for the best music score in a non-musical film, and both Tiomkin and Ned Washington for the best song (the film's "Do Not Forsake Me").

Rated by the critic Alton Cook of the New York *World-Telegram* as "one of the great Westerns of all time," *High Noon* tells of a small town marshal who on the day of his retirement and of his marriage to a Quaker girl chooses to face a vengeful killer. Bosley Crowther, describing Zinnemann's direction as a "splendid job," pointed out, "Mr. Zinnemann has so made his picture that you get the dusty feel of a Western town, the lean and stolid nature of its people . . . and the terrible tension of waiting for violence and death in the afternoon. . . .He has constructed a real pictorial ballad with imagination and skill."

For producer Stanley Kramer, Zinnemann also directed *The Member of the Wedding* (1953), starring the performers who had appeared in the Broadway production, Ethel Waters, Julie Harris, and Brandon de Wilde. The screen version of Carson McCuller's play and novel received mixed reviews, with many critics feeling that the special quality of the story of a sensitive and lonely adolescent was not suitable to the motion picture medium. The *New Yorker* thought that the producer and director had "shown a nice respect for the content of . . . the work" but had limited themselves in the creation," making a film that seemed "too confined." Zinnemann, "for all his cleverness and perception," remarked the *Christian Science Monitor* review, had "not entirely succeeded in transferring unchanged the values of . . . the play and book." In the opinion of the film critic for the *Saturday Review*, however, *The Member of the Wedding* was "a literary work that touches and charms" and the director had "kept his movie intimate and delicate."

One of the most sensational movie successes of 1953 has been Zinnemann's version of James Jones' novel, *From Here to Eternity*. What Zinnemann has done, said the *New Yorker* (August 8, 1953), "is give us a glimpse of the military that is very rare." The critics were unanimous in their applause of Zinnemann's achievement; *Variety* called his direction "solid handling of motion picture dramatics."

Zinnemann, whose directorial style has been called that of a "sensitive realist," believes that the requisite of good directing is versatility. A director "must be open-minded about the world around him," he said in an interview appearing in the New York *Times Magazine*. Elsewhere Zinnemann has been quoted as explaining: "One must try to tell the truth as one sees it. A director does so primarily in visual concept. Words—dialogue—should come second. That's the wonderful advantage of the camera (New York *Times*). In another interview he told a reporter of the New York *Herald Tribune* that he considered the movies artistically allied to the short story—"the single incident that sets off reactions and cuts deep into various aspects of behavior." Zinnemann is short and slender in build, with blue eyes and curly hair. On October 9, 1936, he married Renee Bartlett, an English-born woman who was raised in Chile and later became a resident of California. They have one child, a son, Tim. The director, who continues his interest in music, usually divides his leisure time between violin playing and mountain climbing. He has a natural ear for languages and is fluent in German, English, French, and Spanish, and has a good knowledge of Polish.

References

New Yorker 26:17 Ag 19 '50
N Y Herald Tribune V p1 Ap 9 '50
N Y Times II p5 Ja 25 '53
N Y Times Mag p22 O 26 '52
Parents Mag p32 Ja '51
International Motion Picture Almanac, 1952-53

ZORIN, VALERIAN A(LEXANDRO-VICH) 1902- Soviet Union Government official

Address: Moscow, U.S.S.R.

Valerian A. Zorin, who succeeded Jacob Malik as permanent representative of the U.S.S.R. to the United Nations in October 1952, served in this capacity until April, 1953. The head of the Fourth Central European section of the Russian Ministry of Foreign Affairs in the final two years of World War II, Zorin became the Soviet Union's first postwar Ambassador to Czechoslovakia. He was present in Czechoslovakia in February 1948 and is widely believed to have supervised the political coup during that month which resulted in the establishment of a Communist Government in that country.

Born in 1902, Valerian Alexandrovich Zorin was fifteen years old when the October Revolution established the Bolsheviks in power in Russia in 1917, and twenty when in 1922 he attained what has been described as "a prominent position" on the Central Committee of the Communist Youth League (Comsomol). Active in the youth movement for the next ten years, he was a student for part of this time in the High Communist Institute of Education, being graduated in 1933. The next two years were devoted to postgraduate study; then for six years (1935-41) Zorin was engaged in "party and pedagogical work." In 1941, when the invasion by the Nazis brought Soviet Russia into World War II, Zorin was assigned to the National Commissariat of Foreign Affairs as assistant to the General Secretary, and from 1943 to 1945 was in charge of the Fourth (Central European) Section of the Foreign Ministry.

Zorin attracted international attention as the Soviet Union's first postwar Ambassador to Czechoslovakia. By March 1945 enough of the extreme eastern portion of that country had been freed of the Germans to warrant the return of the Czech Government-in-Exile. President Eduard Beneš visited Moscow at the end of the month for conferences with Soviet officials; proceeding thence to Kosice in Slovakia, which had been selected as a temporary capital pending the liberation of Prague, he was accompanied by Valerian Zorin, who had been named Ambassador Extraordinary and Plenipotentiary of the U.S.S.R. Beneš and Zorin reached Kosice on April 3, 1945, and three days later the Moscow radio announced that Beneš had named an interim government with Zdenek Fierlinger, prewar Czech Ambassador to the Soviet Union, as Premier. "The choice of Fierlinger," stated a dispatch to the New York *Times*, "was interpreted . . . as indicating that the new Cabinet was designed along lines friendly to Russia." The Fierlinger Cabinet included Czech Communist leader, Klement Gottwald, who himself became Premier on July 3, 1946 (and was succeeded by Antonín Zápotocký as Premier and later President).

The Gottwald Government was thus established by the spring of 1947, when Ambassador Zorin left Czechoslovakia for Geneva, Switzerland, to become the delegate of Soviet Russia to the United Nations Economic Commission for Europe. There on May 5 he argued that the Commission should concentrate on "questions of aiding and cooperating with the allied countries that have suffered from invasion." (Michael L. Hoffman of the New York *Times* referred to this speech as a "thinly veiled attack" on the United States policy of aid to Britain and Turkey, neither of which had actually been invaded during the war.) Again in Geneva on July 8, after Soviet Foreign Minister Molotov had walked out of a three-power conference in Paris on European cooperation in the Marshall Plan, Zorin accused Britain and France of having "gone behind the back of the U.S.S.R." to force action on their plan for European aid, and announced that the Soviet Union would "seek cooperation for reestablishment of European economy" on the basis of "mutual recognition of equal rights and guarantees." His concluding statement that Russia had "nothing in common with the erroneous policy pursued at Paris" was taken to mean that the Soviet Union "might seek to form a European cooperative on its own terms" (New York *Times*). Later in the year 1947 Zorin was sent to the United States as a delegate to the United Nations General Assembly. Named to the Assembly's Social, Humanitarian and Cultural Committee, which was considering among other matters the provisional agenda for the forthcoming U.N. International Conference on Freedom of Information and the Press to be held at Geneva, Zorin proposed at Lake Success, New York, on September 26 "world-wide punishment of owners of newspapers that print libelous material about other countries" (New York *Times*). Later, he spoke in support of a Yugoslav proposal to outlaw "false . . . reports calculated . . . to incite to war."

On November 29, 1947, Tass News Agency announced that the Soviet Council of Ministers had appointed Valerian Zorin a Deputy

VALERIAN A. ZORIN

Minister of Foreign Affairs. In December of that year the Czech Government of Klement Gottwald, which had already rejected the Marshall Plan, signed with the U.S.S.R. a "trade agreement for $500 million worth of goods" which "drew the Czechs closer to the Russian planned economy" (*Americana Annual*). After about two months, on February 20, 1948, a "crisis" was brought about in Czechoslovakia through the resignation from the Gottwald Cabinet of a number of non-Communist ministers in protest against growing Communist control of the police. Premier Gottwald demanded that the vacated posts be filled by Communists, but President Beneš refused. When former Ambassador Zorin arrived in Prague, the Minister of the Interior Nosek and Defense Minister Svoboda (both Communists) reportedly discovered a plot for an armed coup against the government. In the week that followed "the historic political parties were largely suppressed" and "under the guidance of Interior Minister Vaclav Nosek hundreds of prominent public figures were jailed or went into exile" (*Americana Annual*). By February 28 Beneš had yielded to Gottwald's demands, and on the next day Zorin returned to Moscow. A "single list" Soviet-type election on May 30 resulted in Communist control of Czechoslovakia; on June 5 Zorin made another visit to Prague, and on June 7 President Beneš resigned. (He died September 3). Meanwhile (April 1948) Deputy Foreign Minister Zorin had allegedly worked out a so-called "Zorin Plan" for the guidance of Italian Communists in the event that they won the election to be held in that month. The Rome newspaper *Tempo* published a summary of the alleged "Plan" a few days before the balloting. According to the New York *Times* correspondent Arnaldo Cortesi, the plan, as outlined in *Tempo*, included "the immediate conclusion of a military alliance with Russia and

Yugoslavia, strict dependence of Italy on Yugoslavia, which would become a pattern for Italian social life, economy, and foreign policy; strict control over the press, radio and movies, and elimination of all priests who do not swear devotion to the Communist state and Communist principles."

Appointed to succeed Jacob Malik as the permanent Soviet representative to the United Nations in New York in October 1952, Zorin made his first appearance at a meeting of the twelve-nation Disarmament Commission on October 1. Here the chief Soviet delegate moved to have the Kremlin's report to the Commission discussed in open instead of closed meetings, and lost by a vote of 9 to 2, with one abstention. In plenary session of the General Assembly on October 23, Zorin argued that a memorandum circulated by Secretary General Trygve Lie with a view to limiting the length of Assembly session was "openly designed" to infringe on "the rights of the so-called minority" and that the U.N. Secretariat was controlled by the United States. Under the system of alphabetical rotation by countries, he assumed his first chairmanship of a U.N. body on November 1, when he succeeded Selim Sarper of Turkey as chairman for one month of the Disarmament Commission. On December 11 the Soviet Union voted against a proposal of the Special Political Committee of the General Assembly to ask Israel and Arab states to begin negotiations to settle differences resulting from the Palestine war. At this time Zorin accused the United States of operating "corridor maneuvers" in the Middle East for the purpose of organizing a Near Eastern bloc against the Communist nations. Later in the month when a vote was taken in the Security Council regarding negotiation of the India-Pakistan dispute over Kashmir, Zorin charged Britain and the United States with delaying settlement of the Kashmir issue in order to advance "imperialist" objectives. These countries intended, he said, to set up military bases in Kashmir from which to strike at Russia.

In April 1953, after Andrei Y. Vishinsky was assigned as permanent representative of the new Malenkov Government in Moscow to the United Nations, Zorin returned to Russia where he is serving as Deputy Foreign Minister.

When Zorin arrived in the United States with his wife in September 1952, he was described as heavy-set and gray-haired. William R. Frye of the *Christian Science Monitor*, observing the chief Soviet delegate at a U.N. meeting, thought him self-possessed, less "tempestuous" than his predecessor. Zorin was decorated with the Order of Lenin in 1945 and has also been awarded the Medal for Distinguished Work in the Great Patriotic War, as well as the Workers' Order of the Red Banner.

References

    Christian Sci Mon p6 O 4 '52
    Newsweek 40:43 S 8 '52 por
    Time 60:29 S 8 '52 por
    International Who's Who, 1952
    World Biography (1948)
    World Diplomatic Directory (1950)

ZWICKY, FRITZ (tsvĭg'ē) Feb. 14, 1898-
Astronomer; physicist
Address: b. c/o California Institute of Technology, Pasadena 4, Calif.; c/o Aerojet Engineering Corporation, Azusa, Calif.; h. 2065 Oakdale St., Pasadena 10, Calif.

Astronomer, physicist, inventor of jet engines, Fritz Zwicky is a versatile physical scientist who offered the theory that supernovae—enormously brilliant exploding stars—occur more frequently than had been suspected and who furnished a physical explanation for the phenomenon. Since coming to the United States from Switzerland in 1927, Zwicky has been associated with the California Institute of Technology. During World War II he directed the research of the Aerojet Engineering Corporation.

One of three children (two boys and a girl) of Fridolin and Franziska (Wrcek) Zwicky, Fritz Zwicky was born on February 14, 1898. His birthplace was Varna, Bulgaria, where his father, an accountant engaged in international trade, was the Norwegian consul. Reared in Switzerland, which he considers his homeland, Zwicky has retained Swiss citizenship during almost three decades of residence in the United States.

After graduation in 1916 from a Zurich secondary school, Fritz Zwicky entered the Federal Institute of Technology (Eidgenische Technische Hochschule), where he majored in mathematics and physics. During his senior year he was secretary of the Swiss Society for Social Reform, which he has characterized as "a large national Swiss political and philanthropic organization." Receiving his B.S. degree in 1920, Zwicky was appointed a research assistant, and in 1922 wrote his doctoral dissertation *On the Theory of Ionic Crystals*. He had published at least one paper earlier, "The Second Virial Coefficient of the Rare Gases" (1921). This and later papers by Zwicky on equations of state of gases, liquids, and solids, behavior of slow electrons and ions in gases, and the physics of crystals, were described by abstracters as "purely mathematical." Zwicky has said that in choosing his lifework he was most strongly influenced by Professors A. Einstein, H. Weyl, P. Scherrer, and A. Stodola. (Weyl is a noted mathematician, and Scherrer later became president of the Swiss Atomic Energy Commission.)

Zwicky remained at the Zurich institute until 1925 when he went to the California Institute of Technology on a Rockefeller International Education Board fellowship. There he became assistant professor of theoretical physics in 1927 and from 1929 to 1942 held the position of associate professor. On his arrival in California, it is told, one of his first questions to president Robert A. Millikan (the 1923 Nobel Prize winner in physics) concerned the availability of mountains to climb. When Millikan indicated 5,700-foot Mount Wilson, Zwicky replied, "Ja, I see the foothills." Recounting this anecdote, *People Today* commented, "That's his attitude toward the impossible in science."

Since 1925 Zwicky has written about 150 papers for Swiss, German, English, and Amer-

DR. FRITZ ZWICKY

ican journals. Many have appeared in the *National Academy of Science Proceedings* and in the *Astrophysical Journal*. One issue of the former (July 1926) contained two of his contributions, "Transfer of Energy from Electrons to Atoms," based on ordinary mechanical principles, and "Quantum Theory and the Behavior of Slow Electrons in Gases." He also wrote on pressure effects in solids, reflection of electrons from crystal lattices, and the specific heat of electrolytes.

Through the early 1930's Zwicky continued to produce papers on such questions of terrestrial physics as solid state, gaseous ionization, and thermodynamics. In the late 20's he had begun also to devote time to cosmological questions, under titles like "On the Thermodynamic Equilibrium in the Universe" (July 1928). "On the Red Shift of Spectral Lines through Interstellar Space" (October 1929) is one of his early astronomical papers in a field which he lists among his major interests.

Better known is Zwicky's work on supernova, novae, and cosmic rays. (Novae are stars which flare up briefly to thousands or billions of times their usual brightness and then fade to their original luminosity. Supernovae are several billion times brighter than the sun.) The May 1934 issue of N.A.S. *Proceedings* carried two contributions by astronomers Walter Baade and Fritz Zwicky, "On Super-Novae" and "Cosmic Rays from Super-Novae," in which the writers come to the conclusion that supernovae are a different class of stellar explosion from the ordinary novae, and occur in our stellar system about once in three centuries. Because this theory was greeted by some astronomers with skepticism and "mild amusement," theoretician Zwicky undertook to prove his point experimentally. Using the powerful photographic telescope of the Mount Wilson Observatory, he made a systematic survey of the extragalactic nebulae, or island universes,

ZWICKY, FRITZ—*Continued*

looking for supernovae explosions. On February 16, 1937, his plates showed a brilliant flash in the nebula which is catalogued as N.G.C. 4157, four million light-years (24 trillion miles) from the earth. Zwicky's article announcing the discovery appeared in the *Publications of the Astronomical Society of the Pacific.* Previously, only about twelve supernovae had ever been recorded by man. When Zwicky found his second on August 26, 1937, "It meant," he said, "that we could prove in a simple way with certainty that nuclear chain reactions existed in the universe and that we could set them off here."

Between 1937 and 1941, using the 100-inch Schmidt telescope, Professor Zwicky discovered and photographed 18 supernovae, explosions in distant galaxies, which had all occurred before the emergence of the human race on earth. He proposed what George Gamow characterized as "an entirely novel mechanism of explosion" to explain their occurrence—the tremendously rapid collapse of very large, heavy, hydrogenless stars from the weight of their own outer layers, into a state so dense that a small dust particle from their interiors would weigh several tons. This theory has gained considerable acceptance and has been elaborated upon by Gamow and Schoenberg as resulting in the formation of large numbers of neutrons. Zwicky continued his research on novae, supernovae, clusters, and other astronomical matters, including cosmic and atomic rays; he has also published articles on the philosophy of science. When he received an advance in rank at the California Institute of Technology in 1942, it was from associate professor of physics to professor of astrophysics. He was also appointed astronomer at the institute's Mount Wilson and Palomar Mountain observatories in 1947.

Meanwhile, Zwicky had become prominent in the field of jet propulsion. As director of research for Aerojet Engineering Corporation at nearby Azusa, California (1943-49), he invented some of the earliest and most advanced jet engines for aircraft and directed the work of a large research department. Since 1949 he has been the company's chief research consultant. Zwicky served as technical representative of the United States Air Force in Germany and Japan in 1945 and 1946 and was author of the book *Certain Phases of War Research in Germany*, which was issued by the Air Force in 1946. He was also a member of the Air Force scientific advisory board until 1949. Before his company's underwater and underground jets were invented, Zwicky had proposed in 1947 a system of morphological classification and nomenclature for jets which was published concurrently in *Aeronautical Engineering Review* and *Aviation.* The author called this "a new principle of scientific engineering and its illustration in the field of propulsive power plants." In addition to providing a standard terminology, his method of classification was intended to reveal possible types which had not yet been invented. In 1949 Zwicky received a patent on a jet engine which operates under water. He was awarded the Presidential Medal of Freedom by President Truman in the same year.

Among Zwicky's present research interests is space travel—"We first throw a little something into the skies," he has said, "then a little more, then a shipload of instruments, then ourselves." Believing that the entire earth could now be exploded by what he calls "very sloppy experimental procedure" in nuclear fusion, the professor thinks scientists should be concerned with "how to stabilize the earth against this eventuality," a stabilization he thinks difficult, "but not nearly so difficult as changing human nature." Zwicky also expects "plans for making the planetary bodies habitable by changing them intrinsically and by changing their positions relative to the sun" (*Collier's*, May 7, 1949). In November 1952 he offered observational proof of his theory that there are stars outside of galaxies, by presenting photographs showing faint luminous bridges connecting three distant galaxies. In the November issue of the *Publications of the Astronomical Society of the Pacific*, Zwicky suggested that there may be clouds of intergalactic matter that are not stars.

In an interview with the press in August, 1953, Dr. Zwicky disclosed that he had fired off a one-pound, copper cone-shaped charge and found that its particles traveled at a velocity "only slightly below the seven miles per second needed to escape the earth's gravity" (*Time*, August 24, 1953). The astrophysicist estimates that man could—with the material at hand—send a small piece of metal hurtling onto the surface of the moon. As a platform for his first "little something tossed into space" Zwicky is counting on high-rising balloons or military-type rockets.

Zwicky was married in 1932 to Dorothy Vernon, daughter of California State Senator Edgar J. Gates. His present wife is the former Anna Margaritha Zuercher, a cashier in Switzerland before their marriage on October 15, 1947; the couple has three daughters, Margrit, Franziska, and Barbara. Half an inch over six feet tall, the hazel-eyed, brown-haired Swiss weighs 175 pounds. He has been described by *Life* as "tempestuous, imaginative" and as a scientist who "has always been regarded by some staid colleagues as a controversial man—part genius, part eccentric." The astronomer-physicist is founder and chairman of the Committee for Aid to War-Stricken Scientific Libraries; he is also a trustee of the Pestalozzi Foundation of America. Among the scientific associations to which he belongs are the American Physical Society (fellow), the Swiss Physical Society (fellow), and the American Astronomical Society (member). Fond of mountain climbing and skiing, he often skis to work on snow-topped Mount Wilson and has retained membership in French and Swiss Alpine clubs.

References

Collier's 123:64 My 7 '49 por
Lit Digest 118:13 Ag 25 '34
People Today 1:16 Je 20 '50 pors
American Men of Science (1949)
International Who's Who, 1952
Who Knows—And What (1949)
Who's Who in America, 1952-53
Who's Who in Switzerland, 1950-51
World Biography (1948)

BIOGRAPHICAL REFERENCES

Consulted by the research staff of CURRENT BIOGRAPHY.

American Catholic Who's Who, 1952-53
American Medical Directory, 1950
American Men in Government (1949)
American Men of Science (1949)
American Women, 1939-40
America's Young Men, 1938-39
ASCAP Biographical Dictionary of Composers, Authors, and Publishers (1952)
Author's and Writer's Who's Who (1948-49)

Baker, T. ed. Biographical Dictionary of Musicians (1940)
Baseball Register (1953)
Biographical Directory of the American Congress, 1774-1949 (1950)
Blue Book of American Aviation, 1942
British Film Annual, 1949
Burke's Landed Gentry (1952)
Burke's Peerage, Baronetage, and Knightage (1953)
Business Executives of America (1950)

Canadian Who's Who, 1949-51
Catholic Who's Who, 1952
Chemical Who's Who, 1951
Chi è? (1948)
Congressional Directory (1952)

Dictionnaire Biographique des Artistes Contemporains, 1910-30
Dictionnaire Biographique Français Contemporain (1950)
Dictionnaire de Biographie Française (1933-)
Dictionnaire National des Contemporains (1936)
Directory of American Scholars (1951)
Directory of Medical Specialists (1951)
Directory of Medical Women, 1949
Directory of the American Political Science Association, 1948

Ewen, D. ed. Composers of Today (1936); Living Musicians (1940); Men and Women Who Make Music (1949)

Grove, G. Dictionary of Music and Musicians (1940)

Hoehn, M. ed. Catholic Authors (1952)
Hvem er Hvem? (1950)

Indian and Pakistan Year Book and Who's Who, 1948
International Motion Picture Almanac, 1952-53
International Press Who's Who; New Zealand, 1938
International Who's Who, 1953
International Who's Who in World Medicine, 1947
International World Who's Who (1949)
Italian-American Who's Who (1946)

Japan Who's Who, 1950

Kelly's Handbook to the Titled, Landed and Official Classes, 1951
Kraks Blaa Bog (1950)
Kunitz, S. J., and Haycraft, H. eds. Junior Book of Authors (1951); Twentieth Century Authors (1942)

Leaders in Education (1948)

Martindale-Hubbell Law Directory, 1952
Musicians' International Directory and Biographical Record (1949-50)

Nalanda Year-Book and Who's Who in India and Pakistan, 1951-53
National Cyclopædia of American Biography Current Volumes A-H (1926-52)
Near and Middle East Who's Who, 1945-46
Nobel Prize Winners (1938)

Prominent Personalities in American Methodism (1945)

Quem é Alguém (1947)

Religious Leaders of America, 1941-42

Salter, J. T. ed. Public Men in and Out of Office (1946)

Slavonic Encyclopaedia (1949)
South African Who's Who, 1952

Thompson, O. ed. International Cyclopedia of Music and Musicians (1949)

Universal Jewish Encyclopedia (1948)

Variety Radio Directory, 1940-41
Vem är Det, 1949
Vem och Vad, 1948

Webster's Biographical Dictionary (1951)
Wer ist Wer? (1951)
Wer ist's? (1935)
Who is Who in Music, 1951
Who Knows—and What (1949)
Who's Important in Medicine, 1945
Who's Who, 1953
Who's Who in Alaska, 1947
Who's Who in America, 1952-53
Who's Who in American Art, (1953)
Who's Who in American Education, 1951-52
Who's Who in American Jewry, 1938-39
Who's Who in Art (1952)
Who's Who in Australia, 1950
Who's Who in Aviation, 1942-43
Who's Who in Canada, 1949-50
Who's Who in Central and East-Europe, 1935-36
Who's Who in Chicago and Illinois (1950)
Who's Who in Colored America, 1950
Who's Who in Commerce and Industry (1951)
Who's Who in Egypt and the Middle East, 1952
Who's Who in Engineering, 1948
Who's Who in Government, 1932-33
Who's Who in India, 1946-47
Who's Who in Japan, 1940-41
Who's Who in Labor (1946)
Who's Who in Latin America Pts 1-7 (1946-51)
Who's Who in Law, 1937
Who's Who in Library Service (1943)
Who's Who in New England (1949)
Who's Who in New York, 1952
Who's Who in New Zealand (1951)

679

Who's Who in Philosophy (1952)
Who's Who in Railroading, 1946
Who's Who in Switzerland, 1950-51
Who's Who in the Clergy, 1941-42
Who's Who in the East (1951)
Who's Who in the Major Leagues (1947)
Who's Who in the Midwest (1952)
Who's Who in the Nation's Capital, 1938-39

Who's Who in the South and Southwest (1952)
Who's Who in the State of Israel, 1949
Who's Who in the Theatre (1952)
Who's Who in the United Nations (1951)
Who's Who in the West (1951)
Who's Who in Transportation and Communication, 1942-43
Who's Who in United States Politics (1950)
Who's Who of the Allied Governments, 1943

Wie is Dat? 1948
Wier, A. E. ed. Macmillan Encyclopedia of Music and Musicians (1938)
Winchester's Screen Encyclopedia (1948)
Women of Achievement (1940)
World Biography (1948)
World Diplomatic Directory, 1951

Yearbook of the United Nations, 1952
Yost, E. American Women of Science (1943)

PERIODICALS AND NEWSPAPERS CONSULTED

A. L. A. Bul—American Library Association Bulletin $1.50; free to members. American Library Assn, 50 E Huron St, Chicago 11

Adult Ed J—Adult Education Journal $2. American Assn for Adult Education, 525 W 120th St, New York 27
Formerly Journal of Adult Education

Adv Age—Advertising Age $2. Advertising Publications, Inc, 200 E. Illinois St, Chicago 11

Adv & Sell—Advertising and Selling $4. Moore Pub Co, Inc, 48 W 38th St, New York 18

Am Artist—American Artist $5. Watson-Guptill Publications, Inc, 24 W 40th St, New York 18
Formerly Art Instruction

Am Assn Univ Women J—Journal of the American Association of University Women $1.50 American Assn of University Women, 1634 I St, N W, Washington 6, D.C.

Am Collector—American Collector $3. Collectors Pub Co, Inc, 432 Fourth Ave, New York 16

Am Federationist—American Federationist $2. American Federation of Labor, 901 Massachusetts Ave, Washington 1, D.C.

Am Hist R—American Historical Review $5; free to members. American Historical Assn, Macmillan Co, 60 Fifth Ave, New York 11

Am Home—American Home $2.50. American Home Magazine Corp, Forest Hills, New York

Am Mag—American Magazine $3. Crowell-Collier Pub Co, Springfield, Ohio

Am Mercury—American Mercury $3. American Mercury, Inc, 11 E 36th St, New York 16

Am Phot—American Photography $2.50. American Photographic Pub Co, 553 6th Ave, New York 1

Am Pol Sci R—American Political Science Review $10, free to members. American Political Science Assn, 1785 Mass. Ave, NW, Washington, D.C.

Am Scand R—American Scandinavian Review $3; free to members. American Scandinavian Foundation, 116 E 64th St, New York 21

Am Scholar—American Scholar $3. United Chapter of Phi Beta Kappa, Phi Beta Kappa Hall, Williamsburg, Va.

Am Sociol R—American Sociological Review $5. American Sociological Society, New York University, Washington Sq, New York 3

America—America $6. America Press, 70 E 45th St, New York 17

Américas—Américas $3. Pan American Union, 17th St and Constitution Ave, NW, Washington 6, D.C.

Ann Am Acad—Annals of the American Academy of Political and Social Science $5; free to members. 3937 Chestnut St, Philadelphia 4

Apollo—Apollo, the Magazine of the Arts for Connoisseurs and Collectors 42s. 10 Vigo St, Regent St, London, W 1. ($6.50 18 E 48th St, New York 17)

Arch Forum—Architectural Forum $12; $5.50 to firms and governments. Time, Inc, 540 N Michigan Ave, Chicago 11

Arch Rec—Architectural Record $4.50. F. W. Dodge Corp, 119 W 40th St, New York 18

Art Bul—Art Bulletin $10. College Art Assn, Inc, 625 Madison Ave, New York 22

Art Digest—Art Digest $5. Art Digest, Inc, 116 E 59th St, New York 22

Art N—Art News $9. Art Foundation, Inc, 136 E 57th St, New York 22

Arts & Arch—Arts and Architecture $5. John D. Entenza, 3305 Wilshire Blvd, Los Angeles 5

Asiatic R—Asiatic Review £1. East and West, Ltd, 3 Victoria St, London, SW 1

Atlan—Atlantic Monthly $6. Atlantic Monthly Co, 8 Arlington St, Boston 16

Automotive Ind—Automotive Industries $2. Chilton Co, 56th & Chestnut Sts, Philadelphia 39
Formerly Automotive and Aviation Industries

Aviation W—Aviation Week $6. McGraw-Hill Pub Co, Inc, 330 W 42d St, New York 36

Banking—Banking $4. American Bankers Assn, 12 E 36th St, New York 16

Bet Hom & Gard—Better Homes & Gardens $2.50. Meredith Pub Co, 1714 Locust St, Des Moines 3, Iowa

Book-of-the-Month Club N—Book-of-the-Month Club News, free to members. Book-of-the-Month Club, Inc, 345 Hudson St, New York 14

Books Abroad—Books Abroad $4. University of Oklahoma Press, Norman, Okla.

Bronx Home News. See N Y Post

Bsns W—Business Week $6. McGraw-Hill Pub Co, Inc, 330 W 42d St, New York 36

Bul Bibliog—Bulletin of Bibliography and Dramatic Index $3. F. W. Faxon Co, 83 Francis St, Boston 15

Bul Museum Modern Art. See New York City. Museum of Modern Art Bul

Bul Pan Am Union. See Américas

Calif Arts & Arch—California Arts & Architecture. See Arts and Architecture

Canad Forum—Canadian Forum $2. Canadian Forum, Ltd, 16 Huntley St, Toronto 5

Canad Hist R—Canadian Historical Review $3. University of Toronto Press, Toronto 5

Cath Lib World—Catholic Library World $5; free to members. Catholic Library Assn, 209 Vine Ave, Park Ridge, Ill.

Cath N—Catholic News $3. C. H. Ridder, 22 N William St, New York 7

Cath School J—Catholic School Journal $3. Bruce Pub Co, 400 N Broadway, Milwaukee 1, Wis.

Cath World—Catholic World $4. Paulist Press, 401 W 59th St, New York 19

Chem & Eng N—Chemical and Engineering News $6. American Chemical Society, 1155 16th St, N W, Washington 6, D.C.

Christian Cent—Christian Century $6. Christian Century Press, 407 S Dearborn St, Chicago 5

Christian Sci Mon—Christian Science Monitor (Atlantic edition) $14, including the Magazine. Christian Science Pub Soc, 1 Norway St, Boston 15

Christian Sci Mon Mag—Christian Science Monitor Weekly Magazine Section. Christian Science Pub Soc, 1 Norway St, Boston 15

Civil Eng—Civil Engineering $5. American Society of Civil Engineers, 33 W 39th St, New York 18

Col Engl—College English $4. University of Chicago Press, 5750 Ellis Ave, Chicago 37

Collier's—Collier's $5. Crowell-Collier Pub Co, Springfield, Ohio

Commonweal—Commonweal $7. Commonweal Pub Co, Inc, 386 Fourth Ave, New York 16

Cong Digest—Congressional Digest $6. Congressional Digest Corp, 1631 K St, N W, Washington 6, D.C.

Connoisseur—Connoisseur 43s. Connoisseur, Ltd, 28 & 30 Grosvenor Gardens, London, SW $1 ($8.50 The Connoisseur 250 W 55th St, New York 19)

Contemp—Contemporary Review $9.50. British Periodicals Ltd, 46-47 Chancery Lane, London, WC 2

Coronet—Coronet $3. Esquire, Inc, Coronet Bldg, Boulder, Colo.

Cosmopolitan—Cosmopolitan $3.50. Hearst Magazines, Inc, 250 W 55th St, New York 19

Cue—Cue (Manhattan edition) $4.50. Cue Pub Co, Inc, 6 E 39th St, New York 16

Cur Hist ns—Current History $4. Events Pub Co, Inc, 108-10 Walnut St, Philadelphia 6

Cur Opinion—Current Opinion (discontinued)

Dance—Dance Magazine $3.75. Rudor Pub Co, 416 W 33d St, New York 1

Design—Design $4. Design Pub Co, 337 S High St, Columbus 15, Ohio

Dublin R—Dublin Review 15s. Burns Oates & Washbourne, Ltd, 28 Ashley Pl, London, SW 1 ($4 International News Co, 131 Varick St, New York 13)

Ed & Pub—Editor and Publisher $5. Charles T. Stuart, 1475 Broadway, New York 18

Educ—Education $4. Palmer Co, 370 Atlantic Ave, Boston 10

El Engl—Elementry English $3.50. National Council of Teachers of English, 211 W 68th St, Chicago 21
Formerly Elementary English Review

Engl J—English Journal $4. University of Chicago Press, 5750 Ellis Ave, Chicago 37

Esquire—Esquire $6. Esquire, Inc, 488 Madison Ave, New York 22

Etude—Etude $3. Theodore Presser Co, Bryn Mawr, Pa.

Facts on File—Facts on File $45. Person's Index, Facts on File, Inc, 516 Fifth Ave, New York 36

Far Eastern S—Far Eastern Survey $6. 1 E 54th St, New York 22

Finance—Finance $5. Finance Pub Corp, 20 N Wacker Dr, Chicago 6

Flying—Flying $3. Ziff-Davis Pub Co, 64 E Lake St. Chicago 1

For Affairs—Foreign Affairs $6. Council on Foreign Relations, Inc, 58 E 68th St, New York 21

For Policy Rep—Foreign Policy Reports $5. (to libraries subscription includes Foreign Policy Bulletins and 6 headline books); $4. to F. P. A. members. Foreign Policy Assn, Inc, 22 E 38th St, New York 16

Forbes—Forbes $4. B. C. Forbes & Sons Pub Co, Inc, 80 Fifth Ave, New York 11

Fortnightly—Fortnightly $6.50. Fortnightly Review, 570 Harrow Rd, London, W 9

Fortune—Fortune $12.50 Time, Inc, 9 Rockefeller, Plaza, New York 20

Forum—Forum $4. Events Pub Co, Inc, 108-10 Walnut St, Philadelphia 6
Forum combined with Current History from May 30, 1940, to August 31, 1945; resumed publication as an independent magazine in September of 1945.

Free World—Free World.
Merged with United Nations World.

Good H—Good Housekeeping $3.50. Hearst Magazines, Inc, 250 W 55th St, New York 19

Harper—Harper's Magazine $5. Harper & Bros, 49 E 33d St, New York 16

Harper's Bazaar—Harper's Bazaar $5. Hearst Magazines, Inc, 572 Madison Ave, New York 22

Holiday—Holiday $5. Curtis Pub Co, Independence Sq, Philadelphia 5

Home & F See House B

Horn Bk—Horn Book $3. Horn Book, Inc, 585 Boylston St, Boston 16

House & Gard—House and Garden $5. Condé Nast Publications, Inc, Boston Post Rd, Greenwich, Conn.

House B—House Beautiful $5. Hearst Magazines, Inc, 572 Madison Ave, New York 22

Illus Lond N—Illustrated London News £5 1s. 1 New Oxford St, London, WC 1 (American edition $16. British edition $18. International News Co, 131 Varick St, New York 13)

Ind Woman—Independent Woman $1.50. National Federation of Business and Professional Women's Clubs, Inc, 1819 Broadway, New York 19

Inland Ptr—Inland Printer $4. The Inland Printer, 309 W Jackson Blvd, Chicago 6

Inter-American—Inter-American.
Merged with United Nations World, February 1947.

J Am Med Assn—Journal of the American Medical Association $8. Am Med Assn, 535 N Dearborn St, Chicago 10

J Home Econ—Journal of Home Economics $5. American Home Economics Assn, 1600 20th St, NW, Washington 9, D.C.

J Negro Hist—Journal of Negro History $4. Association for the Study of Negro Life and History, 1538 Ninth St, N W, Washington 1, D.C.

Knickerbocker—The Knickerbocker $3. The Netherlands Pub Co, 50 Rockefeller Plaza, New York 20

Ladies' Home J—Ladies' Home Journal $3. Curtis Pub Co, Independence Sq, Philadelphia 5

Liberty—Liberty $2.50. Holmes Pub Corp, 270 Park Ave, New York 17

Library J—Library Journal $6. R. R. Bowker Co, 62 W 45th St, New York 36

Life—Life $6. Time, Inc, 9 Rockefeller Plaza, New York 20

Life & Letters To-day—Life and Letters To-day 20s. 430 Strand, London WC 2 ($5. International News Co, 131 Varick St, New York 13)

Lit Digest—Literary Digest (discontinued)

Lon Studio. See Studio

Look—Look $3.50. Cowles Magazines, Inc, 488 Madison Ave, New York 22

Mademoiselle—Mademoiselle $3.50. Street & Smith Publications, Inc, 575 Madison Ave, New York 22

Mag Art—Magazine of Art $6; free to members. American Federation of Arts, 1262 N Hampshire Ave, N W, Washington 6, D.C.

Mag of Wall Street—Magazine of Wall Street $12.50. Ticker Pub Co, 90 Broad St, New York 4

Mo Labor R—Monthly Labor Review $4.50. Supt. of Documents, Washington 25, D.C.

Motion Pict—Motion Picture $1.20. Fawcett Publications, Inc, 67 W 44th St, New York 36

Mus Am—Musical America $4. Musical America Corp. 113 W 57th St, New York 19

Mus Courier—Musical Courier $3. Music Periodicals Corp, 119 W 57th St, New York 19

Mus Q—Musical Quarterly $4. G. Schirmer, Inc, 3 E 43d St, New York 17

Musician—Musician $3. Fellowship Concerts Service, Inc, 545 5th Ave, New York 17

N Y Herald Tribune—New York Herald Tribune $22, including Sunday edition. New York Tribune, Inc, 230 W 41st St, New York 36

N Y Post—New York Post $16.50, including Sunday edition. New York Post, Inc, 75 West St, New York 6
Bronx Home News consolidated with N Y Post February 16, 1948

N Y State Ed—New York State Education $2. New York State Teachers Assn, 152 Washington Ave, Albany 6

N Y Sun. See N Y World-Telegram

N Y Times—New York Times $19.50, including Sunday edition. New York Times Co, 229 W 43d St, New York 36

N Y Times Book R—New York Times Book Review $3. New York Times Co, 229 W 43d St, New York 36

N Y Times Index—New York Times Index $35. New York Times Co, 229 W 43d St, New York 36

N Y Times Mag—New York Times Magazine $7.50. (Complete Sunday edition; not sold separately) New York Times Co, 229 W 43d St, New York 36

N Y World-Telegram—New York World-Telegram and Sun $15. N Y World-Telegram Corp, 125 Barclay St, New York 15
N Y Sun consolidated with N Y World-Telegram January 5, 1950

Nat Ed Assn J—Journal of the National Education Association $5. free to members. National Education Assn, 1201 16th St, N W, Washington 6, D.C.

Nat Geog Mag—National Geographic Magazine $5. National Geographic Soc, 1146 16th St, N W, Washington 6, D.C.

Nat R—National Review 36s. Rolls House, 2 Bream's Bldgs, Chancery Lane, London, EC 4 ($8.50 International News Co, 131 Varick St, New York 13)

Nation—The Nation $7. The Nation Associates, Inc, 20 Vesey St, New York 7

Nation's Bsns—Nation's Business $15 (3 years). Chamber of Commerce of the United States, 1615 H St, N W, Washington 6, D.C.

Natur Hist—Natural History $5. American Museum of Natural History, 79th St and Central Park West, New York 24

Nature—Nature £4 10s; single numbers 1s 6d. Macmillan & Co, Ltd, St Martin's St, London, WC 2 ($22.50; single numbers 50c. Macmillan Co, 60 Fifth Ave, New York 11)

Nature Mag—Nature Magazine $4. American Nature Assn, 1214 16th St, N W, Washington 6, D.C.

New Eng Q—New England Quarterly $4. New England Quarterly, Hubbard Hall, Bowdoin College, Brunswick, Me.

New Repub—New Republic $6.30. Editorial Publications, Inc, 1416 F St, NW, Washington, D.C.

New Statesm & Nation—New Statesman and Nation—Week-end Review 32s 6d. 10 Great Turnstile, London, WC 1 ($7 International News Co, 131 Varick St, New York 13)

New York City. Museum of Modern Art Bul—Bulletin of the Museum of Modern Art 15c to 25c a copy; free to members. Museum of Modern Art, 11 W 53d St, New York 19

New Yorker—New Yorker $7. F-R. Pub Corp, 25 W 43d St, New York 36

Newsweek—Newsweek $6.50. Weekly Publications, Inc, Newsweek Bldg, 152 W 42d St, New York 36

19th Cent—Nineteenth Century and After $8.75. Constable & Co, Ltd, 10 Orange St, London, WC 2

Opera N—Opera News $4; free to members. Metropolitan Opera Guild, Inc, 654 Madison Ave, New York 21

Parents Mag—Parents' Magazine $3. Parents' Institute, Inc, 52 Vanderbilt Ave, New York 17

Parnassus—Parnassus (discontinued)

Pathfinder—Pathfinder $2. Farm Journal, Inc, Washington Sq, Philadelphia 5

Photoplay—Photoplay $3.60 (two years) Macfadden Publications, Inc, 205 E 42d St, New York 17
Combined with Movie Mirror

Poetry—Poetry $5. 232 E Erie St, Chicago 11

Pol Sci Q—Political Science Quarterly $6; free to members. Academy of Political Science, Columbia University, New York 27

Pop Mech—Popular Mechanics Magazine $3.50. Popular Mechanics Co, 200 E Ontario St, Chicago 11

Pop Sci—Popular Science Monthly $3. Popular Science Pub Co, Inc, 353 Fourth Ave, New York 10

Progres Educ—Progressive Education $4.25. American Education Fellowship, 19-27 N. Jackson St., Danville, Ill.

Pub W—Publishers' Weekly $6. R. R. Bowker Co, 62 W 45th St, New York 36

Q R—Quarterly Review 31s 4d. J. Murray, 50 Albemarle St, London, W 1. ($6.50 International News Co, 131 Varick St, New York 13)

Queen's Q—Queen's Quarterly $3. Queen's University, Kingston, Canada

R of Rs—Review of Reviews (discontinued)

Read Digest—Reader's Digest $3. Reader's Digest Assn, Inc, Pleasantville, N.Y.

Ref Shelf—Reference Shelf $7 per volume of six bound numbers, published irregularly. H. W. Wilson Co, 950-972 University Ave, New York 52

Rotarian—Rotarian $2. Rotary International, 35 E Wacker Dr, Chicago 1

Roy Inst Brit Arch J—Journal of the Royal Institute of British Architects £2 postpaid. The Institute, 66 Portland Pl, London, W 1

Sales Management—Sales Management $6. Sales Management, Inc, 386 Fourth Ave, New York 10

Sat Eve Post—Saturday Evening Post $6. Curtis Pub Co, Independence Sq, Philadelphia 5

Sat Night—Saturday Night $4 (in Canada) $6 (in United States). Consolidated Press, Ltd, Birks Bldg, Montreal, Canada

Sat R—Saturday Review $6. Saturday Review Associates, Inc, 25 W 45th St, New York 36

Sch & Soc—School and Society $7; free to members of the Society for the Advancement of Education, Inc, 15 Amsterdam Ave, New York 23

Sch R—School Review $4.50. University of Chicago Press, 5750 Ellis Ave, Chicago 37

Scholastic—Senior Scholastic (High School Teacher edition) $2 (teacher ed. only); school group rate (two or more subscriptions to one address) $1.20 for special eds. $1.50 for combined ed. Scholastic Corp, 7 E 12th St, New York 3

Sci Am—Scientific American $5. Scientific American, Inc, 2 W 45th St, New York 36

Sci Mo—Scientific Monthly $7.50. American Assn for the Advancement of Science, 1515 Massachusetts Ave, N W, Washington 5, D.C.

Sci N L—Science News Letter $5.50. Science Service, Inc, 1719 N St, N W, Washington 6, D.C.

Science ns—Science (news series) $7.50. American Assn for the Advancement of Science, 1515 Massachusetts Ave, NW, Washington 5, D.C.

Scrib Mag—Scribner's Magazine (discontinued)

Sign—The Sign $3. Passionist Missions, Inc, Union City, N.J.

So Atlan Q—South Atlantic Quarterly $3. Duke University Press, Durham, N.C.

Spec—Spectator 30s. 99 Gower St, London, WC 1 ($7 International News Co, 131 Varick St, New York 13)

Sport—Sport $3. Macfadden Publications, Inc, 205 E 42nd St, New York 17

Sporting N—Sporting News $8. Sporting News Pub Co, 20-18 Washington Ave, St. Louis, Mo.

Stage—Stage (discontinued)

Stage Pict—Stage Pictorial (discontinued)

Studio—Studio $6. Studio Publication, Inc, 381 Fourth Ave, New York 16 (30s; The Studio, Ltd, 66 Chandos Pl, London, WC 2)

Sunset Mag—Sunset Magazine $2. Lane Pub Co, Menlo Park Calif.

Survey—Survey $5. Survey Associates, Inc, 112 E 19th St, New York 3

Survey Graphic. See Survey

Survey Midmonthly. See Survey

Theatre Arts—Theatre Arts $5. Theatre Arts, Inc, 130 W 56th St, New York 19
This Week—This Week Magazine. Distributed each Sunday with different newspapers. United Newspapers Magazine Corp, 420 Lexington Ave, New York 17. In New York included in Sunday edition of New York Herald Tribune.
Time—Time $6. Time, Inc, 9 Rockefeller Plaza, New York 20
Town and Country—Town and Country $7.50. Hearst Magazines, Inc, 572 Madison Ave, New York 22
Travel—Travel $4.50. Travel Mag, Inc, 45 W. 57th St, New York 19

U N Bul—United Nations Bulletin $4.50. International Documents Service, Columbia University Press, 2960 Broadway, New York 27
U N World—United Nations World $4. U N World, Inc, 319 E 44th St, New York 17
U S Bur Labor. See Mo Labor R
U S Bur Labor Bul—United States Bureau of Labor Statistics. Bulletins. Free to libraries. Bureau of Labor Statistics, Washington, D.C. Purchase orders, Supt. of Documents. Washington 25, D.C.
U S News—United States News & World Report $5. United States News Pub Corp, 24th & N Sts, NW, Washington 7, D.C.
U S Office Educ Bul—United States Office of Education. Bulletins. Free to libraries. Office of Education, Washington, D.C. Purchase orders, Supt. of Documents, Washington 25, D.C.

Va Q R—Virginia Quarterly Review **$3**. University of Virginia, 1 West Range, Charlottesville, Va.
Variety—Variety $10. Variety, Inc, 154 W 46th St, New York 36
Vital Speeches—Vital Speeches of the Day $5. City News Pub Co, 33 W 42d St, New York 36
Vogue—Vogue (Incorporating Vanity Fair) $7.50. Condé Nast Publications, Inc, Greenwich, Conn. and 420 Lexington Ave, New York 17

Washington (D.C.) Post—Washington Post $10.80. P. L. Graham, Pub, 1337 E St, N W, Washington 4, D.C.
Wilson Lib Bul—Wilson Library Bulletin $2. H. W. Wilson Co, 950-972 University Ave, New York 52
Woman's Home C—Woman's Home Companion $2.50. Crowell-Collier Pub Co, 640 Fifth Ave, New York 19
World Rep—World Report. See U S News
World's Work—World's Work (discontinued)
Writer—The Writer $3. The Writer, Inc, 8 Arlington St, Boston 16

Yale R—Yale Review $3.50. 143 Elm St, New Haven 7, Conn.

NECROLOGY

This is a list of biographees' obituaries which are in this Yearbook, including those of late 1952. Deaths which occurred in late 1953 are recorded in the early 1954 issues of CURRENT BIOGRAPHY.

Andrews, Bert (biog 1948)
Asaf, Ali (biog 1947)

Borgese, G(iuseppe) A(ntonio) (biog 1947)

Carol II, former King of Romania (biog 1940)
Cox, E(dward) Eugene (biog 1943)
Croce, Benedetto (biog 1944)

Davis, Harvey N(athaniel) (biog 1947)
Dufy, Raoul (Ernest Joseph) (biog 1951)

Eaton, Charles A(ubrey) (biog 1945)

Feller, Abraham H(oward) (biog 1946)
Ferrier, Kathleen (biog 1951)
Flynn, Edward J(oseph) (biog 1940)

Gottwald, Klement (biog 1948)
Granville, William Spencer Leveson-Gower, 4th Earl (biog 1950)
Green, William (biog 1942)

Haas, Francis J(oseph), Bishop (biog 1943)
Hannagan, Steve (biog 1944)
Haywood, Allan S(haw) (biog 1952)
Hedin, Sven Anders (biog 1940)
Henderson, E(lmer) L(ee) (biog 1950)
Hepburn, Mitchell F(rederick) (biog 1941)

Horney, Karen (biog 1941)

Jeffers, William M(artin) (biog 1942)
Johnson, Osa (biog 1940)

Kenny, Elizabeth (biog 1942)
Knutson, Harold (biog 1947)
Kuniyoshi, Yasuo (biog 1941)

La Follette, Robert M(arion, Jr.) (biog 1944)
Lahey, Frank H(oward) (biog 1941)
Lee, Clark (Gould) (biog 1943)
Loudon, Alexander (biog 1942)

McCarty, Dan(iel Thomas, Jr.) (biog 1953)
McGraw, Curtis W(hittlesey) (biog 1950)
Mack, Nila (biog 1952)
Marin, John (biog 1949)
Medina Angarita, Isaías (biog 1942)
Mendelsohn, Eric (biog 1953)
Merriam, Charles E(dward) (biog 1947)
Minor, Robert (biog 1941)
Moulton, F(orest) R(ay) (biog 1946)
Munn, Frank (biog 1944)

Orlando, Vittorio Emanuele (biog 1944)

Pasvolsky, Leo (biog 1945)
Piñero, Jesús T(oribio) (biog 1946)
Pitkin, Walter B(oughton) (biog 1941)

Plastiras, Nicholas (biog 1950)
Prokofiev, Serge (Sergeyevich) (biog 1941)
Pugmire, Ernest I(vison) (biog 1945)

Rasmussen, Gustav (biog 1947)
Reuter, Ernst (biog 1949)
Richardson, Seth (Whitley) (biog 1948)
Rundstedt, Karl (Rudolf Gerd) von (biog 1941)

Sabin, Florence R(ena) (biog 1945)
Sadak, Necmeddin (biog 1950)
Sayre, Morris (biog 1948)
Shields, James P. (biog 1951)
Shinn, Everett (biog 1951)
Spalding, Albert (biog 1944)
Stalin, Joseph (biog 1942)
Struther, Jan (biog 1941)
Sugrue, Thomas (Joseph) (biog 1948)

Taft, Robert A(lphonso) (biog 1948)
Thomas, Elbert D(uncan) (biog 1942)
Thorpe, Jim (biog 1950)
Tobey, Charles W(illiam) (biog 1951)
Tobin, Maurice J(oseph) (biog 1946)

Vinson, Fred(erick) M(oore) (biog 1943)

Wagner, Robert F(erdinand) (biog 1941)
Wainwright, Jonathan M(ayhew) (biog 1942)

CLASSIFICATION BY PROFESSION—1953

Agriculture

Benson, Ezra Taft
Brenton, W(oodward) Harold
Fairchild, David (Grandison)
Figueres Ferrer, José (Pepe)
Heintzleman, B. Frank
Hepburn, Mitchell F(rederick)
   obit
Hope, Clifford R(agsdale)
Lincoln, Murray D(anforth)
McCarty, Dan(iel Thomas, Jr.)
Marzotto, Gaetano, Count

Architecture

Mendelsohn, Eric
Troost, Laurens

Art

Archipenko, Alexander
Brackman, Robert
Davis, Gladys Rockmore
Dufy, Raoul (Ernest Joseph)
   obit
Grant, Gordon (Hope)
Hartnell, Norman (Bishop)
Honeywell, Annette
Huntington, Anna Hyatt
Knaths, (Otto) Karl
Kuniyoshi, Yasuo obit
Loewy, Raymond (Fernand)
MacIver, Loren (Newman)
Marin, John obit
Matisse, Henri
Pereira, I(rene) Rice
Shinn, Everett obit
Tamayo, Rufino
Utrillo, Maurice

Aviation

Allen, William M(cPherson)
Auriol, Jacqueline
Baker, George T(heodore)
Plesman, Albert
Ramsey, DeWitt C(linton)
Stump, Felix B(udwell)
Swirbul, Leon A.
Talbott, Harold E(lstner)
Twining, Nathan F(arragut)

Business

Anderson, R(obert) B(ernerd)
Baker, George T(heodore)
Bevis, Palmer
Boles, Ewing T(homas)
Bowditch, Richard L(yon)
Brenton, W(oodward) Harold
Coleman, John S(trider)

Curtice, Harlow H(erbert)
DeButts, Harry A(shby)
Dulles, John Foster
Erikson, Leonard F.
Fletcher, C(yril) Scott
Fruehauf, Roy (August)
Gaither, H(orace) Rowan, Jr.
Hall, Joyce C(lyde)
Hammond, Godfrey
Hannagan, Steve obit
Hartnell, Norman (Bishop)
Heintzleman, B. Frank
Humphrey, George M(agoffin)
Jeffers, William M(artin) obit
Josephs, Devereux C(olt)
Kestnbaum, Meyer
Kohler, Walter J(odok), Jr.
La Follette, Robert M(arion,
   Jr.) obit
Land, Edwin H(erbert)
Lincoln, Murray D(anforth)
Loewy, Raymond (Fernand)
Lyttelton, Oliver
Philbrick, Herbert A(rthur)
Plesman, Albert
Rand, William M(cNear)
Reynolds, R(ichard) S(amuel)
Roberts, C(harles) Wesley
Robertson, Walter S(pencer)
Sayre, Morris obit
Schram, Emil
Sligh, Charles R(obert), Jr.
Stevens, Robert T(en Broeck)
Stolk, William C.
Sullivan, A(loysius) M(ichael)
Talbott, Harold E(lstner)
Trefflich, Henry (Herbert Fred-
   erick)
Waller, Fred(eric)
Weeks, Sinclair
White, William

Dance

Bettis, Valerie (Elizabeth)
Champion, Marge (Marjorie
   Celeste Belcher) and Gower
Eglevsky, André
Kaye, Nora
LeClercq, Tanaquil
Limón, José

Diplomacy

Aldrich, Winthrop W(illiams)
Andrade, Victor (Manuel)
Cabot, John M(oors)
Davis, John W(illiam)
Dillon, C(larence) Douglas
Dulles, John Foster
Fatemi, Hossein
Gibson, Hugh (Simons)
Hallstein, Walter
Hammarskjöld, Dag (Hjalmar
   Agne Carl)

Köprülü, (Mehmet) Fuat
Krishna Menon, V(engalil)
   K(rishnan)
Loudon, Alexander obit
Luce, Clare Boothe
Makins, Sir Roger (Mellor)
Munro, Leslie Knox
Orlando, Vittorio Emanuele
   obit
Petitpierre, Max
Rasmussen, Gustav obit
Robertson, Walter S(pencer)
Royen, Jan Herman van
Saleh, Allah-Yar
Smith, Walter Bedell
Yang, You Chan
Yeh, George K(ung-)C(hao)
Zaroubin, Georgi N(ikolaevich)
Zorin, Valerian A(lexandrovich)

Education

Adkins, Bertha S(heppard)
Anderson, Gaylord W(est)
Bakke, E(dward) Wight
Bell, Bernard Iddings, Rev. Dr.
Bevis, Palmer
Borgese, G(iuseppe) A(ntonio)
   obit
Buber, Martin
Bugher, John C(lifford)
Burns, Arthur F(rank)
Caldwell, Sarah C(ampbell)
Croce, Benedetto obit
Davis, Harvey N(athaniel) obit
De Kiewiet, Cornelis W(illem)
Edman, Irwin
Ewing, (William) Maurice
Fletcher, C(yril) Scott
Gaither, H(orace) Rowan, Jr.
Gallagher, Buell Gordon
Haas, Francis J(oseph), Bishop
   obit
Hallstein, Walter
Hartman, Louis F(rancis), Rev.
Horwich, Frances (Rappaport)
Hussein, Taha
Jung, Carl Gustav
Kallen, Horace M(eyer)
Kenyatta, Jomo
Kerr, Walter F(rancis)
Koch, Fred(erick Henry), Jr.
Komarovsky, Mirra
Köprülü, (Mehmet) Fuat
Latourette, Kenneth S(cott)
Laurel, José P(aciano)
Leonard, Mrs. Newton P(eck-
   ham)
Litchfield, Edward H(arold)
Ludington, Flora B(elle)
McLintock, (George) Gordon
Mercer, Samuel A(lfred)
   B(rowne), Rev. Dr.
Merriam, Charles E(dward)
   obit

Millett, John D(avid)
Moulton, F(orest) R(ay) obit
Munro, Leslie Knox
Nason, John W(illiam)
Overholser, Winfred
Paz Estenssoro, Victor
Pearson, Jay F(rederick) W(esley)
Petitpierre, Max
Pitkin, Walter B(oughton) obit
Pollard, William G(rosvenor), Rev.
Pusey, Nathan M(arsh)
Redfield, Robert
Riley, Susan B.
Romanoff, Alexis L(awrence)
Rose, William C(umming)
Sabin, Florence R(ena) obit
Steacie, E(dgar) W(illiam) R(ichard)
Storey, Robert G(erald)
Thomas, Elbert D(uncan) obit
Troost, Laurens
White, Gilbert F(owler)
Yeh, George K(ung-)C(hao)
Zwicky, Fritz

Engineering

Bowditch, Richard L(yon)
Cousteau, J(acques-)Y(ves)
Davis, Harvey N(athaniel) obit
Herzog, Maurice
Ley, Willy
Loewy, Raymond (Fernand)
Nichols, William T(homas)
Rickover, Hyman G(eorge)
Talbott, Harold E(lstner)
Troost, Laurens

Finance

Aldrich, Winthrop W(illiams)
Beyen, J(ohan) W(illem)
Boles, Ewing T(homas)
Brenton, W(oodward) Harold
Dillon, C(larence) Douglas
Gidney, Ray M(illard)
Humphrey, George M(agoffin)
Josephs, Devereux C(olt)
Pella, Giuseppe
Robertson, Walter S(pencer)
Schäffer, Fritz
Schram, Emil

Government— Foreign

Andrade, Victor (Manuel)
Arbenz Guzman, Jacobo
Asaf, Ali obit
Ben-Zvi, Isaac
Bennett, W(illiam) A(ndrew) C(ecil)
Beyen, J(ohan) W(illem)
Burns, Sir Alan
Carol II, former King of Romania obit
Chiang Kai-shek

Churchill, Sir Winston (Leonard Spencer)
Croce, Benedetto obit
Emmet, Evelyn (Violet Elizabeth)
Fatemi, Hossein
Figueres Ferrer, José (Pepe)
Foot, Sir Hugh (Mackintosh)
Frost, Leslie M(iscampbell)
Gottwald, Klement obit
Granville, William Spencer Leveson-Gower, 4th Earl obit
Hallstein, Walter
Hammarskjöld, Dag (Hjalmar Agne Carl)
Heeney, A(rnold) D(anford) P(atrick)
Hepburn, Mitchell F(rederick) obit
Hussein, Taha
Köprülü, (Mehmet) Fuat
Kraft, Ole Björn
Krishna Menon, V(engalil) K(rishnan)
Laurel, José P(aciano)
Loudon, Alexander obit
Lyttelton, Oliver
Makins, Sir Roger (Mellor)
Medina Angarita, Isaías obit
Muñoz Marín, Luis
Munro, Leslie Knox
Neville, Sir Robert A(rthur) R(oss)
Nkrumah, Kwame
Ollenhauer, Erich
Orlando, Vittorio Emanuele obit
Paz Estenssoro, Victor
Pella, Giuseppe
Penney, Sir William George
Petitpierre, Max
Plastiras, Nicholas obit
Rance, Sir Hubert Elvin
Rasmussen, Gustav obit
Reuter, Ernst obit
Royen, Jan Herman van
Sadak, Necmeddin obit
Saleh, Allah-Yar
Salote Tupou, Queen of Tonga
Scelba, Mario
Schäffer, Fritz
Smallwood, Joseph R(oberts)
Sokolovsky, Vassily D(anilovich)
Stalin, Joseph obit
Steacie, E(dgar) W(illiam) R(ichard)
Teitgen, Pierre-Henri
Whitton, Charlotte (Elizabeth)
Wu, K(uo) C(heng)
Yang, You Chan
Yeh, George K(ung-)C(hao)
Zápotocký, Antonín
Zaroubin, Georgi N(ikolaevich)
Zorin, Valerian A(lexandrovich)

Government— United States

Aldrich, Winthrop W(illiams)
Anderson, R(obert) B(ernerd)

Anderson, Sigurd
Barnes, Stanley N(elson)
Bell, Elliott V(allance)
Benson, Ezra Taft
Bugher, John C(lifford)
Burns, Arthur F(rank)
Cabot, John M(oors)
Cox, E(dward) Eugene obit
Crosser, Robert
Davis, John W(illiam)
Dillon, C(larence) Douglas
Dulles, John Foster
Durkin, Martin P(atrick)
Eaton, Charles A(ubrey) obit
Emerson, Lee E(arl)
Erikson, Leonard F.
Fairchild, David (Grandison)
Feller, Abraham H(oward) obit
Gamble, Ralph A(bernethy)
Gibson, Hugh (Simons)
Gidney, Ray M(illard)
Gough, Lewis K(etcham)
Hagerty, James C.
Hall, Leonard W(ood)
Halley, Rudolph
Hart, Edward J(oseph)
Hauge, Gabriel (Sylvest)
Heintzleman, B. Frank
Hobby, Oveta Culp
Hogan, Frank S(mithwick)
Hope, Clifford R(agsdale)
Howard, Mrs. Charles P(agelsen)
Howrey, Edward F.
Humphrey, George M(agoffin)
Jackson, Henry M(artin)
Jeffers, William M(artin) obit
Kaufman, Irving R(obert)
King, Samuel Wilder
Knutson, Harold obit
Kohler, Walter J(odok), Jr.
La Follette, Robert M(arion, Jr.) obit
Litchfield, Edward H(arold)
Lubin, Isador
Luce, Clare Boothe
McCarty, Dan(iel Thomas, Jr.)
Madden, Ray J(ohn)
Merriam, Charles E(dward) obit
Pastore, John O(rlando)
Pasvolsky, Leo obit
Persons, Wilton B(urton)
Philbrick, Herbert A(rthur)
Piñero, Jesús T(oribio) obit
Rand, William M(cNear)
Reed, Daniel A(lden)
Richardson, Seth (Whitley) obit
Robertson, Walter S(pencer)
Rogers, Will, Jr.
Simpson, Richard M(urray)
Smith, Bruce
Smith, Walter Bedell
Stennis, John C(ornelius)
Stevens, Robert T(en Broeck)
Stratton, William G(rant)
Taft, Robert A(lphonso) obit
Talbott, Harold E(lstner)
Thomas, Elbert D(uncan) obit
Tobey, Charles W(illiam) obit
Tobin, Maurice J(oseph) obit

Velde, Harold H(immel)
Vinson, Fred(erick) M(oore) obit
Wagner, Robert F(erdinand) obit
Weeks, Sinclair

Industry

Allen, William M(cPherson)
Anderson, John W(illiam)
Blackall, Frederick S(teele), Jr.
Bowditch, Richard L(yon)
Coleman, John S(trider)
Curtice, Harlow H(erbert)
DeButts, Harry A(shby)
Fruehauf, Roy (August)
Hood, Clifford F(iroved)
Humphrey, George M(agoffin)
Jeffers, William M(artin) obit
Kestnbaum, Meyer
Kohler, Walter J(odok), Jr.
McCormack, Emmet J.
Marzotto, Gaetano, Count
Ramsey, DeWitt C(linton)
Reynolds, R(ichard) S(amuel)
Shockley, William
Sligh, Charles R(obert), Jr.
Stolk, William C.
Swirbul, Leon A.

International Relations

Aldrich, Winthrop W(illiams)
Andrade, Victor (Manuel)
Asaf, Ali obit
Beyen, J(ohan) W(illem)
Burns, Sir Alan
Cabot, John M(oors)
Churchill, Sir Winston (Leonard Spencer)
Davis, John W(illiam)
Dillon, C(larence) Douglas
Dulles, John Foster
Emmet, Evelyn (Violet Elizabeth)
Erikson, Leonard F.
Fatemi, Hossein
Feller, Abraham H(oward) obit
Gibson, Hugh (Simons)
Hallstein, Walter
Hammarskjöld, Dag (Hjalmar Agne Carl)
Heeney, A(rnold) D(anford) P(atrick)
Köprülü, (Mehmet) Fuat
Kraft, Ole Björn
Krishna Menon, V(engalil) K(rishnan)
Litchfield, Edward H(arold)
Loudon, Alexander obit
Lubin, Isador
Luce, Clare Boothe
Lyttelton, Oliver
Makins, Sir Roger (Mellor)
Munro, Leslie Knox
Nason, John W(illiam)

Orlando, Vittorio Emanuele obit
Pasvolsky, Leo obit
Petitpierre, Max
Rasmussen, Gustav obit
Reuther, Victor (George)
Robertson, Walter S(pencer)
Royen, Jan Herman van
Sadak, Necmeddin obit
Saleh, Allah-Yar
Smith, Walter Bedell
Yang, You Chan
Yeh, George K(ung-)C(hao)
Zaroubin, Georgi N(ikolaevich)
Zorin, Valerian A(lexandrovich)

Journalism

Alvarez, Walter C(lement)
Andrews, Bert obit
Barton, George A(rthur)
Bell, Elliott V(allance)
Benchley, Nathaniel (Goddard)
Costain, Thomas B(ertram)
Crosby, John (Campbell)
Dangerfield, George (Bubb)
Fatemi, Hossein
Fischer, John
Freeman, Lucy (Greenbaum)
Gallagher, William M.
Hagerty, James C.
Hannagan, Steve obit
Hauge, Gabriel (Sylvest)
Kerr, Walter F(rancis)
Kraft, Ole Björn
Lee, Clark (Gould) obit
McCrary, Jinx (Falkenburg)
McCrary, Tex
Marshall, S(amuel) L(yman) A(twood)
Minor, Robert obit
Mowery, Edward J(oseph)
Munro, Leslie Knox
Murrow, Edward R(oscoe)
Parsons, Harriet (Oettinger)
Peterson, Virgilia
Pitkin, Walter B(oughton) obit
Roberts, C(harles) Wesley
Royster, Vermont C(onnecticut)
Smallwood, Joseph R(oberts)
Sugrue, Thomas (Joseph) obit
Whitehead, Don(ald Ford)
Whitton, Charlotte (Elizabeth)

Labor

Allen, William L.
Bakke, E(dward) Wight
Brewer, Roy M(artin)
Durkin, Martin P(atrick)
Green, William obit
Hayes, A(lbert) J.
Haywood, Allan S(haw) obit
McDonald, David J(ohn)
Quill, Michael J(oseph)
Reuther, Victor (George)
Shields, James P. obit
Tobin, Maurice J(oseph) obit

Wagner, Robert F(erdinand) obit

Law

Aldrich, Winthrop W(illiams)
Allen, William M(cPherson)
Anderson, R(obert) B(ernerd)
Anderson, Sigurd
Asaf, Ali obit
Barnes, Stanley N(elson)
Beyen, J(ohan) W(illem)
Cothran, James W.
Cox, E(dward) Eugene obit
Crosser, Robert
Davis, John W(illiam)
Dulles, John Foster
Emerson, Lee E(arl)
Feller, Abraham H(oward) obit
Frost, Leslie M(iscampbell)
Gaither, H(orace) Rowan, Jr.
Goldman, Frank
Hall, Leonard W(ood)
Halley, Rudolph
Hallstein, Walter
Hart, Edward J(oseph)
Heeney, A(rnold) D(anford) P(atrick)
Hogan, Frank S(mithwick)
Howrey, Edward F.
Jackson, Henry M(artin)
Kaufman, Irving R(obert)
Laurel, José P(aciano)
Leibowitz, Samuel S(imon)
Madden, Ray J(ohn)
Miller, Marshall E.
Orlando, Vittorio Emanuele obit
Pastore, John O(rlando)
Petitpierre, Max
Richardson, Seth (Whitley) obit
Schäffer, Fritz
Stennis, John C(ornelius)
Storey, Robert G(erald)
Taft, Robert A(lphonso) obit
Teitgen, Pierre-Henri
Velde, Harold H(immel)
Vinson, Fred(erick) M(oore) obit

Literature

Andrews, Roy Chapman
Asaf, Ali obit
Benavente (y Martínez), Jacinto
Benchley, Nathaniel (Goddard)
Borgese, G(iuseppe) A(ntonio) obit
Bradbury, Ray (Douglas)
Buber, Martin
Churchill, Sir Winston (Leonard Spencer)
Clark, Eugenie
Costain, Thomas B(ertram)
Cousteau, J(acques-)Y(ves)
Croce, Benedetto obit
Douglas, Marjory Stoneman

Edman, Irwin
Fairchild, David (Grandison)
Fischer, John
Hedin, Sven Anders obit
Herzog, Maurice
Hussein, Taha
Kallen, Horace M(eyer)
La Farge, Oliver (Hazard Perry)
Latourette, Kenneth S(cott)
Ley, Willy
Luce, Clare Boothe
Peterson, Virgilia
Struther, Jan obit
Sugrue, Thomas (Joseph) obit
Sullivan, A(loysius) M(ichael)
Wood, Peggy

Medicine

Alvarez, Walter C(lement)
Anderson, Gaylord W(est)
Bugher, John C(lifford)
Henderson, E(lmer) L(ee) obit
Horney, Karen obit
Jung, Carl Gustav
Lahey, Frank H(oward) obit
McCarthy, Kenneth C(ecil)
McCormick, Edward J(ames)
Martin, A(rcher) J(ohn) P)orter)
Overholser, Winfred
Rhoads, C(ornelius) P(ackard)
Robitzek, Edward H(einrich)
Sabin, Florence R(ena) obit
Selye, Hans (Hugo Bruno)
Synge, Richard L(aurence) M(illington)
Yang, You Chan

Military

Chiang Kai-shek
Cothran, James W.
Galloway, Irene O(tillia)
Gough, Lewis K(etcham)
Hamblet, Julia E.
Hobby, Oveta Culp
McCarthy, Kenneth C(ecil)
Marshall, S(amuel) L(yman) A(twood)
Medina Angarita, Isaías obit
Miller, Marshall E.
Navarre, Henri (Eugène)
Neville, Sir Robert A(rthur) R(oss)
Persons, Wilton B(urton)
Rance, Sir Hubert Elvin
Rundstedt, Karl (Rudolf Gerd) von obit
Santelmann, William F(redrick Henry)
Smith, Walter Bedell
Sokolovsky, Vassily D(anilovich)
Stevens, Robert T(en Broeck)
Talbott, Harold E(lstner)
Twining, Nathan F(arragut)
Wainwright, Jonathan M(ayhew) obit

Motion Pictures

Arden, Eve
Bankhead, Tallulah (Brockman)
Barrault, Jean-Louis
Bettis, Valerie (Elizabeth)
Booth, Shirley
Cantinflas
Champion, Gower
Champion, Marge (Marjorie Celeste Belcher)
Cousteau, J(acques-)Y(ves)
Crosby, Bing
Davis, Bette
Day, Laraine
Dietrich, Marlene
Fletcher, C(yril) Scott
Hampden, Walter (Dougherty)
Hayward, Susan
Hope, Bob
Hull, Josephine (Sherwood)
Johnson, Osa obit
Lancaster, Burt(on Stephen)
Lean, David
Liebman, Max
Lynn, Diana
McCrary, Jinx (Falkenburg)
Miner, Worthington (C.)
O'Hara, Maureen
Page, Geraldine
Parsons, Harriet (Oettinger)
Renaud, Madeleine
Thorndike, Dame Sybil
Waller, Fred(eric)
Watson, Lucile
Young, Alan
Zinnemann, Fred

Music

Bloch, Ernest
Edwards, Joan
Einem, Gottfried von
Ferrier, Kathleen obit
Hilsberg, Alexander
London, George
Munn, Frank obit
Novaes (Pinto), Guiomar
Pinza, Ezio
Prokofiev, Serge (Sergeyevich) obit
Reiner, Fritz
Santelmann, William F(redrick Henry)
Spalding, Albert obit
Stokowski, Leopold (Anton Stanislaw)
Stravinsky, Igor (Fëdorovich)
Vaughan Williams, Ralph
Warren, Leonard

Naval

Anderson, R(obert) B(ernerd)
Cousteau, J(acques-)Y(ves)
Harp, Edward B(laine), Jr.
King, Samuel Wilder
McLintock, (George) Gordon
Ma, Chi-Chuang
Ramsey, DeWitt C(linton)
Rickover, Hyman G(eorge)
Stump, Felix B(udwell)

Philosophy

Bhave, Vinoba
Buber, Martin
Edman, Irwin
Kallen, Horace M(eyer)

Politics

Adkins, Bertha S(heppard)
Anderson, Sigurd
Andrade, Victor (Manuel)
Arbenz Guzman, Jacobo
Bell, Elliott V(allance)
Ben-Zvi, Isaac
Bennett, W(illiam) A(ndrew) C(ecil)
Benson, Ezra Taft
Chiang Kai-shek
Churchill, Sir Winston (Leonard Spencer)
Cox, E(dward) Eugene obit
Croce, Benedetto obit
Crosser, Robert
Davis, John W(illiam)
Dillon, C(larence) Douglas
Eaton, Charles A(ubrey) obit
Emerson, Lee E(arl)
Emmet, Evelyn (Violet Elizabeth)
Fatemi, Hossein
Figueres Ferrer, José (Pepe)
Flynn, Edward J(oseph) obit
Frost, Leslie M(iscampbell)
Gamble, Ralph A(bernethy)
Gottwald, Klement obit
Hall, Leonard W(ood)
Halley, Rudolph
Hart, Edward J(oseph)
Hepburn, Mitchell F(rederick) obit
Hobby, Oveta Culp
Hogan, Frank S(mithwick)
Hope, Clifford R(agsdale)
Howard, Mrs. Charles P(agelsen)
Humphrey, George M(agoffin)
Jackson, Henry M(artin)
Kenyatta, Jomo
King, Samuel Wilder
Knutson, Harold obit
Kohler, Walter J(odok), Jr.
Köprülü, (Mehmet) Fuat
Kraft, Ole Björn
Krishna Menon, V(engalil) K(rishnan)
La Follette, Robert M(arion, Jr.) obit
Laurel, José P(aciano)
Luce, Clare Boothe
Lyttelton, Oliver
McCarty, Dan(iel Thomas, Jr.)
Madden, Ray J(ohn)
Merriam, Charles E(dward) obit
Minor, Robert obit
Muñoz Marín, Luis
Nkrumah, Kwame
Ollenhauer, Erich
Orlando, Vittorio Emanuele obit

Pastore, John O(rlando)
Paz Estenssoro, Victor
Pella, Giuseppe
Piñero, Jesús T(oribio) obit
Plastiras, Nicholas obit
Reed, Daniel A(lden)
Reuter, Ernst obit
Richardson, Seth (Whitley) obit
Roberts, C(harles) Wesley
Rogers, Will, Jr.
Sadak, Necmeddin obit
Saleh, Allah-Yar
Scelba, Mario
Simpson, Richard M(urray)
Smallwood, Joseph R(oberts)
Stalin, Joseph obit
Stennis, John C(ornelius)
Stratton, William G(rant)
Taft, Robert A(lphonso) obit
Talbott, Harold E(lstner)
Teitgen, Pierre-Henri
Thomas, Elbert D(uncan) obit
Tobey, Charles W(illiam) obit
Tobin, Maurice J(oseph) obit
Velde, Harold H(immel)
Vinson, Fred(erick) M(oore) obit
Wagner, Robert F(erdinand) obit
Weeks, Sinclair
Whitton, Charlotte (Elizabeth)
Wu, K(uo) C(heng)
Yang, You Chan
Yeh, George K(ung-)C(hao)
Zápotocký, Antonín
Zaroubin, Georgi N(ikolaevich)
Zorin, Valerian A(lexandrovich)

Publishing

Bell, Elliott V(allance)
Costain, Thomas B(ertram)
Fatemi, Hossein
Fischer, John
Hammond, Godfrey
Hobby, Oveta Culp
Kanter, Albert L(ewis)
McGraw, Curtis W(hittlesey) obit
Muir, Malcolm
Roberts, C(harles) Wesley
Rogers, Will, Jr.

Radio

Arden, Eve
Bankhead, Tallulah (Brockman)
Booth, Shirley
Crosby, Bing
Crosby, John (Campbell)
Day, Laraine
Dietrich, Marlene
Edwards, Joan
Hampden, Walter (Dougherty)
Hope, Bob
Linkletter, Art(hurGordon)
Lynn, Diana
McCrary, Jinx (Falkenburg)

McCrary, Tex
Mack, Nila obit
Munn, Frank obit
Murrow, Edward R(oscoe)
Page, Geraldine
Parsons, Harriet (Oettinger)
Pinza, Ezio
Smallwood, Joseph R(oberts)
Struther, Jan obit
Young, Alan

Religion

Alexei, Patriarch of Russia
Bell, Bernard Iddings, Rev. Dr.
Benson, Ezra Taft
Bhave, Vinoba
Buber, Martin
Dibelius, Otto (Friedrich Karl), Bishop
Eaton, Charles A(ubrey) obit
Gallagher, Buell Gordon
Goldman, Frank
Haas, Francis J(oseph), Bishop obit
Hall, Raymond S(tewart), Rev. Dr.
Harp, Edward B(laine), Jr.
Hartman, Louis F(rancis), Rev.
Latourette, Kenneth S(cott)
Léger, Paul-Émile, Cardinal
McIntyre, James Francis (Aloysius), Cardinal
Martin, William C(lyde), Bishop
Mercer, Samuel A(lfred) B(rowne), Rev. Dr.
Pollard, William G(rosvenor), Rev.
Pugmire, Ernest I(vison) obit
Reinartz, F(rederick) Eppling, Rev. Dr.
Scott, (Guthrie) Michael, Rev.
Stepinac, Alojzije, Cardinal
Thomas, Elbert D(uncan) obit

Science

Alvarez, Walter C(lement)
Andrews, Roy Chapman
Clark, Eugenie
Davis, Harvey N(athaniel) obit
Einstein, Albert
Ewing, (William) Maurice
Fairchild, David (Grandison)
Hedin, Sven Anders obit
Land, Edwin H(erbert)
Ley, Willy
Martin, A(rcher) J(ohn) P(orter)
Moulton, F(orest) R(ay) obit
Nichols, William T(homas)
Pearson, Jay F(rederick) W(esley)
Penney, Sir William George
Pollard, William G(rosvenor), Rev.
Robitzek, Edward H(einrich)
Romanoff, Alexis L(awrence)
Rose, William C(umming)

Sabin, Florence R(ena) obit
Selye, Hans (Hugo Bruno)
Shockley, William
Steacie, E(dgar) W(illiam) R(ichard)
Synge, Richard L(aurence) M(illington)
Wigner, Eugene P(aul)
Zwicky, Fritz

Social Science

Bakke, E(dward) Wight
Ben-Zvi, Isaac
Burns, Arthur F(rank)
Croce, Benedetto obit
Dangerfield, George (Bubb)
Gaither, H(orace) Rowan, Jr.
Hauge, Gabriel (Sylvest)
Hedin, Sven Anders obit
Horney, Karen obit
Johnson, Osa obit
Jung, Carl Gustav
Kenyatta, Jomo
Komarovsky, Mirra
La Farge, Oliver (Hazard Perry)
Litchfield, Edward H(arold)
Lubin, Isador
Mercer, Samuel A(lfred) B(rowne), Rev. Dr.
Merriam, Charles E(dward) obit
Overholser, Winfred
Pasvolsky, Leo obit
Redfield, Robert
Riley, Susan B.
Sadak, Necmeddin obit
Smith, Bruce
Vogt, William
White, Gilbert F(owler)

Social Service

Bevis, Palmer
Emmet, Evelyn (Violet Elizabeth)
Hall, Raymond S(tewart), Rev. Dr.
Leonard, Mrs. Newton (Peckham)
Lincoln, Murray D(anforth)
Martin, William C(lyde), Bishop
Marzotto, Gaetano, Count
Pugmire, Ernest I(vison) obit
Rockefeller, John D(avidson) 3d
Schram, Emil
Scott, (Guthrie) Michael, Rev.
Tolstoy, Alexandra (Lvovna)
Whitton, Charlotte (Elizabeth)

Sports

Barton, George A(rthur)
Campanella, Roy
Herzog, Maurice
McCrary, Jinx (Falkenburg)

Maglie, Sal(vatore Anthony)
Mantle, Mickey (Charles)
Munn, Clarence L(ester)
Roberts, Robin (Evan)
Shantz, Robert Clayton
Thorpe, Jim obit
Zatopek, Emil

Technology

Land, Edwin H(erbert)
Ley, Willy
Shockley, William
Stokowski, Leopold (Anton
   Stanislaw)
Stolk, William C.
Troost, Laurens
Waller, Fred(eric)
Zwicky, Fritz

Television

Arden, Eve
Bankhead, Tallulah (Brockman)
Bettis, Valerie (Elizabeth)
Champion, Gower
Champion, Marge (Marjorie
   Celeste Belcher)
Crosby, John (Campbell)
Day, Laraine
Hampden, Walter (Dougherty)

Hope, Bob
Horwich, Frances (Rappaport)
Liebman, Max
Linkletter, Art(hur Gordon)
Lynn, Diana
McCrary, Jinx (Falkenburg)
McCrary, Tex
Miner, Worthington (C.)
Murrow, Edward R(oscoe)
Page, Geraldine
Peterson, Virgilia
Wood, Peggy
Young, Alan

Theatre

Anderson, Maxwell
Arden, Eve
Bankhead, Tallulah (Brockman)
Barrault, Jean-Louis
Benavente (y Martínez), Jacin-
   to
Bettis, Valerie (Elizabeth)
Booth, Shirley
Cantinflas
Champion, Gower
Champion, Marge (Marjorie
   Celeste Belcher)
Dalrymple, Jean
Davis, Bette
Dietrich, Marlene

Hampden, Walter (Dougherty)
Hull, Josephine (Sherwood)
Inge, William (Motter)
Kerr, Walter F(rancis)
Koch, Fred(erick Henry), Jr.
Liebman, Max
Luce, Clare Boothe
Lynn, Diana
Mack, Nila obit
Minor, Worthington (C.)
Page, Geraldine
Pinza, Ezio
Renaud, Madeleine
Thorndike, Dame Sybil
Watson, Lucile

Other Classifications

Bliss, Henry E(velyn)
Churchill, (Clementine Ogilvy
   Hozier Spencer), Lady
Eisenhower, Mrs. Dwight
   D(avid)
Kenny, Elizabeth obit
Margaret, Princess of Great
   Britain
Rombauer, Irma (von) S(tark-
   loff)

BIOGRAPHIES OF WOMEN—1953

Adkins, Bertha S(heppard)
Arden, Eve
Atkinson, Oriana (Torrey) (WLB)
Auriol, Jacqueline

Bankhead, Tallulah (Brockman)
Barnes, Margaret Campbell (WLB)
Bettis, Valerie (Elizabeth)
Booth, Shirley

Caldwell, Sarah C(ampbell)
Champion, Marge (Marjorie Celeste Belcher)
Churchill, (Clementine Ogilvy Hozier Spencer), Lady
Clark, Eugenie
Crockett, Lucy Herndon (WLB)

Dalrymple, Jean
Davis, Bette
Davis, Gladys Rockmore
Day, Laraine
Dietrich, Marlene
Douglas, Marjory Stoneman
Du Jardin, Rosamond (Neal) (WLB)·

Edwards, Joan
Eisenhower, Mrs. Dwight D(avid)
Emmet, Evelyn (Violet Elizabeth)

Freeman, Lucy (Greenbaum)

Galloway, Irene O(tillia)
Goertz, Arthémise (WLB)

Hamblet, Julia E.
Hayward, Susan
Hobby, Oveta Culp
Honeywell, Annette
Horwich, Frances (Rappaport)
Howard, Mrs. Charles P(agelsen)
Hull, Josephine (Sherwood)
Huntington, Anna Hyatt

Jenkins, Sara (WLB)

Kaye, Nora
Kennelly, Ardyth (WLB)
Komarovsky, Mirra

Lawrence, Mildred (WLB)
LeClercq, Tanaquil
Leonard, Mrs. Newton P(eckham)
Luce, Clare Boothe
Ludington, Flora B(elle)
Lynn, Diana

McCrary, Jinx (Falkenburg)
MacIver, Loren (Newman)

McSwigan, Marie (WLB)
Margaret (Rose), Princess of Great Britain

Novaes (Pinto), Guiomar

O'Hara, Maureen

Page, Geraldine
Parsons, Harriet (Oettinger)
Pereira, I(rene) Rice
Peterson, Virgilia

Renaud, Madeleine
Riley, Susan B.
Ritner, Ann (Gilliland) (WLB)
Rombauer, Irma (von) S(tarkloff)

Salote Tupou, Queen of Tonga
Seton, Anya (WLB)
Stolz, Mary Slattery (WLB)

Thorndike, Dame Sybil
Tolstoy, Alexandra (Lvovna)

Watson, Lucile
Whitton, Charlotte (Elizabeth)
Wood, Peggy

CUMULATED INDEX—1951-1953

This is a three-year cumulation of all names which have appeared in CURRENT BIOGRAPHY from 1951 through 1953. The dates after names indicate monthly issues and/or Yearbooks in which biographies and obituaries are contained.

For the index to 1940-1950 biographies, see CURRENT BIOGRAPHY 1950 Yearbook; that eleven-year cumulated index is also available separately. Inquire of the publisher for price.

Abbell, Maxwell Jul 51
Abdullah, Mohammad Nov 52
Abdullah Ibn Hussein, King of Jordan biog Jun 48 obit Sep 51
Adamic, Louis biog Yrbk 40 obit Oct 51
Adams, Arthur S(tanton) Jan 51
Adams, Sherman Nov 52
Adkins, Bertha S(heppard) May 53
Adler, Mortimer J. Sep 52
Ahlgren, Mildred Carlson See Ahlgren, Mrs. O. A. Jul 52
Ahlgren, Mrs. Oscar A(lexander) Jul 52
Ala, Hussein May 51
Aldrich, Winthrop W(illiams) Mar 53
Alexei, Patriarch of Russia Mar 53
Ali, Mohammed Oct 52
Allen, Gracie See Burns, G. and Allen, G. Mar 51
Allen, Raymond B(ernard) Mar 52
Allen, Stephen Valentine See Allen, S. Jul 51
Allen, Steve Jul 51
Allen, William L. Sep 53
Allen, William M(cPherson) Mar 53
Allyson, June Jan 52
Almond, Edward M(allory) Mar 51
Alphand, Hervé Nov 51
Alsop, Joseph W(right), Jr. Oct 52
Alsop, Stewart (Johonnot Oliver) Oct 52
Alvarez, Walter C(lement) Sep 53
Ambedkar, B(himrao) R(amji) Nov 51
Anderson, Carl D(avid) Jan 51
Anderson, Gaylord W(est) Feb 53
Anderson, John W(illiam) Jul 53
Anderson, Leroy Sep 52
Anderson, Maxwell Sep 53
Anderson, R(obert) B(ernerd) Jun 53
Anderson, Sigurd Sep 53
Andrade, Victor (Manuel) Feb 53
Andrewes, Sir William (Gerrard) Sep 52
Andrews, Bert biog Sep 48 obit Oct 53
Andrews, Roy Chapman Jul 53

Andrews, Stanley Jun 52
Araki, Eikichi Oct 52
Arbenz Guzman, Jacobo Sep 53
Archipenko, Alexander Sep 53
Arden, Eve Sep 53
Armstrong, George E(llis) Apr 52
Armstrong, Harry G(eorge) Jul 51
Arnaz, Desi See Ball, L. and Arnaz, D. Sep 52
Asaf Ali biog Jun 47 obit May 53
Asgeirsson, Asgeir Sep 52
Ashton, Frederick May 51
Asimov, Isaac (WLB) Yrbk 53
Aswell, James (WLB) Yrbk 51
Atkinson, Oriana (Torrey) (WLB) Yrbk 53
Auriol, Jacqueline Sep 53
Avenol, Joseph (Louis Anne) biog Jan-Feb 40 obit Oct 52
Aydelotte, Frank Apr 52

Babson, Naomi Lane (WLB) Yrbk 52
Backman, Jules Apr 52
Bacon, Selden D(askam) May 52
Baker, George T(heodore) Jun 53
Bakke, E(dward) Wight Sep 53
Ball, Lucille and Arnaz, Desi Sep 52
Ball, Stuart S(coble) Jul 52
Ball, Zachary (WLB) Yrbk 53
Bankhead, Tallulah (Brockman) Jan 53
Barcelona, Count of See Juan Carlos, Count of Barcelona Oct 51
Barnes, Albert C(oombs) biog Mar 45 obit Sep 51
Barnes, Margaret Campbell (WLB) Yrbk 53
Barnes, Stanley N(elson) Sep 53
Barrault, Jean-Louis and Renaud, Madeleine Mar 53
Bartlett, E(dward) L(ewis) Jun 51
Barton, George A(rthur) May 53
Barzin, Leon (Eugene) May 51
Bateson, Mrs. Gregory See Mead, M. May 51
Batista (y Zaldívar), Fulgencio Apr 52
Bausher, Mrs. J. Lee See Jordan, M. (WLB) Yrbk 51
Becker, Mrs. Harry J. See Freeman, L. (G.) Oct 53
Beecham, Sir Thomas Jan 51
Belkin, Samuel Nov 52

Bell, Bernard Iddings, Rev. Dr. Apr 53
Bell, E.liott V(allance) Mar 53
Bell, Margaret Elizabeth (WLB) Yrbk 52
Bellamy, Ralph Nov 51
Ben-Zvi, Isaac Apr 53
Benavente (y Martínez), Jacinto Jun 53
Benchley, Nathaniel (Goddard) Sep 53
Bender, George H(arrison) Jan 52
Bendetsen, Karl R(obin) May 52
Bengough, Percy R(obert) Apr 51
Bennett, Henry G(arland) biog Feb 51 obit Feb 52
Bennett, Ivan L(overidge) Nov 52
Bennett, W(illiam) A(ndrew) C(ecil) May 53
Benson, Ezra Taft Feb 53
Bernstein, Philip S(idney) Nov 51
Berra, Lawrence (Peter) May 52
Berra, Yogi See Berra, L. P. May 52
Berry, James Gomer See Kemsley, J. G. B., 1st Viscount Jan 51
Bettis, Valerie (Elizabeth) May 53
Bevin, Ernest biog Sep 40 Jun 49 obit May 51
Bevis, Palmer Apr 53
Beyen, J(ohan) W(illem) Feb 53
Bhave, Vinoba Sep 53
Bigart, Homer Jun 51
Binder, Carroll May 51
Bingham, Hiram Mar 51
Birnie, William A(lfred) H(art) Sep 52
Björnsson, Sveinn biog Aug 44 obit Mar 52
Blackall, Frederick S(teele), Jr. Jan 53
Blake, Francis G(ilman) biog Jan 43 obit Mar 52
Blamey, Sir Thomas (Albert) biog Jun 42 obit Jul 51
Blank, Theodor Sep 52
Bliss, Henry E(velyn) Sep 53
Bliss, Raymond W(hitcomb) Jan 51
Bloch, Ernest Sep 53
Blodgett, Katharine Burr May 52
Boatner, Haydon L(emaire) Jul 52
Boheman, Erik (Carlson) Mar 51
Boles, Ewing T(homas) Apr 53

Fry, Christopher Feb 51

Fuller, Charles E(dward), Rev. Dec 51

Funston, G(eorge) Keith Jul 51

Furman, N(athaniel) Howell Dec 51

Fyan, Loleta D(awson) Dec 51

Fyfe, Sir David (Patrick) Maxwell Dec 51

Fyfe, H(enry) Hamilton biog Yrbk 40 obit Jul 51

Gaer, Joseph (WLB) Yrbk 51

Gainza Paz, Alberto Apr 51

Gaither, H(orace) Rowan, Jr. May 53

Gallagher, Buell Gordon May 53

Gallagher, William M. Oct 53

Galloway, Irene O(tillia) May 53

Gallup, George (Horace) Dec 52

Gamble, Ralph A(bernethy) Jan 53

Gamow, George Oct 51

Garbett, Cyril Forster, Archbishop of York Feb 51

Gardner, Matthias B(ennett) Jun 52

Garfield, John biog Apr 48 obit Jul 52

Garland, Judy Dec 52

Garroway, Dave May 52

Garroway, David Cunningham See Garroway, D. May 52

Gasparotti, Mrs. John J. See Seifert, E. (WLB) Yrbk 51

Gauss, Christian biog Apr 45 obit Dec 51

Gehrmann, Don(ald Arthur) Oct 52 See correction page 664 Yrbk 52

George VI, King of Great Britain biog Mar 42 obit Mar 52

Giannini, L(awrence) M(ario) biog Nov 50 obit Oct 52

Gibson, Hugh (Simons) Jan 53

Gidney, Ray M(illard) Oct 53

Gilbreth, Mrs. Frank Bunker See Gilbreth, L. (E.) M. Sep 51

Gilbreth, Lillian (Evelyn) M(oller) Sep 51

Gilmer, Elizabeth Meriwether See Dix, D. biog Jan-Jun 40 obit Feb 52

Glubb, John Bagot Sep 51

Goedhart, G(errit) J(an) van Heuven See Heuven Goedhart, G. J. van Oct 52

Goertz, Arthémise (WLB) Yrbk 53

Goldman, Frank Jan 53

Goldsborough, T(homas) Alan biog Jun 48 obit Jul 51

Goldstine, Herman H(eine) Nov 52

Golschmann, Vladimir Apr 51

Goodwin, Robert C(lifford) May 51

Gore, Albert (Arnold) Jan 52

Gorrie, Jack (Osborne) Mar 52

Goshorn, Clarence B(aker) biog Mar 50 obit Jan 51

Gottwald, Klement biog Apr 48 obit Apr 53

Gough, Lewis K(etcham) Jan 53

Gould, Ronald Nov 52

Gow, James (Ellis) biog Mar 44 obit Mar 52

Graham, Billy, Rev. See Graham, W. F., Rev. Apr 51

Graham, Elinor (Mish) (WLB) Yrbk 52

Graham, Evarts A(mbrose) Feb 52

Graham, Frank P(orter) Jul 51

Graham, William Franklin, Rev. Apr 51

Granik, (S.) Theodore Dec 52

Grant, Gordon (Hope) Jun 53

Granville, William Spencer Leveson-Gower, 4th Earl biog Sep 50 obit Sep 53

Graves, Alvin C(ushman) Dec 52

Greco, José Mar 52

Grede, William J. Feb 52

Green, William biog Mar 42 obit Jan 53

Greenbaum, Lucy See Freeman, L. (G.) Oct 53

Grey, J(ames) D(avid) Sep 52

Grieder, Naomi Lane Babson See Babson, N. L. (WLB) Yrbk 52

Griffin, R(obert) Allen Feb 51

Grogan, John Joseph Dec 51

Gropius, Walter (Adolf) Mar 52

Gross, Ernest A(rnold) Feb 51

Guillaume, Augustin (Léon) Jan 52

Gumpert, Martin Dec 51

Guzman, Jacobo Arbenz See Arbenz, J. Guzman Sep 53

Haas, Francis J(oseph), Bishop biog Aug 43 obit Oct 53

Haber, Heinz Dec 52

Hagerty, James C. Mar 53

Hahn, Otto Mar 51

Hall, Joyce C(lyde) May 53

Hall, Leonard W(ood) Jul 53

Hall, Raymond S(tev.art), Rev. Dr. Oct 53

Halley, Rudolph Jun 53

Hallinan, Vincent (W.) Oct 52

Hallstein, Walter Oct 53

Hamblet, Julia E. Oct 53

Hammarskjöld, Dag (Hjalmar Agne Carl) May 53

Hammond, Godfrey Oct 53

Hampden, Walter (Dougherty) May 53

Handlin, Oscar Jul 52

Handy, Thomas T(roy) Sep 51

Hannagan, Steve biog Aug 44 obit Mar 53

Hannah, John A(lfred) Oct 52

Harber, W. Elmer Mar 51

Hardie, S(teven) J(ames) L(indsay) Jul 51

Harding, Allan Francis See Harding, Sir J. Oct 52

Harding, Sir John Oct 52

Harnoncourt, René d' See D'Harnoncourt, R. Sep 52

Harp, Edward B(laine), Jr. Oct 53

Harriman, E(dward) Roland (Noel) Mar 51

Harrison, William K(elly), Jr. Jul 52

Hart, Edward J(oseph) Feb 53

Hartman, Louis F(rancis), Rev. Jan 53

Hartnell, Norman (Bishop) May 53

Harvey, E(dmund) Newton May 52

Haskell, William N(afew) biog Feb 47 obit Sep 52

Hauge, Gabriel (Sylvest) Oct 53

Havill, Edward (WLB) Yrbk 52

Hawkins, Harry C(alvin) Apr 52

Hayden, Carl T(rumbull) Jul 51

Hayes, A(lbert) J. Oct 53

Hayward, Susan May 53

Haywood, Allan S(haw) biog May 52 obit Apr 53

Heald, Henry Townley Feb 52

Hébert, F(elix) Edward Nov 51

Hedin, Sven Anders biog May 40 obit Jan 53

Heeney, A(rnold) D(anford) P(atrick) Jun 53

Heidenstam, Rolf (Magnus) von Oct 51

Heintzleman, B. Frank Jun 53

Hektoen, Ludvig biog Dec 47 obit Sep 51

Henderson, E(lmer) L(ee) biog Jun 50 obit Oct 53

Hendrickson, Robert C. Nov 52

Henie, Sonja Jan 52

Hepburn, Mitchell F(rederick) biog Dec 41 obit Feb 53

Herod, William Rogers Mar 51

Hershey, Lewis B(laine) Jun 51

Herzog, Maurice Jul 53

Heuven Goedhart, G(errit) J(an) van Oct 52

Heyman, Mrs. Marcus A. See Komarovsky, M. Oct 53

Hickman, Herman (Michael, Jr.) Nov 51

Higgins, Andrew J(ackson) biog May 43 obit Sep 52

Higgins, Marguerite Jun 51

Hightower, John M(armann) Nov 52

Hilaly, Ahmed Naguib Jul 52

Hilsberg, Alex(ander) Oct 53

Hilton, Frank C. Jul 52

Hinshaw, (John) Carl (Williams) Jul 51

Hobby, Oveta Culp Feb 53

Hobby, Mrs. William (Pettus) See Hobby, O. C. Feb 53

Hogan, Frank S(mithwick) Sep 53

Holland, (George) Kenneth Mar 52

Hollenbeck, Don Feb 51

Holliday, Judy Apr 51

Holt, Hamilton biog Dec 47 obit May 51

Homer, Arthur B(artlett) Jul 52

Honeywell, Annette Jul 53

Hood, Clifford F(iroved) Apr 53

Hook, Sidney Oct 52

Hoopes, Darlington Sep 52

Hope, Bob Oct 53

Hope, Clifford R(agsdale) May 53

Hope, Leslie Townes See Hope, B. Oct 53

Horne, John E(lmer) Dec 52

Horney, Karen biog Aug 41 obit Jan 53

Hornsby, Rogers Sep 52

Horsbrugh, Florence Feb 52

Horwich, Frances (Rappaport) Oct 53

Horwich, Mrs. Harvey L. See Horwich, F. (R.) Oct 53

Houtte, Jean van Mar 52

Howard, Mrs. Charles P(agelsen) Jul 53

Howard, Elizabeth (WLB) Yrbk 51

Howard, Katherine (Montague) G(raham) See Howard, Mrs. C. P. Jul 53

Howorth, Mrs. Joseph Marion See Howorth, L. S. Oct 51

Howorth, Lucy Somerville Oct 51

Howrey, Edward F. Jul 53

Hudleston, Edmund C(uthbert) May 51

Hulcy, Dechard A(nderson) Sep 51

Hull, Josephine (Sherwood) Oct 53

Hume, Edgar Erskine biog Aug 44 obit Mar 52

Humphrey, George M(agoffin) Feb 53

Humphrey, Helen F. Nov 52

Hunt, Lester C(allaway) Mar 51

Hunt, Mabel Leigh (WLB) Yrbk 51

Hunter, Croil Jul 51

Hunter, Kim May 52

Huntington, Anna Hyatt Oct 53

Huntington, Mrs. Archer M(ilton) See Huntington, A. H. Oct 53

Hussein, Taha Oct 53

Hyatt, Anna See Huntington, A. H. Oct 53

Ibáñez (del Campo), Carlos Dec 52

Ibarra, José María Velasco See Velasco Ibarra, J. M. Nov 52

Ickes, Harold L(e Claire) biog Jul 41 obit Mar 52

Impellitteri, Vincent R(ichard) Feb 51

Inge, William (Motter) Jun 53

Ingram, Jonas H(oward) biog Apr 47 obit Oct 52

Inverchapel of Loch Eck, Archibald John Kerr Clark Kerr, 1st

Baron biog Dec 42 obit Sep 51

Ironside, Henry Allan biog Feb 45 obit Feb 51

Irving, Frederick A(ugustus) Mar 51

Irwin, Helen G. Oct 52

Irwin, Robert B(enjamin) biog Mar 48 obit Jan 52

Iverson, Kenneth R(oss) Apr 51

Jackson, C(harles) D(ouglas) Oct 51

Jackson, Henry M(artin) Oct 53

Jackson, William H(arding) Mar 51

Jagendorf, Moritz (Adolf) (WLB) Yrbk 52

Jansen, William Oct 51

Jeanmaire, Renée Nov 52

Jeffers, William M(artin) biog Nov 42 obit Apr 53

Jenkins, Sara (WLB) Yrbk 53

Jenner, William E(zra) Jun 51

Jennings, B(enjamin) Brewster May 51

Jensen, Mrs. Oliver See Stafford, J. (WLB) Yrbk 51

Johnson, David M(offat) Jul 52

Johnson, Joseph T(ravis) Feb 52

Johnson, Lyndon B(aines) Jan 51

Johnson, Osa biog Apr 40 obit Feb 53

Johnston, Alvanley biog Jun 46 obit Nov 51

Johnston, Olin D(eWitt) Nov 51

Johnston, Wayne A(ndrew) May 51

Jooste, G(erhardus) P(etrus) Apr 51

Jordan, Mildred (WLB) Yrbk 51

Josephs, Devereux C(olt) Jul 53

Jouvet, Louis biog Oct 49 obit Oct 51

Joy, C(harles) Turner Jun 51

Juan Carlos, Count of Barcelona Oct 51

Jung, Carl Gustav Oct 53

Kahmann, (Mable) Chesley (WLB) Yrbk 52

Kai-shek, Chiang See Chiang Kai-shek May 53

Kalich, Mrs. Jacob See Picon, M. Jun 51

Kallen, Horace M(eyer) Oct 53

Kenau, Johnstone See Kenyatta, J. Oct 53

Kanin, Garson Oct 52

Kanter, Albert L(ewis) Jul 53

Karfiol, Bernard biog Nov 47 obit Oct 52

Karsh, Yousuf Dec 52

Katz-Suchy, Juliusz Jun 51

Kaufman, Irving R(obert) Apr 53

Kaye, Danny Nov 52

Kaye, Nora Jan 53

Kee, John biog Jun 50 obit Jun 51

Keller, James (Gregory), Rev. Oct 51

Kelley, Augustine B(ernard) Apr 51

Kemsley, James Gomer Berry, 1st Viscount Jan 51

Kennelly, Ardyth (WLB) Yrbk 53

Kenny, Elizabeth biog Oct 42 obit Jan 53

Kenyatta, Jomo Oct 53

Kerr, Sir Archibald (John Kerr) Clark See Inverchapel of Loch Eck, Archibald John Kerr Clark Kerr, 1st Baron biog Dec 42 obit Sep 51

Kerr, Walter F(rancis) Oct 53

Kersten, Charles J. Sep 52

Kestnbaum, Meyer May 53

Kettering, Charles Franklin Dec 51

Khan, Liaquat Ali biog Jun 48 obit Dec 51

Khoury, Bechara El- Dec 51

Kiewiet, Cornelis W(illem) de See de Kiewiet, C. W. Jul 53

Kilgallen, Dorothy, and Kollmar, Dick Feb 52

Killion, George (Leonard) Nov 52

Kim Il Sung Sep 51

Kimball, Dan A(ble) Sep 51

Kimball, Lindsley F(iske) Jul 51

Kimble, George H(erbert) T(inley) Oct 52

Kimpton, Lawrence A(lpheus) Jun 51

Kindelberger, J(ames) H(oward) Mar 51

King, Cecil R(hodes) Feb 52

King, Samuel Wilder Oct 53

Kirby, Rollin biog Dec 44 obit Jun 52

Kirk, Grayson L(ouis) May 51

Kirstein, Lincoln (Edward) Dec 52

Kitchell, Iva Dec 51

Kitson, Harry Dexter Apr 51

Kluckhohn, Clyde (Kay Maben) Nov 51

Knaths, (Otto) Karl Jul 53

Knight, O(rie) A(lbert) Jun 52

Knutson, Harold biog Jan 47 obit Oct 53

Koch, Fred(erick Henry), Jr. Oct 53

Kohler, Walter J(odok), Jr. Jan 53

Kollmar, Dick See Kilgallen, D. and Kollmar, D. Feb 52

Kollmar, Richard Tompkins See Kilgallen, D. and Kollmar, D. Feb 52

Kollmar, Mrs. Richard Tompkins See Kilgallen, D. and Kollmar D. Feb 52

Kollontay, Alexandra (Mikhailovna) biog Oct 43 obit Apr 52

Komarovsky, Mirra Oct 53

Konstantinu, Mrs. Ilias See Clark, E. Sep 53

Konstanty, Casimer James See Konstanty, J. Apr 51

Konstanty, Jim Apr 51

Köprülü, (Mehmet) Fuat Jun 53

Körner, Theodor Jul 51

Kotschnig, Walter M(aria) Oct 52

Koussevitzky, Serge biog Nov 40 obit Jul 51

Kraft, Ole Björn Feb 53

Kramer, Stanley (E.) May 51

Kramm, Joseph Jul 52

Krasna, Norman May 52

Krebs, Richard Julius Herman See Valtin, J. biog Apr 41 obit Jan 51

Krekeler, Heinz L(udwig) Dec 51

Krishna Menon, V(engalil) K(rishnan) Mar 53

Kubelik, Rafael Feb 51

Kuniyoshi, Yasuo biog Jun 41 obit Jun 53

La Cava, Gregory biog Dec 41 obit Apr 52

La Farge, Oliver (Hazard Perry) Jan 53

La Follette, Robert M(arion, Jr.) biog May 44 obit Apr 53

Lagerkvist, Pär (Fabian) Jan 52

Lahey, Frank H(oward) biog Mar 41 obit Sep 53

Lahr, Bert Jan 52

Lancaster, Burt(on Stephen) Jul 53

Land, Edwin H(erbert) Nov 53

Lane, Carl D(aniel) (WLB) Yrbk 51

Langer, William Feb 52

Larson, Jess Jun 51

Laski, Marghanita (WLB) Yrbk 51

Latourette, Kenneth S(cott) Nov 53

Lattre de Tassigny, Jean (Joseph Marie Gabriel) de biog Jan 45 obit Feb 52

Laurel, José P(aciano) Jun 53

Lauritzen, Jonreed (WLB) Yrbk 52

Lawrence, Mrs. Clarence A. See Lawrence, M. (WLB) Yrbk 53

Lawrence, Ernest O(rlando) Jan 52

Lawrence, Gertrude biog Aug 40 Sep 52 obit Oct 52

Lawrence, Mildred (WLB) Yrbk 53

Lawton, Frederick J(oseph) Mar 51

Layton, Mrs. Roy F(rancis) Jan 52

Lean, David May 53

Leavey, Edmond H(arrison) May 51

Lebrun, (Fede)rico Sep 52

LeClercq, Tanaquil Jul 53

Lee, Canada biog Dec 44 obit Jun 52

Lee, Clark (Gould) biog Dec 43 obit Apr 53

Lee, Laurence F(rederick) Jun 52

Léger, Paul-Émile, Cardinal May 53

Leibowitz, Samuel S(imon) Jan 53

Leighton, Margaret (Carver) (WLB) Yrbk 52

Lemonnier, André (Georges) Nov 52

Leonard, Lucille P(utnam) See Leonard, Mrs. N. P. Feb 53

Leonard, Mrs. Newton P(eckham) Feb 53

Lequerica y Erquiza, José Félix de Jun 51

Letourneau, Jean Oct 52

Levant, Oscar Oct 52

Levi, Carlo Dec 52

Leviero, Anthony H(arry) Sep 52

Ley, Willy Feb 53

Liaquat Ali Khan See Khan, L. A. biog Jun 48 obit Dec 51

Liddel, Urner May 51

Liebman, Max Apr 53

Limb, Ben C. Jan 51

Limón, José Jun 53

Lincoln, Murray D(anforth) Mar 53

Lindemann, Frederick Alexander, 1st Baron Cherwell See Cherwell, F. A. L., 1st Baron Mar 52

Linkletter, Art(hur Gordon) Nov 53

Linlithgow, Victor Alexander John Hope, 2d Marquess of biog Jan 42 obit Feb 52

Litchfield, Edward H(arold) Nov 53

Litvinov, Maxim (Maximovitch) biog Dec 41 obit Feb 52

Lloyd, (John) Selwyn (Brooke) Apr 52

Lloyd, Wesley P(arkinson) Jan 52

Lloyd-George, Gwilym Nov 52

Locke, Edwin A(llen), Jr. Jan 52

Loewy, Raymond (Fernand) Jun 53

London, George Nov 53

Long, Oren E(thelbirt) Sep 51

Long, Russell B(illiu) Dec 51

Lord, Mary Stimson Pillsbury See Lord, Mrs O. B. Oct 52

Lord, Mrs. Oswald B(ates) Oct 52

Loudon, Alexander biog Jul 42 obit Mar 53

Lovett, Robert A(bercrombie) Nov 51

Loynd, Harry J. Feb 52

Lubin, Isador Jan 53

Luce, Clare Boothe Apr 53

Ludington, Flora B(elle) Nov 53

Lundeberg, Harry Nov 52

Lynn, Diana Nov 53

Lysenko, T(rofim) D(enisovich) Oct 52

Lyttelton, Oliver Jan 53

Ma Chi-Chuang Jul 53

Ma, G. John See Ma Chi-Chuang Jul 53

McCarthy, Kenneth C(ecil) Nov 53

McCarthy, Leighton (Goldie) biog Oct 42 obit Nov 52

McCarty, Dan(iel Thomas, Jr.) biog Jul 53 obit Dec 53

McConnell, F(owler) B(eery) Jul 52

McCormack, Emmet J. Jul 53

MacCormick, Austin H(arbutt) Jul 51

McCormick, Edward J(ames) Nov 53

McCormick, Edward T(heodore) May 51

McCormick, Lynde Dupuy Feb 52

McCrary, Jinx (Falkenburg) See McCrary, T. and J. (F.) Jul 53

McCrary, John Reagan, Jr. See McCrary, T. and J. (F.) Jul 53

McCrary, Tex and Jinx (Falkenburg) Jul 53

McDaniel, Glen May 52

McDaniel, Hattie biog Sep 40 obit Dec 52

McDermott, Michael J(ames) Feb 51

McDonald, David J(ohn) Jun 53

Macdonald, John Ross See Millar, K. (WLB) Yrbk 53

McElroy, Neil H(osler) Apr 51

McFarland, Ernest W(illiam) Jan 51

McGranery, James P(atrick) May 52

McGraw, Curtis W(hittlesey) biog Jun 50 obit Nov 53

McIntyre, James Francis (Aloysius), Cardinal Feb 53

MacIver, Loren (Newman) Nov 53

Mack, Nila biog Dec 52 obit Mar 53

Mack, Ted Apr 51

McKay, David O(man) Jun 51

Mackay, John A(lexander) Feb 52

McKeldin, Theodore R(oosevelt) Oct 52

Mackenzie, C(halmers) J(ack) Jun 52

McKinney, Frank E(dward) Jan 52

McLean, Robert Nov 51

McLintock, (George) Gordon Nov 53

McMahon, (James O')Brien biog Dec 45 obit Sep 52

McMillan, Edwin M(attison) Feb 52

McSwigan, Marie (WLB) Yrbk 53

MacVeagh, Lincoln Jun 52

Macy, Edith Dewing See Macy, Mrs. E. W. Dec 52

Macy, Mrs. Edward W(arren) Dec 52

Madden, Ray J(ohn) Apr 53

Maggiolo, Walter A(ndrew) Jul 52

Maglie, Sal(vatore Anthony) Jun 53

Papagos, Alexander Nov 51

Parker, Roy H(artford) Oct 51

Parsons, Harriet (Oettinger) Jan 53

Pastore, John O(rlando) Apr 53

Pasvolsky, Leo biog May 45 obit Jun 53

Pate, Maurice Jun 51

Patel, Vallabhbhai (Jhaverbhai) biog Mar 48 obit Jan 51

Paton, Alan Jun 52

Patterson, Robert P(orter) biog Oct 41 obit Mar 52

Paulding, Mrs. C. Gouverneur See Peterson, V. Dec 53

Payne, Frederick G. Dec 52

Paz, Alberto Gainza See Gainza Paz, A. Apr 51

Paz, Hipólito Jesús Jan 52

Paz Estenssoro, Víctor May 53

Pearson, Jay F(rederick) W(esley) Dec 53

Pella, Giuseppe Nov 53

Peng Teh-huai Dec 51

Penney, Sir William George Feb 53

Pereira, I(rene) Rice Nov 53

Perkins, R(ichard) Marlin Oct 51

Perlman, Philip B(enjamin) Jul 52

Perón, (Maria) Eva (Duarte) de biog Mar 49 obit Sep 52

Perrin, Francis (Henri) Jul 51

Persons, Wilton B(urton) May 53

Pétain, Henri Philippe biog Aug 40 obit Sep 51

Peterson, Virgilia Dec 53

Petit, Roland Apr 52

Petitpierre, Max Dec 53

Petsche, Maurice biog Nov 49 obit Nov 51

Philbrick, Herbert A(rthur) Mar 53

Pholien, Joseph Feb 51

Pibul Songgram, Luang Sep 51

Picon, Molly Jun 51

Pinay, Antoine Apr 52

Pine, David A(ndrew) Jun 52

Piñero, Jesús T(oribio) biog Oct 46 obit Jan 53

Pinza, Ezio Dec 53

Pitkin, Walter B(oughton) biog Oct 41 obit Mar 53

Placzek, Mrs. A. K. see Struther, J. biog Jan 41 obit Oct 53

Plastiras, Nicholas biog May 50 obit Oct 53

Plaza (Lasso), Galo Oct 51

Plesman, Albert Mar 53

Poindexter, Joseph B(oyd) biog Jan 42 obit Jan 52

Pollard, William G(rosvenor), Rev. Mar 53

Poole, DeWitt C(linton) biog Nov 50 obit Oct 52

Popkin, Zelda (WLB) Yrbk 51

Popovic, Vladimir Feb 52

Porter, Mrs. Elizabeth K(err) Oct 52

Porter, Mrs. Eugene Vandergrift See Porter, Mrs. E. K. Oct 52

Powers, Marie Jan 51

Priest, Ivy (Maude) Baker Nov 52

Priest, Mrs. Roy F(letcher) See Priest, I. (M.) B. Nov 52

Prokofiev, Serge (Sergeyevich) biog Nov 41 obit Apr 53

Pugh, (Herbert) Lamont Mar 51

Pugmire, Ernest I(vison) biog Apr 45 obit Sep 53

Pusey, Merlo J(ohn) Jul 52

Pusey, Nathan M(arsh) Dec 53

Putnam, Roger L(owell) Jan 52

Quill, Michael J(oseph) Mar 53

Quo Tai-chi biog May 46 obit Apr 52

Rabaut, Louis Charles Jan 52

Rackmil, Milton R. Nov 52

Raddall, Thomas (Head) (WLB) Yrbk 51

Radhakrishnan, Sir Sarvepalli Jun 52

Ralls, Charles C. Jan 51

Ramsey, DeWitt C(linton) Jan 53

Ramspeck, Robert (C. Word) Jun 51

Rance, Sir Hubert Elvin Dec 53

Rand, William M(cNear) May 53

Randall, Clarence B(elden) Jun 52

Randolph, A(sa) Philip Oct 51

Rappard, William E(mmanuel) Oct 51

Rasmussen, Gustav biog Dec 47 obit Nov 53

Rathbone, Basil Mar 51

Rau, Sir Benegal Narsing Dec 51

Razmara, Ali biog Oct 50 obit Mar 51

Reavey, Mrs. George See Pereira, I. R. Nov 53

Redfield, Robert Dec 53

Reed, Daniel A(lden) May 53

Reed, Ralph T(homas) Apr 51

Reichstein, Tadeus Feb 51

Reid, Helen Rogers May 52

Reid, Mrs. Ogden Mills See Reid, H. R. May 52

Reinartz, F(rederick) Eppling, Rev. Dr. Jul 53

Reiner, Fritz Dec 53

Remorino, Jerónimo Sep 51

Renaud, Madeleine See Barrault, J. and Renaud, M. Mar 53

Renner, Karl biog Sep 45 obit Jan 51

Reuter, Ernst biog Oct 49 obit Dec 53

Reuther, Victor (George) Dec 53

Reynolds, Albert Pierce See Reynolds, A. Jun 52

Reynolds, Allie Jun 52

Reynolds, R(ichard) S(amuel) Feb 53

Rhoads, C(ornelius) P(ackard) Mar 53

Richards, James P(rioleau) Sep 51

Richardson, Seth (Whitley) biog Feb 48 obit May 53

Richter, Conrad (Michael) Jun 51

Rickenbacker, Eddie See Rickenbacker, E. V. Feb 52

Rickenbacker, Edward Vernon Feb 52

Rickover, Hyman G(eorge) May 53

Riddell, R(obert) Gerald biog Sep 50 obit Apr 51

Ridenour, Nina Apr 51

Riiser-Larsen, Hjalmar Nov 51

Riley, Susan B. Feb 53

Riley, William E(dward) Nov 51

Ritner, Ann (Gilliland) (WLB) Yrbk 53

Roberts, C(harles) Wesley Apr 53

Roberts, Robin (Evan) Dec 53

Robertson, Walter S(pencer) Dec 53

Robinson, Boardman biog Dec 41 obit Oct 52

Robinson, Ray Mar 51

Robinson, Sugar Ray See Robinson, R. Mar 51

Robitzek, Edward H(einrich) Dec 53

Robson, Flora Jan 51

Rockefeller, John D(avison) 3d Jun 53

Rockefeller, Nelson A(ldrich) Mar 51

Rodgers, Richard Apr 51

Rogers, Will, Jr. Dec 53

Romanoff, Alexis L(awrence) Dec 53

Rombauer, Irma (von) S(tarkloff) Dec 53

Romberg, Sigmund biog Mar 45 obit Dec 51

Roome, Mrs. Charles O. See Goertz, A. (WLB) Yrbk 53

Root, Oren Jul 52

Rootes, Sir William (Edward) Nov 51

Rooth, Ivar Dec 52

Rose, William C(umming) Mar 53

Rosenbach, A(braham) S(imon) W(olf) biog May 46 obit Sep 52

Rosenberg, Mrs. Anna M(arie) Jan 51

Rosenfield, Harry N(athan) Apr 52

Ross, Charles (Griffith) biog Jun 45 obit Jan 51

Ross, Harold W(allace) biog May 43 obit Jan 52

Ross, Nancy Wilson (WLB) Yrbk 52

Royen, Jan Herman van Dec 53

Royster, Vermont C(onnecticut) Dec 53

Ruffin, William H(aywood) Feb 51

Struble, Arthur D(ewey) Nov 51

Struther, Jan biog Jan 41 obit Oct 53

Stump, Felix B(udwell) Jan 53

Sugrue, Thomas (Joseph) biog Jun 48 obit Feb 53

Sullivan, A(loysius) M(ichael) Dec 53

Sullivan, Ed(ward Vincent) Sep 52

Summerfield, Arthur E(llsworth) Sep 52

Swirbul, Leon A. Apr 53

Synge, Richard L(aurence) M(illington) Nov 53

Szyk, Arthur biog Nov 46 obit Oct 51

Taber, Gladys (Leonae Bagg) (WLB) Yrbk 52

Taft, Robert A(lphonso) biog May 40 Apr 48 obit Oct 53

Talal, former King of Jordan Jan 52

Talbott, Harold E(lstner) Jul 53

Tallant, Robert (WLB) Yrbk 53

Tallchief, Maria Nov 51

Tamayo, Rufino Mar 53

Tassigny, Jean (Joseph Marie Gabriel) de Lattre de See Lattre de Tassigny, J.J.M.G. de biog Jan 45 obit Feb 52

Taylor, Elizabeth Jul 52

Taylor, Robert May 52

Taylor, Mrs. William Bolling See Young, M. Jun 52

Teague, Olin E(arl) Mar 52

Tebbel, John (William) (WLB) Yrbk 53

Teitgen, Pierre-Henri Jan 53

Templer, Sir Gerald (Walter Robert) Jul 52

Tewson, Sir (Harold) Vincent Feb 52

Thakin Nu See Nu, T. Dec 51

Theiler, Max Jan 52

Thomas, Elbert D(uncan) biog Oct 42 obit Mar 53

Thomas, Lowell (Jackson) Jan 52

Thomas, Sir (William) Miles (Webster) Jan 52

Thompson, Ruth Nov 51

Thorek, Max Jan 51

Thorndike, Dame Sybil Dec 53

Thorneycroft, (George Edward) Peter Dec 52

Thorpe, Jim biog Nov 50 obit May 53

Thye, Edward J(ohn) Oct 51

Thyssen, Fritz biog May 40 obit Mar 51

Tillstrom, Burr May 51

Tishler, Max Mar 52

Tobey, Charles W(illiam) biog Jun 41 Jul 51 obit Oct 53

Tobin, Maurice J(oseph) biog Jun 46 obit Oct 53

Tolstoy, Alexandra (Lvovna) Apr 53

Torp, Oscar (Fredrik) Dec 52

Towers, Graham F(ord) Feb 52

Toy, Henry, Jr. May 52

Traubel, Helen Feb 52

Trautman, George M(cNeal) Oct 51

Trefflich, Henry (Herbert Frederick) Jan 53

Troost, Laurens Jan 53

Turpin, Randolph See Turpin, R. Sep 51

Turpin, Randy Sep 51

Twining, Nathan F(arragut) Dec 53

U Nu See Nu, T. Dec 51

Ulbricht, Walter Jul 52

Ullman, Mrs. Egon V. See Kennelly, A. (WLB) Yrbk 53

Utrillo, Maurice Sep 53

Valtin, Jan biog Apr 41 obit Jan 51

Van Heuven Goedhart, G(errit) J(an) See Heuven Goedhart, G. J. van Oct 52

Van Houtte, Jean See Houtte, J. van Mar 52

Van Royen, Jan Herman See Royen, J. H. van Dec 53

Vance, Marguerite (WLB) Yrbk 51

Vandenberg, Arthur H(endrick) biog Nov 40 Jun 48 obit May 51

Vardaman, James K(imble), Jr. Apr 51

Vargas, Getulio Dornelles May 51

Varnay, Astrid May 51

Vaughan Williams, Ralph Dec 53

Velasco Ibarra, José María Nov 52

Velde, Harold H(immel) Mar 53

Vinson, Fred(erick) M(oore) biog Aug 43 obit Nov 53

Vogt, William Mar 53

Von Braun, Wernher Jan 52

Von Einem, Gottfried See Einem. G. von Jul 53

Von Heidenstam, Rolf (Magnus) See Heidenstam, R. M. von Oct 51

Von Mannerheim, Carl Gustaf Emil, Baron See Mannerheim, C. G. E., Baron von biog Apr 40 obit Feb 51

Von Rundstedt, Karl (Rudolf Gerd) See Rundstedt, K. (R. G.) von biog Nov 41 obit Apr 53

Voronoff, Serge biog Jan 41 obit Oct 51

Wadsworth, James W(olcott) biog Jul 43 obit Sep 52

Wagner, Robert F(erdinand) biog May 41 obit Jun 53

Wainwright, Jonathan M(ayhew) biog May 42 obit Nov 53

Wald, Jerome Irving See Wald, J. May 52

Wald, Jerry May 52

Walker, Paul A(tlee) May 52

Walker, Walton H(arris) biog Sep 50 obit Jan 51

Wallenstein, Alfred (Franz) Apr 52

Waller, Fred(eric) Feb 53

Walter, Francis E(ugene) Jun 52

Walton, Ernest Thomas Sinton Mar 52

Wampler, (ElRey) Cloud Dec 52

Warburton, Herbert B(irchby) Nov 51

Warne, William E(lmo) Nov 52

Warren, Leonard Dec 53

Waterman, Alan T(ower) Jun 51

Waters, Ethel Mar 51

Watson, Lucile Dec 53

Wayne, John Feb 51

Weaver, Warren Apr 52

Webster, H(arold) T(ucker) biog Mar 45 obit Nov 52

Weeks, Sinclair Mar 53

Weil, Richard. Jr. Jul 51

Weizmann, Chaim biog Nov 42 Nov 48 obit Dec 52

Werner, Max biog Dec 43 obit Feb 51

Wheelwright, Jere (Hungerford, Jr.) (WLB) Yrbk 52

Wherry, Kenneth S(picer) biog Apr 46 obit Jan 52

Whipple, Fred Lawrence May 52

Whitaker, Douglas (Merritt) Nov 51

White, Alexander M(oss) Jul 51

White, Gilbert F(owler) Mar 53

White, Wallace H(umphrey), Jr. biog May 48 obit May 52

White, William Jan 53

Whitehead, Don(ald Ford) Dec 53

Whitman, Walter G(ordon) Feb 52

Whitney, Courtney Jun 51

Whitton, Charlotte (Elizabeth) Apr 53

Wickenden, (Leonard) Dan(iel) (WLB) Yrbk 51

Wigner, Eugene P(aul) Apr 53

Wilder, Billy Feb 51

Williams, Camilla Jun 52

Williams, Emlyn Apr 52

Williams, John J(ames) Jan 52

Williams, Ralph Vaughan See Vaughan Williams, R. Dec 53

Williams, Robert R(ampatnam) Sep 51

Willis, Paul S. Jan 51

Wilson, Charles E(dward) Feb 51

Wilson, Donald R(andolph) Jan 52

Wilson, Dorothy Clarke (WLB) Yrbk 51

Wilson, I(rving) W(hite) Jul 52

Wilson, Leroy A(ugust) biog Apr 48 obit Jul 51

Wilt, Fred(erick Loren) Oct 52

Wiman, Dwight Deere biog Jun 49 obit Feb 51

ADDENDA

PAGE 116:

It was announced on October 15, 1953 that Sir Winston Churchill would receive the $35,000 Nobel Prize for literature from the Swedish Academy of Literature.

(5844)